The
Princeton
Review

The Best Northeastern Colleges

224 Great Schools to Consider

By Robert Franek,
Tom Meltzer, Christopher Maier, Carson Brown,
Julie Doherty, and Andrew Friedman

Random House, Inc.

New York

www.PrincetonReview.com

The Princeton Review, Inc.
2315 Broadway
New York, NY 10024
E-mail: bookeditor@review.com

© 2005 by The Princeton Review, Inc.

ISBN 0-375-76481-X

Publisher: Robert Franek
Editors: Erik Olson and Lisa Marie Rovito
Designer: Scott Harris
Production Editor: Christine LaRubio

Manufactured in the United States of America.

9 8 7 6 5 4 3 2 1

FOREWORD

Every year, about two million high school graduates go to college. To make sure they end up at the *right* school, they spend several billion dollars on the admissions process. This money pays for countless admissions officers and counselors, a bunch of standardized tests (and preparation for them), and many books similar to—but not as good as—this one.

It's so expensive because most admissions professionals have a thing about being in control. As a group, colleges resist almost every attempt to standardize or otherwise simplify the process. Admissions officers want you to believe that every admissions decision that they render occurs within systems of weights, measures, and deliberations that are far too complex for you to comprehend. They shudder at the notion of having to respond to students and their parents in down-to-earth language that might reveal the arbitrary nature of a huge percentage of the admissions and denials that they issue during each cycle. That would be admitting that good luck and circumstance play a major part in many successful applications. So, in flight from public accountability, they make the process a lot more mysterious than it needs to be.

Even the most straightforward colleges hide the information you would want to know about the way they'll evaluate your application: What grades and SATs are they looking for? Do their reported SAT averages include minority students, athletes, and legacies (kids whose parents went to their school)? Exactly how much do extracurricular activities count? What percentage of the aid that they give out is in loans and what percentage is in grants?

We couldn't get answers to these questions from many colleges. In fact, we couldn't get answers to *any* questions from some schools. Others who supplied this information to us for earlier editions of this guide have since decided that they never should have in the first place. After all, knowledge is power.

Colleges seem to have the time and money to create beautiful brochures that generally show that all college classes are held under a tree on a beautiful day. Why not just tell you what sort of students they're looking for, and what factors they'll use to consider your application?

Until the schools demystify the admissions process, this book is your best bet. It's not a phone book containing every fact about every college in the country. And it's not a memoir written by a few graduates describing their favorite dining halls or professors. We've given you the facts you'll need to apply to the best schools in the northeast. And enough information about them—which we gathered from hundreds of counselors and admissions officers and tens of thousands of college students—to help you make a smart decision about which school to attend.

One note: We don't talk a lot about majors. This is because most high school students really don't know what they want to major in—and the ones who do almost always change their minds by the beginning of junior year. Choosing a school because of the reputation of a single department is often a terrible idea.

If you're interested in learning about majors and the colleges that offer them, pick up our *Guide to College Majors* or visit our website, www.PrincetonReview.com, where we explain majors and list the colleges that offer them.

As complicated and difficult as the admissions process is, we think you'll love college itself—especially at the schools listed in this book.

Good luck in your search.

John Katzman
June 2005

ACKNOWLEDGMENTS

Each year we assembly an awe inspiringly talented group of colleagues who work together to produce our guidebooks; this year is no exception. Everyone involved in this effort—authors, editors, data collectors, production specialists, and designers—gives so much more than is required to make *The Best 224 Northeastern Colleges* an exceptional student resource guide. This new edition yields the essentials of what prospective college students really want: the most honest, accessible, and pertinent information on the Northeastern colleges they are considering attending for the next four years of their lives. My sincere thanks go to the many who contributed to this tremendous project. I am proud to note here that we have again successfully provided an uncompromising look into the true nature of each profiled college or university based on the opinions of each institution's current students. I know our readers will benefit from our cumulative efforts.

A special thank you goes to our authors, Tom Meltzer, Christopher Maier, Carson Brown, Julie Doherty, and Andrew Friedman for their dedication in sifting through tens of thousands of surveys to produce the essence of each school profiled. Very special thanks go to Erik Olson, Director of Guidebook Publications, Lisa Marie Rovito and Spencer Foxworth, Editors, for their editorial commitment and vision. Erik deserves special thanks for the managerial role he took in working directly with our student survey team, establishing protocol with an unblinking eye on providing balanced narrative profiles. Lisa Marie and Spencer have quickly become assets to our editorial department. They met the challenges of this book head on, I am grateful for their thoughtful and careful reading.

Michael Palumbo, Student Survey Manager, has been a dedicated TPR staffer since 1999. This is Michael's second year at the helm of the student survey process, and we have all profited from his presence. Michael is a gifted communicator, he understands our survey/collection process and works exceptionally well with school administrators and students alike. A warm and special thank you goes to our Student Surveyor Administrator, Jen Adams. Jen is in the trenches everyday, her spirit never wavers, and her work—consistently excellent.

My continued thanks go to our data collection pros, Ben Zelevansky, and Perry Medina, for their successful efforts in collecting and accurately representing the statistical data that appear with each college profile. A sincere thank you goes to Ben Zelevansky for all the needed work he completed for data generation and his competence in book pours.

The enormity of this project and its deadline constraints could not have been realized without the calm presence of our production team, Scott Harris, Production Manager; Christine LaRubio, Production Editor; and Ricky Marson, Copy Editor. Their unconditional dedication, focus, and most importantly, careful eyes, continue to inspire and impress me. They deserve great thanks for their flexible schedules and uncompromising efficiency.

Special thanks also go to Jeanne Krier, our Random House publicist, for the work she has done on this book and the overall series since its inception. Jeanne continues to be my trusted colleague, media advisor, and friend. I would also like to make special mention of Tom Russell, our publisher, for his continuous investment and faith in our ideas.

Lastly, I thank John Katzman, Mark Chernis, and Young Shin for their steadfast confidence in this book and our publishing department, and for always being the champions of student opinion. It is a pleasure to work with each of you.

Again, to all who contributed so much to this publication, thank you for your efforts; they do not go unnoticed.

Robert Franek
Publisher
Lead Author—The Best 224 Northeastern Colleges

CONTENTS

PART 1: INTRODUCTION 1

How We Produce This Book 1
How This Book Is Organized 3
Glossary 10

PART 2: THE SCHOOLS 11

PART 3: THE STATS 460

PART 4: INDEX BY STATE 559

About the Authors 569

PART 1: INTRODUCTION

HOW WE PRODUCE THIS BOOK

Welcome to the second edition of *The Best Northeastern Colleges*, one-fourth of our *Best* regional series. Our decision to produce this series was fueled by a desire to raise awareness of academically excellent but lesser-known regional colleges for those looking to study within a specific geographic area. Many of the schools within these pages are nationally competitive institutions of higher learning; we therefore also include their profiles in the 2006 edition of our best-selling *The Best 361 Colleges*. In fact, for these regional guides, we employ the same methodology for collecting student surveys and distilling them into college profiles as we do for *The Best 361 Colleges*. An important difference between this series and *The Best 361 Colleges*, however, is that we do not include any ranking lists.

But why are some of the outstanding schools in this book *not* included in *Best 361*? For one or both of two possible reasons. First, it may be because—at this time—they have a regional, rather than a national, focus. That is, they draw their students primarily from the state in which they are located, or from bordering states. A second possible reason is that—again, at this time—they have not met the rather rigorous standards for inclusion in *The Best 361 Colleges*. Is that meant as a snub to the schools that didn't make it into *Best 361*? Absolutely not. There are more than 3,000 institutions of higher learning in the United States, and *The Best 361 Colleges* profiles the top 10 percent, academically, of those schools. *Best Northeastern Colleges*, on the other hand, offers student opinion—driven information on all of the top colleges in eleven states and the District of Columbia. The eleven states are: Connecticut, Delaware, Maine, Maryland, Massachusetts, New Hampshire, New Jersey, New York, Pennsylvania, Rhode Island, and Vermont.

For each school, we provide both in-depth statistical data (on admissions, financial aid, student body demographics, and academics) and narrative descriptions of academic and social life based on the opinions of the very students who attend them.

We avoided using any sort of mathematical calculations or formulas to determine which colleges and universities to include in *Best Northeastern Colleges*. We aim to provide an inclusive cross-section of colleges: large and small, public and private, all-male and all-female, historically black colleges and universities, science and technology—focused institutions, nontraditional colleges, highly selective and virtually open-door admissions, great buys and the wildly expensive. All are institutions well worth considering. Though not every college included will appeal to every student, this guide represents the top 226 colleges in the Northeastern states.

Each college we surveyed this year had to meet two criteria: first, they had to meet our standards for academic excellence, and second, we had to be able to survey their students anonymously, either through our online survey (http://survey.review.com) or through our paper survey, which we distribute and collect during an on-campus visit.

Surveying thousands of students on hundreds of campuses is a mammoth undertaking, but the launch of our online student survey, available 24/7, has made it possible for students to complete a survey anytime and anywhere an Internet-enabled computer can be found.

So how do we do it? All colleges and universities we plan to visit are notified through established campus contacts that we wish to arrange a survey; we depend on these contacts for assistance in identifying common, high-traffic areas on campus in which to distribute our paper survey and to help us make any necessary arrangements as required by campus policies. When possible, and when the college is willing, our contacts will arrange for an e-mail to be sent to the entire student body encouraging them to fill out our online survey. (In recent years, many schools have chosen to send an e-mail to the entire student body, which in some cases yielded astonishing results.) Many of the colleges included in *Best Northeastern Colleges* were surveyed this past year, but not *all*; each is surveyed *at least* once every three years. The reality is that, unless there's been some grand upheaval at a campus, we've found that there's little change in student opinion from one year to the next. Colleges that wish to be resurveyed prior to their turn in the regular survey cycle are accommodated with an earlier visit if at all possible.

The survey itself is extensive, divided into four fundamental sections—"About Yourself," "Your School's Academics/Administration," "Students," and "Life at Your School"—that collectively include more than 70 questions. We ask about everything imaginable, from "How many out-of-class hours do you spend studying each day?" to "How widely used is beer?" Most questions are multiple-response in nature, but several offer students the opportunity to expand on their answers with narrative responses. These narrative responses are the source of the student quotes that appear throughout each college profile in *Best Northeastern Colleges*.

Once the surveys have been completed and the responses stored in our database, each college is given a grade point average (GPA) for its students' answers to each multiple-response question. It is these GPAs that enable us to compare student opinions from college to college, and to gauge which aspects of the complete experience at each college rate highest and lowest according to the institution's own students. (They are also the basis for three of the ratings—Quality of Life, Financial Aid, and Academic—that appear at the top of each college profile.) Once we have this information in hand, we write the individual college profiles. Student quotes within the profiles are not chosen for their extreme nature, humor, or singular perspective—in all cases the intention is that they represent closely the sentiments expressed by the majority of survey respondents from the college or that they illustrate one side or another of a mixed bag of student opinion (in which case the counterpoint will also appear within the text). And of course, if a student's quote accomplishes this *and* is noteworthy for it's wittiness, it'll definitely make it into the guide.

The profiles in general seek to accomplish that which a college admissions viewbook by its very nature can never really hope to achieve—to provide a (relatively) uncensored view of life at a particular college, and acknowledge that even the best colleges have their shortcomings. Though some college administrators find this book hard to accept, most have come to recognize that college officials no longer enjoy the luxury of controlling every word that students hear or read about their institutions and that the age of consumerism in the college search process is here to stay.

Our survey is qualitative and anecdotal. While this approach sometimes means we blow a result—such as when we surveyed at Stephens College during the week the administration was debating the abolition of women's studies as a major at that small women's college and *(surprise!)* the survey results indicated an unhappy student body—most of our results are confirmed by feedback we get from alums, current students, counselors, and prospective students who visit the campuses. In order to help guard against the likelihood that we produce an entry that's way off the mark, we send administrators at each school a copy of the entry we intend to publish prior to its actual publication date, with ample opportunity to respond with corrections, comments, and/or outright objections. In every case in which we receive a reply, we take careful steps to ensure that we review their suggestions and make appropriate changes when warranted.

Far more important than what college administrators think is what *you* think. Take our information on colleges as you should take information from all sources—as input that reflects the values and opinions of others, which may be helpful to you as you *form your own opinions*. This guide is not an end point from which you should cull your list of possible colleges but rather a starting point, a tool that can help you to probe the surface and get a sense of the college experience. You must do your own investigation, refer to other sources, visit the campuses, and develop your own list of best colleges. Only then will this book be the useful tool that it is intended to be.

How This Book Is Organized

Each of the colleges and universities listed in this book has its own two-page spread. To make it easier to find information about the schools of your choice, we've used the same format for every school. Look at the sample pages below:

ADELPHI UNIVERSITY

LEVERMORE HALL 114, SOUTH AVENUE, GARDEN CITY, NY 11530 ▪ ADMISSIONS: 516-877-3050
FAX: 516-877-3039 ▪ E-MAIL: ADMISSIONS@ADELPHI.EDU ▪ WEBSITE: WWW.ADELPHI.EDU

Ratings
Quality of Life: 76   Academic: 69   Admissions: 63   Financial Aid: 89

Academics

With "small classes" and "extremely helpful" faculty, students at Adelphi University are able to sink their teeth into their chosen majors with close guidance from their profs. The most popular majors are business management, education, psychology, and nursing, though Adelphi offers a cast of award-winning programs, including fine arts, performing arts, health, social welfare, environmental sciences, physical education, and communicative disorders. One sophomore chose Adelphi because of its dual degree program that will allow her to earn a BS in psychology and a master's in elementary education in just five years. The university also offers "good internship opportunities" and, for its more ambitious students, a nationally regarded honors college. To land in this esteemed program, students must meet a list of rigorous academic requirements and fare well in an interview with one of the college's deans or professors. In contrast to Adelphi's "excellent" and "approachable" faculty the administration is generally described as deceptive and distant. A sophomore offers this example: she "wrote a letter of concern" to the big man on campus, and in return, "all I received from the president was a three sentence letter." Regarding the admissions staff, a frustrated freshman quips, "Adelphi puts on a big show for its prospective students, but nothing is overexactly as they describe it." A senior from Vicenza, Italy shakes her head at comments like these: "Adelphi gives you a chance to discover who you are and what you want to be."

Life

The location of Adelphi University, in Long Island's Garden City, gives students easy access to the bustle of New York City while rooting them in "a comfortable environment that would make anyone feel at home." The problem is that many people already have homes nearby, so campus life shrinks considerably after class time ends. "The hardest time is on the weekends," notes a freshman. "Everyone goes home, so there's not much to do. It's your typical suitcase school." But on-campus students who seek out extracurricular entertainment can take advantage of the more than 60 active student organizations and a number of popular athletic programs that the university offers. Every year, a carnival called Spring-In takes over one of the greens at Adelphi and attracts a healthy portion of the student population. The university also sponsors lectures, performances, and art exhibits. When students get bored on a dead weekend on Adelphi's "dry campus" (no alcohol allowed at all, even for of-age students)" they don't have to venture too far to find "diners and bowling and pool halls and clubs." And, of course, Adelphi students—like any college students—have the uncanny ability to simply "hang out with friends" and, yes, "study."

Student Body

More than 9 out of every 10 Adelphi students come from New York, and many are commuters native to Long Island. In general, "people keep to themselves" here. "It would be better if more people lived on campus," says a student since there would be a stronger sense of belonging and a stronger impetus for conversation. If you run into the right people at Adelphi, you'll discover that students "are friendly and eager to chat with you"; turn down

> **SURVEY SAYS . . .**
> Diverse students interact
> Students are happy. Classes are small
> Instructors are good teachers

22 ▪ THE BEST NORTHEASTERN COLLEGES

---

another corridor, and you may get the impression that "students here are about as friendly as rabid dogs." Some praise the diverse student body, made up of "people from many different countries and cultures," but the ladies of Adelphi are concerned with the comparatively small number of guys on campus—a mere 30 percent. "More boys," pleads a female business major. Tellingly, none of the fellas complain.

ADMISSIONS

Very important factors considered by the admissions committee include: secondary school record. Important factors considered include: class rank, standardized test scores, essay, extracurricular activities, talent/ability, character/personal qualities, and volunteer work. Other factors considered include: recommendations, interview, alumni/ae relation, and work experience. SAT I or ACT required. TOEFL required of all international applicants. High school diploma or GED is required. High school was required/recommended: 4 English recommended, 3 math recommended, 3 science recommended, 2 foreign language recommended, 4 social studies recommended.

The Inside Word

Adelphi sets its admissions standards relatively low, providing a great opportunity for the high school underachiever seeking access to quality programs. For accomplished candidates there's Adelphi's exclusive Honors College, which admits select students "with grade point averages of 3.5 or better and SAT's of 1200 or higher." Most Adelphi undergraduates originate from the immediate area; the performing arts program is one of a few here that attract students from across the nation.

FINANCIAL AID

Students should submit FAFSA and state aid form. Priority filing deadline is March 1. Need-based scholarship/grants offered: Pell, SEOC, state scholarship/grants, private scholarships, the school's own gift aid, United Negro College Fund, and Endowed, and restricted funds (donor funds) Loan aid offered: FFEL Subsidized Stafford, FFEL Unsubsidized Stafford, FFEL PLUS, Federal Perkins, Federal Nursing, and alternative loans. Federal Work-Study Program available. Institutional employment available. Applicants will be notified of awards on a rolling basis beginning on or about March 1. Off-campus job opportunities are good.

FROM THE ADMISSIONS OFFICE

"Adelphi University has a rich history, an exciting present, and a limitless future. Founded in 1896, Adelphi University is Long Island's oldest private co-educational institution of higher learning. In September 2002, Adelphi was named *Business U's* top pick in the education industry, an honor that places the university at the top of a field of 19 colleges and universities and 126 school districts on Long Island. The publication cited our increased enrollment, a new off-campus center, community outreach programs, and innovative joint degree programs. As Adelphi grows, our academic programs evolve to reflect the needs and interests of our more than 6,900 students from 40 states and more than 55 countries. Recent program additions include criminal justice administration, computer management and information sciences, and school psychology. In response to increasing enrollment, Adelphi's main 75-acre campus will include a sixth residence hall by fall 2003. Students may join Adelphi's 55-plus student organizations, including fraternities, sororities, and academic honor societies. Our student-athletes compete in 16 Division I and II intercollegiate sports as well as in an array of intramural activities. Students also benefit from Long Island's many resources, and are a 45-minute train ride from New York City. Adelphi's College of Arts and Sciences; Honors and University Colleges; Derner Institute of Advanced Psychological Studies; and Schools of Business, Education, and Social Work offer more than 100 undergraduate and graduate programs of study at our main Garden City campus and at off-campus locations in Hauppauge, Manhattan, and Poughkeepsie."

For even more information on this school, turn to page TK of the "Stats" section.

THE SCHOOLS ▪ 23

Each spread has several components. First, at the very top of the spread you will see the school's address, telephone and fax numbers for the admissions office, the telephone number for the financial aid office, and the school's website and/or e-mail address. Next, you will find the school's ratings in four categories: Quality of Life, Academics, Admissions, and Financial Aid, which are described further below. Then you will see our "Survey Says . . ." bubble and the first three sections—"Academics," "Life," and "Student Body"—which are drawn primarily from student survey responses for that particular college. Then comes the "Admissions" section with information on how the admissions office weighs the different components of your application; followed by the "Inside Word" on admissions, academics, life, or demographics at that school; "Financial Aid" application pointers; and an institution- authored message under the title "From the Admissions Office." Finally, at the end of the profile is the page number on which the school's statistical data appears. Here's an explanation of each part:

1. Contact Information

Includes school address, admissions phone and fax numbers, financial aid phone number, admissions e-mail address, and school website.

2. Quality of Life Rating

How happy students are with their lives outside the classroom. This rating is given on a scale of 80 to 99. The ratings were determined using the results of our surveys. We weighed several factors, including students' overall happiness; the beauty, safety, and location of the campus; comfort of dorms; food quality; and ease in dealing with the administration. Note that even if a school's rating is in the low 80s, it does not mean that the quality of life is horrible—there are no "failing" schools. A low ranking just means that the school placed low compared with others in our *Best* regional series. This individual rating places each college on a continuum for purposes of comparing all colleges within this edition of the series only. Though similar, these ratings are not intended to be compared directly to those within any other edition, as our ratings computations are refined and change somewhat annually.

3. Fire Safety Rating

This rating measures how well prepared a school is to prevent or respond to campus fires, specifically in residence halls, on a scale of 60-99.

We asked all the schools we annually collect data from to answer several questions about their efforts to ensure fire safety for campus residents. Each school's responses to eight of those questions were considered when calculating its Fire Safety Rating. The questions were developed in consultation with the Center for Campus Fire Safety (www.campusfire.org <http://www.campusfire.org>) and cover: 1) the percentage of residence hall rooms protected by an automatic sprinkler system, 2) the percentage of residence hall rooms equipped with a smoke alarm that is connected to a supervised fire alarm system, 3) the action most often taken when a residence hall fire alarm is activated, 4) whether the school requires fire-resistance ratings on dorm room furniture, 5) the number of hours per student per year of fire prevention/evacuation training the school provides, 6) whether the school requires all students living in on-campus residences to receive fire extinguisher training, 7) whether certain fire-unsafe items or activities(e.g., candles, smoking) are banned in dorm rooms and 8) how often fire safety rules-compliance inspections are conducted in the school's residence halls.

Schools that did not report answers to any of the questions receive a Fire Safety Rating of 60*. The schools have an opportunity to update their fire safety data every year and will have their fire safety ratings re-calculated and published annually.

Each individual rating places a college on a continuum for purposes of comparing all colleges within this academic year only. Though similar, these ratings are not intended to be compared directly to those that appeared on PrincetonReview.com in any prior academic year or within any Princeton Review print publication, except for *Complete Book of Colleges, 2006 Edition* and *The Best 361 Colleges, 2006 Edition,* as our ratings computations are refined and change somewhat annually.

4. Academic Rating

On a scale of 60 to 99, how hard students work at the school and how much they get back for their efforts. The ratings are based on results of our surveys of students and administrators. Factors weighed included how many hours students study and the quality of students the school attracts; we also considered students' assessments of their professors' abilities and helpfulness. This individual rating places each college on a continuum for purposes of comparing all colleges within this edition only. Though similar, these ratings are not intended to be compared directly to those within any other edition, as our ratings computations are refined and change somewhat annually.

5. Admissions Rating

How competitive admission is at the school, on a scale of 60 to 99. This rating is determined by several factors, including the class rank of entering freshmen, their test scores, and the percentage of applicants accepted. By incorporating all these factors, our competitiveness rating adjusts for "self-selecting" applicant pools. University of Chicago, for example, has a very high competitiveness rating, even though it admits a surprisingly large proportion of its applicants. Chicago's applicant pool is self-selecting; that is, nearly all the school's applicants are exceptional students. This individual rating places each college on a continuum for purposes of comparing all colleges within this edition only. Though similar, these ratings are not intended to be compared directly to those within any other edition, as our ratings computations are refined and change somewhat annually.

6. Financial Aid Rating

Based on school-reported data on financial aid awards to students and students' satisfaction with the aid they receive as collected on our survey with the financial aid they receive. Again, this is on a scale of 60 to 99. This individual rating places each college on a continuum for purposes of comparing all colleges within this edition only. Though similar, these ratings are not intended to be compared directly to those within any other edition, as our ratings computations are refined and change somewhat annually.

Nota Bene

If a 60* appears as any school's rating, it means that the school reported so few of the rating's underlying data points by our deadline that we were unable to calculate an accurate rating for it. In such cases, the reader is advised to follow up with the school about the specific measures each rating takes into account.

7. Survey Says . . .

Our "Survey Says" list, located under the ratings on each school's two-page spread, is based entirely on the results of our student surveys. In other words, the items on this list are based on the opinions of the students we surveyed at those schools (not on any numerical analysis of library size, endowment, etc.). Items listed are those that are unusually popular or unpopular on that campus. Some of the terms that appear on the list are not entirely self-explanatory; these terms are defined below.

Diverse students interact: We asked whether students from different class and ethnic backgrounds interacted frequently and easily. When students' collective response is "yes," the heading "Diverse students interact" appears on the list. When student response indicates there are not many interactions between students from different class and ethnic backgrounds, the heading "Students are cliquish" appears on the list.

Cheating: We asked students how prevalent cheating is at their school. If students reported cheating to be rare, "No one cheats" shows up on the list.

Students are happy: This category reflects student responses to the question "Overall, how happy are you with your school?"

TAs teach upper-level classes: At some large universities, you'll continue to be taught by teaching assistants even in your upper-level courses. It is safe to assume that when "Lots of TAs teach upper-level courses" appears on the list, TAs also teach a disproportionate number of intro courses as well.

Students are very religious or **Students aren't religious:** We asked students how religious they and their peers are. Their responses are reflected in this category.

Diverse student body: We asked students whether their student body is made up of a variety of ethnic groups. This category reflects their answers, and shows up as "Diversity lacking on campus" or "Ethnic diversity on campus."

Town-gown relations: We asked students whether they got along with local residents; their answers are reflected by this category.

7. Academics, Life, and Student Body
The first three sections summarize the results of the surveys we distributed to students at the school. The "Academics" section reports how hard students work and how satisfied they are with the education they are getting. It also often tells you which academic departments our respondents rated favorably. Student opinion regarding administrative departments often works its way into this section, as well. The "Life" section describes life outside the classroom and addresses questions ranging from "How nice is the campus?" and "How comfortable are the dorms?" to "How popular are fraternities and sororities?" The "Student Body" section tells you about what type of student the school usually attracts and how the students view the level of interaction between various groups, including those of different ethnic origins. All quotes in these three sections are from students' written responses to our open-ended surveys. We choose quotes based on the accuracy with which they reflect our overall survey results for that school.

8. Admissions
This section tells you what aspects of your application are most important to the school's admissions officers. It also lists the high school curricular prerequisites for applicants, which standardized tests (if any) are required, and special information about the school's admissions process (e.g., Do minority students and legacies, for example, receive special consideration? Are there any unusual application requirements for applicants to special programs?).

9. The Inside Word
This section contains our own insights into each school's admissions process, student-body demographics, life on campus, or unique academic attributes.

10. Financial Aid
This section summarizes the financial aid process at the school—what forms you need and what types of aid and loans are available. (More information about need-based aid is listed under "Financial Facts" in the school's statistical profile at the back of the book.) While this section includes specific deadline dates as reported by the colleges, we strongly encourage students seeking financial aid to file all forms—federal, state, and institutional—as soon as they become available. In the world of financial aid, the early birds almost always get the best worms (provided, of course, that they're eligible for a meal!).

11. From the Admissions Office
This section contains text supplied by the colleges in response to our invitation that they use this space to "speak directly to the readers of our guide."

12. For More Information
We refer you to the page number in our school statistics section where you can find detailed statistical information for the particular school you're reading about.

SCHOOL STATISTICS

This section, located in the back of the book, contains various statistics culled from our student surveys and from questionnaires school administrators fill out. Keep in mind that not every category will appear for every school, since in some cases the information is not reported or not applicable. Please note that ratings for Quality of Life, Academics, Admissions, and Financial Aid are explained on pages 10-11.

If a school has completed each and every data field (and not all do), the headings will appear in the following order:

ADELPHI UNIVERSITY

CAMPUS LIFE

Quality of Life Rating	76
Type of school	private
Affiliation	none
Environment	urban

STUDENTS

Total undergrad enrollment	3,291
% male/female	29/71
% from out of state	11
% from public high school	75
% live on campus	26
% in (# of) fraternities	6 (3)
% in (# of) sororities	6 (6)
% African American	12
% Asian	4
% Caucasian	51
% Hispanic	7
% international	4

ACADEMICS

Academic Rating	69
Calendar	semester
Student/faculty ratio	14:1
Profs interesting rating	
Profs accessible rating	
% profs teaching UG courses	100
% classes taught by TAs	0
Avg lab size	10-19 students
Avg reg class size	20-29 students

MOST POPULAR MAJORS
social work
social sciences
business administration/management

SELECTIVITY

Admissions Rating	63
# of applicants	3,703
% of applicants accepted	66
% of acceptees attending	27

FRESHMAN PROFILE

Range SAT Verbal	460-560
Average SAT Verbal	533
Range SAT Math	460-590
Average SAT Math	536
Minimum TOEFL	550
Average HS GPA	3.3
% graduated top 10% of class	17
% graduated top 25% of class	46
% graduated top 50% of class	89

DEADLINES

Nonfall registration?	yes

FINANCIAL FACTS

Financial Aid Rating	89
Tuition	$16,100
Room and board	$7,050
Books and supplies	$1,000
Avg frosh grant	$5,553
Avg frosh loan	$3,219

294 ■ THE BEST NORTHEASTERN COLLEGES

Type of school: Whether the school is public or private.

Affiliation: Any religious order with which the school is affiliated.

Environment: Whether the campus is located in an urban, suburban, or rural setting.

Total undergrad enrollment: The total number of degree-seeking undergraduates who attend the school.

% male/female through **# countries represented:** The demographic breakdown of the full-time undergraduate student body, a listing of what percentage of the student body lives on campus, the percentage belonging to Greek organizations, and finally, the number of countries represented by the student body.

Calendar: The school's schedule of academic terms. A "semester" schedule has two long terms, usually starting in September and January. A "trimester" schedule has three terms, one usually beginning before Christmas and two after. A "quarterly" schedule has four terms, which go by very quickly: the entire term, including exams, usually lasts only nine or ten weeks. A "4-1-4" schedule is like a semester schedule, but with a month-long term in between the fall and spring semesters. (Similarly, a "4-4-1" has a short term following two longer semesters.) When a school's academic calendar doesn't match any of these traditional schedules we note that by saying "other." For schools that have "other" as their calendar, it is best to call the admissions office for details.

Student/faculty ratio: The ratio of full-time undergraduate instructional faculty members to all undergraduates.

Profs interesting rating: Based on the answers given by students to the survey question, "In general, how good are your instructors as teachers?"

Profs accessible rating: Based on the answers given by students to the survey question, "In general, how accessible are your instructors outside the classroom?"

% profs teaching UG courses: Largely self-explanatory; this category shows the percentage of professors who teach undergraduates and doesn't include any faculty whose focus is solely on research.

% classes taught by TAs: Many universities that offer graduate programs use graduate students as teaching assistants (TAs). They teach undergraduate courses, primarily at the introductory level. This category reports on the percentage of classes that are taught by TAs instead of regular faculty.

Avg lab size; Avg reg class size: College-reported figures on class size averages for regular courses and for labs/discussion sections.

Most Popular Majors: The three most highly-enrolled majors at the school.

% of applicants accepted: The percentage of applicants to which the school offered admission.

% of acceptees attending: The percentage of those who were accepted who eventually enrolled.

 # accepting a place on wait list: The number of students who decided to take a place on the wait list when offered this option.

% admitted from wait list: The percentage of applicants who opted to take a place on the wait list and were subsequently offered admission. These figures will vary tremendously from college to college and should be a consideration when deciding whether to accept a place on a college's wait list.

# of early decision applicants: The number of students who applied under the college's early decision or early action plan.

% accepted early decision: The percentage of early decision or early action applicants who were admitted under this plan. By the nature of these plans, the vast majority who are admitted wind up enrolling. (See the early decision/action description on the next page for more detail.)

Range/Average SAT Verbal, Range/Average SAT Math, Range/Average ACT Composite: The average and the middle 50 percent range of test scores for entering freshmen. Don't be discouraged from applying to the school of your choice even if your combined SAT scores are 80 or even 120 points below the average because you may still have a chance of getting in. Remember that many schools emphasize other aspects of your application (e.g., your grades, how good a match you make with the school) more heavily than test scores.

Minimum TOEFL: The minimum test score necessary for entering freshmen who are required to take the TOEFL (Test of English as a Foreign Language). Most schools will require all international students or non-native English speakers to take the TOEFL in order to be considered for admission.

Average HS GPA: We report this on a scale of 0.0 to 4.0 (occasionally colleges report averages on a 100 scale, in which case we report those figures). This is one of the key factors in college admissions. Be sure to keep your GPA as high as possible straight through until graduation from high school.

% graduated top 10%, top 25%, top 50% of class: Of those students for whom class rank was reported, the percentage of entering freshmen who ranked in the top tenth, quarter, and half of their high school classes.

Early decision/action deadlines: The deadline for submission of application materials under the early decision or early action plan. Early decision is generally for students for whom the school is a first choice. The applicant commits to attending the school if admitted; in return, the school renders an early decision, usually in December or January. If accepted, the applicant doesn't have to spend the time and money applying to other schools. In most cases, students may apply for early decision to only one school. Early action is similar to early decision, but less binding; applicants need not commit to attending the school and in some cases may apply early action to more than one school. The school, in turn, may not render a decision, choosing to defer the applicant to the regular admissions pool. Each school's guidelines are a little different, and the policies of a few of the most selective colleges in the country have changed quite dramatically recently. Some colleges offer more than one early decision cycle, so it's a good idea to call and get full details if you plan to pursue one of these options.

Early decision, early action, priority, and regular admission deadlines: The dates by which all materials must be postmarked (we'd suggest "received in the office") in order to be considered for admission under each particular admissions option/cycle for admission for the fall term.

Early decision, early action, priority, and regular admission notification: The dates by which you can expect a decision on your application under each admissions option/cycle.

Nonfall registration: Some schools will allow applicants or transfers to matriculate at times other than the fall term—the traditional beginning of the academic calendar year. Other schools will only allow you to register for classes if you can begin in the fall term. A simple "yes" or "no" in this category indicates the school's policy on nonfall registration.

Tuition, In-state tuition: The tuition at the school, or for public colleges, for a resident of the school's state. In-state tuition is usually much lower than out-of-state tuition for state-supported public schools.

Out-of-state tuition: For public colleges, the tuition for a nonresident of the school's state. This entry appears only for public colleges, since tuition at private colleges is generally the same regardless of state of residence.

Room and board: Estimated room and board costs.

Books and supplies: Estimated annual cost of necessary textbooks and/or supplies.

% frosh receiving aid: According to the school's financial aid department, the percentage of all degree-seeking freshmen who applied for financial aid, were determined to have financial need, and received any financial aid, need-based or otherwise.

% undergrads receiving aid: According to the school's financial aid department, the percentage of all degree-seeking undergrads who applied for financial aid, were determined to have financial need, and received any financial aid, need-based or otherwise.

Avg frosh grant: The average grant or scholarship amount awarded to freshmen.

Avg frosh loan: The average amount of loans disbursed to freshmen.

If you have any questions, comments, or suggestions, please contact us at Editorial Department, Admissions Services, 2315 Broadway, New York, NY 10024, or e-mail us at bookeditor@review.com. We appreciate your input and want to make our books as useful to you as they can be.

GLOSSARY

ACT: Like the SAT I but less tricky. Many schools accept either SAT or ACT scores; if you consistently get blown away by the SAT, you might want to consider taking the ACT instead.

College-prep curriculum: 16 to 18 academic credits (each credit equals a full year of a high school course), usually including 4 years of English, 3 to 4 years of social studies, and at least 2 years each of science, mathematics, and foreign language.

Core curriculum: Students at schools with core curricula must take a number of required courses, usually in such subjects as world history and/or western civilization, writing skills, and fundamental math and science.

CSS/Financial Aid PROFILE: The College Scholarship Service PROFILE, an optional financial aid form required by some colleges in addition to the FAFSA.

Distribution, or general education requirements: Students at schools with distribution requirements must take a number of courses in various subject areas, such as foreign language, humanities, natural science, and social science. Distribution requirements do not specify which courses you must take, only which types of courses.

FAFSA: The Free Application for Federal Student Aid. Schools are required by law to accept the FAFSA; some require that applicants complete at least one other form (usually a CSS/Financial Aid PROFILE or the college's own form) to be considered for financial aid.

GDI: "Goddamned independent," a term frequently used by students in fraternities and sororities to describe those not in fraternities and sororities.

Greek system, Greeks: Fraternities and sororities and their members.

Humanities: These include such disciplines as art history, drama, English, foreign languages, music, philosophy, and religion.

Merit-based grant: A scholarship (not necessarily full) given to students because of some special talent or attribute. Artists, athletes, community leaders, and geniuses are typical recipients.

Natural sciences: These include such disciplines as astronomy, biology, chemistry, genetics, geology, mathematics, physics, and zoology.

Need-based grant: A scholarship (not necessarily full) given to students because they would otherwise be unable to afford college. Student need is determined on the basis of the FAFSA. Some schools also require the CSS PROFILE and/or institutional applications.

Priority deadline: Some schools will list a deadline for admission and/or financial aid as a "priority deadline," meaning that while they will accept applications after that date, all applications received prior to the deadline are assured of getting the most thorough, and in some instances potentially more generous, appraisal possible.

RA: Residence assistant (or residential advisor). Someone, usually an upperclassman or graduate student, who supervises a floor or section of a dorm, usually in return for free room and board. RAs are responsible for enforcing the drinking and noise rules.

SAT I: A college entrance exam required by many schools.

SAT II: Subject Tests: Subject-specific exams administered by the Educational Testing Service (the SAT people). These tests are required by some, but not all, admissions offices. English Writing and Math Level I or IIC are the tests most frequently required.

Social sciences: These include such disciplines as anthropology, economics, geography, history, international studies, political science, psychology, and sociology.

Work-study: A government-funded financial aid program that provides assistance to financial aid recipients in return for work in the school's library, labs, etc.

PART 2

THE SCHOOLS

ADELPHI UNIVERSITY

LEVERMORE HALL 114, SOUTH AVENUE, GARDEN CITY, NY 11530 • ADMISSIONS: 516-877-3050
FAX: 516-877-3039 • E-MAIL: ADMISSIONS@ADELPHI.EDU • WEBSITE: WWW.ADELPHI.EDU

Ratings
Quality of Life: 64   Academic: 70   Admissions: 82   Financial Aid: 61

Academics

With "small classes" and "extremely helpful" faculty, students at Adelphi University are able to sink their teeth into their chosen majors with close guidance from their professors. The most popular majors are business management, education, psychology, and nursing, though Adelphi offers a cast of award-winning programs, including fine arts, performing arts, health, social welfare, environmental sciences, physical education, and communicative disorders. One sophomore chose Adelphi because of its dual degree program that will allow her to earn a BS in psychology and a master's in elementary education in just five years. The university also offers "good internship opportunities" and, for its more ambitious students, a nationally regarded honors college. To land in this esteemed program, students must meet a list of rigorous academic requirements and fare well in an interview with one of the college's deans or professors. In contrast to Adelphi's "excellent" and "approachable" faculty, the administration is generally described as deceptive and distant. Regarding the admissions staff, a frustrated freshman quips, "Adelphi puts on a big show for its prospective students, but nothing is ever exactly as they describe it." A senior from Vicenza, Italy, shakes her head at comments like these: "Adelphi gives you a chance to discover who you are and what you want to be."

> **SURVEY SAYS . . .**
> *Small classes*
> *Lots of beer drinking*
> *(Almost) everyone smokes*

Life

The location of Adelphi University, in Long Island's Garden City, gives students easy access to the bustle of New York City while rooting them in "a comfortable environment that would make anyone feel at home." The problem is that many people already have homes nearby, so campus life shrinks considerably after class time ends. "The hardest time is on the weekends," notes a freshman. "Everyone goes home, so there's not much to do. It's your typical suitcase school." But on-campus students who seek out extracurricular entertainment can take advantage of the more than 60 active student organizations and a number of popular athletic programs that the university offers. Every year, a carnival called Spring-In takes over one of the greens at Adelphi and attracts a healthy portion of the student population. The university also sponsors lectures, performances, and art exhibits. When students get bored on a dead weekend on Adelphi's "dry campus (no alcohol allowed at all, even for of-age students)," they don't have to venture too far to find the nightlife they're looking for in "diners and bowling and pool halls and clubs." And, of course, Adelphi students—like any college students—have the uncanny ability to simply "hang out with friends" and, yes, "study."

Student Body

More than 9 out of every 10 Adelphi students come from New York, and many are commuters native to Long Island. In general, "people keep to themselves" here. "It would be better if more people lived on campus," says a student, since there would be a stronger sense of belonging and a stronger impetus for conversation. If you run into the right people at Adelphi, you'll discover that students "are friendly and eager to chat with you"; turn down another corridor, and you may get the impression that students aren't interested in meeting anyone new. Some praise the diverse student body, made up of "people from many different countries and cultures," but the ladies of Adelphi are concerned with the comparatively small number of guys on campus—a mere 30 percent. "More boys," pleads a female business major. Tellingly, none of the fellas complain.

ADMISSIONS

Very important factors considered include: Secondary school record. *Important factors considered include.* Character/personal qualities, class rank, essays, extracurricular activities, standardized test scores, talent/ability, volunteer work. *Other factors considered include:* alumni/ae relation, interview, recommendations, work experience, SAT Reasoning or ACT required; TOEFL required of all international applicants. High school diploma is required and GED is accepted. *Academic units recommended:* 4 English, 3 math, 3 science, 2 foreign language, 4 Social Studies, History, English, Math, Science, or Foreign Language.

The Inside Word

Adelphi sets its admissions standards relatively low, providing a great opportunity for the high school underachiever seeking access to quality programs. For accomplished candidates there's Adelphi's exclusive Honors College, which admits select students "with grade point averages of 3.5 or better and SAT's of 1200 or higher." Most Adelphi undergraduates originate from the immediate area; the performing arts program is one of a few here that attract students from across the nation.

INANCIAL AID

Students should submit: FAFSA, state aid form. The Princeton Review suggests that all financial aid forms be submitted as soon as possible after January 1. *Need-based scholarships/grants offered:* Pell, SEOG, state scholarships/grants, private scholarships, the school's own gift aid, United Negro College Fund, Endowed and restricted funds (donor funds). *Loan aid offered:* FFEL Subsidized Stafford, FFEL Unsubsidized Stafford, FFEL PLUS, Federal Perkins, Federal Nursing, non-federal (private) alternative loans. Applicants will be notified of awards on a rolling basis beginning on or about 3/1. Federal Work-Study Program available. Institutional employment available. Off-campus job opportunities are good.

FROM THE ADMISSIONS OFFICE

"Adelphi University has a rich history, an exciting present, and a limitless future. Founded in 1896, Adelphi University is Long Island's oldest private co-educational institution of higher learning. In September 2002, Adelphi was named *Business LI*'s top pick in the education industry, an honor that places the university at the top of a field of 19 colleges and universities and 126 school districts on Long Island. The publication cited our increased enrollment, a new off-campus center, community outreach programs, and innovative joint degree programs. As Adelphi grows, our academic programs evolve to reflect the needs and interests of our more than 6,900 students from 40 states and more than 55 countries. Recent program additions include criminal justice administration, computer management and information sciences, and school psychology. In response to increasing enrollment, Adelphi's main 75-acre campus will include a sixth residence hall by fall 2003. Students may join Adelphi's 55-plus student organizations, including fraternities, sororities, and academic honor societies. Our student-athletes compete in 16 Division I and II intercollegiate sports as well as in an array of intramural activities. Students also benefit from Long Island's many resources, and are a 45-minute train ride from New York City. Adelphi's College of Arts and Sciences; Honors and University Colleges; Derner Institute of Advanced Psychological Studies; and Schools of Business, Education, and Social Work offer more than 100 undergraduate and graduate programs of study at our main Garden City campus and at off-campus locations in Hauppauge, Manhattan, and Poughkeepsie."

For even more information on this school, turn to page 460 of the "Stats" section.

ALBRIGHT COLLEGE

PO Box 15234, 13th and Bern Streets, Reading, PA 19612-5234 • Admissions: 800-252-1856
Fax: 610-921-7294 • E-mail: ALBRIGHT@ALB.EDU • Website: WWW.ALBRIGHT.EDU

Ratings
Quality of Life: 70   Academic: 84   Admissions: 79   Financial Aid: 74

Academics

SURVEY SAYS . . .
Small classes
Students are friendly
Frats and sororities dominate social scene
(Almost) everyone smokes

For nearly half a century, Albright College has been a national leader in interdisciplinary education, encouraging its students to combine fields of study to augment an existing major or to create a new one. That tradition continues today; nearly half of all Albright students graduate with interdisciplinary, combined, or multiple majors. This "individualized education" affords students "a great deal of opportunities to conduct their own research" in order to foster "a new way of thinking" (this, not coincidentally, is the school's motto). One senior writes that his interdisciplinary program of study taught him "to 'think outside the box' in all of the areas of academe." The flip side to such broad-based learning is occasionally "missing out on some specialized courses;" but overall, students are grateful to receive a "well-rounded education with its basis in real-life, people-to-people interaction." Albright's approach works in part because "you really get individualized attention" here, thanks to "small class sizes" and professors who "treat you with respect and the level of responsibility that comes with being a college student." Experiential learning is also part of the mix; internships, community placements, and independent studies enhance Albright's academic offerings. Students here give top marks to the theater, English, philosophy, business, biology/premed, and psychology departments. High on their wish list is a facilities upgrade; writes a junior: "The conditions of the school are not good. The dormitories need fixing up; maintenance and computers are very slow; and there are not enough classrooms, teachers, or classes offered each semester."

Life

Underclassmen at Albright have no choice but to get out of their rooms and absorb a little culture every now and then; the school's "experience event" program requires students to attend 16 such events (which include concerts, theatrical productions, art exhibitions, panel discussions, and stand-up comedy acts) during their first two years here. Most seem to enjoy these events; but a few cynics suggest that attendance is mandatory because the events "aren't of interest." Students report that "life on campus is pretty active during the week with all the organizational stuff." Greek life is also "pretty popular on campus," and the college offers many "sports nights, intramurals, formals, coffeehouse/poetry readings, dances, and day trips—all available for free or at a nominal fee." On weekends, "we plan things so people don't feel that they have to go home, but we still have those people—especially freshman—who run home sometimes." Additionally, because of the school's "proximity to Philadelphia and King of Prussia," students always have the option of partaking in "great night life."

Student Body

Students write that "it's kind of hard" to characterize "a typical kid" because "everybody is involved in so many different things." The "outgoing and happy" undergrads here are "usually very approachable." Students describe their schoolmates as "involved" and "determined to succeed." While many often belong to small "core groups" defined by field of study and organizational affiliations, a junior reminds us that "the majority of the groups interact with one another on a regular basis, and students can belong to a number of groups at the same time." Fortunately, "the popular feeling on the campus is that no matter what type of person you are or wish to be, there is somewhere that you will fit in and people that will welcome you." Remarks a senior: "It is fun to get to know the students here at Albright."

ADMISSIONS

Very important factors considered include: Secondary school record. *Important factors considered include:* Character/personal qualities, class rank, essays, recommendations, standardized test scores. *Other factors considered include:* Alumni/ae relation, extracurricular activities, talent/ability, volunteer work, work experience. SAT Reasoning or ACT required. High school diploma is required, and GED is accepted. *Academic units required:* 4 English, 3 math, 3 science (2 science lab), 2 foreign language, 2 history, 1 social studies, 1 academic elective. *Academic units recommended:* 4 English, 4 math, 4 science (3 science lab), 3 foreign language, 3 history, 1 social studies, 1 academic elective.

The Inside Word

Albright is currently pursuing a major capital campaign that should enable it to expand program offerings and attract more quality applicants in the not-too-distant future. The next few years may provide a window for a few less-qualified students to sneak in under the radar, but after that, expect admissions criteria at this fine liberal arts school to grow more rigorous.

FINANCIAL AID

Students should submit: FAFSA. The Princeton Review suggests that all financial aid forms be submitted as soon as possible after 1/1. *Need-based scholarships/grants offered:* Pell, SEOG, state scholarships/grants, private scholarships, the school's own gift aid. *Loan aid offered:* FFEL Subsidized Stafford, FFEL Unsubsidized Stafford, FFEL PLUS, Federal Perkins, private educational loans. Applicants will be notified of awards on or about 2/8. Federal Work-study Program available. Institutional employment available. Off-campus job opportunities are good.

FROM THE ADMISSIONS OFFICE

"**Academics:** Founded in 1856, Albright College is recognized as a national leader in interdisciplinary study. Nearly half of our students opt for combined or interdisciplinary majors . . . . while still graduating in four years. Last year, students chose 143 different combinations of majors—from art/biology and psychology/business to education/theatre and sociology/Latin American studies. But whether students select one major or combine fields, Albright's faculty work closely with students to create experiences that reflect individual talents, interests, and career goals.

"**Atmosphere**: Albright College is renowned for its openness and warmth. Students who visit Albright rate it as one of the friendliest small liberal arts colleges anywhere. Albright students have a strong sense of community, based on friendliness, tolerance, and mutual support. These are the common ties that bind the community and make Albright an easy place for students to be heard and have an impact.

"**Outcomes:** An Albright education is designed to help students develop their individual voices and visions and become skilled problem solvers and communicators. Albright graduates leave with the knowledge, skills, and confidence to succeed.

"**Location:** The Albright campus is located one hour west of Philadelphia in a tree-lined suburb of Reading, Pennsylvania, a metropolitan area of 250,000.

"**Scholarships and Financial Aid:** Albright is pledged to help make its education affordable. This is evident in Albright's inclusion in Barron's Best Buys in College Education and in our generous need-based financial aid awards and numerous merit scholarships (ranging from $5,000 per year to full tuition)."

For even more information on this school, turn to page 460 of the "Stats" section.

ALFRED UNIVERSITY

ALUMNI HALL, ONE SAXON DRIVE, ALFRED, NY 14802-1205 • ADMISSIONS: 607-871-2115
FAX: 607-871-2198 • FINANCIAL AID: 607-871-2159 • E-MAIL: ADMWWW@ALFRED.EDU • WEBSITE: WWW.ALFRED.EDU

Ratings
Quality of Life: 85   Academic: 83   Admissions: 74   Financial Aid: 92

Academics

Alfred University is a private school with a twist. The School of Engineering and the School of Art and Design receive state funding, resulting in reduced tuition for both New Yorkers and out-of-state students (although state residents receive a larger discount for the art school). The state-funded programs are "what Alfred is known for." The School of Engineering is famous for its glass and ceramics

> **SURVEY SAYS . . .**
> *Small classes*
> *Campus feels safe*
> *Frats and sororities are unpopular or nonexistent*

program and is, in fact, one of the few schools in the nation offering a degree in ceramic engineering. Students don't attend Alfred only for the art and engineering programs; they are also drawn to the business and English departments. Alfred provides a cozy community that students, professors, and administrators enjoy. One student says, "There is excellent interaction between students and professors; and with small classes, the faculty can devote more time to each individual student." Alfred is the kind of place where "about half our professors, maybe more, want to go by first name." One student reports, "Within a few months of being here, I had met the president of the university and the chairman of the board of trustees. I am now on a first-name basis with the president and the dean of students. I babysit the dean of students' kids." No wonder students tell us that "the level of personal connection here, all across the board, is exceptional."

Life

Small-town life can be a rough go for college students, especially in the wintry landscape of upstate New York, but fortunately "Alfred provides desperately needed entertainment. The school seems to realize that its position in the world (an hour away from civilization) requires some extra effort as far as keeping the students from going stir-crazy, and they really pull through." The school "is really good about bringing different performers and movies into town every weekend," while "art shows, visiting lecturers in every division," and "over a hundred clubs and activities" help round out the schedule. There are also activities that students enjoy in the snow, since "[they] get enough of it." One student explains, "Traying, or stealing dining hall trays and riding them down the dangerously steep hill between upper and lower campus, is a perennial favorite. I've seen [people do it in the] nude, in subzero weather, too." Even with all these activities, the small-town experience does occasionally get to people. One student writes, "Alfred is not without its small-town quirks. One of our theater professors, who has lived several places but is a devoted Alfred-ite, is throwing the town's one stoplight a thirtieth birthday party this summer." Students with cars remind us that "within thirty to sixty minutes' radius are most of the major entertainments you could want—movies, a mall or two, bowling, places to volunteer if you're so inclined, restaurants, and places to cut loose and dance."

Student Body

Alfred University, students tell us, "is like a bizarro high school where the artsy kids outnumber the football players. There are so many different social groups here. You have sporty kids, walking tapestries (dreaded neo-hippies), artsy indie rock kids, D&D [Dungeons and Dragons] kids, intellectuals, [and] engineering nerds. They tend to be somewhat cliquey, but everyone can find their place in Alfred." While some may say "it's not all artsy here," there are plenty of art students, and they tend to stick out in the crowd—when they're anywhere near the crowd, that is. "You don't always see a lot of them because they keep really strange hours," explains one nonartsy student. "Minorities and LGBT kids are well-represented on campus and in campus leadership positions," and "there's even peaceful coexisting with (neighboring) Alfred State. We rib them, and they probably rib us, but we have [Alfred] State kids in some of our extracurricular groups, and until I was told they weren't [Alfred] University kids, I would never have known the difference."

ADMISSIONS

Very important factors considered include: Character/personal qualities, class rank, extracurricular activities, recommendations, secondary school record. *Important factors considered include:* Essays, standardized test scores, volunteer work, work experience. *Other factors considered include:* Interview, minority status, talent/ability. SAT Reasoning or ACT required. TOEFL required of all international applicants. High school diploma is required, and GED is accepted. *Academic units required:* 4 English, 2 math, 2 science (2 science lab), 2 social studies. *Academic units recommended:* 4 math, 3 science (3 science lab), 3 social studies.

The Inside Word

There's no questioning the high quality of academics at Alfred, especially in their internationally known ceramics program. Still, the university's general lack of name recognition and relatively isolated campus directly affect both the applicant pool and the number of admitted students who enroll, and thus keeps selectivity relatively low for a school of its caliber. (The exception is clearly in ceramic arts, where candidates will face a very rigorous review.) If you're a back-to-nature type looking for a challenging academic environment, Alfred could be just what the doctor ordered. And if you're a standout academically, you may find that they're generous with financial aid, too—they are serious about competing for good students.

FINANCIAL AID

Students should submit: FAFSA, institution's own financial aid form, state aid form, noncustodial (divorced/separated) parents' statement, business/farm supplement. The Princeton Review suggests that all financial aid forms be submitted as soon as possible after 1/1. *Need-based scholarships/grants offered:* Pell, SEOG, state scholarships/grants, private scholarships, the school's own gift aid. *Loan aid offered:* FFEL Subsidized Stafford, FFEL Unsubsidized Stafford, FFEL PLUS, Federal Perkins, college/university loans from institutional funds, private alternative loans. Applicants will be notified of awards on a rolling basis beginning on or about 2/15. Federal Work-study Program available. Institutional employment available. Off-campus job opportunities are poor.

FROM THE ADMISSIONS OFFICE

"The admissions process at Alfred University is the foundation for the per-sonal attention that a student can expect from this institution. Each applicant is evaluated individually and can expect genuine, personal attention at Alfred University."

For even more information on this school, turn to page 460 of the "Stats" section.

ALLEGHENY COLLEGE

OFFICE OF ADMISSIONS, MEADVILLE, PA 16335 • ADMISSIONS: 800-521-5293
FAX: 814-337-0431 • FINANCIAL AID: 800-835-7780 • E-MAIL: ADMISS@ALLEGHENY.EDU • WEBSITE: WWW.ALLEGHENY.EDU

Ratings
Quality of Life: 76   Academic: 88   Admissions: 89   Financial Aid: 87

Academics

For students ready to hit the books hard, Allegheny College offers great rewards; explains one undergrad, "We have a huge workload here, with a lot of reading and a ton of writing. It really prepares you for graduate school and taking many upper-level courses at one time." The experience also benefits those looking to move directly into the business world after graduation because of its "great opportunities in experiential learning." As one student puts it, "Allegheny's strengths are its ample amounts of opportunity to excel both in and out of the classroom. The college provides numerous internship opportunities in addition to solid career services." Before they can reap the rewards of their degrees, though, Allegheny undergrads must complete a rigorous curriculum, one they praise for its "openness to individuality. It gave me the option of self-designing a major." Professors at Allegheny "are not only personally interested in you as a student, but in your personal well-being as well. You can't skip a class without a professor noticing and worrying about you, and you can be sure that they will go out of their way to help you whether or not you fall behind in class or are having a personal problem." Students say a larger school could not provide this kind of "professor–student connection." Administrators also integrate themselves wholly into the school community. Notes one undergrad, "Students will greet the dean or president from across campus and there is a great deal of interaction between administrators and students. No one is too important to make personal connections with students."

> **SURVEY SAYS . . .**
> *Small classes*
> *Lab facilities are great*
> *Athletic facilities are great*
> *Students are friendly*
> *Students are happy*
> *Lots of beer drinking*

Life

A heavy workload keeps Allegheny students very busy during the week, so much so that, come the weekend, most look for a way "to relieve the stress caused by the demands of the school." Sometimes that involves drinking, sometimes not. Students report that "provisions by the school to crack down on off-campus parties in the past year have made social life pretty dull," making it harder—though certainly not impossible—to blow off some steam with a brew or four. Because of the new policy enforcement, "the greater portion of the campus community is more secluded from one another, with smaller groups of friends forming." This is especially true in the winter months, "when many students seem to hibernate," or hole up in the coffee house, "a hotspot for concerts, open mic nights, and general chillin,' the school's newly renovated and expanded campus center has also increased late night programming." The campus is considerably more active "in the early fall and late spring months, during which campus-wide activities from sports to college-run activities become much more common." Hometown Meadville—which some describe as "a bit backward"—is a quiet, low- to middle-income town, some of whose locals "resent the students who pay all this money to go to school and drive around in nice cars and wear nice clothes," according to Allegheny undergrads. As a result, students "band together to fight boredom" and "head up to Erie to go shopping or to Port Erie's Bayfront district for nightlife." Pittsburgh is an occasional destination, "but only for concerts or other big events."

Student Body

"Everyone is involved in a variety of activities" at Allegheny, students report. "No one is just involved in religious life or just involved in Greek life. Therefore, it's not hard to fit in somewhere." Agrees one undergrad, "We have athletes, sorority and fraternity members, very religious people, very artsy dreadlocked students, students heavily involved with the radio station and music department, etc. There are so many things to get involved in that it's hard to classify students." A common thread is that on this "politically opinionated campus, people can get pretty heated. Political and philosophical debates randomly occur." When not involved in a hot-button conversation, just about everyone "is studious to the point that it nags them during the week."

ADMISSIONS

Very important factors considered include: Class rank, secondary school record. *Important factors considered include:* Character/personal qualities, extracurricular activities, interview, recommendations, standardized test scores. *Other factors considered include:* Alumni/ae relation, essays, geographical residence, minority status, talent/ability, volunteer work, work experience. SAT Reasoning or ACT required. TOEFL required of all international applicants. High school diploma is required, and GED is accepted. *Academic units required:* 4 English, 3 math, 3 science, 2 foreign language, 3 social studies, 1 academic elective.

The Inside Word

Don't be deceived by the fairly high admit rate here—Allegheny draws a strong pool of academically well-qualified applicants, and candidate evaluation is rigorous and personalized. The admissions staff strongly recommends campus visits and interviews; students who visit the campus prior to Allegheny's application deadline receive application fee waivers. Given the highly personalized nature of candidate evaluation, we'd suggest both the visit and taking the most challenging courses in high school to be as competitive in the applicant pool as possible.

FINANCIAL AID

Students should submit: FAFSA. The Princeton Review suggests that all financial aid forms be submitted as soon as possible after 1/1. *Need-based scholarships/grants offered:* Pell, SEOG, state scholarships/grants, private scholarships, the school's own gift aid. *Loan aid offered:* FFEL Subsidized Stafford, FFEL Unsubsidized Stafford, FFEL PLUS, Federal Perkins, state loans, private loans from commercial lenders. Applicants will be notified of awards on a rolling basis beginning on or about 3/1. Federal Work-study Program available. Institutional employment available. Off-campus job opportunities are excellent.

FROM THE ADMISSIONS OFFICE

"We're proud of Allegheny's beautiful campus and cutting-edge technologies. And we know that our professors are leading scholars who pride themselves even more on being among the best teachers in the United States. But it's our students who make Allegheny the unique and special place that it is.

"Allegheny attracts students with unusual combinations of interests, skills, and talents. How do we characterize them? Although it's impossible to label our students, they do share some common characteristics. You'll find an abiding passion for learning and life, a spirit of camaraderie, and shared inquiry that spans across individuals as well as areas of study. And you'll see over and over again such a variety of interests and passions and skills that, after a while, those unusual combinations don't seem so unusual at all.

"Allegheny is not for everybody. If you find labels reassuring, if you're looking for a narrow technical training, if you're in search of the shortest distance between point A and point B, then perhaps another college will be better for you.

"But, if you recognize that everything you experience between points A and B will make you appreciate point B that much more; if you've noticed that when life gives you a choice between two things, you're tempted to answer both or simply yes; if you start to get excited because you sense there is a college willing to echo the resounding YES then we look forward to meeting you."

For even more information on this school, turn to page 461 of the "Stats" section.

AMERICAN UNIVERSITY

4400 MASSACHUSETTS AVENUE, NW, WASHINGTON, DC 20016-8001 • ADMISSIONS: 202-885-6000
FAX: 202-885-1025 • FINANCIAL AID: 202-885-6100 • E-MAIL: AFA@AMERICAN.EDU • WEBSITE: WWW.AMERICAN.EDU

Ratings
Quality of Life: 85   **Academic:** 84   **Admissions:** 93   **Financial Aid:** 80

Academics

"So many academic and social opportunities" await one at American University, thanks in large part to its location in northwest Washington, DC. Students have to be self-starters to take advantage of those opportunities, however; no one will hold your hand and accompany you to the threshold of learning here. "If you know what you want out of American University (AU), you will get it," explains one student. Professors ("about half are brilliant, and half are just okay," reports one undergrad) often have multiple commitments beyond campus. "We have lots of adjuncts who have super-professional experiences, but who are inaccessible outside class," warns one student. Adds another, "Professors are not always approachable. Some have an attitude with students if they ask for help [or] if students do not agree with their views." Students don't feel completely ignored on the matter of their instructors, though, as "the school really takes the students' feedback on the professors very seriously," which means bad teachers often quietly and mysteriously disappear. And the faculty has plenty of bright lights, dedicated teachers who "are really amicable and cordial and are willing to help students. And many are leaders in their fields." Students generally dislike the administration, perceiving it as "much more concerned with the outward appearance of the school" than with current students' concerns. Some are willing to concede, however, "Although our president rules the school like a banana republic, he has brought about much-needed improvements in the community." The business department draws kudos, though science facilities reportedly need some TLC. The study abroad program and internship opportunities earn students' universal praise.

> **SURVEY SAYS . . .**
> *Small classes*
> *Students love Washington, DC*
> *Great off-campus food*
> *Campus feels safe*
> *Political activism is popular*
> *(Almost) everyone smokes*

Life

"DC is a great city to go to school," AU students agree. "The city is the school's most valuable asset; it's got a life of its own, in contrast to many college towns. It really makes going to school here exciting." Students love Dupont Circle and the nearby neighborhood of Adams Morgan ("a big attention drawer because there are so many restaurants, clubs, bars, and poetry places") but find plenty to do all over town. As one student told us, "There are so many other things to do in DC! There are dozens of clubs and hundreds of unique restaurants, many of which specialize in cultural goods." Another enthusiastic undergraduate adds, "It is not possible to go a single day without experiencing at least one aspect of a different culture." The city picks up the slack for the AU campus, which is often dormant: "Campus life itself isn't as exciting as a Big Ten school or something," concedes one student, "but that's because we're in a big city that actually has places to go [to] and hang out [in]." The campus is officially dry, a fact that further encourages this outwardly oriented student body to look for gathering places beyond the campus gates. With DC at the university's doorstep, partying away from school is a no-brainer. Students note that this is the type of campus where "we're more likely to attend Election Night parties than Super Bowl parties."

Student Body

The "idealistic, smart, concerned" students at American University are "extremely politically involved. People here are passionate about various issues, due in no small part to our location." Most are to the left end of the political spectrum; one disaffected undergrad writes, "The typical student is a liberal tree-hugger who thinks he/she has an open mind but actually doesn't." A large international population ("lots of diplomats' kids"), along with smaller minority populations, engenders a diversity that is "wonderful; it makes political science classes quite invigorating!" When we asked what the typical American University student was like, we typically got one of two responses. Some balked at the request: "This school is way too diverse to pinpoint the typical student," while others described a white kid from the "middle to upper middle class, interested in international relations, [who] likes trying new things [and is] interested in community service."

ADMISSIONS

Very important factors considered include: Secondary school record, standardized test scores. *Important factors considered include:* Class rank, essays, extracurricular activities, recommendations, volunteer work. *Other factors considered include:* Alumni/ae relation, character/personal qualities, geographical residence, interview, minority status, talent/ability, work experience. SAT Reasoning or ACT required. TOEFL required of all international applicants. High school diploma is required, and GED is accepted. *Academic units required:* 4 English, 3 math, 2 science (2 science lab), 2 foreign language, 2 social studies, 3 academic electives. *Academic units recommended:* 4 English, 4 math, 4 science (2 science lab), 3 foreign language, 4 social studies, 1 academic elective.

The Inside Word

Washington, DC, is indeed a tremendous attraction for students who aspire to careers in government, politics, and other areas of public service. Georgetown skims most of the cream of the crop off the top of this considerable pool of prospective students, but American does quite nicely. Because the university is nationally known, it also has formidable competition outside its own backyard, and, as a result, its yield of admits who enroll is on the low side. This necessitates a higher admit rate than one might expect at a school with considerable academic strength and an impressively credentialed faculty. If you're an active leadership type with a strong academic record the admissions process should be fairly painless—American offers a great opportunity for a quality educational experience without having to plead for admission.

FINANCIAL AID

Students should submit: FAFSA, institution's own financial aid form. Regular filing deadline 2/15. The Princeton Review suggests that all financial aid forms be submitted as soon as possible after 1/1. *Need-based scholarships/grants offered:* Pell, SEOG, state scholarships/grants, private scholarships, the school's own gift aid. Academic merit scholarships: Presidential scholarships, dean's scholarships, leadership scholarships, Phi Theta Kappa scholarships (transfers only), tuition exchange scholarships, United Methodist scholarships, and other private/restricted scholarships are awarded by the Undergraduate Admissions Office. Most scholarships do not require a separate application and are renewable for up to 3 years if certain criteria are met. *Loan aid offered:* Direct Subsidized Stafford, Direct Unsubsidized Stafford, Direct PLUS, FFEL PLUS, Federal Perkins, college/university loans from institutional funds. Applicants will be notified of awards on or about 4/1. Federal Work-study Program available. Institutional employment available. Off-campus job opportunities are excellent.

FROM THE ADMISSIONS OFFICE

"Ideas, action, and service—at AU, you interact regularly with decision makers and leaders in every profession and corner of the globe. You'll be academically challenged in a rich multicultural environment. Our expert teaching faculty provide a strong liberal arts education, characterized by small classes, the use of cutting-edge technology, and an interdisciplinary curriculum in the arts, education, humanities, social sciences, and sciences. Not just a political town, Washington, DC offers a variety of research, internship, and community service opportunities in every field. Our AU Abroad Program, with over 50 international locations, lets you expand your studies into international settings. The Princeton Review selected AU for the 2005 edition of *America's Best Value Colleges*. AU was one of 77 schools, and the only one from DC, selected as a 'best value' for its combination of outstanding academics, moderate tuition, and financial aid packages."

For even more information on this school, turn to page 461 of the "Stats" section.

AMHERST COLLEGE

Campus Box 2231, PO Box 5000, Amherst, MA 01002 • Admissions: 413-542-2328
Fax: 413-542-2040 • Financial Aid: 413-542-2296 • E-mail: admissions@amherst.edu • Website: www.amherst.edu

Ratings

Quality of Life: 97   **Academic:** 98   **Admissions:** 98   **Financial Aid:** 99

Academics

Amherst College goes against the national trend of imposing a regimented undergraduate curriculum and does not make its students take a single required course. Students approvingly say, "The requirement-free curriculum has been wonderful. Nearly everyone experiments in a range of departments on their own anyhow, and except in a few large introductory classes, the students are always there by

> **SURVEY SAYS . . .**
> *Small classes*
> *Athletic facilities are great*
> *Campus feels safe*
> *Students are happy*

choice." It takes a special type of student body to handle this large amount of academic freedom, but fortunately Amherst has just such an undergraduate population. As one student explains, "There is no such thing as 'too intellectual' here. I came to college dreaming of late-night intellectual discussions that would degenerate into fantastical idealism or dramatic fanatical stances, and I got them." Students enjoy a close academic community with "insanely accessible professors. They live across the street from the dorm and have students over on a regular basis. In fact, there is a program in which you can take them out for a meal financed by the school." Professors "do an excellent job [of] balancing their outside research and projects with their teachings. Their priority seems to be with the students." Amherst also boasts an "amazing alumni network." One student adds, "All my friends have gotten jobs doing what they want, where they want."

Life

Amherst is an "awesome college town" in "an area full of education and culture," especially since there are many colleges and universities nearby. Course work can be grueling: "Generally, people work during the week and party on the weekends. But partying comes in all forms. You can go to a keg party, or you can go to a coffeehouse. There's something for everyone and always something that doesn't involve drinking." Because Amherst lacks a Greek scene, "Social life is much more varied than at most other schools. Parties are always happening at different locations with different themes and sources of entertainment, and everyone's always welcome." Campus activities include "movies, plays, a cappella concerts (we are the singing school!), lectures, and meetings. There's also a movie theater nearby that people go to a lot." Also, "most people participate in team or club sports," and extracurricular clubs are popular. One undergraduate says, "With so many clubs and activities and [an] overall accepting atmosphere here at Amherst, it's hard not to fit in." Students love that Amherst "is a very close-knit campus. There is only one dining hall and everyone has to purchase a meal plan, so everyone pretty much eats every meal there. This allows you to see and interact with people every day." They're less pleased with the local weather. Students warn, "It can get pretty cold in the winter, so it takes more willpower to go out."

Student Body

Amherst is home to "two different types of students. One [type of student] is rich, white, and preppy. The other [type of student] is just a normal, funky, smart kid." Both groups are very bright. At Amherst "[students] are surrounded by the future leaders of the country and benefit from their ideas in class discussion[s], during lab[s], or over tea at the local coffee shop. There's always someone to debate with and always someone to help you out." The population boasts "a lot of racial diversity, and everyone interacts well together." One student agrees, "Students of different backgrounds tend to mix a lot more here than elsewhere." Politically, "most students are moderate-left wingers. However, there is a noticeable conservative contingent on campus." Many are "surprised to find how many student athletes there are. It seems that nearly everyone is on one of our varsity, club, or intramural teams or played in high school."

Human Values, Center for, Marx Hall, G2
Information: Orange Key Guide Service,
    Frist Campus Center, G3; Public Safety,
    Stanhope Hall, E1; Communications Office,
    22 Chambers St., D1
International Center, Frist Campus Center, G3
Jewish Life, Center for, G3
Library, Firestone, F1
Limousine (to Newark Airport), Nassau Inn,
    Palmer Square, E1
Lost and found, Public Safety, Stanhope Hall, E1
Ombuds Office, 179 Nassau St., G1
Parking: visitor, garage, lot 7, E5 (campus
    shuttle stop); parking information, Public
    Safety, Stanhope Hall, E1
President, Nassau Hall, E1
Princeton Alumni Weekly, 194 Nassau St., H1
Princeton Institute for the Science and
    Techology of Materials, Bowen Hall, I2
Princeton Weekly Bulletin (and calendar
    of events), Communications Office,
    22 Chambers St., D1
Prospect House (and Gardens), F2

Provost, Nassau Hall, E1
Registrar, West College, E2
Restrooms: Frist Campus Center, G3;
    Stanhope Hall, E1; West College, E2
Security, Public Safety, Stanhope Hall, E1
Snack bar, Frist Campus Center, G3
Taxi, Nassau St., E1
Teacher Preparation, Program in,
    41 William St., H2
Telephones: Frist Campus Center, G3;
    Nassau Street, E1; Stanhope Hall, E1
Theatre: Berlind, D4; Garden, G1; Intime,
    Murray-Dodge Hall, F2; McCarter, D4
Tours, Orange Key Guide Service,
    Frist Campus Center, G3
Train station (Dinky), D4
Treasurer, New South, E4
Women's Center, Frist Campus Center, G3
Woodrow Wilson School of Public and
    International Affairs, Robertson Hall, G2

Princeton University operator: 609-258-3000
Emergency: 911

Fisher Hall, H2
Fitzrandolph Observatory, J5
Forbes College Addition, D5
Forbes College, C5
Foulke Hall, D2
Frick Laboratory, G2
Friend Center, H1
Frist Campus Center, G3
Gauss Hall, F4
Graduate College-Old, B5
Graduate College-New, A4
Green Hall, G1
Guyot Hall, G3
Hamilton Hall, D1
Henry Hall, D3
Henry House, F1
Holder Hall, E1
Hoyt Laboratory, H1
Jadwin Gymnasium, I6
Jadwin Hall, H4
Jewish Life, Center for, G3
Joline Hall, D1
Jones Hall, F3
Lenz Tennis Center, F6
Little Hall, E2
Lockhart Hall, D2

Lourie-Love Hall, F4
Maclean House, E1
MacMillan Building, E5
Madison Hall, D1
Marx Hall, G2
McCarter Theatre, D4
McCormick Hall, F2
McCosh Hall, G2
McCosh Health Center, G3
McDonnell Hall, H4
Moffett Laboratory, G4
Mudd Library, I2
Murray-Dodge Hall, F2
Nassau Hall, E1
New South Building, E4
Notestein Hall, H3
Palmer House, C1
Parking Garage (Campus), E5
Parking Garage (Prospect
    Avenue), J2
Patton Hall, F3
Peyton Hall, H4
Princeton Stadium, I4
Princeton University Press, H2
Prospect House, F3

Pyne Hall, E3
Robertson Hall, G2
Schultz Laboratory, G4
Scully Hall, F4
Shea Rowing Center, G1
Spelman Halls, E3
Springdale Golf Club, C4
Stanhope Hall, E1
Stephens Fitness Center, E3
Tennis Pavilion, E4
Thomas Laboratory, G4
Train Station (Dinky), D4
Undergraduate Dormitory, F5
University Store, D2
Von Neumann Hall, J2
Walker Hall, F3
Wallace Hall, H2
Warehouse, D4
West College, E2
Whig Hall, F2
Wilcox Hall, F4
Witherspoon Hall, E2
Woolworth Music Center, G3
Wu Hall, F4
Wyman House, A5

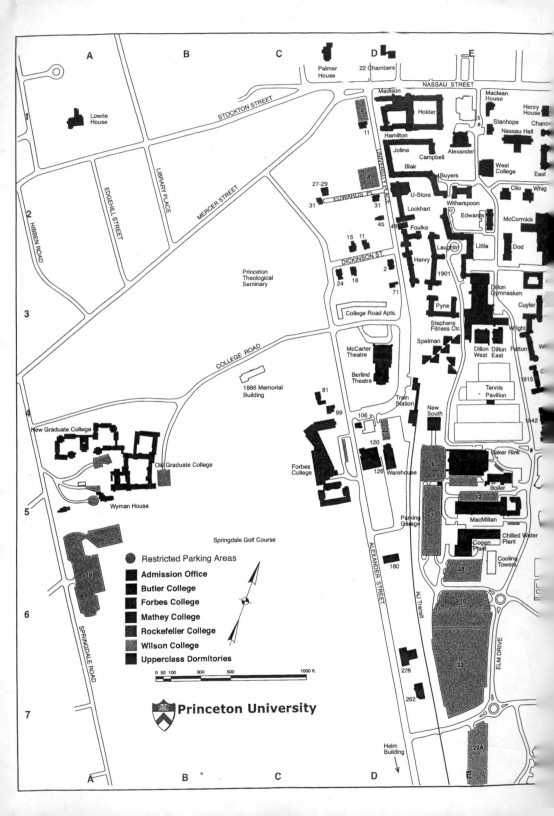

Princeton University

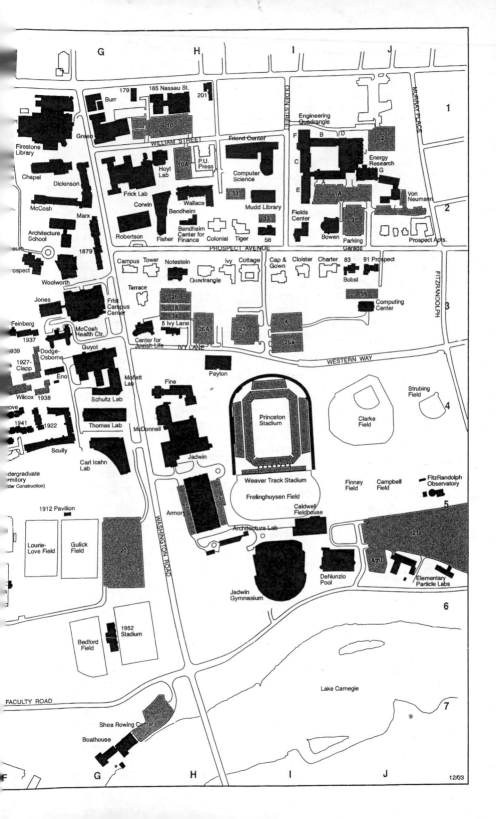

PrincetonUniversity

Administration: Dean of Admission,
  West College, E2; VP for Campus Life,
  Nassau Hall, E1; Dean of the Chapel,
  Murray-Dodge Hall, F2; of the College,
  West College, E2; of the Faculty, Nassau
  Hall, E1; of the Graduate School, Nassau
  Hall, E1; of Undergraduate Students,
  West College, E1
Admission: undergraduate, West College,
  E2; graduate, Nassau Hall, E1
Alumni Council, Maclean House, E1
Architecture, School of, G2
Art Museum, F2
Athletic event ticket office,
  Jadwin Gym, I6
Auditoriums: Betts, School of
  Architecture, G2; Dodds, Robertson
  Hall, G2;
  Helm, 50 McCosh Hall, G2;
  Richardson, Alexander Hall, E1;
  Taplin, Fine Hall, H4;
  Wood, 10 McCosh Hall, G2
Bookstore, Princeton University Store
  (U-Store), D2

Bus tickets, newsstand kiosk,
  Palmer Square, E1
Career Services, 201 Nassau St., H1
Community and State Affairs,
  22 Chambers St., D1
Daily Princetonian, 48 University Place
Employment, Human Resources,
  New South, E4
Engineering and Applied Science,
  School of, I1
Exhibits: Art Museum, F2; Firestone
  Library, F1; Mudd Library, I2
Fields Center for Equality and Cultural
  Understanding, 86 Olden St., I2
Financial aid, undergraduate,
  West College, E2
Food, phones, restrooms:
  Frist Campus Center, G3
Garden Theatre, G1
Gardens, Prospect, F3
Gymnasiums: Dillon, E3; Jadwin, I6
Health Center, McCosh, G3
Housing Office, MacMillan Building, E5

Building Directory

2 Dickinson Street, D3
22 Chambers Street, D1
48 University Place, D2
71 University Place, D3
91 Prospect Avenue, J3
99 Alexander Street, C4
106 Alexander Street, D4
120 Alexander Street, D4
126 Alexander Street, D5
179 Nassau Street, G1
180 Alexander Street, D6
185 Nassau Street, H1
201 Nassau Street, H1
228 Alexander Street, D7
262 Alexander Street, D7
1879 Hall, G2
1901-Laughlin Hall, E3
1903 Hall, F3
1912 Pavilion, G5
1915 Hall, F4
1922 Hall, F4
1927-Clapp Hall, F4
1937 Hall, F3
1938 Hall, F4
1939 Hall, F3

1940 Hall, F4
1941 Hall, F4
1942 Hall, F4
1952 Stadium, G6
Alexander Hall, E1
Architecture Laboratory, H5
Architecture School, G2
Armory, H5
Art Museum, F2
Baker Rink, E5
Bendheim Center for Finance, H2
Bendheim Hall, H2
Berlind Theatre, D4
Blair Hall, D2
Boathouse, G7
Bobst Hall, J3
Boiler House, E5
Bowen Hall, I2
Brown Hall, F3
Burr Hall, G1
Buyers Hall, E2
Caldwell Fieldhouse, I5
Campbell Hall, E1
Carl Icahn Laboratory, G4
Chancellor Green, F1
Chapel, F2

Chilled Water Plant, E5
Clio Hall, E2
Cogeneration Plant, E5
College Road Apartments,
Computer Science, I2
Computing Center, J3
Cooling Towers, E6
Corwin Hall, H2
Cuyler Hall, F3
DeNunzio Pool, I6
Dickinson Hall, G2
Dillon Gymnasium, E3
Dod Hall, E2
Dodge-Osborn Hall, F3
East Pyne, F2
Edwards Hall, E2
Elementary Particle
  Laboratory, J6
Elm Club, I2
Engineering Quadrangle, I1
Eno Hall, F4
Feinberg Hall, F3
Fields Center, I2
Fine Hall, H4
Firestone Library, F1

ADMISSIONS

Very important factors considered include: Character/personal qualities, essays, extracurricular activities, recommendations, secondary school record, standardized test scores, talent/ability. *Important factors considered include:* Alumni/ae relation, class rank, volunteer work. *Other factors considered include:* Geographical residence, state residency, work experience. SAT Reasoning and SAT Subject Tests or ACT required. TOEFL required of all international applicants. High school diploma or equivalent is not required. *Academic units recommended:* 4 English, 4 math, 3 science (1 science lab), 4 foreign language, 2 social studies, 2 history.

The Inside Word

Despite an up-and-down fluctuation in application totals at most highly selective colleges over the past couple of years, Amherst remains a popular choice and very competitive. You've got to be a strong match all-around, and given their formidable applicant pool, it's very important that you make your case as direct as possible. If you're a special-interest candidate such as a legacy or recruited athlete, you may get a bit of a break from the admissions committee, but you'll still need to show sound academic capabilities and potential. Those without such links have a tougher task. On top of taking the toughest courses available to them and performing at the highest of their abilities, they must be strong writers who demonstrate that they are intellectually curious self-starters who will contribute to the community and profit from the experience. In other words, you've got to have a strong profile and a very convincing application to get admitted.

FINANCIAL AID

Students should submit: FAFSA, CSS/Financial Aid PROFILE, noncustodial (divorced/separated) parents' statement, business/farm supplement, income tax and W-2 forms (submitted through IDOC). The Princeton Review suggests that all financial aid forms be submitted as soon as possible after 1/1. *Need-based scholarships/grants offered:* Pell, SEOG, state scholarships/grants, private scholarships, the school's own gift aid. *Loan aid offered:* Direct Subsidized Stafford, Direct Unsubsidized Stafford, Direct PLUS, Federal Perkins, college/university loans from institutional funds. Applicants will be notified of awards on or about 4/1. Federal Work-study Program available. Institutional employment available. Off-campus job opportunities are good.

FROM THE ADMISSIONS OFFICE

"Amherst College looks, above all, for men and women of intellectual promise who have demonstrated qualities of mind and character that will enable them to take full advantage of the college's curriculum. . . . Admission decisions aim to select from among the many qualified applicants those possessing the intellectual talent, mental discipline, and imagination that will allow them most fully to benefit from the curriculum and contribute to the life of the college and of society. Whatever the form of academic experience—lecture course, seminar, conference, studio, laboratory, independent study at various levels—intellectual competence and awareness of problems and methods are the goals of the Amherst program, rather than the direct preparation for a profession."

For even more information on this school, turn to page 462 of the "Stats" section.

ARCADIA UNIVERSITY

450 SOUTH EASTON ROAD, GLENSIDE, PA 19038 • ADMISSIONS: 215-572-2910 • FAX: 215-572-4049
E-MAIL: ADMISS@ARCADIA.EDU • WEBSITE: WWW.ARCADIA.EDU

Ratings
Quality of Life: 81 **Academic:** 81 **Admissions:** 79 **Financial Aid:** 71

Academics

"Study-abroad is a very big thing" at Arcadia University, a small liberal arts school outside of Philadelphia. Students here can choose from a variety of compelling study-abroad options, including "opportunities to study in Australia, London, Spain, and Italy." Arcadia's First Year Study Abroad program sends select freshmen to London or Scotland for their first semester. And for those who prefer a briefer international experience, Arcadia's London Preview "sends students to London during spring break" at incredibly cheap

rates. Explains one junior: "This introductory experience allows students to see whether they would like to study abroad in the future." Students praise the overseas programs, writing that going abroad is "an experience that is once-in-a-lifetime and very easy to do here, so many people take advantage of the chance." When they're not globetrotting, Arcadia undergrads enjoy studying with "incredible" professors who "interact with students constantly. If students are interested in research, they not only show them how to do research, but also help to get students published prior to graduation." The school's proximity to Philadelphia means that internships are "available to upperclassmen if they are interested in a hands-on experience in their chosen major." Students report that Arcadia "is good for science majors," and the school also demonstrates strength in education, fine arts, and business.

Life

The Arcadia campus, students tell us, "can be fun at times and at others extremely boring." The school does a good job of bringing in outside entertainment, such as "comedians, musicians, and movie nights" as well as organizing "dances with varying themes, such as a black light dance, a Halloween dance, a winter-themed dance, and Cotillion, a prom-like dance." Arcadia encourages its students to be active in clubs and organizations; reports a junior: "If you are a martial arts enthusiast, there's a club for you. If you show horses, there's an equestrian club. There's the Student Government Organization, the Student Programming Board, several multicultural and ethnic clubs, and there are clubs designed for specific majors." Then there's the men's soccer team, "one of the best in the state," which "students really support." Even so, there are plenty of times when "there's nothing to do on campus," students concede; observes one, "The campus is pretty quiet over the weekends, especially on Saturdays." Fortunately, "Philly is not far from school, just 30 minutes by train." A number of students also like to "hop onto trains and visit New York City." Students stick close to campus on the last weekend of October, though, so they can catch "the very popular Mr. Beaver contest, a male beauty pageant that is always fun to participate in and watch."

Student Body

The typical Arcadia student is "most likely a female. There is a high concentration of females at Arcadia," because the school "began as an all-female academy." Typical students take their studies "moderately seriously" and are "involved in one or two clubs." Those who aren't in clubs are often "pretty involved in sports." Arcadia has a sizeable homosexual student population and hosts "many international students because of the strong study abroad program." "We do draw in foreign students and other ethnicities," writes a senior, "but there's still a predominately white, female population." That said, "there isn't a problem with discrimination" on campus, students report.

ADMISSIONS

Very important factors considered include: Secondary school record. *Important factors considered include:* Class rank, essays, extracurricular activities, recommendations, standardized test scores. *Other factors considered include:* Alumni/ae relation, character/personal qualities, interview, talent/ability, volunteer work, work experience. SAT Reasoning or ACT required. TOEFL required of all international applicants. High school diploma is required, and GED is accepted. *Academic units recommended:* 4 English, 3 math, 3 science (3 science lab), 2 foreign language, 2 social studies, 2 history.

The Inside Word

Changing the name of the school from Beaver College to Arcadia University has already paid handsome dividends: enrollment has increased by 20 percent since the switch. Expect admissions to grow more competitive here in the next few years as more high school seniors hear about this "new school."

FINANCIAL AID

Students should submit: FAFSA, institution's own financial aid form. The Princeton Review suggests that all financial aid forms be submitted as soon as possible after 1/1. *Need-based scholarships/grants offered:* Pell, SEOG, state scholarships/grants, private scholarships, the school's own gift aid. *Loan aid offered:* FFEL Subsidized Stafford, FFEL Unsubsidized Stafford, FFEL PLUS, Federal Perkins, college/university loans from institutional funds. Applicants will be notified of awards on a rolling basis beginning on or about 2/15.

FROM THE ADMISSIONS OFFICE

"Arcadia University is a coeducational, private, comprehensive university founded in 1853 and located on a 71-acre private estate in Glenside, Pennsylvania, just 25 minutes from Center City Philadelphia. As a student at Arcadia University, your education expands beyond the classroom. Our study abroad programs, international faculty, and global vision of education combine to create an environment that affords you a world of opportunities. Our Center for Education Abroad is top ranked, and students have the opportunity to study in England, Equatorial Guinea, Scotland, Wales, Ireland, Northern Ireland, Australia, Greece, Korea, Italy, Spain, and New Zealand. Freshmen at Arcadia have the unique opportunity to spend spring break in London or Scotland for only $245. The London/Scotland Preview Program introduces students to overseas study and travel. Students may choose from more than 60 different undergraduate programs and 12 graduate degrees. Our 12:1 student/faculty ratio enables students to work closely with faculty for academic advising, research, and publication activities.

For even more information on this school, turn to page 462 of the "Stats" section.

The Art Institute of Boston at Lesley University

700 Beacon Street, Boston, MA 02215-2598 • Admissions: 617-585-6700 • Fax: 617-437-1226
E-mail: ADMISSIONS@AIBOSTON.EDU • Website: WWW.AIBOSTON.EDU

Ratings
Quality of Life: 72   **Academic:** 67   **Admissions:** 60   **Financial Aid:** 62

Academics

Artists looking to be "the best artists they are capable of being" in an environment where "the learning is intense" find a home at the Art Institute of Boston—a small, private professional art college affiliated with Lesley University. Freshmen at AIB are immersed in the fine arts through the school's "intense" Foundation Program, which focuses on drawing, visual perception, and principles of design, with the exception of photography students, who follow a different foundation sequence designed for their field of study. To ensure that students learn the context of their work as well as their craft, AIB requires a wide array of liberal arts classes constituting one third of all undergraduate credits. The school's affiliation with Lesley University affords students a solid selection of liberal arts electives as well. Ultimately, however, students go to AIB to get their hands dirty, and AIB gives them plenty of opportunities to do so. Facilities include a well-stocked printmaking studio, a clay lab with several kilns, a wood shop, color and black-and-white darkrooms, an extensive assortment of lenses and lighting options, computer labs for design and animation, and galleries. AIB undergrads praise their professors, telling us "the faculty is fun, very understanding, and generally organized." AIB undergrads add, "It helps that [the professors] are all working artists." That's what enables them to "embrace individual responses to projects." Instructors "are really willing to help outside of the class," a major plus considering that "studio classes can be crowded in the first year or two." Students at AIB also appreciate that "the school is usually very good about asking students what they want and helping with getting it, such as new shuttle schedules, new food service, etc."

> **SURVEY SAYS . . .**
> *Small classes*
> *Students love Boston, MA*
> *Intercollegiate sports are unpopular*
> *or nonexistent*
> *Intramural sports are unpopular or nonexistent*
> *Frats and sororities are unpopular or nonexistent*
> *(Almost) everyone smokes*

Life

Artists are generally happiest when they're at work, so it should come as no surprise that AIB undergraduates describe life at the school as filled with "work, work, work. The weeks are so busy that it's hard to fit everything into the weekends." When they can tear themselves away from their studios, computers, and darkrooms, students enjoy a limited schedule of on-campus events, including lectures, exhibitions, coffeehouses, and seven varsity sports as well as intramural sports including dodgeball. Mostly, however, they take advantage of their location in Boston which is "within walking distance of both Fenway Park and the Museum of Fine Arts." Boston is a tremendous college town, with nearly a quarter-million students at seventy different institutions. The city accommodates them with good cheap eats, tons of excellent music venues and movie theaters, and shopping for people of all income levels. Navigable by pedestrians, Boston is one of the few places in the United States where you can get along pretty easily without an automobile.

Student Body

Students explain that "AIB is an art school, so everyone is pretty unique. It doesn't matter if you fit in; it's all about producing art. That's the one thing everyone has in common." A photography major says, "[I am at AIB because it's] a place where I can do what I love 24/7." The school is home to a substantial number of transfer students; some tried attending larger universities and were dissatisfied, while others simply needed a few years of college to meet AIB's admissions requirements. Either way, "most students went to good high schools." Making art is expensive and plenty of "people work on the side" to help offset the cost of their supplies. The student body also includes many international students from around the globe.

ADMISSIONS

Very important factors considered include: Character/personal qualities, secondary school record, talent/ability. *Important factors considered include:* Essays, interview, recommendations, standardized test scores. *Other factors considered include:* Alumni/ae relation, extracurricular activities, geographical residence, minority status, state residency, volunteer work, work experience. TOEFL required of all international applicants. High school diploma is required, and GED is accepted. *Academic units required:* 4 English. *Academic units recommended:* 4 English, 2 social studies, 2 history, 2 academic electives, 2 studio art, 1 math, 1 science, 1 foreign language.

The Inside Word

"Your artistic potential, academic performance, and personal commitment are of primary importance in your application," according to the school's website. That's also where to find detailed portfolio guidelines. Study them carefully—then consult with your art teacher before selecting the works for your portfolio. Visit the campus and schedule an interview if at all possible.

FINANCIAL AID

Students should submit: FAFSA, institution's own financial aid form. The Princeton Review suggests that all financial aid forms be submitted as soon as possible after 1/1. *Need-based scholarships/grants offered:* Pell, SEOG, state scholarships/grants, private scholarships, the school's own gift aid. *Loan aid offered:* FFEL Subsidized Stafford, FFEL Unsubsidized Stafford, FFEL PLUS, Federal Perkins, state loans. Applicants will be notified of awards on a rolling basis beginning on or about 4/1. Federal Work-study Program available. Institutional employment available. Off-campus job opportunities are excellent.

FROM THE ADMISSIONS OFFICE

"Founded in 1912, the Art Institute of Boston at Lesley University is a professional college of visual arts, offering program and course work designed to prepare students to be creative professionals. Graduates go on to successful careers as illustrators, animators, graphic designers, Web designers, photographers, exhibiting fine artists, art teachers, and art therapists.

"AIB provides students with an intimate, challenging, and supportive environment that balances personal artistic expression with practical professional preparation.

Studio classes are small and intimate—with an average of 14 students per instructor—which allows for personal attention and an emphasis on self-exploration. Internships and freelance opportunities provide students with significant professional experience and they also benefit from University-sponsored activities such as major exhibitions, student exhibits, lectures, art auctions, special event–related parties, as well as a visiting artist program that brings prominent artists to the campus for lectures and workshops. As a part of Lesley, AIB students benefit from access to the resources of a major University while maintaining the experience of a small, private art college.

"The school offers international learning opportunities in Holland, Florence, Ireland, and Paris. Students may also take an intensive yearlong course of study and studio work in New York City, and can also take classes at the Boston Architectural Center and the Maine Photographic Workshop. The Art Institute of Boston was selected to join the New Media Centers Program, a consortium of higher education institutions and digital technology companies dedicated to advancing learning through new media."

For even more information on this school, turn to page 463 of the "Stats" section.

ASSUMPTION COLLEGE

500 SALISBURY STREET, WORCESTER, MA 01609-1296 • ADMISSIONS: 888-882-7786 • FAX: 508-799-4412
E-MAIL: ADMISS@ASSUMPTION.EDU • WEBSITE: WWW.ASSUMPTION.EDU

Ratings
Quality of Life: 75   Academic: 80   Admissions: 81   Financial Aid: 72

Academics

SURVEY SAYS . . .
Small classes
Lab facilities are great
Great computer facilities
Frats and sororities are unpopular
or nonexistent
Lots of beer drinking
Hard liquor is popular

Assumption College, a Catholic liberal arts school with pre-professional programs in Worcester, Massachusetts, provides to its 2,100 predominantly regional students "a small community" with "a friendly face wherever you go." "Class sizes are very small" at Assumption, and this "enables a lot of one-on-one attention between the teacher and student." This is important because the workload can be demanding. A sophomore agrees and says, "We have high standards for admissions and high standards to keep scholarships." Assumption professors "are very intelligent and usually personable," and most of them "genuinely care" about their students. One undergrad writes, "I really feel like they're teaching me more than simply the curriculum. Many of them encourage thinking outside the box and respectful discussion or debate. They choose reading materials that provoke reactions and deep thought." All students must complete general education requirements that "make them take a large number of courses from different disciplines in order to give them a feel for everything and help them decide what it is they want to do." But students need not worry about getting the help they need: "Professors provide plenty of office hours, and the academic support center is excellent." One sophomore writes, "My academic experience has been great. I have gotten nearly every class I have signed up for, and I plan to study abroad."

Life

"Assumption is pretty relaxed and low-key," students tell us. Some students spend weekends "drinking in dorms with friends," while others report that they keep busy with campus events: "There are a lot of activities on campus, if you like dances, comedians, bingo, and concerts." Many students are involved in sports; the intramural scene is hopping, and there is enthusiasm for the school's intercollegiate teams—although they are often overmatched by their Division II rivals. Still others feel the allure of hometown Worcester, lauding its "many different clubs and bars." One student explains, "The school is located on the outskirts of Worcester, so it's far enough from the city that I feel safe, but it's close enough so that I can still find things to do to keep busy." As is the case at many religiously affiliated schools, Assumption "has a great deal of community service involvement." One undergrad sums up, "I think that there is always something to do around campus, no matter what you enjoy doing. Chapel choir, intramurals, student government, campus ministry, campus activities board, volunteering . . . the list goes on and on. The key to finding your 'place' here at Assumption is getting involved."

Student Body

The "extremely friendly people from New York, Massachusetts, Connecticut, and Rhode Island wearing Boston Red Sox hats and North Face coats" who make up the majority of students at Assumption are largely "middle-class." Many of them are Catholic as well, although students report that Assumption "is not overly religious." That said, "the Campus Ministry Program provides an array of awesome programs for students who are very interested in their spirituality." Most Assumption students "try to achieve a perfect balance between academics and social endeavors." Although the student body overall is "warm and welcoming, friendly, and interested in a variety of things there is a definite lack of diversity on campus."

ADMISSIONS

Very important factors considered include: Class rank, essays, secondary school record, standardized test scores. *Important factors considered include:* Recommendations. *Other factors considered include:* Alumni/ac relation, character/personal qualities, extracurricular activities, geographical residence, interview, minority status, talent/ability, volunteer work, work experience. SAT Reasoning or ACT required. TOEFL required of all international applicants. High school diploma is required, and GED is accepted. *Academic units required:* 4 English, 3 math, 2 science, 2 foreign language, 2 history, 5 academic electives.

The Inside Word

Assumption takes the "personal qualities" of its applicants into consideration, looking closely at candidates' co-curricular activities, leadership experiences, and commitment to community service. Essays and letters of recommendation, both required, are also considered important indicators of character. Spend some extra time on the nonacademic part of your application, and choose your recommenders carefully.

FINANCIAL AID

Students should submit: FAFSA. The Princeton Review suggests that all financial aid forms be submitted as soon as possible after 1/1. *Need-based scholarships/grants offered:* Pell, SEOG, state scholarships/grants, private scholarships, the school's own gift aid. *Loan aid offered:* FFEL Subsidized Stafford, FFEL Unsubsidized Stafford, FFEL PLUS, Federal Perkins, state loans, college/university loans from institutional funds. Applicants will be notified of awards on a rolling basis beginning on or about 2/15.

FROM THE ADMISSIONS OFFICE

"The strength of Assumption College can be found in its ongoing commitment to its student-centered mission. This mission provides an intellectual, social, and spiritual environment designed to attract, retain, and graduate students who pursue ethical professional careers and personal lives based on values undergirded by both faith and reason.

"President Tom Plough is fond of saying that 'Assumption features what I call close encounters of the Assumption kind; that is, the relationships between faculty and students and staff here often approach the quality levels of those found in a stable, extended family.' The active engagement of faculty and staff with students in and out of the classroom is a strategic strength of Assumption College. It is relatively easy for graduating seniors to find faculty and staff who know them so well that highly personalized letters of reference to potential employers and graduate schools can be obtained with ease.

"Assumption is explicitly in the business of building compassion, competence, and character through active and aggressive outreach to students. Early attention, availability, interaction, and follow-up with individual students is a top priority

"As Assumption moves into its second century (the college just celebrated its centennial in 2004), the college focuses its efforts on providing the resources and facilities its faculty and students need to attain their educational outcomes. It remains primarily residential, believing that the residential learning environment, properly designed, is the superior education model for assisting students to ask the broadest questions at the deepest levels."

For even more information on this school, turn to page 463 of the "Stats" section.

BABSON COLLEGE

MUSTARD HALL, BABSON PARK, MA 02457-0310 • ADMISSIONS: 800-488-3696 • FAX: 781-239-4006
FINANCIAL AID: 781-239-4219 • E-MAIL: UGRADADMISSION@BABSON.EDU • WEBSITE: WWW.BABSON.EDU

Ratings
Quality of Life: 79   Academic: 88   Admissions: 93   Financial Aid: 95

Academics

Entrepreneurship is the name of the game at Babson College. The college has strengths in other areas, surely, but most students arrive here hoping to learn the secret of establishing America's next Jiffy Lube or Continental Polymers (both of whose founders teach here). Babson stresses "hands-on experience" with a curriculum that "really plunges you into the real world, rather than teaching you theories. During [the] first year, you actually start a business and then learn how to manage it." (A few naysayers dismiss the freshman project as "small time. The businesses tends to be more of peddle-shops than anything.") Starting a business is only part of a rigorous freshman year that students uniformly refer to as "business boot camp." Warns one undergrad, "Free time is very hard to come by at Babson. You'll always have a business plan to write, a group meeting to go to, or reading to do for a class." Professors are admired for their experience and expertise ("They are typically seasoned businessmen and businesswomen who have a genuine desire to teach students how to be successful in the real world"). While some here complain that "at times Babson can focus too much on 'street smarts' at the expense of 'book smarts'" and others assert that "Babson needs to improve the quality and quantity of the liberal arts curriculum," most here believe the school's assets far outweigh its drawbacks. As one student put it, "From great speakers, like the head of the NYSE, to programs like the Rocket Pitch Event, Business Plan Competition, and entrepreneurship conferences . . . Babson students get what they pay for."

Life

Even though the Babson campus offers "tons of sports events, plays, concerts," and numerous active organizations (including Babson Dance Ensemble, the Babson Players, Student Government, and the Campus Activities Board), most students here agree that "There's lots of stuff offered on campus, but with such a diverse [international] population, it's hard to please everyone. Babson students are so spoiled in so many ways; we get very whiny and complain about things a lot, even though we have it so amazingly good." Some blame the situation on the school's small size; others finger the "super anal" campus police; still others say it's the grueling academic schedule ("Being both happy and successful at Babson requires 36 hours a day"). Fortunately, the school is "not quite in Boston, but close enough to all the action," at least for the majority of students who have cars (for those who don't, the college offers a weekend shuttle service). "Boston is the choice destination for partying," students tell us, warning that "clubs can set you back $100 in one night with cover charges, drinks, and shared cab fare." Students praise Babson's "small, beautiful campus" and the "extremely safe, lovely neighborhood" surrounding it.

Student Body

The typical Babson undergrad is either "a white suburbanite from an East Coast private school" or "an international who smokes, is always on his/her cell phone, and wears designer threads." Students are "very conservative" and "extremely competitive," leading some to complain that "there are too many unfriendly people here. No one says hello when you walk by them, and if you initiate a greeting, it is seldom returned." Reports one undergrad, "Many students are individualistic in nature. They could happily survive on a deserted island with a computer, a cell phone, and caffeine." Given the school's focus on entrepreneurship, it is unsurprising that many here are also very materialistic. "If you want to be criticized for not ordering every new gadget in Maxim magazine or for not having more than one car on campus, this is the place for you," is how one sardonic student here puts it.

ADMISSIONS

Very important factors considered include: Secondary school record, standardized test scores. *Important factors considered include:* Class rank, essays, recommendations. *Other factors considered include:* Alumni/ae relation, character/personal qualities, extracurricular activities, geographical residence, interview, minority status, state residency, talent/ability, volunteer work, work experience. SAT Reasoning or ACT required. SAT Subject Tests recommended. High school diploma is required, and GED is accepted. *Academic units required:* 4 English, 3 math, 3 science (2 science lab), 2 foreign language, 2 social studies, 1 history. *Academic units recommended:* 4 English, 4 math, 3 science (2 science lab), 4 foreign language, 3 social studies, 1 precalculus.

The Inside Word

Minority representation, including that of women, remains low, which makes for a very advantageous situation for such candidates. In this age of corporate "downsizing," it has become much more commonplace for students to pursue college programs that lead directly to career paths, and Babson has benefited handsomely from this trend. When this trend and the college's fine reputation are combined, the result is a relatively challenging admissions process despite a relatively modest freshman academic profile. On top of this, the college is also recruiting further afield than in the past. Be wary of overconfidence when applying.

FINANCIAL AID

Students should submit: FAFSA, CSS/Financial Aid PROFILE, noncustodial (divorced/separated) parents' statement, business/farm supplement, federal tax returns, W-2 forms, and verification worksheet. Regular filing deadline 2/15. The Princeton Review suggests that all financial aid forms be submitted as soon as possible after 1/1. *Need-based scholarships/grants offered:* Pell, SEOG, state scholarships/grants, the school's own gift aid. *Loan aid offered:* FFEL Subsidized Stafford, FFEL Unsubsidized Stafford, FFEL PLUS, Federal Perkins, state loans. Applicants will be notified of awards on or about 4/1. Federal Work-study Program available. Institutional employment available. Off-campus job opportunities are good.

FROM THE ADMISSIONS OFFICE

"In addition to theoretical knowledge, Babson College is dedicated to providing its students with hands-on business experience. The Foundation Management Experience (FME) and Management Consulting Field Experience (MCFE) are two prime examples of this commitment. During the FME, all freshmen are placed into groups of 30 and actually create their own businesses that they operate until the end of the academic year. The profits of each FME business are then donated to the charity of each group's choice.

"MCFE offers upperclassmen the unique and exciting opportunity to work as actual consultants for private companies and/or nonprofit organizations in small groups of three to five. Students receive academic credit for their work as well as invaluable experience in the field of consulting. FME and MCFE are just two of the ways Babson strives to produce business leaders with both theoretical knowledge and practical experience."

For even more information on this school, turn to page 463 of the "Stats" section.

BARD COLLEGE

OFFICE OF ADMISSIONS, ANNANDALE-ON-HUDSON, NY 12504 • ADMISSIONS: 845-758-7472
FAX: 845-758-5208 • FINANCIAL AID: 845-758-7526 • E-MAIL: ADMISSION@BARD.EDU • WEBSITE: WWW.BARD.EDU

Ratings
Quality of Life: 76   Academic: 95   Admissions: 96   Financial Aid: 85

Academics

Bard College, a Hudson Valley school that puts the "liberal" in "liberal arts," is a bastion of nonconformity and intellectualism. Professors and academics, students tell us, "are both pretty amazing. All the professors seem willing to bend over backward for the students while being respectable members of academia in general." Undergrads may also love the faculty because "the professors are a reflection of the student body: a combination of above-it-all artists, leftist intellectuals, and downright nerds." Students here love the school's "general looseness, which makes it easy to do things—start a club, get a tutorial, make your own major, whatever." Recounts one student, "I wanted to transfer credits so I walked into the registrar's office and was out in five minutes. I wanted a Hebrew tutorial, I found the professor in his office, and he arranged it. . . . Every time I've needed anything, people have graciously given me their time and their advice, minus formality and bureaucracy." According to students, the only exception to the rule is course registration, "which is a nightmare. Professors sit in their offices, and it's first come, first served. Registration opens at noon. People camp out outside the offices up to six hours ahead of time. It's like a Star Wars premiere."

> **SURVEY SAYS . . .**
> *Small classes*
> *Students aren't religious*
> *Campus feels safe*
> *Frats and sororities are unpopular*
> *or nonexistent*
> *Political activism is popular*
> *(Almost) everyone smokes*

Life

Because Bard "isn't really on top of any town—you have to drive 5 to 10 [miles] to hit anything more than a fruit stand," the school "tries to be its own entertainment." The campus scene is enjoyable, if subdued, according to most; explains one undergrad, "For fun we have intellectual conversations, go to the movies, go to campus events, go to see bands, hang out in the library, drive around, go to thrift stores or to Wal- Mart, hang out in the campus center . . . and surf the Internet." There are "always movies at the theatre on weekends, and there are often theatrical productions, art openings, concerts, and lectures" as well. Even so, "It's the party/music scene that runs the place." There "are a lot of herbal activities" here, though "for the most part, people respect themselves and one another and do not overuse." Many traditional college diversions are absent here; as one student puts it, "These arc things people are not into: football, television, dating, and fast food. Things people are into: dance parties, leftist politics, New York City, organic vegetables, and doing their own thang."

Student Body

When conservatives complain about PC campuses and ultraliberal students, they might well be specifically describing Bard. It's the kind of place where students tell you that "we are more concerned with the terrorism for which our government is responsible than the terrorism that targets the United States," and mean it. "There is no typical Bard student" undergrads tell us, but most feel right at home here among the "leftist white woman who goes to Green Party rallies weekly" and the "friendly white guys with dreadlocks . . . whose joys include learning, music, and getting stoned with close friends." Bard students describe themselves as cerebral, telling us that "a certain level of intellectualism prevails here, and you really feel that the people you are talking to know what they are talking about, and have done research on these topics. Debates get heated, but that's essential to really get to the depth of an issue anyway." Undergrads appreciate the fact that "There is a really high percentage of international students, which gives the Americans a different perspective of the world."

ADMISSIONS

Very important factors considered include: Character/personal qualities, essays, extracurricular activities, recommendations, secondary school record, talent/ability, volunteer work. *Important factors considered include:* Work experience. *Other factors considered include:* Alumni/ae relation, class rank, geographical residence, interview, minority status, religious affiliation/commitment, standardized test scores, state residency. TOEFL required of all international applicants. High school diploma is required, and GED is accepted. *Academic units recommended:* 4 English, 4 math, 4 science, 4 foreign language, 4 social studies, 4 history.

The Inside Word

Applicants tend to be cerebral sorts. Bard is highly selective, but the match counts more than having the right numerical profile.

FINANCIAL AID

Students should submit: FAFSA, CSS/Financial Aid PROFILE, state aid form, noncustodial (divorced/separated) parents' statement, business/farm supplement. Regular filing deadline 2/15. The Princeton Review suggests that all financial aid forms be submitted as soon as possible after 1/1. *Need-based scholarships/grants offered:* Pell, SEOG, state scholarships/grants, private scholarships, the school's own gift aid. *Loan aid offered:* FFEL Subsidized Stafford, FFEL Unsubsidized Stafford, FFEL PLUS, Federal Perkins, college/university loans from institutional funds (for international students only). Applicants will be notified of awards on or about 4/1. Federal Work-study Program available. Institutional employment available. Off-campus job opportunities are good.

FROM THE ADMISSIONS OFFICE

"An alliance with Rockefeller University, the renowned graduate scientific research institution, gives Bardians access to Rockefeller's professors and laboratories and to places in Rockefeller's Summer Research Fellows Program. Almost all our math and science graduates pursue graduate or professional studies; 90 percent of our applicants to medical and health professional schools are accepted.

"The Globalization and International Affairs (BGIA) Program is a residential program in the heart of New York City that offers undergraduates a unique opportunity to undertake specialized study with leading practitioners and scholars in international affairs and to gain internship experience with international-affairs organizations. Topics in the curriculum include human rights, international economics, global environmental issues, international justice, managing international risk, and writing on international affairs, among others. Internships/tutorials are tailored to students' particular fields of study.

"Student dormitory and classroom facilities are in Bard Hall, 410 West 58th Street, a newly renovated 11-story building near the Lincoln Center District in New York City."

For even more information on this school, turn to page 464 of the "Stats" section.

BARNARD COLLEGE

3009 BROADWAY, NEW YORK, NY 10027 • ADMISSIONS: 212-854-2014 • FAX: 212-854-6220
FINANCIAL AID: 212-854-2154 • E-MAIL: ADMISSIONS@BARNARD.EDU • WEBSITE: WWW.BARNARD.EDU

Ratings
Quality of Life: 97   Academic: 94   Admissions: 97   Financial Aid: 94

Academics

Barnard College, the all-women's liberal arts school associated with Columbia University, "offers students the best of both worlds: the seclusion and intimacy of a small liberal arts college within a tremendous research university and one of the greatest cities in the world." Women here explain that "because Barnard students have complete cross-registration privileges at Columbia, full access to all of its resources and libraries, and upon graduation receive a degree from the University, we enjoy the full benefits of an Ivy League education, without the punishment of having to take Columbia's core curriculum, pass a swim test, or eat at the lousy Columbia dining room." Students here also get more of a small-college experience than do their Columbia peers; explains one student, "While the Columbia professors can be arrogant and pompous, most of the Barnard professors are really nice, down-to-earth people." Administrators are "unequivocally dedicated to finding rapid, individualized solutions to students' problems." Because the school is in New York City, "there are amazing opportunities here; the city really is our learning lab!" In short, "Barnard is really great as a small school to act as your home base. From here, you can explore the university and the city as much as you want. You have to take the initiative, but if you do, you can find a way to do anything you want. And Barnard is so supportive, you'll be able to find someone on campus who's willing to help."

> **SURVEY SAYS . . .**
> *No one cheats*
> *Great library*
> *Students love New York, NY*
> *Great off-campus food*
> *Campus feels safe*

Life

"Life at school is dominated by studies." Undergraduates agree that "most students here spend at least 60 percent of their week on schoolwork." Still, to the degree allowed by their academic workload, "most undergraduates make a conscious effort to take advantage of NYC through internships, nightlife, museums, and exhibits. Many of us love to just spend an afternoon walking down Broadway and shopping." The campus is a magnet for high-powered speakers and prestigious events; reports one student, "There are always rallies or lectures going on that are highly attended. In the past year, Janeane Garofalo, John Edwards, Anna Quindlen, and Alice Walker have spoken on campus, to name a few." Barnard is located in Morningside Heights, "a neighborhood that thrives very much on the college community." Students here miss out a bit on the classic college experience, but they don't mind; explains one undergrad, "Barnard feels that, since we are in the city, they don't need to create a community for us. Therefore, occasionally I feel like I'm just living in the city and taking classes. It's definitely worth it, though, and my friends and I make our own college touch!" Women here also warn that "Barnard's facilities could use drastic remodeling. With the exception of a few recently renovated lecture spaces, the classrooms are in need of major technological and aesthetic updates. New resident halls need to be built because many of the existing buildings are too old."

Student Body

Barnard, like its hometown, is a magnet for the idiosyncratic. Explains one student, "New York is a place that allows people to be anyone they want to be. You can wear a zebra-striped bikini in the middle of winter on a snow covered street here and people would hardly look twice… [but] because we go to school in such an eclectic place, I don't think it's possible to describe a 'typical' Barnard student." Some here try all the same; they tell us that Barnard students are "driven, intelligent, cosmopolitan young women who come from every corner of the country and throughout the world, from different socioeconomic backgrounds, and varying life experiences." Because of a dual degree program with the Jewish Theological Seminary, "there are many Orthodox Jews here" who "typically socialize only with other Orthodox Jews." There's also a large, less insular Asian population. There are "many feminists and lesbians, too, but fewer than one might expect."

ADMISSIONS

Very important factors considered include: Essays, recommendations, secondary school record, standardized test scores. *Important factors considered include:* Class rank, extracurricular activities, talent/ability, volunteer work. *Other factors considered include:* Alumni/ae relation, character/personal qualities, geographical residence, interview, minority status, state residency, work experience. SAT Reasoning and SAT Subject Tests or ACT required. TOEFL required of all international applicants. High school diploma or equivalent is not required. *Academic units recommended:* 4 English, 3 math, 3 science (2 science lab), 3 foreign language, 3 history.

The Inside Word

As at many top colleges, early decision applications have increased at Barnard—although the admissions standards are virtually the same as for their regular admissions cycle. The college's admissions staff is open and accessible, which is not always the case at highly selective colleges with as long and impressive a tradition of excellence. The admissions committee's expectations are high, but their attitude reflects a true interest in who you are and what's on your mind. Students have a much better experience throughout the admissions process when treated with sincerity and respect—perhaps this is why Barnard continues to attract and enroll some of the best students in the country.

FINANCIAL AID

Students should submit: FAFSA; institution's own financial aid form; CSS/Financial Aid PROFILE; state aid form; noncustodial (divorced/separated) parents' statement; business/farm supplement; parents' individual, corporate, and/or partnership federal income tax returns. Regular filing deadline 2/1. The Princeton Review suggests that all financial aid forms be submitted as soon as possible after 1/1. *Need-based scholarships/grants offered:* Pell, SEOG, state scholarships/grants, private scholarships, the school's own gift aid. *Loan aid offered:* FFEL Subsidized Stafford, FFEL Unsubsidized Stafford, FFEL PLUS, Federal Perkins, state loans, college/university loans from institutional funds. Applicants will be notified of awards on or about 4/1. Federal Work-study Program available. Institutional employment available. Off-campus job opportunities are excellent.

FROM THE ADMISSIONS OFFICE

"Barnard College, a small, distinguished liberal arts college for women that is affiliated with Columbia University, and located in the heart of New York City. The college enrolls women from all over the United States, Puerto Rico, and the Caribbean. More than thirty countries, including France, England, Hong Kong, and Greece, are also represented in the student body. Students pursue their academic studies in over 40 majors and are able to cross-register at Columbia University."

For even more information on this school, turn to page 464 of the "Stats" section.

BATES COLLEGE

23 CAMPUS AVENUE, LEWISTON, ME 04240-9917 • ADMISSIONS: 207-786-6000 • FAX: 207-786-6025
FINANCIAL AID: 207-786-6096 • E-MAIL: ADMISSIONS@BATES.EDU • WEBSITE: WWW.BATES.EDU

Ratings
Quality of Life: 87   **Academic:** 93   **Admissions:** 96   **Financial Aid:** 93

Academics

Those seeking "a high-paced rigorous academic college with a low-key, laid-back, and fun student body and campus life" should consider Maine's Bates College, a small liberal arts school that "focuses on students becoming critically and creatively thinking citizens of the world" through first-year seminars, mandatory senior projects, and a range of departmental, interdisciplinary, and student-designed majors. Undergrads report that departments in economics, biology, chemistry, religion, philosophy, and English are all "very good," with academics that "are challenging indeed, but not to the point where they interfere with all the other enjoyable aspects of life here." Professors are exemplars of exclusive, small-school pedagogy; they "are always willing to chat about classes, internship possibilities, future jobs, graduate school, further readings to be done and just about life." This is because "teaching is their main priority, and as a result they have an invested interest in their students that facilitates meaningful and personal relationships." Another adds student, "The feeling of community fostered at Bates is unparalleled. The students are truly welcoming, and the professors seem to really enjoy their jobs. The administration really gives the students a say in what happens at their college."

> **SURVEY SAYS . . .**
> *Small classes*
> *Great library*
> *Students are friendly*
> *Frats and sororities are unpopular*
> *or nonexistent*
> *Lots of beer drinking*

Life

"You can really develop into a complete person at Bates, through involvement in athletics, community service, and supportive relationships with faculty and staff. At Bates you don't have to choose between activities; you can do it all if you decide that is what you want." Adds another undergrad, "I can't think of a single person who isn't busy 24 hours a day, but by choice. People fill up their lives with things that are important to them, whether it be academics, sports, student government, political activism, outdoor activities, or clubs. Many people can't choose just one." "Student organizations are easy to become involved in here. For instance, anyone, regardless of experience or major, may try out for a play, and most likely will land a part." Students also love outdoor activities, especially "skiing at Sunday River in the winter," but also "varsity or club sports, which even those who aren't quite athletic enjoy. Bates really emphasizes an overall sort of health of mind and body." Parties "are quite common on the weekends, especially in the wood-frame houses that serve as one housing option." And while "there isn't much to do in the Lewiston-Auburn area," that hardly matters because "Bates does an excellent job of providing entertainment on the weekends for students." As one undergrad puts it, "Students rarely leave campus for the weekends; no one wants to leave because there is so much going on here!" When students feel they just have to get away, "Bates pays for buses to nearby cities like Freeport, Portland and Boston."

Student Body

Far from big-city pressures, Bates students can afford the luxury of being "laid-back and willing to take time to chat with friends over coffee, read the newspaper, go to plays, become engaged in the community and be active politically. Students value not only the academic experience they are offered at Bates, but take advantage of other fashions of learning." The student body includes "a lot of pseudo-hippies who cruise around campus pedaling their junkyard bikes with their Birkenstock-ed feet while toting their Nalgenes, who then spend their holidays in palatial mansions," and also has its share of "New Englander Ralph Lauren-wearing preppies." One student explains, "Bates combines hippies with Cape Cod kids, athletes with intellectuals. Everyone is a dork in his or her own way, and everyone's passionate about something ridiculous, and totally unpredictable." Students speculate that "Bates has one of the more vocal gay/bisexual populations out there," and proudly report that "straight students (even those who might come in with some prejudices in this regard) interact with them freely and openly. This is one instance where one really sees Bates overcoming prejudice."

ADMISSIONS

Very important factors considered include: Character/personal qualities, class rank, essays, extracurricular activities, interview, recommendations, secondary school record, talent/ability. *Other factors considered include:* Alumni/ae relation, geographical residence, minority status, standardized test scores, volunteer work, work experience. TOEFL required of all international applicants. High school diploma is required, and GED is not accepted. *Academic units required:* 4 English, 3 math, 2 science (1 science lab), 2 foreign language, 3 social studies, 3 history. *Academic units recommended:* 4 English, 4 math, 3 science (1 science lab), 4 foreign language, 3 social studies, 3 history.

The Inside Word

With or without test scores, the admissions office will weed out weak students who show little or no intellectual curiosity. Students with high SAT scores should always submit them. If you are curious about Bates, it is important to have solid grades in challenging courses; without them, you are not a viable candidate for admission. Tough competition for students between the college and its New England peers has intensified greatly over the past couple of years; Bates is holding its own. It remains a top choice among its applicants, and as a result selectivity is on the rise.

FINANCIAL AID

Students should submit: FAFSA, CSS/Financial Aid PROFILE, noncustodial (divorced/separated) parents' statement, business/farm supplement. Regular filing deadline 2/1. The Princeton Review suggests that all financial aid forms be submitted as soon as possible after 1/1. *Need-based scholarships/grants offered:* Pell, SEOG, state scholarships/grants, private scholarships, the school's own gift aid. *Loan aid offered:* FFEL Subsidized Stafford, FFEL Unsubsidized Stafford, FFEL PLUS, Federal Perkins, state loans, alternative loans. Applicants will be notified of awards on or about 4/1. Federal Work-study Program available. Institutional employment available. Off-campus job opportunities are good.

FROM THE ADMISSIONS OFFICE

"Bates College is widely recognized as one of the finest liberal arts colleges in the nation. The curriculum and faculty challenge students to develop the essential skills of critical assessment, analysis, expression, aesthetic sensibility and independent thought. Founded by abolitionists in 1855, Bates graduates have always included men and women from diverse ethnic and religious backgrounds. Bates highly values its study abroad programs, unique calendar (4-4-1), and the many opportunities available for one-on-one collaboration with faculty through seminars, research, service-learning, and the capstone experience of senior thesis.

"Co-curricular life at Bates is rich; most students participate in club or varsity sports; many participate in performing arts; and almost all students participate in one of more than 90 student-run clubs and organizations. About 40 percent of students participate in career internships, and more than two-thirds of alumni enroll in graduate study within 10 years.

"The Bates College admissions staff reads applications very carefully; the high school record and the quality of writing are of particular importance. Applicants are strongly encouraged to have a personal interview, either on campus or with an alumni representative. Students who choose not to interview may place themselves at a disadvantage in the selection process. Bates offers tours, interviews and information sessions throughout the summer and fall. Drop-ins are welcome for tours and information sessions. Please call ahead to schedule an interview."

For even more information on this school, turn to page 465 of the "Stats" section.

BENNINGTON COLLEGE

OFFICE OF ADMISSIONS AND FINANCIAL AID, BENNINGTON, VT 05201 • ADMISSIONS: 800-833-6845
FAX: 802-440-4320 • FINANCIAL AID: 802-440-4325 • E-MAIL: ADMISSIONS@BENNINGTON.EDU • WEBSITE: WWW.BENNINGTON.EDU

Ratings
Quality of Life: 69   **Academic:** 87   **Admissions:** 87   **Financial Aid:** 70

Academics

Bennington College has long been committed to "honoring individuality and the power to create your own education." Students at this unconventional school "don't ever officially declare majors," nor do they take final exams. "We do final projects instead," explained one undergrad. "I got to do a project imitating the style of my favorite poet and a psychological study about student drinking on campus. I feel so involved with my classes!" Instead of grades, most students receive written evaluations of their work, however, all students have the option to receive grades in addition. Bennington's curriculum "is really dependent on the makeup of the faculty" because "there are not a lot of professors" and also because "the teachers 'teach what keeps them up at night.'" Profs here are "brilliant, amazing people who deeply care about their students;" undergrads also praise the Field Work Term ("a great program of going out for eight weeks to intern or work in your field or a field that you're interested in learning more about"). The visual arts program is one of the school's undisputed strengths. The VAPA (Visual and Performing Arts) center is "open 24/7, and every studio, work space, or lab is open to everyone." Music and language arts instruction also receive praise; the sciences, on the other hand, are considered relatively weak. Many here worry that the student body is growing too rapidly ("We have 200 more students here this year than we had last year") without a proportionate increase in the faculty. "We need more professors," writes a typical student. "If the school is going to continue to accept more students, the college is going to change. Normalization is beginning, and that's sad."

> **SURVEY SAYS . . .**
> *Small classes*
> *Students aren't religious*
> *Campus feels safe*
> *Intercollegiate sports are unpopular or nonexistent*
> *Frats and sororities are unpopular or nonexistent*
> *Theater is popular*
> *(Almost) everyone smokes*

Life

Bennington's "small and secluded" campus is "absolutely beautiful. Imagine the most beautiful haven you have ever been to; that is Bennington in early May. Imagine Norman Rockwell paintings; that is our winter and fall." Students enjoy the luxury of living in actual houses rather than dormitories. "We have both colonial-style houses built in the 1930s and modern houses that were built in 2001 and were featured in architecture magazines," writes one student. All the same, because of the school's remote location, "most people have a really hard time adjusting to life, myself included. If you stick it out, it gets better. There's a positive side to it: if I were in a larger city I would not be devoting as much time to my academics, which is the reason I came here." Bennington is "very isolated from the town, so there are a lot of on-campus events to keep one interested." Students mention "people screening independent films, stand-up comedy shows, and bands playing" as entertainment options. And "students are very supportive about attending others' performances." Undergrads also "tend to have small parties in their rooms, and every weekend, a house always throws a party." Because "constantly being on campus can get claustrophobic," "people with cars try to leave for the weekend." Many head to the Williams College campus, about a half-hour drive to the south.

Student Body

Bennington students range from "vegan, environmentally conscious punks that pretend to be hippies to a significant group of students extremely passionate about their work." The tiny student body "gets oppressive at times, but is very comforting at others. You can say 'I was with Patrick,' and everyone will know who you are talking about." Students tend to subdivide into cliques: "I have a small but very lovable group of friends; that's the tendency here, to form cliques of friends . . . it's just the nature of a small school like this," explains one student. The atmosphere here is politically and socially liberal; "sexuality, religion, social class—none of that matters. I swear, it's like a hippie commune utopia or at least another dimension from *The Matrix*," is how one student describes it.

ADMISSIONS

Very important factors considered include: Character/personal qualities, class rank, essays, interview, recommendations, secondary school record, standardized test scores, talent/ability, volunteer work. *Important factors considered include:* Extracurricular activities. *Other factors considered include:* Alumni/ae relation, minority status, work experience. SAT Reasoning or ACT required. SAT Subject Tests recommended. TOEFL required of all international applicants. High school diploma is required, and GED is accepted. *Academic units recommended:* 4 English, 3 math, 3 science, 3 foreign language, 3 social studies.

The Inside Word

. For intellectually curious students Bennington can be a godsend, but for those who lack self-motivation it can represent a sidetracking of progress toward a degree. Admissions standards remain rigorous, and enrollment is on an upswing. Candidates will encounter a thorough review process that places great emphasis on matchmaking, which means that strong essays and solid interviews are a must. Intellectual types whose high school grades are inconsistent with their potential will find an opportunity for forgiveness if they can write well and demonstrate self-awareness and a capacity to thrive in the college's self-driven environment. Minority students are rarities in the applicant pool and thus enjoy "most-favored candidate" status—provided they fit Bennington's profile.

FINANCIAL AID

Students should submit: FAFSA, institution's own financial aid form, CSS/Financial Aid PROFILE, noncustodial (divorced/separated) parents' statement, parent and student federal tax returns and W-2 forms. CSS/Financial Aid PROFILE for early decision applicants only. Regular filing deadline 2/15. The Princeton Review suggests that all financial aid forms be submitted as soon as possible after 1/1. *Need-based scholarships/grants offered:* Pell, SEOG, state scholarships/grants, private scholarships, the school's own gift aid. *Loan aid offered:* FFEL Subsidized Stafford, FFEL Unsubsidized Stafford, FFEL PLUS, college/university loans from institutional funds. College/university loans from institutional fund for international students only. Applicants will be notified of awards on or about 4/1. Federal Work-study Program available. Institutional employment available. Off-campus job opportunities are good.

FROM THE ADMISSIONS OFFICE

"The educational philosophy of Bennington is rooted in an abiding faith in the talent, imagination, and responsibility of the individual; thus, the principle of learning by practice underlies every major feature of a Bennington education. We believe that a college education should not merely provide preparation for graduate school or a career, but should be an experience valuable in itself and the model for lifelong learning. Faculty, staff, and students at Bennington work together in a collaborative environment based upon respect for each other and the power of ideas to make a difference in the world. We are looking for intellectually curious students who have a passion for learning, are willing to take risks, and are open to making connections."

For even more information on this school, turn to page 465 of the "Stats" section.

BENTLEY COLLEGE

175 FOREST STREET, WALTHAM, MA 02452-4705 • ADMISSIONS: 781-891-2244 • FAX: 781-891-3414
FINANCIAL AID: 781-891-3441 • E-MAIL: UGADMISSION@BENTLEY.EDU • WEBSITE: WWW.BENTLEY.EDU

Ratings
Quality of Life: 87   **Academic:** 83   **Admissions:** 89   **Financial Aid:** 78

Academics

Bentley College, a business-focused school just outside Boston, "is all about making sure you have a career when you graduate, not just a job. They don't teach you useless textbook information just to impress people with how much you know. Most of what you learn is something that will help you advance, either as a business professional or as a person." Students agree that this practical approach is what makes Bentley special. One student writes, "It's like what my marketing professor taught me, 'Mass customization: You get what you need.' This school focuses on knowledge to take with you in life and gives you limitless options as to where you want it to go." Bentley professors are "really good in terms of teaching and [providing] assistance outside the classroom" and they make sure there is "a good balance between class work and homework." As one student puts it, "The overall academic environment is challenging but not rigorous. There is no need to study on Friday and Saturday night." Add "technological resources that are some of the best," an administration that "is very open to student suggestion and input," and the school's "connections with companies so you can get a job or an internship," and people are left asking themselves what else they could possibly need. Oh, yeah: "proximity to Boston."

> **SURVEY SAYS . . .**
> *Small classes*
> *Great computer facilities*
> *Great library*
> *Campus feels safe*
> *Lots of beer drinking*
> *Hard liquor is popular*

Life

With an active campus set near a big college town, Bentley College offers its students the best of all possible social worlds. One undergraduate says, "Life here is great; not only is the campus fifteen minutes from Harvard Square by an hourly shuttle, but [also] there is a very active party scene at Bentley." Students "love to have fun, but never at the expense of grades. People who party even a little too hard tend to drop out very quick." Although many students drink, those who choose to abstain "are respected for it and have fun on campus as well." That fun includes involvement in Bentley's intramural and intercollegiate athletic programs. "There are also many extracurricular activities to participate in, so students are rarely bored. There's always a school-sponsored event every night of the week, generally more on weekends. There is a pub and [a] coffeehouse, which host weekly events such as movies, comedians, and musicians." Students who decide to just chill at home think "the dorms are outstanding, so living conditions after you are a freshman are nice." Beyond campus is the city of Boston, which is "a great college city. Going into the city to eat, shop, or just hang out is great for the weekends. [There are] great museums, lots of culture, and, of course, all the other colleges."

Student Body

There are plenty of "cookie-cutter business students" at Bentley; they're the type of kids who are "hardworking, Type A personality individuals [who are] looking for a predominantly business education and who are very career-focused." Many students who attend the school come from money. One student agrees and adds, "Typical Bentley student[s have] heavy wallet[s] in their Abercrombie pants, although [they are] sometimes [kept] in the center console[s] of their BMW[s]." A huge international population means "the campus is very diverse," but many wish the gender demographic would change. One male student complains, "There are a lot more males on the campus than females." The student body can be somewhat cliquish. One undergraduate explains, "There are three types of students at Bentley College: the jock, the Greek, and neither of the above. Everyone knows their group and is happy with it because you end up with people like yourself."

ADMISSIONS

Very important factors considered include: Secondary school record, standardized test scores. *Important factors considered include:* Character/personal qualities, class rank, essays, extracurricular activities, interview, recommendations, talent/ability, volunteer work, work experience. *Other factors considered include:* Alumni/ae relation, geographical residence, minority status, state residency. SAT Reasoning and SAT Subject Tests or ACT required. TOEFL required of all international applicants. High school diploma is required, and GED is accepted. *Academic units recommended:* 4 English, 4 math, 3 science (3 science lab), 3 foreign language, 3 social studies.

The Inside Word

If you're a solid B student, there's little challenge to encounter in the admissions process here. The college's appealing greater Boston location and career-oriented academic strengths account for a sizable applicant pool and the moderate selectivity that it enjoys.

FINANCIAL AID

Students should submit: FAFSA, CSS/Financial Aid PROFILE, noncustodial (divorced/separated) parents' statement, business/farm supplement. Regular filing deadline 2/1. The Princeton Review suggests that all financial aid forms be submitted as soon as possible after 1/1. *Need-based scholarships/grants offered:* Pell, SEOG, state scholarships/grants, private scholarships, the school's own gift aid. *Loan aid offered:* FFEL Subsidized Stafford, FFEL Unsubsidized Stafford, FFEL PLUS, Federal Perkins, state loans. Applicants will be notified of awards on a rolling basis beginning on or about 3/25. Federal Work-study Program available. Institutional employment available. Off-campus job opportunities are excellent.

FROM THE ADMISSIONS OFFICE

"Bentley, a business university, blends the breadth and technological strength of a large university with the values and student focus of a small college. Students who are interested in business professions can choose from a wide variety of programs, including accountancy, finance, marketing, and management—all with a strong foundation in information technology. A Bentley education includes outstanding preparation in the arts and sciences, a faculty of dynamic teachers with real-world research and consulting experience, and a vibrant campus teeming with athletic, social, and cultural opportunities. Ethics and social responsibility are woven throughout the school's curriculum; Bentley's Service-Learning program is ranked among the top 20 in the United States. Students also study abroad and pursue internships at leading companies in the U.S. and overseas.

"Concepts and theories that students learn in the classroom come alive in several hands-on, high-tech learning laboratories—each among the first of its kind in higher education: the financial Trading Room, Center for Marketing Technology, Accounting Center for Electronic Learning and Business Measurement, Center for Languages and International Collaboration and the Design and Usability Testing Center. The Mobile Computing program provides all Bentley freshmen with a fully-loaded, network-ready laptop computer.

"New athletic and recreation facilities complement the 22 varsity teams in Division I and II, and the extensive intramural and recreational sports programs. Boston and Cambridge, just minutes from campus, are accessible via the school's free shuttle. Both cities are great resources for internships, job opportunities, cultural events, and social life. "

For even more information on this school, turn to page 466 of the "Stats" section.

BOSTON COLLEGE

140 COMMONWEALTH AVENUE, DEVLIN HALL 208, CHESTNUT HILL, MA 02467-3809 • ADMISSIONS: 617-552-3100
FAX: 617-552-0798 • FINANCIAL AID: 800-294-0294 • E-MAIL: UGADMIS@BC.EDU • WEBSITE: WWW.BC.EDU

Ratings
Quality of Life: 94   **Academic:** 88   **Admissions:** 96   **Financial Aid:** 93

Academics

Students praise the strong academics, the competitive athletic teams, the lively social scene, and the premium location that all combine to create a remarkable all-around college experience at Boston College. For many, though, BC's greatest asset is the "strong spiritual presence [that] shows how positive an influence religion can have on one's life." Don't worry; "They don't try to make anybody be Catholic" here. Rather, the school "simply reflects the Jesuit ideals of community, spirituality, and social justice," and these ideals pervade both the curriculum and the academic community. True to the Jesuit ideal of "educating the entire person," BC requires a thorough core curriculum "including philosophy, theology, and language requirements" rounded out by "strong [but optional] programs, such as internships and studying abroad." Beyond the core curriculum, "BC offers something for everyone. If you go here, you are with business students, nursing students, education majors, and arts and science majors." And even though this is a fairly large school, students insist that "you never feel like a number here. Yes, you have to be independent and seek out your professors. But when you do seek them out, you get incredible individualized attention." One undergrad sums it up like this: "BC's strength is a mix of everything. It may not be an Ivy League school in academics or win national championships everywhere in NCAA athletics, but it is a 'jack of all trades' when it comes to academics, athletics, art, and social activity."

Life

There is a "real spirit of volunteerism and giving back to the community [that] is one of BC's greatest strengths," many students here tell us, reporting that "there are about a million volunteer groups on campus, as well as a bunch of immersion trips to different places, the most renowned of which is the Appalachia group trip." Students here "really care about the world outside of Chestnut Hill. In a way, even the notion of studying abroad has turned into a question of 'How can I help people while there?' BC's Jesuit mission is contagious." Not all extracurricular life at BC is so altruistic, however; students here love to have fun in "the greatest location of any college ever! We are on the T [train] so we can get into the city of Boston whenever we like, but we are in suburbia so we can relax without all of the gimmicks of city life." Undergrads love to explore Boston, a city with "tons of great museums, historical sights, restaurants and a lot of great concerts," that also happens to be "such a big college town. It's easy to meet kids that go to BU, Harvard, Emerson, Northeastern or any of the other universities in the area." Closer to campus, BC has "great sports. Our football team has won five bowl games in a row and basketball is, at this writing, ranked 9th in the nation. The ice hockey team is consistently ranked high nationally," and students turn out to support their Eagles in both men's and women's athletics.

Student Body

Boston magazine once described the BC student body as "a J. Crew catalogue with a slight hangover," and while students protest that "there are a number of students who do not conform to such a vision of the student body," they also admit that "there are a lot of preppy people at our school. Girls usually wear skirts and Uggs (unless it's freezing out, but it has to be very, very cold), and boys usually wear jeans and t-shirts or collared cotton shirts." And yes, "the typical BC student is white, Catholic, usually from the Northeast, who probably had family that went to BC," but with 9,000 undergrads, "we have students from all sorts of backgrounds, religions, sexual orientations." BC students tend to be extremely ambitious; they are "those super-involved people in high school who were three-season team captains, class president, and straight-A students. [They] have carried over that focus and determination into college."

ADMISSIONS

Very important factors considered include: Secondary school record, standardized test scores. *Important factors considered include:* Alumni/ae relation, character/personal qualities, class rank, essays, extracurricular activities, recommendations, religious affiliation/commitment, talent/ability, volunteer work. *Other factors considered include:* Minority status, work experience. SAT Reasoning and SAT Subject Tests or ACT required. TOEFL required of all international applicants. High school diploma is required, and GED is accepted. *Academic units recommended:* 4 English, 4 math, 4 science (4 science lab), 4 foreign language.

The Inside Word

While applications to BC in general have increased over the past couple of years, early action applications have risen more dramatically. Standards remain high, and we more than recommend a strong college-preparatory curriculum in high school—it's a must to have a shot. With a large percentage of its students coming from Catholic high schools such applicants are treated well, but there is little room for relaxation in the process. Applicants need to show strong SAT reasoning and SAT subject scores, but keep the tests in perspective—BC is interested in the whole package.

FINANCIAL AID

Students should submit: FAFSA, CSS/Financial Aid PROFILE, noncustodial (divorced/separated) parents' statement, business/farm supplement, parent and student tax returns and W-2 forms. The Princeton Review suggests that all financial aid forms be submitted as soon as possible after 1/1. *Need-based scholarships/grants offered:* Pell, SEOG, state scholarships/grants, private scholarships, the school's own gift aid. *Loan aid offered:* FFEL Subsidized Stafford, FFEL Unsubsidized Stafford, FFEL PLUS, Federal Perkins, Federal Nursing, state loans. Applicants will be notified of awards on or about 4/1. Federal Work-study Program available. Off-campus job opportunities are excellent.

FROM THE ADMISSIONS OFFICE

"Boston College students achieve at the highest levels with honors last year including two Rhodes scholarship winners, nine Fulbrights, and one each for Marshall, Goldwater, Madison, and Truman Post-Graduate Fellowship Programs. Junior Year Abroad and Scholar of the College Program offer students flexibility within the curriculum. Facilities opened in the past 10 years include: the Merkert Chemistry Center, Higgins Hall (housing the Biology and Physics departments), three new residence halls, the Yawkey Athletics Center, the Vanderslice Commons Dining Hall, the Hillside Cafe, and a state-of-the-art library. Students enjoy the vibrant location in Chestnut Hill with easy access to the cultural and historical richness of Boston."

For even more information on this school, turn to page 466 of the "Stats" section.

BOSTON UNIVERSITY

121 Bay State Road, Boston, MA 02215 • Admissions: 617-353-2300 • Fax: 617-353-9695
Financial Aid: 617-353-2965 • E-mail: admissions@bu.edu • Website: www.bu.edu

Ratings
Quality of Life: 82   Academic: 85   Admissions: 94   Financial Aid: 86

Academics

Boston University (BU), "an intense academic school in the perfect, fun, intense college city" of Boston, knows how to wring the most out of its premier location. "Professors utilize the city [by] leading field trips to the Museum of Fine Arts, the Museum of Science, and a French film festival at Coolidge Corner, to name a few." Internships abound, aided by the school's "enormous alumni network" in its hometown. And of course, the allure of a world-class city helps BU attract luminaries to the faculty, including poet Robert Pinsky, physicist and Nobel laureate Sheldon Glashow, and biomedical engineer and MacArthur Grant recipient Jim Collins. Students say, "We have an amazing faculty and [amazing] resources. BU is very good about getting world-renowned writers, philosophers, and political figures to teach or engage in programs here at BU." Of course, not every class is taught by a Nobel laureate or even by a full professor; in fact, "the classes are too often taught by graduate students. Plus, there are too few sections of each class." Although this problem exists, most agree that their instructors "seem like really nice people. They all have office hours and encourage the students to come and visit." One student offers prospective undergraduates advice: "Go into this college as an 'undeclared' major. There is no changing majors without major paperwork and a high GPA."

> **SURVEY SAYS . . .**
> *Students love Boston, MA*
> *Great off-campus food*
> *Campus feels safe*
> *Students are happy*
> *Student publications are popular*
> *Lots of beer drinking*
> *(Almost) everyone smokes*

Life

Boston University does not offer the classic campus-focused college experience because life "is very much centered [in] the city. Attending school is just part of your life at BU. There are so many other things going on in the area that you could go weeks without attending a BU party." The Boston club scene is a huge draw for BU students, as are the city's many bars, restaurants, stores, museums, theaters, concert halls, and ballets. There's a ton of colleges in town, so there's always a party—many parties—to be found. One place where students won't find parties is in BU dorms; the school's strict visitation policies ensure that. Many students complain that "the rules are way too strict," but others appreciate that the rules show "how focused our administration is on stressing academics to the students here." Campus is a term students rarely use since "Boston University doesn't really have a closed campus; the entire school is basically integrated with the city." However, the campus does offer "great fitness facilities with a swimming pool, ice-skating rink, weight rooms, cardio rooms, and classes in things from yoga to aerobics to Zen meditation to ice skating." You'll also find "lots of quiet places to read." Boston University's big intercollegiate sport is men's hockey, which some students follow religiously.

Student Body

Because "BU is huge," "there are all types of people here." Students say, "The school is so large that fitting in is not really an issue." The university's reputation as a haven for Louis Vuitton-toting rich girls may be undeserved; one student says, "These people are the loud stereotypes. BU is so large that the atypical people dominate my social life rather than the bland Abercrombie types that dominate the sidewalk on the way to class." While "most of the students at this school are from wealthy American families, there is a fair percentage of minority students, particularly Asians and Indians/Pakistanis." "Everyone gets along," although "there may not be too much interaction between the majority and minority." A lopsided female-to-male ratio means that "guys get along quite easily with each other because there is no competition." Students also report that "sexual orientation is not a big issue on this campus. Many people are openly homosexual, and they are accepted."

ADMISSIONS

Very important factors considered include: Secondary school record. *Important factors considered include:* Class rank, essays, recommendations, standardized test scores. *Other factors considered include:* Alumni/ae relation, character/personal qualities, extracurricular activities, volunteer work, work experience. SAT Reasoning and SAT Subject Tests or ACT required. TOEFL required of all international applicants. High school diploma is required, and GED is accepted. *Academic units required:* 4 English, 3 math, 3 science (3 science lab), 2 foreign language, 3 social studies. *Academic units recommended:* 4 English, 4 math, 4 science (4 science lab), 4 foreign language, 4 social studies.

The Inside Word

Boston is one of the nation's most popular college towns, and BU benefits tremendously. The university's last few entering classes have been chock-full of high-caliber students; despite a general decline in applications at colleges in the Northeast, it will continue to be competitive to gain admission to BU, as applications keep a steady upward trend and entering class size is kept in check. Those who aren't up to traditional standards are sometimes referred to the less selective College of General Studies, which allows students to continue on to other divisions of the university once they prove themselves academically—but standards here are rising.

FINANCIAL AID

Students should submit: FAFSA, CSS/Financial Aid PROFILE, state aid form, noncustodial (divorced/separated) parents' statement, business/farm supplement. Regular filing deadline 2/15. The Princeton Review suggests that all financial aid forms be submitted as soon as possible after 1/1. *Need-based scholarships/grants offered:* Pell, SEOG, state scholarships/grants, private scholarships, the school's own gift aid. *Loan aid offered:* Direct Subsidized Stafford, Direct Unsubsidized Stafford, Direct PLUS, Federal Perkins, state loans. Applicants will be notified of awards on a rolling basis beginning on or about 3/15. Federal Work-study Program available. Institutional employment available. Off-campus job opportunities are excellent.

FROM THE ADMISSIONS OFFICE

"Boston University (BU) is a private teaching and research institution with a strong emphasis on undergraduate education. We are committed to providing the highest level of teaching excellence, and fulfillment of this pledge is our highest priority. Boston University has 11 undergraduate schools and colleges offering 250 major and minor areas of concentration. Students may choose from programs of study in areas as diverse as biochemistry, theater arts, physical therapy, elementary education, broadcast journalism, international relations, business, and computer engineering. BU has an international student body, with students from every state and more than 100 countries. In addition, opportunities to study abroad exist through 44 semester-long programs, spanning 26 cities and 18 countries on six continents."

For even more information on this school, turn to page 467 of the "Stats" section.

BOWDOIN COLLEGE

5000 COLLEGE STATION, BRUNSWICK, ME 04011-8441 • ADMISSIONS: 207-725-3100 • FAX: 207-725-3101
FINANCIAL AID: 207-725-3273 • E-MAIL: ADMISSIONS@BOWDOIN.EDU • WEBSITE: WWW.BOWDOIN.EDU

Ratings
Quality of Life: 95   Academic: 94   Admissions: 98   Financial Aid: 97

Academics

Bowdoin College offers an intensive liberal arts education in "an incredibly friendly, supportive, and challenging learning environment." This is "a beautiful place where students work hard at the things they love, not because they are competing with someone but because they want to do well." The school is especially "strong in the sciences,

> **SURVEY SAYS . . .**
> *Small classes*
> *Great food on campus*
> *Lots of beer drinking*

with great lab facilities and research opportunities;" few departments don't garner raves from students. Throughout the school, professors "are first-class teachers who are here because they want to teach. They go out of their way to have study groups and sessions that prepare the students well. They also unobtrusively go out of their way to make sure that each student is successful and comfortable." Regarding administrations, students say, "[They] do a great job of letting us know that the reason they're there is for us, and they really follow through on that. Every single one, from secretaries to the president of the college, is receptive and very visible on campus." Add "excellent internship and study abroad resources, willingness of alumni to stay in touch and help current students, and the dedication the school has for increasing diversity," and what more could a prospective freshman ask for from an undergraduate institution? Perhaps a "great outreach program; the school gets every student in touch with at least one faculty member who knows them well, so every student has a way out, a person to vent to in times of discomfort."

Life

Students describe Bowdoin as "a work-hard, play-hard type of place. Classes are really hard, and the students really like to wind down come Friday night. It's easy to get alcohol, but there's never a ton of abuse here." Students needn't drink for lack of things to do; our survey respondents describe an active campus outside of class. There is an unusually "high involvement in sports at Bowdoin, which keeps students active and well-rounded." Many undergraduates claim that "most students play a varsity sport." For entertainment, "the Campus Activities Board has a budget of $120,000-plus exclusively for booking acts at the school, [which] averages to about one event per week: theater groups, musical groups, and comedians." The school also "brings a lot of speakers and lecturers." Parties take place mostly in the social houses. One student says, "[Social houses] are basically frats without the exclusivity. [They] usually have a cool theme or band, but most everyone is downstairs at the keg. I don't drink, but I still go to these parties." Hometown Brunswick "is charming, with great restaurants, two movie theaters, a coffeehouse," and a few other student-friendly establishments. But "town-gown relations aren't the greatest as a result of the parties and noise." The school is conveniently located "fifteen to twenty minutes from Freeport, and if you're a shopper, this is heaven. Burberry, Coach, The North Face, Starbucks, Bath and Body Works, Abercrombie and Fitch outlet, Banana Republic, Gap outlet, they're all there." A little farther away is Portland, of which at least one student writes, "I'd take this city over Manhattan anyday: cobblestone streets, cute shops, great restaurants, and good parking. It's fabulous and right on the water!"

Student Body

Students proudly tell us that at Bowdoin, "everyone seems to be the kid in high school who played three varsity sports: ran the yearbook, newspaper, or student government: and worked hard to get good grades." These "intelligent, funny, socially active, and motivated" students are "primarily concerned with their academic success, putting academics before everything else." This explains why "they're so stressed out." The preppy contingent is large; an undergraduate explains, "There is definitely a certain J. Crew/Abercrombie and Fitch look to the majority of students." However, the student body "varie[s] socioeconomically." Although "mostly white," the student body "has become much more diverse in the past four years."

ADMISSIONS

Very important factors considered include: Character/personal qualities, class rank, essays, extracurricular activities, recommendations, secondary school record, talent/ability. *Important factors considered include:* Alumni/ae relation, geographical residence, minority status, volunteer work, work experience. *Other factors considered include:* Interview, standardized test scores, state residency. TOEFL required of all international applicants: High school diploma is required, and GED is not accepted. *Academic units recommended:* 4 English, 4 math, 4 science (3 science lab), 4 foreign language, 4 social studies.

The Inside Word

This is one of the 20 or so most selective colleges in the country. Virtually everyone who applies is well-qualified academically, which means criteria besides grades and test scores become critically important in candidate review. Who you are, what you think, where you are from, and why you are interested in Bowdoin are the sorts of things that will determine whether you get in, provided you meet their high academic standards.

FINANCIAL AID

Students should submit: FAFSA, institution's own financial aid form, CSS/Financial Aid PROFILE, noncustodial (divorced/separated) parents' statement, business/farm supplement. Regular filing deadline 2/15. The Princeton Review suggests that all financial aid forms be submitted as soon as possible after 1/1. *Need-based scholarships/grants offered:* Pell, SEOG, state scholarships/grants, private scholarships, the school's own gift aid. *Loan aid offered:* FFEL Subsidized Stafford, FFEL Unsubsidized Stafford, FFEL PLUS, Federal Perkins, state loans, college/university loans from institutional funds. Applicants will be notified of awards on or about 4/5. Federal Work-study Program available. Institutional employment available. Off-campus job opportunities are good.

FROM THE ADMISSIONS OFFICE

"Each year Bowdoin sponsors myriad events, including performances by bands, comedians, artists, and dancers as well as lectures and film series, community service events, and the occasional scavenger hunt. Performers who have appeared at the college recently include Savion Glover, Dar Williams, Guster, Wynton Marsalis, and Mos Def. Speakers have included David Sedaris, Adrienne Rich, Robert Reich, Spike Lee, Nobel Laureate Thomas Cech, and playwright Tony Kushner. The college has more than 100 active student organizations. About 70 percent of students participate in community service during their time at Bowdoin, and the college's many volunteer programs allow students to interact with the Brunswick community. Club and intramural sports and the Outing Club enable students to get involved in physical fitness without having to be star athletes. Bowdoin is determined to be a place that brings together people from widely diverse ethnic and economic backgrounds, from different parts of the country and the world, and with divergent political beliefs, a full range of religious identities, and broad academic interests."

For even more information on this school, turn to page 467 of the "Stats" section.

BRANDEIS UNIVERSITY

415 SOUTH STREET, MS003, WALTHAM, MA 02454 • ADMISSIONS: 781-736-3500 • FAX: 781-736-3536
FINANCIAL AID: 781-736-3700 • E-MAIL: SENDINFO@BRANDEIS.EDU • WEBSITE: WWW.BRANDEIS.EDU

Ratings
Quality of Life: 84   **Academic:** 90   **Admissions:** 96   **Financial Aid:** 60

Academics

"Big enough [so you can] always meet new people, [yet] small enough [so you can] always see a friend," is how one English major describes Brandeis University. Most students agree that Brandeis gives them a taste of the research-oriented life usually found at a large university while letting them enjoy the comforts of a small liberal arts college. Students give rave reviews of their professors. One undergraduate writes, "Brandeis professors aren't just given a list of their students' names at the beginning of the semester. They're also given their pictures. And many of them, even in large lecture classes, make an effort to study those pictures and learn students' names. I think that's a statement on the relative involvement professors here have with students." Many of the faculty members at Brandeis are "illustrious professors who are often experts and distinguished people in their fields," but they also bring a sense of humor to the classroom. For example, a music and psychology double major recommends that newcomers look out for one of her music theory professors because he "balances a piano bench on his head." Another excellent benefit at Brandeis is that students are encouraged to take classes from a wide variety of disciplines. A third-year biology major boasts, "I've managed to take theater, neuroscience, music, and philosophy courses without conflict." But don't think that fun is the same as easy. Academics at Brandeis are "very competitive," and "students need to be highly motivated to succeed."

Life

"If you're looking for a big party school with outstanding sports, don't come here," warns a junior. "But if you're looking for a small liberal arts university with an intelligent, inquisitive student body [who balances] work and fun, this is the place for you." Students have long complained that the opportunities for fun at Brandeis are limited, but in recent years there's been "an amazing initiative taking place by students and administrators to make Brandeis more fun." Many students like to take a shuttle into Boston so they can get a little crazy; however, there are other diversionary outlets available. One undergraduate says, "In the time that I've been here, I've gotten to go skydiving, learn[ed] how to knit, learn[ed] to work a state-of-the-art sound system, [paid] $5.00 to see musical acts like Ben Folds, walk[ed] around an on-campus art museum, edit[ed] my own literary magazine, and participate[d] in all kinds of cool events in Boston and on campus, all because of the opportunities provided by the school." Performance groups are very popular— "a cappella groups are huge on campus!"—but there are also plenty of events and clubs that appeal to other interests. One student adds, "And if there isn't an activity that satisfies you, then charter your own club!" Students even report that the campus's "boxlike architecture and drab décor are undergoing some improvements." Students also do their best to take advantage of the New England winters. A senior says, "We sled down Library Hill on cafeteria trays."

Student Body

"While most people like to say they can define the typical Brandeis student (Jewish, from a suburb, upper-middle class), so many of my friends don't fit that stereotype," reports one student. It's true that "the university was established on Jewish ideals" and that "there is a decent Jewish population" at Brandeis, but "you can find anyone into anything, I promise," writes a junior. She continues, "I've done everything from pagan rituals to orthodox services to cutting friends' hair to dressing guys in drag." While one English major is exaggerating when she says, "The typical Brandeis student is a George W. Bush-loathing, wannabe gangsta that enjoys philosophy, tofu, and Birkenstocks," she's hinting at something that holds much of this student body together: Even when the wind's not blowing, the student body leans to the left politically. And regarding the political thing, Brandeis boasts "a pretty strong activist community."

ADMISSIONS

Very important factors considered include: Class rank, secondary school record. *Important factors considered include:* Character/personal qualities, essays, extracurricular activities, recommendations, standardized test scores, talent/ability, volunteer work, work experience. *Other factors considered include:* Alumni/ae relation, interview, minority status. SAT Reasoning and SAT Subject Tests or ACT required. TOEFL required of all international applicants. High school diploma is required, and GED is accepted. *Academic units recommended:* 4 English, 3 math, 1 science (1 science lab), 3 foreign language, 1 history, 4 academic electives.

The Inside Word

While the university has a reputation for quality, the low yield of admits who actually choose to attend Brandeis results in a higher acceptance rate than one might expect. Weak students will still find it difficult to gain admission. The option of submitting ACT scores instead of SAT and SAT II: Subject Test scores should be the hands-down choice of any candidate who doesn't have to take SAT IIs for any other reason.

FINANCIAL AID

The Princeton Review suggests that all financial aid forms be submitted as soon as possible after 1/1.

FROM THE ADMISSIONS OFFICE

"Education at Brandeis is personal, combining the intimacy of a small liberal arts college and the intellectual power of a large research university. Classes are small and are taught by professors, 98 percent of whom hold the highest degree in their fields. They give students personal attention in state-of-the-art resources, giving them the tools to succeed in a variety of post-graduate endeavors.

"This vibrant, freethinking, intellectual university was founded in 1948. Brandeis University reflects the values of the first Jewish Supreme Court Justice Louis Brandeis, which are passion for learning, commitment to social justice, respect for creativity and diversity, and concern for the world.

"Brandeis has an ideal location on the commuter rail nine miles west of Boston; state-of-the-art sports facilities; and internships that complement interests in law, medicine, government, finance, business, and the arts. Brandeis offers generous university scholarships and need-based financial aid that can be renewed for four years."

For even more information on this school, turn to page 467 of the "Stats" section.

BROWN UNIVERSITY

Box 1876, 45 Prospect Street, Providence, RI 02912 • Admissions: 401-863-2378 • Fax: 401-863-9300
Financial Aid: 401-863-2721 • E-mail: admission_undergraduate@brown.edu • Website: www.brown.edu

Ratings
Quality of Life: 95   **Academic:** 83   **Admissions:** 99   **Financial Aid:** 96

Academics

"It's like the school has a motto," writes a typical Brown University undergrad, "and that motto is: 'It's your money. Why should we choose your classes?'" Thanks to the school's open curriculum, "being at Brown means you will never again have to take a class if you don't want to." Students who flock here are the type who yearn for such academic freedom; they "love the open curriculum and the chance it gives us to really invest ourselves in what we're most interested in. Brown allows you to explore academically without punishing you for it." Brown also "allows students to choose how we are evaluated in our classes by choosing to take any class S/NC (Satisfactory/No Credit). This says a lot about the learning philosophy of the school, which is mainly focused on the process of learning rather than simply the results." Brown professors "are engaging, challenging us as students and as participants in the learning process," and are "very accessible, dedicated to undergraduate students and usually pretty funny outside the classroom." Students appreciate that "a lot of the introductory classes are taught by brilliant professors. The concentration is truly on the undergraduates." Administrators, "as strange as it seems, are also incredibly accessible." Sums up one student, "Everything is at your fingertips, but you have to reach out for it. At Brown, very few things will simply come to you, but you can be sure that if you want it, it will be there."

> **SURVEY SAYS . . .**
> *No one cheats*
> *Students are friendly*
> *Great off-campus food*
> *Students are happy*
> *Political activism is popular*

Life

"The social scene is a lot like the academic scene" at Brown "in that there is a huge variety of options, and people tend to experience most of them. From hanging out to cocktail parties, from hippies partying in their co-ops to kids studying in the library, from fraternity parties to watching a movie, everything you can imagine doing for fun happens." Students agree that "Brown is a school that definitely parties, and Wednesday night through Sunday students here are partying," but not until they get their schoolwork done. Academics are demanding and students here work hard, but "aside from exams and major assignments, life is laid-back. That isn't to say the students lack passion or drive—quite the opposite—but there's a marked lack of nervous tension." Undergrads find plenty of time for extracurriculars, populating "over 150 extracurricular clubs and activities," including "great theater and music" opportunities. They also enjoy "free lectures by everyone from Spike Lee to Mikhail Gorbachev, free concerts, free comedy show, plays. We have anything and everything. There is almost too much going on." And then there's Providence, "a nice location with all sorts of cool night clubs and restaurants that don't make it easy to be bored on a Saturday night. There are hot spots like Fish Company, where people drink and dance, and there's Thayer Street, with anything a college student could ever need, from groceries, books, and clothes to videos, bikes, and clubs." Brown undergrads also take advantage of the fact that "Boston and New York City are relatively close by."

Student Body

Most Brown undergrads are "individual, free-thinking, and eager to learn." They are "very smart, have a keen knowledge of current affairs, and can talk about Plato, FDR, or biology," but "they don't have swelled heads. They're generally pretty well-grounded, open to new ideas, and fun." Like the New Englanders who surround them, "they tend to be very liberal and very politically active. It is a necessity to be up-to-date on current events, as discussions and debates take place from dorm rooms to the gym to the cafeteria." The "typically small 'outsider' communities (e.g. GLBT students) here have a lot of support on campus and generally hang out together." While "Brown has a reputation as a hippie school, it really isn't: There are people who fit into every social niche, and although it's not always easy to find the right people right away, they're out there."

ADMISSIONS

Very important factors considered include: Character/personal qualities, secondary school record, talent/ability. *Important factors considered include:* Class rank, essays, extracurricular activities, recommendations. *Other factors considered include:* Alumni/ae relation, geographical residence, interview, minority status, standardized test scores, state residency, volunteer work, work experience. SAT Reasoning and SAT Subject Tests or ACT required. TOEFL required of all international applicants. High school diploma is required, and GED is not accepted. *Academic units required:* 4 English, 3 math, 3 science (2 science lab), 3 foreign language, 2 history, 1 academic elective. *Academic units recommended:* 4 English, 4 math, 4 science (3 science lab), 4 foreign language, 2 history, 1 academic elective.

The Inside Word

The cream of just about every crop applies to Brown. Gaining admission requires more than just a superior academic profile from high school. Some candidates, such as the sons and daughters of Brown graduates (who are admitted at virtually double the usual acceptance rate), have a better chance for admission than most others. Minority students benefit from some courtship, particularly once admitted. Ivies like to share the wealth and distribute offers of admission across a wide range of constituencies. Candidates from states that are overrepresented in the applicant pool, such as New York, have to be particularly distinguished in order to have the best chance at admission. So do those who attend high schools with many seniors applying to Brown, as it is rare for several students from any one school to be offered admission.

FINANCIAL AID

Students should submit: FAFSA, CSS/Financial Aid PROFILE, noncustodial (divorced/separated) parents' statement, business/farm supplement. Regular filing deadline 2/1. The Princeton Review suggests that all financial aid forms be submitted as soon as possible after 1/1. *Need-based scholarships/grants offered:* Pell, SEOG, state scholarships/grants, private scholarships, the school's own gift aid. *Loan aid offered:* Direct Subsidized Stafford, Direct Unsubsidized Stafford, Direct PLUS, Federal Perkins, state loans, college/university loans from institutional funds. Applicants will be notified of awards on or about 4/1. Federal Work-study Program available. Institutional employment available. Off-campus job opportunities are excellent.

FROM THE ADMISSIONS OFFICE

"It is our pleasure to introduce you to a unique and wonderful place of learning: Brown University. Founded in 1764, Brown is a private, coeducational, Ivy League university in which the intellectual development of undergraduate students is fostered by a dedicated faculty on a traditional New England campus."

For even more information on this school, turn to page 468 of the "Stats" section.

BRYANT UNIVERSITY

1150 Douglas Pike, Smithfield, RI 02917 • Admissions: 401-232-6100 • Fax: 401-232-6741
Financial Aid: 401-232-6020 • E-mail: admissions@bryant.edu • Website: www.bryant.edu

Ratings
Quality of Life: 84   **Academic:** 77   **Admissions:** 84   **Financial Aid:** 70

Academics

Bryant University offers some majors outside of business and management, but students tell us that pursuing one of those majors would be like ordering a dinner salad at a steakhouse. Students report that "every class, including the liberal arts classes...will involve business in one way or another." Another trumpets, "All my sociology, psychology, even ecology classes somehow discussed the business world within them!" Technologically, the school goes all-out, with "an enormous amount of resources on campus, including a simulated trading floor of the NYSE. Also, the entire campus is now wireless, so students can connect to the Internet with their laptops anywhere." Studying in such technologically advanced facilities means that "students can relate classes to the real world. We really do live in a business environment." The school's "student-centered" approach distinguishes it as well; "Everything on campus is designed to help out the student body, from the student programming, to the facilities, to the faculty. It is a very nurturing environment," explains one undergrad. Students also appreciate the "strong alumni relations, which help with internships and job placement." Solid programs in accounting, finance, marketing, and management have earned Bryant "a strong academic reputation. The school challenges its students to think creatively, both alone and in group settings, to reach goals."

> **SURVEY SAYS . . .**
> Small classes
> Great computer facilities
> Great library
> Athletic facilities are great
> Campus feels safe
> Lots of beer drinking
> Hard liquor is popular

Life

Because many "students at Bryant have——on top of a full course load—a job and/or internship, are members of a minimum of two organizations and/or sports, and hold some type of position of leadership," undergraduates "have little free time during the week." The campus is a very work-friendly environment, students tell us; "The abundance of technology on our campus——television monitors in almost every corner that you look, VOIP phones in the dorm rooms, wireless internet connectivity all over campus—creates an environment where students can work hard, relax a little, and work some more." The "very clean and well-landscaped [campus] is basically in the middle of the woods," providing "peace to study," but with the benefit "of a great city not far away." While weekdays are devoted to work and clubs, "Thursday through Sunday there are parties, or people going out to Providence who you can catch a ride with, with more studying on the weekends at intermittent times."

Student Body

"Since it's a business school with all serious business students for the most part, it excludes a wide diversity of people and their quirks," Bryant students observe. "Every day, either you're dressing in a business suit or you're in your daily clothing (mainly Abercrombie and Fitch and North Face and other high-end brand names, such as Burberry, Gucci, Seven, etc)." In other words, "idiosyncrasy is not encouraged; business etiquette and manners are a must at most times in this school." Most here are "preppy and financially stable. There are not many people who come from non-wealthy backgrounds." They can be cliquish; explains one student, "people rarely leave their own groups and the drama caused by much of it can get annoying by senior year." The school "has a sizeable population of international students, including students from China, India, Spain, South Africa, Turkey, and Italy. These students, many of whom belong to the Multicultural Student Union, are among the most active members of the Bryant community and take part in a number of events to educate Bryant students and faculty about different races and cultures."

ADMISSIONS

Very important factors considered include: Character/personal qualities, class rank, essays, recommendations, secondary school record, standardized test scores. *Important factors considered include:* Alumni/ae relation, extracurricular activities, talent/ability. *Other factors considered include:* Geographical residence, interview, minority status, volunteer work, work experience. SAT Reasoning or ACT required. TOEFL required of all international applicants. High school diploma is required, and GED is accepted. *Academic units required:* 4 English, 4 math, 3 science (2 science lab), 2 foreign language, 2 history/social sciences. *Academic units recommended:* 4 history/social sciences.

The Inside Word

If you're a solid student you should meet little trouble getting into Bryant. The university's admissions effort has brought in qualified applicants from across the country, but the heaviest draw remains from New England. Students attending Bryant will receive a solid business education as well as precious connections in the corporate worlds of Providence and Boston.

FINANCIAL AID

Students should submit: FAFSA. Regular filing deadline 2/15. The Princeton Review suggests that all financial aid forms be submitted as soon as possible after 1/1. *Need-based scholarships/grants offered:* Pell, SEOG, state scholarships/grants, private scholarships, the school's own gift aid. *Loan aid offered:* Direct Subsidized Stafford, Direct Unsubsidized Stafford, FFEL PLUS, Federal Perkins. Applicants will be notified of awards on or about 3/24. Federal Work-study Program available. Institutional employment available. Off-campus job opportunities are good.

FROM THE ADMISSIONS OFFICE

"Bryant is a student-centered University that provides the resources that students need to acquire knowledge, develop character, and achieve success—as they define it. In addition to a first-class faculty, state-of-the-art facilities, and advanced technology, Bryant offers stimulating classroom dynamics; internship opportunities at more than 300 companies; 60 student clubs and organizations; varsity, intramural, and club sports for men and women; and many opportunities for community service and leadership development.

"Bryant is the right choice for individuals seeking the best combination of a business and liberal arts education and offers degrees in Applied Psychology, Business Administration, Communication, Information Technology, International Business, and Liberal Studies. All of our academic programs blend the theoretical with the practical to make our graduates uniquely prepared to excel. Bryant's rigorous academic standards have been recognized and accredited by NEASC and AACSB International.

"Technology is a fundamental component of the learning process at Bryant. Every entering freshman is provided with an IBM laptop for personal use. Students exchange their laptop for a new one in their junior year, which they will own upon graduation. Bryant University was ranked 2nd of the "Top 25 Most Connected Campuses," by The Princeton's Review in October 2004 on Forbes.com.

"Bryant is situated on 392 acres of beautiful New England countryside and offers an array of cultural, social, and co-curricular educational activities right on campus. Bryant is only 15 minutes from Providence, one hour from Boston, and three hours from New York City and all of the attractions and opportunities available in these major metropolitan areas."

For even more information on this school, turn to page 468 of the "Stats" section.

Bryn Mawr College

101 North Merion Avenue, Bryn Mawr, PA 19010-2899 • Admissions: 610-526-5152
Fax: 610-526-7471 • Financial Aid: 610-526-5245 • E-mail: admissions@brynmawr.edu • Website: www.brynmawr.edu

Ratings
Quality of Life: 95   **Academic: 90**   **Admissions: 95**   **Financial Aid: 97**

Academics

"In order to excel at Bryn Mawr, you need to be willing to do more work than you've ever done in your life," under-grads at this small, prestigious all-women's college warn. Most are. They "challenge themselves, always doing their individual best" to meet the demands of the school's "insanely rigorous, but rewarding, academics." Why? One student writes, "I feel that the hours and hours of work are worthwhile. The students know that their work isn't just

busy work and that there are high standards; that pushes us to improve and learn in a way that wouldn't oth-erwise be possible." Bryn Mawr's "great track record for sending students to medical school" attests to the suc-cess of the school's approach; students' devotion to the school does likewise. Undergrads here especially appre-ciate the important role they play in running the school. Explains one student, "With the oldest self-governing association in the entire country, Bryn Mawr prides itself on the close communication between everyone in the community, from the president of the college to the incoming freshmen, each year." A student-administered honor code, one of the school's many treasured traditions, "makes taking final exams incredibly easy. Almost all exams are self-scheduled, so you can take them when you're ready, not when they're assigned." Additionally, "The student curriculum committee is very active in fulfilling the students' needs and desires for the academic process." Academic partnerships with Haverford, Swarthmore, and U Penn heavily supplement the "some-times pitiful course selection" here.

Life

"Because Bryn Mawr is all women, the social life is different from the traditional college experience," students here explain. "When you're a freshman, traditions like Lantern Night, Hell Week, and Parade Night really make you feel like a part of 'the sisterhood' of Bryn Mawr." Undergrads also point out that except for the aforemen-tioned traditions, "you really have to go off campus if you want to party. Fortunately there are so many colleges in such close proximity, including Villanova, Haverford, Swarthmore, and Penn, that you can always go out to a party if you want to, and you get to come home to a clean and quiet dorm." Many here report that "we spend most weekends in Philadelphia." For those who stick around campus on weekends, activities "usually include watching a movie and ordering out or going to some campus activity." The surrounding town, students agree, "is pretty boring." On a more positive note, "the campus is gorgeous. Imagine a Welsh castle," one undergrad suggests.

Student Body

"The only really common feature to Bryn Mawr women is an intense commitment to our studies. Other than that, everyone here really does their own thing," students agree. Even so, they see some dominant strains with-in their ranks; they detect, for example, a strong contingent of women who are "preppy, liberal, and open to homosexuality. Because it is an all-girls school, there are a lot of gay students, and those who aren't gay are accepting of the gay community." There are also conspicuous minorities of "high school misfits who come here to fit in, as well as students who take Harry Potter a little too seriously. They wear capes every day." Women here agree that "the community is overwhelmingly liberal politically, and the more moderate or conservative approaches or viewpoints of an issue can get lost in the majority at times. It would be nice to see more diversi-ty of political opinion at Bryn Mawr." Otherwise, Bryn Mawr students "run the gamut from the well-groomed New Jersey girl, to the vegan Girl Scout, to the hairy rugby player."

ADMISSIONS

Very important factors considered include: Essays, recommendations, secondary school record. *Important factors considered include:* Extracurricular activities. *Other factors considered include:* Class rank, interview, standardized test scores, talent/ability, volunteer work, work experience. SAT Reasoning and SAT Subject Tests or ACT required. TOEFL required of all international applicants. High school diploma is required, and GED is accepted. *Academic units required:* 2 academic electives. *Academic units recommended:* 4 English, 3 math, 2 science (1 science lab), 3 foreign language, 2 social studies, 2 history.

The Inside Word

Do not be deceived by Bryn Mawr's admit rate; its student body is among the academically best in the nation. Outstanding preparation for graduate study draws an applicant pool that is well prepared and intellectually curious. The admissions committee includes eight faculty members and four seniors. Each applicant is reviewed by four readers, including at least one faculty member and one student.

FINANCIAL AID

Students should submit: FAFSA, CSS/Financial Aid PROFILE, noncustodial (divorced/separated) parents' statement, business/farm supplement, student and parent federal tax returns. Regular filing deadline 2/4. The Princeton Review suggests that all financial aid forms be submitted as soon as possible after 1/1. *Need-based scholarships/grants offered:* Pell, SEOG, state scholarships/grants, the school's own gift aid. *Loan aid offered:* FFEL Subsidized Stafford, FFEL Unsubsidized Stafford, FFEL PLUS, Federal Perkins. Applicants will be notified of awards on or about 3/23. Off-campus job opportunities are excellent.

FROM THE ADMISSIONS OFFICE

"One wouldn't ordinarily assume that a small institution could offer as diverse a range of opportunities as many large universities, or that a campus that looks like the English countryside could exist within 20 minutes of downtown Philadelphia, but Bryn Mawr is far from ordinary. Prepare to be surprised. Innovative, creative, and purposeful, the students at Bryn Mawr inspire their peers as much and as often as any faculty member. Spirited intellectual inquiry, a commitment to academic excellence, and a desire to impact the world in a meaningful way are the hallmarks of this community of equals. Students at Bryn Mawr learn by doing and lead by example. They take full advantage of all that Bryn Mawr has to offer, including internship opportunities, an active Alumnae Association, a lively Community Service office and a consortium of schools that includes Haverford, Swarthmore, and the University of Pennsylvania. Bryn Mawr's Student Government Association is the oldest in the country and students participate in every aspect of the college's decision-making process, serving as representatives to Admissions, The Honor Board, The Curriculum Committee, and even The Board of Trustees. Bryn Mawr is a demanding and caring place where both ideas and individuals matter."

For even more information on this school, turn to page 469 of the "Stats" section.

BUCKNELL UNIVERSITY

FREAS HALL, LEWISBURG, PA 17837 • ADMISSIONS: 570-577-1101 • FAX: 570-577-3538
FINANCIAL AID: 570-577-1331 • E-MAIL: ADMISSIONS@BUCKNELL.EDU • WEBSITE: WWW.BUCKNELL.EDU

Ratings
Quality of Life: 82   **Academic:** 91   **Admissions:** 95   **Financial Aid:** 96

Academics

Among an elite tier of small East Coast schools, Bucknell University prides itself on providing plenty of attention to its undergraduates. "Professors are always accessible and willing to help," confirms a junior. "I once missed a week of classes because I was sick—my professor called me in and spent three hours catching me up on everything I missed." But this isn't a simple case of babysitting. An accounting major explains, "The faculty challenge you on so many levels, and their commitment to our education is clear." This competitive student body of 3,000-plus can choose from over 50 majors and over 60 minors. Students say, "The academics are outstanding." Their review of the administration isn't as good, due in large part to recent anti-alcohol policies that have upset many students. But other students remind us that not everything is foul in the administrative wings. Online registration, a recent project, "makes things much easier," a sophomore says. The administration also makes sure that the "gorgeous campus" doesn't lose its luster. One theater major describes Bucknell as "a country club on the Susquehanna River."

> **SURVEY SAYS . . .**
> *Small classes*
> *Great library*
> *Athletic facilities are great*
> *Campus feels safe*
> *Frats and sororities dominate social scene*
> *Lots of beer drinking*

Life

Bucknell is "located in the heart of central Pennsylvania," and it boasts a huge Greek scene. The student body's motto is "work hard, play hard," and much of the hard playing takes place "on frat row." As one student puts it, Bucknell students are "fratastically fun." A freshman adds that "for those who don't drink, there are tons of activities available." One of his classmates says, "The school works hard to bring in comedians, have concerts, or [provide] other recreational activities." The school just completed a $32 million expansion and renovation of its athletic facilities, and exercise enthusiasts report that "they are well used." Other on-campus perks include a poetry center, an observatory, and an eighteen-hole golf course. Although it may not be the most exciting place in the world, Lewisburg, Bucknell's host community, "is beautiful, quaint, and safe." But the social life at Bucknell provides enough excitement. Besides, these students don't need any more distractions. One student reminds us that the first part of the Bucknell creed is to work hard: "Lots of time spent studying," she says.

Student Body

"I've never been to a place with such a large percentage of cool and attractive people," raves a junior from New Jersey. A number of students corroborate this opinion and describe their classmates as look-alikes for models in "a J. Crew catalog." While this student body hails from all over the United States and more than 40 foreign countries, an education major tells us that you'll find a large number of students from "New Jersey, Pennsylvania, or California." No matter where they come from, those who arrive in Lewisburg find themselves in what students affectionately refer to as the "Bucknell Bubble." A student explains the bubble as a place where students are "disconnected from the real problems of the world." One business management major claims, "There could be more diversity here at Bucknell;" however, another undergraduate adds, "Each freshman class seems to be a bit more diversified."

ADMISSIONS

Very important factors considered include: Character/personal qualities, class rank, secondary school record, standardized test scores, talent/ability. *Important factors considered include:* Extracurricular activities, minority status, recommendations, volunteer work. *Other factors considered include:* Alumni/ae relation, essays, geographical residence, interview, religious affiliation/commitment, work experience. SAT Reasoning or ACT required. TOEFL required of all international applicants. High school diploma is required, and GED is accepted. *Academic units required:* 4 English, 3 math, 2 science, 2 foreign language, 2 social studies, 2 history, 1 academic elective. *Academic units recommended:* 4 English, 4 math, 3 science, 4 foreign language, 2 social studies, 2 history, 1 academic elective.

The Inside Word

Each application is read by two admissions officers. If you are serious about attending Bucknell, you'll need to take the most competitive courses available at your high school and have strong grades and test scores. Still, overconfidence or a so-so match can throw a wrench in the plans of some; recent trends show larger numbers on the university's wait list and a track record of increased competitiveness for admission.

FINANCIAL AID

Students should submit: FAFSA, CSS/Financial Aid PROFILE, noncustodial (divorced/separated) parents' statement. Regular filing deadline 1/1. The Princeton Review suggests that all financial aid forms be submitted as soon as possible after 1/1. *Need-based scholarships/grants offered:* Pell, SEOG, state scholarships/grants, private scholarships, the school's own gift aid. *Loan aid offered:* FFEL Subsidized Stafford, FFEL Unsubsidized Stafford, FFEL PLUS, Federal Perkins. Applicants will be notified of awards on or about 4/1. Federal Work-study Program available. Off-campus job opportunities are poor.

FROM THE ADMISSIONS OFFICE

"Bucknell combines the personal experience of a small residential liberal arts college and the wide choices offered by a larger university. The College of Arts and Sciences and College of Engineering offer 53 majors and 64 minors. A college-like university enrolling 3,350 undergraduates and 150 graduate students. Bucknell offers many opportunities for learning in and out of the classroom. Engineering students take part in music ensembles, theater productions, and poetry readings. Arts and sciences students enroll in engineering courses. With a student/faculty ratio of 12:1, students gain exceptional first-hand experience by collaborating with faculty on serious research projects. Students complement their classroom experience with more than 150 student organizations, including competition in the prestigious Division I Patriot League. Together, these opportunities allow Bucknell students to learn how to think critically and to develop their leadership skills, preparing them to make a difference in their local communities and in the world."

For even more information on this school, turn to page 469 of the "Stats" section.

CALIFORNIA UNIVERSITY OF PENNSYLVANIA

250 UNIVERSITY AVENUE, CALIFORNIA, PA 15419 • ADMISSIONS: 724-938-4404 • FAX: 724-938-4564
FINANCIAL AID: 724-938-4415 • E-MAIL: INQUIRY@CUP.EDU • WEBSITE: WWW.CUP.EDU

Ratings
Quality of Life: 67   **Academic:** 70   **Admissions:** 70   **Financial Aid:** 62

Academics

Students brag that California University of Pennsylvania strives to provide students with "a premium education at an affordable cost." As one student explains, "All of my professors are very knowledgeable. They are excellent teachers. My advisor is tough enough to keep me on track but very understanding and helpful. Classes are medium

> **SURVEY SAYS . . .**
> *Small classes*
> *Lots of beer drinking*
> *(Almost) everyone smokes*

sized, but never too big." Cal U has an "excellent reputation for its education department," and is "one of the best schools in the area [of] special education." The school has "a very good art department that is rapidly growing," and "a very good graphic communications program." Students find that their professors are "very informed and easily accessible outside the classroom. The courses are challenging, but most offer out-of-class experiences such as seminars and guest speakers that can enhance your learning experience and your grade." Students also rave about the women's basketball team, which is "the number one Champion for Division II NCAA." Areas in need of improvement include the registration process. "It is nearly impossible, even as an upperclassman, to get into the classes needed for graduation without having to get signed into them," warns one undergrad.

Life

The town of California "isn't very big, so many students venture to the surrounding areas for fun. The good thing about this location is that there are many places within short driving distance." Pittsburgh, for example, is just an hour's drive north of campus. "There are bars here in town, but people venture to Pittsburgh and Morgantown most of the time." Students who stay on campus "play a lot of video games," "watch movies, go to parties, make trips to Wal-Mart, watch Futurama or Family Guy, and go out to eat." Wednesday and Thursday seem to be the big party nights, since many students go home on weekends. Undergrads report that "the student activities board is very active. There is usually something happening every week." Recent events have featured "The Pittsburgh Symphony Orchestra, and Coretta Scott King, widow of Martin Luther King, Jr." While some students find the low-key vibe of the area less than exciting, other students say that it is "very conducive to studying because there is not that much distraction or traffic."

Student Body

Cal U students most often describe themselves as "friendly," "laid-back," and "accepting." Undergrads report that "there is a good variety of people at Cal U. There are people into athletics, into theater, into visual art, into science, and into nothing." There are "party people and the people who take college more seriously." A sizeable portion of the student body is made up of commuters and nontraditional students, who "fit in just like the regular students." As one student puts it, "The students here are mostly good natured, good-hearted people. I really haven't seen people being rude, discriminatory, or bad natured. There are students who seclude themselves and don't associate with others, but if you approach them, they are normal, nice people."

ADMISSIONS

Very important factors considered include: Class rank, secondary school record, standardized test scores. *Other factors considered include:* Essays, extracurricular activities, interview, recommendations, talent/ability, work experience. SAT Reasoning Test required. TOEFL required of all international applicants. High school diploma is required, and GED is accepted. *Academic units required:* 4 English, 3 math, 1 science (1 science lab), 2 social studies, 2 history, 6 academic electives, 1 arts and humanities. *Academic units recommended:* 4 English, 3 math, 1 science (1 science lab), 2 foreign language, 2 social studies, 2 history, 6 academic electives, 1 arts and humanities.

The Inside Word

Standardized test scores and high school transcripts are the most important factors in the admissions decision here. Essays and diversity issues are also factors. Early admission requires a high-school GPA of 3.0 and a minimum PSAT or SAT score of 1050.

FINANCIAL AID

Students should submit: FAFSA. The Princeton Review suggests that all financial aid forms be submitted as soon as possible after 1/1. *Need-based scholarships/grants offered:* Pell, SEOG, state scholarships/grants, private scholarships, the school's own gift aid. *Loan aid offered:* FFEL Subsidized Stafford, FFEL Unsubsidized Stafford, FFEL PLUS, Federal Perkins. Off-campus job opportunities are excellent.

FROM THE ADMISSIONS OFFICE

"California University, a proud member of the Pennsylvania State System of Higher Education, has a mission to build character and careers. Character education is a part of every classroom, lived in every residence hall and on every playing field. Career building is an ongoing, four-year process. Students participate in hands-on learning and research, and gain invaluable real-world experience through co-ops and internships. Cal U's unique Career Advantage Program provides a checklist for career success beginning with the freshman year and continuing through graduation.

"Each bachelor's degree requires a minimum of 120 semester hours of credit including a general education requirement of 51 credits. An honors program provides an opportunity for an enhanced educational experience to students who meet the criteria.

"All classes are taught by teaching faculty members. The student-faculty ratio is 20:1. Doctorates are held by more than 74 percent of the full-time faculty.

"Cal U is recognized as a leader in providing premiere student living options. Two locations, the lower and the upper campus, provide students with the Suite Life, a whole new experience in university living.

"California University welcomes applications from all qualified persons regardless of race, religion or national origin. All applicants should submit an application form, an official high school transcript which includes class rank (or GED certificate and scores), and SAT or American College Test (ACT) scores. Transfer students must submit official transcripts from all colleges and universities attended. A nonrefundable application fee of $25 must accompany the application. Students can apply and pay online at www.cup.edu."

For even more information on this school, turn to page 470 of the "Stats" section.

CARNEGIE MELLON UNIVERSITY

5000 FORBES AVENUE, PITTSBURGH, PA 15213 • ADMISSIONS: 412-268-2082 • FAX: 412-268-7838
FINANCIAL AID: 412-268-2068 • E-MAIL: UNDERGRADUATE-ADMISSIONS@ANDREW.CMU.EDU • WEBSITE: WWW.CMU.EDU

Ratings
Quality of Life: 66   **Academic:** 91   **Admissions:** 96   **Financial Aid:** 76

Academics

The students of Carnegie Mellon University proudly report that their school fulfills the fundamental mission of the university: to offer excellent instruction in a wide variety of fields while also promoting cutting-edge research. "Of all the schools I've seen, no other is as well known in so many different fields: architecture, engineering, drama, science, design, music, and business, just to name a few," is how one undergrad put it, adding, "If you couldn't decide what path to take in life, you could still come to Carnegie Mellon and have a world-class education in almost any interest." Students warn, "Academically, this school will push you to your limit." As one puts it, "Carnegie Mellon is a very research-oriented university. . . . It has truly opened doors for me that I did not know were available. The professors are actively involved in the topics in which they teach. There is no such thing as a 'basic' course at Carnegie Mellon." The school does a good job of recognizing the demands it makes, however, and "in many departments, professors actually coordinate their tests and papers so that there is very little overlap in workloads between classes." It's just such little touches that so endear Carnegie Mellon to its students. Another example: "The Business School's administration loves to send us notes about various types of opportunities for internships, jobs, and lectures through email." Students are also unanimous in their praise for online services: "You can register online, check your grades online, often get assignments online, and even check what movie is playing at school online," reports an undergrad.

> **SURVEY SAYS . . .**
> *Registration is a breeze*
> *Lab facilities are great*
> *Great computer facilities*
> *Diverse student types on campus*
> *Lots of beer drinking*

Life

Because of Carnegie Mellon's intense academic demands, "people here think about school 90 percent of the time. The other 10 percent is divided among when they're going to sleep next [and] how they're going to blow off some stress." Fortunately, there are lots of options for that scant 10 percent. Hometown Pittsburgh "is a great city if you let it be. There are many theaters, museums, and sporting events. Shops and great restaurants are all really close, and we get bus passes as students, so you can get anywhere." There are also many nearby bars, "most of which don't card." On campus, "people go to the fraternities on weekends." Also popular are one-dollar movies ("shown from Thursday to Sunday, which are a real great getaway from work, and they get good, recent movies") and student-produced plays. Student clubs and organizations also have their boosters; writes one student, "Carnegie Mellon has a lot of really fun, quirky organizations. My two favorites are the Kiltie Band and KGB. The Kiltie Band is our band for nonmajors. As The Band Without Pants, we wear our kilts proudly, cheer giddily, click our heels, and beep when we back up. Talent for music and/or marching is not a requirement. KGB stands for Keeping Geeks Busy. Each semester, they host Capture the Flag with Stuff, a game that always attracts a large crowd." Although "there are sports games going on, no one ever knows when or cares to go."

Student Body

"There are a few types that are typical," at Carnegie Mellon; identifiable factions include: "a large number of tech, math, and computer geeks . . . strange art students, loud drama students, and many Asian student groups." Most are "hardworking, bright, ambitious," and shy. Reports one undergrad, "Students here would be considered very friendly if they weren't so reserved. You'll find that the person who sits next to you in lecture is always really nice if either of you ever overcomes your shyness enough to say hello." Politically "there is a large minority of very left-wing, extremely active students who are responsible for most of what occurs on campus. Most students, however, are apathetic and very absorbed in their studies."

ADMISSIONS

Very important factors considered include: Secondary school record, standardized test scores. *Important factors considered include:* Alumni/ae relation, character/personal qualities, class rank, extracurricular activities, recommendations, talent/ability, volunteer work, work experience. *Other factors considered include:* Essays, interview, minority status. SAT Reasoning or ACT required. TOEFL required of all international applicants. High school diploma is required, and GED is accepted. *Academic units required:* 4 English, 4 math, 3 science (3 science lab), 2 foreign language, 3 academic electives. *Academic units recommended:* 4 English, 4 math, 3 science (3 science lab), 2 foreign language, 4 academic electives.

The Inside Word

The Office of Admission reports that it uses "no cutoffs [and] no formulas" in assessing its applicant pool. Don't get too excited—that doesn't necessarily mean that applicants are looked at in a more personal fashion. Applications have seesawed here over the past couple of years, and to temper the effects of a decline in application totals on selectivity, Carnegie Mellon maintains a huge wait list. A very low yield of admits who enroll keeps selectivity moderate, but you've got to have strong numbers to gain admission.

FINANCIAL AID

Students should submit: FAFSA, institution's own financial aid form, parent and student federal tax returns, parent W-2 forms. Regular filing deadline 5/1. The Princeton Review suggests that all financial aid forms be submitted as soon as possible after 1/1. *Need-based scholarships/grants offered:* Pell, SEOG, state scholarships/grants, private scholarships, the school's own gift aid. *Loan aid offered:* FFEL Subsidized Stafford, FFEL Unsubsidized Stafford, FFEL PLUS, Federal Perkins, GATE Student Loan. Applicants will be notified of awards on or about 3/15. Federal Work-study Program available. Institutional employment available.

FROM THE ADMISSIONS OFFICE

"Carnegie Mellon is a private, coeducational university with approximately 5,100 undergraduates; 3,300 graduate students; and 778 full-time faculty members. The university's 103-acre campus is located in the Oakland area of Pittsburgh, five miles from downtown. The university is composed of seven colleges: the Carnegie Institute of Technology (engineering), the College of Fine Arts, the College of Humanities and Social Sciences (combining liberal arts education with professional specializations), the Tepper School of Business (undergraduate business and industrial management), the Mellon College of Science, the School of Computer Science, and the H. John Heina III School of Public Policy and Management."

For even more information on this school, turn to page 470 of the "Stats" section.

CATHOLIC UNIVERSITY OF AMERICA

CARDINAL STATION, WASHINGTON, DC 20064 • ADMISSIONS: 202-319-5305 • FAX: 202-319-6533
FINANCIAL AID: 202-319-5307 • E-MAIL: CUA-ADMISSIONS@CUA.EDU • WEBSITE: WWW.CUA.EDU

Ratings
Quality of Life: 67   Academic: 73   Admissions: 85   Financial Aid: 69

Academics

The Catholic University of America (CWA) is "a spiritual place with an excellent academic setting" where "the professional schools—engineering, architecture, and nursing—are outstanding." The school successfully combines the best aspects of a large university and a small liberal arts college. The university's Washington, DC setting provides access to government research projects, which in turn drive the school's cutting-edge School of Engineering. In all CUA schools, undergraduates are provided ample opportunity to participate in research. Music, theater, media studies, and theology are among the other departments praised by students. All undergraduates must complete CUA's core curriculum, which demonstrates "a deep respect for the classics." One student tells us, "This is one of the few places where Aristotle is always right, and Saint Thomas Aquinas is spoken of on a first-name basis." The university's professors provide "individual attention that allows each student to find a personal niche" and "will go above and beyond the call of duty to help you turn your dream into reality." The administration, however, "has a communication problem with the students, is too slow, [and] leaves much room for improvement." Undergraduates appreciate the fact that "the school is extremely strong in promoting its religious ideals and beliefs. There are many opportunities to get involved religiously."

> **SURVEY SAYS . . .**
> *Small classes*
> *Students are friendly*
> *Frats and sororities are unpopular*
> *or nonexistent*
> *Lots of beer drinking*
> *Hard liquor is popular*

Life

Students at CUA enjoy a campus that has "so much to do," and a hometown that's "the best city in the world." Students extol the campus's endless "dance lessons, vocal/instrumental lessons, student government, special-interest clubs, service organizations, sports, dances, open-mic nights, choirs, club-sponsored activities, literary contests, movie nights, [and] stimulating lectures." Of special note is the school's "outstanding music program. Students perform musical plays, showcases, and concerts free or [for a low] admission. [Both students and] people from the area come to see these students perform." The campus itself "is so beautiful and really easy to take walks at any time of the year. Everything is not too spread out, so you can easily walk across campus just to spend time with friends." Moreover, DC "provides a wealth of opportunities, especially since the Metro is right next to the campus. Just a few Metro stops away is Union Station with restaurants and shopping, the Capitol, and tons of museums. With Dupont Circle, Adams Morgan, Chinatown, and Capitol Hill, there's plenty to do and 10,000 places to eat." That's especially good to know since "the university food is gross."

Student Body

Undergraduates at CUA "are very similar to one another. Pretty much everyone is white, Catholic, from a middle- or upper-middle-class family somewhere in the Northeast. Most come from Maryland, Pennsylvania, New York, New Jersey, and Massachusetts." The great number of Irish Catholics leads one student to quip that they "look like Conan O'Brien's offspring. It's 'Irish Catholic extreme with a little Italian flavor.'" It "seems almost as if there is a dress code at CUA, since everyone wears pretty much the same thing: jeans always, sweatpants and hooded sweatshirts when the weather gets colder, and flip-flops are a requirement, even into November." Although the school has a religious affiliation and places a general emphasis on faith, one student reports, "Not everyone is religious. The people who are seem to be trying to make up for those of us heathens and then some." The student body is nearly politically homogeneous; writes one student, "It tries to be the Catholic University, but it should be called the Conservative Republican University."

ADMISSIONS

Very important factors considered include: Character/personal qualities, essays, recommendations, secondary school record, standardized test scores, volunteer work. *Important factors considered include:* Class rank, extracurricular activities, interview, talent/ability. *Other factors considered include:* Alumni/ae relation, minority status, work experience. SAT Reasoning or ACT required. SAT Subject Tests recommended. TOEFL required of all international applicants. High school diploma is required, and GED is not accepted. *Academic units recommended:* 4 English, 3 math, 3 science (1 science lab), 2 foreign language, 4 social studies, 1 history.

The Inside Word

This is not the place to try radical approaches to completing your admissions application: smooth sailing for solid students and even friendlier for candidates from distant states or unique high schools.

FINANCIAL AID

Students should submit: FAFSA. Regular filing deadline 2/1. The Princeton Review suggests that all financial aid forms be submitted as soon as possible after 1/1. *Need-based scholarships/grants offered:* Pell, SEOG, state scholarships/grants, private scholarships, the school's own gift aid, federal nursing scholarships. *Loan aid offered:* FFEL Subsidized Stafford, FFEL Unsubsidized Stafford, FFEL PLUS, Federal Perkins, Federal Nursing, commercial loans. Applicants will be notified of awards on a rolling basis beginning on or about 4/1. Federal Work-study Program available. Institutional employment available. Off-campus job opportunities are excellent.

FROM THE ADMISSIONS OFFICE

"The Catholic University of America's friendly atmosphere, rigorous academic programs, and emphasis on time-honored values attract students from most states and more than 30 foreign countries. Its 144-acre, tree-lined campus is only 10 minutes from the nation's capital. Distinguished as the national university of the Catholic Church in the United States, CUA is the only institution of higher education established by the U.S. Catholic bishops; however, students from all religious traditions are welcome.

"CUA offers undergraduate degrees in more than 60 major areas in six schools of study. Students enroll into the School of Arts and Sciences, Architecture, Nursing, Engineering, Music, or Philosophy. Additionally, CUA students can concentrate in areas of pre-professional study including law, dentistry, medicine, or veterinary studies.

"With Capitol Hill, the Smithsonian Institution, NASA, the Kennedy Center, and the National Institutes of Health among the places students obtain internships, firsthand experience is a valuable piece of the experience that CUA offers. Numerous students also take the opportunity in their junior year to study abroad at one of Catholic's 17 country program sites. Political science majors even have the opportunity to do a Parliamentary Internship in either England or Ireland. With the campus just minutes away from downtown via the Metrorail rapid transit system, students enjoy a residential campus in an exciting city of historical monuments, theaters, festivals, ethnic restaurants, and parks."

For even more information on this school, turn to page 471 of the "Stats" section.

CENTRAL CONNECTICUT STATE UNIVERSITY

1615 STANLEY STREET, NEW BRITAIN, CT 06050 • ADMISSIONS: 800-832-3200 • FAX: 862-832-2295
E-MAIL: ADMISSIONS@CCSU.EDU • WEBSITE: WWW.CCSU.EDU

Ratings
Quality of Life: 69   Academic: 70   Admissions: 70   Financial Aid: 64

Academics

Central Connecticut State University is a public mid-sized liberal arts and sciences institution where professors supplement book knowledge with life experience. One student notes, "My business law professor is a civil lawyer, and my public speaking professor is an executive for a major pharmaceutical company. I love how they teach us about real-world situations, so I know that I will be better prepared than most other students at different colleges." Many students describe their professors as "down-to-earth," "knowledgeable," and eager to help students succeed, although it should be noted that "while some professors are very easy to reach outside of class and seem as though they really do want to help students pass their class, others are impossible to reach." CCSU undergrads rave about the "highly recognized" education program, which is accredited by the National Council for Accreditation of Teacher Education (NCATE). The honors program is also regarded as "absolutely outstanding." While "excellent online services" streamline registration and bill-paying processes, the rest of the administration can pose annoying hurdles because it is "extremely disorganized."

> **SURVEY SAYS . . .**
> *Small classes*
> *Great computer facilities*
> *Diverse student types on campus*
> *(Almost) everyone smokes*

Life

CCSU offers a variety of clubs and activities that make the campus "a great place to be during weekdays." There are "plenty of good places to eat within walking distance, and the mall in Farmington is but a short bus ride away." Some students take advantage of "free weekly movies in the Welte Auditorium," attend sporting events, and hang out in the student center, which features a pool hall and several plasma TVs. Because CCSU is largely a commuter school, "Weekends are boring unless you have a car and can get into Hartford." CCSU is "a supposedly dry campus," so on-campus parties generally consist of "five to eight people in a dorm room just hanging out drinking beer." As one student explains, "People either have a group of friends with whom they regularly interact, go home for the weekends, or play an absurd amount of computer/console-based video games."

Student Body

"The student population at Central is very diverse, but very welcoming," the predominantly local undergrads of CCSU here tell us. Students are described as "laid-back," "friendly," and "really down-to-earth." Says one undergrad, "The typical student on campus goes to school full time and has a job on the side to help pay for school and other expenses. They work very hard to do well in school and be able to take care of themselves. There is a comfortable respect and admiration among these students because they can all relate to how everyone feels when it comes to having to work hard to get the education they want." CCSU students "like to have fun, but they also know what they need to do to accomplish their goals."

ADMISSIONS

Very important factors considered include: Secondary school record. *Important factors considered include:* Class rank, standardized test scores. *Other factors considered include:* Essays, extracurricular activities, interview, minority status, recommendations, state residency, talent/ability. SAT Reasoning Test required. TOEFL required of all international applicants. High school diploma is required, and GED is accepted. *Academic units required:* 4 English, 3 math, 2 science (1 science lab), 2 social studies, 1 history. *Academic units recommended:* 1 math, 3 foreign language.

The Inside Word

CCSU has fairly generous admissions standards, meaning that the average college-bound high school senior should gain entrance here without much difficulty. Borderline candidates should schedule an interview with the Admissions Office and take the opportunity to present themselves as highly motivated candidates.

FINANCIAL AID

Students should submit: FAFSA. Regular filing deadline 9/24. The Princeton Review suggests that all financial aid forms be submitted as soon as possible after 1/1. *Need-based scholarships/grants offered:* Pell, SEOG, state scholarships/grants, the school's own gift aid. *Loan aid offered:* Direct Subsidized Stafford, Direct Unsubsidized Stafford, Direct PLUS, FFEL PLUS, Federal Perkins. Applicants will be notified of awards on or about 3/24. Federal Work-study Program available. Institutional employment available. Off-campus job opportunities are good.

FROM THE ADMISSIONS OFFICE

"Selected as one of the 'Great Colleges for the Real World' and honored as a 'Leadership Institution' by the Association of American Colleges & Universities, CCSU stands as a national example of quality undergraduate education. Offering more than 100 majors in 82 fields of study in its four schools, CCSU also provides a wide array of special curricular opportunities to enrich learning.

"As exemplified in the University's slogan, 'Start with a dream. Finish with a future!' CCSU is committed to preparing students for success in whatever field they choose. The offices of career services and cooperative education provide interesting career-related work experience plus opportunities to make connections with hundreds of participating employers. Nearly 70 percent of participating students are offered permanent, career-starting positions with their co-op employers upon graduation.

"CCSU's campus is attractive, with new and renovated buildings adding to the classic collegiate 'look' of its historical architecture. Academic buildings feature state-of-the-art, fully networked 'smart classrooms.' A newly renovated and expanded student center provides lounges, conference and game rooms, dining and information services, a bookstore, and a range of other support services. With 120 student clubs and organizations covering a broad spectrum of interests, there is a wealth of opportunities to meet new people, broaden horizons, and develop leadership skills. Athletics are a big part of campus life, and students enjoy a state-of-the-art fitness center with training rooms, a swimming pool, a track, and tennis and basketball courts. And CCSU's 18 Division I sports teams provide exciting opportunities to play or watch."

For even more information on this school, turn to page 471 of the "Stats" section.

CHATHAM COLLEGE

WOODLAND ROAD, PITTSBURGH, PA 15232 • ADMISSIONS: 412-365-1290 • FAX: 412-365-1609
E-MAIL: ADMISSIONS@CHATHAM.EDU • WEBSITE: WWW.CHATHAM.EDU

Ratings
Quality of Life: 89   Academic: 86   Admissions: 84   Financial Aid: 87

Academics

Chatham College, "a liberal arts women's college that focuses on leadership and service," specializes in "a 'world-ready' approach to education" that "prepares women to take over the world." Providing small classes, "excellent resources, especially for a school of its size," and "a fantastic environment in which academic and personal growth are highly regarded," Chatham is all about the personal touches that inspire students to achieve great things. As one student recounts, "My advisor sat with me for an hour, examining my educational interests and plotting every direction I could go for both the upcoming year and beyond. The professors here go to great lengths to make sure students achieve their goals." Adds another, "The professors seem to live on campus. You can always catch them in their offices or in the dining hall. The administration also has an open-door policy, and you can always seem to meet with them. Both administrators and professors care about you as an individual. If you did well in a soccer game or if your name was mentioned in the local newspaper, you'll be sure to get a personalized letter of congratulations." "Great leadership opportunities" round out the picture at this "very challenging" liberal arts school where "you have to learn time-management to balance your school and activity schedule."

> **SURVEY SAYS . . .**
> *Small classes*
> *Students are friendly*
> *Students love Pittsburgh, PA*
> *Great off-campus food*
> *Campus feels safe*
> *Frats and sororities are unpopular*
> *or nonexistent*

Life

Chatham's campus, students tell us, is "secluded in its own land of trees and mansions," making it "one of the most beautiful places to go to college." Despite the urban address, Chatham's environment "makes it easy to get away from the city of Pittsburgh, or the college scene for that matter, because it looks and feels very secluded (even though it's not)." Explains one student, "Once I came and saw the beautiful campus, I knew I wanted to attend Chatham. It feels like home here. Everyone, including students, faculty and staff, goes out of his or her way to help you with anything. There are so many activities on campus, and it really is quite easy to get involved." For those so inclined, "there is a good opportunity to participate in Division III athletics, as many of the teams are short-handed. It really enriches the college experience." Chatham's central location offers easy access to Squirrel Hill, Shadyside, and Oakland, three of Pittsburgh's more fashionable residential and retail neighborhoods. Not much further off are the excellent dining and nightlife offered by the Strip District (so named for its geographical outline, not for any untoward activity that takes place there) and the Southside. Men are in no short supply in Pittsburgh, women here assure us, and those seeking their company can hit the town or head to one of the city's many other colleges, which include University of Pittsburgh and Carnegie Mellon University within walking distance.

Student Body

The "outgoing, involved, friendly, happy" typical Chatham woman is "open-minded, democratic, and hard-working and ventures off-campus often. The bulk of the students exhibit these characteristics. There aren't many outliers." Students note that "the student body is very diverse in percentages, many of the students coming from other countries and states." They also point out that "every student, regardless of their beliefs, interests, and personality, finds a place here," although the leftward political tilt of the student body makes Chatham a slightly less hospitable place for outspoken conservatives. And they caution that "since it is small, everyone knows everyone and their business."

ADMISSIONS

Very important factors considered include: Secondary school record. *Important factors considered include:* Essays, standardized test scores. *Other factors considered include:* Alumni/ae relation, character/personal qualities, class rank, extracurricular activities, interview, recommendations, talent/ability, volunteer work, work experience. SAT Reasoning or ACT required. TOEFL required of all international applicants. High school diploma is required, and GED is accepted. *Academic units required:* 4 English, 2 math, 2 science, 3 social science. *Academic units recommended:* 4 English, 3 math, 3 science, 2 foreign language, 3 social science.

The Inside Word

Chatham's single-sex demographic turns off some potential undergraduates. As a result, Chatham presents underachieving women a unique opportunity for admittance to a fine liberal arts college. Cooperative learning programs provide access to nine colleges and universities in Pittsburgh, including UPitt and Carnegie Mellon.

FINANCIAL AID

Students should submit: FAFSA. The Princeton Review suggests that all financial aid forms be submitted as soon as possible after 1/1. *Need-based scholarships/grants offered:* Pell, SEOG, state scholarships/grants, private scholarships, the school's own gift aid. *Loan aid offered:* FFEL Subsidized Stafford, FFEL Unsubsidized Stafford, FFEL PLUS, Federal Perkins, alternative loans. Applicants will be notified of awards on a rolling basis beginning on or about 2/15. Federal Work-study Program available. Institutional employment available. Off-campus job opportunities are good.

FROM THE ADMISSIONS OFFICE

"Chatham College's World-Ready Women are excited about learning about themselves and about their place in this world. More importantly, they are ready to make their mark on this world. Focused on preparing students for the future, a Chatham College education emphasizes the environment, global issues, and women's leadership. "Chatham is the college for independent women who have a desire to succeed. Undergraduate students may earn both their bachelor's and master's degrees from Chatham in as few as five years through our Accelerated Masters Program, or through a partnership with Carnegie Mellon University's Heinz School of Public Policy.

"Each year members of the senior class complete a year long independent research project known as the Senior Tutorial. Eighty-five percent of Chatham students take advantage of the countless internship opportunities available to them, with most students participating in at least two. In addition, almost three-quarters of the senior class participated in service-learning last year, with more than 46,000 total hours completed by Chatham students.

"Chatham students may participate in the Rachel Carson Institute, established to honor the legacy of Chatham alumna Rachel Carson. The Center concentrates on the impact of environmental degradation on women's health and other issues. Likewise, the Pennsylvania Center for Women, Politics, and Public Policy exposes students to civic engagement through interaction with top-level practitioners in government, public policy, and related fields.

"Finally, each year the Global Focus Program explores the politics, geography, cultures, and perceptions of particular global region. Recent Global Focus topics include Latin America and the Communities of Islam."

For even more information on this school, turn to page 472 of the "Stats" section.

CHESTNUT HILL UNIVERSITY

9601 GERMANTOWN AVENUE, PHILADELPHIA, PA 19118-2693 • ADMISSIONS: 215-248-7001 • FAX: 215-248-7082
FINANCIAL AID: 215-248-7182 • E-MAIL: CHCAPPLY@CHC.EDU • WEBSITE: WWW.CHC.EDU

Ratings
Quality of Life: 65   **Academic:** 73   **Admissions:** 72   **Financial Aid:** 82

Academics

The times they are a-changin' at Chestnut Hill College, a one-time all-women's college that broke the gender barrier in the autumn of 2003. Reports one student, "The school is rapidly changing for the better as a result of coeducation. There is much more to do, and a new breed of student is arriving on campus." Many things haven't changed at CHC, though. The school remains "a small-classroom school with professors and Sisters of Saint Joseph" provid-

> **SURVEY SAYS . . .**
> *Small classes*
> *Students love Philadelphia, PA*
> *Frats and sororities are unpopular*
> *or nonexistent*
> *(Almost) everyone smokes*

ing "a structured Catholic environment" and "great academics" to "educate critical thinkers." CHC professors generally split time between the school and other area colleges. Even so, they are "easy to get in touch with. There's a strong sense of interconnection between teachers and students" here. Students also note with approval that "none of the classes are taught by TAs, and that is good." CHC's Philadelphia location means students have "great access to outside resources," including internship and cooperative education opportunities. All CHC undergraduates must complete a demanding liberal-arts-intensive core curriculum focused on global perspectives, various modes of intellectual analysis, and interdisciplinary study.

Life

Chestnut Hill provides "a nice, quiet environment" in northwest Philadelphia in which students can concentrate without distraction on their studies. Some actually find it a little too quiet. "Chestnut Hill is solely academic, there is no such thing as a social environment here," complains one undergrad. Others report a slightly more animated extracurricular scene, noting that "the student government tries to keep students involved and entertained, offering activities throughout the week." Adds one undergrad, "There are many student clubs and organizations, and if there is interest in one that doesn't exist, students are welcome to start their own club." Still, just about everyone here admits that "people go home a lot on weekends," in part because "the rules on campus are so strict," and in part simply because "the campus is not much of a campus. It's very small." Fortunately, CHC offers easy access to Philadelphia, where students go to movies, museums, and Phillies and Eagles games." The city is awash with great restaurants, fun clubs, wonderful cultural outlets, lively bars, and a full slate of professional athletic teams.

Student Body

2003 brought a significant demographic shift to the CHC student body; that's the year the school admitted men for the first time, breaking a 78-year-old, women-only tradition. Today, four in five students is female, but that ratio promises to balance out in coming years. When it does, the school should remain "a small community where everyone is connected" and a home to "a diverse group of people from different religions, countries, and economic statuses." They are "a sneakers and sweatpants kind of group" who "typically play a sport or two, join clubs, and study hard." The CHC student body includes students from Austria, Canada, the Congo, the Czech Republic, France, Ghana, Japan, Kazakhstan, Kenya, the Ukraine, the United Arab Emirates, and the West Indies.

ADMISSIONS

Very important factors considered include: Essays, secondary school record. *Important factors considered include:* Character/personal qualities, class rank, extracurricular activities, interview, recommendations, standardized test scores. *Other factors considered include:* Alumni/ae relation, talent/ability, volunteer work, work experience. SAT Reasoning or ACT required. TOEFL required of all international applicants. High school diploma is required, and GED is accepted. *Academic units recommended:* 4 English, 3 math, 3 science, 2 foreign language, 4 social studies.

The Inside Word

Admissions officers rank high school transcript and personal essays as the most important factors in determining who gets into Chestnut Hill. Some extra sweat invested into those personal essays could help an applicant overcome less-than-impressive standardized test scores. A good interview can also help a lot here.

FINANCIAL AID

Students should submit: FAFSA. Regular filing deadline 4/15. The Princeton Review suggests that all financial aid forms be submitted as soon as possible after 1/1. *Need-based scholarships/grants offered:* Pell, SEOG, state scholarships/grants, private scholarships, the school's own gift aid. *Loan aid offered:* FFEL Subsidized Stafford, FFEL Unsubsidized Stafford, FFEL PLUS, Federal Perkins. Applicants will be notified of awards on a rolling basis beginning on or about 1/31.

FROM THE ADMISSIONS OFFICE

"Chestnut Hill College provides students with an opportunity for the highest quality education needed to achieve personal and professional success. We offer 28 majors and 27 minors that can lead to countless career opportunities. Over 82% of our faculty possess the highest degree in their field. They are professors who share a love for learning and readily make themselves available outside of class. There are also opportunities to study abroad and create individualized majors. "College is much more than declaring a major or cramming for finals. Joining others who share your passion is an ideal way to expand your horizons and build on your classroom education. At Chestnut Hill College there are over 25 organizations devoted to a variety of student interests— everything from the biology club to Amnesty International. There are also 14 NCAA Division III teams, with plans to expand the number of sports offered. If your sports pursuits are of an individual nature, you can go horseback riding, mountain-biking in Fairmount Park, or rollerblading from the Philadelphia suburbs to the Art Museum.

"At Chestnut Hill College, we pride ourselves on our philosophy of holistic education. We believe that a curriculum should go beyond the lecture hall, off the reading list and out of the library. It should emphasize growth of the whole person not only through a liberal arts education, but also through an exciting social life, a healthy spiritual life, and a well-rounded active life, therefore exposing students to the best college has to offer."

For even more information on this school, turn to page 472 of the "Stats" section.

CHEYNEY UNIVERSITY OF PENNSYLVANIA

CHEYNEY AND CREEK ROADS, CHEYNEY, PA 19319 • ADMISSIONS: 610-399-2275 • FAX: 610-399-2099
E-MAIL: JBROWN@CHEYNEY.EDU • WEBSITE: WWW.CHEYNEY.EDU

Ratings
Quality of Life: 63   Academic: 60   Admissions: 60   Financial Aid: 77

Academics

Priding themselves on being students at "America's first black college," the undergraduates at Cheyney University of Pennsylvania explain that their school is "about blacks coming together to build up a community." At the center of this community are the professors who "are like family" to the students who they mentor. One biology major promises, "The teachers are very committed to the students." While some are content with teacher's commitments, others complain that there are a few "unqualified staff and faculty" who can spoil the experience for some students. One evenhanded undergraduate recalls, "I've had some professors that I feel should teach middle school…and I've had some really good ones." To expand in the university's academics, some undergraduates recommend that the admissions office be a little more selective. Wide acceptance, though, is the point of a Cheyney education, according to some. As one undergraduate puts it, "One of the greatest strengths of our school is encouraging campus love." Some of the most popular programs include social sciences, business, education, communications, and psychology.

> **SURVEY SAYS . . .**
> Small classes
> Great library
> Great off-campus food
> Frats and sororities dominate social scene
> Very little drug use

Life

Located on a 275-acre campus between Philadelphia and Wilmington, Delaware, Cheyney draws both strong resident and commuter populations—with each of these populations relating to the University differently. "I commute," writes one senior, "and usually leave campus after classes, but I do spend one full day per week on campus. I enjoy many opportunities for student interaction and even hang out with some of my teachers while doing work for class. It's great." One place that draws a healthy student crowd, both resident and commuter alike, is the Student Activity Center. Here, distractions are not hard to come by. The students who choose to live on campus find plenty of other ways to enjoy their free time, including the age-old college pastime—partying. "I have a 3.45 GPA," writes a business student, "and I play as hard as I work." While libations are quite common in and around campus, many students seek out nightlife in Wilmington (15 miles away) or Philadelphia (25 miles away). Both New York, NY and Washington, DC, can also be reached in less than two hours.

Student Body

Cheyney draws in approximately a 98 percent black population. A senior from Philadelphia writes, "The typical student is African American and very contemporary in style and opinion." By this, she means that Cheyney's undergraduates enjoy looking good and maintaining a collective "free spirit." Though the undergraduate population at Cheyney is only around 1,100, it's tough to package these students into neat boxes. This is largely because many students come from diverse communities in major Mid-Atlantic urban centers such as Philadelphia, Wilmington, and New York. Some students come to Cheyney for the social life, while others keep their noses in the books. An elementary education student complains that "many students at Cheyney are not focused on their education. They sit around on campus smoking, drinking, and carrying on." An accounting major, however, believes just the opposite, "Focused on grades," he says of his classmates, "demanding excellence."

ADMISSIONS

Very important factors considered include: Recommendations, secondary school record. *Important factors considered include:* Class rank, essays, extracurricular activities, interview, standardized test scores, state residency. *Other factors considered include:* Minority status, talent/ability. SAT Reasoning, SAT Subject Tests, or ACT required. TOEFL required of all international applicants. High school diploma is required, and GED is accepted. *Academic units required:* 4 English, 3 math, 2 science, 2 foreign language, 2 history.

The Inside Word

Previous academic performance counts most at the Cheyney Admissions Office. The application lists letters of recommendation as optional. Make sure to submit them anyway, as those who do not provide letters of recommendation are at a distinct disadvantage to those who do.

FINANCIAL AID

Students should submit: FAFSA. The Princeton Review suggests that all financial aid forms be submitted as soon as possible after 1/1. *Need-based scholarships/grants offered:* Pell, SEOG, state scholarships/grants, private scholarships, the school's own gift aid. *Loan aid offered:* FFEL Subsidized Stafford, FFEL Unsubsidized Stafford, FFEL PLUS, Federal Perkins. Applicants will be notified of awards on a rolling basis beginning on or about 4/1. Federal Work-study Program available. Institutional employment available. Off-campus job opportunities are good.

For even more information on this school, turn to page 472 of the "Stats" section.

CITY UNIVERSITY OF NEW YORK—BARUCH COLLEGE

UNDERGRADUATE ADMISSIONS, ONE BERNARD BARUCH WAY BOX H-0720, NEW YORK, NY 10010
ADMISSIONS: 646-312-1400 • FAX: 646-312-1361 • E-MAIL: ADMISSIONS@BARUCH.CUNY.EDU • WEBSITE: WWW.BARUCH.CUNY.EDU

Ratings
Quality of Life: 74   **Academic:** 61   **Admissions:** 60   **Financial Aid:** 68

Academics

The City University's Baruch College consists of three schools: the Weissman School of Arts and Sciences, the School of Public Affairs, and the Zicklin School of Business. The last, housed in a brand new state-of-the-art facility called the Vertical Campus, is home to Baruch's most popular and highest profile programs, including what students believe is "the best public school for accounting in the state of New York." Business students here also benefit from their facility's "fantastic equity trading floor" and a Manhattan location that offers "endless networking possibilities" and "popular and accessible internships." While Zicklin may be the best known of Baruch's colleges, Weissman is the one most universally used; it administers the common core curriculum, a 60-credit sequence consisting of required courses, and broad-ranging distribution requirements. Students here tell us that "generally, professors are easily accessible after class, and depending on the class, professors will hold discussions and not just lecture. Students are also encouraged to participate and ask and answer questions, even in a 500-student intro class." The administration, on the other hand, "is a nightmare, with long lines outside the bursar and registrar's office constantly."

> **SURVEY SAYS . . .**
> *Great computer facilities*
> *Great library*
> *Athletic facilities are great*
> *Diverse student types on campus*
> *Students love New York, NY*
> *Very little drug use*

Life

Baruch is a commuter campus, and, as one student puts it, "No residence halls means that on-campus life is pretty much nonexistent." Adds another, "When classes are over, people go back home to their own friends." The exception is student clubs, which exist "for anything from pre-law to hip-hop;" these, however, meet only once a week. Between classes, students enjoy some accommodating facilities, especially in the brand-new Vertical Campus. Baruch students have access to "a nice new gym that is free of charge," a "great library with comfy chairs for taking a nap," and the Vertical Campus' third-floor common area "where everyone hangs out during club hours. Every day you meet new people (that's the best part). We play games, cards, listen to music, watch TV, talk to each other, and sometimes study. This helps take our mind off of school for a few hours." And if there's enough time between classes, they head out into Manhattan. The school's Gramercy Park location puts students in the middle of great shopping, dining, and just-wandering-around-and-staring-at-cool-stuff terrain. When students do socialize, "they usually go to bars or clubs after school is over. Many students at Baruch also work while they go to school, however, so sometimes it can be hard to coordinate schedules with your friends."

Student Body

Baruch "is a microcosm of many of the different neighborhoods of New York City," students report, the kind of place where "you will meet people from countries you never heard of before." Undergrads agree that "The diversity is a big plus. It helps bring a cornucopia of thought and ideas" to almost every class. Students don't get much chance to get close, however, since Baruch "is a commuter school, with many people working full-time jobs or commuting for hours from the far reaches of Long Island or upstate New York. People come to class, then they leave right after." Explains one undergrad, "Students primarily view each other as potential business contacts, not potential friends. It's definitely possible to make friends, but it would be a lot easier at a school with dorms than at this, a commuter school."

ADMISSIONS

Very important factors considered include: Secondary school record, standardized test scores. *Important factors considered include:* Essays, recommendations. *Other factors considered include:* Alumni/ae relation, character/personal qualities, class rank, extracurricular activities, interview, talent/ability, work experience. SAT Reasoning or ACT required. TOEFL required of all international applicants. High school diploma is required, and GED is accepted. *Academic units required:* 4 English, 3 math, 2 science (2 science lab), 2 foreign language, 4 social studies. *Academic units recommended:* 4 math, 3 foreign language, 1 academic elective.

The Inside Word

Interest in Baruch has risen greatly in recent years, and so too have admissions standards. Applications are processed through the University Application Processing Center, which handles applications for all CUNY campuses, so don't expect much in the way of individualized attention. Applying early will improve your chances.

FINANCIAL AID

Students should submit: FAFSA, state aid form. Regular filing deadline 4/30. The Princeton Review suggests that all financial aid forms be submitted as soon as possible after 1/1. *Need-based scholarships/grants offered:* Pell, SEOG, state scholarships/grants, the school's own gift aid, city merit scholarships. *Loan aid offered:* Direct Subsidized Stafford, Direct Unsubsidized Stafford, Direct PLUS, Federal Perkins. Applicants will be notified of awards on a rolling basis beginning on or about 4/1. Federal Work-study Program available. Institutional employment available. Off-campus job opportunities are excellent.

For even more information on this school, turn to page 479 of the "Stats" section.

CITY UNIVERSITY OF NEW YORK—BROOKLYN COLLEGE

2900 BEDFORD AVENUE, BROOKLYN, NY 11210 • ADMISSIONS: 718-951-5001
FINANCIAL AID: 718-951-5051 • E-MAIL: ADMINGRY@BROOKLYN.CUNY.EDU • WEBSITE: WWW.BROOKLYN.CUNY.EDU

Ratings
Quality of Life: 65   **Academic:** 70   **Admissions:** 82   **Financial Aid:** 93

Academics

It's "all about getting a quality, low-cost education" at Brooklyn College, a New York City school that serves a large undergraduate population of both traditional and nontraditional students. About 16 percent of undergraduates here major in business. Computer and information sciences, boosted by "very up-to-date technology," attract a sizable percentage of students, too. Psychology, education, and pre-medical studies are also popular programs.

> **SURVEY SAYS . . .**
> *Small classes*
> *Great computer facilities*
> *Great library*
> *Diverse student types on campus*
> *Very little drug use*

Undergrads report that it's rough going at first at BC; frequent griping by students has led to a change in the core requirements that have been deemed "too numerous," and "the professors who teach core courses are not the greatest." Things get much better once students find an area of specialization; explains one, "Until I found a program that I could tailor to my needs, I found BC to be a cold place lacking interest in its students. Now I realize that once students find their key supporting office or department, we actually have a chance to accomplish wonderful things." Professors here include "everything from a former truck driver to a top experienced CPA.... There are also professors from every background and religion." Although some teachers in the sciences and technology "don't really speak much English," students generally are impressed with the quality of the faculty, telling us that instructors "push us to do our best" and "foster a great environment for academic quality and success." Undergrads also appreciate the "great tutors" and "helpful writing center;" they complain, however, that "the school needs to do a better job helping students find jobs when they graduate;" the college has recently responded to these complaints with the creation of a Career Development Center. Those in the honors program tell us that "courses are compelling and challenging, fully preparing you to be at the top of your grad-school class."

Life

Brooklyn College "does not have too much of a social life outside of fraternities and sororities," in large part because there is no residential life here. The school's location in Midwood, a quiet, unhip neighborhood, also stifles extracurricular life. Students tell us that "there are basketball games, parties, and fashion shows, but relative to the number of students here, they are not that well attended." Perhaps the most popular extracurricular outlets on campus are the many interest- and background-related clubs and organizations, which "get together frequently and are very accepting no matter what your race, gender, or ethnicity." Students also like the student center, which "has fun games, sports, and other activities." Otherwise, undergrads visit campus to attend classes and study, then typically head home or off to another part of New York City for diversion. Manhattan and other areas are, fortunately, easy to reach by subway. Undergrads note that the BC campus is "quite beautiful" and that "library facilities are great." Sports facilities, on the other hand, "must improve," and improve they will when the college's West Quad Building opens its doors in 2007.

Student Body

The "busy, hurried" undergrads of Brooklyn College are "generally mature and look forward to earning their degrees." They are "very street-smart" and typically "in a rush to graduate, so they focus more on receiving their credentials than on participating in student life." Notes one student, "As a commuter college, BC is merely a brief stopping point for most of us." Students here "represent the plurality of ethnicities that make up Brooklyn," the most populous, and by some accounts, diverse of the Big Apple's five boroughs. As one student puts it, "There are so many different types of students in terms of race, ethnicity, and religion. In addition, the day students differ from the night students who all tend to be working full-time jobs." Undergrads here are impressed that "Brooklyn College graduates go on to do great things," like Eugene Shenderov, a 2005 Rhodes Scholar, who is the second BC student to win the prestigious award. "Perhaps it's that tough Brooklyn attitude they help us build."

ADMISSIONS

Very important factors considered include: Secondary school record, standardized test scores. *Other factors considered include:* Recommendations. SAT Reasoning Test and ACT required. TOEFL required of all international applicants. High school diploma is required, and GED is accepted. *Academic units recommended:* 4 English, 3 math, 3 science, 3 foreign language, 4 social studies, 4 academic electives.

The Inside Word

Like other CUNY schools, Brooklyn College provides easy access to a college education for students who want one. Brooklyn raises the bar, however, with superior offerings in the arts and sciences. You don't have to have a spotless academic record to get into Brooklyn College, but once there you will receive a solid and respected education.

FINANCIAL AID

Students should submit: FAFSA, state aid form. The Princeton Review suggests that all financial aid forms be submitted as soon as possible after 1/1. *Need-based scholarships/grants offered:* Pell, SEOG, state scholarships/grants, private scholarships, the school's own gift aid. *Loan aid offered:* Direct Subsidized Stafford, Direct Unsubsidized Stafford, Direct PLUS, Federal Perkins. Applicants will be notified of awards on or about 5/1.

FROM THE ADMISSIONS OFFICE

"Brooklyn College, a premier public liberal arts college founded in 1930, ranked sixth this year in the Princeton Review's America's Best Value Colleges. In the 2003 edition of the Princeton Review's The Best 351 Colleges the college ranked first in the country for its "Beautiful Campus," and fifth for providing the "Best Academic Bang for Your Buck" and for its friendly diversity on the "Students from Different Backgrounds Interact" list. It again placed among the top five in the guide's 2004 edition.

"Brooklyn College's 15,000 undergraduate and graduate students represent the ethnic and cultural diversity of the borough. And the college's accessibility by subway or bus allows students to further enrich their educational experience through New York City's many cultural events and institutions.

"The college continues on an ambitious program of expansion and renewal. The dazzling new library is the most technologically advanced educational and research facility in the CUNY system. A state-of-the-art student services and physical education building, currently under construction, is scheduled to be completed in 2007.

"Respected nationally for its rigorous academic standards, the college takes pride in such innovative programs as its award-winning Freshman Year College; the Honors Academy, which houses nine programs for high achievers, and the core curriculum. Brooklyn College's strong academic reputation has attracted an outstanding faculty of nationally renowned teachers and scholars. Among the awards they have won are Pulitzers, Guggenheims, Fulbrights, and National Institutes of Health grants. Brooklyn College students also receive such prestigious honors as Fulbright Scholarships, the Beinecke Memorial Scholarship, and the Paul and Daisy Soros Fellowships for New Americans."

For even more information on this school, turn to page 479 of the "Stats" section.

CITY UNIVERSITY OF NEW YORK—HUNTER COLLEGE

695 PARK AVENUE, NEW YORK, NY 10021 • ADMISSIONS: 212-772-4000 • FAX: 212-650-3336
FINANCIAL AID: 212-772-4820 • E-MAIL: ADMISSIONS@HUNTER.CUNY.EDU • WEBSITE: WWW.HUNTER.CUNY.EDU

Ratings
Quality of Life: 67   **Academic:** 66   **Admissions:** 86   **Financial Aid:** 92

Academics

Students describe Hunter College, a branch of the City University of New York located on Manhattan's Upper East Side, as "overcrowded [and having] too much paperwork, [but] the professors are top of the line, which is unexpected because of the low tuition." Don't expect much hand-holding or one-on-one instruction. City bureaucracy and the school being "terribly underfunded translate to poor services for students and huge class sizes." That's not

> **SURVEY SAYS . . .**
> *Diverse student types on campus*
> *Students love New York, NY*
> *Great off-campus food*
> *Political activism is popular*
> *(Almost) everyone smokes*

to say that affordability is Hunter's only asset. On the contrary, the school has many tremendous assets, including its New York City location. Hunter provides fantastic learning opportunities ("One of my evolution labs is held at the American Museum of Natural History, which is neat," reports one undergraduate) and a stellar faculty. Many students commend the selective Honors College, and believe that "it gives you a ton back in return for your sacrifice of a 'normal' college experience, as well as saving you huge amounts of money." It can still be difficult to navigate through a school where administrative bureaucrats "always tell you that, whatever your problem, it's up to someone else to fix it, but recent changes in administration are working on new initiatives to counter this." One nontraditional undergraduate observes, "Hunter is a good environment for mature or older students who have a sense of their future goals, both career and otherwise. However, this is not the place for someone who needs a large network of support from career counselors or other students in order to make major decisions about their college track or career."

Life

Hunter is a commuter school. Even the relatively few students who live in dorms essentially live "off-campus," since the dormitories are located on Hunter's downtown campus, where the Health Professions school is located. Accordingly, "many people go straight home after classes," which stymies campus life. The physical facilities also present an obstacle because of the layout, which "offers nothing to do during three-hour breaks between classes except study." Although there are setbacks, one student says, "Many people are involved in on-campus activities apart from classes, including the large amounts of clubs we have, the student-faculty senate, student government, and just hanging out in the hallways waiting for class." Of course, New York City offers myriad things to do and draws away students who might otherwise remain on campus. Explains one undergraduate, "Living in New York City is incomparable. The city is alive with culture. There is so much to do and see that it can be overwhelming. There are shows, concerts, comedy clubs, various universities, and many other activities to keep the students busy." The school itself is "located in a decent neighborhood near many world-renowned cultural institutions: Carnegie Hall, the Metropolitan [Museum of Art], Central Park, Sotheby's. If you have time to kill, there are also lots of boutiques and little restaurants to eat in. And, in the warm months, you can go to Central Park between classes." The city also offers job seekers "endless networking opportunities, which are extremely helpful."

Student Body

It's not a surprise that Hunter is filled with a wide assortment of people; among the part-timers, full-timers, traditional students, nontraditional students (students who return to school after decades), there are individuals from every possible race and ethnicity, faith, and sexual orientation. "This school is extremely ethnically diverse," students tell us, noting that "all cultures are respectful of one another, and this is very interesting in the classroom." Many students "are first-generation college students, first-generation Americans, or both. Many of them go to outstanding lengths to achieve excellence in academics while supporting families and working part- or full-time jobs." The school is also home to "openly gay and lesbian groups," and according to one student, "they are not treated any differently. That's mostly because we are located in NYC, so most of the students grew up accepting difference." Conservatives warn that "Hunter can be a very hostile place to those on the political right."

ADMISSIONS

Very important factors considered include: Secondary school record, standardized test scores. SAT Reasoning or ACT required. TOEFL required of all international applicants. High school diploma is required, and GED is accepted. *Academic units required:* 2 English, 2 math, 1 science (1 science lab). *Academic units recommended:* 4 English, 3 math, 2 science (2 science lab), 2 foreign language, 4 social studies, 1 visual or performing arts.

The Inside Word

Like other City University of New York (CUNY) schools, Hunter College provides easy access to a college education for students who want one. Hunter raises the bar, however, with its superior offerings in the arts and sciences. You don't have to have a spotless academic record to get into Hunter College; but once you are there, you will receive a solid and respected education.

FINANCIAL AID

Students should submit: FAFSA, state aid form, institutional direct loan request form from direct loan applicants. The Princeton Review suggests that all financial aid forms be submitted as soon as possible after 1/1. *Need-based scholarships/grants offered:* Pell, SEOG, state scholarships/grants, private scholarships, the school's own gift aid. *Loan aid offered:* Direct Subsidized Stafford, Direct Unsubsidized Stafford, Direct PLUS, Federal Perkins, alternative loans. Applicants will be notified of awards on a rolling basis beginning on or about 5/15. Federal Work-study Program available. Institutional employment available. Off-campus job opportunities are good.

FROM THE ADMISSIONS OFFICE

"Located in the heart of Manhattan, Hunter offers students the stimulating learning environment and career-building opportunities you might expect from a college that's been a part of the world's most exciting city since 1870. The largest college in the City University of New York, Hunter pulses with energy. Hunter's vitality stems from a large, highly diverse faculty and student body. Its schools—Arts and Sciences, Education, the Health Professions, and Social Work—provide an affordable first-rate education. Undergraduates have extraordinary opportunities to conduct high-level research under renowned faculty, and many opt for credit-bearing internships in such exciting fields as media, the arts, and government. The College's high standards and special programs ensure a challenging education. The Block Program for first-year students keeps classmates together as they pursue courses in the liberal arts, pre-health science, pre-nursing, pre-med, or honors. A range of honors programs is available for students with strong academic records, including the highly competitive tuition-free Hunter CUNY Honors College for entering freshmen and the Thomas Hunter Honors Program, which emphasizes small classes with personalized mentoring by the most outstanding faculty. Qualified students also benefit from Hunter's participation in minority science research and training programs, the prestigious Andrew W. Mellon Minority Undergraduate Program, and many other passports to professional success."

For even more information on this school, turn to page 480 of the "Stats" section.

CITY UNIVERSITY OF NEW YORK—QUEENS COLLEGE

65-30 KISSENA BOULEVARD, FLUSHING, NY 11367 • ADMISSIONS: 718-997-5000 • FAX: 718-997-5617
FINANCIAL AID: 718-997-5101 • E-MAIL: ADMISSIONS@QC.EDU • WEBSITE: WWW.QC.EDU

Ratings
Quality of Life: 67   Academic: 71   Admissions: 80   Financial Aid: 88

Academics

The appeal of Queens College can be summed up in four words: "Great education, cheap price." Students say their college has "the best academic reputation of all the CUNY schools." Academic requirements place "a strong emphasis on the liberal arts, intended to create a well-rounded student." The faculty "encourages students to excel and seek their help." An evenhanded senior writes, "Although professors don't spoon-feed you, they really care about you as an individual and make you feel like you matter."

> **SURVEY SAYS . . .**
> *Small classes*
> *Great library*
> *Diverse student types on campus*
> *Very little beer drinking*
> *Very little hard liquor*
> *Very little drug use*

Instructors set a rigorous academic standard and "sometimes expect too much from you, which can be stressful." Undergraduates typically encounter "a mix of great teachers and awful ones;" to sort it out, "you just need to ask around." Tight city and state budgets mean lab equipment better suited as museum pieces and "a few academic departments where it is virtually impossible for students to register for classes." An upperclassman writes, "Many students have to delay graduation because they cannot get in to the classes they need on time." Despite these snags, students believe that "you can get an amazing education if you try." The abundant resources of New York City are "used to enrich classes" and to compensate for any outdated or limited campus resources. Although students say "the administration is kind and cooperative," several people agree that Queens is "not a student-friendly school, although [they] see signs that it is slowly changing."

Life

Because a large percentage of Queens College students commute, people may expect a dismal campus social scene. It's true that "once classes are over, most students don't spend a lot of time on campus." However, as part of the "growing student life," midday "free hour" events bring everyone together for parties, speakers, discussion groups, or food before they head for home. One student says, "Free hour is the best thing that happened to collegiate education because it forces you to slow down and appreciate life." Students also commonly congregate in the cafeteria or student union. Another student explains that "clubs provide a viable substitute for residential life at Queens." People get "very active in clubs and after-school activities" to forge a sense of social connection. Many extracurricular activities reflect the international flavor of the campus, such as the popular dance performances put on by the Hindi Student Council. Some organizations "exist only in theory" and need to be revived by some fresh blood. A casual crew of Frisbee enthusiasts can typically be found on the lawn against the backdrop "of the spectacular midtown Manhattan skyline."

Student Body

In today's higher education landscape, Queens College stands out as a paragon of diversity. In fact, "it's one of the most diverse student populations of all campuses nationwide." Pick an ethnicity, culture, nation of origin, or religion, and you will most likely find it at the school. The student body "reflects the global population and the population of the great city [that] it is located in." Most students appreciate the resulting atmosphere. One student agrees, "The diversity is a great benefit to anyone who comes here. It opens up your eyes and mind to new cultures and customs." This "eclectic group" shows more signs of internal intermingling than other campuses that claim to have similar student body demographic numbers. "For the most part, different groups mix both in class and out of it." Intercultural exchange happens naturally: "All the students are glad to share with you something about their culture." With such a degree of heterogeneity, it's hardly surprising that "very few people feel left out." Students "on both extremes, from overachievers to slackers," come together in this "friendly and cheerful environment."

ADMISSIONS

Very important factors considered include: Secondary school record, standardized test scores. SAT Reasoning or ACT required. TOEFL required of all international applicants. High school diploma is required, and GED is accepted. *Academic units required:* 4 English, 3 math, 2 science (2 science lab), 3 foreign language, 4 social studies. *Academic units recommended:* 4 English, 3 math, 3 science (3 science lab), 3 foreign language, 4 social studies.

The Inside Word

Applicants to Queens follow the usual CUNY application procedures, which have gotten tougher with the implementation of updated high school curriculum requirements. Candidates for the Aaron Copeland School of Music must also successfully pass through a rigorous audition process. CUNY admissions requirements are currently undergoing close scrutiny; beware of the possibility of further changes.

FINANCIAL AID

Students should submit: FAFSA, state aid form. The Princeton Review suggests that all financial aid forms be submitted as soon as possible after 1/1. *Need-based scholarships/grants offered:* Pell, SEOG, state scholarships/grants, private scholarships, the school's own gift aid. *Loan aid offered:* Direct Subsidized Stafford, Direct Unsubsidized Stafford, Direct PLUS, Federal Perkins. Applicants will be notified of awards on a rolling basis beginning on or about 5/1. Federal Work-study Program available. Off-campus job opportunities are excellent.

FROM THE ADMISSIONS OFFICE

"New York State Governor George Pataki calls Queens College "the jewel of the City University of New York system" for two good reasons: its faculty and its students. Faculty members, who have received prestigious awards such as the Emmy, Guggenheim, and Fulbright, are renowned for their commitment to scholarship and teaching. Interaction among students, who come from 140 nations, and a fast-growing student life program also create a dynamic learning environment.

"Queens College, ranked as the 6th "Best Bargain Public College" by The Princeton Review in 2005, offers nationally recognized programs in many fields, including the Aaron Copland School of Music. In fall 2003, a Bachelor of Business Administration degree was introduced, providing business career preparation grounded in the liberal arts and sciences. A Bachelor of Science degree in graphic design was added in fall 2004. Aspiring teachers benefit from the Education Division's innovative programs (Queens College educates more teachers than any college in the tri-state area). Queens College also participates in the CUNY Honors College and offers its own Honors programs in the arts and humanities, sciences, and social sciences to qualified students. It is also the only CUNY college that participates in Division II sports.

"A commuter college with a residential feel, Queens boasts a beautiful, 77-acre campus lined with trees surrounding grassy open spaces and a traditional quad. In 2003, the completely renovated Powdermaker Hall, the major classroom building, reopened with state-of-the-art technology throughout. In fact, in an Intel survey that ranks the top 100 schools for wireless computing access, Queens College places 13th in the nation"

For even more information on this school, turn to page 480 of the "Stats" section.

CLARK UNIVERSITY

950 MAIN STREET, WORCESTER, MA 01610 • ADMISSIONS: 508-793-7431 • FAX: 508-793-8821
FINANCIAL AID: 508-793-7478 • E-MAIL: ADMISSIONS@CLARKU.EDU • WEBSITE: WWW.CLARKU.EDU

Ratings
Quality of Life: 71   **Academic:** 82   **Admissions:** 89   **Financial Aid:** 89

Academics

"Clark is geared toward providing every student with the opportunity for personal growth," students at this prestigious liberal arts school report. The school achieves this goal "by offering a wide and fascinating variety of courses, programs, travel opportunities, and events that inform and intrigue." The solid academic community on campus is key to the Clark experience; a "group of mentors (your professors, the administration, and your peers)" is "always willing to help" students deal with the "extremely challenging classes" that make up the Clark curriculum. Writes a typical undergrad, "I know all my professors and all my professors know me (even in my larger classes)." Classes that are "usually small in size" are "intimate enough to give you a chance to connect with professors" who "really do want their students to actually understand the material, not just know it to succeed on tests. They also take a personal interest in the students; several friends have gone to their professors' houses for dinner (as first-year students)." This closeness between professors and students encourages "opportunities to get involved with research," a real boon to students' curriculum vitaes. Research is further promoted by Clark's constant efforts at self-improvement; students tell us that the school "keeps adding new facilities that are up-to-date so that learning can be more hands-on." Psychology and the hard sciences are standout offerings here; political science, government, and history are all also reportedly strong.

> **SURVEY SAYS . . .**
> *Small classes*
> *Frats and sororities are unpopular*
> *or nonexistent*
> *Lots of beer drinking*
> *Hard liquor is popular*

Life

"Clark is a small school with a very strong sense of community" where "you can sit down at a random table in the cafeteria and the odds are that you'll know at least one other person at the table." Writes one undergrad, "I can count on one hand the number of meals I've eaten alone this semester." Students love how Clark "retains its community feel without feeling cramped. The opportunities for community service, studying abroad, and internships provide plenty of opportunities to broaden oneself socially, and there are other ways to get away from people if one wants to be alone or lose oneself." Otherwise, "If you leave your room at all, ever, you will have a social life here, and that doesn't have to mean drinking or drugs, since there's a lot more to life here. There's also very little pressure to drink if you don't." If you do drink, you'll find plenty of company, as "people party a good amount. Going to local bars after parties is very popular. Hard liquor and beer is always around and never cheap beer or hard liquor, always good stuff." Other diversions include "sports, movies, theatre performances, comedy sketches, and lectures. Mostly indoor stuff, because Worcester gets really cold in the winter." Hometown Worcester has other problems; it "isn't the best city to go to school in, despite having eight colleges here. There's very little to do off campus on weekends unless you go to Boston."

Student Body

"We have a really unique combination of preppy, hippie, artsy, jock and everything in between" at Clark, students tell us, "most people fit into more than one category." Asked which category is represented with the greatest frequency, most here will tell you that "it's the student who looks like he's just returning from Woodstock: Birkenstocks, bandanas, grubby-looking, loose clothing, reeking of weed." Everyone is welcome, we're told; writes one outlier, "I myself am a practicing Republican ROTC cadet who abstains from nearly every vice, and I have no trouble fitting in." Clark undergrads appreciate that "students are focused more on learning than on competition with one another, so there are very few cutthroats about grades." Students tend to be bright and curious, so "it's easy to get involved in a very long conversation about some class topic, which is how a recent study session was extended from three to seven hours."

ADMISSIONS

Very important factors considered include: Character/personal qualities, recommendations, secondary school record, standardized test scores. *Important factors considered include:* Essays, extracurricular activities, talent/ability, volunteer work. *Other factors considered include:* Alumni/ae relation, class rank, geographical residence, interview, minority status, work experience. SAT Reasoning and SAT Subject Tests or ACT required. TOEFL required of all international applicants. High school diploma is required, and GED is accepted. *Academic units recommended:* 4 English, 3 math, 3 science (2 science lab), 2 foreign language, 2 social studies, 2 history.

The Inside Word

Clark is surrounded by formidable competitors, and its selectivity suffers because of it. Most B students will encounter little difficulty gaining admission. Given the university's solid academic environment and access to other member colleges in the Worcester Consortium, it can be a terrific choice for students who are not up to the ultra-competitive admission expectations of "top-tier" universities.

FINANCIAL AID

Students should submit: FAFSA, CSS/Financial Aid PROFILE. The Princeton Review suggests that all financial aid forms be submitted as soon as possible after 1/1. *Need-based scholarships/grants offered:* Pell, SEOG, state scholarships/grants, the school's own gift aid. *Loan aid offered:* FFEL Subsidized Stafford, FFEL Unsubsidized Stafford, FFEL PLUS, Federal Perkins, state loans, college/university loans from institutional funds. Applicants will be notified of awards on or about 3/31. Federal Work-study Program available. Institutional employment available. Off-campus job opportunities are good.

FROM THE ADMISSIONS OFFICE

"At Clark University, you are respected for challenging convention, for trying out new ideas and skills, and for inspiring new ways of thinking. You learn how social change is made, and you get to be a part of it. Individual development is nurtured by a dedicated faculty who encourages hands-on learning. Founded in 1887, Clark is home to students from more than 57 countries and 44 states."

For even more information on this school, turn to page 473 of the "Stats" section.

CLARKSON UNIVERSITY

Box 5605, Potsdam, NY 13699 • Admissions: 315-268-6479 • Fax: 315-268-7647
Financial Aid: 315-268-7699 • E-mail: admissions@clarkson.edu • Website: www.clarkson.edu

Ratings
Quality of Life: 62   Academic: 70   Admissions: 86   Financial Aid: 90

Academics

"Academics and hockey are the greatest strengths at Clarkson University," a tech-heavy school in upstate New York where it sometimes seems that "99 percent of us are here for business, engineering, or science." For many here, Clarkson's chief appeal is the way it opens doors for graduates; explains one student, "Clarkson has a very good name… alumni have gone on to become CEOs or own their own company. Employers come here to recruit because

they know the Clarkson student is likely to be successful." This is because Clarkson grads have conquered a curriculum that "is challenging even for people who are skilled in math, science, and engineering." It's so challenging, in fact, that "teamwork is essential here. It is the only way we can successfully learn all the material." Undergrads appreciate Clarkson's "interdisciplinary approach to all learning, as well as the emphasis on leadership" in the curriculum. They're less enamored of the liberal arts offerings, noting that the departments are small and classes are few. Professors get wildly mixed reviews, which actually puts them in the upper stratum of tech instructors, whose marks are usually quite low. Students warn that "the school often has new professors teaching classes in which they are unprepared to teach. Most of the time they are very well-qualified individuals but do not yet have the ability to properly teach a classroom full of students." Better teachers here "have a genuine interest in their students' succeeding, and enjoy their jobs."

Life

Located in Potsdam, NY, Clarkson "is in the middle of nowhere." Some see that as an asset; one such student explains, "It forces you to meet people and make friends to have fun. And since it is in the middle of nowhere, it is easier to get work done…there are fewer things to distract you from doing your work." Others see a downside; "Unless you are an avid hunter/fisherman, your options for not getting bored doing the same exact thing week after week are very poor. Remember the movie Groundhog Day? Life here is comparable." Compounding the challenges of extracurricular life here are the heavy workload and the fact that "it's freezing up there for about half of the school year," which drives many students "to bars, Canada, dinner, or hockey games. Or we stay in, playing video games or hanging out with friends." Some feel the school could do more to improve things; one undergrad observes, "There isn't enough money spent on bringing events to campus. Every year they bring the same comedians, the same small bands. The only event that seems to be any good is the spring concert, but that's about it." As a result, "Most of the students spend their free time hanging with friends and drinking." Sums up one student, "When I'm not working…I drink. We are a technical school that certainly knows how to party. There isn't much else to do up here."

Student Body

"There are typically two groups at Clarkson," students tell us. There are "those focused on learning and interested in having a good time; and, there are those solely focused on learning." Most Clarkson students share "a drive to succeed, an ability to learn in multi-disciplinary environments, and a strong career/graduate study focus." This focus can be overwhelming at times; "Even in party atmospheres you will find numerous conversations regarding nothing but academic-related topics. Not enough separation between 'business and pleasure,' so to speak." Like many tech-oriented schools, "Clarkson needs more women. The ratio is so completely horrible that it is probably the top of every male student's list of what needs improving here." Scattered among the student population are "a number of athletes and quite a few outdoorsy people."

ADMISSIONS

Very important factors considered include: Interview, secondary school record. *Important factors considered include:* Class rank, extracurricular activities, recommendations, standardized test scores, volunteer work. *Other factors considered include:* Alumni/ae relation, character/personal qualities, essays, talent/ability, work experience. TOEFL required of all international applicants. High school diploma is required, and GED is accepted. *Academic units required:* 4 English, 3 math, 2 science. *Academic units recommended:* 4 math, 3 science.

The Inside Word

Clarkson's acceptance rate is too high for solid applicants to lose much sleep about gaining admission. Serious candidates should interview anyway. If you are particularly solid and really want to come here, it could help you get some scholarship money. Women and minorities will encounter an especially friendly admissions committee.

FINANCIAL AID

Students should submit: FAFSA, institution's own financial aid form, state aid form. The Princeton Review suggests that all financial aid forms be submitted as soon as possible after 1/1. *Need-based scholarships/grants offered:* Pell, SEOG, state scholarships/grants, private scholarships, the school's own gift aid, HEOP. *Loan aid offered:* Direct Subsidized Stafford, Direct Unsubsidized Stafford, Direct PLUS, Federal Perkins, college/university loans from institutional funds, GATE. Applicants will be notified of awards on or about 3/23.

FROM THE ADMISSIONS OFFICE

"Clarkson is an independent, coeducational university with a strong focus on technology-based fields. It offers innovative programs in business, engineering, science, liberal arts, and health sciences. Clarkson is known for having a friendly, personal campus where professors are accessible. The academic environment is highly collaborative and interdisciplinary. A rigorous curriculum emphasizes team project-based learning and creative problem solving. Students develop collaboration, communication, and leadership skills along with versatility and hands-on management experience. They also enjoy opportunities for faculty-mentored research experience. Health sciences (including physical therapy) and health-oriented engineering are increasing in emphasis at Clarkson. With input from leading corporations, the business curriculum has been recently redesigned to develop skills needed in today's changing, global marketplace.

"Clarkson is nationally recognized for the effectiveness of its team, project-based learning programs. The university has won the Boeing Outstanding Educator Award and the Corporate and Foundation Alliance Award for team project-based learning and the IBM Linux Scholar Challenge (an international, open-source, computer programming competition). In business, Clarkson was a finalist for the National Undergraduate Entrepreneurship Education Award, and the program in Supply Chain Management is ranked in the nation's top 20 by *U.S. News* and *World Report*."

For even more information on this school, turn to page 473 of the "Stats" section.

COLBY COLLEGE

4800 MAYFLOWER HILL, WATERVILLE, ME 04901-8848 • ADMISSIONS: 207-872-3168 • FAX: 207-872-3474
FINANCIAL AID: 207-872-3168 • E-MAIL: ADMISSIONS@COLBY.EDU • WEBSITE: WWW.COLBY.EDU

Ratings
Quality of Life: 83   **Academic:** 92   **Admissions:** 96   **Financial Aid:** 94

Academics

This small, close-knit liberal arts college draws praise from students for its rigorous but caring approach to academics. It's a place where devoted professors "invite students to dinner" and learning happens "for learning's sake." Small classes are one of Colby's biggest draws. "It's all about personal attention from professors," writes a freshman. One junior warns, "But watch out. If you've screwed up in one class, future profs will know." Professors get high grades for their teaching and accessibility, which together foster a

> **SURVEY SAYS . . .**
> *Small classes*
> *Great food on campus*
> *Frats and sororities are unpopular*
> *or nonexistent*
> *Lots of beer drinking*

"love for learning" in undergraduates. "What stands out about the professors is that most are the rare combination of brilliant mind and brilliant teacher," writes one student. "I know most of my professors and the deans on a personal level, and I have felt challenged by every course that I have taken," adds another student. This makes Colby an intense place to go to school, and students work a lot and study hard. Students must not only complete their major requirements but also fulfill a hefty load of distribution requirements to graduate. The popular "Jan Plan" lets students take an extra month long term of focused or independent study in January, often accompanied by an internship. The administration, however, is often criticized for being unresponsive to student concerns and input. "While they want to do what's best for the campus, their goals and ideals are antiquated," writes one senior.

Life

"Friends and a sense of community drive life at Colby," writes one senior. Students live together in coed, mixed-class dorms. Everything centers around the campus, which is "constructed on a gorgeous wooded hill near the Kennebec River in Central Maine." And since "there isn't a ridiculous amount to do" in these remote environs, "Colby works hard to fill the day with countless events, lectures, discussions, and concerts. People can study hard, party, take advantage of the beautiful outdoors, and most do all three." Students go hiking in autumn and spring, skiing in winter, and participate in traditional outdoor sports like lacrosse. Writes one senior, "People like to unwind after our incredibly stressful weeks with movies, skiing, and partying." Booze flows freely and drug use is not unheard of at Colby. The "alcohol-centered social scene" usually takes place at small dorm parties or at the few local pubs. Students make sure to add that they not only play hard but also they work hard. But drinkers beware: "This school is too small to have a private life," and "if you do something, everyone will know the details in a day or two."

Student Body

While the prototypical Colby student may be "white and from 20 minutes outside of Boston," undergrads are quick to point out that their "campus is very open to diversity and ready to embrace it." The administration recently launched a major push for diversity and it appears to have gained some initial success. "The diversity has increased a lot since my freshman year," notes a senior. "There are also a lot more international students." A junior adds, "We have students here that dress in business suits and bow ties while others walk around in capes." Most students, however, settle for the more general description of "preppy students who enjoy the outdoors and enjoy having a good time." Although this means that the student body can often look like a small army of "J. Crew models," students assure us that there is "an abundance of clubs on campus for all kinds of people. It's easy to find your niche." Both intellectual and adventurous, Colby students for the most part are "enthusiastic, gregarious, and well balanced."

ADMISSIONS

Very important factors considered include: Character/personal qualities, secondary school record. *Important factors considered include:* Class rank, essays, extracurricular activities, interview, minority status, recommendations, standardized test scores, talent/ability. *Other factors considered include:* Alumni/ae relation, geographical residence, state residency, volunteer work, work experience. SAT Reasoning or ACT required. TOEFL required of all international applicants. High school diploma or equivalent is not required. *Academic units recommended:* 4 English, 3 math, 2 science (2 science lab), 3 foreign language, 2 social studies, 2 academic electives.

The Inside Word

Colby continues to be both very selective and successful in converting admits to enrollees, which makes for a perpetually challenging admissions process.

INANCIAL AID

Students should submit: FAFSA, either institutional application or CSS/Financial Aid PROFILE and institutional supplement. Regular filing deadline 2/1. The Princeton Review suggests that all financial aid forms be submitted as soon as possible after 1/1. *Need-based scholarships/grants offered:* Pell, SEOG, state scholarships/grants, private scholarships, the school's own gift aid. *Loan aid offered:* Direct Subsidized Stafford, Direct Unsubsidized Stafford, Direct PLUS, FFEL Subsidized Stafford, FFEL Unsubsidized Stafford, FFEL PLUS, Federal Perkins, state loans, college/university loans from institutional funds, alternative loans. Applicants will be notified of awards on or about 4/1. Off-campus job opportunities are fair.

FROM THE ADMISSIONS OFFICE

"Colby offers world-class academic programs, a supportive community atmosphere, and rich opportunities after graduation. Colby prepares students by giving them a broad foundation of knowledge and intellectual tools, experience as active participants in a diverse community of scholars, and opportunities to engage the world. The depth of student-faculty interaction and collaboration is extraordinary, and the college is recognized as a national leader in undergraduate research and project-based learning. Colby's commitment to global reach earned the college a 2005 Senator Paul Simon Award for internationalizing the campus. The award recognizes the international content of the curriculum, the college's emphasis on study abroad, and the international diversity of the student body and faculty. Colby's strong commitment to environmental stewardship was recognized in 2004 with an EPA Environmental Merit Award and a Maine Governor's Award for Environmental Excellence. The challenging academic experience is complemented by an active community life featuring 100 student-run organizations, more than 50 athletic and recreational choices, and many leadership and volunteer opportunities—all on one of the nation's most beautiful campuses. Colby graduates succeed, finding their places at the finest medical and other graduate schools, top Wall Street firms, and in the arts, government service, social service, education, and nonprofit organizations."

For even more information on this school, turn to page 474 of the "Stats" section.

COLGATE UNIVERSITY

13 OAK DRIVE, HAMILTON, NY 13346 • ADMISSIONS: 315-228-7401 • FAX: 315-228-7544
FINANCIAL AID: 315-228-7431 • E-MAIL: ADMISSION@MAIL.COLGATE.EDU • WEBSITE: WWW.COLGATE.EDU

Ratings
Quality of Life: 83   Academic: 93   Admissions: 97   Financial Aid: 98

Academics

Colgate University is the type of undergraduate institution that inspires fierce loyalty among students and alumni; as one undergrad puts it, "From the student athletes, professors, artists, political activists, to the maintenance people and administration, the majority of Colgate loves the school. People go into Colgate with numerous loves and passions and leave the University with Colgate as a new-found passion." A combination of factors spur this devotion: a beautiful campus, an accomplished and caring faculty, a bright and goal-oriented student body, and a strong sense of community forged at least in part by the school's geographic isolation. Students here report that "the academics are intense, but not overwhelming because the students are intelligent enough to handle the workload," and they praise the liberal arts core curriculum and distribution requirements that "serve as an excellent base for students to pursue other academic interests." They also love the "great study abroad opportunities; if you want to go anywhere in the world you generally can, and the trips are quite affordable." The Outdoor Education Program, through which "nearly 70 percent of students participate in physical education classes, Back Yard Adventures or the Pre-Orientation trip, Wilderness Adventure," is popular, too. Most of all, students love how Colgate prepares them for success in the real world. "Colgate fosters the education of students outside the classroom as well as inside the classroom. Therefore, when students leave Colgate they have great interpersonal skills," explains one student. Another goes on to say, "The 'Colgate Connection' is probably one of the school's greatest benefits, as alumni are very helpful in finding and offering careers for graduates."

> **SURVEY SAYS . . .**
> *Small classes*
> *Everyone loves the Raiders*
> *Lots of beer drinking*
> *Hard liquor is popular*

Life

Colgate's hometown of Hamilton is a "small town that, without Colgate students, has only around 3,000 people." The good news is that "administrators recognize that our location in a small rural community may be construed as a weakness, so they do a great job to make up for this with a profusion of programs on campus. There is always something to do, and if you leave Hamilton for even one day, you feel you've missed out on incredible things." Colgate's geographic isolation is also tempered by the school's "ridiculously beautiful campus, like a country club," its "awesome dorms," and its "clean and comfortable facilities." Intercollegiate sports are big here; "Good Division I athletics are also a rarity among liberal arts colleges, but unlike larger schools, the athletes here are also some of the best students," brags one undergrad. The school is well known for its lively party scene, but students point out that "Colgate has something for just about everyone, including special events, newly opened restaurants, dance halls and the improved movie theater." And "although people party, they know how to keep up with their schoolwork and do well academically." Overall, Colgate undergrads "work hard in school, but also look to have a good time outside the classroom. Whether that means joining groups, playing sports, or going out with their friends, Colgate students like to have fun."

Student Body

Colgate draws an accomplished student body; "the typical Colgate student was captain of a sports team, homecoming king or queen, president of the class, and an excellent student at his or her high school. At Colgate, this translates to a student body of incredibly bright, talented and congenial students," explains one student. Undergrads tell us that "while everyone is really smart, people aren't pretentious about it. You don't feel lower than anyone else, but rather challenged to expand your mind and develop your knowledge and talents." Undergrads tend to be on the preppy side and are typically athletic; it's no surprise, then, that "the gym is one of the hot spots on campus." Colgate "has a reputation as a conservative school, but in fact the bent of the campus is moderately liberal, if anything. While there is a very vocal, organized conservative element, most people seem to be either moderate or left-of-center."

ADMISSIONS

Very important factors considered include: Class rank, secondary school record. *Important factors considered include:* Character/personal qualities, essays, extracurricular activities, recommendations, standardized test scores, talent/ability, volunteer work, work experience. *Other factors considered include:* Alumni/ae relation, geographical residence, minority status. SAT Reasoning or ACT required. TOEFL required of all international applicants. High school diploma is required, and GED is accepted. *Academic units required:* 4 English, 3 math, 3 science (2 science lab), 3 foreign language, 2 social studies, 1 history. *Academic units recommended:* 4 English, 4 math, 4 science (3 science lab), 4 foreign language, 2 social studies, 3 history.

The Inside Word

Like many colleges, Colgate caters to some well-developed special interests. Athletes, minorities, and legacies (the children of alums) are among the most special of interests and benefit from more favorable consideration than applicants without particular distinction. Students without a solid, consistent academic record, beware— the university's wait list leans toward jumbo size.

FINANCIAL AID

Students should submit: FAFSA, CSS/Financial Aid PROFILE, noncustodial (divorced/separated) parents' statement, business/farm supplement. Regular filing deadline 1/15. The Princeton Review suggests that all financial aid forms be submitted as soon as possible after 1/1. *Need-based scholarships/grants offered:* Pell, SEOG, state scholarships/grants, the school's own gift aid. *Loan aid offered:* FFEL Subsidized Stafford, FFEL Unsubsidized Stafford, FFEL PLUS, Federal Perkins. Applicants will be notified of awards on or about 4/1. Federal Work-study Program available. Off-campus job opportunities are good.

FROM THE ADMISSIONS OFFICE

"Students and faculty alike are drawn to Colgate by the quality of its academic programs. Faculty initiative has given the university a rich mix of learning opportunities that includes a liberal arts core, 51 academic concentrations, and a wealth of Colgate faculty-led, off-campus study programs in the United States and abroad. But there is more to Colgate than academic life, including more than 100 student organizations, athletics and recreation at all levels, and a full complement of living options set within a campus described as one of the most beautiful in the country. A new center for community service builds upon the tradition of Colgate students interacting with the surrounding community in meaningful ways. Colgate students become extraordinarily devoted alumni, contributing significantly to career networking and exploration programs on and off campus. For students in search of a busy and varied campus life, Colgate is a place to learn and grow."

For even more information on this school, turn to page 474 of the "Stats" section.

COLLEGE OF THE ATLANTIC

105 EDEN STREET, BAR HARBOR, ME 04609 • ADMISSIONS: 800-528-0025 • FAX: 207-288-4126
FINANCIAL AID: 207-288-5015 • E-MAIL: INQUIRY@ECOLOGY.COA.EDU • WEBSITE: WWW.COA.EDU

Ratings
Quality of Life: 95   **Academic:** 90   **Admissions:** 88   **Financial Aid:** 94

Academics

"It is all about being a better citizen in the world," say the environmentally and politically conscious undergrads of College of the Atlantic, a tiny college whose "strengths include environmental sciences, biology, social sciences, philosophy, and psychology, as well as a tight community [that promotes] intellectual stimulation." COA fosters community spirit and responsibility through its administration, which "is mainly done by committees consisting of students, faculty, and staff, where everyone's opinion counts in decision making." Students love feeling plugged in to the deliberative process and say that the one-for-all approach here also engenders a pervasive feeling of

> **SURVEY SAYS . . .**
> *Small classes*
> *No one cheats*
> *Students are friendly*
> *Campus feels safe*
> *Intercollegiate sports are unpopular or nonexistent*
> *Frats and sororities are unpopular or nonexistent*
> *Student government is popular*

"trust—we don't have locks on our mailboxes, and you can leave your laptop unattended for hours, and it will still be there when you get back." The school allows students "lots of freedom—freedom to take the classes we want, and freedom in those classes to direct our own studies." As one student tells us, "there is so much flexibility here. COA has very few requirements, and they really aren't a big deal." Students praise profs as "energetic and enthusiastic and constantly involved in the students' lives and their learning." Reports one undergrad, "there are posters by each phone on campus, which list the on-campus extension as well as the home phone number of each faculty and staff member. We can call them whenever we need to regarding school, campus committees, and/or personal matters."

Life

Bar Harbor, COA's hometown, may be the perfect antithesis of a college town; during the summer it's a hopping vacation resort, but during the school year "almost all the stores close up" and students "need to find their own entertainment." Bar Harbor is famous for its bracing winters: "It is gray and miserable," notes one undergrad who wishes she were somewhere else. Many here, though, are winter-philes who tout the range of available snow-related activities, which include "skating, cross-country skiing, and snowshoeing." The dearth of in-town options and the small student body combine to create a very subdued campus social scene; "this is not the place for those looking to party, drink, or do lots of drugs (or slack off, for that matter)," explains one student. For fun, "people like cooking together, playing cards, hanging out, going to contra dances, watching movies," and spending as much time outside as they can. Everyone here praises nearby Acadia National Park, "the best backyard a college student could ask for. Finding favorite beautiful hikes, walks, or study spots has become a four-year goal," reports one student. Students party on Tuesdays ("There are no classes on Wednesdays, so Tuesday night is the big social period," explains one student) and on weekends. "Parties are never big, but often fun." Students also want the world to know that "the food is SOOOOO good here! There's no corporate 'food service'—it's just people that work in the kitchen and concoct really tasty (and healthy) food."

Student Body

"Some people think this school is a bunch of granola-eating, flower-child, pot-smoking hippies, but that's not the way it is," reports one COA undergrad. "The typical COA student has a lot of individuality. We're not all cookie-cutter Rastafarians. We're all atypical." Agrees another student, "The COA student tries to be different . . . just like everyone else. There is no 'in' to fit into, just a lot of cliques." Those cliques, students tell us, include "hippies, lobstermen, city kids, trendy people . . . just about every category one could imagine." Students do, on the whole, tend to be "environmentally and socially sensitive" and "liberal in political thought," the type who attend "protests and drive an ancient Volvo or VW with a political bumper sticker and a Darwin fish." "There are quite a few international students, especially from Europe and Asia," at COA, and "they get along well with the rest of the students, but most tend to hang out [primarily] with each other."

ADMISSIONS

Very important factors considered include: Essays, extracurricular activities, interview, recommendations, secondary school record, volunteer work. *Important factors considered include:* Character/personal qualities, talent/ability. *Other factors considered include:* Alumni/ae relation, class rank, minority status, standardized test scores, work experience. TOEFL required of all international applicants. High school diploma is required, and GED is accepted. *Academic units required:* 4 English, 3 math, 2 science (2 science lab), 2 social studies. *Academic units recommended:* 4 English, 4 math, 3 science (2 science lab), 2 foreign language, 2 social studies, 2 history, 1 academic elective.

The Inside Word

COA's academic emphasis results in a highly self-selected applicant pool. Fortunately for the college, its focus on human ecology strikes a chord that is timely in its appeal to students. Enrolling here is definitely opting to take an atypical path to higher education. Admissions evaluations emphasize what's on your mind over what's on your transcript, which makes thoughtful essays and an interview musts for serious candidates. It also makes the admissions process a refreshing experience in the relatively uniform world of college admission. The admissions committee includes a few current students who have full voting rights as members.

FINANCIAL AID

Students should submit: FAFSA, institution's own financial aid form, noncustodial (divorced/separated) parents' statement, business/farm supplement. Regular filing deadline 2/15. The Princeton Review suggests that all financial aid forms be submitted as soon as possible after 1/1. *Need-based scholarships/grants offered:* Pell, SEOG, private scholarships, the school's own gift aid. *Loan aid offered:* FFEL Subsidized Stafford, FFEL Unsubsidized Stafford, FFEL PLUS, Federal Perkins. Applicants will be notified of awards on or about 4/1.

FROM THE ADMISSIONS OFFICE

"College of the Atlantic was created three decades ago at a time when it was becoming evident that conventional education was inadequate for citizenship in our increasingly complex and technical society. The growing interdependence of environmental and social issues and the limitations of academic specialization demanded a wider vision. COA's founders created a pioneering institution dedicated to the interdisciplinary study of human ecology, a college in which students overcome narrow points of view and integrate knowledge across traditional academic lines."

For even more information on this school, turn to page 475 of the "Stats" section.

COLLEGE OF THE HOLY CROSS

ADMISSIONS OFFICE, 1 COLLEGE STREET, WORCESTER, MA 01610-2395 • ADMISSIONS: 508-793-2443
FAX: 508-793-3888 • FINANCIAL AID: 508-793-2265 • E-MAIL: ADMISSIONS@HOLYCROSS.EDU • WEBSITE: WWW.HOLYCROSS.EDU

Ratings
Quality of Life: 65   **Academic:** 89   **Admissions:** 94   **Financial Aid:** 93

Academics

"Academics are very difficult, but very worth the effort" at College of the Holy Cross (HC), a small liberal arts school with "a total sense of community—almost family—just like the admissions propaganda claims." Professors pile on so much work that the school allows students to take only four classes per semester. Even with this limit, "the work is by all means tough. There's a lot of studying, but it really pays off in the real world." The grading system is equally demanding. Fortunately, HC's stringent standards are well

> **SURVEY SAYS . . .**
> *Small classes*
> *Frats and sororities are unpopular*
> *or nonexistent*
> *Lots of beer drinking*
> *Hard liquor is popular*

known to the outside world. "A hiring manager from one of the big accounting firms told me the company considers a 3.0 at Holy Cross [equal to] a 3.5 at other schools," explained one student. Students gripe, but they appreciate the results. Wrote one, "I may hate actually being at school, but having Holy Cross on my resume has gotten me a great summer internship, is allowing me to intern in DC for the spring semester, and will even indirectly lead into being accepted [by] a reputable law school." They also appreciate the "close personal attention you can receive from professors. I have never had a problem getting extra help from a professor on papers or assignments." This is due in part to the "exclusively undergraduate environment. There are no grad students teaching the classes, and the 'good' professors are also available to everyone, not just upper-level or graduate students." "Active alumni support" further sweetens the deal.

Life

At HC, "everyone works their butt off, but also needs to let off steam. It's a really hard school with very high expectations. The stress can be too much at times." Students "work like mad Sunday through Wednesday" and then start letting off that steam on Thursday, usually at a kegger ("HC is a keg school," students tell us). Alternatives are few. "While the student programming people may put on events that try to bring students together, these events rarely draw many (Spring Weekend and the Opportunity Knocks dance are the exceptions)." Hometown Worcester "does not offer a lot despite the high number of colleges in the area. The city is also not very fond of college students." Nonetheless, a few intrepid souls venture out into the city and report that "dining in Worcester is amazing—many great restaurants. There are usually many choices of things to do here between film series, music performances, theatre, and varsity sports." They warn those who'd follow in their footsteps not to reveal their status as HC students. Undergrads praise their "absolutely gorgeous" campus but warn that its famous picturesque hill "is a real pain in the ass, especially in winter." Intercollegiate athletics, "especially men's and women's basketball teams, are hugely popular," as are intramurals. When escape is essential, students head to Boston or Providence.

Student Body

"There are no surprises" in the Holy Cross student body. "It is a small, private, liberal arts college with a Jesuit identity in New England. Therefore, the population is mostly white, middle class, Irish or Italian Catholics." As one student puts it, "A certain type of person, I believe, looks at Holy Cross. This type of person wants a small school in a suburb, with preppy students, small classes, and religion. I am not sure why minorities don't choose Holy Cross; I believe it is because this school just isn't what they want. It is nobody's fault." HC has made some inroads into minority populations through its outreach programs, students here report. The typical HC undergrad is "friendly, outgoing" and conservative. "Religion is big, sports are bigger, and drinking is the biggest." Students like that fact that HC "is a small community, which is nice because you can generally say 'Hi' to anyone and you know them."

ADMISSIONS

Very important factors considered include: Class rank, secondary school record, standardized test scores. *Important factors considered include:* Alumni/ae relation, character/personal qualities, essays, extracurricular activities, interview, recommendations. *Other factors considered include:* Geographical residence, minority status, talent/ability, volunteer work, work experience. SAT Reasoning and SAT Subject Tests or ACT required. TOEFL required of all international applicants. High school diploma is required, and GED is accepted. *Academic units recommended:* 4 English, 4 math, 4 science, 3 foreign language, 2 social studies, 2 history, 1 academic elective.

The Inside Word

The applicant pool at Holy Cross is strong; students are well advised to take the most challenging courses available to them in secondary school. Everyone faces fairly close scrutiny, but as is the case virtually everywhere, the College does have its particular interests. The admissions committee takes good care of candidates from the many Catholic high schools that are the source of dozens of solid applicants each year.

FINANCIAL AID

Students should submit: FAFSA, CSS/Financial Aid PROFILE, noncustodial (divorced/separated) parents' statement, business/farm supplement, parent and student federal tax returns. Regular filing deadline 2/1. The Princeton Review suggests that all financial aid forms be submitted as soon as possible after 1/1. *Need-based scholarships/grants offered:* Pell, SEOG, state scholarships/grants, private scholarships, the school's own gift aid. *Loan aid offered:* FFEL Subsidized Stafford, FFEL Unsubsidized Stafford, FFEL PLUS, Federal Perkins, MDFA. Applicants will be notified of awards on or about 4/1.

FROM THE ADMISSIONS OFFICE

"When applying to Holy Cross, two areas deserve particular attention. First, the essay should be developed thoughtfully, with correct language and syntax in mind. That essay reflects for the Board of Admissions how you think and how you can express yourself. Second, activity beyond the classroom should be clearly defined. Since Holy Cross [only has] 2,800 students, the chance for involvement/participation is exceptional. The Board reviews many applications for academically qualified students. A key difference in being accepted is the extent to which a candidate participates in-depth beyond the classroom—don't be modest; define who you are."

For even more information on this school, turn to page 475 of the "Stats" section.

COLLEGE MISERICORDIA

301 LAKE STREET, DALLAS, PA 18612 • ADMISSIONS: 570-674-6264 • FAX: 570-675-2441
E-MAIL: ADMISS@MISERICORDIA.EDU • WEBSITE: WWW.MISERICORDIA.EDU

Ratings

Quality of Life: 80   **Academic:** 79   **Admissions:** 74   **Financial Aid:** 73

Academics

Most schools promise to provide the skills you need to get a job after graduation. College Misericordia, however, goes one step further. Its "Guaranteed Placement Program "ensures participants will receive a paid internship in their chosen field if they do not obtain a job offer or acceptance to grad school within six months of earning their undergraduate degree. One student gushes, "I love the 'Guaranteed Placement Program,' which says we are guar-

> **SURVEY SAYS . . .**
> *Small classes*
> *Great library*
> *Athletic facilities are great*
> *Frats and sororities are unpopular*
> *or nonexistent*

anteed a job after graduation." Quite simply, "it works." The College goes the extra mile in other areas too. Its Learning Resource Center, for example, serves as an academic safety net. As one undergraduate tells us, "If any students have problems in just about any course, tutoring is available in the LRC, which is a plus. The extra help is incredible." Students also report that, "Service is a huge aspect of every part of Misericordia. We have to complete service projects not only in our curriculum for our degree, but also in many of our classes." Such programs would probably flounder at a large school, but Misericordia is small enough to attend to each student's needs. As one student sums it up, "The size of Misericordia is really what it's all about. The smallness means you can really know your classmates, professors, and the staff—it provides so many opportunities for education."

Life

There are plenty of school- and student-organized activities on the Misericordia campus, students tell us. "Sometimes there is so much going on at Misericordia, its difficult to take part in everything you desire," writes one undergraduate. "For fun on campus there are socials [dances] and Karaoke nights. There's also bingo, mud wrestling, hikes, and rappelling down buildings; all sorts of things are available to us." Also, "Sports like soccer, field hockey and lacrosse are pushed here, and our teams do well." Students who enjoy such activities rave about their extracurricular lives here; others are less enthusiastic. As one such student puts it, "Life on campus is quiet, almost dull. The area surrounding campus is made up of no fewer than seven cemeteries. We have very quiet neighbors." Others have noticed that some spend their weekend life off campus. "Many students commute or live close, so many students go home on the weekends." As a result, parties are infrequent. Some escape to town, one student claims, and "you have to drive 10 to 20 minutes to get to the city," so not everyone has this option. The college does, however, arrange organized student activities and provide shuttle service to local attractions each weekend.

Student Body

Students of the college have claimed that the predominantly "white, Catholic, upper-middle class" students of Misericordia are "the type who get involved because a big percentage of our school is involved in clubs or service." They also "typically study a lot, because many are physical therapy and occupational therapy majors . . . but they still have fun here." One student notes, "Regardless of race, gender, or religion, every student is very into academics." Race, gender, and religious diversity, by the way, are not all it could be, students admit. "There are many students who are different, but not many who are 'diverse'," one student says. "Students who are different fit in as much as they choose to." There is a large preppy contingent here, as well as a sizeable 'jock' population, and some believe "the two groups run the place."

ADMISSIONS

Very important factors considered include: Character/personal qualities, secondary school record. *Important factors considered include:* Class rank, extracurricular activities, interview, standardized test scores, volunteer work. *Other factors considered include:* Essays, minority status, recommendations, work experience. SAT Reasoning or ACT required. TOEFL required of all international applicants. High school diploma is required, and GED is accepted. *Academic units required:* 4 English, 4 math, 4 science, 4 social studies.

The Inside Word

Intended field of study figures into the admissions decision at Misericordia; the school is small and only has so many spots for students in each discipline. Because the school practices rolling admissions, it makes sense to apply here as early as possible to avoid being closed out of your chosen department.

FINANCIAL AID

Students should submit: FAFSA, institution's own financial aid form. Regular filing deadline 5/1. The Princeton Review suggests that all financial aid forms be submitted as soon as possible after 1/1. *Need-based scholarships/grants offered:* Pell, SEOG, state scholarships/grants, private scholarships, the school's own gift aid, federal nursing scholarships. *Loan aid offered:* FFEL Subsidized Stafford, FFEL Unsubsidized Stafford, FFEL PLUS, Federal Perkins, Federal Nursing, state loans. Applicants will be notified of awards on a rolling basis beginning on or about 3/15. Federal Work-study Program available. Institutional employment available. Off-campus job opportunities are good.

FROM THE ADMISSIONS OFFICE

"From your first day of classes until you graduate, you'll know what College Misericordia's expects from you—nothing but the best. When you graduate, you'll be prepared to excel in your career, lead others, and serve the community both professionally and personally. Classes are small, often with as few as 10 students in advanced areas. Overall, the student-faculty ratio is 11:1, ensuring personalized attention. Students choose from 30 majors in four academic divisions. Some of the majors in high-demand careers include nursing, physical therapy, biology (pre-med and pre-vet) and speech-language pathology as well as education and sport management. CM's "Trinity of Learning" concept offers students an effective mix of quality academics, professional preparation and service leadership. The student is at the center of everything we do. At CM, you'll find a supportive environment. The National Survey of Student Engagement (NSSE), shows that our students perform better academically and are more satisfied. In fact, 96 percent of our seniors would choose us if they had to do it all over again. At College Misericordia, education also means socialization. We believe that there is life outside of the classroom, and that those experiences are an integral part of a college education. CM has two dozen clubs and social organizations. The Student Government Association sponsors a multitude of activities throughout the year, focused on student fun and involvement. As a Division III school, College Misericordia competes in the Pennsylvania Athletic Conference (PAC). We currently have 19 men's and women's varsity sports."

For even more information on this school, turn to page 475 of the "Stats" section.

COLLEGE OF MOUNT SAINT VINCENT

6301 RIVERDALE AVENUE, RIVERDALE, NY 10471 • ADMISSIONS: 718-405-3267 • FAX: 718-549-7945
E-MAIL: ADMISSNS@MOUNTSAINTVINCENT.EDU • WEBSITE: WWW.MOUNTSAINTVINCENT.EDU

Ratings
Quality of Life: 68   Academic: 68   Admissions: 77   Financial Aid: 68

Academics

Situated along the Hudson River in the Riverdale section of the Bronx, the College of Mount Saint Vincent offers a pleasant mix of cloistered academia and big-city living to its small student body. Undergrads here enjoy "a community where everyone is willing to help each other grow as a student and as a person," which stands in contrast to the sometimes impersonal city Mount Saint Vincent calls home. Here "faculty and administrators are amazing. They are my friends, mentors, and sometimes my second parents." Academics are solid too, with particular strengths in nursing and forensic science. A broad core curriculum means students receive "a mix of liberal arts and major studies to prepare you for the real world." Students describe the academic experience as "a great way to mature and transcend into the workplace. Every day is a journey, good or bad, but lessons are learned." Mount Saint Vincent has a long-standing partnership with nearby Manhattan College, which allows both schools to offer a wider range of academic options than they otherwise could.

> **SURVEY SAYS . . .**
> *Small classes*
> *Diverse student types on campus*
> *Students love Riverdale, NY*
> *Frats and sororities are unpopular or nonexistent*
> *Lots of beer drinking*
> *(Almost) everyone smokes*

Life

"Life is pretty quiet" on the Mount Saint Vincent campus, where the number of planned on-campus extracurricular activities is relatively small; "This college needs more things for the students to do," complains one student. Some say there's more here than meets the eye, but that you have to dig to find the fun. "If you do not become active in the activities going on around campus, you will be bored," advises one student. "Go to an RA-run event, go to the shows, get involved. You'll probably be pleasantly surprised." Of course, "with New York City just 10 miles away," students don't really need campus events to distract them. "The possibilities in the city are endless," undergrads correctly point out. Unfortunately, Mount Saint Vincent is beyond the reach of the subway, which means students must take bith a free shuttle bus and the subway, or Metro North—which is more expensive and runs less frequently—to reach Midtown. As a result, "a lot of people just hang around campus." Undergrads appreciate that "the school makes dorm life available to anyone who wants it," although some warn that housing space is tight; an unhappy junior in our survey was placed in a triple. Welcome to New York!

Student Body

The "hard-working" undergrads of Mount Saint Vincent include "a variety of nationalities' as well as "a diverse range of ethnicity, seriousness, academic achievement, and motivation." Like the city that it calls home, Mount Saint Vincent is a true melting pot, with substantial white, Hispanic, African American, and Asian populations. Gender diversity is a little less representative of the general population. Although the school went coed over 30 years ago, the vestiges of its days as an all-women's school remain in the three-to-one girl–guy ratio; the split is a little more even over at Mount Saint Vincent's partner school, Manhattan College. Students here also warn that "residents and commuters really do not interact. More activities should be planned to fix that." When they do interact, students find their peers "friendly and cool to hang out with."

ADMISSIONS

Very important factors considered include: Character/personal qualities, recommendations, secondary school record, standardized test scores. *Important factors considered include:* Essays, extracurricular activities, interview. *Other factors considered include:* Alumni/ae relation, class rank, volunteer work, work experience. SAT Reasoning or ACT required. TOEFL required of all international applicants. High school diploma is required, and GED is accepted. *Academic units required:* 4 English, 2 math, 2 science, 2 foreign language, 3 social studies, 3 academic electives. *Academic units recommended:* 3 math, 3 science, 3 foreign language, 4 social studies.

The Inside Word

Mount Saint Vincent does not set terribly high admissions standards, but space is limited at this small school, so candidates are well advised to apply early. Applications are processed on a rolling basis, with decisions rendered within two weeks of submission. The admissions staff at this small school is helpful and attentive.

FINANCIAL AID

Students should submit: FAFSA, state aid form. The Princeton Review suggests that all financial aid forms be submitted as soon as possible after 1/1. *Need-based scholarships/grants offered:* Pell, SEOG, state scholarships/grants, private scholarships, the school's own gift aid. *Loan aid offered:* FFEL Subsidized Stafford, FFEL Unsubsidized Stafford, FFEL PLUS, Federal Perkins, Federal Nursing. Applicants will be notified of awards on a rolling basis beginning on or about 3/1.

FROM THE ADMISSIONS OFFICE

"Overlooking the Hudson River, Mount Saint Vincent's beautiful 70-acre campus is just minutes away from all that New York City offers. With a $20 million building plan underway for the next four years, the College will experience major enhancements in its athletic, residence, and academic facilities and programs.

"The student body is rich in religious, ethnic, and cultural diversity, and a strong sense of community prevails on campus. Small classes, the personal attention the 13:1 student/faculty ratio affords, and an outstanding faculty all provide students with an exceptional learning environment. Leading-edge, quality academic programs include over 60 majors and concentrations to select from, such as business, communications, nursing, and education. Majors in accounting, graphic design, and theatre are planned additions to the curriculum.

"Students take advantage of real-world opportunities and experiences through internships with leading New York businesses like MTV, the NBA, and Merrill Lynch as well as healthcare organizations like Sloan Kettering and New York Hospital. The 32 clubs and organizations, campus radio and TV stations, and several intramural sports offer students many choices for extracurricular activities. In addition, the college has a strong NCAA Division III athletics program, with seven men's and nine women's athletic teams, including the recent additions of men's and women's lacrosse and men's baseball."

For even more information on this school, turn to page 476 of the "Stats" section.

THE COLLEGE OF NEW JERSEY

PO BOX 7718, EWING, NJ 08628-0718 • ADMISSIONS: 609-771-2131 • FAX: 609-637-5174
FINANCIAL AID: 609-771-2211 • E-MAIL: ADMISS@VM.TCNJ.EDU • WEBSITE: WWW.TCNJ.EDU

Ratings

Quality of Life: 85   **Academic:** 86   **Admissions:** 92   **Financial Aid:** 76

Academics

For "a price-is-right education with good professors, small class sizes, and extracurricular activities," many are turning to The College of New Jersey, a state liberal arts school "with a lot of potential" that "is just now really starting to expand." While still developing—one manifestation of which is the nonstop construction on campus—the school is already well on its way to "giving the typical college life that one has always dreamed about." All the key elements of a great education are here. Classes are "small enough for close attention by professors in class, large enough to constantly meet new people." The school offers "wonderful resources, if you are aware of them. For example, TCNJ has a lot of academic and job placement services that are there, just never utilized by the students." Most important, TCNJ is home to "a lot of smart students" and a faculty who, "on the whole, are available for guidance and help outside of class." Academics are demanding but satisfying here; as one student reported, "I have found that many of my classes have been a lot of work, but that I have come out of them with more knowledge than I would have expected." Students report that "the administration is surprisingly open-minded and constantly exploring new directions for the institution," but warn that day-to-day administrative tasks "often seem very unorganized. . . . You may be sent to a few different departments for the answer to one question."

> **SURVEY SAYS . . .**
> *Small classes*
> *Lab facilities are great*
> *Students are friendly*
> *Campus feels safe*
> *Students are happy*
> *Lots of beer drinking*

Life

Most at TCNJ agree that "social life is not as great as you will find in a big college town or a larger school. This is a suitcase college." While "there are parties many weekends at either a fraternity/sorority or sports team house, the scene gets pretty boring pretty quickly," according to many. The biggest party night here, surprisingly, is Tuesday, "because many people don't have any classes on Wednesday until late in the day (12:30–5:00 is reserved for club meetings, and also sometimes lecturers and things of that nature)." Weekends, in contrast, "can seem kinda desolate." Those who are satisfied with campus life are usually those deeply involved in the Greek scene and student clubs and organizations; as one such student put it, "There are so many great opportunities to take advantage of in terms of organizations and internships!" Sporting events occasionally mobilize the campus, with the annual football game against archrival Rowan the unquestioned highlight of the athletic schedule. "Tailgating for the Rowan game is a must for any fan of football or beer," reports one sports enthusiast. "I know it's not Penn State or anything like that, but it's still a great time." TCNJ's campus is "beautiful, except for the persistent construction." Hometown Ewing, on the other hand, is "lame. It requires some effort to find stuff to do off campus." One suggestion for spicing things up here: "TCNJ should also promote more interaction with other schools such as Rider, which is five miles away, yet I do not know one student from there."

Student Body

The undergrads of TCNJ are "very hardworking and dedicated to academics," but also know how to "maintain a balance between schoolwork and social life." They are an active bunch; explains one undergrad, "Most TCNJ students were involved in high school in something, often a high school sport. So, while the average TCNJ student had a good GPA and SAT score, she was also involved in extracurricular activities." Upon arriving at TCNJ, this student "becomes affiliated with some organization, whether a sorority or fraternity or a student group like government. This student likely wears Abercrombie & Fitch/American Eagle/Gap/Express clothing, [and] is Caucasian and Catholic with a middle- to upper-middle-class background and permanent residence in New Jersey." While the college is "trying to bring kids in from other states and add to the diversity," currently "diversity among the student population is not as great as I think the college would like to brag it is."

ADMISSIONS

Very important factors considered include: Character/personal qualities, class rank, secondary school record, standardized test scores, talent/ability. *Important factors considered include:* Essays, extracurricular activities, recommendations, volunteer work. *Other factors considered include:* Alumni/ae relation, geographical residence, interview, minority status, state residency, work experience. SAT Reasoning and SAT Subject Tests or ACT required. TOEFL required of all international applicants. High school diploma is required, and GED is accepted. *Academic units required:* 4 English, 2 math, 2 science (2 science lab), 2 foreign language, 2 social studies.

The Inside Word

A new name and new-found visibility have given a boost to the applicant pool at The College of New Jersey, but selectivity remains at about the level it has been for the past few years. Since the pool is somewhat better than in prior years, this still translates into a stronger entering class.

FINANCIAL AID

Students should submit: FAFSA. Regular filing deadline 10/1. The Princeton Review suggests that all financial aid forms be submitted as soon as possible after 1/1. *Need-based scholarships/grants offered:* Pell, SEOG, state scholarships/grants, private scholarships, the school's own gift aid, federal nursing scholarships. *Loan aid offered:* Direct Subsidized Stafford, Direct Unsubsidized Stafford, Direct PLUS, FFEL Subsidized Stafford, FFEL Unsubsidized Stafford, FFEL PLUS, Federal Perkins, Federal Nursing, state loans. Applicants will be notified of awards on a rolling basis beginning on or about 7/15.

FROM THE ADMISSIONS OFFICE

"Twin lakes form the border of the The College of New Jersey campus, which is set on 289 acres of wooded and landscaped grounds in suburban Ewing Township, New Jersey. TCNJ offers more than 40 baccalaureate degree programs in seven schools: art, media, and music; culture and society; business; education; engineering; nursing; and science. The campus is residential, with nearly two-thirds of the full-time students housed on campus. Classes are small and are all taught by faculty members: there are no graduate teaching assistants. The college is strongly committed to retaining and graduating the students it enrolls. This commitment is reflected in the high return rate of entering students, which has consistently been over 90 percent for the past five years."

For even more information on this school, turn to page 476 of the "Stats" section.

COLUMBIA UNIVERSITY

535 WEST 116TH STREET, NEW YORK, NY 10027 • ADMISSIONS: 212-854-2521 • FAX: 212-894-1209
FINANCIAL AID: 212-854-3711 • E-MAIL: UGRAD-ADMISS@COLUMBIA.EDU • WEBSITE: WWW.COLUMBIA.EDU

Ratings

Quality of Life: 92   **Academic:** 95   **Admissions:** 99   **Financial Aid:** 92

Academics

Columbia University's largest undergraduate school, Columbia College is an "academic powerhouse" that boasts offerings in a staggering array of disciplines, and one of the nation's few core curricula that students actually love. Even so, "how many schools can boast world-class education and location in the greatest city in the world? One: Columbia." Students here warn that "Columbia truly is hands-off. It's sink or swim, and you are the only person who can help yourself. Advising is minimal and the administration is a celebration of red tape." However, "for the independent-minded student, Columbia is the perfect environment." Central to the CU experience is the Core Curriculum, a sequence that immerses students in western philosophy, literature, and the fine arts. Many here will tell you that the Core "changed my life. It's a great feeling to read something junior year for another class and realize that I know where the ideas originated, and how they progressed." Profs here "are all extremely talented," and "accessible and knowledgeable," "but they also make sure that you understand that they are humans too, and not super people." Sums up one undergrad, "You will not have a laid-back, happy-go-lucky type of life at Columbia. Instead of spending your time on sculptured lawns with faculty mapping out the way to go, you will get on a crowded subway, push your way into. Some may think this kind of college experience is terrible. Columbia students are those who think it's the only way to go."

> **SURVEY SAYS . . .**
> Great computer facilities
> Great library
> Diverse student types on campus
> Students love New York, NY
> Great off-campus food
> Campus feels safe
> Students are happy

Life

Columbia's campus, a six-block-square urban oasis in the middle of New York's Morningside Heights neighborhood (Harlem is just to the north), includes 36 acres of open, grassy space for sunbathers and ultimate Frisbee™ fanatics. Few students linger long on campus when classes and studying are done, however; instead, they set off to explore the overstuffed metropolis that is their home. "One night on the weekends, you might go to a party with friends, a concert on campus, a Columbia-sponsored event; another night, you might go to a Broadway show, a club downtown, a Yankees game." The city provides access to "so many resources and opportunities off-campus. It's wonderful. I found a great internship this summer and since I am only a subway ride away, I can continue to work part-time during the school year." As one student put it, "In my New York City history class, we (150 students) take a bike ride through New York City, leaving campus at 11:00 p.m and returning at 7a.m. in the morning. In my art history class, we go to the Met; in my music class we go to Lincoln Center. Can you easily do this kind of thing at Yale or Harvard? No, you cannot. Yale has New Haven, Harvard has Boston, and Columbia has New York City. Make your choice."

Student Body

Columbia students are "stalwart NYC fans, and support hasn't flagged since 9/11. Students thrive on the city. They don't fear it." Some are from the Big Apple, while many others have merely adopted its mien; they are "very New York: they are not exceedingly polite, but can be; they mind their own business and don't butt into yours." These "extremely independent" students, according to one undergrad, "love being urbane, tortured intellectuals." Fortunately, "most students are like this and thus get along." Diversity is a bragging point for CU. Some here, however, caution that "in terms of a demographic breakdown, Columbia is diverse, but there is far less interaction than one might expect." Conservatives warn that CU "is downright über-liberal. 'Left-wing' is probably an understatement."

ADMISSIONS

Very important factors considered include: Character/personal qualities, class rank, essays, recommendations, secondary school record, standardized test scores. *Important factors considered include:* Extracurricular activities, talent/ability. *Other factors considered include:* Alumni/ae relation, geographical residence, interview, minority status, volunteer work. SAT Reasoning and SAT Subject Tests or ACT required. TOEFL required of all international applicants. High school diploma is required, and GED is accepted. *Academic units recommended:* 4 English, 4 math, 4 science (4 science lab), 4 foreign language, 4 history, 4 academic electives.

The Inside Word

Columbia's application increases continue to outpace the rest of the Ivy League, and as a result the university keeps moving higher up in the Ivy pecking order. Crime is down in New York City, the football team wins (while still in baby-blue uniforms, no less!), and Columbia has become even more appealing. It's less selective than the absolute cream of the Ivy crop, but offers the advantage of being a bit more open and frank in discussing the admissions process with students, parents, and counselors—refreshing amid the typical shrouds of Ivy mystique.

FINANCIAL AID

Students should submit: FAFSA, institution's own financial aid form, CSS/Financial Aid PROFILE, noncustodial (divorced/separated) parents' statement, business/farm supplement, parent and student income tax returns. Regular filing deadline 2/10. The Princeton Review suggests that all financial aid forms be submitted as soon as possible after 1/1. *Need-based scholarships/grants offered:* Pell, SEOG, state scholarships/grants, private scholarships, the school's own gift aid. *Loan aid offered:* FFEL Subsidized Stafford, FFEL Unsubsidized Stafford, FFEL PLUS, Federal Perkins, alternative loans. Applicants will be notified of awards on or about 4/1. Federal Work-study Program available. Institutional employment available. Off-campus job opportunities are good.

FROM THE ADMISSIONS OFFICE

"Columbia maintains an intimate college campus within one of the world's most vibrant cities. After a long day exploring the bustling streets of the Big Apple, the coziness of home waits within the Columbia gates. Nobel Prize-winning professors will challenge you in class discussions and sit down for a one-on-one afterward. The Core Curriculum attracts intensely free-minded students, eager to explore ideas. The discussions in the classrooms are only the beginning of your education. Like the music that wafts from our concert halls, ideas spill out from the classrooms, filling the lawns and electrifying the air. Friendships formed in the residence halls solidify during a game of Frisbee on South Lawn or over bagels on "The Steps," Columbia's urban beach. From your first day on campus, you will be part of our community."

For even more information on this school, turn to page 477 of the "Stats" section.

CONNECTICUT COLLEGE

270 MOHEGAN AVENUE, NEW LONDON, CT 06320 • ADMISSIONS: 860-439-2200 • FAX: 860-439-4301
FINANCIAL AID: 860-439-2200• E-MAIL: ADMIT@CONNCOLL.EDU • WEBSITE: WWW.CONNCOLL.EDU

Ratings
Quality of Life: 72   **Academic:** 89   **Admissions:** 94   **Financial Aid:** 95

Academics

Students at Connecticut College assert that their professors have "done cool things, and they bring those experiences to the classroom." Instructors are approachable and "truly are concerned with our education," and this dedication is complemented by the deans, "who are excellent, understanding people." The small academic setting affords undergraduates very personal attention. "In one class, the professor, one of the associate Deans of the college, scheduled a meeting with every student in our 100-plus person

SURVEY SAYS . . .
Small classes
Students are friendly
Frats and sororities are unpopular
or nonexistent
Lots of beer drinking
Hard liquor is popular

class to talk about the take home exam." Another student writes, "Some of my professors are now my personal confidants, and I can go to them for my academic or personal needs." This type of nurturing means that "even though I'm not an exceptional student, [I'm able] to do independent research during my freshman year." Top programs include dance, chemistry, biological sciences, religion, and psychology, and many students also laud the well-organized study abroad programs. The career center receives solid praise, particularly for the variety of "internships that focus on community action, international issues, and the environment."

Life

In general, students at "Conn" feel "pretty pampered" in their "playground for trust-fund babies." The weekend social scene centers largely on alcohol, and several students believe "sometimes it's hard to take part in college activities without being a part of the drinking scene." Those who do indulge "look forward to the huge campus-wide parties, like Festivus or Floralia, which are reason alone to come here—think Woodstock but less hippie." The school organizes Thursday Night Events (TNE's) that draw large numbers of freshmen and sophomores. And an organization called MOBROC (Musicians Organized for Band Rights On Campus), which sets up practice space and a performance venue for campus bands, provides another mainstay of nightlife. ("It's a big deal, but almost underground scene. No other East Coast school has an organization like it.") Alternatives to drinking include "playing out on Harkness Green," attending the "very popular a capella concerts," watching the "amazing student theater productions," "cheering for mediocre sports teams," or venturing in to New London, a town that "takes some time to learn to love."

Student Body

The stereotypical Conn student grew up "just outside Boston" (or somewhere else in New England, New Jersery, or New York) "helps to "keep J. Crew in business," "gets Tiffany's for Christmas," and "drives a Volkswagen with a ski rack on top." Even in this land of self-described WASPs, a few deviants manage to survive, including "our fair share of hippies, punks, straight edge, and D and D magic kids." Reportedly, these atypical students "flock together, just like the rest of the minorities on campus." Many students lament the lack of diversity at Conn, crying, "This is not the real world!" Surveys do point out however, that "a great deal is being done on administrative and student levels to deal with issues of diversity on campus." In the meantime, they content themselves with a "substantial international student population." Some people say the student body is "very supportive of students with differing sexual orientations," while others claim "gays and minorities are segregated." In the end, most students agree, "You basically know everyone on campus, at least by association, [which] makes for a very comfortable, caring environment."

ADMISSIONS

Very important factors considered include: Character/personal qualities, essays, extracurricular activities, minority status, recommendations, secondary school record. *Important factors considered include:* Alumni/ae relation, class rank, interview, standardized test scores, talent/ability, volunteer work, work experience. *Other factors considered include:* Geographical residence, SAT Subject Tests required. TOEFL required of all international applicants. High school diploma is required, and GED is accepted. *Academic units recommended:* 4 English, 4 math, 4 science (3 science lab), 2 foreign language, 2 social studies, 3 history, 3 academic electives.

The Inside Word

Late in 1994, Connecticut became the most recent college to drop the SAT I as a requirement for admission, citing the overemphasis that the test receives from the media and, in turn, students. The college is judicious about keeping their acceptance rate as low as possible. Candidates undergo a rigorous review of their credentials and should be strong students in order to be competitive. Still, the college's competition for students is formidable.

FINANCIAL AID

Students should submit: FAFSA, CSS/Financial Aid PROFILE, noncustodial (divorced/separated) parents' statement, business/farm supplement, federal tax returns, federal W-2 forms. Regular filing deadline 1/15. The Princeton Review suggests that all financial aid forms be submitted as soon as possible after 1/1. *Need-based scholarships/grants offered:* Pell, SEOG, state scholarships/grants, the school's own gift aid. *Loan aid offered:* FFEL Subsidized Stafford, FFEL Unsubsidized Stafford, FFEL PLUS, Federal Perkins, college/university loans from institutional funds. Applicants will be notified of awards on or about 4/1. Federal Work-study Program available. Institutional employment available. Off-campus job opportunities are good.

FROM THE ADMISSIONS OFFICE

"Distinguishing characteristics of the diverse student body at this small, highly selective college are honor and tolerance. Student leadership is pronounced in all aspects of the college's administration from exclusive jurisdiction of the honor code and dorm life to active representation on the president's academic and administrative cabinets. Differences of opinion are respected and celebrated as legitimate avenues to new understanding. Students come to Connecticut College seeking opportunities for independence and initiative and find them in abundance."

For even more information on this school, turn to page 477 of the "Stats" section.

COOPER UNION

30 COOPER SQUARE, NEW YORK, NY 10003 • ADMISSIONS: 212-353-4120 • FAX: 212-353-4342
FINANCIAL AID: 212-353-4130 • E-MAIL: ADMISSIONS@COOPER.EDU • WEBSITE: WWW.COOPER.EDU

Ratings
Quality of Life: 73   **Academic:** 87   **Admissions:** 98   **Financial Aid:** 93

Academics

You'll get a "free education" at Cooper Union—everyone receives a full-tuition scholarship for all four years—"but you have to pay it off with hard labor in the classroom." Cooper's "intense, engaging programs in engineering, art, and architecture" are the only options on the menu here; "while this seems narrow," explains one freshman, it "allows for more focus on those fields. As long as you're interested in one of the majors…you will receive one of the best educations in the country." The professors overall earn

> **SURVEY SAYS . . .**
> *Small classes*
> *Athletic facilities need improving*
> *Students are friendly*
> *Diverse student types on campus*
> *Students love New York, NY*
> *Great off-campus food*

kudos for being "intelligent, accessible, [and] excellent," but a number of students complain that there are "too many adjunct professors," who are "underpaid" and teach "straight from the textbook." All professors expect a lot from students—"they can be quite sadistic toward the end of the semester, heaping more work on you than you could possibly handle," warns one electrical engineer—but "you never feel as if any of your effort is in vain." A number of students gripe about getting "mediocre grades" in exchange for "sweat" and "your immortal soul"—but just as many also point out that "you will leave knowing everything in your field about as well as it is possible to know it" and boast that Cooper students benefit from virtually "guaranteed job placement" after graduation. With "lots of work and little time," students learn to share the load: "We all work together to get projects done and to study for exams," explains one student. "I have spent the night before most of my major upper-level exams studying with about half, or more, of my classmates." That team spirit dissipates, though, come registration time, which "involves waiting on line on a cold New York City sidewalk from 2 a.m. to 9 a.m. just to get required classes, let alone electives." Some say that this "physical registration" is a consequence of Cooper's "free tuition," and gripe that "there's no money left" for such conveniences as mailing "bills or grades." That said, time after time we read that Cooper's greatest incentive "is that it's free." In that regard, "Cooper's strength is also its drawback."

Life

"The overall school experience is pretty much academic" at Cooper Union, as "there is not much time to have any fun." That said, "the experience is about who surrounds you in your classes," notes a senior. When students can make free time, they usually like to get away from Cooper. As one puts it, "I associate school with hard work." "The school consists of five buildings in the middle of the East Village," and the surrounding neighborhood is famous for its funky shops, cheap eateries, theaters, bars, and live music venues; conveniently located subways can whisk students just about anywhere in the five boroughs at any time of day. On campus, "The school organizes several events that may seem kind of ridiculous but often prove to be lots of fun, such as ice cream and karaoke night, study break (a lunch party during finals), and Peter Cooper's birthday celebration." Whether on or off campus, "there is always something happening at school where people can eat and interact."

Student Body

"Everyone at Cooper fits into one of three distinct groups: engineers, artists, or architects," undergrads here tell us. "We are very divided by major. For the most part, no one is left out of their respective group, but the groups don't mix well." Observes one student, "The engineering students tend to be the most strange and have all done very well in their high school careers and have very noticeable and unique talents. Art students tend to follow unique trends and are more creative and reclusive. Architecture students can be considered the link between engineering and art students." The average Cooper student is "a tad quirky with a nerdy sense of humor." "You'll find no cheerleader, jock, or regular, whimsical university students. Cooper students tend to all be extremely intelligent, ambitious, and studious individuals"—with an emphasis on individual.

ADMISSIONS

Very important factors considered include: Secondary school record, standardized test scores, talent/ability. *Important factors considered include:* Essays. *Other factors considered include:* Character/personal qualities, extracurricular activities, recommendations, volunteer work, work experience. SAT Reasoning or ACT required. TOEFL required of all international applicants. High school diploma is required, and GED is accepted. *Academic units required:* 4 English, 1 math, 1 science, 1 social studies, 1 history, 8 academic electives. *Academic units recommended:* 4 English, 4 math, 4 science, 2 foreign language, 4 social studies.

The Inside Word

It is ultra-tough to gain admission to Cooper Union, and will only get tougher. Loads of people apply here, and national publicity and the addition of dorms have brought even more candidates to the pool. Not only do students need to have top academic accomplishments but also they need to be a good fit for Cooper's offbeat milieu.

FINANCIAL AID

Students should submit: FAFSA, CSS/Financial Aid PROFILE, state aid form. Regular filing deadline 4/15. The Princeton Review suggests that all financial aid forms be submitted as soon as possible after 1/1. *Need-based scholarships/grants offered:* Pell, SEOG, state scholarships/grants, private scholarships, the school's own gift aid. *Loan aid offered:* FFEL Subsidized Stafford, FFEL Unsubsidized Stafford, FFEL PLUS, Federal Perkins, college/university loans from institutional funds. Applicants will be notified of awards on or about 6/1. Federal Work-study Program available. Institutional employment available. Off-campus job opportunities are excellent.

FROM THE ADMISSIONS OFFICE

"Each of the three schools, architecture, art, and engineering, adheres strongly to preparation for its profession and is committed to a problem-solving philosophy of education in a unique, scholarship environment. A rigorous curriculum and group projects reinforce this unique atmosphere in higher education and contribute to a strong sense of community and identity in each school. With McSorley's Ale House and the Joseph Papp Public Theater nearby, Cooper Union remains at the heart of the city's tradition of free speech, enlightenment, and entertainment. Cooper's Great Hall has hosted national leaders, from Abraham Lincoln to Booker T. Washington, from Mark Twain to Samuel Gompers, from Susan B. Anthony to Betty Friedan, and more recently, President Bill Clinton."

For even more information on this school, turn to page 478 of the "Stats" section.

CORNELL UNIVERSITY

410 THURSTON AVENUE, ITHACA, NY 14850 • ADMISSIONS: 607-255-5241 • FAX: 607-255-0659
FINANCIAL AID: 607-255-5145 • E-MAIL: ADMISSIONS@CORNELL.EDU • WEBSITE: WWW.CORNELL.EDU

Ratings
Quality of Life: 83   **Academic:** 89   **Admissions:** 97   **Financial Aid:** 94

Academics

With seven colleges and "a course catalog that is upwards of 680 pages long," Cornell University offers "unlimited resources and opportunities for undergraduates." Students say that "if you want to study it, you almost certainly can" at Cornell. Options include not only the expected arts, sciences, and engineering programs, but also standout offerings in hospitality administration, human ecology, industrial and labor relations, and agricultural science. All the

> **SURVEY SAYS . . .**
> *Great computer facilities*
> *Great library*
> *Great food on campus*
> *Great off-campus food*
> *Lots of beer drinking*

choices create numerous opportunities for undergraduates; explains one student, "Cornell has so many academic facilities that it is very easy to get involved with research opportunities even as an undergraduate. I have been doing research in my major since the beginning of my sophomore year." (Research at Cornell, by the way, is abetted by "one of the [largest] most unified libraries in the world, with tons of workspace and tons of research materials.") Professors are very accommodating to undergraduates; explains one student, "I expected to find professors who were only concerned with their lab work and cared nothing about the students. And I am not going to lie: A few of the professors are like that. But the great majority [of them] really care about their students, offering help to whoever needs it and being generally concerned about their well-being." Although "the workload is very heavy, there is an unlimited amount of resources to help—profs, TAs, help centers, tutors, and fellow students." Undergraduates speak highly about their classmates, telling us that they "are pretty passionate about what they do, and there isn't a lack of intellectual or stimulating conversation. People aren't afraid to be smart here."

Life

Most Cornell students report a heavy workload that seriously eats into free time. Engineers report, "You go through the day expecting to spend some of the time in class (assuming you wake up in time and spend the thirty minutes walking to class in two feet of snow) and the rest in the library. When it's 2:00 a.m., then it's about time to go home, knowing you are one day closer to the weekend." Some students say, "The tough workweeks make Cornell a good party school on the weekends. Our weekends are short—just Friday and Saturday nights for the most part, unlike the Wednesday through Saturday weekends of some schools." The campus hosts numerous social sub-scenes, including a large Greek system (especially popular with underclassmen), a restaurant and bar scene (for upperclassmen), "the athletic crowd, [and] the theater crowd; there're about a million crowds, actually, each reflecting a million different interests." Being that Cornell is a large school, "there's really a lot to do on campus: There's a movie theater and a bowling alley on campus, and it seems like every weekend there [is an] a cappella concert or dance show going on." Students have mixed feelings about Ithaca but are unanimous in their praise of the campus, which they say "provides a glorious atmosphere."

Student Body

The allure of the Ivy League, the presence of lower-cost state-funded divisions, and generous financial aid packages contribute to a population that is "diverse beyond belief." One undergraduate adds, "I live on campus and have become friends with two students from Lebanon, one from Mexico City, and one from Jordan just in this last semester. There is a great variety of beliefs, political and otherwise, a great amount of tolerance and through that a great opportunity to learn about alternative cultures, beliefs, and ideas." While many students come from within New York State, "that doesn't lend itself to there being a 'typical' student because New York varies so greatly from one area to the next." Academically, "there are basically two types of students at Cornell: the social type and the studious type. The social type hits up the frat parties and typically joins a house as a freshman, then moves on to apartment parties and bars as they grow older. The studious type is only seen in class or the library. There isn't much in-between."

ADMISSIONS

Very important factors considered include: Essays, extracurricular activities, recommendations, secondary school record, standardized test scores, talent/ability. *Important factors considered include:* Class rank. *Other factors considered include:* Alumni/ae relation, character/personal qualities, geographical residence, interview, minority status, state residency, volunteer work, work experience. SAT Reasoning and SAT Subject Tests or ACT required. TOEFL required of all international applicants. High school diploma or equivalent is not required. *Academic units required:* 4 English, 3 math. *Academic units recommended:* 3 science (3 science lab), 3 foreign language, 3 social studies, 3 history.

The Inside Word

Cornell is the largest of the Ivies, and its admissions operation is a reflection of the fairly grand scale of the institution: complex and somewhat intimidating. Candidates should not expect contact with admissions to reveal much in the way of helpful insights on the admissions process, as the university seems to prefer to keep things close to the vest. Only applicants with top accomplishments, academic or otherwise, will be viable candidates. The university is a very positive place for minorities, and the public status presents a value that's hard to beat.

FINANCIAL AID

Students should submit: FAFSA, institution's own financial aid form, CSS/Financial Aid PROFILE, noncustodial (divorced/separated) parents' statement, business/farm supplement, prior year tax forms. Regular filing deadline 2/11. The Princeton Review suggests that all financial aid forms be submitted as soon as possible after 1/1. *Need-based scholarships/grants offered:* Pell, SEOG, state scholarships/grants, private scholarships, the school's own gift aid. *Loan aid offered:* Direct Subsidized Stafford, Direct Unsubsidized Stafford, Direct PLUS, FFEL Subsidized Stafford, FFEL Unsubsidized Stafford, FFEL PLUS, Federal Perkins, college/university loans from institutional funds, Key Bank alternative loan. Applicants will be notified of awards on or about 4/1. Federal Work-study Program available. Institutional employment available. Off-campus job opportunities are good.

FROM THE ADMISSIONS OFFICE

"Cornell University, an Ivy League school and land-grant college located in the scenic Finger Lakes region of central New York, provides an outstanding education to students in seven small to midsize undergraduate colleges: Agriculture & Life Sciences; Architecture, Art, & Planning; Arts & Sciences; Engineering; Hotel Administration; Human Ecology; and Industrial & Labor Relations. Cornellians come from all 50 states and more than 100 countries, and they pursue their academic goals in more than 100 departments. The College of Arts and Sciences, one of the smallest liberal arts schools in the Ivy League, offers more than forty majors, most of which rank near the top nationwide. Applied programs in the other six colleges also rank among the best in the world.

"Other special features of the university include a world-renowned faculty; 4,000 courses available to all students; an extensive undergraduate research program; superb research, teaching, and library facilities; a large, diverse study abroad program; and more than 600 student organizations and 36 varsity sports. Cornell's campus is one of the most beautiful in the country; students pass streams, rocky gorges, and waterfalls on their way to class. First-year students make their home on North Campus, a living-learning community that features a special advising center, faculty-in-residence, a fitness center, and traditional residence halls as well as theme-centered buildings such as Ecology House. Cornell University invites applications from all interested students and uses the Common Application exclusively with a short required Cornell Supplement."

For even more information on this school, turn to page 478 of the "Stats" section.

DARTMOUTH COLLEGE

6016 McNUTT HALL, HANOVER, NH 03755 • ADMISSIONS: 603-646-2875 • FAX: 603-646-1216
FINANCIAL AID: 603-646-2451 • E-MAIL: ADMISSIONS.OFFICE@DARTMOUTH.EDU • WEBSITE: WWW.DARTMOUTH.EDU

Ratings
Quality of Life: 97   Academic: 96   Admissions: 98   Financial Aid: 97

Academics

Regarded as "the undergraduate school of the Ivies" because of the minimal and unobtrusive presence of graduate students, Dartmouth College seems to offer it all: "a beautiful campus, nurturing professors, a great library, world-class cultural performances and lectures, comfortable dorms, tasty food, and most importantly, bright, enthusiastic, and spirited peers with whom to share it all." Students praise the school's focus on undergraduates; one student says, "You get a lot of attention from professors, but still have the benefits of having graduate students around for class help sessions and as general resources." Professors at Dartmouth "are great scholars in their field. [And they] can actually teach instead of just being smart." If they couldn't teach, undergraduates assure us "they wouldn't be at Dartmouth." The school also offers "great opportunities to do research and internships, awesome lab facilities, [and] tremendously strong academics." And that's not all. "The factor most people tend to overlook is the strong alumni base. It's so easy to get internships while you're there, and after school the connections you make are invaluable."

> **SURVEY SAYS . . .**
> Great computer facilities
> Great library
> Campus feels safe
> Frats and sororities dominate social scene
> Lots of beer drinking

Life

Undergraduates agree that "life is like summer camp" at Dartmouth. Students explain that "you're in a beautiful place, living with your best friends and having as much fun as you can. The only difference is going to class and studying, both things Dartmouth students take very seriously." Students are understandably happy to be at Dartmouth, and that helps generate "an incredible sense of community. As soon as you get here, you immediately feel like you're part of a group." Greek life adds to the community spirit. Students regard it as "an amazing compliment to the sometimes arduous demands of academia" and praise the Greek houses' "welcoming atmosphere and the 'come one, come all' attitude at their parties." That's good news for Independents, since "the Greek scene is pervasive and positive." Students note that "there's never any pressure to drink" and that there are a lot of things to do on campus. The Hop has shows and movies every night, the skating rink has open skate all winter long, and there are all kinds of lectures and discussions put on by the college and by groups on campus. Everyone goes to home games, especially hockey; intramural sports are big; there are several newspapers and literary publications; there are dance and a cappella groups, [and] the list goes on." Campus grounds include a golf course and ski way and excellent rock-climbing areas and hiking trails. In short, the school's outdoorsy reputation is well deserved.

Student Body

Dartmouth students look alike, for reasons that have nothing to do with their backgrounds. "The average Dartmouth student is usually too bundled up in warm clothes to distinguish them from everyone else," undergraduates clarify. However, "once you get past the ten layers of clothing that everyone wears, Dartmouth students are a bunch of extraordinarily bright, sexually charged, procrastinating, sensitive comedians who go out of their way to make you feel like the most important person in the world." They tend to be "outdoorsy people, but there are also those who aren't athletic at all, and everyone fits in fine." Dartmouth students "are either very liberal or very conservative." One student adds, "The campus is politically active. When talking to my friends at other schools, they are always amazed to hear how many people at Dartmouth are involved and aware of politics, both national and global." However, they never let political differences spoil the genial atmosphere. Students are "friendly, eloquent, and generally very happy."

ADMISSIONS

Very important factors considered include: Character/personal qualities, class rank, essays, extracurricular activities, recommendations, secondary school record, standardized test scores. *Important factors considered include:* Talent/ability, volunteer work. *Other factors considered include:* Alumni/ae relation, geographical residence, interview, minority status, work experience. SAT Reasoning and SAT Subject Tests or ACT required. TOEFL required of all international applicants. High school diploma or equivalent is not required. *Academic units recommended:* 4 English, 4 math, 4 science, 3 foreign language, 3 social studies.

The Inside Word

Applications for the class of 2007 were up 15 percent from the previous year's totals, making this small-town Ivy more selective in choosing who gets offered a coveted spot in the class. As is the case with those who apply to any of the Ivies or other highly selective colleges, candidates are up against (or benefit from) many institutional interests that go unmentioned in discussions of appropriate qualifications for admission. This makes an already stressful process even more so for most candidates.

FINANCIAL AID

Students should submit: FAFSA, CSS/Financial Aid PROFILE, noncustodial (divorced/separated) parents' statement, business/farm supplement, current W-2 forms or federal tax returns. Regular filing deadline 2/1. The Princeton Review suggests that all financial aid forms be submitted as soon as possible after 1/1. *Need-based scholarships/grants offered:* Pell, SEOG, state scholarships/grants, the school's own gift aid. *Loan aid offered:* FFEL Subsidized Stafford, FFEL Unsubsidized Stafford, FFEL PLUS, Federal Perkins, college/university loans from institutional funds. Applicants will be notified of awards on or about 4/15. Federal Work-study Program available. Institutional employment available.

FROM THE ADMISSIONS OFFICE

"Dartmouth's mission is to endow students with the knowledge and wisdom needed to make creative and positive contributions to society. The college brings together a breadth of cultures, traditions, and ideas to create a campus that is alive with ongoing debate and exploration. The educational value of such discourse cannot be underestimated. From student-initiated round table discussions that attempt to make sense of world events to the late-night philosophizing in a dormitory lounge, Dartmouth students take advantage of their opportunities to learn from each other. The unique benefits of sharing in this interchange are accompanied by a great sense of responsibility. Each individual's commitment to the principles of community ensures the vitality of this learning environment."

For even more information on this school, turn to page 480 of the "Stats" section.

DELAWARE VALLEY COLLEGE

700 EAST BUTLER AVENUE, DOYLESTOWN, PA 18901-2697 • ADMISSIONS: 215-489-2211
FAX: 215-230-2968 • E-MAIL: ADMITME@DEVALCOL.EDU • WEBSITE: WWW.DEVALCOL.EDU

Ratings
Quality of Life: 61   **Academic:** 66   **Admissions:** 74   **Financial Aid:** 77

Academics

Delaware Valley College, students agree, "is a great agricultural school" as well as "a good school for people who want to get involved with animals or education." Writes one animal science major, "I have thoroughly enjoyed the majority of academic courses that I have enrolled in while at Del Val; they have provided me with excellent hands-on experience with both large and small animals that I would not have attained at a larger university." Students here appreciate the fact that "the classes are small enough that you get a lot of one-on-one attention if you need it" and that "the majority of the professors here are so open-minded and willing to discuss things that the students want to talk about as well as general lecture topics." Students praise professors for "knowing what they are talking about and not being too caught-up in their degree. They are down to earth and treat you like a friend." Writes one undergrad, "Professors are frequently available to the students outside of the classroom setting for help with class work, exam reviews, job searches, or personal matters." Some students feel that "less popular majors (e.g., criminal justice) do not get any support from the school, while there is loads of funding and support for the agricultural-based majors."

> **SURVEY SAYS . . .**
> *Class discussions are rare*
> *Small classes*
> *Lots of beer drinking*
> *Hard liquor is popular*
> *(Almost) everyone smokes*

Life

Students on the "beautiful campus" of Delaware Valley College tell us that life at their school is "all about friends—hanging out, going out, even studying in groups makes everything better. If you're not out with someone or doing something, there's not much else to be doing!" Commenting both on campus life and the surrounding town of Doylestown, a typical student told us that "it is pretty boring because there really isn't much to do [other than] taking a 45-minute drive to Philadelphia." As a result, students say, "Parties are the nightly thing, especially if you're in a frat/sorority. Drugs are very popular, and security really doesn't care to deal with them." Writes one student, "I think the student population as a whole is a normal college-age group who are experiencing freedom for the first time. The school does not stress responsibility for actions, and I do not feel they assist with the maturity of the students. Del Val is quite a party school, and [the administration] lets a lot of mischief go on." Undergrads also note that "Del Val is basically a suitcase college. The weekends are generally small groups of friends hanging out. The big night on campus is Thursdays."

Student Body

Undergrads report that "most people at Del Val are very 'upper class' or 'farmers.' These two groups clash slightly, but most often they get along." There are points of tension: writes one 'upper class' student, "I was extremely offended at the fact that many students wave their Confederate flags with pride, not taking into consideration that it may be offensive to other students. On the other hand, if I waved a flag that said 'All Ag students are hicks,' I would get into an unbelievable amount of trouble." Others tell us that "the worst things here are the cliques. We have the sorority sisters, the agricultural science people, the equine science girls, the frat brothers, and then everybody else. For the most part we all get along, but I wish there was more 'crossing over the lines' between groups."

ADMISSIONS

Very important factors considered include: Class rank, secondary school record, standardized test scores. *Important factors considered include:* Recommendations. *Other factors considered include:* Alumni/ae relation, essays, extracurricular activities, interview, talent/ability, volunteer work, work experience. SAT Reasoning or ACT required. TOEFL required of all international applicants. High school diploma is required, and GED is accepted. *Academic units required:* 3 English, 2 math, 2 science (1 science lab), 2 social studies, 6 academic electives.

The Inside Word

Delaware Valley admits students on a rolling basis. Apply early for the popular agricultural programs, as they can fill quickly. Candidates with weak academic records may be admitted through the CHOICES program; this program accepts freshman conditionally, pending completion of a required introductory curriculum.

FINANCIAL AID

Students should submit: FAFSA. The Princeton Review suggests that all financial aid forms be submitted as soon as possible after 1/1. *Need-based scholarships/grants offered:* Pell, SEOG, state scholarships/grants, private scholarships, the school's own gift aid. *Loan aid offered:* FFEL Subsidized Stafford, FFEL Unsubsidized Stafford, FFEL PLUS, Federal Perkins, alternative loans. Applicants will be notified of awards on a rolling basis beginning on or about 1/15.

For even more information on this school, turn to page 481 of the "Stats" section.

DICKINSON COLLEGE

PO Box 1773, CARLISLE, PA 17013-2896 • ADMISSIONS: 717-245-1231 • FAX: 717-245-1442
FINANCIAL AID: 717-245-1308 • E-MAIL: ADMIT@DICKINSON.EDU • WEBSITE: WWW.DICKINSON.EDU

Ratings
Quality of Life: 79   **Academic:** 89   **Admissions:** 92   **Financial Aid:** 91

Academics

Offering "an intense and global curriculum" driven by a study abroad program "unsurpassed by most institutions," Dickinson College pursues a mission of "preparing future leaders to become important movers and shapers in America and abroad." A focus on matters international is just one way in which Dickinson is "constantly defining itself as a revolutionary institution." The school also has "a strong tradition of encouraging students to go beyond the things that are familiar and comfortable, and to engage the world around them" through field work and participation in faculty research. The workload here can be tough; warns one undergraduate, "Academically, Dickinson can be a bit overwhelming, as much is demanded from each student; however, all the work will be worth it in the long run." Help is always available: "The classes tend to be pretty small, which creates a good learning environment. The professors are great [and] would love nothing more than to meet with every student in every one of their classes." Reviews of administrators are mixed, but most appreciate the personal touches, like the fact that "the president of the college has open hours at a café where students can just come in and talk to him." Despite a few complaints about the brass being "much more concerned with image than with students, something is working [since] we've jumped a lot in the rankings" in recent years. Add up all the plusses here and you'll understand why "Dickinson is getting harder and harder to get into. Suddenly, when I go home people recognize where I go to school."

> **SURVEY SAYS . . .**
> *Small classes*
> *Great computer facilities*
> *Great library*
> *Lots of beer drinking*

Life

How you react to life at Dickinson depends largely on how you react to Carlisle, Dickinson's hometown. There are those who "love small towns like this one, which has tons of good restaurants. The biggest thing in the town is the 24-hour Super Wal-Mart, which sits atop a hill on the edge of town. For fun, there are a few things to do in the town, including dining, movies, and a bowling alley." Undergrads "who are 21 go out to the couple of bars and mix it up with the townies." Then there are those who insist adamantly that Carlisle "is not a college town" and "of campus there is virtually nothing to do." Most students fill their time by "getting involved in lots of different organizations, volunteer networks, and special housing activities," immersing themselves in Greek life, and hitting the party scene. Many students warn, however, that "the Dickinson Department of Public Safety is constantly on the prowl for underage drinking," and getting busted almost invariably results in a citation. But "if students don't like to be around [partying], there are always numerous things happening on campus that do not involve alcohol on the weekends and weeknights. There are always two or three evening lectures per week, as well as midnight movies, dry-dance parties, comedians, concerts—you name it, it has probably been done at Dickinson."

Student Body

Most students agree that at first glance, "Dickenson looks very preppy—the Louis Vuitton bags, popped collars, guys in pastels—but there is more to it than that. It took a bit of searching, but there are plenty of people here who run against the grain—and they all fit in fine. There may not be a ton of interaction between the sorority girls and the hippie kids, but there isn't any animosity." Since the late 1990's, Dickinson has aggressively recruited beyond its traditional core constituencies and has even established safe havens for targeted demographics: Arts Haüs, a residential community for "alternative punk kids," and Tree House, for environmentally conscious (i.e., hippie) students. Undergrads detect "a more politically active, alternative sub-culture 'within the limestone walls' that is rapidly emerging." The school is also home to "a large homosexual population, which is accepted by all students [and] many international students coming from numerous foreign countries." Sums up one junior, "The school is doing a great deal to make the campus more diverse. In my three years, I would say they have been successful in recruiting a more diverse student body, economically and ethnically."

ADMISSIONS

Very important factors considered include: Extracurricular activities, minority status, secondary school record, talent/ability, volunteer work. *Important factors considered include:* Alumni/ae relation, class rank, recommendations, standardized test scores, work experience. *Other factors considered include:* Character/personal qualities, essays, geographical residence, interview, state residency. SAT Reasoning or ACT recommended. TOEFL required of all international applicants. High school diploma is required, and GED is accepted. *Academic units required:* 4 English, 3 math, 3 science (2 science lab), 2 foreign language, 2 social studies, 2 academic electives. *Academic units recommended:* 3 foreign language.

The Inside Word

Dickinson's admissions process is typical of most small liberal arts colleges. The best candidates for such a place are those with solid grades and broad extracurricular involvement—the stereotypical "well-rounded student." Admissions selectivity is kept in check by a strong group of competitor colleges that fight tooth and nail for their cross-applicants.

FINANCIAL AID

Students should submit: FAFSA, CSS/Financial Aid PROFILE, state aid form, noncustodial (divorced/separated) parents' statement, business/farm supplement. Regular filing deadline 2/1. The Princeton Review suggests that all financial aid forms be submitted as soon as possible after 1/1. *Need-based scholarships/grants offered:* Pell, SEOG, state scholarships/grants, private scholarships, the school's own gift aid. *Loan aid offered:* FFEL Subsidized Stafford, FFEL Unsubsidized Stafford, FFEL PLUS, Federal Perkins, college/university loans from institutional funds. Applicants will be notified of awards on or about 3/20. Federal Work-study Program available. Institutional employment available. Off-campus job opportunities are good.

FROM THE ADMISSIONS OFFICE

"College is more than a collection of courses. It is about crossing traditional boundaries, about seeing the inter-relationships among different subjects, about learning a paradigm for solving problems, about developing critical thinking and communication skills, and about speaking out on issues that matter. Dickinson was founded to be different from the 15 colleges that existed in our nation before it: to provide a "useful" education, where students would learn by doing, through hands-on experiences and engagement with the community the region, the nation and the world. And this is truer today than ever, with workshop science courses replacing traditional lectures, fieldwork experiences in community studies where students take oral histories, and 12 study centers abroad in nontourist cities where students, under the guidance of a Dickinson faculty director, experience a true international culture. Almost 80 percent of the student body studies abroad, preparing them to compete and succeed in a complex global world."

For even more information on this school, turn to page 481 of the "Stats" section.

DREW UNIVERSITY

36 MADISON AVENUE, MADISON, NJ 07940-1493 • ADMISSIONS: 973-408-3739 • FAX: 973-408-3068
FINANCIAL AID: 973-408-3112 • E-MAIL: CADM@DREW.EDU • WEBSITE: WWW.DREW.EDU

Ratings
Quality of Life: 81   Academic: 85   Admissions: 85   Financial Aid: 79

Academics

Both as a small school with university resources and as a suburban school with easy access to big cities, Drew University successfully straddles divergent universes to fashion a unique undergraduate experience. With fewer than 2,000 undergrads, Drew can offer "perfect class sizes" that "really allow professors to teach their material well and students to get immediate feedback on questions they have." Explains one student, "Because of Drew's small size, professors and administrators are highly accessible. They go out of their way to make sure that you understand what you're being taught, that you feel like you're going in the right direction. They even e-mail you with clarifications at midnight about that day's lecture because they couldn't sleep, worried you might be confused." Despite the small-school vibe, Drew offers some big-school amenities, including "wonderful opportunities to study abroad, breadth requirements that cause students to take classes they might not think about taking, which can often open up doors for them, [and] strong job placement and internship programs." Some students warn, "Because Drew is so small, some upper-level classes are only offered every other year, which can make planning a major difficult. This is only true in the smaller departments, however, such as math and physics."

> **SURVEY SAYS . . .**
> *Small classes*
> *Frats and sororities are unpopular
> or nonexistent*
> *Theater is popular*
> *Student publications are popular*

Life

"Drew has an extremely good balance between socializing and studying," students agree, pointing out that "we work hard during the week, but on any Thursday, Friday, or Saturday night, it is easy to find a party and drink, if that's what you want to do. It's just as easy, however, to stay in with friends and watch a movie or just hang out. The chill factor here is pretty high." Because "the alcohol policy is very lenient (it's basically 'If we don't see it, it's not happening'), alcohol is a popular pastime." Parties often occur in "The Suites," a residence for upperclassmen and are frequently hosted by male athletic teams. Some undergrads warn that these parties "are not always open to everyone," and "if you want to party and get drunk, it helps to be an athlete or friends with a large group of them." There is a lot more to life at Drew than drinking and working, though. The school boasts a very active theater department: "Theater is a very big part of Drew life. Students are more supportive of theatrical events than of most sporting events." Hometown Madison is "an art-oriented town, so there is a lot of opportunity for cultural activities," although be forewarned that "the town goes to sleep at 6:00 P.M." Fortunately, "New York City is close by, although it's harder to get there than the school would have you believe. Still, it's nice to be isolated in a safe suburb where you can be in NYC in an hour."

Student Body

"There are two main groups within the Drew student population," according to students: "the athletes and their friends" and the "artsy" crowd. The former congregate in such popular social science departments as political science, economics, and psychology; the latter dominate the theater department. Most students are active within the campus community, as "Drew is a predominantly student-run school. Students decide the activities, help work on policies, and generally run campus life. Drew is a campus of leaders, which is what makes it so exciting." Students are also active politically, with the balance tipped to the left; observes one student, "Drew can best be understood by viewing the movie *P.C.U.*—minus the Republicans." Drew's relatively high price tag, coupled with its proximity to northeastern wealth centers, means that "many students are loaded—sons and daughters of governors and ambassadors whose families have at least two houses somewhere around the world." The school "has a large gay population, and they tend to stick together but have no problems getting along with other students."

ADMISSIONS

Very important factors considered include: Secondary school record. *Important factors considered include:* Class rank, standardized test scores. *Other factors considered include:* Alumni/ae relation, character/personal qualities, essays, extracurricular activities, interview, minority status, recommendations, talent/ability, volunteer work, work experience. SAT Reasoning or ACT required. TOEFL required of all international applicants. High school diploma or equivalent is not required. *Academic units recommended:* 4 English, 3 math, 2 science, 2 foreign language, 2 social studies, 2 history, 3 academic electives.

The Inside Word

Drew suffers greatly from the annual mass exodus of New Jersey's college-age residents and a lack of recognition by others. Application totals have significantly increased in recent years, but the university must begin to enroll more of its admitted students before any significant change in selectivity will occur. This makes Drew a great choice for solid students, and easier to get into than it should be given its quality.

FINANCIAL AID

Students should submit: FAFSA, CSS/Financial Aid PROFILE. Regular filing deadline 2/15. The Princeton Review suggests that all financial aid forms be submitted as soon as possible after 1/1. *Need-based scholarships/grants offered:* Pell, SEOG, state scholarships/grants, private scholarships, the school's own gift aid. Non-need-based (college administered): State, academic, creative arts/performance. *Loan aid offered:* FFEL Subsidized Stafford, FFEL Unsubsidized Stafford, FFEL PLUS, Federal Perkins, state loans. Applicants will be notified of awards on or about 3/31. Federal Work-study Program available. Institutional employment available. Off-campus job opportunities are excellent.

FROM THE ADMISSIONS OFFICE

"At Drew, great teachers are transforming the undergraduate learning experience. With a commitment to teaching, Drew professors have made educating undergraduates their top priority. With a spirit of innovation, they have brought the most advanced technology and distinctive modes of experiential learning into the Drew classroom. The result is a stimulating and challenging education that connects the traditional liberal arts and sciences to the workplace and to the world."

For even more information on this school, turn to page 482 of the "Stats" section.

DREXEL UNIVERSITY

3141 CHESTNUT STREET, PHILADELPHIA, PA 19104 • ADMISSIONS: 215-895-2400 • FAX: 215-895-5939
FINANCIAL AID: 215-895-2535 • E-MAIL: ENROLL@DREXEL.EDU • WEBSITE: WWW.DREXEL.EDU

Ratings
Quality of Life: 63   Academic: 73   Admissions: 87   Financial Aid: 63

Academics

"Learning in both the classroom and the workplace" is the focus of Drexel's co-op experience. Students alternate between academic quarters on campus and full-time jobs with university-approved employers. Co-op, which commences upon the completion of freshman year (exactly when it begins varies by program), is required of all majors in computer science, design arts, engineering, and information science and technology, as well as undergraduates selecting the co-op option in the Colleges of Arts and Sciences and Business. Students report, "The co-op program gives you a taste of what life will be like working at a full-time job, which can help you in deciding what you want to do when you graduate." They also appreciate "the money you make through co-op, since it helps with the cost of going to school." Drexel's strongest areas are in engineering, technology, and business disciplines. "This is definitely not a liberal arts school," students warn. According to undergraduates, Drexel professors are a mixed bag. The school "offers some of the greatest professors in the country. However, these professors are contrasted by some of the worst in the country." Many "are working professionals in their field, so they know exactly what they're talking about," but they are not always accessible and aren't all adept instructors. Students report, "Overall, the academic experience teaches you to deal with work on your own and not be 'hand-fed.' You can do well or terribly, depending on how you, the student, wish to do." Students are unanimous regarding their distaste for the administration, purveyors of the famous (or infamous) "Drexel shaft." Writes one student, "The offices and administrators: Who? What? They are entirely inaccessible."

> **SURVEY SAYS . . .**
> *Great computer facilities*
> *Diverse student types on campus*
> *Great off-campus food*
> *Student publications are popular*
> *Lots of beer drinking*
> *Hard liquor is popular*
> *(Almost) everyone smokes*

Life

"Life at Drexel is different than at most schools due to co-op," which leaves "only half the student body on campus at any given time." With students coming and going from campus with such frequency, "there is little to no interest in student organizations;" "intramurals must fight the scheduling problems of a quarter system and students on co-op." The Greeks are stymied by a restrictive administration ("[the administration] does not allow fraternities to hold many functions"). Students would probably make a greater effort to drum up a campus life if Philadelphia and several other more active college campuses weren't so close to Drexel. Students tell us that "living in the city is great. If you get bored, you and your friends can just go wander around the city. You can go to the zoo, comedy clubs, art galleries, and museums." Philadelphia also has "four major sports teams that are great to watch" and "plenty of great bars." In addition, Drexel "is literally right next to University of Pennsylvania and the University of the Sciences in Philadelphia and about ten minutes from Temple, so there is always something to do with college-aged people." Aesthetes should be forewarned that Drexel's campus is made entirely of concrete. Students add, "The last nice piece of grass between buildings recently became a building."

Student Body

Although Drexel "isn't as diverse as some other schools, there are many minorities, and people seem to get along pretty well." Students say, "The majority of kids here are from Pennsylvania." Drexel's engineering focus means that "most of the student body is male and more conservative than many other schools." Undergraduates are rarely politically active. "Instead of worrying about politics and social causes as much, people are more concerned about their careers," students tell us. While some students are typically "bookwormish, somewhat intelligent, antisocial (keep door closed and/or play popular network computer games all day), there [are] also a good amount of cool, social people, too." The student body includes many legacies, as supported by a student who said that many students "have a parent or sibling who has attended the university."

ADMISSIONS

Very important factors considered include: Class rank, essays, secondary school record, standardized test scores. *Important factors considered include:* Character/personal qualities, extracurricular activities, interview, recommendations, talent/ability. *Other factors considered include:* Alumni/ae relation, volunteer work, work experience. SAT Reasoning or ACT required. TOEFL required of all international applicants. High school diploma is required, and GED is accepted. *Academic units required:* 3 math, 1 science (1 science lab). *Academic units recommended:* 1 foreign language.

The Inside Word

Drexel's distinct nature creates a high level of self-selection in the applicant pool, and most decent students are admitted.

FINANCIAL AID

Students should submit: FAFSA. The Princeton Review suggests that all financial aid forms be submitted as soon as possible after 1/1. *Need-based scholarships/grants offered:* Pell, SEOG, state scholarships/grants, private scholarships, the school's own gift aid, United Negro College Fund. *Loan aid offered:* FFEL Subsidized Stafford, FFEL Unsubsidized Stafford, FFEL PLUS, Federal Perkins, Federal Nursing, college/university loans from institutional funds. Applicants will be notified of awards on a rolling basis beginning on or about 3/15.

FROM THE ADMISSIONS OFFICE

"Since its inception in 1891, Drexel University has gained national recognition among colleges and universities for its academic excellence, experiential education program (Drexel co-op), technological expertise, and curricular innovation. In 1998, Drexel began operating one of the Philadelphia region's premier medical and health sciences schools, MCP Hahnemann University. In April, Drexel's Board of Trustees unanimously voted to approve merging MCP Hahnemann into Drexel University.

"With the addition of the nation's largest private medical school, an outstanding college of nursing and health professions, and one of only two schools of public health in Pennsylvania, Drexel University now comprises 12 academic colleges and schools. By this summer, we will offer 175 degree programs to some 11,500 undergraduates and 4,200 graduate students. Alumni will number 90,000, and the size of the full-time faculty will exceed 1,000.

"The post-merger Drexel will join the fewer than 50 private universities classified by the Carnegie Foundation as Doctoral/Research Universities-Extensive, which include Carnegie Mellon, MIT, Caltech, and Penn. Drexel also joins the top 100 U.S. universities in federal research expenditures and market value of endowment. Another benefit of this merger is that qualified Drexel applicants can now pursue four new accelerated dual-degree programs in the health sciences: the bachelor's/MD in medicine; bachelor's/master's in nursing; bachelor's/doctor of physical therapy; and bachelor's/master's for physician assistants.

"By combining our expertise in advanced technology and cooperative education with academic programs in medicine and health-related fields, we can now offer our students a unique set of skills with which to succeed in today's ever-changing world."

For even more information on this school, turn to page 482 of the "Stats" section.

DUQUESNE UNIVERSITY

600 FORBES AVENUE, PITTSBURGH, PA 15282 • ADMISSIONS: 412-396-5000 • FAX: 412-396-5644
FINANCIAL AID: 412-396-6607 • E-MAIL: ADMISSIONS@DUQ.EDU • WEBSITE: WWW.DUQ.EDU

Ratings
Quality of Life: 80   **Academic:** 75   **Admissions:** 81   **Financial Aid:** 79

Academics

Duquesne University offers a first-rate education at a relatively low cost. (The school's tuition is roughly two-thirds that charged by crosstown rival Carnegie Mellon University.) Undergraduates tout their school's commitment to "teaching Catholic values to accompany its excellent academic tradition." The excellent offerings in business and the health sciences are very popular. The professors who teach this program's courses "come from the professional world, and they bring years of business experience into the classroom." Professors in the health sciences "really make a point to get to know you personally and remember you years later. They are always open to meet with you, even when they're not currently your professor, and help in any way they can." Academics are generally difficult, although "the core classes are usually pretty easy and help boost your GPA." For the more challenging upper-level courses, "There are many people—students, tutors, and professors—who are willing to help." This support network helps to make this large university, which comprises ten schools, feel a little smaller and friendlier. An "amazing library and great research materials" also ease students' academic burdens.

> **SURVEY SAYS . . .**
> *Small classes*
> *Great off-campus food*
> *Campus feels safe*
> *Lots of beer drinking*
> *(Almost) everyone smokes*

Life

Duquesne is located in Pittsburgh's Central Business District, a site that provides easy access to all that the city offers. One student says, "The location of the school is one of its biggest strengths. It is located in one of the nicest parts of uptown Pittsburgh yet is just a short drive or walk to many exciting activities in the downtown area." The Southside "is right across the river, which works out really nicely for students. If you are old enough to drink, that is probably the best place to go." Another student adds, "The shopping is great at Station Square, and there are a ton of restaurants as well." Despite its urban setting, "Once you get on campus, you feel like you are in the suburbs. It's good, and everyone feels safe at school." Students love "the convenience of the campus buildings and things necessary for students. Although it has a small campus, Duquesne really makes the most of its space. There is beautiful landscaping, and the buildings are arranged nicely enough to leave students areas to just hang out and chill." While the party scene is pretty quiet—"we really have no frats on campus. The frats we go to are on Mount Washington and one that is closer to the Hill District, which isn't that convenient"—students can and do head over to University of Pittsburgh or Carnegie Mellon University, where parties are much more plentiful. About half the students live on campus, and "there is a fair amount of people who will go home almost every weekend."

Student Body

"Most students at Duquesne are white, middle- to upper-class private school kids who come from the eastern part of the United States, most from the general Pittsburgh area," students tell us. Some students "don't like the fact that there is very little diversity. Everyone seems so identical in their views. It is hard to have interesting class discussions with students who think so locally instead of globally." Although "the school can be a little cliquey," undergraduates are famously polite—"the strange thing is, here, everyone holds the door open for everyone! I have literally had to run to the door because someone was way up ahead holding it and waiting for me." Duquesne students "work hard but nothing too excessive. They like to party on the weekends and study on the weeknights." A large portion of the student population lives off campus; these students "have most interaction with other commuter students. The commuter council is a great organization for commuters to get involved in and helps the commuters to be more active on campus."

ADMISSIONS

Very important factors considered include: Essays, recommendations, secondary school record, standardized test scores. *Important factors considered include:* Character/personal qualities, class rank, extracurricular activities, interview, talent/ability, volunteer work. *Other factors considered include:* Alumni/ae relation, work experience. SAT Reasoning or ACT required. High school diploma is required, and GED is accepted. *Academic units required:* 4 English, 2 math, 2 science, 2 foreign language, 2 social studies, 4 academic electives.

The Inside Word

With such a high admit rate, the admissions process should create little anxiety in all but the weakest candidates.

FINANCIAL AID

Students should submit: FAFSA, institution's own financial aid form. Regular filing deadline 5/1. The Princeton Review suggests that all financial aid forms be submitted as soon as possible after 1/1. *Need-based scholarships/grants offered:* Pell, SEOG, state scholarships/grants, private scholarships, the school's own gift aid, United Negro College Fund. *Loan aid offered:* FFEL Subsidized Stafford, FFEL Unsubsidized Stafford, FFEL PLUS, Federal Perkins, Federal Nursing, private alternative loans. Applicants will be notified of awards on a rolling basis beginning on or about 3/1.

FROM THE ADMISSIONS OFFICE

"Duquesne University was founded in 1878 by the Holy Ghost Fathers. Although it is a private, Roman Catholic institution, Duquesne is proud of its ecumenical reputation. The total University enrollment is 9,803. Duquesne University's attractive and secluded campus is set on a 48-acre hilltop ('the bluff') overlooking the large corporate metropolis of Pittsburgh's Golden Triangle. It offers a wide variety of educational opportunities, from the liberal arts to modern professional training. Duquesne is a medium-size university striving to offer personal attention to its students while having the versatility and opportunities of a true university. A deep sense of tradition is combined with innovation and flexibility to make the Duquesne experience both challenging and rewarding. The Palumbo Convocation/Recreation Complex features a 6,300-seat arena, home court to the university's Division I basketball teams; racquetball and handball courts, weight rooms, and saunas. Extracurricular activities are recognized as an essential part of college life, complementing academics in the process of total student development. Students are involved in nearly 100 university-sponsored activities, and Duquesne's location gives students the opportunity to enjoy sports and cultural events both on campus and citywide. There are six residence halls with the capacity to house 3,574 students."

For even more information on this school, turn to page 483 of the "Stats" section.

ELIZABETHTOWN COLLEGE

LEFFLER HOUSE, ONE ALPHA DRIVE, ELIZABETHTOWN, PA 17022 • ADMISSIONS: 717-361-1400
FAX: 717-361-1365 • E-MAIL: ADMISSIONS@ETOWN.EDU • WEBSITE: WWW.ETOWN.EDU

Ratings
Quality of Life: 92   **Academic:** 86   **Admissions:** 87   **Financial Aid:** 80

Academics

Students love the "small, friendly, and supportive atmosphere" of Elizabethtown College and value its "service-oriented programs and the personal attention offered by the professors." The classes are "small" and "the professors are extremely friendly and work closely with students." One student explains, "Most of my classes have approximately eight students in them. If I do have a class with more than 20 students, it's usually a core course, and it's probably the only one with that many people." Students describe their aca-

demic experience as "pleasant [and] somewhat demanding." One undergrad remarks, "Professors really strive to help you with problems. There are tutors and writing consultants available at the Learning Center. Everyone wants you to do well academically." Students speak highly of Elizabethtown's "very good business program,"" excellent biology department," and "great occupational therapy program." Undergrads also appreciate that Elizabethtown "offers many chances to work in community service and opportunities to study overseas." The administration is generally described as "helpful and informative." However, one student points out, "Many of the students would agree that the administration is too old-fashioned in their thinking, but I feel that this experience would be felt at any college."

Life

Elizabethtown's campus "is gorgeous," students say, but point out that the location is "in the middle of Amish country, so there is not much to do off-campus in the immediate surrounding area." One undergrad says, "The town has some nice things to do such as eating at good restaurants and going to the movies at a good movie theater." Most students feel that the school offers "plenty of activities" to keep them entertained. "SWEET, the organization that is in charge of campus entertainment, holds dances every other week. Dances are a big part of E-town," says one student. "There are movies and other activities on campus every month," and " the Park City mall 'isn't very far away." In addition, "a lot of students spend their free time during the week playing poker with their friends or having parties. When it snows, many students have a good time sledding and playing in the snow." The school has a "strict alcohol policy," but "if you are into partying, then you can find parties." One student explains, "There is more partying going on than some realize, but I wouldn't call it a party school."

Student Body

"There is definitely an 'E-town personality,'" explains one student. "A typical E-town student is hardworking and very friendly. Most everyone is from Pennsylvania. If you're from out of state, you're definitely a minority." Students note that there is not much racial diversity on-campus, although "there are also minorities and exchange students" and "all the students basically get along with one another." Most students "come from the middle- to upper-middle-class. Women outnumber men on a 2:1 ratio and most students are Roman Catholic, but religion is not the end-all, be-all on campus." In fact, the majority of students seem pretty happy with their lives at the school. One undergrad comments, "The greatest thing about E-town is the sense of community. You can trust everyone here. Students leave their wallets and cell phones lying on chairs in the cafeteria to save their seats and don't worry about anyone stealing them." Another student adds, "'We're all here to help one another, not hurt one another.'"

ADMISSIONS

Very important factors considered include: Secondary school record. *Important factors considered include:* Class rank, interview, minority status, recommendations, standardized test scores, volunteer work. *Other factors considered include:* Alumni/ae relation, character/personal qualities, essays, extracurricular activities, geographical residence, religious affiliation/commitment, state residency, talent/ability, work experience. SAT Reasoning or ACT required. TOEFL required of all international applicants. High school diploma is required, and GED is accepted. *Academic units required:* 4 English, 3 math, 2 science (2 science lab), 2 foreign language, 2 social studies, 2 history. *Academic units recommended:* 4 English, 4 math, 4 science (3 science lab), 2 foreign language, 2 social studies, 2 history, 2 academic electives.

The Inside Word

The admissions office at Elizabethtown strongly encourages you to tell "what experiences are uniquely yours and how [they] will distinguish you from other applicants." The popular occupational therapy and allied health programs fill quickly, so if you are interested in these options, apply early.

FINANCIAL AID

Students should submit: FAFSA, institution's own financial aid form, federal tax records. The Princeton Review suggests that all financial aid forms be submitted as soon as possible after 1/1. *Need-based scholarships/grants offered:* Pell, SEOG, state scholarships/grants, private scholarships, the school's own gift aid. *Loan aid offered:* FFEL Subsidized Stafford, FFEL Unsubsidized Stafford, FFEL PLUS, Federal Perkins, state loans. Applicants will be notified of awards on a rolling basis beginning on or about 3/1.

FROM THE ADMISSIONS OFFICE

"The most important aspect of the admissions program is to admit graduates of Elizabethtown College. The entire focus of the admissions process is determining if a student is a good fit for E-town and if E-town is a good fit for the student. We pride ourselves on our 'conversational interviews' as a way to set a student at ease so that we can discover their potential to contribute to our community. Applicants are assessed in three areas: academic fit, co-curricular fit, and social fit. Integrity, diversity, academic excellence, and a commitment to services are qualities that are highly valued.

"E-town distinguishes itself from its peers through its commitment to personal attention, experiential learning, and diverse curriculum and a historic commitment to human service. The college is also one of the few small, regional colleges to have recently graduated a Rhodes Scholar. The campus visit will set E-town apart from other places as you experience the beautiful campus and surrounding area. Campus visitors are welcomed year-around.

"E-town is likely one of the finest colleges that you don't know enough about."

For even more information on this school, turn to page 483 of the "Stats" section.

ELMIRA COLLEGE

One Park Place, Elmira, NY 14901 • Admissions: 607-735-1724 • Fax: 607-735-1718
E-mail: admissions@elmira.edu • Website: www.elmira.edu

Ratings
Quality of Life: 69   Academic: 86   Admissions: 88   Financial Aid: 76

Academics

Elmira College offers "very strong academic programs (the three most recognized are its education, biology, and speech and hearing departments)" to its solid regional student body. The unusual academic calendar consists of two twelve-week terms followed by a six-week term known as Term III, during which students are able to explore their field of study via nontraditional means such as studying abroad, independent study, internships, student teaching, and specially tailored on-campus course work. Another

unique feature is the school's Encore performing arts requirement, which gives credit to students for attending music and theater performances. In addition, "every freshman is required to do 60 hours of community service, which seems tedious at first but is very, very, very rewarding." Students say the professors at the school are "overall very good." Many students do feel, however, that they would be better served if Elmira spent "less money on image and more on resources." "New desks and classroom equipment are desperately needed, and Elmira wastes so much money on unnecessary things." Students also suggest that "getting rid of Saturday morning classes for freshmen would" improve their college experience.

Life

Elmira College is steeped in traditions that help create a "very close-knit community and a sense of campus pride." One student says, "We have amazing school spirit. Our school colors are everywhere (purple walls, doors, fountains, and salt for the walkways) and so is our school shape, the octagon." While most students enjoy the "amazing sense of community" that Elmira sustains, some think the traditions that help foster it occasionally "go overboard." Hockey and other team sports "are very well-supported at Elmira." Students can "easily form their own clubs, such as the recently formed Paintball and Ultimate Frisbee™ Clubs," or participate in over 90 other clubs and organizations the school has to offer. The Student Activities Board "sponsors activities every weekend like movies, plays, games, bands, and comedians." Since Elmira is a small town in upstate New York, "there is not much around for city life." However, the city does offer "bars within walking distance of campus, like 501 or the Branch. For nonalcoholic fun, the Arnot Mall is about 15 minutes from campus, and it has a theater." Several students warn that the community surrounding the school is "sketchy." One undergrad explains, "Walking downtown to a certain area is all right, but any time after 5:00 P.M., you really need to walk with a group of people."

Student Body

"The first thing people notice about EC is that everyone seems so friendly here. No matter who you are, there's always someone to wave to or say a quick hello, even if you've never met them before." Students mention that the school "isn't as ethnically diverse as some," with "white, middle- to upper-class" females making up the majority. "The male-to-female ratio is about 3:7, and there are very few black or Hispanic students, although we do have many Asian students." Elmira also has "a large percentage of gay and lesbian students." Overall, most agree that all students "are treated equally." One undergrad describes the typical Elmira College student as "very studious, very friendly, and very concerned with the needs of others." Another student confirms this, saying that "the typical student at EC is overachieving and over-involved."

ADMISSIONS

Very important factors considered include: Character/personal qualities, class rank, secondary school record. *Important factors considered include:* Essays, extracurricular activities, recommendations, standardized test scores. *Other factors considered include:* Alumni/ae relation, geographical residence, interview, minority status, talent/ability, volunteer work, work experience. SAT Reasoning or ACT required. TOEFL required of all international applicants. High school diploma is required, and GED is accepted. *Academic units required:* 4 English, 3 math, 3 science (2 science lab), 3 social studies, 1 history, 2 academic electives. *Academic units recommended:* 2 foreign language.

The Inside Word

Elmira admissions officers consider the full application package carefully and pay especially close attention to candidates' essays. Notes the admissions office, "The 'fit' between the student and the college is the most important factor." Vegetarians take note: PETA named Elmira one of the nation's 10 most vegetarian-friendly campuses.

FINANCIAL AID

Students should submit: FAFSA, state aid form, state aid forms if applicable (NY, VT, RI). Regular filing deadline 6/30. The Princeton Review suggests that all financial aid forms be submitted as soon as possible after 1/1. *Need-based scholarships/grants offered:* Pell, SEOG, state scholarships/grants, private scholarships, the school's own gift aid. *Loan aid offered:* FFEL Subsidized Stafford, FFEL Unsubsidized Stafford, FFEL PLUS, Federal Perkins, college/university loans from institutional funds, GATE, alternative loans. Applicants will be notified of awards on a rolling basis beginning on or about 2/1. Federal Work-study Program available. Institutional employment available.

FROM THE ADMISSIONS OFFICE

"This year marks the sesquicentennial anniversary of Elmira College. After 15 decades of excellence, Elmira College remains rooted in the liberal arts and sciences, enriching its students' inquiry and analysis of their world, communication skills, and civic and ethical responsibility. The College also requires every student to complete a career-related internship, knowing that this hands-on experience helps 98 percent of June graduates to secure jobs in their desired field of employment or enter graduate or professional school by Labor Day each year. More than one-third of the student body studies abroad with Elmira College professors during the six-week Spring Term. The College's 12:1 student-faculty ratio allows the academic experience to be both rigorous and individualized. No classes are taught by teaching assistants. Committed to the residential college experience, on-campus housing is guaranteed all four years for undergraduates. Elmira College alumni are loyal, offering internships for students and demonstrating unwavering commitment through giving generously of their time, professional expertise, and financial resources."

For even more information on this school, turn to page 483 of the "Stats" section.

EMERSON COLLEGE

120 BOYLSTON STREET, BOSTON, MA 02116-4624 • ADMISSIONS: 617-824-8600 • FAX: 617-824-8609
FINANCIAL AID: 617-824-8655 • E-MAIL: ADMISSION@EMERSON.EDU • WEBSITE: WWW.EMERSON.EDU

Ratings
Quality of Life: 84   Academic: 82   Admissions: 91   Financial Aid: 87

Academics

"It's about communications and performance arts" at Emerson College, a school that "is great for passionate, talented people because not only will they be accepted for who they are but they will also be celebrated and will get the connections they need to survive in the real world." Because of the school's singular focus, "the majority of the learning time at Emerson is not spent in the classroom, but in rehearsal, at a film shoot, or going to press with their headline story." Professors are usually professionals, "people who have been in the field and want to teach now for one reason or another." Professors bring real world experience to the classroom and empathize with their students. "Our professors understand what a tough field we might be getting ourselves into," writes one undergraduate, "especially those people who choose to go into the entertainment industry, and our professors take it as seriously as we do." Better still, "in many cases, they invite students to participate in their work outside of the college." Students get their hands dirty early, and as such, "Emerson tries to get freshmen using equipment (video and other media, not film) as soon as possible." Explains one undergraduate, "Most students finish all their general education requirements within their first year and a half (if not sooner) and get to spend the rest of their time at Emerson focusing on what they love." You may not write as many term papers as you would at another school, but that doesn't mean you won't work hard. One student explains, "While at larger schools you may write 20-page term papers at the end of every course, at Emerson you're more likely to do a video. They take as long, trust me."

> **SURVEY SAYS . . .**
> *Small classes*
> *Students love Boston, MA*
> *College radio is popular*
> *Theater is popular*
> *(Almost) everyone smokes*

Life

"Life at Emerson revolves around activities at the school," students report and add that "most people are usually working on a theater piece or a television show, or some other kind of art that relates to their education, but also counts as their fun activity." "There is always some student production or a comedy show to see [as well as] a giant movie theater on our campus grounds, which Emerson kids probably support solely." There are also "the campus television and radio station, which run 24 hours a day, so students are always there." And that's just within the confines of Emerson; step off school grounds (the term "campus" doesn't really apply), and you'll quickly discover that "Boston is an amazing place to live, [and it is] one of the best cities in the world for college students." The city offers "plenty to do, including concerts at the Hatch Shell, Red Sox Games, a movie theater next door, and everything in Boston only a few subway stops away." The only downside is that "things close pretty early because Boston is so conservative."

Student Body

"There is no typical student" at Emerson, undergraduates report. One student explains, "If you take your high school artsy kid, the band geek, the theater chic, and the overachieving student leader, you've got Emerson, but without the stereotypes and with more homosexuality." Many students confirm that Emerson's "rather large gay community is totally accepted" by the school's "population of creative people. People at Emerson are actors and actresses, advertising gurus, and entertainment reporters. I have met the coolest people who have exposed me to cultural scenes that I never knew existed." Students dream big: "Everyone thinks they are going to be the next big thing, and some people are a bit pretentious about it." Emerson students also lean far left politically, "enough that a Texas Democrat could feel like Jesse Helms." A high tuition and limited endowment means that "the student body is limited to mostly upper-middle-class and above students whose parents can afford to pay for the school. Were Emerson a public college with half the tuition, it would be a very diverse, very politically correct institution."

ADMISSIONS

Very important factors considered include: Secondary school record, standardized test scores. *Important factors considered include:* Character/personal qualities, essays, extracurricular activities, recommendations, talent/ability. *Other factors considered include:* Alumni/ae relation, class rank, interview, minority status, volunteer work, work experience. SAT Reasoning or ACT required. TOEFL required of all international applicants. High school diploma is required, and GED is accepted. *Academic units required:* 4 English, 3 math, 3 science, 3 foreign language, 3 social studies. *Academic units recommended:* 4 English, 3 math, 3 science, 3 foreign language, 3 social studies, 4 academic electives.

The Inside Word

Being in Boston does more for Emerson's selectivity than do rigorous admissions standards.

FINANCIAL AID

Students should submit: FAFSA, institution's own financial aid form, noncustodial (divorced/separated) parents' statement, business/farm supplement, tax returns. The Princeton Review suggests that all financial aid forms be submitted as soon as possible after 1/1. *Need-based scholarships/grants offered:* Pell, SEOG, state scholarships/grants, private scholarships, the school's own gift aid. *Loan aid offered:* FFEL Subsidized Stafford, FFEL Unsubsidized Stafford, FFEL PLUS, Federal Perkins, state loans. Applicants will be notified of awards on or about 4/1. Federal Work-study Program available. Institutional employment available. Off-campus job opportunities are excellent.

FROM THE ADMISSIONS OFFICE

"Founded in 1880, Emerson is one of the premier colleges in the United States for the study of communication and the performing arts. Students may choose from more than two dozen undergraduate and graduate programs supported by state-of-the-art facilities and a nationally renowned faculty. The campus is home to WERS-FM, the oldest noncommercial radio station in New England; the historic 1,200-seat Cutler Majestic Theatre; and Ploughshares, the award-winning literary journal for new writing. A new 11-story performance and production center houses expanded performance and rehearsal space, a theater design/technology center, makeup lab, and television studios with editing and control rooms.

"Located on Boston Common in the heart of the city's Theater District, the Emerson campus is walking distance from the Massachusetts State House, historic Freedom Trial, Newbury Street shops, financial district, and numerous restaurants and museums. Emerson's 2,800 undergraduate and 900 graduate students come from over 50 countries and 45 states and territories. There are more than 60 student organizations and performance groups, 13 NCAA Division III intercollegiate teams, student publications, and honor societies. The college also sponsors programs in Los Angeles, Kasteel Well (The Netherlands), summer film study in Prague, and course cross-registration with the six-member Boston ProArts Consortium."

For even more information on this school, turn to page 484 of the "Stats" section.

EMMANUEL COLLEGE

400 THE FENWAY, BOSTON, MA 02115 • ADMISSIONS: 617-735-9715 • FAX: 617-735-9801
E-MAIL: ENROLL@EMMANUEL.EDU • WEBSITE: WWW.EMMANUEL.EDU

Ratings
Quality of Life: 92   **Academic:** 82   **Admissions:** 78   **Financial Aid:** 73

Academics

Emmanuel College is "a perfect [mix] of big city with a small school," students at this "small Catholic school right in the middle of Boston" say. This "community of learning, challenge, compassion, service, and friendship that prepares students to become spiritual and smart members of society" aims "to educate students in a dynamic learning environment, shaped by a liberal arts curriculum, rooted in strong human values and a Catholic heritage." Students add, "Emmanuel doesn't force Catholicism on students, but rather helps with instilling good ethics and morals." Professors "show great concern and interest in students' academic growth" and are "very accessible and try to make class interesting by keeping the students engaged through discussion." Although it is a small school, Emmanuel can offer students a fairly wide variety of choices thanks to its participation in the Colleges of the Fenway, a consortium of six area schools that together offer more than 3,000 courses.

> **SURVEY SAYS . . .**
> *Small classes*
> *Students love Boston, MA*
> *Great off-campus food*
> *Frats and sororities are unpopular*
> *or nonexistent*
> *Student government is popular*

Life

"Having a school in Boston is fantastic," undergrads at Emmanuel say and add, "There is something for everyone at any time. People here can easily go off campus to shop, eat, visit museums, clubs, anything." Emmanuel is located "in the shadows of Fenway Park, and [students] live and die with the success and failure of the Red Sox." The location "is perfect. Almost everything in the city is within walking distance, including the neighboring colleges such as Boston University and Northeastern." Undergrads head to those other campuses, or to some of their Colleges of the Fenway neighbors, to party, since "Emmanuel is a dry campus and not a lot of parties occur here. There are plenty around the immediate area, so it's no big deal." Campus life has picked up since the school went coed in 2000, with "new clubs and organizations popping up left and right" and "the addition of a lot of new facilities and activities. '[The school has] built a new athletic facility and new residence halls, increased enrollment, and added sports." While obviously happy with these changes, several respondents complain that the library's collection "is in extreme need of updating (they are told that is coming)." Students report that "because [this is] a Catholic college, the religious element is present, but because [students] are so diverse, it is more spiritual. There is no pressure to be Catholic or attend Mass, yet Campus Ministry is a popular group and does a lot for the community."

Student Body

"Everyone is unique" at Emmanuel, where "there are students that are very religious, not at all religious, very into sports, not at all into sports, those that love art, music and theater, and those that don't care about such things. There is a good balance of types here. Everyone can find a group that they get along well with." Different types of students "all tend to hang out with others like them, but people intermingle as well." Most students "are involved with at least one organization or sports team" and "get their work done on the weekdays but party on the weekends." The student body is largely drawn "from the New England suburbs or the city of Boston itself." Emmanuel has a roughly 3:1 female to male ratio, and with total enrollment increasing "at an incredible rate," students hope this will balance out soon.

ADMISSIONS

Very important factors considered include: Essays, recommendations, secondary school record, standardized test scores. *Other factors considered include:* Alumni/ae relation, character/personal qualities, class rank, extracurricular activities, interview, volunteer work, work experience. SAT Reasoning or ACT required. TOEFL required of all international applicants. High school diploma is required, and GED is accepted. *Academic units required:* 4 English, 3 math, 2 science (2 science lab), 2 foreign language, 2 social studies.

The Inside Word

Emmanuel admissions officers consider each candidate carefully. The application offers them plenty of information, including two writing samples, extracurricular commitments, and work experience. If you're serious about attending Emmanuel, pay attention to these extras; they could be the difference between admission and rejection.

FINANCIAL AID

Students should submit: FAFSA, institution's own financial aid form. The Princeton Review suggests that all financial aid forms be submitted as soon as possible after 1/1. *Need-based scholarships/grants offered:* Pell, SEOG, state scholarships/grants, private scholarships, the school's own gift aid. *Loan aid offered:* FFEL Subsidized Stafford, FFEL Unsubsidized Stafford, FFEL PLUS, Federal Perkins, state loans. Applicants will be notified of awards on a rolling basis beginning on or about 3/15. Federal Work-study Program available. Institutional employment available. Off-campus job opportunities are good.

FROM THE ADMISSIONS OFFICE

"Emmanuel College, founded in 1919, prepares men and women with the skills to succeed in tomorrow's world and the social conscience to make a difference in that world. An excellent liberal arts education, shaped by human values and a Catholic heritage, and a strong career development and internship program define the Emmanuel College experience. At Emmanuel, students become engaged learners in small interactive classes and develop leadership skills through participation in campus life. The city of Boston provides an extended classroom, opportunities for community service, and exciting internships with the city's most prestigious, leading-edge employers. And because we recognize the critical importance of information technology, our students have full access to a robust IT network right on campus! A vigorous mind built on an ethical foundation is the hallmark of today's Emmanuel College student."

For even more information on this school, turn to page 484 of the "Stats" section.

EUGENE LANG COLLEGE

65 WEST 11TH STREET, NEW YORK, NY 10011 • ADMISSIONS: 212-229-5665 • FAX: 212-229-5355
FINANCIAL AID: 212-229-8930 • E-MAIL: LANG@NEWSCHOOL.EDU • WEBSITE: WWW.LANG.EDU

Ratings
Quality of Life: 83   **Academic:** 87   **Admissions:** 83   **Financial Aid:** 66

Academics

The Eugene Lang College "offers a space for various kinds of interdisciplinary learning, critical thinking, and nontraditional study, often placing the responsibility for a fine education on its independent students." Those who thrive here are individuals who "want to push themselves and truly challenge themselves academically. Professors say they teach at Lang because of the students, and there is a true sense of students' wanting to explore and learn for education's sake rather than to simply 'get ahead' in life." As "one of very few schools in the nation that has seminar-style learning" where "you're not just crammed into a lecture hall with 300 other students and talked at," Lang promotes "the ability to freely express yourself in all levels, whether individually, intellectually, or politically." Classes here "tend to have really long, poetic titles like Hearing Art, Seeing Music, and the like," and "the material one learns at Lang is different then what would be core at another college, which is why the school attracts an interesting group of people and what makes for interesting conversations." Professors vary in teaching skills, but "the good professors who know a lot and know how to teach in 'the Lang style' (i.e., able to go off on tangents within the discussion and not lose focus of the bigger picture) are absolutely amazing." Because the school stresses independence, "you get out of Lang what you put into it. If you take advantage of what it has to offer, it can be one of the most rewarding and unique academic experiences in the country."

> **SURVEY SAYS . . .**
> Class discussions encouraged
> Small classes
> Students love New York, NY
> Great off-campus food
> Intercollegiate sports are unpopular
> or nonexistent
> Frats and sororities are unpopular
> or nonexistent
> Political activism is popular
> (Almost) everyone smokes

Life

"There is not much in the way of common space" in Eugene Lang's small facility, "so gatherings among students pretty much take to the streets." And they do take place: "We meet up with each other outside of the classroom and find that they have more in common than just a school. Often we are involved in the same music/art scene or political groups that exist outside of the school. The school just offers a starting point for relationships." Students spend most of their free time exploring New York City, where "there is always something to do that you've never done, or even heard of, before." The school is located on the northern end of Greenwich Village, the center of the city's youth social life. Public transportation makes the rest of Manhattan, and the other four boroughs of the city, easily accessible. Observes one undergrad, "Life in the city is incredible. Every possible opportunity is open to you. Living in the city allows me to apply the concepts I'm learning in the classroom to the world immediately around me through internships in politics, law, communications, etc." New York also "offers much more real interaction than the forced 'You like X college sports team? I love X college sports team,' interaction that so many colleges pride themselves on," students insist.

Student Body

Lang undergrads are "independent, analytical, passionate" and "more urban, academic, and aware than your average college student." Although "the 'typical' Lang student is often characterized as a pierced and tattooed hipster," Lang also "has students who listen to Britney Spears, were very popular in high school, and played multiple varsity sports but know what they want in education, so they came to Lang." Adds one undergrad, "You really can't be too weird or too normal for this place." Most Lang students "are extremely politically aware and very liberal." Lang boasts "an incredible amount of diversity in age, ethnicity, background, sexual identity, etc.," and students are cool with that.

ADMISSIONS

Very important factors considered include: Essays, recommendations, secondary school record. *Important factors considered include:* Character/personal qualities, interview, standardized test scores, talent/ability, volunteer work. *Other factors considered include:* Alumni/ae relation, class rank, extracurricular activities, geographical residence, minority status, work experience. SAT Reasoning or ACT required. TOEFL required of all international applicants. High school diploma is required, and GED is accepted. *Academic units required:* 4 English. *Academic units recommended:* 3 math, 3 science, 2 foreign language, 3 social studies, 2 history.

The Inside Word

The college draws a very self-selected and intellectually curious pool, and applications are up. Those who demonstrate little self-motivation will find themselves denied.

FINANCIAL AID

Students should submit: FAFSA, state aid form. The Princeton Review suggests that all financial aid forms be submitted as soon as possible after 1/1. *Need-based scholarships/grants offered:* Pell, SEOG, state scholarships/grants, private scholarships, the school's own gift aid. *Loan aid offered:* FFEL Subsidized Stafford, FFEL Unsubsidized Stafford, FFEL PLUS, Federal Perkins, college/university loans from institutional funds. Applicants will be notified of awards on a rolling basis beginning on or about 3/1. Federal Work-study Program available. Institutional employment available. Off-campus job opportunities are good.

FROM THE ADMISSIONS OFFICE

"Eugene Lang College offers students of diverse backgrounds an innovative and creative approach to a liberal arts education, combining stimulating classroom activity of a small, intimate college with rich resources of a dynamic, urban university—New School University. The curriculum at Lang College is challenging and flexible. Class size, limited to eighteen students, promotes energetic and thoughtful discussions and writing is an essential component of all classes. Students design their own program of study within one of thirteen interdisciplinary concentrations in the Social Sciences and Humanities. They also have the opportunity to pursue a five-year BA/BFA, BA/MA, or BA/MST at one of the university's six other divisions. Our Greenwich Village location means that all the cultural treasures of the city—museums, libraries, music, theater—are literally at your doorstep."

For even more information on this school, turn to page 485 of the "Stats" section.

FAIRFIELD UNIVERSITY

1073 North Benson Road, Fairfield, CT 06824 • Admissions: 203-254-4100 • Fax: 203-254-4199
Financial Aid: 203-254-4125 • E-mail: admis@mail.fairfield.edu • Website: www.fairfield.edu

Ratings
Quality of Life: 81   **Academic:** 81   **Admissions:** 89   **Financial Aid:** 74

Academics

Fairfield University, "a small Jesuit University that provides so many opportunities because of its great resources and faculty," achieves the Jesuit ideal of "educating the whole person" through a "strong core curriculum" and extracurricular programs that "put the focus on finding balance in life." Through its four undergraduate divisions, Fairfield offers a wide range of choices to its relatively small student body, further accommodating students with "small class sizes" and "lots of class discussions, which is awesome because we get to see stuff from a different perspective." Students explain that "since we are a liberal arts school, we get a taste of everything, which is so much fun" and report that "we have really good nursing, business, and arts and science programs." One biology major writes, "I chose this school because it had an excellent science program. Now I get to study with a professor who worked on the Human Genome Project." Course work here "is tough and certainly requires studying," as professors "are understanding people but at the same time, take no crap. They are there to help us learn, and that is completely obvious. Overall, it is a challenging environment where a serious student can feel comfortable."

Life

Fairfield "is an extremely social school, both on and off campus. It's the antithesis of a suitcase school. Students tend to be very involved in a wide range of activities and the great social scene." Undergrads here enjoy a good party, whether it's at the beach, or the townhouses on campus. One student writes, "There are parties every night. You must be social in order to get the full experience at Fairfield." Many are apparently happy with only a partial experience; they skip the party scene, participating instead in "the many Fairfield University Student Association (FUSA)-sponsored events such as bowling, Broadway shows, Mega-Bingo, semi-formals, concerts, and comedians." Explains one student, "FUSA makes sure to plan things every single Thursday, Friday, and Saturday. There is always something to do." Campus ministry is also very active and very popular, as are such quiet diversions as "shopping in Westport or Greenwich or just hanging out with friends." The Stags, Fairfield's intercollegiate squads, compete in 19 men's and women's sports. Students here love that "it's easy enough to get to New York City," either by car or public transportation.

Student Body

The Fairfield stereotype is that "everyone falls into one of two basic categories: those who show up for class dressed like it's a Saturday night and they're going to a club, or those who get to class and look as though they need directions to the country club. If you don't fall into one of these categories in some sense, you are not Fairfield material." There is some debate here over the accuracy of Fairfield's nickname "J. Crew U"—while those who insist "there are many different kinds of people that go here," they'll point out that "the majority of the people here are white, though." Many of our respondents suggest that Fairfield needs to improve its lack of diversity: "Most of the kids on campus are white [though] the minorities are usually the most popular kids around." One sophomore's advice to "freshmen who come to me complaining of the social homogeny here: There are absolutely wonderful students who attend this school. Your challenge—and this is really not so hard—is to find them." Homogenous or not, Fairfield undergrads tend to be "smart, but not brainy" and often "have a strong interest in professional sports." Overall, "everyone is very friendly and get along well with one another."

ADMISSIONS

Very important factors considered include: Class rank, essays, recommendations, secondary school record, standardized test scores. *Important factors considered include:* Extracurricular activities. *Other factors considered include:* Alumni/ae relation, character/personal qualities, geographical residence, interview, minority status, talent/ability, volunteer work, work experience. SAT Reasoning or ACT required. TOEFL required of all international applicants. High school diploma is required, and GED is not accepted. *Academic units required:* 4 English, 3 math, 3 science (3 science lab), 2 foreign language, 3 social studies. *Academic units recommended:* 4 English, 4 math, 4 science (3 science lab), 4 foreign language, 4 social studies, 1 history. It is highly recommended that music majors submit portfolios and theater majors submit resumes.

The Inside Word

Solid support from Catholic high schools goes a long way toward stocking the applicant pool. Important to note: Steady increases in the number of admission applications has nicely increased selectivity in recent years. Fairfield's campus and central location combined with improvements to the library, campus center, classrooms, athletic facilities, and campus residences, make this a campus worth seeing.

FINANCIAL AID

Students should submit: FAFSA, CSS/Financial Aid PROFILE, business/farm supplement. The Princeton Review suggests that all financial aid forms be submitted as soon as possible after 1/1. *Need-based scholarships/grants offered:* Pell, SEOG, state scholarships/grants, private scholarships, the school's own gift aid, United Negro College Fund. *Loan aid offered:* FFEL Subsidized Stafford, FFEL Unsubsidized Stafford, FFEL PLUS, Federal Perkins, Federal Nursing, state loans, private alternate loans. Applicants will be notified of awards on a rolling basis beginning on or about 4/1. Federal Work-study Program available. Institutional employment available. Off-campus job opportunities are good.

FROM THE ADMISSIONS OFFICE

"Fairfield University's primary objectives are to develop of the creative intellectual potential of its students and to foster in them ethical and religious values, and a sense of social responsibility. The Jesuit tradition inspires habits of heart and mind, and creates an educational experience which is both personal and powerful. Students learn in a supportive environment with faculty committed to individual development and personal enrichment. As the key to the lifelong process of learning, Fairfield has developed a core curriculum to introduce all students to the broad rand of liberal learning. Students choose from 32 majors and 19 interdisciplinary minors. They also have outstanding internships opportunities in Fairfield County and New York City. Fairfield grads wishing to continue their education are highly successful in gaining graduate and professional school admission, while others pursue extensive job opportunities throughout the region. Thirty three Fairfield students have been tapped as Fulbright scholars in the last ten years."

For even more information on this school, turn to page 485 of the "Stats" section.

FORDHAM UNIVERSITY

441 EAST FORDHAM ROAD, THEBAUD HALL, NEW YORK, NY 10458 • ADMISSIONS: 718-817-4000
FAX: 718-367-9404 • FINANCIAL AID: 718-817-3800 • E-MAIL: ENROLL@FORDHAM.EDU • WEBSITE: WWW.FORDHAM.EDU

Ratings
Quality of Life: 75   Academic: 84   Admissions: 90   Financial Aid: 71

Academics

Fordham University has campuses in the Bronx and Manhattan and "is all about the Jesuit tradition" of education. That tradition "places the total emphasis on working on a student-by-student basis, tailoring to each student's strengths and weaknesses" and "focuses on development of the whole person, not just on academics." Central to the Jesuit approach is Fordham's thorough core curriculum, which takes "almost two full years to complete." Some students describe it as "amazing because it introduces you to a wide variety of disciplines and topics," but others feel the core requirements are too onerous and too remote from their career goals. Comments one such student, "I understand that they want people to be thinkers, but all the core manages to do is make people feel as though their first two years are a meaningless waste of time." The Jesuit focus on individuals is facilitated by small class sizes. "When I first got here," writes one undergraduate, "I was amazed at how small classes were and how 'real' professors were teaching my classes. I've even been able to work on research projects with some of them and do an independent study—as a sophomore—with another." Close contact with influential professors and the school's urban setting translate into "great jobs and internships," something appreciated by the entire student body. Many warn that the school needs a major tech upgrade, telling us that "technology is far behind that of many schools" of lesser academic caliber and that "dorm Internet connections are slower than dialup."

> **SURVEY SAYS . . .**
> *Small classes*
> *Great library*
> *Great off-campus food*
> *Campus feels safe*
> *Frats and sororities are unpopular or nonexistent*
> *Lots of beer drinking*
> *Hard liquor is popular*

Life

Fordham's Rose Hill campus in the Bronx, students tell us, is "the best location possible: It's close to the city, but far enough away for it not to be a distraction." It also boasts "the most gorgeous campus in New York City," which is "completely gated, and you need a school ID to get on to campus and into dorms after 6:00 P.M." Although the surrounding area "isn't the best neighborhood," it has lots to offer (above and beyond "teaching students street smarts"), including the New York Botanical Garden and the Bronx Zoo. Manhattan is a 15-minute subway ride away and provides "an unlimited source of entertainment." On campus, there's not much of a party scene "because the rules are very strict," so "many people go to local bars, to parties at off-campus apartments," or to Manhattan for fun. One student explains, "Life at school centers around a balance of classwork, activities in the city (Broadway plays, going out to eat, shopping, going to see other performing arts and concerts, Yankee games) and activities on campus (community service in local hospitals, watching our basketball and football games, and participating in the university band). Life can be as full as you choose to make it."

Student Body

The predominantly "upper-middle-class Irish or Italian Catholic" students at Fordham University "fall into one of two categories: resident students and commuters." Residents can be divided into "a few basic types of people: preppy, athletic, and/or trendy," while commuters "mostly hang out together, and they tend to be much more ethnically diverse than the resident students. Somehow, everyone manages to fit into a very multifaceted Fordham," in part because "students are very respectful and friendly to each other." Many are active outside the classroom; reports one undergraduate, "the typical student at Fordham not only goes to class, but [also] is involved in extracurricular activities both on and off campus, whether clubs on campus, or an internship, or working a part-time job." Adds another student, "Global Outreach is one of the most popular programs on campus. You travel to an impoverished area (national and foreign) and, with a group of other students, help out for a few days. What kind of student gives up his/her spring break to teach orphans in Romania or the poor in El Salvador? [A] Fordham student!"

ADMISSIONS

Very important factors considered include: Class rank, secondary school record, standardized test scores. *Important factors considered include:* Character/personal qualities, essays, extracurricular activities, recommendations, talent/ability. *Other factors considered include:* Alumni/ae relation, geographical residence, interview, minority status, volunteer work, work experience. SAT Reasoning or ACT required. TOEFL required of all international applicants. High school diploma is required, and GED is accepted. *Academic units required:* 4 English, 3 math, 3 science, 2 foreign language, 2 social studies, 2 history, 6 academic electives. *Academic units recommended:* 4 English, 4 math, 4 science, 3 foreign language, 2 social studies, 2 history, 6 academic electives.

The Inside Word

Candidates are reviewed by a committee made up of admissions officers, faculty, administrators, and deans. Admission to Fordham is quite competitive and a solid flow of applicants from metropolitan area Catholic schools keeps their student profile sound.

FINANCIAL AID

Students should submit: FAFSA, CSS/Financial Aid PROFILE, noncustodial (divorced/separated) parents' statement, business/farm supplement. Regular filing deadline 2/1. The Princeton Review suggests that all financial aid forms be submitted as soon as possible after 1/1. *Need-based scholarships/grants offered:* Pell, SEOG, state scholarships/grants, private scholarships, the school's own gift aid. *Loan aid offered:* FFEL Subsidized Stafford, FFEL Unsubsidized Stafford, FFEL PLUS, Federal Perkins. Applicants will be notified of awards on or about 4/1. Federal Work-study Program available. Institutional employment available. Off-campus job opportunities are excellent.

FROM THE ADMISSIONS OFFICE

"Fordham University offers a distinctive, values-centered educational experience that is rooted in the Jesuit tradition of intellectual rigor and personal attention. Located in New York City, Fordham offers to students the unparalleled educational, cultural and recreational advantages of one of the world's greatest cities. Fordham has three residential campuses in New York—the tree-lined, 85-acre Rose Hill in the Bronx, the cosmopolitan Lincoln Center campus in the heart of Manhattan's performing arts center, and the scenic Marymount campus located on the banks of the Hudson River in Tarrytown, New York. The university's state of the art facilities and buildings include one of the most technologically advanced libraries in the country. Fordham offers to its students a variety of majors, concentrations, and programs that can be combined with an extensive career planning and placement program. More than 2,600 organizations in the New York metropolitan area offer students internships that provide hands-on experience and valuable networking opportunities in fields such as business, communications, medicine, law, and education."

For even more information on this school, turn to page 486 of the "Stats" section.

FRANKLIN & MARSHALL COLLEGE

PO Box 3003, Lancaster, PA 17604-3003 • Admissions: 717-291-3953 • Fax: 717-291-4381
Financial Aid: 717-291-3991 • E-mail: admission@fandm.edu • Website: www.fandm.edu

Ratings
Quality of Life: 71   **Academic:** 88   **Admissions:** 91   **Financial Aid:** 97

Academics

"The workload is tremendous" at Franklin & Marshall College, a small private college that produces "great acceptance rates into graduate and professional schools." The school's "great reputation for its premed program" as well as "its success in placing graduates in top law schools" are among the reasons students endure the "make-you-or-break-you academics" here; the fact that "the school is ded-

icated to helping students get interesting opportunities, such as internships, study-abroad programs, and independent research programs" is another attraction. And then there are the professors, identified by many as "the bright spot of the school. They are all very kind and helpful and enjoy teaching." Writes one student, "The professors enliven the classroom and their accessibility outside of the classroom makes the academic experience at F&M that much better." Good grades are hard to come by at F&M. Warns one undergrad, "F&M is known for its grade deflation. Professors do not inflate grades here. Students understand this and work hard." As one student puts it, "My parents must think I goof off sometimes when I come out with Bs, yet I work more than I ever have. Getting an A– here for me is like finding the Holy Grail." But after they've put in their long hours of study, "students realize how much they have truly learned, and how it was all worth it in the end. The results of the strong liberal arts education can be seen in F&M's extremely high number of acceptances to graduate, medical, and law schools."

Life

F&M has a long history of active Greek life on campus, despite the fact that the school "de-recognized" Greek organizations in 1988. In 2004, F&M brought the Greeks back into the fold, which should mean the popular system should grow even more popular in coming years. Even before the re-recognition, "frat parties were a huge part of campus life," in part due to a perceived lack of alternatives; many here feel that hometown Lancaster, PA, "is a pretty small city with not too much for a college student to do." Of course, F&M's famous academic workload pretty well takes care of students' weekdays. "Most students have no time for anything but work during the week, but party hardy when they get the chance on the weekend," undergrads agree. Come Friday afternoon, students "hang out and party at the off-campus frat houses or apartments," or they "enjoy events such as concerts, movies, comedy shows, lectures, and debates, which the college does a great job of setting up." A few adventurous undergrads venture into Lancaster, which we're told "has a few alternative venues, including the independent movie theater Zoetropolis, Chameleon Club, and Tally-Ho (a local gay club)." Lancaster also has "some excellent restaurants for when parents come up with the money to buy those kinds of dinners" and "great local shopping with a couple of big outlet malls." Many here "do volunteer work around the community," often in conjunction with their Greek organizations.

Student Body

"There are a significant number of your stereotypical Abercrombie frat boys and sorority girls" at F&M, "but there are also representatives of just about every other socio-demographic group you could think of," including "a very strong international population representing about 60 different countries." Notes one student, "My four best friends here are a Shia Muslim from Tanzania, a New York Catholic, a minister's daughter, and an extremely rural Baha'i." The sameness of much of the school's "conservative, preppy, middle-class majority" is further counterbalanced by "a lot of atypical students: gays, nerds, a few potheads, people with different religious beliefs. Most of them are considered very interesting to talk to and some of them are very popular on campus." Many who attend here "are not only capable academically but are also extremely talented in other areas such as sports, theater, and music."

ADMISSIONS

Very important factors considered include: Character/personal qualities, class rank, secondary school record. *Important factors considered include:* Essays, extracurricular activities, interview, minority status, recommendations, standardized test scores, talent/ability, volunteer work. *Other factors considered include:* Alumni/ae relation, geographical residence, work experience. SAT Reasoning or ACT required. TOEFL required of all international applicants. High school diploma is required, and GED is accepted. *Academic units required:* 4 English, 3 math, 2 science (2 science lab), 2 foreign language, 1 social studies, 2 history, 1 arts/music/theater. *Academic units recommended:* 4 math, 3 science (3 science lab), 4 foreign language, 3 social studies, 3 history.

The Inside Word

Applicants who are serious about attending the college should definitely interview; it will also help to make it known that F&M is one of your top choices. The college loses a lot of its admits to competitor colleges and will take notice of a candidate who is likely to enroll.

FINANCIAL AID

Students should submit: FAFSA, institution's own financial aid form, CSS/Financial Aid PROFILE, noncustodial (divorced/separated) parents' statement, business/farm supplement. Regular filing deadline 3/1. The Princeton Review suggests that all financial aid forms be submitted as soon as possible after 1/1. *Need-based scholarships/grants offered:* Pell, SEOG, state scholarships/grants, private scholarships, the school's own gift aid. *Loan aid offered:* FFEL Subsidized Stafford, FFEL Unsubsidized Stafford, FFEL PLUS, Federal Perkins, college/university loans from institutional funds. Applicants will be notified of awards on or about 3/15. Federal Work-study Program available. Off-campus job opportunities are good.

FROM THE ADMISSIONS OFFICE

"Franklin & Marshall students choose from a variety of fields of study, traditional and interdisciplinary, that typify liberal learning. Professors in all of these fields are committed to a common purpose, which is to teach students to think, speak, and write with clarity and confidence. Whether the course is in theater or in physics, the class will be small, engagement will be high, and discussion will dominate over lecture. Thus throughout their four years, beginning with the First Year Seminar, students at Franklin & Marshall are repeatedly invited to active participation in intellectual play at high levels. Our graduates consistently testify to the high quality of an F&M education as a mental preparation for life."

For even more information on this school, turn to page 486 of the "Stats" section.

FRANKLIN W. OLIN COLLEGE OF ENGINEERING

OLIN WAY NEEDHAM, MA 02492-1245 • ADMISSIONS: 781-292-2222 • FAX: 781-292-2210
FINANCIAL AID: 781-292-2364 • E-MAIL: INFO@OLIN.EDU • WEBSITE: WWW.OLIN.EDU

Ratings
Quality of Life: 99　　**Academic:** 98　　**Admissions:** 99　　**Financial Aid:** 99

Academics

For students at Franklin W. Olin College of Engineering, the best school to attend is the one they get to create. This young and "constantly evolving" technical institution hopes to receive accreditation in 2006, when the first graduating class earns their degrees. Now, students have the opportunity to "actively shape an innovative new school." At this nascent stage, "It's impossible for everything to run perfectly smooth," but students focus on "what a difference we're making for future students and how much we're learning about learning itself." Suggestions regarding curriculum and class structure are implemented swiftly. "Feedback is a huge and serious deal around here," resulting in hands-on projects, collaborative work, and creative problem solving. One student writes, "Freshmen get busy building miniature solar car racers during the first semester." A normal day could involve "software modeling, building parts in the machines shop, and programming." In the interest of training well-rounded individuals, AHS (arts, humanities, social sciences) classes are used to balance science/engineering and business/entrepreneurship courses in the "Olin Triangle." Students may also take courses through neighboring Brandeis, Babson, and Wellesley. Students regard their professors as "a team of superheroes who save us from the harshness of a typical engineering education with their passion for teaching." They interact on a personal, first-name basis in order to "establish a nurturing community for learning." It's all part of "participating in the greatest engineering teaching experiment of our time." These grand aspirations extend beyond school, to careers dedicated to "constantly striving to improve the world through innovation."

> **SURVEY SAYS . . .**
> *Small classes*
> *No one cheats*
> *Lab facilities are great*
> *Great computer facilities*
> *Students are friendly*
> *Dorms are like palaces*
> *Campus feels safe*
> *Intercollegiate sports are unpopular or nonexistent*
> *Frats and sororities are unpopular or nonexistent*

Life

With Olin's grinding workload, students know that balance is the key to survival. They need an outside pastime to turn to when the o-chem gets ugly. The school actively encourages "Passionate Pursuits" by offering nondegree credit and funds for pursuing an extracurricular interest. Envision this: A student shaves his head, a drunken rite of passage at many schools, but rather than pop a keg stand, everyone gathers 'round to discuss the friction coefficient of growing hair. Conversely, "it's not unusual to do physics until ten on Friday night and then go out." One student reports, "If parties are your thing, this is a great environment. It's very safe, supportive, and respectful." For the majority, social life means "watching a lot of movies together rather than getting completely plastered every night." Olin claims to breed "less stress than other tech schools," keeping things light with a well-timed practical joke or spontaneous sing-along. Recently, a school-wide game of capture the flag managed to drag most people away from the widespread hobby of "playing Halo on XBox." Rumors also persist that a bouncy castle materialized outside of a dormitory for a study break one weekend.

Student Body

Actually meeting the entire Olin student body would not take much longer than reading this paragraph. This tight group of 216 "awesome, awesome people" might just be "the most social bunch of nerds you'll ever find." One student says her peers walk the line between "socially adept geeks and brainy cool kids." Others also emphasize these future engineers of America "have good people skills and know how to have fun." These are engineering students who put down their protractors and "do everything from glass-blowing to swing dancing to professional theater." The only evident common denominator is that everyone "is passionate about something outside of school." Because they all get to know each other, "people here really understand and appreciate diversity and crazy and wild personalities." The group accommodates "variety in political beliefs, social lives, and ambition." Ultimately, a strong bond unites the Olin population since they share "a commitment to build [their] school together."

ADMISSIONS

Very important factors considered include: Character/personal qualities, essays, extracurricular activities, recommendations, secondary school record, talent/ability. *Important factors considered include:* Class rank, interview, minority status, standardized test scores, volunteer work. *Other factors considered include:* Geographical residence, state residency, work experience. SAT Reasoning and SAT Subject Tests or ACT required. High school diploma is required, and GED is accepted. *Academic units required:* 4 English, 4 math, 3 science (3 science lab), 2 foreign language, 2 social studies, 2 history.

The Inside Word

Although Franklin W. Olin College of Engineering is an extremely young institution—it first opened its doors to students in fall 2002—admissions is as tough as it gets. Students are judged not only on high school course work and standardized test scores but also on personal character. Students who exhibit creativity, passion, and an entrepreneurial spirit are favored over their less adventurous peers. Olin strives for gender balance; therefore, female applicants currently enjoy an admit rate about three times that of male applicants.

FINANCIAL AID

Students should submit: FAFSA. Regular filing deadline 4/15. The Princeton Review suggests that all financial aid forms be submitted as soon as possible after 1/1. *Need-based scholarships/grants offered:* the school's own gift aid. Applicants will be notified of awards on a rolling basis beginning on or about 3/25. Off-campus job opportunities are good.

FROM THE ADMISSIONS OFFICE

"Every admitted student at Olin College receives a $130,000 four-year full-tuition scholarship. The endowment to support these scholarships, as well as the funds to build a brand new state-of-the-art campus, was provided by F. W. Olin Foundation. This commitment, in excess of $450 million, is among the largest grants in the history of U.S. higher education. It is the intention of the founders that this scholarship will be offered in perpetuity. "The selection process at Olin College is unique to college admission. Each year a highly self-selecting pool of approximately 600 applications is reviewed on traditional selection criteria. Approximately 160 finalists are invited to one of two Candidates' Weekends in February and March. These candidates are grouped into five person teams for a weekend of design and build exercises, group discussions and interviews with Olin students, faculty, and staff. Written evaluations and recommendations for each candidate are prepared by all Olin participants and submitted to the faculty admission committee. The committee admits about 100 Candidates to yield a freshman class of 75. The result is that the freshman class is ultimately chosen on the strength of personal attributes such as leadership, cooperation, creativity, communication, and their enthusiasm for Olin College. "A waiting list of approximately 20 is also established. Any wait list Candidate who is not offered a spot in the class may defer enrollment for one year—with the guarantee of the Olin Scholarship. Wait list students are strongly encouraged do something unusual, exciting, and productive during their sabbatical year."

For even more information on this school, turn to page 487 of the "Stats" section.

THE GEORGE WASHINGTON UNIVERSITY

2121 I STREET NW, SUITE 201, WASHINGTON, DC 20052 • ADMISSIONS: 202-994-6040
FAX: 202-994-0325 • FINANCIAL AID: 202-994-6620 • E-MAIL: GWADM@GWIS2.CIRC.GWU.EDU • WEBSITE: WWW.GWU.EDU

Ratings
Quality of Life: 76   **Academic:** 82   **Admissions:** 94   **Financial Aid:** 91

Academics

"As advertised when you first visit [George Washington University (GW)], one of the [university's] greatest strengths lies in the fact that GW is located literally in the middle of Washington, DC. If you're political, this is the place to be." The university places a heavy emphasis on internships that land many of these politically oriented students in congressional offices on Capitol Hill or at lobbying firms on K Street. Students enjoy this "combination of practical and theoretical" learning and the great faculty. Not only are many faculty members well versed in both the pro-

> **SURVEY SAYS . . .**
> Students love Washington, DC
> Great off-campus food
> Dorms are like palaces
> Campus feels safe
> Student publications are popular
> Political activism is popular
> Hard liquor is popular

fessional and academic aspects of their disciplines but also "they wrote the textbook they use." "The school's amazing professors in the fields of economics, international affairs," and other globally relevant disciplines draw rave reviews from the student body. But some students grumble that the university could better its arts and science programs with more funding and a wider breadth of offerings. Many students opt for time away from GW's main campus (in the Foggy Bottom neighborhood of the District) to spend a year or more at the university's residential Mount Vernon campus, located just fifteen minutes away from the main campus. At Mount Vernon, students have full access to the courses and events of Foggy Bottom but can take advantage of a more traditional campus and smaller classes. The Mount Vernon campus recently initiated an honors program that mirrors the respected program already in place at Foggy Bottom. If students could change one thing about GW, it would probably be the administration. Grumbles one student, "GW, in classic Washington style, is a mountain of red tape."

Life

While GW's urban location does not offer students the sprawling acreage and groves of trees that you find on many rural college campuses, the university's grounds "in the heart of DC" provide a comfortable nesting ground for this student body. "I say with absolute certainty that our six city blocks feel like as much of a campus as 20 acres of grass would," asserts one undergraduate. Still, some students complain about the lack of a social scene and school spirit within those city blocks. "GW's not a big party school," due in part to the "strict laws of DC" and the tight campus regulations. But, as almost any student will tell you, the real fun happens in the city—and that's fine with them. "There are many shopping areas around GW, as well as bars, clubs, restaurants, jazz clubs, etc." "Whether playing Frisbee on the mall, looking at a Picasso at the Smithsonian, or shopping in Georgetown, there's something for everyone," says one satisfied student. And for those with a taste for the exotic, "one amazing aspect of DC is that you can indulge in a lot of different cuisines from around the world." If the world's finest museums, most popular public parks, and most recognizable monuments aren't appealing, students can just relax in their comfortable dorms. "In my freshman dorm," a student tells us, "I have a kitchen and a bathroom that is shared with three roommates."

Student Body

It's probably not surprising that many of the students who choose to attend school "three blocks west of the White House and three blocks north of the Vietnam War Memorial" are politically active. And taken as a whole, this student body leans heavily to the left. Within that left-leaning mass, you will find "all sorts of colors, sizes, religious and political affiliations, and sexual preferences represented." A student from the rural Midwest opines that the attitude on campus is "very tolerant," adding, "It's not atypical to see interracial couples, Jews and Arabs as friends, and two fraternity presidents dating each other." A satisfied first-year student says, "Maybe it's just that I have stars in my freshman eyes, but to me it seems like one big, happy family here."

ADMISSIONS

Very important factors considered include: Secondary school record. *Important factors considered include:* Class rank, essays, extracurricular activities, interview, recommendations, standardized test scores, talent/ability, volunteer work. *Other factors considered include:* Alumni/ae relation, character/personal qualities, geographical residence, minority status, work experience. SAT Reasoning or ACT required. TOEFL required of all international applicants. High school diploma is required, and GED is not accepted. *Academic units required:* 4 English, 2 math, 2 science (1 science lab), 2 foreign language, 2 social studies. *Academic units recommended:* 4 English, 4 math, 4 science, 4 foreign language, 4 social studies.

The Inside Word

The low percentage of admitted students who enroll at GW works to keep the admit rate relatively high. For strong students, this is definitely a low-stress admissions process. The university's location and access to faculty with impressive credentials are the main reasons for GW's sound freshman profile.

FINANCIAL AID

Students should submit: FAFSA, CSS/Financial Aid PROFILE. Regular filing deadline 2/1. The Princeton Review suggests that all financial aid forms be submitted as soon as possible after 1/1. *Need-based scholarships/grants offered:* Pell, SEOG, state scholarships/grants, the school's own gift aid. *Loan aid offered:* FFEL Subsidized Stafford, FFEL Unsubsidized Stafford, FFEL PLUS, Federal Perkins. Applicants will be notified of awards on a rolling basis beginning on or about 3/24. Federal Work-study Program available. Institutional employment available. Off-campus job opportunities are excellent.

FROM THE ADMISSIONS OFFICE

"At GW, we welcome students who show a measure of impatience with the limitations of traditional education. At many universities, the edge of campus is the real world, but not at GW, where our campus and Washington, DC are seamless. We look for bold, bright students who are ambitious, energetic, and self-motivated. Here, where we are so close to the centers of thought and action in every field we offer, we easily integrate our outstanding academic tradition and faculty connections with the best internship and job opportunities of Washington, DC. A generous scholarship and financial assistance program attracts top students from all parts of the country and the world."

For even more information on this school, turn to page 487 of the "Stats" section.

GEORGETOWN UNIVERSITY

37TH AND P STREETS, NW, WASHINGTON, DC 20057 • ADMISSIONS: 202-687-3600 • FAX: 202-687-5084
FINANCIAL AID: 202-687-4547 • WEBSITE: WWW.GEORGETOWN.EDU

Ratings
Quality of Life: 85   **Academic:** 93   **Admissions:** 98   **Financial Aid:** 94

Academics

It's impossible to separate the virtues of a Georgetown education with the opportunities afforded by the school's Washington, DC, location. The "out-of-this-world" internship opportunities include positions at "all kinds of businesses and law firms"; reports one seasoned senior, a considerable number of students "have a congressional internship during their time at Georgetown." Washington also provides a never-ending source of amazing faculty; boasts another senior, "I've had a 25-person class with Donna Brazile, a 50-person class with Madeleine Albright, and a

> **SURVEY SAYS . . .**
> Students love Washington, DC
> Great off-campus food
> Students are happy
> Frats and sororities are unpopular
> or nonexistent
> Political activism is popular
> Lots of beer drinking

10-person class with Ron Faucheaux (editor of Campaigns and Elections magazine)." In the words of a first-year, "It is not uncommon after class to go back to your room, turn on CNN or MSNBC, and see your professor." With so many power brokers floating about, "Georgetown is easily the best school for finding a mentor: there are genius Jesuits, serving diplomats, authors, and other luminaries walking about campus every day, not only waiting to be approached, but approaching you." Assures one international political economy major, "even though they are busy, they are always available if you need help." Students point out that "Georgetown is also a great place to come if you want to study anything international or go abroad. Half of the junior class goes abroad, and the school offers or is affiliated with a lot of programs that support direct matriculation into a local university." While best known for its programs in the liberal arts, foreign affairs, language, and nursing, Georgetown, in the words of a senior, "embodies a unique combination of true academic commitment, social and political awareness, rich tradition, a diverse student body, and all the crazy fun of college."

Life

"Georgetown has a great social life," undergrads here agree; the school offers "tons of on- and off-campus parties as well as bars within walking distance." Extracurricular options include numerous "a cappella and theater groups on campus," and students can choose to attend any of the frequent on-campus lectures and readings. And, of course, there's always Hoyas basketball, which enjoys a fanatical following among the student body. Students like to spend free time in Washington, DC, which they hail as "an amazing place to live." The District "has a ton of free museums, exhibits, plays, and concerts." Reports one student, "I have been dancing for free at the Kennedy Center, seen concerts just a few minutes into Pennsylvania Avenue, visited museums (also free), eaten great food throughout DC, volunteered in after-school programs, and gone running along the canal and through the monuments at night. The public transportation in DC makes it easy to go anywhere without a car." Georgetown takes the edge off urban living with a campus that's "isolated by walls and gates…we've got all the fun of the city in a homier atmosphere." Prospective students should take note that "the cost of living in Georgetown as a whole is high, so you're definitely better off either having a job or learning to manage your money fast!"

Student Body

"You hear a lot about 'Joe and Jane Hoya,' the typical preppy types" at Georgetown—and while "there is definitely a strong presence of the rich boarding school students," there are "way more students from public schools of every stripe, from countries ranging from Romania to India to Spain, from all kinds of socioeconomic backgrounds, and with all kinds of interests." Although Georgetown is religiously affiliated, "this is not your typical Catholic university"; there is "lots of diversity across cultural, ethnic, and religious categories." A common thread among students is that they are all "very ambitious and driven. Also, most people tend to have either lived in another country, know more than two languages, or have traveled a lot. In general there's a big interest in learning about diverse cultures." Not surprisingly, most here "are highly political" and "conscious of international affairs." While students' views may differ, a sophomore promises, "There is a place for everyone on campus."

ADMISSIONS

Very important factors considered include: Character/personal qualities, class rank, essays, recommendations, secondary school record, standardized test scores, talent/ability. *Important factors considered include:* Extracurricular activities, interview, volunteer work. *Other factors considered include:* Alumni/ae relation, geographical residence, minority status, state residency, work experience. SAT Reasoning or ACT required. SAT Subject Tests recommended. TOEFL required of all international applicants. High school diploma is required, and GED is accepted. *Academic units required:* 4 English, 2 math, 2 science, 2 foreign language, 2 social studies, 2 history. *Academic units recommended:* 4 English, 4 math, 4 science (1 science lab), 4 foreign language, 4 social studies.

The Inside Word

It was always tough to get admitted to Georgetown, but in the early 1980s Patrick Ewing and the Hoyas created a basketball sensation that catapulted the place into position as one of the most selective universities in the nation. There has been no turning back since. GU gets almost 10 applications for every space in the entering class, and the academic strength of the pool is impressive. Virtually 50 percent of the entire student body took AP courses in high school. Candidates who are wait-listed should hold little hope for an offer of admission; over the past several years Georgetown has taken very few off their lists.

FINANCIAL AID

Students should submit: FAFSA, CSS/Financial Aid PROFILE, noncustodial (divorced/separated) parents' statement, business/farm supplement, tax returns. Regular filing deadline 2/1. The Princeton Review suggests that all financial aid forms be submitted as soon as possible after 1/1. *Need-based scholarships/grants offered:* Pell, SEOG, state scholarships/grants, private scholarships, the school's own gift aid. *Loan aid offered:* FFEL Subsidized Stafford, FFEL Unsubsidized Stafford, FFEL PLUS, Federal Perkins, Federal Nursing. Applicants will be notified of awards on or about 4/1.

FROM THE ADMISSIONS OFFICE

"Georgetown was founded in 1789 by John Carroll, who concurred with his contemporaries Benjamin Franklin and Thomas Jefferson in believing that the success of the young democracy depended upon an educated and virtuous citizenry. Carroll founded the school with the dynamic, Jesuit tradition of education, characterized by humanism and committed to the assumption of responsibility and action. Georgetown is a national and international university, enrolling students from all 50 states and over 100 foreign countries. Undergraduate students are enrolled in one of four undergraduate schools: the College of Arts and Sciences, School of Foreign Service, Georgetown School of Business, and Georgetown School of Nursing and Health Studies. All students share a common liberal arts core and have access to the entire university curriculum."

For even more information on this school, turn to page 487 of the "Stats" section.

GETTYSBURG COLLEGE

ADMISSIONS OFFICE, EISENHOWER HOUSE, GETTYSBURG, PA 17325-1484 • ADMISSIONS: 717-337-6100 • FAX: 717-337-6145
FINANCIAL AID: 717-337-6611 • E-MAIL: ADMISS@GETTYSBURG.EDU • WEBSITE: WWW.GETTYSBURG.EDU

Ratings
Quality of Life: 87   Academic: 91   Admissions: 94   Financial Aid: 98

Academics

"By far, the greatest strength of Gettysburg College is the small class size maintained in practically every subject and level," say students at this small southern Pennsylvania school. It's the small details that distinguish the Gettysburg experience for most undergraduates. One student says, "Class time isn't solely in the lecture hall. My classes have occurred at organic farms, state parks, and Chincoteague and Assateague Islands. They truly mean it when they chal-

> **SURVEY SAYS . . .**
> Small classes
> Lab facilities are great
> Great library
> Frats and sororities dominate social scene
> Lots of beer drinking

lenge you to 'live outside the box' at Gettysburg." Students really appreciate "professors who make a habit out of responding to written papers in a personal way to highlight the strengths and weaknesses of the paper, with suggestions on how to develop the topic for further research. Because of the personalized attention received (largely due to the small classes and dedication of faculty), it is almost impossible for a student not to succeed here." Students also appreciate "the academic honor code [that] allows students the ability to take unproctored tests in the location of their choice and allows students the freedom to leave their laptops and other belongings alone in the library, college union building, dining hall, and dorm without having to worry about theft." Strong programs include the sciences, music, history, psychology, and business. Gettysburg "has a very popular abroad program that is easy to do, with programs in a wide variety of locations."

Life

"There is a lot to do on campus and off" at Gettysburg College, undergraduates report. One student reports, "You can take in a movie at the historic Majestic Theater or walk around the battlefields on the outskirts of campus. In the spring there are always tourists and reenactors walking the streets of town; it's like going to school in a living history museum, which I love." Underclassmen are most often drawn to the school's popular fraternity parties, which "are open to anyone on campus," although male underclassmen have a better chance of getting in if they arrive with one or more females. While many students love the Greek scene, others warn that "the parties get old quickly." To provide alternatives, the school "really tries to promote other activities on campus besides drinking on weekends. They show recent movies; have popular bands, such as Good Charlotte, come to campus; host popular comedians; [and] have dance parties in the on-campus nightclub." Many students participate in community service. One student says, "Community service is big, not surprising considering the great resources of the Center for Public Service. Students travel to places like Nicaragua, Native American reservations, Birmingham, Alabama, New York City, the Chesapeake Bay, and other places for community service-learning trips." Hometown Gettysburg, while small, offers many tourist attractions (outlet malls, miniature golf, battlefields) as well as "the most consistent display of beautiful sunsets year-round. You have never seen a sunset until you have witnessed one from the battlefields, which connect to campus."

Student Body

The "Gettysburg cliché" is the "J. Crew U. student: white, upper- or upper-middle class, who joins a sorority or a fraternity." According to students, there is some truth to the cliché. "I never expected to see so many Range Rovers and BMWs on a college campus," writes one nonplussed undergraduate, but adds, "Things have changed a bit in the past two years as they've raised the admissions standards." Now students "don't feel as overwhelmed by Abercrombie in the dining hall anymore." Most undergraduates "are involved on campus in the Greek life system, clubs, athletics, etc." There's a large jock group. Politically, students are very conservative. "Maybe this is selfish," writes one undergraduate, "but I think there should be more than just conservatives at the school. I think the school could improve with a little more diversity of thought and self-expression."

ADMISSIONS

Very important factors considered include: Class rank, recommendations, secondary school record. *Important factors considered include:* Character/personal qualities, essays, extracurricular activities, interview, standardized test scores, talent/ability, volunteer work. *Other factors considered include:* Alumni/ae relation, geographical residence, minority status, work experience. SAT Reasoning or ACT required. TOEFL required of all international applicants. High school diploma is required, and GED is accepted. *Academic units required:* 4 English, 3 math, 3 science (3 science lab), 3 foreign language, 3 social studies, 3 history. *Academic units recommended:* 4 English, 4 math, 4 science (4 science lab), 4 foreign language, 4 social studies, 4 history.

The Inside Word

Gettysburg's small size definitely allows for a more personal approach to admission. The admissions committee puts a lot of energy into matchmaking, and last year it paid off with its largest freshman class in its history. Most Gettysburg types are good students and also match up well with competitor colleges, which makes this accomplishment even more laudable. Look for a somewhat more selective profile as a result.

FINANCIAL AID

Students should submit: FAFSA, CSS/Financial Aid PROFILE, noncustodial (divorced/separated) parents' statement, business/farm supplement. The Princeton Review suggests that all financial aid forms be submitted as soon as possible after 1/1. *Need-based scholarships/grants offered:* Pell, SEOG, state scholarships/grants, private scholarships, the school's own gift aid. *Loan aid offered:* FFEL Subsidized Stafford, FFEL Unsubsidized Stafford, FFEL PLUS, Federal Perkins, college/university loans from institutional funds. Applicants will be notified of awards on or about 3/30. Federal Work-study Program available. Institutional employment available. Off-campus job opportunities are good.

FROM THE ADMISSIONS OFFICE

"Four major goals of Gettysburg College to best prepare students to enter the twenty-first century, include: first, to accelerate the intellectual development of our first-year students by integrating them more quickly into the intellectual life of the campus; second, to use interdisciplinary courses combining the intellectual approaches of various fields; third, to encourage students to develop an international perspective through course work, study abroad, association with international faculty, and a variety of extracurricular activities; and fourth, to encourage students to develop (1) a capacity for independent study by ensuring that all students work closely with individual faculty members on an extensive project during their undergraduate years and (2) the ability to work with their peers by making the small group a central feature in college life."

For even more information on this school, turn to page 488 of the "Stats" section.

Gordon College

255 Grapevine Road, Wenham, MA 01984-1899 • Admissions: 866-464-6736 • Fax: 978-867-4682
E-mail: admissions@hope.gordon.edu • Website: www.gordon.edu

Ratings
Quality of Life: 96   **Academic:** 87   **Admissions:** 88   **Financial Aid:** 72

Academics

Gordon College is a nondenominational Christian liberal arts school that, according to its mission statement, "strives to graduate men and women distinguished by intellectual maturity and Christian character, committed to a lifestyle of service, and prepared for leadership roles worldwide." According to one student, "as far as Christian colleges go, Gordon puts the 'liberal' back into a 'liberal arts' education. The professors and student body are thinkers as well as people of faith." Students rave about the "life-changing" La Vida outdoor education requirement, which is a two-week adventure in Adirondack State Park. Additionally, the school's "excellent" Gordon-at-Oxford program allows students to spend a year studying abroad in Oxford, England. GC undergrads insist that "Gordon is not a 'soft' school—you can be a straight-A student in high school and still find Gordon sufficiently challenging and exciting." Another student adds, "The academic load is pretty demanding, but totally doable. The professors are incredible and are open to using different methods of teaching besides your standard boring lecture." Gordon's administration "is very efficiently run and does quite a good job balancing fund-raising with quality of life/academic experience for students." However, a few students did point out that the "science labs and library could stand some improvement."

> **SURVEY SAYS . . .**
> *Campus feels safe*
> *Frats and sororities are unpopular*
> *or nonexistent*
> *Very little drug use*

Life

"The location of Gordon is great," says one student. "I love the hometown New England feel, complemented by the city of Boston only 30 minutes away." The campus "is surrounded by woods, but minutes away from town, and a short drive to shopping and groceries. Salem is only ten minutes away, as is Beverly. Both offer different shops and entertainment." Thanks to "the Campus Events Council, intramural sports, residence hall activities, and guest speakers, there's never a shortage of things to see or do." All of these activities center on the school's "no-tolerance for drugs and alcohol policy that really aids in the building of this community." The campus also has a large number of ministries and Bible study groups. In warmer months, students appreciate the fact that "Gordon is two miles from the ocean and local beaches" of the Massachusetts North Shore. For fun, most students enjoy "hanging out, watching movies, going out to the movies, going out to dinner, heading to Boston, playing Laser Tag™, swing dancing (very popular and very fun), going to plays, going to the beach, attending sports games, playing video games, and ringing the large bell on campus to annoy everyone." Several students say, "It's difficult to do anything off campus if you don't have a car. You NEED a car!!" How else will you "go apple picking, go on a weekend ski trip, and go into Boston to visit a museum or aquarium?"

Student Body

The GC student body is primarily made up of "white, middle-class Christians," though it was recently recognized for its efforts in recruiting ethnic minorities. Students describe themselves as "intelligent, spiritual, curious, ambitious, friendly, sociable, and fun loving." There is "a growing number of minority and international students, who are very integrated life on campus. Students are also warmly welcoming toward missionary kids and others from different backgrounds." What Gordon lacks in ethnic diversity it makes up for in the diversity of student interests and personalities. "Gordon has lots of little social subgroups," says one student. "Often these groups arise by department or major." Another student adds, "There's some great artistic underground here if you look for it—awesome theater people, writers, and socially awkward artists." GC students typically "go to the majority of their classes, and participate in at least one extracurricular activity whether it is a sport, ministry, or club." One undergrad notes that students "sometimes can be too conservative, but the liberals on campus make their voices heard as well."

ADMISSIONS

Very important factors considered include: Character/personal qualities, essays, interview, recommendations, religious affiliation/commitment, secondary school record, standardized test scores. *Important factors considered include:* Class rank, extracurricular activities. *Other factors considered include:* Alumni/ae relation, minority status, talent/ability, volunteer work, work experience. SAT Reasoning or SAT Subject Tests required. TOEFL required of all international applicants. High school diploma is required, and GED is accepted. *Academic units required:* 4 English, 2 math, 2 science (1 science lab), 2 foreign language, 2 social studies, 5 academic electives. *Academic units recommended:* 4 English, 3 math, 3 science (3 science lab), 4 foreign language, 3 social studies, 5 academic electives.

The Inside Word

Interviews are required at Gordon, presumably so admissions officers can gauge candidates' readiness for the rigorous curriculum and high level of religious commitment. Students interested in studying social work must meet a second, more rigorous set of admissions requirements in addition to general requirements.

FINANCIAL AID

Students should submit: FAFSA, CSS/Financial Aid PROFILE, state aid form. Regular filing deadline 3/1. The Princeton Review suggests that all financial aid forms be submitted as soon as possible after 1/1. *Need-based scholarships/grants offered:* Pell, SEOG, state scholarships/grants, private scholarships, the school's own gift aid. *Loan aid offered:* FFEL Subsidized Stafford, FFEL Unsubsidized Stafford, FFEL PLUS, Federal Perkins, state loans, college/university loans from institutional funds. Applicants will be notified of awards on a rolling basis beginning on or about 4/15. Federal Work-study Program available. Institutional employment available. Off-campus job opportunities are excellent.

For even more information on this school, turn to page 488 of the "Stats" section.

GOUCHER COLLEGE

1021 DULANEY VALLEY ROAD, BALTIMORE, MD 21204-2794 • ADMISSIONS: 410-337-6100
FAX: 410-337-6354 • FINANCIAL AID: 410-337-6141 • E-MAIL: ADMISSIONS@GOUCHER.EDU • WEBSITE: WWW.GOUCHER.EDU

Ratings
Quality of Life: 86   **Academic:** 86   **Admissions:** 88   **Financial Aid:** 77

Academics

"Despite its practically unknown name in the college world," Goucher College offers "rigorous but manageable academics" to its small, dedicated student body. Undergraduates at this Baltimore school extol its "balance of academics, clubs/activities, and social events. It's a great place to learn," in part because students can receive so much personal attention from their professors. "Leaders are nurtured at Goucher, and it's difficult to just slip by unnoticed. One has to work to be ignored," writes one student. Psychology and English are the most popular programs, collectively claiming about one-quarter of the student body. Pre-meds rate the biology department favorably, while performing artists give the dance program high grades. Students report that professors "are the best. They are easily accessible, knowledgeable, and willing to help you better yourself." Administrators "are extremely accessible, as well, and want to have direct contact with the students. How many college presidents have open hours so students can come in and chat?" Goucher is also proud of its study abroad program. The college "fosters an international/worldly view in students by requiring [them] to study abroad or [take] an internship." Students also love the Service Learning Program, which provides "so many opportunities to serve the community and make a difference in the world."

Life

"Everyone talks about the 'Goucher Bubble,'" students say, "and it's completely true that people just hang out on campus at the Gopher Hole (the campus coffeehouse) or hang out in the dorms. Although Goucher is very close to a big city and a 10-to-15-minute walk to town, people don't leave campus that much." Some students get "really involved on campus with many different clubs, organizations, and jobs," while others "tend to strive for social consciousness" by immersing themselves in political causes. Other students "just hang out with friends and play video games and poker." However, they don't party hard—at least not on campus. Students tell us that "if you are looking for a party school as seen on MTV and in the movies, this isn't it. If you want to go to a great school for learning and interesting people, Goucher is it." Fortunately, students can head to Towson University, a little over a mile down the road, when they seek a more party-oriented student body. They can also head into Towson itself, an upscale, northern enclave of Baltimore that "offers movie theaters, a four-story mall, restaurants, and other stores. It's a fun place to escape to." The Collegetown Shuttle bus connects Baltimore's major college campuses, giving students access to most areas of the city; even so, many students insist that a car is a necessity. One student cautions, "If you have a car, all of Baltimore is your playground. If you don't, I hope you like hanging out with your friends in your dorm room."

Student Body

Goucher students are "generally the kids who were 'outside the box' in high school, and they all fit together well at Goucher. The atypical students are the ones who would be perceived as 'typical' anywhere else." Undergraduates tend to break off into cliques defined either by major or by "type," for example, "punky kids, quirky kids, dancers, environmentalists, etc." One student says, "Different students have hardly any problems mixing together in social and academic situations," and overall students feel that "Goucher is amazing because it has such a strong community. Everyone knows everyone and loves it." Students tend to be "extremely liberal and want to be politically aware." One undergraduate observes, "We see ourselves as tolerant and open-minded, but when students express views that are not liberal, they are not always welcomed." Men constitute a minority at this former all women's college.

ADMISSIONS

Very important factors considered include: Recommendations, secondary school record. *Important factors considered include:* Essays, extracurricular activities, standardized test scores, talent/ability. *Other factors considered include:* Alumni/ae relation, character/personal qualities, class rank, interview, volunteer work, work experience. SAT Reasoning or ACT required. TOEFL required of all international applicants. High school diploma is required, and GED is accepted. *Academic units required:* 4 English, 3 math, 2 science (2 science lab), 2 foreign language, 2 social studies. *Academic units recommended:* 3 social studies.

The Inside Word

Goucher is in serious battle for the students to which it is best-suited and often fills the role of safety to some of the region's strongest colleges. Although the college is a solid choice in its own right, its admissions profile reflects modest competitiveness as a result of these circumstances.

FINANCIAL AID

Students should submit: FAFSA, CSS/Financial Aid PROFILE, noncustodial (divorced/separated) parents' statement, business/farm supplement. Regular filing deadline 2/15. The Princeton Review suggests that all financial aid forms be submitted as soon as possible after 1/1. *Need-based scholarships/grants offered:* Pell, SEOG, state scholarships/grants, private scholarships, the school's own gift aid. *Loan aid offered:* Direct Subsidized Stafford, Direct Unsubsidized Stafford, Direct PLUS, Federal Perkins, college/university loans from institutional funds. Applicants will be notified of awards on or about 4/1.

FROM THE ADMISSIONS OFFICE

"A Goucher liberal arts education aims to prepare students for the real world. The college integrates thought and action, combining a strong liberal arts curriculum with hands-on learning in off-campus settings through internships, fieldwork, study abroad, and independent projects. Students can choose majors in 18 departments and four interdisciplinary areas, or they may design their own individualized program of study. Small classes taught by skilled faculty, strong international studies programs, and research with faculty are other key characteristics. Goucher has impressive resources in technology, including a campus fully wired for access to the Internet and the World Wide Web. Goucher's merit scholarship program is one of the top programs in the nation, offering strong students awards ranging from partial tuition to full tuition plus room and board."

For even more information on this school, turn to page 489 of the "Stats" section.

GROVE CITY COLLEGE

100 CAMPUS DRIVE, GROVE CITY, PA 16127-2104 • ADMISSIONS: 724-458-2100 • FAX: 724-458-3395
FINANCIAL AID: 724-458-2163 • E-MAIL: ADMISSIONS@GCC.EDU • WEBSITE: WWW.GCC.EDU

Ratings
Quality of Life: 77   **Academic:** 84   **Admissions:** 95   **Financial Aid:** 62

Academics

The Grove City College (GCC) environment allows students to be "continually challenged to learn more—more about my field of studies, more about the world around me, more about my faith, and more about myself." This "Ivy League school in disguise" runs according to a "Christian viewpoint that is refreshing and open-minded." Some students feel that the religious bent makes "almost every course become in some way, shape, or form a theology course." One respondent feels that the school's "pride in a 'rigorous curriculum' translates into standards that sometimes border on the ridiculous." Amid the challenging course work, students work with professors who are "inconceivably intelligent and brilliant in their fields" and "not afraid to stand up for liberty and truth." Undergraduates feel personally supported by the faculty, noting that instructors "go out of their way to help students understand material without robbing them of the learning experience." Students embrace their core curriculum, eager to "dabble in everything from physics to Spanish to philosophy, no matter what your major." Several students think "it seems that faculty and students mesh well, while the administration isolates itself." Reportedly, students and professors alike "voice their displeasure concerning administrative direction." On the one hand, a common sentiment goes, "Administration needs to get with the times and realize we're big boys and big girls and we can handle ourselves." On the other hand, one student writes, "Where else can you watch the president of the college team up with faculty members for a basketball game against students?" In the end, the school succeeds in "giving support to students in many ways, which lightens the academic load."

> **SURVEY SAYS . . .**
> Small classes
> Students are friendly
> Diversity lacking on campus
> Students are very religious
> Campus feels safe
> Low cost of living
> Intramural sports are popular
> Very little drug use

Life

A defining factor of Grove is the "definite focus on God." That means "Calvin and Luther are generally on the tip of the tongue here," and "we do have parties, just minus the alcohol." Employing a well-used double negative, one student writes "the party scene isn't nonexistent," but typically, students partake in "snowball fights, movie nights, Bible study, intermural bowling, ice cream socials, square dancing, lots of long conversations," and other activities that "don't involve breaking the law." Some students think that Greeks don't do much besides "wear matching sweatshirts," but others say, "Greek life gives variety, friendship, and fun that the campus does not offer." The anti-Greek faction goes so far as to say that fraternities and sororities are "the cause of all drinking and sex that goes on." "Intervisitation," that fated time when men and women are allowed to be in the same residences at the same time, means that "the freshmen dorms get loud and stay loud until 12:45 A.M." That early collegiate bedtime hints at the "atmosphere bordering on repressive at times." All told, certain students remark suggestively, "Don't let the Norman Rockwell facade fool you."

Student Body

Students offer three basic descriptions of TGs, or "typical Grovers." The first camp, "the home-schooled, very sheltered kids who go home every weekend and are engaged by sophomore year," give the campus its reputation, but many students will tell you that students are not as marriage-obsessed as outsiders believe. These kids are the ones "who would ask, 'What are hallucinogens?'" one student explains. Another group comprises "the normal, Nalgene bottle–carrying, Christian summer camp–working, service-oriented students." The leftovers are those who "slack off, drink, and get off campus." In general, most undergrads are "white, suburban, Christian Republicans." Many students point out, "We're diverse in our Christian denominations, but not our ethnicities," to the degree that "there are more amputees than minorities on this campus." In this "homogenous group," "there are a few gays/lesbians, and they probably don't fit in well." Reportedly, atypical students are "acknowledged as individuals and accepted for [whom] they are." The cumulative effect is "so many people who enjoy being around each other so much."

ADMISSIONS

Very important factors considered include: Character/personal qualities, essays, extracurricular activities, interview, religious affiliation/commitment, secondary school record, standardized test scores. *Important factors considered include:* Recommendations, talent/ability. *Other factors considered include:* Alumni/ae relation, class rank, geographical residence, minority status, state residency, volunteer work, work experience. SAT Reasoning or ACT required. TOEFL required of all international applicants. High school diploma is required, and GED is accepted. *Academic units recommended:* 4 English, 3 math, 3 science (2 science lab), 3 foreign language, 2 social studies, 2 history.

The Inside Word

If you're looking for a northeastern college with a Christian orientation, Grove City is a pretty good choice, but it's getting tougher to get in as we speak. Applications and standards are on the rise, and the college is fast becoming the newest addition to the lofty realm of the highly selective. Minorities are in short supply and will encounter a somewhat friendlier admissions process. All students should definitely follow the college's recommendation and interview.

FINANCIAL AID

Students should submit: Institution's own financial aid form, state aid form. Regular filing deadline 4/15. The Princeton Review suggests that all financial aid forms be submitted as soon as possible after 1/1. *Need-based scholarships/grants offered:* State scholarships/grants, private scholarships, the school's own gift aid. *Loan aid offered:* Private, alternative loans. Applicants will be notified of awards on a rolling basis beginning on or about 3/15. Institutional employment available. Off-campus job opportunities are good.

FROM THE ADMISSIONS OFFICE

"A good college education doesn't have to cost a fortune. For decades, Grove City College has offered a quality education at costs among the lowest nationally. Since the 1990s, increased national academic acclaim has come to Grove City College. Grove City College is a place where professors teach. You will not see graduate assistants or teacher's aides in the classroom. Our professors are also active in the total life of the campus. More than 100 student organizations on campus afford opportunity for a wide variety of cocurricular activities. Outstanding scholars and leaders in education, science, and international affairs visit the campus each year. The environment at GCC is friendly, secure, and dedicated to high standards. Character-building is emphasized and traditional Christian values are supported."

For even more information on this school, turn to page 489 of the "Stats" section.

HAMILTON COLLEGE

198 COLLEGE HILL ROAD, CLINTON, NY 13323 • ADMISSIONS: 800-843-2655 • FAX: 315-859-4457
FINANCIAL AID: 800-859-4413 • E-MAIL: ADMISSION@HAMILTON.EDU • WEBSITE: WWW.HAMILTON.EDU

Ratings
Quality of Life: 74   Academic: 95   Admissions: 95   Financial Aid: 95

Academics

According to a studious junior, Hamilton affords a "gruel-ing but fulfilling education" in a "rigorous yet nurturing" environment. The college "really produces great writers and great thinkers," another student comments, and sever-al respondents highlight the strength of the school's writ-ing program, designed to ensure that graduates can wield the pen as effectively as the institution's namesake,

> **SURVEY SAYS . . .**
> *Small classes*
> *Great library*
> *Lots of beer drinking*
> *Hard liquor is popular*

Alexander Hamilton. The college's "very helpful and available" professors conduct classes in a "hands-on" manner and hold students to "very high standards." Luckily, instructors "really communicate the material well" and are always "there for you if you have a problem." The faculty has a reputation for being "eager to meet with students to help prepare for exams or write papers." They also develop camaraderie with their wards: "Only at Hamilton can you go to the pub and have a beer with your professor." Other students concur: "Your teacher is your best friend," and "professors are constantly having entire classes over for dinner." The small classes "concentrate on discussion," which means "you are expected to participate." A music major waxes, "I adore the fact that we call all the professors in our department by their first names." The administra-tion is said to be "exceedingly accessible" as well as "concerned with student opinion and open to suggestions." Hamilton's president holds a weekly "open hour" to meet with students, and most "administrators know stu-dent names." In this supportive atmosphere, students aver that "if you have a vision, Hamilton will provide the funding and assistance to [help you] achieve your goals."

Life

For students sometimes it seems that life at Hamilton consists of "nothing but work and alcohol." Students attribute the drinking culture on campus to the fact that "it is always ass-cold winter" in central New York. Although "beer is readily available" and many students say they "drink for fun," a sophomore wants you to know that "drinking isn't compulsory, just common" in Clinton. While some students wish for "more things for people who don't drink to do," others point out "alternatives like movies, dance, theater, comedy, and other low-key activities." Fraternities and sororities are considered "integral" to Hamilton social life, and many stu-dents agree that things "would be better if the Greeks still had houses." Students also venture off campus in search of a colder beer. "Three words: The Village Tavern," a senior writes, referring to one of the two bars in town and the scene of many a Hamilton student's fond college memories. Students report that their adopted hometown of Clinton "is the textbook definition of boring," but nonetheless wish for improved town-gown relations. One student notes, "Being isolated on 'the Hill' can sometimes warp students' perception of the real world."

Student Body

A large number of respondents share the sentiment that "a small percentage of the students account for the Hamilton image of rich, white, and preppy." While the Greek population may be the most visible and "some-times it seems like everyone is from old-money Greenwich," students emphasize that other types do coexist in Clinton. In general, "the majority of people are friendly, open-minded, and intelligent," and "most people smile, even if they don't know you," contributing to a "nice sense of community." Currently, students note the decid-edly "homogeneous population" when it comes to race and ethnicity. One junior tells us, "I'm not sure that minorities feel welcome." But other students observe, "Hamilton's diversity is increasing. It has come a long way in a few years." According to a senior, "Even though Hamilton is sort of über-whitey land, it's clear that admissions and the administration are trying very hard to diversify the campus."

ADMISSIONS

Very important factors considered include: Class rank, recommendations, secondary school record. *Important factors considered include:* Character/personal qualities, essays, extracurricular activities, interview, minority status, standardized test scores. *Other factors considered include:* Alumni/ae relation, geographical residence, talent/ability, volunteer work, work experience. TOEFL required of all international applicants. High school diploma or equivalent is not required. *Academic units recommended:* 4 English, 3 math, 3 science, 3 foreign language, 3 social studies.

The Inside Word

Gaining admission to Hamilton is difficult and would be more so if the college didn't lose many of its shared applicants to competitor schools. The college's position as a popular safety for the top tier of northeastern colleges has always benefited the quality of its applicant pool, but it translates into a tough fight when it comes to getting admits to enroll. Although selectivity has risen significantly of late, Hamilton remains in the position of losing many of its best candidates to other, more prestigious schools. Students who view Hamilton as their first-choice college should definitely make it plain to the admissions committee—such news can often be influential, especially under circumstances like those mentioned here.

FINANCIAL AID

Students should submit: FAFSA, institution's own financial aid form, CSS/Financial Aid PROFILE, state aid form, noncustodial (divorced/separated) parents' statement, business/farm supplement. Regular filing deadline 1/1. The Princeton Review suggests that all financial aid forms be submitted as soon as possible after 1/1. *Need-based scholarships/grants offered:* Pell, SEOG, state scholarships/grants, private scholarships, the school's own gift aid. *Loan aid offered:* FFEL Subsidized Stafford, FFEL Unsubsidized Stafford, FFEL PLUS, Federal Perkins, college/university loans from institutional funds. Applicants will be notified of awards on or about 4/1. Federal Work-study Program available. Institutional employment available.

FROM THE ADMISSIONS OFFICE

"One of Hamilton's most important characteristics is the exceptional interaction that takes place between students and faculty members. Whether in class or out, they work together, challenging one another to excel. Academic life at Hamilton is rigorous, and emerging from that rigor is a community spirit based on common commitment. It binds together student and teacher and stimulates self-motivation, thus making the learning process not only more productive but also more enjoyable and satisfying. Hamilton's Bristol Scholars program is merit-based, offering ten half-tuition scholarships. Both the Bristol and the need-based Schambach scholars program also offer special research opportunities with faculty on campus. National merit finalists also receive $2,000 a year."

For even more information on this school, turn to page 490 of the "Stats" section.

HAMPSHIRE COLLEGE

ADMISSIONS OFFICE, 893 WEST STREET, AMHERST, MA 01002 • ADMISSIONS: 413-559-5471
FAX: 413-559-5631 • FINANCIAL AID: 413-559-5484 • E-MAIL: ADMISSIONS@HAMPSHIRE.EDU • WEBSITE: WWW.HAMPSHIRE.EDU

Ratings
Quality of Life: 80   Academic: 88   Admissions: 87   Financial Aid: 92

Academics

Independent study and self-designed majors are the norm at Hampshire College, a small Pioneer Valley liberal arts school that "takes you up on your wager that all you need is academic freedom." Hampshire freshmen must complete the recently added First Year Program. ("Actual academic requirements for this year's freshman class have turned Hampshire mainstream," gripes one old-timer.) After that, students are pretty much on their own, although they must complete a concentration and an advanced study project. Most students meet the last two requirements through curricula of their own choosing. "Academically, Hampshire is

> **SURVEY SAYS . . .**
> *Small classes*
> *No one cheats*
> *Students aren't religious*
> *Intercollegiate sports are unpopular*
> *or nonexistent*
> *Frats and sororities are unpopular*
> *or nonexistent*
> *Political activism is popular*

a place where you can do whatever you want, as long as you are able to find a few professors who are willing to work with you on your self-constructed major," explains one student. Although the school is small, students' options are broadened considerably by Hampshire's participation in the Five-College Consortium, which allows students to cross-register at Amherst, Smith, University of Massachusetts, and Mount Holyoke. Some here warn that "Hampshire's academic structure is not for everyone. It's very well suited for people who have a strong idea of what they would like to study, but don't want to squeeze their interests into the confines of traditional majors. It's also good for people who want to explore several interests. However, if you're easily distracted and need someone to point you in a clear, well-defined direction, then Hampshire is probably not the place for you."

Life

"There's not much centralized activity" at Hampshire College, students here agree. As one student put it, "Everything is pretty laid-back and easygoing. People are really into the work they are doing, and they spend a lot of time thinking about that and talking to others about it." While campus is usually quiet, the other four area colleges and the towns of Amherst and Northampton offer all the action most students want. "If you're bored, it's your own fault," writes one undergrad. "The Pioneer Valley is a happening little place. Amherst and Northampton are both funky little college towns with lots to do in nice weather. There's excellent shopping at numerous vintage stores. The Pearl Street nightclub has cheap concerts every week. Ani DiFranco, Carrot Top, BB King, and Sonic Youth have been to Northampton at least once, to name a few." Furthermore, "if you want to escape, you can do that too. There are miles and miles of hiking trails within walking distance of campus, as well as biking trails. I knew that I wasn't going to have a car, so the free bus system was a humongous plus." Activity reaches its lowest ebb "during the long, hard winters." "That's when we start smoking marijuana," explains one student. Campus movies—"Indie, hip-hop, action, anime, classic low camp; we tend to like movies we can laugh with (or at least at)"—are also very popular.

Student Body

The "talented, artistic, quixotic, eccentric, and highly motivated" undergrads of Hampshire include a large group of "those kids in elementary school who were caught trying to dissect the pencil sharpener during math class. We're horrible at following rules." While students like to regard themselves as entirely unique, there is "definitely a stereotype of the pot-smoking, Phish-loving, hippie activist kid at Hampshire, and for the most part, I would say it's true." Critics might accuse these students of being self-absorbed; "I think that's true," agrees one undergrad. "We all spend a ridiculous amount of time thinking about ourselves and what we do, which makes us an incredibly self-aware (if sometimes egocentric) group of people." Politically, "Hampshire students are ultra-liberal. While many would claim that we are an open-minded community because all kinds of lifestyles and ethnic groups are accepted, just try bringing in a conservative speaker to campus, and students will be there quicker than the lifespan of a Hollywood marriage to protest, disrupt, and cause mayhem."

Students are proud to report that Hampshire is extremely GLBT-friendly.

ADMISSIONS

Very important factors considered include: Essays, recommendations, secondary school record. *Important factors considered include:* Character/personal qualities, extracurricular activities, talent/ability. *Other factors considered include:* Alumni/ae relation, class rank, interview, minority status, standardized test scores, volunteer work, work experience. TOEFL required of all international applicants. High school diploma or equivalent is not required. *Academic units recommended:* 4 English, 4 math, 4 science (2 science lab), 3 foreign language, 2 social studies, 2 history.

The Inside Word

Don Quixote would be a fairly solid candidate for admission to Hampshire. The admissions committee (and it really is one, unlike at many colleges) looks to identify thinkers, dreamers, and the generally intellectually curious. It is important to have a solid record from high school, but high grades only go so far toward impressing the committee. Those who are denied usually lack self-awareness and are fairly poor communicators. Candidates should expect their essays to come under close scrutiny.

FINANCIAL AID

Students should submit: FAFSA, institution's own financial aid form, CSS/Financial Aid PROFILE, noncustodial (divorced/separated) parents' statement. Regular filing deadline 2/1. The Princeton Review suggests that all financial aid forms be submitted as soon as possible after 1/1. *Need-based scholarships/grants offered:* Pell, SEOG, state scholarships/grants, private scholarships, the school's own gift aid. *Loan aid offered:* Direct Subsidized Stafford, Direct Unsubsidized Stafford, FFEL PLUS, Federal Perkins. Applicants will be notified of awards on or about 4/1. Off-campus job opportunities are good.

FROM THE ADMISSIONS OFFICE

"Students tell us they like our application. It is less derivative and more open-ended than most. Rather than assigning an essay topic, we ask to learn more about you as an individual and invite your ideas. Instead of just asking for lists of activities, we ask you how those activities (and academic or other endeavors) have shown some of the traits that lead to success at Hampshire (initiative, independence, persistence, for example). This approach parallels the work you will do at Hampshire, defining the questions you will ask and the courses and experiences that will help you to answer them, and integrating your interests."

For even more information on this school, turn to page 490 of the "Stats" section.

HARTWICK COLLEGE

PO Box 4020, Oneonta, NY 13820-4020 • Admissions: 888-427-8925 • Fax: 607-431-4138
E-mail: admissions@hartwick.edu • Website: www.hartwick.edu

Ratings
Quality of Life: 75   **Academic:** 83   **Admissions:** 74   **Financial Aid:** 89

Academics

For a small school, Hartwick College offers a surprisingly wide selection of both typical and unique programs. Students praise the school's English, education, nursing, music, management, and biology programs—all pretty standard fare at small liberal arts schools. Most small

> **SURVEY SAYS . . .**
> *Small classes*
> *Lots of beer drinking*

schools, however, don't also have a "920-acre plot of land with a huge lake and woods and cabins" that serves as a natural laboratory to facilitate environmental studies. And not every small school has an observatory to enhance its astronomy program. Did we also happen to mention the "incredible international J-term program, in which the entire campus basically leaves for a month for study around the world"? At Hartwick, undergrads enjoy all of these big-school amenities in the context of "a close-knit community. Students, staff, faculty, and professors come together to create a comfortable, safe, and healthy environment." The curriculum at Hatwick includes "a heavy stress on liberal arts, meaning that the college pushes you to take a little bit of everything so you can be a well-rounded student and person. The idea behind it is that you can broaden your horizons and [it can] possibly introduce you to something that you could study for a major." Still on the fence? Perhaps the fact that "laptops are included in the cost of tuition" will seal the deal.

Life

Hartwick's hillside campus "captivates almost every prospective student with its amazing views of the landscape," and students never lose their love for its beauty, even when they tire of "the incredible and awful number of stairs" they must climb to get to class. The hills must serve as an effective means of exercise, as much of the student body is "fairly athletic, [and] the school takes athletics very seriously," fielding excellent women's water polo and field hockey teams as well as a strong men's soccer team. Lacrosse and football are also very popular. Hartwick has an active Greek scene as well as strong performing-arts communities. In fact, the campus hosts a variety of activities, and "if you can't find exactly what you want, you can form your own club for whatever you're interested in." Downtown Oneonta "also has its own life, from the nighttime scene to its charming stores, restaurants, and cafés." Cooperstown and the Baseball Hall of Fame "are located nearby and are popular." Occasionally students even hop on a bus to make the four-hour trip to New York City. While most residents live on campus, a lucky few board at Pine Lake "in a lakeside cabin heated by a wood stove. The community at Pine Lake is very environmentally conscious."

Student Body

"There are a lot of different student types" on the Hartwick campus because "the programs that attract the most students—fine arts and medicine—are so different." Students note that "it is really great to see the interaction among all these different types of students who may not have gotten to know one another so well outside of Hartwick College." They add that the interaction is "facilitated by Curriculum XXI," a core curriculum that places students from different departments together in required courses. Many students "are involved in sports, clubs, or theater [and] try to maintain balance in their lives by always keeping some time in the schedule for relaxation and fun." Hartwick hosts "a significant gay and lesbian population, which tends to be accepted [and] is involved in music and theater." The majority of the student population leans to the left, politically.

ADMISSIONS

Very important factors considered include: Class rank, secondary school record. *Important factors considered include:* Essays, extracurricular activities, recommendations. *Other factors considered include:* Alumni/ae relation, character/personal qualities, geographical residence, interview, minority status, standardized test scores, state residency, talent/ability, volunteer work, work experience. TOEFL required of all international applicants. High school diploma is required, and GED is accepted. *Academic units recommended:* 4 English, 3 math, 3 science (2 science lab), 3 foreign language, 2 social studies, 2 history.

The Inside Word

With stiff area competition from both state universities and more prestigious private colleges, Hartwick cannot afford to be as selective as it would like. The school thus offers a great opportunity to underachievers looking to start over at a challenging liberal arts college.

FINANCIAL AID

Students should submit: FAFSA, institution's own financial aid form, state aid form. Regular filing deadline 2/1. The Princeton Review suggests that all financial aid forms be submitted as soon as possible after 1/1. *Need-based scholarships/grants offered:* Pell, SEOG, state scholarships/grants, private scholarships, the school's own gift aid. *Loan aid offered:* FFEL Subsidized Stafford, FFEL Unsubsidized Stafford, FFEL PLUS, Federal Perkins, Federal Nursing, alternative loans. Applicants will be notified of awards on or about 3/15. Federal Work-study Program available. Institutional employment available. Off-campus job opportunities are excellent.

FROM THE ADMISSIONS OFFICE

"The foundation of a Hartwick education is learning by doing. Students are actively involved in learning, whether it's managing a 'virtual' business, engaging in transcultural nursing in Jamaica, or designing and building environmentally friendly houses on the college's Pine Lake campus. Many Hartwick students conduct research with their professors, sometimes resulting in students co-authoring articles for journals in their disciplines. This hands-on learning helps 96 percent of graduating seniors find jobs or enter graduate or professional school within six months of graduation. Another program unique to Hartwick that leads to the high placement rate in MetroLink. This award-winning annual program takes students to New York, Boston, and Washington D.C. for a weeklong experience in 'shadowing' professionals in those cities. Established Metrolink sites include the Boston Red Sox, Saatchi & Saatchi advertising, the Bronx Zoo, the FBI, and the Smithsonian Institution. Recent full-semester internships have included the National Baseball Hall of Fame, the New York Mets, John Hancock Insurance, the U.S. Congress, and many others."

For even more information on this school, turn to page 491 of the "Stats" section.

HARVARD COLLEGE

Info 2 pm ... ...

BYERLY HALL, 8 GARDEN STREET, CAMBRIDGE, MA 02318 • ADMISSIONS: 617-495-1551 • FAX: 617-495-8821
FINANCIAL AID: 617-495-1581 • E-MAIL: COLLEGE@FAS.HARVARD.EDU • WEBSITE: WWW.FAS.HARVARD.EDU

Ratings
Quality of Life: 89   Academic: 96   Admissions: 99   Financial Aid: 95

Academics

"Harvard has distinguished faculty, an extremely accomplished and diverse student body, a million and one extracurriculars, and very generous alumni," a student at this ne plus ultra of American academia explains, adding "What more could you ask for from a school?" What more, indeed? With "unparalleled academics" and "a huge endowment that really allows Harvard to give its students every available resource," Harvard has it all for the aspiring

> **SURVEY SAYS . . .**
> *Registration is a breeze*
> *Great library*
> *Students love Cambridge, MA*
> *Student publications are popular*

intellectual. By throwing in Cambridge and Boston, have we discovered academic nirvana? Close, but not quite. Students complain that "Harvard would benefit from a more active advising system, because a substantial number of courses, including many options for fulfilling requirements under the core program, are offered only once every two years, and many students don't realize this." Even so, the pros far outweigh the cons here. Students especially love the "high number of tutorials and seminars, which are always taught by a professor to a small group of students. They are a great chance to find a mentor." They're also pretty psyched about "interacting with and learning from world experts in almost every subject" and their access to "the best university library in America." Four in five students admitted here attend; that figure pretty much says it all.

Life

"In terms of life in general, there is a lot of studying" at Harvard, "but letting it rule your life means you miss out on so many experiences. The happiest Harvard students are probably those who do their schoolwork but make sure that they have a life outside of it. Otherwise, you never meet people and you stress yourself out." Cambridge and Boston offer plenty of opportunities to get out, but "unfortunately, it's too easy to just get stuck on campus, especially since there's always something going on." Students report that "there is always a cultural show, musical concert, movie showing, information session, graduate-school talk, or colloquium to attend, and the hardest part is balancing all of the work with all the other interesting options on campus." Student clubs and organizations pull double duty, "serving a strong social function; for example, the board of the Gilbert and Sullivan Players has lots of meetings and produces shows, but then we throw about six parties a semester." Undergrads here tell us that "most people do one or two extracurriculars, often pretty intensely. There's not that frantic volunteering for everything that distinguishes the future Harvard student in high school. Once we get in, we skip the resume padders and only do the stuff we're actually into doing." Just about everyone here "lives on campus in the huge suites," and "since we are allowed to have parties with alcohol in our suites, that is a popular social activity."

Student Body

Harvard can handpick top candidates to create the degree of student diversity it wants, so it should come as no surprise that "there is no 'typical' student here. You get someone from West Philly who is the first person in his family to go to college; you have the daughter of a Saudi prince, who will be married to a 60-year-old oil baron after graduation; you get 'development cases' and legacies, with surnames like Kilroy and Lynch; and you get a range of students from blue- to white-collar backgrounds." Explains one student, "The admissions process goes to great lengths to find students that they feel will add to the community at Harvard. As a result, even a simple meal in the dining hall is always an entertaining part of the day, just laughing and goofing off with friends, or even debating about political issues." Undergrads here tend to be "multitalented, overextended, articulate," and "secure in their own fabulousness, so they really don't brag, and they'll totally be happy for you if you do something cool."

ADMISSIONS

Very important factors considered include: Character/personal qualities, extracurricular activities, recommendations, secondary school record, talent/ability. *Important factors considered include:* Class rank, essays, interview, standardized test scores. *Other factors considered include:* Alumni/ae relation, geographical residence, minority status, volunteer work, work experience. SAT Reasoning or ACT required. High school diploma or equivalent is not required. *Academic units recommended:* 4 English, 4 math, 4 science, 4 foreign language.

The Inside Word

It just doesn't get any tougher than this. Candidates to Harvard face dual obstacles—an awe-inspiring applicant pool and, as a result, admissions standards that defy explanation in quantifiable terms. Harvard denies admission to the vast majority, and virtually all of them are top students. It all boils down to splitting hairs, which is quite hard to explain and even harder for candidates to understand. Rather than being as detailed and direct as possible about the selection process and criteria, Harvard keeps things close to the vest—before, during, and after. They even refuse to admit that being from South Dakota is an advantage. Thus the admissions process does more to intimidate candidates than to empower them. Moving to a common application seemed to be a small step in the right direction, but with the current explosion of early decision applicants and a super-high yield of enrollees, things are not likely to change dramatically.

FINANCIAL AID

Students should submit: FAFSA, CSS/Financial Aid PROFILE, noncustodial (divorced/separated) parents' statement, business/farm supplement, tax returns. The Princeton Review suggests that all financial aid forms be submitted as soon as possible after 1/1. *Need-based scholarships/grants offered:* Pell, SEOG, state scholarships/grants, private scholarships, the school's own gift aid. *Loan aid offered:* Direct Subsidized Stafford, Direct Unsubsidized Stafford, Direct PLUS, Federal Perkins, state loans, college/university loans from institutional funds. Applicants will be notified of awards on or about 4/1. Federal Work-study Program available. Institutional employment available. Off-campus job opportunities are excellent.

FROM THE ADMISSIONS OFFICE

"The admissions committee looks for energy, ambition, and the capacity to make the most of opportunities. Academic ability and preparation are important, and so is intellectual curiosity—but many of the strongest applicants have significant nonacademic interests and accomplishments as well. There is no formula for admission, and applicants are considered carefully, with attention to future promise."

For even more information on this school, turn to page 491 of the "Stats" section.

HAVERFORD COLLEGE

370 LANCASTER AVENUE, HAVERFORD, PA 19041 • ADMISSIONS: 610-896-1350 • FAX: 610-896-1338
FINANCIAL AID: 610-896-1350 • E-MAIL: ADMITME@HAVERFORD.EDU • WEBSITE: WWW.HAVERFORD.EDU

Ratings
Quality of Life: 98   **Academic:** 98   **Admissions:** 97   **Financial Aid:** 80

Academics

Haverford College "is the quintessence of the liberal arts experience: superb academics with an emphasis on teacher/student interaction." Originally a Quaker school, Haverford has "never forgotten its Quaker roots" and accordingly "is a community committed to the ideals of taking responsibility for your actions." This is a "high-pressure academic environment" but also "cooperative and nonthreatening." Students warn, "The sciences and math here are hard core; the humanities are somewhat less challenging," though "professors who are brilliant people and who truly care about their students" are there to ensure

> **SURVEY SAYS . . .**
> *Small classes*
> *No one cheats*
> *Lab facilities are great*
> *Students are friendly*
> *Campus feels safe*
> *Students are happy*
> *Frats and sororities are unpopular or nonexistent*

undergraduates' success. Haverford's Honor Code plays a prominent role in fostering a sense of unity; "the honor code here is amazing; it promotes a lot of trust and freedom in the community, which the students love," explains one undergrad. Students receive the red carpet treatment from the moment they arrive; "Haverford knows how to take care of freshmen," explains one undergrad. "When you come here, you get Customs People (like RAs, except cooler), Honor Code Orienteers, an Upper Class Advisor, Peer Awareness Facilitators, a faculty advisor, and a dean. So there are a million people whom you can go to for help and advisement." For those students with wanderlust, "Our study abroad office is excellent! I'm studying at the London School of Economics this year thanks to my accessible, helpful, and alarmingly organized study abroad dean." Students speak in similarly glowing terms about the rest of the administration, noting also the large degree of autonomy afforded them in running the school. Explains one student, "In terms of the administrators, Haverford is mostly run by the students. We start our own organizations. We allocate where the Student Council funds go."

Life

Haverford's rigorous curriculum means that "during the week, work pretty much dominates everything. Even if, by luck, you do not have work to do, all of your friends do, so you are pretty much bound to stay in the dorm." Students unwind on weekends, enjoying "a lot of activities, like dances, plays, concerts, and musicals. Last weekend, we had a play, a formal dance, a musical performance, and an improv group. It's pretty easy to find activities to keep you busy." While some here take advantage of nearby Philadelphia ("good history and culture, as well as a club scene and places like South Street to hang out at"), most tend to stick close to campus. And what a campus! "It's so beautiful that it's practically unbearable," gushes one undergrad. Parties here are generally low-key and usually involve alcohol and other substances; as with academics, the Honor Code applies. Reports one student, "I'm impressed by the leniency and respectfulness of security and the administration vis-à-vis drinking and substance use. They definitely trust students to be responsible for themselves and for one another, and I think that for the most part, that trust is well placed." Students report an active intramural sports program, lots of clubs and organizations (with ample opportunities to start your own), and a fair amount of political activity, most of which leans leftward.

Student Body

As befits an elite liberal arts school, Haverford is home to a student body "good at more things than you can count on your fingers and toes, and interested in just about everything." More than one student confided that "the typical student is a cool dork: someone with really funky interests and life experiences who loves sharing and learning, even if s/he's not amazing at performing or shmoozing a crowd." Most "probably own a pair of Birkenstocks but aren't quite as leftist as they make themselves out to be." Complains one conservative, "Haverford is accepting of anyone except for non-left-wingers." While most feel that "there is a good amount of diversity here," especially for such a small, expensive school, many also report that the school needs to make an "effort to increase the diversity."

ADMISSIONS

Very important factors considered include: Character/personal qualities, recommendations, secondary school record, standardized test scores. *Important factors considered include:* Class rank, essays, extracurricular activities, volunteer work. *Other factors considered include:* Alumni/ae relation, geographical residence, interview, minority status, talent/ability, work experience. TOEFL required of all international applicants. High school diploma is required, and GED is accepted. *Academic units required:* 4 English, 3 math, 1 science (1 science lab), 3 foreign language, 1 social studies. *Academic units recommended:* 4 math, 2 science.

The Inside Word

Candidate evaluation at Haverford is quite thorough, and the applicant pool is sizable and strong. Applicants who are successful through the initial academic review are then carefully considered for the match they make with the college. This part of the process is especially important at small schools like Haverford, and students should definitely spend some time assessing the reasons for their interest in attending before responding to essays and interviewing. Interviewing is a must.

FINANCIAL AID

Students should submit: FAFSA, CSS/Financial Aid PROFILE, state aid form, noncustodial (divorced/separated) parents' statement, business/farm supplement. Regular filing deadline 1/31. The Princeton Review suggests that all financial aid forms be submitted as soon as possible after 1/1. *Need-based scholarships/grants offered:* Pell, SEOG, state scholarships/grants, private scholarships, the school's own gift aid. *Loan aid offered:* FFEL Subsidized Stafford, FFEL Unsubsidized Stafford, FFEL PLUS, Federal Perkins. Applicants will be notified of awards on or about 4/8. Federal Work-study Program available. Institutional employment available. Off-campus job opportunities are good.

FROM THE ADMISSIONS OFFICE

"Haverford strives to be a college in which integrity, honesty, and concern for others are dominant forces. The college does not have many formal rules; rather, it offers an opportunity for students to govern their affairs and conduct themselves with respect and concern for others. Each student is expected to adhere to the Honor Code as it is adopted each year by the Students' Association. Haverford's Quaker roots show most clearly in the relationship of faculty and students, in the emphasis on integrity, in the interaction of the individual and the community, and through the college's concern for the uses to which its students put their expanding knowledge. Haverford's 1,100 students represent a wide diversity of interests, backgrounds, and talents. They come from public, parochial, and independent schools across the United States, Puerto Rico, and twenty-eight foreign countries. Students of color are an important part of the Haverford community."

For even more information on this school, turn to page 491 of the "Stats" section.

HOBART AND WILLIAM SMITH COLLEGES

639 SOUTH MAIN STREET, GENEVA, NY 14456 • ADMISSIONS: 315-781-3472 • FAX: 315-781-3471
FINANCIAL AID: 315-781-3315 • E-MAIL: HOADM@HWS.EDU • WEBSITE: WWW.HWS.EDU

Ratings
Quality of Life: 74   Academic: 87   Admissions: 87   Financial Aid: 92

Academics

"Immense study abroad opportunities, great internships, [and] an emphasis on interdisciplinary courses, majors, and minors" are among the chief attributes of Hobart and William Smith Colleges (HWS), a pair of associated single-sex colleges that share a campus, faculty, and administration. Students appreciate the "small, personal classes" that "require student involvement." This intimate setting helps to foster "a great sense of community." One student explains, "Everyone is friendly here—profs, students, and administration. Profs actually care about happiness of the students." Accordingly, instructors—who "provide both liberal and conservative viewpoints and encourage you to think outside of the box"—receive high grades from their students. Undergraduates especially praise their accessibility; one student says, "Teachers have met with me outside their office hours and been at school for extra help sessions as late as 10:00 p.m. because students still had questions," though it hasn't kept students from winning one Rhodes and five Goldwater scholarships over the past six years. As is the case with many small schools, "some programs are underfunded." Most students accept these limitations as the cost of close, caring instruction. One science student explains, "HWS is very supportive of work done off campus. I personally have done research at a different, larger university."

> **SURVEY SAYS . . .**
> *Small classes*
> *Great computer facilities*
> *Great library*
> *Everyone loves the Statesmen*
> *Lots of beer drinking*
> *Hard liquor is popular*

Life

Students report that the school is home to many different social scenes. Because "athletic programs are top notch," one scene revolves around sports; at least a few students say they're too busy studying and practicing to do much else. Another scene focuses on the "many organizations here that are easy to get involved with, and every organization is eager to have help." There's also the orbit of the "Student Life Office that coordinates many events on campus; FolkFest and HWS Day draw almost all of the student body out." The largest scene of all, however, is the party scene. HWS kids "have parties in their rooms or they go out together to the frats, which always have parties. The downtown bars are very popular, too." One student adds, "There is a large group of people that just think about Wednesday night, Friday night, and Saturday night parties and going to the bars." The campus "is absolutely beautiful, especially in the warm weather. When spring comes around, everyone comes together on the quad and you couldn't imagine being happy anywhere else." Hometown Geneva is "a small town with very few good restaurants and places to hang out. Many of us like to take weekend trips to Ithaca, Rochester, and Syracuse."

Student Body

Hobart and William Smith has a reputation as a stronghold of rich preppies, and while the stereotype has some basis in truth, it doesn't tell the whole story. One student says, "People like to characterize the typical 'Smithy'—the rich stuck-up girl—as the norm at our school. And there are a lot of people like this, probably more so than other schools. But there are also so many different people with unique personalities, and once you take your concentration away from the negative and become open to people, you realize that the majority of students are really nice." Another student points out, "upper-class students seem to stand out more. However, according to all the data they feed us, a large percentage of us are on financial aid!" One student describes the various ways everyone spends their time: "There are students here that go to class and do their work and chill at night. Then there are those students that get involved, set up new clubs, compete in athletics, and organize study groups. All students on this campus [can] find a group/club for them to get involved with and easily fit in."

ADMISSIONS

Very important factors considered include: Essays, secondary school record. *Important factors considered include:* Character/personal qualities, class rank, extracurricular activities, recommendations, standardized test scores, volunteer work, work experience. *Other factors considered include:* Alumni/ae relation, geographical residence, interview, minority status, talent/ability. SAT Reasoning or ACT required. TOEFL required of all international applicants. High school diploma is required, and GED is accepted. *Academic units required:* 4 English, 3 math, 3 science (2 science lab), 2 foreign language, 2 social studies, 2 history, 2 academic electives. *Academic units recommended:* 3 foreign language, 4 academic electives.

The Inside Word

Hobart and William Smith lose a lot of students to their competitors, who are many and strong. This helps open up the gates a bit for more candidates. However, the schools' location, right on Seneca Lake, offers students a great place to study.

FINANCIAL AID

Students should submit: FAFSA, CSS/Financial Aid PROFILE, state aid form, noncustodial (divorced/separated) parents' statement, parent and student tax returns. Regular filing deadline 2/1. The Princeton Review suggests that all financial aid forms be submitted as soon as possible after 1/1. *Need-based scholarships/grants offered:* Pell, SEOG, state scholarships/grants, private scholarships, the school's own gift aid. *Loan aid offered:* FFEL Subsidized Stafford, FFEL Unsubsidized Stafford, FFEL PLUS, Federal Perkins. Applicants will be notified of awards on or about 4/1. Federal Work-study Program available. Off-campus job opportunities are fair.

FROM THE ADMISSIONS OFFICE

"Hobart and William Smith Colleges seek students with a sense of adventure and a commitment to the life of the mind. Inside the classroom, students find the academic climate to be rigorous, with a faculty that is deeply involved in teaching and working with them. Outside, they discover a supportive community that helps to cultivate a balance and hopes to foster an integration among academics, extracurricular activities, and social life. Hobart and William Smith, as coordinate colleges, have an awareness of gender differences and equality and are committed to respect and a celebration of diversity."

For even more information on this school, turn to page 492 of the "Stats" section.

HOFSTRA UNIVERSITY

ADMISSIONS CENTER, BERNON HALL, HEMPSTEAD, NY 11549 • ADMISSIONS: 516-463-6700
FAX: 516-463-5100 • FINANCIAL AID: 516-463-6680 • E-MAIL: HOFSTRA@HOFSTRA.EDU • WEBSITE: WWW.HOFSTRA.EDU

Ratings
Quality of Life: 62   **Academic:** 76   **Admissions:** 84   **Financial Aid:** 67

Academics

For many who attend this up-and-coming university on Long Island, "Hofstra's growing academic reputation is its strength. It seems everywhere you turn, somebody tells you what a great school Hofstra is." Students are especially proud of the school's offerings in business, history, education, English, and communications. They also love that "the location is great for job opportunities" although some students complain that "the career center caters too much to business majors (and not enough [to] everyone else!)."

> **SURVEY SAYS . . .**
> *Small classes*
> *Great computer facilities*
> *Great library*
> *Lots of beer drinking*
> *Hard liquor is popular*
> *(Almost) everyone smokes*

You will find different types of professors at Hofstra. Students report, "Half of the professors are interested in teaching, and half of them could care less." Some people blame the spotty teaching on the student body; "professors are into the class if the students show a genuine interest." The administration receives a universal thumbs-down from undergraduates. One student adds, "You have better luck [of] getting something done [at] the DMV." However, in recent years, the school has taken note of this and have begun making universal improvements in student services.

Life

Much of Hofstra's active social scene revolves around Greek organizations and the bars surrounding the campus. "Time management is very important," writes one conscientious student. "Because we have so many bars close by, partying can take over one's life." Although "there are no Greek houses on campus, "fraternites and sororities sponsor many campus social events, most of which are well attended." Support for team sports, however, is not strong: "We have more winning teams than not amongst our intercollegiate teams, but nobody seems to care. Even for Homecoming, only half the stadium gets filled. That's just pathetic." Some students find the situation on and around campus stultifying; one student says, "The lack of campus life and activity is very depressing," a few students on the flip side, claim that "the greatest strength of the school is that everything is there for you—the clubs, sports, career services—you just have to go and seek them." Many students board the Long Island Railroad and trek into nearby New York City. While several students don't claim to be happy, a few stalwart Hofstra boosters claim, "there aren't really a lot of valid reasons for this unhappiness. The school has a lot to offer if students would just get off their asses and take advantage of it." Among other things, students can enjoy the "beautiful campus," complete with an arboretum.

Student Body

Students report that Hofstra has more than its fair share of status-conscious students. "Students always attend classes as if they are a fashion show, wearing Gucci and Armani and acting like they are in their late twenties," writes one student. Another student agrees, "It is common to see a Hofstra student with a cell phone in one hand and a cigarette in the other. And don't forget their Mercedes, BMW, or Expedition blasting the latest song." Most students hail "from Long Island, Boston, or New Jersey," and everyone here, we're told, "fits into one of four groups: Greek, commuter, jock, and 'other.'" Regarding the temperament of their peers, student opinion varies from "most are really friendly" to "they're New Yorkers, so they just seem unfriendly until you get to know them."

ADMISSIONS

Very important factors considered include: Class rank, essays, recommendations, secondary school record, standardized test scores. *Important factors considered include:* Character/personal qualities, extracurricular activities, interview, talent/ability. *Other factors considered include:* Alumni/ae relation, geographical residence, minority status, volunteer work, work experience. SAT Subject Tests recommended. TOEFL required of all international applicants. High school diploma is required, and GED is accepted. *Academic units required:* 4 English, 3 math, 3 science (1 science lab), 2 foreign language, 3 social studies. *Academic units recommended:* 4 math, 4 science, 3 foreign language, 4 social studies.

The Inside Word

Hofstra wants to be national and has positioned itself very well with impressive facilities, appealing program offerings, solid athletic teams, and an effective national ad campaign. As a result, Hofstra's current student profile has increased dramatically. Presently, Hofstra is a solidly competitive regional university; it is a school to watch in the future.

FINANCIAL AID

Students should submit: FAFSA, state aid form. The Princeton Review suggests that all financial aid forms be submitted as soon as possible after 1/1. *Need-based scholarships/grants offered:* Pell, SEOG, state scholarships/grants, private scholarships, the school's own gift aid. *Loan aid offered:* FFEL Subsidized Stafford, FFEL Unsubsidized Stafford, FFEL PLUS, Federal Perkins. Applicants will be notified of awards on a rolling basis beginning on or about 3/15. Federal Work-study Program available. Institutional employment available. Off-campus job opportunities are excellent.

FROM THE ADMISSIONS OFFICE

"Hofstra University is a nationally-recognized university, which offers all the benefits of a traditional college experience, including challenging academic programs with small classes and faculty devoted to teaching, and a vibrant campus life. Hofstra enrolls students from almost every state and 59 foreign countries. Students choose from over 130 undergraduate programs in arts and sciences, business, communications, education and allied human services, and honors studies.

"A distinctive aspect of the Hofstra experience is our focus on teaching. All of our classes are taught by faculty, which includes recipients of top academic honors including National Endowment for the Humanities fellows, Guggenheim fellows, an Emmy Award winner, and major grant recipients. Thanks to a student/faculty ratio of 14:1 and average class size of 23, students work closely with their professors.

"Complementing the classroom experience is the incomparable resource of New York City, just 25 miles from campus. Our students make full use of the city for internships and as a social and cultural outlet.

"Hofstra's students have the resources they need, including a library with 1.2 million volumes and a wealth of technology resources for learning and research, including grid computing and wireless access. Students may study abroad on five continents and over 25 countries. Over 120 clubs and organizations provide students with the opportunity to become involved in a broad array of activities, as does Hofstra's 18 NCAA Division I athletic programs. There are 37 residence halls at Hofstra that offer a variety of living arrangements."

For even more information on this school, turn to page 492 of the "Stats" section.

HOOD COLLEGE

401 ROSEMONT AVENUE, FREDRICK, MD 21701 • ADMISSIONS: 301-696-3400 • FAX: 301-696-3819
E-MAIL: ADMISSIONS@HOOD.EDU • WEBSITE: WWW.HOOD.EDU

Ratings

Quality of Life: 84   **Academic:** 86   **Admissions:** 87   **Financial Aid:** 86

Academics

Hood College touts itself as "a great place to be smart," a sentiment with which its students overwhelmingly agree. Professors are "understanding and helpful, yet challenging. They make students think, question, analyze, and be critical about everything, including what they teach." Students say, "You get a very individualized education. You can't slack off in class because your professor will see you when your class has only ten people." The Hood College Honor Code is widely regarded as another of the school's greatest assets. According to the school's website, the Honor Code ensures that "all members of the college assume the obligation to maintain the principles of honesty, responsibility, and intellectual integrity in all student activities." The Honor Code also allows students to schedule their own final exams by choosing from a list of dates and times. One student explains, "The academic honor system makes me feel more like an adult who paid to go to school and is trusted, rather than having someone dictate how I must complete papers and exams." Another student adds, "Very few cheat because of the Honor Code." The administration "has an open-door policy and sticks to it." Hood has seen an increase in enrollment in recent years, causing concern about the school's ability to maintain its 10:1 student/teacher ratio "The student population is increasing, and the school just doesn't seem big enough to accommodate the number of students expected to enroll in the upcoming years," notes one undergrad.

> **SURVEY SAYS . . .**
> *Small classes*
> *No one cheats*
> *Lab facilities are great*
> *Frats and sororities are unpopular or nonexistent*

Life

Hood College is situated in Frederick, Maryland, "only an hour from Baltimore and 45 minutes to DC." Frederick has "a lot of very good restaurants and shops downtown, [and] day trips to Baltimore and DC are pretty common. Some of the students get together and go clubbing in DC. Others go hiking in the many different local and state parks around the area." Hood offers "a wide range of clubs and campus events, lectures, field trips, even school-sponsored parties (age 21 and over can drink). Hood is also very politically active. A good political discussion can be had any day of the week." Students describe the school as "not a huge party school, [where] drinking is common but not excessive." Some students suggest that the school "should make public transportation to and from local malls and Metro stations easier." One student explains, "It's hard to get around Frederick because of the bad transportation system."

Student Body

The typical student at Hood College "is weighed down with work, but also possesses a determination to get it done, get it right, and still have fun." Because the school, which was once an all-women's school, just recently went coed, "females outnumber males by about 3:1." Some older students complain that because of this switch, "the atmosphere at Hood is changing fast," and the college is "losing some of what made it very unique; this is less of an issue with younger students," however. Despite its predominantly white female population, students find there is enough diversity on campus to suit them. One student says, "Hood is well-known for its exchange student program, and we have many students from many different countries. There are many students of different ethnicities, as well as a small gay and lesbian population." At Hood, "everyone gets along and talks to everyone else regardless of their differences."

ADMISSIONS

Very important factors considered include: Secondary school record, standardized test scores. *Important factors considered include:* Character/personal qualities, class rank, essays, extracurricular activities, interview, recommendations, talent/ability. *Other factors considered include:* Alumni/ae relation, minority status, volunteer work, work experience. SAT Reasoning or ACT required. TOEFL required of all international applicants. High school diploma is required, and GED is accepted. *Academic units required:* 4 English, 3 math, 3 science (2 science lab), 2 foreign language, 3 social studies, 1 academic elective.

The Inside Word

Applications to Hood for 2004–2005 were up 40 percent from previous years. The school recently offered "legacies" (the children/grandchildren of alumnae) a great incentive to apply: get in and your freshman tuition will equal whatever your parent or grandparent paid their freshman year.

FINANCIAL AID

Students should submit: FAFSA. The Princeton Review suggests that all financial aid forms be submitted as soon as possible after 1/1. *Need-based scholarships/grants offered:* Pell, SEOG, state scholarships/grants, private scholarships, the school's own gift aid. *Loan aid offered:* Direct Subsidized Stafford, Direct Unsubsidized Stafford, Direct PLUS, FFEL Subsidized Stafford, FFEL Unsubsidized Stafford, FFEL PLUS, Federal Perkins. Applicants will be notified of awards on or about 3/1. Federal Work-study Program available. Institutional employment available. Off-campus job opportunities are good.

FROM THE ADMISSIONS OFFICE

"Hood College has experienced several changes in recent years. In August of 2003, men were enrolled as residential students for the first time (men attended as commuters in the undergraduate and graduate programs since 1973). While some campus traditions have changed to reflect the new student body, the transition to coeducation has been smooth. Student enrollment has increased in recent years, yet classes remain small and students have ample opportunity to meet with faculty outside of class for advising, discussion, and individual research projects. The college opened its new science and technology center in 2002, with state-of-the-art laboratories designed specifically for biology, biochemistry, chemistry, and environmental science. Both the classroom (average class size is 14) and the extracurricular environment focus on active student learning. Hood students also develop and practice critical thinking skills in every class and every campus activity. Along with the obvious social and cultural advantages of Hood's proximity to Washington, DC and Baltimore, students have an abundant array of internships in government and industry. On campus, students have the opportunity to get involved in numerous clubs, activities and organizations from community service, literary, and artistic groups to intramurals and NCAA Division III intercollegiate sports. About one-third of Hood's students compete in 17 varsity athletic teams, and several Hood teams are multi-year champions in their respective sports. Hood's lively and involved student body is diverse, including more than one-fifth who are students of color."

For even more information on this school, turn to page 493 of the "Stats" section.

HOUGHTON COLLEGE

PO Box 128, Houghton, NY 14744 • Admissions: 800-777-2556 • Fax: 585-567-9522
E-mail: admissions@houghton.edu • Website: www.houghton.edu

Ratings
Quality of Life: 89   **Academic:** 84   **Admissions:** 82   **Financial Aid:** 71

Academics

Houghton College, a small Christian liberal arts school in Western New York, is hailed by students for its "rigorous academics, religious devotion, and a warm community feel." Students report "the smallness of the school also lends itself to a more personal atmosphere in the classroom—an atmosphere open to sharing and discussion instead of just listening to lectures." Students enjoy the school's "awesome music program, good premed program, good business program, [and] superb" English and education departments. Houghton also has "one of the top,

if not the top, equestrian programs in the nation, with Olympic-level coaching available and upper-level professors." One student adds, "Houghton is completely wired: Everyone has a laptop computer and a school e-mail address." "I can get in touch with anybody from a janitor to the president of the college just by e-mail, and I virtually always get a reply within a day." Students find that "professors are always ready to answer questions, discuss issues, and clarify assignments both during and after classes. They are open about their Christian faith, and they challenge students to be open-minded and discerning." Another student adds, "I have not yet had an instructor who was unavailable for individual tutoring."

Life

Houghton College is "smack-dab in the middle of rural Western New York, on a gorgeous campus." One student says, "Since we are a good distance from the cities, we create our own fun on campus." Some students have a difficult time with Houghton's rural locale—"it often becomes a bubble," says one, and "it's difficult to ascertain all that is going on in the outside world." But another student counters, "In my opinion, it is quite a plus! Not having the distractions of a busy city life causes students to interact with one another more. Relationships and friendships are built that will last a lifetime." For fun, students "watch movies, play cards, and play pool; hang out together in the Daily Grind coffee shop or Big Al's snack shop and talk about all aspects of life; [and] spend a lot of time outdoors, biking, hiking, running, skiing, or canoeing." Students report, "Drugs, alcohol, tobacco, and social dancing are prohibited on campus, "so we enjoy doing activities without needing to get drunk or high." Students who wish to escape their rural setting "drive the hour and a half to Buffalo, Niagara Falls, or Rochester. Sometimes just going to Wal-Mart (a minimum drive of 30 minutes) is an exciting thing."

Student Body

Students say the typical Houghton undergrad "is Caucasian and from New York or nearby states like Pennsylvania. Over 60 percent of the school is female. There is a wide amount of diversity with different ethnicities at Houghton, but they still represent a relatively small population of the school." Students add, "The different ethnicities and backgrounds blend beautifully at Houghton with very little discrimination." In general, Houghton students describe themselves as "goal-oriented, intelligent, religious, friendly, [and] accepting." The student body "is a close-knit, caring community that goes out of its way to befriend students and make them feel at home." "Every time I return from a break," says one happy student, "the college says 'welcome home.'"

ADMISSIONS

Very important factors considered include: Character/personal qualities, class rank, religious affiliation/commitment, secondary school record. *Important factors considered include:* Essays, recommendations, standardized test scores. *Other factors considered include:* Alumni/ae relation, extracurricular activities, interview, minority status, talent/ability, volunteer work, work experience. SAT Reasoning or ACT required. TOEFL required of all international applicants. High school diploma is required, and GED is accepted. *Academic units recommended:* 4 English, 3 math, 2 science (2 science lab), 2 foreign language, 1 social studies, 2 history.

The Inside Word

Houghton is a deeply Christian evangelical school. Students not committed to proselytizing will not be happy here. Admissions counselors know that and will block the applications of those who, in their view, are "bad fits" with the college.

FINANCIAL AID

Students should submit: FAFSA. The Princeton Review suggests that all financial aid forms be submitted as soon as possible after 1/1. *Need-based scholarships/grants offered:* Pell, SEOG, state scholarships/grants, private scholarships, the school's own gift aid. *Loan aid offered:* FFEL Subsidized Stafford, FFEL Unsubsidized Stafford, FFEL PLUS, Federal Perkins, college/university loans from institutional funds, private alternative loans. Applicants will be notified of awards on a rolling basis beginning on or about 3/15. Federal Work-study Program available. Institutional employment available. Off-campus job opportunities are poor.

FROM THE ADMISSIONS OFFICE

"Since 1883, Houghton College has provided a residential educational experience that integrates high-quality academic instruction with the Christian faith. Houghton is selective in admission, attracting a very capable student body from 25 countries and 40 states. The college receives widespread national recognition for the quality of its student profile, faculty, and facilities. Enrolling 1,200 full-time students, Houghton is located on a beautiful 1,300-acre campus in western New York. The college's campus includes a 386-acre equestrian center as well as cross-country and downhill ski trails. Houghton's campus combines classic-style architecture with state-of-the-art technology and facilities, including a campuswide computer network and Internet access. All first-year students and transfers receive laptop computers and printers. Houghton's traditional liberal arts curriculum offers more than 40 majors and programs. Numerous study abroad programs are available, including Houghton's own offerings in Tanzania, Australia, Eastern Europe, and London. The First-Year Honors Program offers highly qualified students the opportunity to study in England during the second semester of their first year with 25 of their peers and two Houghton faculty members. There is a strong pre-professional orientation, with 30 to 35 percent of graduates moving on to graduate or professional school upon graduation. Houghton alumni can be found teaching at 175 colleges and universities around the United States and abroad."

For even more information on this school, turn to page 493 of the "Stats" section.

HOWARD UNIVERSITY

2400 SIXTH STREET NW, WASHINGTON, DC 20059 • ADMISSIONS: 202-806-2700 • FAX: 202-806-4462
FINANCIAL AID: 202-806-2800 • E-MAIL: ADMISSION@HOWARD.EDU • WEBSITE: WWW.HOWARD.EDU

Ratings
Quality of Life: 66   **Academic:** 83   **Admissions:** 88   **Financial Aid:** 68

Academics

A school with "a rich legacy" that "continues to produce successful leaders," Howard University is truly "one of the nation's most prestigious historically black universities." The history is worth noting; the parade of impressive Howard graduates includes Nobel-Prize winning author Toni Morrison and former UN ambassador and civil-rights activist Andrew Young. So too is the present; Howard is well-regarded for its "excellent biology program" and other premed majors, as well as for communications and business. With its outstanding reputation, Howard "attracts

big companies that come looking for strong black students to employ, which makes it slightly easier for us as blacks to find jobs in today's market." Observes one undergrad, "We profit from an incredible amount of networking with large and prominent companies." Students also benefit from the school's location in DC, "a city where there are an unlimited number of resources open to students." Undergrads report that "academics at Howard are unparalleled; professors are masters of their skills, and the students are not here to play around, but to actually learn and earn their education." The school's famously bureaucratic administration remains true to its reputation; "Anything dealing with administration and student services tends to be long and unnecessarily tedious," students warn. They also caution that "the facilities definitely need upgrading."

Life

"During the week, most people's main priority is their classes" at Howard, "but weekends are a time to [take a] break." "There is always something to do in Washington DC," including "going to eat in exotic restaurants, watching movies, going to museums, and visiting other colleges and universities in the area." The school is "located literally in the middle of Washington, DC. It sits on top of a large hill (a rarity in the area), giving us a view of the city's landmarks." The surrounding neighborhood "was once considered the black Georgetown, the side of town for wealthy black intellectuals who were affiliated with Howard. They built large, fashionable row houses.... The area turned into a ghetto, though, when people began to move into the newer suburbs out of the city. Within the last few years, the neighborhood has been revitalized, and people are buying and fixing the abandoned mansions and row houses. It's still somewhat dangerous, especially at night, but it is coming around. It's wonderful to witness the growth of this neighborhood (with my school's help)." On campus there is "a wide array of student organizations available. There is something for everybody, and we have people from all types of cultural and socioeconomic backgrounds." Many involve community service, as "the students are aware of the struggles faced by minorities, and many study to make a difference in the lives of the disadvantaged. Many students take part in volunteer programs such as elementary tutoring." There's also "Greek life, parties, choirs, the arts, our great school newspaper, mock trials, student government, you name it." Homecoming, we're assured, "is a very big event every year, with lots of celebrities."

Student Body

The "outgoing, fashionable, confident" undergrads of Howard are "predominantly black," but "this doesn't mean we are all African American. Besides coming from all over the United States, we come from Africa, Trinidad, Jamaica, Haiti, and everywhere else." Americans contribute mightily to the geographic diversity, since "Black people are not all the same, in case you didn't know. Black students from New Orleans act completely differently than black students from New York, etc. Howard is one big melting pot of black culture, and I love that!" Most here "came from a high school where they were probably popular, were class presidents or held some sort of leadership role in some student activity, and think they can take over the world." Adds one student, "We are definitely leaders by nature. As different as we are, we all think that we can and will be the best at something. We all have a drive that cannot be taught, just developed."

ADMISSIONS

Very important factors considered include: Class rank, secondary school record, standardized test scores. *Important factors considered include:* Character/personal qualities, recommendations. *Other factors considered include:* Alumni/ae relation, essays, extracurricular activities, talent/ability, volunteer work, work experience. SAT Reasoning or ACT required. SAT Subject Tests recommended. TOEFL required of all international applicants. High school diploma is required, and GED is accepted. *Academic units required:* 4 English, 2 math, 2 science, 2 foreign language, 2 social studies, 2 history. *Academic units recommended:* 4 English, 3 math, 4 science (2 science lab), 2 foreign language, 2 social studies, 2 history, 4 academic electives.

The Inside Word

A large applicant pool and solid yield of acceptees who enroll is a combination that adds up to selectivity for Howard. Pay strict attention to the formula.

FINANCIAL AID

Students should submit: FAFSA. The Princeton Review suggests that all financial aid forms be submitted as soon as possible after 1/1. *Need-based scholarships/grants offered:* Pell, SEOG, state scholarships/grants, private scholarships, the school's own gift aid, federal nursing scholarships. *Loan aid offered:* Direct Subsidized Stafford, Direct PLUS, FFEL Subsidized Stafford, FFEL Unsubsidized Stafford, FFEL PLUS, Federal Perkins, Federal Nursing, state loans, college/university loans from institutional funds. Applicants will be notified of awards on a rolling basis beginning on or about 4/1. Federal Work-study Program available. Institutional employment available. Off-campus job opportunities are excellent.

FROM THE ADMISSIONS OFFICE

"Since its founding, Howard has stood among the few institutions of higher learning where African Americans and other minorities have participated freely in a truly comprehensive university experience. Thus, Howard has assumed a special responsibility to prepare its students to exercise leadership wherever their interest and commitments take them. Howard has issued approximately 99,318 degrees, diplomas, and certificates to men and women in the professions, the arts and sciences, and the humanities. The university has produced and continues to produce a high percentage of the nation's African American professionals in the fields of medicine, dentistry, pharmacy, engineering, nursing, architecture, religion, law, music, social work, education, and business. There are more than 8,906 students from across the nation and approximately 85 countries and territories attending the university. Their varied customs, cultures, ideas, and interests contribute to Howard's international character and vitality. More than 1,598 faculty members represent the largest concentration of African American scholars in any single institution of higher education."

For even more information on this school, turn to page 494 of the "Stats" section.

Immaculata University

1145 King Road, PO Box 642, Immaculata, PA 19345-0642 • Admissions: 610-647-4400 • Fax: 610-640-0836
E-mail: admiss@immaculata.edu • Website: www.immaculata.edu

Ratings
Quality of Life: 88   **Academic:** 72   **Admissions:** 60   **Financial Aid:** 74

Academics

In September of 2005, the Women's College of Immaculata University becomes the College of Undergraduate Studies and opens its doors to male students. There is no reason, however, to expect a change in the College's nurturing environment, which is known for its supportive faculty and administration. Students claim that "many of Immaculata's professors live on campus like the students, so they're available for a friendly dinner, and they're always open to drop-ins and quick chats. The administration has its doors open almost all day for quick fixes and responds to our needs as students." Immaculata is also distinguished by "some rare programs, like Family and Consumer Science," "a strong music therapy program," and "an Education certification program that outshines that of many of the local universities," according to some. A student adds that "traditional classes are not offered on Wednesdays, so the students get that day off to get some homework done and/or work, and go to observations and internships."

> **SURVEY SAYS . . .**
> Small classes
> Great computer facilities
> Great library
> Students are friendly
> Campus feels safe
> Very little drug use

Life

Most here agree that the social scene at Immaculata "could use some livening up. This campus is totally dead on the weekends." While it's hard to say whether social life here is dead because so many students go home on weekends, or vice versa, the enrollment of male students in the fall of 2005 should give the on campus social scene a boost. While one student claims that Immaculata is "located in the middle of a cornfield," Philadelphia, along with "many other universities, [is] close by, so often on the weekends we go out and get to experience life at other schools." Other students say there are "really strict policies on when people can come and visit." All in all, the result is "a very peaceful campus, which is great to come back to after a night out."

Student Body

Students enjoy the small campus intimacy Immaculata University provides. "The great thing about being at Immaculata is that everyone knows your name," explains one student. Undergraduates are typically "outgoing and friendly, have eclectic talents, and are involved in various unrelated groups and organizations." The student body is also predominantly white. One student claims, "While there is some racial and cultural diversity, most are Caucasian. Economically, many of the students are from upper-middle class families." Most students are "very into religion," which can be a source of friction with the current "large gay percentage here, which probably has something to do with it being a women's college."

ADMISSIONS

Very important factors considered include: Secondary school record. *Important factors considered include:* Standardized test scores, talent/ability. *Other factors considered include:* Alumni/ae relation, class rank, interview, recommendations. SAT Reasoning or ACT required. SAT Subject Tests recommended. TOEFL required of all international applicants. High school diploma is required, and GED is accepted. *Academic units required:* 4 English, 2 math, 2 science (1 science lab), 2 foreign language, 2 social studies, 4 academic electives.

The Inside Word

Admission to Immaculata is not overly competitive. Borderline candidates, however, should pull out all the stops by requesting an interview, submitting the optional writing sample, and, if possible, finding an alumnus to endorse them.

FINANCIAL AID

Students should submit: FAFSA, institution's own financial aid form. Regular filing deadline 4/15. The Princeton Review suggests that all financial aid forms be submitted as soon as possible after 1/1. *Need-based scholarships/grants offered:* Pell, SEOG, state scholarships/grants, private scholarships, the school's own gift aid, United Negro College Fund. *Loan aid offered:* FFEL Subsidized Stafford, FFEL Unsubsidized Stafford, FFEL PLUS, Federal Perkins. Applicants will be notified of awards on a rolling basis beginning on or about 2/1.

For even more information on this school, turn to page 494 of the "Stats" section.

INDIANA UNIVERSITY OF PENNSYLVANIA

216 PRATT HALL, INDIANA, PA 15705 • ADMISSIONS: 724-357-2230 • FAX: 724-357-6281
FINANCIAL AID: 415-357-2218 • E-MAIL: ADMISSIONS_INQUIRY@GROVE.IUP.EDU • WEBSITE: WWW.IUP.EDU

Ratings
Quality of Life: 72   **Academic:** 74   **Admissions:** 79   **Financial Aid:** 73

Academics

The Robert E. Cook Honors College is what distinguishes Indiana University of Pennsylvania (IUP) from your typical big-box state university. Reports one honors student, "The Honors College allows students to take interesting discussion-based classes instead of the standard liberal studies freshman classes. These honor classes are never lecture-based and have made me a much better writer and thinker." Students' only complaint about the honors program concerns its limited scope; as one student told us, "My academic experience has been pretty good; however, there needs to be more honors courses and an honors program in each academic college." Beyond the Honors College, "the rest of the university is pretty much only concerned with partying." While profs "are easily accessible and encouraging," they face "a huge obstacle: a student body with too much laziness." Since the Honors College covers only some of students' course work, all students must take at least some courses outside the college. Reports one student, "Required classes are large, freakishly easy, and completely made up of lecture time. My honors classes are absolutely excellent, with discussion 60 percent of the time." Even so, IUP offers plenty of challenges to those willing to step up to the plate. Sums up one undergrad, "IUP might not have ten sets of all the newest equipment, but it does train me in everything I need to know and gives me additional chances to learn outside of the school through its numerous internship and study abroad programs."

> **SURVEY SAYS . . .**
> *Small classes*
> *Frats and sororities dominate social scene*
> *Student publications are popular*
> *Lots of beer drinking*
> *(Almost) everyone smokes*

Life

Hometown Indiana, students at IUP tell us, "is not the place for city people who like a lot of excitement and nightclubs." The town "offers a myriad of bars but very little else." It is the birthplace of film legend Jimmy Stewart, and many feel "it could very well be named 'Jimmy Stewart-ville' for all the paraphernalia: the Jimmy Stewart Museum, the sign coming into town proclaiming that Indiana, Pennsylvania is the birthplace of Jimmy Stewart, and the showings of It's a Wonderful Life during the holidays at the local theater." Irreverent IUP undergrads occasionally "steal away in the middle of the night to put a dress and hat on the Jimmy Stewart statue, which proudly stands in front of the courthouse," giving you some idea of how little else there is to do here. Students tell us IUP was once a big party school, but that "life in general at IUP is changing. They have increased the police force in order to better enforce drug and alcohol laws." To fill the void, "IUP offers many student organizations and musical events from an anime club to equestrian team to dance squad to sororities and fraternities. If you have an interest, IUP is a good place to pursue it." Otherwise, students seek quiet entertainment of their own devising or, more often, pack up and go home when their last class ends. Pittsburgh is only an hour's drive away.

Student Body

With over 12,000 undergraduates, "there are students from all walks of life here at IUP. . . . The majority are related by the fact that they come from a middle-income family and are here to get the best education they can for their dollar." Many "are from within a 60-mile radius of the school," an area that is "very conservative Christian and not generally accepting of liberal viewpoints." IUP also has "a large population of African Americans and foreign students from all around the world, like Asia, Africa, and Europe." Students warn, however, "There is a visual segregation between the African American community and the rest of the campus," however, the school is working to be more embrasive of cultural/ethnic differences through student groups and initiatives. Most here "are more concerned with getting a job and money than being educated," according to their critics.

ADMISSIONS

Very important factors considered include: Secondary school record. *Important factors considered include:* Class rank, standardized test scores, talent/ability. *Other factors considered include:* Alumni/ac relation, character/personal qualities, essays, extracurricular activities, interview, recommendations, volunteer work, work experience. SAT Reasoning or ACT required. TOEFL required of all international applicants. High school diploma is required, and GED is accepted. *Academic units recommended:* 4 English, 3 math, 3 science, 2 foreign language, 2 social studies, 1 history, 1 academic elective.

The Inside Word

IUP is impressive in many ways and should command more attention than it does. As a state school, it provides Pennsylvania residents with a great education at a rock-bottom price. Students applying to IUP with an average academic record will have little trouble getting admitted. Once on campus, students will find an unexpectedly diverse population who hail from many states and countries.

FINANCIAL AID

Students should submit: FAFSA. The Princeton Review suggests that all financial aid forms be submitted as soon as possible after 1/1. *Need-based scholarships/grants offered:* Pell, SEOG, state scholarships/grants, private scholarships, the school's own gift aid, United Negro College Fund. *Loan aid offered:* FFEL Subsidized Stafford, FFEL Unsubsidized Stafford, FFEL PLUS, Federal Perkins, private alternative loans. Applicants will be notified of awards on or about 3/15. Federal Work-study Program available. Institutional employment available. Off-campus job opportunities are good.

FROM THE ADMISSIONS OFFICE

"At IUP, we look at each applicant as an individual, not as a number. That means we'll review your application materials very carefully. When reviewing applications, the primary focus of the admissions committee is on the student's high school record and SAT scores. In addition, the committee often reviews the optional personal essay and letters of recommendations submitted by the student to help aid in the decision-making process. We're always happy to speak with prospective students. Call us toll free at 800-422-6830 or 724-357-2230 or e-mail us at admissions-inquiry@iup.edu."

For even more information on this school, turn to page 494 of the "Stats" section.

IONA COLLEGE

715 NORTH AVENUE, NEW ROCHELLE, NY 10801 • ADMISSIONS: 914-633-2502 • FAX: 914-633-2642
E-MAIL: ICAD@IONA.EDU • WEBSITE: WWW.IONA.EDU

Ratings
Quality of Life: 72   **Academic:** 77   **Admissions:** 85   **Financial Aid:** 62

Academics

Iona College is a small Catholic liberal arts school just north of the Big Apple. "The business program is good," claims one student at the college. It "benefits greatly from being so close to New York City. Internships are available for many majors, particularly business, criminal justice, and mass communication." Location also helps with job placement after graduation, students tell us. Professors "are very good at teaching us because most of them actually worked in the field themselves, and therefore they know what they are talking about from experience." Many, especially adjunct professors, are still active in their fields. Some students point out that the downside of this is that "it is sometimes difficult to get in touch with them. However, for the most part full-time professors are accessible." Students can also seek one-on-one instruction at the Rudin Center, "where you can get tutors for any subject if you need help." Undergraduates appreciate and claim that "Iona keeps its classes small. Even the freshman lecture classes are no larger than 40 students. The administrators "are easy to become friendly with and are so supportive of the students." They also love the exclusive Honors Program in which "class registration and class availability cater to you."

> **SURVEY SAYS . . .**
> *Small classes*
> *Great computer facilities*
> *Great off-campus food*
> *Everyone loves the Gaels*
> *Lots of beer drinking*
> *Hard liquor is popular*
> *(Almost) everyone smokes*

Life

Extracurricular life at Iona is hampered by a large commuter population. As one undergraduate explains, "The campus is really alive from 9:00 A.M.–4:00 P.M. during weekdays, but then all the commuters leave and it gets quiet again." Furthermore, "A lot of the residents go home on weekends, and those of us who remain are forced to be creative to keep busy." According to most, this creativity usual consists of heading for a neighborhood bar. "This is a bar school," students concede, and "most Iona college students spend their weekends—Wednesday through Saturday nights—at the local bars." Some here note that, "Iona offers many activities to encourage a sober, positive environment. However, they tend to be less popular." One undergraduate writes, "We could use some more variety, and a lot more programming on the weekend. Then maybe more people would stick around for the weekends." That would give students more time to enjoy the "beautiful campus, which is very easy to get around," become involved in the "very strong campus ministries department, the excellent cross-country team" and "fun basketball games." Of course, with New York City so close by, Iona will always have a tough time competing for students' attention. As one undergraduate explains, "Iona is located a hop, skip, and a 20-minute train ride from the City."

Student Body

Student reports state that a typical student at Iona is "white and middle-class," and many are "Italian or Irish" and "from either Long Island, Staten Island, Queens, Brooklyn, New Jersey, or way upstate New York." Most agree "the only separation that really takes place is residents versus commuters." One student sums it up by saying, "Students are from very diverse backgrounds, but most are friendly. One downfall is that because of the surrounding area [the wealthy suburbs of New York City], many students are extremely materialistic." Another student adds, "Everybody has spent too much time in the tanning bed and carries a Nextel in a fake designer bag."

ADMISSIONS

Very important factors considered include: Secondary school record. *Important factors considered include:* Character/personal qualities, class rank, essays, extracurricular activities, interview, standardized test scores, volunteer work. *Other factors considered include:* Alumni/ae relation, geographical residence, recommendations, talent/ability, work experience. SAT Reasoning or ACT required. TOEFL required of all international applicants. High school diploma is required, and GED is accepted. *Academic units required:* 4 English, 3 math, 2 science (2 science lab), 2 foreign language, 1 social studies, 1 history, 4 academic electives. *Academic units recommended:* 4 English, 4 math, 3 science (2 science lab), 2 foreign language, 1 social studies, 1 history, 3 academic electives.

The Inside Word

According to the school's website, "Personal characteristics and potential to succeed are highly valued," by Iona's admissions committee. Emphasize those personality traits and experiences that make you a unique and compelling individual as you complete the application. A solid high school transcript is a necessity here.

INANCIAL AID

Students should submit: FAFSA, institution's own financial aid form, state aid form. The Princeton Review suggests that all financial aid forms be submitted as soon as possible after 1/1. *Need-based scholarships/grants offered:* Pell, SEOG, state scholarships/grants, private scholarships, the school's own gift aid. *Loan aid offered:* FFEL Subsidized Stafford, FFEL Unsubsidized Stafford, FFEL PLUS, Federal Perkins, alternative loans. Applicants will be notified of awards on a rolling basis beginning on or about 12/20.

For even more information on this school, turn to page 495 of the "Stats" section.

ITHACA COLLEGE

100 Job Hall, Ithaca, NY 14850-7020 • Admissions: 607-274-3124 • Fax: 607-274-1900
Financial Aid: 607-274-3131 • E-mail: admission@ithaca.edu • Website: www.ithaca.edu

Ratings
Quality of Life: 77   **Academic:** 81   **Admissions:** 86   **Financial Aid:** 80

Academics

With a "world-recognized music school," a stellar "communications department with amazing facilities," and "extremely strong programs in theater and physical therapy," Ithaca College stakes out a lot of high ground for a school of its size. Perhaps the school strives to achieve so much because of its formidable cross-town competition: Ithaca shares its namesake hometown with Cornell University. IC "offers a wide variety of majors [that] do a good job of opening your eyes to new ideas and the world." Business programs are popular, and many come for the "great programs in the entertainment industry. In the music school, the a cappella groups are so cool to go

> **SURVEY SAYS . . .**
> Great off-campus food
> Frats and sororities are unpopular
> or nonexistent
> Musical organizations are popular
> College radio is popular
> Theater is popular
> Student publications are popular
> Lots of beer drinking
> Hard liquor is popular

watch." The "fabulous" theater department "has a program in London for theater students and non-theater majors in theater. It's an amazing experience." The equally distinguished communications program is home to an active radio station and award-wining TV station. "Newswatch16, Ithaca College's own locally broadcasted news program won a College Emmy in the fall of 2003 for a spectacular broadcast." In all areas, professors "are very accessible and, because the class sizes are small, they actually know you." Teachers "love class discussions more than just lecturing, and there is always time for questions. Those who exert the extra effort to participate will generally excel more than those who sit in the shadows." At IC "you won't get lost in a sea of people, but it's large enough to offer diverse classes and lots of extracurriculars" as well as "a study abroad program that totally rocks!!!"

Life

"Everyone has fun on the weekends" at Ithaca College, "either through the college or through someone who is having a party. If not, you can travel two minutes to Cornell frats and party there, or go downtown and have tons of fun listening to music or eating out." There's "a lot of culture on and off campus—tons of music, theater, hippie stuff, political happenings." Variety reigns: "One day there's a sold-out football game; the next there's a gay pride rally or a drum circle on the quad." The weather dictates extracurricular life to some extent. "The first month or two of the fall semester, the weather is breathtaking and you get to experience all the beauty the Ithaca area has to offer. You can go hiking, cliff-jumping, camping, swimming, fishing, explore the head shops in the Commons, or just lay outside on one of the many grassy quads and relax in the sun—then the first snowstorm hits and everything changes. Your list of possible activities shortens drastically—unless you're a ski enthusiast, you're basically forced into hibernation until the last month or so of school, when the weather finally gets nice again." Intercollegiate athletics are "a big thing at IC. Even though we're only Division III, students get psyched for football games and such. Intramural and club sports are also big." But "even more people are into our musical and non-sporty exploits. If there was an NCAA thing for band and choir, we would be at the top of Division I."

Student Body

"Ithaca has several different types of 'typical students," undergrads here tell us. "As far as groups go, there seem to be the jocks, the preps, and the hippies. But even if you don't fit into these groups, you will fit in someplace else." Besides, at IC "jocks and hippies interact much more than they would at another school." While the "majority are white, come from privilege, don't have strong religious backgrounds, and are liberal and well-informed in politics," there are also plenty "who come from very religious backgrounds, and those who are conservative and/or Republican, those who are politically apathetic, a mixture of ethnic/minority students and foreign students, all of whom get along with the majority students, [and] a large gay community that seems to be generally accepted by the population. There is very little discrimination on this campus." Students see "an even spread of Protestant,

Catholic, and Jewish faith students. There is even a strict 'Kosher Kitchen' in one of the campus dining halls."

ADMISSIONS

Very important factors considered include: Secondary school record, standardized test scores. *Important factors considered include:* Character/personal qualities, class rank, essays, extracurricular activities, interview, recommendations, talent/ability. *Other factors considered include:* Alumni/ae relation, volunteer work, work experience. SAT Reasoning or ACT required. TOEFL required of all international applicants. High school diploma is required, and GED is accepted. *Academic units required:* 4 English, 3 math, 3 science, 2 foreign language, 3 social studies, 1 academic elective.

The Inside Word

Ithaca has enjoyed a renaissance of interest from prospective students of late, and its moderately competitive admissions profile has been bolstered as a result. In addition to a thorough review of academic accomplishments, candidates are always given close consideration of their personal background, talents, and achievements. Programs requiring an audition or portfolio review are among the college's most demanding for admission; the arts have always been particularly strong.

FINANCIAL AID

Students should submit: FAFSA, CSS/Financial Aid PROFILE required of early decision applicants by 11/1. The Princeton Review suggests that all financial aid forms be submitted as soon as possible after 1/1. *Need-based scholarships/grants offered:* Pell, SEOG, state scholarships/grants, private scholarships, the school's own gift aid. *Loan aid offered:* FFEL Subsidized Stafford, FFEL Unsubsidized Stafford, FFEL PLUS, Federal Perkins, college/university loans from institutional funds. Applicants will be notified of awards on a rolling basis beginning on or about 2/15. Federal Work-study Program available. Off-campus job opportunities are good.

FROM THE ADMISSIONS OFFICE

"Ithaca College was founded in 1892 as a music conservatory, and it continues that commitment to performance and excellence. Its modern, residential 750-acre campus, equipped with state-of-the-art facilities, is home to the schools of Business, Communications, Health Sciences and Human Performance, Humanities and Sciences, and Music and our new Division of Interdisciplinary and International Studies. With more than 100 majors—from biochemistry to business administration, journalism to jazz, philosophy to physical therapy, and special programs in Washington, DC, Los Angeles, London, and Australia—students enjoy the curricular choices of a large campus in a personalized, smaller school environment. And Ithaca's students benefit from an education that emphasizes active learning, small classes, collaborative student-faculty research, and development of the whole student. Located in central New York's spectacular Finger Lakes region in what many consider the classic college town, the college has 25 highly competitive varsity teams, more than 130 campus clubs, two radio stations and a television station, as well as hundreds of concerts, recitals, and theater performances annually."

For even more information on this school, turn to page 495 of the "Stats" section.

JOHNS HOPKINS UNIVERSITY

3400 NORTH CHARLES STREET/140 GARLAND, BALTIMORE, MD 21218 • ADMISSIONS: 410-516-8171
FAX: 410-516-6025 • FINANCIAL AID: 410-516-8028 • E-MAIL: GOTOJHU@JHU.EDU • WEBSITE: WWW.JHU.EDU

Ratings
Quality of Life: 66   **Academic:** 86   **Admissions:** 98   **Financial Aid:** 89

Academics

Johns Hopkins has earned a top reputation as an "excellent and challenging" university, with students who believe their school is "second to none." They value the "contacts you can make" with top professionals in a wide variety of fields. Professors, known to be "experts in their respective areas," take the time to "learn names, talk with students, and give them great advice," according to a student in the political science department, who adds, "Get to know them—it's worthwhile." Another student gushes, "I love the way instructors care about us," making themselves "generally available to offer help outside of class." One student in the "phenomenal" accelerated nursing program calls the course load "highly intense," which leaves "barely any time for social life." The most common complaint logged at Johns Hopkins concerns the perception that professors and administration alike prioritize research over teaching, leading some students to moan that professors think "undergraduates are peons who don't matter much." Students want to see more support for the arts at the school and say that professors in the humanities focus more on their role as teachers than their counterparts in the sciences. The administration, which "needs to be more helpful and understanding," in the words of a few respondents, "prioritizes engineering and medical research" over the needs of undergraduates. Current students remind prospective attendees that they will have to be "proactive to get the best education," but the rewards include the "immense amount of opportunity available for students with good ideas."

> **SURVEY SAYS . . .**
> *Lab facilities are great*
> *Great computer facilities*
> *Great library*
> *Athletic facilities are great*
> *Diverse student types on campus*
> *Students are happy*
> *Lots of beer drinking*
> *Hard liquor is popular*

Life

In the "highly educational environment" of Johns Hopkins, it may seem that "there's not a lot to do besides fraternity parties and homework." Students report, "You have to find your own fun, but it isn't hard to do." Those who have a difficult time entertaining themselves can always fall back on the "instant social life that erupts when you join a fraternity." One undergrad writes, "We generally don't go out more than once or twice a week, but when we do, we live it up." A freshman majoring in international relations appreciates that "there's enough that you can find stuff to do but not so much that it is a distraction." Though one student whines that "Baltimore is a ghetto," many students head downtown when "there isn't much to do on campus." An upperclassman reassures students, "Once you are old enough for bars, it gets better," especially for those with wheels. Many surveys note the brand-spanking-new athletic center, which entices students to play sports and attend to their cardiovascular systems during study breaks. Some students say the school could improve in terms of "clubs and anything school supported," but others offer, "If you want to build a new social outlet, the money [from the school] is available."

Student Body

A typical student who chooses Johns Hopkins might be described as "overly ambitious," "introverted," and "hardworking." To some people, the assortment of "too many weirdos" that makes up the student body displays "little personality." On the one hand, a few students accuse their group of peers, in general, of being "ruled too much by their parents' wishes." On the other hand, one student tells us, "People surprise me (in a good way) every day." Even if "kids could be cooler," respondents agree that "most are good people" and "everyone tends to work together." Accusations of blandness aren't universal; some students boast that "everyone here has done interesting things." While many students say, "We all get along," the population seems to "lack of a sense of unified community," and at times "cultural barriers are very hard to break through."

ADMISSIONS

Very important factors considered include: Character/personal qualities, essays, recommendations, secondary school record. *Important factors considered include:* Class rank, extracurricular activities, standardized test scores, talent/ability, volunteer work. *Other factors considered include:* Alumni/ae relation, geographical residence, interview, minority status, state residency, work experience. SAT Reasoning or ACT required. SAT Subject Tests recommended. TOEFL required of all international applicants. High school diploma is required, and GED is accepted. *Academic units recommended:* 4 English, 4 math, 3 science (2 science lab), 4 foreign language, 3 social studies, 3 history, 2 foreign language for engineering majors.

The Inside Word

The admissions process at Hopkins demands to be taken seriously. Competition with the best colleges and universities in the country keeps the acceptance rate artificially high. Make certain that your personal credentials—essays, recommendations, and extracurricular activities—are impressive.

FINANCIAL AID

Students should submit: FAFSA, CSS/Financial Aid PROFILE, noncustodial (divorced/separated) parents' statement, business/farm supplement, prior and current year federal tax returns. Regular filing deadline 2/15. The Princeton Review suggests that all financial aid forms be submitted as soon as possible after 1/1. *Need-based scholarships/grants offered:* Pell, SEOG, state scholarships/grants, private scholarships, the school's own gift aid. *Loan aid offered:* Direct Subsidized Stafford, Direct Unsubsidized Stafford, FFEL PLUS, Federal Perkins, college/university loans from institutional funds. Applicants will be notified of awards on or about 4/1.

FROM THE ADMISSIONS OFFICE

"The Hopkins tradition of preeminent academic excellence naturally attracts the very best students in the nation and from around the world. The Admissions Committee carefully examines each application for evidence of compelling intellectual interest and academic performance as well as strong personal recommendations and meaningful extracurricular contributions. Every applicant who matriculates to Johns Hopkins University was found qualified by the Admissions Committee through a 'whole person' assessment, and every applicant accepted for admission is fully expected to graduate. The Admissions Committee determines whom they believe will take full advantage of the exceptional opportunities offered at Hopkins, contribute the most to the educational process of the institution, and be the most successful in using what they have learned and experienced for the benefit of society."

For even more information on this school, turn to page 496 of the "Stats" section.

JUNIATA COLLEGE

ENROLLMENT OFFICE, 1700 MOORE ST., HUNTINGDON, PA 16652 • ADMISSIONS: 877-586-4282
FAX: 814-641-3100 • FINANCIAL AID: 814-641-3142 • E-MAIL: ADMISSION@JUNIATA.EDU • WEBSITE: WWW.JUNIATA.EDU

Ratings

Quality of Life: 85   Academic: 88   Admissions: 88   Financial Aid: 76

Academics

"Science is definitely big" at Juniata College, a small, rural liberal arts college in central Pennsylvania, and the school clearly plans to keep it that way. Juniata recently opened a new science center with "state-of-the-art lab facilities and high tech gadgets [that] give students hands-on opportunities to really dive into research. There are great opportunities to prepare for graduate school." But "science isn't the only thing that we offer," students insist; many want you to know that "Juniata also has a much-overlooked yet highly competent education program" and that "you can't go wrong with English, communication, history, foreign languages, or philosophy," although a few warn that "certain departments are really small, and don't receive the support that the sciences have." Through a unique Program of Emphasis (POE) option, Juniata undergrads "can personalize their own program to get a better educational experience." One student writes, "Juniata's Program of Emphasis is a major strength. Students are able to have their major and involve other classes that they may be interested in. For an example, we have students who are computer science majors and also have an emphasis on acting. By allowing students to combine classes that may not be required, they can experience many different things." No matter what undergrads choose to study, "This school is about challenging yourself and your view on the world in preparation for becoming part of it."

> ### SURVEY SAYS . . .
> *Small classes*
> *Lab facilities are great*
> *Students are friendly*
> *Campus feels safe*
> *Low cost of living*
> *Frats and sororities are unpopular or nonexistent*

Life

Because Juniata "is located in beautiful Huntingdon, PA," "there are a lot of things to do outdoors, such as hiking, camping, and biking [but] the town is predominantly residential, so with the exception of the bowling alley and movie theater, there is not much to do here." The college fills the void by "offering wonderful extracurricular activities, from the academic groups such as the Null Set (the mathematics club) and the Barristers Club (for pre-law students), to AWOL (our gay-straight alliance), to the Japanese Club and dozens of others." There's also "a very active campus ministry," as well as "concerts, speakers, shows, and screenings on campus all the time. It is impossible to do everything." Juniata's athletic teams "are another strength. Our men's and women's volleyball teams have both recently won NCAA championships...and our field hockey team is becoming one of the strongest in the nation." Furthermore, the JC calendar is peppered with "several unique traditions, such as Mountain Day, Mr. Juniata, Storming of the Arch, and Madrigal Tenting. These allow the entire Juniata community to get out and have fun with each other." When students seek larger crowds, they travel to Altoona or State College, each about a half-hour's drive away.

Student Body

The "self-driven" undergrads of Juniata "really love what they're studying, and it becomes their life. Once you've accepted that, the school really opens up to you. Everyone is equally interested in their own POE, so you find yourself in really interesting conversations about anything from science to politics to religion. It's great." A large proportion of "the kids who attend here play a varsity or club sport," so a "typical student at Juniata is an athlete." He or she is also "liberal, and proud of it. If you walked around here the day before Election Day 2004 and thought that this campus was a reflection of the rest of the country, you would think that there is no way in hell that George Bush would win the election." Most undergrads "are from Pennsylvania or the surrounding mid-Atlantic states," with a split of "half 'hicks,' half city kids." Although "this is mostly a middle- to upperclass, white, Christian campus...the new Office of Diversity has begun bringing in a promising increase in people of different ethnic and religious backgrounds, as well as different sexual orientations."

ADMISSIONS

Very important factors considered include: Character/personal qualities, essays, extracurricular activities, recommendations, secondary school record, standardized test scores. *Important factors considered include:* Alumni/ae relation, interview, minority status, talent/ability, volunteer work. *Other factors considered include:* Class rank. SAT Reasoning or ACT recommended. TOEFL required of all international applicants. High school diploma is required, and GED is accepted. *Academic units required:* 4 English, 3 math, 3 science (2 science lab), 2 foreign language, 1 social studies, 3 history. *Academic units recommended:* 4 English, 4 math, 4 science (2 science lab), 2 foreign language, 1 social studies, 3 history.

The Inside Word

Like at many traditional liberal arts schools, the admissions process at Juniata is a personal one. The school wants students who will decide to attend Juniata and stay for the next fours years. Among Juniata's bragging rights are that a staggering 40 percent of students graduate with a degree in science, 60 percent of undergrads design their own major, and 78 percent participate in internships.

FINANCIAL AID

Students should submit: FAFSA. Regular filing deadline 3/1. The Princeton Review suggests that all financial aid forms be submitted as soon as possible after 1/1. *Need-based scholarships/grants offered:* Pell, SEOG, state scholarships/grants, private scholarships, the school's own gift aid. *Loan aid offered:* FFEL Subsidized Stafford, FFEL Unsubsidized Stafford, FFEL PLUS, Federal Perkins, college/university loans from institutional funds. Applicants will be notified of awards on a rolling basis beginning on or about 2/1. Federal Work-study Program available. Institutional employment available. Off-campus job opportunities are fair.

FROM THE ADMISSIONS OFFICE

"This is an exciting time to be a part of the Juniata community. Whether students are designing their own programs of study, participating in internships, studying abroad, volunteering for local charities, leading student organizations, or working on individual research, Juniata students learn early in their education how to make things happen.

"Juniata's unique approach to learning has a flexible, student-centered focus. With the help of two advisors, over half of Juniata's students design their own majors (called the "Program of Emphasis" or "POE"). Those who choose a more traditional academic journey still benefit from the assistance of two faculty advisors and interdisciplinary collaboration between multiple academic departments.

"In addition, all students benefit from the recent, significant investments in academic facilities that help students actively learn by doing. For example, the new Halbritter Performing Arts Center houses an innovative theatre program where theatre professionals work side by side with students; the Sill Business Incubator provides $5,000 in seed capital to students with a desire to start their own business; the LEEDS-certified Shuster Environmental Studies Field Station, located on nearby Raystown Lake, gives unparalleled hands-on study opportunities to students; and the von Liebig Center for Science provides opportunities for student/faculty research surpassing those available at even large universities.

"The benefits of Juniata's quality educational environment are apparent. Seventy-five percent of the students who enter Juniata graduate; of those, an impressive 91 percent do so in four years. Upon graduation, 95 percent of the graduates who apply to medical, veterinary, dental, and law school are accepted, and 96 percent of those seeking jobs are employed within six months of graduation.

"As the 2003 Middle States Accreditation Team noted, "Juniata is truly a student-centered college. There is a remarkable cohesiveness in this commitment—faculty, students, trustees, staff, and alumni, each from their own vantage point, describe a community in which the growth of the student is central." This cohesiveness creates a dynamic learning environment that enables students to think and grow intellectually, to evolve in their academic careers, and to graduate as active, successful participants in the global community."

For even more information on this school, turn to page 496 of the "Stats" section.

KEENE STATE COLLEGE

229 MAIN STREET, KEENE, NH 03435 • ADMISSIONS: 603-358-2276 • FAX: 603-358-2767
E-MAIL: ADMISSIONS@KEENE.EDU • WEBSITE: WWW.KEENE.EDU

Ratings
Quality of Life: 70   **Academic:** 74   **Admissions:** 73   **Financial Aid:** 70

Academics

"Keene State is what you make of it," students at this former teachers' college in New Hampshire tell us, explaining that "it is a good school if you make it a good school, [and] it is a party school if you make it a party school." Students who do the latter jokingly refer to KSC as "Kinda Sorta College," and many find a way to slip through the cracks long enough to earn a degree. Others, however, report that there's a fine and challenging education to be had at Keene

State, and all you have to do is go looking for it. Education remains Keene State's forte. One student writes, "Keene State is still geared toward education majors as a holdover from when it was strictly a teachers' college. As an education major, I love this. The administration and professors do their best to make the full schedule of an education major doable." Students report that the business program is also strong, that there are "excellent teachers in the math department," and that the sciences benefit from "a gorgeous science center." Classes in most departments "are generally small, which allows for better classroom discussions and less confusion with class material."

Life

"The greatest strengths of KSC are its size and the ease that students can get around and do things both on campus and in the city of Keene itself," according to the many students who love Keene State's small-town charms. Some students do complain that "there isn't much [to do], especially when you are under twenty-one [in this] beautiful but small New England town," but the majority of students loves the setting. Keene has "gorgeous scenery [and offers] great skiing," and the school works hard to provide diversion by "offering a lot of trips, everything from tubing to paintball to Six Flags. They also have a lot of events in the Night Owl Café, which is a hangout spot on campus. Events such as open mic night, parties during baseball and football games, and comedy nights are also frequent." There's a heavy party scene—"if you're a partier, this is the school for you because there are parties in different places every night and always plenty of people going with you"—but "there is plenty to do for other people who aren't into the party scene." Students report that "the school tries very hard to diminish the reputation of 'party school,' and they are headed in the right direction; however, they cannot totally control the students."

Student Body

The student body at Keene State consists "mostly of white middle-class students from New England; therefore, it is no surprise that ethnicity is not something that is diverse" at the school, students agree. About half of all students originate from outside New Hampshire; most of them come from Connecticut, Massachusetts, and other nearby states. Women outnumber men by a margin of roughly 3:2. While "there is a fair percentage of students who are motivated to get degrees in useful fields and are at Keene for financial or transportation reasons," there are also "many students who it seems didn't do well in high school and just want to have a good time." Students tend to be cliquish: "You have the jocks, nerds, bookworms, and the average Joes, and each person fits in with their own clique."

ADMISSIONS

Very important factors considered include: Secondary school record. *Important factors considered include:* Essays, interview, recommendations, standardized test scores. *Other factors considered include:* Alumni/ae relation, character/personal qualities, class rank, extracurricular activities, minority status, talent/ability, volunteer work, work experience. SAT Reasoning or ACT required. TOEFL required of all international applicants. High school diploma is required, and GED is accepted. *Academic units required:* 4 English, 3 math, 3 science (1 science lab), 2 social studies, 2 academic electives.

The Inside Word

Keene State takes the time to look at your admissions application, primarily in an effort to justify admitting otherwise substandard candidates. The gatekeepers here want to invite you in; all you have to do is give them a good reason.

FINANCIAL AID

Students should submit: FAFSA. Regular filing deadline 3/1. The Princeton Review suggests that all financial aid forms be submitted as soon as possible after 1/1. *Need-based scholarships/grants offered:* Pell, SEOG, state scholarships/grants, private scholarships, the school's own gift aid. *Loan aid offered:* FFEL Subsidized Stafford, FFEL Unsubsidized Stafford, FFEL PLUS, Federal Perkins, college/university loans from institutional funds. Federal Work-study Program available. Institutional employment available. Off-campus job opportunities are fair.

For even more information on this school, turn to page 497 of the "Stats" section.

KUTZTOWN UNIVERSITY OF PENNSYLVANIA

ADMISSIONS OFFICE, 15200 KUTZTOWN ROAD, KUTZTOWN, PA 19530-0730 • ADMISSIONS: 610-683-4060
FAX: 610-683-1375 • E-MAIL: ADMISSION@KUTZTOWN.EDU • WEBSITE: WWW.KUTZTOWN.EDU

Ratings
Quality of Life: 72 Academic: 73 Admissions: 73 Financial Aid: 78

Academics

Kutztown University is a midsize liberal arts school that "combines the benefits of a state college with the intimacy and comfort of a private school." Students rave about the school's "phenomenal" art department, "excellent" English department, "one of the best [electronic media programs] in the country," and its "one-of-a-kind education program, [whose] dual major with special education and elementary education" is quite popular. Education majors also appreciate that the school provides them with "field experiences prior to student teaching that enable [them] to really be pre-

> **SURVEY SAYS . . .**
> *Small classes*
> *Great computer facilities*
> *Great library*
> *Diverse student types on campus*
> *Lots of beer drinking*
> *(Almost) everyone smokes*

pared." The school's enrollment has increased in recent years, causing some growing pains. One student explains, "When I started here in 2001, there were approximately 7,000 students. Now, in 2005, there are almost 9,500. The stress these extra students are putting on the campus is beginning to take place. Temporary classrooms had to be brought in and most of my general education classes are completely full." Still, students are largely satisfied with the education they receive at Kutztown. Professors are "dedicated to their students. They don't put up with laziness or irresponsibility, but if you have a genuine excuse, or need extra attention, they bend over backward for you." One student says, "Overall, with all the assistance and resources available (including multiple computer labs), if students are serious about their education, it is nearly impossible to not succeed."

Life

"Kutztown is a small rural town centered around the university." Students describe life in Kutztown as "pretty slow," and report that many students leave campus on the weekends—a time when they say "the university has very little activities for students." Students who stick around, however, say that "normally, [they] can find something to keep [them] busy." For fun, students head to "local places down the street to eat, such as Momma's Pizza, the Uptown Espresso bar, and Woogie's Famous Hotdogs." Students also "hang out in dorms, play video games, [and] go to the movie theater." Occasionally the school brings in "comedians or hypnotists [or has] open mic nights, [and] casino nights." Road trips are a popular diversion, as well. The cities of Allentown and Reading are "about a half hour away, [and] Dorney Park is down the road about thirty to forty minutes." Because Kutztown has a dry campus, "most students either attend off-campus parties regularly, or if they are over 21 they tend to spend their weekends (and Thursdays) at a bar in town." Although a few students describe their college lives as "boring," other students find the small-town environment comfortable. One student suggests, "People have to be creative, willing to explore, and be okay with just hanging out with friends."

Student Body

Kutztown students are "laid-back, friendly, [and] active" individuals who are "looking to have fun, but to also get the kind of education they need." The "dorms are big so you meet a lot of people. There's a very homelike feel, and it's easy to be comfortable here." Students feel that the diversity of the student body is one of the school's greatest strengths. "This campus has been focusing on diversity for the last four years," one undergrad explains, "and has actually gone out of its way to find more diverse people to attend the university." The student body is a jumble of "business-minded people, creative people, science-buffs, athletes, international students, minorities, [and] nontraditional students." Political, social, and religious views "seem to run the gamut." One student says, "Whether you're a goth, a jock, or a geek, you can usually find a good place to fit in. Everyone interacts well and that makes it an easy place to fit in and make new friends."

ADMISSIONS

Very important factors considered include: Class rank, secondary school record, standardized test scores. *Other factors considered include:* Character/personal qualities, extracurricular activities, geographical residence, interview, minority status, recommendations, state residency, talent/ability, volunteer work, work experience. SAT Reasoning and SAT Subject Tests or ACT required. TOEFL required of all international applicants. High school diploma is required, and GED is accepted. *Academic units recommended:* 4 English, 3 math, 3 science, 2 foreign language, 2 social studies.

The Inside Word

Kutztown makes the vast majority of its admissions decisions based solely on GPA and standardized test scores. Candidates who think they may be on the cusp can, and should, include a personal essay, a list of extracurricular activities, and letters of recommendation with their applications.

FINANCIAL AID

Students should submit: FAFSA. The Princeton Review suggests that all financial aid forms be submitted as soon as possible after 1/1. *Need-based scholarships/grants offered:* Pell, SEOG, state scholarships/grants, private scholarships, the school's own gift aid. *Loan aid offered:* FFEL Subsidized Stafford, FFEL Unsubsidized Stafford, FFEL PLUS, Federal Perkins. Applicants will be notified of awards on a rolling basis beginning on or about 3/30. Federal Work-study Program available. Institutional employment available. Off-campus job opportunities are excellent.

FROM THE ADMISSIONS OFFICE

"In a recent independent survey, 93 percent of students and recent alumni rated their education at Kutztown University as excellent or good in regard to their overall college experience, the quality of instruction they received, and the quality of the faculty. Kutztown offers excellent academic programs through its undergraduate Colleges of Liberal Arts and Sciences, Visual and Performing Arts, Business, and Education and through its graduate studies program. A wide range of student support services complements the high-quality classroom instruction.

"In addition, Kutztown students have the advantage of a well-rounded program of athletic, cultural, and social events. At Kutztown, there are clubs, organizations, and activities to satisfy nearly every taste. Currently, 8,524 full-time and part-time students are enrolled at the university. About half of the full-time undergraduates live in residence halls; the rest live at home or in apartments in nearby communities.

"Kutztown University's attractive 325-acre campus includes a mix of old and new buildings, including stately Old Main, the historic building known to generations of Kutztown's students; Golden Bear Village West, a modern townhouse complex; and the Student Union Building. A new state-of-the-art science facility is set to open in fall 2003.

"The university's graduate program awards the Master of Science, Master of Art, Master of Education, Master of Business Administration, Master of Library Science, Master of Public Administration, and Master of Social Work degrees."

For even more information on this school, turn to page 497 of the "Stats" section.

La Roche College

9000 Babcock Boulevard, Pittsburgh, PA 15237 • Admissions: 412-536-1272 • Fax: 412-536-1820
E-mail: admissions@laroche.edu • Website: www.laroche.edu

Ratings
Quality of Life: 71   Academic: 67   Admissions: 74   Financial Aid: 76

Academics

La Roche College, a Roman Catholic liberal arts school north of downtown Pittsburgh, is "a small community of students representing over 20 countries," states one student. The college strives to maintain a unique learning environment in which students of many cultures can intermingle and learn from one another. The school's Pacem In Terris Institute, offers scholarships to outstanding students in war-torn nations and contributes to the school's commendable diversity. Regardless of the diverse backgrounds, LRC students agree, "The strength of the school is its small size." One student explains, "In a small class with at most 33 other students, you really get a personalized education. Another great quality is that you can possibly have the same teacher more than once, leading to a better student/teacher relationship. My advisor is excellent and gives me very good tips for choosing courses that will make my resume look better." Students speak highly of LRC's business and graphic design programs and their "top-of-the-line" instructors. The professors at La Roche "are easy to talk to and usually will meet with you outside of class or will refer you to someone who can help you. Administration is a little slow but does a good job." One student adds, "There are also many offices dedicated just to your academic improvement. If you care about your academic standing, there is no reason for you to do poorly if you take advantage of the free services." On the downside, several students mention, "The facilities that house the design department could be vastly improved upon in comparison to the rest of the campus."

Life

LaRoche College students "have the luxury of being very close to the city of Pittsburgh," which is just "a fifteen-minute car ride" from campus, many students claim. Those without cars report that a trip into the city takes "about an hour on public transportation." The residence halls are "extremely comfortable, with air conditioning, wall-to-wall carpeting, large accommodations, and a personal shower, sink, and toilet in each room. Cable and micro-fridges are free to each student." Students report that "La Roche is not a party school. However, those who feel the need to party can always head into Oakland where Pitt, CMU, Carlow & Chatham." Students know how to have a good time. Other than that, some state, "There are many activities planned for students that live on campus," including "swing dance and salsa lessons, karaoke, ski trips, dances, trips to operas and plays in downtown Pittsburgh, foam parties, movie nights, bingo, hypnotists, and comedy shows." Another student adds, "With the Catholic affiliation there are many opportunities for community service, which I find rewarding."

Student Body

A typical LaRoche student stands firmly behind the belief that, "There is no typical student at LRC." The campus is "extremely diverse in race, culture, religion and aspirations," one student explains. "I have gained a strong cultural and religious awareness that I do not believe is found on larger campuses. My friends are not all American—many are from Jordan, Africa, and often the Middle East. There are many younger students, as well as nontraditional students like myself. I believe everyone has an equal chance of fitting in." Another student adds, "The classroom could have people from three different continents at the same time, which really spurs up interesting conversations."

ADMISSIONS

Very important factors considered include: Character/personal qualities, essays, interview, recommendations, secondary school record, standardized test scores. *Important factors considered include:* Extracurricular activities, talent/ability. *Other factors considered include:* Volunteer work, work experience. SAT Reasoning or ACT required. High school diploma is required, and GED is accepted. *Academic units required:* 4 English, 3 math, 3 science (2 science lab), 3 social studies, 2 history. *Academic units recommended:* 4 English, 4 math, 3 science (2 science lab), 2 foreign language, 3 social studies, 3 history.

The Inside Word

Don't skip the optional essay in the La Roche application; the school will take it as a sure sign that you're not seriously interested in attending. Applicants are asked to specify their intended area of study on the application. Competition is strongest in the school's popular design majors.

FINANCIAL AID

Students should submit: FAFSA. Regular filing deadline 5/1. The Princeton Review suggests that all financial aid forms be submitted as soon as possible after 1/1. *Need-based scholarships/grants offered:* Pell, SEOG, state scholarships/grants, private scholarships, the school's own gift aid. *Loan aid offered:* FFEL Subsidized Stafford, FFEL Unsubsidized Stafford, FFEL PLUS, Federal Perkins, private loans. Applicants will be notified of awards on a rolling basis beginning on or about 2/15. Federal Work-study Program available. Institutional employment available. Off-campus job opportunities are good.

FROM THE ADMISSIONS OFFICE

"You have the power to change your world. Choose a college that will help you make the most of the opportunities that lie ahead. Discover how La Roche College's 21st-century approach to individualized education will take you exactly where you want to go.

"At La Roche, our faculty prides itself on getting to know you as an individual and understanding the educational goals you have set for yourself. We keep our classes small, allowing for personal attention. We also put the latest technology at your fingertips with our "smart" classrooms. The SMARTBoard lets your professor play a DVD or browse the Internet by simply touching a screen. When you're ready to select a course of study, you can choose from more than 50 undergraduate degree programs that combine thoughtful, engaging classroom instruction with "real-world" experiences.

"'Ad Lucem Per Amorem'" is Latin for 'To Light Through Love,' and it is also La Roche College's motto. It is a reminder of the College's Catholic heritage. Founded in 1963, La Roche College originally served as an institution of higher learning for women preparing to enter religious life. Today, the College enrolls young men and women from nearly 25 states and more than 20 countries; students come with different ideas about the world, and they become members of a growing global community.

"The La Roche campus is located on 80 acres of rolling hills and is ranked as one of the safest four-year private college campuses in the nation. Our apartment-style suites offer the comforts of home, including a refrigerator, a microwave and a bathroom right in your room. The College supports more than 30 student organizations and ten varsity sports in NCAA Division III. La Roche's proximity to Pittsburgh, PA puts you at the doorstep of a world-class city, providing plenty of internship and career opportunities.

"When it comes to financing a quality La Roche education, we have a host of competitive merit-based scholarships and need-based awards. Contact our admissions office and find out for yourself how a La Roche education offers *learning that brings your world together.* Call us at 412-536-1272 (toll-free 1-800-838-4LRC) or e-mail us at admissions@laroche.edu. You can also visit our website at www.laroche.edu."

For even more information on this school, turn to page 498 of the "Stats" section.

LABORATORY INSTITUTE OF MERCHANDISING

12 EAST 53RD STREET, NEW YORK, NY 10022 • ADMISSIONS: 212-752-1530 • FAX: 212-317-8602
E-MAIL: ADMISSIONS@LIMCOLLEGE.EDU • WEBSITE: WWW.LIMCOLLEGE.EDU

Ratings
Quality of Life: 71   Academic: 64   Admissions: 73   Financial Aid: 90

Academics

The Laboratory Institute of Merchandising aims to provide its students with "real-world" experience in all aspects of the fashion industry. A small private college in the heart of Manhattan, LIM is "surrounded by every major designer and every major department store" claims one student. Students appreciate the school's close-knit atmosphere. "I love that I can see the Dean whenever I need to," writes one student. "The small class size makes it easy for the teacher to get to know you on a more personal level." Another student adds, "You're never addressed by your social security number, rather by your nickname...semester meetings with your advisor are required, so you always know what you have to do to reach your desired goal." Professors are "people from the industry, experienced and very knowledgeable." They are routinely described as caring, informative, and friendly. The academic program at LIM primarily focuses on student's careers after they graduate. Students are required to do internships with various companies to ensure that they make the necessary connections to get a foot in the door. As for student complaints, one student writes, "I rarely feel challenged, which doesn't make me work as hard as I should." Another common complaint is that the administration is unorganized, old-fashioned, and unrealistic. One student explains, "There is no choice in schedule, you are handed one to deal with, like it or not. You must register in person and the only way to receive your grades is through the good ole U.S. Postal Service." In response to these concerns, LIM is currently implementing a new Student Information System which will allow students to register and check grades online.

Life

One of the strong points of the institute is the Manhattan setting. "Attending LIM, you will always have something to do on your down time," writes one student. LIM consists of three buildings and five floors of a college dormitory, but lacks an actual campus. "If you want to live in the city," one student explains, "you'll have to find a place yourself." As a result of this, many students feel they "don't really have 'the college experience.'" Although LIM does have its share of clubs, there are no athletic teams, sororities, or fraternities. "Clubs are held during the permanent lunch hour," one student says. According to another, "Most of the students go shopping between classes, eat, or talk on their phones. For fun, I've joined some of the clubs, I work, surf the Internet at school, read magazines, make jewelry, and go clubbing." Students often mention that the school's facilities are somewhat lacking. "We need lockers," declared several students.

Student Body

LIM is regarded as a specialty school, and therefore, most students have a lot in common with each other. A typical student "dresses well, loves to shop, and studies hard." One student writes, "There is mostly a white female population at the school. Some come from money, others do not, but there are your few snobs and others that are very down-to-earth." Some students describe the student body as cliquey, but others disagree.

ADMISSIONS

Very important factors considered include: Interview, secondary school record. *Important factors considered include:* Character/personal qualities, class rank, essays, recommendations, standardized test scores. *Other factors considered include:* Alumni/ae relation, extracurricular activities, talent/ability, volunteer work, work experience. SAT Reasoning or ACT required. TOEFL required of all international applicants. High school diploma is required, and GED is accepted.

The Inside Word

A personal interview is required at LIM; arrive prepared to enthusiastically explain why fashion merchandising is your passion and purpose in life. Two strong letters of recommendation will also boost your chances of admission.

FINANCIAL AID

Students should submit: FAFSA, institution's own financial aid form. The Princeton Review suggests that all financial aid forms be submitted as soon as possible after 1/1. *Need-based scholarships/grants offered:* Pell, SEOG, state scholarships/grants, the school's own gift aid. *Loan aid offered:* Direct Subsidized Stafford, Direct Unsubsidized Stafford, Direct PLUS. Applicants will be notified of awards on a rolling basis beginning on or about 2/15. Federal Work-study Program available. Institutional employment available. Off-campus job opportunities are excellent.

FROM THE ADMISSIONS OFFICE

"LIM College, the College for the Business of Fashion, has been educating leaders in the fashion industry for more than 65 years. Located in the heart of Manhattan, just steps from Fifth Avenue, LIM takes full advantage of its New York City campus and believes that the most powerful ways to learn is to harvest experience from industry professionals. From day one, LIM incorporates real-world experience into a unique hands-on curriculum.

"With four specialized majors in Fashion Merchandising, Marketing, Management, and Visual Merchandising, a 9:1 student to faculty ratio, and an average class size of 19, LIM understands the value of personal attention. LIM is dedicated to preparing its students for the fashion industry and with over 90 percent career placement upon graduation, LIM graduates move forward and upward into exciting careers.

"LIM's highly regarded faculty, a diverse group of industry professionals and educators, bring the business of fashion into LIM's classrooms. An advisory board comprised of top-level business executives also counsel the college on the latest fashion business developments in retail, maufacturing, product development, public relations, marketing, publishing, and visual merchandising.

"Early on, LIM students are exposed to the fashion industry through field tips, an active guest lecture series and two five week full-time internships. In their senior year, students complete a co-op, an entire semester of full-time work in the industry along with a capstone project which incorporates aspects of all four years of their education."

For even more information on this school, turn to page 498 of the "Stats" section.

LAFAYETTE COLLEGE

118 MARKLE HALL, EASTON, PA 18042 • ADMISSIONS: 610-330-5100 • FAX: 610-330-5355
FINANCIAL AID: 610-330-5055 • E-MAIL: ADMISSIONS@LAFAYETTE.EDU • WEBSITE: WWW.LAFAYETTE.EDU

Ratings
Quality of Life: 70   Academic: 89   Admissions: 95   Financial Aid: 95

Academics

"Lafayette's small size and exclusively undergraduate population create tight bonds between professors and students and open the door for research opportunities," students at this small-but-mighty liberal arts school tell us. That's true at many small schools; few others of this size can claim that "the small size does not prevent students from enjoying Division I sports, a nationally recognized engineering program, and great resources and facilities." Lafayette students can and do; they justifiably boast a "great math department, excellent programs in the sciences and engineering, [and] very good classes in the humanities and social sciences, which are under-noticed and underappreciated because of the well-known engineering programs." Students here benefit from a "strong emphasis on class discussion, individual attention from professors, [and] widely available internships and research opportunities with professors." Internships and externships are plentiful thanks in part to "a ton of alumni connections, people who have really stayed involved in the school after they graduated. They can provide resources, connections, ideas, opportunities and more. The sheer number of active alumni is amazing, and their willingness to interact with us is great." Lafayette also offers a number of "popular, widely used study-abroad programs," including six full-semester faculty-led opportunities (in Belgium, Greece, France, Germany, Spain, and Ghana).

> **SURVEY SAYS . . .**
> Small classes
> Lab facilities are great
> Great computer facilities
> Great library
> Athletic facilities are great
> Lots of beer drinking

Life

Lafayette "is located on a hill above downtown Easton, isolating most students on campus, or at least those without cars." Some here tell us that "there is not much to do on top of the hill except drink," which is why "weekends are spent partying." Not everyone feels that way, though. Some are glad to be secluded from Easton, which they describe as "a tad sketchy at night," and they're perfectly happy to remain on their "beautiful campus, with its amazing attention paid to planting and replanting color-coordinated flowers." Others tout the many alcohol-free options available; writes one student, "There is always something to do at Lafayette. There are movies, speakers, comedians, and singing groups available for students. Community service and sporting events are also popular." Because the school is so small, "there are endless opportunities to get involved. If there is an association you want to start, start it! If there is a play you want to write and/or produce, do it! If you have a great new business idea, go for it. Lafayette professors and administrators are very supportive of students' creativity." The campus and the region do a good job of pulling in top-flight entertainment; reports one undergrad, "The amount of performing arts we get at both the Williams Center for the Arts (which is the art and music and theater building) and at the State Theater for the Arts is immense. At Williams, you get a ton of great classical and jazz music. At the State Theater, you get comedians such as Jon Stewart, Jeff Foxworthy, Bill Engvall, Larry 'The Cable Guy', Ron White, Drew Carey, as well as plays such as The Full Monty and The Graduate."

Student Body

"The typical student at Lafayette is very concerned with academics"—you can't last here very long if you're not—"but able to go out and have fun at the same time." He or she also makes time for extracurriculars; observes one student, "The typical Lafayette student has a full plate. Not only is he or she a serious academic student but at the same time is involved in some sort of club or organization on campus, whether it be sports, volunteering, music, or academic-related." Students tell us that "Lafayette is not very diverse, but minorities do have organizations that hold events for the whole campus. The typical student is middle- to upper-class, white, and has generally not had to work for much in their lives, but the student body as a whole is very friendly and accepting." Undergrads tend to be "politically conservative and most are religiously affiliated."

ADMISSIONS

Very important factors considered include: Secondary school record. *Important factors considered include:* Alumni/ae relation, character/personal qualities, class rank, essays, extracurricular activities, minority status, recommendations, standardized test scores, talent/ability, volunteer work. *Other factors considered include:* Geographical residence, interview, work experience. SAT Reasoning or ACT required. TOEFL required of all international applicants. High school diploma or equivalent is not required. *Academic units recommended:* 4 English, 3 math, 2 science (2 science lab), 2 foreign language, 5 academic electives.

The Inside Word

Applications are reviewed three to five times and evaluated by as many as nine different committee members. In all cases, students who continually seek challenges and are willing to take risks academically win out over those who play it safe to maintain a high GPA.

FINANCIAL AID

Students should submit: FAFSA, CSS/Financial Aid PROFILE, noncustodial (divorced/separated) parents' statement, business/farm supplement. Regular filing deadline 2/1. The Princeton Review suggests that all financial aid forms be submitted as soon as possible after 1/1. *Need-based scholarships/grants offered:* Pell, SEOG, state scholarships/grants, private scholarships. *Loan aid offered:* FFEL Subsidized Stafford, FFEL Unsubsidized Stafford, FFEL PLUS, Federal Perkins, state loans, college/university loans from institutional funds, HELP loans to parents. Applicants will be notified of awards on or about 4/1. Federal Work-study Program available. Institutional employment available. Off-campus job opportunities are good.

FROM THE ADMISSIONS OFFICE

"We choose students individually, one by one, and we hope that the ones we choose will approach their education the same way, as a highly individual enterprise. Our first-year seminars have enrollments limited to 15 or 16 students each in order to introduce the concept of learning not as passive receipt of information but as an active, participatory process. Our low average class size and 11:1 student/teacher ratio reflect that same philosophy. We also devote substantial resources to our Marquis Scholars Program, to one-on-one faculty-student mentoring relationships, and to other programs in engineering within a liberal arts context, giving Lafayette its distinctive character, articulated in our second-year seminars exploring values in science and technology. Lafayette provides an environment in which its students can discover their own personal capacity for learning, personal growth, and leadership."

For even more information on this school, turn to page 498 of the "Stats" section.

LANCASTER BIBLE COLLEGE

PO Box 83403, 901 Eden Rd., Lancaster, PA 17608 • Admissions: 717-560-8271 • Fax: 717-560-8213
E-mail: admissions@lbc.edu • Website: www.lbc.edu

Ratings
Quality of Life: 91   **Academic:** 83   **Admissions:** 80   **Financial Aid:** 69

Academics

"Lancaster Bible College exists for the purpose of educating Christian men and women to live according to a Biblical worldview and to serve through professional Christian ministries," declare some students. One student adds, "The greatest strength of the school is the singularity of focus. LBC is all about teaching the Bible and preparing students for ministry. That's it. My advice would be that if you aren't interested in those two things, don't come here." According to our survey, respondents claimed, "The academics are good for basic instruction in Bible and the basic skills of life like English, math, and science." Many praise the education department as well. Nearly all would agree that they "learn more about philosophy and theology than most secular students, and we enjoy discussion in and out of the classroom, mostly because what we are studying is about our lives." Students tell us that administrators and professors "are wonderful. They are so willing to help the students at any time. We can go to them with anything, school-related or not." Notes one undergraduate, "Overall, the professors are here because they want to be, and that makes a huge difference in the way they teach—they actually care."

> **SURVEY SAYS . . .**
> *Small classes*
> *Frats and sororities are unpopular or nonexistent*
> *Very little beer drinking*
> *Very little hard liquor*
> *(Almost) no one smokes*
> *Very little drug use*

Life

"Because the school is smaller," Lancaster students warn, "it sometimes lacks organized on-campus activities." As a result, most of the fun here is of the quiet, subdued variety. "We do everything from bowling to coffeehouses and concerts to road trips. We like shopping at the outlets and doing outdoors things. Most of the time, though, we just hang out with friends and go for dinner, or shop, or talk." Students immerse themselves in extracurricular clubs, service projects, and prayer and Bible-study groups, so they are constantly kept busy. One student notes, "Getting actively involved in Christian service is a strength of this school. We have abundant opportunities: abroad, domestic, urban, or rural." Sporting events are popular, but when there isn't one to attend, "weekends can be pretty boring, since many students go home." Beyond the campus some state, "there are big cities within a day's drive" and, of course, hometown Lancaster, about which students are divided. Some call it "a great town with lots of cultural things to do and lots of great places to work," while others describe it as "a rural area mostly known for the Amish and farming."

Student Body

Lancaster Bible College is a small undergraduate population sharing an unusual singularity of purpose for a "close-knit student body". We all have one thing in common," students here point out, "We love the Lord!" Nearly all are "white, middle class, very friendly, [and] serious about God. We have a lot of students whose parents are or were missionaries, and a lot whose parents are ministers." Students here state they "take studying and going to classes seriously." However, they also realize there is more to life than this. A typical student has a lot of opportunity to become involved within the school and within the community. Also, they have opportunities to "have fun as well." Most who choose to come here fit in fine, undergraduates tell us, adding that "those who don't leave after the first year."

ADMISSIONS

Very important factors considered include: Character/personal qualities, essays, recommendations, religious affiliation/commitment, secondary school record, standardized test scores. *Important factors considered include:* Extracurricular activities. *Other factors considered include:* Class rank, interview, talent/ability, volunteer work. SAT Reasoning or ACT required. TOEFL required of all international applicants. High school diploma is required, and GED is accepted.

The Inside Word

Because LBC prepares students for the ministry, personal character is a major factor. The school assesses character by reviewing applicants' personal written biographies and the letter of recommendation from a pastor; choose your recommender carefully.

FINANCIAL AID

Students should submit: FAFSA, state aid form. The Princeton Review suggests that all financial aid forms be submitted as soon as possible after 1/1. *Need-based scholarships/grants offered:* Pell, SEOG, state scholarships/grants, private scholarships, the school's own gift aid, Office of Vocational Rehabilitation Blindness and Visual Services Awards. *Loan aid offered:* FFEL Subsidized Stafford, FFEL Unsubsidized Stafford, FFEL PLUS, Federal Perkins, alternative loans. Applicants will be notified of awards on a rolling basis beginning on or about 3/15. Federal Work-study Program available. Institutional employment available. Off-campus job opportunities are excellent.

For even more information on this school, turn to page 499 of the "Stats" section.

LEBANON VALLEY COLLEGE

101 NORTH COLLEGE AVENUE, ANNVILLE, PA 17003-6100 • ADMISSIONS: 717-867-6181
FAX: 717-867-6026 • E-MAIL: ADMISSION@LVC.EDU • WEBSITE: WWW.LVC.EDU

Ratings
Quality of Life: 77   Academic: 82   Admissions: 80   Financial Aid: 82

Academics

"Lebanon Valley College is a wonderful college if you enjoy a more personalized setting," say students at this Methodist-affiliated, liberal arts school. One student notes, "Since the school is smaller, you have a chance to know students and faculty on a non-academic level. You have better student-to-professor ratios and have better access to networking in your profession." Students at LVC speak highly of the music, elementary education, science, and mathe-

> **SURVEY SAYS . . .**
> *Small classes*
> *Great library*
> *Athletic facilities are great*
> *Low cost of living*
> *Musical organizations are popular*

matics departments. "We have one of the only and best music recording technology programs, as well as one of the best digital communications programs," reports one student. Undergrads also appreciate how "LVC is also always trying to improve the campus for students, such as the new basketball gym, senior housing, and the new space for the computer science and digi-comm programs that are being built." Students "feel welcomed by the faculty and staff" at LVC. One student agrees, "The faculty knows and remembers you. The classes are small and you can talk to your professors if you have any problems or questions." In addition, "everyone is very helpful, from the financial aid office helping you get the loans you need to the dean of students taking time to meet with every student who gets into trouble." The drawback some find is that the school's modest size can make it feel overprotective. One student says, "I think that the administration is a bit too strict in some of its rules, but that is also because it is such a small campus located in a very small town." Overall, however, students appreciate the challenges that LVC presents. One math major explains, "I find that the mathematics department, while very difficult and demanding, is actually very talented and extraordinarily successful. Many graduates get jobs or are accepted to graduate school right out of college."

Life

Students describe life in Annville, Pennsylvania, as "quiet, serene, [and] relaxing." A few students describe life on campus as "boring." One student explains, "In Annville, there is very little to do. LVC makes up for this by sponsoring activities almost every Friday for the students to go to. Also, there are dances almost every Saturday in the UG, aka The Underground—a small dining hall that doubles as a nightclub and recreation room." The school also offers free outings to students including, "trips to NYC, Ocean City [in Maryland], Baltimore, or Washington DC, and shorter trips to Hershey Park (only 15 minutes away!), ice skating, and bowling." LVC also has "a great fitness center," and a variety of organizations such as "groups for Republicans, Democrats, gay support groups, multicultural groups, athletic groups, and community service organizations." Intramural sporting events are also a popular attraction. One student says, "If you want to find something to do, it takes a little effort, but not much."

Student Body

LVC undergrads are "down-to-earth people who enjoy having a good time, but who are also serious when it comes to grades." The students at LVC have been described as "conservative, somewhat religious, [and] from a fairly wealthy background." Overall they say the school is "mostly white, although the incoming classes are becoming more diverse. The white students get along well with the minorities on campus." Students report that there is also "a small population of homosexual or bisexual students on campus." Most students seem to agree that it is fairly easy to find a comfortable niche on campus, for example, "studious [groups], jocks, party-hardy [students], religious [students], preps, anime [fans], liberals, [and] conservatives." One student explains, "Overall we all get into our own groups and mesh well with the other groups."

ADMISSIONS

Very important factors considered include: Class rank, secondary school record. *Important factors considered include:* Character/personal qualities, extracurricular activities, interview, standardized test scores, talent/ability. *Other factors considered include:* Alumni/ae relation, essays, geographical residence, minority status, recommendations, state residency, volunteer work, work experience. SAT Reasoning or ACT required. TOEFL required of all international applicants. High school diploma is required, and GED is accepted. *Academic units required:* 4 English, 2 math, 1 science, 2 foreign language, 1 social studies. *Academic units recommended:* 3 science (2 science lab), 3 foreign language.

The Inside Word

Lebanon Valley looks primarily at high school grades and curriculum. If you're a B student in the top half of your class, the school's website reports, you have a very good chance of gaining admittance. Students in the top 30 percent of their graduating class are eligible for generous scholarships.

FINANCIAL AID

Students should submit: FAFSA, institution's own financial aid form. The Princeton Review suggests that all financial aid forms be submitted as soon as possible after 1/1. *Need-based scholarships/grants offered:* Pell, SEOG, state scholarships/grants, private scholarships, the school's own gift aid. *Loan aid offered:* FFEL Subsidized Stafford, FFEL Unsubsidized Stafford, FFEL PLUS, Federal Perkins. Applicants will be notified of awards on a rolling basis beginning on or about 3/1. Federal Work-study Program available. Institutional employment available. Off-campus job opportunities are good.

FROM THE ADMISSIONS OFFICE

"Lebanon Valley College encourages applications from students who have taken a challenging college-prep program in high school and performed well. Typical successful applicants have had 3 years of science, 3 of math, and 2 of a foreign language, in addition to English and social studies. While high school grading systems vary widely, we look for applicants to have at least a B average and rank in the top half of their class. Our outstanding, nationally recognized scholarship program complements this process. The College offers scholarships worth up to 50 percent of the value of tuition to students accepted for admission who ranked in the top 30 percent of their high school class. The scholarships are based on the class rank decile, with awards of one-quarter tuition going to those in the third decile, one-third to those in the second decile, and one-half to those in the top 10 percent of their class. Standardized test scores give students from high schools that do not provide a class rank access to the scholarships; during the interview process, the college provides an opportunity for students with a minimum combined SAT critical reading and math score of 1100 to apply for these scholarships. Admission decisions for each class are made on a rolling basis beginning in mid-October. Students offered admission are also informed of their scholarship award based on class rank information received on the high school transcript. Students whose class rank improves during their senior year will be considered for an increased award."

For even more information on this school, turn to page 499 of the "Stats" section.

LEHIGH UNIVERSITY

27 MEMORIAL DRIVE WEST, BETHLEHEM, PA 18015 • ADMISSIONS: 610-758-3100 • FAX: 610-758-4361
FINANCIAL AID: 610-758-3181 • E-MAIL: ADMISSIONS@LEHIGH.EDU • WEBSITE: WWW.LEHIGH.EDU

Ratings
Quality of Life: 64 **Academic:** 77 **Admissions:** 96 **Financial Aid:** 88

Academics

Nearly half the students at prestigious Lehigh University study either engineering or business; a select few even combine the two through the "excellent and very selective integrated business and engineering honors program." These disciplines are undoubtedly the marquee attractions at this demanding midsize school, but other programs certainly stand out. Lehigh is "strong in architecture" and "has very competitive science programs," students tell us. The humanities, on the other hand, "could be expanded a bit more," although the school hopes to improve this with the new Arts Leigh initiative. In the most popular disciplines, "the work is extremely tough and you need to constantly keep on top of it all," with "some classes being mostly project-based, while others are mostly test-based." Grading can be a source of stress, as "your entire grade is based on a huge curve, especially in the science, math and engineering classes, so you never know how well you are doing until your grades are posted at the end of the semester." Fortunately, "the faculty here are generally extremely helpful, and any of the professors are more than willing to set up meeting times with students to discuss problems or to provide you with extra help." Undergrads also love that "Lehigh has amazing research facilities and brilliant professors with tons of real-world experience. As an example, one chemistry professor created a method to remove arsenic from wells in India and Bangladesh, and then helped incorporate that into the freshman engineering class." Such assets play well with area businesses, translating into "great opportunities for internships and great job placement rates for graduates."

Life

Lehigh, with its "heavy workload and active social life . . . embodies the 'work hard, play hard' mantra. We party here like there is no tomorrow," students tell us. Partying on 'The Hill,' "where all frat and sorority houses are situated, is the main attraction when we aren't studying, which is rare," but parties in non-Greek off-campus housing are also common, and "the two social groups don't really mix or interact." There are activities for non-drinkers—"There's swing dancing Saturday nights, and guest singers and poetry readings at Lamberton Hall" as well as "some good concerts and comedians on weekends"—but "even these events are mostly attended by people who drink, (before they) go to them, then go out and party afterwards." During the week "there is so much for the students to get involved with, which creates a lot of opportunities to partake in leadership roles and develop in many ways as a human being." College athletics are big, with the annual square-off against nearby Lafayette as the highlight of each season. Although hometown Bethlehem "has some wonderful places for students to go and is very affordable," many here prefer either to hang near campus or "take the bus to Philly for some real city entertainment. It's really convenient."

Student Body

Lehigh's "typically athletic" students "want to do well in class but also love to party." They all shop at the same places, procuring uniforms consisting of some combination of "khakis, Polos with popped collars, North Face fleece, Gucci, Prada, Coach, Dooney & Bourke, pointy boots, Ugg boots, and rainbow sandals. We are prepped out and name branded to the max; this is Lehigh." Some here observe that "the school is trying to diversify" and that "the freshman were more diverse in 2004–2005. Lots of freshman have 'fros, and you notice. You can identify the punk kids and the handful of goth kids; everyone knows who you are if you look different." Students tend to be apolitical; explains one undergrad, "Politics is not a big topic, and current events tend to not be known. You end up in the 'Lehigh Bubble' here." An added benefit of attending Lehigh is that the campus landscape guarantees a daily workout; most undergrads "have great legs from climbing our mountain day in and day out!"

ADMISSIONS

Very important factors considered include: Recommendations, secondary school record. *Important factors considered include:* Character/personal qualities, essays, extracurricular activities, standardized test scores, talent/ability, volunteer work. *Other factors considered include:* Alumni/ae relation, class rank, minority status, work experience. SAT Reasoning or ACT required. TOEFL required of all international applicants. High school diploma or equivalent is not required. *Academic units required:* 4 English, 3 math, 2 science (2 science lab), 2 foreign language, 2 social studies, 3 academic electives.

The Inside Word

Lots of work at bolstering Lehigh's public recognition for overall academic quality has paid off—liberal arts candidates will now find the admissions process to be highly selective. Students without solidly impressive academic credentials will have a rough time getting in regardless of their choice of programs, as will unenthusiastic but academically strong candidates who have clearly chosen Lehigh as a safety.

FINANCIAL AID

Students should submit: FAFSA, CSS/Financial Aid PROFILE, noncustodial (divorced/separated) parents' statement, business/farm supplement. Regular filing deadline 2/1. The Princeton Review suggests that all financial aid forms be submitted as soon as possible after 1/1. *Need-based scholarships/grants offered:* Pell, SEOG, state scholarships/grants, private scholarships, the school's own gift aid, United Negro College Fund. *Loan aid offered:* FFEL Subsidized Stafford, FFEL Unsubsidized Stafford, FFEL PLUS, Federal Perkins, college/university loans from institutional funds, private educational alternative loans. Applicants will be notified of awards on or about 3/30. Off-campus job opportunities are excellent.

FROM THE ADMISSIONS OFFICE

"Lehigh University is located 50 miles north of Philadelphia and 75 miles southwest of New York City in Bethlehem, Pennsylvania, where a cultural renaissance has taken place with the opening of more than a dozen ethnic restaurants, the addition of several boutiques and galleries, and Lehigh's new Campus Square residential/retail complex. Lehigh combines learning opportunities of a large research university with the personal attention of a small, private college, by offering an education that integrates courses from four colleges and dozens of fields of study. Students customize their experience to their interests by tailoring majors and academic programs from more than 2,000 courses, changing majors, carrying a double major, or taking courses outside their college or major field of study. Lehigh offers unique learning opportunities through interdisciplinary programs such as music and engineering and computer science and business (www.lehigh.edu/specialprograms). The arts are essential to the learning experience and are integrated throughout the curriculum. Students develop their imagination and creativity while acquiring skills that will complement their professional development. Students have access to world-class faculty who offer their time and personal attention to help students learn and succeed. Students gain hands-on, real world experience and take part in activities that build confidence and help them develop as leaders. Lehigh's vibrant campus life offers many social and extracurricular activities. Choose from 140 clubs and social organizations or 25 intercollegiate sports teams or become one of the 3,500 students (75 percent) who participate in intramural and club programs."

For even more information on this school, turn to page 500 of the "Stats" section.

LESLEY COLLEGE AT LESLEY UNIVERSITY

LESLEY COLLEGE: 29 EVERETT STREET, CAMBRIDGE, MA 02138 • ADMISSIONS: 617-349-8800
FAX: 617-349-8810 • E-MAIL: UGADM@MAIL.LESLEY.EDU • WEBSITE: WWW.LESLEY.EDU

Ratings
Quality of Life: 70   **Academic:** 77   **Admissions:** 77   **Financial Aid:** 72

Academics

A small school in Cambridge, Massachusetts, Lesley College is committed to the "professional empowerment and engagement in social change of the community and world." Boasting popular programs in Education and Art Therapy, Lesley attracts many undergraduates with an interest in politics, community organizing, education, and justice. However, in all its major fields, Lesley encourages practical applications of the academic experience through a number of avenues, including a mandatory internship requirement for undergraduate majors. A freshman enthuses, "If you have been dreaming of a school where you can learn how to effectively improve people's everyday lives, Lesley is the place to come." At Lesley, faculty brings practical, real-world experience to the classroom. A junior tells us, "The professors are all professionals in the fields they teach. They are able to share their personal experiences in order to foster our growth and knowledge in our particular major or class of interest." In that vein, personal growth is a big part of the educational experience at Lesley, and faculty promotes a "focus on self-awareness as an impetus for social change." A sophomore shares: "My professors exceed my expectations in every respect—specifically through their ability to connect with students and cater to their individual needs." As a result, students admit that the Lesley experience can occasionally be "very touchy-feely, let's-get-to-know-you." However, this friendly attitude is generally appreciated, permeating every aspect of campus life. A happy freshman tells us, "You can talk to pretty much anyone here, from kitchen staff to the deans to the president. By the end of the first year, you recognize almost everybody." Despite their reputed friendliness, there are widespread complaints that "the registrar, bursar, and financial aid office are completely disorganized," leading to a lot of headaches for undergrads.

> **SURVEY SAYS . . .**
> *Small classes*
> *Students love Cambridge, MA*
> *Great off-campus food*
> *Frats and sororities are unpopular*
> *or nonexistent*
> *(Almost) everyone smokes*

Life

On the small Lesley campus, "students work, sleep, eat, and play together." As a result, there is a "real sense of community and friendship" amongst Lesley students. The students body is fairly active in the local community, and "there is always a club to join or an activity or demonstration to attend." In addition, "sports are huge here" and most men and women participate in at least one club team or intramurals. On-campus social life is generally low-key and, in addition to hanging out and studying together, "the student activities department brings in musical acts, recently-released movies, and fun weeks." However, students warn that "Lesley is not a party school" and the campus quiets down considerably on the weekends, when many students go home or leave campus in search of more raucous social outlets. For the festive crew, "Boston clubs and bars are popular," as are parties at one of the many neighboring colleges. On that note, many say that one of the school's greatest assets is its location in the consummate college town of Cambridge, Massachusetts. A freshman enthuses, "Being so close to Boston is amazing. There is always something to do a few minutes away in Harvard Square."

Student Body

Lesley students describe each other as "outgoing, politically active, and open-minded." Given the school's interest in promoting a practical education, it's not surprising that Lesley students are mostly "career-oriented girls" who take a proactive approach to their education and future as well as the improvement of their community. Insists a freshman, "Most students are genuinely interested in learning new things and creating positive change." On that note, there is a strong political and activist vibe at Lesley, mostly promoted by the school's majority of "left-wing, liberal democrats" who dominate the faculty and student population. In addition to their homogenous political views, Lesley students tend to come from similar economic and personal backgrounds. Students admit that there isn't a lot of ethnic or cultural diversity on campus; however, there is, to some extent, "a mixture in ethnic, religious, and social ways." Under any circumstance, Lesley is a tolerant and open environment where "everyone is really interesting and they share their own personal views."

ADMISSIONS

Very important factors considered include: Character/personal qualities, interview, secondary school record, talent/ability. *Important factors considered include:* Essays, extracurricular activities, recommendations, standardized test scores, volunteer work. *Other factors considered include:* Alumni/ae relation, class rank, geographical residence, minority status, work experience. SAT Reasoning or ACT required. TOEFL required of all international applicants. High school diploma is required, and GED is accepted. *Academic units required:* 4 English, 3 math, 3 science (2 science lab), 1 social studies, 1 history, 7 academic electives. *Academic units recommended:* 4 English, 3 math, 3 science (2 science lab), 2 foreign language, 2 social studies, 2 history, 4 academic electives.

The Inside Word

The majority of Lesley undergrads major in education or psychology. This means that admissions officers are looking for candidates with more than just a strong academic background; they are also looking for evidence of compassion, patience, and a passion for working with and helping people.

FINANCIAL AID

Students should submit: FAFSA, institution's own financial aid form. The Princeton Review suggests that all financial aid forms be submitted as soon as possible after 1/1. *Need-based scholarships/grants offered:* Pell, SEOG, state scholarships/grants, private scholarships, the school's own gift aid. *Loan aid offered:* FFEL Subsidized Stafford, FFEL Unsubsidized Stafford, FFEL PLUS, Federal Perkins, state loans. Applicants will be notified of awards on a rolling basis beginning on or about 3/15. Federal Work-study Program available. Institutional employment available. Off-campus job opportunities are excellent.

FROM THE ADMISSIONS OFFICE

"Lesley College prepares men and women for careers and lives that make a difference, providing students with the skills and knowledge to make a positive difference and create hope. Central to this mission is a commitment to broad liberal arts preparation, career-focused field placements and internships, and true integration of theory and practice.

"Lesley College combines the advantages of an intimate learning community with all of the academic and co-curricular resources of a large university. That includes access to the professionals and programs of the Art Institute of Boston at Lesley, and a wide-ranging array of graduate programs and academic centers. The Lesley campus is steps away from bustling Harvard Square, in the heart of America's premiere college town. The exciting cultural and educational resources of the Boston area are not just an added social benefit to college life; involvement in the community is an important aspect of the Lesley undergraduate experience.

"Lesley graduates are creative problem-solvers, highly qualified professionals, confident life-long learners, and engaged citizens, active in their workplaces and communities. They believe individuals—working collaboratively—can make a difference. Whether they choose to enter professional fields or pursue graduate studies, their undergraduate experiences at Lesley prepare them for leadership and success. In classrooms, human service settings, government, non-profit organizations and corporations, the environment, and the arts, Lesley graduates are working daily to improve the lives of others and the world around them."

For even more information on this school, turn to page 500 of the "Stats" section.

LOYOLA COLLEGE IN MARYLAND

4501 NORTH CHARLES STREET, BALTIMORE, MD 21210 • ADMISSIONS: 410-617-5012 • FAX: 410-617-2176
FINANCIAL AID: 410-617-2576 • WEBSITE: WWW.LOYOLA.EDU

Ratings
Quality of Life: 89   **Academic:** 83   **Admissions:** 89   **Financial Aid:** 93

Academics

"Loyola is about the community experience, which can be seen in the way faculty and students are truly involved in the community," students at this small Jesuit liberal arts college in Baltimore report. Community service is just one of many ways in which a Loyola education embodies Jesuit ideals. The school also pursues the Jesuit raison d'être of educating the "whole person" through a thorough core curriculum that "pushes students to their full potential, requiring us to take classes that we would not necessarily choose to take" in such disciplines as writing, social science, philosophy, and theology. Professors here strive to create "an excellent environment for learning and discussion" in which "there is a general sense that everyone wants you to succeed. They let you know that they are willing to help you in whatever way they can, and they really mean it." This sense of community extends beyond the classroom; notes one undergraduate, "Professors do not just go home at the end of the day. They are present at school sporting events, concerts, plays and much more. They really make an effort to get to know all students." Students also appreciate the "unbeatable study abroad program" and the way "professors try to incorporate cultural aspects of Baltimore into their classes. There are often trips to see plays, museum visits, and community service events incorporated into the class." The school's location offers not only numerous cultural outlets, but also "many opportunities to network with high business executives and land great internships."

> **SURVEY SAYS . . .**
> Small classes
> Athletic facilities are great
> Dorms are like palaces
> Frats and sororities are unpopular or nonexistent
> Lots of beer drinking
> Hard liquor is popular

Life

Loyola students enjoy an "amazingly beautiful campus for such a great location. We're right in Baltimore, but away from the hustle and bustle of downtown in a suburban atmosphere." The campus hosts a wide range of activities, including "great annual events with huge turnouts, such as Loyolapalooza, the Fall Football Classic, and Crabfests," as well as "midnight breakfasts, basketball games, and other weekend activities [like] excellent school concerts with great bands and comedians," all of which help to fill up students' extracurricular calendars. Many undergraduates also cite Baltimore's "many museums, coffee shops, restaurants, the Inner Harbor and sporting events," as well as easy access to DC and Annapolis when joking that "there is almost too much to do here." Then there are those who love the area bars. Those who favor the bar scene—and there are quite a few of them—insist that "Loyola is a bar school. Everybody loves the Baltimore bars and everyone loves going to them. You can always be sure to find fellow Loyola students at any bar in Baltimore on any day of the week." Others temper their assessment, telling us, "A good amount of us do take advantage of the bar scene, but we are not out of control. There are plenty of activities to do aside from drinking." What students don't do is party in their "awesome dorms, [since] the college is looking to bust anyone and everyone for the slightest infringement on the rules."

Student Body

"Popped collars, Ugg boots, J. Crew, Abercrombie, American Eagle, flip-flops, and a North Face jacket" are all acceptable components of the unofficial Loyola uniform. Students also point out that "Although everyone may look the same, they really are different people. You can tell based on the variety of groups and clubs the campus offers." While many students here are admittedly materialistic—"There is the unspoken desire to outdo each other: Who has the most expensive car, who wears the better clothes, who has the best sunglasses"—they are "friendly and outgoing" and also have an altruistic side; "Volunteering is huge," many tell us. Although "the racial and social diversity at Loyola has increased greatly over the last few years," the student body remains "very homogeneous."

ADMISSIONS

Very important factors considered include: Secondary school record. *Important factors considered include:* Standardized test scores. *Other factors considered include:* Alumni/ae relation, character/personal qualities, class rank, essays, extracurricular activities, minority status, recommendations, talent/ability, volunteer work, work experience. SAT Reasoning or ACT required. TOEFL required of all international applicants. High school diploma is required, and GED is accepted. *Academic units required:* 4 English, 3 math, 3 science, 2 history. *Academic units recommended:* 4 English, 4 math, 4 science, 3 history.

The Inside Word

Loyola is to be commended for notifying outstanding candidates of acceptance early in the applicant review cycle without demanding an early commitment in return. Traditional Early Decision plans are confusing, archaic, and unreasonable to students. A binding commitment is a huge price to pay to get a decision four months sooner. This is obviously one place that cares.

FINANCIAL AID

Students should submit: FAFSA, CSS/Financial Aid PROFILE, noncustodial (divorced/separated) parents' statement, business/farm supplement. Regular filing deadline 2/15. The Princeton Review suggests that all financial aid forms be submitted as soon as possible after 1/1. *Need-based scholarships/grants offered:* Pell, SEOG, state scholarships/grants, private scholarships, the school's own gift aid. *Loan aid offered:* Direct Subsidized Stafford, Direct Unsubsidized Stafford, FFEL PLUS, Federal Perkins, college/university loans from institutional funds. Applicants will be notified of awards on or about 4/1. Federal Work-study Program available. Institutional employment available. Off-campus job opportunities are good.

FROM THE ADMISSIONS OFFICE

"To make a wise choice about your college plans, you will need to find out more. We extend to you these invitations. Question-and-answer periods with an admissions counselor are helpful to prospective students. An appointment should be made in advance. Admissions office hours are 9 A.M. to 5 P.M., Monday through Friday. College day programs and Saturday information programs are scheduled during the academic year. These programs include a video about Loyola, a general information session, a discussion of various majors, a campus tour, and lunch. Summer information programs can help high school juniors to get a head start on investigating colleges. These programs feature an introductory presentation about the college and a campus tour."

For even more information on this school, turn to page 501 of the "Stats" section.

LYCOMING COLLEGE

700 COLLEGE PLACE, WILLIAMSPORT, PA 17701 • ADMISSIONS: 570-321-4026 • FAX: 570-321-4317
E-MAIL: ADMISSIONS@LYCOMING.EDU • WEBSITE: WWW.LYCOMING.EDU

Ratings
Quality of Life: 84   **Academic:** 82   **Admissions:** 80   **Financial Aid:** 75

Academics

Practical experiences figure prominently at Lycoming College, a small liberal arts and sciences school in north central Pennsylvania where "biology and psychology are the two largest majors." Four in five students complete an internship, independent study, honors project, or other practical experience during their tenure at the school. One student notes, "The greatest strength of Lycoming would

> **SURVEY SAYS . . .**
> *Small classes*
> *Athletic facilities are great*
> *Lots of beer drinking*

have to be the experiences that the students have outside of campus; for example, the internships and open opportunities that aren't provided at a larger university." Small classes are also a mainstay of Lycoming life; students approve of the "well-rounded, close-knit" vibe on campus facilitated by a "good teacher-to-student ratio that makes you feel welcome and that you are a person, not just a number." Professors "try to make class interesting and get [students] motivated. Most value class participation heavily. The more ideas thrown out to the class, the better atmosphere it creates. They even make themselves available outside of class if [students] have problems." Course selection is limited by the school's size, but most students are willing to concede breadth of selection for personal attention. The school allows students to broaden their curricula by taking some classes at other institutions.

Life

"The weekends are good fun" at Lycoming, with students enjoying "lots of parties, but not your typically Penn State kind of party. They're more low-key (but still pretty crazy)." Weekends are also the time for "movies, karaoke, concerts, comedians, dances, and lots of other fun things on campus. There is almost always something to do if you are just willing to look around." There is "heavy participation in various clubs on campus and a wide variety of clubs to fit almost any interest you might have, from dance to crew to religion." Lycoming's Greek organizations "are fairly popular on campus, [although] there is a college and city policy against off-campus housing, so Greeks are placed in dorms like any other students." Greeks and non-Greeks alike are "very active in community service." Intramural and intercollegiate sports are also very popular; the women's soccer team recently recorded its single-season high for victories, going 12-4-1. Students' opinions of hometown Williamsport are split. Some tell us that "there isn't much to do on the weekends because it isn't much of a college town; things close pretty early at night." Others say just the opposite: "There are plenty of things to do in Williamsport. There are restaurants, a movie theater, bowling alleys, and a big mall."

Student Body

While overwhelmingly Caucasian, the Lycoming student body "is pretty diverse in terms of student interests. Musicians, athletes, and frat boys and girls all [coexist] in one happy group. Everyone meshes pretty well, everyone is accepting, and really, [they] are all pretty down-to-earth." The exceptions are the athletes, who some say consider themselves better than their peers. One student agrees and grumbles, "The football players parade around campus like they are first-class and everyone should bow to them." Many Lycoming undergrads are "from small rural towns, of the Methodist faith, and very conservative." American Eagle is their outfitter of choice, but "many students just wear sweats or their pajamas to class because everything is pretty laid-back." While "they are for the most part very studious," Lycoming students "also like to have fun."

ADMISSIONS

Very important factors considered include: Secondary school record. *Important factors considered include:* Character/personal qualities, class rank, interview, standardized test scores. *Other factors considered include:* Alumni/ae relation, essays, extracurricular activities, recommendations, talent/ability, volunteer work, work experience. SAT Reasoning or ACT required. TOEFL required of all international applicants. High school diploma is required, and GED is accepted. *Academic units required:* 4 English, 3 math, 2 science (2 science lab), 2 foreign language, 3 social studies, 2 academic electives. *Academic units recommended:* 4 English, 4 math, 3 science (3 science lab), 3 foreign language, 4 social studies, 3 academic electives.

The Inside Word

B students with above-average standardized test scores should clear all Lycoming admission hurdles without trouble. Those who don't meet these qualifications can improve their chances considerably by visiting the campus, interviewing, and expressing a strong interest in attending the college.

FINANCIAL AID

Students should submit: FAFSA, institution's own financial aid form, state aid form. The Princeton Review suggests that all financial aid forms be submitted as soon as possible after 1/1. *Need-based scholarships/grants offered:* Pell, SEOG, state scholarships/grants, private scholarships, the school's own gift aid. *Loan aid offered:* FFEL Subsidized Stafford, FFEL Unsubsidized Stafford, FFEL PLUS, Federal Perkins, state loans. Applicants will be notified of awards on a rolling basis beginning on or about 3/15. Off-campus job opportunities are excellent.

FROM THE ADMISSIONS OFFICE

"At a time when many colleges have tried to become all things to all people, Lycoming has chosen to remain a traditional, undergraduate, residential, liberal arts college. What makes Lycoming different is the way it chooses to deliver its curriculum—in small classes taught by highly credentialed, well-seasoned, full-time professors. 'It's how we teach, not what we teach that is special here,' says Professor Mel Zimmerman, chair of the faculty. 'It's the way we respond to questions, the comments we write on papers, and the way we interact with students outside the classroom that makes this school so appealing.' Staying true to who we are is the reason we've been in business since 1812."

For even more information on this school, turn to page 501 of the "Stats" section.

MANHATTAN COLLEGE

MANHATTAN COLLEGE PARKWAY, RIVERDALE, NY 10471 • ADMISSIONS: 718-862-7200 • FAX: 718-862-8019
E-MAIL: ADMIT@MANHATTAN.EDU • WEBSITE: WWW.MANHATTAN.EDU

Ratings

Quality of Life: 72   **Academic:** 63   **Admissions:** 60   **Financial Aid:** 65

Academics

Manhattan College, a private Lasallian Catholic school that is actually located several miles north of Manhattan, New York, does a solid job of "preparing its students for outstanding job opportunities in teaching, business, and engineering." Undergrads at the school agree that the school's "greatest strength is its size. It's small enough that professors and administrators know you personally, [which is] especially useful when it comes to finding internships or jobs because there are plenty of people who can write great recommendations for you." A solid "network of alumni

[and] a very strong career service department that will help you with jobs upon graduation and during senior year" also contribute in this area. Students appreciate that "there are no teachers' assistants at Manhattan, so you are always taught by a professor or PhD [and] professors are always there to help. When you walk by their offices, [all the] professors [have their doors open]. They are extremely welcoming and generous with their time." As a bonus, "the teachers are all very technologically aware. A large portion of teachers uses PowerPoint or other digital slides on a weekly basis when giving lectures."

Life

While "campus life can be active at times" at Manhattan College, most students spend little extracurricular time on campus; the allure of downtown Manhattan, just a short subway ride away, is too great. Students tell us, "There is not much partying in the dorms [so] the best place for students to go is into New York City. There is so much to do in the city that no one has an excuse to be bored." The IRT stops right outside the campus gate to whisk students to Columbus Circle, Times Square, and Greenwich Village; bus service takes students to Fordham and Yonkers, two other popular destinations. Closer to campus are Van Cortlandt Park "where you can go for a run, play golf, or just relax;" the surrounding Riverdale and Fieldstone neighborhoods, "which are pretty wealthy, so it is sometimes nice to walk around and look at the houses, and there are also good babysitting opportunities;" and some local bars that have become traditional student haunts. The campus itself "is small but beautiful. They use it a lot for movies and television shows." When lounging around the dorm, "the satellite TV access, including five HBO stations is well-appreciated and widely utilized all around campus." Lots of students rally to support the men's basketball team, a frequent participant in the NCAA tournament.

Student Body

Students detect "two very different groups" on the Manhattan College campus. "The residents are mostly all from the tristate area from Catholic upbringings, which means that many went to the same school and/or share the same lifestyles," explains one undergrad, "whereas majority of the commuters are from urban areas and seem out of touch with the residents." Most students tell us that the student body at the school is "mostly white" [with a mix] of African Americans, Hispanics, and Asians. People's backgrounds range from middle-class to upper-class. Everyone fits in fine and gets along well around campus." They "are either dressed really well [and have] real Louis Vuitton bags or [are] bumming it out with sweatpants by Abercrombie. There are a variety of styles from punk to preppy and everything in between."

ADMISSIONS

Very important factors considered include: Secondary school record, standardized test scores. *Important factors considered include:* Class rank, essays, extracurricular activities, interview, recommendations. *Other factors considered include:* Alumni/ae relation, character/personal qualities, talent/ability, volunteer work, work experience. SAT Reasoning or SAT Subject Tests required. TOEFL required of all international applicants. High school diploma is required, and GED is accepted. *Academic units required:* 4 English, 3 math, 2 science, 2 foreign language, 3 social studies, 2 academic electives. *Academic units recommended:* 4 English, 4 math, 3 science, 3 foreign language, 3 social studies.

The Inside Word

Manhattan's engineering program may be one of the undiscovered gems of the region. Because of heavy competition from other area engineering schools, however, the college cannot afford to be as selective as it might wish, thus presenting a golden opportunity to prospective engineers who slacked off a bit in high school.

FINANCIAL AID

Students should submit: FAFSA. Regular filing deadline 4/1. The Princeton Review suggests that all financial aid forms be submitted as soon as possible after 1/1. *Need-based scholarships/grants offered:* Pell, SEOG, state scholarships/grants, private scholarships, the school's own gift aid. *Loan aid offered:* Direct Subsidized Stafford, Direct Unsubsidized Stafford, Direct PLUS, FFEL Subsidized Stafford, FFEL Unsubsidized Stafford, FFEL PLUS, Federal Perkins. Applicants will be notified of awards on or about 3/1. Federal Work-study Program available. Institutional employment available. Off-campus job opportunities are good.

FROM THE ADMISSIONS OFFICE

"Manhattan College has surpassed its 150th anniversary—a milestone in its commitment to providing students a person-centered educational experience characterized by high academic standards and reflection on values and principles. At 150 years and counting, the college continues to improve its academic programs and offerings to properly serve the next generation of students. For instance, the school of business in 2004 received accreditation by the Association to Advance Collegiate Schools of Business (AACSB) International, boosting the College's solid reputation among business programs worldwide. Also, the school of education recently won a New York State grant to start a graduate program in autism studies, a growing field of interest among education majors. While the College does its part to reinvent itself to remain a top choice among college-bound students, certain things will never change, such as the personal attention students receive from their professors and the College's Lasallian dedication to helping students nurture their spiritual side."

For even more information on this school, turn to page 501 of the "Stats" section.

MANHATTANVILLE COLLEGE

2900 PURCHASE STREET, ADMISSIONS OFFICE, PURCHASE, NY 10577 • ADMISSIONS: 914-323-5124
FAX: 914-694-1732 • E-MAIL: ADMISSIONS@MVILLE.EDU • WEBSITE: WWW.MVILLE.EDU

Ratings
Quality of Life: 80   **Academic:** 77   **Admissions:** 83   **Financial Aid:** 75

Academics

Ask students to describe the Manhattanville experience, and they'll likely use the word "family" time and again. "Manhattanville is a family. Professors' and administrators' doors are always open," writes a typical student. Giving rise to this homey atmosphere are "small and personal classrooms that contribute to a very engaging learning experience between yourself, your professor, and your classmates, all giving and taking equally and efficiently."

SURVEY SAYS . . .
Small classes
Diverse student types on campus
Frats and sororities are unpopular
or nonexistent
(Almost) everyone smokes

The success of such an approach, of course, hinges on the quality of the faculty. Fortunately, "The professors are incredible, very down-to-earth. They greet you when they see you, and they give their home phone numbers so you can contact them at any time." Crowed one student, "My profs make me feel important so that I want to work harder for them." Upper-level administration is equally accessible. In fact, many students singled out President Berman as one of Manhattanville's greatest assets. "The president holds monthly dinners at his house, and many of us stay for hours to discuss various issues, both personal and school-related. He also attends most student events. How many other college students can say that they see and interact with the school's president at least once a week?" Students report that "The education department has made quite a name for itself and is helpful getting jobs for grad students," but add that the school is strong in many areas. Wrote one student, "Manhattanville offers a great liberal arts education, with strength in a variety of departments, from drama to computer science." A few warned that the small departments are very small; chemistry majors, for example, cross-register at SUNY at Purchase for a few of their classes.

Life

There's "not much to do on campus" at Manhattanville, students here agree, attributing the subdued social scene to several factors. Many report that "Security is ridiculously tight," and "there are no Greeks on campus, so there isn't even a place to have huge parties." The most compelling reason, perhaps, is that "most people go to New York City for fun. It is only 45 minutes by train" or on the free Valiant bus service provided by the school. Being "the most amazing cultural activity center in the world," students find no lack of things to do in the city. Campus fun consists of quiet activities; explains one undergrad, "There's pretty much always someone's room to go hang out in. Watching movies, playing video games, watching TV, playing guitar, drinking, playing Frisbee or lacrosse, and just talking are what people do—among a few other things—to have fun." Undergrads also tell us that "major sporting events and theater productions are lots of fun and are well attended." As one student summarizes, "Situated in a rich Westchester suburb, the campus is beautifully serene. Yet within 10 minutes of the campus is the center of Westchester County, offering plenty of great food, shopping, and night life."

Student Body

The "smart, sociable," "athletic, easygoing" undergrads of Manhattanville generally hail from New York and Connecticut, although there is also a sizeable international student population. Wrote one local, "The greatest strengths [of] my school are the extreme levels of diversity. There are students from Europe, [Asia], the Middle East, and the Caribbean. I have never known so many international people before!" A few complain, however, that "while there is diversity, students are segregated into their own groups." Others gripe that their classmates are "highly concerned with materialistic issues."

ADMISSIONS

Very important factors considered include: Secondary school record, standardized test scores. *Important factors considered include:* Essays, extracurricular activities, interview, recommendations. *Other factors considered include:* Alumni/ae relation, character/personal qualities, geographical residence, talent/ability, volunteer work, work experience. SAT Reasoning or ACT required. TOEFL required of all international applicants. High school diploma is required, and GED is accepted. *Academic units required:* 4 English, 3 math, 2 science, 2 social studies, 5 academic electives.

The Inside Word

More than 30 years after going coed, this former women's college is still predominantly female and is still looking to boost its male population. The fact that the school accepts only half its male applicants speaks more to the quality of the applicant pool than to its selectiveness; if male and female candidates of equal qualifications are vying for the last seat in the freshman class, it will go to the male.

FINANCIAL AID

Students should submit: FAFSA, state aid form. The Princeton Review suggests that all financial aid forms be submitted as soon as possible after 1/1. *Need-based scholarships/grants offered:* Pell, SEOG, state scholarships/grants, private scholarships, the school's own gift aid. *Loan aid offered:* FFEL Subsidized Stafford, FFEL Unsubsidized Stafford, FFEL PLUS, Federal Perkins. Applicants will be notified of awards on a rolling basis beginning on or about 3/1. Federal Work-study Program available. Institutional employment available. Off-campus job opportunities are excellent.

FROM THE ADMISSIONS OFFICE

"Manhattanville's mission—to educate ethically and socially responsible leaders for the global community—is evident throughout the College, from academics to athletics to social and extracurricular activities. With 1,500 undergraduates from 53 nations and 37 states, our diversity spans geographic, cultural, ethnic, religious, socioeconomic, and academic backgrounds. Students are free to express their views in this tight-knit community, where we value the personal as well as the global. Any six students with similar interest can start a club, and most participate in a variety of campus-wide programs. Last year, students engaged in more than 19,000 hours of community service and social justice activity. Study abroad opportunities include not only the most desirable international locations, but also a semester-long immersion for living, studying, and working in New York City. In the true liberal arts tradition, students are encouraged to think for themselves and develop new skills—in music, the studio arts, on stage, in the sciences, or on the playing field. With more than 50 areas of study and a popular self-designed major, there is no limit to our academic scope. Our Westchester county location, just 35 miles north of New York City, gives students an edge for jobs and internships. Over the past few years, Manhattanville has been rated among the '100 Most Wired,' the '100 Most Undeservedly Under-Appreciated,' the '320 Hottest,' and in U.S. News & World Report's first tier. Last year, the men's and women's ice hockey teams were ranked #1 in the nation for Division III."

For even more information on this school, turn to page 502 of the "Stats" section.

MARIST COLLEGE

3399 NORTH ROAD, POUGHKEEPSIE, NY 12601-1387 • ADMISSIONS: 845-575-3226 • FAX: 845-575-3215
E-MAIL: ADMISSIONS@MARIST.EDU • WEBSITE: WWW.MARIST.EDU

Ratings
Quality of Life: 84   **Academic:** 82   **Admissions:** 89   **Financial Aid:** 71

Academics

Marist College's "simply spectacular" library, called "one of the nicest and most modern with a very high student-to-Internet connection ratio," stands as a testament to the college's commitment to academics. The professors count among "the most devoted I have ever met" and are "active participants in their field outside of class." One of the school's "greatest strengths is the interaction between professor and student," causing one student to point out, "Getting together to watch college hoops with your professor is not something you can do at every school." Most students save their criticism for the "mediocre assistant professors." Snipes one malcontent, "Adjunct professors in foundation courses are destroying the academic continuity of the college." "I rarely get into the classes I need for my major," is a common complaint, but most agree: "I go to classes because I enjoy them." The most popular and renowned programs include communications, business, education, fashion, IT, and the Public Praxis Program, "an exceptional blend of philosophy courses and community service." The Marist administration is composed of "consummate professionals" who also happen to be "very strict. They try to act like our parents." On the positive side, students share their residence halls with "mentors who help us with any problems we have, even if it's not related to academics." The school enjoys a "good reputation with surrounding businesses" and "many connections with large companies, especially IBM." The "great internship program" ensures that Marist undergrads are "well prepared for jobs after graduation."

Life

Many students characterize Marist as a "big bar school," as opposed to your run-of-the-mill "party school," and thus, an ID (of any degree of authenticity) is "crucial." Though the school hosts no on-campus sororities or fraternities, everybody apparently "knows how to have a good time while getting their work done." According to many, the surrounding town of Poughkeepsie is "very ghetto" and "economically challenged and in need of student involvement." Undergrads consider the school's strict guest policy, with its roots in Marist's Catholic past, "old-fashioned," making dorms "like a prison, especially for freshmen." Opines one, "We are college students, and having curfew for visiting other students is just inexplicable." A system based on "Priority Points," awarded for all types of campus involvement, dictates the on-campus housing lottery, and some students "think that this is a great thing." Others bitterly note, "This college needs to actually reward the students who spend a majority of their time going to class and studying." In terms of activities, many respondents praise the school-sponsored "bus trips to Broadway shows for only $25. You can't beat that!" The city looms only 90 minutes away, and closer to home, the "Hudson Valley has a large amount of history to explore."

Student Body

Among the population of 4,000, "there isn't a lot of diversity, culturally or socially." Many students are "white, middle-class Catholics," often from Long Island; one student notes, "Sometimes I look around campus and feel like I'm looking at a mirror." Students call for "more minority-oriented events" but still believe "the minority community mixes in very well with everyone, even though there are very few of us." "I know it's cheesy when you see kids of all different types playing Frisbee and laughing on the green outside in brochures," comments a student, "but it really does happen here." Perfect harmony is confronted by obstacles like "segregation between 'normal' students and athletes" and the perception that "commuters are generally not as valued as live-in students." Generally, however, friendliness abounds at Marist, where "everyone says 'hi' to everyone," which "makes you feel like a rock star."

ADMISSIONS

Very important factors considered include: Class rank, essays, recommendations, secondary school record, standardized test scores. *Important factors considered include:* Character/personal qualities, extracurricular activities, geographical residence, minority status, state residency, talent/ability, volunteer work, work experience. *Other factors considered include:* Alumni/ae relation. SAT Reasoning or ACT required. TOEFL required of all international applicants. High school diploma is required, and GED is accepted. *Academic units required:* 4 English, 3 math, 3 science (2 science lab), 2 social studies, 1 history, 2 academic electives. *Academic units recommended:* 4 math, 4 science (3 science lab), 2 foreign language.

The Inside Word

As the school's housing policy indicates, Marist places a strong emphasis on civic responsibility. Candidates who show a strong record of community service and leadership activities will have a definite leg up in the admissions process here.

FINANCIAL AID

Students should submit: FAFSA, institution's own financial aid form. Regular filing deadline 5/1. The Princeton Review suggests that all financial aid forms be submitted as soon as possible after 1/1. *Need-based scholarships/grants offered:* Pell, SEOG, state scholarships/grants, private scholarships, the school's own gift aid. *Loan aid offered:* FFEL Subsidized Stafford, FFEL Unsubsidized Stafford, FFEL PLUS, Federal Perkins, alternative loans. Applicants will be notified of awards on or about 3/15. Federal Work-study Program available. Institutional employment available. Off-campus job opportunities are excellent.

FROM THE ADMISSIONS OFFICE

"Marist is a 'hot school' among prospective students. We are seeing a record number of applications each year. But the number of seats available for the freshman class remains the same, about 950. Therefore, becoming an accepted applicant is an increasingly competitive process. Our recommendations: Keep your grades up, score well on the SAT, participate in community service both in and out of school, and exercise leadership in the classroom, athletics, extracurricular activities, and your place of worship. We encourage a campus visit. When prospective students see Marist—our beautiful location on a scenic stretch of the Hudson River, the quality of our facilities, the interaction between students and faculty, and the fact that everyone really enjoys their time here—they want to become a part of the Marist College community. We'll help you in the transition from high school to college through an innovative first-year program that provides mentors for every student. You'll also learn how to use technology in whatever field you choose. We emphasize three aspects of a true Marist experience: excellence in education, service to others, and the pursuit of higher human values. At Marist, you will get a premium education, develop your skills, have fun and make lifelong friends, be given the opportunity to gain valuable experience through our internship and study abroad programs, and be ahead of the competition for graduate school or work."

For even more information on this school, turn to page 502 of the "Stats" section.

MARLBORO COLLEGE

PO Box A, South Road, Marlboro, VT 05344 • Admissions: 802-258-9236 • Fax: 802-257-4154
Financial Aid: 802-257-4333 • E-mail: admissions@marlboro.edu • Website: www.marlboro.edu

Ratings
Quality of Life: 86   Academic: 99   Admissions: 88   Financial Aid: 75

Academics

Finally, a school that offers, "a great undergrad program for students who would rather be in grad school." Tiny, remote Marlboro College "seeks to nurture critical thinking, effective writing, and engaged citizens" through a program that emphasizes closely supervised independent study and the ideal of self-government. The apex of Marlboro's nontraditional education is "the Plan," which requires students to design their own junior- and senior-year curricula, culminating in a senior research paper. Under the Plan, students "attend one-on-one tutorials with professors in which we spend the entire class asking all of the questions we want to ask and exploring the subjects we want to learn about." One undergrad writes, "The encouragement of critical thinking on both an academic and a social level is incredible here." Freshman and sophomore years are dedicated to more traditional classroom study; classes are "engaging and interesting, everyone is encouraged to speak, and every class is a lively discussion." Professors and administrators are not only mentors and facilitators of learning, but also serve as peers and friends, students tell us. Classes are small—the school has a student/faculty ratio of 8 to 1—a benefit that outweighs some of the drawbacks of the school's size, which "requires Marlboro to be very economical. While there are ways to make up for what the bigger universities have to offer, we must think realistically and be cost-conscious."

> **SURVEY SAYS . . .**
> *Small classes*
> *No one cheats*
> *Frats and sororities are unpopular*
> *or nonexistent*
> *Student government is popular*

Life

Located "on a tiny hill in Vermont at least 20 minutes from the nearest town," Marlboro "really is in the middle of nowhere." Students learn to adapt to the low excitement level here. As one student explains, "I didn't realize that there was nothing to do here until my friend came to visit me. He was saying, 'Okay! Let's go do something!' and I realized that showing him the library and playing a round of ping-pong had already exhausted all of our options." One student warns, "It's a little boring. You are responsible for making your own entertainment. People try, but how many times can you go to see different mutations of the same band, and that annoying kid from next door reading his erotic beat poetry at the open mic?" Schoolwork keeps students busy a good part of the time, and many even appreciate how the lack of distraction facilitates academics. When it's time to unwind, "people hang out, watch movies, and play video games. Some people get completely plastered." An appreciation for the outdoors helps. Anyone who's willing can "take advantage of rock climbing, whitewater paddling, snowboarding, hiking, caving, mountain biking, cross-country skiing, and snowshoeing. None of it is more than 45 minutes away, and we have a great outdoor program (that loans equipment to students at no cost) which makes it easy for people to learn these things."

Student Body

"Atypical is typical, but not in an obnoxious way," Marlboro students report, pointing out that "we bathe; some girls even shave!" Notes one student, "Sometimes our nonconformity is manifest in our clothes, be it flashy hipness, dirty hippieness, caps with hoods, or just the standard drag-queen apparel." Students are fond of saying that everyone here "is really bright in some way or another." They "often come from alternative educational institutions—Waldorf schools, home schools, and special high schools of different kinds—so they sort of have that 'I'm not doing it the mainstream way' attitude about them." Most "are quite liberal in their thinking and are encouraged to share their views." Among their ranks are "many bisexual and gay students, but anyone can talk to anyone else. It's very open." Diversity here "is less focused on race than it is on sexuality and socioeconomics, where it truly is diverse. The geography and current demographic seems to be unappealing to some minority groups, which drives the administrators nuts." As one undergrad puts it, "The only segment of student demographics less represented than students of color are students of conformity."

ADMISSIONS

Very important factors considered include: Character/personal qualities, essays, secondary school record. *Important factors considered include:* Class rank, extracurricular activities, interview, recommendations, standardized test scores, talent/ability, volunteer work, work experience. *Other factors considered include:* Alumni/ae relation, geographical residence, state residency. SAT Reasoning or ACT required. TOEFL required of all international applicants. High school diploma is required, and GED is accepted. *Academic units required:* 4 English, 3 math, 3 science, 3 social studies. *Academic units recommended:* 4 English, 3 math, 3 science (1 science lab), 3 foreign language, 3 social studies, 3 history, 3 academic electives.

The Inside Word

Don't be misled by Marlboro's high acceptance rate; the College's applicant pool consists mainly of candidates who are sincerely interested in a nontraditional path to their BA or BS. They also possess sincere intellectual curiosity, and students who don't should not bother applying. The admissions process here is driven by matchmaking and a search for those who truly want to learn. For the right kind of person, Marlboro can be a terrific college choice.

FINANCIAL AID

Students should submit: FAFSA, CSS/Financial Aid PROFILE, state aid form, noncustodial (divorced/separated) parents' statement. Regular filing deadline 3/1. The Princeton Review suggests that all financial aid forms be submitted as soon as possible after 1/1. *Need-based scholarships/grants offered:* Pell, SEOG, state scholarships/grants, private scholarships, the school's own gift aid. *Loan aid offered:* FFEL Subsidized Stafford, FFEL Unsubsidized Stafford, FFEL PLUS, college/university loans from institutional funds. Applicants will be notified of awards on or about 4/1. Federal Work-study Program available. Institutional employment available. Off-campus job opportunities are fair.

FROM THE ADMISSIONS OFFICE

"Marlboro College is distinguished by its curriculum, praised in higher education circles as unique; it is known for its self-governing philosophy, in which each student, faculty, and staff has an equal vote on many issues affecting the community; and it is recognized for its 60-year history of offering a rigorous, exciting, self-designed course of study taught in very small classes and individualized study with faculty. Marlboro's size also distinguishes it from most other schools. With 300 students and a student/faculty ratio of 8 to 1, it is one of the nation's smallest liberal arts colleges. Few other schools offer a program where students have such close interaction with faculty, and where community life is inseparable from academic life. The result, the self-designed, self-directed Plan of Concentration, allows students to develop their own unique academic work by defining a problem, setting clear limits on an area of inquiry, and analyzing, evaluating, and reporting on the outcome of a significant project. A Marlboro education teaches you to think for yourself, articulate your thoughts, express your ideas, believe in yourself, and do it all with the clarity, confidence and self-reliance necessary for later success, no matter what postgraduate path you take."

For even more information on this school, turn to page 503 of the "Stats" section.

MARYLAND INSTITUTE COLLEGE OF ART

1300 MOUNT ROYAL AVENUE, BALTIMORE, MD 21217 • ADMISSIONS: 410-225-2222 • FAX: 410-225-2337
E-MAIL: ADMISSIONS@MICA.EDU • WEBSITE: WWW.MICA.EDU

Ratings

Quality of Life: 79   Academic: 89   Admissions: 90   Financial Aid: 71

Academics

The Maryland Institute College of Art gives the nation's blossoming young artists a place to "discover their own voice, skills, and self," according to one student. In the words of one undergraduate, "It's work, work, work—but amazing work, work, work." Instructors "respect their students and treat their art seriously [by] showing interest in our work and our progress." With "class size usually under 20," students have close contact with their talented and hard-working mentors. One student observes, "All the people want to be here, including the faculty." Some people call for higher academic standards and improved liberal arts courses, but a MICA freshman points out, "We have

a resident philosopher. What more do you want?" Many students cite the college's top reputation, calling it the "most intriguing art program on the east coast." The superb painting and printmaking departments and facilities receive high marks, the design and commercial art programs less so. Students feel the need for increased career counseling and job placement assistance. Perhaps they will receive it, since the administration is described as "compassionate and considerate of the student body." All in all, a second-year student sums up his academic experience this way, "I feel I have definitely improved as an artist, student, and person because of the people I have interacted with here."

Life

A common credo among the college students is that "life is art, art is life." It seems as though many students don't stray too far from their studios unless dragged. People list working on projects, talking about art, and learning new techniques as their pastimes of choice. The photographers take pictures, and the painters go to art galleries. Even the animation majors are researching their future careers in their free time. They state, "We go to each others' houses and play video games." Another diversion that is more popular than some would think is "thinking about the existential dilemma and how post-structuralism ruined our lives." Occasionally, students have been known to "have potlucks and whine about our sexual frustration." Others choose to do yoga, skateboard, visit other schools and go to New York. Additional activity options include root beer float parties, knitting, extreme spelling bees, and pie-eating contests. Students want the administration to "ease up on the house parties" because truly, in the words of a senior, "everyone could be having more fun."

Student Body

It may be stereotypical, but this art-school crew cultivates two main loves—wearing thrift store clothes and analyzing everything. It seems MICA students have become so alternative that they've inadvertently circled back to create a new norm. In other words, "Everyone is atypical, so no one is weird," claims one student. Thrown into this "left-wing play pen for artists," students find an accepting community that is full of life. Respondents describe their cohorts as "creative, open-minded, ambitious, curious, and goal-oriented," as well as amazingly talented. Students declare that because "our one common interest, art, brings us together," they perceive very few boundaries between groups. A senior calls the student body "very diverse ethnically, sexually, and financially," but someone else points out that "the minority crowd could expand a bit." As expected in an environment all about self-expression, "Everyone believes they are unique snowflakes."

ADMISSIONS

Very important factors considered include: Secondary school record, talent/ability. *Important factors considered include:* Class rank, essays, extracurricular activities, interview, standardized test scores. *Other factors considered include:* Alumni/ae relation, character/personal qualities, minority status, recommendations, volunteer work. TOEFL required of all international applicants. High school diploma is required, and GED is accepted. *Academic units required:* 4 English, 2 math, 2 science (1 science lab), 4 social studies, 3 history, 6 academic electives, 2 studio art. *Academic units recommended:* 4 English, 3 math, 3 science (1 science lab), 4 social studies, 4 history, 5 academic electives, 2 studio art.

The Inside Word

Admission to the Maryland Institute is competitive and takes not only artistic and academic achievement into account, but also extracurricular achievement and personal qualities. That said, without a killer portfolio, no one has much chance of getting in here.

FINANCIAL AID

Students should submit: FAFSA, institution's own financial aid form. Regular filing deadline 3/1. The Princeton Review suggests that all financial aid forms be submitted as soon as possible after 1/1. *Need-based scholarships/grants offered:* Pell, SEOG, state scholarships/grants, private scholarships, the school's own gift aid. *Loan aid offered:* FFEL Subsidized Stafford, FFEL Unsubsidized Stafford, FFEL PLUS, Federal Perkins. Applicants will be notified of awards on or about 4/15. Federal Work-study Program available. Institutional employment available. Off-campus job opportunities are good.

FROM THE ADMISSIONS OFFICE

"Maryland Institute College of Art attracts some of the most talented, passionate, and serious visual art and design faculty and students in the world. The college is a universe of artists, designers, and scholars who celebrate the creative process, the majesty of the arts, and the mind-expanding pursuit of knowledge. To maintain this community of artists, admission is highly competitive. Successful applicants are men and women who have made a commitment to art, and demonstrated this commitment by developing a serious portfolio of artwork. In selecting from among the many outstanding applications we receive for a limited number of places, MICA's Admission Committee considers a comprehensive set of factors. Central to our evaluations are the artistic and academic qualifications of our candidates, but we also consider extracurricular activities and achievements, art experience beyond required classroom instruction, and personal qualities. The portfolio is the most meaningful indicator of serious artistic commitment, ability, and potential to succeed in MICA's rigorous studio environment. Your artwork reflects your visual sensitivity, intellectual curiosity and creativity, motivation and self-discipline, and previous experience in the visual arts. Portfolios are evaluated on an individual basis, in the context of the specific educational background and experiences of each applicant. Our evaluation of your academic performance is determined by grades, level of classwork, test scores, and class rank. The required essay is also seriously considered."

For even more information on this school, turn to page 503 of the "Stats" section.

MARYMOUNT COLLEGE OF FORDHAM UNIVERSITY

100 MARYMOUNT AVENUE, TARRYTOWN, NY 10591-3798 • ADMISSIONS: 914-332-8295 • FAX: 914-332-7442
E-MAIL: MCENROLL@FORDHAM.EDU • WEBSITE: WWW.FORDHAM.EDU

Ratings
Quality of Life: 65   Academic: 84   Admissions: 78   Financial Aid: 70

Academics

Marymount College strives to "empower young women by providing an education that emphasizes feminist values," according to one student. Many students agree that the mostly female environment (very few men are enrolled as degree-seeking students in a part-time adult evening program held on the campus) allows students to keep the focus on academics. Previously an independent institution, Marymount is now part of Fordham University. "The

> **SURVEY SAYS . . .**
> *Small classes*
> *Diverse student types on campus*
> *Frats and sororities are unpopular*
> *or nonexistent*
> *(Almost) everyone smokes*

administration was more accessible before the merge, but that was bound to happen," writes a senior. Some respondents feel their school "falls short of what Fordham stands for academically." However, the majority of students say the college strikes an effective balance between challenge and hand-holding. For instance, attendance counts significantly in final grades, yet "professors treat you as an adult," the student says. They "talk to you, not at you," during lectures commonly described as "interactive." Another senior acknowledges that her four years of solid academic progress rest on "the hard work and effort of my professors." Overall, the faculty forms a "great support system" that "welcomes feedback" from undergraduates. Class deans are considered "a good source of help and information," and know students by their names. Advisors also demonstrate "a passion for helping students get classes that they will like and that will enrich their minds." It's evident that students enjoy their subject matter when "classroom conversation seeps into the dorms and cafeteria." Marymount succeeds in its purpose of "preparing women for a successful life beyond college, with no limitations of age, economic status, ethnic background, or interests."

Life

From their location near the Tappan Zee Bridge overlooking the Hudson River, Marymount students live a suburban life filled with "cute local hang-outs," as described by some. There are also frequent excursions to New York City, either on the MetroNorth rail line or the Ram Van—a school-run shuttle. On campus, social life barely registers, though a few optimists claim that "activities are getting a lot better." For now, most people flee on the weekends, heading for home or the other Fordham campuses in the Bronx (Rose Hill) and Manhattan (Lincoln Center). "There are so many interesting events going on at Rose Hill and Lincoln Center and hardly any here," students agree. Active student organizations, such as Latinas Unidas, the Black Student Union, and the drama club, do their part to combat the social void. Campus Ministry organizes recurring community service outings as well as "at least three different [masses] in any given week." Since every night is girls' night, Marymount women love to "host sleepovers and junk food parties with plenty of hot cocoa and instant mac and cheese in our dorm rooms." Some claim that a mellow social life definitely "leaves enough room to be silly and immature at times."

Student Body

The student body at the college is "as diverse as diverse can be," notes one student. Many African American and Latina students arrive from New York City, while others are international students representing countries such as Brazil, China, Nepal, and the Ukraine. "Everyone brings their own stories, experiences, uniqueness, and perspective on life to the proverbial table." Identifiable identity groups include "the intellectuals, the future politicians, the laid-back athletes, the fashion-savvy snobs, the musicians, and writers, and even the students who are like junior mothers to their friends." Together, they make up a small, nurturing community where "you can define yourself and be yourself without worrying about being judged." Members of this "sociable and down to earth" sorority relish "being women and feeling the freedom to be tastefully and gracefully crude at times."

ADMISSIONS

Very important factors considered include: Secondary school record, standardized test scores. *Important factors considered include:* Character/personal qualities, essays, extracurricular activities, recommendations. *Other factors considered include:* Alumni/ae relation, class rank, interview, volunteer work, work experience. SAT Reasoning or ACT required. TOEFL required of all international applicants. High school diploma is required, and GED is accepted. *Academic units required:* 4 English, 3 math, 2 science (2 science lab), 2 foreign language, 3 social studies, 2 academic electives. *Academic units recommended:* 4 math, 4 social studies, 3 academic electives.

The Inside Word

Admission to this women's college is not highly competitive. Students with shortcomings in their application profile may be able to turn the admissions decision their way by contacting the school and convincingly expressing a desire to attend. A strong personal essay can really help.

FINANCIAL AID

Students should submit: FAFSA. The Princeton Review suggests that all financial aid forms be submitted as soon as possible after 1/1. *Need-based scholarships/grants offered:* Pell, SEOG, state scholarships/grants, private scholarships, the school's own gift aid. *Loan aid offered:* Direct Subsidized Stafford, Direct Unsubsidized Stafford, Direct PLUS, FFEL Subsidized Stafford, FFEL Unsubsidized Stafford, FFEL PLUS, Federal Perkins. Applicants will be notified of awards on a rolling basis beginning on or about 3/31.

FROM THE ADMISSIONS OFFICE

"Marymount College, founded in 1907 by the Religious of the Sacred Heart of Mary, is an independent, four-year liberal arts college in the Catholic tradition. It remains true to its original mission to equip and empower women to achieve their full potential, preparing them for leadership roles in a rapidly changing society.

"Building upon a long relationship, Marymount consolidated with Fordham University in July 2002, becoming the University's fifth undergraduate college. At Marymount College of Fordham University, students benefit from the academic resources of a major university and the opportunities of New York City at a small, student-centered Catholic liberal arts college. The supportive faculty and values-laden education build a strong foundation for excellence both in the classroom and in life.

"While many students commute to the school, the Marymount campus remains largely residential. Approximately 62 percent of its nearly 850 students live in one of three residence halls on the campus, which overlooks the Hudson River from its scenic perch in the Westchester County village of Tarrytown, NY. Located 25 miles north of Manhattan, the school's proximity to the unmatched cultural and professional opportunities of New York City attracts many students.

"In addition, the Core Curriculum is designed to develop the habits of mind and heart that are the hallmarks of a strong liberal arts education. Courses blend reverence for tradition with openness to new challenges and new ways of knowing and engaging the world, providing students with the foundation they need for lifelong learning."

For even more information on this school, turn to page 504 of the "Stats" section.

MASSACHUSETTS INSTITUTE OF TECHNOLOGY

77 MASSACHUSETTS AVENUE, CAMBRIDGE, MA 02139 • ADMISSIONS: 617-253-4791
FAX: 617-253-1986 • FINANCIAL AID: 617-253-4971 • E-MAIL: ADMISSIONS@MIT.EDU • WEBSITE: WWW.MIT.EDU

Ratings
Quality of Life: 88   **Academic:** 96   **Admissions:** 99   **Financial Aid:** 96

Academics

Research heavyweight MIT "is the ultimate academic powerhouse," its students brag. MIT is the type of place where
"almost everyone, including the teachers, loves to learn for
the sake of learning, and you end up loving MIT for what
it gives you while hating it for the work you have to do to
succeed." Sure, "it's hard to get into and hard to stay in,"
but the rewards for all the difficult work include "professors who are just as eager to teach in their field as they are
to research in it." The Undergraduate Research

Opportunities Program puts students in the lab "doing cutting-edge work in almost any field. This can be invaluable, giving students a chance to get a real feel for what life is like in their chosen field, to learn a great deal, make good contacts with prestigious faculty members, and even earn a little cash." Not every professor here is entirely obliging. One student writes, "As is likely the case at most schools, professors range from excellent to terrible, but if you ask around, you can usually figure out which ones to avoid." The overarching spirit of MIT is one of cooperation. As one student puts it, "If you are willing to put in the work, there is always a way to get enough help to complete all assignments." Undergraduates appreciate how "The name 'MIT' opens many doors for internships and full-time jobs." They also love the freshman year grading system of pass/no record.

Life

MIT students have plenty of entertainment options available to them: Greek parties, lectures, clubs, on-campus performances and art shows, online gaming, and, of course, all that the city of Boston has to offer. The problem, however, "is that it's hard to enjoy yourself when you know that on Monday you have 54 hours of work that needs to be completed." Students do occasionally find time to close the books, though, and when they do, many head to the school's popular fraternities and sororities to unwind. Or they may undertake projects with the folks they live with. One student says, "Whether people live in the dorms, fraternities, sororities, or independent living groups, they almost always find an extremely close, tight-knit community there. Many MIT students end up managing budgets of tens, if not hundreds of thousands of dollars, in their living groups or other clubs. They build, fix, or maintain houses they live in or cabins in the woods. They plan shows and events that draw hundreds of people." Beyond campus are Cambridge and Boston. The latter "is an amazing city, although if you want to have time to take advantage of it more than once a month, go to Boston University. If you're not at a party Friday night, chances are you're in lab or studying in your dorm room," or shooting the breeze with a fellow student. "MIT is the only place where you will find yourself staying up until three in the morning debating the (hypothetical) chemical interactions of urine in a Brita filter based on various chemical models," explains one student.

Student Body

"There's a guy upstairs who unlocks his room with a thumbprint scanner," writes one MIT undergraduate, allowing us a peek into how many standard deviations from the norm some students fall into. While some students assert that "nearly all students at MIT are nerds," others take exception to this characterization. We're inclined to believe the student who tells us the following: "We have jocks/frat boys (who are really nerds inside), sorority girls (also nerds inside), theater people (nerds), artists (nerds), athletes (nerds), and even out-right, full-on nerds." Undergraduates proudly report that "many MIT students will take a 'break' from work to help other people with their problem sets. This helpful nature combined with the ease of finding intelligent and interesting people to spend time with makes this institute worth attending." The diverse population includes "a very large number of people of Asian or Indian descent."

ADMISSIONS

Very important factors considered include: Character/personal qualities, secondary school record. *Important factors considered include:* Class rank, extracurricular activities, interview, recommendations, standardized test scores, talent/ability. *Other factors considered include:* Alumni/ae relation, essays, geographical residence, minority status, volunteer work, work experience. SAT Reasoning or ACT required. High school diploma or equivalent is not required. *Academic units recommended:* 4 English, 4 math, 4 science, 2 foreign language, 2 social studies.

The Inside Word

High academic achievement, lofty test scores, and the most rigorous high school courseload possible are prerequisites for a successful candidacy. Among the most selective institutions in the country, MIT's admissions operation is easily one of the most down-to-earth and accessible. Over the years they have shown both a sense of humor in admissions literature and an awareness that applying to such a prestigious and demanding place creates a high level of anxiety in students. Their relaxed and helpful approach does much to temper such stress.

FINANCIAL AID

Students should submit: FAFSA, CSS/Financial Aid PROFILE, noncustodial (divorced/separated) parents' statement, business/farm supplement, parents' complete federal income tax returns, including W-2 forms, from prior year. Regular filing deadline 2/1. The Princeton Review suggests that all financial aid forms be submitted as soon as possible after 1/1. *Need-based scholarships/grants offered:* Pell, SEOG, state scholarships/grants, private scholarships, the school's own gift aid. *Loan aid offered:* Direct Subsidized Stafford, Direct Unsubsidized Stafford, Direct PLUS, Federal Perkins, college/university loans from institutional funds. Applicants will be notified of awards on or about 3/15. Federal Work-study Program available. Institutional employment available. Off-campus job opportunities are excellent.

FROM THE ADMISSIONS OFFICE

"The students who come to the Massachusetts Institute of Technology are some of America's—and the world's—best and most creative. As graduates, they leave here to make real contributions—in science, technology, business, education, politics, architecture, and the arts. From any class, many will go on to do work that is historically significant. These young men and women are leaders, achievers, producers. Helping such students make the most of their talents and dreams would challenge any educational institution. MIT gives them its best advantages: a world-class faculty, unparalleled facilities, remarkable opportunities. In turn, these students help to make the institute the vital place it is. They bring fresh viewpoints to faculty research: More than three-quarters participate in the Undergraduate Research Opportunities Program. They play on MIT's 41 intercollegiate teams as well as in its 15 musical ensembles. To their classes and to their out-of-class activities, they bring enthusiasm, energy, and individual style."

For even more information on this school, turn to page 504 of the "Stats" section.

MERCYHURST COLLEGE

ADMISSIONS, 501 E. 38TH STREET, ERIE, PA 16546 • ADMISSIONS: 800-825-1926 • FAX: 814-824-2071
E-MAIL: ADMISSIONS@MERCYHURST.EDU • WEBSITE: WWW.MERCYHURST.EDU

Ratings
Quality of Life: 76   Academic: 82   Admissions: 79   Financial Aid: 90

Academics

When the Sisters of Mercy founded Mercyhurst College, they envisioned a small, Catholic liberal arts college promoting "the values of truth, individual integrity, human dignity, service, and justice." Today, students apply themselves to the "challenging but not impossible" course work within a religious context. Professors are known for their personable and supportive styles as much as their high curves. They encourage students "to ask questions and

> **SURVEY SAYS . . .**
> *Small classes*
> *Frats and sororities are unpopular*
> *or nonexistent*
> *Student government is popular*
> *Lots of beer drinking*

think abstractly and analytically," rather than force-feeding facts. The faculty's down-to-earth approach "helps [students] along the way rather than making [them] feel like [they'll] never reach their genius, elite status." A junior writes, "They encourage you to stop by outside of class at least once so that they can get a feel for how you think the class is going." Students survive "common core" liberal arts requirements that many consider "more difficult than the major requirements." Several "unique and nationally recognized" academic programs stand out, including intelligence studies (formerly the research/intelligence analyst program), a program which trains future intelligence analysts in government or the private sector, and archaeology. Career services helps students "secure good internships and prepare solid resumes;" a senior says, "If it weren't for them, I don't know where I would be heading in terms of career." The administration, however, "could stand to be more honest with the student body."

Life

Aside from the lake-effect snow, students love their lively town of Erie, who look off-campus for most of their entertainment. Students attend minor league hockey and baseball games or haunt the "corner bar where you can go for dancing, live bands, and great specials." Cultural events like the winter jazz series, the Erie Playhouse, and the Warner Theater, "which often hosts concerts and comedians," also attract the Mercyhurst crowd. The student government runs free shuttles to the mall and Lake Erie beaches. The Erie police force turns a blind eye to off-campus parties, in contrast to campus cops who "will bust anyone and everyone they can." Students face "significant punishments" when caught breaking the rules, creating a disciplinary atmosphere "comparable to a boarding school." An older student reports, "Last year, there were a ton of parties, but this year is the complete opposite." Vegas Night, karaoke, themed movie events, dodge ball tournaments, and Mercyhurst's 25 intercollegiate athletic teams keep students out of trouble. Most students agree, "We live in Mercy World, and it's a great place to be."

Student Body

"Upper middle-class, white, suburban" students make up the vast majority at Mercyhurst; therefore, most people agree, "the student body could be more diverse." "People worry a lot about their grades and what path to take in life and school," says a sophomore. Avid people watchers may be disappointed by the fact that the "general dress code consists of jeans, T-shirts, sweatpants, sweaters, and hoodies." Most people come from the tristate area, particularly Pittsburgh and Cleveland suburbs, "except for the sports teams," which often attract international students from "Canada, the UK, or Ireland." It is the high percentage of student athletes and internationals that make the Mercyhurst population distinctive. A junior observes, "Everyone seems to have a friend from another country, and it seems like one in four people play a varsity sport." A senior summarizes his peers, "Take a high school student, make him or her less dramatic and trivial, and expand his or her mind with new perspectives and knowledge, and there is your Mercyhurst student."

ADMISSIONS

Very important factors considered include: Secondary school record. *Important factors considered include:* Character/personal qualities, class rank, interview, standardized test scores, talent/ability. *Other factors considered include:* Alumni/ae relation, essays, extracurricular activities, geographical residence, minority status, recommendations, religious affiliation/commitment, state residency, volunteer work, work experience. SAT Reasoning or ACT required. TOEFL required of all international applicants. High school diploma is required, and GED is accepted. *Academic units recommended:* 4 English, 3 math, 3 science (1 science lab), 2 foreign language, 2 social studies, 2 history.

The Inside Word

The trick at Mercyhurst is learning how to successfully navigate the administrative rigmarole necessary for achieving your academic goals. To gain entrée to this Catholic school with its second North East campus, impress upon the admissions committee your desire and ability to take advantage of the school's varied academic opportunities.

FINANCIAL AID

Students should submit: FAFSA. Regular filing deadline 5/1. The Princeton Review suggests that all financial aid forms be submitted as soon as possible after 1/1. *Need-based scholarships/grants offered:* Pell, SEOG, state scholarships/grants, private scholarships, the school's own gift aid. *Loan aid offered:* FFEL Subsidized Stafford, FFEL Unsubsidized Stafford, FFEL PLUS, Federal Perkins. Applicants will be notified of awards on a rolling basis beginning on or about 2/15. Federal Work-study Program available. Institutional employment available. Off-campus job opportunities are good.

FROM THE ADMISSIONS OFFICE

"Mercyhurst College is a community of students who have come to expect a vibrant and challenging higher education experience. From its humble beginnings in 1926 to the current explosive growth in both size and reputation, Mercyhurst is a college full of tradition but not afraid of change.

"The motto Carpe Diem permeates throughout the college's history! The best illustration may be our collection of academic programs. In the last 20 years, Mercyhurst has had the foresight to add the cutting-edge fields of research intelligence, forensic science, and archaeology. We've also become home to very strong visual and performing arts programs such as dance, music, and art. Our 50 majors and 67 concentrations, both traditional and unique, have helped Mercyhurst draw students from 40 states and 20 countries, and earn nationwide respect.

"Our campus is covered with beautiful buildings and landscaping, making it a comfortable place to spend your college years. After a year in one of four residence halls, upperclassmen live in one of the more than 300 college-owned apartments on the east side of campus. Living on campus has its perks. Students who venture out most any night on campus will find athletic events, concerts, and interesting guest speakers. An excellent recreation center, 25 varsity sports, and 50 student organizations offer other extra-curricular options for our active students.

"In selecting a student for admission, Mercyhurst looks for evidence of academic ability and readiness as demonstrated by high school course work, grades earned, performance on standardized tests, and personal characteristics that relate to a student's ability to succeed."

For even more information on this school, turn to page 505 of the "Stats" section.

MERRIMACK COLLEGE

OFFICE OF ADMISSION, AUSTIN HALL, NORTH ANDOVER, MA 01845 • ADMISSIONS: 978-837-5100
FAX: 978-837-5133 • E-MAIL: ADMISSION@MERRIMACK.EDU • WEBSITE: WWW.MERRIMACK.EDU

Ratings
Quality of Life: 76   Academic: 77   Admissions: 82   Financial Aid: 84

Academics

Roman Catholic–affiliated Merrimack College is a "close-knit" Augustinian community "devoted to learning, community service, and helping its students become involved in every way possible to prepare them for the career world." The faculty at Merrimack is the school's greatest strength, students tell us. Professors are "effective, demanding, yet fair, and they listen to students. Their doors are always open if you need help." One student elaborates, "All of the tenured professors that I have had were wonderful, particularly those who teach philosophy, religion, and the fine arts. They really know their stuff, they know how to communicate their knowledge effectively, and they genuinely seem to like the students." The administration "is very involved on a personal basis with the student body," explains another student. "If at any time I had been confronted with a conflict necessitating administrative help or assistance from one of my professors, I always was given thorough, personalized attention and guidance quickly and kindly." Merrimack is well-known for its "state-of-the-art" Girard School of Business, which students say "is all about working in groups and applying our education to real-world situations." The "great sports medicine program" is another curricular highlight. Undergrads appreciate Merrimack's "great academic support services, like tutoring labs, for each subject [and] very good volunteer programs." One sticking point students mentioned was that "since it is a smaller private school, there are not many classes available for students to get into. Many times, students do not get into the classes that they want to take, or the ones they need to take to fill their general requirements, until junior or senior year."

> **SURVEY SAYS . . .**
> *Small classes*
> *Lots of beer drinking*
> *Hard liquor is popular*

Life

"During the week, life at Merrimack is strongly focused on academics," students tell us, "The weekends are generally quieter than they are on most campuses, due to the strict alcohol policies," but, there are still plenty of parties. Some Merrimack students complain that "it is hard to have a good time when public safety is continuously breaking up parties even if the students present are of age." The party scene aside, "there is always something going on such as contests, movie nights, concerts, weekend retreats (M.O.R.E.), and other activities." Students are also "really into football and hockey games" and can often be seen playing impromptu games of Ultimate Frisbee™ and Wiffle™ ball. "The proximity of Boston is a huge benefit" as well; "trips to Red Sox, Patriots, and Celtics games occur frequently through different organizations at the school." Freshmen aren't allowed to have cars at Merrimack, and some students wish that Merrimack would "make it easier to get off campus. The shuttle service does not run that often and makes it hard to get around, making it necessary to pay for a cab."

Student Body

"The typical student here at Merrimack College is somewhat intelligent, athletic, outgoing, and very friendly. Most of the kids here know how to have a good time and make the best out of what we have." A large portion of the student body is "white, middle-class, and likely from New England, if not Massachusetts." Students say that the school "would benefit from a more diverse community," but also mention that "Merrimack has been busy marketing the school to more non-white, non-Anglo students, and it's beginning to show. Like anything else that's new, it takes time and patience to make those kinds of changes." Regardless of their backgrounds, "Merrimack students create an environment of safety, friendship, community, and even a feeling of extended family."

ADMISSIONS

Very important factors considered include: Essays, secondary school record, standardized test scores. *Important factors considered include:* Character/personal qualities, class rank, recommendations. *Other factors considered include:* Alumni/ae relation, extracurricular activities, geographical residence, interview, talent/ability, volunteer work, work experience. SAT Reasoning and SAT Subject Tests or ACT required. TOEFL required of all international applicants. High school diploma is required, and GED is accepted. *Academic units required:* 4 English, 3 math, 3 science (3 science lab), 2 foreign language, 2 social studies, 2 history, 1 academic elective. *Academic units recommended:* 4 English, 4 math, 4 science (4 science lab), 3 foreign language, 2 social studies, 2 history, 1 academic elective.

The Inside Word

Applicants should seriously consider applying to Merrimack through the Early Action program if they are interested in merit scholarships. It guarantees priority registration and financial aid for those accepted, provides a variety of school-related discounts, and best of all, is nonbinding.

FINANCIAL AID

Students should submit: FAFSA. Regular filing deadline 2/1. The Princeton Review suggests that all financial aid forms be submitted as soon as possible after 1/1. *Need-based scholarships/grants offered:* Pell, SEOG, state scholarships/grants, private scholarships, the school's own gift aid. *Loan aid offered:* FFEL Subsidized Stafford, FFEL Unsubsidized Stafford, FFEL PLUS, Federal Perkins, state loans, college/university loans from institutional funds, alternative loans. Applicants will be notified of awards on a rolling basis beginning on or about 3/1. Federal Work-study Program available. Institutional employment available. Off-campus job opportunities are fair.

FROM THE ADMISSIONS OFFICE

"Merrimack has become an increasingly competitive and demanding college with greater expectations of our talented students. For the fourth year in a row, *U.S. News & World Report* named Merrimack a Top 10 regional school.

"Student request for admission has increased by more than 70 percent in only four years and freshman residency has grown to 85 percent. To meet the growing demand, many new facilities have been added within the past four years, including an award-winning campus and recreation center, a state-of-the-art center for the arts, and two new residence halls for freshmen and sophomores. A new hockey rink and extensive landscaping designs are putting the finishing touches on an already beautiful campus.

"Co-operative Education is a popular work/study option for all of our students and many are taking advantage of study opportunities around the world, including the most popular placements in Australia, Italy, and Great Britain.

"Merrimack continues to improve its 34 major course offerings in all three of our divisions: Liberal Arts, Science/Engineering, and the Girard School of Business and International Commerce. This makes our college, with its 2,150 students, a most desirable choice for academic preparation. Our student/faculty ratio of 12:1 not only allows close contact with faculty, but also great dialogue with fellow students—a hallmark of the Merrimack curriculum."

For even more information on this school, turn to page 505 of the "Stats" section.

MESSIAH COLLEGE

ONE COLLEGE AVENUE, GRANTHAM, PA 17027 • ADMISSIONS: 717-691-6000 • FAX: 717-796-5374
E-MAIL: ADMISS@MESSIAH.EDU • WEBSITE: WWW.MESSIAH.EDU

Ratings
Quality of Life: 89   **Academic:** 84   **Admissions:** 88   **Financial Aid:** 71

Academics

As a Christian institution, "faith is central to the Messiah College education, but it is not forced on students excessively." Some students call their school "very freethinking compared to other institutions of similar faith," while others say that those who are in charge "'aren't very open-minded about radical issues that have been the beginnings of great things." The administration's personnel is currently in transition but still "makes an effort to get in touch with the students through pizza nights with the president and similar activities." Professors haven't lost touch with what it's like to be an overextended, stressed-out college student and "leave room for personal needs in their classroom policies." Faculty members "keep it real with the students" and often "have lunch with [them] and a group of friends, even if it's just to talk about life, God, or politics." Very few fail classes because "if [a student's] grade is even bordering a D, the professors here will contact [that student] day and night to try to help." Messiah "doesn't brainwash students with Christian rhetoric" but equips them to think critically. According to a senior in international relations, "I've found my faith deepened through the process because the analytical questioning takes place in an affirming context."

> **SURVEY SAYS . . .**
> *Small classes*
> *Frats and sororities are unpopular or nonexistent*

Life

Messiah students challenge the assumption that attending a Christian college means succumbing to boredom. "We're not missing out on life. In fact, being here has made me all the more appreciative of life because of the profound understanding of a higher purpose," says a freshman. One student finds social life "reminiscent of childhood: innocent and silly." A junior writes, "My best memories consist of mud sliding, rope swinging, 'eighties dance parties, and sledding on Cemetery Hill." The campus stays busy through the year with Fall Festival, Superbowl parties, and semester kickoff events. Music fans can find small "coffeehouse" shows in the new Student Union or catch "high-profile performers like Bob Dylan and Counting Crows" brought in by the student government. Division III athletic action draws faithful crowds, especially to cheer for the men's soccer squad and final-four field hockey team. People turn out for Saturday night line dancing at the Tractor Twang with students from Dickinson and Gettysburg colleges. Thursday night brings Powerhouse, "a wonderful worship event," where students can really get their praise on. "Other than that," a senior tells us, "we chill."

Student Body

What makes Messiah different from every other WASP-y, affluent Christian school lies in the Peace Church roots. The school's mission statement and "strong contingent of pacifists" drive the student body's "propensity for social activism and involvement." Although most students identify as politically conservative, "It's not in such a way that we tow the party line on all major issues." Beliefs "represent every part of the spectrum, [while the] strong common bond" of Christianity ensures "a large availability of spiritual and emotional support." A freshman recalls, "Everyone I have met on campus, notably the upperclassmen, has been open toward me and invited me to activities." School rules impose the only limits on bonding. "I feel that I miss out on the opportunity to build certain friendships because the opposite gender is not allowed on the floor most of the time." Fellowship still flourishes over meals and within residence halls. The tight community helps "the average Messiah student to make better choices and develop a stronger character than the average college student."

ADMISSIONS

Very important factors considered include: Character/personal qualities, class rank, extracurricular activities, recommendations, religious affiliation/commitment, secondary school record, standardized test scores, talent/ability. *Important factors considered include:* Essays, volunteer work. *Other factors considered include:* Alumni/ae relation, interview, minority status, work experience. TOEFL required of all international applicants. High school diploma is required, and GED is accepted. *Academic units required:* 4 English, 2 math, 2 science (2 science lab), 2 foreign language, 2 social studies, 4 academic electives. *Academic units recommended:* 4 English, 3 math, 3 science (3 science lab), 2 foreign language, 2 social studies, 2 history, 4 academic electives.

The Inside Word

Admissions officers at Messiah are looking for students who are not only a good academic fit but who will also fit in well with the school's devoutly religious community. Those who embrace "the evangelical spirit rooted in the Anabaptist, Pietist, and Wesleyan traditions of the Christian Church" will be most comfortable here.

FINANCIAL AID

Students should submit: FAFSA. The Princeton Review suggests that all financial aid forms be submitted as soon as possible after 1/1. *Need-based scholarships/grants offered:* Pell, SEOG, state scholarships/grants, private scholarships, the school's own gift aid. *Loan aid offered:* Direct Subsidized Stafford, Direct Unsubsidized Stafford, Direct PLUS, Federal Perkins, Federal Nursing. Applicants will be notified of awards on a rolling basis beginning on or about 3/15. Federal Work-study Program available. Institutional employment available. Off-campus job opportunities are good.

FROM THE ADMISSIONS OFFICE

"Messiah College is a place where education involves a student's intellect, character, and Christian faith. Students receive a superb higher education and also discover a higher calling as they prepare for lives of service, leadership, and reconciliation.

"As a community of learners, Messiah gives academics a high priority. More than 2,800 students from 38 states and 25 countries receive a thorough liberal arts foundation and pursue their choice of more than 50 liberal or applied majors.

"Messiah students learn in many settings. Whether they are involved in student government, a national championship–quality athletic tram, or a community service project, students apply what they have learned. Co-curricular activities and organizations provide a laboratory for testing values and convictions. These opportunities for character development at Messiah are as diverse as the students who bring their gifts and abilities. The 20 intercollegiate athletic teams, academic clubs, student publications, the radio station, music and theatre ensembles, and leadership development programs are just a few of the opportunities available.

"For the person of faith, rigorous intellectual study demands a similar response from the heart. Messiah College faculty and administration mentor students toward spiritual maturity. Students explore their faith while asking the difficult questions of life.

"Interested students should visit during their sophomore or junior year of high school either individually or during one of the various open house events. Applications for admission are considered on a rolling basis."

For even more information on this school, turn to page 505 of the "Stats" section.

MIDDLEBURY COLLEGE

THE EMMA WILLARD HOUSE, MIDDLEBURY, VT 05753 • ADMISSIONS: 802-443-3000 • FAX: 802-443-2056
FINANCIAL AID: 802-443-5158 • E-MAIL: ADMISSIONS@MIDDLEBURY.EDU • WEBSITE: WWW.MIDDLEBURY.EDU

Ratings
Quality of Life: 98   Academic: 99   Admissions: 98   Financial Aid: 95

Academics

Academically one of the most rigorous programs in the country, "top-rate" Middlebury College, tucked away in rural Vermont (about three and a half hours' drive to Boston, 45 minutes to Burlington, and two hours to Montreal) manages to offer the resources, facilities, and faculty excellence of a much larger school—while keeping enrollment for undergrads at around 2,300. Nationally recognized language, writing, and theater programs share the spotlight with a top-notch science curriculum— which has benefited in recent years from the construction of a new science center. One student is thrilled that "professors here actually teach. They manage classes, advising, and research demands seamlessly." Despite "tons of homework" and tough classes, students say there's little of the "cutthroat competition" that might characterize other schools of Middlebury's caliber. It might have something to do with the pristine location of "Club Midd," their "laid-back" atmosphere, and an excellent alumni network that makes finding a job after graduation a whole lot easier. Or it might be the result of a bit of grade inflation (some kids complain that "if you're smart, you can get A's and B's hardly doing any work"). But most likely, it's just Middlebury's special blend of a quality program, personal attention, and something a little more nebulous one student calls "attitude." In any case, Middlebury's got it. Sums up a senior, "Academically, I've been challenged, but also have had time to breathe and have fun."

> ### SURVEY SAYS . . .
> *Small classes*
> *Lab facilities are great*
> *Athletic facilities are great*
> *Campus feels safe*

Life

You'd think that at a place that gets "so cold your nostrils freeze together" folks would be spending most of their time inside. Not so at Club Midd! "We own our own ski mountain," notes a junior, one of the reasons why, come winter, most students head outside for fun. With skiing, hiking, rock climbing, mountain biking, kayaking, and fishing right in the college's backyard, you can see why "year round people are involved in outdoor activities." "Almost everyone is athletic one way or another," adds another senior. The school's facilities say as much—students can choose between a hockey rink, fitness center, pool, golf course, and "snow bowl" for fun. It's no surprise, then, that "sports are a major preoccupation here." The "work hard, play hard" ethos extends into socializing, too. A senior explains: "As opportunities for nightlife are virtually nonexistent, we drink. While fun, this does take its toll on one's health." And though there doesn't seem to be a shortage of school-sponsored activities and clubs (social houses and a "commons"-style dorm system provide social opportunities for underclassmen), some students complain that the Middlebury experience "varies between having amazing times to wanting to get the hell out of here." What's more, besides the professed lack of academic competition, "life can be very stressful," notes a junior; "everyone around is an overachiever, star athlete, talented musician, and very attractive."

Student Body

"Students here come from every corner of the world and every New England prep school," jokes a first-year on the subject of Middlebury's fairly homogenous student body (69 percent of its undergrads self-identify as "Caucasian"). A junior gives his take on the situation: "They're cool but the same. This is what I heard before I got here, and this is definitely true. [M]ost are rich and white" and from somewhere "just outside of Boston." Still, it's the people that most students say make the Middlebury experience what it is. Take it from this sophomore: "The main reason I fell in love with Midd was the students. At no other school did I see so many happy, outgoing students." Concludes a classmate, "The majority of the students are really smart and really cool, which makes a small school not feel that way."

ADMISSIONS

Very important factors considered include: Character/personal qualities, class rank, extracurricular activities, secondary school record, talent/ability. *Important factors considered include:* Essays, minority status, recommendations, standardized test scores. *Other factors considered include:* Alumni/ae relation, geographical residence, interview, volunteer work, work experience. SAT Reasoning Test, SAT Subject Tests, and ACT required. High school diploma or equivalent is not required. *Academic units recommended:* 4 English, 4 math, 3 science (3 science lab), 4 foreign language, 3 social studies.

The Inside Word

While Middlebury benefits tremendously from its age-old position as an Ivy League safety, it is nonetheless a very strong and demanding place in its own right. Middlebury has a broad national applicant pool and sees more ACT scores than most eastern colleges, so submitting ACT scores to Middlebury is a more comfortable option than at most eastern schools.

FINANCIAL AID

Students should submit: CSS/Financial Aid PROFILE, state aid form, noncustodial (divorced/separated) parents' statement, business/farm supplement. Regular filing deadline 12/31. The Princeton Review suggests that all financial aid forms be submitted as soon as possible after 1/1. *Need-based scholarships/grants offered:* Pell, SEOG, state scholarships/grants, private scholarships, the school's own gift aid. *Loan aid offered:* Direct Subsidized Stafford, Direct Unsubsidized Stafford, Direct PLUS, Federal Perkins, college/university loans from institutional funds. Applicants will be notified of awards on or about 4/1. Federal Work-study Program available. Institutional employment available. Off-campus job opportunities are good.

FROM THE ADMISSIONS OFFICE

"The successful Middlebury candidate excels in a variety of areas including academics, athletics, the arts, leadership, and service to others. These strengths and interests permit students to grow beyond their traditional 'comfort zones' and conventional limits. Our classrooms are as varied as the Green Mountains, the Metropolitan Museum of Art, or the great cities Russia and Japan. Outside the classroom, students informally interact with professors in activities such as intramural basketball games and community service. At Middlebury, students develop critical thinking skills, enduring bonds of friendship, and the ability to challenge themselves."

For even more information on this school, turn to page 506 of the "Stats" section.

MONMOUTH UNIVERSITY

ADMISSION, MONMOUTH UNIVERSITY, 400 CEDAR AVENUE, WEST LONG BRANCH, NJ 07764-1898
ADMISSIONS: 732-571-3456 • FAX: 732-263-5166 • E-MAIL: ADMISSION@MONMOUTH.EDU • WEBSITE: WWW.MONMOUTH.EDU

Ratings
Quality of Life: 73   **Academic:** 75   **Admissions:** 75   **Financial Aid:** 70

Academics

West Long Branch, New Jersey's, Monmouth University "is a comfortably-sized school (not too big, but not too small) with helpful faculty and staff members and many opportunities for real-world experience." Most students find professors to be "fair, knowledgeable, and most importantly, willing to compromise," although some note that "the quality of professors varies from class to class." Overall, students agree that "the quality of instruction at Monmouth is good." The 'school's new president, Paul Gaffney, "is very interested in student affairs and can be seen regularly at campus events. He has even helped incoming freshmen move into their dorms"." One student adds, "The lower-level administrators 'aren't as impressive, but do treat students as human beings, which is always nice." Communications is a popular major at Monmouth; many students were lured to the school by its impressive $13 million Jules L. Plangere Jr. Center for Communication and Instructional Technology, a "state-of-the-art facility" that features a "brand-new five million dollar TV studio and radio production studio." Monmouth students have wrestled with in-person class registration hassles in the past, but students report, "We have online registration now (thank God!), so no more waiting in line, although sometimes the servers are slow on the first day of registration."

> **SURVEY SAYS . . .**
> *Small classes*
> *Lots of beer drinking*
> *Hard liquor is popular*
> *(Almost) everyone smokes*

Life

"Monmouth is in perfect proximity to the beach or the city," undergrads tell us. "A person can hop on the train and be in New York City in 45minutes or drive two minutes up the road and be at the beach." Students seeking other means of entertainment "go to bars, clubs, an athletic event, Greek house, or hang out in their room or apartment." There are "great local clubs like The Stone Pony and the Groove Lounge, and there are also coffeehouses like Starbucks and The Ink Well." Students also frequent the local mall, which is ten minutes away. In addition, the university sponsors "a lot of events on campus, from concerts to guest speakers." Monmouth is somewhat of a suitcase school; "a lot of people go home on the weekend because they live so close." Students feel confident in the campus security at Monmouth. One student writes, "Security is always around. I can walk from my car at one in the morning and feel safe. I also feel safe when walking from my night classes."

Student Body

Monmouth undergrads are split down the middle when it comes to describing the student body. Some students can be described as "rich...preppy...cliquey...Gucci [and] Armani-obsessed." On the flipside, undergrads describe their fellow students as "friendly, involved, outgoing, [and] fun." Most students agree that most Monmouth undergrads are from "white, upper-middle class" backgrounds. One student explains, "There are a lot of upper-class students who come from wealth. The people I've met are generally all nice and friendly. But I've heard stories that say otherwise. I think it depends on who you meet. There are intelligent, hardworking students, and others who aren't. It's a mix of many different people." Another student adds, "There are lots of different groups of kids on campus and all types of people fit in. You just have to find your group. Monmouth is a lot like high school."

ADMISSIONS

Very important factors considered include: Secondary school record, standardized test scores. *Other factors considered include:* Alumni/ae relation, character/personal qualities, class rank, essays, extracurricular activities, interview, recommendations, volunteer work, work experience. SAT Reasoning or ACT required. TOEFL required of all international applicants. High school diploma is required, and GED is accepted. *Academic units required:* 4 English, 3 math, 2 science (1 science lab), 2 history, 5 academic electives. *Academic units recommended:* 2 foreign language, 2 social studies.

The Inside Word

B students with average standardized test scores should have little trouble getting into Monmouth University. Stiff competition from the area's many quality schools forces MU to accept more students, and less-qualified students, than it otherwise would.

FINANCIAL AID

Students should submit: FAFSA. The Princeton Review suggests that all financial aid forms be submitted as soon as possible after 1/1. *Need-based scholarships/grants offered:* Pell, SEOG, state scholarships/grants, private scholarships, the school's own gift aid. *Loan aid offered:* Direct Subsidized Stafford, Direct Unsubsidized Stafford, Direct PLUS, Federal Perkins, state loans, college/university loans from institutional funds. Applicants will be notified of awards on a rolling basis beginning on or about 2/4. Federal Work-study Program available. Institutional employment available. Off-campus job opportunities are excellent.

FROM THE ADMISSIONS OFFICE

"Monmouth University is a leading independent institution of higher learning, emphasizing teaching and scholarship at undergraduate and graduate levels. The University is committed to helping men and women pursue and achieve a wide variety of bachelor's and master's programs. Monmouth is dedicated to serving its students and actively manages its resources to keep up with its growth. Because of this, the University still offers small classes that are taught by professors who focus on the student's learning and career preparation. Seven schools within the University provide a variety of academic programs. There are bachelor's degree programs in arts and sciences and in professional areas of business, computer science, criminal justice, education, nursing, social work, and software engineering. Master's-level programs include business administration, computer science, corporate and public communication, criminal justice, education, electronic engineering, history, liberal arts, nursing, psychological counseling, social work, and software engineering. Monmouth faculty members are respected scholars, artists, scientists, and professionals, all of whom are committed to helping students achieve their fullest potential. The University's beautiful and historic 153-acre campus is located in attractive, residential West Long Branch, New Jersey, near the ocean and close to New York City and Philadelphia. Monmouth University also enjoys proximity to high-technology firms and financial institutions and a thriving business-industrial sector. Monmouth offers a high-tech learning environment, professors who meet the highest standards for teaching and academic excellence, and the vibrant life of a large university combined with the individual attention typical of small liberal arts colleges."

For even more information on this school, turn to page 506 of the "Stats" section.

Moore College of Art & Design

20th Street and The Parkway, Philadelphia, PA 19103-1179 • Admissions: 215-965-4014 • Fax: 215-568-3547
E-mail: admiss@moore.edu • Website: www.moore.edu

Ratings
Quality of Life: 74   Academic: 71   Admissions: 60   Financial Aid: 62

Academics

Students searching for a place that's "all about artistic girl power" find a prize in Moore College of Art and Design. Current students mention the demanding workload more often than anything else. The first year brings a "very intense foundations program" to whip entering students' technique into shape. A textile design major writes, "You learn more than you ever imagined, but you give up sleep, too." Students believe this fierce pace "prepares us for a professional workload." Many of these young artists share a career-oriented attitude, emphasizing the curriculum's focus on teaching "how to apply my craft in the working world." Major programs include fashion design, art history, 2-D and 3-D fine arts, illustration, interior design, and art education. Professors set high standards to best nurture their students. Some students claim that professors "expect a lot, and there's a lot of homework assigned." A junior comments that thanks to her professors, "My art skills have grown measurably, and my interest in art and art-making is more acute than ever." Even beyond the realm of art, "they teach that there's more to life than getting a job." For undergraduates set on a creative career, the college offers "a supportive area to learn, grow as an artist, and mature into a strong woman."

> **SURVEY SAYS . . .**
> Small classes
> No one cheats
> Students love Philadelphia, PA
> Campus feels safe
> Intercollegiate sports are unpopular or nonexistent
> Intramural sports are unpopular or nonexistent
> Frats and sororities are unpopular or nonexistent

Life

"There is fun only when created in order to procrastinate or shroud ourselves from the huge amount of work assigned," writes one student. To most, however, spending all of their time and money on art isn't necessarily a bad thing. One student explains, "I don't do anything except go to school, which is fun, getting to do what I love every day." Masters of time management succeed in "working hard, but having fun regardless." Philadelphia, with its "clubs, museums, galleries, shopping, and Chinatown," usually plays a central role in the diversions students permit themselves. One satisfied student writes, "For fun, I wander this glorious city." Students are working to cultivate more on-campus diversion, including "better organization for school events" and "something to give purpose to our spirit week, like a mascot."

Student Body

When characterizing this group of young women artists, the most commonly drawn image is that of a "stressed out art student working her ass off nonstop." Despite the busy schedules, a "sense of sisterhood" emerges. One student writes, "We're not just a group of individuals, we're a community." Students praise their "awesome residential assistants and student leaders" for fostering this feeling of connection. Genuine relationships form since people are "open to many things, yet feel strongly about their beliefs." A high degree of tolerance comes from the fact that "we are all individuals, and we appreciate individualism." In their personalities and opinions as well as their art, "We are able to express ourselves freely." Not a bad place to end up for "all the artistic, imaginative so-called weirdos you knew in high school."

ADMISSIONS

Very important factors considered include: Character/personal qualities, interview, secondary school record, standardized test scores, talent/ability. *Important factors considered include:* Essays, extracurricular activities, recommendations. *Other factors considered include:* Class rank, volunteer work, work experience. SAT Reasoning Test recommended; SAT Reasoning or SAT Subject Tests required. TOEFL required of all international applicants. High school diploma is required, and GED is accepted.

The Inside Word

Portfolio submission is the critical stage of the Moore admissions process. All students who live within 100 miles of the school must submit to an on-campus interview; portfolios are reviewed at this time. Those outside the radius who can visit campus to interview should do so as well. An in-person presentation of the portfolio is more impressive than a set of slides.

FINANCIAL AID

Students should submit: FAFSA. The Princeton Review suggests that all financial aid forms be submitted as soon as possible after 1/1. *Need-based scholarships/grants offered:* Pell, SEOG, state scholarships/grants, private scholarships, the school's own gift aid. *Loan aid offered:* FFEL Subsidized Stafford, FFEL Unsubsidized Stafford, FFEL PLUS, Federal Perkins, alternative loans. Applicants will be notified of awards on a rolling basis beginning on or about 3/1. Federal Work-study Program available. Institutional employment available. Off-campus job opportunities are excellent.

For even more information on this school, turn to page 507 of the "Stats" section.

MORAVIAN COLLEGE

1200 MAIN ST., BETHLEHEM, PA 18018 • ADMISSIONS: 800-441-3191 • FAX: 610-625-7930
FINANCIAL AID: 610-861-1330 • E-MAIL: ADMISSIONS@MORAVIAN.EDU • WEBSITE: WWW.MORAVIAN.EDU

Ratings
Quality of Life: 85   **Academic:** 84   **Admissions:** 81   **Financial Aid:** 75

Academics

The sixth-oldest undergraduate institution in the United States (founded in 1742), there's no arguing that Moravian College is "a historic institution." But this small eastern Pennsylvanian liberal arts school also knows how to keep up with the times; through its Learning in Common general education curriculum, Moravian exposes all undergraduates to a broad range of skills taught within a multidisciplinary framework, preparing them, in theory, to adapt to

rapid and dramatic changes in the world, no matter what fields they choose to pursue. Undergraduates appreciate the approach, telling us that there are "few, if any, colleges that rival our curriculum." Students also give high marks to the business, education, nursing, art, and music departments (the last two of which are housed separately, on the school's Priscilla Payne Hard Campus). Professors here "are mostly all amazing. These teachers get to know their students and make sure that they are available to the students, and our classes are small, allowing engaging, open, free discussion." While the school is small—"If you went to a small high school, Moravian isn't going to be a big shift for you"—academic options are unusually broad thanks to the school's participation in the Lehigh Valley Association of Independent Colleges, which allows students to take classes and use the libraries at Lafayette College, Lehigh University, Muhlenberg College, DeSales University, and Cedar Crest College. The school works hard to offer "an infinite number of opportunities for students, such as on-campus jobs, internships, [and] study abroad programs."

Life

"The greatest strength of Moravian is combining the emphasis on academics with enjoying college life," undergraduates tell us, observing that "everyone here realizes that students don't want to study 100 percent of the time, so the workload is reasonable, sports are very important, and there are many on-campus activities." Those activities include "plenty of concerts, plays, and speakers, as well as movies and athletic events." Student clubs and organizations are popular, with a number of students involved in numerous extracurricular endeavors. Fraternities and sororities figure into the mix. While "there's always a party" somewhere, "there's always another option, too, [so] there's no excuse for anyone being bored and not making friends" here. Those on a budget appreciate that "most of the activities are free of charge, or there's a student discount" and that "a lot of the fun around here comes from just hanging out with friends whenever you can, and there is almost always time for that." All these activities dovetail into a renewed sense of campus vitality. "While Moravian was once considered to be a 'suitcase' college, these days more and more students stay on campus. They feel they miss out on too much leaving for the weekend." Students are also fond of Bethlehem, describing its downtown as "a lovely, scenic area that is good for light shopping and browsing. Our school provides trips to the mall and grocery store, which are always fun breaks to take with friends."

Student Body

Many Moravian students see themselves in the context of their closest neighbors; writes one undergrad, "Moravian is surrounded by Lehigh, Lafayette and Muhlenberg, which are known as more prissy schools, where the students are a lot more stuck up. There isn't a lot of priss at Moravian." Here, "the typical student comes from the Mid-Atlantic region, grew up in suburbia, and is often of a middle-class background." Most are "very friendly; they smile and say 'hi' to one another." Observers detect a clear difference between students on the Main Campus and their counterparts on the Priscilla Payne Hard Campus, who are relatively "more artsy, more open-minded, dress different, and are more city-smart."

ADMISSIONS

Very important factors considered include: Character/personal qualities, class rank, secondary school record. *Important factors considered include:* Essays, extracurricular activities, interview, recommendations, standardized test scores, volunteer work. *Other factors considered include:* Alumni/ae relation, geographical residence, talent/ability, work experience. SAT Reasoning or ACT required. TOEFL required of all international applicants. High school diploma is required, and GED is accepted. *Academic units required:* 4 English, 3 math, 2 science (2 science lab), 2 foreign language, 4 social studies. *Academic units recommended:* 4 math, 3 foreign language.

The Inside Word

Moravian is a small liberal arts school with all the bells and whistles. Applicants will find a pretty straightforward admissions process—solid grades and test scores are required. Counselors will look closely to find the extras—community service, extracurricular activities—that make students stand out from the crowd. Moravian has many programs that should not be overlooked, including music, education, and the sciences.

FINANCIAL AID

Students should submit: FAFSA, CSS/Financial Aid PROFILE, noncustodial (divorced/separated) parents' statement, business/farm supplement, copies of parent and student W-2 and 1040 forms. Regular filing deadline 3/15. The Princeton Review suggests that all financial aid forms be submitted as soon as possible after 1/1. *Need-based scholarships/grants offered:* Pell, SEOG, state scholarships/grants, private scholarships, the school's own gift aid. *Loan aid offered:* FFEL Subsidized Stafford, FFEL Unsubsidized Stafford, FFEL PLUS, Federal Perkins. Applicants will be notified of awards on a rolling basis beginning on or about 4/1. Federal Work-study Program available. Institutional employment available. Off-campus job opportunities are good.

FROM THE ADMISSIONS OFFICE

"Founded in 1742, Moravian is proud of its history as one of America's oldest and most respected liberal arts colleges. The low student/faculty ratio allows for an immediate and unusually close bond. The Moravian family, comprising current students and faculty, as well as alumni and emeritus professors, praises the college as a supportive environment for learning, personal exploration, and character development. The overarching emphasis of our curriculum is on scholarship enriched by self-discovery. In the last five years, Moravian has produced four Fulbright scholars, a Goldwater scholar, a Rhodes finalist, a Truman Scholar finalist, and three NCAA Postgraduate Scholars. Its robust varsity athletic program has produced All-American student athletes, Academic All-Americans, national champions, a national Player of the Year, and several Olympic hopefuls. In the fall of 2005, the college will dedicate Rocco Calvo Field, a state of the art synthetic multi-sport field and the eight lane Timothy Breidegam Olympic track. At the heart of the campus is a new $20 million academic building. It houses 15 new classrooms, four faculty departments, laboratories, research facilities, and "smart" classrooms for easy technological interface. In 2004, the college established a unique Leadership Center, the goal of which is to engage the campus community is discussion, discovery, and dialogue about the many aspects of leadership as applied to the academic disciplines, professions, the community, and campus organizations. The college welcomes inquiries from students eager to participate in an environment of self-directed, life-long learning."

For even more information on this school, turn to page 507 of the "Stats" section.

MOUNT HOLYOKE COLLEGE

50 COLLEGE STREET, SOUTH HADLEY, MA 01075 • ADMISSIONS: 413-538-2023 • FAX: 413-538-2409
FINANCIAL AID: 413-538-2291 • E-MAIL: ADMISSIONS@MTHOLYOKE.EDU • WEBSITE: WWW.MTHOLYOKE.EDU

Ratings
Quality of Life: 90   **Academic:** 95   **Admissions:** 93   **Financial Aid:** 98

Academics

"Empowering" is a word the women of Mount Holyoke often use when describing their school. Holyoke's "nurturing environment" means that "no matter who you are, what your interests, background, ethnicity, or religion, you are treated as an intelligent woman who has the right to be listened to. No place could be more supportive," one student says. The school is nurturing, but not mollycoddling; students warn that "academically, Mount Holyoke College is challenging. You cannot get behind and expect to catch up." Not that students mind; they tell us that "Mount Holyoke's academic reputation, and the fact that it lives up to that reputation, is commendable," and that its trial by fire makes its students "stronger writers, thinkers, friends, students, daughters, sisters, but most of all, better people." Holyoke's offerings are augmented by its participation in the Five College Consortium, "which allows students to take classes at any of the other four institutions (Smith, Amherst, Hampshire, UMass) around the Pioneer Valley. I love having that kind of freedom, and like being able to vary my classroom environments," writes one student. Another education-broadening experience is the school's popular study abroad program. Still, other opportunities present themselves in the many independent study options available. One student reports, "Professors are sincerely interested in developing student research projects and helping students find and partake in projects that sincerely interest them."

> **SURVEY SAYS . . .**
> *Small classes*
> *Lab facilities are great*
> *Great library*
> *Diverse student types on campus*
> *Campus feels safe*
> *Frats and sororities are unpopular
> or nonexistent*

Life

The Mount Holyoke campus is quiet—not dead, mind you, just quiet—a situation most students appreciate. As one undergraduate puts it, "One of the greatest strengths of this school is that you are able to study without any distraction, but if you choose to party you are able to." Hometown South Hadley is similarly quiet, although students are less enthusiastic about its lack of activity. "South Hadley is about as sad as you get for a college town," students tell us, although rarely without also pointing out that "Amherst and Northampton, two towns with plenty of shopping and other things of interest, are close by and easily reached by the PVTA (our bus system)." The campus may not always be bustling, but it is always beautiful. Students lovingly describe "greens surrounded only by classic brick buildings, covered in ivy." One rapturous undergraduate writes, "In the fall, the colors welcome students. In the winter, the skating rink is within walking distance of many sledding hills and cross-country skiing trails. In the spring, the lakes are home to baby geese and the campus is covered in flowers." Holyoke is also home to the "best golf course and equestrian center ever, dorms like palaces, [which have] dining rooms right downstairs [serving] food that's better than any other school I've been to, with a wide variety of choices and special attention paid to vegetarians and vegans," writes one enthusiastic student. Beyond campus, "There's plenty to do in the Pioneer Valley: hiking, climbing, and camping. And Boston is only an hour and a half away."

Student Body

Mount Holyoke women "fall into all sorts of categories, whether it be because of their style in clothing, what they like to do outside of the classroom, or sexual orientation." Students feel that a "large international population also provides for a very diverse atmosphere," as does the sizable lesbian contingent. If there is common ground among all students, it is that they are "outgoing super-achievers who spend far more time in the library than they do at parties." Undergraduates "are generally serious about their work, interested in their world, and politically left." Students pride themselves on their tolerance, although campus conservatives complain that it's selective. One undergraduate tells us, "A word to the wise, unless you agree with the vast majority on campus—or at least the vocal majority—keep your mouth shut or wear flame-retardant clothing."

ADMISSIONS

Very important factors considered include: Class rank, essays, recommendations, secondary school record. *Important factors considered include:* Character/personal qualities, extracurricular activities, interview, talent/ability, volunteer work, work experience. *Other factors considered include:* Alumni/ae relation, geographical residence, minority status, standardized test scores. TOEFL required of all international applicants. High school diploma is required, and GED is accepted. *Academic units recommended:* 4 English, 3 math, 3 science (3 science lab), 3 foreign language, 3 history, 1 academic elective.

The Inside Word

Mount Holyoke has benefited well from the renaissance of interest in women's colleges; selectivity and academic quality are on the rise. Considering that the college was already fairly selective, candidates are well advised to take the admissions process seriously. Matchmaking is a significant factor here; strong academic performance, well-written essays, and an understanding of and appreciation for "the Mount Holyoke experience" will usually carry the day.

FINANCIAL AID

Students should submit: FAFSA, CSS/Financial Aid PROFILE, noncustodial (divorced/separated) parents' statement, business/farm supplement. Regular filing deadline 2/1. The Princeton Review suggests that all financial aid forms be submitted as soon as possible after 1/1. *Need-based scholarships/grants offered:* Pell, SEOG, state scholarships/grants, private scholarships, the school's own gift aid. *Loan aid offered:* Direct Subsidized Stafford, Direct Unsubsidized Stafford, Direct PLUS, Federal Perkins, college/university loans from institutional funds. Applicants will be notified of awards on or about 4/1. Federal Work-study Program available. Institutional employment available. Off-campus job opportunities are good.

FROM THE ADMISSIONS OFFICE

"Did you know that the majority of students who choose Mount Holyoke do so simply because it is an outstanding liberal arts college? After a semester or two, they start to appreciate the fact that Mount Holyoke is a women's college, even though most Mount Holyoke students never thought they'd go to a women's college when they started their college search. Students talk of having 'space' to really figure out who they are. They speak about feeling empowered to excel in traditionally male subjects such as science and technology. They talk about the remarkable array of opportunities—for academic achievement, career exploration, and leadership— and the impressive, creative accomplishments of their peers. If you're looking for a college that will challenge you to be your best, most powerful self and to fulfill potential, Mount Holyoke should be at the top of your list."

For even more information on this school, turn to page 508 of the "Stats" section.

MUHLENBERG COLLEGE

2400 WEST CHEW STREET, ALLENTOWN, PA 18104-5596 • ADMISSIONS: 484-664-3200 • FAX: 484-664-3234
FINANCIAL AID: 484-664-3175 • E-MAIL: ADMISSION@MUHLENBERG.EDU • WEBSITE: WWW.MUHLENBERG.EDU

Ratings
Quality of Life: 75   Academic: 86   Admissions: 93   Financial Aid: 94

Academics

Students praise the "amazing" theater and science departments at Muhlenberg College. Notes one undergrad, "The single greatest strength [of this school] is the reputation of the science departments. The rigor I have faced here as a biology major, although at times extremely tough, has been also very rewarding." Muhlenberg also boasts "excellent" departments of English and history; the business and philosophy departments here "aren't too shabby either."

Indeed, Muhlenberg has a lot to offer for an institution with less than 3,000 students. Undergrads appreciate how "the small student body allows the professors to tailor the education for each student." As one student told us, "The best part about my school is its smallness—something I thought I would hate about Muhlenberg turned out to be what makes it so great." Another benefit of the school's small size: "Since we don't have a graduate school, we don't have any graduate students, so undergrads have opportunities to do research." Prospective students are forewarned that "this is a tough school to get into and to stay in, due to a heavy workload." While profs pile on the work, they are also "extremely approachable and welcome you to speak with them about anything, not just class work. They can help you succeed in school if you take the initiative to get to know them." Sums up one student here: "Muhlenberg is what you make of it; if you're ambitious, the school will be good to you; if you're not, most likely you'll get swept along for the ride."

Life

The "beautiful and safe" Muhlenberg campus provides a serene setting to counteract students' hectic academic schedules. "Life is very busy," notes one student. "The best days are the ones where you have a spare hour or two to sit out on the lawn and read or study with some friends when the weather is nice. The front lawn is great; it always gets crowded with kids just hanging out in the spring and fall or playing in the snow in the winter." An active social scene, however, is not part of what clutters most kids' calendars. There are school-sponsored activities offered, but "most are lame," and as far as the Greek scene goes, the frats "are now either kicked off campus or on probation, so now we are becoming a bar and house party school." Hometown Allentown offers little. Explains one undergrad, "Allentown is technically a city, but don't expect it to be like Manhattan. The college is located in the middle of the suburbs, and most people don't go downtown." Adds another, "I wish they would just pick up the whole damn school and move it out of Allentown." Students enjoy "a few sporting events, mainly men's soccer and women's rugby." Even so, most who can do so seek entertainment elsewhere, often in Philadelphia or New York City. Unfortunately, "freshmen are not allowed to have cars on campus due to major lack of parking space and the rule is pretty strictly enforced," which is why they "tend to flock to the fraternities or hang out in their dorm rooms."

Student Body

Muhlenberg's student body is predominantly white and affluent, students here agree. Detractors describe their peers as people "who have never worked in their lives, drive BMWs and have exorbitant allowances." They "tend to be conservative" and cliquish; reports one, "I don't think anyone really goes out of their way to make new friends once they have found their clique. That's not to say people aren't friendly, though. Overall, the students all get along with each other." Theater majors tend to be the major exception to the preppy, conservative stereotype; their ranks include a disproportionate number of iconoclasts as well as gay students. Despite its Lutheran affiliation, "most kids here are Roman Catholic or Jewish."

ADMISSIONS

Very important factors considered include: Character/personal qualities, secondary school record, talent/ability. *Important factors considered include:* Class rank, essays, extracurricular activities, interview, recommendations, standardized test scores, volunteer work. *Other factors considered include:* Alumni/ae relation, geographical residence, minority status, work experience. TOEFL required of all international applicants. High school diploma is required, and GED is accepted. *Academic units required:* 4 English, 3 math, 2 science (2 science lab), 2 foreign language, 2 history, 1 academic elective. *Academic units recommended:* 4 math, 3 science, 4 foreign language, 2 social studies.

The Inside Word

Muhlenberg's inquiries and applications continue to increase, which serves to reinforce its selectivity. Competition for students among small Pennsylvania liberal arts colleges is quite heated, and the college is among the more competitive of the lot.

FINANCIAL AID

Students should submit: FAFSA, institution's own financial aid form, CSS/Financial Aid PROFILE, noncustodial (divorced/separated) parents' statement. Regular filing deadline 2/15. The Princeton Review suggests that all financial aid forms be submitted as soon as possible after 1/1. *Need-based scholarships/grants offered:* Pell, SEOG, state scholarships/grants, private scholarships, the school's own gift aid. *Loan aid offered:* FFEL Subsidized Stafford, FFEL Unsubsidized Stafford, FFEL PLUS, Federal Perkins, private loans. Applicants will be notified of awards on or about 4/1.

FROM THE ADMISSIONS OFFICE

"Listening to our own students, we've learned that most picked Muhlenberg mainly because it has a long-standing reputation for being academically demanding on one hand, but personally supportive on the other. We expect a lot from our students, but we also expect a lot from ourselves in providing the challenge and support they need to stretch, grow, and succeed. It's not unusual for professors to put their home phone numbers on the course syllabus and encourage students to call them at home with questions. Upperclassmen are helpful to underclassmen. 'We really know about collegiality here,' says an alumna who now works at Muhlenberg. 'It's that kind of place.' The supportive atmosphere and strong work ethic produce lots of successes. The pre-med and pre-law programs are very strong, as are programs in theater arts, English, psychology, the sciences, business, and accounting. 'When I was a student here,' recalls Dr. Walter Loy, now a professor emeritus of physics, 'we were encouraged to live life to its fullest, to do our best, to be honest, to deal openly with others, and to treat everyone as an individual. Those are important things, and they haven't changed at Muhlenberg.' "

For even more information on this school, turn to page 508 of the "Stats" section.

NAZARETH COLLEGE

4245 EAST AVENUE, ROCHESTER, NY 14618-3790 • ADMISSIONS: 585-389-2860 • FAX: 585-389-2826
E-MAIL: ADMISSIONS@NAZ.EDU • WEBSITE: WWW.NAZ.EDU

Ratings
Quality of Life: 96   **Academic:** 87   **Admissions:** 81   **Financial Aid:** 89

Academics

Not many schools inspire students to reflect on the role of "independence and interdependence" in society as much as Nazareth College. Beyond job skills, a junior in nursing says, "[I've learned who I am and how to be a better person, all because of the environment at Naz." The curriculum challenges each student to "find out what [he or she is] capable of doing within a community of faculty, staff, and students." Many students choose Nazareth specifically for the "huge

benefit of small class size and individual attention from professors," although certain people think there's such a thing as too small. One student says, "I understand why some students compare it to high school in terms of size and the way the teachers care about the students." Personal attention can also go too far and feel "suffocating at times." A math student attributes his high GPA to "more support than I ever could have expected" from the department's faculty, "probably the greatest group of people I've ever met." The administration responds to the vocal student body and affords "a lot of opportunities for student leadership" within its structure. A senior majoring in physical therapy says, "Everyone who works for this campus is so flexible and makes sure that the student population is satisfied and happy. If you have complaints, you see changes right away."

Life

Many current Nazareth students remember the sense of destiny they felt the first time they set foot on campus, and the love simply grows upon matriculation. Others arrive "expecting the party life and diversity of a bigger campus" and don't take to the mellow social life of "constantly hanging out in 'one another's apartments." An underclassman explains, "We range from laid-back movie nights to full-blown gatherings where we listen to music, play games, and have fun." Alternatives to drunken spectacles include comedians, casino nights, bands, mixers, hypnotists, formals, a stroll along the Erie Canal, or "a friendly game of Jell-O Twister." Beyond the purely social life, "Most students at Nazareth are very involved through residential life, the Undergraduate Association, admissions, or athletics." Partners for Learning, which "assists inner-city school children with tutoring and reading assistance," is just one example of the many opportunities for community service. Shuttles whisk students through the local malls and grocery stores on Sundays and also provide "affordable twenty-four-hour 'Zip-Trips' to New York City" when urban attractions call.

Student Body

Nazareth sells itself on the intimate community that forms among students, and the current class truly lives it: "You learn alongside your best friends, who become like family to you within the first semester." Admittedly, "the close-knit atmosphere of Nazareth 'isn't for everyone." Some students complain of cliques, but a school this small implodes into one big clique, after all—"If you don't know a person, 'it's very likely that one or more of your friends do." The high percentage of women could be attributed to the "strength of programs that are generally female-oriented." Reports indicate that students "fit a hardworking, middle-class mold," but "cookie-cutter" can be a good thing when "friendly, involved, and dedicated" are the norm. The recent opening of a Student Diversity Resource Center corresponds with "the visible growth in diversity on campus in the past couple of years." A sophomore sees her friends "establish close relationships with people who are and are not similar to them." To get the right idea of Nazareth College, just imagine "a really nice high school where everyone knows your name."

ADMISSIONS

Very important factors considered include: Class rank, secondary school record, standardized test scores. *Important factors considered include:* Essays, interview, recommendations. *Other factors considered include:* Alumni/ae relation, character/personal qualities, extracurricular activities, geographical residence, minority status, state residency, talent/ability, volunteer work, work experience. SAT Reasoning or ACT required. TOEFL required of all international applicants. High school diploma is required, and GED is accepted. *Academic units required:* 4 English, 3 math, 3 science (2 science lab), 3 foreign language, 3 social studies. *Academic units recommended:* 4 English, 4 math, 4 science, 4 foreign language, 4 social studies.

The Inside Word

Admissions officers at Nazareth College are looking for candidates who will enhance the college community as a whole. This means that a special talent in athletics, music, the arts, or leadership areas counts; it can be especially helpful to candidates whose academic records are less than exemplary.

FINANCIAL AID

Students should submit: FAFSA. Regular filing deadline 5/1. The Princeton Review suggests that all financial aid forms be submitted as soon as possible after 1/1. *Need-based scholarships/grants offered:* Pell, SEOG, state scholarships/grants, private scholarships, the school's own gift aid. *Loan aid offered:* FFEL Subsidized Stafford, FFEL Unsubsidized Stafford, FFEL PLUS, Federal Perkins. Applicants will be notified of awards on a rolling basis beginning on or about 2/20. Federal Work-study Program available. Institutional employment available. Off-campus job opportunities are excellent.

FROM THE ADMISSIONS OFFICE

"Campus expansion is creating more opportunities for Nazareth students in what they study, where they reside, and how they play. Information Technology prepares students for careers in demand by all organizations. New campus apartments plus a growing number of single rooms provide more living choices for our growing student body. Soccer, lacrosse, and track athletes will compete in the new 2,200 seat stadium. Recreational athletes will love running on the 400-meter, all-weather oval.

"More students from more places are choosing Nazareth College. The 2002 freshman came from throughout the United States and abroad. In turn, more of our students seek opportunities for international study and internships. The new Center for International Education creates 'two-way traffic' for study; participants are students wishing to come to the United States as well as U.S. students seeking an international experience. The new Center for Teaching Excellence assists Nazareth and other college faculty in honing their classroom skills. Recent campus speakers have included space shuttle astronaut Pamela Melroy, olympic gold medallist Billy Mills, anthropologist Meave Leakey, Marriott CEO Bill Marriott Jr., and former surgeon general of the United States Dr. David Satcher."

For even more information on this school, turn to page 509 of the "Stats" section.

NEUMANN COLLEGE

One Neumann Drive, Aston, PA 19014 • Admissions: 610-558-5616 • Fax: 610-558-5652
E-mail: neumann@neumann.edu • Website: www.neumann.edu

Ratings
Quality of Life: 69   **Academic:** 66   **Admissions:** 65   **Financial Aid:** 82

Academics

In Aston, Pennsylvania—just west of Philadelphia and north of Wilmington, Delaware—Neumann College contributes to the heavy concentration of colleges and universities in the Delaware Valley. While it is in the suburbs, it's not exactly "in the middle of nowhere," as one freshman claims. This "small Catholic college" offers men and women the chance to study in nearly 20 fields—including tracks in pre-law and

> **SURVEY SAYS . . .**
> *Small classes*
> *Frats and sororities are unpopular*
> *or nonexistent*
> *(Almost) everyone smokes*

premed—and all students are required to complete a core of liberal arts courses. The most recent additions to the curriculum include majors in athletic training and criminal justice. One student refers to the faculty as "extraordinary . . . . Imagine your few favorite teachers from high school that really made an impact on you—now imagine a whole college full of them!" Adds a sophomore, "Their focus is entirely unselfish and they give 100 percent." And the accolades extend to the administration, as well. A junior asks, "Where else does the administration not only know your face and name, but also knows your favorite candy?" She's got us there.

Life

With a healthy population of commuting students from around the Delaware Valley, Neumann must cater to its resident and nonresident students. "There is not much to do at Neumann," says one commuter, echoing the impressions of other nonresidents. But, of course, the commuters aren't around campus at night or on weekends, and residents report that students who seek fun are able to find it. After all, Philadelphia and Wilmington are nearby. And on campus, friends are not tough to come by. "We are so small that you know most of the people," a sophomore says. Friends often venture to "parties or to the mall," as well as taking advantage of the "high number of activities" that the college offers. For instance, six arts groups are available for creative minds, and 15 NCAA teams cater to the athletes. (Athletes would be even happier if the college would "get a rugby team.") Most griping at Neumann is focused on three aspects of life: parking, food, and rules. Commuters and residents alike would be able to stave off their ulcers if the college would find more spots to park their cars. Students also report that on bad days, the cafeteria food is less than satisfactory. But the biggest point of contention is rules. "Be less strict," begs a nursing major, referring to the policies like the "dry campus" rule that drives many partiers to off-campus soirees.

Student Body

"Good people!" That's what you'll find at Neumann College. Most students here come from the Pennsylvania-Delaware-New Jersey tri-state area, and many choose to commute to school from their hometowns. But even good people can stand to grow up a little more. A seasoned senior explains, "The maturity level (among students) on this campus is lower than what I would expect from an institution of higher learning." This is partially because groups of friends transfer their cliquey attitudes directly from high school to this nearby college. But every group has its luster and its rust, its good days and its bad days. "It's like a big family," says a freshman.

ADMISSIONS

Very important factors considered include: Extracurricular activities, recommendations, secondary school record, talent/ability. *Important factors considered include:* Alumni/ae relation, character/personal qualities, class rank, interview, standardized test scores. *Other factors considered include:* Minority status, religious affiliation/commitment, volunteer work. SAT Reasoning or ACT required. TOEFL required of all international applicants. High school diploma is required, and GED is accepted. *Academic units required:* 4 English, 2 math, 2 science, 2 foreign language, 2 social studies, 4 academic electives. *Academic units recommended:* 4 English, 2 math, 3 science, 2 foreign language, 2 social studies, 4 academic electives.

The Inside Word

Admission to Neumann College is not highly competitive. Admission to specific departments, which occurs during sophomore year, can be more competitive, depending on the popularity of the department. Check with the admissions office about the popularity of your intended major before applying if you already know what field you plan to enter.

FINANCIAL AID

Students should submit: FAFSA. The Princeton Review suggests that all financial aid forms be submitted as soon as possible after 1/1. *Need-based scholarships/grants offered:* Pell, SEOG, state scholarships/grants, private scholarships, the school's own gift aid, federal nursing scholarships. *Loan aid offered:* Direct Subsidized Stafford, Direct Unsubsidized Stafford, Direct PLUS, FFEL Subsidized Stafford, FFEL Unsubsidized Stafford, FFEL PLUS, Federal Nursing. Applicants will be notified of awards on a rolling basis beginning on or about 3/1. Federal Work-study Program available. Institutional employment available. Off-campus job opportunities are good.

FROM THE ADMISSIONS OFFICE

"Neumann College offers the ideal educational setting. As a small college, it provides students with the personal attention and support they seek. Dedicated faculty teach and assist our students in developing their thinking, writing, communication, and technical skills. As a Catholic College in the Franciscan tradition, Neumann College supports the spiritual, social, and athletic development of students. Neumann College's academic majors most often include experiential components, allowing students to blend classroom study and real work experiences. Neumann College graduates are well on their way to career advancement, having benefited from a tailored curriculum, personal advisement, support, and field experiences that offer them the competitive edge. Freshmen begin career exploration right away through the Academic Resource and Career Counseling Center.

"Campus life is a real strength of Neumann College. Three new suite-style residence halls are home to almost 600 residents. Residence halls are totally wired. Designed to offer the advantage of living in a community while supporting privacy and independence, the Living Learning Centers combine academic space and recreational, health, and fitness facilities all under one roof. Two modern dining facilities offer a variety of meal plans including a late-night serving at 10 p.m.

"There's always plenty to do at Neumann. The advantages of nearby Philadelphia and a variety of on-campus activities and programs fill the student's schedule. Neumann College offers 15 intercollegiate sports (NCAA), 6 performing arts groups, and dozens of student clubs and organizations. Students planning for college are always invited to visit and see Neumann College first-hand."

For even more information on this school, turn to page 509 of the "Stats" section.

NEW JERSEY INSTITUTE OF TECHNOLOGY

UNIVERSITY HEIGHTS, NEWARK, NJ 07102 • ADMISSIONS: 973-596-3300 • FAX: 973-596-3461
FINANCIAL AID: 973-596-3480 • E-MAIL: ADMISSIONS@NJIT.EDU • WEBSITE: WWW.NJIT.EDU

Ratings
Quality of Life: 61   **Academic:** 70   **Admissions:** 80   **Financial Aid:** 78

Academics

Mathematics, science, technology, and architecture offerings all shine at New Jersey Institute of Technology, a "leader in the field of technology in the tri-state area" whose public-school pricing allows students to "graduate without the bank owning our first-borns, which is a definite plus." As at many prestigious tech-oriented schools, "The professors are generally hired for research rather than

> **SURVEY SAYS . . .**
> *Small classes*
> *Great computer facilities*
> *Diverse student types on campus*
> *Campus feels safe*

teaching ability, [so] there are some who cannot teach, and they aren't that great at grading assignments or handing back papers, either." Students hasten to add that "There are also plenty of great professors who work hard for the students" and "a handful are wonderful teachers" as well as "good people. Many are tied to industry, which really helps in the long run." In the short run, too, since those connections help provide "so many opportunities in research and internships." The demanding undergraduate curriculum means "You have to be serious about studies if you are choosing NJIT. There is no time for fun and games." Students groan about the demands made on them but also recognize the benefits; "NJIT is an intense academic university that allows students to be prepared for the working world," explains one architect. Another plus of studying at NJIT is "how well the students interact, especially during exam time. Seniors help juniors, who help sophomores, who help freshman. It's helpful when someone who has taken the courses you're taking at the moment can put things into perspective, and give you hints about what may be on the test."

Life

NJIT is "not the best school socially, but few engineering schools are," students here concede. Since "a lot of classes give amazing amounts of homework, it is hard to have a normal social life. Most nights are spent doing homework late, then getting a few hours of fun before passing out." Extracurricular life has improved recently with the addition of new recreation facilities; one student notes, "The game room has been improved, with pool tables, bowling, and arcades, and a much-needed pub on campus." The Institute also boasts "a pretty good gym to work out in, and a brand new soccer field." Undergrads note optimistically that "Our team sports are all performing better, and the students are starting to feel a sense of competition building. There are plenty of parties on Thursday nights on campus, organized by frats or clubs." And, of course, "Possibilities are endless because New York City is minutes away" by affordable public transportation, opening the door to "major league sports, world-class museums, and theater." Hometown Newark, although much maligned by students and locals, offers "great food and restaurants less than half a mile away from campus, in the Ironbound section." Students also appreciate how the "small classes and campus make a 'small-town' atmosphere during the semester," even though they also acknowledge that "the campus is ugly; there's not a lot of green space here."

Student Body

"There are two types of students at NJIT," writes one student, elaborating: "The first are the ones who are involved with athletics, clubs, organizations, and other things. The others are the antisocial ones. These people stay in their dorms and play computer games all day." How many of each category populate this campus? One student offers some pertinent data: "Class attendance dropped 32 percent the day Halo 2 came out." Like the region surrounding it, "NJIT is a total melting pot; the mix of ethnic backgrounds of students is diverse." While many say the various groups interact well, just as many others describe the student body as "clusters of ethnic groups isolated from each other." Because of curricular demands, "Everyone is pretty smart. But you also have the very smart people." When asked in what ways his school could stand to improve, one succinct information technologist wrote "GIRLS!" reflecting a sentiment running through much of the student body. The male to female ratio is about 4:1.

ADMISSIONS

Very important factors considered include: Class rank, secondary school record, standardized test scores. *Other factors considered include:* Alumni/ae relation, character/personal qualities, essays, extracurricular activities, geographical residence, interview, minority status, recommendations, religious affiliation/commitment, state residency, talent/ability, volunteer work, work experience. SAT Reasoning or ACT required. TOEFL required of all international applicants. High school diploma is required, and GED is accepted. *Academic units required:* 4 English, 4 math, 2 science (2 science lab). *Academic units recommended:* 2 foreign language, 1 social studies, 1 history, 2 academic electives.

The Inside Word

NJIT is a great choice for students who aspire to technical careers but don't meet the requirements for better known and more selective universities. To top it off, it's a pretty good buy.

FINANCIAL AID

Students should submit: FAFSA. Regular filing deadline 5/15. The Princeton Review suggests that all financial aid forms be submitted as soon as possible after 1/1. *Need-based scholarships/grants offered:* Pell, SEOG, state scholarships/grants, private scholarships, the school's own gift aid. *Loan aid offered:* Direct Subsidized Stafford, Direct Unsubsidized Stafford, Direct PLUS, FFEL Subsidized Stafford, FFEL Unsubsidized Stafford, FFEL PLUS, Federal Perkins, state loans, college/university loans from institutional funds. Federal Work-study Program available. Off-campus job opportunities are good.

FROM THE ADMISSIONS OFFICE

"Talented high school graduates from across the nation come to NJIT to prepare for leadership roles in architecture, business, engineering, medical, legal, science, and technological fields. Students experience a public research university conducting more than $75 million in research that maintains a small-college atmosphere at a modest cost. Our attractive 45-acre campus is just minutes from New York City and less than an hour from the Jersey shore. Students find an outstanding faculty and a safe, diverse, caring learning and residential community. All dormitory rooms have sprinklers. NJIT's academic environment challenges and prepares students for rewarding careers and full-time advanced study after graduation. The campus is computing-intensive. For five consecutive years, Yahoo! Internet Life ranked NJIT among America's Most Wired Universities."

For even more information on this school, turn to page 509 of the "Stats" section.

NEW YORK UNIVERSITY

22 WASHINGTON SQUARE NORTH, NEW YORK, NY 10011 • ADMISSIONS: 212-998-4500 • FAX: 212-995-4902
FINANCIAL AID: 212-998-4444 • E-MAIL: ADMISSIONS@NYU.EDU • WEBSITE: WWW.NYU.EDU

Ratings
Quality of Life: 81   Academic: 85   Admissions: 95   Financial Aid: 75

Academics

When people rave about the strong academics at New York University (NYU), they are often referring to one of the many colleges under the university's umbrella. The Tisch School of the Arts and The Stern School of Business have established themselves as frontrunners in their respective fields, but undergraduates urge us not to forget about the other schools: The College of Arts and Science, the Gallatin School of Individualized Study, The Steinhardt School of Education, The Ehrenkranz School of Social Work, The

> **SURVEY SAYS . . .**
> *Great library*
> *Diverse student types on campus*
> *Students love New York, NY*
> *Great off-campus food*
> *Hard liquor is popular*
> *(Almost) everyone smokes*

College of Nursing, and The School of Continuing and Professional Studies. Furthermore, each school has its own feel. So what do all students enjoy regardless of their undergraduate school? The university's enviable location in Lower Manhattan, and its long history of academic excellence attracts, across the board, some the world's most accomplished scholars. While some of the faculty can be difficult to find outside of class, "many professors are wonderful teachers and easily accessible." Another undergraduate adds, "I like the professors here because they have passion." Yet, because NYU is a large school in America's biggest city, the students who get the most out of their academic experiences are the ones who are able to take the reins. As one student explains, "It is a school and environment where the chances of success are dependent solely on the student's ability to avoid distractions, [maintain] motivation to achieve his/her goals, and [use] his/her creative ability to map the different roads that can lead to [those] goals, as in the real world." Even the go-getters who thrive at NYU have trouble cutting through the red tape that has become a symbol of the university's administration. As one student puts it, trying to get in touch with the proper people in the administration to get something done "is like trying to get attention from inanimate objects."

Life

Student life at New York University boils down to an equation: "NYU = NYC." As one student further explains, "NYU students use the city as their playground." In Greenwich Village, where the heart of the campus is located, "the possibilities for any kind of social life are endless." And that's not counting the rest of the city. "For fun, what don't we do?" poses an eager undergraduate. "There are dance clubs, [a countless number] of bars, museums, tons of great restaurants, shopping (if you have money), Broadway, off-Broadway, off-off-Broadway, sports (Yankees, Mets, Knicks, Giants, and so on), Central Park, random ethnic festivals and street fairs, all sorts of cool neighborhoods, fabulous people-watching, and even just walking down the street is completely fascinating." However, the amenities of city life do come at a cost. "Campus life plays a minimal role in student life," explains one student. Because the university buildings and the student residences are quite spread out, there is not a strong sense of community at NYU. "If you're looking for a school with a football team and cheerleaders and people who wave flags and paint faces to show their pride," says one undergraduate, "NYU is not the place for you." That said, "Joining a club or simply making an effort to say hi will easily get you friends," promises another student.

Student Body

"There is no typical student at NYU," students explain. "NYU has everything: the Ivy League go-getting types, the vegan protestors, the hard working recent immigrants, a big vibrant Jewish community, a vocal African American community, a huge LGBT community, an Arab community—everything, really." In general, it is fair to say that the NYU community "does tilt to the left," though "the typical 'Sternie' business student is politically conservative and comes from a wealthy family." It is important to remember that the student body at each school will take a slightly different shape. "The one thing that almost all NYU students have in common is that they love New York City." One great benefit of all of this diversity, as one student puts it, is that after a little while at NYU, "the concept of discrimination seems ultimately foreign."

ADMISSIONS

Very important factors considered include: Secondary school record, standardized test scores. *Important factors considered include:* Character/personal qualities, class rank, essays, extracurricular activities, recommendations, talent/ability. *Other factors considered include:* Alumni/ae relation, minority status, volunteer work, work experience. SAT Reasoning or ACT required. SAT Subject Tests recommended. TOEFL required of all international applicants. High school diploma is required, and GED is accepted. *Academic units required:* 4 English, 3 math, 3 science (2 science lab), 2 foreign language, 4 history. *Academic units recommended:* 4 math, 3 science (3 science lab).

The Inside Word

NYU is more selective than most large private universities but, except for a few particularly choosy programs, no more personal in its evaluation of candidates. A solid GPA and test scores go further toward getting in than anything else. Still, the university is very serious about projecting a highly selective image, and it's dangerous to take your application too lightly. Since the completion of several major dormitories in the late 1980s, NYU has turned its attention to increasing the national profile of its student body. Applications have increased by more than half over the past five years.

FINANCIAL AID

Students should submit: FAFSA, state aid form, early decision applicants may submit an institutuional form for an estimated award. Regular filing deadline 2/15. The Princeton Review suggests that all financial aid forms be submitted as soon as possible after 1/1. *Need-based scholarships/grants offered:* Pell, SEOG, state scholarships/grants, private scholarships, the school's own gift aid. *Loan aid offered:* FFEL Subsidized Stafford, FFEL Unsubsidized Stafford, FFEL PLUS, Federal Perkins, Federal Nursing. Applicants will be notified of awards on a rolling basis beginning on or about 4/1. Federal Work-study Program available. Off-campus job opportunities are excellent.

FROM THE ADMISSIONS OFFICE

"NYU is distinctive both in the quality of education we provide and in the exhilarating atmosphere in which our students study and learn. As an undergraduate in one of our eight small- to medium-size colleges, you will enjoy a small faculty/student ratio and a dynamic, challenging learning environment that encourages lively interaction between students and professors. At the same time, you will have available to you all the resources of a distinguished university dedicated to research and scholarship at the highest levels, including a curriculum that offers over 2,500 courses and 160 programs of study and a faculty that includes some of the most highly regarded scholars, scientists, and artists in the country. New York University is a vital, vibrant community. There is an aura of energy and excitement here, a sense that possibilities and opportunities are limited only by the number of hours in a day. The educational experience at NYU is intense, but varied and richly satisfying. You will be actively engaged in your own education, both in the classroom and beyond."

For even more information on this school, turn to page 510 of the "Stats" section.

NIAGARA UNIVERSITY

BAILO HALL, PO BOX 2011, NIAGARA UNIVERSITY, NY 14109 • ADMISSIONS: 716-286-8700 • FAX: 716-286-8710
E-MAIL: ADMISSIONS@NIAGARA.EDU • WEBSITE: WWW.NIAGARA.EDU

Ratings
Quality of Life: 69 **Academic:** 71 **Admissions:** 75 **Financial Aid:** 78

Academics

Niagara University is regarded as "a small, Catholic university in a great location, focusing primarily on the majors of education and business, and offering a lot of personal attention" to its approximately 2,700 undergraduate students. The school is well-known for its College of Hospitality and Tourism Management. Students in all disciplines appreciate the school's strong Vincentian traditions, which emphasize the importance of community service and charity. "The greatest strengths of this school are its

> **SURVEY SAYS . . .**
> *Small classes*
> *Great computer facilities*
> *Everyone loves the Purple Eagles*
> *Lots of beer drinking*
> *Hard liquor is popular*
> *(Almost) everyone smokes*

sense of community, commitment to service-learning, great academics, and wonderful faculty," explains one undergraduate. Professors here receive high marks for being "very involved with their students and accessible. They are interested in the students' learning as opposed to simply grades." Reports one student, "The professors, for the most part, are interesting, knowledgeable, and truly help you understand the material. They all have at least six office hours throughout the week, and if you can't see them during those hours, they are also available by appointment." The lower-level administrators with whom students come into contact most often "can make things very difficult and make you feel like you do not know anything," but at the top things get better, as "The Dean and the Dean's assistant are usually available, very personable, and friendly and always willing to help."

Life

Life in Niagara Falls offers the students of Niagara University a wide assortment of diversions, students here agree. "There are always different activities or events that go on, on or off campus," reports one student. "We go to a Buffalo Bills game, a Buffalo Sabres game, and go sledding and tubing." Canada, which is "only about 5 minutes away," is "a wonderland and the place to go for bars and other night activities—it's always a vacation in Canada. Of course, there are also countless bars in Niagara Falls and Buffalo." One student states that many love the "nearby outlet mall, which wrecks havoc on my credit card but is well worth it." On campus, "We have concerts once a month where local bands/groups perform, and there is always some kind of athletic event that goes on." Furthermore, "campus activities coordinates activities on and off campus usually once a week. Our theater department puts on performances all the time." All in all, "Life at school is pretty good. Everything on campus is within walking distance, and it's good to walk, especially when it gets nice out." Nice weather, however, isn't all that often—the the average high temperature is below freezing and stays that way much of the entire winter in Niagara Falls.

Student Body

Like many universities, Niagara draws a student body with diverse interests. "We have the theater department, business, [and] education [department]. Then we have all the different sports teams. There is somewhere for all students to fit into," explains one undergraduate. In terms of demographics, the student body is considerably more homogeneous. A student adds that the typical student here is "Caucasian and from New York," and "can be civil but cliquish," and as a result "those diverse students from lower socioeconomic statuses often times stick together" and don't join the mainstream. Students are enthusiastic about athletics, and while "not everyone is a jock, those who aren't are perhaps overshadowed by the strong focus on the athletic program."

ADMISSIONS

Very important factors considered include: Secondary school record. *Important factors considered include:* Interview, recommendations, standardized test scores. *Other factors considered include:* Alumni/ae relation, character/personal qualities, class rank, essays, extracurricular activities, talent/ability, volunteer work. SAT Reasoning or ACT required. TOEFL required of all international applicants. High school diploma is required, and GED is accepted. *Academic units required:* 4 English, 2 math, 2 science, 2 foreign language, 2 social studies, 4 academic electives.

The Inside Word

Niagara has a high admissions rate, but that's because the applicant pool to this school is self-selecting. Those with no chance of getting in generally don't bother to apply. Above-average high school grades and test scores are a prerequisite to admission.

FINANCIAL AID

Students should submit: FAFSA, state aid form. The Princeton Review suggests that all financial aid forms be submitted as soon as possible after 1/1. *Need-based scholarships/grants offered:* Pell, SEOG, state scholarships/grants, private scholarships, the school's own gift aid. *Loan aid offered:* Direct Subsidized Stafford, Direct Unsubsidized Stafford, Direct PLUS, Federal Perkins, Federal Nursing, state loans, college/university loans from institutional funds. Applicants will be notified of awards on a rolling basis beginning on or about 3/1. Federal Work-study Program available. Institutional employment available. Off-campus job opportunities are excellent.

FROM THE ADMISSIONS OFFICE

"'A great place to be!' is the way one undergraduate describes his experience at Niagara University (NU), and he isn't alone. Our 2,700 undergraduates find that NU provides over 50 academic, career-oriented and pre-professional programs housed within the College of Arts and Sciences, College of Business Administration, College of Education and the College of Hospitality and tourism Management. In addition, the university offers an undeclared program, academic exploration, and the Higher Educational Opportunity Program. NU students have the opportunity to enrich their programs with internships, co-ops, overseas study, honors, and community service work. At NU, it is not unusual for students to get involved in an original research project or work with faculty members on special research assignments.

"Best of all, NU combines the diverse academic opportunities usually associated with a larger university with the close personal attention of a smaller institution. With a 16 to 1 student-faculty ratio and an average class size of 25, students can ask questions in the classroom and develop rapport with faculty members who are accomplished in their fields. NU's faculty is dedicated and accessible. More importantly NU faculty members genuinely care about the academic and personal growth of their students. Their commitment to teaching is their primary concern.

"To compliment academic life on campus, NU offers a variety of academic, social, cultural, or service organizations. Couple these with a Division I, intramural, and recreational sports programs, there is something for everyone to cheer about at NU.

"NU's suburban campus is located a few minutes from the world-famous Niagara Falls and short drives from Buffalo and Toronto. This affords students with the opportunity to take advantage of all the sights and sounds of the area. "

For even more information on this school, turn to page 510 of the "Stats" section.

NORTHEASTERN UNIVERSITY

360 HUNTINGTON AVENUE, 150 RICHARDS HALL, BOSTON, MA 02115 • ADMISSIONS: 617-373-2200
FAX: 617-373-8780 • FINANCIAL AID: 617-373-3190 • E-MAIL: ADMISSIONS@NEU.EDU • WEBSITE: WWW.NEU.EDU

Ratings
Quality of Life: 82   **Academic:** 79   **Admissions:** 92   **Financial Aid:** 65

Academics

For "incorporating classroom learning with real world application in the middle of a great city," Northeastern University is hard to beat. That's because of the school's celebrated cooperative education (co-op) program, which "gives students a chance to try out jobs in the 'real world' and adjust their career paths accordingly. Co-op gives you the chance to meet new friends, both students and professionals, make some money, and build your resume." "Co-op is the reason many people are at this school," students agree, pointing out that "Through the co-op program stu-

> **SURVEY SAYS . . .**
> *Great computer facilities*
> *Great library*
> *Athletic facilities are great*
> *Students love Boston, MA*
> *Great off-campus food*
> *Lots of beer drinking*
> *Hard liquor is popular*

dents are able to bring more to the table than the average college student. Many of the upperclassman have had experience working within their major beyond serving coffee and copying files for the higher-ups." They warn, however, that "co-ops are not just handed to you, and you must not assume that you will be guaranteed a co-op just by being a NU student. Many friends of mine have suffered through a semester working at the mall on 'no-op.'" A large school, NU excels in a number of areas; students report that health science, business, engineering, and criminal justice are all solid here. As at many large schools, the bureaucracy can be overwhelming; many students reference "the NU shuffle," explaining that "no one is ever willing to help you with a problem. All they're trained to do is send you to someone else." Advisors are in unfortunately short supply, as "each advisor has hundreds of students. Getting a meeting with them is like pulling teeth. Once you get closer to graduation and advisors become more important to you, you get little help, if any."

Life

"Campus life is very small at NU," students tell us explaining, "We have a city to play in. Why waste time on campus where there's not much to do?" NU, located in the heart of Boston, is "in a great area in terms of proximity to places to eat and places to have fun. We are just a few minutes' walk away from Fenway Park and the surrounding bars, as well as Newberry Street, the Prudential Center, and Copley Square." The city is "a lot of fun during the day, with shopping and museums and other tourist attractions," and it's just as fun at night, especially if you're over 21. "Life at Northeastern is all about bars," confides one student. When the weekend rolls around, "many students go out to parties, which can be found ongoing every night," or they "go to basketball and hockey games." They also "take weekend road trips to Cape Cod or just bike and rollerblade around the city, weather permitting, see a lot of movies, [or] just explore the city and goof around." Although "the majority of the school parties," students who are "not into drinking" will "definitely find a niche, and it won't be hard."

Student Body

Undergraduates report that "the vast majority of the school is comprised of people very concerned with their appearance and club life." At a school this size though, those outside the "vast majority" constitute a sizeable population, so "you can hang out with a bunch of different people from different groups, and you all get along well." There are students from all socioeconomic, ethnic, and racial backgrounds contentedly "all mixed together." Atypical students "have many resources and clubs available that cater to their ethnicity, sexual orientation, etc."

ADMISSIONS

Very important factors considered include: Secondary school record. *Important factors considered include:* Character/personal qualities, class rank, essays, extracurricular activities, recommendations, standardized test scores, talent/ability. *Other factors considered include:* Alumni/ae relation, geographical residence, minority status, volunteer work, work experience. SAT Reasoning or SAT Subject Tests required. TOEFL required of all international applicants. High school diploma is required, and GED is accepted. *Academic units required:* 4 English, 3 math, 3 science (2 science lab), 2 foreign language, 3 social studies, 2 history. *Academic units recommended:* 4 math, 4 science (4 science lab), 4 foreign language.

The Inside Word

Northeastern is one of the Boston area's most selective schools which makes it a desirable school for students who want a college experience in an urban environment. Northeastern has a large applicant pool and a low acceptance rate. Northeastern's admissions process relies on a comprehensive review process where personal qualities and interests are as important as academic achievement.

FINANCIAL AID

Students should submit: FAFSA, CSS/Financial Aid PROFILE. The Princeton Review suggests that all financial aid forms be submitted as soon as possible after 1/1. *Need-based scholarships/grants offered:* Pell, SEOG, state scholarships/grants, private scholarships, the school's own gift aid, federal nursing scholarships. *Loan aid offered:* FFEL Subsidized Stafford, FFEL Unsubsidized Stafford, FFEL PLUS, Federal Perkins, Federal Nursing, state loans, MEFA, TERI, Signature, No Interest Loan (NIL), CitiAssist. Applicants will be notified of awards on a rolling basis beginning on or about 2/15. Federal Work-study Program available. Institutional employment available. Off-campus job opportunities are excellent.

FROM THE ADMISSIONS OFFICE

"Northeastern students take charge of their education in a way you'll find nowhere else because a Northeastern education is like no other. We integrate challenging liberal arts and professional studies with the world's largest cooperative education program, where undergraduates alternate semesters of full-time study with semesters of paid work in fields relevant to their professional interests and major, giving them nearly two years of professional experience upon graduation. Northeastern's dynamic of academic excellence and workplace experience means that our students are better prepared to succeed in the lives they choose. On top of that, they experience all of this on a beautifully landscaped, 67-acre campus in the heart of Boston, where culture, commerce, civic pride, and college students from around the globe are all a part of the mix."

For even more information on this school, turn to page 511 of the "Stats" section.

PACE UNIVERSITY

1 PACE PLAZA, NEW YORK, NY 10038 • ADMISSIONS: 212-346-1323 • FAX: 212-346-1040
E-MAIL: INFOCTR@PACE.EDU • WEBSITE: WWW.PACE.EDU

Ratings
Quality of Life: 74   **Academic:** 74   **Admissions:** 79   **Financial Aid:** 67

Academics

"Business, business, business," is the mantra at Pace University. Pace has much to offer, including professors who are "currently working in their fields and pull real-life experiences into the classroom." With one of the University's two main campuses located in the heart of New York City's financial district (the Pleasantville/Briarcliff campus is located in mid-Westchester county, about 45 minutes from the city by train), Pace also offers great access to internships in the field. For non-business students, however, things are

> **SURVEY SAYS . . .**
> *Small classes*
> *Diverse student types on campus*
> *Students love New York, NY*
> *Great off-campus food*
> *Campus feels safe*
> *(Almost) everyone smokes*

less peachy. "Professors are experienced in their fields, but a lot of them are not good teachers," writes one undergraduate. While some professors are "always available outside of the classroom [and are] constantly checking their e-mails to respond to students' questions, [there are] too many adjunct and part-time professors, [many of whom] aren't available outside of class and are difficult to contact." For students who find "the academics here not to be challenging enough," there is the honors program, "which does have devoted students that really care." Pace's price tag should not scare aware prospective students because the school does provide "great financial aid packages." Surprisingly enough, if you actually have to go the financial aid office, you will encounter "the most unorganized and rude people in the world." The administration in general doesn't receive much praise from students. "There is a line for everything," complains one student. Another student adds, "[The administration] seems unable to fix a problem. You go where you think they will fix it and they send you somewhere else, and they send you somewhere else, and so on."

Life

Life outside of the classroom is considerably different for students at Pace's New York City and Pleasantville/Briarcliff campuses. The NYC students consider the city to be their classroom, in part because facilities are limited and there isn't much of a campus feel. "If you want the city life without the whole traditional college campus, come to Pace," advises one New York City student. "We go to class and then party, shop, see plays, whatever." An average weekend might involve a trip to "Central Park, SoHo, Times Square, Chinatown, and [Pace students] always [seem to] be at the South Street Seaport." Students report life in Pleasantville and Briarcliff Manor, NY (the two parts of campus are connected by shuttle bus service) to be more subdued. This is more by necessity than choice, however, as many undergrads feel that campus "partying policies are too strictly enforced." As a result, "Pace [in Westchester] is a bar school, not a party school." A handful of students get involved with clubs and organizations (a small but very visible group goes Greek), while the rest content themselves with "eating out, [seeing] movies, bowling, and shopping" in Pleasantville. The few that stay on campus over the weekend describe the scene as "boring and very quiet, but overall pleasant." Both NYC and Westchester students report that there "isn't a lot of school spirit at Pace. Because it is a commuter school, it is difficult to develop relationships."

Student Body

Overall, Pace is a diverse place, though most of its diversity can be found on the New York City campus. A large contingent of international students attends Pace in the city, and many more students are either "immigrants or the children of immigrants." Fortunately, "for the most part, all students, regardless of race, gender, religion, or sexual [preferences], get along very well together." The Westchester campus, because of it's location in an affluent suburb of the city, draws a less eclectic student body. At both campuses students report that their peers "are basically split into dormers and commuters." Commuters tend to be career-oriented, less interested in extracting a college experience. One student agrees, "As a commuter I don't really get involved. I go to school and come home."

ADMISSIONS

Very important factors considered include: Secondary school record, standardized test scores. *Important factors considered include:* Class rank. *Other factors considered include:* Alumni/ae relation, character/personal qualities, essays, extracurricular activities, recommendations, talent/ability, volunteer work, work experience. SAT Reasoning or ACT required. TOEFL required of all international applicants. High school diploma is required, and GED is accepted. *Academic units required:* 4 English, 3 math, 2 science (2 science lab), 2 foreign language, 1 social studies, 2 history, 2 academic electives. *Academic units recommended:* 4 English, 4 math, 2 science (2 science lab), 3 foreign language, 2 social studies, 2 history, 3 academic electives.

The Inside Word

High school grades and test scores are the most important factors in Pace admissions decisions. Other factors are considered but have comparatively minor impact on the school's final decision.

FINANCIAL AID

Students should submit: FAFSA, state aid form. The Princeton Review suggests that all financial aid forms be submitted as soon as possible after 1/1. *Need-based scholarships/grants offered:* Pell, SEOG, state scholarships/grants, private scholarships, the school's own gift aid. *Loan aid offered:* Direct Subsidized Stafford, Direct Unsubsidized Stafford, Direct PLUS, Federal Perkins, Federal Nursing. Applicants will be notified of awards on a rolling basis beginning on or about 4/1. Federal Work-study Program available. Institutional employment available. Off-campus job opportunities are excellent.

For even more information on this school, turn to page 511 of the "Stats" section.

PENNSYLVANIA STATE UNIVERSITY—UNIVERSITY PARK

201 SHIELDS BUILDING, UNIVERSITY PARK, PA 16802-3000 • ADMISSIONS: 814-865-5471
FAX: 814-863-7590 • FINANCIAL AID: 814-865-6301 • WEBSITE: WWW.PSU.EDU/ADMISSIONS

Ratings
Quality of Life: 83   Academic: 75   Admissions: 90   Financial Aid: 64

Academics

State universities are typically gigantic institutions, and they fall into two broad categories: the type that students grumblingly trundle through, and the type that students absolutely love. Penn State is of the latter variety. It is one of those gargantuan schools that somehow instills a profound pride of place in its undergraduates. Students brag of "top-notch facilities and academics, superior sports programs, an excellent social scene, and the beautiful campus and friendly college town atmosphere. All these make PSU second-to-none in the U.S. for overall undergraduate experience." Even the common complaints about large schools are soft-pedaled by students. One tells us, "People say that 'you are only a number at Penn State.' I would like to clarify this and say that 'you are only a number if you choose to be a number.'" Another student agrees with this sentiment: "Penn State is stereotyped as a school with little access to faculty, but that is farthest from the truth. Faculty and such go out of their way to help with your needs." Perhaps the greatest source of student satisfaction, however, is the "incredible alumni network. We have the number one dues-paying alumni network in the world, with over 146,000 members." No wonder "Penn State is known as Happy Valley, and nothing describes this place better."

> **SURVEY SAYS . . .**
> *Great library*
> *Athletic facilities are great*
> *Everyone loves the Nittany Lions*
> *Intramural sports are popular*
> *Frats and sororities dominate social scene*
> *Student publications are popular*
> *Lots of beer drinking*
> *Hard liquor is popular*

Life

"With 35,000 students, there's never a dull moment" at Penn State, where there are "opportunities to get involved with anything you can ever imagine. Even though it's a large school, if you get involved, it does not seem big at all." Topping students' lists of favorite activities is "Penn State football, which definitely takes over the campus during the fall semester. Sports in Happy Valley are huge!" Partying is a close second. Undergraduates report that "every night revolves around which fraternities are hosting parties, and which other organizations are invited that night. Independents get to drink for free, and there are no cover charges." The University offers a nonalcoholic option (called Late Night Penn State), "but that usually involves cotton candy and the pathetic theater clubs singing songs from their latest shows. It's more fun to sit in your room and watch TV." On-campus concerts are a better alternative, since "world-class artists such as Aerosmith, Garth Brooks, Cher, and the Red Hot Chili Peppers can be seen at the Bryce Jordan Center, number one among ticket sales for a college venue in the world." Of course, it's not all fun and games; students have to study, too. "The workload is a lot, but there's enough time to get it done before it's time to go out and party," students cheerfully report. Is there anything about PSU they don't love? "The weather sucks at University Park! It snows from October through April and rains any other time," offers one undergraduate.

Student Body

There are many towns in the United States with populations smaller than the undergraduate count at PSU, so it's not surprising that "you will find almost every type of student you can imagine here." While "the majority are white and middle class, there are also thousands of international students here from countries such as China, India, and Japan, and a large African American population as well." The diversity leads one student to conclude, "If a student complains about not having any friends at Penn State, they are just antisocial." While undergraduates come in all shapes, shades, and sizes, the archetypal Nittany Lion is "white, in good shape, into the party scene, preppy or a jock, and pretty all-American." Most students agree that "students of different races don't interact often. It's not because they don't want to or are rude to one another, they just don't tend to mix all that much."

ADMISSIONS

Very important factors considered include: Secondary school record, standardized test scores. *Other factors considered include:* Alumni/ae relation, character/personal qualities, class rank, essays, extracurricular activities, recommendations, talent/ability, volunteer work, work experience. SAT Reasoning or ACT required. TOEFL required of all international applicants. High school diploma is required, and GED is accepted. *Academic units required:* 4 English, 3 math, 3 science, 2 foreign language, 3 social studies.

The Inside Word

Penn State is deluged with applicants (they claim to receive more SAT score reports than any other college in the country), which makes it especially important for candidates to have better-than-average grades and test scores. Although a personal essay and information on extracurricular activities are requested, the university's formula focuses on the numbers. At schools this large it's hard for the admissions process to be more individualized.

FINANCIAL AID

Students should submit: FAFSA. The Princeton Review suggests that all financial aid forms be submitted as soon as possible after 1/1. *Need-based scholarships/grants offered:* Pell, SEOG, state scholarships/grants, private scholarships, the school's own gift aid. *Loan aid offered:* FFEL Subsidized Stafford, FFEL Unsubsidized Stafford, FFEL PLUS, Federal Perkins, college/university loans from institutional funds, private loans. Applicants will be notified of awards on a rolling basis beginning on or about 2/15. Federal Work-study Program available. Off-campus job opportunities are good.

FROM THE ADMISSIONS OFFICE

"Unique among large public universities, Penn State combines the nearly 35,000-student setting of its University Park campus with 20 academically and administratively integrated undergraduate locations—small-college settings ranging in size from 600 to 3,400 students. Each year, more than 60 percent of incoming freshmen begin their studies at these residential and commuter campuses, while nearly 40 percent begin at the University Park Campus. The smaller locations focus on the needs of new students by offering the first two years of most Penn State baccalaureate degrees in settings that stress close interaction with faculty. Depending on the major selected, students may choose to complete their degree at University Park or one of the smaller locations. Your application to Penn State qualifies you for review for any of our campuses. Your two choices of location are reviewed in the order given. Entrance difficulty is based, in part, on the demand. Due to its popularity, the University Park campus is the most competitive for admission."

For even more information on this school, turn to page 512 of the "Stats" section.

POLYTECHNIC UNIVERSITY

6 METROTECH CENTER, BROOKLYN, NY 11201-2999 • ADMISSIONS: 718-260-3100 • FAX: 718-260-3446
E-MAIL: ADMITME@POLY.EDU • WEBSITE: WWW.POLY.EDU

Ratings
Quality of Life: 72   Academic: 72   Admissions: 87   Financial Aid: 79

Academics

Students in search of hardcore engineering, mathematics, and computer science may well find a home at the Polytechnic Institute of Brooklyn. Students tell us that Poly "is an academically sound school, and only people who really know what they are doing get degrees from this place, at least in the technical programs. Also, the school is really trying its best to keep up with the marketplace, adding some classes and majors to help reflect trends in the industry." Students warn that "if you don't really know your stuff, you don't have much of a chance of passing many classes, so you gotta have a grip on the source material," pointing out that only half of the students in most freshman classes graduate from Poly. Notes one student, "If your idea of a fun Friday night is finishing up a computer programming assignment followed by reading three chapters of quantum physics, Polytechnic is perfect for you." Students have a few bones to pick with the faculty and administration; they caution that many professors don't speak English as a first language ("75 percent is a safe estimate"), making lectures difficult, and that the administration is poor (one student refers to the staff in the bursar's office, student accounts, and financial aid as "just plain lazy"). One final warning: "It is impossible to transfer out of Poly without losing a large amount of credits (because the classes are so specialized), so you feel as if you're 'trapped' in Poly without a way out." Despite its drawbacks, "Polytechnic University is a well-established, competitive university with extremely rigorous coursework. My academic experience at this school had given me the incentive that you can always try harder, and the harder you try, the more you can achieve."

> SURVEY SAYS . . .
> *Small classes*
> *Lab facilities are great*
> *Great computer facilities*
> *Students are friendly*
> *Diverse student types on campus*
> *Different types of students interact*
> *Great off-campus food*
> *Dorms are like palaces*
> *Campus feels safe*
> *Very little drug use*

Life

Be forewarned: "Poly doesn't allow for much of a social life. The workload will keep most of the students in an effective lockdown all but a few times during the semester." Social life here is further stymied by the fact that "95 percent of us do not live on campus, because the only dorms until this upcoming summer have been part of NYU's campus in Manhattan. Most people come for classes and then go home right after." Adds another student, "The standard organizations (a.k.a. frats) are not really active. Only one of them actively holds parties." Commuters find little reason to hang around after class, because "the campus isn't very nice looking, and the main academic building is a converted safety razor factory." On a positive note, "the school is involved in construction projects, including the creation of a new academic building and dorm." Undergrads tell us that "for fun, we have to be proactive and gather some friends together to go do stuff," and that in New York City, "there are more than enough places to go have some fun." The school's location, in Brooklyn's downtown Metrotech complex, is within walking distance of Brooklyn Heights, home to many fine shops, restaurants, and a waterfront promenade. The Brooklyn Bridge is less than a mile from campus, meaning a mere 15-minute stroll leads students to great neighborhoods like Little Italy and Chinatown in lower Manhattan.

Student Body

Poly students are "extremely diverse in race, culture, and nationality and everyone is very accepting of other cultures and ethnicities." As one student put it, "I mean, we're in Brooklyn, NYC. Of course it's a pretty diverse group, and everyone tends to respect one another. It's the Poly philosophy: we're better than the rest of the population, and therefore we stick together. It's all the techno-brainwashing you go through your first year. You tend to bond easily with other techies." Students also bring diverse attitudes to the classroom. Writes one undergrad, "Some of the students are extremely high strung, and others are extremely loose. Some are extremely obsessed about their school work, and some are rather flippant about it. For the most part, they are friendly, helpful, and hardworking, but not obsessive."

ADMISSIONS

Very important factors considered include: Secondary school record, standardized test scores. *Important factors considered include:* Class rank. *Other factors considered include:* Essays, interview, recommendations. SAT Reasoning or ACT required. TOEFL required of all international applicants. High school diploma is required, and GED is accepted. *Academic units required:* 4 English, 4 math, 4 science, 3 social studies, 2 academic electives. *Academic units recommended:* 2 foreign language.

The Inside Word

Your chops as a techie must be sharp to meet the effort required by Polytechnic's academics. You'll need to be self-motivated, too; La Isla Manhattan, with its zillions of distractions, is only stone's throw away. But if you can handle big-city life, it's worth the effort to gain admittance and take advantage of this campus's accessibility to interests both professional and personal.

FINANCIAL AID

Students should submit: FAFSA. The Princeton Review suggests that all financial aid forms be submitted as soon as possible after 1/1. *Need-based scholarships/grants offered:* Pell, SEOG, state scholarships/grants, private scholarships, the school's own gift aid. *Loan aid offered:* FFEL Subsidized Stafford, FFEL Unsubsidized Stafford, FFEL PLUS, Federal Perkins, college/university loans from institutional funds. Applicants will be notified of awards on a rolling basis beginning on or about 2/1. Federal Work-study Program available. Institutional employment available. Off-campus job opportunities are good.

For even more information on this school, turn to page 512 of the "Stats" section.

PRINCETON UNIVERSITY

PO Box 430, Admission Office, Princeton, NJ 08544-0430 • Admissions: 609-258-3060
Fax: 609-258-6743 • Financial Aid: 609-258-3330 • Website: www.princeton.edu

Ratings

Quality of Life: 98   **Academic:** 88   **Admissions:** 99   **Financial Aid:** 99

Academics

Princeton undergrads are adamant that their school is the "best place to get an undergraduate education," boasting as it does "a combination of comprehensive resources, exceptional faculty, and brilliant students." Unlike many other prestigious universities, "the focus is all on under-graduate education" at Princeton, which has no business, law, or medical schools. There are fewer than 2,000 gradu-ate students (all master's), enabling Princeton to ensure undergraduates access to "Nobel laureates who teach you and give you appointments" as well as "a wealth of aca-demic, monetary, and social resources that students benefit from during and after their studies on campus." With fewer

> **SURVEY SAYS . . .**
> *No one cheats*
> *Lab facilities are great*
> *Great computer facilities*
> *Great library*
> *Athletic facilities are great*
> *School is well run*
> *Campus feels safe*
> *Students are happy*
> *Lots of beer drinking*

grads to elbow them out of the way, undergrads tell us that "the professors treat us like colleagues. They make themselves available and are intensely interested in the ideas of undergraduates." There is "an emphasis on independent undergraduate research, and funding is ample," as are resources at the library, which "has an amazing number and variety of books and other resources." The administration "truly runs like butter. From the application process to enrolling to being enrolled…. If you made an error in one of these processes, to my experience, it's sometimes corrected for you!" No wonder one Princeton undergrad sums up the experience here this way: "They spoil you with amazing resources, world-class professors, beautiful architecture, great people, fun social life, and the inability of the school to say no to anything that you want."

Life

Eating clubs, a phenomenon unique to Princeton, "are the center of social life" at this "country-club like school." One student explains how they work: "During day time, the club houses serve as a place for upperclassmen to dine. (You don't have to join one because they are a bit costly.) Clubs range from those permanently soaked in beer and alcohol to some that are the most pretentious things one may lay an eye on, with gold lined and embossed plates, cutlery and serviettes, and waiters to serve food to the students." All 11 eating clubs are locat-ed on Prospect Avenue, known to students simply as "the Street," and they function not only as dining halls but also as bars and party sites. Many hail the clubs "as great places to party because there is always somewhere to fit in. Because everyone parties on one street it is impossible to go out and not see someone you know." Others dismiss the clubs as "pretentious and pompous," especially the selective "bicker" clubs "in which current mem-bers choose new members," much as a Greek house screens pledges. Campus life tends to stay contained with-in the campus, as the surrounding town "closes up at 10 P.M.," but students are content with the situation. "Since everyone lives on campus and 'the Street' is so close, there is virtually no reason to need a car," explains one student. Adds another, "The best part is that even though Princeton is a small town, there is a train station on campus that takes you to Philly or New York in 45 minutes. Students use the 'dinky,' as the train's called, all the time."

Student Body

"Sure, Princeton's a bit East Coast preppy," undergrads here admit, "but everyone is unique and has her own style, which is totally welcomed and accepted. Princeton is a very kind, low-key, and charming place." It's also a place full of extremely accomplished people. Writes one student, "I have friends who are Presidential Scholars, stayed with the UN Secretary General in Paris over fall break, produced hip hop CDs, or represented different countries at the Olympics. Back home, I would have thought it amazing if I could meet just one of these peo-ple. If I stopped thinking of my friends as friends and thought of what they have accomplished, it's mind bog-gling, and a little humbling." Thanks to "a generous financial aid system," "not everyone is a spoiled rotten, BMW-driving, snooty rich kid. We have students from very diverse backgrounds."

ADMISSIONS

Very important factors considered include: Character/personal qualities, class rank, essays, extracurricular activities, recommendations, secondary school record, standardized test scores, talent/ability. *Important factors considered include:* Alumni/ae relation, geographical residence, volunteer work, work experience. *Other factors considered include:* Interview, minority status. SAT Reasoning and SAT Subject Tests or ACT required. High school diploma or equivalent is not required. *Academic units recommended:* 4 English, 4 math, 3 science, 4 foreign language, 2 social studies, 2 history.

The Inside Word

Princeton is much more open about the admissions process than the rest of their Ivy compatriots. The admissions staff evaluates candidates' credentials using a 1–5 rating scale, common among highly selective colleges. Princeton's recommendation to interview should be considered a requirement, given the ultra-competitive nature of the applicant pool. In addition, three SAT IIs are required; no joke, indeed.

FINANCIAL AID

Students should submit: FAFSA, institution's own financial aid form, noncustodial (divorced/separated) parents' statement. Regular filing deadline 2/1. The Princeton Review suggests that all financial aid forms be submitted as soon as possible after 1/1. *Need-based scholarships/grants offered:* Pell, SEOG, state scholarships/grants, private scholarships, the school's own gift aid. *Loan aid offered:* FFEL Subsidized Stafford, FFEL Unsubsidized Stafford, FFEL PLUS, Federal Perkins, college/university loans from institutional funds. Applicants will be notified of awards on or about 4/1.

FROM THE ADMISSIONS OFFICE

"Methods of instruction [at Princeton] vary widely, but common to all areas is a strong emphasis on individual responsibility and the free interchange of ideas. This is displayed most notably in the wide use of preceptorials and seminars, in the provision of independent study for all upperclass students and qualified underclass students, and in the availability of a series of special programs to meet a range of individual interests. The undergraduate college encourages the student to be an independent seeker of information and to assume responsibility for gaining both knowledge and judgment that will strengthen later contributions to society."

For even more information on this school, turn to page 513 of the "Stats" section.

PROVIDENCE COLLEGE

River Avenue and Eaton Street, Providence, RI 02918 • Admissions: 401-865-2535 • Fax: 401-865-2826
Financial Aid: 401-865-2286 • E-mail: pcadmiss@providence.edu • Website: www.providence.edu

Ratings

Quality of Life: 72   Academic: 83   Admissions: 92   Financial Aid: 73

Academics

Providence College (PC), a small, Catholic, liberal arts school run by the Dominicans, is two schools in one. For the majority of students, it is a proving ground, an academic boot camp where success translates into "the ability to find work in their specialized fields very soon after graduation because of the school's reputation with employers." For a smaller group of students, it's the locus of intellectual fulfillment for its own sake. One student tells us, "Once I discovered the 10 percent of the students who are actually intellectually stimulating it became great." Nowhere is this divide more apparent than in students' attitude toward the Development of Western Civilization, a demanding two-year sequence of survey courses covering the canon of "great books" as well as the history of the arts. Many here dismiss the sequence as a waste of time. Others however, praise this centerpiece of the curriculum, telling us that it "is taught in such a way that makes me want to learn more and apply what I learn to my own life. I feel like I am not only growing as a student, but as a person." As an added bonus, students tell us, "The traditional CIV scream at midnight in the quad the night before the CIV final can make it worth the work. Fireworks, streaking, water-balloon fights, you get the picture." Those considering PC should know that this is a serious Catholic school, as one student explains, "This school has a very Catholic influence. In CIV, for example, philosophy is studied as how it can be applied to the Catholic belief. Plus, the core requirements are very Catholic-centered."

> ### SURVEY SAYS . . .
> *Small classes*
> *Diversity lacking on campus*
> *Students are happy*
> *Everyone loves the Friars*
> *Intramural sports are popular*
> *Frats and sororities are unpopular or nonexistent*
> *Lots of beer drinking*
> *Hard liquor is popular*

Life

Students laughingly and lovingly refer to PC as "Party College," telling us "the school definitely lives up to its nickname." Most students, "whether of age or not, go to local bars to hang out any given night of the week or clubbing, [so] a fake ID is as necessary as oxygen." Second on students' extracurricular to-do list is hanging out in downtown Providence, which is "fantastic. The downtown area of Providence is a good time with a large selection of excellent restaurants, good shopping, and fun bars and clubs. We often go to Providence Place Mall or the ever popular Thayer Street to mix with the Brown and RISD crowd on weekends." Undergraduates also love that Providence is "an hour from the beach, Boston is an hour and NYC is only three hours away, so if for some reason you need to get away, it is possible." Intercollegiate athletics are popular. One student writes, "Having a sports program that is nationally recognized is also cool. Going to the hockey and basketball games gives students something to do that's entertaining and provides a lot of school spirit."

Student Body

At PC, "The student body has a strong community and familial vibe. We get along great." And why wouldn't they, most students ask. "We're all the same." Nearly all of our survey respondents agree that, "PC is overwhelmingly white. Students tend to be Catholics from New England." They also look as though they "stepped right off the pages of an Abercrombie and Fitch catalog. It would be shocking to see someone who didn't look practically just like everyone else. They are typically athletic, involved partiers, but very much your average preppy college student." Cliquishness is common. "Although most students here are friendly, there is not very much interaction between social groups beyond the friendly conversations. Basically, everyone finds a group of friends and sticks with them, morning through night, for the next four years," notes one student. As for religion, "Masses are quite well attended, although this doesn't always translate into moral behavior during the other six days of the week."

ADMISSIONS

Very important factors considered include: Secondary school record. *Important factors considered include:* Character/personal qualities, essays, extracurricular activities, recommendations, standardized test scores, volunteer work, work experience. *Other factors considered include:* Alumni/ae relation, class rank, geographical residence, minority status, religious affiliation/commitment, state residency, talent/ability. SAT Reasoning or ACT required. TOEFL required of all international applicants. High school diploma is required, and GED is not accepted. *Academic units required:* 4 English, 4 math, 3 science (2 science lab), 3 foreign language, 2 social studies, 2 history. *Academic units recommended:* 4 English, 4 math, 4 science (3 science lab), 3 foreign language, 1 social studies, 2 history.

The Inside Word

Providence's reputation for quality is solidly in place among above-average graduates of northeastern Catholic high schools, who account for almost a quarter of the applicant pool. The strength of these candidates is one of the primary factors that allow the college to be choosy about who gets in. Successful candidates usually project a well-rounded, conservative image.

FINANCIAL AID

Students should submit: FAFSA, CSS/Financial Aid PROFILE. Regular filing deadline 2/1. The Princeton Review suggests that all financial aid forms be submitted as soon as possible after 1/1. *Need-based scholarships/grants offered:* Pell, SEOG, state scholarships/grants, private scholarships, the school's own gift aid. *Loan aid offered:* Direct Subsidized Stafford, Direct Unsubsidized Stafford, Direct PLUS, FFEL Subsidized Stafford, FFEL Unsubsidized Stafford, FFEL PLUS, Federal Perkins. Applicants will be notified of awards on or about 4/1. Off-campus job opportunities are excellent.

FROM THE ADMISSIONS OFFICE

"Infused with the history, tradition, and learning of a 700-year-old Catholic teaching order, the Dominican Friars, Providence College offers a value-affirming environment where students are enriched through spiritual, social, physical, and cultural growth as well as through intellectual development. Providence College offers over 35 programs of study leading to baccalaureate degrees in business, education, the sciences, arts, and humanities. Our faculty is noted for a strong commitment to teaching. A close student/faculty relationship allows for in-depth classwork, independent research projects, and detailed career exploration. While noted for the physical facilities and academic opportunities associated with larger universities, Providence also fosters personal growth through a small, spirited, family-like atmosphere that encourages involvement in student activities and athletics."

For even more information on this school, turn to page 513 of the "Stats" section.

QUINNIPIAC UNIVERSITY

Mount Carmel Avenue, 275 Mount Carmel Avenue, Hamden, CT 06518 • Admissions: 203-582-8600
Fax: 203-582-8906 • E-mail: admissions@quinnipiac.edu • Website: www.quinnipiac.edu

Ratings
Quality of Life: 77   Academic: 81   Admissions: 87   Financial Aid: 65

Academics

Students looking for a medium-sized university with career-focused programs and a liberal arts foundation should consider Quinnipiac University (QU). Though the school's undergraduate population is a substantial 5,000, Quinnipiac offers the academic support and personal attention typical of small colleges. Students report that "class sizes are usually under 20" and "the professors make an effort to learn not only your name, but who you really are." Undergrads say that QU professors "are there to teach you, help you, and get to know you, not to fail you or know you by a number." In fact, it is through many channels that the school displays its dedication to helping students succeed, and many note that the school's Learning Center "has tutors, who have been an essential component to hard science classes" and can be a "big help" if you are struggling with academics. Some students, however, feel that the classes at Quinnipiac could stand to be more competitive. In the words of one: "I have been satisfied but not challenged at Quinnipiac." Additionally, many debate the school's use of numerous adjunct professors. While some students claim "the part-time teachers are not devoted to your studies," others insist "the adjuncts here are incredible. They bring their real world experience to the classroom." Regarding majors, "physical therapy, communications, and pre-med here are all very strong and hard to get into." Though administrators are "friendly and personable" when you get them one-on-one, the overall structure is plagued by a "lack of communication between the different departments in the school."

> **SURVEY SAYS . . .**
> *Small classes*
> *Great computer facilities*
> *Great library*
> *Campus feels safe*
> *Lots of beer drinking*
> *Hard liquor is popular*
> *(Almost) everyone smokes*

Life

Students say that "one of QU's greatest strengths is its location: 10 minutes away from Connecticut's cultural center and geographically right between New York and Boston." In addition, there is a "state park directly across from the campus," "the beautiful Sleeping Giant Mountain, which provides a beautiful backdrop for campus every season." Students say they like to take advantage of "concerts, plays, coffeehouses, lectures, restaurants, shopping" in nearby New Haven, as well as the town's "Thirsty Thursdays," which "are almost always happening." For recreation, students say, "it's really relaxing to climb Sleeping Giant or to sit out on the quad and drink a milkshake." In addition, "there are so many different organizations to be involved in, and that creates more opportunity to meet new people and form great friendships." Though students advise that "there is very little academic or intellectual conversation outside the classroom," they also note that "studying is pretty important to most people here." One undergrad summarizes life: "During the week the library is usually full. However, come the start of the weekend (usually Thursday nights) many students choose to drink." On that note, students tell us that, "beer pong, partying, and cigarette smoking are favorite pastimes."

Student Body

"Many of the students at Quinnipiac are alike: well-dressed, upper-middle-class people," according to one undergrad. "Everyone's personality is very similar," adds another. Considering these observations, it's no surprise that students also report that "there is very little diversity" at QU. Not everyone's complaining, however. Opines one undergrad: "I like my classmates because so many of them are just like me. Sometimes I wish it were more diverse, but then at the same time I think the reason everyone gets along so well is because we're all so much alike." Characterization of the student body runs from "shallow and materialistic" to "warm" and "friendly," but many agree, "Like everywhere else there are certain groups, but they are always interacting with each other, and it's easy to make friends with them all."

ADMISSIONS

Very important factors considered include: Secondary school record. *Important factors considered include:* Class rank, essays, recommendations, standardized test scores. *Other factors considered include:* Alumni/ae relation, extracurricular activities, interview, minority status, volunteer work, work experience. SAT Reasoning or ACT required. TOEFL required of all international applicants. High school diploma is required, and GED is accepted. *Academic units required:* 4 English, 3 math, 3 science (2 science lab), 2 social studies, 3 academic electives. *Academic units recommended:* 2 foreign language.

The Inside Word

Quinnipiac boasts a wide range of opportunities for study and social pursuits in a geographic locale equidistant from multiple cultural centers, not to mention a very responsive faculty.

FINANCIAL AID

Students should submit: FAFSA. The Princeton Review suggests that all financial aid forms be submitted as soon as possible after 1/1. *Need-based scholarships/grants offered:* Pell, SEOG, state scholarships/grants, private scholarships, the school's own gift aid, federal nursing scholarships. *Loan aid offered:* FFEL Subsidized Stafford, FFEL Unsubsidized Stafford, FFEL PLUS, Federal Perkins, Federal Nursing, state loans. Applicants will be notified of awards on a rolling basis beginning on or about 2/15. Federal Work-study Program available. Institutional employment available. Off-campus job opportunities are good.

FROM THE ADMISSIONS OFFICE

"The appeal of Quinnipiac University continues to grow each year. Our students come from a variety of states and backgrounds. Seventy-five percent of the freshman class is from out-of-state. Students come from 25 states and 18 countries. Nearly 30 percent of current undergraduates plan to stay at Quinnipiac to complete their graduate degree.

"As admission becomes more competitive and our enrollment remains stable, the university continues to focus on its mission: to provide outstanding academic programs in a student-oriented environment on a campus with a strong sense of community. The development of an honors program, a highly-regarded emerging leaders student life program, and a 'writing across the curriculum' initiative in academic affairs, form the foundation for excellence in business, communications, health sciences, education, liberal arts and law.

"The University is state of the art in technology—with a fully digital high-definition production studio in the School of Communications; the Terry Goodwin '67 Financial Technology Center which provides a high-tech simulated trading floor in the School of Business; a critical care lab for our nursing and physician assistant majors, and a computer program that requires all incoming students to purchase a university recommended laptop with wireless capabilities supported by a campus-wide network."

"More than 70 student organizations, 21 Division I teams (The 'Bobcats'), recreation and intramurals in a newly expanded recreation/fitness center, community service, student publications, and a strong student government offer a variety of outside of class experiences to the student body. Clubs such as the International Student Club, Hillel, Community Action Project, Habitat for Humanity, Christian Fellowship, and others get students involved in campus life. Multicultural awareness is supported through the Black Student Union, Asian/Pacific Islander Association, Latino Cultural Society, and GLASS.

"An active alumni association reflects the strong connection Quinnipiac has with its graduates, and they give the faculty high marks for career preparation.

"An outstanding location and campus atmosphere make Quinnipiac a great choice. "

For even more information on this school, turn to page 513 of the "Stats" section.

RAMAPO COLLEGE OF NEW JERSEY

505 RAMAPO VALLEY ROAD, MAHWAH, NJ 07430 • ADMISSIONS: 201-684-7300 • FAX: 201-684-7964
E-MAIL: ADMISSIONS@RAMAPO.EDU • WEBSITE: WWW.RAMAPO.EDU

Ratings
Quality of Life: 83   Academic: 77   Admissions: 89   Financial Aid: 70

Academics

Ramapo College, a small, public, liberal arts school north-west of New York City, stresses "four pillars" of undergraduate education: an interdisciplinary curriculum, international education, intercultural understanding, and experiential learning opportunities. Like most universities, Ramapo is divided into distinct schools, each responsible for teaching a related set of disciplines and each requiring students to complete a rigorous interdisciplinary core curriculum. The

> **SURVEY SAYS . . .**
> *Small classes*
> *Great computer facilities*
> *Athletic facilities are great*
> *Dorms are like palaces*
> *(Almost) everyone smokes*

Ramapo experience is enhanced through "great study abroad options that are open to all regardless of year," including a wide variety of semester, winter break, and summer programs. Through "wonderful cooperative study programs in the surrounding area," Ramapo provides experiential learning that "allows students to receive credit as well as money." For many, however, Ramapo's greatest strength lies not in its pedagogical pillars but in "the relationship it has with its students. Professor and administrators care what we are thinking about and the needs that we have. Your professors all know your names in class and special one-on-one attention is always available during office hours, which are made well-known. By being personable, the school creates a friendly and inviting atmosphere that allows for personal growth and fosters success." Added bonuses include "the availability of a lot of free academic assistance [and] newly renovated classrooms that are up on the newest technology."

Life

Ramapo occupies "an excellent location [that] is not far from New York City, yet it is set in the Ramapo mountains." Hometown Mahwah "is a beautiful town, consisting of middle to upper-class families. Route 17 is just down the road where two malls and many other shopping centers and restaurants are located." Outdoor enthusiasts note that "not even a mile down the road is a huge reservation that many students frequent to spend time outdoors, hike, and study." Ramapo's campus is a pretty one "and there are constant changes going on to make it even more so." To boot, dormitories "are spectacular and are only getting better. They are large, roomy, and fully equipped. Like nothing I've ever seen, almost hotel-like." A new recreation center "is crazy good, with a full gym, new basketball courts, game rooms, etc." About the only thing missing from the Ramapo campus is an active extracurricular life, especially on weekends when "too many people go home." Students inform us that "the main downfall of Ramapo is the nightlife. The campus is in a rural area, making activities in town and around campus almost nonexistent." One problem, according to one student, is that "the school doesn't offer fraternities and sororities housing, so that hurts. Also the lack of a football team hurts, as it would definitely draw students." On the up side, "the city is only 45 minutes away, making for an enjoyable ride."

Student Body

The kids of Ramapo "wear comfy clothes to class, are on their computers and AIM all the time, study and do homework during free time, and drink occasionally." They are, in other words, "your typical college kids." While some consider Ramapo "a hippie school," others point out that "while there are several countercultural people here, there are also plenty jocks, preppies, and basic, average-looking, non-made-up people. Everyone seems to find a group [because] there are so many clubs on campus that are open campus-wide that almost everyone can find a place to fit in." The school's "many international students" include people from Argentina, the Bahamas, Bulgaria, China, Mauritius, Poland, South Korea, Tanzania, and Trinidad and Tobago.

ADMISSIONS

Very important factors considered include: Class rank, secondary school record, standardized test scores. *Important factors considered include:* Character/personal qualities, essays, extracurricular activities, recommendations, talent/ability. *Other factors considered include:* Alumni/ae relation, geographical residence, state residency, volunteer work, work experience. SAT Reasoning Test required. TOEFL required of all international applicants. High school diploma is required, and GED is accepted. *Academic units required:* 4 English, 3 math, 3 science (2 science lab), 2 foreign language, 4 social studies, 2 academic electives.

The Inside Word

A young institution, Ramapo desires applicants who can define its future heritage, people from all over the world who will capitalize on both its quiet campus and convenient location near New York City.

FINANCIAL AID

Students should submit: FAFSA. The Princeton Review suggests that all financial aid forms be submitted as soon as possible after 1/1. *Need-based scholarships/grants offered:* Pell, SEOG, state scholarships/grants, private scholarships, the school's own gift aid. *Loan aid offered:* Direct Subsidized Stafford, Direct Unsubsidized Stafford, Direct PLUS, Federal Perkins, state loans. Applicants will be notified of awards on or about 4/1.

FROM THE ADMISSIONS OFFICE

"Students admitted to Ramapo College for fall 2004 had an average SAT score of 1164 and ranked in the top 19 percent of their graduating class. Applications to the freshman class were the highest in the history of the college; admission was offered to fewer than half (40 percent) of the freshman applicants. Ramapo students come from all 21 counties in New Jersey as well as 23 states and more than 60 countries. Ninety percent of freshmen and more than 60 percent of all full-time students live on campus, for a total of 2,500 residential students.

"Ranked number one among public comprehensive colleges in the north, Ramapo College of New Jersey is sometimes mistaken for a private college. This is, in part, due to its unique interdisciplinary academic structure, its size of around 5,600 students, and its pastoral setting. Ramapo offers bachelors' degrees in the arts, business, humanities, social sciences, and the sciences as well as in professional studies, which include pre-law, premed, nursing, and social work. In addition, the college offers teacher certification at the elementary and secondary school levels.

"Undergraduate students choose to concentrate their studies in one of five schools: Business; American and International Studies; Contemporary Arts; Theoretical and Applied Science; and Social Science and Human Services. Of the 700 course offerings and 40 academic programs, the most popular are business administration, communications, psychology, nursing, information systems, and computer science."

For even more information on this school, turn to page 514 of the "Stats" section.

REGIS COLLEGE

235 WELLESLEY STREET, WESTON, MA 02493-1571 • ADMISSIONS: 781-768-7100 • FAX: 781-768-7071
E-MAIL: ADMISSION@REGISCOLLEGE.EDU • WEBSITE: WWW.REGISCOLLEGE.EDU

Ratings
Quality of Life: 79   Academic: 83   Admissions: 72   Financial Aid: 68

Academics

Regis College, a small Catholic liberal arts and sciences school for women, "is about living within a community of educated and devoted women who all want the most out of life and constantly make a difference in the lives of others." Some of Regis College's most popular programs are communications, graphics and art, museum studies, music, and theater. The school's English and nursing programs are also quite popular. Whatever their academic pursuits may be, students are urged to take advantage of RC's many Boston-area internship opportunities. Students complete roughly 150 internships per year, some of which are required by their majors. Most students enjoy the "individual attention" that RC's small classes provide. According to one student, "The largest class size that I have had at Regis has been forty students, with my average class size being around twelve to fifteen students." Professors and administrators routinely take the time to interact with students outside of the classroom. One undergraduate says, "Our president eats in the same cafeteria that the students eat in, we can call our dean of students by her first name, and we know all of the staff by their names, and they know the students." "Our professors know students who aren't even in their own classes, and that is what [sets apart] Regis from other schools."

> **SURVEY SAYS . . .**
> *Small classes*
> *Diverse student types on campus*
> *Students love Weston, MA*
> *Frats and sororities are unpopular*
> *or nonexistent*

Life

Regis College is "in a great location—only 12 miles from Boston—and the town's surrounding [campus] has a great deal of things to do." Public transportation is available for students who want to venture off campus. For on-campus fun, RC students may participate in the "many clubs and organizations that are available to them. There is a wide array to choose from, and organizations range in size and popularity." In addition, "there are many activities run on the weekends. Dances and movies are common attractions." One student raves, "I think that I really have become spoiled in my time at Regis. With dorms in such close proximity to classrooms, the student union building, athletic facilities, and the library, walking around the beautiful campus is easy and enjoyable."

Student Body

The RC student body is "very diverse, considering it is a private all-women's college." What these diverse students share in common is their dedication to their studies and their desire to be involved. "The school seems to attract students who genuinely care about school and about others," one student comments. The school's student body includes "athletes, the nerds and bookworms, the very religious, and the Glee Clubbers." Students were quick to point out that RC has atypical students who don't fit into any of the common stereotypes. However, one undergraduate explains, "Regis is such a small school that there is no competition between cliques. I have never come across anyone who feels left out or alone. Everyone fits into the Regis community because Regis students are the most kind, accepting, and most generous people I have ever met." Still, you can't please everyone, as is evident from one student's futile plea: "We need BOYS!!"

ADMISSIONS

Very important factors considered include: Character/personal qualities, essays, recommendations, secondary school record, standardized test scores. *Important factors considered include:* Class rank, extracurricular activities, interview, talent/ability, volunteer work, work experience. *Other factors considered include:* Alumni/ae relation. SAT Reasoning or ACT required. TOEFL required of all international applicants. High school diploma is required, and GED is accepted. *Academic units required:* 4 English, 3 math, 2 science (1 science lab), 2 foreign language, 2 social studies, 2 history, 3 academic electives. *Academic units recommended:* 4 English, 3 math, 3 science (1 science lab), 2 foreign language, 2 social studies, 2 history, 4 academic electives.

The Inside Word

Regis processes applications on a rolling basis and encourages early submissions. The school accepts the common application, making it a great last-minute add-on college for students who have already completed that form.

FINANCIAL AID

Students should submit: FAFSA, institution's own financial aid form. The Princeton Review suggests that all financial aid forms be submitted as soon as possible after 1/1. *Need-based scholarships/grants offered:* Pell, SEOG, state scholarships/grants, private scholarships, the school's own gift aid, federal nursing scholarships. *Loan aid offered:* FFEL Subsidized Stafford, FFEL Unsubsidized Stafford, FFEL PLUS, Federal Perkins, state loans. Applicants will be notified of awards on a rolling basis beginning on or about 3/15. Federal Work-study Program available. Institutional employment available. Off-campus job opportunities are fair.

For even more information on this school, turn to page 514 of the "Stats" section.

RENSSELAER POLYTECHNIC INSTITUTE

110 EIGHTH STREET, TROY, NY 12180-3590 • ADMISSIONS: 518-276-6216 • FAX: 518-276-4072
FINANCIAL AID: 518-276-6813 • E-MAIL: ADMISSIONS@RPI.EDU • WEBSITE: WWW.RPI.EDU

Ratings
Quality of Life: 61   **Academic:** 76   **Admissions:** 91   **Financial Aid:** 89

Academics

In recent years Rensselaer Polytechnic Institute, the venerable math/science/engineering heavyweight of the Hudson Valley, has made "strong efforts to diversify the school into a university, rather than [being satisfied with its stature as] a technical institute. Arts programs, both electronic and conventional, are now receiving funding, along with new biotechnology programs." The goal—to "transform RPI to Rensselaer, a one-word synonym for an Ivy League-quality school"—has both champions and critics among the student body, who either praise "new programs that will help us provide the world with graduates very driven to do great things" or assert that "RPI is not and never could or should be a more liberal school. RPI is engineering and it should stay that way." While attempting to broaden the curriculum, Rensselaer remains "a very technology-oriented school that deals with cutting-edge innovations in science and engineering" and "emphasizes diversity, integrity, and above all, leadership in the context of a world-class research university." The workload here is tremendous and the concepts taught difficult to master, but students are protected by an institutional safety net; one engineer explains, "The learning assistance center has an early detection system that warns students who are below average and offers assistance. If they notice the slightest drop in performance, they will contact you in regards to what's up." For many here, "RPI's greatest strengths are its variety of options for students to gain experience in their field. We have an excellent career development center, a study abroad program, undergraduate research programs, internships and co-ops, which are very popular." Placement services are excellent thanks to "many corporate connections; alumni are always coming back and recruiting and many large and small companies love to recruit here."

Life

"Fraternity life is huge on campus," report RPI students, who note that the school is home to over 30 Greek organizations. "If you're a girl you're associated with at least one. If you're a guy who isn't associated with one, you don't have much of a social life." Explains one student, "Everyone either goes to frat parties on the weekend or stays in and plays video games." Not that there aren't other options; as one undergraduate points out, "If you want to do something on campus and be involved, it's incredibly easy to do so. The people who say otherwise are just apathetic. Between movie nights on campus, union sponsored events, fraternity and sorority events, and downtown, there are tons of things to do." Everyone agrees that "hockey is king here; everyone goes and it is amazing to watch." The team competes in NCAA Division I; RPI's 22 other varsity teams play in Division III and are not as enthusiastically supported. When regarding hometown Troy, students are mixed. While some claim that "the city is devoid of all life and fun," others assert that "downtown Troy, although not the best place to hang out at night, is pretty cool. There are some beautiful buildings and some neat shops and small eateries." An even-handed student avers, "While the city of Troy is improving, it has a long way to go before it becomes a suitable location for Rensselaer."

Student Body

"The former stereotype for RPI, as everyone knows, was that we tend to be kind of nerdy bookworms, and that we are not very involved in campus activities." Students also tell us "that is no longer true. Students are now much more involved in things all over campus, from our excellent football and hockey teams, to our 150plus clubs and activities, to new programs popping up all over campus." The school hasn't switched over entirely, of course; as one student explains, "Fifty percent of us are computer nerds who play video games and have their own social networks. The other 50 percent are normal college students who like to party and have a fun time." While the male-female ratio is quite unbalanced here, "It's not as big of a problem as it is made out to be, due to the closeness of other colleges, especially Russell Sage, an all-girls school.

ADMISSIONS

Very important factors considered include: Secondary school record. *Important factors considered include:* Character/personal qualities, class rank, extracurricular activities, standardized test scores. *Other factors considered include:* Alumni/ae relation, essays, geographical residence, minority status, recommendations, talent/ability, volunteer work, work experience. SAT Reasoning or ACT required. TOEFL required of all international applicants. High school diploma is required, and GED is accepted. *Academic units required:* 4 English, 4 math, 3 science, 2 social studies. *Academic units recommended:* 4 science, 3 social studies.

The Inside Word

Although scores and numbers may not be the only consideration of the admissions committee at RPI, it is important to remember that you have to have high ones in order to stay in the running for admission. Here in Troy and at many other highly selective colleges and universities, the first review weeds out those who are academically weak and without any special considerations. Underrepresented minorities and women are high on the list of desirables in the applicant pool here, and go through the admissions process without any hitches if reasonably well qualified.

FINANCIAL AID

Students should submit: FAFSA. The Princeton Review suggests that all financial aid forms be submitted as soon as possible after 1/1. *Need-based scholarships/grants offered:* Pell, SEOG, state scholarships/grants, private scholarships, the school's own gift aid, GATES Millennium Scholarship. *Loan aid offered:* FFEL Subsidized Stafford, FFEL Unsubsidized Stafford, FFEL PLUS, Federal Perkins, college/university loans from institutional funds. Applicants will be notified of awards on or about 3/25. Federal Work-study Program available. Institutional employment available. Off-campus job opportunities are good.

FROM THE ADMISSIONS OFFICE

"The oldest degree-granting technological research university in North America, Rensselaer was founded in 1824 to instruct students to apply 'science to the common purposes of life.' Rensselaer offers more than 100 programs and 1,000 courses leading to bachelor's, master's, and doctoral degrees. Undergraduates pursue studies in architecture, engineering, humanities and social sciences, management and technology, science, and information technology (IT). A pioneer in interactive learning, Rensselaer provides real-world, hands-on educational opportunities that cut across academic disciplines. Students have ready access to laboratories and attend classes involving lively discussion, problem solving, and faculty mentoring.

"New programs and facilities are enriching the student experience. The Office of First-Year Experience provides programs for students and their primary support persons that begin even before students arrive on campus. The new $80-million Biotechnology and Interdisciplinary Studies Center offers space for scientific research and discovery, while newly renovated residence halls, wireless computing network, and studio classrooms create a fertile environment for study and learning. The $100 million Experimental Media and Performing Arts Center opening in 2008 will encourage students to explore and create at the intersection of engineering and the arts.

"Rensselaer offers recreational and fitness facilities plus numerous student-run organizations and activities, including fraternities and sororities, a newspaper, a radio station, drama and musical groups, and more than 130 clubs. In addition to intramural sports, NCAA varsity sports include a Division I men's ice hockey team and 22 Division III men's and women's teams in 13 sports. Women's ice hockey is being elevated to Division I."

For even more information on this school, turn to page 515 of the "Stats" section.

RICHARD STOCKTON COLLEGE OF NEW JERSEY

Jim Leeds Road, PO Box 195, Pomona, NJ 08240 • Admissions: 609-652-4261 • Fax: 609-748-5541
E-mail: admissions@stockton.edu • Website: www.stockton.edu

Ratings

Quality of Life: 73   Academic: 75   Admissions: 83   Financial Aid: 77

Academics

"Strong programs and electives, [a] laid-back vibe where professors ask you to call them by first name, [and] great value" all draw students to Richard Stockton College of New Jersey, a midsize public liberal arts school. Students point out that "by being a liberal arts college, there's a lot of variety in the classes Stockton offers. And in most cases, the professors are very knowledgeable and excited about

> **SURVEY SAYS . . .**
> *Small classes*
> *Great computer facilities*
> *Great library*
> *(Almost) everyone smokes*

the subject, which makes learning enjoyable." Departments earning students' approval include biology, chemistry, criminal justice, and education. Stockton also offers a number of uncommon disciplines, including a minor in Holocaust and genocide studies, a "very strong marine biology program with a lot of field research, [an] excellent environmental studies program," and a minor in new media studies, "a growing field." Stockton is also "one of those schools that has a good visual arts program and a performing arts program without being a strictly arts-only school," thereby allowing artists to receive solid training along with a well-rounded education. Stockton undergrads praise the small-school vibe, bragging that "professors care about how [they] do in their class." Other amenities include "a career services department that can help you with your [career] resume, graduate school resume, and personal statement letter to graduate school. They can help you find a job, and they are so helpful at whatever you need them for."

Life

Location is a huge determinant of quality of life at Stockton. First, there's the campus itself, "situated in the woods on a campus of 1,600 acres of land, most of which is not permitted to be built on." It is, by all accounts, "a beautiful campus, and the school does pretty good keeping it that way." Then there's the convenience factor—Stockton "is right off the Garden State Parkway"—and the surrounding area, which has "a lot of civic events and entertainment nearby, for example, Atlantic City and the Ocean City boardwalk. And it's not far from Philadelphia. Students do not feel cut off from the rest of the world here." Atlantic City and Philly not only provide entertainment but also "pretty good internships. Many of the business students end up working in the casinos. [Atlantic City] has good placements for social work students too." On campus, "there are always events happening in the Performing Arts Center, and the fraternities and sororities often hold interesting events like a lip sync and talent show." But "sadly, there is little to nothing to do most weekends, or if there is, the events aren't advertised enough." The school's Division III intercollegiate athletic teams draw decent support from students. The men's soccer team, which won an NCAA title in 2001, is especially popular.

Student Body

The typical Stockton undergrad "is a friendly, white, middle-class New Jersey resident with a car and a good GPA who is involved with extracurricular activities," but Stockton is also home to "many atypical students who fit in because there are so many student organizations on campus. Plus, we have support to start up our own clubs if we do not find something we like." Students describe themselves as "down-to-earth, outgoing and friendly," with some majors dominated by constant studiers and others by laid-back partiers. The majority of the student body is "pretty liberal," both politically and socially. One student writes, "There are a lot of diverse people here from many religions, regions, cultures, and the like. They seem to fit in all right. The biggest common denominator among the students is that most go home on the weekends, or they commute."

ADMISSIONS

Very important factors considered include: Class rank, secondary school record, standardized test scores. *Important factors considered include:* Essays, extracurricular activities. *Other factors considered include:* Alumni/ae relation, character/personal qualities, recommendations, talent/ability, volunteer work, work experience. SAT Reasoning or ACT required. TOEFL required of all international applicants. High school diploma is required, and GED is accepted. *Academic units required:* 4 English, 3 math, 2 science (2 science lab), 2 social studies, 5 academic electives.

The Inside Word

Stockton, named after New Jersey's representative at The Continental Congress and a POW of the British Army in 1776, is equally attractive for the on-campus or commuting student. Its strong academic reputation demands that applicants demonstrate their ability to match the school's standards of academic hunger and social diversity.

FINANCIAL AID

Students should submit: FAFSA. The Princeton Review suggests that all financial aid forms be submitted as soon as possible after 1/1. *Need-based scholarships/grants offered:* Pell, SEOG, state scholarships/grants. *Loan aid offered:* FFEL Subsidized Stafford, FFEL Unsubsidized Stafford, FFEL PLUS, Federal Perkins, state loans. Applicants will be notified of awards on a rolling basis beginning on or about 4/1. Federal Work-study Program available. Institutional employment available. Off-campus job opportunities are excellent.

FROM THE ADMISSIONS OFFICE

"Stockton College of New Jersey offers the atmosphere and rigorous academics of the very finest private institutions, at a surprisingly affordale cost. Stockton's outstanding faculty includes a Pulitzer Prize winner, two Fulbright Scholars, and the recipient of an Academy Award, several Emmy Awards, and a Grammy Award. Awards don't tell the whole story, though. Stockton's faculty is dedicated to teaching excellence and student success.

"Student life at Stockton is second to none. Our sports teams are nationally ranked, including the 2001 National Division III men's soccer champions. We recently opened a state-of-the-art, $17 million sports center that includes a fully equipped fitness center, and there are new arts and science, health science, and student housing buildings. Stockton's beautiful campus was voted one of the state's Top Ten Architectural Treasures by New Jersey Monthly Magazine. Our pristine 1,600 acres are located within the Pinelands national preserves, including four lakes as well as trails for hiking and biking—all within a 10-minute drive to the popular southern New Jersey beach resorts. The numerous attractions of Philadelphia and New York City are easily accessible as well.

"Stockton features small class sizes, professors who are friendly and accessible, and student organizations to serve every interest. For the student seeking a total college experience at the most reasonable cost possible, Stockton College of New Jersey offers the best of both worlds. Stockton truly lives up to its slogan: 'An Environment for Excellence.'"

For even more information on this school, turn to page 515 of the "Stats" section.

RIDER UNIVERSITY

2083 LAWRENCEVILLE ROAD, LAWRENCEVILLE, NJ 08648-3099 • FAX: 609-896-5042
E-MAIL: ADMISSIONS@RIDER.EDU • WEBSITE: WWW.RIDER.EDU

Ratings
Quality of Life: 71   Academic: 78   Admissions: 74   Financial Aid: 72

Academics

Rider University, its undergrads tell us, "is about teaching you the necessary knowledge for your intended major while really focusing on making and sharpening the skills that make you stand out as a leader." For one in three students here, that major is business-related, an area in which Rider excels. Students praise the College of Business Administration, singling out DAARSTOC—"an executive skill-building organization that has prepared me more for the business world than any other organization possibly could

have"—for its unique contribution to their education. Business undergrads also appreciate "the opportunities to get involved" through internships and volunteer work, telling us that they "foster your leadership development and prepare you for the real world by teaching you and allowing you to practice the 'soft skills' that are essential to success in any career." The School of Education, part of the College of Liberal Arts, Education, & Sciences, offers an excellent program in elementary education, while the science departments, which "provide so many opportunities to do work-study lab work" are also among the most popular with students. Throughout the university, Rider emphasizes a cross-curricular approach to instruction. Students recognize the benefits; writes one, "Every class basically coexists with [all of the] others, and when you're a senior, you see how all your courses come full circle to give you a better understanding of your major." Professors here "truly care and will do anything to help you succeed, whether it's helping you outside of the classroom with certain material, or helping you to get an internship or full-time job."

Life

Rider is "centrally located between NYC and Philly," giving students plenty of reasons to flee campus in search of fun, and when the weekends arrive many—although certainly not all—do just that. A number of students return home on weekends, giving Rider its "suitcase college" reputation. An increasing number are sticking around, though, and that number is bound to increase further in coming years when new residence halls "with apartment and suite-style rooms [and the] multimillion dollar student recreation center currently under construction" open. On and around campus, "Our student entertainment council is allocated a lot of money and uses it wisely. Between movies, concerts, comedians, and themed Bronc Buffets, there is so much to do you can't possibly make all the events." Parties are frequent and well-attended; notes one undergrad, "Fraternities have parties on the weekend, but Rider does its best to offer the student body options on the weekends. Don't you worry, we do our fair share of partying, but that's just not all we're about." Hometown Lawrenceville "is not much of a town, everything is a drive away. There is nowhere to walk to."

Student Body

Rider undergrads tend to be "rich kids from New Jersey with nice cars," although "great financial aid packages" bring in talented students from other economic strata. Most here take a pragmatic approach to education; they will put in exactly the amount of work required to get good grades, but rarely more. "Not too many are particularly studious, except when mid-terms and finals roll around; then, everyone is a Rhodes Scholar," explains one undergrad. Without an impending academic deadline, the majority here would "prefer to party, hang out with friends, and have a good time four or five nights a week." A substantial minority bucks the trend, though; writes one from among their ranks, "The typical student at Rider unfortunately overshadows how amazing the top 30 percent of Rider students are. The majority are uninformed and really don't take ownership in their University. But the top 30 percent are so amazing that I feel they could beat the top 30 percent in leadership ability and performance in jobs anywhere, because they are all so driven, passionate, and prepared."

ADMISSIONS

Very important factors considered include: Class rank, secondary school record, standardized test scores. *Important factors considered include:* Essays, recommendations. *Other factors considered include:* Alumni/ae relation, character/personal qualities, extracurricular activities, interview, talent/ability, volunteer work, work experience. SAT Reasoning or ACT required. TOEFL required of all international applicants. High school diploma is required, and GED is accepted. *Academic units required:* 4 English, 2 math. *Academic units recommended:* 3 math, 3 science, 3 foreign language, 2 social studies, 2 history.

The Inside Word

In the admissions world there are two all-important mandates: recruit the college's home state, and recruit JERSEY! As a school in the Garden State, Rider deserves some special attention for the diverse group of students it brings in each year. Students who wish to attend need to have a solid academic record and good test scores. A few bumps in your academic past, however, shouldn't pose too much of a threat.

FINANCIAL AID

Students should submit: FAFSA. Regular filing deadline 6/1. The Princeton Review suggests that all financial aid forms be submitted as soon as possible after 1/1. *Need-based scholarships/grants offered:* Pell, SEOG, state scholarships/grants, private scholarships, the school's own gift aid. *Loan aid offered:* FFEL Subsidized Stafford, FFEL Unsubsidized Stafford, FFEL PLUS, Federal Perkins, state loans, college/university loans from institutional funds, alternative loans. Applicants will be notified of awards on a rolling basis beginning on or about 4/15. Federal Work-study Program available. Institutional employment available. Off-campus job opportunities are good.

For even more information on this school, turn to page 516 of the "Stats" section.

ROBERTS WESLEYAN COLLEGE

2301 WESTSIDE DRIVE, ROCHESTER, NY 14624-1997 • ADMISSIONS: 585-594-6400 • FAX: 585-594-6371
E-MAIL: ADMISSIONS@ROBERTS.EDU • WEBSITE: WWW.ROBERTS.EDU

Ratings
Quality of Life: 87   Academic: 82   Admissions: 80   Financial Aid: 74

Academics

Methodist-affiliated Roberts Wesleyan College serves a dual mission, according to students; they tell us that it is "a good Christian college that provides the support and tools you need to do well academically and to develop as a well-rounded individual." Faculty and administrators are "knowledgeable, approachable, compassionate, and challenging," as well as "a vital part of making Roberts feel like a connected Christian community." In fact, students add that "many of the administrative staff eat in the cafeteria, and are often seen walking around campus. Faculty members [also] make themselves available outside of class for help with courses, general questions, and mentoring." Students do have suggestions to improve the school. One student says, "Class buildings should be renovated," and another student adds, "The school could update some of its science facilities." Several students believe that these necessary improvements will happen soon. Writes one, "The college is currently working to upgrade the library, dormitories, and strengthen its already strong academic departments. The administration is taking the necessary steps to improve the school."

> **SURVEY SAYS . . .**
> *Small classes*
> *Students are friendly*
> *Students get along with local community*
> *Frats and sororities are unpopular*
> *or nonexistent*
> *Very little drug use*

Life

Aside from studying, students involve themselves in activities such as going to chapel, participating in athletics (soccer in particular), and enjoying the entertainment options that nearby Rochester provides. "There is always some place to eat," one student writes. "Roberts seems like a school with a good balance of fun and learning." Popular student leisure activities include trips to Rochester, going to the movies, shopping, participating in school clubs and organizations, and participating in school sporting events. One student says, "A quarter of the students do sports of some sort." Another student adds, "School life here is very active. There is pride in our sports teams." Not surprisingly, dorm rules are strictly enforced. One undergraduate says, "We have strict open dorm hours, such as guys are allowed in girls' rooms only on Tuesdays, Thursdays, and weekends from 7:00 P.M. to 10:00 P.M. I had more freedom at home."

Student Body

Students routinely describe RWC's student body as "a big family." One student explains, "A typical student is one who is friendly, has a passion for God, and is not uncomfortable with meeting new people. There are a few atypical students who are not as outgoing or straightforward, and they find their niche with either similar people or find that they can enjoy friendships with others that are not like them." Although the average student is white and Christian, one undergraduate says, "About 15 percent of the population does not fall into these categories. I am one, not being a Christian. I feel that I completely fit in even though my religious views are very different from those of the majority." Even so, you can't please all of the students all of the time. "More guys are needed," complains one student.

ADMISSIONS

Very important factors considered include: Character/personal qualities, essays, recommendations, secondary school record, standardized test scores. *Important factors considered include:* Class rank, extracurricular activities, interview, religious affiliation/commitment. *Other factors considered include:* Alumni/ae relation, geographical residence, minority status, state residency, talent/ability, volunteer work, work experience. SAT Reasoning or ACT required. TOEFL required of all international applicants. High school diploma is required, and GED is accepted. *Academic units required:* 4 English, 2 math, 1 science (1 science lab), 2 social studies, 1 history, 2 academic electives. *Academic units recommended:* 3 math, 3 science (3 science lab), 3 foreign language, 3 social studies.

The Inside Word

One in four students admitted to Roberts Wesleyan had high school GPAs below 3.0. It is possible to gain admission to this strong regional school without having excelled in high school; possible—but not easy. Successful borderline applicants will have to demonstrate that they bring something valuable to the table, such as athletic ability, artistic talent, or an unusual background or life history.

FINANCIAL AID

Students should submit: FAFSA, institution's own financial aid form, state aid form. The Princeton Review suggests that all financial aid forms be submitted as soon as possible after 1/1. *Need-based scholarships/grants offered:* Pell, SEOG, state scholarships/grants, private scholarships, the school's own gift aid. *Loan aid offered:* FFEL Subsidized Stafford, FFEL Unsubsidized Stafford, FFEL PLUS, Federal Perkins. Applicants will be notified of awards on a rolling basis beginning on or about 3/15. Federal Work-study Program available. Institutional employment available. Off-campus job opportunities are good.

FROM THE ADMISSIONS OFFICE

"A Roberts Wesleyan education is beneficial beyond just the first job—Roberts instills in students the knowledge and skills needed for a lifetime of learning and success. At Roberts Wesleyan College, we look for students who are interested in a Christian liberal arts education with plenty of professional opportunities. Students who would benefit from small class sizes, numerous internship options, a close-knit Christian community, and strong academic programs are encouraged to apply.

"Roberts Wesleyan College is a vital part of Rochester NY's exceptional mix of educational opportunities. With nearly 2,000 students and a tradition of excellence since 1866, Roberts Wesleyan is a dynamic leader among American liberal arts colleges with a Christian worldview.

"Roberts Wesleyan offers over 50 undergraduate programs, with graduate programs in education, school psychology and counseling, counseling in ministry, social work, and management. Roberts also offers undergraduate degree-completion programs for working adults in nursing (classroom-based) and organizational management (classroom and online). Northeastern Seminary on the Roberts campus offers Master of Divinity, Master of Arts in Theology, and Doctor of Ministry degrees.

"Roberts Wesleyan is accredited by the Middle States Association of Colleges and Schools, the National Association of Schools of Music, the National Association of Schools of Art and Design, the National League of Nursing, the Council for Social Work Education, and the Association of Collegiate Business Schools and Programs."

For even more information on this school, turn to page 516 of the "Stats" section.

ROCHESTER INSTITUTE OF TECHNOLOGY

60 LOMB MEMORIAL DRIVE, ROCHESTER, NY 14623 • ADMISSIONS: 716-475-6631 • FAX: 716-475-7424
FINANCIAL AID: 716-475-2186 • E-MAIL: ADMISSIONS@RIT.EDU • WEBSITE: WWW.RIT.EDU

Ratings
Quality of Life: 68   **Academic:** 79   **Admissions:** 88   **Financial Aid:** 91

Academics

Come to the Rochester Institute of Technology (RIT) for what students call "a great technical education with a side of liberal arts and almost anything else that you desire." The school "utilizes the newest and most advanced technologies," thanks to sponsorships and partnerships with "corporate giants like Xerox, Kodak, and Bausch and Lomb." Not only do engineers and scientists reap the benefits of this techno-paradise, but art students also prosper. One writes, "Some programs really feel rewarding and

> **SURVEY SAYS . . .**
> *Small classes*
> *Lab facilities are great*
> *Great computer facilities*
> *Great library*
> *Athletic facilities are great*
> *Great off-campus food*

involving here, like the film and animation program, and other arts programs give creative bohemians some experience with twenty-first-century technology." The result of all this high-tech training is that "RIT is well known in the business world; and 90 percent of grads are hired within six months. That's only the graduates, of course. Not everyone makes it through," since "the academic environment is strenuous and it is very easy to get behind," thanks in large part to the quarterly academic calendar. Fortunately, most professors "are readily available outside of the classroom, and are very friendly." The administration, in contrast, is seen as aloof, less concerned about addressing current students' complaints than about raising money and planning for the school's long-term future. That future, by the way, could be very different from the present. One undergraduate explains, "The college of engineering and the college of science want the university to become a research institution, while the college of liberal arts, imaging arts, and the school for the deaf fear that growth in graduate programs would negatively affect the quality of undergraduate education."

Life

"Most RIT students study, study, study," undergraduates tell us. "Art students are running around working on projects, and engineers spend late nights in the labs." Students' desire to succeed and the quarter system combine to create an "incredibly stressful" atmosphere, "especially toward the end of the quarter." Some try to relieve stress with alcohol, and most succeed despite the school's "many restrictions on alcohol." Undergrads evade the restrictions by heading off campus to student apartments for parties. Once an extracurricular sinkhole, RIT is currently "making some ground on the social elements. They've recently added a number of social venues, including a popular coffee shop, and a recently opened field house which has helped bring concerts and other events to campus. Some students have even developed affection for their wintry hometown. One student writes, "When I first came to Rochester, I was disheartened by the industrial 'rust belt' look of it. But the longer I live here, the more I love it. It's a place I could see myself settling down in for the first few years after college." Another undergraduate shares this sentiment: "Nightlife in Rochester is pretty good. I usually go to independent film theaters and ethnic restaurants off campus." College hockey is "popular, and draws substantial, rowdy crowds on weekends," and is likely to become even bigger as the men's team enters the NCAA Division I in 2005.

Student Body

Despite its reputation as a "geek" school, "RIT has an interesting mix of scientists, engineers, business students, arts students, and liberal arts students." The heavy science and engineering presence, however, means "RIT attracts a disproportionately high number of, for lack of a better word, dorks. However, there are a fair share of balanced individuals." Among other interesting facts about the school's student body, RIT's partnership with the National Technical Institute for the Deaf "translates into about 10 to 15 percent of the students being hearing impaired." One student tells us that "there are so many diverse cultures, and that really amazed me when I got here." Unfortunately, "this is not a very social campus," and students tend to stick within small groups defined by major, ethnicity, hearing status, and/or sexual preference.

ADMISSIONS

Very important factors considered include: Secondary school record. *Important factors considered include:* Class rank, standardized test scores. *Other factors considered include:* Alumni/ae relation, character/personal qualities, essays, extracurricular activities, geographical residence, interview, minority status, recommendations, talent/ability, volunteer work, work experience. SAT Reasoning or ACT required. TOEFL required of all international applicants. High school diploma is required, and GED is accepted. *Academic units required:* 4 English, 2 math, 2 science (1 science lab), 4 social studies, 10 academic electives. *Academic units recommended:* 4 English, 3 math, 3 science (2 science lab), 3 foreign language, 4 social studies, 5 academic electives.

The Inside Word

RIT is not as competitive as the top tier of technical schools, but its location and contacts with major research corporations make it a top choice for many students. The acceptance rate is deceptively high when considered in conjunction with the student academic profile and the high yield of admitted students who enroll. There is a strong element of self-selection at work in the applicant pool; the successful candidate is one who is solid academically and ready to hit the ground running.

FINANCIAL AID

Students should submit: FAFSA, state aid form. Regular filing deadline 3/15. The Princeton Review suggests that all financial aid forms be submitted as soon as possible after 1/1. *Need-based scholarships/grants offered:* Pell, SEOG, state scholarships/grants, private scholarships, the school's own gift aid. *Loan aid offered:* Direct Subsidized Stafford, Direct Unsubsidized Stafford, Direct PLUS, Federal Perkins, private bank loans. Applicants will be notified of awards on a rolling basis beginning on or about 3/15. Federal Work-study Program available. Institutional employment available. Off-campus job opportunities are excellent.

FROM THE ADMISSIONS OFFICE

"A nationally respected leader in professional and career-oriented education, RIT has been described as one of America's most imitated institutions and has been recognized as one of the nation's leading universities. RIT has also been rated the number one comprehensive university in the East for its scientific and technology programs. RIT's strength lies in its dedication to providing superior career preparation for today's students. This has attracted excellent faculty to RIT and has led to the development of academic programs that combine small classes and an emphasis on undergraduate teaching, modern classroom facilities, and work experience gained through the university's cooperative education program. Few universities provide RIT's variety of career-oriented programs. Our eight colleges offer outstanding programs in business, engineering, art and design, science and mathematics, liberal arts, photography, hotel management, computer science, and other areas. RIT's National Technical Institute for the Deaf (NTID) is the world's largest mainstreamed college program for the deaf and hearing impaired."

For even more information on this school, turn to page 517 of the "Stats" section.

ROGER WILLIAMS UNIVERSITY

One Old Ferry Road, Bristol, RI 02809 • Admissions: 401-254-3500 • Fax: 401-254-3557
E-mail: admit@rwu.edu • Website: www.rwu.edu

Ratings
Quality of Life: 74   **Academic:** 77   **Admissions:** 79   **Financial Aid:** 82

Academics

"Imagine waking up every morning looking out to Mount Hope Bay, in a small New England town, a half hour from Providence and Newport and an hour and change from Boston, where the faculty is extremely friendly and available, teachers' assistants don't exist, and your biggest class is 25 students." Welcome to Roger Williams University on the coast of Rhode Island. Many students gush over the "smart and helpful" professors, although a healthy number of undergrads add that RWU's academic quality "varies

from class to class and professor to professor." Discussion, debate, and hands-on learning are emphasized in RWU's classrooms. One chemistry major says, "I love the fact that this school thinks undergraduate research is important and gives us a chance to present our research at regional conferences." Something these undergrads don't love, however, is the red tape that seems to ensnare the campus. "The administration is very hard to contact, and deans tend to keep redirecting you to places," says a psychology major. "It took me 10 (10!!!) walks across campus to get a simple scheduling issue resolved." With the ups and downs in the administration and in the academic buildings, "self-motivators" do well at RWU. When the RWU experience clicks, undergrads enjoy "the perfect combination of liberal arts and professional career preparation."

Life

"The campus beauty is one of the greatest strengths" of Roger Williams University. Perched at the edge of the Mount Hope/Narragansett Bay, the campus offers breathtaking views—views that lucky students take in through their dormitory windows. Aside from the surrounding scenery, however, dorms leave much to be desired. Often cramped and rarely cleaned, the dorms seem "like dirty closets," according to one sophomore. Fortunately for the unfortunate dorm dwellers, there are plenty of reasons to venture out. Providence and Newport are each less than half an hour away. "Hop on the RIPTA [public bus transportation] and enjoy what those cities have to offer," suggests a freshmen, who, like all first-year students at RWU, does not have a car on campus. Whether students head off to the Providence clubs or find parties close to campus, Roger Williams undergrads take nightlife quite seriously. As a computer science major puts it, "Most people here have not had a sober weekend while at Roger Williams; [therefore,] people kind of need to learn to have fun without the booze!" And, of course, many people do. Nearly 75 clubs and organizations exist at RWU, as well as 16 varsity sports and a range of intramurals, including the much-loved dodge ball competitions.

Student Body

Students at RWU describe one another as "friendly, open, [and, of course, as people who know] how to have fun." According to one senior, you're always bumping into people who are "willing to smile and say hello." The friendships begin at the university's "awesome orientation program," and because many students are "involved in one or more clubs or sports"—and because these undergrads gather frequently for parties—the friendships continue to grow stronger. Nearly 80 percent of the student body ventures to Roger Williams from out-of-state, particularly the New England and Mid-Atlantic states. However, these undergrads do grumble that "the school definitely needs to work on improving the diversity." But change is on the horizon, a sophomore predicts: "My school is still fighting to lose its reputation as 'Rich White University.' The campus is [becoming] much more diverse and the curriculum is becoming ever more challenging. It's only a matter of time."

ADMISSIONS

Very important factors considered include: Essays, secondary school record, standardized test scores, talent/ability. *Important factors considered include:* Character/personal qualities, class rank, extracurricular activities. *Other factors considered include:* Interview, recommendations, volunteer work, work experience. SAT Reasoning or ACT required. High school diploma is required, and GED is accepted. *Academic units required:* 4 English, 3 math, 3 science (2 science lab), 3 social studies, 2 history. *Academic units recommended:* 4 math.

The Inside Word

Admission to the school's well-regarded architecture program is competitive; all other programs are much less so. Architecture candidates must apply by February 1 and would be well advised to spend considerable effort on their portfolios.

FINANCIAL AID

Students should submit: FAFSA, CSS/Financial Aid PROFILE. Regular filing deadline 2/1. The Princeton Review suggests that all financial aid forms be submitted as soon as possible after 1/1. *Need-based scholarships/grants offered:* Pell, SEOG, state scholarships/grants, private scholarships, the school's own gift aid. *Loan aid offered:* FFEL Subsidized Stafford, FFEL Unsubsidized Stafford, FFEL PLUS, Federal Perkins, state loans. Applicants will be notified of awards on or about 3/15. Federal Work-study Program available. Off-campus job opportunities are excellent.

FROM THE ADMISSIONS OFFICE

"Located on a beautiful, waterfront campus in historic Bristol, Rhode Island, Roger Williams University is a leading liberal arts university in New England. Our modern, safe, 140-acre campus places you among many nearby resources and attractions. You'll enjoy the region's engaging lifestyles and vibrant cultures. Also, our campus is easily accessible from urban centers such as Providence, Boston, and New York by car or other transportation.

"We offer 35 challenging academic majors through a liberal arts college, five professional schools, graduate programs, and the state's only law school. Accredited by the New England Association of Schools and Colleges, Roger Williams University has 3,300 full-time undergraduates. We're just the right size to offer you the friendliness and attention of a small liberal arts college, but with the professional tracks and research opportunities of a larger university. It's the best of both worlds. You'll also benefit from an array of support services to ease your arrival and make your years here comfortable and enjoyable. We give you what you're looking for—a high-quality education within an ideal academic setting that encompasses excellent facilities, recreation, athletics, and social life. Modern academic and support facilities are within walking distance of residence halls. Students have access to first-rate resources including libraries, state-of-the-art computer centers, and other advantages such as design and art studios. A Roger Williams University education gives you the chance to become a complete person who is successfully able to bridge transitions to a rewarding career and gratifying life."

For even more information on this school, turn to page 517 of the "Stats" section.

ROSEMONT COLLEGE

1400 Montgomery Ave., Rosemont, PA 19010 • Admissions: 610-526-2966 • Fax: 610-520-4399
E-mail: admissions@rosemont.edu • Website: www.rosemont.edu

Ratings

Quality of Life: 73   **Academic:** 79   **Admissions:** 82   **Financial Aid:** 77

Academics

At Rosemont, a tiny women's college in suburban Pennsylvania, "everyone knows everyone." Boasting an excellent student/faculty ratio, "class sizes are generally around 15 students," and you can expect to receive, "a large amount of personal attention," from the school's talented faculty. At Rosemont, teachers are friendly, open, and prioritize relationships with their students over personal accomplishments. A freshman shares, "The teachers here are the best thing the school has going for it; they are extremely accessible and very dedicated to teaching. Most have published, but they are foremost teachers." Adds another, "They know everyone in the class and try to get a sense of who you are." In addition to the faculty, "the administration does its best to reach the students' needs and respond to the feedback," creating a very student-oriented academic experience. A freshman sums up the atmosphere: "The dean of students is awesome, the President is the sweetest, nicest woman. Everyone is worried about you, you, you." Some complain the school is too accommodating, letting classroom rigor fall to the lowest common denominator. A freshman tells us, "Rosemont should make students work on a more academic level. In many cases, classes are burdened by extreme spectrums in academic capability." A senior adds, "Rosemont lacks an intellectual environment where students are continually challenged, not only by professors, but by fellow peers." However, a freshman insists, "If a challenge is desired, one must take the initiative in reaching out for that challenge."

> **SURVEY SAYS . . .**
> Small classes
> Diverse student types on campus
> Students love Rosemont, PA
> Great off-campus food
> Intramural sports are unpopular or nonexistent
> Frats and sororities are unpopular or nonexistent

Life

When class is over, Rosemont girls take full advantage of the "five other colleges all within a few blocks from each other," frequenting the coed parties at neighboring institutions. (Otherwise, the "hot-guy deprivation often leads to an attraction to the (not-so-hot) campus facilities guys.) Beyond parties, a sophomore tells us, "I go to the movies, or shopping at the local shops and the King of Prussia Mall. We also watch a lot of DVDs and I work off campus at the Bryn Mawr Hospital." A junior says, "When we stay in, we could be doing anything from drinking to watching movies to just sitting around and talking." While most students enjoy their life at Rosemont, many say, "there are very few campus-wide activities and, whenever there are, they are very poorly advertised." That's because "The Grind, which I suppose can be considered our student center, really doesn't provide the students with much entertainment. There isn't really any place on campus a student can go to just hang out. There are not a lot of parties, either—not many in the dorms, at least." Of particular concern to those who hail from far away or out-of-state is the fact that "most people go home on the weekends, and there are little to no campus activities on the weekends." Laments a junior from California, "Rosemont could really benefit from fostering school spirit on campus."

Student Body

While you might not expect it from a private women's college, Rosemont is described as, "an ethnically and culturally diverse place," made up of, "students of all different interests, races, and tastes." A freshman attests, "Although we are a small community, the diversity on campus and within students is impressive." While "some girls walk around looking as though they're always ready to go clubbing, others wander through the day in comfortable pajamas and sweats." Trouble comes, some claim, with an underlying tension between minority groups. "There is not a great deal of racism, just not a close intermingling of racial groups," says a junior. However, most report that the campus is surprisingly integrated. A senior shares, "The tight-knit community is a major strength of my school. There is a lot of room to grow." Despite their diverse backgrounds, Rosemont students might describe the "typical student as a strong, smart, active female. She wants to pursue everything she can and she wants to be an independent person." Students also describe their classmates as generally social and outgoing. "Rosemonsters are friendly and can easily create groups of friends and mingle amongst others as well," says a senior.

ADMISSIONS

Very important factors considered include: Class rank, interview, secondary school record. *Important factors considered include:* Essays, extracurricular activities, recommendations, standardized test scores, talent/ability, volunteer work. *Other factors considered include:* Alumni/ae relation, character/personal qualities, work experience. SAT Reasoning or SAT Subject Tests required. TOEFL required of all international applicants. High school diploma is required, and GED is accepted. *Academic units required:* 4 English, 3 math, 3 science (2 science lab), 1 social studies, 1 history, 7 academic electives. *Academic units recommended:* 4 English, 3 math, 3 science (2 science lab), 2 foreign language, 2 social studies, 2 history, 4 academic electives.

The Inside Word

Rosemont's admissions staff wants to ensure that its students are a perfect fit for both classroom and community. While high school transcript, standardized test scores, and letters of recommendation are all major considerations, pros here strongly suggest a campus visit and admissions interview.

FINANCIAL AID

Students should submit: FAFSA. The Princeton Review suggests that all financial aid forms be submitted as soon as possible after 1/1. *Need-based scholarships/grants offered:* Pell, SEOG, state scholarships/grants, private scholarships, the school's own gift aid. *Loan aid offered:* FFEL Subsidized Stafford, FFEL Unsubsidized Stafford, FFEL PLUS, Federal Perkins, alternative loans offered, payment plans offered. Applicants will be notified of awards on a rolling basis beginning on or about 2/15. Federal Work-study Program available. Institutional employment available. Off-campus job opportunities are good.

FROM THE ADMISSIONS OFFICE

"Current Rosemont students tell us that the college provides them with an excellent education, that their experience is empowering, and that at Rosemont they meet friends they will keep for life. Rosemont has provided a unique educational experience for almost 85 years and continues to seek to enroll women interested in the liberal arts who have the capacity and desire to pursue a rigorous academic program. Students are considered without regard to race, religion, disability, or ethnic or national origin. A candidate for admission must present a satisfactory record of scholastic ability and personal integrity from an accredited high school as well as acceptable scores on the SAT I or ACT. The student must have an official copy of her high school transcript sent to Rosemont's Office of Admissions. An applicant's secondary school preparation should include 16 college preparatory courses. Applicants are expected to carry a full academic program during their senior year of high school. Two recommendations are required in support of the student's application. Applications for admission are accepted on a rolling basis. A personal interview with a member of the admissions staff is strongly recommended as an important part of the application process. Prospective students are also encouraged to make arrangements to visit classes, meet Rosemont students, and whenever possible, stay overnight.

"To arrange for an interview and a tour, or to receive additional information, students should contact the Office of Admissions."

For even more information on this school, turn to page 518 of the "Stats" section.

ROWAN UNIVERSITY

201 MULLICA HILL ROAD, GLASSBORO, NJ 08028 • ADMISSIONS: 856-256-4200 • FAX: 856-256-4430
E-MAIL: ADMISSIONS@ROWAN.EDU • WEBSITE: WWW.ROWAN.EDU

Ratings
Quality of Life: 61   **Academic:** 73   **Admissions:** 86   **Financial Aid:** 66

Academics

Undergraduates at Rowan University enjoy "a small-school feeling at a university level." Students dole out praises for the school's talented faculty, saying that the majority are genuinely "dedicated to teaching their students." While some complain about the school's extensive general education requirements, students love the support they receive within their major field. In fact, each academic department at Rowan functions like a small support group, and students form close, personal relationships with their professors. "I absolutely love my department's

> **SURVEY SAYS . . .**
> *Small classes*
> *No one cheats*
> *Lab facilities are great*
> *Students aren't religious*
> *Lots of beer drinking*
> *Hard liquor is popular*
> *(Almost) everyone smokes*

professors. I always feel able to talk to them about anything at all," says a junior. A biology major adds, "The biology department has some of the best teachers that I have ever had and probably will ever have. They care about their students and want them to succeed." Overall, students give the Rowan facilities, campus, and location a thumbs-up, pointing out, among other things, that "the labs—whether for science, engineering, or business (including economics)—are top-notch." Rowan's administration gets slightly less enthusiastic reviews from our respondents, primarily where budgetary issues are concerned. One representative student says diplomatically, "The administration has their own vision for the college and does not take advice from the students into much consideration."

Life

While they like to have a good time, most Rowan undergrads tend to maintain a fairly levelheaded lifestyle in college, dividing time between school, work, and relaxation. A sophomore summarizes life at Rowan: "You make friends, you go to class, you do your work, and on weekends, you have some fun. It's a balance of playtime and work time." For the former, Rowan students tend to blow off steam at bars and frat parties. A senior reports, "If you like to party, Rowan is a great place to go. You can find someone and somewhere to go almost every night of the week." However, many lament the fact that "drinking seems to be the main activity for fun" and that the surrounding city of Glassboro "is not as college-friendly as a small town should or could be," offering few entertainment opportunities for students under 21. For students looking for a sober Saturday night, "the school offers concerts and comedians for entertainment" as well as movie and craft nights, and "the mall is about 15 minutes away, with movie theaters and plenty of chain restaurants." On top of that, nearby Philly is a mecca of entertainment and cultural options.

Student Body

There is something of a divide between Rowan's two major student populations. With the school community divided between commuter students and residents, undergrads tell us that "students at Rowan fall into two types: bookworms or socialites." A senior explains a fair number of students are commuters, "who you will never see outside the classroom. The rest of us that live in and around campus are pretty homogenous. Everyone goes to the same parties, hangs with the same group." Indeed, when it comes to the party crew, "athletics and Greeks dominate on our campus," although students reassure us that "everyone fits in somewhere. There is a club, a major, a sport, for everyone." Even so, many admit that there isn't much cultural or socioeconomic diversity at Rowan. A senior says, "There is a smaller percentage of minorities in the classroom. In most cases, there are one to three minorities to a class."

ADMISSIONS

Very important factors considered include: Class rank, secondary school record, standardized test scores. *Important factors considered include:* Extracurricular activities, recommendations, talent/ability. *Other factors considered include:* Alumni/ae relation, character/personal qualities, minority status, volunteer work, work experience. SAT Reasoning or SAT Subject Tests required. TOEFL required of all international applicants. High school diploma is required, and GED is accepted. *Academic units required:* 4 English, 3 math, 2 science (2 science lab), 2 social studies, 5 academic electives.

The Inside Word

Not heretofore known as having a tight admissions process, Rowan is starting to look beyond New York and New Jersey for candidates who want to contribute to its forward scholastic momentum.

FINANCIAL AID

Students should submit: FAFSA. The Princeton Review suggests that all financial aid forms be submitted as soon as possible after 1/1. *Need-based scholarships/grants offered:* Pell, SEOG, state scholarships/grants, private scholarships, the school's own gift aid. *Loan aid offered:* Direct Subsidized Stafford, Direct Unsubsidized Stafford, Direct PLUS, state loans. Applicants will be notified of awards on a rolling basis beginning on or about 3/15.

FROM THE ADMISSIONS OFFICE

"Rowan University is a selective, progressive public university with the funds and public support to transform itself into a top regional university. It is using these resources to improve the academic quality of the university while keeping tuition affordable. Because of its large endowment, the University is able to compete with private colleges and produce direct benefits for students. The university is in the midst of a $530 million 10-year plan to expand the campus, improve facilities, and hire more faculty. By implementing a comprehensive plan for enrollment management, Rowan University will maintain its reputation as a high-quality, moderate-price university.

"These efforts have caught the attention of organizations that evaluate colleges and universities nationwide. U.S. News & World Report ranks Rowan University in the 'Top Tier' of Northern Regional Universities. *Kiplinger's* named Rowan University one of the '100 Best Buys in Public Colleges and Universities.'

"At Rowan, students have access to the resources of a large university without sacrificing the personal attention and small class size of a private college. All classes are taught by professors, not teaching assistants. The university enrolls more than 9,600 students among six colleges (Business, Communication, Education, Engineering, Fine & Performing Arts, and Liberal Arts & Sciences). Students can choose from 36 undergraduate majors and 30 graduate programs leading to master's and doctoral degrees."

For even more information on this school, turn to page 518 of the "Stats" section.

Rutgers University—New Brunswick

65 DAVIDSON ROAD, PISCATAWAY, NJ 08854-8097 • ADMISSIONS: 732-932-4636 • FAX: 732-445-0237
FINANCIAL AID: 732-932-7057 • E-MAIL: ADMISSIONS@ASB-UGADM.RUTGERS.EDU • WEBSITE: WWW.RUTGERS.EDU

Ratings
Quality of Life: 64   Academic: 72   Admissions: 87   Financial Aid: 75

Academics

What to expect from this large state school? Quality education at an "incredibly affordable price," students say. The New Brunswick campus alone encompasses twelve separate colleges, each with its own focus. Among them are historic Rutgers' College, the environmentally focused Cook College, the all-women's Douglass College, the well-regarded School of Engineering, plus schools in nursing, pharmacy, public policy, communication, and business. With so much to choose from, it takes a real self-starter to make the most of a Rutgers experience. "The school has a lot to offer if you can find it," writes a sophomore. "The pro-

> **SURVEY SAYS . . .**
> Great computer facilities
> Great library
> Athletic facilities are great
> Diverse student types on campus
> Student publications are popular
> Lots of beer drinking
> Hard liquor is popular
> (Almost) everyone smokes

fessors are some of the best in their fields," adds another student. It's not surprising, then, that students want more face time with professors—and less with their TAs. But some programs give you more individual attention than others. One senior writes, "Since I am a physics major, most of my classes are around ten people and my professors are available almost all the time." For students in majors with higher enrollments, however, "good luck getting the classes you want." This brings us to the so-called "RU Screw," which has come to symbolize all the ways individual students feel ignored or overlooked by the school's administration—everything from slow bus service among campuses to rude front office staff. One student, takes a more levelheaded approach: "Although many people complain about the 'RU Screw,' there's bound to be some frustration when an administration has to handle over 20,000 undergraduates." The recent creation of the Office of the Ombudsperson seeks to help students resolve their campus difficulties, and is a step in the right direction.

Life

One clever senior describes this place as a "small community with a large population." According to another student there is no shortage of opportunity for extracurricular activities. "There are a thousand and one different activities to join, so there's no excuse for not getting involved in something. At the beginning of every fall semester, there's a huge involvement fair on College Avenue where all the organizations set up tables to attract people." One student has discovered that New Brunswick "is very suburban, but it's like a mini city. There are clubs and lounges downtown, but dorming is probably the quickest way to meet people and have friends for life." A sophomore adds, "Hanging out in the dorms can be fun. It is not always necessary to go off campus. Since there is more than one campus, you can always find something to do or somewhere to go." At Rutgers, "partying is prominent," and students have the option to join a number of fraternities and sororities. Aside from partying, though, students have football games, the annual Rutgers and Spring Fests, free movie nights, and guest comedians to keep them entertained. Still, for some students that is not enough to make up for sleepy New Brunswick. They are left to mourn the "dead social life on weekends." One thing most students lament together is the overcrowded and painfully slow inter-campus bus system. "Transportation definitely needs to improve," one freshman warns.

Student Body

Students differ across the various New Brunswick colleges, whose populations tend to be self-selecting. In the engineering school, for example, you'll find a more scientific crowd. In the Douglass College, you'll find only women. One student puts it this way: "There are academically oriented students, socially-oriented students, and students that fall in the middle." With such a large student population, the campus itself is ethnically and socioeconomically diverse. But getting all those groups to mix is not always easy. "Different races hardly associate with each other!" complains one junior. Nevertheless, says another student, there are "limitless chances to meet a variety of different people—everyone can find their niche."

ADMISSIONS

Very important factors considered include: Class rank, secondary school record, standardized test scores. *Other factors considered include:* Essays, extracurricular activities, geographical residence, interview, minority status, recommendations, state residency, talent/ability, volunteer work, work experience. SAT Reasoning or ACT required. TOEFL required of all international applicants. High school diploma is required, and GED is accepted. *Academic units required:* 4 English, 3 math, 2 science, 2 foreign language, 5 academic electives. *Academic units recommended:* 4 math, 2 foreign language.

The Inside Word

New Jersey residents are finally acknowledging that the flagship of their state university system is among the finest public universities in the nation. As a result, getting in keeps getting tougher every year as more and more New Jersey residents elect to stay home for college.

FINANCIAL AID

Students should submit: FAFSA. The Princeton Review suggests that all financial aid forms be submitted as soon as possible after 1/1. *Need-based scholarships/grants offered:* Pell, SEOG, state scholarships/grants, private scholarships, the school's own gift aid, outside scholarships. *Loan aid offered:* Direct Subsidized Stafford, Direct Unsubsidized Stafford, Direct PLUS, Federal Perkins, state loans, college/university loans from institutional funds, other educational loans. Applicants will be notified of awards on a rolling basis beginning on or about 2/1. Federal Work-study Program available. Institutional employment available. Off-campus job opportunities are good.

FROM THE ADMISSIONS OFFICE

"Rutgers, The State University of New Jersey, one of only 61 members of the Association of American Universities, is a research university, which attracts students from across the nation and around the world. What does it take to be accepted for admission to Rutgers University? There's no single answer to that question. Our primary emphasis is on your past academic performance as indicated by your high school grades (particularly in required academic subjects), your class rank, the strength of your academic program, your standardized test scores on the SAT or ACT, any special talents you may have, and your participation in school and community activities. We seek students with a broad diversity of talents, interests, and backgrounds. Above all else, we're looking for students who will get the most out of a Rutgers education—students with the intellect, initiative, and motivation to make full use of the opportunities we have to offer."

For even more information on this school, turn to page 518 of the "Stats" section.

SACRED HEART UNIVERSITY

5151 PARK AVENUE, FAIRFIELD, CT 06825 • ADMISSIONS: 203-371-7880 • FAX: 203-365-7607
E-MAIL: ENROLL@SACREDHEART.EDU • WEBSITE: WWW.SACREDHEART.EDU

Ratings
Quality of Life: 73   **Academic:** 76   **Admissions:** 80   **Financial Aid:** 72

Academics

Solid departments in business and marketing, psychology, criminal justice, and "a great nursing program" make Sacred Heart University a popular destination for many students in Connecticut and the surrounding region. "Amazing sports programs" and an emphasis on high-tech learning—all students are issued a laptop (included in the cost of tuition) that connects them to the school's wireless network—are also major benefits at this small Roman Catholic school. Undergraduates tell us that "the greatest strength of our school would be the student-to-teacher ratio. Because the ratio is so close, it allows the students to get more one-on-one attention, and it enables [them] to do better in the class." Students say, "[Professors are] extremely knowledgeable and interested in what they are teaching. That brings our interest level up and it allows us to learn and connect easier with the teacher as [much] as the material." The core curriculum "focuses much of its efforts in teaching values and ethics," which students appreciate. An honors program serves students with a pronounced interest in the liberal arts. Its centerpiece is a list of "30 Things You Should Hear, See, and Read." The list ranges from Plato and the Bible, to Miles Davis and Alfred Hitchcock.

> **SURVEY SAYS . . .**
> *Small classes*
> *Great computer facilities*
> *Athletic facilities are great*
> *Everyone loves the Pioneers*
> *Lots of beer drinking*
> *(Almost) everyone smokes*

Life

"The sports teams seem to hold the campus together," SHU students tell us. The school is home to 32 men's and women's competitive teams, many of which draw large, enthusiastic crowds. Students also love the "impressive athletic facilities." The school offers lots of entertainment, including "comedians, concerts, and bingo where you can win some awesome prizes." Alcohol is prohibited on campus. Students say, "[for parties we] go to houses in the area, or we go to the bars. There are a lot of them; this is a real bar school." They also sometimes head down the road to Bridgeport or New Haven. Some students warn, "Everyone needs a car. There is absolutely nothing within walking distance." Life is best during early fall and late spring, when students can enjoy the campus' great landscaping. One student adds, "Plus, when it's warm enough, the beach is a short drive away. It's pretty relaxing to study for spring finals on the beach." Most students find time to take on "a lot of community service. It's nice to see that kids our age care so much about their community." For a great daytrip or weekend fun, "It's just a short train ride into NYC for shows, shopping, or just to go enjoy the city."

Student Body

Sacred Heart "is actually a very big sports school. A lot of the students are student athletes." The student body also includes "your preps, your loners, [and] your bookworms. There is a variety of people here." Most students are white Catholics who grew up in New England. Many students also come from well-off families and are not shy about letting others know it. One undergraduate says, "The typical look is Abercrombie with Coach bags and salon-tanned skin. When you walk on the campus, you get the feeling that the students have some money. However, there are people that are different, and they mix in with no problem."

ADMISSIONS

Very important factors considered include: Secondary school record. *Important factors considered include:* Character/personal qualities, class rank, essays, extracurricular activities, geographical residence, interview, recommendations, standardized test scores, state residency, volunteer work. *Other factors considered include:* Alumni/ae relation, minority status, religious affiliation/commitment, talent/ability, work experience. SAT Reasoning or ACT required. TOEFL required of all international applicants. High school diploma is required, and GED is accepted. *Academic units required:* 4 English, 3 math, 3 science (1 science lab), 2 foreign language, 3 social studies, 3 history, 3 academic electives. *Academic units recommended:* 4 English, 4 math, 4 science (2 science lab), 4 foreign language, 4 social studies, 4 history, 4 academic electives.

The Inside Word

Interviews are not required at Sacred Heart, but they are "strongly recommended." If you are serious about attending this school, make it your business to schedule an interview and show up ready to impress. Over half of all undergraduates major in business here, so dress conservatively for the interview, just to be on the safe side.

FINANCIAL AID

Students should submit: FAFSA, CSS/Financial Aid PROFILE. The Princeton Review suggests that all financial aid forms be submitted as soon as possible after 1/1. *Need-based scholarships/grants offered:* Pell, SEOG, state scholarships/grants, private scholarships, the school's own gift aid, federal nursing scholarships. *Loan aid offered:* FFEL Subsidized Stafford, FFEL Unsubsidized Stafford, FFEL PLUS, Federal Perkins, state loans, alternative loans. Applicants will be notified of awards on a rolling basis beginning on or about 3/1. Federal Work-study Program available. Institutional employment available. Off-campus job opportunities are excellent.

FROM THE ADMISSIONS OFFICE

"Sacred Heart University, distinguished by the personal attention it provides its students, is a thriving, dynamic university known for its commitment to academic excellence, cutting-edge technology and community service. The second-largest Catholic university in New England, Sacred Heart University continues to be innovative in its offerings to students; recently launched programs include Connecticut's first Doctoral program in Physical Therapy and a new campus in Ireland. The key to Sacred Heart's mission is a focus on real-world learning situations that add fire to students' future goals. "Learning is about living—it's about experiencing." This means concrete, real-life study. Drawing on the rich resources both in Connecticut and in New York City, students are connected with research and internship experiences ranging from co-ops at international advertising agencies for marketing students, to joint research with faculty on life in the Long Island Sound for biology majors. These experiential learning opportunities are complemented by a rich student life program offering over 80 clubs and organizations, including strong music programs, media clubs, and academic groups. To navigate all of the opportunities available, all freshmen are assigned a mentor who works with students one-on-one to ensure that students focus on their holistic development and on the learning process both in and out of the classroom. Mentors also act as a support system during the transition to college. We are a liberal arts university in the Catholic intellectual tradition and that means we work from the person first."

For even more information on this school, turn to page 519 of the "Stats" section.

Saint Anselm College

100 Saint Anselm Drive, Manchester, NH 03102-1310 • Admissions: 888-4ANSELM
Fax: 603-641-7550 • Financial Aid: financial_aid@anselm.edu • Website: www.anselm.edu

Ratings
Quality of Life: 75   Academic: 85   Admissions: 85   Financial Aid: 74

Academics

"There is a really strong sense of community among students, faculty, and the monastic community" at Saint Anselm College, a small, Benedictine, liberal arts school in frosty New England. Students love "the one-on-one support of professors and the mentorship they provide," telling us, "if you are looking toward graduate study, you will stand out among other candidates due to the freedom you have to get involved with professors' work here." Notes one undergrad, "When people here say their doors are always open, they really mean it. Countless times I have been able to walk right into the offices of the Dean, the Dean of Students, any professor, and even the President. Their commitment to the students is absolutely unquestionable." Most here love "the very strong humanities program," a required two-year sequence that "teaches you to think about what is important in life. The overarching theme of the program is 'portraits of human greatness.' It provides discussion on things many normally would not think about." Required philosophy and theology classes as well as an intermediate-level language requirement all "help you become a more well-rounded person." Saint A's is notoriously tough academically; "I have never had to work so hard in my life for a good grade, but I have also never enjoyed learning as much as I am enjoying it here," writes one student. Observes another, "Saint A's is nicknamed 'Saint C's.' It is extremely difficult to receive an 'A' here, which makes the students work harder to be the few who do receive them."

> **SURVEY SAYS . . .**
> *Great library*
> *Diversity lacking on campus*
> *Great food on campus*
> *Lots of beer drinking*

Life

Saint Anselm "is a beautiful, small, and homey school" where "you are truly welcomed when you get here." After that, it's time to get to work. "You cannot have too much of a social life here at St. Anselm because the course requirements are so challenging," students warn, but "that's not to say you can't have fun." Students report that "from Monday to Thursday there isn't a whole lot that goes on unless you join a club or sport." Weekends are more active, as there's "always something entertaining to do, from open mic nights, to trips into Boston/NYC, to gingerbread house-building contests. These are always student-run and student-funded." You'll also "find a party if you're on a mission to find one, but it will most likely be off-campus [because] the rules on campus are so strict that it feels like you're in ninth grade again." Students often make the trip into Manchester, which "has a lot going on, from our semi-pro hockey team, the Manchester Monarchs (only $11 a ticket), to bars and clubs that hold college nights specifically targeting Saint A's students," as well as "a mall, places to eat, go bowling, and see movies." There's a lot of good skiing in the area, too, and Boston isn't too far down the road. Community service is big; in fact, "about 80 percent of students and faculty are involved to some degree." One student sums up life this way: "Our school is infamous for strict inter-visitation hours, an arduous humanities program, hours of reading, severe grade deflation, and monks around the campus."

Student Body

The "mostly white, Irish Catholic" undergrads of Saint Anselm "are more than likely to talk with a Boston accent," as "most kids are from Boston or from small towns in New England." Prep-school grads are strongly represented, but so are public-school students. Explains one undergrad, "There are mainly two groups of students: the ones who received excellent aid packages and the ones whose parents are very well-off. The wealth of some students can be a put-off to others" and there are a few reports of rudeness between the two groups. Most here "are hard-working, friendly, and love being involved. By involved, I do not just mean in volunteer work (though we have a large amount of that on campus), but involved in intramural sports, clubs, and other activities." While "there aren't many atypical students…those who are here are welcomed."

ADMISSIONS

Very important factors considered include: Character/personal qualities, secondary school record. *Important factors considered include:* Class rank, essays, recommendations, standardized test scores, talent/ability. *Other factors considered include:* Alumni/ae relation, extracurricular activities, geographical residence, interview, minority status, volunteer work, work experience. SAT Reasoning or ACT required. TOEFL required of all international applicants. High school diploma is required, and GED is accepted. *Academic units required:* 4 English, 3 math, 3 science (3 science lab), 2 foreign language, 2 social studies, 1 history, 3 academic electives. *Academic units recommended:* 4 math, 4 science, 4 foreign language, 2 history.

The Inside Word

St. Anselm gets a predominately regional applicant pool, and Massachusetts is one of its biggest suppliers of students. An above average-academic record should be more than adequate to gain admission.

FINANCIAL AID

Students should submit: FAFSA, CSS/Financial Aid PROFILE. Regular filing deadline 3/15. The Princeton Review suggests that all financial aid forms be submitted as soon as possible after 1/1. *Need-based scholarships/grants offered:* Pell, SEOG, state scholarships/grants, private scholarships, the school's own gift aid. *Loan aid offered:* FFEL Subsidized Stafford, FFEL Unsubsidized Stafford, FFEL PLUS, Federal Perkins, GATE student loans. Applicants will be notified of awards on or about 3/15. Federal Work-study Program available. Institutional employment available. Off-campus job opportunities are excellent.

FROM THE ADMISSIONS OFFICE

"Why St. Anselm? The answer lies with our graduates. Not only do our alumni go on to successful careers in medicine, law, human services, and other areas, but they also make connections on campus that last a lifetime. With small classes, professors are accessible and approachable. The Benedictine monks serve not only as founders of the college, but as teachers, mentors, and spiritual leaders.

"St. Anselm is rich in history, but certainly not stuck in a bygone era. In fact, the college has launched a $50 million fundraising campaign, which will significantly increase funding for financial aid, academic programs, and technology. New initiatives include the New Hampshire Institute of Politics, where the guest list includes every major candidate from the 2000 presidential race, as well as other political movers and shakers. Not a political junkie? No problem. The NHIOP is a diverse undertaking that also involves elements of psychology, history, theology, ethics, and statistics.

"St. Anselm encourages students to challenge themselves academically and to lead lives that are both creative and generous. On that note, more than 40 percent of our students participate in community service locally and globally. Each year, about 150 students take part in Spring Break Alternative to help those less fortunate across the United States and Latin America. High expectations and lofty goals are hallmarks of a St. Anselm College education, and each student is encouraged to achieve his/her full potential here. Why St. Anselm? Accept the challenge and soon you will discover your own answers."

For even more information on this school, turn to page 519 of the "Stats" section.

SAINT JOSEPH COLLEGE

1678 ASYLUM AVENUE, WEST HARTFORD, CT 06117 • ADMISSIONS: 866-44-CTSJC • FAX: 860-233-5695
E-MAIL: ADMISSIONS@MERCY.SJC.EDU • WEBSITE: WWW.SJC.EDU

Ratings
Quality of Life: 75   **Academic:** 78   **Admissions:** 69   **Financial Aid:** 63

Academics

"Whenever people ask me where I go to college and I tell them Saint Joseph College, they automatically say 'Wow, that's a great nursing school,'" writes one student, adding, "I never even have to tell them what I go to SJC for." While this small, Catholic, all-women's college has other strong areas—its science programs, for example, are "rigorous" and its "teacher preparation/education programs are well regarded"—nursing tops the list. It's a challenging program, one that "lots of students fail out of," but for women seeking nursing opportunities in the Hartford area, SJC can be a real ticket puncher. All students at SJC must complete a number of challenging requirements, including completing a writing portfolio. Even so, outside of the school's premier disciplines, "there is an interesting mix of serious students and those who seem less goal-oriented. This is largely influenced by the demands of several academic disciplines that are pursued more fervently by a handful of students." SJC professors "are wonderful" and the classes "are nice and small, even the lectures;" but the administration, unfortunately, "is extremely unorganized" and occasionally a bit tightfisted. One student explains, "We have to fight tooth and nail just to get simple things that everyone should have like paper towels." Students also cite difficulty in getting the school to fix the "horrid food [and] terrible Internet situation."

> **SURVEY SAYS . . .**
> *Small classes*
> *Athletic facilities are great*
> *Students love West Hartford, CT*
> *Frats and sororities are unpopular*
> *or nonexistent*
> *Very little drug use*

Life

"Everybody knows everybody else; it's like a small-town atmosphere" at Saint Joseph, and like most small towns, "it can get really quiet here," especially on weekends when "just about everyone goes home." One undergrad says, "The atmosphere is good for doing homework, but it stinks when you're bored. There's just really not a lot to do on campus on the weekends." Restrictive visitation rules, and "confined living quarters" result in students throwing parties at off-campus locations, especially "the dance clubs of West Hartford." One student adds, "We'll sometimes just go out to eat in West Hartford or Hartford with a bunch of people, just to get away and relax." For the most part, students are not fans of the cafeteria food. On a positive note, SJC's campus "is beautiful and immaculately maintained." While West Hartford and Hartford may not be some students' idea of fun destinations, New Haven, Boston, and New York City are all within reasonable driving distances, at least for day trips.

Student Body

The typical student at SJC "is female, traditional college aged, and quite mainstream in her ideals, dress/grooming, recreational pursuits, and social habits." Women at Saint Joseph take a similar no-nonsense approach to school. Students say, "For the most part, we actually want to be here and actually do the work." Many students live close enough to commute, which hampers the development of an active extracurricular scene. Again, "guys have to be out of the dorms by 11:30 P.M. on weekdays and 1:30 A.M. on the weekends. I think this is the reason why a lot of people leave on the weekends, and a big reason why there is a lack of a social life on this campus." Students seem happy with the level of diversity and say, "There are many Asian, Latina, and black students" at the school, as well as a considerable number of nontraditional students.

ADMISSIONS

Very important factors considered include: Secondary school record, standardized test scores. *Other factors considered include:* Alumni/ae relation, character/personal qualities, essays, extracurricular activities, interview, recommendations, volunteer work. SAT Reasoning or ACT required. TOEFL required of all international applicants. High school diploma is required, and GED is accepted. *Academic units recommended:* 4 English, 3 math, 3 science, 2 foreign language, 2 social studies, 2 history.

The Inside Word

Good thing the campus lies within walking distance of the Hartford scene, as on-campus students still need off-campus mobility to pursue all the school's academic and extracurricular avenues. Saint Joseph is a visually beautiful school unless you find a dearth of boys aesthetically displeasing.

FINANCIAL AID

Students should submit: FAFSA. Regular filing deadline 6/30. The Princeton Review suggests that all financial aid forms be submitted as soon as possible after 1/1. *Need-based scholarships/grants offered:* Pell, SEOG, state scholarships/grants, private scholarships, the school's own gift aid. *Loan aid offered:* FFEL Subsidized Stafford, FFEL Unsubsidized Stafford, FFEL PLUS, Federal Perkins, state loans, Connecticut Family Education Loan Program. Applicants will be notified of awards on a rolling basis beginning on or about 2/1.

FROM THE ADMISSIONS OFFICE

"Saint Joseph College was founded in 1932 by the Sisters of Mercy to provide higher education opportunities for women. Over the years, the college has remained true to this vision, offering students solid professional training grounded in a tradition rich in the liberal arts. Consistently cited on the national level for the quality of its academic programs, Saint Joseph College is committed to responding to the needs of an ever-changing society. Today, the college serves the needs of a diverse, intergenerational student body while remaining true to its original mission.

"The beautiful 84-acre West Hartford campus houses The Women's College, the coeducational Prime Time Program and Graduate School, and The Gengras Center. Located one block from campus is the renowned School for Young Children, one of the earliest childhood centers in the state. The School for Young Children also serves as an on-site laboratory for preschool teacher training. The college's newest facility, The Carol Autorino Center for the Arts and Humanities, houses a 350-seat auditorium, five art galleries to showcase the college's extensive fine arts collections, classrooms, faculty offices, and more. The campus is easily accessible and offers ample parking, residence halls, dining facilities, the Pope Pius XII Library with more than 133,700 volumes and online resources, The O'Connell Athletic Center, and a state-of-the-art Information Technology Network Center."

For even more information on this school, turn to page 520 of the "Stats" section.

SAINT JOSEPH'S UNIVERSITY

5600 CITY AVENUE, PHILADELPHIA, PA 19131 • ADMISSIONS: 888-BE-A-HAWK • FAX: 610-660-1314
E-MAIL: ADMIT@SJU.EDU • WEBSITE: WWW.SJU.EDU

Ratings
Quality of Life: 78   Academic: 80   Admissions: 90   Financial Aid: 74

Academics

To appreciate Saint Joseph's University, students need to embrace liberal arts education for its breadth. Those who resist the strict curriculum outline complain that "half of [the] classes will have absolutely nothing to do with your major, and more than 10 percent of your courses will be religion and philosophy." One savvy student says, "If you make friends with your professors and advisors, miracles can happen" in terms of requirements. One premed student, illustrating the slight friction between the College of

Arts and Science and the business school, says, "Business majors can usually be found crying about the one large presentation they have to do at the end of any given semester." Course rigor clearly varies across disciplines. Some students believe "you work for your grades," while others think "it is fairly easy, and you can get away with a lot." On the topic of the attendance policy, one marketing major says, "If a student can miss class and still do well, it should be celebrated, not penalized." For those who do skip, "tutors and note takers are very effective and always available." The administration succeeds "at its job of growing SJU" but is not so great at managing student life. As Saint Joseph's strives to "catch up to Georgetown and Boston College," it enjoys good local standing. "An SJU degree in Philly is like gold," says a sophomore in sociology. Although "a lot of cheaper schools can provide a comparable education, [the] networking provided by alumni" give graduates an edge. A junior agrees, "I'm in no rush to leave, but it is hard to stay when they make doing well and finding a job so easy."

Life

Jesuits may run the school, but the students have no interest in living like monks. Even as resident advisors police dorm life, "there is always alcohol in almost every room." Students wish that administrators would understand that "people are going to drink and have parties no matter what." The course load permits students "to go out on weeknights and still manage their schedules." In some ways, SJU is "actually very reserved compared to the other colleges in the area." Frats are not considered cool at SJU, which leaves the twenty-one and under crew unsure of what to do. A program called "SJU 'til 2" offers Friday and Saturday night alternatives to drinking and partying. School spirit is evident in high basketball game attendance and the proliferation of SJU gear.

Student Body

The classic SJU student is not only well rounded but also well dressed. For some, a moneyed childhood gave the false impression that "most people in America have the same chances they were blessed with." Designer labels, "shamelessly on display," correlate with particular cliques. Groups of friends from the area's Catholic high schools quickly seek one another out. By one summary, "Everyone loves bars. Everyone loves George W. Bush. Everyone loves the basketball team." Others try to correct what they see as a misperception of uniformity at their school. "Just because SJU kids 'don't have blue hair or tons of body piercings doesn't mean that they aren't free-thinkers." Rainbow Week celebrates the diversity of sexual minorities, but gay students don't push it with overt activism or public displays of affection. Some students have seen minorities transfer out of the school—"life for minority students can range from terrible to okay"—and others believe that no matter how outlying, "you will find a group of friends; it is guaranteed."

ADMISSIONS

Very important factors considered include: Class rank, essays, recommendations, secondary school record, standardized test scores. *Other factors considered include:* Alumni/ae relation, character/personal qualities, extracurricular activities, talent/ability, volunteer work, work experience. SAT Reasoning or ACT required. TOEFL required of all international applicants. High school diploma is required, and GED is not accepted. *Academic units required:* 4 English, 3 math, 2 science (1 science lab), 2 foreign language, 1 history, 2 academic electives. *Academic units recommended:* 4 English, 3 math, 3 science (1 science lab), 2 foreign language, 1 social studies, 1 history, 2 academic electives.

The Inside Word

Despite a growing applicant pool, the credentials that enrolled students generally bring to the table have not changed much in recent years. Those with GPAs above 3.5 and SAT scores above 1200 should not face many problems gaining admission as long as they take the application process seriously.

FINANCIAL AID

Students should submit: FAFSA. Regular filing deadline 5/1. The Princeton Review suggests that all financial aid forms be submitted as soon as possible after 1/1. *Need-based scholarships/grants offered:* Pell, SEOG, state scholarships/grants, private scholarships, the school's own gift aid. *Loan aid offered:* FFEL Subsidized Stafford, FFEL Unsubsidized Stafford, FFEL PLUS, Federal Perkins. Applicants will be notified of awards on a rolling basis beginning on or about 2/15. Federal Work-study Program available. Institutional employment available. Off-campus job opportunities are good.

FROM THE ADMISSIONS OFFICE

"Founded by the Society of Jesus in 1851, Saint Joseph's University advances the professional and personal ambitions of men and women by providing a demanding, yet supportive, educational experience. One of only 142 schools with a Phi Beta Kappa chapter and AACSB business school accreditation, Saint Joseph's is home to 3,950 full-time undergraduates and 3,300 graduate, part-time and doctoral students. Steeped in the 450-year Jesuit tradition of scholarship and service, the university strives to be recognized as the preeminent Catholic comprehensive university in the Northeast."

For even more information on this school, turn to page 520 of the "Stats" section.

SAINT MICHAEL'S COLLEGE

One Winooski Park, Colchester, VT 05439 • Admissions: 802-654-3000 • Fax: 802-654-2591
E-mail: ADMISSION@SMCVT.EDU • Website: WWW.SMCVT.EDU

Ratings
Quality of Life: 95   **Academic:** 87   **Admissions:** 85   **Financial Aid:** 79

Academics

The inclusive atmosphere at Saint Michael's college is "all about creating a comfortable, caring place for students, professors, visitors, and neighboring people." First-year students quickly find themselves in seminars, and "lecture-based classes always leave room for questions." An English major appreciates that professors "aren't afraid to teach pas-

> **SURVEY SAYS . . .**
> *Small classes*
> *Frats and sororities are unpopular*
> *or nonexistent*

sionately." A junior majoring in sociology adds, "[They keep in touch] even while I was abroad or home for the summer. They would e-mail me articles I might enjoy or just say hello." Students expected conservative teachers at a Catholic school but found "90 percent liberals" instead. The broad-minded approach encourages students "to challenge yourself, your peers, professors, and leaders around the world." The faculty spans "geniuses who deserve to be at a better school and charlatans who somehow got tenure." SMC isn't considered a school for science majors, "unless you're interested in theory." Subsequently, physics majors find themselves in "classes of one or four people." The college's main strength lies in international business; the mandated religion courses "are more like ethical discussions than anything else." Students report that they can easily find help from their classmates. "The student-staffed tutoring program and writing center are both well run and provide a comfortable environment for improving 'academics." As an institution "devoted to social justice and community service," much of the learning "happens outside of the classroom." The college prioritizes "a high level of awareness regarding world events" among its students.

Life

Burlington, Vermont, considered "the best location imaginable," wins 'SMC students over with its quaint waterfront and blooming music scene. "Church Street is so interesting and quaint with tons of cool stores and interesting side shops." When May finals roll around, "everyone loves to go down to North Beach and sunbathe. Some daring [students] even go in Lake Champlain." Students survive the winters by participating in winter sports and drinking. The school-subsidized twenty-five dollar season passes to 'Smuggler's Notch ski resort helps students save money for the bars. The 21 and under crowd gets drunk before and after the alcohol-free dances or makes the trek to Montreal. Of the "forty groups with substantial budgets on campus," MOVE attracts the most students, putting more than 85 percent to work in community service at some point during their SMC career. Many students sign up for "correctional volleyball," where they play with local inmates. The popular Wilderness Program leads hiking and climbing outings, even a kayaking trip to Maine. An upperclassman says, "There is no way you could ever be bored on this campus."

Student Body

Students find that their school "lives up to all the hype about having a friendly and supportive community." For example, "everyone hugs at 'SMC. Whenever you see anyone you know, you are a greeted by a big hug." Even a Republican Yankees fan from Vermont claims to get along with the majority of "Democrat Red Sox fans from Massachusetts." Among the 2,000 students, we find common ground in a shared enthusiasm for winter sports and (mostly left-wing) political action. A senior says, "Most students do volunteer work, enjoy low-key partying, and care about grades but more about experiences."

ADMISSIONS

Very important factors considered include: Class rank, secondary school record. *Important factors considered include:* Character/personal qualities, essays, extracurricular activities, recommendations, standardized test scores, talent/ability. *Other factors considered include:* Alumni/ae relation, geographical residence, interview, minority status, volunteer work, work experience. SAT Reasoning or ACT required. TOEFL required of all international applicants. High school diploma is required, and GED is accepted. *Academic units required:* 4 English, 3 math, 3 science (2 science lab), 3 foreign language, 3 social studies. *Academic units recommended:* 4 English, 4 math, 4 science (3 science lab), 4 foreign language, 4 social studies.

The Inside Word

The school is as selective as it is because it trusts students to live up to its Catholic and academic standards without a lot of handholding after admittance. The noninterventionist attitude on campus spills over into nearby Burlington, but keep in mind that Vermont as a whole is strict about underage drinking.

FINANCIAL AID

Students should submit: FAFSA, institution's own financial aid form, parent and student federal tax forms and W-2 forms. Regular filing deadline 3/15. The Princeton Review suggests that all financial aid forms be submitted as soon as possible after 1/1. *Need-based scholarships/grants offered:* Pell, SEOG, state scholarships/grants, private scholarships, the school's own gift aid. *Loan aid offered:* FFEL Subsidized Stafford, FFEL Unsubsidized Stafford, FFEL PLUS, Federal Perkins. Applicants will be notified of awards on a rolling basis beginning on or about 4/1. Federal Work-study Program available. Institutional employment available. Off-campus job opportunities are excellent.

FROM THE ADMISSIONS OFFICE

"With nearly 95 percent of undergraduates living on campus, Saint Michael's College is committed to creating a life-changing educational experience for a diverse student population from throughout the United States and the world. Striking the perfect balance between a busy college town and a spectacular outdoor wilderness, our 440-acre campus is located between Lake Champlain and the majestic Green Mountains, just outside Burlington, Vermont's largest city and home to four colleges, including the University of Vermont. When not excelling in one of the fine academic programs that places Saint Michael's in the top tier of *U.S. News & World Report* rankings, three out of four students spend their time in our wide-reaching Wilderness Programs, in our extensive service program, or in recreational and Northeast-10 sports. Wilderness Programs bring students into the great Vermont outdoors for river rafting, sea kayaking, rock- and ice-climbing, hiking, skiing, snowboarding, and other adventure sports as well as survival training from beginner to advanced certification levels. MOVE, our student-led volunteer corps run in concert with our Edmundite Campus Ministry, earned Saint Michael's a place in history as the 32nd Point of Light for engendering lifelong community service. Some 625 students rack up 42,000 hours of service a year building houses through Habitat for Humanity; working as tutors, youth mentors, and companions for the elderly; and fighting hunger and homelessness. One in four students takes part in 21 NCAA Division II intercollegiate sports (all but six in the Northeast-10 Conference). Meeting the needs of a diverse student population also means providing healthy living options, including GREAT Housing, through which 20 percent of students choose to create and live in a drug- and alcohol-free environment."

For even more information on this school, turn to page 520 of the "Stats" section.

SALISBURY UNIVERSITY

Admissions Office, 1101 Camden Avenue, Salisbury, MD 21801 • Admissions: 410-543-6161
Fax: 410-546-6016 • Financial Aid: 410-543-6165 • E-mail: admissions@salisbury.edu • Website: www.salisbury.edu

Ratings

Quality of Life: 81   **Academic:** 76   **Admissions:** 83   **Financial Aid:** 66

Academics

"Small, personable, and beautiful" Salisbury University, a state school on Maryland's Eastern Shore, is "large enough to be diverse, yet small enough to walk anywhere you need to go." Students here love that "teachers get to know you as students rather than a number, and they are able to help you at a more personable level." Salisbury is probably best known for its Perdue School of Business, the most popular program among undergraduates. Students report that "the school is about teaching students how to become more professional and giving them the skills to be successful in the real world of business." Also noteworthy is the Henson School of Science, which recently received a boost via a new facility "with incredible resources and great technology that provide a flood of information." And don't forget education, Salisbury's longest-running program; "Salisbury was originally a teacher's school before it opened its doors to other majors," undergrads remind us. Students across programs laud the "great internship opportunities, excellent study-abroad programs, and professors who are dedicated and open minded." As at all smaller schools and nearly all state-funded schools, not all aspects of academic life are first-rate. Arts and music students complain that "the school constantly underfunds us," and everyone agrees that "the library is ancient and small, only two floors with mostly old reference books no one uses." An honors program offers top students "small, almost entirely discussion-based classes."

> **SURVEY SAYS . . .**
> *Small classes*
> *Lab facilities are great*
> *Great computer facilities*
> *Students are happy*
> *Lots of beer drinking*

Life

"Salisbury is a big party school," many students tell us, and apparently locals agree: The "farmer's town" of Salisbury recently passed restrictions on off-campus housing intended to curtail the party scene. As you might guess, town-gown relations aren't the best. One student reports, "The locals hate us; we do not get along whatsoever. They are not willing to accept the fact that we are here and we are not leaving." The school and students are trying to address the problem by scheduling more appealing on-campus events and providing services such as SafeRide, a "student-run drunk bus that gets the kids home safe, for free, and without getting written up." But there's more going on at Salisbury besides the parties. Students can dabble in "over 100 active student organizations" including "a student-run program called SOAP that schedules movies, comedians and other interesting stuff" as well as "school-sponsored trips, activities, and on-campus festivals." Athletics are solid, as "Salisbury is among the top teams in Division III in almost every sport." When the weather is nice, students frequently take the half-hour drive to Ocean City and other beach resort areas. Annapolis, Baltimore, and DC are the nearest large cities, but most here agree that "they are a bit far" for regular visits.

Student Body

Students tell us that at Salisbury, "everyone fits in somewhere." That includes "those who want to party and drink all the time, those who like to study all the time, those who study all week and party and drink on the weekends, and those who just like to chill out and have fun." One junior tells us her motto is: "Study hard so you can party harder." Most students are "very laid back and dress comfortably," like those who enjoying coming to "class in his or her pajamas, yet who still manages to finish the work that is supposed to be done." Salisbury's students, generally speaking, are "active in either a social group, fraternity, or club...study for about two hours a day outside of class," and "come from Maryland, Delaware, or New Jersey." While there are "a lot of white, middle-class preppy types" here, they mix in with "students from all over the world, so it's very diverse and interesting." Out of all of this come "a lot of unique or atypical students, especially in the art, anthropology, biology, philosophy, and music departments." Some students detect a divide between the minority (on-campus residents) and the majority (commuters), pointing out that "people who live on campus have a lot more time to interact with one another."

ADMISSIONS

Very important factors considered include: Secondary school record, state residency. *Important factors considered include:* Alumni/ae relation, class rank, extracurricular activities, geographical residence, standardized test scores, talent/ability. *Other factors considered include:* Character/personal qualities, essays, interview, minority status, recommendations, volunteer work, work experience. SAT Reasoning or ACT required. TOEFL required of all international applicants. High school diploma is required, and GED is accepted. *Academic units required:* 4 English, 3 math, 3 science (2 science lab), 2 foreign language, 3 social studies. *Academic units recommended:* 4 English, 4 math, 4 science (3 science lab), 3 foreign language, 3 social studies, 3 academic electives.

The Inside Word

As a part of the new wave of public institutions of higher learning focusing their energies on undergraduate research, Salisbury has seen its admissions standards and the quality of its freshman class steadily improve over the past few years. As a result, candidate review is also more personalized than the formula-driven approaches of most public colleges. The admissions committee will pay close attention to the match you make with the university, evaluating your entire background instead of simply your numbers—though most students are strong academically to begin with.

FINANCIAL AID

Students should submit: FAFSA. The Princeton Review suggests that all financial aid forms be submitted as soon as possible after 1/1. *Need-based scholarships/grants offered:* Pell, SEOG, state scholarships/grants, the school's own gift aid. *Loan aid offered:* Direct Subsidized Stafford, Direct Unsubsidized Stafford, Direct PLUS, Federal Perkins. Applicants will be notified of awards on a rolling basis beginning on or about 4/1. Federal Work-study Program available. Institutional employment available. Off-campus job opportunities are good.

FROM THE ADMISSIONS OFFICE

"Friendly, convenient, safe, and beautiful are just a few of the words used to describe the campus of Salisbury University. The campus is a compact, self-contained community that offers the full range of student services. Beautiful, traditional-style architecture and impeccably landscaped grounds combine to create an atmosphere that inspires learning and fosters student pride. Located just 30 minutes from the beaches of Ocean City, Maryland, SU students enjoy a year-round resort social life as well as an inside track on summer jobs. Situated less than two hours from the urban excitement of Baltimore and Washington, DC, greater Salisbury makes up for its lack of size—its population is about 80,000—by being strategically located. Within easy driving distance of a number of other major cities, including New York City, Philadelphia, and Norfolk, Salisbury is the hub of the Delmarva Peninsula, a mostly rural region flavored by the salty air of the Chesapeake Bay and Atlantic Ocean."

For even more information on this school, turn to page 521 of the "Stats" section.

SALVE REGINA UNIVERSITY

100 Ochre Point Avenue, Newport, RI 02840-4192 • Admissions: 401-341-2908 • Fax: 401-848-2823
E-mail: sruadmis@salve.edu • Website: www.salve.edu

Ratings
Quality of Life: 81   **Academic:** 80   **Admissions:** 85   **Financial Aid:** 70

Academics

"An excellent 'under the radar' academic institution," Salve Regina is a Catholic school that "has deeply adopted the ideals of its founding Sisters of Mercy; [this is] not necessarily a Catholic mission, but a humanitarian one. They are all dedicated to the betterment of ourselves and of one another, and Salve students graduate with a love of life and a desire to make the world a better place, particularly for those less fortunate." In keeping with its mission, Salve excels in service-oriented professions such as education and nursing. Business, theater arts, and psychology are also reportedly popular with undergrads. In most disciplines, "professors are terrific. They are always willing to meet with [students] if [they] need extra help or just want to go over a paper. They make classes interesting and get to know each student in their classes." In addition, because "no class has more than 35 students, you are not a number, [but] a name" at Salve. One student explains, "If you like small classroom settings instead of lecture halls, Salve is a great school to attend." Another adds, "Here, there are people who support your decisions, no matter what. Plus, who wouldn't mind a class with an ocean view?"

> **SURVEY SAYS . . .**
> *Small classes*
> *Great library*
> *Students love Newport, RI*
> *Great off-campus food*
> *Frats and sororities are unpopular*
> *or nonexistent*

Life

Salve is "located on the cliffs of Newport, facing the ocean," lending a beach-resort vibe to extracurricular life. Sophomore and upperclass student residences are largely repurposed mansions and cottages; these are definitely not your standard-issue college dormitories. Although residence hall regulations "are more strict than at most schools—[administrators] are really strict about drinking, and they're also very strict about opposite sex visitors in the dorms"—students tell us that "it doesn't stop you from having fun. Most parties happen off campus, and they are very easy to get to." Newport is considered a major social asset, with "so much to do." One student says, "We go dancing, we go to the bars, and there are a lot of tourist things to do." For those who seek a more sedate social scene, "the school provides a ton of things to do on weekends. It tries to keep the kids entertained." While the school's Newport address allows for "plenty of swimming and tanning at the beach," it also means that "it can be very windy and cold," especially during the long New England winters. True to the school's Sisters of Mercy mission, community service projects are very big.

Student Body

Many describe themselves as "glad to be here." The typical Salve undergrad is a "combination of studious and fun-loving," ready to do whatever is necessary to keep up grades but also not immune to the appeal of Newport. Undergrads tend to be female (by about a 2:1 ratio) and "preppy, but nice; very attractive and well-groomed; [and] occasionally snobby." Diversity is not the school's strong suit; one student calculates, "[About] 97 percent of the campus is white, 1 percent is black, 1 percent is Asian and 1 percent is 'other.'" A senior majoring in English says, "We are leaders, example setters, dedicated to academia, community service, and the future of mankind. I honestly don't think that there are many students who do not fit that role."

ADMISSIONS

Very important factors considered include: Class rank, secondary school record, standardized test scores. *Important factors considered include:* Character/personal qualities, essays, extracurricular activities, minority status, recommendations, talent/ability, volunteer work, work experience. *Other factors considered include:* Alumni/ae relation. SAT Reasoning or ACT required. TOEFL required of all international applicants. High school diploma is required, and GED is accepted. *Academic units required:* 4 English, 3 math, 2 science (2 science lab), 2 foreign language, 1 social studies, 4 academic electives.

The Inside Word

Don't be fooled by the easy admissions because Salve Regina students are challenged to reach higher once admitted to achieve their undergraduate and professional goals. This picturesque campus affords you the perfect opportunity to kick back and . . . study. Partying takes place outside Salve's walls, in Newport and Providence.

FINANCIAL AID

Students should submit: FAFSA, CSS/Financial Aid PROFILE, noncustodial (divorced/separated) parents' statement, business/farm supplement. The Princeton Review suggests that all financial aid forms be submitted as soon as possible after 1/1. *Need-based scholarships/grants offered:* Pell, SEOG, state scholarships/grants, private scholarships, the school's own gift aid. *Loan aid offered:* FFEL Subsidized Stafford, FFEL Unsubsidized Stafford, FFEL PLUS, Federal Perkins, Federal Nursing, state loans, college/university loans from institutional funds, private loans. Applicants will be notified of awards on a rolling basis beginning on or about 3/1. Off-campus job opportunities are excellent.

FROM THE ADMISSIONS OFFICE

"Salve Regina University is a small university with big opportunity. Located on one of the most beautiful campuses in the country, Salve Regina's historic oceanfront campus is a place where students feel at home. Students study and live in historic mansions, yet receive an education that prepares them for modern careers and a lifetime of serving their communities. Salve offers excellent pre-professional and liberal arts programs (most popular are business, education, administration of justice, and biology). The classes are small and are all taught by professors (no grad assistants). Salve's small size also makes it easy for students to get involved on campus with clubs, activities, athletics, or intramurals. At Salve, it is easy to become a leader—even in your first year.

"Newport offers the perfect location for students who love history, sailing, and the outdoors. Students can surf, ocean kayak from First Beach, or bike ride on the famous Ocean Drive. Newport also hosts several festivals throughout the year. All students get a free statewide trolley/bus pass that takes them throughout Newport or to Providence, only 30 minutes away.

"Admission to Salve Regina is competitive. The Admissions Office looks at several factors in reviewing applications. Most important are applicants' day-to-day academic work and the level of the courses they have taken. Recommendation letters and test scores are also reviewed, as are leadership positions and community involvement."

For even more information on this school, turn to page 521 of the "Stats" section.

SARAH LAWRENCE COLLEGE

One Mead Way, Bronxville, NY 10708-5999 • Admissions: 914-395-2510 • Fax: 914-395-2676
Financial Aid: 914-395-2570 • E-mail: SLCADMIT@MAIL.SLC.EDU • Website: WWW.SLC.EDU

Ratings
Quality of Life: 68   **Academic:** 96   **Admissions:** 93   **Financial Aid:** 87

Academics

Sarah Lawrence gives students "the ability to choose: choose your classes, choose your don (advisor), choose to do everything, or choose to do one specific thing. It's all about having the freedom to design your own academic plan, to make your own choices about your own life." With no core curriculum and no formal majors, SLC students are limited in their class selections here only by catalog listings and their own areas of interests. SLC undergrads take three classes per semester. There are few exams; rather, students write lots of short papers for class plus "15- to 35-page semester-long papers" based on their work in conferences, "semi-weekly one-on-one meetings with professors." Undergrads can request to see their grades, but many bypass that option and choose to focus on the thorough written evaluations they receive for each course. Most here love the freedom, although a few warn that "you can create a very unfocused academic program and screw yourself over on transferring to another school" if you aren't careful. Also, "no grades for some students tends to translate into 'I don't have to do anything if I don't want to,'" a problem especially for those who have trouble self-motivating. For those amenable to the system—particularly those interested in theater, dancing, studio arts, writing, philosophy, and education, the school's strongest areas—SLC can be the perfect place, a school that "deeply encourages a personal creativity and fosters accomplishment. While you're here, you can really do anything academically or creatively. It is this freedom that truly allows you to bloom into a creative and intelligent adult."

> **SURVEY SAYS . . .**
> *Class discussions encouraged*
> *Small classes*
> *No one cheats*
> *Frats and sororities are unpopular*
> *or nonexistent*
> *Theater is popular*
> *Political activism is popular*
> *(Almost) everyone smokes*

Life

Undergrads at SLC tend to congregate in small groups, often to enjoy a quiet evening discussing school, cooking dinner, and watching movies. New York City is close by, so "going to the city for concerts, shopping, and museum-hopping" is regularly added to many students' day planners. On campus, "there's always something of interest going on, whether it be a classical music performance, a theater show, an ice cream social, or Ultimate Frisbee™." Political activism is also big. Parties, however, are infrequent; "Large, open parties have to be registered with the college, which makes the social situation a little weird," students tell us. So, too, does the lopsided female to male ratio—which, coupled with the small student body, is seen as a severe limitation to social life by quite a few students. SLC's campus "is beautiful and cozy, with lots of trees, grass, boulders, and pathways. Most of the dorms are also beautiful," although some complain that "the older buildings are falling apart on the inside. They need to be refurbished." Town–gown relations with Bronxville and nearby Yonkers could be better; writes one student, "We could try to create more to do in the town of Bronxville, as relations are somewhat strained. In reality, there's not much of a relationship at all."

Student Body

"With the school motto being 'You are different; so are we,' the atypical student is the typical student" at Sarah Lawrence. Adds another, "Sarah Lawrence is made up of the kids who didn't have anywhere to sit at lunch in high school, and we all get along famously, even the people who don't fit into that category." Undergrads are "for the most part highly intelligent and are able to bring up conversations that not only are thought-provoking, but also a lot of fun to participate in." They "are creatively inclined and politically aware. Students usually have an academic area of interest along with an artistic passion." Some feel that "the school could stand to be a little more politically diverse. A few more Republicans wouldn't hurt things." The student body includes "a large number of students who are either gay, lesbian, bisexual, or queer. There are a good number of straight students too, however, and there is little discrimination over sexual orientation, whatever that orientation may be." Some women complain of "an overdose of estrogen here. The hetero males who do go to SLC are spoiled by the abundance of female students."

ADMISSIONS

Very important factors considered include: Character/personal qualities, essays, recommendations, secondary school record. *Important factors considered include:* Extracurricular activities, talent/ability, volunteer work, work experience. *Other factors considered include:* Alumni/ae relation, class rank, geographical residence, interview, minority status. TOEFL required of all international applicants. High school diploma or equivalent is not required. *Academic units required:* 4 English, 2 math, 2 science, 2 foreign language, 2 history. *Academic units recommended:* 4 English, 4 math, 4 science, 4 foreign language, 4 social studies, 4 history.

The Inside Word

The public generally views Sarah Lawrence as an artsy "alternative" college. The college itself avoids this image, preferring instead to evoke an impression that aligns them with more traditional and prestigious northeastern colleges such as the Ivies, Little Ivies, and former Seven Sisters. Both the total number of applicants and the selectivity of the admissions process have increased over the past few years.

FINANCIAL AID

Students should submit: FAFSA, CSS/Financial Aid PROFILE, noncustodial (divorced/separated) parents' statement. Regular filing deadline 2/1. The Princeton Review suggests that all financial aid forms be submitted as soon as possible after 1/1. *Need-based scholarships/grants offered:* Pell, SEOG, state scholarships/grants, private scholarships, the school's own gift aid. *Loan aid offered:* FFEL Subsidized Stafford, FFEL Unsubsidized Stafford, FFEL PLUS, Federal Perkins. Applicants will be notified of awards on or about 4/1.

FROM THE ADMISSIONS OFFICE

"Students who come to Sarah Lawrence are curious about the world, and they have an ardent desire to satisfy that curiosity. Sarah Lawrence offers such students two innovative academic structures: the seminar/conference system and the arts components. Courses in the humanities, social sciences, natural sciences, and mathematics are taught in the seminar/conference style. The seminars enroll an average of 11 students and consist of lecture, discussion, readings, and assigned papers. For each seminar, students also have private tutorials, called conferences, where they conceive of individualized projects and shape them under the direction of professors. Arts components let students combine history and theory with practice. Painters, printmakers, photographers, sculptors and filmmakers, composers, musicians, choreographers, dancers, actors, and directors work in readily available studios, editing facilities, and darkrooms, guided by accomplished professionals. The secure, wooded campus is 30 minutes from New York City, and the diversity of people and ideas at Sarah Lawrence make it an extraordinary educational environment."

For even more information on this school, turn to page 522 of the "Stats" section.

SETON HALL UNIVERSITY

400 SOUTH ORANGE AVENUE, SOUTH ORANGE, NJ 07079-2697 • ADMISSIONS: 973-761-9332
FAX: 973-275-2040 • FINANCIAL AID: 973-761-9332 • E-MAIL: THEHALL@SHU.EDU • WEBSITE: WWW.ADMISSIONS.SHU.EDU

Ratings
Quality of Life: 62   **Academic:** 74   **Admissions:** 80   **Financial Aid:** 66

Academics

Students at Seton Hall praise their school's pre-profession-al and career-specific programs. The education depart-ment, for example, "has a wonderful staff who are readily available and very resourceful," writes one future teacher. A nursing student reported having "an overall good expe-rience with my professors." And a business student bragged that everyone in the b-school is "helpful, nice, and accessible." Students generally praise the deans as "very personable," and report that priests "are very nice too." There's general approbation of the full-time professors, who "work hard to help the students" and who, "because of our wireless campus and email system, are very accessible day or night!" Despite all these assets, Seton Hall also receives some very loud complaints from its undergraduates. "Registration and the money aspect are horrible," most here agree. They also warn that "advisors are the worst part of the entire process. They either don't know what they're doing or they just don't care." Others grouse that "the instructors for the core classes haven't been the best quality" and that "a lot of adjunct professors arrive here after a long day's work at their other job and don't teach us anything." Summing up both the good and bad here, one student writes, "At Seton Hall you can find small class sizes, pro-fessors who care, students who are willing to help each other and a feeling like you belong to a really big fam-ily. Seton Hall has its problems with parking for commuters, living spaces for residents, long lines at the finan-cial aid office, and even longer lines at the bookstore to buy high-priced books."

Life

"A lot of parties go on at Seton Hall" even though the university "has worked really hard to prevent students from doing the typical party scene." Notes one student, "At the beginning of last year, Seton Hall started put-ting pressure on the South Orange Police. The parties are at Greek houses, which are off campus, and now most parties get broken up by the cops." The university crackdown is the result of frequent complaints from the school's neighbors; notes one student bluntly, "The town of South Orange hates college students." As a result, students either hit the frat parties or "travel away from campus, and usually away from South Orange if they plan to do most things." The net result is that many students feel that "Seton Hall University has absolutely no social life for a student who cares naught for alcohol." A good portion of the student body goes home after class-es; as one student put it, "On the weekends the place is so deserted." Many who stick around "just take the train to New York City, which isn't that expensive or hard to get to. It's only a 20-minute ride, so it's what most of us do for fun here. We head for a bar or club in the city." About the only time the campus truly comes togeth-er is to watch the Pirates shoot hoops.

Student Body

Seton Hall is "a very ethnically and culturally diverse school," but by nearly all accounts, students separate themselves into ethnic and racial enclaves. Students typically "are from New York or New Jersey. They are Catholic and either white or Hispanic. On the weekends, everyone goes home, so the campus is deserted except for out-of-state and international students." Mr. Blackwell would probably side with those who complained that their classmates "wear way too much makeup and try to be J. Lo or Ja Rule. It's sick." Added another crit-ic, "Black pants, tight shirts, and the 'Jersey' look, which is trendy, set the tone. There's Coach, Fendi, Gucci, and Tiffany's everywhere. These people think they're upper class." Undergrads tend to be "uninterested in politics at the local, state, and national levels." Most are "involved in at least one extracurricular activity, have a part-time job, and know when to have fun and when to buckle down to do their work."

ADMISSIONS

Very important factors considered include: Essays, recommendations, secondary school record, standardized test scores. *Important factors considered include:* Extracurricular activities, volunteer work, work experience. *Other factors considered include:* Character/personal qualities, class rank, interview, talent/ability. SAT Reasoning or ACT required. TOEFL required of all international applicants. High school diploma is required, and GED is accepted. *Academic units required:* 4 English, 3 math, 1 science, 2 foreign language, 2 social studies, 4 academic electives.

The Inside Word

Getting into Seton Hall shouldn't be too stressful for most average students who have taken a full college-prep curriculum in high school. In the New York metropolitan area there are a lot of schools with similar characteristics, and collectively they take away the large proportion of Seton Hall's admits. Above average students who are serious about the university should be able to parlay their interest into some scholarship dollars, over 300 full scholarships this year.

FINANCIAL AID

Students should submit: FAFSA. The Princeton Review suggests that all financial aid forms be submitted as soon as possible after 1/1. *Need-based scholarships/grants offered:* Pell, SEOG, state scholarships/grants, private scholarships, the school's own gift aid. *Loan aid offered:* FFEL Subsidized Stafford, FFEL Unsubsidized Stafford, FFEL PLUS, Federal Perkins, state loans. Applicants will be notified of awards on a rolling basis beginning on or about 3/1. Federal Work-study Program available. Institutional employment available. Off-campus job opportunities are excellent.

FROM THE ADMISSIONS OFFICE

"As the oldest and largest diocesan university in the United States, Seton Hall University is committed to providing its students with a diverse environment focusing on academic excellence and ethical development. Outstanding faculty, a technologically advanced campus, and a values-centered curriculum challenge Seton Hall students. Through these things and the personal attention students receive, they are prepared to be leaders in their professional and community lives in a global society. Seton Hall's campus offers students up-to-date facilities, including an award-winning library facility opened in 1994 and the state-of-the art Kozlowski Hall, which opened in 1997. The university has invested more than $25 million in the past five years to provide its students and faculty with leading edge information technology. The Mobile Computing Program is widely recognized as one of the nation's best. In 1999 and 2000, Seton Hall was ranked as one of the nation's Most Wired universities by Yahoo! Internet Life magazine. Recent additions to Seton Hall's academic offerings include the School of Diplomacy and International Relations and a number of dual-degree health sciences programs, including physical therapy, physician assistant, and occupational therapy."

For even more information on this school, turn to page 522 of the "Stats" section.

SETON HILL UNIVERSITY

1 SETON HILL DRIVE, GREENSBURG, PA 15601 • ADMISSIONS: 724-838-4255 • FAX: 724-830-1294
E-MAIL: ADMIT@SETONHILL.EDU • WEBSITE: WWW.SETONHILL.EDU

Ratings
Quality of Life: 70   **Academic:** 77   **Admissions:** 75   **Financial Aid:** 74

Academics

Seton Hill is a school that is undergoing a major transition. A few years back, the school began aggressively recruiting male students and billing itself as coeducational; it had previously called itself a women's college, although it did admit some men. In summer 2002, the school received university status, a move intended to reflect its increased focus on graduate study. Understandably, the changes have aroused strong reactions, especially from students who were admitted when Seton Hill was still "predominantly a liberal arts college, built on visual and performing arts, as well as science and more traditional programs." Now the school is "becoming an influential, coeducational university, and the focus is much less on furthering the arts and sciences and more on publicity." One student complains, "It's supposed to be a community atmosphere, but that is rapidly changing as it becomes a university. Many of the traditions remain, but many more are changing." Even critics, however, concede that many essential elements remain unchanged. Seton Hill still offers "a great liberal arts curriculum and a great physician assistant program, an outstanding program in music and a wonderful education department, great career possibilities, [and access to a faculty that is] very approachable. The professors are just as interested in your success as you are. Attending Seton Hill is a challenging but rewarding experience."

> **SURVEY SAYS . . .**
> *Small classes*
> *Frats and sororities are unpopular*
> *or nonexistent*
> *(Almost) everyone smokes*

Life

Seton Hill is located in the mountains of Western Pennsylvania, approximately 35 miles east of Pittsburgh. One undergraduate warns, "We live on a hill, and it makes it very difficult to get off campus." That's a problem because "for fun, you need to have a car to appreciate anything in the town. Most activities touted on the campus website are off campus." The campus isn't entirely dead. There is the school's burgeoning athletic program, occasional arts productions, and an active party scene. One student says, "There really is nothing fun for a person like me to do here. I don't drink, and I don't party, and because we are up on this hill with nothing around us that is all that students here do for fun. As a result, I spend a lot of time in my room studying, which isn't so bad, I guess."

Student Body

The Seton Hill student body is also undergoing change. One student explains, "There's a great divide here. Upperclassmen are mostly women who came here for an experience geared toward women. Underclassmen are increasingly chosen for their athletic ability." One undergraduate predicts that "soon, the typical student will be an athlete," which seems likely considering that the past two freshman classes have been composed of an average of over 50% athletes. Notes another student, "If not involved in athletics, a lot of students are involved in the many types of clubs offered here on campus. The typical student is goal-oriented and actively involved in some extracurricular activity." Not surprisingly, undergraduates at this Catholic school consider themselves religious.

ADMISSIONS

Very important factors considered include: Interview, secondary school record. *Important factors considered include:* Character/personal qualities, class rank, extracurricular activities, standardized test scores, talent/ability. *Other factors considered include:* Alumni/ae relation, essays, recommendations, volunteer work, work experience. SAT Reasoning or ACT recommended. TOEFL required of all international applicants. High school diploma is required, and GED is accepted. *Academic units required:* 4 English, 2 math, 1 science (1 science lab), 2 social studies, 4 academic electives. *Academic units recommended:* 4 English, 2 math, 1 science (1 science lab), 2 foreign language, 2 social studies, 4 academic electives.

The Inside Word

At Seton Hill, every application is thoroughly reviewed by two admissions counselors. The goal appears to be to find some reason to admit—this school is more interested in giving you an opportunity rather than denying you one—so do your best to accentuate all your positives. Any unusual skill, any unique area of interest, any commitment to the community may be enough to turn you from a "maybe" to a "yes" here.

FINANCIAL AID

Students should submit: FAFSA, institution's own financial aid form. The Princeton Review suggests that all financial aid forms be submitted as soon as possible after 1/1. *Need-based scholarships/grants offered:* Pell, SEOG, state scholarships/grants, private scholarships, the school's own gift aid, United Negro College Fund. *Loan aid offered:* FFEL Subsidized Stafford, FFEL Unsubsidized Stafford, FFEL PLUS, Federal Perkins, college/university loans from institutional funds. Applicants will be notified of awards on a rolling basis beginning on or about 11/1. Federal Work-study Program available. Institutional employment available. Off-campus job opportunities are good.

FROM THE ADMISSIONS OFFICE

"Seton Hill University is an innovative center for learning, offering a variety of educational opportunities to diverse populations within and beyond the Southwestern Pennsylvania region. Seton Hill University produces graduates possessing the values and perspectives inherent in a Catholic education, capable of accomplishment and leadership in the workplace and their communities.

"Undergraduates choose from over 30 areas of study including the sciences, humanities, business, education, and visual and performing arts. At the graduate level, Seton Hill University grants master's degrees in art therapy, special education, writing popular fiction, marriage and family therapy, physician assistant, elementary education, business administration, and instructional design. For working adults, Seton Hill University offers an Adult Degree Program in which students can complete an undergraduate degree in four years or less by attending only on Saturdays. In addition, Seton Hill hosts over 50 international students from 20 different countries in both graduate and undergraduate study. It is the aim of Seton Hill University to do everything possible to provide each student with a complete and fulfilling academic experience that will serve as the foundation for a lifetime of learning.

"Seton Hill University offers basketball, cross country, equestrian, field hockey, golf, lacrosse, soccer, softball, tennis, and volleyball for women and baseball, basketball, cross country, equestrian, football, golf, lacrosse, soccer, and tennis for men. Scholarship money is available for most sports."

For even more information on this school, turn to page 523 of the "Stats" section.

SHIPPENSBURG UNIVERSITY OF PENNSYLVANIA

OLD MAIN 105, 1871 OLD MAIN DRIVE SHIPPENSBURG UNIVERSITY, SHIPPENSBURG, PA 17257-2299
ADMISSIONS: 717-477-1231 • FAX: 717-477-4016 • E-MAIL: ADMISS@SHIP.EDU • WEBSITE: WWW.SHIP.EDU

Ratings
Quality of Life: 72   **Academic: 74**   **Admissions: 76**   **Financial Aid: 70**

Academics

Shippensburg, in the words of a seasoned sophomore, "is about learning who you are, seeing where you fit in, finding what you love to do, and having fun on the way." Students at "Ship" may not be the most scholarly—"We have to be forced to do any type of intellectually stimulating activity"—but they "get the job done" and care deeply about their career prospects. A woman studying public relations writes, "I have been a part of Ship Partners, which

> **SURVEY SAYS . . .**
> Small classes
> Frats and sororities dominate social scene
> Lots of beer drinking
> Hard liquor is popular
> (Almost) everyone smokes

is a PR firm run by the students here and overseen by advisors. Not many other schools have that." Those pursuing work in elementary education, business, criminal justice, and medicine also find strong programs here. The small class sizes and specialized attention belie the fact that Ship is a public institution with a user-friendly sticker price. "I transferred here from a small private school, and I see no difference in the caliber of instruction." Many teachers have earned a reputation for diligence and compassion. A math student says, "They have become an inspiration to me." A public administration major writes, "When I am doing poorly in a class I will get e-mails, letters, or phone calls from my professors, counselors, or the dean of my major." (Advisors "who are not committed to helping their students with scheduling" and the lack of assistance from the financial aid office are reported downsides.) But for students who want a small school with a secure learning environment, Shippensburg is worth checking out.

Life

A good indicator of a school's attitude is its dedication to recreation, and it's tough to beat Ship in this department. The hallowed sand volleyball courts stand as a symbol of laid-back, active life at Ship. Students extend their athletic glory days with facilities for basketball, roller hockey, tennis, baseball and softball, swimming, track, football, Frisbee™, and soccer. "People are always out practicing or playing in one sport or another." The weekend social fare features "overcrowded frat parties" and run-ins with the "overly aggressive police force." A common opinion is that "the typical student at Shippensburg likes to party Thursday through Saturday but studies hard enough to do well in their courses." Greeks insist they are inclusive and sometimes partake in activities other than drinking. Those who are unaffiliated tend to disagree: "All people talk about is parties and how drunk people were—it gets tedious." The religious contingent and student government do plan alternative activities, "designed to help people understand the diverse nature of the world and our society." As far as the super-rural location, students either love it or hate it. The "hometown feel," leafy campus, and stunning views of farmland and the Blue Mountains woo some visitors immediately. But a disenchanted freshman reports, "I actually went and sat in a cornfield with a friend for fun."

Student Body

At first glance, the white, clean-cut, right-leaning Shippensburg population may look like "a homogenous bunch of hicks." But a freshman points out that when you look closer, it's actually a place "where rich kids and rednecks come together in harmony." Kids from Philly and Pittsburgh mingle with the majority, who typically grew up within a two-hour drive of campus, deeper into nowhere. As one junior makes clear, "Minorities are definitely the minority." Nontraditional students integrate easily on the whole, and commuters mix well with residents. A senior summarizes most reasonably when he says, "Students are generally friendly, although sometimes it is difficult to break through the social barriers of ethnicity and religion. If you can do this (and you can!), there is a wealth of diverse and interesting people here at Ship."

ADMISSIONS

Very important factors considered include: Class rank, secondary school record, standardized test scores. *Important factors considered include:* Character/personal qualities. *Other factors considered include:* Essays, extracurricular activities, interview, recommendations, volunteer work, work experience. SAT Reasoning or SAT Subject Tests required. TOEFL required of all international applicants. High school diploma is required, and GED is accepted. *Academic units recommended:* 4 English, 3 math, 3 science (3 science lab), 2 foreign language, 3 social sciences.

The Inside Word

It's a university with small-college access to people and resources, giving you more opportunity than you need to succeed. But if your turnoffs include a strong Greek system and a sizable commuter population, Shippensburg might not shape up . . . and you may end up shipping out.

FINANCIAL AID

Students should submit: FAFSA. The Princeton Review suggests that all financial aid forms be submitted as soon as possible after 1/1. *Need-based scholarships/grants offered:* Pell, SEOG, state scholarships/grants, private scholarships, the school's own gift aid. *Loan aid offered:* FFEL Subsidized Stafford, FFEL Unsubsidized Stafford, FFEL PLUS, Federal Perkins, college/university loans from institutional funds, alternative loans. Applicants will be notified of awards on a rolling basis beginning on or about 2/15. Federal Work-study Program available. Institutional employment available. Off-campus job opportunities are excellent.

FROM THE ADMISSIONS OFFICE

"Shippensburg University's student-focused philosophy remains its hallmark and its strength. That philosophy has enabled the university to be ranked among the best universities in the region for more than a decade by national publications. By maintaining a student focus, the university has been able to achieve some notable goals, including an increase in minority enrollment over the past five years, results of efforts to recruit and retain students of color from throughout the region, including Philadelphia.

"The university has also taken the lead in providing students with alternatives to drinking, including cultural and social programming that offers concerts, films, and internationally known guest speakers such as Danny Glover, Bob Ballard, and James Earl Jones. The university hosts the University-Community Alcohol Coalition Project. Through the Project, representatives from various local, state, and regional agencies and organizations work together to reduce illegal use and abuse of alcohol and drugs. That coalition, which includes students, provides guidance on programming to inform and educate students about drinking, including surveys that show that the number of students who drink is far less than students think. Other efforts include expansion of weekend programming and late-night programming throughout the week. The student-run Activities Program Board also regularly sponsors cultural trips to various major cities on the East Coast. "

For even more information on this school, turn to page 523 of the "Stats" section.

SIENA COLLEGE

515 LOUDON ROAD, LOUDONVILLE, NY 12211 • ADMISSIONS: 518-783-2423 • FAX: 518-783-2436
FINANCIAL AID: 518-783-2427 • E-MAIL: ADMIT@SIENA.EDU • WEBSITE: WWW.SIENA.EDU

Ratings

Quality of Life: 76   Academic: 76   Admissions: 84   Financial Aid: 72

Academics

According to its students, a Siena education is an experience with plenty of benefits and drawbacks. On the one
hand, "most of the professors are very good people and
easy to talk to and get along with." Like the professors, the
friars (this college has Franciscan roots) "often take time
out of their own schedules to interact [with], empathize
[with], and lead Siena students." Nonetheless, many students feel that their classroom experiences are limited. One
student says that she has "noticed many professors [who]

are not enthusiastic about teaching," and many of the adjunct faculty members "are not worth your time and
effort." Of course, we hear different reports from the three schools within the college: the School of Liberal Arts,
the School of Business, and the School of Science. Overall, students tell us that liberal arts professors are especially knowledgeable, a degree in business carries substantial regional weight, and delving into a science major
provides very rewarding challenges as well as a lot of work. Each student's college career begins with the two-
semester Foundations Sequence—a thorough examination of a number of classic and contemporary texts. Core
courses at other colleges often draw complaints, but not here. What does draw the most complaints at Siena is
the administration. One student explains, "Time after time, since I've arrived here, decisions have been made
regarding student life or academics with minimal to no consultation of students." If you end up at Siena, you
might want to follow the advice of this student: "If you do not treat the administration as the enemy from day
one, they will listen to you and respect you."

Life

Siena College has a quiet campus in Loudonville, a small town in upstate New York. Albany is just a couple
miles up the road, so students looking for nightlife off campus will often pile into cabs and head to the capital
city for the clubs and bars. But if a good party is what students are after—and, more often than not, it is—there's
no need to leave campus. "Siena is a party school," one student assures us, "don't let anybody tell you otherwise." The real on-campus action takes place at "the many townhouse parties," where the upperclassmen live.
The student body appreciates athletics and makes sure that the campus gym facilities are well used. A range of
other on-campus activities are available for students, though they receive mixed reviews. A less-than-enthusi-
astic student comments, "It would seem that the target age group for most campus-sponsored activities is 12-
16." Others, however, are excited about the fact that "there are a lot of activities for students to get involved in
or attend." The more popular events include the annual Winter Weekend and Sienafest. When exactly is Winter
Weekend held? Well, "there are only two seasons in Loudonville: September and winter," as one student wryly
puts it. In other words, Winter Weekend is not in September.

Student Body

When a student tells us that "it seems that most everyone is the same at Siena," what she means is that Siena's
student body is an overwhelmingly Caucasian and Catholic crowd with conservative views and roots in New
York State. "Conformity is the name of the game here at good ol' S-I-E-N-A," an undergraduate remarks. Some
students believe that the college is heavy on cliques, but a classmate qualifies that argument, claiming that
"there are no cliques at Siena because everyone is the same!" Along these lines, a student offers this stylistic
breakdown of the student body: "Basically, there are three types of students at Siena," she says, "Abercrombie,
Gap, and Banana Republic." Though students do not deny having superficial streaks, they quickly point out
that "most everyone is friendly," and that one beneficial result of so much homogeneity is that disputes between
student groups are rare.

ADMISSIONS

Very important factors considered include: Secondary school record. *Important factors considered include:* Extracurricular activities, standardized test scores, talent/ability. *Other factors considered include:* Alumni/ae relation, character/personal qualities, class rank, essays, geographical residence, interview, minority status, recommendations, state residency, volunteer work, work experience. SAT Reasoning or ACT required. TOEFL required of all international applicants. High school diploma is required, and GED is accepted. *Academic units required:* 4 English, 3 math, 3 science (3 science lab), 1 social studies, 3 history. *Academic units recommended:* 4 English, 4 math, 4 science (3 science lab), 3 foreign language, 1 social studies, 3 history.

The Inside Word

Students who have consistently solid grades should have no trouble getting admitted. There is hot competition for students between colleges in New York State; Siena has to admit the large majority of its applicants in order to meet freshman class enrollment targets.

FINANCIAL AID

Students should submit: FAFSA, state aid form. The Princeton Review suggests that all financial aid forms be submitted as soon as possible after 1/1. *Need-based scholarships/grants offered:* Pell, SEOG, state scholarships/grants, private scholarships, the school's own gift aid. *Loan aid offered:* FFEL Subsidized Stafford, FFEL Unsubsidized Stafford, FFEL PLUS, Federal Perkins. Applicants will be notified of awards on or about 4/1. Off-campus job opportunities are good.

FROM THE ADMISSIONS OFFICE

"Siena is a coeducational, independent liberal arts college with a Franciscan tradition. It is a community where the intellectual, personal, and social growth of all students is paramount. Siena's faculty calls forth the best Siena students have to give—and the students do the same for them. Students are competitive, but not at each other's expense. Siena's curriculum includes 23 majors in three schools—liberal arts, science, and business. In addition, there are over a dozen pre-professional and special academic programs. With a student/ faculty ratio of 14:1, class size ranges between 15 and 35 students. Siena's 152-acre campus is located in Loudonville, a suburban community within two miles of the New York State seat of government in Albany. With 15 colleges in the area, there is a wide variety of activities on weekends. Regional theater, performances by major concert artists, and professional sports events compete with the activities on the campus. Within 50 miles are the Adirondacks, the Berkshires, and the Catskills, providing outdoor recreation throughout the year. Because the capital region's easy, friendly lifestyle is so appealing, many Siena graduates try to find their first jobs in upstate New York."

For even more information on this school, turn to page 524 of the "Stats" section.

SIMMONS COLLEGE

300 THE FENWAY, BOSTON, MA 02115 • ADMISSIONS: 617-521-2051 • FAX: 617-521-3190
FINANCIAL AID: 617-521-2001 • E-MAIL: UGADM@SIMMONS.EDU • WEBSITE: WWW.SIMMONS.EDU

Ratings
Quality of Life: 86   Academic: 85   Admissions: 84   Financial Aid: 77

Academics

At Simmons College, its all-female, grade-conscious setting demonstrates that "the girls are here to learn." A senior admits, "It might sound cheesy, but the school is really about helping students find their voice." Professors facilitate this process by "treating everyone with respect, dignity, and compassion." Students feel their teachers are "actually on our side, ready to help with almost anything." Extensive office hours and prompt e-mail responses indicate professors' high level of accessibility. "When you find an

> **SURVEY SAYS . . .**
> *Small classes*
> *Students love Boston, MA*
> *Great off-campus food*
> *Frats and sororities are unpopular*
> *or nonexistent*

amazing professor, you can be sure that s/he is available to you in a big way," writes a senior. The political science, international relations, and communications departments rank high with students, while the nursing and physical therapy programs benefit from proximity to some of the nation's top hospitals. "When I look out my window, I see Beth Israel Deaconess Medical Center, and one block down are the rest of the great hospitals in the Longwood Medical Area." This practical training bridges academic work and professional preparation. "All of my professors in the nursing program have wanted me to succeed and have advised me in my career choices." A few departments, such as music and psychology, could use a few more faculty members to cover class demand. Complaints surface regarding Culture Matters (officially the "Multidisciplinary Core Course"), a class required of all first year students. But in most classes, students notice a payoff. "I've seen an amazing improvement in my writing, class participation, and overall attention to detail in my reading." The school places "a high premium on making sure everyone feels comfortable," so that education can be a personal experience. "By the time we graduate, we're far more self-confident."

Life

Be warned: "This is a learning environment, not a place to party or make out with the newest meat from MIT." It's true that on-campus life can feel like "a bizarre combination of a nunnery and Sesame Street." Entertainment veers towards that sleepover-party image of single-sex institutions, complete with "pajamas, movies, and drinks." If Simmons were located in the boonies, the regimen of knitting, Ms. Pac-Man, political rallies, and field hockey could get old. But it's in the middle of Boston, a "huge college-oriented city" that beckons with Newbury Street shopping, hip coffee shops, Red Sox games, and the male-female ratio of the real world. "The school buys bulk discounted tickets to plays and musicals and even the ballet." Participation in the Colleges of Fenway Consortium links the school to its neighbors, though some students seem to have thought before they enrolled that Simmons would host more coed events. Students like coming home to Simmons as much as they like getting away. "It always feels like a safe and secure place to study after a long weekend out." A fair number of entering students seem to experience a rough adjustment period but grow to love the school after getting accustomed and involved.

Student Body

Simmons women see themselves as open-minded, overachieving feminists who are "just as engaging at a party as in the classroom." Students routinely take on crazy class-hours, club leadership positions, and multiple majors. Recently, the vibe of the school has started to shift "from being all about grades to being more about community." The small, liberal student body accepts lesbianism readily—"You become very accustomed to same-sex relationships"—but "Republicans or Yankees fans might want to tread carefully." Many student activists organize around political issues of gender, race, and class. They note a divide between students "on a first-name basis with every financial aid officer and those whose parents can afford a small island in the Pacific." They are also sensitive to the fact that "there are more cleaning people than students of color." However, a junior points out, "With each incoming class, Simmons becomes more and more diverse." Ultimately, students cultivate "solidarity around being a woman," whether that woman is moneyed Cape Cod stock or a gender-bending punk.

ADMISSIONS

Very important factors considered include: Secondary school record. *Important factors considered include:* Character/personal qualities, class rank, essays, recommendations, standardized test scores. *Other factors considered include:* Extracurricular activities, interview, talent/ability, volunteer work, work experience. SAT Reasoning or ACT required. TOEFL required of all international applicants. High school diploma or equivalent is not required. *Academic units required:* 4 English, 3 math, 3 science, 3 foreign language, 3 social studies, 3 history. *Academic units recommended:* 4 English, 4 math, 3 science, 4 foreign language, 4 social studies, 3 history.

The Inside Word

Most of the best women's colleges in the country are in the Northeast, including those Seven Sister schools (roughly the female equivalent of the formerly all-male Ivies) that remain women's colleges. The competition for students is intense, and although Simmons is a strong attraction for many women, there are at least a half-dozen competitors who draw the better students away. For the majority of applicants there is little need for anxiety while awaiting a decision. Its solid academics, Boston location, and bountiful scholarship program make Simmons well worth considering for any student opting for a women's college.

FINANCIAL AID

Students should submit: FAFSA, noncustodial (divorced/separated) parents' statement, business/farm supplement, parents' income tax return. The Princeton Review suggests that all financial aid forms be submitted as soon as possible after 1/1. *Need-based scholarships/grants offered:* Pell, SEOG, state scholarships/grants, private scholarships, the school's own gift aid. *Loan aid offered:* FFEL Subsidized Stafford, FFEL Unsubsidized Stafford, FFEL PLUS, Federal Perkins, state loans, college/university loans from institutional funds. Applicants will be notified of awards on or about 3/15. Federal Work-study Program available. Institutional employment available. Off-campus job opportunities are good.

FROM THE ADMISSIONS OFFICE

"Simmons believes passionately in an 'educational contract' that places students first and helps them build successful careers, lead meaningful lives, and realize a powerful return on their investment.

"Simmons is truly a 100-year-old university in Boston, with a tradition of providing women with a collaborative environment that stimulates dialogue, enhances listening, catalyzes action, and spurs personal and professional growth.

"Simmons honors this contract by delivering a quality education and measurable success through our singular approach to professional preparation, intellectual exploration, and community orientation."

For even more information on this school, turn to page 524 of the "Stats" section.

SIMON'S ROCK COLLEGE OF BARD

84 ALFORD ROAD, GREAT BARRINGTON, MA 01230 • ADMISSIONS: 413-528-7312 • FAX: 413-528-7334
FINANCIAL AID: 413-528-7297 • E-MAIL: ADMIT@SIMONS-ROCK.EDU • WEBSITE: WWW.SIMONS-ROCK.EDU

Ratings
Quality of Life: 70   Academic: 77   Admissions: 60   Financial Aid: 70

Academics

Tiny Simon's Rock College of Bard, which admits exceptional high school sophomores and juniors to its college-level program, "is a fantastic opportunity for students who were either bored in high school (the overachievers) or the really smart kids who never did a damn thing, but want to now. Hating high school isn't enough, though; you really have to work hard here." With barely 400 enrollees, "there are usually only about eight people in a class. You can take the class wherever you want it to go. And if you can't, you can stay after and talk it over with the teacher one-on-one."

> **SURVEY SAYS . . .**
> *Small classes*
> *Athletic facilities are great*
> *Students aren't religious*
> *Campus feels safe*
> *Frats and sororities are unpopular or nonexistent*
> *(Almost) everyone smokes*

The school offers students the freedom "to do independent study or take a 300-level course as a freshman or do practically anything else. All you have to do is ask." Notes one student, "This school is really one giant test of one's own motivation and determination." Although "there isn't a huge variety of majors and classes available," students tell us that "every semester when the course catalog comes out, it's never a question of finding interesting courses to take; it's always a matter of working them into a workable schedule." They also explain that "because of the interdisciplinary nature of academics here, the limited number of majors isn't a huge problem." Furthermore, "if something you want to study isn't being covered, it's remarkably easy to set up a tutorial dedicated to that subject because professors are extraordinarily available and receptive."

Life

"Life at Simon's Rock can be very boring since it's located in a small town," undergrads at this tiny college concede, "but you can find happiness with your friends and student life staff." Diversion comes primarily in the form of "a peculiar form of 'hanging out'—Simon's Rock should really be a verb rather than a noun. This sort of hanging out involves either being outside smoking or inside watching the Fight Club DVD a lot and having conversations that range from the emotionally charged to goofy to intellectual." Go-getters note that "the schools is always really helpful to students. Since many of the students are younger, some too young to drive, they offer town trips every day, and on weekends they often take groups to go ice-skating, bowling, roller skating, miniature golfing, or just to the movies. They also have mall trips, and student groups often go to other colleges to meet other students and to get ideas as to how to incorporate Simon's Rock into the larger college community." Many, however, don't take advantage of these opportunities, instead resorting to immersion in computer games, pot-smoking, or pure tedium. Location and the size of the school are major roadblocks to a more active social scene. "It would be nice if there were stronger campus organizations, but it's difficult for that to happen given the small size of the school and the demanding nature of the classes," explains one student. Notes another, "The location of the school doesn't help one bit." It's so secluded that "there's no television reception, and cell phones are useless, too."

Student Body

Traditionally regarded as a lefty-weirdo haven, Simon's Rock "seems to be getting more conservative and preppy with each entering class." The transition is a slow one, however. According to one student, "the average Simon's Rock student probably smokes both cigarettes and marijuana, is interested in arts and humanities, considers him- or herself to be politically active, and is probably vegetarian or vegan." And oddballs still predominate; as one student put it, "We all come from something abnormal, due to the fact that we are entering college a year or two early. And these abnormalities, although strikingly different, form a common bond." Adds another, "The townies call us 'the freaks on the hill.' My mom calls us 'the patients.'" Because it's a school of 400 students, "everyone knows everybody."

ADMISSIONS

Very important factors considered include: Character/personal qualities, essays, interview, recommendations, talent/ability. *Important factors considered include:* Extracurricular activities, secondary school record, standardized test scores, volunteer work. *Other factors considered include:* Alumni/ae relation, minority status, work experience. SAT Reasoning or ACT required. TOEFL required of all international applicants. High school diploma or equivalent is not required. *Academic units recommended:* 2 English, 2 math, 2 science (1 science lab), 2 foreign language, 2 social studies, 2 history, 2 academic electives.

The Inside Word

There is no other college like Simon's Rock in the country, and no other similar admissions process. Applying to college doesn't get any more personal, and thus any more demanding, than it does here. If you're not ready to tap your potential as a thinker in college beginning with completion of the application, avoid Simon's Rock. Simply hating high school isn't going to get you in. Self-awareness, intellectual curiosity, and a desire for more formidable academic challenges than those typically found in high school will.

FINANCIAL AID

Students should submit: FAFSA, CSS/Financial Aid PROFILE, noncustodial (divorced/separated) parents' statement, business/farm supplement, parent and student federal taxes, federal verification worksheet. The Princeton Review suggests that all financial aid forms be submitted as soon as possible after 1/1. *Need-based scholarships/grants offered:* Pell, SEOG, state scholarships/grants, the school's own gift aid. *Loan aid offered:* FFEL Subsidized Stafford, FFEL Unsubsidized Stafford, FFEL PLUS, Federal Perkins, state loans, alternative educational loans. Applicants will be notified of awards on a rolling basis beginning on or about 2/15. Federal Work-study Program available. Institutional employment available. Off-campus job opportunities are good.

TFROM THE ADMISSIONS OFFICE

"Simon's Rock is dedicated to one thing: to allow bright, highly motivated students the opportunity to pursue college work leading to the AA and BA degrees at an age earlier than our national norm."

For even more information on this school, turn to page 524 of the "Stats" section.

SKIDMORE COLLEGE

815 NORTH BROADWAY, SARATOGA SPRINGS, NY 12866-1632 • ADMISSIONS: 518-580-5570
FAX: 518-580-5584 • FINANCIAL AID: 518-580-5750 • E-MAIL: ADMISSIONS@SKIDMORE.EDU • WEBSITE: WWW.SKIDMORE.EDU

Ratings

Quality of Life: 85   **Academic:** 89   **Admissions:** 93   **Financial Aid:** 93

Academics

Skidmore College puts the emphasis on the "arts" in "liberal arts college." Nearly one in five undergraduates major in the visual or performing arts. The school also does a fine job developing future arts patrons through its popular business major. Undergraduates speak favorably of both the yin and yang of their school's academic offerings. Business "is a great program jumpstarted through real-life case studies and interactions among executives," while the arts departments benefit from "the high quantity of artists, which fuels the place and gives it this energy for invention and enthusiasm for exploration." Small classes—"the largest 'lecture' class is about 25 to 30 students"—foster strong student-teacher bonds, which in turn allow for "endless opportunities, although they require student initiative." Many students tell us that "Skidmore is a very challenging school academically." A vocal minority, however, complain and "wish that the academics were more challenging and that professors had less tolerance for average work." An undergraduate concludes, "Skidmore provides an academically rigorous environment, but only for those students who choose to challenge and dedicate themselves to their studies."

> **SURVEY SAYS . . .**
> *Small classes*
> *Great off-campus food*
> *Frats and sororities are unpopular or nonexistent*
> *Lots of beer drinking*

Life

Weather permitting, the Skidmore campus is a beehive of activity. As one student explains, "We have athletic events, movies, theatrical performances, art galleries, restaurants, political rallies, famous speakers, and interesting people to talk to. I have never had so many unique and exciting things to do in my life." Those seeking a party will find it. Those who want to avoid the party scene are able to. One undergraduate writes, "There are a lot of hard-core party people, a lot of chill, easygoing party people, and a lot of sober party people. Everyone is looking to have a good time on weekends, but that could mean getting trashed or it could mean watching movies with friends." Whatever your preference, "because of Skidmore's small size, a student can really be anything he or she wants to be. If you've always wanted to be in a band, you can do that here. If you want to start your own publication, you can do that, too. It just takes some motivation." Furthermore, if you just want to relax and do nothing, you can enjoy the "gorgeous campus, [dormitories] known for their big room size," or the town of Saratoga Springs, which is "only a short walk away." The town has "great shopping and fabulous restaurants," students report. Outdoorsy types appreciate their "access to endless amounts of Adirondack and Green Mountain hiking. In the winter, the skiing is awesome." Because of the harsh winters, social life is "really dependent on weather. Wintertime, which is most of the school year, is kinda gloomy, but when it's nice out everyone gets really happy, and there's a lot of stuff to do."

Student Body

The Skidmore student body has "a huge mix of kids, from WASPs to JAPs to athletes to stoners." The school is geographically diverse. "Many people are from New York State (and NYC) or the Boston area, but there are many people from the Midwest, Mid-Atlantic, New England, and the West Coast as well," students tell us. Artists and business majors are the two most prominent archetypes. One undergraduate explains, "If you're a business major, you are probably wealthy, white, drink a lot, probably Republican, and probably play sports. If you're an art major, you are wealthy, white, probably gay, from New York City, a pot-smoker, and don't like to be categorized." Another student notes that "there are plenty of students who fit neither stereotypes and still mix in well with the school's atmosphere." The business students are about the only Republicans. The rest of the student body leans pretty far to the left politically.

ADMISSIONS

Very important factors considered include: Recommendations, secondary school record. *Important factors considered include:* Character/personal qualities, class rank, essays, extracurricular activities, standardized test scores, talent/ability, volunteer work, work experience. *Other factors considered include:* Alumni/ae relation, geographical residence, interview, minority status. SAT Reasoning or ACT required. TOEFL required of all international applicants. High school diploma is required, and GED is accepted. *Academic units recommended:* 4 English, 4 math, 4 science (3 science lab), 4 foreign language, 4 social studies.

The Inside Word

Although Skidmore overlaps applicants with some of the best colleges and universities in the Northeast, it's mainly viewed as a safety. Still, this makes for a strong applicant pool, and those students who do enroll give the college a better-than-average freshman academic profile. The entire admissions operation at Skidmore is impressive and efficient, proof that number two does indeed try harder.

FINANCIAL AID

Students should submit: FAFSA, CSS/Financial Aid PROFILE. Regular filing deadline 1/15. The Princeton Review suggests that all financial aid forms be submitted as soon as possible after 1/1. *Need-based scholarships/grants offered:* Pell, SEOG, state scholarships/grants, the school's own gift aid. *Loan aid offered:* FFEL Subsidized Stafford, FFEL Unsubsidized Stafford, FFEL PLUS, Federal Perkins. Applicants will be notified of awards on or about 4/1. Federal Work-study Program available. Institutional employment available. Off-campus job opportunities are fair.

FROM THE ADMISSIONS OFFICE

"New for 2005 is Skidmore's First Year Experience (FYE), a year-long curricular, residential, and programmatic initiative that immediately engages each first-year student with a faculty mentor-advisor, with 14 other students in an innovative Scribner Seminar, and with the entire College via a thematically-linked series of artistic, cultural, and social events. FYE's centerpiece, 40 distinctive Scribner Seminars—ranging from African cinema, to the ethics of tobacco and alcohol advertising, to the biotech revolution—encourage each student to actively and creatively participate in his or her own learning. Individual seminar instructors will also function as faculty mentor-advisors for those 15 students, and will provide both a curricular and co-curricular perspective not only on the specific seminar topic but the liberal arts in general. In most cases, students will live in residence halls in close proximity to other students in their seminar.

"Even prior to arrival on campus, first-year students will have been in telephone contact with summer advisors, selected their preferred Scribner Seminar, explored summer reading intended to provide a thematic umbrella for all students, and gotten to know—at least virtually—their seminar classmates.

"The First-Year Experience is just the beginning of the expectation that students will creatively craft an experience leading to intensive work in a major field of study. It is also a singular manifestation of Skidmore's commitment to the belief that Creative Thought Matters—that every life, career, and endeavor is made more profound with creative ability at its core."

For even more information on this school, turn to page 525 of the "Stats" section.

SLIPPERY ROCK UNIVERSITY OF PENNSYLVANIA

OFFICE OF ADMISSIONS, MALTBY CENTER, SLIPPERY ROCK, PA 16057 • ADMISSIONS: 724-738-2015
FAX: 724-738-2913 • E-MAIL: APPLY@SRU.EDU • WEBSITE: WWW.SRU.EDU

Ratings
Quality of Life: 71   **Academic:** 73   **Admissions:** 75   **Financial Aid:** 86

Academics

For students who are seeking a public education in a small-er-than-state school setting, Slippery Rock University is a solid choice. With just under 6,000 undergrads, Slippery Rock can offer students "manageable class sizes [and] a friendly classroom atmosphere." The school is large enough, however, to offer a variety of strong programs, with particular strength in education, physical therapy, music, and recreation and leisure facilities management.

> **SURVEY SAYS . . .**
> *Small classes*
> *Great library*
> *Athletic facilities are great*
> *Lots of beer drinking*
> *(Almost) everyone smokes*

Most undergrads at the school are firmly focused on their career goals. One student observes, "Academics can easily become second to professional development activities on campus, and that is a good thing." Classes "are challenging but not too difficult," and the school provides safety nets for students who fall behind. One student reports, "This school is made for everyone to succeed, and if you don't, you can only blame yourself. We have a writing center where you can go and get consulting on your paper, and our library is state-of-the-art and they know of all of the projects and project requirements ahead of time so they are always a great resource of information. There are also peer tutors that you can request." Undergrads see a bright future for their school, telling us that "Slippery Rock is a growing school, and with the growing population the school will continue to expand and improve its facilities."

Life

Slippery Rock "is a very athletic school," students brag, telling us that their "sports teams are very good, and it makes students want to go to these sports events to cheer their teams onto victory, which helps bring about school spirit." Students not only cheer the teams on with "Rock Pride," but also are active themselves, taking advantage of "a fairly new student recreation center that includes an Olympic-size pool, four basketball courts, a rock climbing wall, workout equipment (both free weights and machines), various nightly fitness classes, and organized intramural sports." Many can indulge their athletic proclivities and get credit for it too, thanks to SRU's popular exercise science and physical education departments. Slippery Rock offers students "over 100 organizations to join; they're one of the great strengths of the school." The university also "does a good job of keeping its students aware of the activities going on around campus. There are posters and sidewalk chalk everywhere displaying clubs and Greek life and many other events." That's especially helpful since "there's not that much to do in the town of Slippery Rock." One student explains, "It stinks that we have to drive 30 minutes to reach a Wal-Mart or Target and even a movie theater!" The good news is that "Downtown is being completely redone. It is looking great, [and] the community and the students interact with one another."

Student Body

SRU "is made up of the typical Western Pennsylvania population, meaning not much ethnic diversity. Yet everyone has a chance to fit in." They are "mostly the children of working-class homes [who] wear hoodies, jeans, T-shirts, and tennis shoes or flip flops" to class. Because many come from the Pittsburgh area, "they are more used to the fast-paced life, with everything at their fingertips. Slippery Rock has that small-town country feel that is more laid-back and peaceful in a natural way. There are country people mixing with a lot of city and urban people, but everyone seems to get along fine. Every student is different because of his or her background, but college is a place where you experience new cultures." And even if you don't exactly blend into the mainstream, "It's not like high school, where someone who expresses [him or herself with] crazy piercings and wild dress is looked down upon. These people aren't looked at any differently from the next person."

ADMISSIONS

Very important factors considered include: Secondary school record, standardized test scores. *Important factors considered include:* Talent/ability. *Other factors considered include:* Alumni/ae relation, character/personal qualities, class rank, essays, extracurricular activities, interview, minority status, recommendations, volunteer work, work experience. SAT Reasoning or ACT required. TOEFL required of all international applicants. High school diploma is required, and GED is accepted. *Academic units recommended:* 4 English, 3 math, 3 science (2 science lab), 2 foreign language, 2 social studies.

The Inside Word

The sameness of the students' socio-economic/ethnic makeup may give you pause as an applicant, but the undergrads' collective will and involvement in school activities in and out of class are factors that fall solidly in Slippery Rock's favor.

FINANCIAL AID

Students should submit: FAFSA. The Princeton Review suggests that all financial aid forms be submitted as soon as possible after 1/1. *Need-based scholarships/grants offered:* Pell, SEOG, state scholarships/grants, private scholarships, the school's own gift aid. *Loan aid offered:* FFEL Subsidized Stafford, FFEL Unsubsidized Stafford, FFEL PLUS, Federal Perkins. Applicants will be notified of awards on a rolling basis beginning on or about 3/15. Federal Work-study Program available. Institutional employment available. Off-campus job opportunities are excellent.

FROM THE ADMISSIONS OFFICE

"A rock solid education. A classic residential campus. A safe, small-town setting. An affordable life-long value. Committed, caring faculty. A once-in-a-lifetime experience.

"Slippery Rock University is a comprehensive university of 7,500 students and a member of the State System of Higher Education of Pennsylvania. It is comprised of the following colleges: Education; Humanities, Fine and Performing Arts; Business, Information, and Behavioral Sciences; Health, Environment, and Science; and Graduate Studies and Research. The 600-acre campus is located in western Pennsylvania less than an hour north of Pittsburgh in a safe, relaxed, small-town community. An honors program, academic support services, and learning communities are available to foster student success in a learner-centered environment. Students participate in over 100 co-curricular and extracurricular activities. Intercollegiate and intramural sports, concerts, plays, lectures, and other cultural activities are popular.

"Slippery Rock University offers many bachelor's and master's degrees in numerous majors, minors, and program tracks in a plethora of academic disciplines. The university also offers a Doctor of Physical Therapy degree.

"For additional information regarding admission, scheduling a campus visit, or any other aspect of the University, visit our website at www.sru.edu."

For even more information on this school, turn to page 525 of the "Stats" section.

SMITH COLLEGE

7 COLLEGE LANE, NORTHAMPTON, MA 01063 • ADMISSIONS: 413-585-2500 • FAX: 413-585-2527
FINANCIAL AID: 413-585-2530 • E-MAIL: ADMISSIONS@SMITH.EDU • WEBSITE: WWW.SMITH.EDU

Ratings
Quality of Life: 95   Academic: 94   Admissions: 94   Financial Aid: 96

Academics

"Fantastic academics" that demand "insane amounts of studying and work" have always been the signature feature of a Smith education, and the women who attend this elite Northeastern school wouldn't have it any other way. One student explains, "Classes are so incredibly challenging, you work your ass off to succeed, but you do it because the professors are so great and because the work is interesting." With no core requirements to fulfill, Smithies "can spend much more time taking classes they are interested in. It makes you feel like you are getting more out of your college education." So too do professors who "really care and are willing to explain, discuss, re-explain and work with you until you have a solid grasp of the material." An "amazing library" is among Smith's many resources; what students can't find here in the library or course catalog, they can easily seek out at one of the other member schools in the Five College Consortium (Amherst, Mount Holyoke, Hampshire, and UMass); shuttle buses carry students among the different campuses. As one student sums up, Smith is "unabashedly a women's college, devoted to providing incredible education and opportunities to women from around the globe."

> **SURVEY SAYS . . .**
> *Small classes*
> *Great library*
> *Great off-campus food*
> *Dorms are like palaces*
> *Frats and sororities are unpopular*
> *or nonexistent*

Life

Smith undergrads adore the school's unique housing system, under which "students live in a beautiful 19th-century house with 40 of their closest friends." Almost all of the "amazing" dorms "have hardwood floors and big windows" and typically include "dining rooms with kitchen staffs." The system not only allows students to manage their stressful academics in comfort, but also provides them with a ready support network of peers. The houses are just one of many traditions that unite the Smith community; Friday afternoon tea is another. Reports one student, "The kitchen staff bakes cookies and all sorts of pastries and it's a nice time to unwind after the week. We also have candlelight dinner every Thursday night and dinner is served family style as opposed to buffet." Extracurricular life at Smith tends to be on the quiet side, and students approve; writes one, "Being at Smith you get the best of all worlds. Parties here tend to be smaller, lower-key events, but having the Five College connection you get your choice of any party you'd want. Go to UMass for frats and big dance parties. Go to Hampshire for a more chill, laid-back vibe. Go to Amherst for something a little more formal." The campus also hosts regular "dances, poetry readings, movies, lectures, cultural events, you name it." Hometown Northampton, "just a five-minute walk from campus," also shoulders some of the burden. The town "is full of extremely unique stores, boutiques, indie movie theatres, concert venues, bars, coffee houses, and restaurants."

Student Body

If people who "use the word 'hegemony' in everyday conversation" and who cherish "freedom from the oppressive hetero-normative patriarchy "—or even know what that means—sound like your kind of folks, you may be a Smith woman. Smithies are "typically politically active, love to learn, and champion about four different causes. They are quirky and dorky but love to go out and have a good time. And they want to save the world." The crusading can occasionally be overbearing—"Smith students can be vicious when defending their own beliefs and ideas and attacking those who disagree with them," warns one woman, but overall students regard one another as "caring" and "supportive." Like hometown Northampton, "Smith is a very gay-friendly environment"—students report that there are "a lot of lesbians" on campus, and "quite a few 'boys.'" Straight undergrads think "it's important to stress how easy it is to meet guys. Many hetero women are scared to come here because they believe the stereotype about Smith being solely a haven for man-hating lesbians. It really is not true."

ADMISSIONS

Very important factors considered include: Character/personal qualities, recommendations, secondary school record. *Important factors considered include:* Class rank, essays, extracurricular activities, interview, standardized test scores, talent/ability. *Other factors considered include:* Alumni/ae relation, minority status, volunteer work, work experience. SAT Reasoning or ACT required. TOEFL required of all international applicants. High school diploma or equivalent is not required. *Academic units recommended:* 4 English, 3 math, 3 science (3 science lab), 3 foreign language, 2 history.

The Inside Word

Don't be fooled by the relatively high acceptance rate at Smith (or at other top women's colleges). The applicant pool is small and highly self-selected, and it's fairly tough to get admitted. Only women who have taken the most challenging course loads in high school and achieved at a superior level will be competitive.

FINANCIAL AID

Students should submit: FAFSA, CSS/Financial Aid PROFILE, noncustodial (divorced/separated) parents' statement, business/farm supplement. Regular filing deadline 2/1. The Princeton Review suggests that all financial aid forms be submitted as soon as possible after 1/1. *Need-based scholarships/grants offered:* Pell, SEOG, state scholarships/grants, private scholarships, the school's own gift aid. *Loan aid offered:* Direct Subsidized Stafford, Direct Unsubsidized Stafford, FFEL PLUS, Federal Perkins, state loans, college/university loans from institutional funds. Applicants will be notified of awards on or about 4/1. Federal Work-study Program available. Institutional employment available. Off-campus job opportunities are good.

FROM THE ADMISSIONS OFFICE

"Smith students choose from 1,000 courses in more than 50 areas of study. There are no specific course requirements outside the major; students meet individually with faculty advisers to plan a balanced curriculum. Smith programs offer unique opportunities, including the chance to study abroad, or at another college in the United States, and to learn firsthand about the federal government. The Ada Comstock Scholars Program encourages women beyond the traditional age to return to college and complete their undergraduate studies. Smith is located in the scenic Connecticut River valley of western Massachusetts near a number of other outstanding educational institutions. Through the Five College Consortium, Smith, Amherst, Hampshire, and Mount Holyoke colleges and the University of Massachusetts enrich their academic, social, and cultural offerings by means of joint faculty appointments, joint courses, student and faculty exchanges, shared facilities, and other cooperative arrangements. Smith is the only women's college to offer a major in engineering; it's also the only college in the country that offers a guaranteed paid internship program ("Praxis")."

For even more information on this school, turn to page 526 of the "Stats" section.

ST. BONAVENTURE UNIVERSITY

PO Box D, Saint Bonaventure, NY 14778 • Admissions: 716-375-2400 • Fax: 716-375-4005
Financial Aid: 716-375-2528 • E-mail: admissions@sbu.edu • Website: www.sbu.edu

Ratings
Quality of Life: 69   Academic: 77   Admissions: 74   Financial Aid: 78

Academics

One rough translation of the Italian buona ventura is "the good journey," and this has become the operant metaphor for an education at Saint Bonaventure University, a small Franciscan university in upstate New York. Reports one undergraduate here, "Since I've begun 'the good journey,' I've found that every professor I've ever encountered is the most down-to-earth person who would do anything in order for you to earn the grade you desire." Indeed, students here agree that "the professors are really caring and are here because they love their jobs and they love the students." Undergrads are especially excited about the journalism program, pointing out that "a lot of the mass communications faculty have years of experience in the job place, which is helpful." Historically, they've been generally less enthusiastic about Clare College, the university division through which Bona administers its challenging and catholic core curriculum. Notes a typical student, "Clare College is a little too demanding for the 100-level courses and required courses it offers, but overall it is something that the school prides itself on, and I feel privileged to have gone through it." Part of the problem with Clare is the disconnect between its admirable goal of broad intellectual inquiry and most students' desire to focus on career-related subjects; observes one student, "Sometimes the atmosphere on campus reflects a lack of concern over educational studies, and it feels as though people often forget that they are at a liberal arts school." Those who 'get it' praise Bona's efforts to "provide a broad education about the world while also providing that very precise education about your major and learning values at the same time."

> **SURVEY SAYS . . .**
> *Small classes*
> *Students are friendly*
> *Everyone loves the Bonnies*
> *Frats and sororities are unpopular or nonexistent*
> *College radio is popular*
> *Lots of beer drinking*
> *Hard liquor is popular*

Life

Bona is "in the middle of nowhere, and it's freezing outside for about 70 percent of the school year," so students "do the same thing anyone else would do under the circumstances; we drink with friends." Students agree that Bona is "definitely a party school. While on campus parties are tough to pull off, there is a party off campus every night. Almost anyone can get into the local bars and there are many houses off campus that have triple keggers nightly." Some here even express incredulity that Bona fell off our list of the nation's biggest party schools; "Don't worry, we will be back on it next year," students assure us. We'll see. Bona undergrads also tell us that "besides partying, our school offers many programs and clubs that you can participate in. Many students go up to Mt. Irenaeus for a relaxing and spiritual weekend. There are always floor programs going on and there is a club for each major which take field trips." The radio station is very popular; college sports are big too. Bona has "tons of intramural sports that are fun to participate in. Every semester there are a few tournaments of various sports where you can arrange to have you and friends on a team together. It is fun just to be social."

Student Body

"Most students are white, Catholic, and come from middle-class families" at Bona, and while "there are not many atypical students, those who are fit in fine, thanks to our Franciscan values." Many "live within two hours of campus" and have bonded with the school—usually through its sports teams—long before attending the school. Writes one student, "If you go anywhere off campus wearing your Bona gear, someone is likely to yell 'Go Bonas' at you. It's an instant bond." Most here "have both party animal and Catholic tendencies," although there are some who lean more toward the former." Most everyone here "is interested in, and usually active in, some sort of sport."

ADMISSIONS

Very important factors considered include: Character/personal qualities, interview, recommendations, secondary school record. *Important factors considered include:* Essays, extracurricular activities, standardized test scores, talent/ability, volunteer work. *Other factors considered include:* Alumni/ae relation, class rank, work experience. SAT Reasoning or ACT required. TOEFL required of all international applicants. High school diploma is required, and GED is accepted. *Academic units required:* 4 English, 3 math, 3 science, 2 foreign language, 4 social studies. *Academic units recommended:* 4 English, 3 math, 3 science (3 science lab), 2 foreign language, 4 social studies.

The Inside Word

Saint Bonaventure is a safety for many students applying to more selective Catholic universities, but it does a good job of enrolling a sizable percentage of its admits. Most solid students needn't worry about admission; even so, candidates who rank St. Bonnie as a top choice should still submit essays and interview.

FINANCIAL AID

Students should submit: FAFSA, institution's own financial aid form, state aid form. The Princeton Review suggests that all financial aid forms be submitted as soon as possible after 1/1. *Need-based scholarships/grants offered:* Pell, SEOG, state scholarships/grants, private scholarships, the school's own gift aid. *Loan aid offered:* FFEL Subsidized Stafford, FFEL Unsubsidized Stafford, FFEL PLUS, Federal Perkins, college/university loans from institutional funds. Applicants will be notified of awards on a rolling basis beginning on or about 4/1. Federal Work-study Program available. Institutional employment available. Off-campus job opportunities are excellent.

FROM THE ADMISSIONS OFFICE

"The Saint Bonaventure University family has been imparting the Franciscan tradition to men and women of a rich diversity of backgrounds for more than 130 years. This tradition encourages all who become a part of it to face the world confidently, respect the earthly environment, and work for productive change in the world. The charm of our campus and the inspirational beauty of the surrounding hills provide a special place where growth in learning and living is abundantly realized. The Richter Student Fitness Center, scheduled to be completed in 2004, will provide all students with state-of-the-art facilities for athletics and wellness. Academics at Saint Bonaventure are challenging. Small classes and personalized attention encourage individual growth and development for students. Saint Bonaventure's nationally known Schools of Arts and Sciences, Business Administration, Journalism/Mass Communication, and Education offer majors in 31 disciplines. The School of Graduate Studies also offers several programs leading to the master's degree."

For even more information on this school, turn to page 526 of the "Stats" section.

St. John's College

PO Box 2800, Annapolis, MD 21404 • Admissions: 410-626-2522 • Fax: 410-269-7916
Financial Aid: 410-626-2502 • E-mail: admissions@sjca.edu • Website: www.sjca.edu

Ratings

Quality of Life: 93   Academic: 98   Admissions: 90   Financial Aid: 76

Academics

"The only elective at St. John's College is your choice to attend," explains one student. "From there on out, the program will teach you everything you thought you knew." That's because the entire curriculum at SJC is required, a four-year survey of intellectual history that "starts at the beginning (ancient Greece) and works its way through the years to modern times. Starting from Euclidian geometry, we end up at relativity. Starting at Aristotelian biology, we end up at quantum mechanics and genetics. The school

teaches you that you can only learn where you are by understanding where you have been." Classes here "are all discussion-based; there are no lectures, and classes are never larger than 20 students." Faculty members are referred to as "tutors" rather than professors; they must teach every subject in the curriculum and primarily "serve as guides to learning and add to the discussion. They are, as Socrates says, midwives to ideas." Tutors "come from a wide variety of deeply academic backgrounds, but their specializations have little to do with our curriculum. In the classroom, they are glorified students, as puzzled as the rest of us." The result is "an unbelievable academic community" in which "philosophy is not a game, but rather a crucial guide for living." St. John's is the perfect student for those "ready to confront history's original thinkers directly" and those who want to "teach themselves how to think, how to read and digest information, and how to appreciate the beauty of the written word."

Life

"Class discussions often spill into out-of-class venues" at St. John's, where "on a beautiful sunny day you'll be struck by the vast numbers of people reading outside on the lawns, benches, chairs and steps of the quad, front and back campus." There's a rhythm to life on this campus; "Monday and Thursday nights are largely taken up by seminar (All students have seminar 8–10 P.M.), and though there is often drinking, hanging out on the quad, and animated discussion afterwards, there isn't much in the way of organized activity." However, "every other Saturday night from 10:30 P.M. until 2 A.M. there are waltz parties, which consist mostly of swing dancing, though waltz, polka, and tango are also played." Also, "the college Film Society shows movies almost every Saturday night." A student group called Reality "organizes occasional non-waltz parties such as Oktoberfest, a Halloween Party, and a weekend of debauchery at the end of the year." Student organizations include a theater group, a chorus, an orchestra, a society called Melee that "battles with swords made of plastic piping wrapped in foam," a group called Mabel the Swimming Wonder Monkey that "watches bad movies and mocks them," and a sizeable Christian Fellowship. The highlight of the year, according to most, is the fall croquet match against the Naval Academy. Some here tell us they never leave campus; others report that "trips to Baltimore and Washington, DC are frequent, as well as small groups of students going to concerts."

Student Body

St. John's students report "a definite feeling among students that we've all been Johnnies all our lives, but just didn't have a name for it before." The community here is tight, both because it "is fairly self-selecting, so that most students who come here are invested in their education and self-improvement," and also because "we have a common ground that unites us in the shared curriculum. We're not fragmented by major." An "egalitarian intramural sports program that does not exclude any students and the lack of fraternities and politically partisan groups" also helps. This eclectic group includes "students who graduated at the top of their class in high school, some at the bottom, and some who left high school to come to college."

ADMISSIONS

Very important factors considered include: Essays. *Important factors considered include:* Alumni/ae relation, character/personal qualities, interview, recommendations, secondary school record. *Other factors considered include:* Class rank, extracurricular activities, minority status, standardized test scores, talent/ability, volunteer work, work experience. TOEFL required of all international applicants. High school diploma is required, and GED is accepted. *Academic units required:* 3 math, 2 foreign language. *Academic units recommended:* 4 English, 4 math, 3 science (3 science lab), 4 foreign language, 2 social studies, 2 history.

The Inside Word

St. John's has one of the most personal admissions processes in the country. The applicant pool is highly self-selected and extremely bright, so don't be fooled by the high acceptance rate—every student who is offered admission deserves to be here. Candidates who don't give serious thought to the kind of match they make with the college and devote serious energy to their essays are not likely to be successful.

FINANCIAL AID

Students should submit: FAFSA, CSS/Financial Aid PROFILE, noncustodial (divorced/separated) parents' statement, business/farm supplement. The Princeton Review suggests that all financial aid forms be submitted as soon as possible after 1/1. *Need-based scholarships/grants offered:* Pell, SEOG, state scholarships/grants, the school's own gift aid. *Loan aid offered:* FFEL Subsidized Stafford, FFEL Unsubsidized Stafford, FFEL PLUS, Federal Perkins, college/university loans from institutional funds. Applicants will be notified of awards on a rolling basis beginning on or about 11/1. Federal Work-study Program available. Institutional employment available. Off-campus job opportunities are excellent.

FROM THE ADMISSIONS OFFICE

"The purpose of the admission process is to determine whether an applicant has the necessary preparation and ability to complete the St. John's program satisfactorily. The essays are designed to enable applicants to give a full account of themselves. They can tell the committee much more than statistical records reveal. Previous academic records show whether an applicant has the habits of study necessary at St. John's. Letters of reference, particularly those of teachers, are carefully read for indications that the applicant has the maturity, self-discipline, ability, energy, and initiative to succeed in the St. John's program. St. John's attaches little importance to 'objective' test scores, and no applicant is accepted or rejected because of such scores."

For even more information on this school, turn to page 527 of the "Stats" section.

St. John's University—Queens

8000 UTOPIA PARKWAY, JAMAICA, NY 11439 • ADMISSIONS: 718-990-2000 • FAX: 718-990-5728
E-MAIL: ADMISSIONS@STJOHNS.EDU • WEBSITE: WWW.STJOHNS.EDU

Ratings

Quality of Life: 66   **Academic:** 70   **Admissions:** 82   **Financial Aid:** 72

Academics

St. John's attracts high-caliber students thanks in part to the challenging academic programs and "strong alumni base and emphasis on ethics in the Catholic tradition." Once on campus, students find professors who are "very knowledgeable and, above all, very personable." With a student-faculty ratio of 18:1, small class sizes ensure "a lot of attention from my professor;" this personal approach extends to student advisors, as "there's plenty of academic advisement for anyone who needs it." The computer science, government and politics, and pharmacy departments receive high marks from undergraduates. This academic rigor doesn't lead to "the fierce, cutthroat competition between students you see at other schools." Students laud the generous financial aid offered by the school and also praise the "attentive" and "helpful" administration. Throw in "superior computer facilities" and a well-run freshman center, and students start gushing, "My academic experience has been a triumphant one thus far."

> **SURVEY SAYS . . .**
> *Small classes*
> *Diverse student types on campus*
> *Everyone loves the Red Storm*
> *(Almost) everyone smokes*

Life

"I'm involved in a lot of volunteer groups at school, and most of the people I know are too," writes an altruistic student. "St. John's really encourages giving back to the community." Other students spend their time at "comedy shows, talent shows, fashion shows," or other free activities sponsored by the student life committee. Sports are another common obsession: "If you want to play basketball, well then, you've found your haven." The location in New York City is also commonly cited as a huge plus: "What isn't there to do in NYC?" Sometimes students lament the strong commuter component of campus life, and even among the 2,500 residents, many go home every weekend: "It's still a commuter school no matter how many dorms there are." Most agree, however, that "overall the campus vibe is good here." Those who do live at St. John's tell us that Jamaica Estates offers "off-campus restaurants, pizza joints, delis, cafes, bars, shops, diners. There is a lot of nightlife in Queens and even more in Manhattan."

Student Body

Many students share the sentiment, "I love how diverse this school is!" Apparently, St. John's admits "students from almost every single background" who still manage to "get along really well." Maybe this is because "Queens is the most ethnically diverse county in the country," reflecting the student body from "many different nations." Yet onn the other hand, certain students paint a less harmonious picture with comments like, "My sexual orientation has left me ostracized" and "I just wish that people were more open-minded about certain topics here."

ADMISSIONS

Very important factors considered include: Secondary school record. *Important factors considered include:* Class rank, essays, recommendations, standardized test scores. *Other factors considered include:* Character/personal qualities, extracurricular activities, interview, talent/ability, work experience. SAT Reasoning or ACT required. TOEFL required of all international applicants. High school diploma is required, and GED is accepted. *Academic units required:* 4 English.

The Inside Word

St. John's should receive strong consideration from anyone looking for a large institution with good facilities and resources, as well as a good connection to the community, even amidst the sometimes maddening spread of New York City. Socioeconomic and ethnic diversity ensure a place for you within the student body.

FINANCIAL AID

Students should submit: FAFSA, state aid form. The Princeton Review suggests that all financial aid forms be submitted as soon as possible after 1/1. *Need-based scholarships/grants offered:* Pell, SEOG, state scholarships/grants, private scholarships, the school's own gift aid. *Loan aid offered:* FFEL Subsidized Stafford, FFEL Unsubsidized Stafford, FFEL PLUS, Federal Perkins. Applicants will be notified of awards on a rolling basis beginning on or about 3/15. Off-campus job opportunities are excellent.

FROM THE ADMISSIONS OFFICE

"Why not have it all? Students at St. John's University enjoy the very best of college life: world-class academics, lively campus community, high-tech resources, and the know-how to succeed.

"Founded by the Vincentian Fathers in 1870, St. John's offers a residential college experience in dynamic New York City. Hailing from 38 states and 148 countries, students pursue nearly 100 majors in pharmacy and allied health, the arts, the natural and applied sciences, business, and education. Our professors are leading scholars, 90 percent of whom hold a PhD or other comparable degree.

"St. John's blends classroom learning, confidence-building skills, and real-world experience:

• With a WiFi network and laptops for new students, St. John's is the only New York university in Intel's top ten "Most Unwired Colleges."

• Through our Discover New York course, students see plays, tour museums, and visit ethnic neighborhoods to experience the arts, business, and history in action.

• Across the New York area and around the globe, our students gain experience through supervised service activities in Academic Service Learning.

• Guided by professors with global connections, students earn course credit in Europe, Africa, and Asia through our Study Abroad Program.

• And our Big East, Division I men's and women's athletic teams keep students cheering.

"St. John's has three residential New York campuses: our 105-acre campus in Queens, New York; our picturesque Staten Island campus; and our Manhattan campus, in the heart of the Financial District. There are also graduate centers in Oakdale, New York, and Rome, Italy."

For even more information on this school, turn to page 527 of the "Stats" section.

St. Lawrence University

Payson Hall, Canton, NY 13617 • Admissions: 315-229-5261 • Fax: 315-229-5818
Financial Aid: 315-229-5265 • E-mail: admissions@stlaw.edu • Website: www.stlawu.edu

Ratings
Quality of Life: 76   **Academic:** 88   **Admissions:** 89   **Financial Aid:** 86

Academics

St. Lawrence students love the "really comfortable, home-like atmosphere" engendered by "the size of the student body and the relative isolation of our campus from any real cities." Small class sizes are the norm at this small liberal arts college in the "north country" of New York State, meaning that "classes are discussion seminars rather than lectures. This allows students to make a more personal connection—not only with their fellow students, but also with their fellow professors." Professors "are all passionate about their subjects, easy to talk to, have good senses of humor, and available outside of class. If you can't make it to their office hours, they are willing to schedule a meeting time." Add "great research, independent projects, internships, and study abroad opportunities in 14 countries" as well as "a great diversity of classes offered here that makes it is almost impossible to not become enriched," and you'll understand why students here feel so favorably about SLU academics. But wait; there's more! Students also tell us that "the alumni connections are amazing and a great thing to have later on after college, especially for internships or actual jobs."

> **SURVEY SAYS . . .**
> *Small classes*
> *Great library*
> *Athletic facilities are great*
> *Students are happy*
> *Everyone loves the Saints*
> *Lots of beer drinking*

Life

"At St. Lawrence, there isn't much to do for fun except make your own fun." Some students here immerse themselves in campus life; writes one, "It's most important to be extremely active and try to enjoy what the campus has to offer to the fullest. From intramurals to the student government, there is always something to interest everyone." Students enthusiastically support their Division I hockey teams, which "add interest on an otherwise dull campus in the dead of winter," and enjoy special events like Peak Weekend ("It's for those who hike, I mean really hike, and those who just like to own hiking stuff. The Outing Club, the second oldest after Dartmouth, attempts to get college students on all 36 high peaks in the Adirondacks") and Snowbowl ("lots of sledding and beer"). Most students eventually find their way to SLU's lively party scene. "We do drink a lot," confesses one student. "The school tries to hide it, but St. Lawrence students can handle their booze almost any night of the week and still keep pace with the demanding academic program." For many, "the social scene at St. Lawrence gets a little monotonous. The area doesn't have much to offer, and the main weekend activities revolve around drinking with friends." Many warn that winters are long and exceedingly cold. Road trips to Canada, especially to Ottawa or Montreal, are popular diversions.

Student Body

St. Lawrence has long had a reputation as a preppy haven. Students here tell us that about half the student body fits that stereotype; writes one, the typical "Larry" likes "wearing his polo shirt with the collar turned up, [wearing] a North Face fleece, and carrying a Nalgene bottle. A Muffy, the female Larry, can be spotted with her Vera Bradley bags, Tiffany's heart bracelet, and an inordinate number of shoes." Admits one majority student, "St. Lawrence plays into the hands of the classic prep, so many of us seem to come from New England boarding schools, while the remainder are from upscale areas. We look and act like we stepped right out of the pages of *The Official Preppy Handbook*, and most of us seem proud of it." However, "there are also environmentalists, hippies, the outdoors people, and everyone else" at SLU, although "there aren't many punks and skaters, and people of these types tend to find themselves the token 'oddball' of the dorm." Everyone seems to agree that "we are quite a 'white' school and are lacking a bit in diversity." Many here are "involved in everything. I can't think of anyone who doesn't have extracurriculars. There is an organization for anything you can imagine." Many are active in community service.

ADMISSIONS

Very important factors considered include: Character/personal qualities, recommendations, secondary school record. *Important factors considered include:* Class rank, essays, extracurricular activities, interview, minority status. *Other factors considered include:* Alumni/ae relation, geographical residence, standardized test scores, talent/ability, volunteer work, work experience. TOEFL required of all international applicants. High school diploma is required, and GED is accepted. *Academic units recommended:* 4 English, 4 math, 4 science, 4 foreign language, 2 social studies, 2 history.

The Inside Word

St. Lawrence has a rough time convincing students to commit to spending four years in relative isolation. Serious competition from many fine northeastern colleges also causes admissions standards to be less selective than the university would like. This makes St. Lawrence an especially good choice for academically sound but average students who are seeking an excellent small college experience and/or an outdoorsy setting.

FINANCIAL AID

Students should submit: FAFSA, institution's own financial aid form, noncustodial (divorced/separated) parents' statement, income tax returns/W-2 forms. Regular filing deadline 2/15. The Princeton Review suggests that all financial aid forms be submitted as soon as possible after 1/1. *Need-based scholarships/grants offered:* Pell, SEOG, state scholarships/grants, the school's own gift aid. *Loan aid offered:* Direct Subsidized Stafford, Direct Unsubsidized Stafford, FFEL Subsidized Stafford, FFEL Unsubsidized Stafford, FFEL PLUS, Federal Perkins, college/university loans from institutional funds, GATE Student Loan Program. Applicants will be notified of awards on or about 3/30. Federal Work-study Program available. Institutional employment available. Off-campus job opportunities are poor.

FROM THE ADMISSIONS OFFICE

"St. Lawrence is an independent, nondenominational, liberal arts and sciences university located in northern New York. The student body of 2,000 men and women choose from among more than 30 majors and minors; classes are small, with an emphasis on experiential learning, interdisciplinary study, and independent research. St. Lawrence is a residential college where living and learning are combined through the First-Year Program, theme cottages, and international study. St. Lawrence students are well rounded and involved, with many drawn to the 1,000-acre campus for the opportunity it provides for outdoor recreation. The campus, located in the town of Canton, is halfway between the Adirondack Park and the city of Ottawa. Students are active in various organizations centered on the arts, politics, community service, and athletics, with 32 intercollegiate teams offered. St. Lawrence alumni are loyal and active, providing internships for undergraduates and demonstrating their commitment through giving generously of their time and resources."

For even more information on this school, turn to page 527 of the "Stats" section.

St. Mary's College of Maryland

ADMISSIONS OFFICE, 18952 EAST FISHER ROAD, ST. MARY'S CITY, MD 20686-3001 • ADMISSIONS: 800-492-7181 • FAX: 240-895-5001
FINANCIAL AID: 240-895-3000 • E-MAIL: ADMISSIONS@SMCM.EDU • WEBSITE: WWW.SMCM.EDU

Ratings
Quality of Life: 91   Academic: 86   Admissions: 89   Financial Aid: 82

Academics

As the state's public honors college (it's "not a Catholic college," clarifies one junior), St. Mary's College of Maryland offers its 2,000 undergrads the work-heavy, personalized education of a private school at public-school prices—a fact that regularly places the college among the "best buys" in higher education. Students describe the professors as "really awesome people" who are "passionate about their area of focus," and extol their "willingness to help or even just talk with students outside class time." "You're almost always on a first-name basis with them and have their home phone numbers and email addresses," boasts one double major. While "not every professor is going to be absolutely fantastic," we see many variations of the refrain: "The professors rock!" While SMCM's administration receives an array of kudos, it also takes a few knocks. A diplomatic junior writes that though administration members "do their best" to maintain dialog with students, they're often "too removed from the concerns of the students." Because of an enrollment increase a couple of years ago, students occasionally grumble about "understaffed" departments, "temporary professors," or "a shortage of classes and housing." Construction, most likely a result of such growth, grates on many students' nerves—but such are the (temporary) growing pains of small colleges trying to bulk up. Overall, students seem content, describing their education as "challenging but stimulating" and their workload as "heavy." One sophomore writes, "I have learned, laughed, and worked like crazy...but it's all been worth it." A final piece of advice for prospective students: "Take a lot of AP classes and do well on the AP exams...this will help you place out of a number of general education requirements that are not nearly as strong as many other classes."

> **SURVEY SAYS . . .**
> Small classes
> Students are friendly
> Campus feels safe
> Low cost of living
> Students are happy
> Frats and sororities are unpopular
> or nonexistent

Life

Because the "beautiful" SMCM campus lies along the St. Mary's River in the heart of Maryland's Chesapeake Bay region, water sports and other outdoor recreational activities are inescapable here. "You can take out boats, kayaks, etc. just by giving them your student ID," boasts a junior. "Calvert Cliffs is just down the road, too, which is a pretty awesome place to hike." The campus location clearly has its benefits. But "we live in the boonies," admits a sophomore. SMCM is "not located near any big cities or areas that have a lot of off-campus activities" (historic St. Mary's City adjoins the campus; and Washington, DC, is a two-hour drive)—so students rely on campus life to keep them busy. There's "a lot of political activism," "widespread environmental interest," a "wealth of clubs and recreational opportunities," popular athletic programs on the intramural, club, and varsity levels, and, of course, classes to keep these undergrads well occupied. Although some say they drink on weekends, they're quick to add that there are "a lot of students" who don't "party/drink" and that there is "little or no pressure to drink if you're not into it." Overall, the students "lead pretty balanced lives." "Everyone here is all about having fun," says a junior, "but [they] are really serious about getting their work done too."

Student Body

Students describe their classmates as "open," "down-to-earth," "laid back," and write that the only attribute "typical" of a Seahawk is uniqueness. In the cafeteria, "you can witness a girl wearing Abercrombie & Fitch sitting with a farm girl, a goth, a hippie, and they are all hysterically laughing." Another thing you'll notice in the cafeteria: SMCM has a "large vegan/vegetarian population." Students are "on the whole more likely to be liberal"; and at SMCM, "closed minded behavior is usually not taken well by most students." Students are so trusting of each other that "no one locks any doors on campus... Knocking is just not a St. Mary's thing to do!" If undergrads could shake a magic wand, they'd like to see SMCM become more "ethnically diverse." "The school is made up of mostly white, higher-income level kids," says a senior. That said, everyone is "accepted and accepting."

ADMISSIONS

Very important factors considered include: Essays, secondary school record, standardized test scores. *Important factors considered include:* Extracurricular activities, recommendations, talent/ability. *Other factors considered include:* Alumni/ae relation, character/personal qualities, class rank, geographical residence, interview, minority status, state residency, volunteer work, work experience. SAT Reasoning or ACT required. TOEFL required of all international applicants. High school diploma is required, and GED is accepted. *Academic units required:* 4 English, 3 math, 3 science (2 science lab), 1 social studies, 2 history, 7 academic electives. *Academic units recommended:* 4 English, 4 math, 4 science (3 science lab), 4 foreign language, 1 history, 8 academic electives.

The Inside Word

There are few better choices than St. Mary's for better-than-average students who are not likely to get admitted to one of the top 50 or so colleges in the country. It is likely that if funding for public colleges is able to stabilize, or even grow, that this place will soon be joining the ranks of the best. Now is the time to take advantage, before the academic expectations of the admissions committee start to soar.

FINANCIAL AID

Students should submit: FAFSA. Regular filing deadline 3/1. The Princeton Review suggests that all financial aid forms be submitted as soon as possible after 1/1. *Need-based scholarships/grants offered:* Pell, SEOG, state scholarships/grants, private scholarships, the school's own gift aid. *Loan aid offered:* FFEL Subsidized Stafford, FFEL Unsubsidized Stafford, FFEL PLUS, Federal Perkins. Applicants will be notified of awards on or about 4/1. Federal Work-study Program available. Institutional employment available. Off-campus job opportunities are good.

FROM THE ADMISSIONS OFFICE

"St. Mary's College of Maryland occupies a distinctive niche and represents a real value in American higher education. It is a public college, dedicated to the ideal of affordable, accessible education but committed to quality teaching and excellent programs for undergraduate students. The result is that St. Mary's offers the small college experience of the same high caliber usually found at prestigious private colleges, but at public college prices. Designated by the state of Maryland as 'a public honors college,' one of only two public colleges in the nation to hold that distinction, St. Mary's has become increasingly attractive to high school students. Admission is very selective."

For even more information on this school, turn to page 528 of the "Stats" section.

STATE UNIVERSITY OF NEW YORK AT ALBANY

1400 WASHINGTON AVENUE, ALBANY, NY 12222 • ADMISSIONS: 518-442-5435 • FAX: 518-442-5383
FINANCIAL AID: 518-442-5757 • E-MAIL: UGADMISSIONS@ALBANY.EDU • WEBSITE: WWW.ALBANY.EDU

Ratings
Quality of Life: 61   **Academic:** 65   **Admissions:** 85   **Financial Aid:** 71

Academics

SUNY—Albany is an excellent example of a typical large state university. Its assets include broad course offerings in a wide range of departments and world-class research, "especially in the fields of science and nanotechnology." One student agrees, "There is so much to take and learn about." The school's location in New York's capital also "offers a lot of opportunities for political science and business majors." Reports one business undergraduate, "Major

> **SURVEY SAYS . . .**
> *Great library*
> *Diverse student types on campus*
> *Lots of beer drinking*
> *Hard liquor is popular*
> *(Almost) everyone smokes*

firms come up here to recruit, making it easy to obtain an internship and eventually a job." The downside of Albany is that many feel that "you are a number here. Unless you make a point to let your professors know your name, they don't care." Warns one student, "Albany puts a lot of responsibility on the student; there is no hand-holding. Professors are available, resources are accessible, and involvement is possible, but it is entirely on the student to sink or swim." Most professors "do their best to try to help you if you have a problem; however, they are very busy and have many students." Some professors, unfortunately, seem to be "here to do research, not to teach." Students advise that "the study groups on campus are very helpful, and not all students take advantage of them." Weighing the good and bad, most students would probably agree that Albany offers "a quality education with a reasonable price tag."

Life

Students at Albany overwhelmingly agree that "campus life is pretty boring around these parts." Nearly everyone tells us that the bars are the place to be, even for underclassmen, especially since "the bars rarely check ID." The location is so crucial to social life that, by junior year, many students "move downtown by the bars." Many students warn that "Albany is a good school, but the partying can take over your normal good student. You have to be mature to learn to balance both." Teetotalers have few options; writes one, "If you don't drink, then you basically don't have a social life. I don't drink, so I don't have a life." The harsh winters don't help social situations. "The snowstorms and coldness make Albany a very tough place to live, and sometimes students are very depressed," explains one student. Some students find refuge in "political groups such as NYPIRG [New York Public Interest Research Group], and minority groups such as ASIA [Albany State Indian Alliance], which are very popular on campus." Others seek out the city's nonalcoholic offerings, which include "great restaurants. Many people go to them if they have the money." An upgrade to the school's athletic program, many students believe, might offer an attractive alternative to the bar scene; but for now, "students get in free to our football games, and still no one goes. The school definitely has no school spirit, especially with the athletics."

Student Body

With only 7.8 percent of students coming from outside of the state, the key to understanding the student body of SUNY—Albany is an understanding of the body politic of New York State. It is plain to most undergraduates that despite its upstate location, the student population at SUNY—Albany more closely reflects the demographics of New York City and Long Island, as "there is a very strong Jewish population on this campus," as well as "a lot of African American and Hispanic" students. Undergraduates also tell us that "since the school is so [large], it allows for everyone to fit into their own clique." However, some students detect "a little bit of tension between Long Islanders, [students from] New York City (any of the five boroughs), and Upstaters."

ADMISSIONS

Very important factors considered include: Character/personal qualities, class rank, secondary school record, standardized test scores. *Important factors considered include:* Essays, recommendations. *Other factors considered include:* Alumni/ae relation, extracurricular activities, geographical residence, minority status, talent/ability, volunteer work, work experience. SAT Reasoning or ACT required. TOEFL required of all international applicants. High school diploma is required, and GED is accepted. *Academic units required:* 4 English, 2 math, 2 science (2 science lab), 1 foreign language, 3 social studies, 2 history, 5 academic electives. *Academic units recommended:* 4 math, 3 science (3 science lab), 3 foreign language.

The Inside Word

While the SUNY system's budgetary woes have abated to a degree, funding uncertainties continue to be a problem. Applications and standards are on the rise. Albany is the third most selective SUNY campus. Perhaps the university's status as the training camp site for the New York Giants will bring both revenue and facilities to aid a turnaround. Without increased private funding, Albany is likely to remain a relatively easy path into a SUNY university center.

FINANCIAL AID

Students should submit: FAFSA, NY State residents should apply for TAP onliine at www.hesc.com. Regular filing deadline 4/15. The Princeton Review suggests that all financial aid forms be submitted as soon as possible after 1/1. *Need-based scholarships/grants offered:* Pell, SEOG, state scholarships/grants. *Loan aid offered:* FFEL Subsidized Stafford, FFEL Unsubsidized Stafford, FFEL PLUS, Federal Perkins. Applicants will be notified of awards on a rolling basis beginning on or about 3/15. Federal Work-study Program available. Institutional employment available. Off-campus job opportunities are excellent.

FROM THE ADMISSIONS OFFICE

"Increasing numbers of well-prepared students are discovering the benefits of study in SUNY Albany's nationally ranked programs and are taking advantage of outstanding internship and employment opportunities in Upstate New York's "Tech Valley." The already strong undergraduate program will be enhanced, beginning with the expansion of the journalism program, while accelerated degree options enable ambitious students to earn a combined bachelor's/master's in one of 30 fields. Nine schools and colleges, including the nation's first College of Nanoscale Science and Engineering, offer bachelor's, master's, and doctoral programs on three different campuses, to more than 11,000 undergraduates and 5,000 graduate students. An award-winning advisement program helps students take advantage of all these options by customizing the undergraduate experiences. More than two-thirds of Albany graduates go on for advanced degrees, and acceptance to law and medical school is above the national average. Student life on campus includes 150 clubs, honors societies, and other groups, and 19 Division I varsity teams. With 13 other colleges in the Region, Albany is a great college town, adjacent to spectacular natural and recreational centers of New York and New England."

For even more information on this school, turn to page 530 of the "Stats" section.

STATE UNIVERSITY OF NEW YORK AT BINGHAMTON

PO Box 6000, BINGHAMTON, NY 13902-6001 • ADMISSIONS: 607-777-2171 • FAX: 607-777-4445
FINANCIAL AID: 607-777-2428 • E-MAIL: ADMIT@BINGHAMTON.EDU • WEBSITE: WWW.BINGHAMTON.EDU

Ratings
Quality of Life: 62   **Academic:** 75   **Admissions:** 92   **Financial Aid:** 83

Academics

Branded as Binghamton University, SUNY at Binghamton is "a top-rate school that's way more competitive than most private schools in the northeast, and you get it at a state school price," students here report. Undergrads tell us that "Your quality of education really depends on what school you will be in," adding that BU boasts "a good management program," a "strong science department, especially in biology, psychology, and the premed programs," a "very strong political science program offering a popular major called politics, philosophy, and law that yields high law school acceptance rates," and "engineering and nursing programs that give the students what they need." Workloads also vary by school, from "killer math and science classes" and "very hard classes in the special schools (engineering, management, and nursing)," to "everything else, which is okay though still competitive." Similarly, professors can range from good to bad, from the requisite "science profs so caught up in their own research they seem to see teaching as an annoying obligation" and "math TAs who do not speak English" to "social science teachers who really care" and "management profs who demand the best and in return pass along their industry connections." For most students, the administration is either a whipping boy or an afterthought; writes one student, "Academics appear to run themselves. I don't see the administration worrying about them at all; they are too preoccupied with admissions, housing, and their precious up-and-coming basketball team!"

> **SURVEY SAYS . . .**
> *Great computer facilities*
> *Great library*
> *Diverse student types on campus*
> *Campus feels safe*
> *Lots of beer drinking*
> *Hard liquor is popular*
> *(Almost) everyone smokes*

Life

Just about everyone at BU agrees that "Binghamton is not the most exciting city in the world. Many would argue that the only reason the town is still around after almost all of the big employers packed up and left is the university." How this affects student life varies; some look at the town and conclude that "there are not many places that students can go. There are bars, frats, and movies, and these places get old quick." Others discover "some little gems in Binghamton, such as galleries on Washington Street, the Art Mission, and the Lost Dog Cafe for local music and a nice break from the bars." It's the same story on campus; while some complain that "there isn't much to do but drink," others counter that "there is so much to do on campus, but most people are too lazy to explore the different clubs and activities. I feel bad for the students who are missing out on the wide array of on-campus activities, because I know so many of them waste their time drinking either in their dorm rooms or at frat parties." Students "who wish to remain sober have Late Nite Binghamton, which offers free music, movies, drinks, and others games and/or crafts every night on the weekends." Things may perk up here in the future; school spirit is on the rise because "we've recently moved up to Division I in the NCAA."

Student Body

As you might expect at a school with more than 10,000 undergrads, "there is a wide array of students at Binghamton University." Their ranks include "many students from down in Long Island, New York City, and the suburbs," as well as "students from upstate New York." Upstate students tell us "it is very easy to feel a little alienated because upstate is regarded as heinously uncool by the downstaters and also because a lot of students arrive with a whole network of friends already in place." While geographic diversity is limited mostly to the different regions of New York State, "there is plenty of ethnic diversity here. The Black and Latino Student Unions are both very active groups on campus. The Hillel is also very active as there is a large Jewish population. Asian students make up a large minority. Different groups do not necessarily interact, but there is no tension among groups, either."

ADMISSIONS

Very important factors considered include: Secondary school record, standardized test scores. *Important factors considered include:* Class rank, essays, extracurricular activities, recommendations, volunteer work. *Other factors considered include:* Alumni/ae relation, character/personal qualities, geographical residence, minority status, state residency, talent/ability, work experience. SAT Reasoning or ACT required. TOEFL required of all international applicants. High school diploma is required, and GED is accepted. *Academic units required:* 4 English, 3 math, 2 science, 3 foreign language, 2 social studies. *Academic units recommended:* 4 math, 3 science, 3 foreign language, 3 history.

The Inside Word

Binghamton's admissions process is highly selective, but fairly simple. Candidates go through a process that considers an applicant's grades, course selections, and SAT or ACT results. Out-of-state enrollment is small for a public university of Binghamton's reputation, but the University's enrollment management strategy includes enhancing efforts to recruit students from further afield.

FINANCIAL AID

Students should submit: FAFSA, state aid form. The Princeton Review suggests that all financial aid forms be submitted as soon as possible after 1/1. *Need-based scholarships/grants offered:* Pell, SEOG, state scholarships/grants, private scholarships, the school's own gift aid. *Loan aid offered:* Direct Subsidized Stafford, Direct Unsubsidized Stafford, Direct PLUS, Federal Perkins, Federal Nursing, college/university loans from institutional funds. Applicants will be notified of awards on a rolling basis beginning on or about 3/15.

FROM THE ADMISSIONS OFFICE

"SUNY—Binghamton University has established itself as the premier public university in the northeast, because of our outstanding undergraduate programs, vibrant campus culture and committed faculty. Students are academically motivated, but there is a great deal of mutual help as they compete against the standard of a class rather than each other. Faculty and students work side by side in research labs or on artistic pursuits. Achievement, exploration and leadership are hallmarks of a Binghamton education. Add to that a campuswide commitment to internationalization that includes a robust study abroad program, cultural offerings, languages and international studies, and you have a place where graduates leave prepared for success."

For even more information on this school, turn to page 530 of the "Stats" section.

STATE UNIVERSITY OF NEW YORK AT BUFFALO

15 CAPEN HALL, BUFFALO, NY 14260 • ADMISSIONS: 888-UB-ADMIT • FAX: 716-645-6411
FINANCIAL AID: 866-838-7257 • E-MAIL: UB-ADMISSIONS@BUFFALO.EDU • WEBSITE: WWW.BUFFALO.EDU

Ratings
Quality of Life: 70   Academic: 70   Admissions: 86   Financial Aid: 78

Academics

"It is so easy to make connections that will help you later in life" at SUNY at Buffalo (aka University at Buffalo, or UB), a "flagship SUNY school" that students feel offers "the equivalent of a private school education for the price of a public school." One student tells us, "Academically, UB is something to be respected. The engineering and business programs are worthwhile, and the school takes pride in upholding their excellence." Students in our survey also offer rave reviews of the biology department (and other science programs), the architecture program, and offerings in communication. UB provides "a noncompetitive learning environment (good thing) that prepares you well for life beyond the university, whether that be grad school [or] work." The school also offers "a lot of freedom to make your own choices academically" and "great access to internship opportunities." The curriculum is demanding but, in most areas, not grueling. One student adds, "If you study and do your homework, you should have no problem getting through here." While most students find that professors are "not very approachable," outgoing students report otherwise. Writes one, "Professors here are surprisingly accessible if you are willing to do a little work."

> **SURVEY SAYS . . .**
> *Great computer facilities*
> *Great library*
> *Diverse student types on campus*
> *Student publications are popular*
> *Lots of beer drinking*
> *Hard liquor is popular*
> *(Almost) everyone smokes*

Life

The university's two campuses—the urban South Campus, home to students in the medical and architectural sciences, and the suburban North Campus, home to most other undergraduates—have distinct cultures. Most students agree that South is the place to be. It's where "all the good partying is," plus "Main Street on the South Campus has tons of bars and pizzerias to visit." North Campus, by contrast, "is a cement wasteland situated within the cultural void that is Amherst, New York." Students who live on North Campus (many complain that school buses connecting the campuses don't run often enough) "have little opportunity to escape suburbia's death grip, so they never realize how very wrong their perceptions of Buffalo as a boring, uncool city are." Students who have cars (or the tenacity to wait in the cold for the bus) reap the benefits of Buffalo's "coffeehouses, art galleries, museums, unparalleled architecture, nightlife (includes bars that stay open until 4:00 a.m.), fantastic restaurants, concerts, shopping, and the like." Campus comes alive for special events. Students report that "the Student Association tries to play a large part in daily life. And with a budget of about $2.2 million, they bring huge acts to school (like No Doubt, Dave Matthews, Ja Rule, LL Cool J, Jimmy Fallon, [and] Dave Chapelle)." Intercollegiate athletics are not that popular. Explains one student, "We do have a large division of athletics, but our football team is terrible, and, despite the unparalleled efforts of our administration, nobody really cares about sports."

Student Body

The student body at UB is extremely diverse. Writes one, "There are so many different people here and not just race-wise or concerning sexual orientation or religion. People here are so different than [who] I knew in high school—there are hippies, computer obsessives, musicians, Republicans, card players, and artists." Adds another, "You have every kind of student here. You have lazy ones who just want to get drunk and high. You have the hardworking kids who are going to Harvard for grad school. You have upper-middle-class kids, and you have kids who are dirt poor. With ethnicity you have a model UN when it comes to UB." Students observe that "although many people tend to congregate into groups based on ethnicity, they do not intentionally exclude others. I feel welcome in any group of people regardless of race, and I think many of my fellow students would agree."

ADMISSIONS

Very important factors considered include: Class rank, secondary school record, standardized test scores. *Other factors considered include:* Character/personal qualities, essays, extracurricular activities, geographical residence, minority status, recommendations, talent/ability, volunteer work, work experience. SAT Reasoning or ACT required. TOEFL required of all international applicants. High school diploma is required, and GED is accepted. *Academic units recommended:* 4 English, 3 math, 3 science, 3 foreign language, 4 social studies.

The Inside Word

Buffalo was formerly a private university and was absorbed into the SUNY system. Its admissions process reflects this private heritage to the extent possible (applications are centrally processed for the entire system in Albany). It's one of the few SUNY schools with a freshman academic profile higher than its published admissions standards. Although Binghamton is academically the most selective of the SUNY University Centers, Buffalo is in many ways closer to what other states refer to as the flagship of the state system.

FINANCIAL AID

Students should submit: FAFSA. The Princeton Review suggests that all financial aid forms be submitted as soon as possible after 1/1. *Need-based scholarships/grants offered:* Pell, SEOG, state scholarships/grants, private scholarships, the school's own gift aid, federal nursing scholarships. *Loan aid offered:* Direct Subsidized Stafford, Direct Unsubsidized Stafford, Direct PLUS, Federal Perkins, Federal Nursing, college/university loans from institutional funds. Applicants will be notified of awards on a rolling basis beginning on or about 2/1.

FROM THE ADMISSIONS OFFICE

"The University at Buffalo (UB) is among the nation's finest public research universities—a learning community where you'll work side by side with world-renowned faculty, including Nobel, Pulitzer, National Medal of Science, and other award winners. As the largest, most comprehensive university center in the State University of New York (SUNY) system, UB offers more undergraduate majors than any public university in New York or New England. With opportunities for joint degrees and combined five-year bachelor's and master's degrees, you'll be free to chart an academic course that meets your individual goals—you can even design your own major. Our unique University Honors and University at Buffalo Scholars scholarship programs offer an enhanced academic experience, including opportunities for independent study, advanced research, and specialized advisement. The university is committed to providing the latest information technology—and is widely considered to be one of the most wired universities in the country. UB also places a high priority on offering an exciting campus environment. With nonstop festivals, Division I sporting events, concerts, and visiting lecturers, you'll have plenty to do outside of the classroom. We encourage you and your family to visit campus to see UB up close and in person. Our Visit UB campus tours and presentations are offered year-round."

For even more information on this school, turn to page 531 of the "Stats" section.

STATE UNIVERSITY OF NEW YORK AT STONY BROOK

OFFICE OF ADMISSIONS, STONY BROOK, NY 11794-1901 • ADMISSIONS: 631-632-9898 • FAX: 631-632-9898
FINANCIAL AID: 631-632-6840 • E-MAIL: UGADMISSIONS@NOTES.CC.SUNYSB.EDU • WEBSITE: WWW.STONYBROOK.EDU

Ratings
Quality of Life: 62   **Academic:** 73   **Admissions:** 89   **Financial Aid:** 67

Academics

With its solid reputation in the sciences, mathematics, and engineering, Stony Brook University has developed into one of the best known schools in New York's State university system. Students tell us that this reputation is well deserved; writes one, "They put a lot of money into science programs, so you get a decent science- or engineering-related education. The professors are brilliant, too. Not all of them are good teachers, but still it's an honor to be taught by them, and usually, all you have to do is glance through the textbook to clarify something you didn't understand." Students also love that "it is very easy for students to get involved in research." The school's assets help soften the blow of its deficiencies, which include teacher assistants "from other countries, so it is often very difficult to understand or talk to them;" the school's large size; and an administration that sometimes seems "equivalent to chaos. There is no communication between departments who should be working together." The most prestigious programs are also the most rigorous. Students say, "We have a variety of curriculums with different degrees of 'challengingness,' depending on the prerequisites and concepts covered."

> **SURVEY SAYS . . .**
> *Great computer facilities*
> *Great library*
> *Diverse student types on campus*
> *Lots of beer drinking*
> *(Almost) everyone smokes*

Life

The charms of extracurricular life at Stony Brook are apparently lost on many of its students. One student explains, "There are so many things to do on campus, [that] it's crazy; but many students don't take advantage of them." Agrees a junior, "It took me two years to realize how much the campus has to offer. There are many clubs and organizations to participate in, [as well as] choirs and theater; and if you are into parties, there is an array of parties on and off campus." Adds another student, "Student Activities has something planned every Wednesday afternoon: advising sessions, career opportunities, homecoming kickoffs, barbecues, [and] DJs. The athletic programs at Stony Brook are excellent, especially the facilities. The recently completed stadium and the relatively new athletic arena are in excellent condition. Our beloved Seawolves collegiate sports and intramurals keep most athletic people busy." Beyond campus, "Port Jefferson is a great place for fun; and for the students [who are twenty-one or older], there are pubs and great restaurants. There is also a mall and many other stores. It's a busy town." Kids still gripe about life on campus primarily because close to "half the students are commuters, and a large portion of the students who actually live on campus are from the city, and the train station is right on campus. So, the campus is mostly dead on weekends because almost everyone goes home."

Student Body

"There is really no typical student" at Stony Brook, students tell us, "yet there are common groups of students. For example, there are the strongly academic-oriented students, always studying, spending little time at social events; there are the students who mix studying with pleasure; and then there are those students who party more than they study. Everyone somehow finds their place at Stony Brook." Many students who fall into the first group make up the school's powerhouse science and math departments. Students tell us that a surprising number of them are international students. The large international population means that "everyone on campus is so different; there is an overwhelming number of ethnic backgrounds and religions on campus." Also, about half of the students "are commuters who have lived in the area their entire lives."

ADMISSIONS

Very important factors considered include: Secondary school record, standardized test scores. *Important factors considered include:* Class rank. *Other factors considered include:* Alumni/ae relation, character/personal qualities, essays, extracurricular activities, interview, recommendations, talent/ability, volunteer work, work experience. SAT Reasoning or ACT required. TOEFL required of all international applicants. High school diploma is required, and GED is accepted. *Academic units required:* 4 English, 3 math, 3 science, 2 foreign language, 4 history. *Academic units recommended:* 4 English, 4 math, 4 science, 3 foreign language, 4 history.

The Inside Word

Graduate programs continue to receive national accolades, and the New York State legislature has been somewhat kinder to SUNY of late. Stony Brook's athletic programs have moved to NCAA Division I, America East Conference, in hopes of generating greater visibility and increases in applications. For the near future, admission will remain relatively easy for solid students.

FINANCIAL AID

Students should submit: FAFSA. The Princeton Review suggests that all financial aid forms be submitted as soon as possible after 1/1. *Need-based scholarships/grants offered:* Pell, SEOG, state scholarships/grants, the school's own gift aid. *Loan aid offered:* FFEL Subsidized Stafford, FFEL Unsubsidized Stafford, FFEL PLUS, Federal Perkins. Applicants will be notified of awards on a rolling basis beginning on or about 3/1. Federal Work-study Program available. Off-campus job opportunities are good.

FROM THE ADMISSIONS OFFICE

"Stony Brook is ranked among the 50 best universities in North America and one of the 150 best universities worldwide in the London Times Higher Education Supplement—placing Stony Brook in the top two percent of all universities in the world. In addition, *Kiplinger's Personal Finance* has ranked Stony Brook one of the "100 Best Values" among public universities.

"*The Wall Street Journal* has ranked us eighth in the nation among public institutions placing students in the elite graduate schools in medicine, law, and business. Our graduates include the leader of the Imaging Team for the Cassini mission to Saturn, the President of Stanford University, a Pulitzer Prize winning investigative journalist for the Washington Post, and a Grammy award-winning performer with the Metropolitan Opera Company, and more than 100,000 others.

"Situated amidst 1,100 lush, wooded acres on the North Shore of Long Island, life at Stony Brook is as rewarding outside the classroom as it is inside. Our students benefit from both the resources of a major research university and the close-knit communities of innovative undergraduate colleges, with a student-faculty ratio of 14:1. Guaranteed campus housing for all four years, students enjoy outstanding recreational facilities that include a new stadium, modern student activities center, and indoor sports complex. In addition, the Staller Center for the Arts offers spectacular theatrical and musical performances throughout the year.

"We invite students who possess both intellectual curiosity and academic ability to explore the countless exciting opportunities available at Stony Brook."

For even more information on this school, turn to page 531 of the "Stats" section.

STATE UNIVERSITY OF NEW YORK COLLEGE AT BROCKPORT

350 NEW CAMPUS DRIVE, BROCKPORT, NY 14420 • ADMISSIONS: 585-395-2751 • FAX: 585-395-5452
E-MAIL: ADMIT@BROCKPORT.EDU • WEBSITE: WWW.BROCKPORT.EDU

Ratings
Quality of Life: 74   **Academic:** 74   **Admissions:** 79   **Financial Aid:** 86

Academics

Although frequently overshadowed by its larger and better-known peers in the SUNY system, Brockport has a lot to offer, including unique programs in computational science, physical education, and dance. Brockport also shines in a number of popular career-track areas, such as psychology, education, nursing, and criminal justice. Students here appreciate the diversity of classes typical of a state university, coupled with atypical "small class sizes and teachers who are available through e-mail and office hours each day." They disapprove, however, of the general education requirements ("They make you feel like you're taking all your high school classes over again") and the computer system ("It needs a dramatic upgrade. Processing is slow, which is very problematic and inconvenient"). Brockport's Honors Program and the Delta College earn high marks. Students report approvingly that the program's emphasis on experiential learning "helps you to decide if your major is right for you, encouraging you to do a series of internships in your major before graduation."

> **SURVEY SAYS . . .**
> *Small classes*
> *Lots of beer drinking*

Life

Brockport, most students agree, is "a nice location, close enough to Rochester to make internships and jobs fairly available, yet far enough away to stay mostly quiet." Some students think it's a little too quiet, in fact. "There are not so many places for entertainment, such as dancing clubs, playing games, etc., and transportation is limited," complains one international undergrad. Drinking is quite popular from Thursday through Saturday, since a number of local bars make it "very easy for anyone to get drunk around here. It's also very easy to have alcohol in the dorms." Off-campus house parties are another popular option when it's party time, which, for most students, is relegated to weekends only. The school is "very sports-oriented," with most students active in intramurals or intercollegiate sports, or, at the very least, as active spectators. "The biggest school pride is our football team, no matter how bad we are," writes one undergrad of his beloved Golden Eagles, who posted an impressive 9–2 record in 2003. The school does a decent job of scheduling concerts and lectures on campus, students tell us. Bowling, school-sponsored day trips, and midnight movies at The Strand are other favorite ways to unwind. While some students gripe that the buildings could "use a facelift" because "they are stuck in the '60s," the "amazing" food that is served here gets rave reviews from many.

Students

"There are a lot of jocks at Brockport because the physical education major is so popular," students tell us, adding that the school's 23 Division III intercollegiate teams further enhance the jock population. But there are also "'smart' math majors, laid-back English majors, sorority girls, fraternity boys, partiers/druggies, religious people, and then your everyday typical people... They all fit in." While most students are white and "from rural areas," the presence of more than 6,000 undergrads allows students who fall outside the norm to find their own comfortable niche, "whether it be within a dorm, religious organization, sexual orientation, racial clique, or other social setting. Religious, racial, and sexual-orientation groups are widespread and generally accepted throughout campus."

ADMISSIONS

Very important factors considered include: Class rank, secondary school record, standardized test scores. *Important factors considered include:* Essays, extracurricular activities, recommendations, talent/ability. *Other factors considered include:* Character/personal qualities, interview, volunteer work, work experience. SAT Reasoning or ACT required. TOEFL required of all international applicants. High school diploma is required, and GED is accepted. *Academic units required:* 4 English, 3 math, 3 science (1 science lab), 4 social studies, 4 academic electives. *Academic units recommended:* 3 foreign language.

The Inside Word

If you make the hike from beyond the greater Buffalo region to see what Brockport has to offer and why it is described as an idyllic college-town experience, you'll find vibrant, if not especially demanding, academic and social lifestyles, owing themselves to a somewhat complacent student body—that is, until you arrive.

FINANCIAL AID

Students should submit: FAFSA, state aid form. The Princeton Review suggests that all financial aid forms be submitted as soon as possible after 1/1. *Need-based scholarships/grants offered:* Pell, SEOG, state scholarships/grants, private scholarships, the school's own gift aid. *Loan aid offered:* Direct Subsidized Stafford, Direct Unsubsidized Stafford, Direct PLUS, Federal Perkins, Federal Nursing, alternative loans. Applicants will be notified of awards on or about 4/15.

FROM THE ADMISSIONS OFFICE

"The SUNY Brockport mission statement puts it in writing: 'SUNY Brockport has the success of its students as its highest priority.' College programs, faculty, staff, and the campus itself all operate with that goal in mind.

"New programs in environmental science, biology, and computational science and the AACSB accreditation for the business programs serve as a complement to the Honors Program and the unique Delta College, the largest study abroad program in SUNY and one of the top ten in the nation. The full range of SUNY Brockport's academic programs offer students a variety of challenging learning options leading to strong post-graduate success. Nearly 25 percent of SUNY Brockport undergraduates go on to graduate school and 93 percent find jobs or are in graduate school within six months of graduation.

"Substantial investments in campus facilities in recent years have included top-to-bottom renovations of the Lennon Hall science center, Hartwell Hall, and Seymour College Union. These, along with other facilities upgrades, make for as vibrant campus life. A spacious suburban campus with easy access to Rochester, Buffalo, and Lake Ontario offers an exciting choice of cultural and outdoor activities.

"Consider SUNY Brockport if you want to study with world-class faculty; be actively involved in cultural, social, and athletic programs; and apply what you've learned to challenges in the real world. We encourage you to visit our campus of more than 300 acres and meet with faculty, staff, and students. It's the best way to discover if our strengths complement your talents and aspirations."

For even more information on this school, turn to page 532 of the "Stats" section.

STATE UNIVERSITY OF NEW YORK COLLEGE AT FREDONIA

178 CENTRAL AVENUE, FREDONIA, NY 14063 • ADMISSIONS: 716-673-3251 • FAX: 716-673-3249
E-MAIL: ADMISSIONS.OFFICE@FREDONIA.EDU • WEBSITE: WWW.FREDONIA.EDU

Ratings
Quality of Life: 69   Academic: 77   Admissions: 82   Financial Aid: 86

Academics

"This school is all about music programs and education programs," Fredonia undergraduates agree, pointing to three applied-music majors and five other music-related disciplines (including music education, which combines Fredonia's two areas of greatest strength) as proof. Eight majors in the graphic arts also have their champions here, as do popular majors in the more "mainstream" disciplines of history, psychology, and business. Students report that Fredonia provides "a positive learning environment" in which to earn "a liberal arts education in a friendly atmosphere" while gaining "good field experience and life experience." Professors score points for "personality" and friendliness, though the instructional quality varies from school to school. Arts professors "treat students with respect and teach us in a way we can understand. They are great." The business school, on the other hand, "could stand to incorporate a few more discussion classes and team activities into the program." Students tell us that the Fredonia administration "runs well but is kind of invisible."

> **SURVEY SAYS . . .**
> Small classes
> Students are friendly
> Musical organizations are popular
> Lots of beer drinking
> Hard liquor is popular
> (Almost) everyone smokes

Life

"A lot of people do different things with their time" at Fredonia, explains one student, adding that "At any school, people are going to go out and get wasted, and that is also true for Fredonia. But you can have a good time without alcohol. The crew at the radio station is a riot, and broomball is one of the most popular sports here on campus. And everyone is a Bills fan! Also, if you're ever in the area: Pizza, Wings 'N' Things has great chicken finger subs." Those who join student clubs tell us that "being in an organization helps with social life and well as community and college networking." Greek life is popular, as are the local bars, which many tell us "are excellent, especially on dollar pint nights, and there are lots of bars to choose from." The large music program means there's always some sort of musical activity occurring, often in conjunction with the theatre program. Students warn that the Fredonia area is "really windy, like Michael-Jackson-video windy," and that the campus could use a makeover since "at least half of the buildings are made of concrete—that's a little tacky."

Student Body

There are "lots of artsy creative people, but also lots of suburban white kids who drink stale beer" at Fredonia. The former are drawn largely from "the many music and art majors," whose numbers include "a lot of hippies and more than a few homosexuals." Some here would divide the entire student body into "two basic types: those interested in knowledge and education, and those interested in television and alcohol." As one student puts it, "Some of us are very active in student groups, and we are the students who tend to do better in class. Others are apathetic in class and out." It's the "atypical students who tend to spend all their time with their heads in computers." Undergrads agree that Fredonia "is mainly a white campus, with an increasing number of Asians and blacks. Fredonia could use more diversity—it's a good thing." Overall, "the nice quality of the people here," sets the tone for life on campus. It's the kind of place where strangers "hold the door for you." Many students originate from "within a couple of hours of the school, which means lots of middle to lower-middle class white kids" who have found their way to this "very liberal campus."

ADMISSIONS

Very important factors considered include: Secondary school record. *Important factors considered include:* Class rank, extracurricular activities, recommendations, standardized test scores. *Other factors considered include:* Alumni/ae relation, character/personal qualities, essays, minority status, talent/ability, volunteer work, work experience. SAT Reasoning or ACT required. TOEFL required of all international applicants. High school diploma is required, and GED is accepted. *Academic units required:* 4 English, 3 math, 3 science, 3 foreign language, 4 social studies. *Academic units recommended:* 4 English, 4 math, 4 science, 3 foreign language, 4 social studies.

The Inside Word

Standardized test scores and high school transcript are the most important factors in the admissions decision here. As with other SUNY schools, all students must apply through the SUNY Application Processing Center. Admissions pros here are looking for students with solid high school academic work and average SAT scores of 1114.

FINANCIAL AID

Students should submit: FAFSA, state aid form. The Princeton Review suggests that all financial aid forms be submitted as soon as possible after 1/1. *Need-based scholarships/grants offered:* Pell, SEOG, state scholarships/grants, private scholarships, the school's own gift aid. *Loan aid offered:* FFEL Subsidized Stafford, FFEL Unsubsidized Stafford, FFEL PLUS, Federal Perkins. Applicants will be notified of awards on a rolling basis beginning on or about 3/15. Federal Work-study Program available. Institutional employment available. Off-campus job opportunities are good.

For even more information on this school, turn to page 532 of the "Stats" section.

STATE UNIVERSITY OF NEW YORK COLLEGE AT GENESEO

1 COLLEGE CIRCLE, GENESEO, NY 14454-1401 • ADMISSIONS: 716-245-5571 • FAX: 716-245-5550
FINANCIAL AID: 716-245-5731 • E-MAIL: ADMISSIONS@GENESEO.EDU • WEBSITE: WWW.GENESEO.EDU

Ratings
Quality of Life: 72   **Academic:** 78   **Admissions:** 93   **Financial Aid:** 60

Academics

Forget every preconception you have about state schools or the SUNY system. SUNY Geneseo bucks nearly every expectation; a small teaching-oriented school on a beautiful campus, "Geneseo is the epitome of college life. The people, the classes, the area, and the campus life are ideal for students coming from every different background, just as long as they are looking to grow as a person and a student." One undergrad gushes, "This is a great school with many opportunities and 'extras' for a great price. Many of the private schools I looked at didn't have half the programs or clubs that Geneseo offers." Although small, Geneseo is big enough to "offer many different majors and is strong in those majors," especially when it comes to the sciences. Professors here "are extremely dedicated to undergraduate learning and are always willing to help (with a few exceptions, of course)." Most have impressive credentials, too. One student writes, "My first year here, one of my professors had worked as a United Nations Advisor, and another had previously run for Congress. Geneseo is a place where you can learn from people who have had real-life experience in their fields." To "stimulate the students' interests," most professors "require a lot of group work and class discussion. They are very accessible and do their best to notify students about due dates, study tips, and resources (which they provide an ample supply of) outside of class through E-mails, office hours, or review sessions." Students note that "TAs don't teach lecture classes. Sometimes they teach labs, but even then they're closely monitored by professors."

> **SURVEY SAYS . . .**
> Small classes
> Students are friendly
> Campus feels safe
> Low cost of living
> Students are happy
> Lots of beer drinking
> Hard liquor is popular

Life

"Geneseo is in the middle of nowhere, so we make our own fun," students tell us, adding that "while there are many jokes about cow tipping, you'll have a hard time finding someone who's actually done it." To keep students engaged, "the clubs and organizations on campus are constantly putting on events. It is very easy to get involved because there is a club for everyone. Geneseo often hosts guest lecturers, and has interesting scholarly events." There are also "some awesome shows put on by the theater and music departments. And all of the events on campus are either free or very low cost." Intramural sports are popular, too, with "broomball being a favorite for everyone," and intercollegiate hockey games that "are well-attended and can be a lot of fun." There's a lively party scene here, but there is also "a large number of students who don't drink at all [and] a new program called 'Late Knight' which provides alcohol-free entertainment on weekend nights." When all else fails, Geneseo's hills draw plenty of thrill-seekers. "You see a lot of students sledding in the winter or mud sliding in the spring." Another draw is the great outdoors at Letchworth State Park, which "is just a few minutes away by car, and is a great place to hike, picnic, or camp. Many students also bring bikes and ride around the campus and surrounding countryside on weekends." And, why not? The surrounding Genesee Valley "is really nice and the sunsets are amazing." When big-city distraction is a necessity, Rochester is not too far away.

Student Body

"Students at Geneseo work really hard; the library is always packed, [but] we also like to have fun and get involved. Everyone I know is part of at least one student organization." Most here "come from Rochester, Buffalo, New York City, or Long Island," and their ranks include "preppy people, people who study, people who are religious, gays, minorities, everything. What's amazing is how people get along so well." Even if the gender scale has a bit of a tilt to it: nearly two out of three students are female. "Boys, obviously, do exist at Geneseo," writes one woman, "but the lack of males is sort of a running joke among the students." "Minority students are few and far between," but the school does have "a very active Asian population, with an Asian theater group among the cultural organizations."

ADMISSIONS

Very important factors considered include: Class rank, secondary school record, standardized test scores. *Important factors considered include:* Essays, extracurricular activities, minority status, recommendations, talent/ability. *Other factors considered include:* Character/personal qualities, volunteer work. SAT Reasoning or ACT required. TOEFL required of all international applicants. High school diploma is required, and GED is accepted. *Academic units recommended:* 4 English, 4 math, 4 science, 4 foreign language, 4 social studies.

The Inside Word

Geneseo is the most selective of SUNY's 13 undergraduate colleges and more selective than three of SUNY's university centers. No formula approach is used here. Expect a thorough review of both your academic accomplishments (virtually everyone here graduated in the top half of their high school classes) and your extracurricular/personal side. Admissions standards are tempered only by a somewhat low yield of admits who enroll; this keeps the admit rate higher than it might otherwise be.

FINANCIAL AID

Students should submit: FAFSA, state aid form. Regular filing deadline 2/15. The Princeton Review suggests that all financial aid forms be submitted as soon as possible after 1/1. *Need-based scholarships/grants offered:* Pell, SEOG, state scholarships/grants, private scholarships, the school's own gift aid. *Loan aid offered:* FFEL Subsidized Stafford, FFEL Unsubsidized Stafford, FFEL PLUS, Federal Perkins, state loans, alternative loans. Applicants will be notified of awards on a rolling basis beginning on or about 3/15. Federal Work-study Program available. Institutional employment available. Off-campus job opportunities are fair.

FROM THE ADMISSIONS OFFICE

"Geneseo has carved a distinctive niche among the nation's premier public liberal arts colleges. Founded in 1871, the college occupies a 220-acre hillside campus in the historic Village of Geneseo, overlooking the scenic Genesee Valley. As a residential campus—with nearly two-thirds of the students living in college residence halls—it provides a rich and varied program of social, cultural, recreational, and scholarly activities. Geneseo is noted for its distinctive core curriculum and the extraordinary opportunities it offers undergraduates to pursue independent study and research with faculty who value close working relationships with talented students. Equally impressive is the remarkable success of its graduates, nearly one-third of whom study at leading graduate and professional schools immediately following graduation."

For even more information on this school, turn to page 533 of the "Stats" section.

STATE UNIVERSITY OF NEW YORK AT NEW PALTZ

75 S MANHEIM BOULEVARD, SUITE 1, NEW PALTZ, NY 12561-2499 • ADMISSIONS: 845-257-3200
FAX: 845-257-3209 • E-MAIL: ADMISSIONS@NEWPALTZ.EDU • WEBSITE: WWW.NEWPALTZ.EDU

Ratings

Quality of Life: 77   Academic: 77   Admissions: 87   Financial Aid: 72

Academics

The New Paltz campus of the State University of New York—rated second in the system behind Geneseo—started as a teacher training facility and retains its "reputation for being a great school for education majors," as long as you know that it often takes more than four years to complete the double major required for subject specialization. Students in other popular programs, including communications, business, and education complain about class availability, leading one to suspect that it is "kept low to keep them in school longer." A senior warns that advisors may not have a grasp on what you're doing so "you need to take care of yourself." Another student explains, "[Professors demonstrate] genuine concern for my education as well as my mental well-being." A triple-majoring senior says, "At least two [professors] have inspired me to pursue a career in their field." Music majors say they "often find [their] teachers playing at the bar on jazz night." While professors "expose [students] to a lot of left-wing stuff," the administration clashes with students politically. On a personal level, however, one student says, "Even when I procrastinated about getting my graduation papers in, my advisor and the chair of the department got my paperwork approved minutes before the deadline." Upon reflection, students appreciate the New Paltz experience as an "opportunity to attend a midsize, fairly priced, respected institution within the context of a friendly, diverse, and liberal town."

> **SURVEY SAYS . . .**
> *Small classes*
> *Diverse student types on campus*
> *Lots of beer drinking*
> *(Almost) everyone smokes*

Life

New Paltz students love their peaceful country life, close to Lake Minnewaska State Park and miles of hiking trails. The town may be "full of cars on the weekends," but many of the locals "were once college students who loved it so much they graduated and never left." One student adds, "I think I'm going to be one of them." Since the students "staged a political coup" and took control of the village board, the Green Party runs local government. Not surprisingly, New Paltz rocked the vote and won a SUNY-wide competition to register the most people in fall 2004. The eight bars in town form the backbone of social life. A senior observes, "It is finals time, and the bars were packed beyond belief last night." Nearly everyone gets decked out for Thursday '80s night at Cabaloosa's, and Tuesdays mean taco specials and cheap movies. Unlike many state schools, students stick around on the weekends instead of heading for home—unless Manhattan is home. On-campus life depends on the "strong Black and Latino Greek life," events like "New Paltz Idol, [and] a lot of just hanging around and playing guitars."

Student Body

Even though property values in New Paltz and the surrounding areas climb steadily, "the college base has not gentrified." The "very diverse yet weirdly cliquey student body" counts heterogeneity and its tolerance as their greatest strengths. The campus sees a confluence of urban "hipsters, rockers, and rappers," Long Island "fake blonds with expensive jewelry, [and the] progressive element." The "odd blend [of] jocks, trendy girls, art students, and slackers" increasingly represents parts of the state besides NYC and Long Island. "Even though it's expanding, everyone knows everyone to some degree."

ADMISSIONS

Very important factors considered include: Secondary school record, standardized test scores. *Other factors considered include:* Class rank, essays, extracurricular activities, recommendations, talent/ability, volunteer work, work experience. SAT Reasoning and SAT Subject Tests or ACT required. TOEFL required of all international applicants. High school diploma is required, and GED is accepted. *Academic units required:* 4 English, 3 math, 3 science (3 science lab), 2 foreign language, 3 social studies. *Academic units recommended:* 4 English, 4 math, 4 science (4 science lab), 4 foreign language, 4 social studies.

The Inside Word

It's a friendly setting in New Paltz, where the distinct closeness and superior academics can fool you into forgetting its state-school structure. The administrative red tape, however, appears quickly enough to remind you it's a SUNY. Be ready as an applicant.

FINANCIAL AID

Students should submit: FAFSA, state aid form. Regular filing deadline 3/15. The Princeton Review suggests that all financial aid forms be submitted as soon as possible after 1/1. *Need-based scholarships/grants offered:* Pell, SEOG, state scholarships/grants, private scholarships, the school's own gift aid, federal nursing scholarships. *Loan aid offered:* Direct Subsidized Stafford, Direct Unsubsidized Stafford, Direct PLUS. Applicants will be notified of awards on a rolling basis beginning on or about 4/1.

FROM THE ADMISSIONS OFFICE

"The State University of New York at New Paltz (SUNY—New Paltz) offers a range of programs unavailable at peer institutions of a similar size. In 1828, New Paltz began with a commitment to liberal arts education and teacher training. Today, the university maintains its original focus and more. Expanding its vision to include a variety of programs in the fine and performing arts, business, nursing, and engineering, it remains a selective and diverse center of higher education at a size that allows students to get to know their professors and collaborate with them on undergraduate-level research projects.

"SUNY—New Paltz maintains the highest of standards. Last year, the college received 11,400 freshman applications for a class of 900. The current acceptance rate is 39 percent, far lower than the national norm—only 5 percent of colleges and universities nationwide have an acceptance rate below 50 percent. Drawing in academically, socially, and artistically gifted applicants from diverse backgrounds, approximately 21 percent of the undergraduate population is comprised of students from traditionally underrepresented groups, and the retention rate is extremely high. Students come here to stay.

"With its scenic location in New York's historic Hudson Valley and proximity to New York City, the campus environment is vibrant; although, students reach out to experience the world beyond New Paltz as well—15 percent of students study abroad, compared to the national four-year university average of 1 percent.

"SUNY New Paltz has received more undergraduate admissions applications than any other SUNY comprehensive college for 14 consecutive years. Liberal arts oriented, the college confers bachelors and masters degrees in education, business, engineering, fine and performing arts, and pre-doctoral certification in education supervision and administration."

For even more information on this school, turn to page 533 of the "Stats" section.

State University of New York College at Oswego

211 Culkin Hall, Oswego, NY 13126 • Admissions: 315-312-2250 • Fax: 315-312-3260
E-mail: admiss@oswego.edu • Website: www.oswego.edu

Ratings

Quality of Life: 71   **Academic:** 72   **Admissions:** 80   **Financial Aid:** 78

Academics

The State University of New York of Oswego is "a big enough school to be diverse but small enough to have a close-knit community," conditions that many students find extremely appealing. They also appreciate how SUNY Oswego offers them "a good education at an affordable price." Undergrads speak especially highly of the popular

business programs, as well as the education program, which snaps up about one in four students. Classes are generally small, "which helps [students] grasp material and have fun" and allows many of them to "develop some great relationships with faculty members and administration that will last a lifetime." Oswego professors "are very up-to-date, with real-life situations and outside ideas that they bring into the classroom [and they] try hard to make their classes enjoyable." Opportunities to build upon your learning after class abound. One student advises, "Getting involved in internships, school clubs, and discussions with professors is key to a good education here. These experiences teach what isn't taught in the classroom." Oswego's "good study abroad options" and Honors Program gives students "access to a higher level of education in a seminar-like atmosphere" are also highly recommended. The latter is especially beneficial for those who wish to avoid the "many students who come here just to party."

Life

For a sizeable portion of the Oswego student body, "life is more about the party after class than the classes themselves. With the numerous bars located in town, it's not hard to see that students would much rather be there than in class." This is a school of over 7,000 undergrads, however, so "while lots of people party, there are also enough people who spend their time on better things that it isn't a huge problem." Oswego has "numerous student organizations that can keep you busy most of the time [and] an active service community." There's also the "gorgeous lake with its beautiful sunsets" to enjoy, weather permitting. Students caution that "the wind will knock you off your feet" and that the persistent swirl of lake-effect snow could leave you feeling like you live in a snow globe. On campus, Greek organizations are popular, both for their parties and for the community they provide. Oswego traditionally fields a competitive ice hockey team, a team that has made the SUNYAC playoffs 27 years running, and winning the division seven times. While "there are not many things to do in Oswego that are close to campus" other than drink in bars, "it's all right because freshmen are allowed to have cars on campus. The closest mall is over a half hour away, though."

Student Body

Oswego draws "lots of kids from rural areas, [typically] from within a few hours of the school," although it also brings in enough students from the New York City suburbs and Long Island to draw attention (not always of the complimentary variety). Undergrads who are at SUNY Oswego for "the full college experience" concede that there are quite a few among them who "are here to party and don't think much about academics," but they tell us that "there are also students who are here for the educational value." One student explains, "Everyone studies together before exams," a time when there is "lots of teamwork." The school attracts "a higher than average number of nontraditional students."

ADMISSIONS

Very important factors considered include: Secondary school record. *Important factors considered include:* Standardized test scores. *Other factors considered include:* Character/personal qualities, class rank, essays, extracurricular activities, interview, minority status, recommendations, talent/ability, volunteer work, work experience. SAT Reasoning or ACT required. TOEFL required of all international applicants. High school diploma is required, and GED is accepted. *Academic units required:* 4 English, 3 math, 3 science (2 science lab), 2 foreign language, 4 social studies. *Academic units recommended:* 4 English, 4 math, 4 science (3 science lab), 4 foreign language, 4 social studies.

The Inside Word

Two camps of students exist at Oswego: those who maximize their opportunities despite obstacles, and those who maximize their complaints about them. You'll be best off here with a flexible and understanding approach and a knack for planning appropriately for those times when you're socked in by a snowstorm.

FINANCIAL AID

Students should submit: FAFSA. The Princeton Review suggests that all financial aid forms be submitted as soon as possible after 1/1. *Need-based scholarships/grants offered:* Pell, SEOG, state scholarships/grants. *Loan aid offered:* FFEL Subsidized Stafford, FFEL Unsubsidized Stafford, FFEL PLUS, Federal Perkins. Applicants will be notified of awards on a rolling basis beginning on or about 4/1.

FROM THE ADMISSIONS OFFICE

"Oswego offers a great higher education value on a beautiful 690-acre lakeside campus in upstate New York, 35 miles northwest of Syracuse. Oswego is small enough to provide a friendly, welcoming environment and big enough to provide wide-ranging academic and social opportunities. The diverse selection of degree programs ranges from accounting to zoology and includes interdisciplinary options like cognitive science and international trade. The schools of education and business have each won the stamp of excellence from the premier accrediting organizations in their field. The weather makes the college popular with future meteorologists—one of Oswego's best-known alumni is the *Today* show's Al Roker. Oswego is noted for its Honors Program, internships, and international study. Ninety percent of the faculty is full time, one of the highest percentages among public colleges, and all courses are taught by faculty, not graduate assistants. More than $100 million dollars in campus construction is under way, which will provide new living accommodations, high-tech classrooms, and recreational facilities. Students participate in 130 clubs and organizations and 23 intercollegiate sports. Half of all students and 90 percent of freshmen live on campus, which has been named one of the safest in the country. Over $2 million in academic merit scholarships are awarded to nearly 30 percent of the entering class in renewable awards worth ranging from $500 to $4,400 per year, and over $60 million in need-based financial aid is awarded. The Oswego Guarantee promises both that room and board costs will not increase during a student's four years on campus and that a student can complete a degree in that time."

For even more information on this school, turn to page 533 of the "Stats" section.

STATE UNIVERSITY OF NEW YORK—PURCHASE COLLEGE

ADMISSIONS OFFICE, 735 ANDERSON HILL ROAD, PURCHASE, NY 10577 • ADMISSIONS: 914-251-6300 • FAX: 914-251-6314
FINANCIAL AID: 914-251-6350 • E-MAIL: ADMISSN@PURCHASE.EDU • WEBSITE: WWW.PURCHASE.EDU

Ratings
Quality of Life: 62 Academic: 79 Admissions: 85 Financial Aid: 66

Academics

Conservatory programs in dance, music, theater arts, film, and professional training in art and design are the main attractions at SUNY—Purchase College, a small state school nestled in the affluent suburbs of New York City. These "world-class conservatory programs at state university prices" mean that "there is a lot of art on campus." But there is more to Purchase than just the arts. One student, who was not admitted to the music conservatory but entered the school of liberal arts and sciences instead, explains, "I wasn't expecting much from the science end because this is an art/music school, but I was surprised. The teachers are really knowledgeable in the fields they

> **SURVEY SAYS . . .**
> Small classes
> Frats and sororities are unpopular
> or nonexistent
> Musical organizations are popular
> Theater is popular
> Student publications are popular
> Political activism is popular
> (Almost) everyone smokes

teach." Students also note that "the academic support on campus is excellent, although a lot of students do not take advantage of this. The resource staff at the library is phenomenal and will help you find what you need even if it's not in the library." Although many students have complained about a lack of organization in the administration and large amounts of red tape, the school has responded by establishing a student advising center, streamlining the student affairs office and building a new academic services facility that will centralize all student services.

Life

Purchase is home to a vibrant arts scene. One student says, "We have one of the best performing arts centers in the United States, as well as plenty of art shows, dance shows, theater shows, and opera recitals. We have a nationally recognized museum on campus, as well as good discussions by some very influential people." There are also "a lot of on-campus bands, many 'zines written by students, and student art showings." In short, Purchase is the kind of place where "there is practically no one at basketball games, but the ballet is packed." Political and arts organizations are popular, students tell us, but there's not much of a party scene. When students want that type of fun, they generally hop a bus or train and head for New York City. Many students also take advantage of the athletic facility and the wide array of athletic programs. "Aesthetes" that they are, students have plenty of complaints about campus design. "Everything is brown brick. It's very gloomy and depressing, with few flowers and shrubs, just trees. Landscaping and some paint could go a long way here," observes one critic. Students also report that many facilities are in need of a serious upgrade.

Student Body

Purchase students pride themselves on their dedication, their iconoclasm, and their idiosyncrasies. One undergraduate says, "The typical conservatory student here is a bleary-eyed, sleep-deprived, stressed-out workaholic completely in love with their chosen career path. The typical nonconservatory student perceives him/herself as an artist, a rebel, a revolutionary, a unique individual, and an independent thinker." More often than not, the student "has at least one of the following: a clashing/weird, funky fashion sense; piercings; tattoos; five different colors in their hair; a unique hairstyle; paint splattered all over them." Nearly all respondents expressed admiration for and a sense of belonging in the student body as a whole. Purchase "is very diverse, with a large number of homosexual students, politically and socially liberal students, politically and socially conservative students, art students, academics, dancers, actors, etc. Everyone fits in because there are no two people alike."

ADMISSIONS

Very important factors considered include: Essays, secondary school record, standardized test scores. *Important factors considered include:* Recommendations. *Other factors considered include:* Extracurricular activities, interview, talent/ability. SAT Reasoning Test required. TOEFL required of all international applicants. High school diploma is required, and GED is accepted.

The Inside Word

The overall admit rate at Purchase College is low, athough admissions requirements vary greatly depending on the academic program. Almost all applicants wishing to major in the visual or performing arts must audition or submit a portfolio. Admission is less competitive for candidates wishing to major in the liberal arts or sciences.

FINANCIAL AID

Students should submit: FAFSA, state aid form. The Princeton Review suggests that all financial aid forms be submitted as soon as possible after 1/1. *Need-based scholarships/grants offered:* Pell, SEOG, state scholarships/grants, private scholarships, the school's own gift aid. *Loan aid offered:* FFEL Subsidized Stafford, FFEL Unsubsidized Stafford, FFEL PLUS, Federal Perkins. Applicants will be notified of awards on a rolling basis beginning on or about 3/1. Federal Work-study Program available. Institutional employment available. Off-campus job opportunities are excellent.

FROM THE ADMISSIONS OFFICE

"A highly selective college, Purchase College provides a total educational experience, that mirrors the supportive environment of a private college at public college prices. Purchase is the only public 4-year college that fuses the educational goals and traditions of the liberal arts with arts conservatories in music, dance, theater, film, design technology, and a school of art and design. Conservatory programs stress professional training, close cohort–based education providing apprenticeships with professionals and opportunities in the New York arts scene.

"At Purchase you will find a unique arts atmosphere for liberal arts students as well as conservatory students. Attend student performances, or go to the five-theater Performing Arts Center and The Neuberger Museum of Art (the country's eighth largest campus art museum) for the arts and entertainment. Involve yourself in distinctive curricular and cocurricular experiences, have access to the latest in technology, obtain internships, and avail yourself of the services of career development. You can choose from a wide array of majorsin the humanities, sciences and social sciences or disciplinary fields as journalism, creative writing, environmental science or new media. And there are pre-professional programs in law, medicine, and education.

"If you want to study abroad you can participate in summer programs in Italy, France, or Spain. Live and learn with your friends by joining a residential Learning Community or a Freshman Interest Group. As a high achieving student, you could be eligible for a Presidential or Merit scholarship. Purchase College is situated on 500 acres in suburban Westchester County. Come visit us!

"Admissions requirements vary with each program in the college and can include auditions, portfolio reviews, essays, writing samples, and interviews."

For even more information on this school, turn to page 534 of the "Stats" section.

STEVENS INSTITUTE OF TECHNOLOGY

CASTLE POINT ON HUDSON, HOBOKEN, NJ 07030 • ADMISSIONS: 800-458-5323 • FAX: 201-216-8348
FINANCIAL AID: 201-216-5194 • E-MAIL: ADMISSIONS@STEVENS-TECH.EDU • WEBSITE: WWW.STEVENS-TECH.EDU

Ratings
Quality of Life: 75   Academic: 72   Admissions: 89   Financial Aid: 71

Academics

"Academic expectations are high" at Stevens Institute of Technology, a New Jersey engineering, science, and mathematics stronghold. According to undergraduates, "engineering students are required to take more credits than at nearly any other school." Anyone who "manages to graduate from Stevens with an engineering or science degree," students tell us, "can handle anything. The stress level that students experience here is extremely high." Another engineering student adds, "Many students actually feel relieved by the time they graduate because they know that

> SURVEY SAYS . . .
> *Small classes*
> *Diverse student types on campus*
> *Students love Hoboken, NJ*
> *Great off-campus food*
> *Campus feels safe*
> *Frats and sororities dominate social scene*
> *Lots of beer drinking*

they won't be working as hard in the 'real world.'" Students endure this academic rigor, so they can have access to "great internships and co-op jobs," enjoy the "high level of name recognition in the engineering world," and have access to the "very strong opportunities to make good money after graduation." As at most science and tech schools, professors are probably brilliant; we say "probably" because many students don't understand them well enough to say for sure. That's because "most of them don't speak English too well or just can't communicate properly with the class." Although "some professors are not very helpful—they are intimidating to approach, succinct with any answers, not understanding the question perhaps—others are so amazingly generous with their time that it actually makes you feel good that someone would sit down for you and only you (not several students) for an hour of their time to help you with your assignment."

Life

The school's location, students agree, is "perfect. It is close to New York City without actually being in New York City (no dealing with traffic and noise), and it's right on the Hudson River, overlooking the city. Hoboken is a fun place to be, too." One student explains, "Anything you need to wind down is available. We have the river and pier for scenery, New York City for the city, and Hoboken for great food and charm." Of course, there are also campus goings-on, which include "the outdoor club and gym for physical activities, artistic outlets with the theater, choir, so many sports, so many cultural clubs, tutoring, and reviews." Therefore, "student life at Stevens is all in the hands of the student." Students say "Greek life is very active and plays a huge role in the social activity on campus." The campus also hosts numerous shows. Undergraduates tell us that "there has been huge growth in the number of campus activities since the creation of the Entertainment Committee, which works to make sure students get big-name professional entertainment right on campus, as well as movies and carnivals." The only thing that is scarce is spare time and someone to enjoy it with. Many male students feel there is "no time to spend on girls" because of the school and its demanding curriculum; that's okay though, as there are "no girls to spend time on."

Student Body

Many Stevens students remind us that it "is an engineering and computer science school. As such, you get the geeks and the dorks and the nerds. Everyone here is a bit shy of mainstream in some way, shape, or form, and it works wonderfully." Other students argue that "while there may be a few dorks on campus, they are the exception, not the norm. Many students are on varsity athletic teams and are involved with many extracurricular activities." There is probably a little bit of both student types. One student says, "The student body at Stevens can be generalized into two groups. The first half sits in their rooms with Star Wars figurines playing Dungeons and Dragons. The other half [is made up of] fun, outgoing people who get their work done, but know how to let loose and have a good time." Stevens is ethnically and geographically diverse, but male students say that its male-female ratio is "horrible."

ADMISSIONS

Very important factors considered include: Character/personal qualities, essays, interview, recommendations, secondary school record. *Important factors considered include:* Class rank, extracurricular activities, standardized test scores, talent/ability, volunteer work, work experience. *Other factors considered include:* Alumni/ae relation. SAT Reasoning or ACT required. TOEFL required of all international applicants. High school diploma is required, and GED is not accepted. *Academic units required:* 4 English, 4 math, 3 science (3 science lab), 2 history. *Academic units recommended:* 4 English, 4 math, 4 science (4 science lab), 2 foreign language, 2 social studies, 2 history, 4 academic electives.

The Inside Word

Stevens is indeed impressive and legitimately near the top of the "second tier" of technical schools. Above-average students who would run into difficulty trying to gain admission to the MITs and Caltechs of the world will find a much more receptive admissions process here. Given its solid reputation and metropolitan New York location, it's an excellent choice for techies who want to establish their careers in the area.

FINANCIAL AID

Students should submit: FAFSA. The Princeton Review suggests that all financial aid forms be submitted as soon as possible after 1/1. *Need-based scholarships/grants offered:* Pell, SEOG, state scholarships/grants, private scholarships, the school's own gift aid. *Loan aid offered:* Direct Subsidized Stafford, Direct Unsubsidized Stafford, Direct PLUS, Federal Perkins, state loans, signature loans, TERI Loans, NJ CLASS, CitiAssist. Applicants will be notified of awards on a rolling basis beginning on or about 3/30. Federal Work-study Program available. Off-campus job opportunities are excellent.

FROM THE ADMISSIONS OFFICE

"The quality and achievements of our graduates are the greatest hallmarks of a Stevens education. Almost all of our students have had technical, pre-professional experience outside the classroom during their undergraduate years. Among other benefits, this enables them to be the finest candidates for prestigious graduate schools or positions of employment in industry. The most striking indication of this is that most of our graduates receive a job offer prior to graduation, and Stevens has been ranked eleventh among the Top 550 institutions that produce presidents, vice presidents, and directors of U.S. companies. In 2003, Stevens was ranked as the number one 'Most Connected Campus' in the nation by The Princeton Review, and again in 2004 as one of the "Nation's Most Entrepreneurial Campuses." Stevens was also recognized by the Sloan Consortium for 'Excellence in Institution-Wide Online Teaching and Learning Programming." However, outstanding academics need to be balanced with an outstanding campus life, and at Stevens students will find more than 70 student organizations and 22 NCAA Division III athletics teams. Plus, with our Hoboken location overlooking the Hudson River and New York City skyline, Stevens offers a campus environment like no other."

For even more information on this school, turn to page 528 of the "Stats" section.

Stonehill College

320 Washington Street, Easton, MA 02357-5610 • Admissions: 508-565-1373 • Fax: 508-565-1545
E-mail: admissions@stonehill.edu • Website: www.stonehill.edu

Ratings
Quality of Life: 88   Academic: 87   Admissions: 92   Financial Aid: 73

Academics

A Catholic-affiliated institution, Stonehill College "is a place where you can grow academically as well as challenge your mind, body, and spirit on a daily basis." The pervasive "sense of community" at Stonehill allows for students to attack their studies in a "challenging [but] comfortable" environment. "Stonehill really prides itself on the involvement of its administration and professors," says a history major. The college's faculty members "are required to hold as many office hours as class hours they have each week," which means that professors are never difficult to find. And just in case the office hours aren't convenient, students usually receive a professor's "work phone, home phone, cell phone, e-mail address, and screen name." Class sizes stay small—"no larger than twenty-five," promises a sophomore—and discussion is always crucial. Professors "encourage everyone to share their opinions, thoughts, or ideas, and be active in the classroom," assures a math major. Among "Stonehill's greatest strengths," says a junior, are "its internship and study-abroad programs." Add it all up, says a sophomore, and you have a "rigorous and challenging" college experience that "prepares students for graduate school and life after college."

> **SURVEY SAYS . . .**
> Small classes
> Great library
> Dorms are like palaces
> Campus feels safe
> Frats and sororities are unpopular or nonexistent
> Student government is popular
> Lots of beer drinking

Life

Student life is alive and well at Stonehill College's "beautiful" campus in Easton, Massachusetts. "People don't go home on the weekends," says a junior. "There is so much going on here that people don't want to miss out on something." Much of the action is spurred by the "very active Student Government and great Student Activities Program," which combine to ensure that entertainment is always available. During a recent two-day stretch, reports a philosophy major, "we had Mr. Stonehill, which is our male beauty pageant, a hypnotist, an art gallery opening, a Japanese drum group, and a school dance." But don't forget, a junior reminds us, "that academics come before anything else," which means the library is not a barren building. Neither are the campus town houses empty on a Thursday, Friday, or Saturday night. Estimates a sophomore, "Thursday through Sunday morning, about 85 percent of the school is partying on campus." In those rare moments when the Stonehill life just isn't cutting it, students are glad to know that Providence, Cape Cod, and Newport "provide exciting off-campus destinations." And don't forget about Boston, which is just "a stone's throw away."

Student Body

Some students still refer to Stonehill as "Clonehill" because of the racially and economically homogenous clustering of undergrads that pass through the college's gates. One sophomore says that students are "pretty much Caucasian, well-dressed, and wealthy." Another student adds that students are "mostly middle-class to upper-middle class students coming from New England." Others bristle at that nickname, suggesting that "everyone here is diverse in their own ways [and although] everyone wears the same style of clothes and in general tend to look alike, there are those that do not conform and they are not considered outcasts or frowned upon." While it's true that "Stonehill could stand to improve in the diversity department," they seem to be doing quite well as far as morale is concerned. "Everyone is always smiling," says one student, and nearly "every individual participates strongly in both co-curricular and extracurricular activities." At the end of the day, a senior says, "everyone here has one thing in common: They chose to attend Stonehill." Could 2,600 undergraduates be wrong?

ADMISSIONS

Very important factors considered include: Class rank, secondary school record, standardized test scores. *Important factors considered include:* Character/personal qualities, essays, extracurricular activities, recommendations, talent/ability. *Other factors considered include:* Alumni/ae relation, geographical residence, minority status, volunteer work, work experience. SAT Reasoning or ACT required. TOEFL required of all international applicants. High school diploma is required, and GED is accepted. *Academic units required:* 4 English, 3 math, 1 science (1 science lab), 2 foreign language, 3 history, 3 academic electives. *Academic units recommended:* 4 English, 4 math, 3 science (2 science lab), 3 foreign language, 3 history, 3 academic electives.

The Inside Word

This Beantown stronghold exercises strict policies, but students can easily find social outlets off campus. The pursuit of any of the 30 majors in this family atmosphere is contagious, though you might not feel as much a part of the family if you're not white, Catholic, and Irish.

FINANCIAL AID

Students should submit: FAFSA, CSS/Financial Aid PROFILE, noncustodial (divorced/separated) parents' statement, business/farm supplement, verification form (provided by institution). Regular filing deadline 2/1. The Princeton Review suggests that all financial aid forms be submitted as soon as possible after 1/1. *Need-based scholarships/grants offered:* Pell, SEOG, state scholarships/grants, private scholarships, the school's own gift aid. *Loan aid offered:* Direct Subsidized Stafford, Direct Unsubsidized Stafford, Direct PLUS, Federal Perkins, state loans, GATE/Stonehill. Applicants will be notified of awards on or about 4/1. Federal Work-study Program available. Institutional employment available. Off-campus job opportunities are good.

FROM THE ADMISSIONS OFFICE

"Founded in 1948 by the Congregation of Holy Cross, Stonehill's mission is to provide education of the highest caliber, grounded in the liberal arts, comprehensive in nature, and nurtured by Catholic intellectual and moral ideas. Stonehill College is a selective, private, coeducational Catholic college enrolling 2,100 full-time students. Located 20 miles south of Boston on a 375-acre campus with easy access to Boston, we offer 30 challenging majors in the liberal arts, business, and science degree programs. Stonehill also offers students 35 minor programs as well as the opportunity to double major. The college's programs, through an involved and engaging faculty and a commitment to hands-on learning, aim to foster effective communication, critical-thinking, and problem-solving skills in all our students. An Honors Program, undergraduate research opportunities, and area internships enrich the educational experience of many students.

"To gain experience internationally, our students may study abroad, spending four to nine months living and studying in another part of the world. Full-time internships in Dublin, London, Brussels, Paris, Montreal, and Zaragoza, Spain, allow highly motivated students to gain valuable work experience while earning academic credit. On campus, more than 85 percent of our students live in first-rate residence halls that feature large rooms and well-designed layouts. Stonehill's 20 Division II varsity sports, over 60 clubs and organizations, as well as intramural and recreational sports programs provide students with many ways to become involved. Stonehill provides its students with a powerful environment for learning where students are safe, known, and valued."

For even more information on this school, turn to page 529 of the "Stats" section.

SUFFOLK UNIVERSITY

8 ASHBURTON PLACE, BOSTON, MA 02108 • ADMISSIONS: 617-573-8460 • FAX: 617-742-4291
EMAIL: ADMISSION@ADMIN.SUFFOLK.EDU • WEBSITE: WWW.SUFFOLK.EDU

Ratings
Quality of Life: 91   **Academic:** 73   **Admissions:** 70   **Financial Aid:** 66

Academics

"Suffolk University is about diversity and a solid education in an ideal location," agree students at this comprehensive university in downtown Boston. A large international population—enhanced by Suffolk's permanent campuses in Madrid, Spain, and Dakar, Senegal—accounts for much of the diversity. Nontraditional students also add to the mix ("This school is all about second chances," explains one undergrad who returned to school after a long layoff). All here appreciate how "the school is very dedicated to its students," offering small classes and going the extra mile to line up co-op and internship opportunities. Students in management- and government-related areas especially benefit from the school's downtown location and its strong ties to city businesses and government. Suffolk undergrads , however, save their highest praise for the faculty, whom they describe as "a fantastic resource, always willing to help anyone who asks for it. They also do their best to challenge students in classes without setting them up for failure." Brags one student, "Many [adjunct faculty] teach at schools such as Harvard or Boston College. I definitely feel like I'm getting the same education as I would at Ivy League schools but in much smaller classes." Not to mention that they're getting it at a much lower price. Students also appreciate how "the administration is easily accessible and open to student feedback."

> **SURVEY SAYS . . .**
> *Small classes*
> *Diverse student types on campus*
> *Students love Boston, MA*
> *Great off-campus food*

Life

Suffolk does not have a traditional, enclosed campus; rather, the school consists of a collection of buildings scattered across Boston's Beacon Hill neighborhood, not far from the Government Center and the famous Boston Commons. Few people mind, however, because the city of Boston itself offers undergraduates a rich bounty of experiences. Students tell us that "there is so much to do here, from theater to dining to Red Sox games to movies. Boston is such a cultural city!" Beantown is also home to numerous other colleges and universities (Boston University, Boston College, Harvard, MIT, and Emerson, to name just a few), making it "a giant college campus with endless possibilities!" A new dorm opened in fall 2003 that will double the school's residential capacity. Students hope that the increase in residents will result in a more cohesive, active student body.

Student Body

"Suffolk's greatest strength is the diversity" of its student body. "Everyday I seem to meet someone from another country. Just the other day I met someone from Bolivia," writes one student. Internationals are a significant percentage of the population here and "seem to fit in quite well." Suffolk is also home to "a fairly large constituency of adult professionals who have returned to school (often attending night classes intermixed with 'traditional' students)," as well as "a large gay population." Most students come from the New England/New York area" and are of the down-to-earth variety; "there's not a lot of blue-blood here," explains one student. "But that's a good thing, I think. Understand that blue-bloods aren't discouraged or ostracized, just not the norm." Students are generally practical and goal-oriented, the type of people who "get the job done and still make time to spend with friends."

ADMISSIONS

Very important factors considered include: Secondary school record. *Important factors considered include:* Character/personal qualities, class rank, essays, extracurricular activities, recommendations, standardized test scores, volunteer work, work experience. *Other factors considered include:* Alumni/ae relation, geographical residence, interview, state residency. SAT Reasoning or ACT required. TOEFL required of all international applicants. High school diploma is required, and GED is accepted. *Academic units required:* 4 English, 3 math, 2 science (1 science lab), 2 foreign language, 1 history, 4 academic electives. *Academic units recommended:* 4 English, 4 math, 3 science (2 science lab), 3 foreign language, 1 social studies, 2 history, 4 academic electives.

The Inside Word

Graduating senior Paul Fisette says, "They tell me the real world is a terrible place we will be magically transported to on May 23 after receiving our diploma. Before you get too disheartened, I offer a glimmer of hope! We aren't graduating from a secluded 1,000 acre university; we are graduating from Suffolk and what people often do not realize is that we have been kicking the real world square in the teeth since the moment we arrived here. While our friends at other schools complained about the cafeteria food, we were working to pay for school, take night classes, while balancing this with a semblance of a social life. No complaints! I belong to a school where things haven't been handed to people on a silver platter, where we learned as much through living in Boston as we did sitting in a classroom. So as for the real world, I say bring it on. We're ready!"

FINANCIAL AID

Students should submit: FAFSA, institution's own financial aid form. Regular filing deadline 4/1. The Princeton Review suggests that all financial aid forms be submitted as soon as possible after 1/1. *Need-based scholarships/grants offered:* Pell, SEOG, state scholarships/grants, private scholarships, the school's own gift aid. *Loan aid offered:* Direct Subsidized Stafford, Direct Unsubsidized Stafford, Direct PLUS, Federal Perkins. Applicants will be notified of awards on a rolling basis beginning on or about 3/1. Federal Work-study Program available. Off-campus job opportunities are good.

FROM THE ADMISSIONS OFFICE

"Ask any student, and they'll tell you: the best thing about Suffolk is the professors. They go the extra mile to help students to succeed. Suffolk faculty members are noted scholars and experienced professionals, but first and foremost, they are teachers and mentors. Suffolk's faculty is of the highest caliber. Ninety-four percent of the faculty hold PhDs. Suffolk maintains a 12:1 student/faculty ratio with an average class size of 19.

"The university was selected as one of the "Best 201" colleges by the Best 201 Colleges for the Real World (2001/2002) and one of Barron's Best Buys in College Education. Career preparation is a high priority at Suffolk. Many students work during the school year in paid internships, co-op jobs, or work-study positions. Suffolk has an excellent job placement record. More than 94 percent of recent graduates are either employed or enrolled in graduate school at the time of graduation.

"The university's academic programs emphasize quality teaching, small class size, and real-world career applications, and an international experience. There are more than 30 study abroad sites available to students. The undergraduate academic program offers more than 70 majors and 1,000 courses."

For even more information on this school, turn to page 529 of the "Stats" section.

SUSQUEHANNA UNIVERSITY

514 UNIVERSITY AVENUE, SELINSGROVE, PA 17870 • ADMISSIONS: 570-372-4260 • FAX: 570-372-2722
FINANCIAL AID: 570-372-4450 • E-MAIL: SUADMISS@SUSQU.EDU • WEBSITE: WWW.SUSQU.EDU

Ratings
Quality of Life: 79   **Academic:** 81   **Admissions:** 84   **Financial Aid:** 77

Academics

Susquehanna University, a Lutheran affiliated institution situated in central Pennsylvania, boasts "a great teacher-to-student ratio and a close-knit community that comes from having only 2,000 students on campus." The size of the school, students here tell us, "allows you to try many new and different things that you would miss out on at a bigger university" and "makes us a little community where you know so many people. You get to know your professors very well, feel extremely comfortable going to see them out-

> **SURVEY SAYS . . .**
> *Small classes*
> *Great computer facilities*
> *Great library*
> *Athletic facilities are great*
> *Students are friendly*
> *Lots of beer drinking*

side of class, and get the attention and help that you need." Students report that SU's business program "is wonderful and challenging." The music, writing, and arts programs here also earn students' praise, while natural science programs benefit from "lots of opportunities for undergraduate research." Students also appreciate the school's "amazing dedication in finding us internships and jobs" and how SU "encourages us to study abroad and in different specialty programs to learn as much as we can in different environments." The school is "looking to the future with building initiatives. The music and arts building was finished two years ago and new athletic fields were created last year. The campus center (and cafeteria) are being renovated over summer 2005." Additionally, a new residence hall is scheduled to open in fall 2006 and the science department is reportedly "working on plans for a second science building." Observes one student, "The university is continually improving, in both aesthetics and in the quality of education."

Life

"Extracurricular activities are very strong" at SU. Students tell us that "there is a great network of volunteer organizations that work on campus and throughout the local area, from on-campus recycling to mentoring at the middle school. Club sports are also strong," as are the school's Division III intercollegiate athletics. Greek life is also big, with approximately one in four students pledging. Campus organizations "offer a variety of events like movies, spring weekend parties, and different social events." And because the school is small, "you can be involved with a lot of different activities at the same time." The high level of campus activity is necessary, because hometown Selinsgrove "is a nice small town, but it has nothing in the way of entertainment and girls, and the mall sucks—so stock up before you get here." Many students address the boredom of rural seclusion by partying hard, a situation the administration has tried to address recently with predictable results: Plenty of students complain that "we expected a college and instead we got a babysitting service." Undergrads here also gripe that the school is currently overcrowded, with a lot of 'forced triples' in freshman dorms. They report that those renovations are coming along "slowly, so we'll see what it will look like next year."

Student Body

"Susquehanna, located in rural central Pennsylvania, undoubtedly lacks diversity," students write. "The average student is of one of two varieties: white, middle-class, Pennsylvania farm children or white, upper-middle-class kids from in or around New York City." Those from the area "often leave on weekends, especially during freshman year, which is annoying because it makes it hard to get to know them." SU undergrads know how to "strike the balance between academics with extracurricular activities. We are involved in athletics, community service, religious groups and Greek life." Undergrads note "the presence of certain cliques here; for instance, music and drama production, sorority girls, sports teams, frats, etc. However, these groups are not set in stone and many people have many different friends in numerous cliques." Most students here "dress preppy and carry cell phones," but "there is always someone dressed in sweats or pajama, too. There are also some atypical students who wear goth or bohemian-style clothing, but that doesn't usually seem to affect how they fit in."

ADMISSIONS

Very important factors considered include: Class rank, secondary school record, standardized test scores. *Important factors considered include:* Character/personal qualities, essays, extracurricular activities, interview, minority status, recommendations, talent/ability, volunteer work. *Other factors considered include:* Alumni/ae relation, geographical residence, religious affiliation/commitment, state residency, work experience. TOEFL required of all international applicants. High school diploma is required, and GED is accepted. *Academic units required:* 4 English, 3 math, 3 science (2 science lab), 2 foreign language, 1 social studies, 1 history, 2 academic electives. *Academic units recommended:* 4 English, 4 math, 4 science (3 science lab), 3 foreign language, 3 social studies, 2 history, 3 academic electives.

The Inside Word

Susquehanna is about as low profile as universities come in the age of MTV. Getting in is made easier by the serious competition the university faces from numerous like institutions in the region, some with significantly better reputations.

FINANCIAL AID

Students should submit: FAFSA, CSS/Financial Aid PROFILE, business/farm supplement, parent and student federal tax documents. Regular filing deadline 5/1. The Princeton Review suggests that all financial aid forms be submitted as soon as possible after 1/1. *Need-based scholarships/grants offered:* Pell, SEOG, state scholarships/grants, private scholarships, the school's own gift aid. *Loan aid offered:* FFEL Subsidized Stafford, FFEL Unsubsidized Stafford, FFEL PLUS, Federal Perkins, college/university loans from institutional funds. Applicants will be notified of awards on a rolling basis beginning on or about 2/15. Federal Work-study Program available. Institutional employment available. Off-campus job opportunities are good.

FROM THE ADMISSIONS OFFICE

"Students tell us they are getting both a first-rate education and practical experience to help them be competitive upon graduation. Faculty, especially in psychology, marketing, and the sciences, regularly encourage students in their research. Students also do internships at such sites as the White House, Continental Insurance, Estee Lauder, State Street Global Advisors, and Cable News Network. About 90 percent of our graduates go on for advanced degrees or get jobs in their chosen field within six months of graduation. Keeping up with the latest in information technology is easy for our students now that all residence hall rooms have connections to the computer network. Even though the university has six micro-computing laboratories, including one open 24 hours a day, many students find it convenient to use their own PCs to 'surf the 'Net' from their rooms. Small classes, the opportunity to work closely with professors, and the sense of campus community all contribute to the educational experience here. More than 100 student organizations provide lots of opportunity for leadership and involvement in campus life."

For even more information on this school, turn to page 534 of the "Stats" section.

SWARTHMORE COLLEGE

500 COLLEGE AVENUE, SWARTHMORE, PA 19081 • ADMISSIONS: 610-328-8300 • FAX: 610-328-8580
FINANCIAL AID: 610-328-8358 • E-MAIL: ADMISSIONS@SWARTHMORE.EDU • WEBSITE: WWW.SWARTHMORE.EDU

Ratings
Quality of Life: 87   **Academic:** 99   **Admissions:** 98   **Financial Aid:** 97

Academics

"A Swarthmore day is a 28-hour day," notes one student, reflecting on the notoriously heavy workload at this elite liberal arts school. Don't let the reputation scare you off, though; as one student explained, "Academics at Swat are hard; everyone knows that coming in. But that doesn't mean they aren't enjoyable." Furthermore, "Swarthmore has a tremendous support network anchored by the professors and administration (as well as other students).

> **SURVEY SAYS . . .**
> *Small classes*
> *Great library*
> *Campus feels safe*
> *Low cost of living*
> *Political activism is popular*

When help is needed, there is always someone to turn to." The support is essential, since "the overall stress level here is high from balancing classes, activities, and social life." What do students get in return for their fretting and sweating? Academic freedom, for one; "students at Swarthmore manage to study anything and everything that interests them and may do so [to] whatever depth they choose." They also get "campus resources, including many public computers, electronics in the classroom, and free transportation to nearby campuses and Philadelphia to name a few." And let's not forget professors who "love to really get to know their students. They email you back within an hour, invite you to their homes for dinner, ask you to baby-sit for their kids, and always schedule appointments out of their office hours." Finally, students here enjoy an environment in which "learning is the goal, not the means." One thing they don't get, though, is an easy A; "As one of our T-shirts says: 'Anywhere else it would have been an A.'"

Life

Life at Swarthmore, most here agree, is "intense. Between the challenging classes, extracurricular commitments, and small community, people here tend to stress a lot and complain frequently. However, just about everybody who makes it through to graduation looks back on their four (or five or six) years as the most incredible time in their life." On top of their mountain of schoolwork, students "tend to be very involved in campus life and in a wide range of activities. People can be in student government and active in a minority organization and in a play, all at the same time." Accordingly, students have to get their fun on the run and learn to enjoy little pleasures. "Swatties love to have discussions," writes one student. "They will talk about a subject, everything from the gender politics of *Wuthering Heights* to the imagery of *Lord of the Rings*, for hours on end." They also "love walking around the gorgeous campus and taking walks in the acres of [the] well-kept arboretum around us." When it's time to party, Swatties do it for free: all on-campus activities are paid for out of the student activity fund. Notes one student, "It's quite possible to go months without spending money on things to do." Others, however, warn that "campus events are enjoyable for the first two years, but after that get a little old." That's when students head off campus, not to surrounding Swarthmore, which is "a pretty small suburb," but to Philadelphia. There's a train stop "at the foot of campus" that runs kids straight downtown.

Student Body

The "brilliant, creative, engaging, and always ready for a discussion on anything and everything" students of Swarthmore maintain "a very high level of intellectual and social idealism." This social idealism manifests itself in a pervasive political leftism; "almost everyone is so far left politically/ideologically that the Democratic party seems right-wing," explains one undergrad. Many here are "over-involved. A typical Swattie is involved in a ludicrous number of extracurriculars: clubs, sports, volunteering, committees (besides all the work for class!)." Also, "whether a jock or a partygoer, a published writer or world traveler, everyone at Swarthmore has a little bit of dork deep down inside of them, and it's the common bond between us all." As one student put it, "People are unconcerned with matters of fashion, pop culture, and sometimes hygiene." Most Swatties "come from an upper-middle-class background."

ADMISSIONS

Very important factors considered include: Character/personal qualities, class rank, essays, recommendations, secondary school record, standardized test scores. *Important factors considered include:* Extracurricular activities. *Other factors considered include:* Alumni/ae relation, geographical residence, interview, minority status, talent/ability, volunteer work, work experience. SAT Reasoning and SAT Subject Tests or ACT required. High school diploma or equivalent is not required.

The Inside Word

Swarthmore is as good as they come; among liberal arts colleges there is none better. Candidates face an admissions process that is appropriately demanding and thorough. Even the best qualified of students need to complete their applications with a meticulous approach—during candidate evaluation, serious competition is just another file away. Those who are fortunate enough to be offered admission usually have shown the committee that they have a high level of intellectual curiosity, self-confidence, and motivation.

FINANCIAL AID

Students should submit: FAFSA, institution's own financial aid form, CSS/Financial Aid PROFILE, state aid form, noncustodial (divorced/separated) parents' statement, business/farm supplement, federal tax return, W-2 forms, year-end paycheck stub. Regular filing deadline 2/15. The Princeton Review suggests that all financial aid forms be submitted as soon as possible after 1/1. *Need-based scholarships/grants offered:* Pell, SEOG, state scholarships/grants, private scholarships, the school's own gift aid. *Loan aid offered:* FFEL Subsidized Stafford, FFEL Unsubsidized Stafford, FFEL PLUS, Federal Perkins, state loans, college/university loans from institutional funds. Applicants will be notified of awards on or about 4/1. Federal Work-study Program available. Institutional employment available. Off-campus job opportunities are good.

FROM THE ADMISSIONS OFFICE

"Swarthmore is a highly selective college of liberal arts and engineering, located 11 miles southwest of Philadelphia. Founded as a coeducational institution in 1864, it is nonsectarian but reflects many traditions and values of its Quaker founders and attracts students who are engaged in the community as well as the classroom. Swarthmore's Honors Program provides an option to study in small seminars during the junior and senior years. A small school by deliberate policy, Swarthmore has an enrollment of about 1,450, with a student/faculty ratio of 8:1. It attracts students from 50 states and 46 countries."

For even more information on this school, turn to page 535 of the "Stats" section.

SYRACUSE UNIVERSITY

201 TOLLEY, ADMINISTRATION BUILDING, SYRACUSE, NY 13244 • ADMISSIONS: 315-443-3611
FINANCIAL AID: 315-443-1513 • E-MAIL: ORANGE@SYR.EDU • WEBSITE: WWW.SYRACUSE.EDU

Ratings
Quality of Life: 64   Academic: 83   Admissions: 91   Financial Aid: 86

Academics

At Syracuse University (SU), the spotlight shines on internal schools with uncontestable national reputations. The
Newhouse School of Communications and The Maxwell
School of Citizenship & Public Affairs are two such places.
Students enrolled in other top departments, such as religion, information studies, bioengineering, and architecture, beg to make their voice heard and direct our attention
to "a number of specialized areas that many people overlook." A student in the "extremely prestigious" art program

tells us, "Work is very independent, and attention is focused on technical improvement and process."
Consistently, no matter a student's school allegiance, professors are hailed for their dedication, accessibility, and
plain old teaching savvy. The university demonstrates "dedication and attention to all undergraduates," and
students enrolled in the honors program enjoy access to top faculty, smaller classes, and early registration.
Many students report "strong connections with faculty, in class, outside of class, and working together on projects." Complaints arise surrounding certain "student teachers," but for the most part teacher assistants have
reputations for being "very devoted to helping [students] understand the material." Students rely on "word-of
mouth to find the best classes." Popular opinion says the environment "is not big on intellectualism," but most
students feel stimulated during their time at Syracuse and graduate as "independent thinkers."

Life

Let it snow—Syracuse students don't care! Yes, much of that cold manna from the heavens falls on Syracuse
town, but as one student puts it, "there's always a ton of stuff going on around campus: concerts, movies, speakers, etc." For those who do like to play outside, "Skiing is popular." Otherwise, "people stick to indoor activities—like partying." At Syracuse "the Greek scene is hot," while hordes of students descend upon the Marshall
Street bar and restaurant scene. This, along with athletics, galvanizes student experiences. Orangemen basketball—the 2003 national champions—draws rowdy crowds, as do football and lacrosse games. When the weather gets them down, students fortify their spirits with "bowling, hiking, shopping downtown, and taking day
trips to local lakes." One student pithily notes, "there really is everything available to you here; transportation
is as easy as pie, policies flexible, and friends of plenty." Crouse Hill attracts a late-night sledding crowd.
"Quilting groups" and service fraternities offer more wholesome activities. Students participate in the "thriving visual and performing arts community" or the *Daily Orange*, the popular student newspaper thought by
many people to be "the best institution on campus." "A great social life is available here to any student, no matter what he or she is interested in." The university's combination of solid academics and opportunities for
amusement results in "the true college experience."

Student Body

Undergraduates have many different opinions about what the typical student at Syracuse is like. Many students
say that the most visible group "comes from a lot of money and enjoys partying." Others note a seemingly disproportionate number of Long Islanders and "Soprano country" kids. But the numbers don't lie; Syracuse has
strong diversity numbers, both ethnic and geographic. Although inherent diversity exists, students note that,
"no one communicates outside their own group." The university tries to facilitate interaction, however, with
"good programs for sexual orientation, gender, and racial equality." A senior comments, "There seems to be a
high level of openness and no real pressure to conform to any popular standard." One student says, "I lived on
a floor with hippies, frat guys, and architecture students, and it was still calm." Another student adds, "We're
a melting pot of aspiring youth stuck in winter. We're like, 'Why not just all accept each other?'"

ADMISSIONS

Very important factors considered include: Character/personal qualities, class rank, essays, interview, recommendations, secondary school record, standardized test scores, talent/ability. *Important factors considered include:* Extracurricular activities. *Other factors considered include:* Minority status, volunteer work, work experience. SAT Reasoning or ACT required. TOEFL required of all international applicants. High school diploma is required, and GED is accepted. *Academic units required:* 4 English, 3 math, 3 science (3 science lab), 2 foreign language, 3 social studies, 5 academic electives. *Academic units recommended:* 4 English, 3 math, 3 science (3 science lab), 3 foreign language, 3 social studies, 5 academic electives.

The Inside Word

Syracuse is a nationally recognized university which draws a large applicant pool. At the same time, it has reduced the size of the freshman class, so the university has gotten more selective over the past few years. Most above-average students should still be strong candidates; although many weaker students are also able to benefit from Syracuse's individualized admissions process, they must show true promise in order to have a shot. Candidates for the Newhouse School will encounter even greater competition for admission.

FINANCIAL AID

Students should submit: FAFSA, CSS/Financial Aid PROFILE, noncustodial (divorced/separated) parents' statement, business/farm supplement. Regular filing deadline 2/1. The Princeton Review suggests that all financial aid forms be submitted as soon as possible after 1/1. *Need-based scholarships/grants offered:* Pell, SEOG, state scholarships/grants, the school's own gift aid. *Loan aid offered:* FFEL Subsidized Stafford, FFEL Unsubsidized Stafford, FFEL PLUS, Federal Perkins. Applicants will be notified of awards on or about 4/1.

FROM THE ADMISSIONS OFFICE

"Syracuse University is set on a beautiful residential campus that encompasses more than 200 acres and 170 buildings. Situated on a hill, overlooking downtown Syracuse, the school gives students the opportunity to enjoy the traditional college environment while realizing the social and recreational opportunities of a medium-size city.

"Syracuse University is committed to priorities that place its students first and foremost in importance. Small classes, intensive advising, emphasis on transition to college in the first year, and active learning characterize a systematic approach to assuring a productive teaching and learning environment. Improved classroom opportunities through smaller classes provide students with close attention from faculty.

"In virtually every aspect of students' lives at Syracuse, choices abound. The range of courses available, opportunities for study abroad and internships, the scope of residential living possibilities, the array of co-curricular and extracurricular clubs and organizations (there are nearly 300), and the opportunity to participate in the Honors Program makes SU an exciting place to attend. Students at Syracuse University have the choice of more than 200 undergraduate majors and nearly 70 undergraduate minors. Syracuse combines the best characteristics of a research institution with a traditional focus on the highest quality teaching, advising, and mentoring. It is a student-centered research university and is committed to giving students the very best educational experiences available."

For even more information on this school, turn to page 535 of the "Stats" section.

TEMPLE UNIVERSITY

1801 NORTH BROAD STREET, PHILADELPHIA, PA 19122-6096 • ADMISSIONS: 215-204-7200
FAX: 215-204-5694 • FINANCIAL AID: 215-204-8760 • E-MAIL: TUADM@MAIL.TEMPLE.EDU • WEBSITE: WWW.TEMPLE.EDU

Ratings
Quality of Life: 83   **Academic:** 78   **Admissions:** 82   **Financial Aid:** 78

Academics

Temple students love their school for its ability to integrate "a good education with significant life experiences." The school has earned a "great scholastic reputation" while prioritizing "real-life, hands-on experience with internships, co-ops, and experiential learning that prepare you for life beyond college." Many students agree that Temple helps students "develop thinking skills, ask questions, and wake up to see what the reality is." Professors are praised for "incorporating things from outside of the classroom into the lectures and discussions." Instructors both "know their material" and find "effective ways to relate it to the stu-

> **SURVEY SAYS . . .**
> Great computer facilities
> Great library
> Athletic facilities are great
> Diverse student types on campus
> Great off-campus food
> Campus feels safe
> Lots of beer drinking
> (Almost) everyone smokes

dents." The University's heterogeneous student body is reflected in the faculty, "a diverse, intelligent group" that "finds delight in sharing their knowledge with us." In particular, students gush about the professors and classes in the honors program. Honors classes "tend to be smaller, more interesting, and contain people who seem to actually enjoy learning." These courses provide "an atmosphere where discussions create more learning than a lecture would." The "extremely supportive" professors involved in the program "go out of their way to keep in contact with the students." For those not enrolled in the honors program, "course selection and advising can be difficult." One student values that Temple "can also be very interesting and experimental with its class offerings." As far as logistics go, one respondent writes, " I have had no problem contacting [the] administration when I need help with a problem." Though a few students say "The bureaucracy sucks," most agree that "the education can be magic," not to mention affordable.

Life

Temple's urban location largely defines the campus' feel. Though the school organizes "free good food, movies, guest speakers, parties, festivals, and cultural bus trips," most students choose to make their own fun in surrounding Philadelphia, "which is easy because we are directly connected to public transportation." Undergraduates agree, "From theater and museums to shops, clubs, and cafés, Philly has a lot to do." Students just have to "be able to take care of themselves in the city" since the surrounding area is described as "dodgy." One respondent articulates both sides of the issue: "Temple's main strength is the fact that it is in Philadelphia, but this takes away much of the close-knit campus feel." Certain issues do bring people together: "Political activism has become more popular recently, especially concerns over the government and foreign affairs." Fraternities pitch in on the weekend social scene, throwing parties attended mainly by underclassmen and those who live on campus. Commuters claim to have a "completely different life" than their resident counterparts, marked mainly by parking headaches.

Student Body

One student sums it up when she writes, "We call it Diversity University." Repeatedly, surveys emphasize that the undergraduate population includes students from every imaginable racial, ethnic, religious, and class background. A few unifying factors do emerge: "A typical student is a fairly hardworking, goal-oriented, middle-class American looking to carve out a future for his or herself." But as soon as you think you have a beat on it, someone says, "It is impossible to define a typical student because Temple is full of every different type of person." Students appreciate the diversity, claiming that the mix of "various backgrounds challenges opinions and feeds into active class discussions." In this "huge melting pot," respondents claim, "everyone's differences become their connection to other people." Certain students shatter the utopian image by telling us, "Most people seem to stick to their own groups, dictated by either major, race, [or] economic status." Other people call the campus "annoyingly anonymous" because it is "very much a commuter school." Despite these minor grumbles,

Temple students predominantly "look past the stereotypes" and accept their peers "for whom they are and what they are trying to achieve."

ADMISSIONS

Very important factors considered include: Class rank, secondary school record. *Important factors considered include:* Standardized test scores. *Other factors considered include:* Alumni/ae relation, character/personal qualities, essays, extracurricular activities, recommendations, talent/ability, volunteer work, work experience. SAT Reasoning or ACT required. TOEFL required of all international applicants. High school diploma is required, and GED is accepted. *Academic units required:* 4 English, 3 math, 2 science (1 science lab), 2 foreign language, 2 social studies, 1 history, 1 academic elective. *Academic units recommended:* 4 English, 4 math, 3 science (2 science lab), 2 foreign language, 2 social studies, 2 history, 3 academic electives.

The Inside Word

Nearly 50 percent of Temple's applicants are from outside Pennsylvania, 25 percent are from the Philadelphia area, and 25 percent from elsewhere in Pennsylvania. Admissions standards are moderately selective in general (60 percent acceptance rate), but candidates for the College of Music, in particular, face a rigorous review.

FINANCIAL AID

Students should submit: FAFSA. The Princeton Review suggests that all financial aid forms be submitted as soon as possible after 1/1. *Need-based scholarships/grants offered:* Pell, SEOG, state scholarships/grants, private scholarships, the school's own gift aid, federal nursing scholarships. *Loan aid offered:* FFEL Subsidized Stafford, FFEL Unsubsidized Stafford, FFEL PLUS, Federal Perkins, Federal Nursing, college/university loans from institutional funds. Applicants will be notified of awards on a rolling basis beginning on or about 2/15. Federal Work-study Program available. Institutional employment available. Off-campus job opportunities are excellent.

FROM THE ADMISSIONS OFFICE

"Temple combines the academic resources and intellectual stimulation of a large research university with the intimacy of a small college. The university experienced record growth in attracting new students from all 50 states and over 125 countries: up 60 percent in three years. Students choose from 130 undergraduate majors. Special academic programs include honors, learning communities for first-year undergraduates, co-op education, and study abroad. Temple has seven regional campuses, including Main Campus and the Health Sciences Center in historic Philadelphia, suburban Temple University, Ambler, and overseas campuses in Tokyo and Rome. Main Campus is home to the Tuttleman Learning Center, with 1,000 computer stations linked to Paley Library. The Center is a hub for emerging learning technologies and is designed for the high-tech students of today and tomorrow. The Liacouras Center is a state-of-the-art entertainment, recreation, and sports complex that hosts concerts, plays, trade shows, and college and professional athletics. It also includes the Independence Blue Cross Student Recreation Center, a major fitness facility for students now and in the future. Students can also take advantage of the new Student Fieldhouse. The university has constructed two new dorms, built to meet an unprecedented demand for main campus housing."

For even more information on this school, turn to page 536 of the "Stats" section.

THIEL COLLEGE

75 COLLEGE AVENUE, GREENVILLE, PA 16125 • ADMISSIONS: 724-589-2345 • FAX: 724-589-2013
E-MAIL: ADMISSION@THIEL.EDU • WEBSITE: WWW.THIEL.EDU

Ratings
Quality of Life: 70   **Academic:** 76   **Admissions:** 71   **Financial Aid:** 74

Academics

Thiel College is "a down-to-earth, small-town, liberal arts school located between Erie and Pittsburgh, Pennsylvania," affiliated with the Evangelical Lutheran Church in the United States. Students at the school brag about "a very good business department" and strong programs in art, education, English, and religion. They're especially proud of the results Thiel produces for its graduates. One undergraduate says, "We have a 98 percent

> **SURVEY SAYS . . .**
> *Small classes*
> *Students are friendly*
> *Diverse student types on campus*
> *Lots of beer drinking*
> *(Almost) everyone smokes*

placement rate into jobs or graduate schools within eight months of the student graduating." Thiel's small-school status allows students to "be big fish in little ponds rather than working real hard in larger schools just to be little fish in big ponds." It also provides "great opportunities in [their] respective majors, including many opportunities to do internships." One undergrad observes, "Students always have someone to help them, and help is never far away when we need it. We're not just a number like at some other school." Professors "will put in extra time to make sure that all of the students understand the material and will go the extra mile to arrange competitive academic scholarships to reward hard work." An Honors Program features "fabulous classes [and] thought-provoking discussions" for the academically elite.

Life

Thiel is located in "the rather quiet rural community" of Greenville, Pennsylvania, a place that most students agree offers "very little to do." One student writes, "You basically have to create your own fun around here. There aren't big malls, movie theaters, and clubs to go to." There are positive aspects to the location, however. "The campus is in a rather quiet rural community that you can feel safe walking around in after dark." One student says, "While there's not much to do in Greenville, there is lots of stuff to do in neighboring cities. We travel into Sharon, Hermitage, Boardman, and Youngstown a lot on the weekends." Some see another benefit to Greenville: "With so little to do, it's easier for me to concentrate on studies. To compensate for the small-town atmosphere, there are a lot of student activities like bus trips to concerts and baseball games. The majority of these activities are free to students. [Otherwise] for fun, students generally go out to eat and to the movies. A lot of people frequent the local bars, as well. Football is a religion [on campus], as well as wrestling, so [they] tend to frequent these events for fun."

Student Body

The "nice, courteous, respectful, studious, and social" undergrads at Thiel are generally the type of students who "choose Thiel because they are seeking the security and familiarity of a small-campus atmosphere." One student says, "You get a hello or smile anytime you walk down the sidewalk." While Thiel "does not tend to attract stellar academics," undergraduates at Thiel "tend to be dedicated enough to graduate in good standing [while also] understanding that it is also important to be a part of a club, team, or group to help get to know yourself and others." Thiel is small, but "the campus encompasses all races and nationalities with a decent contingency of international representation with very little obvious tension," although there isn't "necessarily a large amount of general interaction [among] the groups."

ADMISSIONS

Very important factors considered include: Secondary school record. *Important factors considered include:* Character/personal qualities, class rank, essays, extracurricular activities, interview, recommendations, standardized test scores, talent/ability. *Other factors considered include:* Alumni/ae relation, volunteer work, work experience. SAT Reasoning or ACT required. TOEFL required of all international applicants. High school diploma is required, and GED is accepted. *Academic units recommended:* 4 English, 2 math, 2 science (2 science lab), 2 foreign language, 3 social studies.

The Inside Word

Opportunities to get involved are ripe for the taking here, especially for students looking to kick-start the campus's interest in politics and diversity. If your interests match Thiel's strong, if unorthodox, structure, this Ohio Valley school is worth serious consideration.

FINANCIAL AID

Students should submit: FAFSA. Regular filing deadline 5/1. The Princeton Review suggests that all financial aid forms be submitted as soon as possible after 1/1. *Need-based scholarships/grants offered:* Pell, SEOG, state scholarships/grants, private scholarships, the school's own gift aid. *Loan aid offered:* FFEL Subsidized Stafford, FFEL Unsubsidized Stafford, FFEL PLUS, Federal Perkins, college/university loans from institutional funds. Applicants will be notified of awards on a rolling basis beginning on or about 2/1. Federal Work-study Program available. Off-campus job opportunities are fair.

FROM THE ADMISSIONS OFFICE

"Exclusively ranked by *U.S. News & World Report* as a top-five Best Value among northeastern comprehensive colleges, Thiel is a place where classes are smaller, personal attention is given in and out of the classroom, and friendships are easily formed—all at a fraction of the cost of other private liberal arts schools. Our professors and administrators are easily accessible and involved in students' development academically and personally, one of the reasons why Thiel graduates are so successful. In fact, 98 percent of graduates have a job or are enrolled in graduate school within eight months of graduation. Faculty and administration help new students successfully adapt to college life through Thiel's First-Year Experience program. Thiel's enrollment is growing, as are facilities and resources such as the Mouganis Instructional Media Center. The recently constructed Howard Miller Student Center is the hub of campus life, with lounges, support services offices, an engaging bookstore, art galleries, the Options convenience store, Starbucks bistro, and a world-class dining hall. Also new to campus are a unique Center for Excellence in Greek Life, a multi-sport athletic complex, the state-of-the-art fitness center, and new townhouse-style apartments. Thiel's "everywhere" campuswide networking features high-speed Internet access, cable television, and enhanced telephones with voice-mail. Thiel's students become leaders and active participants in more than 50 organizations, and more than half our students take advantage of study abroad and internship opportunities. Personalized financial aid benefits more than 95 percent of Thiel students, making Thiel's values-based education an affordable investment in your future. Apply free online at www.thiel.edu."

For even more information on this school, turn to page 536 of the "Stats" section.

TOWSON UNIVERSITY

8000 YORK ROAD, TOWSON, MD 21252-0001 • ADMISSIONS: 1-888-4TOWSON • FAX: 410-704-3030
E-MAIL: ADMISSIONS@TOWSON.EDU • WEBSITE: WWW.DISCOVER.TOWSON.EDU

Ratings
Quality of Life: 70   **Academic:** 71   **Admissions:** 81   **Financial Aid:** 69

Academics

Towson University's location—just outside of Baltimore and a quick drive to Washington, DC—is one of its chief benefits, allowing students to supplement their education with a wide range of internships, professional observation opportunities, and cultural interactions. Towson is the academic home of around 12,000 full-time undergrads, as well as nearly 2,000 part-timers. Despite these substantial numbers, this public university manages to provide "individualized attention right from the start." One student boasts that professors "know me by name and are willing at the drop of a hat to assist me in any problem that comes my way." Most class sizes remain small, and according to one satisfied undergrad, "the majority of my professors involve the students in [their] lectures by asking thought-provoking questions and letting us pretty much determine the structure of the class." The most popular majors at Towson are business administration, elementary education, mass communication, psychology, and biology; students have also urged us to point out the strong programs in art, English, health, and theater and vocal performance. Most complaints lodged by Towson students are in regards to the measly funding that the state of Maryland offers to its second-largest institution and the fact that Towson is temporarily without a president. One student assures, "While we do not have a president, the faculty and student body still run smoothly."

> **SURVEY SAYS . . .**
> *Small classes*
> *Students love Towson, MD*
> *Great off-campus food*
> *Student publications are popular*
> *Lots of beer drinking*
> *Hard liquor is popular*
> *(Almost) everyone smokes*

Life

At Towson University, "if you want to drink and party, you can; if you want to study all night, you can; if you like to just relax with your friends, you can." After all, Towson is a sizable university at the edge of a major metropolitan area. On campus, Greek life is reportedly popular, and "there's a lot to get involved in as far as extracurricular activities" are concerned. And while some go home on the weekends, students tell us that "anything you could be interested in is probably just a few blocks away" from campus, including a mall, a movie theater, and places to eat. And for a taste of urban life, Baltimore is just down the road. "Almost everyone goes into Baltimore at least once a week for something," says a student. One of the biggest Baltimore draws is the club scene. "There's a different Baltimore club to go to each night of the week" and "they all have 'college nights' on different days." To ensure safe travel, "free buses are available every weekend to and from the clubs." Other students take to the city for the museums, the shopping, the sporting events, and the restaurants. "There is *always* something to do in Towson and Baltimore," one student reports.

Student Body

Towson pulls a substantial portion of its student population from its northern neighbors, New Jersey and New York, but Maryland natives make up the majority of the student body. "Many people here have their own groups of friends even before they start attending" college, so cliques are somewhat prevalent. But "whether students live on campus and work part time or commute from home [or] work full-time attending classes at night or join a sorority on campus, all kinds of students mix here." When asked about diversity, students assure us that "there are many different kinds of people," while the student body is nonetheless a "majority white population." Just add to that mix the more than 800 international students from 96 countries that Towson enrolls and you'll find that a multitude of experiences are possible here.

ADMISSIONS

Very important factors considered include: Class rank, secondary school record. *Important factors considered include:* Recommendations, standardized test scores, talent/ability. *Other factors considered include:* Character/personal qualities, essays. SAT Reasoning Test required. High school diploma is required, and GED is accepted. *Academic units required:* 4 English, 3 math, 3 science (3 science lab), 2 foreign language, 3 social studies, 6 academic electives. *Academic units recommended:* 4 English, 4 math, 3 science (3 science lab), 4 foreign language, 4 social studies.

The Inside Word

Towson's large size doesn't seem to present a problem for students; solid facilities and resources within walking and driving distance make TU and its 30 undergrad majors a great option.

FINANCIAL AID

Students should submit: FAFSA. The Princeton Review suggests that all financial aid forms be submitted as soon as possible after 1/1. *Need-based scholarships/grants offered:* Pell, SEOG, state scholarships/grants, private scholarships, the school's own gift aid. *Loan aid offered:* Direct Subsidized Stafford, Direct Unsubsidized Stafford, Direct PLUS, Federal Perkins. Applicants will be notified of awards on a rolling basis beginning on or about 4/10.

FROM THE ADMISSIONS OFFICE

"Towson University is one of the most dynamic college communities in the country, offering academic programs that provide a solid liberal arts foundation and preparation for jobs and graduate school. Founded in 1866, Towson University today is nationally recognized for programs in the arts, sciences, business, communications, health professions, and education and computer science. *U.S. News & World Report* names Towson as one of the best regional public universities in the United States and Kiplinger's magazine counts us among America's great schools with reasonable cost. Students choose from more than 60 undergraduate majors and 37 graduate programs. Towson offers a student-centered learning environment with big-school choices and small-school personal attention. We encourage students to pursue learning inside and outside the classroom— through internships, student organizations, extracurricular activities, and research projects with faculty.

"An NCAA Division I program, Towson fields intercollegiate athletic teams in 23 sports. Our 24-acre sports complex includes University Stadium, home of Tiger football, field hockey, track, and lacrosse. The Tiger basketball, volleyball, and gymnastics teams compete at the 5,000-seat Towson Center. Athletic facilities include an NCAA-regulation swimming pool, gymnasiums, a sand volleyball court, tennis courts, a fitness center, and racquetball and squash courts.

"A member of the University System of Maryland, we enroll more than 17,000 students on our 328-acre campus located just eight miles north of downtown Baltimore. Local attractions include the National Aquarium, Oriole Park at Camden Yards, the Maryland Science Center, the Walters Art Museum, and historic Fells Point. The campus is a 10-minute walk to suburban shops, restaurants, movie theaters, and bookstores."

For even more information on this school, turn to page 537 of the "Stats" section.

TRINITY COLLEGE (CT)

300 SUMMIT STREET, HARTFORD, CT 06016 • ADMISSIONS: 860-297-2180 • FAX: 860-297-2287
FINANCIAL AID: 860-297-2046 • E-MAIL: ADMISSIONS.OFFICE@TRINCOLL.EDU • WEBSITE: WWW.TRINCOLL.EDU

Ratings
Quality of Life: 63   Academic: 89   Admissions: 94   Financial Aid: 94

Academics

Because of a flurry of recent administrative changes (the school has had four presidents in four years), Connecticut's Trinity College appears to be a school in constant flux. Students paint a different picture; they describe an upbeat institution that is progressing toward a more rigorous academic program without losing sight of what has made the school popular (small class sizes, caring professors, and solid liberal arts and sciences). Students tell us, "Trinity fosters interpersonal growth by allowing for the formation of close relationships with faculty and peers in a small-school environment. There is a more pronounced academic atmosphere than there has been in the past because the college is admitting a different type of student: one that is more focused, ambitious, and goal-oriented." One student describes professors as "extremely demanding with an exception or two," and adds, "But they are also the most accessible and engaging I have ever had, which fosters great professor/student interaction." Undergraduates also praise Trinity's curricular innovations. One student writes, "For freshmen seminars, the best are the 'reacting to the past' seminars, where students reenact historically important controversial events, such as the French Revolution. These seminars are very popular with students and project all sides of past political events in a way that allows students to learn much more and become more interested and involved in class." Another student reports, "[The school] offers great major flexibility. I'm designing my own major in human rights."

> **SURVEY SAYS . . .**
> *Small classes*
> *Great computer facilities*
> *Great library*
> *Lots of beer drinking*
> *Hard liquor is popular*

Life

Students agree that Trinity was a huge party school in the not-so-distant past. Many students still swear that "Trinity is a party school. It is hard to find other people who do not drink." An increasing number of students, however, counter that "Trinity may have once been a party school, but it is far from being true now. The days of 'raging 24/7' are over because the amount of work the professors assign is too much if [you] would like to graduate with 'good' grades." For the most part, students still agree that there's not much more to do except to party "[because of] the size of the school and the fact that it is in such a bad neighborhood that you really don't want to venture outside." Brave students who do venture off campus tell us that "Hartford offers many opportunities for fun" and many opportunities to engage in community service. Hartford's "central location in the Northeast puts us about an hour-and-a-half away from Boston and New York." On campus, there's Cinestudio, "an awesome movie theater that shows great independent and second-run movies" and "a great emphasis on sports, both intercollegiate and intramural."

Student Body

Trinity has long been known as a holding pen for "rich, snobby prep school kids." These "pink Polo with popped collar" kids may be the most instantly recognizable group on campus, but they are hardly the only ones who attend the school. In recent years, Trinity has stepped up efforts to diversify the student body, with noticeable results. Writes one senior, "In my time at Trinity, I have seen a transformation in the type of student. In the beginning, they were all rich, lazy prep school kids with exceptions, now there are not as many lazy, rich prep school kids. I see many more minorities, many, many more students in the library at all times, and an overcohesiveness among the student body." There can't be that many slackers; nearly one in five students proceed directly to grad school upon matriculating. Perhaps this is why one student says, "Most students at Trinity are engaged and interesting. Everyone has something in particular in which they are the best at, whether it be acting, writing, science, or even our five-time national champion squash team!"

ADMISSIONS

Very important factors considered include: Secondary school record. *Important factors considered include:* Character/personal qualities, class rank, essays, extracurricular activities, interview, minority status, recommendations, standardized test scores, talent/ability. *Other factors considered include:* Alumni/ae relation, geographical residence, volunteer work, work experience. TOEFL required of all international applicants. High school diploma is required, and GED is accepted. *Academic units required:* 4 English, 3 math, 2 science (2 science lab), 2 foreign language, 2 history.

The Inside Word

Trinity's Ivy safety status and well-deserved reputation for academic quality enables it to enroll a fairly impressive student body, but many of its best applicants go elsewhere. The price tag is high, and the college's competitors include a large portion of the best schools in the country. Minority candidates with sound academic backgrounds will encounter a most accommodating admissions committee.

FINANCIAL AID

Students should submit: FAFSA, CSS/Financial Aid PROFILE, noncustodial (divorced/separated) parents' statement, federal income tax returns. Regular filing deadline 2/1. The Princeton Review suggests that all financial aid forms be submitted as soon as possible after 1/1. *Need-based scholarships/grants offered:* Pell, SEOG, state scholarships/grants, private scholarships, the school's own gift aid. *Loan aid offered:* Direct Subsidized Stafford, Direct Unsubsidized Stafford, Direct PLUS, FFEL Subsidized Stafford, FFEL Unsubsidized Stafford, FFEL PLUS, Federal Perkins, college/university loans from institutional funds. Applicants will be notified of awards on or about 4/1. Federal Work-study Program available. Institutional employment available. Off-campus job opportunities are good.

FROM THE ADMISSIONS OFFICE

"An array of distinctive curricular options—including an interdisciplinary neuroscience major and a professionally accredited engineering degree program, a unique Human Rights Program, a tutorial college for selected sophomores, a Health Fellows Program, and interdisciplinary programs such as the Cities Program, Interdisciplinary Science Program, and InterArts—is one reason record numbers of students are applying to Trinity. In fact, applications are up 80 percent over the past five years. In addition, the college has been recognized for its commitment to diversity; students of color have represented approximately 20 percent of the freshman class for the past four years, setting Trinity apart from many of its peers. Trinity's capital city location offers students unparalleled 'real world' learning experiences to complement classroom learning. Students take advantage of extensive opportunities for internships for academic credit and community service, and these opportunities extend to Trinity's global learning sites in cities around the world. Trinity's faculty is a devoted and accomplished group of exceptional teacher-scholars; our 100-acre campus is beautiful; Hartford is an educational asset that differentiates Trinity from other liberal arts colleges; our global connections and foreign study opportunities prepare students to be good citizens of the world; and our graduates go on to excel in virtually every field. We invite you to learn more about why Trinity might be the best choice for you."

For even more information on this school, turn to page 537 of the "Stats" section.

TUFTS UNIVERSITY

BENDETSON HALL, MEDFORD, MA 02155 • ADMISSIONS: 617-627-3170 • FAX: 617-627-3860
FINANCIAL AID: 617-627-3528 • E-MAIL: ADMISSIONS.INQUIRY@ASE.TUFTS.EDU • WEBSITE: WWW.TUFTS.EDU

Ratings
Quality of Life: 90   **Academic:** 89   **Admissions:** 97   **Financial Aid:** 94

Academics

The boilerplate description of Tufts University—that it's the school for kids who couldn't get into one of the Ivies—may be accurate; however, this description places too much emphasis on Tufts's silver medal standing and downplays that Tufts is everyone's second choice precisely because its offerings are competitive with those of the Ivies. Tufts has a renowned faculty. One student agrees, "I can't say how often I hear their names on NPR or read in magazines that one has discovered or written something or other." The school is especially highly regarded in the field of international relations. Students say, "The presence of the Fletcher

> **SURVEY SAYS . . .**
> Great computer facilities
> Great library
> Great food on campus
> Great off-campus food
> Campus feels safe
> Students are happy
> Student publications are popular
> Lots of beer drinking

School of Law and Diplomacy on campus means that not only are classes available to advanced students but [also] important people in the international relations field often come for lectures." Pre-medical studies, engineering, and the liberal arts are also strong at Tufts. Unlike many Ivies, Tufts focuses on its undergraduates; "TAs only teach labs and study groups, while professors teach the actual classes." One undergraduate reports, "You could be the only freshman in a classroom filled with sophomores and juniors and your professor would still ask you your opinion, know your name, and treat you [as] a friend when he or she sees you in the dining hall." This "small-college" vibe extends right up to the top; the school's president "makes it a priority to be personally involved with students. Living right on campus, he is an advisor to undergraduates, has kids at his house for dinner or to go running, and is always available for appointments." Students also praise the career services at Tufts.

Life

The Tufts curriculum places heavy demands on students. Undergraduates report that "life at school revolves around classes. In general, most Tufts students take their grades very seriously." Students still manage to find some time during their busy weeks to blow off steam. One undergraduate says, "I love Tufts because I love being around intelligent people and being able to have an intellectual discussion, to go to a class and then spend a couple hours talking about the subjects, whether philosophy or international relations, with my friends. I'm just as happy staying in as going out." Other students enjoy the "absolutely gorgeous" campus in their spare time, while others run off to "well-publicized, interesting guest lectures, a cappella concerts," student-produced plays and art exhibits, and "large-scale, free campus events, such as Tuftonia's Day Fireworks, the Naked Quad Run, and Spring Fling." Freshmen also flock to "incredibly crowded frat parties," although as students grow older the allure of these shindigs wanes. Boston is only a few minutes away, so "on weekends, a good part of the student population takes the T into the city. Boston is a great resource for fun and entertainment." Students appreciate that they can enjoy a night in the big city, then retreat to the "safe suburban environment" of Medford.

Student Body

Students concede that "with a private school in the 'burbs of Boston, you're going to have your Prada shoes and Gucci bags," but quickly add that they are "impressed with how much diversity there actually is within the student body." They also note that "underrepresented minorities on campus seem to be comfortable and have a strong presence," but that different populations are "very self-segregated, which is frustrating." In all, just about everyone "can find a place here." One student adds, "What makes Tufts unique is that there are frats that attract a certain type of student as well as places like Oxfam Cafe, which serves vegetarian/vegan cuisine, where a different crowd of students hang out." Undergraduates also report that "there is a lot of political activism on campus."

ADMISSIONS

Very important factors considered include: Secondary school record. *Important factors considered include:* Character/personal qualities, class rank, essays, extracurricular activities, minority status, recommendations, standardized test scores, talent/ability, volunteer work, work experience. *Other factors considered include:* Alumni/ae relation, geographical residence, interview. SAT Reasoning and SAT Subject Tests or ACT required. TOEFL required of all international applicants. High school diploma is required, and GED is accepted. *Academic units recommended:* 4 English, 3 math, 2 science, 3 foreign language, 2 history.

The Inside Word

Tufts has little visibility outside the Northeast and little personality either. Still it manages to attract and keep an excellent student body, mostly from right inside its own backyard. In order to be successful, candidates must have significant academic accomplishments and submit a thoroughly well-prepared application—the review is rigorous, and the standards are high.

FINANCIAL AID

Students should submit: FAFSA, CSS/Financial Aid PROFILE, noncustodial (divorced/separated) parents' statement, business/farm supplement, parent and student federal income tax returns. Regular filing deadline 2/15. The Princeton Review suggests that all financial aid forms be submitted as soon as possible after 1/1. *Need-based scholarships/grants offered:* Pell, SEOG, state scholarships/grants, private scholarships, the school's own gift aid. *Loan aid offered:* FFEL Subsidized Stafford, FFEL Unsubsidized Stafford, FFEL PLUS, Federal Perkins, state loans, college/university loans from institutional funds. Applicants will be notified of awards on or about 4/1. Federal Work-study Program available. Institutional employment available. Off-campus job opportunities are good.

FROM THE ADMISSIONS OFFICE

"Tufts University, on the boundary between Medford and Somerville, sits on a hill overlooking Boston, five miles northwest of the city. The campus is a tranquil New England setting within easy access by subway and bus to the cultural, social, and entertainment resources of Boston and Cambridge. Since its founding in 1852 by members of the Universalist church, Tufts has grown from a small liberal arts college into a nonsectarian university of over 7,000 students. By 1900 the college had added a medical school, a dental school, and graduate studies. The University now also includes the Fletcher School of Law and Diplomacy, the Graduate School of Arts and Sciences, the School of Veterinary Medicine, the School of Nutrition, the Sackler School of Graduate Biomedical Sciences, and the Gordon Institute of Engineering Management."

For even more information on this school, turn to page 538 of the "Stats" section.

UNION COLLEGE

GRANT HALL, SCHENECTADY, NY 12308 • ADMISSIONS: 518-388-6112 • FAX: 518-388-6986
FINANCIAL AID: 518-388-6123 • E-MAIL: ADMISSIONS@UNION.EDU • WEBSITE: WWW.UNION.EDU

Ratings
Quality of Life: 70   Academic: 90   Admissions: 94   Financial Aid: 96

Academics

A renowned engineering program and widely available opportunities for study abroad are the marquee features at Union College, a small liberal arts school in upstate New York. It is almost impossible to slack off and get by at Union: "You need to do your work, and professors notice if you're not in class. Attendance is key," warns one student. Another adds, "There are a lot of classes that require writing papers and research reports." Even so, students know

how good they have it. "There is a great deal of communication and cooperation between the administration and the students," writes one undergraduate. "The sense of community is something I didn't feel at any other school I visited." Another student agrees, "Union does a good job of making sure everything runs smoothly and overall [does] a good job of making [itself] 'student (and parent)-friendly.'" Union profs earn high marks from students, who tell us, "The professors are what makes Union such an excellent institution. The overall academic experience is highly positive [because professors] go beyond the duty of holding required office hours. They usually invite students over to their homes for dinner." Add in the "great resources [and] a study abroad program that something like 75 percent of the students take advantage of," and the Union College picture is certainly complete.

Life

Everyone agrees that Union College is "a big school for frat parties on the weekend. Social life is based around fraternities, football games, and our men's ice hockey team." While almost everyone acknowledges that weekends are pretty wild, most also point out that "at Union, there is a partylike atmosphere at certain times that make the school seem like a party school, but during the week most people are in tune to their school work." Beyond the frats, "there are lots of other possibilities," although reportedly very few students take advantage of them. They include "movies that play every weekend, comedians who come, and bands. There are countless clubs, ranging from community service to ballroom dancing, and plenty of opportunities for free meals. There are also places to ski/snowboard nearby. Albany is pretty close, as well, and there are many things to do there." Some dismiss hometown Schenectady as "too dangerous," but others disagree. One such dissenter writes, "People who visit think that the town of Schenectady looks like it's dying. But they're wrong—it isn't the biggest or the best college town, but there's a lot to do: restaurants, a museum, a library, shopping, even one of the oldest theaters in the country, Proctor's Theater, which gets Broadway shows." One student finds another positive about Union; "The campus is beautiful. Whether it is fall, winter, or spring, the campus looks amazing."

Student Body

The preppier the school, the more students' descriptions of one another focus on their wardrobes. At Union, nearly every respondent categorized classmates by what was in their closets. "Girls wear a lot of Lilly Pulitzer and bows in their hair, and the boys are all Abercrombie models with their faded jeans. Everyone looks alike," writes one student. "It's all Polo collars turned up, Vera Bradley bags, name-brand everything," offers another. Once they finish their fashion reviews, students also note, "Almost no one here is from anywhere other than New York, New Jersey, Connecticut, or greater Boston," and that their classmates are "friendly, intelligent, at class on time, always ready for class discussions and lectures, and after class partying with friends." Union College students perceive their classmates as having major ambitions for their post-college years.

ADMISSIONS

Very important factors considered include: Class rank, secondary school record. *Important factors considered include:* Character/personal qualities, extracurricular activities, recommendations, standardized test scores. *Other factors considered include:* Alumni/ae relation, essays, geographical residence, interview, minority status, state residency, talent/ability, volunteer work, work experience. SAT Reasoning or ACT required. TOEFL required of all international applicants. High school diploma is required, and GED is not accepted. *Academic units required:* 4 English, 3 math, 2 science (2 science lab), 2 foreign language, 1 social studies, 1 history. *Academic units recommended:* 4 English, 4 math, 4 science (4 science lab), 4 foreign language, 2 social studies, 2 history.

The Inside Word

In this age of MTV-type admissions videos and ultra-glossy promotional literature, Union is decidedly more low-key than most colleges. The college is a bastion of tradition and conservatism and sticks to what it knows best when it comes to recruitment and admission. Students who are thinking about Union need to be prepared with as challenging a high school curriculum as possible and solid grades across the board.

FINANCIAL AID

Students should submit: FAFSA, CSS/Financial Aid PROFILE, state aid form, noncustodial (divorced/separated) parents' statement, business/farm supplement. Regular filing deadline 2/1. The Princeton Review suggests that all financial aid forms be submitted as soon as possible after 1/1. *Need-based scholarships/grants offered:* Pell, SEOG, state scholarships/grants, private scholarships, the school's own gift aid. *Loan aid offered:* FFEL Subsidized Stafford, FFEL Unsubsidized Stafford, FFEL PLUS, Federal Perkins, college/university loans from institutional funds. Applicants will be notified of awards on or about 4/1. Federal Work-study Program available. Off-campus job opportunities are good.

FROM THE ADMISSIONS OFFICE

"'Breadth' and 'flexibility' characterize the Union academic program. Whether the subject is the poetry of ancient Greece or the possibilities of developing fields such as nanotechnology, Union students can choose among nearly 1,000 courses—a range that is unusual among America's highly selective colleges. Students can major in a single field, combine work in two or more departments, or even create their own organizing theme major. Undergraduate research is strongly encouraged, and more than half of Union's students take advantage of the college's extensive international study program."

For even more information on this school, turn to page 538 of the "Stats" section.

UNITED STATES COAST GUARD ACADEMY

31 MOHEGAN AVENUE, NEW LONDON, CT 06320-8103 • ADMISSIONS: 800-883-8724 • FAX: 860-701-6700
E-MAIL: ADMISSIONS@CGA.USCG.MIL • WEBSITE: WWW.CGA.EDU

Ratings
Quality of Life: 63   **Academic:** 87   **Admissions:** 96   **Financial Aid:** 99

Academics

The United States Coast Guard Academy "brings together a diverse group of people dedicated to a common goal and teaches them how to live and work together to become leaders and to truly function as a team. We all live in the same building, eat the same meals, and go through the same training." If learning "personal discipline and how to balance a lot of responsibility with a heavy class load" sounds appealing to you—and you like the sea—then the CGA may be the right fit for you. Benefits include a free education ("although you put in enough mandatory extracurricular work to work your way though a normal college"), a "guaranteed job for five years after you gradu-

ate," and "incredible summer training programs that include all-expenses-paid trips (on Coast Guard ships) to places like Hawaii, Alaska, and Bermuda." Students can choose from only eight majors (the majority of which have the word 'engineering' in them somewhere), and much of the coursework here is required; "Every cadet has to take mandatory classes of calculus I & II, chemistry I & II, physics I & II, morals and ethics, world & American government, criminal justice, health, static engineering design, basic naval architecture, English and literature, introduction to electrical engineering, and macroeconomics, before and while we are taking our major-area classes. We all leave here very well-rounded." While professors "are tough and push us hard," students enjoy "an incredible support network of teachers, students, mentors, coaches and staff that take an integral role in helping us to achieve our personal and professional goals in and out of the Coast Guard."

Life

"Life is very regimented" at CGA, as students "all live in the same building, wake up at the same time, attend formations, and eat together." The experience "is a mix of military training, academics, and other activities. The first year is all about indoctrination. You will carry about 20+ credit hours, military work (duty and always having your uniform and room ready for inspection), and required activity credits." Even after first year, "We are not given many of the freedoms that most college students have. We aren't allowed to go out on weeknights and the rest of our liberty is restricted." As a result, cadets report, "When we are given the opportunity to go out or go on vacation, we go hard." The strict regulations work for some students, but others "become cynical by the time they have become seniors. Sometimes I regret not experiencing the kind of life that normal college students get to have." Stress relievers include club sports, which "are incredible considering the size of the school." Days out enjoying "the picturesque New England setting" and trips to New York City and Boston also help.

Student Body

"Because of the uniform, there is no discrimination like the petty discrimination of cliques in high school" at CGA. "We are shipmates, no matter where you were from or what you were like in your previous life as a civilian." One student explains, "Since we know we'll be working together for the rest of our military careers, people treat others with the utmost respect. There is no cheating, no stealing, no lying. If someone says they'll do something, they will." Most students are "A-type personalities" who "come from backgrounds in which [they] have always excelled academically, socially, and athletically. A-typical students are those who miss one or more of those traits." One cadet warns, "A-typical students quickly become typical students. We make sure of that!" Those who cannot fit the mold "do not perform well or are discharged."

ADMISSIONS

Very important factors considered include: Character/personal qualities, class rank, extracurricular activities, secondary school record, standardized test scores. *Important factors considered include:* Essays, recommendations, talent/ability. *Other factors considered include:* Alumni/ae relation, interview, volunteer work, work experience. SAT Reasoning or ACT required. TOEFL required of all international applicants. High school diploma is required, and GED is accepted. *Academic units required:* 4 English, 4 math, 3 science (3 science lab).

The Inside Word

The Coast Guard is the smallest service academy, regarded by many as a well-kept secret. Just like the other military service academies, admission is highly selective. Candidates must go through a rigorous admissions process that includes a medical exam and physical fitness evaluation. Those who pass muster join a very proud service. If you're a woman and thinking about a service academy, be aware that the Corps of Cadets at the Coast Guard Academy is 30 percent women!

FINANCIAL AID

The Coast Guard Academy is tuition-free.

FROM THE ADMISSIONS OFFICE

"Founded in 1876, the United State Coast Guard Academy has a proud tradition as one of the finest colleges in the country. When you've earned your four-year bachelor of science degree and a commission as an Ensign, you're prepared professionally, physically, and mentally as a leader and lifelong learner. You'll build friendships to last a lifetime, study with inspiring teachers in small classes, and train during the summer aboard America's Tall Ship EAGLE and the service's newest, most sophisticated ships and aircraft. Top performers spend their senior summer traveling on exciting internships. No Congressional nominations, appointments are awarded competitively on a nationwide basis. Graduates must serve for five years and have unmatched opportunities to attend flight training and graduate school, all funded by the Coast Guard. Your leadership potential and desire to serve your fellow Americans are what counts. Our student body reflects the best America has to offer—with all its potential and diversity!"

For even more information on this school, turn to page 538 of the "Stats" section.

UNITED STATES MERCHANT MARINE ACADEMY

OFFICE OF ADMISSIONS, KINGS POINT, NY 11024-1699 • ADMISSIONS: 516-773-5391 • FAX: 516-773-5390
EMAIL: ADMISSIONS@USMMA.EDU • WEBSITE: WWW.USMMA.EDU

Ratings

Quality of Life: 66   **Academic:** 81   **Admissions:** 94   **Financial Aid:** 98

Academics

Mention sailors and most people think of swearing, drinking, and port-of-call carousing, and while this image applies on rare occasions to students at the United States Merchant Marine Academy (USMMA), the focus here is decidedly on academics. At the beginning of the second semester of freshman year, midshipmen select a major—one of six available: "deck or engine, [meaning Marine Transportation or Marine Engineering] with a few subcategories in each." From that point forward, they have their course schedule laid out by the Academy. "I get one elective in four years," one midshipman notes. The academic program receives high praise, specifically because classroom learning is complemented by "one of four years of actual working experience." That experience comes during Sea Year, and students say, "Sea Year Courses, which are done while training on various merchant ships throughout the world, are the most difficult of the academy's courses." Professors are characterized as "dedicated," some to the point of being "slave drivers." The small classes, lack of TAs, and mandatory class attendance policy ensure that students get the attention they need to manage the "very heavy course load" and regimental requirements. Even deans pitch in and "tutor students when they can." Students submit mixed opinions when it comes to the administration, though the superintendent is widely respected. Some midshipmen perceive an "open door" attitude from administrators, but others claim that the "administration thinks we are whiny brats." Most students look forward to the high-paying careers available to them after graduation and appreciate the "excellent leadership training" they receive at the Academy.

> **SURVEY SAYS . . .**
> *Small classes*
> *Everyone loves the Mariners*
> *Frats and sororities are unpopular*
> *or nonexistent*
> *Political activism is unpopular or nonexistent*
> *Lots of beer drinking*
> *Very little drug use*

Life

"This school is a country club if you disregard the marching," one USMMA student observes. Marching and other regimental activities constitute much of life in Kings Point, prompting some students to feel at times like "inmates" on campus. Some report "sleeping two to four hours a night" to accommodate the intense academic and regimental schedule. Basically, "freshmen don't have lives," but even first-years point out, "We are here to train." As they progress, midshipmen begin to enjoy more "individual freedoms [and] privileges, which are granted based upon seniority and individual performance." To blow off steam, "most people work out nearly every day or play sports." When the weekend rolls around, "it's all about New York City," which is only 20 to 30 minutes away by train. One student writes, "I typically utilize some of our perks, such as free admission to Mets games, the U.S. Open, Yankees games, and David Letterman." Though rumors suggest "a few people have actually gone into museums" during these outings to the Big Apple, students mainly hit the bars, "on the prowl due to the lack of women at school." Other people choose to "sail all over Long Island on the weekends." A common sentiment goes something like, "Life at school is very busy, and there are not many times to just 'chill,' as my regular college friends call it."

Students

The typical USMMA student is reported to be a "white male between the ages of 18 and 22;" only about 100 women attend the Academy. Also, the population includes "very few students that are of a different ethnicity," but one minority student writes frankly, "I have not found this to be a problem." This might be partly due to the pervasive notion that "having people from many different areas of the country and world makes for an increased awareness of life in general and how people act." Respondents agree that "most students have similar political views," which translates to "no hippies." "Everyone becomes 'typical' by necessity because of the regimentation of the school." Strong bonds form during an "indoctrination period" that each incoming class undergoes, the "evident esprit de corps" solidified by the "cramped quarters" and "repressive regime" in which they exist. These solid connections endure after graduates set sail: "The merchant marine community is so small that there is also the advantage of an excellent network of contacts."

ADMISSIONS

Very important factors considered include: Character/personal qualities, secondary school record, standardized test scores. *Important factors considered include:* Class rank, essays, extracurricular activities, geographical residence, recommendations, talent/ability. *Other factors considered include:* Interview, minority status, state residency, volunteer work, work experience. SAT Reasoning or ACT required. TOEFL required of all international applicants. High school diploma is required, and GED is not accepted. *Academic units required:* 4 English, 3 math, 3 science (1 science lab), 8 academic electives. *Academic units recommended:* 4 English, 4 math, 4 science (2 science lab), 2 foreign language, 4 social studies.

The Inside Word

Academic criteria are only part of the admissions game here; you must also meet the Academy's physical requirements. The school catalog has three pages of requirements concerning vision, hearing, weight and body fat percent, skin condition, and respiratory health. You also need to know how to swim.

FINANCIAL AID

Students should submit: FAFSA, institution's own financial aid form. Regular filing deadline 5/1. The Princeton Review suggests that all financial aid forms be submitted as soon as possible after 1/1. *Need-based scholarships/grants offered:* Pell, private scholarships. *Loan aid offered:* FFEL Subsidized Stafford, FFEL Unsubsidized Stafford, FFEL PLUS. Applicants will be notified of awards on a rolling basis beginning on or about 1/31. Off-campus job opportunities are poor.

FROM THE ADMISSIONS OFFICE

"What makes the U.S. Merchant Marine Academy different from the other federal service academies? The difference can be summarized in two phrases that appear in our publications. The first: 'The World Is Your Campus.' You will spend a year at sea—a third of your sophomore year and two-thirds of your junior year—teamed with a classmate aboard a U.S. merchant ship. You will visit an average of 18 foreign nations while you work and learn in a mariner's true environment. You will graduate with seafaring experience and as a citizen of the world. The second phrase is 'Options and Opportunities.' Unlike students at the other federal academies, who are required to enter the service connected to their academy, you have the option of working in the seagoing merchant marine and transportation industry or applying for active duty in the Navy, Coast Guard, Marine Corps, Air Force, or Army. Nearly 29 percent of our most recent graduating class entered various branches of the Armed Forces with an officer rank. As a graduate of the U.S. Merchant Marine Academy, you will receive a Bachelor of Science degree, a government-issued merchant marine officer's license, and a Naval Reserve commission (unless you have been accepted for active military duty). No other service academy offers so attractive a package."

For even more information on this school, turn to page 539 of the "Stats" section.

UNITED STATES MILITARY ACADEMY

600 THAYER ROAD, WEST POINT, NY 10996-1797 • ADMISSIONS: 914-938-4041 • FAX: 914-938-3021
FINANCIAL AID: 914-938-3516 • E-MAIL: 8DAD@EXMAIL.USMA.ARMY.MIL • WEBSITE: WWW.USMA.EDU

Ratings
Quality of Life: 65   **Academic:** 97   **Admissions:** 96   **Financial Aid:** 99

Academics

At West Point, students tell us, "We forge leaders. Not build, not make, not teach; forge. Forging involves heat, pressure, and time." How? For starters, you will pretty much combine a full day's study with another full day's drills and exercise every day, especially during freshman and sophomore years. As one student explains, "The days normally start at 0600 and end at 2400 for most people. Our free time is filled by 'developmental' activities intended to help us become officers. We have no lives until we are in our third year." Not only are underclassmen's daily schedules fully prescribed, but so is their course of study; all classes during the first two years are required general education classes that are "very broad. It is hard to retain information because of the volume of material we have to learn each semester." To make the experience even more challenging, West Point employs the "Thayer method of teaching," in which students "teach themselves the material the night before [as homework], and the teacher explains it if we have any questions" in class. Fortunately, "Instructors are great, and they will make time to provide additional instruction outside the classroom." Still, it is just about as tough a row to hoe as there is. What's the payoff? Only an "awesome campus, free education, awesome academic and military opportunities for all cadets, free room and board, plus a small paycheck each month." Plus, things do ease up a little during the third and fourth years. As one student sums up, "You get a lot done in one day, and at the end of it, you're very proud of everything you're able to accomplish."

> **SURVEY SAYS . . .**
> *Small classes*
> *No one cheats*
> *Great computer facilities*
> *Great library*
> *Campus feels safe*
> *Intramural sports are popular*
> *Frats and sororities are unpopular or nonexistent*
> *Very little drug use*

Life

Many agree that life at West Point is "far stricter than anyone could imagine." For plebes (freshmen) and yearlings (sophomores), "There is essentially no free time during the day. There's mandatory drill (practice marching for parades), mandatory intramurals, chain of command duties, mandatory lectures/meetings, and academia." One plebe notes, "As freshmen, we are only allowed one weekend per semester to get out of here on our own. It gets quite depressing. For a wild Friday or Saturday night, we generally throw in a DVD on our computers and fall asleep around 10:00 p.m." No wonder underclassmen "try to leave on trip sections with different organizations as much as possible to get out of here." It does not stay that way. "Things are a little better your last two years; still, you'll be more than ready to break out at graduation," notes one undergraduate. When upperclassmen have free time, "most people go to a place on campus [where] they are allowed to drink. But they have to be 21, of course. [Others] get involved with the clubs, hang out with friends, [and] have pickup games of football or basketball during the warmer months." Or, understandably enough, they sleep.

Student Body

It takes an exceptional student to get into West Point, and an even more exceptional student to survive its grind. The typical student "is the All-American kid; he played sports and was in all sorts of stuff in high school. Most are religious. All want to be the best, but without screwing other people over." To make it at West Point, you have to "fit into a very small category: physically fit, intelligent, and willing to live a regimented lifestyle." The fitness part is critical. "If you are not physically fit, don't come here," students warn. They are also extremely goal-oriented; they have to be to "handle the suck" that is life for an underclassman. Otherwise, students have little to say about each other's distinguishing traits and for good reason. "A lot of students are the same because we are molded to think similarly." As one wry student puts it, "The typical students at my school all wear the same clothes, have weapons in their rooms, and get graded on how well they beat up their classmates."

ADMISSIONS

Very important factors considered include: Character/personal qualities, class rank, essays, extracurricular activities, recommendations, secondary school record, standardized test scores. *Important factors considered include:* Interview, minority status, talent/ability, volunteer work. *Other factors considered include:* Geographical residence, work experience. SAT Reasoning or ACT required. High school diploma is required, and GED is accepted. *Academic units recommended:* 4 English, 4 math, 2 science (2 science lab), 2 foreign language, 3 social studies, 1 history, 3 academic electives.

The Inside Word

Students considering a candidacy at West Point need to hit the ground running in the second half of their junior year. Don't delay initiating the application and nomination processes; together they constitute a long, hard road that includes not one but several highly competitive elements. Successful candidates must demonstrate strength both academically and physically, be solid citizens and contributors to society, and show true fortitude and potential for leadership. Admissions processes at other top schools can seem like a cakewalk compared to this, but those who get a nomination and pass the physical part of the process have made it through the hardest part.

FINANCIAL AID

The Princeton Review suggests that all financial aid forms be submitted as soon as possible after 1/1. *Need-based scholarships/grants offered:* All cadets are on active duty as members of the United States Army and receive an annual salary of approximately $8,880.20. Room and board and medical and dental care are provided by the U.S. Army. A one-time deposit of $2,400 is required upon admission (if needed, loans for the deposit are available for $100 to $2,400) to help pay for the initial issue of uniforms, books, supplies, equipment, and fees. A cadet's salary pays for uniforms, activities, services, books, sundries, and other personal effects throughout the 4-year experience. Upon graduation, cadets are awarded a bachelor of science degree and are commissioned in the U.S. Army as second lieutenants with a 5-year active duty service obligation. Off-campus job opportunities are poor.

For even more information on this school, turn to page 539 of the "Stats" section.

UNITED STATES NAVAL ACADEMY

117 DECATUR ROAD, ANNAPOLIS, MD 21402 • ADMISSIONS: 410-293-4361 • FAX: 410-295-1815
E-MAIL: WEBMAIL@GWMAIL.USNA.COM • WEBSITE: WWW.USNA.EDU

Ratings
Quality of Life: 90   **Academic:** 92   **Admissions:** 96   **Financial Aid:** 99

Academics

The United States Naval Academy "produces leaders, not just people with book knowledge" through a grueling academic and physical ordeal that forges graduates who are "strong morally, mentally, and physically, able to cope in any place that they are put, and able to overcome any obstacle that lies in their way." This "nonstop competition from start to finish [instills] discipline, time management, and dedication," as well as "great moral and ethical values" in midshipmen. All students receive a full scholarship, but no one here would tell you she or he is getting a free ride; "It is a an expensive education shoved up your rear a nickel at a time," wryly notes one student. "Academics are extremely hard" because, in large part, "there is very little time to do your work, with the military aspect taking up a great deal of time." The USNA offers a "solid curriculum" reinforced by small classes ("even freshmen-level courses never exceed 21 students per class"), tremendous resources ("we have the money to access all kinds of amazing things"), and a solid faculty ("I take classes from a former Chairman of the Joint Chiefs of Staff and other respected professionals"). Sums up one student, "This school sets and maintains a standard unimaginable at other colleges and universities, and the feeling of accomplishment at the end of the day is hard to beat."

> **SURVEY SAYS . . .**
> *Small classes*
> *No one cheats*
> *Lab facilities are great*
> *Great computer facilities*
> *Campus feels safe*
> *Everyone loves the Navy*
> *Intramural sports are popular*
> *Frats and sororities are unpopular*
> *or nonexistent*
> *Very little drug use*

Life

"Every midshipman may complain at one time or another about many aspects of life at the Naval Academy, but overall I believe it is what we want," notes one student at the USNA. "We did not come here for an easy experience. We came here to be the best. And the administration, officers, and professors expect exactly that from us." Be forewarned, that "your first year will be extremely hard here," as "plebe year is something that you'll have to experience in order to believe." For plebes, "life is as restricted as it gets, short of prison. No music and movies, and you can only go out on Saturdays. We have mandatory drill, training, and physical exercise, along with student and military chains of command that restrict weekend liberty and what clothes we can wear, among other things." Throughout all four years, students "do an enormous amount of professional training, from summer training cruises to character development and leadership classes," and they "work out all the time." Campus recreation includes extracurricular activities "of every size and description;" when they get liberty ("you get more each year"), students head to Annapolis or to other nearby campuses. "for fun, there are about 10 bars within walking distance, for those of age." Students agree: it's a rough life, but "even the people who say they hate it rarely ever leave. There's nothing like being in King Hall (our dining hall) with 4,000 other midshipmen banging crab mallets on the table during the annual fall Crab Feast, or walking into Memorial Hall late at night and reading the names of graduates that have died in combat and remembering that 'they have set the course.'"

Student Body

"Contrary to what one might expect, there is a tremendous variety of students," at the United States Naval Academy. "They come from all over the country and many different socioeconomic classes and walks of life. No one can tell what kind of financial background you have; we all wear the same uniform, get the same pay, and get in effect full scholarship and free room and board." Many "were high-school athletes who lettered in two or more varsity sports while having a 3.9 GPA in classes," the type of people who "excelled at almost everything they tried their hand at in high school and continue to excel at USNA." Despite the diversity of backgrounds, "there are almost [no] students who are atypical, because this is not an environment hospitable to them."

ADMISSIONS

Very important factors considered include: Character/personal qualities, class rank, essays, extracurricular activities, interview, recommendations, secondary school record, standardized test scores. *Important factors considered include:* Talent/ability. *Other factors considered include:* Alumni/ae relation, geographical residence, minority status, state residency, volunteer work, work experience. SAT Reasoning or ACT required. TOEFL required of all international applicants. High school diploma or equivalent is not required. *Academic units recommended:* 4 English, 4 math, 2 science (1 science lab), 2 foreign language, 2 history, 1 introductory computer and typing course.

The Inside Word

It doesn't take a genius to recognize that getting admitted to Annapolis requires true strength of character; simply completing the arduous admissions process is an accomplishment worthy of remembrance. Those who have successful candidacies are strong, motivated students, and leaders in both school and community. Perseverance is an important character trait for anyone considering the life of a midshipman—the application process is only the beginning of a truly challenging and demanding experience.

FINANCIAL AID

The Naval Academy is tuition-free.

FROM THE ADMISSIONS OFFICE

"The Naval Academy offers you a unique opportunity to associate with a broad cross-section of the country's finest young men and women. You will have the opportunity to pursue a four-year program that develops you mentally, morally, and physically as no civilian college can. As you might expect, this program is demanding, but the opportunities are limitless and more than worth the effort. To receive an appointment to the academy, you need four years of high school preparation to develop the strong academic, athletic, and extracurricular background required to compete successfully for admission. You should begin preparing in your freshman year and apply for admission at the end of your junior year. Selection for appointment to the academy comes as a result of a complete evaluation of your admissions package and completion of the nomination process. Complete admissions guidance may be found at www.usna.edu."

For even more information on this school, turn to page 540 of the "Stats" section.

UNITY COLLEGE

PO Box 532, Unity, ME 04988-0532 • Admissions: 207-948-3131 • Fax: 207-948-6277
E-mail: admissions@unity.edu • Website: www.unity.edu

Ratings
Quality of Life: 68   Academic: 62   Admissions: 69   Financial Aid: 86

Academics

Some people get to work in the great outdoors, where others only vacation; Unity College students are preparing themselves for just those types of careers. Unity offers programs that produce "professionals who can positively impact the environment." Typical Unity undergraduates feel passionate enough about preserving the environment, but they choose from many different paths to reach their goal. Some students want to "collaboratively work to accomplish environmental awareness through outdoor adventures," while others focus on "sustainability as the ulti-

> **SURVEY SAYS . . .**
> *Small classes*
> *Students are friendly*
> *Students are happy*
> *Frats and sororities are unpopular*
> *or nonexistent*
> *Lots of beer drinking*

mate goal." The college's unique and practical environmental degrees include environmental writing, wildlife care and education, and landscape horticulture. Additionally, Unity is the only institution granting diplomas in conservation law enforcement or a BS in adventure education leadership. The experienced professors "teach here because they love the school." Students call them "partners" and feel they "form an extended family." Because Unity students represent diverse opinions when it comes to environmental policy, "Class discussions can get pretty interesting." Respondents note creative approaches to instruction and "lots of hands-on learning." Furthermore, because of the "small community-learning environment," students can contribute to campus-wide administrative decisions.

Life

When the field surveys and rope courses are complete, Unity students spend every free moment fishing, snowmobiling, hunting, canoeing, dog sledding, white water rafting, or (in some other way) frolicking in Maine's open-air playground. "The Activity Center rents equipment for rock climbing, camping, and skiing," so students can jaunt off to the woods or hit the Appalachian Trail at any time. Small town life is described as "averagely fun," but most people enjoy nights at the local tavern, where a live band plays once a week. Students organize open mic nights, bowling outings, pool tournaments, semiformal events, and movie screenings; "new ideas for fun classes and activities are always flowing." Hockey games draw dedicated fans in the winter. A few odd students "drive twenty minutes to Waterville to buy giant pickles and see who can eat them the fastest." One student sums up the general flavor of the school this way: "It's the only college where a tree can tip over and students rush with their own chainsaws to remove it." Students feel content at Unity, one so much so that he writes, "When I go visit home, I want to go back to Unity after, like, three days. And I have a good home life."

Student Body

"Hippy" and "hick" stand at opposite ends of the Unity personality spectrum and pretty much cover the range of stereotypes that students use to describe their peers. Students are either "tree huggers or Bambi killers, with very little in between." Some people bridge the groups: "I agree more with the rednecks opinion-wise, but I get along better with the hippies." The most visible contingent is the "con-law" students, mostly males with big trucks, Carhartt's, and camouflage hats. So how do the "environmentally conscious and easygoing" vegetarians coexist with students who "kill critters and stuff 'em"? They focus on their "common goal: a healthy Earth." One student writes, "It's really easy to make friends because we all have a love of the outdoors in common." Whether students identify as "brilliant underachievers" or "serious activists," they contribute to the diversity of ideas and lifestyles. Students note a lack of ethnic diversity; one student says, "Once you've been here for a while, you see that there are a lot of very different people."

ADMISSIONS

Very important factors considered include: Essays, interview, recommendations, secondary school record. *Important factors considered include:* Character/personal qualities, extracurricular activities, talent/ability. *Other factors considered include:* Alumni/ae relation, standardized test scores, volunteer work, work experience. SAT Reasoning Test and ACT recommended. TOEFL required of all international applicants. High school diploma is required, and GED is accepted. *Academic units required:* 4 English, 2 science. *Academic units recommended:* 4 math, 2 foreign language, 4 social studies.

The Inside Word

A love of the outdoors is a prerequisite of admission to Unity College, but it isn't the only one. Applicants need two years of lab science and three years of college prep math to be considered here. The school is willing to take a chance on students who scraped by in high school, provided they show promise.

FINANCIAL AID

Students should submit: FAFSA, institution's own financial aid form. Regular filing deadline 4/15. The Princeton Review suggests that all financial aid forms be submitted as soon as possible after 1/1. *Need-based scholarships/grants offered:* Pell, SEOG, state scholarships/grants, private scholarships, the school's own gift aid. *Loan aid offered:* FFEL Subsidized Stafford, FFEL Unsubsidized Stafford, FFEL PLUS. Applicants will be notified of awards on a rolling basis beginning on or about 3/15. Federal Work-study Program available. Off-campus job opportunities are fair.

For even more information on this school, turn to page 540 of the "Stats" section.

UNIVERSITY OF THE ARTS

320 South Broad Street, Philadelphia, PA 19102 • Admissions: 215-717-6049 • Fax: 215-717-6045
E-mail: admissions@uarts.edu • Website: www.uarts.edu

Ratings
Quality of Life: 72   Academic: 78   Admissions: 80   Financial Aid: 74

Academics

It doesn't surprise anyone that the University of the Arts "is about doing, being, feeling, and loving art." The school draws students because it allows them to "find [their] passion and go for it" and "[to] learn the technical skills to aid [their] creativity." Students appreciate that the school gives them latitude to express themselves and "self-guide" their education. University of the Arts takes pride in being "the only university with all creative majors." The dance, photography, graphic design, and crafts departments get singled out often, but students in majors including ceramic arts, art education, sculpture, and industrial design also have good things to say about their programs. Ideally, "all of the majors intermingle," but it seems that more often people "segregate along media lines." The rigorous curriculum, likened to medical school by some, includes a foundation program for all freshmen, which covers the fundamentals of drawing as well as 2-D and 3-D design. Professors receive high marks across the board. Students respect them as practicing artists and working professionals who develop productive relationships with students. Some instructors are described as "a bit nutty and eccentric," but as a group, "their passion is infectious." Students must develop thick skins to survive "crits." One student explains, "Professors critique [us], and we get paranoid about everything." Although students have minor complaints about bureaucracy and tuition hikes, the school succeeds in "training the artist to function in the real world."

> **SURVEY SAYS . . .**
> *Small classes*
> *Great off-campus food*
> *Intercollegiate sports are unpopular or nonexistent*
> *Intramural sports are unpopular or nonexistent*
> *Frats and sororities are unpopular or nonexistent*
> *Theater is popular*
> *(Almost) everyone smokes*

Life

Most students say they spend most of their time in the studio. One student says, "I wake up, go to the studio, work, eat, and sleep again." Even after a long day of "making stuff" and looking at slides, students at the University of the Arts seem to crave more art. A music major says, "For fun, I play music and listen to music." Other students like to "paint and draw with [their] friends" or hit the Philadelphia art galleries, especially when they are free on the first Friday of the month. "Center city Philadelphia is our campus," a junior reminds prospective students and points out that the "buildings dot the Avenue of the Arts." This degree of integration means that "if students want to be part of an organization, it's out in the city, not an on-campus club." Students love the South Street scene and the "great diners, bars, and live music" all around them. One student says, "Most people live and hang out off campus." Reportedly, house parties "art-school style" have many themes; whether they are "pirates, pimps and ho's, or rednecks," give these kids some fabric and a glue gun, and they're set. Some students "wish there were sports and other activities that non-campus residents could be involved in," but most of them are content with student performances, open mic events, and the coffee houses.

Student Body

"There are a lot of typical art students who like to appear atypical" at the University of the Arts. Amid the "more alternative than thou" milieu of art school, "Atypical is typical and vice versa." For example, "jocks and cheerleaders are very rare and don't fit in." So unless you're Ken or Barbie, "It isn't too hard to find a group you relate to." People come in "quirky, artsy-fartsy, [and] intense" personality types, although when superficial distinctions are stripped away, many of them seem to be "middle class, white women from Jersey." One student comments that "everyone is so diverse," but that seems to be in terms of "dancers, musicians, writers, and visual artists." Politically left-leaning, the student population "accepts everyone for who they are," forming "a blend of everyone's unique styles and tastes."

ADMISSIONS

Very important factors considered include: Interview, secondary school record, talent/ability. *Important factors considered include:* Character/personal qualities, class rank, essays, extracurricular activities, standardized test scores. *Other factors considered include:* Alumni/ae relation, minority status, recommendations, volunteer work, work experience. SAT Reasoning or SAT Subject Tests required. TOEFL required of all international applicants. High school diploma is required, and GED is accepted. *Academic units required:* 4 English. *Academic units recommended:* 3 math, 2 science, 2 foreign language, 2 social studies, 2 history, 2 academic electives.

The Inside Word

Like most good arts schools, UArts is not easy to get into. Academic record factors in somewhat here, but demonstration of artistic talent is much more important. For most applicants, the portfolio/audition is the make-or-break moment in the admissions process.

FINANCIAL AID

Students should submit: FAFSA. Regular filing deadline 3/1. The Princeton Review suggests that all financial aid forms be submitted as soon as possible after 1/1. *Need-based scholarships/grants offered:* Pell, SEOG, state scholarships/grants, private scholarships, the school's own gift aid, merit scholarships. *Loan aid offered:* FFEL Subsidized Stafford, FFEL Unsubsidized Stafford, FFEL PLUS, Federal Perkins, alternative loans. Applicants will be notified of awards on or about 3/1. Federal Work-study Program available. Institutional employment available. Off-campus job opportunities are excellent.

FROM THE ADMISSIONS OFFICE

"'Art is central to our everyday lives,' says Miguel-Angel Corzo, President of The University of the Arts. "It drives the media we consume, the design of products we use, the form of the buildings we frequent, the layout of cities in which we live, and the channels through which we communicate." As president of the only university in the nation dedicated exclusively to the visual, performing, communication and media arts, Corzo is committed to advancing this notion by preparing students to apply their strengths to create a better society.

"Located in the heart of Philadelphia on the Avenue of the Arts, U Arts offers 25 majors in a single environment where students inspire each other with their creativity, focus and drive. U Arts students learn through exposure to all the languages of imagination—sound, movement, words, and form. The university offers traditional programs in painting, sculpture, printmaking, and photography as well as state-of-the-art programs in digital video, graphics, and multi-media communication. Its performing arts programs train dancers, musicians, actors and directors for top jobs in entertainment around the country. At the same time, U Arts provides its 2,200 undergraduate students with an education grounded in the liberal arts, through core courses in English, history, and others.

"We help students satisfy their need to create while preparing them to apply their talents and strengths to contribute to society as a whole," says Corzo. 'These characteristics not only are important to success in the arts but to success in society in general.'"

For even more information on this school, turn to page 540 of the "Stats" section.

UNIVERSITY OF CONNECTICUT

2131 HILLSIDE ROAD, U-3088, STORRS, CT 06268-3088 • ADMISSIONS: 860-486-3137 • FAX: 860-486-1476
FINANCIAL AID: 860-486-2819 • E-MAIL: BEAHUSKY@UCONN.EDU • WEBSITE: WWW.UCONN.EDU

Ratings
Quality of Life: 65   Academic: 76   Admissions: 88   Financial Aid: 72

AAcademics

Students at the University of Connecticut's (UConn) flag-ship campus in Storrs tell us that they chose their school for "the wide variety of opportunities it provides its students to get involved and get ahead." Undergrads here also cite as big pluses "undergraduate research, study abroad, career services/internships, cooperative education programs," "more than 100 majors, including an individualized major which allows students to design their own plan of study, and over 300 clubs and activities. There is literally something for everyone." Business administration, music, theater, education, computer science, and engineering are among the disciplines garnering students' specific praise here. As at many large state schools, many warn that "introductory courses are not that great. It gets better as you progress as a student." Profs are "surprisingly helpful when students go to their office hours and tend to return emails the same day," although "with [UConn] being a research university, you sometimes get stuck with professors that are just too intelligent to be teaching." Of course, for the right student, the presence of so many researchers "provides a great experience. You can find numerous opportunities to get involved in professors' research projects." Many here appreciate the fact that "larger lectures are almost always broken into discussion sections of 20–25 students that meet once a week." Being the flagship university for the state of Connecticut doesn't hurt either. Connecticut profited, not once, but twice from state grants of $1 billion each, first in 1996 and then again in 2002. Students directly benefit from this windfall of dough in that every residence hall, academic building, sports facility, program office, etc. is being completely refurbished, torn down and rebuilt, or simply added anew to campus.

> **SURVEY SAYS . . .**
> *Great computer facilities*
> *Great library*
> *Athletic facilities are great*
> *Everyone loves the Huskies*
> *Intramural sports are popular*
> *Student publications are popular*
> *Lots of beer drinking*
> *Hard liquor is popular*

Life

As a large university, UConn has the resources to support a wide variety of campus activities. Big-name acts "come to the university's Jorgensen Auditorium; they're amazing and with student ticket prices are a wonderfully cheap way to see great shows." On a smaller scale, "there are many students who enjoy the concerts of UConn Underground, numerous films, lectures, plays, and other activities going on in the dorms on a nightly basis." Furthermore, "there are so many clubs and organizations to be involved with that if you're bored on campus, it's because of your own laziness." Even so, a surprising number of students here claim that "there is nothing to do here except party." One reason is that many of the nonparty activities end early; explains one student, "UConn has a great campus life, which ends at 10 p.m. every day. Unfortunately because of that, alcohol is a popular late-night substitute. Activities are available . . . if you look hard enough and are open to different cultural and artistic experiences." Don't look in hometown Storrs, though, which "is not a college town. There is nothing to do off campus without driving at least 20 minutes." Do, however, look in the stadiums, arenas, and gymnasiums, as "the University of Connecticut offers strong Division I athletic programs in addition to a vast selection of club and intramural sports." Most here agree that "Spring Weekend is the highlight of the year. Three straight days (starting on a Thursday) of parties with crowds up to and over 10,000 people: just an overall amazing experience."

Student Body

While "the large size of UConn means that there's not one typical student," we're told that most students here "have a good balance of school and social life. They work hard during the week and enjoy the weekend." Many are serious about success but not necessarily about book learning for its own sake; they "know that it's OK to skip at least one or two classes a week and to show up late because no one will say anything." Students are split regarding diversity. While some describe the typical UConn student as "white, middle/upper class, and from Connecticut," others point to "our five cultural centers, [where] it's easy for students to fit in and feel a part of a community."

ADMISSIONS

Very important factors considered include: Class rank, secondary school record, standardized test scores, talent/ability. *Important factors considered include:* Character/personal qualities, essays, extracurricular activities, minority status, recommendations, volunteer work. *Other factors considered include:* Alumni/ae relation, geographical residence, state residency, work experience. SAT Reasoning or ACT required. TOEFL required of all international applicants. High school diploma is required, and GED is accepted. *Academic units required:* 4 English, 3 math, 2 science (2 science lab), 2 foreign language, 2 social studies, 3 academic electives. *Academic units recommended:* 3 foreign language.

The Inside Word

While no formulas or cutoffs may be used at UConn in the admissions process, getting in is still simply a matter of decent courses, grades, and tests. The $2.3 billion building program coupled with the recent high national profiles of the UConn men's and women's basketball teams has resulted in an increase in applications and in turn an increase in selectivity. With an incoming freshman class of more than 3,000, UConn is now holding enrollment steady for eager Huskies-to-be.

FINANCIAL AID

Students should submit: FAFSA. The Princeton Review suggests that all financial aid forms be submitted as soon as possible after 1/1. *Need-based scholarships/grants offered:* Pell, SEOG, state scholarships/grants, private scholarships, the school's own gift aid. *Loan aid offered:* FFEL Subsidized Stafford, FFEL Unsubsidized Stafford, FFEL PLUS, Federal Perkins. Applicants will be notified of awards on a rolling basis beginning on or about 3/1.

FROM THE ADMISSIONS OFFICE

"The University of Connecticut provides students with high quality education, personalized attention, and a wide range of social and cultural opportunities. From award-winning actors to the federal reserve board chair, fascinating speakers and world leaders have lectured on campus within the past year, while students have taken in shows by premier dance, jazz, and rock performers. Transportation to campus events is convenient and safe; most students walk to class or ride university shuttlebuses. Through UCONN 2000 and Twenty-first-Century UConn, landmark building programs totaling $2.3 billion, the university is erecting state-of-the-art academic and residential facilities. Among the projects: A new Center for Undergraduate Education, unifying student support services in one central location and providing speedy answers to student concerns. Because of a variety of innovations like this one, UConn is transforming the undergraduate experience and fast becoming a school of choice for a new generation of achievement-oriented students."

For even more information on this school, turn to page 541 of the "Stats" section.

UNIVERSITY OF DELAWARE

116 HULLIHEN HALL, NEWARK, DE 19716 • ADMISSIONS: 302-831-8123 • FAX: 302-831-6905
FINANCIAL AID: 302-831-8761 • E-MAIL: ADMISSIONS@UDEL.EDU • WEBSITE: WWW.UDEL.EDU/VIEWBOOK

Ratings
Quality of Life: 77   Academic: 79   Admissions: 92   Financial Aid: 78

Academics

What students like most about University of Delaware (UD) is that "despite the fact that it's a pretty big school, it doesn't feel that way." One student says, "The school has done a great job making me feel at home and part of an amazing community of people that care about me personally." That sense of engagement permeates the UD academic experience. One undergraduate writes, "Delaware is about opportunities to work hands-on with faculty, either through the honors program, undergraduate research, senior thesis, or simply additional meetings with professors outside of class." Outside the classroom, students, professors, and administrators "keep in close contact via E-mail [and] WebCT," and professors "are extremely accessible." University of Delaware has "a number of excellent faculty members in all of the major fields and an outstanding research program." Undergraduates are especially sanguine about the "strong majors in business and agriculture, [the] great engineering programs, [and] well-developed arts programs, especially in music and theater." The chemistry department is also something to rave about, as it "is a wonderful place for undergraduates." Students also love all the extras, which include a solid study abroad program, an honors program that "gives you a more hands-on approach and allows a much more personal relationship with professors," and a full slate of extracurricular activities. One student sums up, "University of Delaware prides itself on enriching its students while they are here, not only in academics, but also in life experiences, involvement on campus, and preparing for the future."

Life

"There is always something to do on or around campus," UD undergraduates report. "The campus movie theater shows new movies every weekend, and on Main Street there are billiard halls and a bowling alley. There are also a lot of restaurants to go to in the area," and plenty of parties. Students tell us that "Delaware has always had a party-school reputation, which the university is trying to get away from, but the campus is still a great place to go out and party." Where students party depends on their age. "Frat parties are big for the underclassmen. After you're 21, the school turns into a bar school. Everyone is at certain bars on certain nights." Because most students are serious about success, they "know when to stop and get work done, or study for a test. The biggest challenge is to manage the time between partying and studying, but most people handle it pretty well." Not everyone drinks, of course: "For students who don't drink, there are always other options on campus, such as comedy shows, band performances, and a lot of student-run organizations, over 200 of them. The university offers so many activities and organizations to be involved in; someone can always find something that fits them individually." Student groups also organize plenty of bus trips to Philadelphia, Baltimore, Washington, DC, and New York City. With so much to offer, it is no wonder that some students feel that "University of Delaware has achieved the perfect balance between strong and challenging academic work and social events."

Student Body

"There are so many kids at UD that everyone fits in. Whatever you see yourself as: jock, nerd, whatever, there are people like you at UD," students tell us. Most would also agree, however, that you will fit in with the largest part of the population if you "look like you just walked out of an Abercrombie ad. [There are] lots of preppy kids, mostly white and middle to upper class." In general, students tend to self-segregate. As one student puts it, "While we tend to get along, there isn't necessarily interaction between social groups." One clear divide separates Delaware residents and out-of-staters, who actually compose the majority of the student body. "Out-of-state students are, on the whole, very well off, and show it. In-state students, however, are generally viewed as not as well off." Another divide is the "big split between Greek and non-Greek students." Minorities, most agree, are underrepresented at UD.

ADMISSIONS

Very important factors considered include: Essays, secondary school record, state residency. *Important factors considered include:* Character/personal qualities, class rank, extracurricular activities, geographical residence, recommendations, standardized test scores, talent/ability. *Other factors considered include:* Alumni/ae relation, interview, minority status, volunteer work, work experience. SAT Reasoning or ACT required. TOEFL required of all international applicants. High school diploma is required, and GED is accepted. *Academic units required:* 4 English, 3 math, 3 science (2 science lab), 2 foreign language, 2 social studies, 2 history. *Academic units recommended:* 4 English, 4 math, 4 science (3 science lab), 4 foreign language, 2 social studies, 2 history, 2 academic electives.

Inside Word

Most students applying to Delaware face a moderately selective admissions process focused mainly on grades and tests with some focus on nonacademic characteristics. Those who seek to enter the university's honors program need to be far more thorough in completing their applications and much better prepared academically in order to gain admission. The honors program has high expectations; from what we know, it appears to be well worth it.

FINANCIAL AID

Students should submit: FAFSA. Regular filing deadline 3/15. The Princeton Review suggests that all financial aid forms be submitted as soon as possible after 1/1. *Need-based scholarships/grants offered:* Pell, SEOG, state scholarships/grants, private scholarships, the school's own gift aid. *Loan aid offered:* Direct Subsidized Stafford, Direct Unsubsidized Stafford, Direct PLUS, Federal Perkins, Federal Nursing. Applicants will be notified of awards on or about 3/15. Federal Work-study Program available. Institutional employment available. Off-campus job opportunities are good.

FROM THE ADMISSIONS OFFICE

"The University of Delaware is a major national research university with a long-standing commitment to teaching and serving undergraduates. It is one of only a few universities in the country designated as a land-grant, sea-grant, urban-grant, and space-grant institution. The academic strength of this university is found in its highly selective Honors Program, nationally recognized Undergraduate Research Program, study abroad opportunities on all seven continents, and its successful alumni, including three Rhodes Scholars since 1998. The University of Delaware offers the wide range of majors and course offerings expected of a university, but in spirit it remains a small place where you can interact with your professors and feel at home. The beautiful green campus is ideally located at the very center of the East Coast 'megacity' that stretches from New York City to Washington, DC. All of these elements, combined with an endowment approaching $1 billion and a spirited Division I athletics program, make the University of Delaware a tremendous value."

For even more information on this school, turn to page 541 of the "Stats" section.

THE UNIVERSITY OF MAINE

5713 Chadbourne Hall, Orono, ME 04469-5713 • Admissions: 207-581-1561 • Fax: 207-581-1213
Financial Aid: 207-581-1324 • E-mail: um-admit@maine.edu • Website: www.umaine.edu

Ratings
Quality of Life: 76   Academic: 74   Admissions: 78   Financial Aid: 75

Academics

Combine cheap in-state tuition with top programs, and it's easy to understand why not too many University of Maine students are in any rush to leave the warm embrace (which is at a premium in chilly Maine) of their college after four sweet years. Engineering is tops here, but exciting majors like new media, marine science, and landscape horticulture draw their fair share of undergraduates, too. For those who

> **SURVEY SAYS . . .**
> *Great library*
> *Everyone loves the Black Bears*
> *Lots of beer drinking*
> *Hard liquor is popular*

fear the anonymity of a public school, UM undergrads swear that "It's not overwhelmingly huge." General education classes can be large and impersonal, but a math major writes, "Most of my classes for the past two years have been under 20 people, many under 10. I can actually go to my professors with questions on homework, class, or career." Another undergrad adds, "I have always received attention when I needed it, even in classes of 300-plus." One student who is taking advantage of the tutoring program writes that, thanks to the one-on-one time, "I am now receiving 100's on my tests and quizzes." The administration generally makes a good impression on students from the get-go by "setting up meetings with the first-year students to get to know them and to establish a communication line. If anyone has questions, answers are a phone-call, visit, or e-mail away."

Life

Word on the street is that "people here know how to recreate." Take, for example, flowing pumpkin ale at Oktoberfest, mud volleyball along with campus beautification (in lieu of classes) on Maine Day, and the school-sponsored bonfire celebrating the Red Sox pennant in 2004, which, we are told, "was genius, as it kept the excited student body from doing any damage and gave us all an outlet for our celebratory energy." The Division I athletic teams, hockey in particular, draw a rabid following. "When you say Maine Black Bears, you say all." On the weekends, "You can go dancing at Ushie's or drinking at the Bear Brew, which are almost always packed on Thursdays." Greek life "is slowly getting a better reputation thanks to the fraternities and sororities changing policies and extending out into the community." After the night's revelries are over, kids grab a few hours of sleep before waking in the morning to hike off any hangovers on the extensive network of trails near the campus. There's a lot of alcohol-less cheer to be had at UM too; plenty of people appreciate that "six nights out of the week, somewhere on campus you can find free fun that does not involve alcohol or sports." That means karaoke, comedians, movies in the main lecture hall, board games, and open-mic nights. "There's even a knitting club."

Student Body

The University of Maine's undergraduate population includes a colorful array of more than 8,000 characters: "boozers, stoners, foresters, adventurers, businessmen, and the straight-up Mainers." Just what is a "straight-up Mainer?" The answer depends on whom you ask. Most here agree, though, that he isn't so welcoming to out-of-state folks. That shouldn't upset too many people, though, as only about 15 percent of students hail from beyond the borders of The Pine Tree State. Still, according to students, "every type of person is represented in the student body in some way." A visible Goth contingent mingles with hacky-sacking hippies and anime enthusiasts. Against the backdrop of "white back hill hicks," the "African American athletes from Massachusetts and hockey players from New York or Canada" do stand out. Still, "You can wear what you want, say what you want, think what you want, and it's accepted." Students tend to form cliques "made up of high school friends or people from your area;" in such a small state, people always seem connected by "three or fewer degrees of separation."

ADMISSIONS

Very important factors considered include: Secondary school record. *Important factors considered include:* Class rank, standardized test scores. *Other factors considered include:* Alumni/ae relation, character/personal qualities, essays, extracurricular activities, interview, recommendations, talent/ability, volunteer work, work experience. SAT Reasoning or SAT Subject Tests required. TOEFL required of all international applicants. High school diploma is required, and GED is accepted. *Academic units required:* 4 English, 3 math, 2 science (2 science lab), 2 foreign language, 2 social studies, 3 academic electives, 1 physical education. *Academic units recommended:* 4 English, 4 math, 3 science (3 science lab), 2 foreign language, 3 social studies, 1 history, 3 academic electives, 1 physical education.

The Inside Word

The University of Maine is much smaller than most public flagship universities, and its admissions process reflects this; it is a much more personal approach than most others use. Candidates are reviewed carefully for fit with their choice of college and major, and the committee will contact students regarding a second choice if the first doesn't seem to be a good match. Prepare your application as if you are applying to a private university.

FINANCIAL AID

Students should submit: FAFSA. The Princeton Review suggests that all financial aid forms be submitted as soon as possible after 1/1. *Need-based scholarships/grants offered:* Pell, SEOG, state scholarships/grants, private scholarships, the school's own gift aid. *Loan aid offered:* FFEL Subsidized Stafford, FFEL Unsubsidized Stafford, FFEL PLUS, Federal Perkins, state loans. Applicants will be notified of awards on a rolling basis beginning on or about 3/15. Federal Work-study Program available. Institutional employment available. Off-campus job opportunities are good.

FROM THE ADMISSIONS OFFICE

"The University of Maine offers students a wide array of academic and social programs, including clubs, organizations, professional societies, and religious groups. We strive to help students feel welcome and to provide opportunities for them to become an integral part of the campus community. Visit our beautiful campus and become better acquainted with this community. Take a guided campus tour and learn about campus facilities, services and technologies, and living and dining. Our student tour guides give a firsthand view of the Black Bear experience. During your visit, meet with faculty and admission staff to learn more about your program of interest and our academic climate. The University of Maine's commitment to educational excellence and community building will be reinforced when you visit our campus!"

For even more information on this school, turn to page 542 of the "Stats" section.

UNIVERSITY OF MAINE—FORT KENT

23 University Drive, Fort Kent, ME 04743 • Admissions: 207-834-7500 • Fax: 207-834-7609
E-mail: umfkadm@maine.maine.edu • Website: www.umfk.maine.edu

Ratings
Quality of Life: 72   Academic: 71   Admissions: 62   Financial Aid: 73

Academics

Students consistently praise the Fort Kent campus of the University of Maine for two reasons: its small size and affordable cost. The tight-knit academic community prompts one student to write, "It [gives you an] education in an environment that's similar to family." A freshman far from her Virginia home says, "The professors and administrators made me feel at home." Another student from Cameroon agrees, "As an international student, the administration's welcoming attitude was beyond what I expected." The "accessibility of faculty and staff, even the dean," impresses all the newcomers. Small class sizes "facilitate the learning process" and afford "lots of personal attention from the faculty." An upperclassman tells us, "Professors are friendly and treat you like friends. They look out for their students." Top academic programs include nursing, environmental science, education, and forestry. Students note the "technology available in the classrooms," but some still want "more facilities for research and buildings for studying." And increased enrollment in certain departments has caused some growing pains. An undergraduate says, "[This is my opportunity to] increase my knowledge, make friends, and ensure my future."

> **SURVEY SAYS . . .**
> *Small classes*
> *Registration is a breeze*
> *Great computer facilities*
> *Great library*
> *Students are friendly*
> *Diverse student types on campus*
> *Students get along with local community*

Life

In Northern Maine, "life can be grand," especially for people who love the outdoors. Athletic students tackle the elements year round, with skiing, snowmobiling, and skating in the winter and canoeing, hiking, biking, fishing, and swimming in the summer. "It's great to head out to the local trails and lakes." The Can-Am dog sled race even shows up in Fort Kent. When they can't be outdoors, students hit the gym to work out and play sports. Another great love around the university is soccer, and many students want "more money and support for athletics" in general. Even in this quiet town, students' "main thoughts are usually, 'When can we go out again?'" Locally, the school hosts "a large number of small events, like movies, dances, and pool tournaments." Many people "go to school, work, do homework, [and] spend time with friends." They basically enjoy their "small, homelike atmosphere" and "a good relationship with the surrounding community."

Student Body

Many freshmen are funneled straight from Fort Kent Community High School, while others arrive from Argentina and Lithuania. The collision of Maine natives and "thirty or forty different nationalities" results in much cultural diversity. No matter where they're from, virtually everyone gushes about the "family environment" and "secure and comfortable" campus atmosphere. The small community of students is described as open minded, polite, friendly, and mature. When asked to describe a typical student, a business major writes, "[A typical student is] somebody [who] is involved in their school and community."

ADMISSIONS

Very important factors considered include: Secondary school record. *Important factors considered include:* Essays. *Other factors considered include:* Character/personal qualities, class rank, extracurricular activities, interview, recommendations, standardized test scores, talent/ability, volunteer work, work experience. SAT Reasoning or ACT recommended. TOEFL required of all international applicants. High school diploma is required, and GED is accepted. *Academic units required:* 4 English, 2 math, 2 science (2 science lab), 2 social studies.

The Inside Word

It's possible to get into Fort Kent on high school grades alone, because standardized test scores, letters of recommendation, and an interview are all optional. If you really under-perform on standardized tests, Kent would be a good place to apply without submitting SAT scores.

FINANCIAL AID

Students should submit: FAFSA. The Princeton Review suggests that all financial aid forms be submitted as soon as possible after 1/1. *Need-based scholarships/grants offered:* Pell, SEOG, state scholarships/grants, private scholarships, the school's own gift aid. *Loan aid offered:* FFEL Subsidized Stafford, FFEL Unsubsidized Stafford, FFEL PLUS, Federal Perkins, state loans. Federal Work-study Program available. Institutional employment available. Off-campus job opportunities are good.

For even more information on this school, turn to page 542 of the "Stats" section.

University of Maryland, Baltimore County

1000 Hilltop Circle, Baltimore, MD 21250 • Admissions: 410-455-2291 • Fax: 410-455-1094
Financial Aid: 410-455-2387 • E-mail: admissions@umbc.edu • Website: www.umbc.edu

Ratings
Quality of Life: 70   Academic: 76   Admissions: 86   Financial Aid: 71

Academics

The University of Maryland—Baltimore County is primarily known as a great "science and engineering school" with superb "research opportunities"—but this justly earned reputation tells only part of the story. Many here report that "the humanities are wonderful," even though some concede that they "are not very well funded or respected." Offerings here are enhanced by the "focus on research. There are so many opportunities for students to learn the latest tidbits of up-to-date research done on campus and to work with professors for credit." "The professors seem to be a mixed bag," getting reviews that range from "very inspiring" and "excellent" to "crappy" and "awful," with some falling "in the middle." Students here enjoy "really great opportunities for internships. The proximity to Washington, DC, and Baltimore provides easy access to jobs other people around the country would love to have." UMBC's career services office also facilitates "great placement opportunities. The methods of getting your resume around in your field of interest are easy and very effective." In all areas, UMBC adheres to an "honors college philosophy of smaller classes and more professor interaction."

> **SURVEY SAYS . . .**
> *Great computer facilities*
> *Great library*
> *Diverse student types on campus*
> *Campus feels safe*

Life

Campus life at UMBC has many hurdles to clear. One of the biggest is the campus itself, which students complain "has no atmosphere," griping that "it's just a bunch of buildings" that are "disconnected from the surrounding community." Explains one undergrad, "The campus is not very inviting…There's almost nowhere to relax or study outdoors between classes. The dorms are on the outskirts of campus, [so] the part where classrooms are located is pretty desolate. It's rare to see people socializing, sunbathing, playing Frisbee™, etc. on campus between classes." Compounding these problems is the fact that it has "the reputation of being a commuter campus." A growing number of underclassmen—over 70 percent of last year's freshman class—also live on campus, which has bolstered a sense of community at UMBC. There is fun to be had, though. Several students write that "fun at UMBC usually consists of hanging out at the Commons and eating food, playing in the game room, or just relaxing in a friend's dorm room." Some note optimistically that "campus life is improving, especially with the addition of our on-campus bar," and others point out that the Student Events Board (which "tries to give us something cool to do as much as possible") has booked "many great events, such as Dave Chappelle, Good Charlotte, Kanye West, Third Eye Blind, Tracey Morgan, and most recently, Yellowcard." While "there are many students that go out to drink," this is not true of "everyone by any means." And while "most weekends are still pretty much dead here," students can take comfort in the fact that "Baltimore's Inner Harbor is only five minutes away."

Student Body

With minorities making up about one-third of the student body, UMBC is a "truly diverse" place. "The diversity is wonderful," writes one junior. "It gives everyone a chance to learn about different cultures, religions, etc." A few students also note that while "the ethnic, religious and ideological diversity on the campus means that most people can find some small set of friends or acquaintances with whom they can comfortably spend what free time they have," it also "contributes to a certain cliquishness…which is easily seen by the lack of great interaction between students of different nationalities and races." More than half the students are commuters "like to go to school and go home." While commuters are "typically poorly integrated into the social fabric of the campus," they aren't totally isolated: they have a "commuter lounge where breakfast is offered for free for commuters on Tuesdays and Thursdays." UMBC's students "try to eke out a social existence however they can. Even those who live on-campus, however, are typically mostly dedicated to completing their work, rapidly earning their degrees, and quickly leaving the school."

ADMISSIONS

Very important factors considered include: Secondary school record, standardized test scores. *Important factors considered include:* Class rank, essays, recommendations. *Other factors considered include:* Character/personal qualities, extracurricular activities, interview, talent/ability, volunteer work, work experience. SAT Reasoning or ACT required. TOEFL required of all international applicants. High school diploma is required, and GED is accepted. *Academic units required:* 4 English, 3 math, 3 science (2 science lab), 2 foreign language, 2 social studies, 2 history, 4 academic electives. *Academic units recommended:* 4 English, 4 math, 3 science (2 science lab), 2 foreign language, 2 social studies, 2 history, 4 academic electives.

The Inside Word

The State of Maryland seems blessed with several strong, small, public universities in addition to its flagship campus at College Park. UMBC is one of those to watch; its national visibility and admissions standards are on the rise. Strong students are attracted by UMBC's emphasis on academic achievement. As a result, the admissions committee has grown to expect evidence of challenging academic course work throughout high school from its candidates, preferably at the honors or AP level. This competitive path will give you the best shot for admission if you're an eager learner looking for a campus where the academic experience is engaging.

FINANCIAL AID

Students should submit: FAFSA. The Princeton Review suggests that all financial aid forms be submitted as soon as possible after 1/1. *Need-based scholarships/grants offered:* Pell, SEOG, state scholarships/grants, private scholarships. *Loan aid offered:* FFEL Subsidized Stafford, FFEL Unsubsidized Stafford, FFEL PLUS, Federal Perkins. Applicants will be notified of awards on a rolling basis beginning on or about 3/15. Off-campus job opportunities are excellent.

FROM THE ADMISSIONS OFFICE

"When it comes to universities, a midsized school can be just right. Some students want the resources of a large community. Others are looking for the attention found at a smaller one. With an undergraduate population of 8,000, UMBC can offer the best of both. There are always new people to meet and things to do—from Division 1 sports to more than 170 student clubs. As a research university, we offer an abundance of programs, technology, and opportunities for hands-on experiences. Yet we are small enough that students don't get lost in the shuffle. More than 80 percent of our classes have fewer than 40 students. Among public research universities, UMBC is recognized for its success in placing students in the most competitive graduate programs and careers. Of course, much of the success of UMBC has to do with the students themselves—highly motivated students who get involved in their education."

For even more information on this school, turn to page 543 of the "Stats" section.

UNIVERSITY OF MARYLAND, COLLEGE PARK

MITCHELL BUILDING, COLLEGE PARK, MD 20742-5235 • ADMISSIONS: 301-314-8385 • FAX: 301-314-9693
FINANCIAL AID: 301-314-9000 • E-MAIL: UM-ADMIT@UGA.UMD.EDU • WEBSITE: WWW.MARYLAND.EDU

Ratings

Quality of Life: 69   Academic: 76   Admissions: 93   Financial Aid: 65

Academics

The University of Maryland—College Park (UMCP) contains boosters that proudly proclaim, "[it] has it all: a beautiful campus, a diverse student body (but always plenty of people like yourself), awesome athletics, an incredible array of great classes, and a million and one ways to get involved and pursue what you love." The school is a winner in students' eyes, even when they focus solely on academics. "Maryland has the kind of academic reputation that you'd like to see on a resume," reports one undergraduate. "We have awesome resources available to students, and there are even opportunities to work one-on-one with professors on research projects." Engineering and business offerings earn high marks. The school's proximity to Washington, DC makes it a solid choice for those interested in government and political science as well. Like the federal government (for which many grads will ultimately work), UMCP is "so large that a student is nothing more than a number." (Honors Programs remedy this problem for those ambitious enough to take on some extra work.) To help students deal with their often-impersonal educations, "all courses have an online component, with syllabi, announcements, message boards to contact teachers and other students, and often quizzes and class discussions, which is very helpful." Large classes offer "labs and discussions, usually run by TAs, but they [the TAs] are very knowledgeable and personable. They're also easy to contact and easy to relate to on an academic and personal level." Students conclude that "courses at UMCP are challenging, and many times incredibly difficult, but with great teachers, thousands of campus resources, and some good hard work, it is a great place to be."

> **SURVEY SAYS . . .**
> *Great library*
> *Athletic facilities are great*
> *Diverse student types on campus*
> *Everyone loves the Terrapins*
> *Student publications are popular*
> *Lots of beer drinking*
> *Hard liquor is popular*

Life

"Having a huge campus gives Maryland one advantage over the rest," students tell us. They also point out, "There's everything in the world to do here. From a number one nationally ranked Mock Trial Team to chorus groups and the highly visible Pride Alliance, there's something for everyone, if you can find it." Not to mention the school's many nationally ranked athletic teams. Undergraduates report that "basketball season is particularly fun, as the men's basketball games will make a sports fan out of anyone!" The university's location gets mixed reviews. Students dislike hometown College Park ("ugly and a little dangerous" and say "residents do not like students"), but love the campus (they think it is "beautiful," and there is "easy access to a variety of food") and its proximity to both Baltimore and Washington, DC. One student writes, "If you can't find something to do locally, there are tons of places to go in DC and Baltimore for students of all ages and interests. The metro trains and buses offer ways for students to get around without needing a car. The cities offer so many cultural things to do!"

Student Body

"You definitely see all kinds of people when you are walking across campus" at the University of Maryland. As one student puts it, "Nothing shocks me anymore. Each person seems to find her place, whether it's with the Satanic Mechanics (i.e., Rocky Horror Picture Show people), the Greeks, or the Solar House team." But while "Maryland has a very diverse student population, students tend to gravitate toward students more like them, mostly because the school is so large. It can become somewhat cliquish." Once you learn the lay of the land, "you can really tell where people fit in. All the sorority girls look the same (think headbands, Saucony sneakers, and Juicy Couture sweats). There is definitely a preppy-suburban look to most of the student body. Then there's still a bunch of people who have their own thing. So basically anyone can fit in."

ADMISSIONS

Very important factors considered include: Secondary school record, standardized test scores. *Important factors considered include:* Class rank, essays, recommendations, state residency, talent/ability. *Other factors considered include:* Alumni/ae relation, character/personal qualities, extracurricular activities, geographical residence, minority status, volunteer work, work experience. SAT Reasoning or SAT Subject Tests required. TOEFL required of all international applicants. High school diploma is required, and GED is accepted. *Academic units required:* 4 English, 3 math, 3 science (2 science lab), 2 foreign language, 3 social studies. *Academic units recommended:* 4 math.

The Inside Word

Maryland's initial candidate review process emphasizes academic credentials and preparedness. Through this first review, roughly 20 percent of the applicant pool is either admitted or denied. The remaining 80 percent are then evaluated in depth by admissions officers and reviewed by an admissions committee of seven, who collectively decide upon each candidate. Don't take essays and the compilation of other personal material that is required of applicants lightly. It's uncommon for a large university to devote this kind of attention to candidate selection. Perhaps this explains why so many of the students here made Maryland their first choice.

FINANCIAL AID

Students should submit: FAFSA. The Princeton Review suggests that all financial aid forms be submitted as soon as possible after 1/1. *Need-based scholarships/grants offered:* Pell, SEOG, state scholarships/grants, private scholarships, the school's own gift aid. *Loan aid offered:* FFEL Subsidized Stafford, FFEL Unsubsidized Stafford, FFEL PLUS, Federal Perkins. Applicants will be notified of awards on a rolling basis beginning on or about 4/1.

FROM THE ADMISSIONS OFFICE

"Commitment to excellence, to diversity, to learning—these are the hallmarks of a Maryland education. As the state's flagship campus and one of the nation's leading public universities, Maryland offers students and faculty the opportunity to come together to explore and create knowledge, to debate and discover our similarities and our differences, and to serve as a model of intellectual and cultural excellence for the state and the nation's capital. With leading programs in engineering, business, journalism, architecture, and the sciences, the university offers an outstanding educational value."

For even more information on this school, turn to page 543 of the "Stats" section.

UNIVERSITY OF MASSACHUSETTS—AMHERST

UNIVERSITY ADMISSIONS CENTER, AMHERST, MA 01003 • ADMISSIONS: 413-545-0222
FAX: 413-545-4312 • FINANCIAL AID: 413-545-0801 • E-MAIL: MAIL@ADMISSIONS.UMASS.EDU • WEBSITE: WWW.UMASS.EDU

Ratings
Quality of Life: 68   **Academic:** 69   **Admissions:** 78   **Financial Aid:** 71

Academics

It is no secret to Massachusetts residents that their entire state university system, including its flagship campus at Amherst, has struggled with deep budget cuts in recent years. The school is doing its best under such less-than-ideal fiscal circumstances. As one student reports, "While struggling against major budget deficits in the state, UMass has done an excellent job keeping a strong faculty. And while classes are often too large, many professors compensate for this with abundant office hours and interesting teaching styles." The biggest problem caused by the cuts is "getting into classes that you want can be nearly impossible." One undergraduate explains further, "Students are now informed that they most likely will be here for more then four years because it is so hard to get into courses you want." For those willing to endure these inconveniences, the university has plenty to offer: still-reasonable tuition and fees, a universe of excellent departments, a faculty that includes "many leading thinkers," and access to the Five College Consortium, which broadens available offerings even further. Some appreciate another choice provided by the school: "The ability to choose to party every night or advance one's intellect with the incredible minds that are around (both students and professors alike)." Class sizes vary by major, but "all intro-level classes are large." The University takes a variety of steps to make the experience a little easier. Some professors, for example, "are great when it comes to e-mail response and personal help, if students needed it, [and] most of the text offerings are available on the Internet, which is a big help."

> **SURVEY SAYS . . .**
> *Great library*
> *Students love Amherst, MA*
> *Great off-campus food*
> *Student publications are popular*
> *Lots of beer drinking*
> *Hard liquor is popular*

Life

"I have to give credit for the location of UMass," writes one student of the school's western Massachusetts Pioneer Valley setting. "It's in the middle of nowhere, but there are so many other colleges around it that you can always find people. It's also close to New York City, Boston, Hartford, and skiing up in Vermont." Students have no trouble finding entertainment in Amherst and its environs. The school's hometown offers "Uptown, which is what we call the downtown area, and it is always busy," while nearby Northampton offers a music scene and quaint shops. A little farther down the road sits Springfield, home to numerous dance clubs and the Basketball Hall of Fame. Not that anyone needs to travel that far to find entertainment. The University is home to so many parties that some students refer to the school as "ZooMass." One student explains, "Off-campus keg parties are huge at our school. Smoking marijuana is also very popular." There are also plenty of "intramurals, organizations, political protests," and all the other standard trappings of a large college campus. The Pioneer Valley, many students note, is ideal for "biking and hiking; the area also has awesome places to eat, shop, and just hang out."

Student Body

As at most large universities, there is a little of everything at the University of Massachusetts. Different groups are easily identified by their residences, undergraduates tell us. One student writes, "Those who enjoy normal mainstream culture live in the high-rises of Southwest. (It is also where the booze usually is.) Students who are more socially conscious and are open to diversity live in Central. (It is also where most of the drugs are.) Orchard Hill is usually more quiet and is filled with people who have a hard time in social situations, or those that would rather study than party. Northeast is filled with mainly computer science majors and Asian students. (The Asian-cuisine-influenced dining hall is also there.)" Despite such segregation by domicile, "everyone is forced to mix during the day on campus, and everyone seems to get along well," observes one student. "It is a good social environment, as you can meet any imaginable type of person, from anarchist to über-conservative, and can encounter everything from blank, unintelligent conversation to ones of brilliance that are difficult to wrap one's mind around."

ADMISSIONS

Very important factors considered include: Secondary school record. *Important factors considered include:* Standardized test scores. *Other factors considered include:* Alumni/ae relation, character/personal qualities, class rank, essays, extracurricular activities, geographical residence, minority status, recommendations, talent/ability, volunteer work, work experience. SAT Reasoning or ACT required. TOEFL required of all international applicants. High school diploma is required, and GED is accepted. *Academic units required:* 4 English, 3 math, 3 science (2 science lab), 2 foreign language, 2 social studies, 2 academic electives.

The Inside Word

Gaining admission to UMass is generally not particularly difficult, but an increase in applications last year resulted in the university increasing its selectivity. Still, most applicants with solid grades in high school should be successful. UMass is a great choice for students who might have a tougher time getting in at the other Five College Consortium members.

FINANCIAL AID

Students should submit: FAFSA. The Princeton Review suggests that all financial aid forms be submitted as soon as possible after 1/1. *Need-based scholarships/grants offered:* Pell, SEOG, state scholarships/grants, private scholarships, the school's own gift aid. *Loan aid offered:* Direct Subsidized Stafford, Direct Unsubsidized Stafford, Direct PLUS, Federal Perkins, state loans. Applicants will be notified of awards on a rolling basis beginning on or about 4/1. Federal Work-study Program available. Institutional employment available. Off-campus job opportunities are good.

FROM THE ADMISSIONS OFFICE

"The University of Massachusetts—Amherst is the largest public university in New England, offering its students an almost limitless variety of academic programs and activities. Nearly 100 majors are offered, including a unique program called Bachelor's Degree with Individual Concentration (BDIC) in which students create their own program of study. The outstanding faculty of 1,100 includes novelist John Wideman, Pulitzer Prize winners Madeleine Blais and James Tate, National Medal of Science winner Lynn Margulis, and five members of the prestigious National Academy of Sciences. Students can take courses through the honors program and sample classes at nearby Amherst, Hampshire, Mount Holyoke, and Smith Colleges at no extra charge. Students can take classes in the residence halls with other dorm residents through Residential Academic Programs (RAP), and first-year students may be asked to participate in the Talent Advancement Programs (TAP) in which students with the same majors live and take classes together. And the university's extensive library system is the largest at any public institution in the Northeast. Extracurricular activities include more than 200 clubs and organizations, fraternities and sororities, multicultural and religious centers, and NCAA Division I sports for men and women. Award-winning student-operated businesses, the largest college daily newspaper in the region, and an active student government provide hands-on experiences. About 5,000 students a year participate in the intramural sports program. The picturesque New England town of Amherst offers shopping and dining, and the ski slopes of western Massachusetts and southern Vermont are close by."

For even more information on this school, turn to page 543 of the "Stats" section.

UNIVERSITY OF MASSACHUSETTS—BOSTON

100 MORRISSEY BOULEVARD, BOSTON, MA 02125-3393 • ADMISSIONS: 617-287-6000 • FAX: 617-287-5999
E-MAIL: UNDERGRAD@UMB.EDU • WEBSITE: WWW.UMB.EDU

Ratings
Quality of Life: 71   Academic: 65   Admissions: 60   Financial Aid: 84

Academics

Partiers and slackers, read no further. University of Massachusetts—Boston is definitely not for you because this is a school "about serious learning." It offers "an affordable option for working adults" and traditional-age commuters who want to "get a real education in a great city for a great price." Students are drawn to "great teachers who learned at such recognized local universities as Boston University, Harvard University, and M.I.T., as well as experienced faculty from all over the world, with a range of political identities and religious beliefs."
Nontraditional students in particular appreciate the "rising numbers of evening and weekend classes for working professionals. Under certain circumstances one can take twelve or more credits and still work full-time at regular business hours." As at most state-funded schools, budgetary problems cause numerous bureaucratic snafus as well as backlogs and errors resulting from understaffing. Although you need to bring your scissors to deal with the red tape, one student says, "If you are motivated, this school will provide you with the most comprehensive tools available for a reasonable price."

> **SURVEY SAYS . . .**
> *Small classes*
> *Diverse student types on campus*
> *Students love Boston, MA*
> *Frats and sororities are unpopular*
> *or nonexistent*
> *Very little drug use*

Life

Students caution that the University of Massachusetts—Boston "is not a 'normal' school. It's not the same as your usual college life. Social activities (sports, fraternities, parties) are not the center of extracurricular affairs." The school's "abnormality" stems in large part from the fact that "there are currently no dorms," so everyone is a commuter. Parking is difficult to find and expensive, and "a lot of people have a hard time getting here because of traffic, or they have to wake up early because of where they live." Consequently, they're in no mood to hang around once classes are over. One student says, "My non-class-related life happens exclusively outside the university." However, things could change in coming years. The school opened its first dormitories in August 2004, and plans to make more dorms available in years. One student adds, "The campus is [also] opening a new Student Center, and we currently have a good number of computer labs, cafeterias, and a state-of-the-art fitness facility. The fitness center, while small, is really nice." All these developments may broaden campus life. For now, however, extracurricular activity is confined largely to clubs and organizations. As one student reports, "Casa Latina, Black Student Center, Asian Center, ARMS Center, Women's Center, Queer Student Union, Veteran's Center, et al, go above and beyond to gain the awareness on campus. They have highly motivated coordinators who are visibly in our community trying to make a difference."

Student Body

University of Massachusetts—Boston's undergraduates are "hard-working, diligent, goal-oriented students who are here to better their life by [earning] a degree." Often they are attending school and holding down a full-time job. "Typical students at UMB work numerous hours a week to pay for their college education." Many of these students are nontraditional ones who attend evening classes. There is also a population of traditional students who "usually live at home with parents, although some are in an apartment with other similarly-aged people and are just learning how to live on their own." The school has a "multicultural and diverse atmosphere" that many students consider the school's greatest asset. One student adds, "I've met people from Vermont and people from Africa. I've been in classes with retirees, veterans, single parents, and all sorts of people. It makes for an interesting learning environment."

ADMISSIONS

Very important factors considered include: Character/personal qualities, secondary school record, standardized test scores. *Important factors considered include:* Essays, recommendations. *Other factors considered include:* Extracurricular activities, interview, talent/ability, volunteer work, work experience. SAT Reasoning or ACT required. TOEFL required of all international applicants. High school diploma is required, and GED is accepted. *Academic units required:* 4 English, 3 math, 3 science (2 science lab), 2 foreign language, 2 history, 2 academic electives.

The Inside Word

UMB requires a 500-word essay as part of its application. This is one big school that doesn't just crunch the numbers according to a formula. The school gives you a choice of four essay topics, so if you've already written a good personal essay for another school, you should be able to retrofit it to fit one of the topics.

FINANCIAL AID

Students should submit: FAFSA. The Princeton Review suggests that all financial aid forms be submitted as soon as possible after 1/1. *Need-based scholarships/grants offered:* Pell, SEOG, state scholarships/grants, private scholarships, the school's own gift aid. *Loan aid offered:* Direct Subsidized Stafford, Direct Unsubsidized Stafford, Direct PLUS, Federal Perkins, state loans. Applicants will be notified of awards on or about 4/1. Federal Work-study Program available. Institutional employment available. Off-campus job opportunities are excellent.

For even more information on this school, turn to page 544 of the "Stats" section.

UNIVERSITY OF MASSACHUSETTS—LOWELL

OFFICE OF UNDERGRAD ADMISSIONS, 883 BROADWAY STREET ROOM 110, LOWELL, MA 01854-5104
ADMISSIONS: 978-934-3931 • FAX: 978-934-3086 • E-MAIL: ADMISSIONS@UML.EDU • WEBSITE: WWW.UML.EDU

Ratings
Quality of Life: 65　　　Academic: 76　　　Admissions: 78　　　Financial Aid: 89

Academics

Like many quality state institutions, "the University of Massachusetts—Lowell has strong colleges of nursing and health and science and engineering." Where UML distinguishes itself from the pack is in "certain majors that are pretty much only being [offered] here and nowhere else in the country," such as the unique program in plastics engineering in which "the labs are new, the computers are new,

> **SURVEY SAYS . . .**
> *Small classes*
> *Athletic facilities are great*
> *Diverse student types on campus*
> *Lots of beer drinking*

everyone knows you, you have lots of friends, and there are a lot of people in industry who recognize UML as the only source of qualified students for internships and work." UML also excels in sound recording technology and other music disciplines, and students report that "the humanities programs are very good if the students apply themselves." Some students even feel that "the school is transitioning from [a] science-dominated [one] to one that values and encourages the liberal arts programs by getting outstanding professors and distributing scholarships to deserving students in the humanities programs." Students in all areas enjoy "small class sizes that make professors easily accessible, a great administration who is constantly looking to improve the school, [and] many available internship and research opportunities made possible by the openness of good faculty members. It's up to the student to take advantage of the best of these opportunities, but the opportunities are there."

Life

UML "needs more of a sense of community," many students agree, although most are at a loss as to how to achieve this goal. Because "most of the students here are commuters" (many with at least part-time jobs in addition to their academic responsibilities), it is difficult to engage a good portion of the population in extracurricular activities. The division of the campus into sectors further separates the student body. One student explains, "The campus is divided into North and South. The North is more introverted engineer types and the South is more outgoing, social liberal types." Then there's hometown Lowell, which receives very mixed reviews from students. Few cite it as an incentive to hang around and socialize with classmates. 'Residents generally go home right after their final Friday class, so "weekends are dead." Even so, intrepid entertainment seekers at the school report, "There are a lot of things to do around here if you look for them or make the effort to show up. There are rock concerts every Thursday, and the resident advisors are always trying to do programs to get the students involved with something." 'There is also "a lot of drinking and parties," especially in the dorms on the north side. Students often abscond to nearby Boston or "go to Nashua, New Hampshire, for tax-free shopping."

Student Body

"Since Lowell is large commuter school," undergrads explain, "a typical student would be a day undergrad commuter. They can be seen hanging around the Student Union between classes watching TV and chatting." Most students "find their clique within their major and graduating class, and once their group is established, they tend to try to not step outside its boundaries." Students are generally very businesslike in their approach to academics; they're "trying to be independent, taking their life seriously, and are here to get an education, not just mess around." Many "have off-campus jobs where they work a lot of hours. Everyone is generally working-class."

ADMISSIONS

Very important factors considered include: Secondary school record, standardized test scores. *Important factors considered include:* Class rank, essays, recommendations. *Other factors considered include:* Character/personal qualities, extracurricular activities, interview, talent/ability, volunteer work, work experience. SAT Reasoning or ACT required. TOEFL required of all international applicants. High school diploma is required, and GED is accepted. *Academic units required:* 4 English, 3 math, 3 science (2 science lab), 2 foreign language, 2 social studies, 2 academic electives.

The Inside Word

Solid academic disciplines attract high-caliber students to UML, many of whom strive to meet academic standards that belie moderate admissions requirements.

FINANCIAL AID

Students should submit: FAFSA. The Princeton Review suggests that all financial aid forms be submitted as soon as possible after 1/1. *Need-based scholarships/grants offered:* Pell, SEOG, state scholarships/grants, private scholarships, the school's own gift aid, federal nursing scholarships. *Loan aid offered:* Direct Subsidized Stafford, Direct Unsubsidized Stafford, Direct PLUS, Federal Perkins, state loans. Applicants will be notified of awards on a rolling basis beginning on or about 3/25. Federal Work-study Program available. Institutional employment available. Off-campus job opportunities are good.

For even more information on this school, turn to page 544 of the "Stats" section.

UNIVERSITY OF NEW HAMPSHIRE

4 GARRISON AVENUE, DURHAM, NH 03824 • ADMISSIONS: 603-862-1360 • FAX: 603-862-0077
FINANCIAL AID: 603-862-3600 • E-MAIL: ADMISSIONS@UNH.EDU • WEBSITE: WWW.UNH.EDU

Ratings

Quality of Life: 69   Academic: 73   Admissions: 80   Financial Aid: 71

Academics

"University of New Hampshire captures the social appeal every student wants and provides every academic opportunity he or she needs," students at this midsize state university agree. With "so many students and majors it is impossible not to find some activity or major to interest you." UNH allows students to pursue their ambitions as aggressively as they like. Some choose to take advantage of the "excellent nursing and nutrition programs," "the awesome business school," "a great education program," "strong departments in music and computer science," an

> **SURVEY SAYS . . .**
> *Great library*
> *Athletic facilities are great*
> *Frats and sororities dominate social scene*
> *Lots of beer drinking*
> *Hard liquor is popular*

"incredible aggie school," and "one of the best programs for marine biology on the East Coast." These students tout the "excellent internships and study abroad programs" available here, as well as the "great research opportunities. The business kids are always working on outside projects, and every class I have had has ended with some type of individual research project. There are tons of opportunities for research grants from your sophomore year on. . . . The list is endless." Others pursue an "all play, no work" option, cruising through with a carefully chosen curriculum of easy courses. The presence of this latter group partly accounts for the perception that "UNH is really underrated academically." Undergrads warn that the school "lacks a personal touch at times, but in general, it works well for a university of its size."

Life

"The social scene is great" at UNH, where "the Greek system is strong and very involved in the campus community," and "there are also numerous sports clubs, intramurals, and other groups to get involved in." Undergrads generally "like to party, and the opportunities are plentiful. Along with UMass we're probably the place to go and party if you're going to school in the New England region." Observes one student, "Life is all about going to class in sweats and getting dressed up to drink. Classes later in the day are preferred and drinking isn't reserved just for the weekends; it's a week-long ordeal." While some here pride themselves on their partying prowess, others are not impressed; writes one, "I'm from the South, so I've seen what partying is really like at state schools like Georgia and Tennessee. UNH kind of pales in comparison." No one disputes UNH's primacy in college hockey, though; the men's team "is practically an annual participant in the Frozen Four. It's hard not to get caught up in the excitement of the UNH hockey season." The campus also plays host to "constant theatrical productions, comedians, fairs, and sports. Every weekend movies are playing for 3 bucks in the MUB (Memorial Union Building); they range from Star Wars to sneak previews of movies that aren't in theatres yet." Outdoor enthusiasts enjoy "at least one student-led hiking/ biking/ kayaking/rock climbing/ canoeing/ sky-diving trip per week, organized by the Outing Club." The nearby White Mountains ensure "great skiing," while the charming oceanfront town of Portsmouth and the Kittery Outlets in Maine mean great dining and shopping is just down the road.

Student Body

"Since we are a state university in New England, sort of in the center of the region, our demographics generally reflect that of New England itself," explains one UNH undergrad. Undergrads "are pretty run-of-the-mill, with a lot of them being local suburban kids from Concord and Manchester. There are some extremes—the hippies, the preps, the hicks, the nerds, the wannabe gangstas—but overall, there is not too much diversity at UNH. Just a lot of average-Joes." The student body includes "a lot of jock types. Athletics in all forms (varsity, club, and intramurals) is huge."

ADMISSIONS

Very important factors considered include: Secondary school record. *Important factors considered include:* Class rank, essays, recommendations, standardized test scores, state residency. *Other factors considered include:* Alumni/ae relation, character/personal qualities, extracurricular activities, geographical residence, minority status, talent/ability, volunteer work, work experience. SAT Reasoning or ACT required. TOEFL required of all international applicants. High school diploma is required, and GED is accepted. *Academic units recommended:* 4 English, 4 math, 4 science (4 science lab), 3 foreign language, 3 social studies.

The Inside Word

New Hampshire's emphasis on academic accomplishment in the admissions process makes it clear that the admissions committee is looking for students who have taken high school seriously. Standardized tests take as much of a backseat here as is possible at a large public university.

FINANCIAL AID

Students should submit: FAFSA. The Princeton Review suggests that all financial aid forms be submitted as soon as possible after 1/1. *Need-based scholarships/grants offered:* Pell, SEOG, state scholarships/grants, private scholarships, the school's own gift aid. *Loan aid offered:* FFEL Subsidized Stafford, FFEL Unsubsidized Stafford, FFEL PLUS, Federal Perkins, state loans, college/university loans from institutional funds. Applicants will be notified of awards on a rolling basis beginning on or about 3/1. Federal Work-study Program available. Institutional employment available. Off-campus job opportunities are excellent.

FROM THE ADMISSIONS OFFICE

"The University of New Hampshire is a public university founded in 1866 with an undergraduate population of 11,000 students. UNH offers an excellent education at a reasonable cost to students with a broad range of interests. Over 100 majors, 2,000 courses, and 130 student clubs and organizations are offered. Programs that provide valuable experience include the honors program, undergraduate research, internships, study abroad, and national exchange. UNH's location also caters to a wide range of interests. The campus itself is in a small town setting, surrounded by woods and farms; within 20 minutes is the Atlantic coastline, and just over an hour away are the White Mountains, Boston, and Portland."

For even more information on this school, turn to page 545 of the "Stats" section.

UNIVERSITY OF PENNSYLVANIA

1 COLLEGE HALL, PHILADELPHIA, PA 19104 • ADMISSIONS: 215-898-7507 • FAX: 215-898-9670
FINANCIAL AID: 215-898-1988 • E-MAIL: INFO@ADMISSIONS.UGAO.UPENN.EDU • WEBSITE: WWW.UPENN.EDU

Ratings
Quality of Life: 75   Academic: 92   Admissions: 99   Financial Aid: 94

Academics

The University of Pennsylvania is perhaps best known for its Wharton School of Business ("the number one undergraduate business program in the country," students claim), but this Ivy League institution "is strong in all divisions, a fact that one can take advantage of very easily through dual degree programs across schools." Wharton, the engineering school and science programs "require students to study a lot, as the courses move fast and cover a lot of material," while "students in the College studying liberal arts don't have it as bad." With a world-class faculty in nearly all disciplines, "Penn offers access to the best and brightest minds in the world, people who are always

> **SURVEY SAYS . . .**
> *Registration is a breeze*
> *Great computer facilities*
> *Great library*
> *Athletic facilities are great*
> *Great off-campus food*
> *Student publications are popular*
> *Lots of beer drinking*
> *Hard liquor is popular*

willing and available to discuss any topic, whether or not you are enrolled in one of their classes." Students tell us that "among the Ivies, Penn seems to be the most career-oriented, as fewer students here are on the academia track than at other schools. Many students take jobs right out after graduation rather than go to graduate school, and Penn does an excellent job of placing these students." Indeed, "a very large number of students grab the country's most prestigious jobs for undergrads: investment banking, consulting, and private equity." As at many large schools, "the administration tends to feel a bit remote to most students" and "the school can be a little bureaucratic, with little communication among administrative departments."

Life

There's a common arc to most students' extracurricular lives during their four years at Penn. When they first arrive they stick close to campus; "The social scene for most freshmen consists of frat parties, period," explains one student. As they get older, "they leave the bubble of campus and explore more of Philadelphia. There are a lot of awesome places in the city in terms of the nightlife, but you can't really get in unless you're of age." Options abound both on and off campus; notes one student, "Having Center City (and many bars/clubs/activities) just 20 blocks away is a plus, though there is also tons to do on campus as well." Campus options include "parties, theater, a cappella shows, sporting events, guest lectures, sketch comedy, movie showings, etc." Students point out that "Penn's campus is located in West Philly, which doesn't have the best reputation, but the campus itself is a vast improvement from the local area and security is a moderate concern." They also note that "for being a city school, Penn's campus is so nice, it looks more like a plush suburban park... Walking down Locust Walk (the main artery of campus) one can always see people stopping to say hello to their fellow students, student groups handing out fliers promoting an event or trying to draw attention to an issue, students enjoying an outdoor lunch while sitting at one of the many benches or tables set up outside, or standing in line at one of the lunch trucks (a staple of any Penn student's diet)."

Student Body

"There are distinct stereotypes for each of the four undergraduate schools" at Penn—brainy engineer, ambitious Wharton student, artsy college kid, hard-working nurse—although "generally students from all four schools interact quite smoothly." The student body includes "a surprising number of very religious people, including some staunch Christians and many Jews. There are far fewer agnostics and atheists than you would expect." Penn is known among the Ivies as the school where students unwind most enthusiastically; "Everyone at Penn is very stressed out, all the time, which is why most people have to let loose on the weekend," explains one student. Adds another, "The average Penn student is a thinker and a drinker. Everybody studies really hard all week long and lets loose on the weekends at wild parties. But the students are also insanely smart. On our first day, the dean asked everyone to stand up in the auditorium who had been valedictorian. The number of people who stood up almost scared me to death."

ADMISSIONS

Very important factors considered include: Character/personal qualities, essays, recommendations, secondary school record. *Important factors considered include:* Extracurricular activities, standardized test scores. *Other factors considered include:* Alumni/ae relation, class rank, geographical residence, interview, minority status, talent/ability, volunteer work, work experience. SAT Reasoning and SAT Subject Tests or ACT required. TOEFL required of all international applicants. High school diploma is required, and GED is accepted. *Academic units recommended:* 4 English, 4 math, 4 science, 4 foreign language, 1 social studies, 3 history.

The Inside Word

After a small decline three cycles ago, applications are once again climbing at Penn—the fourth increase in five years. The competition in the applicant pool is formidable. Applicants can safely assume that they need to be one of the strongest students in their graduating class in order to be successful.

FINANCIAL AID

Students should submit: FAFSA, institution's own financial aid form, CSS/Financial Aid PROFILE, state aid form, noncustodial (divorced/separated) parents' statement, business/farm supplement, parent and student federal income tax returns (for verification). The Princeton Review suggests that all financial aid forms be submitted as soon as possible after 1/1. *Need-based scholarships/grants offered:* Pell, SEOG, state scholarships/grants, private scholarships, the school's own gift aid. *Loan aid offered:* FFEL Subsidized Stafford, FFEL Unsubsidized Stafford, FFEL PLUS, Federal Perkins, Federal Nursing, college/university loans from institutional funds, Penn Guaranteed loan. Applicants will be notified of awards on or about 4/1. Federal Work-study Program available. Institutional employment available. Off-campus job opportunities are excellent.

FROM THE ADMISSIONS OFFICE

"The nation's first university, the University of Pennsylvania had its beginnings in 1740, some 36 years before Thomas Jefferson, Benjamin Franklin (Penn's founder), and their fellow revolutionaries went public in Philadelphia with incendiary notions about life, liberty and the pursuit of happiness. Today, Penn continues in the spirit of the Founding Fathers, developing the intellectual, discussion-oriented seminars that comprise the majority of our course offerings, shaping innovative new courses of study, and allowing a remarkable degree of academic flexibility to its undergraduate students.

"Penn is situated on a green, tree-lined, 260-acre, urban campus, four blocks west of the Schuylkill River in Philadelphia. The broad lawns that connect Penn's stately halls embody a philosophy of academic freedom within our undergraduate schools. Newly developed interdisciplinary programs fusing classical disciplines with practical, professional options enable Penn to define cutting-edge academia in and out of the classroom. Students are encouraged to partake in study and research that may extend into many of the graduate and professional schools. As part of our College House system, Penn's Faculty Masters engage students in academic and civic experience while leading residential programs that promote an environment where living and learning intersect around the clock.

"Penn students are part of a dynamic community that includes a traditional campus, a lively neighborhood, and a city rich in culture and diversity. Whether your interests include artistic performance, community involvement, student government, athletics, fraternities and sororities, or cultural and religious organizations, you'll find many different options. Most importantly, students at Penn find that their lives in and out of the classroom compliment each other and are full, interesting and busy. We invite you to visit Penn in Philadelphia. You'll enjoy the revolutionary spirit of the campus and city."

For even more information on this school, turn to page 545 of the "Stats" section.

UNIVERSITY OF PITTSBURGH AT BRADFORD

Office of Admissions - Hanley Library, 300 Campus Drive, Bradford, PA 16701 • Admissions: 814-362-7555 • Fax: 814-362-7578
E-mail: Admissions@www.upb.pitt.edu • Website: www.upb.pitt.edu

Ratings
Quality of Life: 77   Academic: 75   Admissions: 70   Financial Aid: 73

Academics

"I come away from classes thinking I am definitely getting an education here," a Bradford student tells us. This positive attitude toward the university's academics has much to do with the professors, who "never fail to amaze and impress [students]." In general, the professors "believe in an open-door policy," which means that students feel comfortable asking for extra help whenever they need it. The cozy size of the university—about 1,400 students—adds to this sense of comfort. One undergraduate explains, "I would like to stress that Pitt—Bradford may be small, but this size brings about the unique, family-like atmosphere that you will not find in many other places." There are, however, a few students who warn that faculty attention should not be confused with breadth of course offerings. "Sometimes it is difficult to get in the class [you want] because they only offer one [section] a semester," writes one.

> **SURVEY SAYS . . .**
> *Small classes*
> *Great computer facilities*
> *Athletic facilities are great*
> *Campus feels safe*
> *Lots of beer drinking*
> *(Almost) everyone smokes*

Life

The great outdoors is what surrounds the Pitt—Bradford campus. The school sits in northwestern Pennsylvania, near the Allegheny National Forest, and is only a stone's throw from the New York State border. The nearest city of noteworthy size is Buffalo, about 80 miles north. That said, it shouldn't be surprising that many students tell us they spend their free hours doing things like "hunting, fishing, camping, sled riding, sightseeing around the area, and, especially in the fall when the leaves are at their peak, taking pictures." The area is also "ideal for skiers and snowboarders." As many students are either nontraditional commuters or on-campus residents from nearby, it should be noted that a decent percentage of the student population heads away from Bradford at night and on weekends. Of the students that remain on this "small campus in a small town," some say they "drink to have fun," while others laud the considerable programming that the university provides, including "hypnotists, comedians, movies, speakers, sporting events, panel discussions, theme dinners, intramural tournaments, and mock game shows." Wet or dry, we hear that life at Bradford is "all about having fun with your friends."

Student Body

There are two distinct populations at Pitt—Bradford: the traditional students and the nontraditional students. Whereas the traditional students are fresh out of high school and live primarily on or around campus, the nontraditional students have been out in the work force for a while and usually commute from home. According to students from both camps, the traditional and nontraditional students get along very well. One thing that holds this student body together is that almost everyone you bump into is "someone who is from the area." While it's fair to say that Pitt—Bradford isn't the world's most diverse university, undergraduates assure us that you'll find "students from every economic background, varied social upbringing, educational histories, and ethnic backgrounds."

ADMISSIONS

Very important factors considered include: Secondary school record. *Important factors considered include:* Interview, standardized test scores. *Other factors considered include:* Alumni/ae relation, character/personal qualities, class rank, essays, extracurricular activities, recommendations, talent/ability, volunteer work, work experience. SAT Reasoning or ACT required. TOEFL required of all international applicants. High school diploma is required, and GED is accepted. *Academic units required:* 4 English, 2 math, 1 science (1 science lab), 2 foreign language, 1 history, 5 academic electives. *Academic units recommended:* 4 English, 2 math, 2 science (2 science lab), 2 foreign language, 1 history, 5 academic electives.

The Inside Word

The Bradford admissions office looks most closely at high school transcript, standardized test scores, and letters of recommendation. The school also takes into account other factors including extracurriculars, special skills, and potential contribution to the community. With 96 percent of applicants gaining admission, it's clear the school looks hard for reasons to admit.

FINANCIAL AID

Students should submit: FAFSA. The Princeton Review suggests that all financial aid forms be submitted as soon as possible after 1/1. *Need-based scholarships/grants offered:* Pell, SEOG, state scholarships/grants, private scholarships, the school's own gift aid. *Loan aid offered:* FFEL Subsidized Stafford, FFEL Unsubsidized Stafford, FFEL PLUS, Federal Perkins. Applicants will be notified of awards on a rolling basis beginning on or about 4/1. Federal Work-study Program available. Institutional employment available. Off-campus job opportunities are fair.

FROM THE ADMISSIONS OFFICE

"When it comes to picking a college, many students discover that they have to choose between a university where teachers know and care about their students or a world-renowned institution from which they can earn a reputable degree.

"At Pitt-Bradford you don't have to choose. You can have both.

"Your classes will be small and your professors will be highly qualified and dedicated to teaching. As a result, you'll be able to get personalized, one-on-one attention from your professors. They'll not only know your name, they'll know you. So they will be able to help you secure an internship in your chosen field of study or work with you to conduct and, maybe even, publish research. And, if you need a little extra help after class, or if you are interested in a topic and want to know more about it, you and your professor can head back to his or her office to talk or catch a bite in the dining room.

"When students graduate from Pitt-Bradford, they earn a degree from the University of Pittsburgh, one of the premier universities in the world with that degree recognized worldwide. You will foster life-long relationships and friendships and the preparation you need to be successful in life."

For even more information on this school, turn to page 546 of the "Stats" section.

UNIVERSITY OF PITTSBURGH—JOHNSTOWN

450 SCHOOLHOUSE ROAD, 157 BLACKINGTON HALL, JOHNSTOWN, PA 15904 • ADMISSIONS: 814-269-7050
FAX: 814-269-7044 • E-MAIL: UPJADMIT@PITT.EDU • WEBSITE: WWW.UPJ.PITT.EDU

Ratings
Quality of Life: 83   **Academic:** 75   **Admissions:** 71   **Financial Aid:** 63

Academics

The University of Pittsburgh at Johnstown is "great for anyone who is looking for a smaller setting but with most of the advantages of a big college," students at this "challenging school" 60 miles east of Pittsburgh tell us. Fewer than 3,000 full-time undergrads attend UPJ. One student notes, "One of the advantages of going to a smaller school is that most of the professors know you on a first-name basis." Others add that, while small, UPJ is large enough "to offer a good variety of challenging classes." Professors are "very easily accessible to students. Nearly all have an open-door policy, so you can go to them with any questions or concerns. Administrators are easily accessible, too." UPJ enjoys a strong regional reputation in engineering and business (with "a well-developed accounting program"). Students agree that offerings in education, computer science, environmental studies, and psychology are also top quality. A solid internship program means "students get real-world experience that they can carry out into the job force." UPJ undergrads have it good "when it comes to getting career guidance or finding internships. Instructors are happy to give [them] contacts or even to call the contacts themselves."

> **SURVEY SAYS . . .**
> *Small classes*
> *Great library*
> *Students are friendly*
> *Lots of beer drinking*
> *(Almost) everyone smokes*

Life

Students all agree that UPJ's campus "is one of the most beautiful on the East Coast." One student writes, "The campus is set back in the woods with rolling hills and a 600+ acre wildlife preserve and nature area right here on campus. Some mornings with the way the buildings look and the great views, it almost seems like you are walking through a ski resort. It is very beautiful." Dorms and other structures are "done in a sort of rustic-looking flagstone [and] in the winter, every lobby has a fire going, and it is a great place to go sit with a cup of hot chocolate and watch out the windows as the snow falls." Speaking of snow, Johnstown winters are long and cold, students warn. Despite "lots of clubs and organizations that meet during the weekdays," undergrads feel that extracurricular life at UPJ could use a serious boost. One student says, "We need more activities for the students to do. We hardly have any entertainment coming to our school, other than a spring concert." The word on campus is, "if you're a big partier, this school is not for you." The city of Johnstown offers little help, as "it is largely residential. It is nice, with a big middle- and upper-class population, but there is not much to do in Johnstown." As a result, many people "do not stay on campus over the weekend. A lot of those who do stay drink and go to parties at the frat houses. Those who do not drink study, hang out together, or go to the mall or movies."

Student Body

UPJ draws largely from "the white middle-class, [with] a lot of kids from the area and from suburban homes [and many others] from the city of Pittsburgh." Students report, "Minorities make up a small percentage here," with white students constituting over 95 percent of the student body. UPJ undergrads "typically dress down; comfortable is one of the most important words here on campus." UPJ students are "outgoing and lively. They know they are here to get an education, but they also understand that there has to be fun involved." During the week "students will get together to do homework and study, which helps a lot [so] the library is a pretty busy place." One student aptly sums up the school by saying, "It's a great mix of academics and friends." Because so many students are from the area, "a lot of people go home on the weekends."

ADMISSIONS

Very important factors considered include: Class rank, secondary school record. *Important factors considered include:* Interview, standardized test scores. *Other factors considered include:* Character/personal qualities, essays, extracurricular activities, minority status, recommendations, talent/ability, volunteer work, work experience. SAT Reasoning or ACT required. TOEFL required of all international applicants. High school diploma is required, and GED is accepted. *Academic units required:* 4 English, 2 math, 2 science (1 science lab), 2 foreign language, 4 social studies. *Academic units recommended:* 3 math, 2 science (2 science lab).

The Inside Word

The University of Pittsburgh's Johnstown campus—two hours east of the Steel City—is an environment best suited for students who consider themselves hands-on learners who are willing to go the extra mile to interact with peers and professors.

FINANCIAL AID

Students should submit: FAFSA. The Princeton Review suggests that all financial aid forms be submitted as soon as possible after 1/1. *Need-based scholarships/grants offered:* Pell, SEOG, state scholarships/grants, private scholarships, the school's own gift aid. *Loan aid offered:* FFEL Subsidized Stafford, FFEL Unsubsidized Stafford, FFEL PLUS, Federal Perkins. Applicants will be notified of awards on a rolling basis beginning on or about 3/1. Federal Work-study Program available. Institutional employment available. Off-campus job opportunities are excellent.

For even more information on this school, turn to page 546 of the "Stats" section.

UNIVERSITY OF PITTSBURGH—PITTSBURGH

ALUMNI HALL, 4227 FIFTH AVENUE, FIRST FLOOR, PITTSBURGH, PA 15260 • ADMISSIONS: 412-624-7488
FAX: 412-648-8815 • FINANCIAL AID: 412-624-7488 • E-MAIL: OAFA@PITT.EDU • WEBSITE: WWW.PITT.EDU

Ratings
Quality of Life: 80   Academic: 81   Admissions: 89   Financial Aid: 78

Academics

Many University of Pittsburgh students feel "happy that we discovered this amazing yet quite underrated school." They cite the English and science programs as two of the strongest, and one student tells us, "The nursing program is excellent and prepares you for the real world." The university offers "tons of diverse courses in any one semester," and students are encouraged to take a term abroad, "which is the best thing you can do." Some people see Pitt as "primarily a research school," but "it's stated university policy that professors are easy to see." The faculty "urges us to question things and provides an environment where we feel comfortable doing that." These "instructors and mentors" are known for being "passionate about what they teach" and "helpful both during lecture and during their office hours." Students appreciate that they "draw from real world experience as a complement to their academic knowledge." Advisors provide additional academic support: "We meet one-on-one with our advisors at least twice a semester, and mine has always gotten me the classes I needed at the times I needed with the professors I want." The administration receives high marks "for advancing the university, raising money, recruiting strong applicants, and managing public affairs." Though they may "look out for our best interests," administrators are seen as "a bit detached," "extremely inaccessible," and "nearly impossible to reach." Recent tuition hikes only exacerbate this unfavorable assessment. Nonetheless, Pitt provides a scholastic climate where undergraduates "learn so much and grow as people." A senior writes, "It has been quite challenging, but I am thankful for my time here. It just goes to prove that I have a strong degree behind me."

> **SURVEY SAYS . . .**
> Great computer facilities
> Great library
> Athletic facilities are great
> Students love Pittsburgh, PA
> Great off-campus food
> Everyone loves the Panthers
> Student publications are popular
> Lots of beer drinking

Life

The Pitt existence can be "extremely busy with academics, extracurricular activities, internships, part-time jobs, work-study positions, and social life." With more than 300 student organizations, there's room for everyone to "do their own thing." Students love their location in the Oakland section of Pittsburgh, "home to many restaurants and bars, making for a very social atmosphere." Students looking to enrich themselves take advantage of the "Carnegie Museums across the street" and the popular PITT ARTS program, which "provides discounted or free tickets to various cultural events around Pittsburgh." Couple that with free public transit for students, and one student writes, "What can beat free transportation, dinner, a symphony ticket, and dessert afterward?" The only better plan could be cheering on the top-notch football and basketball squads—season tickets set students back only 40 bucks. On campus, "the weekends are full of fun with activities planned through different student organizations and great parties." Though some students claim "the majority of students drink on the weekends," many people think the "novelty of fraternity parties tends to wear off pretty fast."

Student Body

The 17,000 undergarduate students attending Pitt form "a diverse group of students that, from what I have seen, interact easily and on a regular basis." One student observes, "We are amazingly diverse, and everyone is not only respectful, but also curious and excited to learn about and meet new people." Other respondents report that "people of the same ethnic group or background usually hang together." Even with approximately 14 percent of the student body members of minorities, one student points out, "Unfortunately, that is low for a city school." The minority populations organize effectively, in groups including the Black Action Society, Rainbow Alliance, and Asian Students Alliance. Amid this "wide spectrum of students" with a "broad range of interests," most are "friendly, outgoing, involved, motivated, and responsible." Most people seem to find their niche among "academically focused and open-minded" peers.

ADMISSIONS

Very important factors considered include: Class rank, secondary school record, standardized test scores. *Important factors considered include:* Essays, recommendations. *Other factors considered include:* Character/personal qualities, extracurricular activities, geographical residence, interview, minority status, state residency, talent/ability, volunteer work, work experience. SAT Reasoning and SAT Subject Tests or ACT required. TOEFL required of all international applicants. High school diploma is required, and GED is not accepted. *Academic units required:* 4 English, 3 math, 3 science (3 science lab), 1 social studies, 4 academic electives. *Academic units recommended:* 3 foreign language, 3 social studies.

The Inside Word

Applicants to Pitt, as at most large public universities, are admitted primarily on the strength of basic qualifiers like grades and test scores. If you are serious about Pitt, rolling admissions allows you to get a decision earlier than most colleges notify their applicants.

FINANCIAL AID

Students should submit: FAFSA, institution's own financial aid form. Regular filing deadline 6/1. The Princeton Review suggests that all financial aid forms be submitted as soon as possible after 1/1. *Need-based scholarships/grants offered:* Pell, SEOG, state scholarships/grants, private scholarships, the school's own gift aid. *Loan aid offered:* FFEL Subsidized Stafford, FFEL Unsubsidized Stafford, FFEL PLUS, Federal Perkins, Federal Nursing, college/university loans from institutional funds. Applicants will be notified of awards on a rolling basis beginning on or about 3/1. Federal Work-study Program available. Off-campus job opportunities are excellent.

FROM THE ADMISSIONS OFFICE

"The University of Pittsburgh is one of 62 members of the Association of American Universities, a prestigious group whose members include the major research universities of North America. There are nearly 400 degree programs available at the 16 Pittsburgh campus schools (two offering only undergraduate degree programs, four offering graduate degree programs, and ten offering both) and four regional campuses, allowing students a wide latitude of choices, both academically and in setting and style, size and pace of campus. Programs ranked nationally include philosophy, history and philosophy of science, chemistry, economics, English, history, physics, political science, and psychology. The University Center for International Studies is ranked one of the exemplary international programs in the country by the Council on Learning; and the Semester at Sea Program takes students to different ports of call around the world on an ocean liner."

For even more information on this school, turn to page 547 of the "Stats" section.

University of Rhode Island

14 Upper College Road, Kingston, RI 02881-1391 • Admissions: 401-874-7000 • Fax: 401-874-5523
Financial Aid: 401-874-9500 • E-mail: uriadmit@eta1.uri.edu • Website: www.uri.edu/admissions

Ratings
Quality of Life: 64   Academic: 61   Admissions: 60   Financial Aid: 65

Academics

In square miles, Rhode Island is the smallest of the 50 states, but at the University of Rhode Island, a large-scale academic experience is offered to the school's 10,000-plus undergrads. Popular majors include psychology, communication studies, pharmacy, and human development and family studies and "most professors go out of their way to help their students." A junior in the communications studies programs appreciates that "professors actually know what they're talking about. They've had out of the classroom experience and have held jobs in the fields they're teaching. It's reassuring to know that what I'm learning will still be applicable once I leave my classroom." A student in the political science department confirms, "There are some amazing professors that really get you thinking, but others are not so passionate." We've also heard several rumblings from students who've struggled "to understand the professor due to a lack of the English language." Among this community of pre-professional students, though, most feel that they're receiving a strong, vocation-minded education at "a good price." As one student says, URI is all about "preparing students for the real world." In the meantime, students wrangle with an administration that "puts meaning to the quote, 'In the land of the blind, the man with one eye leads.'" "Registering for classes can be a huge pain, [and] "the Internet system is terrible."

> **SURVEY SAYS . . .**
> *Great library*
> *Great off-campus food*
> *Students are happy*
> *Student publications are popular*
> *Lots of beer drinking*
> *Hard liquor is popular*
> *(Almost) everyone smokes*

Life

The Oliver Watson House—the oldest building at URI—was built around 1796, and when students reflect on the relatively dry campus here (students 21+ can drink in their room), they feel as if they're living back in the era of Oliver Watson himself. "Campus liquor rules are very strict," sighs one student. "Everyone goes home on the weekends [because] there isn't much going on." Those who stick around "are here to party," and head to off-campus ragers or cruise into nearby Providence or Newport. If you find the parties, says a sophomore, the "social life at URI can be a lot of sloppy fun." Even if that's not your scene, students assure us there's "a peaceful, friendly environment [on a] beautiful campus" with opportunities to satisfy a range of tastes. Make an effort to "get involved and it's a great place to be." Upwards of 80 campus organizations are offered, and the new, state-of-the-art Ryan Center hosts entertainment and athletic events. The school "definitely takes care of their athletes," and athletics are serious business around here. The Rhode Island Rams' men's basketball team makes a fair share of headlines, and a sophomore asserts, "The ice hockey club team is the best in the nation!" Aside from the "horrific" parking situation—the many students who commute have been known "to skip class because there are literally no spots to park"—students find that life at URI is pretty good; many of them say they chose the school for its beach locale. As one Rhode Island native yelps, "RI born! RI die!"

Student Body

The majority of URI's student body comes from Rhode Island—attracted by the close proximity to home and the nice in-state price—though Massachusetts, New Jersey, Connecticut, and New York contribute noteworthy numbers to the population, too. One student gripes that "local RI students come with their friends from high school and they aren't really interested in making new friends," but at least there's "a mixture of students socioeconomically." Among this mix, "many students are extremely involved in campus life, but there are still those who are apathetic and refuse to do anything outside of themselves." The majority of URI students are "white and middle class," and one senior warns that "ethnic groups do not mix. People here tend to hang out with people who look and act like they do." But this tendency, of course, is not law. A business administration major sums up his experience by saying, "At URI you can enjoy the best of what college life has to offer."

ADMISSIONS

Very important factors considered include: Class rank, secondary school record. *Important factors considered include:* Standardized test scores. *Other factors considered include:* Alumni/ae relation, character/personal qualities, essays, extracurricular activities, geographical residence, interview, minority status, recommendations, state residency, talent/ability, volunteer work, work experience. SAT Reasoning or ACT required. TOEFL required of all international applicants. High school diploma is required, and GED is accepted. *Academic units required:* 4 English, 3 math, 2 science (2 science lab), 2 foreign language, 2 social studies, 5 academic electives. *Academic units recommended:* 4 English, 4 math, 4 science, 4 foreign language, 4 social studies.

The Inside Word

Any candidate with solid grades is likely to find the university's admissions committee to be welcoming. The yield of admits who enroll is low and the state's population small. Out-of-state students are attractive to URI because they are sorely needed to fill out the student body. Students who graduate in the top 10 percent of their class are good scholarship bets.

FINANCIAL AID

Students should submit: FAFSA. The Princeton Review suggests that all financial aid forms be submitted as soon as possible after 1/1. *Need-based scholarships/grants offered:* Pell, SEOG, state scholarships/grants, private scholarships, the school's own gift aid. *Loan aid offered:* Direct Subsidized Stafford, Direct Unsubsidized Stafford, Direct PLUS, Federal Perkins, Federal Nursing, state loans, college/university loans from institutional funds. Applicants will be notified of awards on a rolling basis beginning on or about 3/31. Federal Work-study Program available.

FROM THE ADMISSIONS OFFICE

"Outstanding freshmen candidates with minimum SAT scores of 1150 or ACT composite of 25 who rank in the top third of their high school class are eligible to be considered for a Centennial Scholarship. These merit based scholarships range up to full tuition and are renewable each semester if the student maintains full-time continuous enrollment and a 3.00 average or better. Eligibility requires that a completed admissions application be RECEIVED by our December 15, 2005 Early Action deadline. Applications filed electronically are NOT considered complete until the application fee, official secondary school transcript(s), and SAT or ACT scores are received. To qualify for consideration for the Centennial Scholarship, everything must arrive in the Undergraduate Admissions Office by December 15, 2005. No extra form is required. If a student's residency status changes from out-of-state to regional or in-state, the Centennial award will be reduced because tuition varies on the basis of residency classification. Secondary school students with more than 23 college credits (excluding AP credits) and secondary school graduates who have matriculated at other postsecondary institutions are not eligible for Centennial Scholarships."

For even more information on this school, turn to page 547 of the "Stats" section.

UNIVERSITY OF ROCHESTER

Box 270251, ROCHESTER, NY 14627-0251 • ADMISSIONS: 716-275-3221 • FAX: 716-461-4595
FINANCIAL AID: 716-275-3226 • E-MAIL: ADMIT@ADMISSIONS.ROCHESTER.EDU • WEBSITE: WWW.ROCHESTER.EDU

Ratings
Quality of Life: 78   **Academic:** 88   **Admissions:** 96   **Financial Aid:** 85

Academics

Those seeking "a small, quantitative, team-oriented environment with a lot of diversity, challenges, and customization" might want to consider the University of Rochester (U of R), a math and science heavy hitter that also "has well-recognized economics and political science programs [and] a top-notch optics program." Many students insist that "U of R has strengths in all aspects of the school," reporting that "there is so much diversity within the aca-

demic departments. It's wonderful to have friends in the humanities and also in engineering." Despite its breadth of offerings, U of R maintains a small-school feel. Students think, "It's the perfect size, so that you can see familiar faces." They say professors "are extremely approachable for both academic and nonacademic matters, are very flexible in setting up a meeting, [and] are not only amazing thinkers, but [also] they also genuinely care that you leave the institution with a firm grasp of concepts." Administrators also earn raves because they "seem to genuinely care about the student body. The deans and faculty make sure that they roam the campus and dining halls, and typically invite students to eat with them."

Life

"There are all different types of people who are into all different types of things" at the University of Rochester. In terms of student involvement, "there is definitely a large population of students at Rochester who are not involved with many campus, community, or social activities." However, "there are also a lot of other students who do like to be active and have fun, so you need to get out and do things to meet these people." Many students "work hard during the week, and on the weekends they relax on the fraternity quad, regardless of affiliation." While students observe, "Fraternities and sororities have a large presence on campus," they follow up by saying, "[they] are certainly not the only social outlets." There are also sports—Rochester's Division III standing allows serious scholars to compete at the intercollegiate level and still have time for the copious amount of schoolwork—as well as "dances, balls, movies, and guest speakers." Weather plays a role in determining how active the campus is. Because winters at U of R are very long and very cold, "people tend to stay inside more, and there are more dorm-related activities held." Although the city of Rochester "can be a lot of fun," the school "is not located well in the city. There's a huge cemetery on one side, a large medical center on another, and a river along the other two sides." Unfortunately, some students see the location as a disincentive to leaving campus.

Student Body

University of Rochester is "small enough to find your niche, but large enough to have enough people [so that] you are bound to find a group you like," students tell us. The "smart, intellectual, nicely-dressed" U of R undergraduates "take academics very seriously." They must to survive the challenges of the curriculum. Although the school has taken some knocks for its failure to recruit minorities more successfully, students tell us that "there are plenty of blacks, Hispanics, and Asians on campus" and that "University of Rochester is much more diverse than I would have ever expected. The people one meets around campus are as varied as a large box of Crayolas," in part because they bring "different views and upbringings" to the table. Despite their differences, "all have a common willingness to meet new people and learn to live with those that are different."

ADMISSIONS

Very important factors considered include: Character/personal qualities, interview, secondary school record. *Important factors considered include:* Class rank, essays, minority status, recommendations, talent/ability. *Other factors considered include:* Alumni/ae relation, extracurricular activities, standardized test scores, volunteer work, work experience. SAT Reasoning or ACT required. SAT Subject Tests recommended. TOEFL required of all international applicants. High school diploma is required, and GED is accepted.

The Inside Word

The University of Rochester is definitely a good school, but the competition takes away three-fourths of the university's admits. Many students use Rochester as a safety; this hinders the university's ability to move up among top national institutions in selectivity. It also makes U of R a very solid choice for above-average students who aren't Ivy material.

FINANCIAL AID

Students should submit: FAFSA, CSS/Financial Aid PROFILE, state aid form, noncustodial (divorced/separated) parents' statement, business/farm supplement. Regular filing deadline 2/1. The Princeton Review suggests that all financial aid forms be submitted as soon as possible after 1/1. *Need-based scholarships/grants offered:* Pell, SEOG, state scholarships/grants, the school's own gift aid. *Loan aid offered:* Direct Subsidized Stafford, Direct Unsubsidized Stafford, Direct PLUS, Federal Perkins, Federal Nursing, college/university loans from institutional funds. Applicants will be notified of awards on or about 4/1. Federal Work-study Program available. Institutional employment available. Off-campus job opportunities are excellent.

FROM THE ADMISSIONS OFFICE

"A campus visit can be one of the most important (and most enjoyable) components of a college search. Visiting Rochester can provide you with the opportunity to experience for yourself the traditions and innovations of our university. Whether you visit a class, tour the campus, or meet with a professor or coach, you'll learn a great deal about the power of a Rochester education—with advantages that begin during your undergraduate years and continue after graduation. No other school combines the wealth of academic programs on the personal scale that the University of Rochester offers. Our students achieve academic excellence in a university setting that encourages frequent, informal contact with distinguished faculty. Our faculty-designed 'Rochester Renaissance Curriculum' allows students to spend as much of their time as possible studying subjects they enjoy so much that they stop watching the clock,' says William Scott Green, dean of the undergraduate college. At the heart of the Renaissance Curriculum is the Quest Program. Quest courses are seminar-sized offerings that encourage you to solve problems through investigations and exploration . . . much the same way our faculty do. Working alongside your professor, you will test theories and explore education frontiers on a campus with some of the best resources in the world, driven by a curriculum that is truly unprecedented."

For even more information on this school, turn to page 547 of the "Stats" section.

UNIVERSITY OF SCRANTON

800 LINDEN STREET, SCRANTON, PA 18510 • ADMISSIONS: 570-941-7540 • FAX: 570-941-5928
FINANCIAL AID: 570-941-7700 • E-MAIL: ADMISSIONS@SCRANTON.EDU • WEBSITE: WWW.SCRANTON.EDU

Ratings
Quality of Life: 83   Academic: 82   Admissions: 84   Financial Aid: 70

Academics

With "an outstanding record for admission to graduate programs, not only in law and medicine but also in several other fields," the University of Scranton is a good fit for ambitious students seeking "a Jesuit school in every sense of the word. If you come here, expect to be challenged to become a better person, to develop a strong concern for the poor and marginalized, and to grow spiritually and intellectually." The school manages to accomplish this without "forcing religion upon you, which is nice." Undergraduates

also approve of the mandatory liberal-arts-based curriculum that "forces you to learn about broader things than your own major." Strong majors here include "an amazing occupational therapy program, [an] excellent special education program," business, and biology. "This is a great place for premeds and other sciences," students agree. While the workload can be difficult, "a tutoring center provides free tutoring for any students who may need it, and also provides work-study positions for students who qualify to tutor." Need more help? Professors "are extremely accessible. They will go to any lengths to help you understand material and do well," while administrators "are here for the students, and show that every day inside and outside of the classroom." Community ties here are strong; as one student points out, "The Jesuits live in our dorms, creating an even greater sense of community, because we don't view them as just priests, we view them as real people who can relate on our level."

Life

"There is a whole range of activities to do on the weekends" at University of Scranton, including "frequent trips, dances, and movies that are screened for free." Students tell us that "the school and student organizations provide plenty of options, such as retreats, talent shows, and other various activities." There are also "many intramurals to become involved in, and the varsity sports (specifically the women's) are very successful." Furthermore, "Being a Jesuit school, social justice issues are huge. They are taught in the classroom, and students spend a lot of time volunteering." Hometown Scranton is big enough to provide "movie theaters, two malls, parks, a zoo, a bowling alley, and a skiing/snowboarding mountain." In short, there are plenty of choices for the non-partier at Scranton; the many we heard from in our survey reported busy extracurricular schedules. But those seeking a party won't be disappointed here, either. Scranton undergrads "party a lot, but they balance it with studying. Parties are chances to go out, see people, dance, and drink if you want." You "can find a party any time of day, seven days a week" here, usually with a keg tapped and pouring. Few here feel the party scene is out of hand, however; a typical student writes, "It's very different than at schools with Greek systems. It is a lot more laid back, and all about everyone having a good time."

Students

While "the typical Scranton student is white, Catholic, and from the suburbs," students hasten to point out that "Within this sameness, there is much diversity. There are people who couldn't care at all about religion, and there are people who are deeply religious. Even in the Catholic atmosphere of the school, the school only requires that you learn about Catholicism as it stands. Theology classes…are prefaced with the idea that 'You do not have to believe this!'" Undergrads here are generally "friendly and welcoming. Cliques are pretty much nonexistent, and anyone who would be classified as 'popular' is only considered so because they are extremely friendly, outgoing, and seek out friendships with as many people as possible." Students tend to be on the Abercrombie-preppy side, with lots of undergrads of Italian, Irish, and Polish descent.

ADMISSIONS

Very important factors considered include: Secondary school record. *Important factors considered include:* Class rank, standardized test scores. *Other factors considered include:* Alumni/ae relation, character/personal qualities, essays, extracurricular activities, interview, minority status, recommendations, talent/ability, volunteer work, work experience. SAT Reasoning or ACT required. TOEFL required of all international applicants. High school diploma is required, and GED is accepted. *Academic units required:* 4 English, 3 math, 1 science, 2 foreign language, 2 social studies. *Academic units recommended:* 4 English, 4 math, 2 science, 2 foreign language, 3 social studies.

The Inside Word

Admission to Scranton gets harder each year. A steady stream of smart kids from the tri-state area keeps classes full and the admit rate low. Successful applicants will need solid grades and test scores. As with many religiously affiliated schools, students should be a good match philosophically as well.

FINANCIAL AID

Students should submit: FAFSA. The Princeton Review suggests that all financial aid forms be submitted as soon as possible after 1/1. *Need-based scholarships/grants offered:* Pell, SEOG, state scholarships/grants, private scholarships, the school's own gift aid. *Loan aid offered:* FFEL Subsidized Stafford, FFEL Unsubsidized Stafford, FFEL PLUS, Federal Perkins, Federal Nursing. Applicants will be notified of awards on a rolling basis beginning on or about 3/1.

FROM THE ADMISSIONS OFFICE

"A Jesuit institution in Pennsylvania's Pocono northeast, The University of Scranton is known for its outstanding academics, state-of-the art campus and technology, and exceptional sense of community. Founded in 1888, the university offers more than 80 undergraduate and graduate academic programs of study through five colleges and schools.

"For the tenth consecutive year, U.S. News & World Report named Scranton among the top 10 comprehensive universities in the North. In the 2004 edition, Scranton ranked sixth and was spotlighted among schools in the north with the 'Highest Graduate Rate.'

"The Princeton Review included Scranton among The Best 351 Colleges in the nation in its 2004 edition. Princeton Review also ranked Scranton thirtieth among the nation's most connected campuses in a listing published in Forbes magazine. Intel Corporation focused attention on Scranton's increasing commitment to wireless technology, ranking the university eighty-seventh on its list of the nation's most "Most Unwired Campus Colleges."

"For two consecutive years, USA Today included Scranton students on its All-USA College Academic Team. In 2004, Scranton was the only college in Pennsylvania and the only Jesuit university to have two students listed and to have a student placed on the first academic team.

"In other national recognition, Kaplan Publishing counted Scranton among the nation's 328 Most Interesting Colleges and The Washington Post Magazine included the university in a national list of just '100 Colleges Worth Considering.'

"Students are encouraged to apply early for admission and can do so online with no application fee at www.scranton.edu/apply."

For even more information on this school, turn to page 548 of the "Stats" section.

UNIVERSITY OF SOUTHERN MAINE

37 COLLEGE AVENUE, GORHAM, ME 04038 • ADMISSIONS: 207-780-5670 • FAX: 207-780-5640
E-MAIL: USMADM@USM.MAINE.EDU • WEBSITE: WWW.USM.MAINE.EDU

Ratings
Quality of Life: 72   **Academic:** 74   **Admissions:** 74   **Financial Aid:** 72

Academics

With two residential campuses, a commuter campus, and several satellite learning centers, the University of Southern Maine capably serves the diverse needs of a wide range of area students. The school's rural Gorham campus attracts the lion's share of USM's traditional residential undergraduates, while its downtown Portland campus serves a predominantly commuter population that mixes traditional and nontraditional undergrads. A third campus, in Lewiston–Auburn, serves only commuters and primarily nontraditional students. Most traditional undergrads take

> **SURVEY SAYS . . .**
> *Small classes*
> *Great library*
> *Students love Gorham, ME*
> *Great off-campus food*
> *Lots of beer drinking*
> *(Almost) everyone smokes*

classes on the two residential campuses, a situation they regard as both a blessing and a curse. Explains one, "Because the school has dual campuses and many commuters, USM can offer the resources of a big school with regard to research and exchange of ideas, but with the advantage of small class sizes. In addition, the school community is, in a large part, the greater community, and thus students are highly involved and are vocal concerning local issues." The chief downside is that "a majority of the students attend one campus with a majority of the official things happening on a campus 30 to 40 minutes away." Compounding the problem, "communication and travel between the two is not smooth. If you miss the bus, you're stuck at wherever you are for another 45 minutes, which usually means you miss a class. It can be a real pain." All the same, faculty score high marks across the board. As one junior in political science tells us, "The faculty within my major are awesome. They know what they are talking about and are extremely willing and helpful outside the classroom."

Life

"There's really something for everyone going on all the time" at USM's campuses, particularly in Gorham where the majority of residential students live. Students engage in "nearly every sport you can think of at the great gym facilities" and "get involved in organizations, either related to their field of study like the Classics Student Organization, or they get involved with the various papers like the Freedom Press, or the Ancient." A senior majoring in media studies says, "Most of the people I know get involved in nonprofit groups in Portland." Undergrads also report that "all three campuses have art, music, community interaction, social activities, political groups, and activists," and that "organizations work on putting together events and gust speakers." Students love Portland's downtown nightlife, calling Portland "a fantastic city with a wonderful community that includes and can be separate from the university."

Students

"Most of the students are white," at USM "simply because, well, it's Maine," but once you look beyond race, the school has "a very diverse student body. We all sort of just coexist and fit in." Besides the traditional students, "there is a large contingent of nontraditionals," particularly at the Portland and Lewiston–Auburn campuses, and even some ethnic diversity at Lewiston–Auburn ("the cities have a large population of Somalis," students explain). Sums up one undergrad, "Different campuses mean different profiles of the typical student. There's a 19-year-old Gorham resident freshman who spends all of his time on campus, talking about beer, and who doesn't know the difference between Karl Marx and Groucho Marx, if he's even heard of either. The typical Portland student lives off campus with her husband and four children and works two full-time jobs. But she does go to her classes and can tell you who Fredrick Nietzsche is, if you ask her." Lewiston–Auburn students more closely resemble their peers in Portland.

ADMISSIONS

Very important factors considered include: Class rank, secondary school record, standardized test scores. *Important factors considered include:* Essays, recommendations. *Other factors considered include:* Alumni/ae relation, character/personal qualities, extracurricular activities, geographical residence, interview, minority status, state residency, talent/ability, volunteer work, work experience. SAT Reasoning or ACT required. TOEFL required of all international applicants. High school diploma is required, and GED is accepted. *Academic units required:* 4 English, 3 math, 2 science (2 science lab), 2 foreign language, 2 social studies, 2 history. *Academic units recommended:* 4 math, 3 science (3 science lab), 3 foreign language, 3 social studies, 3 history.

The Inside Word

USM's price tag would be much higher if dollars were equated with the faculty's dedication to the students. The result: A wellspring of educational opportunity.

FINANCIAL AID

Students should submit: FAFSA. The Princeton Review suggests that all financial aid forms be submitted as soon as possible after 1/1. *Need-based scholarships/grants offered:* Pell, SEOG, state scholarships/grants, private scholarships, the school's own gift aid. *Loan aid offered:* FFEL Subsidized Stafford, FFEL Unsubsidized Stafford, FFEL PLUS, Federal Perkins, Federal Nursing, state loans. Applicants will be notified of awards on a rolling basis beginning on or about 3/15. Federal Work-study Program available. Off-campus job opportunities are excellent.

FROM THE ADMISSIONS OFFICE

"At the University of Southern Maine you will find the personalized atmosphere and learning environment of a small, New England, residential college combined with the opportunities typically available only at large, national universities. Our student body of approximately 4,600 full-time undergraduates, 4,000 part-time and nondegree students, and 2,000 graduate students enables us to be large enough to provide a wide range of offerings, yet small enough to offer classes averaging around 22 students. USM offers more than 50 majors and 40 additional academic programs, 25 NCAA Division III athletic teams, and nearly 100 student clubs and organizations, yet our student/faculty ratio is only 13:1.

"Our students come from 35 states and 37 countries. Sixty percent of our entering freshmen choose to live on campus. Almost half of our total full-time undergraduate population resides in university housing, while many upperclassmen choose to live with their classmates in off-campus apartments in the Portland area.

"Within a two-hour drive north of Boston, the vibrant city of Portland is located along the scenic southern Maine coastline, with the Atlantic Ocean on one side and majestic mountains and lakes on the other. Our national reputation as one of the best cities for outdoor recreation; the abundant art, music, and theater scenes; and the 35,000 college students that live within an hour's drive make Portland an ideal location to be a college student."

For even more information on this school, turn to page 548 of the "Stats" section.

UNIVERSITY OF VERMONT

OFFICE OF ADMISSIONS, 194 S. PROSPECT STREET, BURLINGTON, VT 05401-3596 • ADMISSIONS: 802-656-3370
FAX: 802-656-8611 • FINANCIAL AID: 802-656-3156 • E-MAIL: ADMISSIONS@UVM.EDU • WEBSITE: WWW.UVM.EDU

Ratings

Quality of Life: 82   Academic: 77   Admissions: 79   Financial Aid: 79

Academics

The University of Vermont, students tell us, is the perfect size: "Small enough to allow for close relationships between friends and faculty, yet large enough for a diverse academic experience, all while being set in one of the most beautiful locations in the Northeast." Unlike most state universities, the trend at UVM is toward smaller classes, not larger. One student writes, "The class sizes have gotten much smaller over the past few years, and I feel that is very

> **SURVEY SAYS . . .**
> *Students are friendly*
> *Students love Burlington, VT*
> *Great off-campus food*
> *Lots of beer drinking*
> *Hard liquor is popular*

impressive. Sure, we have a few large classes, but the majority of mine have less than 50 students in them." The university excels in areas both mainstream—education, political science, English, nursing, business administration, and sociology—and extraordinary. The university's Rubenstein School for the Environment and Natural Resources, for example, "is wonderful. The school has an amazing diversity of course offerings for the size (100 per class)." The department of animal science, which offers degrees in dairy production, equine sciences, and pre-veterinary medicine, is another standout. If there is any knock on UVM, it's the quality of some of its students; many are drawn to UVM more by the school's surroundings than by a genuine desire for a first-rate education. As one undergraduate puts it, "Overall, the school is hamstrung by its deserved reputation as a party school."

Life

The University of Vermont "is in one of the best college towns in the U.S.," according to students, who love that the university is "a strong academic school but still has a raging social scene." Undergraduates feel they "are typically very focused during the first three days of the week and Sunday. This is the time when people finish up any papers, big projects, and homework. When Thursday arrives, though, it's time to have fun." The town of Burlington "has something for everyone to do: movies, dining, the waterfront, the gym, shopping, and coffee shops." It's especially good "if you like music. All sorts of bands come here; Phish-y stuff to hard-core hip-hop and everything between." Just beyond the town are the mountains, providing all manner of outdoor activity. "A majority of students ski or snowboard often [since] the best skiing and snowboarding on the East Coast is just minutes away." Other students "climb in the Green, White, or Adirondack Mountains, fish nearby trout streams, or simply relax down by the waterfront of Lake Champlain." On campus, "frat parties are popular, but they're very selective as to who they allow in" and often lose their appeal as students get older. Upperclassmen tend to move off campus and "host smaller, more intimate parties with 10 to 25 people [or] hit the bars downtown." The university offers "many intramural, club and varsity athletics, as well as a variety of student organizations." The Canadian city of Montreal "is not too far away for those who need a dose of city life on occasion."

Student Body

The student body at University of Vermont consists of "two main types: preppies and hippies." Skiing and the beautiful location seem to be the chief attractions for preppy undergraduates, who "sport polo shirts (collars up), Patagonia/North Face new seasonal outerwear, designer jeans, shoes, jewelry, and accessories (down to the Louis Vuitton bags). The girls tend to sport pearls and hair ribbons." The hippies, in contrast, favor "Birkenstocks, dreadlocks, hemp necklaces, and glass beads; they speak freely about left-wing politics and marijuana, wear natural scents, and eat vegetarian foods that are organically grown." Many students come from well-off families, leading some to comment caustically that "lots of people preach a simplistic way of life and pretend they are hippies, yet drive SUVs and have a trust fund set up by their parents." A third, more conservative group, consisting largely of native Vermonters, can be found "in the college of business and the department of animal science. Mostly, these students tolerate or ignore the liberals who primarily do the same, although there are some who propagandize in front of the library."

ADMISSIONS

Very important factors considered include: Secondary school record. *Important factors considered include:* Character/personal qualities, class rank, essays, standardized test scores, state residency. *Other factors considered include:* Alumni/ae relation, extracurricular activities, geographical residence, interview, minority status, recommendations, talent/ability, volunteer work, work experience. SAT Reasoning or ACT required. TOEFL required of all international applicants. High school diploma is required, and GED is accepted. *Academic units required:* 4 English, 3 math, 2 science (1 science lab), 2 foreign language, 3 social studies.

The Inside Word

UVM is one of the most popular public universities in the country, and its admissions standards are significantly more competitive for out-of-state students. Nonresidents shouldn't get too anxiety-ridden about getting in; more than half of the student body comes from elsewhere. Candidates with above-average academic profiles should be in good shape.

FINANCIAL AID

Students should submit: FAFSA. The Princeton Review suggests that all financial aid forms be submitted as soon as possible after 1/1. *Need-based scholarships/grants offered:* Pell, SEOG, state scholarships/grants, private scholarships, the school's own gift aid, federal nursing scholarships. *Loan aid offered:* FFEL Subsidized Stafford, FFEL Unsubsidized Stafford, FFEL PLUS, Federal Perkins, Federal Nursing, college/university loans from institutional funds. Applicants will be notified of awards on a rolling basis beginning on or about 3/15. Federal Work-study Program available. Institutional employment available. Off-campus job opportunities are good.

FROM THE ADMISSIONS OFFICE

"The University of Vermont blends the close faculty-student relationships most commonly found in a small liberal arts college with the dynamic exchange of knowledge associated with a research university. This is not surprising because UVM is both. A comprehensive research university offering nearly 100 undergraduate majors and extensive offerings through its Graduate College and College of Medicine, UVM is one of the nation's premier public research universities. UVM prides itself on the richness of its undergraduate experience. Distinguished senior faculty teach introductory courses in their fields. They also advise not only juniors and seniors, but also first- and second-year students, and work collaboratively with undergraduates on research initiatives. Students find extensive opportunities to test classroom knowledge in field through practicums, academic internships, and community service. More than 100 student organizations (involving 80 percent of the student body), 20 Division I varsity teams, 15 intercollegiate club and 14 intramural sports programs, and a packed schedule of cultural events fill in where the classroom leaves off."

For even more information on this school, turn to page 549 of the "Stats" section.

URSINUS COLLEGE

URSINUS COLLEGE, ADMISSIONS OFFICE, COLLEGEVILLE, PA 19426 • ADMISSIONS: 610-409-3200
FAX: 610-409-3662 • FINANCIAL AID: 610-409-3600 • E-MAIL: ADMISSIONS@URSINUS.EDU • WEBSITE: WWW.URSINUS.EDU

Ratings
Quality of Life: 88   Academic: 92   Admissions: 89   Financial Aid: 89

Academics

Ursinus College is justly renowned for its biology and chemistry departments. The school's graduates—about one in eight proceed to medical school—boast an impressive 90-plus percent acceptance rate with medical programs. A program this successful, of course, does a good job of winnowing out any slackers, which explains why "Ursinus has many 'ex-biology' students as well as biology

> **SURVEY SAYS . . .**
> *Small classes*
> *Lab facilities are great*
> *Athletic facilities are great*
> *Lots of beer drinking*

students." Those who survive the ordeal benefit from "some of the best chemistry and biology labs around, where really interesting research is being done by undergraduate students and professors. It's nice to have that opportunity, rather than giving up all the research opportunities to graduate students." "Passionate" professors who "care about you and your education" are very accessible to students," as well as an "administration that runs smoothly." A laptop for every student is also part of the deal. Ursinus isn't exclusively about premeds, either. In fact, just as many graduates go on to law school, thanks to "strong humanities programs, especially in history, politics, philosophy, and religion." A brand-new performing arts center that will open in April 2005, promising a flowering of music, dance, and theater on campus. In all areas, "Ursinus College does a great job at preparing its students for future education or jobs by focusing on independent learning, discussions, and providing a ton of learning resources."

Life

"Ursinus is all about having a great learning atmosphere while at the same time providing a place for sports and many other kinds of social events where one can get a true and complete liberal arts education," undergraduates here agree. Even the overworked premeds occasionally find time to work out, play on a team, participate in a student organization, and attend the occasional frat party, we're told. "Greek organizations run the social life and all the big parties" at Ursinus, with about one-third of all students pledging. At the same time, there are "both registered and unregistered parties every weekend," so there's always a party for unaffiliated students to attend. Students like to drink—beer pong is a popular pastime—and smoke herb, but will point out that "while Ursinus College students do party very hard, they are reasonably responsible about it. The college has very loose rules which allow students to make up for the difficult academics with an active social life, while still being held responsible for their actions." For those who abjure intoxication, "there are usually plenty of non-alcoholic activities on campus to attend like movies, concerts, etc." Just don't expect much from Collegeville (yes, the town's real name) other than a Dunkin' Donuts. That's why when students leave campus, they usually head to Philly about half an hour away. A bus or train can "get you to the hot spots of the city," although automobile is the preferred mode of transportation.

Students

The "motivated and ambitious" undergraduates of Ursinus "have a desire to succeed, but also want to have a good time while in college." Many "are white and from the middle to upper classes of society," but students claim that Ursinus "has a larger minority component than most liberal arts colleges in the this area." We're a good-looking school." Students note however, that "the typical student at Ursinus is generally very well-rounded. There are no typical 'jocks' because so many people play sports, and there are no typical 'nerds' because a lot of the same kids excelling in the playing fields are excelling in the classroom as well." In the past, Ursinus has had a large preppy population ("Most of the kids want to be Abercrombie models"), but these days it's starting to attract "a lot of students who have different tastes." "We're a good looking school," says one. A senior describes her school as "one huge clique. Students here may not be diverse in ethnicity, but they are at least diverse in their interests." Undergrads report approvingly that "the tolerant atmosphere on campus is rather amazing. The Gay-Straight Alliance, for example, is a vivacious group coming up with a lot of activities that involve the whole campus."

ADMISSIONS

Very important factors considered include: Class rank, extracurricular activities, secondary school record. *Important factors considered include:* Alumni/ae relation, essays, minority status, recommendations, standardized test scores, talent/ability, volunteer work, work experience. *Other factors considered include:* Character/personal qualities, geographical residence, interview. TOEFL required of all international applicants. High school diploma is required, and GED is accepted. *Academic units required:* 4 English, 3 math, 1 science (1 science lab), 2 foreign language, 1 social studies, 5 academic electives. *Academic units recommended:* 4 math, 3 science, 4 foreign language, 3 social studies.

The Inside Word

The admission process at Ursinus is very straightforward; about 70 percent of those who apply get in. Grades, test scores, and class rank count for more than anything else, and unless you are academically inconsistent, you'll likely get good news.

FINANCIAL AID

Students should submit: FAFSA, institution's own financial aid form, CSS/Financial Aid PROFILE. Regular filing deadline 2/15. The Princeton Review suggests that all financial aid forms be submitted as soon as possible after 1/1. *Need-based scholarships/grants offered:* Pell, SEOG, state scholarships/grants, private scholarships, the school's own gift aid. *Loan aid offered:* FFEL Subsidized Stafford, FFEL Unsubsidized Stafford, FFEL PLUS, Federal Perkins, college/university loans from institutional funds. Applicants will be notified of awards on or about 4/1. Federal Work-study Program available. Off-campus job opportunities are excellent.

FROM THE ADMISSIONS OFFICE

"Located one-half hour from center-city Philadelphia, the college boasts a beautiful 168-acre campus that includes the Residential Village (renovated Victorian-style homes that decorate the Main Street and house our students) and the nationally recognized Berman Museum of Art. Ursinus is a member of the Centennial Conference, competing both in academics and in intercollegiate athletics with institutions such as Dickinson, Franklin and Marshall, Gettysburg, and Muhlenberg. The academic environment is enhanced with such fine programs as a chapter of Phi Beta Kappa, an Early Assurance Program to medical school with the Medical College of Pennsylvania, and myriad student exchanges both at home and abroad. A heavy emphasis is placed on student research—an emphasis that can only be carried out with the one-on-one attention Ursinus students receive from their professors."

For even more information on this school, turn to page 549 of the "Stats" section.

VASSAR COLLEGE

124 RAYMOND AVENUE, POUGHKEEPSIE, NY 12604 • ADMISSIONS: 845-437-7300 • FAX: 845-437-7063
FINANCIAL AID: 845-437-5320 • E-MAIL: ADMISSIONS@VASSAR.EDU • WEBSITE: WWW.VASSAR.EDU

Ratings
Quality of Life: 79   Academic: 95   Admissions: 97   Financial Aid: 98

Academics

Students say that Vassar's goal is "teaching students to think" and that the college achieves this end by affording undergraduates a high degree of academic freedom. "Vassar trusts that I can achieve my academic goals without strict guidance" is one common sentiment among students. Most students "love that we have no core curriculum," leaving them time to pursue their "genuine interests." Though the "workload is very challenging," students

> **SURVEY SAYS . . .**
> Small classes
> Great library
> Frats and sororities are unpopular
> or nonexistent
> Theater is popular

feel supported by their "impressive, friendly, empathetic," and "very encouraging" professors. "If you had a question for one of my professors after class, she would talk to you for half an hour and not realize how much time had gone by," writes a sophomore. Instructors "love what they do and want you to do well," and the small class sizes "force us to contribute to discussions." Students perceive "significant academic competitiveness" among undergraduates; writes one, "Sometimes Vassar students are a bit too intense about academics." A few complaints arise regarding the "limited number of classes and sections." Certain students groan that the administration "likes to maintain absurd amounts of authority." Still others call for "increased communication between administration and students." But a sophomore offers the following challenge: "Tell me any other college where the president would take the time to e-mail me personally to tell me that she's a fan of my newspaper column." In the end, a student in the American culture department avers that a Vassar education is "about self-development and intellectual glory."

Life

In their fairly isolated location in the Hudson Valley, most students feel "restricted to on-campus activities." Luckily, "on any given Friday, there's usually a concert, lecture, play, and comedy performance." Other students frequent The Mug, the college's dance club and bar, or hit the live music performances at the campus café every Thursday. One student writes, "For fun, most people are drinking," and another adds that students have "no social life if you don't drink or take drugs recreationally." The administration, however, has been "cracking down lately with new party rules," putting a damper on the scene. As an alternative, students happily resort to sledding on cafeteria trays, also known as "tray-ing." When this grows tiresome—or when the snow melts—students take advantage of their "great location close to New York City." Several respondents note the abundant "opportunities for leadership positions and internships" at Vassar, emphasizing that "the activist groups here are great." Surveys repeatedly praise the beautiful campus, the perfect surroundings in which to pursue Vassar students' favorite pastime of all: "finding yourself."

Student Body

The most common opinion regarding the undergraduate population of Vassar goes something like, "An atypical student here is the sort who would be a typical student elsewhere." In a place where students "conform by not conforming," the climate remains "very accepting of individuality," prompting one student to describe her peers as "tolerant, almost to the point of apathy." If forced to pin down a stereotype, one might try one or all of: "hippie, style conscious, smart, left wing, idealist, East-Village-y." Less generous characterizations call students "white, rich kids with holes in their clothes" or "liberal people feeling good about it." Though some people see "no ideological diversity," others are quick to point out that the campus is "getting more conservative" and that "there are spiritual and religious people here." The student body is "very accepting in terms of sexuality," which can be a boon, considering that 60 percent of the population is female. Basically, these "pretty people with lots of talent" will continue to "pride themselves on being unique and involved" and "overthinking virtually everything."

ADMISSIONS

Very important factors considered include: Secondary school record. *Important factors considered include:* Class rank, essays, recommendations, standardized test scores. *Other factors considered include:* Alumni/ae relation, character/personal qualities, extracurricular activities, geographical residence, minority status, talent/ability, volunteer work, work experience. SAT Reasoning and SAT Subject Tests or ACT required. TOEFL required of all international applicants. High school diploma is required, and GED is accepted. *Academic units required:* 4 English, 4 math, 3 science (3 science lab), 3 foreign language, 2 social studies, 2 history, 4 academic electives. *Academic units recommended:* 4 English, 4 math, 3 science (4 science lab), 4 foreign language, 3 social studies, 2 history.

The Inside Word

Vassar is relatively frank about its standards; you won't get much more direct advice from colleges about how to get admitted. The admissions process here follows very closely the practices of most prestigious northeastern schools. Your personal side—essays, extracurriculars, interview, etc.—is not going to do a lot for you if you don't demonstrate significant academic accomplishments. Multiple applicants from the same high school will be compared against each other as well as the entire applicant pool. Males and minorities are actively courted by the admissions staff, and the college is sincere in its commitment.

FINANCIAL AID

Students should submit: FAFSA, institution's own financial aid form, CSS/Financial Aid PROFILE, state aid form, noncustodial (divorced/separated) parents' statement, business/farm supplement. Regular filing deadline 2/1. The Princeton Review suggests that all financial aid forms be submitted as soon as possible after 1/1. *Need-based scholarships/grants offered:* Pell, SEOG, state scholarships/grants, private scholarships, the school's own gift aid. *Loan aid offered:* FFEL Subsidized Stafford, FFEL Unsubsidized Stafford, FFEL PLUS, Federal Perkins, loans for non-citizens with need. Applicants will be notified of awards on or about 3/30. Federal Work-study Program available. Off-campus job opportunities are good.

FROM THE ADMISSIONS OFFICE

"Vassar presents a rich variety of social and cultural activities, clubs, sports, living arrangements, and regional attractions. Vassar is a vital, residential college community recognized for its respect for the rights and individuality of others."

For even more information on this school, turn to page 550 of the "Stats" section.

VILLANOVA UNIVERSITY

800 LANCASTER AVENUE, VILLANOVA, PA 19085-1672 • ADMISSIONS: 610-519-4000 • FAX: 610-519-6450
FINANCIAL AID: 610-519-4010 • E-MAIL: GOTOVU@EMAIL.VILLANOVA.EDU • WEBSITE: WWW.VILLANOVA.EDU

Ratings
Quality of Life: 82   **Academic:** 82   **Admissions:** 92   **Financial Aid:** 71

Academics

Students at Villanova feel that their university "helps everyone to be their best on a personal and academic level." The challenging course work and Catholic environment draw young scholars eager to jump in on "great class discussions" and work with professors who are "easy to approach." Instructors are known to "go out of their way to accommodate students," whether that means "inviting everyone who was going to be on campus over for Thanksgiving" or "giving out their cell phone numbers in case we are screwed on an assignment." This "great rapport" allows professors to "help you learn about the material and about yourself." Undergraduates see that the faculty "reaches out and wants to meet their students," which is part of what helps them all to be "good at their job and enjoy what they're doing." We get mixed reviews regarding the administration, with some students calling them "extremely helpful" and others "a big hassle." Overall, however, the campus seems to "run pretty smoothly," and students feel they are "a face with a name, not a number."

> **SURVEY SAYS . . .**
> *Small classes*
> *Great off-campus food*
> *Campus feels safe*
> *Everyone loves the Wildcats*
> *Lots of beer drinking*

Life

The Villanova lifestyle combines academics with top-notch athletics and plenty of opportunities for fun. The typical schedule runs "learn four days a week, get hammered two days a week, and save the world on the other day." The get-hammered portion is brought to you by your friendly neighborhood frat house. "Greeks provide a great social life, but you don't have to be a brother or a sister to have a good time." Students say, "I always manage to drink in some dorm room," but it can be "hard to have a lot of fun because of strict [alcohol] policies." Some think that "the rules are too strict," but they can still head to "the Brick Bar, which is pretty popular when the beer is cheap." For those not interested in bending the hooch regulations, "there are a lot of non-alcohol activities, too," including "late-night movies," theater performances, supporting the perennially successful basketball team, and listening to the ever-popular radio station. Some undergrads complain that "the campus is secluded," meaning they "must go to Philly for fun," but creative fun seekers claim "the town around campus has some good surprises." Student life is rounded out by "so many volunteer opportunities [that] it's overwhelming." Many people participate in the campus ministry, and many agree that "the religious presence here is completely optional but really adds to the sense of community and charity."

Student Body

A field guide to Villanova students might describe them as "white kids from different suburbs across the country," the progeny of "upper-middle-class, Catholic" families. Sometimes known as "Vanilla-nova," the university is "hurting for diversity," but also seems to be "making good progress to diversify the school." For now, the majority of students either are "pretty preppy, or they're guidos." Certain plebeians call their peers "snobbish" and snipe that "being academic comes second to looking good." The "motivated, bright, and outgoing" population includes "very few atypical students." Those who deviate from the "fun-loving, studious, career-oriented" norm may be few in number, but they "find their own niche." Others argue that within this "family environment" of "involved, intelligent, and witty" students, they do count a "decent number of interesting/quirky people."

ADMISSIONS

Other factors considered include: Alumni/ae relation, character/personal qualities, class rank, essays, extracurricular activities, geographical residence, minority status, recommendations, secondary school record, standardized test scores, volunteer work, work experience. SAT Reasoning or ACT required. TOEFL required of all international applicants. High school diploma is required, and GED is accepted. *Academic units required:* 4 English, 4 math, 4 science (2 science lab), 2 foreign language. *Academic units recommended:* 4 English, 4 math, 4 science (3 science lab), 4 foreign language.

The Inside Word

Villanova has a very solid and growing reputation among Catholic universities nationally, yet is less competitive for admissions than the top tier of schools like Georgetown and Notre Dame. If Villanova is your first choice, be careful. As is the case at many universities, Early Action applicants face higher academic standards than those for the regular pool. This university is a very sound option, whether high on your list of choices or as a safety school.

FINANCIAL AID

Students should submit: FAFSA, institution's own financial aid form. Regular filing deadline 2/7. The Princeton Review suggests that all financial aid forms be submitted as soon as possible after 1/1. *Need-based scholarships/grants offered:* Pell, SEOG, state scholarships/grants, private scholarships, the school's own gift aid. *Loan aid offered:* FFEL Subsidized Stafford, FFEL Unsubsidized Stafford, FFEL PLUS, Federal Perkins, Federal Nursing. Applicants will be notified of awards on or about 4/1. Federal Work-study Program available. Off-campus job opportunities are excellent.

FROM THE ADMISSIONS OFFICE

"The university is a community of persons of diverse professional, academic, and personal interests who in a spirit of collegiality cooperate to achieve their common goals and objectives in the transmission, the pursuit, and the discovery of knowledge. Villanova attempts to enroll students with diverse social, geographic, economic, and educational backgrounds. Villanova welcomes students who consider it desirable to study within the philosophical framework of Christian Humanism. Finally, this community seeks to reflect the spirit of St. Augustine by the cultivation of knowledge, by respect for individual differences, and by adherence to the principle that mutual love and respect should animate every aspect of university life."

—Villanova University

For even more information on this school, turn to page 550 of the "Stats" section.

WAGNER COLLEGE

ONE CAMPUS ROAD, STATEN ISLAND, NY 10301 • ADMISSIONS: 718-390-3411 • FAX: 718-390-3105
FINANCIAL AID: 718-390-3183 • E-MAIL: ADMISSIONS@WAGNER.EDU • WEBSITE: WWW.WAGNER.EDU

Ratings
Quality of Life: 70   **Academic:** 77   **Admissions:** 79   **Financial Aid:** 70

Academics

In theory, the Wagner Plan for the Practical Liberal Arts educates free thinkers who can also pay the rent. Required senior-year internships and active volunteering programs mean "a head start on post-graduation plans." First-year learning communities incorporate experiential learning, creative expression, interdisciplinary connections, and frequent trips to the "classroom of New York City." A freshman writes, "They force you to look at the way two subjects relate to each other in a new way." Some people think

> **SURVEY SAYS . . .**
> *Small classes*
> *Athletic facilities are great*
> *Theater is popular*
> *Lots of beer drinking*
> *Hard liquor is popular*
> *(Almost) everyone smokes*

the four-year-old program still needs to work out a few kinks. "It is difficult for students to have confidence in what they are doing if there is no one to encourage them," an English major writes, referring to the self-guided assignments. Theater is a big thing here, too, but even with its liberal and fine arts focus, Wagner manages to also attract students interested in health professions with top nursing and physician's assistant programs. Regardless of major, writing skills are emphasized. "If you don't like doing papers, this is not the place for you. Even the dance classes have tons of them assigned," students warn. Professors are said to be available for academic advice, problem solving, or casual conversation. Reviews of the efficacy of the administration are mixed, but one sage senior adds some helpful context, noting that "since coming to Wagner the administration has gotten better (more involved) and the professors are still about the same (sometimes you get old, boring ones; other times you get good, interesting ones). The more I've gotten involved on campus, the better my experience has been as a whole"—advice that a student at any college could employ to good effect.

Life

Visually, imagine "a classic TV high school"—a large, well-endowed, private high school—and you've got Wagner College. Students relish their dorm-room views of the skyline of Lower Manhattan and make frequent trips to "the greatest metropolis on Earth." One grumpy junior points out that Wagner is "supposedly close to NYC," but cites the time it takes to get to the Staten Island ferry, ride it, and hop the subway to midtown to back up his case. Commuters mingle with residents, though on-campus students maintain that they "have more fun living the ultimate college life." Nighttime hours are typically reserved for social activities, sometimes involving alcohol, rather than sleeping, resulting in a culture prone to cat-napping. Other popular activities include movie nights, hanging out at the coffee house, and using open studio space for ceramics and sculpture. The annual Wagnerstock festivities bring barbecues, bands, and booths. With only 20 percent Greek participation, it's up to the "theater people" to throw the risqué theme parties, like "Schoolgirls and Professors." Tension does arise between the school's main interests, sports and theater—"two things that don't go together at all." Students at Wagner are the first to admit they love to gripe when opportunity presents itself, but underneath the East Coast attitude, they admit, "We're spoiled here."

Student Body

Pull a Wagner student from the crowd and you'll typically find wrinkled clothes, flip flops, and dark circles under the eyes. A senior psychology major sees everyone as "white, young, and skinny." "A different Coach purse every day seems to be the norm, and when you don't come from that, or have the resources for it, fitting in is a little difficult," reports one woman. A large percentage of Wagner kids "dream of making it on Broadway," and this show-tune-humming theater contingent does feel some animosity from the jocks. "Ultimately, they all get along pretty well. Just don't ask different categories to sit together in the dining hall." Single straight women complain about "a really low ratio of guys to girls" and the fact that "a lot of the guys here are gay." A small-town transplant writes, "Wagner has really opened my eyes to the issues facing the homosexual community." The college's "commitment to teaching us to accept diversity" seems to be working.

ADMISSIONS

Very important factors considered include: Class rank, secondary school record, standardized test scores. *Important factors considered include:* Essays, extracurricular activities, interview, recommendations. *Other factors considered include:* Character/personal qualities, talent/ability, volunteer work, work experience. TOEFL required of all international applicants. High school diploma is required, and GED is accepted. *Academic units required:* 4 English, 3 math, 2 science (1 science lab), 2 foreign language, 1 social studies, 3 history, 6 academic electives.

The Inside Word

Wagner has profited in recent years from a renewed interest in urban colleges. In other words, don't take the application process too lightly. Applicants are met with a college admissions staff dedicated to finding the right students for their school. Wagner's pioneering efforts in experiential learning for all students make its recent resurgence well earned.

FINANCIAL AID

Students should submit: FAFSA, institution's own financial aid form, state aid form. The Princeton Review suggests that all financial aid forms be submitted as soon as possible after 1/1. *Need-based scholarships/grants offered:* Pell, SEOG, state scholarships/grants, private scholarships, the school's own gift aid. *Loan aid offered:* FFEL Subsidized Stafford, FFEL Unsubsidized Stafford, FFEL PLUS, Federal Perkins, Federal Nursing. Applicants will be notified of awards on or about 3/1. Federal Work-study Program available. Institutional employment available. Off-campus job opportunities are good.

FROM THE ADMISSIONS OFFICE

"At Wagner College, we attract and develop active learners and future leaders. Wagner College has received national acclaim (Time magazine, American Association of Colleges and Universities) for its innovative curriculum, 'The Wagner Plan for the Practical Liberal Arts.' At Wagner, we capitalize on our unique geography; we are a traditional, scenic, residential campus, which happens to sit atop a hill on an island overlooking lower Manhattan. Our location allows us to offer a program that couples required off-campus experiences (experiential learning), with 'learning community' clusters of courses. This program begins in the first semester and continues through the senior capstone experience in the major. Fieldwork and internships, writing-intensive reflective tutorials, connected learning, 'reading, writing, and doing' . . . at Wagner College our students truly discover 'the practical liberal arts in New York City.'"

For even more information on this school, turn to page 551 of the "Stats" section.

Washington & Jefferson College

60 South Lincoln Street, Washington, PA 15301 • Admissions: 724-223-6025 • Fax: 724-223-6534
E-mail: admission@washjeff.edu • Website: www.washjeff.edu

Ratings
Quality of Life: 68   **Academic:** 80   **Admissions:** 89   **Financial Aid:** 71

Academics

"High academic standards" and small class sizes, coupled with a student body made up of individuals "very serious about their education" leads to a lot of hard work and accountability for the undergrads of Washington & Jefferson College. While many choose the College for its strong programs in the sciences and the liberal arts, every major at W&J is reportedly difficult. The College's friendly professors, administrators, and staff, however, do their best to help students to succeed and "make you feel as comfy as possi-

> **SURVEY SAYS . . .**
> *Small classes*
> *Great computer facilities*
> *Everyone loves the Presidents*
> *Frats and sororities dominate social scene*
> *Lots of beer drinking*
> *Hard liquor is popular*

ble." Despite the heavy workload, students describe W&J as a "fun, challenging, and nurturing environment" where students are truly mentored and supported by the faculty and staff; writes one freshman, "The professors are amazing. They are always there whenever you are struggling, confused, or just want to talk. Even the administration is available to chat!" While the quality of the academic program is undisputed, some students gripe about the high costs of this private school. In particular, students tell us that "the financial aid department needs some work." Commenting on this state of affairs, a freshman jokes that the College might consider changing its motto to "providing the best education possible for the most amount of money."

Life

When considering student life at W&J, a junior offers this analogy: "It's like a mullet: business in the front, party in the back." Indeed, students say that W&J is the place to go for both a "good education and a good time," as the friendly student body is as social as it is studious. On campus "people are busy with sports, clubs, and fraternities/sororities," of which athletics are particularly popular with students; writes a sophomore, "Our school is all about education…and after education comes sports." During the weekend, the W&J campus comes alive with parties. "After a hard week of stressful classes, most of the people here drink," writes a student. However, undergraduates reassure us that there are "no crazy state-school style parties" at W&J, and most students prioritize books over booze; reports a sophomore, "I like to drink and party on the weekends, but get my homework done during the week." Whether you like the W&J social life or not, you're stuck with it, as undergraduates are required to live on campus.

Students

On the whole, this small campus is home to "nice, studious, involved, and athletic" undergrads, most of whom take their education very seriously. Almost all students claim to be "hard workers" and generally describe their classmates as intelligent and motivated. But the similarities don't end there. A junior reports that "Everyone is pretty typical white, upper-middle class American. We have very few minorities." Another confesses, "The majority of students are cookie-cutter images of each other. There is very little individuality on this campus." Even so, students claim that their classmates are generally accepting and friendly, even if there are very few students who don't fit in. Writes a junior, "Everyone gets along no matter what they look like; a benefit to a small campus." In fact, students insist that W&J, "works like a small community; everyone helps everyone."

ADMISSIONS

Very important factors considered include: Secondary school record. *Important factors considered include:* Character/personal qualities, class rank, essays, extracurricular activities, interview, recommendations, standardized test scores, volunteer work, work experience. *Other factors considered include:* Alumni/ae relation, geographical residence, state residency, talent/ability. SAT Reasoning or ACT required. TOEFL required of all international applicants. High school diploma is required, and GED is accepted. *Academic units required:* 3 English, 3 math, 1 science, 2 foreign language, 6 academic electives.

The Inside Word

W&J puts its facilities and resources within easy reach of students striving to maintain high scholastic standards, and students respond by raising the bar just a little higher when they blow off steam, as well. Minority students and those hailing from far outside the region are raising its level of diversity, too.

FINANCIAL AID

Students should submit: FAFSA. The Princeton Review suggests that all financial aid forms be submitted as soon as possible after 1/1. *Need-based scholarships/grants offered:* Pell, SEOG, state scholarships/grants, private scholarships, the school's own gift aid. *Loan aid offered:* FFEL Subsidized Stafford, FFEL Unsubsidized Stafford, FFEL PLUS, Federal Perkins, college/university loans from institutional funds. Applicants will be notified of awards on a rolling basis beginning on or about 3/1. Federal Work-study Program available. Institutional employment available. Off-campus job opportunities are good.

FROM THE ADMISSIONS OFFICE

"An avalanche of applications has hit Washington & Jefferson College. Last year, W&J shattered the all-time school record for the number of applications for admission. This year's application numbers have already eclipsed last year's total, and the quality of the pool has not been compromised. Incoming freshmen have an average SAT score of above 1140 and a median grade point average of 3.4. A revised curriculum and new academic programs and facilities have contributed to the influx.

"The Office of Admissions welcomes prospective students and their families. Students can schedule a personal interview, tour the campus, spend the night, and attend a class. To schedule a visit, students should contact the office directly or go to the website."

For even more information on this school, turn to page 551 of the "Stats" section.

WASHINGTON COLLEGE

300 WASHINGTON AVENUE, CHESTERTOWN, MD 21620 • ADMISSIONS: 410-778-7700 • FAX: 410-778-7287
E-MAIL: ADM.OFF@WASHCOLL.EDU • WEBSITE: WWW.WASHCOLL.EDU

Ratings

Quality of Life: 71   Academic: 84   Admissions: 90   Financial Aid: 87

Academics

Students say that "individualized attention" is the greatest strength of Chestertown, Maryland's, Washington College (WAC). The small size of this liberal arts school "allows everyone, including professors and the administration, to get to know [students] both inside and outside of the classroom." WAC places a strong emphasis on writing and literature and has a well-respected creative writing program; every

> **SURVEY SAYS . . .**
> *Small classes*
> *Lots of beer drinking*
> *Hard liquor is popular*

year, the school awards the Sophie Kerr Prize to one graduating senior. According to the school's website, the honor is "the largest undergraduate prize in the nation. Last "year's prize was worth over $60,000." Students rave about WAC's Rose O'Neill Literary House, a Victorian home that serves as the hub of the school's literary activities. Undergrads also applaud WAC's "great psych program [and] excellent record of placement into medical schools," and they appreciate the academic freedom that the small school allows them. "You can develop and design your own curriculum and independent research projects, from biology to drama to sociology," one student explains. Furthermore, "the professors are amazing; there is plenty of opportunity to meet with them and to further discuss any issues in class. They are wonderful at helping students advance their careers in their chosen fields. Often they take their students" research to conferences and seminars." The administration is described as "fairly accessible." One student says, "Sometimes, it would be helpful if they allowed students to have more of a voice in school decisions."

Life

Students describe Chestertown as "rural, small, quaint, and beautiful." The town features "one movie theater and two pizza places. You have to make your own entertainment. For a lot of students, this means drinking a lot, but the more creative kids find other ways to keep themselves busy." Students who crave urban entertainment take road trips. "It is an hour and a half drive to Washington, DC and Philadelphia. Annapolis and Baltimore are nearby (an hour or so), as are Newark and Dover (both in Delaware)." Students who choose to stay on and around campus enjoy "watching plays, working out in the gym, swimming, or playing games in the student center. Musicians or comedians come every now and then, and the school invites many speakers, including famous figures such as Howard Dean, Robert Novak, and James Carville." Many students "take advantage of WAC's rural surroundings by either taking part in water sports on the river, horseback riding, biking, or just exploring backcountry roads." Students also "party at off-campus houses or at dorms," but they don't necessarily classify WAC as a party school. One undergrad explains, "There aren't many big, raging parties on a regular basis, but there are preplanned events that get rather large."

Student Body

WAC students are "driven to succeed but know how to relax and have fun." The bulk of the student body "appears to be white, upper-middle class jocks, Greeks, and yuppies in training," one student says, "but there is a good-sized underground with diverse interests from diverse backgrounds." Another student contributes, "We have several individuals on campus who are not very traditional in their choice of dress or behavior, but I don't believe that they're treated any differently because of it." Many students complain that the school lacks ethnic diversity, but other students point out that "a significant percentage of the student population is international, including a number of students from Japan." WAC's gay community "is able to be extremely open about their preferences and no one really bothers them." One student adds, "Since WAC is a liberal arts college, there is an easy mix of different types of students. All of the groups easily intermingle and are friendly across campus. It is a very genuine and pleasant mix of students." '

ADMISSIONS

Very important factors considered include: Interview, secondary school record. *Important factors considered include:* Character/personal qualities, class rank, essays, recommendations, standardized test scores. *Other factors considered include:* Alumni/ae relation, extracurricular activities, geographical residence, minority status, state residency, talent/ability, volunteer work, work experience. SAT Reasoning or ACT required. TOEFL required of all international applicants. High school diploma is required, and GED is accepted. *Academic units required:* 4 English, 3 math, 3 science (2 science lab), 2 foreign language, 4 social studies. *Academic units recommended:* 4 English, 4 math, 4 science (3 science lab), 4 foreign language, 4 social studies.

The Inside Word

Admissions standards are moderately selective at Washington College, the 10th oldest college in the nation, where nearly half of all applicants are from out of state. A strong B student should not encounter many obstacles to admission, but applicants should note that interviews are considered very important factors in the selection process.

FINANCIAL AID

Students should submit: FAFSA, institution's own financial aid form, federal income tax forms. The Princeton Review suggests that all financial aid forms be submitted as soon as possible after 1/1. *Need-based scholarships/grants offered:* Pell, SEOG, state scholarships/grants, private scholarships, the school's own gift aid. *Loan aid offered:* FFEL Subsidized Stafford, FFEL Unsubsidized Stafford, FFEL PLUS, Federal Perkins, college/university loans from institutional funds. Applicants will be notified of awards on a rolling basis beginning on or about 3/1. Federal Work-study Program available. Institutional employment available. Off-campus job opportunities are excellent.

FROM THE ADMISSIONS OFFICE

"Founded in 1782, Washington College is the 10th oldest college in America. George Washington, in whose honor the college was named, served as a trustee from 1784 until 1789 and was awarded the college's first honorary degree. From its inception, Washington College has maintained an unwavering commitment to the liberal arts and sciences. Through diverse curricular offerings, excellent teaching, and engaged learning we develop in our students the habits of analytic thought, aesthetic insight, imagination, ethical sensitivity, and clarity of expression. We choose to maintain an enrollment of approximately 1,250 students and a 12:1 student/faculty ratio. Two-thirds of all WC classes have 20 or fewer students, making it easy for undergrads and their professors to engage in the exchange of information and ideas. Our graduates leave us prepared for admission to graduate and professional schools, able to pursue a wide variety of career options, and ready for lives of responsible citizenship and personal fulfillment.

"Our 112-acre campus is in historic Chestertown on Maryland's Eastern Shore. We are situated in a county with more than 200 miles of waterfront including a beautiful stretch along the Chester River just a short walk from campus. Location is everything and ours is in the very heart of the Chesapeake Bay region, 45 minutes from Annapolis and 90 minutes from Baltimore, Philadelphia, and Washington, DC.

"More than 50 percent of Washington College students are National Honor Society members. The college offers $40,000 scholarships to all NHS members who qualify for admission."

For even more information on this school, turn to page 551 of the "Stats" section.

WEBB INSTITUTE

298 CRESCENT BEACH ROAD, OCEAN COVE, NY 11542 • ADMISSIONS: 516-674-9838
FINANCIAL AID: 516-671-2213 • E-MAIL: ADMISSIONS@WEBB-INSTITUTE.EDU • WEBSITE: WWW.WEBB-INSTITUTE.EDU

Ratings

Quality of Life: 97 **Academic:** 96 **Admissions:** 98 **Financial Aid:** 83

Academics

Offering a full-tuition scholarship to every student and boasting a "100 percent placement rate in grad schools and careers," Long Island's Webb Institute would be the ideal school for everyone, but for one catch: only one major, Naval Architecture and Marine Engineering, is available here. For the "shipbuilders of tomorrow," though, Webb is a dream come true—a "rigorously academic experience tempered by a spirit of cooperation amongst the students and professors who are always willing to help out." Like most engineering schools, Webb demands a lot from its students; writes one, "This school is about keeping a positive

> **SURVEY SAYS . . .**
> *Small classes*
> *No one cheats*
> *Registration is a breeze*
> *Dorms are like palaces*
> *Campus feels safe*
> *Frats and sororities are unpopular or nonexistent*
> *Very little drug use*

attitude in the face of long days and nights of plentiful and difficult work." That task is made easier by the fact that students and faculty form "a tight knit community with strong social bonds. It is not competitive amongst the students, which makes the overall academic experience good." Webb professors "are readily available and often hold review sessions outside of class hours," and while "some introductory professors just don't know how to teach, all courses important to the major are taught by knowledgeable and good professors." Administrators are "readily available and responsive to suggestions, [and] because our school is run on an honor code, the administration has little to do with the overall social lives of the students. So in essence the students run the school." Concludes one engineer, "For the major they offer, it's the best school in the world. The professors are great, the other students are great, and overall the school is great."

Life

"The class load is brutal" at Webb Institute, and "schoolwork has a tendency to take over everything," including leisure time. "We get hours of homework each night," students explain, "so we have to work together and make homework fun in order to survive." All students live together, too, in a remodeled mansion on a 26-acre beachfront estate. As a result, "you get to know your classmates very well because you spend all day with them. All of the classes intermingle a lot too." Webb engineers "joke that we function on our own time zone here. We stay up until 2:00 or 3:00 A.M. regularly, but classes don't start until 9:00 A.M., so we sleep later than the rest of the Eastern Seaboard too." When students can muster some spare time, they enjoy typical college fun. One student reports, "There are many school-sponsored parties every semester, as well as a pub, a TV room, and game room in the main building. Watching movies is pretty popular, as well as video games. Also, there are annual white water rafting and ski trips. Basketball and other sports are played pretty often, just for fun." Because the administration "is very strict about drinking on campus," students head to the local pub or travel into New York City when they feel the need to tie one on. "One must make every effort possible to go to New York City, an easy one-hour train ride away," students insist.

Student Body

"All of the students are very hard working" at Webb, because "if you're not then you won't stay for very long." There are "two types of students at Webb: those who are bookworms and study all the time and are always working, and those who do the work when needed but also enjoy themselves on campus by playing sports or going out and having a good time." As at most engineering schools, most students are male; atypical of engineering schools, nearly all students are white. "We're all nerdy white boys, except for the few nerdy white girls," sums up one student, adding that "minority students aren't social outcasts or anything like that. We don't care what you look like; we care what's going on inside and upstairs. We treat each other with mutual respect."

ADMISSIONS

Very important factors considered include: Class rank, interview, secondary school record, standardized test scores. *Important factors considered include:* Character/personal qualities, recommendations, talent/ability. *Other factors considered include:* Extracurricular activities, volunteer work, work experience. SAT Reasoning Test required or SAT Subject Tests required. High school diploma is required, and GED is not accepted. *Academic units required:* 4 English, 4 math, 2 science (2 science lab), 2 social studies, 4 academic electives.

The Inside Word

Let's not mince words; admission to Webb is mega-tough. Webb's admissions counselors are out to find the right kid for their curriculum—one that can survive the school's rigorous academics. The applicant pool is highly self-selected because of the focused program of study: naval architecture and marine engineering.

FINANCIAL AID

Students should submit: FAFSA. Regular filing deadline 7/1. The Princeton Review suggests that all financial aid forms be submitted as soon as possible after 1/1. *Need-based scholarships/grants offered:* Pell, state scholarships/grants, private scholarships, the school's own gift aid. *Loan aid offered:* FFEL Subsidized Stafford, FFEL Unsubsidized Stafford, FFEL PLUS. Applicants will be notified of awards on or about 8/1. Off-campus job opportunities are good.

FROM THE ADMISSIONS OFFICE

"Webb, the only college in the country that specializes in the engineering field of Naval Architecture and Marine Engineering, seeks young men and women of all races from all over the country who are interested in receiving an excellent engineering education with a full-tuition scholarship. Students don't have to know anything about ships, they just have to be motivated to study how mechanical, civil, structural, and electrical engineering come together with the design elements that make up a ship and all its systems. Being small and private has its major advantages. Every applicant is special and the President will interview all entering students personally. The student/faculty ratio is 6:1, and since there are no teaching assistants, interaction with the faculty occurs daily in class and labs at a level not found at most other colleges. The college provides each student with a high-end laptop computer. The entire campus operates under the Student Organization's Honor System that allows unsupervised exams and 24-hour access to the library, every classroom and laboratory, and the shop and gymnasium. Despite a total enrollment of between 70 and 80 students and a demanding workload, Webb manages to field six intercollegiate teams. Currently more than 60 percent of the members of the student body play on one or more intercollegiate teams. Work hard, play hard and the payoff is a job for every student upon graduation. The placement record of the college is 100 percent every year."

For even more information on this school, turn to page 552 of the "Stats" section.

WELLESLEY COLLEGE

BOARD OF ADMISSION, 106 CENTRAL STREET, WELLESLEY, MA 02481-8203 • ADMISSIONS: 781-283-2270
FAX: 781-283-3678 • FINANCIAL AID: 781-283-2360 • E-MAIL: ADMISSION@WELLESLEY.EDU • WEBSITE: WWW.WELLESLEY.EDU

Ratings
Quality of Life: 96   **Academic:** 98   **Admissions:** 97   **Financial Aid:** 80

Academics

"It's plastered all over campus, but that doesn't make it any less true: 'Wellesley—women who will make a difference in the world.'" Not that Wellesley students need to see their school's unofficial motto (its official motto is *Non ministrari sed ministrare*; "Not to be served, but to serve") to remember their school's mission. It is evidenced in the intensity and scope of the curriculum, the "amazing, inspiring faculty," and the school's success in sending students on to graduate school and careers in a wide variety of areas. Wellesley classes often "resemble high-school classes or seminars, in that the numbers are usually pretty low, and there is more discussion than you would expect in a college class."

> **SURVEY SAYS . . .**
> *Small classes*
> *No one cheats*
> *Lab facilities are great*
> *Great computer facilities*
> *Great library*
> *Diverse student types on campus*
> *Campus feels safe*
> *Frats and sororities are unpopular or nonexistent*

Frequent discussion keeps students honest, ensuring that they keep up with the syllabus. One student adds, "Academics are hard and time-consuming, but so rewarding." Those who put in the hours reap the rewards. Students tell us, "The faculty will do everything to assure you get into grad school and help you prepare for your future, [while] the Alumnae Association is also full of amazing people who are constantly giving us advice and help with internships, jobs, and just Wellesley in general." Students are satisfied with the Wellesley experience, telling us that it is "all about finding out who you are, even when the world tells you something otherwise."

Life

"There is something for everyone at Wellesley College," women at Wellesley report, adding, "Your social life is really what you make of it." While some will "go out on weekends and go to frat parties," others say they "will go into Boston or Cambridge and go out for dinner, or see a concert, or just go shopping." Another majority of students "will stay on campus and watch movies, surf the Internet, order takeout, do homework or laundry, or just stay in and study." Despite students' tendency to "do their own thing," the campus unites for "Wellesley's special traditions, such as Stepsinging (classes compete to have the loudest cheers), Spring Weekend (concerts, cookouts, and other fun activities), Tower Court (our biggest party of the year, guys come from other schools in U-Hauls), and Lake Day (students skip classes and hang out by Lake Waban)." Though Boston and all that it offers are a mere ten miles away, the school "makes a solid effort to entertain students who remain on campus. There are many lecturers throughout the year, and last year [there were] such visitors as Amiri Baraka, Seamus Heaney, and Phyllis Schlafly. There have also been movie screenings outdoors on Severance Green, and other college-sponsored events meant to entertain (or enlighten) the students at Wellesley College." When these hard-working students can cobble together more than a few hours for fun, they often "walk into the town (the 'Ville') or take buses to Cambridge or the T [Boston's subway]."

Student Body

"The typical student in Wellesley is studious, laborious, and loquacious," undergraduates tell us. "One of the things I love about Wellesley," explains one undergraduate, "is that when you arrive for orientation, you see that the women in the seats around you are just the type of people you liked in high school, and that you won't have to deal with the ditzy popular girls or the macho dumb boys here. We have the cream of the crop, the women who take their education seriously and enjoy every minute of it." Wellesley women love "the incredible diversity of the school, including (but not limited to) ethnicity, socioeconomic class, sexual orientation, and race." One student notes, "Women come from all over the world and the country. My roommate is from Florida, my best friend is from Chicago, a girl down the hall is from Thailand, another from South Africa." Most Wellesley women, we're told, are "rather strong-willed and independent," politically to the left, and vocal about their beliefs. "The college can overload on political correctness. Sometimes students at Wellesley are too easily offended and too uptight," warn some.

ADMISSIONS

Very important factors considered include: Essays, recommendations, secondary school record, standardized test scores. *Important factors considered include:* Character/personal qualities, class rank, extracurricular activities. *Other factors considered include:* Alumni/ae relation, geographical residence, interview, minority status, state residency, talent/ability, volunteer work, work experience. SAT Reasoning and SAT Subject Tests or ACT required. TOEFL required of all international applicants. High school diploma or equivalent is not required. *Academic units recommended:* 4 English, 4 math, 3 science (2 science lab), 4 foreign language, 4 social studies, 4 history.

The Inside Word

While the majority of women's colleges have gone coed or even closed over the past two decades, Wellesley has continued with vigor. As a surviving member of the Seven Sisters, the nation's most prestigious women's colleges, Wellesley enjoys even more popularity with students who choose the single-sex option. Admissions standards are rigorous, but among institutions of such high reputation, Wellesley's admissions staff is friendlier and more open than the majority. Their willingness to conduct preliminary evaluations for candidates is especially commendable and in some form or another should be the rule rather than an exception at highly selective colleges.

FINANCIAL AID

Students should submit: FAFSA, institution's own financial aid form, CSS/Financial Aid PROFILE, noncustodial (divorced/separated) parents' statement, business/farm supplement, parents' and student' tax returns and W-2 forms. The Princeton Review suggests that all financial aid forms be submitted as soon as possible after 1/1. *Need-based scholarships/grants offered:* Pell, SEOG, state scholarships/grants, private scholarships, the school's own gift aid. *Loan aid offered:* FFEL Subsidized Stafford, FFEL Unsubsidized Stafford, FFEL PLUS, Federal Perkins, state loans, college/university loans from institutional funds. Applicants will be notified of awards on or about 4/1. Federal Work-study Program available. Institutional employment available. Off-campus job opportunities are good.

FROM THE ADMISSIONS OFFICE

"A student's years at Wellesley are the beginning—not the end—of an education. A Wellesley College degree signifies not that the graduate has memorized certain blocks of material, but that she has acquired the curiosity, the desire, and the ability to seek and assimilate new information. Four years at Wellesley can provide the foundation for the widest possible range of ambitions and the necessary self-confidence to fulfill them. At Wellesley, a student has every educational opportunity. Above all, it is Wellesley's purpose to teach students to apply knowledge wisely and to use the advantages of talent and education to seek new ways to serve the wider community."

For even more information on this school, turn to page 552 of the "Stats" section.

WELLS COLLEGE

Route 90, Aurora, NY 13026 • Admissions: 315-364-3264 • Fax: 315-364-3327
Financial Aid: 315-364-3289 • E-mail: admissions@wells.edu • Website: www.wells.edu

Ratings
Quality of Life: 73   Academic: 88   Admissions: 88   Financial Aid: 84

Academics

The women of Wells College enrolled expecting "a single-sex education" designed to "form a strong community and strong female leaders." Recently, however, they were rocked by the administration's decision to go coed. Most students adamantly believe "the decision will seriously impair the school's ability to achieve its most important goal: teaching women to be independent, free-thinking individuals." Trust between students and administrators has been damaged, "creating an unhealthy divide." The

good news is that professors still enjoy a close relationship with students and employ an honor code that rewards responsibility with freedom. "Students are allowed to take exams out of the classroom and leave it in the professor's office when they're done." Due to small classes, teachers notice class participation and "will approach you afterwards if they think you did well or saw that you were unprepared. Three-hour seminars pause for a mid-session tea break "when the dining hall brings cookies and coffee." Students call for improvements in "our science, art, and music programs, athletic facilities, library sources, and website," but they praise the sociology and language departments. Throw in extensive study abroad opportunities and the "very interesting and very rare" book arts center, and we predict Wells will continue to attract students into their coed halls.

Life

The Wells existence "can be summarized in one word: isolation." Hometown Aurora, shuts down by 8:00 p.m. One student warns: "If you are from NYC, you may be culture shocked" when you find yourself spending "Friday and Saturday nights doing homework." Besides the farms and barns, "there's a bar where the entire senior class congregates on Fridays, a wickedly expensive inn, and a pizza place." At least "the Office of Campus Events is really good about giving us stuff to do. But the most fun comes from the traditions: The Even/Odd rivalry, Junior Blast, Freshman Elves, . . . These are really what give Wells its fabulous life." Civilization, meaning malls and Cornell boys, lies 45 minutes away in Ithaca, but some people prefer to stay put, swimming in Cayuga Lake, sledding down Student Union hill, exploring the local cemetery, and involving themselves with campus organizations. "Being creative and willing to try new things makes for interesting weekends," as long as you can "make your own fun." For the Wells crowd, that can range from "hallway soccer" to a good "wine and Cheez-Its party." Off campus, "there's a 24 hour Wal-Mart that always produces some good stories." Other students emphasize the luxury of "the safe space we have here. You can walk back to your dorm across campus at 3:00 a.m. alone, and your biggest worry is bumping into the campus skunk."

Student Body

"Whether a radical feminist or a quiet feminist, this school is full of feminists," asserts a senior. And plenty of them are happy to show up at their morning classes "in their PJ bottoms, flip-flops, a hoodie, and no make-up." These 400 women are typically "liberal, confident, outgoing, and willing to share [their] thoughts," which might just center on "queer and gender theory." Lesbians represent at Wells, and most students agree that everyone gets along well, regardless of sexual preferences.students come from "working-class, white, New York state families," but wherever they are from, "you will rarely find someone who belonged to the popular crowd in high school." The coed crisis has brought out differences of opinion. "Our amazing sisterhood has fractured, and the community has become more like a brood of disgruntled women," writes one student. Others are optimistic that the student body can "keep the same feeling of community even though it is no longer a women's college."

ADMISSIONS

Very important factors considered include: Extracurricular activities, recommendations, secondary school record, standardized test scores. *Important factors considered include:* Essays, interview. *Other factors considered include:* Alumni/ae relation, character/personal qualities, class rank, talent/ability, volunteer work, work experience. SAT Reasoning or ACT required. TOEFL required of all international applicants. High school diploma is required, and GED is accepted. *Academic units required:* 4 English, 3 math, 2 science (2 science lab), 2 social studies, 2 academic electives. *Academic units recommended:* 4 English, 4 math, 3 science (3 science lab), 2 foreign language, 3 social studies, 3 academic electives.

The Inside Word

Wells is engaged in that age-old admissions game called matchmaking. There are no minimums or cutoffs in the admissions process here. But don't be fooled by the high admit rate. The admissions committee will look closely at your academic accomplishments, but also gives attention to your essay, recommendations, and extracurricular pursuits. The committee also recommends an interview; we suggest taking them up on it.

FINANCIAL AID

Students should submit: FAFSA, CSS/Financial Aid PROFILE for early decision applicants only. The Princeton Review suggests that all financial aid forms be submitted as soon as possible after 1/1. *Need-based scholarships/grants offered:* Pell, SEOG, state scholarships/grants, private scholarships, the school's own gift aid. *Loan aid offered:* FFEL Subsidized Stafford, FFEL Unsubsidized Stafford, FFEL PLUS, Federal Perkins. Applicants will be notified of awards on a rolling basis beginning on or about 3/1.

FROM THE ADMISSIONS OFFICE

"Wells College believes the twenty-first century needs well-educated individuals with the ability, self-confidence, and vision to contribute to an ever-changing world. Wells offers an outstanding classroom experience and innovative liberal arts curriculum that prepares students for leadership in a variety of fields, including business, government, the arts, sciences, medicine, and education. By directly connecting the liberal arts curriculum to experience and career development through internships, off-campus study, study abroad, research with professors, and community service, each student has an ideal preparation for graduate and professional school as well as for the twenty-first century."

For even more information on this school, turn to page 553 of the "Stats" section.

WENTWORTH INSTITUTE OF TECHNOLOGY

550 HUNTINGTON AVENUE, ADMISSIONS OFFICE, BOSTON, MA 02115-5998 • ADMISSIONS: 617-989-4000 • FAX: 617-989-4010
E-MAIL: ADMISSIONS@WIT.EDU • WEBSITE: WWW.WIT.EDU

Ratings
Quality of Life: 70 **Academic:** 70 **Admissions:** 74 **Financial Aid:** 61

Academics

"Hands-on learning" is what draws students to Wentworth Institute of Technology, a Boston school where the "main focus is training students for the professional world in the fields of architecture, engineering, and construction." Undergraduates appreciate "the focus on real-world knowledge. They avoid making students take classes that will have no relevance to them afterward." Students also praise the co-op program, explaining that "it gives students the opportunity to see what it's really like in their chosen field." Wentworth is a school that's not so tough to get into, but much, much more difficult to graduate from. One undergraduate explains, "My school's admission is extremely easy; I believe this is a great thing because it accepts the students who might have potential but didn't show it in high school. But then [the school] weeds them out as the years go." An industrial design major agrees and adds, "We have something called 'sophomore review.' You present all of your best work from the last two years in front of all of your professors and peers. If the review board doesn't think [your work is] good enough, you don't get to move on to junior year. People stay up for four days straight to prepare just to be told they aren't good enough." While the demands are great, help is always available. "The Academic Resource Center offers well-prepared and smart tutors who can help you every single day if you wish. Best of all, it is free."

> **SURVEY SAYS . . .**
> *Small classes*
> *Students love Boston, MA*
> *Great off-campus food*
> *Frats and sororities are unpopular*
> *or nonexistent*
> *Lots of beer drinking*
> *(Almost) everyone smokes*

Life

Students' fields of study determine the amount of free time they have at WIT. "Depending on the major, you will find people very dedicated to their major, and that is what a lot of their time (including free time) is spent on," explains one student. Architects, in particular, tell us that "the degree is very demanding and time-consuming. Professors are pressured by the department head to assign overwhelming amounts of work with the intent of weeding out the less dedicated students. There are a lot of sleepless nights." In other less stressful fields, undergraduates create free time to "enjoy Boston, which has many other colleges, lots of bars, clubs, concerts, and restaurants." They also sometimes "party in off-campus residences." One student remarks, "There are definitely two types of students: the studious ones and the partiers. The partiers party every weekend; the studious students find other constructive ways to enjoy themselves—something pretty easy to do in the city of Boston." For those who find Boston "too expensive," there's also "stuff to do around the dorm, or you can participate in school-sponsored events."

Student Body

Wentworth reportedly "attracts nearly every type of person, from the nerdy computer science kid to the artistic designer." Because of this, students represent "a vast collection of various personalities. This is great because it permits interaction with people on any end of the social/religious/academic/financial/racial spectrum." Even so, many students say, "We're all basically dorks who like computers and fun." Many students conclude that "most of the students are male, white, and [from] working-class families." One student observes, "There are a lot of kids with dreams of MIT, but who couldn't afford it." The male/female ratio, as at most technical colleges, is pretty lopsided.

ADMISSIONS

Very important factors considered include: Secondary school record. *Important factors considered include:* Essays, recommendations, standardized test scores. *Other factors considered include:* Extracurricular activities, interview, volunteer work, work experience. SAT Reasoning or SAT Subject Tests required. TOEFL required of all international applicants. High school diploma is required, and GED is accepted. *Academic units required:* 4 English, 3 math, 1 science (1 science lab). *Academic units recommended:* 4 English, 4 math, 3 science (2 science lab).

The Inside Word

Strength in math and science are obviously the key concerns here. You can help your chances by completing all the optional parts of the application. Extra letters of recommendation, an on-campus visit, and an interview are not required, but they are a great way of saying "I really want to go to Wentworth," which never hurts.

FINANCIAL AID

Students should submit: FAFSA. The Princeton Review suggests that all financial aid forms be submitted as soon as possible after 1/1. *Need-based scholarships/grants offered:* Pell, SEOG, state scholarships/grants, the school's own gift aid. *Loan aid offered:* Direct Subsidized Stafford, Direct Unsubsidized Stafford, Direct PLUS, Federal Perkins, state loans. Applicants will be notified of awards on a rolling basis beginning on or about 3/15. Federal Work-study Program available. Institutional employment available. Off-campus job opportunities are excellent.

FROM THE ADMISSIONS OFFICE

"One of the most affordable colleges in greater Boston, Wentworth Institute of Technology provides the tools today's career-oriented students need to succeed in the marketplace: strong academic programs, cutting-edge labs and studios, and a cooperative education program (co-op) that is one of the largest and most comprehensive of its kind.

"When you join the Wentworth community, you'll find energetic, can-do students from 36 states and 44 countries. You'll find individuals ready to roll up their sleeves and get to work. Most importantly, you'll find fellow students with a strong drive to succeed academically and professionally.

"At Wentworth you get the best of both worlds: small college comforts and big city excitement. You'll find a tree-lined quad, a food court cafeteria, traditional and modern residence halls, recreational facilities, and more on our 35-acre campus. You'll also enjoy easy access to Boston's exciting venues and New England's scenic wonders: walk to Fenway Park, the Museum of Fine Arts, or Copley Place; take a ferry to Cape Cod; hike the White Mountains. Whatever your destination, having the 'T' Green Line and the Ruggles Station stop on the commuter rail right beside campus means you can get into—or out of—Boston easily.

"Wentworth is also a member of the Colleges of the Fenway consortium. This consortium offers the benefits of cross-registration and access to social events, professional activities, libraries, and campus facilities at six colleges within walking distance of one another. The other Colleges of the Fenway members are Emmanuel College, Massachusetts College of Art, Massachusetts College of Pharmacy and Health Sciences, Simmons College, and Wheelock College."

For even more information on this school, turn to page 553 of the "Stats" section.

WESLEYAN UNIVERSITY

The Stewart M. Reid House, 70 Wyllys Avenue, Middletown, CT 06459-0265 • Admissions: 860-685-3000 • Fax: 860-685-3001
Financial Aid: 860-685-2800 • E-mail: admissions@wesleyan.edu • Website: www.wesleyan.edu

Ratings
Quality of Life: 82   Academic: 93   Admissions: 97   Financial Aid: 96

Academics

Prestigious Wesleyan University serves a unique demographic. Students tell us it is "a place for those wacky hippie types who would be interested in participating in a Jewish a cappella group, coteaching at a high school, working towards a 'third path' to break outside of the current binary Israel/Palestine debate, singing in the campus gospel choir, and starring in a rock opera in which he/she/ze runs across the stage screaming his/her/hir lines

wearing nothing but yellow suspenders and a rainbow-colored belt; or, for those who like a good film department." Actually, others find a comfortable niche at Wesleyan as well, but those who love it mostly fall into the general category implied above: creative, active, extremely bright, and more than a little liberal. Undergraduates are a demanding lot. Fortunately, their school delivers, offering solid academics, attentive professors, and a caring (if not always accommodating) administration. Professors "tend to be brilliant. For example, my chemistry teacher can talk intelligently about chemistry, as well as advanced physics, mathematics, and literature. There is an amazing level of experience there. My academic experience has so far been wonderful," explains an undergrad. Coursework is tough. As one student puts it, "The only complaint I have about academics at Wesleyan is that my classes constantly interfere with my extracurricular activities, which is to say classes are hard!" Fortunately, "professors are very encouraging and they want to see their students succeed. They are almost always available if you need to talk to them about homework, a test, or just need help."

Life

Students at Wesleyan "work very hard, but they also know when to have fun. There are parties, concerts, plays, movies, dances, games, protests, and anything else you can think of nearly every time you turn around." There are also "so many different student groups on campus that a lot of people are involved in. These include every activist group you could imagine, many student-run dance groups, a storytelling club, a cappella groups galore, improvisational comedy, etc. There are lots of performances to go to on weekends." And, of course, there are parties, some "big frat parties" and lots of "small parties at students' houses. The wood frame houses that are given to upperclassmen make for a great house party scene." This scene, while active, is not out of hand. "There are definitely a lot of people here who drink, smoke pot, and trip, but no one will ever look down on you if you don't do any of these things," one student tells us. Overall, the "good amount of stuff going on on campus [helps] make up for the relative lack of activity in Middletown," which students say is "not a ghost town, but not a big city, either. It doesn't offer much in the way of entertainment."

Student Body

Thanks to the efforts of its fine admissions department, Wesleyan's student population is one of the most diverse in the nation among highly selective universities. Students recognize the benefits of such a population, telling us, "Wesleyan's greatest strength is its diverse student body. The huge range of perspectives and the intellectual hunger make Wes the vibrant and amazing community that it is." The high degree of selectivity means "Wesleyan students have got their [you-know-what] together like no one you ever meet. They're those ideal college kids who are every bit as intellectual and driven as any Ivy Leaguer, every bit as snobby about it as a Reed student, every bit as hip as a RISD student, and yet as crunchy and earthy as a UC—Berkeley student. It's a campus of total badass intellectuals." Politically, students say, "The atmosphere is open to many views, as long as they're radical."

ADMISSIONS

Very important factors considered include: Class rank, secondary school record. *Important factors considered include:* Alumni/ae relation, character/personal qualities, essays, extracurricular activities, minority status, recommendations, standardized test scores, talent/ability, volunteer work. *Other factors considered include:* Geographical residence, interview, work experience. SAT Reasoning and SAT Subject Tests or ACT required. TOEFL required of all international applicants. High school diploma is required, and GED is not accepted. *Academic units required:* 4 English, 3 math, 3 science, 3 foreign language, 3 social studies. *Academic units recommended:* 4 math, 4 science (3 science lab), 4 foreign language, 4 social studies.

The Inside Word

Wesleyan stacks up well against its very formidable competitors academically, yet due to these same competitors the university admits at a fairly high rate for an institution of its high caliber. Candidate evaluation is nonetheless rigorous. If you aren't one of the best students in your graduating class, it isn't likely that you will be very competitive in Wesleyan's applicant pool. Strong communicators can help open the doors by submitting persuasive essays and interviews that clearly demonstrate an effective match with the university.

FINANCIAL AID

Students should submit: FAFSA, CSS/Financial Aid PROFILE, noncustodial (divorced/separated) parents' statement, business/farm supplement. Regular filing deadline 2/1. The Princeton Review suggests that all financial aid forms be submitted as soon as possible after 1/1. *Need-based scholarships/grants offered:* Pell, SEOG, state scholarships/grants, private scholarships, the school's own gift aid. *Loan aid offered:* FFEL Subsidized Stafford, FFEL Unsubsidized Stafford, FFEL PLUS, Federal Perkins, college/university loans from institutional funds. Applicants will be notified of awards on or about 4/1. Federal Work-study Program available. Off-campus job opportunities are good.

FROM THE ADMISSIONS OFFICE

"Wesleyan faculty believe in an education that is flexible and affords individual freedom and that a strong liberal arts education is the best foundation for success in any endeavor. The broad curriculum focuses on essential communication skills and analytical abilities through course content and teaching methodology, allowing students to pursue their intellectual interests with passion while honing those capabilities. As a result, Wesleyan students achieve a very personalized but broad education. Wesleyan's dean of admission and financial aid, Nancy Hargrave Meislahn, describes the qualities Wesleyan seeks in its students: 'Our very holistic process seeks to identify academically accomplished and intellectually curious students who can thrive in Wesleyan's rigorous and vibrant academic environment; we look for personal strengths, accomplishments, and potential for real contribution to our diverse community.'"

For even more information on this school, turn to page 554 of the "Stats" section.

WEST CHESTER UNIVERSITY OF PENNSYLVANIA

MESSIKOMER HALL, 100 W. ROSEDALE AVENUE, WEST CHESTER, PA 19383 • ADMISSIONS: 610-436-3411
FAX: 610-436-2907 • E-MAIL: UGADMISS@WCUPA.EDU • WEBSITE: WWW.WCUPA.EDU

Ratings
Quality of Life: 74   Academic: 72   Admissions: 80   Financial Aid: 60

Academics

West Chester University of Pennsylvania, a public school that students describe as "small enough and large enough," provides its undergraduates with "a large selection of majors and academics [in] classes that are small enough for you to get individual attention." WCU's "excellent" education programs include solid offerings in music education, physical education ("If you want to be a gym teacher, this place is heaven," writes one student), and special education. Business-related disciplines, sports medicine, and psychology are also popular; chemistry majors brag, "The faculty is phenomenal, as are our lab and research facilities. As undergrads, we get first-hand experience with any and all instrumentation and also have the opportunity to conduct research." In most areas, professors are "so helpful and understanding. [Students] never feel like [they] are in the dark or haven't learned all [they] could." One undergrad explains, "The professors and teachers here really want to see every student succeed, and if you show your dedication to their class, then they will help you in every way possible." Students also appreciate how WCU "really stresses internships. For most departments, [students] must have an internship to graduate." In all these ways, WCU helps undergraduates "get the education needed to further their career in life."

> ### SURVEY SAYS . . .
> Small classes
> Students love West Chester, PA
> Great off-campus food
> Frats and sororities dominate social scene
> Lots of beer drinking
> Hard liquor is popular
> (Almost) everyone smokes

Life

West Chester's location "is perfect," students tell us. One student adds, "Unlike other state schools, West Chester is close to a lot of fun places, including Philadelphia, King of Prussia Mall, and Exton Mall. Downtown West Chester is beautiful and is filled with restaurants, bars, and shops. One could definitely find something to do there on a Friday or Saturday night." The proximity to Philly suits WCU's many pro sports fanatics; "the Phillies, the 76ers, and the Eagles have a huge base of fans here at West Chester," undergrads report. The school is also located close to where most students grew up, and as a result "West Chester is a 'suitcase' school, meaning over 50 percent of the students living in the dorms go home on the weekends." Because the WCU campus "is very clean and doesn't tolerate the underage drinking, parties are all at off-campus houses. Most of the student off-campus living is concentrated in the same area, so it's a community of your peers." One student reports, "The school has a lot of students that party just like any other school, but the school also does its part to make sure that doesn't get out of control. I appreciate how my school handles situations." A "great student activities association" guarantees that "there is always something fun going on" for those who want to stay on campus.

Student Body

"Being so close to a big city like Philadelphia, it is not surprising [that] WCU is a very diverse community," students inform us. "Many kids do come from the city and its surrounding area. Others come from Southern New Jersey. Many come from the counties to the west like Lancaster, York, and Dauphin." WCU undergrads "are pretty much friendly. Students hang out with other students that they associate with, not really by race or gender but by some exterior thing that they have in common, such as a campus organization or residence halls. Because of the many different student organizations on campus and the extent that all of them seem to interact together, you get to meet a lot of different people."

ADMISSIONS

Very important factors considered include: Class rank, secondary school record. *Important factors considered include:* Essays, standardized test scores. *Other factors considered include:* Character/personal qualities, extracurricular activities, minority status, state residency, talent/ability, volunteer work, work experience. SAT Reasoning or ACT required. TOEFL required of all international applicants. High school diploma is required, and GED is accepted. *Academic units required:* 4 English, 3 math, 2 science (1 science lab), 4 history, 3 academic electives. *Academic units recommended:* 4 English, 4 math, 3 science (2 science lab), 2 foreign language, 4 history, 4 academic electives.

The Inside Word

Students from up and down the Northeast Corridor converge on WCU as much for its campus energy as for its strength in the social sciences. Its proximity to Philly and the Big Apple make it attractive for both homebodies and those with wanderlust.

FINANCIAL AID

Students should submit: FAFSA. The Princeton Review suggests that all financial aid forms be submitted as soon as possible after 1/1. *Need-based scholarships/grants offered:* Pell, SEOG, state scholarships/grants, private scholarships, the school's own gift aid. *Loan aid offered:* FFEL Subsidized Stafford, FFEL Unsubsidized Stafford, FFEL PLUS, Federal Perkins, Federal Nursing, state loans. Applicants will be notified of awards on a rolling basis beginning on or about 4/15. Federal Work-study Program available. Institutional employment available. Off-campus job opportunities are good.

FROM THE ADMISSIONS OFFICE

"West Chester University (WCU) has an enrollment of almost 13,000 students, is the second largest of the 14 institutions in the Pennsylvania State System of Higher Education, and the fourth-largest university in the Philadelphia metropolitan area. While the university attracts the majority of its students from Pennsylvania, News Jersey, and Delaware, it also enrolls students from all over the U.S. and over 50 countries. It has become increasingly selective; WCU received more than 10,400 applications for the 1,880 spaces in the fall 2004 freshman class.

"The College of Arts and Sciences offers 40 undergraduate degree programs, including a premedical program, which has placed 95 percent of its graduates in medical schools over the past 24 years. The College of Business and Public Affairs is recognized locally for its assistance to the business community. WCU had the second-best pass rate in the state for first-time candidates of the CPA exam in 1999 and has been number two for seven of the past 13 years. The College of Visual and Performing Arts School of Music offers students the opportunity to learn from and play with award-winning faculty, as well as the opportunity to experiment in the Center for Music Technology, where computers offer another aspect of music education. The College of Health Sciences offers a wide range of programs from public health and nursing to sports medicine. The College of Education prepares more teachers than any other institution in southeastern Pennsylvania.

"Numerous campus groups in music, theatre, athletics, and other activities as well as clubs, fraternities, sororities, service organizations, and honor societies provide students with the opportunity to participate in a full range of programs. The university offers 23 intercollegiate sports and 11 club sports for men and women. WCU offers other innovations as well, including free room and board during summer sessions for those who take a minimum of six credits. The program was proclaimed a 'Great Deal' by *Time* magazine."

For even more information on this school, turn to page 554 of the "Stats" section.

WESTMINSTER COLLEGE (PA)

319 SOUTH MARKET STREET, NEW WILMINGTON, PA 16172 • ADMISSIONS: 800-942-8033
FAX: 724-946-7171 • FINANCIAL AID: 724-946-7102 • E-MAIL: ADMIS@WESTMINSTER.EDU • WEBSITE: WWW.WESTMINSTER.EDU

Ratings
Quality of Life: 78   Academic: 82   Admissions: 80   Financial Aid: 84

Academics

At most schools, if your alarm clock doesn't go off the morning of your final exam, you miss the test, fail the class, and enter therapy. Not so for a freshman at Westminster: "I received a phone call from my professor at quarter after nine saying, 'The exam has started! Where are you? Get down here!'" This type of personal attention is the norm at Westminster, where students site the faculty and adminis-

> **SURVEY SAYS . . .**
> *Small classes*
> *Students are friendly*
> *Frats and sororities dominate social scene*
> *Lots of beer drinking*

trators as one of the school's greatest assets. "My sister who had just graduated introduced me to the professors in her education major. They hugged me, shook my hand, and treated me like family." Clearly, many of the teachers here "relate well to the students and their needs," cultivating a "personal and comfortable atmosphere in the classroom," which extends outside of class as well. It's not unusual to be invited to a professor's house for a meal; even the president hosts picnics and dinners to get to know the students. A sophomore now majoring in communications was appreciative when "the Dean of Academic Affairs took me under his wing last year because I was undecided." Undergrads aspiring to be doctors one day hope to cash in on the school's exceptional medical school acceptance rates. But they don't complete the premed program easily; these students will tell you that "slacking is not an option." Other top programs include English, business, elementary education, and music. In addition, "the education experience in physics here competes with some of the biggest name schools, even though we lack equipment and opportunity." Overall, the Westminster academic experience aims to "expand your views on the world" and make students "think more clearly and analytically." The Career Center "offers amazing career placements, and they are always willing to help students improve resumes and job skills." A graduating senior sums it up well, saying her school is "loaded with people looking to make each student's life a little easier."

Life

"People think we don't do anything here because our college is located in a small, dry town." Rural New Wilmington shuts down at 7:00 P.M., precluding much excitement "unless an Amish revolt should break out." Most people head to nearby megalopolises Grove City and New Castle "because this town is stuck in 1950." On-campus activities occasionally suffer from low attendance, but movies and sports draw a crowd. Religious students take part in "varied opportunities for Christian fellowship and worship. There are organizations for athletes; Gospel Choir and Praise Band for singers and musicians; and Bible study groups, chapel services, a weekly informal, student-led worship, and weekly Vespers for everyone else." Though the campus is "supposedly dry," students still find a way to drink. "I feel that by following the rules and applying myself to my studies I am in the minority of kids who take college seriously," reports a resident assistant. Several students comment that rivalries between fraternities and tensions between Greeks and independent students have been overemphasized in the past. They claim all groups come together "for fun and philanthropy." A chorus of voices also agree that both the food and the parking situations could use some improvement.

Student Body

Westminster students jump to point out that "things have really improved here in terms of diversity, especially in the past two years." For example, "there has been a dramatic spike in the number of open homosexuals and people who support that community. A gay student was even elected as homecoming king." On the other hand, many still complain that the small percentage of minorities is disheartening. Undergraduates separate into straight-laced religious types, rowdy bacchanalian slackers, and a few black-clad "protestors of modern society." Most are Caucasian and come from rural towns in western Ohio or eastern Pennsylvania—with a few Pittsburgh suburbanites mixed in—and families with money and college degrees. Many respondents emphasize "the interpersonal aspect" of the community—the say-hi-to-everyone culture, rooted in Christian conservative values without being all the way religious right.

ADMISSIONS

Very important factors considered include: Interview, secondary school record, standardized test scores. *Important factors considered include:* Character/personal qualities, class rank, essays, recommendations. *Other factors considered include:* Alumni/ae relation, extracurricular activities, minority status, talent/ability, volunteer work, work experience. SAT Reasoning or ACT required. TOEFL required of all international applicants. High school diploma is required, and GED is accepted. *Academic units required:* 4 English, 3 math, 2 science (2 science lab), 2 foreign language, 2 social studies, 1 history, 3 academic electives.

The Inside Word

The vast majority of those who apply to Westminster gain admission, but the applicant pool is strong enough to enable the college to weed out those who don't measure up to the solid entering class academic profile. Candidates who are shooting for academic scholarships should play the admissions game all the way and put a solid effort into the completion of their applications.

FINANCIAL AID

Students should submit: FAFSA, institution's own financial aid form. The Princeton Review suggests that all financial aid forms be submitted as soon as possible after 1/1. *Need-based scholarships/grants offered:* Pell, SEOG, state scholarships/grants, private scholarships, the school's own gift aid. *Loan aid offered:* FFEL Subsidized Stafford, FFEL Unsubsidized Stafford, FFEL PLUS, Federal Perkins. Federal Work-study Program available. Off-campus job opportunities are good.

FROM THE ADMISSIONS OFFICE

"Since its founding, Westminster has been dedicated to a solid foundation in today's most crucial social, cultural, and ethical issues. Related to the Presbyterian Church (U.S.A.), Westminster is home to people of many faiths. Our students and faculty, tradition of campus, and small-town setting all contribute to an enlightening educational experience."

For even more information on this school, turn to page 554 of the "Stats" section.

WHEATON COLLEGE (MA)

OFFICE OF ADMISSION, NORTON, MA 02766 • ADMISSIONS: 508-286-8251 • FAX: 508-286-8271
FINANCIAL AID: 508-286-8232 • E-MAIL: ADMISSION@WHEATONCOLLEGE.EDU • WEBSITE: WWW.WHEATONCOLLEGE.EDU

Ratings
Quality of Life: 69   **Academic:** 91   **Admissions:** 92   **Financial Aid:** 83

Academics

"The greatest strengths of Wheaton are the opportunities that come as a result of being such a small school," students at this New England liberal arts stronghold agree. Those opportunities include "close relationships with faculty, chances to study something independently if the subject is not specifically offered," and the encouragement students receive, "for studying abroad and getting internships,

> **SURVEY SAYS . . .**
> *Small classes*
> *Frats and sororities are unpopular*
> *or nonexistent*
> *Lots of beer drinking*

which is really awesome at the undergraduate level." Students get personal-touch treatment from the moment they arrive. Their first academic experience is the First Year Seminar, "in which students learn to read, write, and study at a college level. It serves as an introductory course for the way most classes will run. The professor of this course will be the student's advisor until that student declares his/her major...Each first-year student is also assigned two upper-class students who serve as mentors to the freshmen, guiding them through their adjustments to college life and answering any questions that need answering. The transition into college life couldn't have been easier because of this program." The personal attention continues right through to graduation and beyond, with help from the exceptional Filene Center, "a career and job placement services office that is the best institution available to students and graduates of Wheaton. It opens many doors for students to obtain internships as well as jobs after college, and from freshman year on they help you build your resume and interests." The school's size also has its drawbacks; "It is very difficult to get into the classes of your choice here, especially if you are a psychology major," warns a student in one of the school's more popular majors.

Life

"Wheaton is cursed by geography," students agree, complaining that hometown Norton "has nothing to offer college students." Couple this with the school's aggressively enforced dry-campus policy and you can see why "Wheaton is a suitcase school. Too many people go home on the weekends, and college shouldn't be like that." Students wish it were otherwise. "You don't get the full experience by going home every weekend," grouses one. On the up side, the school is making efforts to address the situation. One undergrad explains, "The school has tried having dances and more on-campus events, but the reality of it is that campus life over the weekend here will never be fabulous." As a result, students bug out on Fridays, "going into Boston and Providence for dinner or just to hang out." Things are pretty busy during the week, as "there are over 50 student run organizations on campus. Literally, there is something for everybody, and if you don't find a club for you, start one! The process is very easy!" Weekends, however, are a different story. Also, "athletics are a big part of life here, since such a big proportion of students are athletes." A few students note the benefits of living in quiet seclusion: "Our small, suburban town means that students concentrate on their studies, sans distractions, on a beautiful campus," explains one undergrad.

Student Body

"There are no 'typical' students on campus, unless you count white, upper-middle class, sweater-and-jeans wearing, white-teeth blazing, upstanding men and women," jokes a typical Wheatie. This same student adds that "realistically, we are a predominately wealthy, educated student body whose parents are usually educated as well. We have a pitifully small racial and ethnic population, and those who are diverse tend to group together." A former women's school, Wheaton is still predominantly female. Observes one male, "I can't complain about the male to female ratio—67 percent female is 67 percent female no matter how you look at it. The benefits...just think about the benefits." Most undergraduates "fall into the category of liberal when it comes to many issues [and] are very intellectually and artistically active. Students are really encouraged to explore their interests and passions here," regardless of the health impact. "Almost 100 percent of the campus exercises regularly, [yet] many students smoke like chimneys."

ADMISSIONS

Very important factors considered include: Character/personal qualities, essays, extracurricular activities, secondary school record, talent/ability. *Important factors considered include:* Alumni/ae relation, class rank, interview, recommendations, volunteer work, work experience. *Other factors considered include:* Geographical residence, minority status, state residency. TOEFL required of all international applicants. High school diploma is required, and GED is accepted. *Academic units recommended:* 4 English, 4 math, 3 science (2 science lab), 4 foreign language, 2 social studies.

The Inside Word

Wheaton is to be applauded for periodically re-examining its admissions process; some colleges use virtually the same application process eternally, never acknowledging the fluid nature of societal attitudes and institutional circumstances. Approaches that emphasize individuals, or even their accomplishments, over their numbers are unfortunately rare in the world of college admission, where GPA and SAT I reign supreme. Wheaton has an easier time than some colleges in taking this step because it isn't prohibitively selective.

FINANCIAL AID

Students should submit: FAFSA, CSS/Financial Aid PROFILE, noncustodial (divorced/separated) parents' statement, business/farm supplement, parent and student federal tax returns and W-2 forms. Regular filing deadline 2/1. The Princeton Review suggests that all financial aid forms be submitted as soon as possible after 1/1. *Need-based scholarships/grants offered:* Pell, SEOG, state scholarships/grants, private scholarships, the school's own gift aid. *Loan aid offered:* FFEL Subsidized Stafford, FFEL Unsubsidized Stafford, FFEL PLUS, Federal Perkins, state loans, MEFA, TERI, CitiAssist, Signature, and other private loans. Applicants will be notified of awards on or about 4/1. Federal Work-study Program available. Institutional employment available. Off-campus job opportunities are good.

FROM THE ADMISSIONS OFFICE

"What makes for a 'best college'? Is it merely the hard-to-define notions of prestige or image? We don't think so. We think what makes college 'best' and best for you is a school that will make you a first-rate thinker and writer, a pragmatic professional in your work, and an ethical practitioner in your life. To get you to all these places, Wheaton takes advantage of its great combinations: a beautiful, secluded New England campus combined with access to Boston and Providence; a high quality, classic liberal arts and sciences curriculum combined with award-winning internship, job, and community service programs; and a campus that respects your individuality in the context of the larger community. What's the 'best' outcome of a Wheaton education? A start on life that combines meaningful work, significant relationships, and a commitment to your local and global community. Far more than for what they've studied or for what they've gone on to do for a living, we're most proud of Wheaton graduates for who they become."

For even more information on this school, turn to page 555 of the "Stats" section.

WIDENER UNIVERSITY

ONE UNIVERSITY PLACE, CHESTER, PA 19013 • ADMISSIONS: 610-499-4126 • FAX: 610-499-4676
E-MAIL: ADMISSIONS.OFFICE@WIDENER.EDU • WEBSITE: WWW.WIDENER.EDU

Ratings
Quality of Life: 61   Academic: 76   Admissions: 70   Financial Aid: 73

Academics

Students at Widener University, a small university just outside Philadelphia, speak highly of their school's offerings in a variety of professional areas. Programs in engineering, computer science, hospitality management, nursing, and business were all singled out for praise by respondents to our survey. Regardless of the area of study, students tell us that "the academics at the school are always what come first. The administration and professors are always trying to help the students succeed." One undergraduate says, "Widener is a very tough school, but there are many sources available to help you in addition to your professors, like tutors, a writing help center, and a math help center. I really feel at home here, like people are looking out for me and I'm not just another number lost in the bunch at a huge school." Upper-level administrators, including the president, "come to events and talks to the students. Most administrators on campus are willing to help you with your problems." That's a good thing, since "certain aspects of the school, like housing, registration, and financial aid, could be run much more smoothly."

Life

"Weekends are weak," at Widener University, mostly because many residents and all the commuters (about one-third of the student body) disappear come Friday afternoon, and many of "the small number of people who stay on weekends spends the whole time drinking," explains one student. Another student advises, "If you decide to attend Widener, it would be wise to purchase a car." Despite strong efforts on the school's part to provide alcohol-free events every weekend (including trips to sporting events, DJs, and marathons), one of the woebegone car-less students adds, "Often times we simply hang out in our rooms because there is nothing else to do." While Philly and all that a major metropolis has to offer ("South Street, bars in the Old City, clubs, art museums, [and] the list goes on") are just a scant ten-minute car ride away, hometown Chester is merely "a small, economically-depressed city in Southeastern Pennsylvania." The school tries to provide some distraction. One student writes, "The student government always has discount tickets to see plays, movies, and sporting events in Philadelphia." In this regard, Widener's one area of unqualified success is its competitive sports teams. One student brags, "Our football, men's cross-country, and track teams are always near the top in the Middle-Atlantic Conference!" Another student adds, "The campus is beautiful, and it is not uncommon to see a large number of students outside playing sports."

Student Body

Widener draws much of its student body from the area immediately surrounding Philadelphia. One student explains, "The typical student at Widener is an average white kid from a suburb of Philadelphia, Delaware, or New Jersey. There's a strong chance that he or she attended a Catholic high school." Widener undergraduates tend to be fairly well-off, conservative, and politically apathetic, though the school is making concerted efforts to increase student diversity. Many of them are strongly committed to community service and passionate about athletics. Social cliques develop around students' extracurricular interests. One student says, "Most here are involved in a club, sport, or Greek organization. Whichever club, sport, or Greek organization you are involved in most likely makes up your circle of friends."

ADMISSIONS

Very important factors considered include: Secondary school record, standardized test scores. *Important factors considered include:* Class rank. *Other factors considered include:* Alumni/ae relation, character/personal qualities, essays, extracurricular activities, interview, recommendations. SAT Reasoning or ACT required. TOEFL required of all international applicants. High school diploma is required, and GED is not accepted. *Academic units required:* 4 English, 3 math, 3 science, 2 foreign language, 4 social studies, 3 academic electives. *Academic units recommended:* 4 English, 4 math, 4 science (3 science lab), 2 foreign language, 4 social studies, 3 academic electives.

The Inside Word

Widener is a "safety school" for a lot of students who wind up somewhere more competitive. Communicating clearly to the school that Widener is your first choice would definitely help your chances of gaining admission.

FINANCIAL AID

Students should submit: FAFSA, institution's own financial aid form. The Princeton Review suggests that all financial aid forms be submitted as soon as possible after 1/1. *Need-based scholarships/grants offered:* Pell, SEOG, state scholarships/grants, private scholarships, the school's own gift aid. *Loan aid offered:* FFEL Subsidized Stafford, FFEL Unsubsidized Stafford, FFEL PLUS, Federal Perkins. Applicants will be notified of awards on a rolling basis beginning on or about 3/15. Off-campus job opportunities are good.

FROM THE ADMISSIONS OFFICE

"As an entrepreneurial, metropolitan university with an undergraduate enrollment of 2,400 and total student population of more than 6,000, Widener offers the resources of a large research institution within the context of a small academic community. Admission to Widener University is considered competitive. Applicants undergo individual evaluation to determine their potential for academic success. The university bases its decision on the strength of academic preparation, achievement, recommendations, extracurricular activities, personal qualifications, and the pattern of testing on the Scholastic Assessment Test (SAT) of the College Entrance Examination Board (CEEB) or the American College Test (ACT). Excluding those being considered for enrollment in special programs, candidates for admission must be graduates of approved secondary schools. Applicants should also meet additional recommendations for specific degree programs.

"The university gives consideration for admission as early action applicants to students with strong three-year academic records, SAT I scores, and recommendations. Applicants who meet these criteria should submit their applications no later than December 1. Early action applicants will receive an admission decision after 12/15. Students who apply for regular admission for the fall semester will be notified of their admission decision after2/15. Applications received after the priority application deadline of 2/15 will be notified on a rolling basis.

"Widener University welcomes students who wish to transfer from other colleges and universities. Transfer students are given the same consideration as other students for financial aid and campus housing. The university also invites the matriculation of students from other nations."

For even more information on this school, turn to page 555 of the "Stats" section.

WILKES UNIVERSITY

84 W SOUTH ST, WILKES-BARRE, PA 18766 • ADMISSIONS: 570-408-4400 • FAX: 570-408-4904
E-MAIL: ADMISSIONS@WILKES.EDU • WEBSITE: WWW.WILKES.EDU

Ratings
Quality of Life: 61   **Academic:** 71   **Admissions:** 73   **Financial Aid:** 75

Academics

If Wilkes University were a stock and its prospectus credible, now would be the time to invest: Over the next decade, the small, independent, eastern Pennsylvania university looks to increase its ethnic, geographic, and curricular diversity and augment its national reputation by a considerably greater proportion. Students at Wilkes are already noticing the change, reporting improvements to programs in engineering, business, psychology, and the school's most prominent offering: pre-pharmacy, which often leads into

> **SURVEY SAYS . . .**
> *Small classes*
> *Frats and sororities are unpopular*
> *or nonexistent*
> *Lots of beer drinking*
> *Hard liquor is popular*
> *(Almost) everyone smokes*

admission into the professional Nesbitt School of Pharmacy. Some students complain that the upgrades are coming at the expense of other, less sexy departments. "The pharmacy program gets all of the benefits," grouses one undergrad. Growing pains aside, Wilkes undergraduates generally speak very warmly of their school, describing it as "a small, friendly, welcoming community, mixed with excellent academic programs." One student says, "There is always a friendly face, be it a student, faculty member, or staff member, to help you through any problems you may have, and if you involve yourself in the many programs that are offered, you are sure to have a great college experience. Down to earth [professors] really try to help you; they are here for you. The best part is that there is a requirement of five hours for office hours, but every teacher that I have had has been there more." The cherry on the sundae is the widespread perception that "most people honestly care about [a student's] success at Wilkes."

Life

"If you are into partying, there is a wide range to pick from" at Wilkes University, students tell us. Partying is hardly all that goes on, although hometown Wilkes-Barre offers little in the way of an alternative. Although city leaders do have plans in the works to develop the downtown area to cater more towards student needs, students still claim that "there really isn't much to do around here [except go to the mall, and] if you want to get there you need a car." Fortunately, campus organizations pick up some of the slack. One student writes, "The student activities club here is extremely active and puts on a lot of great events, so there is always something to do or friends to see, especially on the weekends, [including] discounted movie tickets almost every Friday, comedians and bands, dances for Homecoming and spring, and a Block Party at the end of the year." Another undergraduate agrees, "The more involved you become the better the campus seems to be." Students are also well-known for being actively involved in community service. A few students feel that "Wilkes University could improve itself greatly by instituting the Greek system. This would allow for an actual social life to be instituted with opportunities for students to meet and interact with others like themselves."

Student Body

Students at Wilkes notice a definite dividing line running through their ranks. "There are two types of typical student," explains one undergrad. "There are those who go to class, have fun, but still get their academics done. And then there are those who don't care about class and spend their college life goofing off. There are generally more of the first type." Another student agrees, "There is a good population of serious students with imaginative goals for their future." All students tend to be preppy. One student says, "I sometimes feel that the average Wilkes student was cut out of an American Eagle mold." However, another student adds, "As far as personality and background of students here, there is a lot of diversity. A lot of freshman come in and feel like they're the outcast and are afraid of 'making contact.' Come mid-freshman year, they realize that everyone is in the same boat as them and everyone basically gets along."

ADMISSIONS

Very important factors considered include: Class rank, secondary school record. *Important factors considered include:* Character/personal qualities, extracurricular activities, interview, recommendations, standardized test scores. *Other factors considered include:* Alumni/ae relation, essays, talent/ability, volunteer work, work experience. SAT Reasoning or ACT required. TOEFL required of all international applicants. High school diploma is required, and GED is accepted. *Academic units required:* 4 English, 3 math, 2 science (2 science lab), 3 social studies, 2 history. *Academic units recommended:* 4 English, 4 math, 4 science (2 science lab), 2 foreign language, 2 social studies, 2 history.

The Inside Word

Wilkes processes applications on a rolling basis and typically renders decisions within two weeks of receiving all application materials. For those who can't stand the suspense of waiting until April, here's your chance to be done with the application process by mid-December.

FINANCIAL AID

Students should submit: FAFSA, institution's own financial aid form. The Princeton Review suggests that all financial aid forms be submitted as soon as possible after 1/1. *Need-based scholarships/grants offered:* Pell, SEOG, state scholarships/grants, private scholarships, the school's own gift aid. *Loan aid offered:* FFEL Subsidized Stafford, FFEL Unsubsidized Stafford, FFEL PLUS, Federal Perkins, Federal Nursing, state loans, college/university loans from institutional funds. Applicants will be notified of awards on a rolling basis beginning on or about 3/1. Federal Work-study Program available. Institutional employment available. Off-campus job opportunities are good.

FROM THE ADMISSIONS OFFICE

"As our students reported, "people honestly care about [a student's] success at Wilkes." This is the basis for deep and meaningful relationships between students and faculty members. Students conduct independent research under the direction of active, faculty scholars. Faculty members can be found interacting with their students in the cafeteria, at campus activities and sporting events, and in the hallways of the academic buildings, as well as in their offices and homes.

"These mentoring relationships, which extend from professional guidance to personal direction, blossom over four years, but don't end at graduation. Instead, alumni report that they stay in contact with their faculty members throughout their professional careers. Consider this recent event. During winter break, one professor drove two senior students to Boston to visit graduate schools. Upon arrival, they met with a Wilkes alumna, herself a former advisee of this professor, who shared her experiences with them. As our students say, "[professors] really try to help you; they are here for you."

"In choosing our students, we look for students who want to actively engage in their personal and professional development. To do so, we look at the entire individual: the academic record and strength of curriculum, community service and active extracurricular life, career goals and motivation for success. Successful students are those who want to learn in collaboration with their peers and professors. They also energetically participate in campus life because they know that learning takes place both in and outside the classroom."

For even more information on this school, turn to page 556 of the "Stats" section.

WILLIAM PATERSON UNIVERSITY

OFFICE OF ADMISSION, 300 POMPTON ROAD, WAYNE, NJ 07470 • ADMISSIONS: 973-720-2125
FAX: 973-720-2910 • E-MAIL: ADMISSIONS@WPUNJ.EDU • WEBSITE: WWW.WPUNJ.EDU

Ratings
Quality of Life: 61   Academic: 66   Admissions: 70   Financial Aid: 69

Academics

William Paterson University is an affordable public school with a friendly, student-oriented teaching staff. The education and nursing programs are well-regarded here, as well as the newly AACSB-accredited Cotsakos College of Business. But students in just about every department say they benefit from William Paterson's attractive combination of low price and quality teaching. With less than 10,000 undergraduates, William Paterson maintains "good class sizes," which makes

it is easy for students to establish direct contact with their instructors, whom they describe as "highly educated and intelligent individuals." In addition, professors are "very personable and nice" and committed to "helping students grow individually and intellectually." They "generally care about their students, and it shows." But while the academic experience at William Paterson is very personal, the bureaucracy is dizzying. A senior explains, "The potential here is enormous, but only when the university truly puts the students first and we are more than numbers." In a similar vein, many of the evening and commuter students feel that the university is not sensitive to their unique situation. One suggests that it "be more actively involved with night students and older students. Have more activities and programs readily available." The university hopes to answer these complaints with a Student Information Center and the newly established Commuter Services department.

Life

From study groups and academic clubs, to movie nights and parties, you can find every aspect of the classic college experience at William Paterson. With so many activities and commitments, life at William Paterson "is about balancing school work and social time." One freshman writes that "life at school is very busy. I'm always on the go—either going to class, meetings, or just out with friends." A junior shares a similar experience, "The typical student is constantly on the move, whether it be going to class or going to study, or going to club meetings." If you like to have a good time, you'll fit right in at William Paterson because come the weekend, students say you're likely to find them at a bar, club, or party with their outgoing classmates. Students warn, however, that "this school is a place where you have to make your own fun," as the university provides few social options and activities (though the Student Center is undergoing major renovations). Suggests a senior, "Campus life is okay, but if the school provided more activities for students, I think campus life would be a lot more exciting and fun."

Student Body

Hailing from across the Garden State, the student body at William Paterson represents a wide range of backgrounds, interests, and experiences; "The school prides itself on diversity and rightly so. People of ethnicity hang out and share experiences all the time," writes a senior. Nonetheless, there are large groups of like-minded students, many of whom tend to stick together socially. Older students are especially aware of such clique-forming; they claim that younger, traditional students dominate the student body, causing them to feel like outsiders. Still, most students agree that their campus is generally very friendly and social; one freshman writes, "The typical student is one who walks around campus with friends by their side, talking and having a good time before and after class."

ADMISSIONS

Very important factors considered include: Secondary school record, standardized test scores. *Important factors considered include:* Class rank. *Other factors considered include:* Alumni/ae relation, character/personal qualities, essays, extracurricular activities, minority status, recommendations, talent/ability, volunteer work. SAT Reasoning or ACT required. TOEFL required of all international applicants. High school diploma is required, and GED is accepted. *Academic units required:* 4 English, 3 math, 2 science (2 science lab), 2 social studies. Additional college preparatory courses (in advanced math, literature, foreign language, and social science) are also required.

The Inside Word

Variety is the spice of life at WPU, where opportunities enable all types of students to satisfy their academic goals. Its location also enables students to tap into the environment that suits them socially, either on or off campus, where New York City awaits.

FINANCIAL AID

Students should submit: FAFSA. Regular filing deadline 4/1. The Princeton Review suggests that all financial aid forms be submitted as soon as possible after 1/1. *Need-based scholarships/grants offered:* Pell, SEOG, state scholarships/grants, the school's own gift aid. *Loan aid offered:* Direct Subsidized Stafford, Direct Unsubsidized Stafford, Direct PLUS, Federal Perkins. Applicants will be notified of awards on a rolling basis beginning on or about 3/1. Federal Work-study Program available. Institutional employment available. Off-campus job opportunities are excellent.

FROM THE ADMISSIONS OFFICE

"William Paterson University's 370-acre, wooded hilltop campus in Wayne, New Jersey, encompasses more than 38 buildings, and a sleek glass-covered Atrium stands within sight of a nineteenth-century Victorian mansion, Hobart Manor. William Paterson has continued to grow with the recent addition of a 150,000-square-foot building set on 50 acres of scenic woodland. This building, 1600 Valley Road, is home to the E*Trade Financial Learning Center—a state-of-the-art facility featuring live real-time datafeeds of financial information. It also features the Russ Berrie Institute for Professional Sales with its advanced Professional Sales laboratory that enables students to practice sales presentations in a real-world setting. A quiet setting with a distinctive collegiate atmosphere, William Paterson University is dotted with sculpture, flowers, and even a waterfall, but is easily transformed into a flurry of activity by nearly 11,500 students. A comprehensive, public, liberal arts institution committed to academic excellence and student success, William Paterson University is accredited by the Middle States Association of Schools and Colleges. It offers 32 undergraduate and 19 graduate degree programs through its five colleges: Arts and Communication, Christos M. Cotsakos College of Business, Education, Humanities and Social Sciences, and Science and Health. William Patterson University provides unique educational offerings that combine classroom learning with real-world experiences, from faculty mentoring and internships, to hands-on research and performance opportunities. It also offers a wide variety of student activities, modern on-campus housing, and the most up-to-date educational facilities."

For even more information on this school, turn to page 556 of the "Stats" section.

WILLIAMS COLLEGE

33 STETSON COURT, WILLIAMSTOWN, MA 01267 • ADMISSIONS: 413-597-2211 • FAX: 413-597-4052
FINANCIAL AID: 413-597-4181 • E-MAIL: ADMISSIONS@WILLIAMS.EDU • WEBSITE: WWW.WILLIAMS.EDU

Ratings
Quality of Life: 96   **Academic:** 99   **Admissions:** 98   **Financial Aid:** 99

Academics

"The academics are quite rigorous—expect to spend six hours a day studying—and the professors definitely challenge you" at Williams College, a small liberal arts school in the northwestern corner of Massachusetts. Undergrads insist, however, that "that's what you come here for." A strong campus community makes Williams "a perfect stepping stone from high school to the real world. If you feel you can become obscenely excited at the sight of a purple cow (our mascot); love to get to know professors, classmates and staff on a personal level; and enjoy sports at all, be it as a spectator, athlete, or would-be athlete, Williams is your nirvana." Undergrads assure us that "there's absolutely no place better for an undergraduate to study any of the hard sciences or art history" and that "math, English, economics, and the visual and performing arts are also very strong." Coursework "really pushes you to delve deep into the material and encourages original thinking," allowing students "to learn a lot, more maybe than you even think possible." Undergrads are especially enthusiastic about Williams' winter study program, "a month where you take one relatively low-stress class and get to go snowboarding and hang out a lot. My friends and I like to think of it as our reward for having lived through finals." One student says, "Williams combines stellar academics with a beautiful campus, friendly atmosphere, and caring administration that jump to make students as happy as possible. I've never seen a happier group of people in my life."

> **SURVEY SAYS . . .**
> *Small classes*
> *Campus feels safe*
> *Everyone loves the Ephs*
> *Frats and sororities are unpopular or nonexistent*

Life

"Williams is in the middle of some very beautiful, although very isolated, countryside" in Williamstown, which "is not exactly a metropolis." Reports one student, "Because Williamstown pretty much closes at 5:00 p.m., the college knows it has to provide all of our entertainment, and it does a pretty great job of it. Movies, plays, concerts, and lectures can be found on campus almost every night of the week, and each weekend a few student organizations get $500 to throw all-campus parties." Athletics occupy the minds of many undergrads; the intercollegiate teams "are particularly strong," "intramural sports are big, as is just playing for fun," and the surrounding area is especially amenable to outdoor fun. One student notes, "We enjoy the outdoors year round. On a random Friday in October, the President continues a two-hundred-year tradition by declaring it 'Mountain Day'; classes are cancelled and the majority of the student body heads to the top of our mountain to enjoy the fall colors, the outdoors, and each other! In Winter, most everyone skis or snowboards at a local ski mountain, 15 minutes away from campus." As one student puts it, "I've never seen so many physically active people in my life. It's actually inspired me to start going to the gym." Williams' strong sense of community receives a boost from the "JA entry system, under which 15 to 25 freshmen live in 'entries' with two 'JAs.' The JAs are basically upperclassmen who volunteer to be cool junior friends to all of the frosh on campus. The entry system eases the transition from high school to college, as you have a core group of friends from the first day of school on." The dorms, we're told, "are awesome, with nice touches that make dorm life very comfortable and non-institutional."

Student Body

Williams undergrads describe themselves as "exceptionally driven and intelligent, yet not dorky or unsociable." Ephs (pronounced "Eefs," short for the school's founder, Ephraim Williams) "love politics, scientific research, reading," and for some, "getting plastered after a rough week." Because of the school's secluded mountain location, "students tend to be outdoors-types, and sports are big, although we don't have typical college 'jocks.' Everyone participates at their level. The presence of sports on campus means that most students are tremendously motivated, disciplined, and hard-working, not to mention fit." While "there is a bit of segregation between the jocks and the artsy students, there isn't ever any tension" between the two groups.

ADMISSIONS

Very important factors considered include: Essays, recommendations, secondary school record, standardized test scores. *Important factors considered include:* Class rank, extracurricular activities, talent/ability. *Other factors considered include:* Alumni/ae relation, character/personal qualities, geographical residence, minority status, volunteer work, work experience. SAT Reasoning and SAT Subject Tests or ACT required. High school diploma or equivalent is not required. *Academic units recommended:* 4 English, 4 math, 3 science (3 science lab), 4 foreign language, 3 social studies.

The Inside Word

As is typical of highly selective colleges, at Williams high grades and test scores work more as qualifiers than to determine admissibility. Beyond a strong record of achievement, evidence of intellectual curiosity, noteworthy nonacademic talents, and a noncollege family background are some aspects of a candidate's application that might make for an offer of admission. But there are no guarantees—the evaluation process here is rigorous. The admissions committee (the entire admissions staff) discusses each candidate in comparison to the entire applicant pool. The pool is divided alphabetically for individual reading; after weak candidates are eliminated, those who remain undergo additional evaluations by different members of the staff. Admission decisions must be confirmed by the agreement of a plurality of the committee. Such close scrutiny demands a well-prepared candidate and application.

FINANCIAL AID

Students should submit: FAFSA, CSS/Financial Aid PROFILE. The Princeton Review suggests that all financial aid forms be submitted as soon as possible after 1/1. *Need-based scholarships/grants offered:* Pell, SEOG, state scholarships/grants, private scholarships, the school's own gift aid. *Loan aid offered:* Direct Subsidized Stafford, Direct Unsubsidized Stafford, Direct PLUS, Federal Perkins, college/university loans from institutional funds. Applicants will be notified of awards on or about 4/1. Federal Work-study Program available. Institutional employment available. Off-campus job opportunities are fair.

FROM THE ADMISSIONS OFFICE

"Special course offerings at Williams include Oxford-style tutorials, where students (in teams of two) research and defend ideas, engaging in weekly debate with a faculty tutor. Annually 30 Williams students devote a full year to the tutorial method of study at Oxford; half of Williams students pursue overseas education. Four weeks of Winter Study each January provide time for individualized projects, research, and novel fields of study. Students compete in 32 Division III athletic teams, perform in 25 musical groups, stage 10 theatrical productions, and volunteer in 30 service organizations. The college receives several million dollars annually for undergraduate science research and equipment. The town offers two distinguished art museums, and 2,200 forest acres—complete with a treetop canopy walkway—for environmental research and recreation."

For even more information on this school, turn to page 557 of the "Stats" section.

WORCESTER POLYTECHNIC INSTITUTE

100 INSTITUTE ROAD, WORCESTER, MA 01609 • ADMISSIONS: 508-831-5286 • FAX: 508-831-5875
FINANCIAL AID: 508-831-5469 • E-MAIL: ADMISSIONS@WPI.EDU • WEBSITE: WWW.WPI.EDU

Ratings
Quality of Life: 77   **Academic:** 85   **Admissions:** 91   **Financial Aid:** 80

Academics

For "engineering taught in terms of both theory and practice, with unique opportunities and special attention paid to undergraduate students," consider Worcester Polytechnic Institute (WPI). Instruction at this student-friendly university centers on the three-project system, "which requires that each student completes three projects in order to graduate. The first is done in the humanities, the second relates science and technology with society and real-world problems, and the third is within your major." The second project, called the Interactive Project, sends

about half the student body abroad "to analyze and solve real-life problems unrelated to their major." One engineer notes, "The global projects have allowed me to gain a more realistic view of the world outside of the United States The project system also promotes gaining practical knowledge in engineering, along with group dynamics and technological problem solving and management. And you can actually help society." As at most tech schools, the workload at WPI is difficult, the challenges are amplified by a quarterly schedule "where we have new classes every seven weeks, [which] makes it impossible to procrastinate." Yet such a schedule offers several noteworthy benefits, like forcing "students to adapt to a daily schedule that more closely resembles the real world." Professors are a mixed bag. "Some are excellent, some are more concerned with research, and some have a language barrier." All, however, "encourage students to utilize office hours for personal and academic concerns."

Life

"There is a big diversity of what people do for fun" at WPI; what they choose to do seems to depend on how anxious they are to abandon their computers. One student writes, "Some people never leave their rooms and play video games all day, while others party every night. It all depends on what you are into." Some are into tinkering. One such student writes, "For fun, we FIX things. We hook up homemade stereo systems to our televisions, we rig washing machines, we program computers, we play Risk, Warcraft, and any other strategy game on the market." Worcester is not a pure Nerdvana, though; there is also "Greek life, which is really big for about a third of campus. Frat parties are a big part of the social scene, but the other half of campus probably wouldn't know what to do with a beer if they saw one." There are also "literally hundreds of organizations with all kinds of people in them. Any interest you have will be represented by a group, some large, some small, but there are always a few people around who are more than willing to share experiences." Students rarely leave campus except to travel to other area schools, since Worcester "doesn't have much to do in terms of nightlife. The clubs aren't safe, and there aren't any late-night diners within walking distance." The campus confines, fortunately, are comfy, since the "dorms are amazing, [and] the food is excellent."

Student Body

"There are two types of typical students at WPI," undergraduates tell us. "The first type is a very outgoing person who has joined at least two or three different clubs and organizations and/or is in a fraternity or sorority. The second type of person is very introverted and doesn't leave his room very often to socialize." Some students are, by their own admission, awfully nerdy. One undergraduate writes, "Looking out the window right now, I see a kid with welder goggles and a foam sword. He is a 'wedge rat.' Perhaps he is socially inept. Fortunately there are many people here just like him." The ratio of males to females is a bit lopsided; "the 25 percent female population consists of mostly engineering majors, so the selection is rather poor. However, with WPI having the only Greek scene in the Worcester area, finding a girl is hardly an issue at large fraternity parties."

ADMISSIONS

Very important factors considered include: Class rank, secondary school record, standardized test scores. *Important factors considered include:* Essays, extracurricular activities, recommendations. *Other factors considered include:* Alumni/ae relation, character/personal qualities, geographical residence, interview, minority status, state residency, talent/ability, volunteer work, work experience. SAT Reasoning or ACT required. SAT Subject Tests recommended. TOEFL required of all international applicants. High school diploma is required, and GED is not accepted. *Academic units required:* 4 math, 2 science (2 science lab). *Academic units recommended:* 4 English.

The Inside Word

Worcester's applicant pool is small but very well qualified. Its high acceptance rate makes it a good safety choice for those aiming at more difficult tech schools and for those who are solid but aren't MIT material. As is the case at most technical institutes, women will meet with a very receptive admissions committee.

FINANCIAL AID

Students should submit: FAFSA, CSS/Financial Aid PROFILE, noncustodial (divorced/separated) parents' statement, parents' and students' prior year federal tax return and W-2 forms. Regular filing deadline 3/1. The Princeton Review suggests that all financial aid forms be submitted as soon as possible after 1/1. *Need-based scholarships/grants offered:* Pell, SEOG, state scholarships/grants, the school's own gift aid. *Loan aid offered:* FFEL Subsidized Stafford, FFEL Unsubsidized Stafford, FFEL PLUS, Federal Perkins, state loans, college/university loans from institutional funds. Applicants will be notified of awards on or about 4/1. Federal Work-study Program available. Institutional employment available. Off-campus job opportunities are good.

FROM THE ADMISSIONS OFFICE

"Projects and research enrich WPI's academic program. WPI believes that in these times simply passing courses and accumulating theoretical knowledge is not enough to truly educate tomorrow's leaders. Tomorrow's professionals ought to be involved in project work that prepares them today for future challenges. Projects at WPI come as close to professional experience as a college program can possibly achieve. In fact, WPI works with more than 200 companies, government agencies, and private organizations each year. These groups provide opportunities where students get a chance to work in real, professional settings. Students gain invaluable experience in planning, coordinating team efforts, meeting deadlines, writing proposals and reports, making oral presentations, doing cost analyses, and making decisions."

For even more information on this school, turn to page 557 of the "Stats" section.

WORCESTER STATE COLLEGE

486 CHANDLER STREET, DEPARTMENT OF ADMISSIONS, WORCESTER, MA 01602-2597 • ADMISSIONS: 508-929-8040 • FAX: 508-929-8183
E-MAIL: ADMISSIONS@WORCESTER.EDU • WEBSITE: WWW.WORCESTER.EDU

Ratings

Quality of Life: 66   Academic: 70   Admissions: 75   Financial Aid: 78

Academics

Worcester State College, "a local resource for those traditional and nontraditional students looking for more education" in central Massachusetts, is "a great, cheap place to go to school" for "open-minded students, most of whom pay their own way and realize the value of an education." Standout programs include business, education, occupational therapy, nursing, and other health- and science-related areas; these programs in particular are abetted by "a whole new science and technology building, recently finished in 2000. The building is remarkable, with state-of-the-

> **SURVEY SAYS . . .**
> *Small classes*
> *Diverse student types on campus*
> *Great off-campus food*
> *Frats and sororities are unpopular*
> *or nonexistent*
> *Lots of beer drinking*
> *(Almost) everyone smokes*

art equipment and even an electron microscope for research purposes." Students appreciate WSC's commitment to keeping class sizes small; one student writes, "I have the opportunity to develop a student-professor relationship and know that the professor will know me as a person, not a number in his/her rank book." There is a drawback, however, to class size limits at WSC: it can be "very hard to find classes to register for that meet [general education] requirements." This is particularly true of classes in some of the smaller departments. Professors in all departments are generally well regarded; they "have a variety of backgrounds with one common goal: To show you what the world is really like in your field. I have had the pleasure of taking many wonderful teachers in my major." Many students agree that some professors "need to [brush up] on explaining problems and making sure the class understands the material." Students also warn that "the campus needs some much overdue repair (some of the buildings inside look like an inner city high school)." Recent efforts to improve this situation include the complete renovation of the College's oldest academic building as well as the construction of a new residence hall which opened in fall of 2004.

Life

WSC is a commuter school—one in three full-time students lives on campus, and many of the students who dorm go home on weekends. Students tell us that "there are a lot of extracurricular groups for people to get involved in and a lot of groups within each major for people to be involved in," and add that "after hours activities supported by the Student Center are fun, such as the graffiti nights and the holiday parties." However, one student says, "There's not too much structured activity here, so you have to be able to make your own fun. Being social is important too, it's the only way to meet people!" On-campus partying is hampered by the rules because "dorm life under 21 is fairly strict. [The school does] have 21+ houses, though, and it's awesome once you're old enough to enjoy those." Kids travel off-campus for good times; one student explains, "For fun, many people go to the dance clubs nearby, or if they are 21, they go to the bars."

Student Body

There is "a good sense of diversity" at WSC, where "[they] have international students, returning adults, students from Worcester, and students from out of state. Fashion-wise, you see everything from business suits to just-rolled-out-of-bed PJs." Most students are from Worcester and the surrounding area; "It's shocking how many people here know each other from high school," one student tells us. That doesn't dilute the school's diversity, however, since "Worcester, Massachusetts is the stir-fry pan of New England. There is so much diversity and culture here that a typical student does not exist." There are many nontraditional students, people "who work or have children and are trying to fit an education into their hectic schedule. This school is wonderful for that."

ADMISSIONS

Very important factors considered include: Secondary school record, standardized test scores. *Other factors considered include:* Essays, extracurricular activities, interview, recommendations, talent/ability. TOEFL required of all international applicants. High school diploma is required, and GED is accepted. *Academic units required:* 4 English, 3 math, 3 science (2 science lab), 2 foreign language, 1 social studies, 1 history, 2 academic electives.

The Inside Word

Your high school transcript is the most important factor in the admissions decision here; standardized test scores are also important. Applicants with poor showings in one or both of these areas can make up their deficiencies through a strong record of work, community service, and extracurricular activity. Letters of recommendation can also help.

FINANCIAL AID

Students should submit: FAFSA, institution's own financial aid form. The Princeton Review suggests that all financial aid forms be submitted as soon as possible after 1/1. *Need-based scholarships/grants offered:* Pell, SEOG, state scholarships/grants, private scholarships, the school's own gift aid. *Loan aid offered:* FFEL Subsidized Stafford, FFEL PLUS, Federal Perkins, state loans. Applicants will be notified of awards on a rolling basis beginning on or about 3/1. Federal Work-study Program available. Institutional employment available.

FROM THE ADMISSIONS OFFICE

"Worcester State College, a public institution located on 58 acres of rolling wooded land in central Massachusetts, offers a wide variety of majors in the areas of liberal arts and sciences, business, teacher education, and the health professions. The college is dedicated to offering affordable undergraduate and graduate programs and to promoting lifelong intellectual growth and career opportunities, and is accredited by the New England Association of Schools and Colleges. The Worcester State College campus is a completely wireless network environment, and the number of online courses has increased by 200% since 2003. Student housing is safely set in the back of campus on a hill that commands a spectacular view of the entire campus. Applications for admission are evaluated on a rolling basis with an application deadline of 6/1. Student guided tours of campus are offered on a weekly basis and two open houses are held in the fall for prospective students and their families. Financial Assistance is offered in the form of grants, loans and campus work. For more information about Worcester State College contact the Office of Admission (508) 929-8793 or visit the website http://www.worcester.edu."

For even more information on this school, turn to page 558 of the "Stats" section.

YALE UNIVERSITY

PO Box 208234, New Haven, CT 06520-8234 • Admissions: 203-432-9316 • Fax: 203-432-9392
Financial Aid: 203-432-2700 • E-mail: student.questions@yale.edu • Website: www.yale.edu/admit

Ratings

Quality of Life: 93   **Academic:** 97   **Admissions:** 99   **Financial Aid:** 97

Academics

"There are too many strengths to name" at Yale University, one of the nation's top undergraduate and graduate institutions, but that doesn't stop undergrads here from trying; they identify "the resources, of course, the marvelous professors, and the students themselves" as some of Yale's biggest assets. As one student puts it, "Coming to Yale means that you will be able to do anything you want to do at the highest caliber. They will make it as easy as they can for you to learn what you want." If the experience sounds a little daunting, that's because it is. Explains one undergrad, "It's intimidating, Yale University. You feel like you have something to prove. Were you the 'mistake' who got in? You challenge yourself for the sake of learning and for the sake of being the best." (And it's comforting to note that "faculty tries to ensure that no one is lost in the wash.") Students' burdens are somewhat lessened by the fact that "you don't really have to deal with the highest levels of the administration, because every residential college has a Master (for residential issues) and a Dean (for academic issues), who you can easily discuss things with, and who will generally help you take care of things in the most efficient way possible."

> **SURVEY SAYS . . .**
> Registration is a breeze
> Great library
> Musical organizations are popular
> Student publications are popular

Life

Yale is extremely demanding academically, but students here still find time for plenty of extracurricular enrichment and fun. Reports one student, "People generally study Monday through Thursday, and oftentimes have extracurriculars in the evenings. On the weekends, people tend to study during the day and go out at night." Undergrads tell us that "art, music, theater, and sports are huge, loved, and well-funded, as are organizations such as the Yale Daily News, the Slavic Chorus (a cappella is huge here), Just Add Water (a comedy troupe), and the fire-juggling club (best Halloween show in the world!)." The campus also sustains "an absolutely ridiculous amount of theatrical and musical events." Students also love the traditional "Masters' Teas, of which there are several every week, with everyone from the Swiss delegate to the United Nations to Eric Schlosser (author of *Fast Food Nation*) to biomedical engineers coming to share their life experiences over tea and chocolates." Yale's campus is "gorgeous" with "jaw-dropping architecture and awesome dorms and dining halls." While New Haven is not held in especially high regard, students appreciate that "there are some excellent clubs and restaurants in town" and that "the city provides easy access to New York," which can be reached by train in about 90 minutes.

Student Body

While "there is no typical Yale student," most agree that "there are two overarching characteristics that everyone here has been blessed with: talent and motivation." Notes one student, "Though we come from different backgrounds and have different interests, it's easy to look around and imagine your classmates being the leaders of the next generation." Professors and peers alike never cease to surprise you and just completely blow you away with their talent and knowledge and personality. Yet at the same time, everyone is down-to-earth. Very few people flaunt their abilities, though they have every right to." Students "tend to have a liberal bent, although any political affiliation (just like any background) is welcomed, and politics carry over from mere discussion into real action: Community programs, public-health advocacy and work, and political campaigns are all vital to campus life." Undergrads are also typically "noncompetitive and very supportive of each other academically and socially." Explains one student, "If I have to miss lecture, I know that first, I can always e-mail my professor and ask for help and second, any one of a dozen friends will gladly not only share notes, but also go over them with me to make sure that I understand them." Thanks to need-blind admissions and generous financial aid, "the economic backgrounds of students are very diverse."

ADMISSIONS

Very important factors considered include: Character/personal qualities, class rank, essays, extracurricular activities, recommendations, secondary school record, standardized test scores, talent/ability. *Other factors considered include:* Alumni/ae relation, geographical residence, interview, minority status, state residency, volunteer work, work experience. TOEFL required of all international applicants. High school diploma or equivalent is not required.

The Inside Word

There is no grey area; Yale is ultra-selective with growing applicant pools each year. And there's nothing to be gained by appealing a denial here—the admissions committee considers all of its decisions final. Yale uses a regional review process that serves as a preliminary screening for all candidates, and only the best-qualified, well-matched candidates actually come before the admissions committee.

FINANCIAL AID

Students should submit: FAFSA, CSS/Financial Aid PROFILE, state aid form, noncustodial (divorced/separated) parents' statement, business/farm supplement, tax returns. Regular filing deadline 3/1. The Princeton Review suggests that all financial aid forms be submitted as soon as possible after 1/1. *Need-based scholarships/grants offered:* Pell, SEOG, state scholarships/grants, private scholarships, the school's own gift aid, United Negro College Fund, Alumni Club Awards. *Loan aid offered:* FFEL Subsidized Stafford, FFEL Unsubsidized Stafford, FFEL PLUS, Federal Perkins, state loans, college/university loans from institutional funds. Applicants will be notified of awards on or about 4/1. Federal Work-study Program available. Institutional employment available. Off-campus job opportunities are good.

FROM THE ADMISSIONS OFFICE

"The most important questions the admissions committee must resolve are 'Who is likely to make the most of Yale's resources?' and 'Who will contribute significantly to the Yale community?' These questions suggest an approach to evaluating applicants that is more complex than whether Yale would rather admit well-rounded people or those with specialized talents. In selecting a class of 1,300 from approximately 19,700 applicants, the admissions committee looks for academic ability and achievement combined with such personal characteristics as motivation, curiosity, energy, and leadership ability. The nature of these qualities is such that there is no simple profile of grades, scores, interests, and activities that will assure admission. Diversity within the student population is important, and the admissions committee selects a class of able and contributing individuals from a variety of backgrounds and with a broad range of interests and skills."

For even more information on this school, turn to page 558 of the "Stats" section.

PART 3: THE STATS

ADELPHI UNIVERSITY

CAMPUS LIFE

Quality of Life Rating	**64**
Fire Safety Rating	**99**
Type of school	private
Environment	metropolis

STUDENTS

Total undergrad enrollment	4,413
% male/female	29/71
% from out of state	8
% % from public high school	77
% live on campus	24
% in (# of) fraternities	3 (2)
% in (# of) sororities	4 (5)
% African American	12
% Asian	5
% Caucasian	46
% Hispanic	9
% international	3
# of countries represented	44

ACADEMICS

Academic Rating	**70**
Calendar	semester
Student/faculty ratio	14:1
Profs interesting Rating	66
Profs accessible Rating	64
% profs teaching UG courses	100
Most common lab size	20-29 students
Most common reg class size	10-19 students

MOST POPULAR MAJORS
business administration/management
education
psychology

SELECTIVITY

Admissions Selectivity Rating	**82**
# of applicants	4,749
% of applicants accepted	70
% of acceptees attending	24

FRESHMAN PROFILE

Range SAT Verbal	500-600
Average SAT Verbal	548
Range SAT Math	500-610
Average SAT Math	558
Projected Range SAT Writing	560-630
Range ACT Composite	22-26
Average ACT Composite	24
Minimum Paper TOEFL	550
Minimum Computer Based TOEFL	213
Average HS GPA	3.3
% graduated top 10% of class	22
% graduated top 25% of class	55
% graduated top 50% of class	90

DEADLINES

Regular notification	rolling
Nonfall registration?	yes

FINANCIAL FACTS

Financial Aid Rating	**61**
Annual tuition	$17,700
Room & Board	$8,900
Books and supplies	$1,000
Required fees	$1,000
% frosh rec. need-based scholarship or grant aid	63
% UG rec. need-based scholarship or grant aid	57
% frosh rec. need-based self-help aid	63
% UG rec. need-based self-help aid	57
% frosh rec. any financial aid	93
% UG rec. any financial aid	88
Avg. frosh grant	$13,800
Avg. frosh loan	$3,276

ALBRIGHT COLLEGE

CAMPUS LIFE

Quality of Life Rating	**70**
Fire Safety Rating	**82**
Type of school	private
Affiliation	Methodist
Environment	city

STUDENTS

Total undergrad enrollment	2,124
% male/female	41/59
% from out of state	34
% from public high school	77
% live on campus	65
% in (# of) fraternities	25 (4)
% in (# of) sororities	30 (3)
% African American	9
% Asian	2
% Caucasian	78
% Hispanic	4
% international	4
# of countries represented	28

ACADEMICS

Academic Rating	**84**
Calendar	4-1-4
Student/faculty ratio	14:1
Professors Interesting Rating	92
Professors Accessible Rating	89
% professors teaching UG courses	100
Most common lab size	10-19 students
Most common regular class size	10-19 students

MOST POPULAR MAJORS
biology/biological sciences
business administration/management
sociology

SELECTIVITY

Admissions Selectivity Rating	**79**
# of applicants	2,991
% of applicants accepted	70
% of acceptees attending	24

FRESHMAN PROFILE

Range SAT Verbal	470-570
Average SAT Verbal	519
Range SAT Math	460-560
Average SAT Math	511
Projected Range SAT Writing	530-610
Average ACT Composite	21
Average HS GPA	3.21
% graduated top 10% of class	21
% graduated top 25% of class	47
% graduated top 50% of class	80

DEADLINES

Regular notification	rolling
Nonfall registration?	yes

FINANCIAL FACTS

Financial Aid Rating	**74**
Annual tuiton	$25,232
Books and supplies	$800
% frosh rec. need-based scholarship or grant aid	85
% UG rec. need-based scholarship or grant aid	70
% frosh rec. need-based self-help aid	75
% UG rec. need-based self-help aid	63
% frosh rec. any financial aid	94
% UG rec. any financial aid	94
Avg. frosh grant	$15,217
Avg. frosh loan	$8,835

ALFRED UNIVERSITY

CAMPUS LIFE

Quality of Life Rating	**85**
Fire Safety Rating	**82**
Type of school	private
Environment	rural

STUDENTS

Total undergrad enrollment	1,971
% male/female	51/49
% from out of state	35
% African American	6
% Asian	2
% Caucasian	76
% Hispanic	4
% international	2

ACADEMICS

Academic Rating	**83**
Calendar	semester
Student/faculty ratio	12:1
Professors Interesting Rating	83
Professors Accessible Rating	84
% professors teaching UG courses	100
Most common lab size	10-19 students
Most common	
regular class size	10-19 students

MOST POPULAR MAJORS
business administration/management
ceramic sciences and engineering
fine/studio arts

SELECTIVITY

Admissions Selectivity Rating	**74**
# of applicants	2,243
% of applicants accepted	73
% of acceptees attending	· 31
# of early decision applicants	45
% accepted early decision	74

FRESHMAN PROFILE

Range SAT Verbal	500-610
Average SAT Verbal	565
Range SAT Math	500-610
Average SAT Math	572
Projected Range SAT Writing	560-640
Range ACT Composite	20-26
Average ACT Composite	24
Minimum Paper TOEFL	550
Minimum Computer Based TOEFL	213
% graduated top 10% of class	15
% graduated top 25% of class	47
% graduated top 50% of class	84

DEADLINES

Early decision application deadline	12/1
Regular notification	rolling
Nonfall registration?	yes

FINANCIAL FACTS

Annual tuition	$20,150
Financial Aid Rating	**92**
% frosh rec. need-based scholarship	
or grant aid	80
% UG rec. need-based scholarship	
or grant aid .	80
% frosh rec. need-based self-help aid	72
% UG rec. need-based self-help aid	74
% frosh rec. any financial aid	92
% UG rec. any financial aid	90

ALLEGHENY COLLEGE

CAMPUS LIFE

Quality of Life Rating	**76**
Fire Safety Rating	**86**
Type of school	private

Affiliation	United Methodist
Environment	town

STUDENTS

Total undergrad enrollment	1,929
% male/female	48/52
% from out of state	34
% from public high school	83
% live on campus	75
% in (# of) fraternities	26 (5)
% in (# of) sororities	28 (4)
% African American	1
% Asian	3
% Caucasian	93
% Hispanic	1
% international	1
# of countries represented	31

ACADEMICS

Academic Rating	**88**
Calendar	semester
Student/faculty ratio	13:1
Professors Interesting Rating	90
Professors Accessible Rating	88
% professors teaching UG courses	100
Most common lab size	10-19 students

MOST POPULAR MAJORS
biology/biological sciences
political science and government
psychology

SELECTIVITY

Admissions Selectivity Rating	**89**
# of applicants	3,279
% of applicants accepted	74
% of acceptees attending	27
# accepting a place on wait list	122
% admitted from wait list	20
# of early decision applicants	72
% accepted early decision	77

FRESHMAN PROFILE

Range SAT Verbal	550-650
Average SAT Verbal	605
Range SAT Math	560-650
Average SAT Math	608
Projected Range SAT Writing	600-670
Range ACT Composite	23-28
Average ACT Composite	26
Minimum Paper TOEFL	550
Minimum Computer Based TOEFL	213
Average HS GPA	3.74
% graduated top 10% of class	43
% graduated top 25% of class	72
% graduated top 50% of class	94

DEADLINES

Early decision application deadline	11/15
Regular application deadline	2/15
Regular notification	4/1
Nonfall registration? ·	yes

FINANCIAL FACTS

Financial Aid Rating	**87**
Annual tuition	$26,650
Room & Board	$6,550
Books and supplies	$800
Required fees	$300
% frosh rec. need-based scholarship	
or grant aid	72
% UG rec. need-based scholarship	
or grant aid	72
% frosh rec. need-based self-help aid	58
% UG rec. need-based self-help aid	60
% frosh rec. any financial aid	98
% UG rec. any financial aid	96
Avg. frosh grant	$15,500
Avg. frosh loan	$3,230

AMERICAN UNIVERSITY

CAMPUS LIFE

Quality of Life Rating	**85**
Fire Safety Rating	**78**
Type of school	private
Affiliation	Methodist
Environment	metropolis

STUDENTS

Total undergrad enrollment	5,731
% male/female	38/62
% from out of state	95
% live on campus	68
% in (# of) fraternities	17 (10)
% in (# of) sororities	18 (13)
% African American	6
% Asian	5
% Caucasian	63
% Hispanic	5
% international	7
# of countries represented	118

ACADEMICS

Academic Rating	**84**
Calendar	semester
Student/faculty ratio	15:1
Professors Interesting Rating	77
Professors Accessible Rating	79
% professors teaching UG courses	95
% classes taught by TAs	5
Most common lab size	10-19 students

MOST POPULAR MAJORS
business administration/management
international relations and affairs
mass communications/media studies

SELECTIVITY

Admissions Selectivity Rating	**93**
# of applicants	12,211
% of applicants accepted	53
% of acceptees attending	19
# of early decision applicants	227

% accepted early decision	61

FRESHMAN PROFILE

Range SAT Verbal	580-690
Average SAT Verbal	620
Range SAT Math	570-660
Average SAT Math	603
Projected Range SAT Writing	620-690
Range ACT Composite	25-29
Average ACT Composite	27
Minimum Paper TOEFL	550
Minimum Computer Based TOEFL	213
Average HS GPA	3.47
% graduated top 10% of class	44
% graduated top 25% of class	82
% graduated top 50% of class	97

DEADLINES

Early decision application deadline	11/15
Regular application deadline	1/15
Regular notification	4/1
Nonfall registration?	yes

FINANCIAL FACTS

Financial Aid Rating	**80**
Annual tuition	$27,552
Room & Board	$10,700
Books and supplies	$600
Required fees	$467
% frosh rec. need-based scholarship or grant aid	39
% UG rec. need-based scholarship or grant aid	37
% frosh rec. need-based self-help aid	46
% UG rec. need-based self-help aid	43
% frosh rec. any financial aid	81
% UG rec. any financial aid	69
Avg. frosh grant	$15,813
Avg. frosh loan	$5,722

AMHERST COLLEGE

CAMPUS LIFE

Quality of Life Rating	**97**
Fire Safety Rating	**60**
Type of school	private
Environment	town

STUDENTS

Total undergrad enrollment	1,638
% male/female	52/48
% from out of state	87
% from public high school	59
% live on campus	98
% African American	9
% Asian	13
% Caucasian	46
% Hispanic	7

% international	6
# of countries represented	31

ACADEMICS

Academic Rating	**98**
Calendar	semester
Student/faculty ratio	8:1
Professors Interesting Rating	98
Professors Accessible Rating	95
% professors teaching UG courses	100
Most common lab size	10-19 students
Most common regular class size	10-19 students

MOST POPULAR MAJORS
economics
English language and literature
political science and government

SELECTIVITY

Admissions Selectivity Rating	**98**
# of applicants	5,489
% of applicants accepted	21
% of acceptees attending	38
# accepting a place on wait list	1,023
% admitted from wait list	8
# of early decision applicants	127
% accepted early decision	38

FRESHMAN PROFILE

Range SAT Verbal	680-770
Average SAT Verbal	722
Range SAT Math	680-780
Average SAT Math	721
Projected Range SAT Writing	680-740
Range ACT Composite	30-33
Average ACT Composite	31
Minimum Paper TOEFL	600
Minimum Computer Based TOEFL	250
% graduated top 10% of class	87
% graduated top 25% of class	99
% graduated top 50% of class	100

DEADLINES

Early decision application deadline	11/15
Regular application deadline	12/31
Regular notification	4/2
Nonfall registration?	no

FINANCIAL FACTS

Financial Aid Rating	**99**
Annual tuition	$30,780
Room & Board	$8,160
Books and supplies	$900
Required fees	$584
% frosh rec. need-based scholarship or grant aid	44
% UG rec. need-based scholarship or grant aid	44
% frosh rec. need-based self-help aid	41
% UG rec. need-based self-help aid	43

Avg. frosh grant	$25,727
Avg. frosh loan	$1,839

ARCADIA UNIVERSITY

CAMPUS LIFE

Quality of Life Rating	**81**
Fire Safety Rating	**60**
Type of school	private
Affiliation	Presbyterian
Environment	village

STUDENTS

Total undergrad enrollment	1,924
% male/female	27/73
% from out of state	30
% from public high school	72
% African American	9
% Asian	3
% Caucasian	75
% Hispanic	2
% international	1
# of countries represented	13

ACADEMICS

Academic Rating	**81**
Calendar	semester
Student/faculty ratio	12:1
Professors Interesting Rating	84
Professors Accessible Rating	78
% professors teaching UG courses	100
Most common lab size	10-19 students

MOST POPULAR MAJORS
education
fine/studio arts

SELECTIVITY

Admissions Selectivity Rating	**79**
# of applicants	2,567
% of applicants accepted	72
% of acceptees attending	27

FRESHMAN PROFILE

Range SAT Verbal	490-610
Average SAT Verbal	530
Range SAT Math	470-590
Average SAT Math	518
Projected Range SAT Writing	550-640
Average ACT Composite	23
Minimum Paper TOEFL	600
Average HS GPA	3.1
% graduated top 10% of class	25
% graduated top 25% of class	44
% graduated top 50% of class	73

DEADLINES

Early decision application deadline	10/15
Regular application deadline	8/1
Regular notification	rolling
Nonfall registration?	yes

FINANCIAL FACTS
Financial Aid Rating   **71**
Annual tuition	$23,990
Room & Board	$9,300
Books and supplies	$800
Required fees	$280
% frosh rec. need-based scholarship or grant aid	70
% UG rec. need-based scholarship or grant aid	70
% frosh rec. need-based self-help aid	74
% UG rec. need-based self-help aid	71
% frosh rec. any financial aid	97
Avg. frosh grant	$13,258
Avg. frosh loan	$2,656

THE ART INSTITUTE OF BOSTON AT LESLEY UNIVERSITY

CAMPUS LIFE
Quality of Life Rating   **72**
Fire Safety Rating   **60**
Type of school	private
Environment	metropolis

STUDENTS
Total undergrad enrollment	1,032
% male/female	19/81
% from out of state	41
% from public high school	82
% live on campus	66
% African American	7
% Asian	5
% Caucasian	63
% Hispanic	4
% international	5
# of countries represented	30

ACADEMICS
Academic Rating   **67**
Calendar	semester
Student/faculty ratio	10:1
Professors Interesting Rating	83
Professors Accessible Rating	70
% professors teaching UG courses	100
Most common lab size	10-19 students

MOST POPULAR MAJORS
graphic design
illustration
photography

SELECTIVITY
Admissions Selectivity Rating   **60**
# of applicants	885
% of applicants accepted	78
% of acceptees attending	34

FRESHMAN PROFILE
Range SAT Verbal	480-600
Average SAT Verbal	530
Range SAT Math	440-550
Average SAT Math	515
Projected Range SAT Writing	540-630
Minimum Paper TOEFL	500
Minimum Computer Based TOEFL	173
Average HS GPA	3.0

DEADLINES
Regular notification 3 weeks after completed application is received
Nonfall registration?   yes

FINANCIAL FACTS
Financial Aid Rating   **62**
Annual tuition	$19,600
Room & Board	$9,950
Books and supplies	$1,575
Required fees	$710
% frosh rec. need-based scholarship or grant aid	52
% UG rec. need-based scholarship or grant aid	34
% frosh rec. need-based self-help aid	68
% UG rec. need-based self-help aid	55
Avg. frosh grant	$4,283
Avg. frosh loan	$3,298

ASSUMPTION COLLEGE

CAMPUS LIFE
Quality of Life Rating   **75**
Fire Safety Rating   **86**
Type of school	private
Affiliation	Roman Catholic
Environment	city

STUDENTS
Total undergrad enrollment	2,164
% male/female	39/61
% from out of state	31
% from public high school	71
% live on campus	90
% African American	1
% Asian	1
% Caucasian	85
% Hispanic	2

ACADEMICS
Academic Rating   **80**
Calendar	semester
Student/faculty ratio	13:1
Professors Interesting Rating	88
Professors Accessible Rating	88
% professors teaching UG courses	100
Most common lab size	20-29 students
Most common regular class size	10-19 students

MOST POPULAR MAJORS
English language and literature
psychology
rehabilitation and therapeutic professions

SELECTIVITY
Admissions Selectivity Rating   **81**
# of applicants	3,538
% of applicants accepted	69
% of acceptees attending	26
# accepting a place on wait list	469
% admitted from wait list	32
# of early decision applicants	50
% accepted early decision	82

FRESHMAN PROFILE
Range SAT Verbal	490-590
Average SAT Verbal	545
Range SAT Math	500-590
Average SAT Math	543
Projected Range SAT Writing	550-620
Range ACT Composite	19-25
Average ACT Composite	22
Minimum Paper TOEFL	200
Minimum Computer Based TOEFL	40
Average HS GPA	3.25
% graduated top 10% of class	15
% graduated top 25% of class	52
% graduated top 50% of class	84

DEADLINES
Early decision application deadline	11/15
Regular application deadline	2/15
Regular notification	continuous until 5/1
Nonfall registration?	yes

FINANCIAL FACTS
Financial Aid Rating   **72**
Annual tuition	$22,260
Room & Board	$8,640
Books and supplies	$850
Required fees	$165
% frosh rec. need-based scholarship or grant aid	72
% UG rec. need-based scholarship or grant aid	71
% frosh rec. need-based self-help aid	65
% UG rec. need-based self-help aid	65
% frosh rec. any financial aid	93
% UG rec. any financial aid	90
Avg. frosh grant	$11,655
Avg. frosh loan	$3,374

BABSON COLLEGE

CAMPUS LIFE
Quality of Life Rating   **79**
Fire Safety Rating   **88**
Type of school	private
Environment	village

STUDENTS

Total undergrad enrollment	1,697
% male/female	60/40
% from out of state	62
% live on campus	83
% in (# of) fraternities	10 (3)
% in (# of) sororities	10 (2)
% African American	3
% Asian	8
% Caucasian	44
% Hispanic	5
% international	17
# of countries represented	59

ACADEMICS

Academic Rating	**88**
Calendar	semester
Student/faculty ratio	13:1
Professors Interesting Rating	89
Professors Accessible Rating	89
% professors teaching UG courses	100
Most common lab size	30-39 students
Most common	
regular class size	10-19 students

MOST POPULAR MAJORS

business administration/management

SELECTIVITY

Admissions Selectivity Rating	**93**
# of applicants	3,064
% of applicants accepted	37
% of acceptees attending	38
# accepting a place on wait list	532
# of early decision applicants	119
% accepted early decision	52

FRESHMAN PROFILE

Range SAT Verbal	560-640
Average SAT Verbal	597
Range SAT Math	600-690
Average SAT Math	655
Projected Range SAT Writing	600-660
Range ACT Composite	26-28
% graduated top 10% of class	53
% graduated top 25% of class	83
% graduated top 50% of class	98

DEADLINES

Early decision application deadline	11/15
Regular application deadline	1/15
Regular notification	4/1
Nonfall registration?	no

FINANCIAL FACTS

Financial Aid Rating	**95**
Annual tuition	$28,832
Room & Board	$10,376
Books and supplies	$856
% frosh rec. need-based scholarship	
or grant aid	42
% UG rec. need-based scholarship	
or grant aid	40
% frosh rec. need-based self-help aid	46
% UG rec. need-based self-help aid	45
% frosh rec. any financial aid	46
% UG rec. any financial aid	45
Avg. frosh grant	$20,589
Avg. frosh loan	$2,686

BARD COLLEGE

CAMPUS LIFE

Quality of Life Rating	**76**
Fire Safety Rating	**80**
Type of school	private
Environment	rural

STUDENTS

Total undergrad enrollment	1,458
% male/female	45/55
% from out of state	76
% from public high school	67
% live on campus	81
% African American	3
% Asian	5
% Caucasian	70
% Hispanic	4
% international	5
# of countries represented	51

ACADEMICS

Academic Rating	**95**
Calendar	4-1-4
Student/faculty ratio	9:1
Professors Interesting Rating	89
Professors Accessible Rating	85
% professors teaching UG courses	100
Most common lab size	10-19 students

MOST POPULAR MAJORS

English language and literature
social sciences
visual and performing arts

SELECTIVITY

Admissions Selectivity Rating	**96**
# of applicants	3,603
% of applicants accepted	36
% of acceptees attending	31
# accepting a place on wait list	267
% admitted from wait list	4

FRESHMAN PROFILE

Range SAT Verbal	650-750
Average SAT Verbal	690
Range SAT Math	590-690
Average SAT Math	630
Projected Range SAT Writing	670-730
Minimum Paper TOEFL	600
Minimum Computer Based TOEFL	250
Average HS GPA	3.5
% graduated top 10% of class	64
% graduated top 25% of class	90
% graduated top 50% of class	99

DEADLINES

Regular application deadline	1/15
Regular notification	4/1
Nonfall registration?	yes

FINANCIAL FACTS

Financial Aid Rating	**85**
Annual tuition	$31,850
Room & board	$9,340
Books and supplies	$750
% frosh rec. need-based scholarship	
or grant aid	53
% UG rec. need-based scholarship	
or grant aid	58
% frosh rec. need-based self-help aid	48
% UG rec. need-based self-help aid	52
% frosh rec. any financial aid	65
% UG rec. any financial aid	68
Avg. frosh grant	$21,464
Avg. frosh loan	$3,434

BARNARD COLLEGE

CAMPUS LIFE

Quality of Life Rating	**97**
Fire Safety Rating	**77**
Type of school	private
Environment	metropolis

STUDENTS

Total undergrad enrollment	2,287
% male/female	0/100
% from out of state	66
% from public high school	52
% live on campus	90
% African American	5
% Asian	17
% Caucasian	67
% Hispanic	7
% Native American	1
% international	3
# of countries represented	40

ACADEMICS

Academic Rating	**94**
Calendar	semester
Student/faculty ratio	10:1
Professors Interesting Rating	91
Professors Accessible Rating	89
% professors teaching UG courses	100
Most common lab size	10-19 students
Most common	
regular class size	fewer than 10 students

MOST POPULAR MAJORS

economics
English language and literature
psychology

SELECTIVITY
Admissions Selectivity Rating **97**

# of applicants	4,380
% of applicants accepted	27
% of acceptees attending	46
# accepting a place on wait list	931
% admitted from wait list	5
# of early decision applicants	167
% accepted early decision	41

FRESHMAN PROFILE

Range SAT Verbal	650-730
Average SAT Verbal	690
Range SAT Math	620-700
Average SAT Math	660
Projected Range SAT Writing	670-720
Range ACT Composite	28-31
Average ACT Composite	30
Minimum Paper TOEFL	600
Minimum Computer Based TOEFL	250
Average HS GPA	3.93
% graduated top 10% of class	72
% graduated top 25% of class	93
% graduated top 50% of class	100

DEADLINES

Early decision application deadline	11/15
Regular application deadline	1/1
Regular notification	4/1
Nonfall registration?	yes

FINANCIAL FACTS
Financial Aid Rating **94**

Annual tuition	$27,064
Room & Board	$10,800
Books and supplies	$1,000
Required fees	$1,276
% frosh rec. need-based scholarship or grant aid	41
% UG rec. need-based scholarship or grant aid	38
% frosh rec. need-based self-help aid	44
% UG rec. need-based self-help aid	41
% frosh rec. any financial aid	55
% UG rec. any financial aid	56
Avg. frosh grant	$24,902
Avg. frosh loan	$3,382

BATES COLLEGE

CAMPUS LIFE
Quality of Life Rating **87**
Fire Safety Rating **60**

Type of school	private
Environment	town

STUDENTS

Total undergrad enrollment	1,743
% male/female	49/51
% from out of state	89
% from public high school	55
% live on campus	90
% African American	2
% Asian	4
% Caucasian	83
% Hispanic	3
% international	6
# of countries represented	72

ACADEMICS
Academic Rating **93**

Calendar	4-4-1
Student/faculty ratio	10:1
Professors Interesting Rating	88
Professors Accessible Rating	95
% professors teaching UG courses	100
Most common lab size	10-19 students
Most common regular class size	10-19 students

MOST POPULAR MAJORS
economics
political science and government
psychology

SELECTIVITY
Admissions Selectivity Rating **96**

# of applicants	4,098
% of applicants accepted	30
% of acceptees attending	38
# accepting a place on wait list	1,055
% admitted from wait list	10
# of early decision applicants	216
% accepted early decision	54

FRESHMAN PROFILE

Range SAT Verbal	630-710
Average SAT Verbal	670
Range SAT Math	640-710
Average SAT Math	672
Projected Range SAT Writing	650-700
Minimum Paper TOEFL	200
Minimum Computer Based TOEFL	40
% graduated top 10% of class	65
% graduated top 25% of class	92
% graduated top 50% of class	100

DEADLINES

Early decision application deadline	11/15
Regular application deadline	1/1
Regular notification	4/1
Nonfall registration?	yes

FINANCIAL FACTS
Financial Aid Rating **93**

Comprehensive fee	$39,900
Books and supplies	$1,750
% frosh rec. need-based scholarship or grant aid	40
% UG rec. need-based scholarship or grant aid	40
% frosh rec. need-based self-help aid	37
% UG rec. need-based self-help aid	39
% frosh rec. any financial aid	40
% UG rec. any financial aid	40
Avg. frosh grant	$21,983
Avg. frosh loan	$3,230

BENNINGTON COLLEGE

CAMPUS LIFE
Quality of Life Rating **69**
Fire Safety Rating **86**

Type of school	private
Environment	village

STUDENTS

Total undergrad enrollment	621
% male/female	34/66
% from out of state	96
% live on campus	97
% African American	1
% Asian	2
% Caucasian	86
% Hispanic	3
% international	4
# of countries represented	18

ACADEMICS
Academic Rating **87**

Calendar	15-week fall and spring terms, 7-week winter work term
Student/faculty ratio	8:1
Professors Interesting Rating	84
Professors Accessible Rating	76
% professors teaching UG courses	100
% classes taught by TAs	2
Most common lab size	10-19 students
Most common regular class size	10-19 students

MOST POPULAR MAJORS
English language and literature
social sciences
visual and performing arts

SELECTIVITY
Admissions Selectivity Rating **87**

# of applicants	842
% of applicants accepted	73
% of acceptees attending	33
# of early decision applicants	39
% accepted early decision	71

FRESHMAN PROFILE

Range SAT Verbal	580-690
Average SAT Verbal	640
Range SAT Math	510-610
Average SAT Math	560
Projected Range SAT Writing	620-690
Range ACT Composite	23-27
Average ACT Composite	25

Minimum Paper TOEFL	550
Minimum Computer Based TOEFL	213
Average HS GPA	3.29
% graduated top 10% of class	23
% graduated top 25% of class	61
% graduated top 50% of class	86

DEADLINES

Early decision application deadline	11/15
Regular application deadline	1/1
Regular notification	4/1
Nonfall registration?	yes

FINANCIAL FACTS

Financial Aid Rating	**70**
Annual tuition	$30,270
Room & Board	$7,710
Books and supplies	$800
Required fees	$800
% frosh rec. need-based scholarship or grant aid	64
% UG rec. need-based scholarship or grant aid	65
% frosh rec. need-based self-help aid	62
% UG rec. need-based self-help aid	63
% frosh rec. any financial aid	72
% UG rec. any financial aid	79
Avg. frosh grant	$19,163
Avg. frosh loan	$2,980

BENTLEY COLLEGE

CAMPUS LIFE

Quality of Life Rating	**87**
Fire Safety Rating	**86**
Type of school	private
Environment	city

STUDENTS

Total undergrad enrollment	4,250
% male/female	58/42
% from out of state	45
% from public high school	71
% live on campus	80
% African American	4
% Asian	7
% Caucasian	69
% Hispanic	4
% international	8
# of countries represented	78

ACADEMICS

Academic Rating	**83**
Calendar	semester
Student/faculty ratio	13:1
Professors Interesting Rating	79
Professors Accessible Rating	84
% professors teaching UG courses	100
Most common lab size	20-29 students

MOST POPULAR MAJORS

business administration/management
finance
marketing/marketing management

SELECTIVITY

Admissions Selectivity Rating	**89**
# of applicants	5,865
% of applicants accepted	45
% of acceptees attending	36
# accepting a place on wait list	936
% admitted from wait list	2
# of early decision applicants	111
% accepted early decision	63

FRESHMAN PROFILE

Range SAT Verbal	540-620
Average SAT Verbal	576
Range SAT Math	580-660
Average SAT Math	623
Projected Range SAT Writing	590-650
Range ACT Composite	23-27
Minimum Paper TOEFL	550
Minimum Computer Based TOEFL	213
% graduated top 10% of class	35
% graduated top 25% of class	76
% graduated top 50% of class	97

DEADLINES

Early decision application deadline	11/15
Regular application deadline	2/1
Regular notification	4/1
Nonfall registration?	yes

FINANCIAL FACTS

Financial Aid Rating	**78**
Annual tuition	$25,330
Room & Board	$9,860
Books and supplies	$920
Required fees	$214
% frosh rec. need-based scholarship or grant aid	53
% UG rec. need-based scholarship or grant aid	48
% frosh rec. need-based self-help aid	48
% UG rec. need-based self-help aid	48
% frosh rec. any financial aid	75
% UG rec. any financial aid	70
Avg. frosh grant	$17,258
Avg. frosh loan	$4,570

BOSTON COLLEGE

CAMPUS LIFE

Quality of Life Rating	**94**
Fire Safety Rating	**99**
Type of school	private
Affiliation	Roman Catholic
Environment	city

STUDENTS

Total undergrad enrollment	9,059
% male/female	47/53
% from out of state	72
% from public high school	60
% live on campus	78
% African American	6
% Asian	9
% Caucasian	74
% Hispanic	7
% international	2
# of countries represented	94

ACADEMICS

Academic Rating	**88**
Calendar	semester
Student/faculty ratio	13:1
Professors Interesting Rating	84
Professors Accessible Rating	83
% professors teaching UG courses	100
Most common lab size	10-19 students

MOST POPULAR MAJORS

Communications and media studies
English language and literature
finance

SELECTIVITY

Admissions Selectivity Rating	**96**
# of applicants	22,451
% of applicants accepted	32
% of acceptees attending	32
# accepting a place on wait list	5,000
% admitted from wait list	3

FRESHMAN PROFILE

Range SAT Verbal	610-700
Average SAT Verbal	650
Range SAT Math	630-710
Average SAT Math	667
Projected Range SAT Writing	640-700
Minimum Paper TOEFL	600
Minimum Computer Based TOEFL	250
% graduated top 10% of class	74
% graduated top 25% of class	95
% graduated top 50% of class	99

DEADLINES

Regular application deadline	1/2
Regular notification	4/15
Nonfall registration?	yes

FINANCIAL FACTS

Financial Aid Rating	**93**
Annual tuition	$28,940
Room & Board	$10,580
Books and supplies	$650
Required fees	$456
% frosh rec. need-based scholarship or grant aid	36

% UG rec. need-based scholarship
or grant aid 37
% frosh rec. need-based self-help aid 36
% UG rec. need-based self-help aid 38
% frosh rec. any financial aid 70
% UG rec. any financial aid 70
Avg. frosh grant $17,638
Avg. frosh loan $4,104

BOSTON UNIVERSITY

CAMPUS LIFE
Quality of Life Rating **82**
Fire Safety Rating **60**
Type of school private
Environment metropolis
STUDENTS
Total undergrad enrollment 15,953
% male/female 40/60
% from out of state 77
% from public high school 70
% live on campus 74
% in (# of) fraternities 3 (8)
% in (# of) sororities 5 (10)
% African American 2
% Asian 13
% Caucasian 58
% Hispanic 5
% international 7
# of countries represented 103

ACADEMICS
Academic Rating **85**
Calendar semester
Student/faculty ratio 15:1
Professors Interesting Rating 72
Professors Accessible Rating 74
% professors teaching UG courses 75
% classes taught by TAs 6
Most common lab size 10-19 students
Most common
regular class size 20-29 students
MOST POPULAR MAJORS
business administration/management
communications and media studies
engineering

SELECTIVITY
Admissions Selectivity Rating **94**
# of applicants 28,240
% of applicants accepted 55
% of acceptees attending 28
# accepting a place on wait list 1,738
% admitted from wait list 3
# of early decision applicants 219
% accepted early decision 47
FRESHMAN PROFILE
Range SAT Verbal 600-690

Average SAT Verbal 643
Range SAT Math 610-700
Average SAT Math 656
Projected Range SAT Writing 630-690
Range ACT Composite 26-30
Average ACT Composite 28
Minimum Paper TOEFL 550
Minimum Computer Based TOEFL 215
Average HS GPA 3.5
% graduated top 10% of class 60
% graduated top 25% of class 92
% graduated top 50% of class 100
DEADLINES
Early decision application deadline 11/1
Regular application deadline 1/1
Regular notification late March
through mid-April
Nonfall registration? yes

FINANCIAL FACTS
Financial Aid Rating **86**
Annual tuition $31,530
Room & Board $10,080
Books and supplies $754
Required fees $436
% frosh rec. need-based scholarship
or grant aid 47
% UG rec. need-based scholarship
or grant aid 43
% frosh rec. need-based self-help aid 43
% UG rec. need-based self-help aid 42
% frosh rec. any financial aid 70
% UG rec. any financial aid 66
Avg. frosh grant $18,844
Avg. frosh loan $3,656

BOWDOIN COLLEGE

CAMPUS LIFE
Quality of Life Rating **95**
Fire Safety Rating **60**
Type of school private
Environment village
STUDENTS
Total undergrad enrollment 1,665
% male/female 51/49
% from out of state 86
% from public high school 53
% live on campus 93
% African American 5
% Asian 11
% Caucasian 72
% Hispanic 6
% Native American 1
% international 3
# of countries represented 29

ACADEMICS
Academic Rating **94**
Calendar semester
Student/faculty ratio 10:1
Professors Interesting Rating 89
Professors Accessible Rating 94
% professors teaching UG courses 100
Most common lab size 10-19 students
Most common
regular class size 10-19 students
MOST POPULAR MAJORS
biology/biological sciences
economics
political science and government

SELECTIVITY
Admissions Selectivity Rating **98**
# of applicants 4,853
% of applicants accepted 24
% of acceptees attending 40
# of early decision applicants 189
% accepted early decision 30
FRESHMAN PROFILE
Range SAT Verbal 640-740
Average SAT Verbal 690
Range SAT Math 650-720
Average SAT Math 690
Projected Range SAT Writing 660-720
Minimum Paper TOEFL 600
Minimum Computer Based TOEFL 250
% graduated top 10% of class 82
% graduated top 25% of class 96
% graduated top 50% of class 100
DEADLINES
Early decision application deadline 11/15
Regular application deadline 1/1
Regular notification 4/5
Nonfall registration? no

FINANCIAL FACTS
Financial Aid Rating **97**
Annual tuition $30,944
Room & Board $8,054
Books and supplies $880
Required fees $682
% frosh rec. need-based scholarship
or grant aid 42
% UG rec. need-based scholarship
or grant aid 46
% frosh rec. need-based self-help aid 37
% UG rec. need-based self-help aid 42
% frosh rec. any financial aid 45
% UG rec. any financial aid 49
Avg. frosh grant $24,041
Avg. frosh loan $3,275

BRANDEIS UNIVERSITY

CAMPUS LIFE
Quality of Life Rating **84**
Fire Safety Rating **60**
Type of school private
Environment village
STUDENTS
Total undergrad enrollment 3,158
% male/female 44/56
% from out of state 75
% from public high school 70
% live on campus 82
% African American 3
% Asian 8
% Caucasian 67
% Hispanic 3
% international 7
# of countries represented 54

ACADEMICS
Academic Rating **90**
Calendar semester
Student/faculty ratio 9:1
Professors Interesting Rating 87
Professors Accessible Rating 83
% professors teaching UG courses 100
Most common lab size 10-19 students
MOST POPULAR MAJORS
computer and information sciences and
support services
political science and government
psychology

SELECTIVITY
Admissions Selectivity Rating **96**
# of applicants 5,831
% of applicants accepted 40
% of acceptees attending 33
# accepting a place on wait list 874
% admitted from wait list 4
# of early decision applicants 222
% accepted early decision 67
FRESHMAN PROFILE
Range SAT Verbal 630-720
Average SAT Verbal 660
Range SAT Math 630-720
Average SAT Math 670
Projected Range SAT Writing 650-710
Range ACT Composite 28-33
Minimum Paper TOEFL 600
Minimum Computer Based TOEFL 250
Average HS GPA 3.85
% graduated top 10% of class 71
% graduated top 25% of class 89
% graduated top 50% of class 100
DEADLINES
Early decision application deadline 1/1

Regular application deadline 1/31
Regular notification 4/15
Nonfall registration? yes
FINANCIAL FACTS
Financial Aid Rating **60**
Annual tuition $30,159
Room & board $8,656
% frosh rec. need-based scholarship
or grant aid 56
% frosh rec. need-based self-help aid 46
Avg. frosh grant $15,825
Avg. frosh loan $3,002

BROWN UNIVERSITY

CAMPUS LIFE
Quality of Life Rating **95**
Fire Safety Rating **60**
Type of school private
STUDENTS
Total undergrad enrollment 5,772
% male/female 46/54
% from out of state 96
% from public high school 60
% live on campus 85
% in (# of) fraternities 15 (10)
% in (# of) sororities 5 (3)
% African American 7
% Asian 13
% Caucasian 51
% Hispanic 7
% Native American 1
% international 6
# of countries represented 72

ACADEMICS
Academic Rating **83**
Calendar semester
Student/faculty ratio 9:1
Professors Interesting Rating 84
Professors Accessible Rating 88
% professors teaching UG courses 100
% classes taught by TAs 13
MOST POPULAR MAJORS
history
international relations and affairs

SELECTIVITY
Admissions Selectivity Rating **99**
# of applicants 15,286
% of applicants accepted 17
% of acceptees attending 58
# accepting a place on wait list 1,400
% admitted from wait list 6
# of early decision applicants 551
% accepted early decision 29
FRESHMAN PROFILE
Range SAT Verbal 650-760

Average SAT Verbal 690
Range SAT Math 660-760
Average SAT Math 700
Projected Range SAT Writing 670-740
Range ACT Composite 27-32
Average ACT Composite 29
Minimum Paper TOEFL 600
Minimum Computer Based TOEFL 250
% graduated top 10% of class 90
% graduated top 25% of class 98
% graduated top 50% of class 100
DEADLINES
Early decision application deadline 11/1
Regular application deadline 1/1
Regular notification 4/1
Nonfall registration? no
FINANCIAL FACTS
Financial Aid Rating **96**
Annual tuition $30,672
Room & Board $8,474
Books and supplies $2,300
Required fees $901
% frosh rec. need-based scholarship
or grant aid 39
% UG rec. need-based scholarship
or grant aid 37
% frosh rec. need-based self-help aid 38
% UG rec. need-based self-help aid 39
Avg. frosh grant $21,600
Avg. frosh loan $4,000

BRYANT UNIVERSITY

CAMPUS LIFE
Quality of Life Rating **84**
Fire Safety Rating **91**
Type of school private
Environment town
STUDENTS
Total undergrad enrollment 3,030
% male/female 60/40
% from out of state 83
% from public high school 80
% live on campus 84
% in (# of) fraternities 11 (6)
% in (# of) sororities 7 (3)
% African American 3
% Asian 3
% Caucasian 84
% Hispanic 3
% international 2
# of countries represented 28

ACADEMICS
Academic Rating **77**
Calendar semester
Student/faculty ratio 16:1

Professors Interesting Rating 79
Professors Accessible Rating 82
% professors teaching UG courses 100
Most common lab size 30-39 students
Most common
regular class size 30-39 students

MOST POPULAR MAJORS
business administration/management
finance
marketing/marketing management

SELECTIVITY
Admissions Selectivity Rating 84
# of applicants 3,879
% of applicants accepted 63
% of acceptees attending 31
# accepting a place on wait list 541
% admitted from wait list 24
# of early decision applicants 48
% accepted early decision 75

FRESHMAN PROFILE
Range SAT Verbal 490-580
Average SAT Verbal 535
Range SAT Math 530-610
Average SAT Math 569
Projected Range SAT Writing 550-620
Range ACT Composite 22-25
Average ACT Composite 24
Minimum Paper TOEFL 550
Minimum Computer Based TOEFL 213
Average HS GPA 3.2
% graduated top 10% of class 13
% graduated top 25% of class 47
% graduated top 50% of class 88

DEADLINES
Early decision application deadline 11/15
Regular application deadline 2/15
Regular notification 3/15
Nonfall registration? yes

FINANCIAL FACTS
Financial Aid Rating 70
Annual tuition $24,762
Room & Board $9,568
Books and supplies $1,000
% frosh rec. need-based scholarship
or grant aid 57
% UG rec. need-based scholarship
or grant aid 48
% frosh rec. need-based self-help aid 60
% UG rec. need-based self-help aid 58
% frosh rec. any financial aid 81
% UG rec. any financial aid 88
Avg. frosh grant $11,274
Avg. frosh loan $4,231

BRYN MAWR COLLEGE

CAMPUS LIFE
Quality of Life Rating 95
Fire Safety Rating 89
Type of school private
Environment metropolis

STUDENTS
Total undergrad enrollment 1,313
% male/female 2/98
% from out of state 80
% from public high school 60
% live on campus 97
% African American 5
% Asian 11
% Caucasian 45
% Hispanic 3
% international 8
# of countries represented 44

ACADEMICS
Academic Rating 90
Calendar semester
Student/faculty ratio 8:1
Professors Interesting Rating 93
Professors Accessible Rating 90
% professors teaching UG courses 100
Most common lab size 10-19 students

MOST POPULAR MAJORS
English language and literature
political science and government

SELECTIVITY
Admissions Selectivity Rating 95
# of applicants 1,926
% of applicants accepted 47
% of acceptees attending 40
# accepting a place on wait list 288
% admitted from wait list 5
# of early decision applicants 97
% accepted early decision 73

FRESHMAN PROFILE
Range SAT Verbal 620-720
Average SAT Verbal 668
Range SAT Math 600-690
Average SAT Math 645
Projected Range SAT Writing 650-710
Average ACT Composite 28
Minimum Paper TOEFL 600
Minimum Computer Based TOEFL 250
% graduated top 10% of class 66
% graduated top 25% of class 93
% graduated top 50% of class 100

DEADLINES
Early decision application deadline 11/15
Regular application deadline 1/15

Regular notification 4/15
Nonfall registration? no

FINANCIAL FACTS
Financial Aid Rating 97
Annual tuition $27,900
Room & Board $9,700
Books and supplies $1,000
Required fees $730
% frosh rec. need-based scholarship
or grant aid 52
% UG rec. need-based scholarship
or grant aid 53
% frosh rec. need-based self-help aid 42
% UG rec. need-based self-help aid 45
% frosh rec. any financial aid 57
% UG rec. any financial aid 59
Avg. frosh grant $22,406
Avg. frosh loan $3,472

BUCKNELL UNIVERSITY

CAMPUS LIFE
Quality of Life Rating 82
Fire Safety Rating 75
Type of school private
Environment rural

STUDENTS
Total undergrad enrollment 3,419
% male/female 50/50
% from out of state 68
% from public high school 68
% live on campus 88
% in (# of) fraternities 35 (11)
% in (# of) sororities 38 (7)
% African American 3
% Asian 6
% Caucasian 84
% Hispanic 2
% international 3
# of countries represented 41

ACADEMICS
Academic Rating 91
Calendar semester
Student/faculty ratio 11:1
Professors Interesting Rating 87
Professors Accessible Rating 89
% professors teaching UG courses 100
Most common lab size 10-19 students
Most common
regular class size 10-19 students

MOST POPULAR MAJORS
biology/biological sciences
business administration/management
economics

SELECTIVITY

Admissions Selectivity Rating **95**

# of applicants	8,324
% of applicants accepted	36
% of acceptees attending	30
# accepting a place on wait list	1,862
% admitted from wait list	4
# of early decision applicants	332
% accepted early decision	49

FRESHMAN PROFILE

Range SAT Verbal	600-670
Average SAT Verbal	636
Range SAT Math	630-710
Average SAT Math	666
Projected Range SAT Writing	630-680
Range ACT Composite	27-31
Average ACT Composite	29
Minimum Paper TOEFL	550
Minimum Computer Based TOEFL	213
% graduated top 10% of class	64
% graduated top 25% of class	93
% graduated top 50% of class	99

DEADLINES

Early decision application deadline	11/15
Regular application deadline	1/1
Regular notification	4/1
Nonfall registration?	no

FINANCIAL FACTS

Financial Aid Rating **96**

Annual tuition	$32,592
Room & Board	$6,872
Books and supplies	$750
Required fees	$196
% frosh rec. need-based scholarship or grant aid	46
% UG rec. need-based scholarship or grant aid	45
% frosh rec. need-based self-help aid	48
% UG rec. need-based self-help aid	51
% frosh rec. any financial aid	49
% UG rec. any financial aid	51
Avg. frosh grant	$17,300
Avg. frosh loan	$4,000

CALIFORNIA UNIVERSITY OF PENNSYLVANIA

CAMPUS LIFE

Quality of Life Rating	**67**
Fire Safety Rating	**60**
Type of school	public
Environment	village

STUDENTS

Total undergrad enrollment	5,350
% male/female	48/52
% from out of state	4
% from public high school	80
% live on campus	30
% in (# of) fraternities	10 (6)
% in (# of) sororities	10 (7)
% African American	5
% Caucasian	70
% Hispanic	1
% international	1
# of countries represented	18

ACADEMICS

Academic Rating **70**

Calendar	semester
Student/faculty ratio	22:1
Professors Interesting Rating	72
Professors Accessible Rating	69
% professors teaching UG courses	98
Most common lab size	20-29 students
Most common regular class size	20-29 students

MOST POPULAR MAJORS
business administration and management
criminal justice/safety studies
education

SELECTIVITY

Admissions Selectivity Rating **70**

# of applicants	3,015
% of applicants accepted	74
% of acceptees attending	47

FRESHMAN PROFILE

Range SAT Verbal	430-520
Average SAT Verbal	492
Range SAT Math	440-530
Average SAT Math	496
Projected Range SAT Writing	500-570
Minimum Paper TOEFL	450
Minimum Computer Based TOEFL	133
Average HS GPA	2.97
% graduated top 10% of class	3
% graduated top 25% of class	13
% graduated top 50% of class	40

DEADLINES

Regular notification	within 2 weeks
Nonfall registration?	yes

FINANCIAL FACTS

Financial Aid Rating **62**

Annual in-state tuition	$4,810
Annual out-of-state tuition	$7,216
Room & Board	$7,164
Books and supplies	$650
Required fees	$1,441
% frosh rec. need-based scholarship or grant aid	59
% UG rec. need-based scholarship or grant aid	52
% frosh rec. need-based self-help aid	66
% UG rec. need-based self-help aid	64
% frosh rec. any financial aid	76
% UG rec. any financial aid	72
Avg. frosh grant	$3,794
Avg. frosh loan	$2,768

CARNEGIE MELLON UNIVERSITY

CAMPUS LIFE

Quality of Life Rating	**66**
Fire Safety Rating	**71**
Type of school	private
Environment	metropolis

STUDENTS

Total undergrad enrollment	5,389
% male/female	61/39
% from out of state	76
% live on campus	84
% in (# of) fraternities	14 (13)
% in (# of) sororities	11 (5)
% African American	5
% Asian	23
% Caucasian	42
% Hispanic	5
% Native American	1
% international	12
# of countries represented	93

ACADEMICS

Academic Rating **91**

Calendar	semester
Student/faculty ratio	10:1
Professors Interesting Rating	75
Professors Accessible Rating	79
Most common lab size	fewer than 10 students
Most common regular class size	20-29 students

MOST POPULAR MAJORS
business administration and management
computer engineering
computer science

SELECTIVITY

Admissions Selectivity Rating **96**

# of applicants	14,114
% of applicants accepted	42
% of acceptees attending	23
# accepting a place on wait list	2,709
% admitted from wait list	4
# of early decision applicants	179
% accepted early decision	53

FRESHMAN PROFILE

Range SAT Verbal	610-710
Average SAT Verbal	657
Range SAT Math	680-770
Average SAT Math	718

Projected Range SAT Writing	640-700
Range ACT Composite	27-32
Average ACT Composite	30
Minimum Paper TOEFL	600
Minimum Computer Based TOEFL	250
Average HS GPA	3.6
% graduated top 10% of class	72
% graduated top 25% of class	95
% graduated top 50% of class	100

DEADLINES

Early decision application deadline	11/15
Regular application deadline	1/1
Regular notification	4/15
Nonfall registration?	no

FINANCIAL FACTS

Financial Aid Rating	**76**
Annual tuition	$31,650
Room & board	$8,916
Books and supplies	$925
% frosh rec. need-based scholarship or grant aid	52
% UG rec. need-based scholarship or grant aid	48
% frosh rec. need-based self-help aid	51
% UG rec. need-based self-help aid	49
% frosh rec. any financial aid	70
% UG rec. any financial aid	66
Avg. frosh grant	$17,446
Avg. frosh loan	$6,200

THE CATHOLIC UNIVERSITY OF AMERICA

CAMPUS LIFE

Quality of Life Rating	**67**
Fire Safety Rating	**85**
Type of school	private
Affiliation	Roman Catholic
Environment	metropolis

STUDENTS

Total undergrad enrollment	2,871
% male/female	44/56
% from out of state	93
% from public high school	50
% live on campus	68
% in (# of) fraternities	1 (1)
% in (# of) sororities	1 (1)
% African American	7
% Asian	3
% Caucasian	71
% Hispanic	5
% international	2
# of countries represented	80

ACADEMICS

Academic Rating	**73**

Calendar	semester
Student/faculty ratio	9:1
Professors Interesting Rating	76
Professors Accessible Rating	75
% professors teaching UG courses	66
% classes taught by TAs	11
Most common lab size	10-19 students
Most common regular class size	20-29 students

MOST POPULAR MAJORS

architecture
(BArch, BA/BS, MArch, MA/MS, PhD)
engineering
political science and government

SELECTIVITY

Admissions Selectivity Rating	**85**
# of applicants	2,744
% of applicants accepted	82
% of acceptees attending	32
# of early decision applicants	85
% accepted early decision	65

FRESHMAN PROFILE

Range SAT Verbal	520-640
Average SAT Verbal	590
Range SAT Math	510-620
Average SAT Math	577
Projected Range SAT Writing	570-660
Range ACT Composite	21-27
Average ACT Composite	24
Minimum Paper TOEFL	560
Minimum Computer Based TOEFL	220
Average HS GPA	3.37
% graduated top 10% of class	22
% graduated top 25% of class	57
% graduated top 50% of class	88

DEADLINES

Regular application deadline	2/1
Regular notification	3/15
Nonfall registration?	yes

FINANCIAL FACTS

Financial Aid Rating	**69**
Annual tuition	$24,800
Room & Board	$9,838
Books and supplies	$1,000
Required fees	$1,200
% frosh rec. need-based scholarship or grant aid	40
% UG rec. need-based scholarship or grant aid	25
% frosh rec. need-based self-help aid	47
% UG rec. need-based self-help aid	42
% frosh rec. any financial aid	98
% UG rec. any financial aid	91
Avg. frosh grant	$10,231
Avg. frosh loan	$6,585

CENTRAL CONNECTICUT STATE UNIVERSITY

CAMPUS LIFE

Quality of Life Rating	**69**
Fire Safety Rating	**84**
Type of school	public
Environment	village

STUDENTS

Total undergrad enrollment	9,016
% male/female	49/51
% from out of state	4
% live on campus	21
% in (# of) fraternities	1
% in (# of) sororities	1 (1)
% African American	8
% Asian	3
% Caucasian	74
% Hispanic	6
% Native American	1
% international	2
# of countries represented	64

ACADEMICS

Academic Rating	**70**
Calendar	semester
Student/faculty ratio	19:1
Professors Interesting Rating	69
Professors Accessible Rating	68
% professors teaching UG courses	100
Most common lab size	20-29 students
Most common regular class size	fewer than 10 students

MOST POPULAR MAJORS

accounting
psychology
teacher education, multiple levels

SELECTIVITY

Admissions Selectivity Rating	**70**
# of applicants	5,198
% of applicants accepted	61
% of acceptees attending	41

FRESHMAN PROFILE

Range SAT Verbal	470-560
Average SAT Verbal	514
Range SAT Math	470-570
Average SAT Math	518
Projected Range SAT Writing	530-600
Minimum Paper TOEFL	500
% graduated top 10% of class	7
% graduated top 25% of class	27
% graduated top 50% of class	68

DEADLINES

Regular application deadline	6/1
Regular notification	rolling
Nonfall registration?	yes

FINANCIAL FACTS

Financial Aid Rating	**64**
Annual in-state tuition	$2,862
Annual out-of-state tuition	$9,264
Room & Board	$7,036
Books and supplies	$750
Required fees	$3,040
% frosh rec. need-based scholarship or grant aid	39
% UG rec. need-based scholarship or grant aid	34
% frosh rec. need-based self-help aid	44
% UG rec. need-based self-help aid	46
% frosh rec. any financial aid	53
% UG rec. any financial aid	54
Avg. frosh grant	$5,306
Avg. frosh loan	$3,031

CHATHAM COLLEGE

CAMPUS LIFE

Quality of Life Rating	**89**
Fire Safety Rating	**71**
Type of school	private
Environment	metropolis

STUDENTS

Total undergrad enrollment	431
% male/female	0/100
% from out of state	20
% from public high school	96
% live on campus	60
% African American	12
% Asian	2
% Caucasian	69
% Hispanic	3
% international	6
# of countries represented	16

ACADEMICS

Academic Rating	**86**
Calendar	4-1-4
Student/faculty ratio	13:1
Professors Interesting Rating	91
Professors Accessible Rating	89
% professors teaching UG courses	78
Most common lab size	fewer than 10 students
Most common regular class size	10-19 students

MOST POPULAR MAJORS
English language and literature
psychology

SELECTIVITY

Admissions Selectivity Rating	**84**
# of applicants	469
% of applicants accepted	62
% of acceptees attending	31

FRESHMAN PROFILE

Range SAT Verbal	510-620
Range SAT Math	470-580
Projected Range SAT Writing	570-650
Range ACT Composite	22-27
Minimum Paper TOEFL	550
Minimum Computer Based TOEFL	210
Average HS GPA	3.45
% graduated top 10% of class	23
% graduated top 25% of class	54
% graduated top 50% of class	88

DEADLINES

Regular notification	rolling
Nonfall registration?	yes

FINANCIAL FACTS

Financial Aid Rating	**87**
Annual tuition	$21,780
Room & Board	$7,050
Books and supplies	$860
Required fees	$216
% frosh rec. need-based scholarship or grant aid	77
% UG rec. need-based scholarship or grant aid	89
% frosh rec. need-based self-help aid	77
% UG rec. need-based self-help aid	91
% frosh rec. any financial aid	95
% UG rec. any financial aid	95
Avg. frosh grant	$12,000
Avg. frosh loan	$2,625

CHESTNUT HILL COLLEGE

CAMPUS LIFE

Quality of Life Rating	**65**
Fire Safety Rating	**60**
Type of school	private
Affiliation	Roman Catholic
Environment	metropolis

STUDENTS

Total undergrad enrollment	973
% male/female	26/74
% from out of state	20
% from public high school	50
% live on campus	65
% African American	41
% Asian	2
% Caucasian	52
% Hispanic	5
% international	1
# of countries represented	12

ACADEMICS

Academic Rating	**73**
Calendar	2 undergrad calendars; semester and 6 sessions that are 8 weeks long

Student/faculty ratio	10:1
Professors Interesting Rating	74
Professors Accessible Rating	67
% professors teaching UG courses	64
Most common lab size	fewer than 10 students
Most common regular class size	10-19 students

MOST POPULAR MAJORS
business administration/management
elementary education and teaching
psychology

SELECTIVITY

Admissions Selectivity Rating	**72**
# of applicants	1,092
% of applicants accepted	72
% of acceptees attending	25

FRESHMAN PROFILE

Range SAT Verbal	440-550
Average SAT Verbal	497
Range SAT Math	420-520
Average SAT Math	478
Projected Range SAT Writing	510-600
Average ACT Composite	20
Minimum Paper TOEFL	500
Average HS GPA	2.95
% graduated top 10% of class	9
% graduated top 25% of class	20
% graduated top 50% of class	55

DEADLINES

Regular notification	rolling
Nonfall registration?	yes

FINANCIAL FACTS

Financial Aid Rating	**82**
Annual tuition	$19,660
Room & Board	$7,500
Books and supplies	$2,045
Required fees	$720
% frosh rec. need-based scholarship or grant aid	71
% UG rec. need-based scholarship or grant aid	69
% frosh rec. need-based self-help aid	71
% UG rec. need-based self-help aid	69
% frosh rec. any financial aid	71
% UG rec. any financial aid	69
Avg. frosh grant	$8,525
Avg. frosh loan	$2,625

CHEYNEY UNIVERSITY OF PENNSYLVANIA

CAMPUS LIFE

Quality of Life Rating	**63**
Fire Safety Rating	**60**
Type of school	public

Environment	village

STUDENTS

Total undergrad enrollment	1,087
% male/female	46/54
% from out of state	17
% live on campus	68
% in (# of) fraternities	5 (4)
% in (# of) sororities	8 (4)
% African American	98
% Hispanic	1
% international	1

ACADEMICS

Academic Rating	**60**
Calendar	semester
Student/faculty ratio	18:1
Professors Interesting Rating	67
Professors Accessible Rating	61
% professors teaching UG courses	89

SELECTIVITY

Admissions Selectivity Rating	**60**
# of applicants	1,164
% of applicants accepted	82
% of acceptees attending	31

FRESHMAN PROFILE

Minimum Paper TOEFL	500

DEADLINES

Regular notification	rolling
Nonfall registration?	yes

FINANCIAL FACTS

Financial Aid Rating	**77**
Annual in-state tuition	$3,792
Annual out-of-state tuition	$9,480
Room & Board	$4,983
Books and supplies	$675
Required fees	$655
% frosh rec. need-based scholarship or grant aid	72
% UG rec. need-based scholarship or grant aid	61
% frosh rec. need-based self-help aid	84
% UG rec. need-based self-help aid	80

CLARK UNIVERSITY

CAMPUS LIFE

Quality of Life Rating	**71**
Fire Safety Rating	**96**
Type of school	private
Environment	city

STUDENTS

Total undergrad enrollment	2,082
% male/female	39/61
% from out of state	60
% from public high school	70
% live on campus	77

% African American	3
% Asian	4
% Caucasian	64
% Hispanic	3
% international	7
# of countries represented	56

ACADEMICS

Academic Rating	**82**
Calendar	semester
Student/faculty ratio	10:1
Professors Interesting Rating	76
Professors Accessible Rating	80
% professors teaching UG courses	100
Most common lab size	10-19 students
Most common regular class size	10-19 students

MOST POPULAR MAJORS

English language and literature
political science and government
psychology

SELECTIVITY

Admissions Selectivity Rating	**89**
# of applicants	4,239
% of applicants accepted	62
% of acceptees attending	20
# accepting a place on wait list	91
% admitted from wait list	12
# of early decision applicants	75
% accepted early decision	83

FRESHMAN PROFILE

Range SAT Verbal	540-660
Average SAT Verbal	593
Range SAT Math	540-645
Average SAT Math	588
Projected Range SAT Writing	590-670
Range ACT Composite	22-28
Average ACT Composite	25
Minimum Paper TOEFL	550
Minimum Computer Based TOEFL	213
Average HS GPA	3.4
% graduated top 10% of class	31
% graduated top 25% of class	72
% graduated top 50% of class	99

DEADLINES

Early decision application deadline	11/15
Regular application deadline	2/1
Regular notification	4/1

FINANCIAL FACTS

Financial Aid Rating	**89**
Annual tuition	$29,300
Room & Board	$5,400
Books and supplies	$800
Required fees	$265
% frosh rec. need-based scholarship or grant aid	58

% UG rec. need-based scholarship or grant aid	58
% frosh rec. need-based self-help aid	54
% UG rec. need-based self-help aid	54
% frosh rec. any financial aid	78
% UG rec. any financial aid	77
Avg. frosh grant	$17,630
Avg. frosh loan	$3,633

CLARKSON UNIVERSITY

CAMPUS LIFE

Quality of Life Rating	**62**
Fire Safety Rating	**78**
Type of school	private
Environment	village

STUDENTS

Total undergrad enrollment	2,717
% male/female	77/23
% from out of state	25
% from public high school	86
% live on campus	77
% in (# of) fraternities	15 (11)
% in (# of) sororities	12 (2)
% African American	2
% Asian	2
% Caucasian	92
% Hispanic	2
% international	2
# of countries represented	41

ACADEMICS

Academic Rating	**70**
Calendar	semester
Student/faculty ratio	16:1
Professors Interesting Rating	64
Professors Accessible Rating	74
% professors teaching UG courses	85
% classes taught by TAs	1
Most common lab size	20-29 students
Most common regular class size	10-19 students

MOST POPULAR MAJORS

civil engineering
mechanical engineering
multi/interdisciplinary studies

SELECTIVITY

Admissions Selectivity Rating	**86**
# of applicants	2,473
% of applicants accepted	86
% of acceptees attending	31
# of early decision applicants	153
% accepted early decision	89

FRESHMAN PROFILE

Range SAT Verbal	520-630
Average SAT Verbal	574
Range SAT Math	570-660

Average SAT Math	619
Projected Range SAT Writing	570-650
Range ACT Composite	23-28
Average ACT Composite	25
Minimum Paper TOEFL	500
Minimum Computer Based TOEFL	213
Average HS GPA	3.51
% graduated top 10% of class	33
% graduated top 25% of class	73
% graduated top 50% of class	93

DEADLINES

Early decision application deadline	12/1
Regular application deadline	3/15
Regular notification	continuous
Nonfall registration?	yes

FINANCIAL FACTS

Financial Aid Rating	**90**
Annual tuition	$25,185
Room & Board	$9,345
Books and supplies	$1,000
Required fees	$400
% frosh rec. need-based scholarship or grant aid	69
% UG rec. need-based scholarship or grant aid	66
% frosh rec. need-based self-help aid	72
% UG rec. need-based self-help aid	75
% frosh rec. any financial aid	86
% UG rec. any financial aid	87
Avg. frosh grant	$13,680
Avg. frosh loan	$6,225

COLBY COLLEGE

CAMPUS LIFE

Quality of Life Rating	**83**
Fire Safety Rating	**69**
Type of school	private
Environment	town

STUDENTS

Total undergrad enrollment	1,820
% male/female	47/53
% from out of state	87
% from public high school	58
% live on campus	93
% African American	1
% Asian	5
% Caucasian	83
% Hispanic	3
% Native American	1
% international	7
# of countries represented	66

ACADEMICS

Academic Rating	**92**
Calendar	4-1-4
Student/faculty ratio	10:1

Professors Interesting Rating	89
Professors Accessible Rating	86
% professors teaching UG courses	100
Most common lab size	10-19 students
Most common regular class size	10-19 students

MOST POPULAR MAJORS
biology/biological sciences
economics
English language and literature

SELECTIVITY

Admissions Selectivity Rating	**96**
# of applicants	4,065
% of applicants accepted	37
% of acceptees attending	34
# accepting a place on wait list	604
% admitted from wait list	9
# of early decision applicants	197
% accepted early decision	40

FRESHMAN PROFILE

Range SAT Verbal	640-720
Average SAT Verbal	676
Range SAT Math	640-710
Average SAT Math	678
Projected Range SAT Writing	660-710
Range ACT Composite	27-31
Average ACT Composite	29
Minimum Paper TOEFL	600
Minimum Computer Based TOEFL	240
% graduated top 10% of class	66
% graduated top 25% of class	92
% graduated top 50% of class	98

DEADLINES

Early decision application deadline	11/15
Regular application deadline	1/1
Regular notification	4/1
Nonfall registration?	yes

FINANCIAL FACTS

Financial Aid Rating	**94**
Comprehensive fee	$41,770
Books and supplies	$600
% frosh rec. need-based scholarship or grant aid	38
% UG rec. need-based scholarship or grant aid	37
% frosh rec. need-based self-help aid	32
% UG rec. need-based self-help aid	32
% frosh rec. any financial aid	39
% UG rec. any financial aid	39
Avg. frosh grant	$23,348
Avg. frosh loan	$2,984

COLGATE UNIVERSITY

CAMPUS LIFE

Quality of Life Rating	**83**

Fire Safety Rating	**82**
Type of school	private
Environment	rural

STUDENTS

Total undergrad enrollment	2,800
% male/female	48/52
% from out of state	65
% from public high school	70
% live on campus	90
% in (# of) fraternities	37 (7)
% in (# of) sororities	30 (4)
% African American	4
% Asian	6
% Caucasian	75
% Hispanic	4
% Native American	1
% international	5
# of countries represented	37

ACADEMICS

Academic Rating	**93**
Calendar	semester
Student/faculty ratio	10:1
Professors Interesting Rating	92
Professors Accessible Rating	93
% professors teaching UG courses	100
Most common lab size	10-19 students
Most common regular class size	10-19 students

MOST POPULAR MAJORS
economics
English language and literature
history

SELECTIVITY

Admissions Selectivity Rating	**97**
# of applicants	6,551
% of applicants accepted	33
% of acceptees attending	34
# accepting a place on wait list	889
% admitted from wait list	5
# of early decision applicants	282
% accepted early decision	60

FRESHMAN PROFILE

Range SAT Verbal	630-710
Average SAT Verbal	666
Range SAT Math	640-720
Average SAT Math	675
Projected Range SAT Writing	650-700
Range ACT Composite	28-32
Average ACT Composite	29
Minimum Paper TOEFL	600
Minimum Computer Based TOEFL	250
Average HS GPA	3.6
% graduated top 10% of class	73
% graduated top 25% of class	95
% graduated top 50% of class	100

DEADLINES

Early decision application deadline	11/15
Regular application deadline	1/15
Regular notification	4/1
Nonfall registration?	no

FINANCIAL FACTS

Financial Aid Rating	**98**
Annual tuition	$31,230
Room & Board	$7,620
Books and supplies	$830
Required fees	$210
% frosh rec. need-based scholarship or grant aid	36
% UG rec. need-based scholarship or grant aid	42
% frosh rec. need-based self-help aid	30
% UG rec. need-based self-help aid	34
% frosh rec. any financial aid	36
% UG rec. any financial aid	44
Avg. frosh grant	$29,338
Avg. frosh loan	$2,296

COLLEGE OF THE ATLANTIC

CAMPUS LIFE

Quality of Life Rating	**95**
Fire Safety Rating	**87**
Type of school	private
Environment	rural

STUDENTS

Total undergrad enrollment	262
% male/female	37/63
% from out of state	80
% from public high school	69
% live on campus	36
% international	19
# of countries represented	36

ACADEMICS

Academic Rating	**90**
Calendar	trimester
Student/faculty ratio	9:1
Professors Interesting Rating	96
Professors Accessible Rating	98
% professors teaching UG courses	100
Most common lab size	10-19 students

MOST POPULAR MAJOR
ecology

SELECTIVITY

Admissions Selectivity Rating	**88**
# of applicants	255
% of applicants accepted	67
% of acceptees attending	40
# accepting a place on wait list	12
% admitted from wait list	33
# of early decision applicants	25
% accepted early decision	76

FRESHMAN PROFILE

Range SAT Verbal	550-680
Average SAT Verbal	624
Range SAT Math	510-620
Average SAT Math	586
Projected Range SAT Writing	600-680
Range ACT Composite	23-31
Average ACT Composite	28
Minimum Paper TOEFL	550
Minimum Computer Based TOEFL	217
Average HS GPA	3.3
% graduated top 10% of class	29
% graduated top 25% of class	69
% graduated top 50% of class	87

DEADLINES

Early decision application deadline	12/1
Regular application deadline	2/15
Regular notification	4/1
Nonfall registration?	yes

FINANCIAL FACTS

Financial Aid Rating	**94**
Annual tuition	$24,870
Room & Board	$6,732
Books and supplies	$500
Required fees	$375
% frosh rec. need-based scholarship or grant aid	84
% UG rec. need-based scholarship or grant aid	81
% frosh rec. need-based self-help aid	83
% UG rec. need-based self-help aid	77
% frosh rec. any financial aid	87
% UG rec. any financial aid	90
Avg. frosh grant	$15,427
Avg. frosh loan	$2,625

COLLEGE OF THE HOLY CROSS

CAMPUS LIFE

Quality of Life Rating	**65**
Fire Safety Rating	**60**
Type of school	private
Affiliation	Roman Catholic
Environment	city

STUDENTS

Total undergrad enrollment	2,718
% male/female	46/54
% from out of state	64
% from public high school	52
% live on campus	88
% African American	3
% Asian	5
% Caucasian	77
% Hispanic	5
% international	2
# of countries represented	18

ACADEMICS

Academic Rating	**89**
Calendar	semester
Student/faculty ratio	11:1
Professors Interesting Rating	85
Professors Accessible Rating	86
% professors teaching UG courses	100
Most common lab size	10-19 students
Most common regular class size	fewer than 10 students

MOST POPULAR MAJORS
economics
English language and literature
psychology

SELECTIVITY

Admissions Selectivity Rating	**94**
# of applicants	4,969
% of applicants accepted	44
% of acceptees attending	32
# accepting a place on wait list	1,045
% admitted from wait list	9
# of early decision applicants	249
% accepted early decision	69

FRESHMAN PROFILE

Range SAT Verbal	580-670
Average SAT Verbal	631
Range SAT Math	580-680
Average SAT Math	629
Projected Range SAT Writing	620-680
Minimum Paper TOEFL	550
Minimum Computer Based TOEFL	213
% graduated top 10% of class	60
% graduated top 25% of class	91
% graduated top 50% of class	99

DEADLINES

Early decision application deadline	12/15
Regular application deadline	1/15
Regular notification	4/1
Nonfall registration?	yes

FINANCIAL FACTS

Financial Aid Rating	**93**
Annual tuition	$30,960
Room & board	$9,220
Books and supplies	$700
% frosh rec. need-based scholarship or grant aid	41
% UG rec. need-based scholarship or grant aid	40
% frosh rec. need-based self-help aid	38
% UG rec. need-based self-help aid	39
% frosh rec. any financial aid	56
% UG rec. any financial aid	56
Avg. frosh grant	$16,424
Avg. frosh loan	$4,980

COLLEGE MISERICORDIA

CAMPUS LIFE

Quality of Life Rating	**80**
Fire Safety Rating	**69**
Type of school	private
Affiliation	Roman Catholic
Environment	town

STUDENTS

Total undergrad enrollment	1,934
% male/female	26/74
% from out of state	16
% from public high school	79
% live on campus	39
% African American	1
% Asian	1
% Caucasian	96
% Hispanic	1

ACADEMICS

Academic Rating	**79**
Calendar	semester
Student/faculty ratio	11:1
Professors Interesting Rating	81
Professors Accessible Rating	85
% professors teaching UG courses	97
Most common lab size	10-19 students
Most common regular class size	10-19 students

MOST POPULAR MAJORS
elementary education and teaching
nursing/registered nurse training
(RN, ASN, BSN, MSN)
physical therapy/therapist

SELECTIVITY

Admissions Selectivity Rating	**74**
# of applicants	1,019
% of applicants accepted	78
% of acceptees attending	40
# accepting a place on wait list	23
% admitted from wait list	87

FRESHMAN PROFILE

Range SAT Verbal	450-530
Average SAT Verbal	499
Range SAT Math	450-550
Average SAT Math	502
Projected Range SAT Writing	520-580
Range ACT Composite	21-28
Average ACT Composite	23
Minimum Paper TOEFL	500
Minimum Computer Based TOEFL	75
Average HS GPA	3.1
% graduated top 10% of class	15
% graduated top 25% of class	40
% graduated top 50% of class	71

DEADLINES

Regular notification	rolling
Nonfall registration?	yes

FINANCIAL FACTS

Financial Aid Rating	**73**
Annual tuition	$17,850
Room & Board	$7,850
Books and supplies	$800
Required fees	$950
% frosh rec. need-based scholarship or grant aid	86
% UG rec. need-based scholarship or grant aid	83
% frosh rec. need-based self-help aid	77
% UG rec. need-based self-help aid	73
% frosh rec. any financial aid	100
% UG rec. any financial aid	98
Avg. frosh grant	$9,518
Avg. frosh loan	$3,566

COLLEGE OF MOUNT SAINT VINCENT

CAMPUS LIFE

Quality of Life Rating	**68**
Fire Safety Rating	**61**
Type of school	private
Affiliation	Roman Catholic
Environment	city

STUDENTS

Total undergrad enrollment	1,360
% male/female	24/76
% from out of state	12
% from public high school	45
% live on campus	48
% African American	12
% Asian	11
% Caucasian	42
% Hispanic	30

ACADEMICS

Academic Rating	**68**
Calendar	semester
Student/faculty ratio	13:1
Professors Interesting Rating	65
Professors Accessible Rating	64
% professors teaching UG courses	100
Most common lab size	20-29 students
Most common regular class size	10-19 students

MOST POPULAR MAJORS
business administration/management
nursing/registered nurse training
(RN, ASN, BSN, MSN)
psychology

SELECTIVITY

Admissions Selectivity Rating	**77**
# of applicants	1,877
% of applicants accepted	71
% of acceptees attending	27

FRESHMAN PROFILE

Range SAT Verbal	470-550
Average SAT Verbal	516
Range SAT Math	460-550
Average SAT Math	508
Projected Range SAT Writing	530-600
Minimum Paper TOEFL	550
Minimum Computer Based TOEFL	213
Average HS GPA	3.1
% graduated top 10% of class	17
% graduated top 25% of class	47
% graduated top 50% of class	77

DEADLINES

Early decision application deadline	11/15
Regular notification	rolling
Nonfall registration?	yes

FINANCIAL FACTS

Financial Aid Rating	**68**
Annual tuition	$19,100
Room & Board	$8,000
Books and supplies	$800
Required fees	$500
% frosh rec. need-based scholarship or grant aid	87
% UG rec. need-based scholarship or grant aid	86
% frosh rec. need-based self-help aid	87
% UG rec. need-based self-help aid	86
% frosh rec. any financial aid	87
% UG rec. any financial aid	86
Avg. frosh grant	$9,000
Avg. frosh loan	$2,625

THE COLLEGE OF NEW JERSEY

CAMPUS LIFE

Quality of Life Rating	**85**
Fire Safety Rating	**82**
Type of school	public
Environment	village

STUDENTS

Total undergrad enrollment	5,840
% male/female	41/59
% from out of state	5
% from public high school	85
% live on campus	65
% in (# of) fraternities	3 (8)
% in (# of) sororities	6 (7)
% African American	6
% Asian	5

% Caucasian 78
% Hispanic 7

ACADEMICS
Academic Rating **86**
Calendar semester
Student/faculty ratio 13:1
Professors Interesting Rating 85
Professors Accessible Rating 86
% professors teaching UG courses 95
Most common lab size 10-19 students
Most common
  regular class size 20-29 students

MOST POPULAR MAJORS
elementary education and teaching
English language and literature

SELECTIVITY
Admissions Selectivity Rating **92**
# of applicants 6,485
% of applicants accepted 48
% of acceptees attending 40
# accepting a place on wait list 466
% admitted from wait list 17
# of early decision applicants 225
% accepted early decision 43

FRESHMAN PROFILE
Range SAT Verbal 575-670
Average SAT Verbal 622
Range SAT Math 595-690
Average SAT Math 639
Projected Range SAT Writing 620-680
Minimum Paper TOEFL 550
Minimum Computer Based TOEFL 215
% graduated top 10% of class 64
% graduated top 25% of class 91
% graduated top 50% of class 100

DEADLINES
Early decision application deadline 11/15
Regular application deadline 2/15
Regular notification rolling
Nonfall registration? yes

FINANCIAL FACTS
Financial Aid Rating **76**
Annual in-state tuition $6,621
Annual out-of-state tuition $11,562
Room & board $8,093
Books and supplies $736
% frosh rec. need-based scholarship
  or grant aid 23
% UG rec. need-based scholarship
  or grant aid 21
% frosh rec. need-based self-help aid 29
% UG rec. need-based self-help aid 33
Avg. frosh grant $3,500
Avg. frosh loan $3,000

COLUMBIA UNIVERSITY—
COLUMBIA COLLEGE

CAMPUS LIFE
Quality of Life Rating **92**
Fire Safety Rating **60**
Type of school private
Environment metropolis

STUDENTS
Total undergrad enrollment 4,115
% male/female 50/50
% from out of state 74
% from public high school 49
% live on campus 97
% African American 9
% Asian 12
% Caucasian 51
% Hispanic 8
% international 6
# of countries represented 54

ACADEMICS
Academic Rating **95**
Calendar semester
Student/faculty ratio 6:1
Professors Interesting Rating 79
Professors Accessible Rating 74
% professors teaching UG courses 100
Most common lab size 10-19 students

MOST POPULAR MAJORS
English language and literature
history
political science and government

SELECTIVITY
Admissions Selectivity Rating **99**
# of applicants 15,006
% of applicants accepted 11
% of acceptees attending 62
# accepting a place on wait list 2,017
% admitted from wait list 2
# of early decision applicants 534
% accepted early decision 32

FRESHMAN PROFILE
Range SAT Verbal 660-760
Average SAT Verbal 706
Range SAT Math 660-760
Average SAT Math 703
Projected Range SAT Writing 670-740
Range ACT Composite 27-32
Average ACT Composite 33
Minimum Paper TOEFL 600
Minimum Computer Based TOEFL 250
Average HS GPA 3.78
% graduated top 10% of class 85
% graduated top 25% of class 98
% graduated top 50% of class 100

DEADLINES
Early decision application deadline 11/1
Regular application deadline 1/2
Regular notification 4/4
Nonfall registration? no

FINANCIAL FACTS
Financial Aid Rating **92**
Annual tuition $30,260
Room & board $9,066
% frosh rec. need-based scholarship
  or grant aid 40
% UG rec. need-based scholarship
  or grant aid 40
% frosh rec. need-based self-help aid 40
% UG rec. need-based self-help aid 42
% frosh rec. any financial aid 42
% UG rec. any financial aid 41
Avg. frosh grant $23,900
Avg. frosh loan $3,282

CONNECTICUT COLLEGE

CAMPUS LIFE
Quality of Life Rating **72**
Fire Safety Rating **60**
Type of school private
Environment town

STUDENTS
Total undergrad enrollment 1,796
% male/female 40/60
% from out of state 76
% from public high school 52
% live on campus 99
% African American 4
% Asian 4
% Caucasian 71
% Hispanic 4
% international 7
# of countries represented 39

ACADEMICS
Academic Rating **89**
Calendar semester
Student/faculty ratio 11:1
Professors Interesting Rating 86
Professors Accessible Rating 86
% professors teaching UG courses 100
Most common lab size 10-19 students
Most common
  regular class size 10-19 students

MOST POPULAR MAJORS
english language and literature
political science and government
psychology

SELECTIVITY
Admissions Selectivity Rating **94**
# of applicants 4,503

% of applicants accepted 34
% of acceptees attending 32
# accepting a place on wait list 973
% admitted from wait list 5
# of early decision applicants 199
% accepted early decision 60

FRESHMAN PROFILE
Range SAT Verbal 620-700
Average SAT Verbal 663
Range SAT Math 630-700
Average SAT Math 665
Projected Range SAT Writing 650-700
Minimum Paper TOEFL 600
Minimum Computer Based TOEFL 250
% graduated top 10% of class 55
% graduated top 25% of class 79
% graduated top 50% of class 99

DEADLINES
Early decision application deadline 11/15
Regular application deadline 1/1
Regular notification 4/1
Nonfall registration? yes

FINANCIAL FACTS
Financial Aid Rating 95
Comprehensive fee $41,975
Books and supplies $800
% frosh rec. need-based scholarship
   or grant aid 38
% UG rec. need-based scholarship
   or grant aid 42
% frosh rec. need-based self-help aid 37
% UG rec. need-based self-help aid 40
% frosh rec. any financial aid 46
% UG rec. any financial aid 43
Avg. frosh grant $24,009
Avg. frosh loan $2,861

COOPER UNION

CAMPUS LIFE
Quality of Life Rating 73
Fire Safety Rating 60
Type of school private
Environment metropolis
STUDENTS
Total undergrad enrollment 903
% male/female 65/35
% from out of state 41
% from public high school 65
% live on campus 20
% in (# of) fraternities 10 (2)
% in (# of) sororities 5 (1)
% African American 5
% Asian 25
% Caucasian 54
% Hispanic 8

% Native American 1
% international 9

ACADEMICS
Academic Rating 87
Calendar semester
Student/faculty ratio 7:1
Professors Interesting Rating 62
Professors Accessible Rating 65
% professors teaching UG courses 100
Most common lab size 10-19 students
Most common
   regular class size 10-19 students

MOST POPULAR MAJORS
architecture
(BArch, BA/BS, MArch, MA/MS, PhD)
electrical, electronics, and communications
engineering
fine arts and art studies

SELECTIVITY
Admissions Selectivity Rating 98
# of applicants 2,414
% of applicants accepted 12
% of acceptees attending 70
# accepting a place on wait list 43
% admitted from wait list 23
# of early decision applicants 53
% accepted early decision 21

FRESHMAN PROFILE
Range SAT Verbal 620-700
Average SAT Verbal 680
Range SAT Math 630-750
Average SAT Math 710
Projected Range SAT Writing 650-700
Minimum Paper TOEFL 600
Minimum Computer Based TOEFL 250
Average HS GPA 3.6
% graduated top 10% of class 80
% graduated top 25% of class 100
% graduated top 50% of class 100

DEADLINES
Early decision application deadline 12/1
Regular application deadline 1/1
Regular notification 4/1
Nonfall registration? no

FINANCIAL FACTS
Financial Aid Rating 93
Annual tuition $27,500
Room & Board $13,000
Books and supplies $1,800
Required fees $1,400
% frosh rec. need-based scholarship
   or grant aid 32
% UG rec. need-based scholarship
   or grant aid 33
% frosh rec. need-based self-help aid 28

% UG rec. need-based self-help aid 31
% frosh rec. any financial aid 100
% UG rec. any financial aid 100
Avg. frosh grant $27,500
Avg. frosh loan $2,519

CORNELL UNIVERSITY

CAMPUS LIFE
Quality of Life Rating 83
Fire Safety Rating 70
Type of school private
Environment town
STUDENTS
Total undergrad enrollment 13,577
% male/female 50/50
% from out of state 60
% live on campus 42
% in (# of) fraternities 27 (49)
% in (# of) sororities 24 (22)
% African American 5
% Asian 16
% Caucasian 58
% Hispanic 5
% international 7
# of countries represented 109

ACADEMICS
Academic Rating 89
Calendar semester
Student/faculty ratio 9:1
Professors Interesting Rating 75
Professors Accessible Rating 75
% professors teaching UG courses 100
Most common lab size 10-19 students
Most common
   regular class size 10-19 students
MOST POPULAR MAJORS
agriculture
business/commerce
engineering

SELECTIVITY
Admissions Selectivity Rating 97
# of applicants 20,822
% of applicants accepted 29
% of acceptees attending 50
# accepting a place on wait list 2,411
% admitted from wait list 7
# of early decision applicants 1,120
% accepted early decision 44

FRESHMAN PROFILE
Range SAT Verbal 630-730
Range SAT Math 660-760
Projected Range SAT Writing 650-720
Range ACT Composite 28-32
Minimum Paper TOEFL 550
Minimum Computer Based TOEFL 250

% graduated top 10% of class	85
% graduated top 25% of class	95
% graduated top 50% of class	99

DEADLINES

Early decision application deadline	11/1
Regular application deadline	1/1
Regular notification	4/1
Nonfall registration?	no

FINANCIAL FACTS

Financial Aid Rating	**94**
Annual tuition	$30,000
Room & Board	$9,882
Books and supplies	$660
Required fees	$167
% frosh rec. need-based scholarship or grant aid	46
% UG rec. need-based scholarship or grant aid	46
% frosh rec. need-based self-help aid	43
% UG rec. need-based self-help aid	47
% frosh rec. any financial aid	48
% UG rec. any financial aid	49
Avg. frosh grant	$21,257
Avg. frosh loan	$10,400

CUNY—BARUCH COLLEGE

CAMPUS LIFE

Quality of Life Rating	**74**
Fire Safety Rating	**60**
Type of school	public
Environment	metropolis

STUDENTS

Total undergrad enrollment	12,493
% male/female	44/56
% from out of state	3
% from public high school	76
% in (# of) fraternities	10 (4)
% in (# of) sororities	10 (4)
% African American	14
% Asian	27
% Caucasian	32
% Hispanic	18
% international	10
# of countries represented	103

ACADEMICS

Academic Rating	**61**
Calendar	semester
Student/faculty ratio	17:1
Professors Interesting Rating	67
Professors Accessible Rating	63
% professors teaching UG courses	95
% classes taught by TAs	1
Most common lab size	20-29 students
Most common regular class size	20-29 students

MOST POPULAR MAJORS
accounting
computer and information sciences
finance

SELECTIVITY

Admissions Selectivity Rating	**60**
# of applicants	9,356
% of applicants accepted	36
% of acceptees attending	51
# of early decision applicants	3
% accepted early decision	14

FRESHMAN PROFILE

Range SAT Verbal	470-580
Average SAT Verbal	520
Range SAT Math	530-630
Average SAT Math	584
Projected Range SAT Writing	530-620
Minimum Paper TOEFL	620
Minimum Computer Based TOEFL	260
Average HS GPA	3.0

DEADLINES

Early decision application deadline	12/13
Regular application deadline	4/1
Regular notification	4/15
Nonfall registration?	yes

FINANCIAL FACTS

Financial Aid Rating	**68**
Annual in-state tuition	$4,000
Annual out-of-state tuition	$8,640
Required fees	$300
% frosh rec. need-based scholarship or grant aid	61
% UG rec. need-based scholarship or grant aid	70
% frosh rec. need-based self-help aid	25
% UG rec. need-based self-help aid	33
% frosh rec. any financial aid	79
% UG rec. any financial aid	75
Avg. frosh grant	$5,380
Avg. frosh loan	$2,350

CUNY—BROOKLYN COLLEGE

CAMPUS LIFE

Quality of Life Rating	**65**
Fire Safety Rating	**60**
Type of school	public
Environment	metropolis

STUDENTS

Total undergrad enrollment	10,789
% male/female	40/60
% from out of state	1
% from public high school	60
% in (# of) fraternities	2 (4)
% in (# of) sororities	2 (6)
% African American	29

% Asian	10
% Caucasian	43
% Hispanic	11
% international	6
# of countries represented	82

ACADEMICS

Academic Rating	**70**
Calendar	semester
Student/faculty ratio	15:1
Professors Interesting Rating	62
Professors Accessible Rating	61
% professors teaching UG courses	80
% classes taught by TAs	2
Most common lab size	20-29 students

MOST POPULAR MAJORS
business administration/management
education
psychology

SELECTIVITY

Admissions Selectivity Rating	**82**
# of applicants	7,083
% of applicants accepted	33
% of acceptees attending	51

FRESHMAN PROFILE

Range SAT Verbal	450-570
Average SAT Verbal	515
Range SAT Math	490-600
Average SAT Math	544
Projected Range SAT Writing	520-610
Minimum Paper TOEFL	500
Minimum Computer Based TOEFL	173
Average HS GPA	3.0
% graduated top 10% of class	14
% graduated top 25% of class	35
% graduated top 50% of class	77

DEADLINES

Regular notification	rolling
Nonfall registration?	yes

FINANCIAL FACTS

Financial Aid Rating	**93**
Annual in-state tuition	$4,000
Annual out-of-state tuition	$8,640
Books and supplies	$800
Required fees	$353
% frosh rec. need-based scholarship or grant aid	75
% UG rec. need-based scholarship or grant aid	71
% frosh rec. need-based self-help aid	74
% UG rec. need-based self-help aid	70
% frosh rec. any financial aid	67
% UG rec. any financial aid	65
Avg. frosh grant	$4,000
Avg. frosh loan	$2,800

CUNY—HUNTER COLLEGE

CAMPUS LIFE

Quality of Life Rating	**67**
Fire Safety Rating	**94**
Type of school	public
Environment	metropolis

STUDENTS

Total undergrad enrollment	14,109
% male/female	30/70
% from out of state	4
% from public high school	70
% live on campus	4
% in (# of) fraternities	1 (2)
% in (# of) sororities	1 (2)
% African American	16
% Asian	17
% Caucasian	39
% Hispanic	21
% international	7
# of countries represented	150

ACADEMICS

Academic Rating	**66**
Calendar	semester
Student/faculty ratio	15:1
Professors Interesting Rating	74
Professors Accessible Rating	65
% professors teaching UG courses	100
Most common lab size	20-29 students
Most common regular class size	20-29 students

MOST POPULAR MAJORS
english language and literature
psychology
sociology

SELECTIVITY

Admissions Selectivity Rating	**86**
# of applicants	12,776
% of applicants accepted	30
% of acceptees attending	49

FRESHMAN PROFILE

Range SAT Verbal	470-570
Average SAT Verbal	520
Range SAT Math	500-590
Average SAT Math	545
Projected Range SAT Writing	530-610
Minimum Paper TOEFL	500
Minimum Computer Based TOEFL	173
Average HS GPA	2.9
% graduated top 10% of class	21
% graduated top 25% of class	48
% graduated top 50% of class	78

DEADLINES

Regular application deadline	3/15
Regular notification	rolling
Nonfall registration?	yes

FINANCIAL FACTS

Financial Aid Rating	**92**
Annual in-state tuition	$4,000
Room & Board	$2,600
Books and supplies	$798
Required fees	$329
% frosh rec. need-based scholarship or grant aid	58
% UG rec. need-based scholarship or grant aid	50
% frosh rec. need-based self-help aid	10
% UG rec. need-based self-help aid	19
% frosh rec. any financial aid	78
% UG rec. any financial aid	52
Avg. frosh grant	$6,158
Avg. frosh loan	$2,309

CUNY—QUEENS COLLEGE

CAMPUS LIFE

Quality of Life Rating	**67**
Fire Safety Rating	**60**
Type of school	public
Environment	metropolis

STUDENTS

Total undergrad enrollment	11,859
% male/female	38/62
% from out of state	1
% from public high school	67
% in (# of) fraternities	1 (3)
% in (# of) sororities	1 (2)
% African American	10
% Asian	19
% Caucasian	48
% Hispanic	17
% international	6
# of countries represented	140

ACADEMICS

Academic Rating	**71**
Calendar	semester
Student/faculty ratio	17:1
Professors Interesting Rating	67
Professors Accessible Rating	63
% professors teaching UG courses	90
% classes taught by TAs	3
Most common lab size	20-29 students

MOST POPULAR MAJORS
accounting
psychology
sociology

SELECTIVITY

Admissions Selectivity Rating	**80**
# of applicants	6,518
% of applicants accepted	42
% of acceptees attending	51

FRESHMAN PROFILE

Range SAT Verbal	440-550
Average SAT Verbal	500
Range SAT Math	490-580
Average SAT Math	535
Projected Range SAT Writing	510-600
Minimum Paper TOEFL	500
Minimum Computer Based TOEFL	200
Average HS GPA	3.2
% graduated top 10% of class	15
% graduated top 25% of class	30
% graduated top 50% of class	82

DEADLINES

Regular notification	rolling
Nonfall registration?	yes

FINANCIAL FACTS

Financial Aid Rating	**88**
Annual in-state tuition	$4,000
Annual out-of-state tuition	$10,800
Required fees	$356
% frosh rec. need-based scholarship or grant aid	69
% UG rec. need-based scholarship or grant aid	47
% frosh rec. need-based self-help aid	56
% UG rec. need-based self-help aid	35
% frosh rec. any financial aid	95
% UG rec. any financial aid	95
Avg. frosh grant	$5,000
Avg. frosh loan	$2,500

DARTMOUTH COLLEGE

CAMPUS LIFE

Quality of Life Rating	**97**
Fire Safety Rating	**60**
Type of school	private
Environment	village

STUDENTS

Total undergrad enrollment	3,998
% male/female	50/50
% from out of state	96
% from public high school	63
% live on campus	83
% in (# of) fraternities	39 (14)
% in (# of) sororities	34 (8)
% African American	7
% Asian	13
% Caucasian	58
% Hispanic	6
% Native American	4
% international	5

ACADEMICS

Academic Rating	**96**

Calendar	quarter
Student/faculty ratio	8:1
Professors Interesting Rating	87
Professors Accessible Rating	92
% professors teaching UG courses	100
Most common lab size	10-19 students
Most common regular class size	10-19 students

SELECTIVITY

Admissions Selectivity Rating	**98**
# of applicants	11,734
% of applicants accepted	19
% of acceptees attending	50
# accepting a place on wait list	1,275
% admitted from wait list	2
# of early decision applicants	384
% accepted early decision	30

FRESHMAN PROFILE

Range SAT Verbal	670-770
Average SAT Verbal	713
Range SAT Math	690-780
Average SAT Math	719
Projected Range SAT Writing	680-740
Average ACT Composite	30
Minimum Paper TOEFL	600
Minimum Computer Based TOEFL	250
Average HS GPA	3.73
% graduated top 10% of class	88
% graduated top 50% of class	100

DEADLINES

Early decision application deadline	11/1
Regular application deadline	1/1
Regular notification	4/10
Nonfall registration?	no

FINANCIAL FACTS

Financial Aid Rating	**97**
Annual tuition	$30,279
Room & Board	$9,000
Books and supplies	$1,122
Required fees	$186
% frosh rec. need-based scholarship or grant aid	47
% UG rec. need-based scholarship or grant aid	47
% frosh rec. need-based self-help aid	45
% UG rec. need-based self-help aid	48
% frosh rec. any financial aid	48
% UG rec. any financial aid	50
Avg. frosh grant	$24,375
Avg. frosh loan	$3,759

DELAWARE VALLEY COLLEGE

CAMPUS LIFE

Quality of Life Rating	**61**
Fire Safety Rating	**72**
Type of school	private
Environment	village

STUDENTS

Total undergrad enrollment	1,744
% male/female	48/52
% from out of state	35
% live on campus	55
% in (# of) fraternities	4 (5)
% in (# of) sororities	5 (3)
% African American	4
% Asian	1
% Caucasian	81
% Hispanic	1
% international	1

ACADEMICS

Academic Rating	**66**
Calendar	semester
Student/faculty ratio	14:1
Professors Interesting Rating	61
Professors Accessible Rating	62
% professors teaching UG courses	100
Most common lab size	10-19 students
Most common regular class size	10-19 students

MOST POPULAR MAJORS
animal sciences
business administration/management
equestrian/equine studies

SELECTIVITY

Admissions Selectivity Rating	**74**
# of applicants	1,489
% of applicants accepted	89
% of acceptees attending	34

FRESHMAN PROFILE

Range SAT Verbal	450-560
Average SAT Verbal	497
Range SAT Math	460-550
Average SAT Math	494
Projected Range SAT Writing	520-600
Range ACT Composite	20-27
Average ACT Composite	21
Minimum Paper TOEFL	500
Minimum Computer Based TOEFL	173
Average HS GPA	3.37
% graduated top 10% of class	12
% graduated top 25% of class	34
% graduated top 50% of class	71

DEADLINES

Regular notification	rolling
Nonfall registration?	yes

FINANCIAL FACTS

Financial Aid Rating	**77**
Annual tuition	$21,038
Room & board	$8,542
% frosh rec. need-based scholarship or grant aid	79
% UG rec. need-based scholarship or grant aid	69
% frosh rec. need-based self-help aid	70
% UG rec. need-based self-help aid	62
Avg. frosh grant	$11,925
Avg. frosh loan	$2,911

DICKINSON COLLEGE

CAMPUS LIFE

Quality of Life Rating	**79**
Fire Safety Rating	**86**
Type of school	private
Environment	city

STUDENTS

Total undergrad enrollment	2,280
% male/female	45/55
% from out of state	67
% from public high school	66
% live on campus	90
% in (# of) fraternities	17 (6)
% in (# of) sororities	26 (4)
% African American	4
% Asian	4
% Caucasian	86
% Hispanic	3
% international	3
# of countries represented	35

ACADEMICS

Academic Rating	**89**
Calendar	semester
Student/faculty ratio	13:1
Professors Interesting Rating	87
Professors Accessible Rating	91
% professors teaching UG courses	100
Most common lab size	10-19 students
Most common regular class size	10-19 students

MOST POPULAR MAJORS
English language and literature
international business
political science and government

SELECTIVITY

Admissions Selectivity Rating	**92**
# of applicants	4,998
% of applicants accepted	49
% of acceptees attending	25
# accepting a place on wait list	270
% admitted from wait list	15
# of early decision applicants	292
% accepted early decision	69

FRESHMAN PROFILE

Range SAT Verbal	600-690
Average SAT Verbal	640

Range SAT Math	590-680
Average SAT Math	634
Projected Range SAT Writing	630-690
Range ACT Composite	26-29
Average ACT Composite	28
Minimum Paper TOEFL	550
Minimum Computer Based TOEFL	250
% graduated top 10% of class	51
% graduated top 25% of class	82
% graduated top 50% of class	98

DEADLINES

Early decision application deadline	11/15
Regular application deadline	2/1
Regular notification	3/31
Nonfall registration?	yes

FINANCIAL FACTS

Financial Aid Rating	**91**
Annual tuition	$31,800
Room & Board	$8,050
Books and supplies	$750
Required fees	$320
% frosh rec. need-based scholarship or grant aid	48
% UG rec. need-based scholarship or grant aid	49
% frosh rec. need-based self-help aid	44
% UG rec. need-based self-help aid	45
% frosh rec. any financial aid	56
% UG rec. any financial aid	58
Avg. frosh grant	$18,250
Avg. frosh loan	$3,466

DREW UNIVERSITY

CAMPUS LIFE

Quality of Life Rating	**81**
Fire Safety Rating	**86**
Type of school	private
Affiliation	Methodist
Environment	village

STUDENTS

Total undergrad enrollment	1,578
% male/female	40/60
% from out of state	43
% from public high school	67
% live on campus	88
% African American	4
% Asian	6
% Caucasian	64
% Hispanic	6
% international	1
# of countries represented	14

ACADEMICS

Academic Rating	**85**
Calendar	semester
Student/faculty ratio	12:1

Professors Interesting Rating	84
Professors Accessible Rating	85
% professors teaching UG courses	100
Most common lab size	10-19 students
Most common regular class size	10-19 students

MOST POPULAR MAJORS
English language and literature
political science and government
psychology

SELECTIVITY

Admissions Selectivity Rating	**85**
# of applicants	3,266
% of applicants accepted	70
% of acceptees attending	18
# accepting a place on wait list	329
% admitted from wait list	23
# of early decision applicants	78
% accepted early decision	89

FRESHMAN PROFILE

Range SAT Verbal	560-670
Average SAT Verbal	615
Range SAT Math	550-650
Average SAT Math	600
Projected Range SAT Writing	600-680
Range ACT Composite	22-29
Average ACT Composite	25
Minimum Paper TOEFL	550
% graduated top 10% of class	37
% graduated top 25% of class	68
% graduated top 50% of class	92

DEADLINES

Early decision application deadline	12/1
Regular application deadline	2/15
Regular notification	3/21
Nonfall registration?	yes

FINANCIAL FACTS

Financial Aid Rating	**79**
Annual tuition	$29,000
Room & Board	$8,010
Books and supplies	$1,090
% frosh rec. need-based scholarship or grant aid	51
% UG rec. need-based scholarship or grant aid	50
% frosh rec. need-based self-help aid	38
% UG rec. need-based self-help aid	41
% frosh rec. any financial aid	85
% UG rec. any financial aid	79
Avg. frosh grant	$19,840
Avg. frosh loan	$14,490

DREXEL UNIVERSITY

CAMPUS LIFE

Quality of Life Rating	**63**

Fire Safety Rating	**60**
Type of school	private
Environment	metropolis

STUDENTS

Total undergrad enrollment	11,544
% male/female	60/40
% from out of state	42
% from public high school	70
% live on campus	38
% in (# of) fraternities	6 (11)
% in (# of) sororities	6 (5)
% African American	10
% Asian	12
% Caucasian	63
% Hispanic	3
% international	6
# of countries represented	105

ACADEMICS

Academic Rating	**73**
Calendar	quarter for most, semester for College of Medicine
Student/faculty ratio	10:1
Professors Interesting Rating	62
Professors Accessible Rating	61
% professors teaching UG courses	100
Most common lab size	10-19 students
Most common regular class size	20-29 students

MOST POPULAR MAJORS
business administration/management
computer and information sciences
information science/studies

SELECTIVITY

Admissions Selectivity Rating	**87**
# of applicants	12,157
% of applicants accepted	73
% of acceptees attending	24
# accepting a place on wait list	519
% admitted from wait list	44

FRESHMAN PROFILE

Range SAT Verbal	540-640
Average SAT Verbal	590
Range SAT Math	560-670
Average SAT Math	620
Projected Range SAT Writing	590-660
Minimum Paper TOEFL	550
Minimum Computer Based TOEFL	213
Average HS GPA	3.51
% graduated top 10% of class	34
% graduated top 25% of class	61
% graduated top 50% of class	91

DEADLINES

Regular application deadline	3/1
Regular notification	rolling
Nonfall registration?	yes

FINANCIAL FACTS
Financial Aid Rating   **63**

Annual tuition	$19,900
Room & Board	$8,600
% frosh rec. need-based scholarship or grant aid	25
% UG rec. need-based scholarship or grant aid	30
% frosh rec. need-based self-help aid	64
% UG rec. need-based self-help aid	64

DUQUESNE UNIVERSITY

CAMPUS LIFE
Quality of Life Rating   **80**
Fire Safety Rating   **78**

Type of school	private
Affiliation	Roman Catholic
Environment	metropolis

STUDENTS

Total undergrad enrollment	5,549
% male/female	41/59
% from out of state	19
% from public high school	75
% live on campus	54
% in (# of) fraternities	16 (9)
% in (# of) sororities	14 (9)
% African American	4
% Asian	1
% Caucasian	82
% Hispanic	1
% international	2
# of countries represented	94

ACADEMICS
Academic Rating   **75**

Calendar	semester
Student/faculty ratio	15:1
Professors Interesting Rating	74
Professors Accessible Rating	74
% professors teaching UG courses	70
% classes taught by TAs	5
Most common lab size	10-19 students
Most common regular class size	20-29 students

MOST POPULAR MAJORS
communications studies/speech communication and rhetoric
marketing/marketing management
psychology

SELECTIVITY
Admissions Selectivity Rating   **81**

# of applicants	3,221
% of applicants accepted	85
% of acceptees attending	44
# of early decision applicants	51
% accepted early decision	93

FRESHMAN PROFILE

Range SAT Verbal	510-600
Average SAT Verbal	557
Range SAT Math	510-610
Average SAT Math	562
Projected Range SAT Writing	570-630
Range ACT Composite	21-26
Average ACT Composite	24
Average HS GPA	3.58
% graduated top 10% of class	27
% graduated top 25% of class	54
% graduated top 50% of class	84

DEADLINES

Early decision application deadline	11/1
Regular application deadline	7/1
Regular notification	rolling
Nonfall registration?	yes

FINANCIAL FACTS
Financial Aid Rating   **79**

Annual tuition	$18,693
Room & Board	$7,820
Books and supplies	$600
Required fees	$1,667
% frosh rec. need-based scholarship or grant aid	71
% UG rec. need-based scholarship or grant aid	63
% frosh rec. need-based self-help aid	66
% UG rec. need-based self-help aid	61
% frosh rec. any financial aid	97
% UG rec. any financial aid	86
Avg. frosh grant	$10,226
Avg. frosh loan	$8,806

ELIZABETHTOWN COLLEGE

CAMPUS LIFE
Quality of Life Rating   **92**
Fire Safety Rating   **60**

Type of school	private
Affiliation	Church of Brethren
Environment	village

STUDENTS

Total undergrad enrollment	2,096
% male/female	35/65
% from out of state	32
% from public high school	80
% live on campus	85
% African American	1
% Asian	2
% Caucasian	82
% Hispanic	1
% international	2
# of countries represented	17

ACADEMICS
Academic Rating   **86**

Calendar	semester
Student/faculty ratio	13:1
Professors Interesting Rating	86
Professors Accessible Rating	87
% professors teaching UG courses	100
Most common lab size	10-19 students
Most common regular class size	10-19 students

MOST POPULAR MAJORS
business administration/management
communications, journalism, and related fields

SELECTIVITY
Admissions Selectivity Rating   **87**

# of applicants	2,923
% of applicants accepted	64
% of acceptees attending	29

FRESHMAN PROFILE

Range SAT Verbal	510-610
Range SAT Math	510-630
Projected Range SAT Writing	570-640
Range ACT Composite	21-26
Minimum Paper TOEFL	525
Minimum Computer Based TOEFL	200
Average HS GPA	3.64
% graduated top 10% of class	30
% graduated top 25% of class	65
% graduated top 50% of class	93

DEADLINES

Regular notification	rolling
Nonfall registration?	yes

FINANCIAL FACTS
Financial Aid Rating   **80**

Annual tuition	$23,710
Room & Board	$6,600
Books and supplies	$700
% frosh rec. need-based scholarship or grant aid	71
% UG rec. need-based scholarship or grant aid	71
% frosh rec. need-based self-help aid	59
% UG rec. need-based self-help aid	61
% frosh rec. any financial aid	95
% UG rec. any financial aid	95

ELMIRA COLLEGE

CAMPUS LIFE
Quality of Life Rating   **69**
Fire Safety Rating   **60**

Type of school	private
Environment	village

STUDENTS

Total undergrad enrollment	1,448
% male/female	29/71
% from out of state	51

% from public high school	65
% live on campus	92
% African American	1
% Caucasian	67
% Hispanic	1
% international	4
# of countries represented	23

ACADEMICS
Academic Rating	**86**

Calendar 2 terms that are 12 weeks long followed by a 6-week term.

Student/faculty ratio	12:1
Professors Interesting Rating	76
Professors Accessible Rating	81
% professors teaching UG courses	100
Most common lab size	fewer than 10 students
Most common regular class size	10-19 students

MOST POPULAR MAJORS
business administration/management
elementary education and teaching
psychology

SELECTIVITY
Admissions Selectivity Rating	**88**
# of applicants	2,149
% of applicants accepted	67
% of acceptees attending	24
# accepting a place on wait list	121
% admitted from wait list	7
# of early decision applicants	71
% accepted early decision	72

FRESHMAN PROFILE
Range SAT Verbal	520-630
Average SAT Verbal	577
Range SAT Math	510-620
Average SAT Math	568
Projected Range SAT Writing	570-650
Range ACT Composite	23-28
Average ACT Composite	26
Minimum Paper TOEFL	500
Minimum Computer Based TOEFL	173
Average HS GPA	3.5
% graduated top 10% of class	30
% graduated top 25% of class	69
% graduated top 50% of class	100

DEADLINES
Early decision application deadline	11/15
Regular application deadline	3/1
Regular notification	rolling
Nonfall registration?	yes

FINANCIAL FACTS
Financial Aid Rating	**76**
Annual tuition	$27,500
Room & Board	$8,700

Books and supplies	$450
Required fees	$900
% frosh rec. need-based scholarship or grant aid	81
% UG rec. need-based scholarship or grant aid	79
% frosh rec. need-based self-help aid	66
% UG rec. need-based self-help aid	66
% frosh rec. any financial aid	82
% UG rec. any financial aid	82
Avg. frosh grant	$15,729
Avg. frosh loan	$5,244

EMERSON COLLEGE

CAMPUS LIFE
Quality of Life Rating	**84**
Fire Safety Rating	**95**
Type of school	private
Environment	metropolis

STUDENTS
Total undergrad enrollment	3,076
% male/female	42/58
% from out of state	63
% from public high school	75
% live on campus	42
% in (# of) fraternities	3 (4)
% in (# of) sororities	3 (3)
% African American	2
% Asian	4
% Caucasian	76
% Hispanic	5
% international	3
# of countries represented	41

ACADEMICS
Academic Rating	**82**
Calendar	semester
Student/faculty ratio	15:1
Professors Interesting Rating	70
Professors Accessible Rating	78
% professors teaching UG courses	97
% classes taught by TAs	3
Most common lab size	10-19 students
Most common regular class size	10-19 students

MOST POPULAR MAJORS
cinematography and film/video production
creative writing
visual and performing arts

SELECTIVITY
Admissions Selectivity Rating	**91**
# of applicants	4,584
% of applicants accepted	48
% of acceptees attending	32
# accepting a place on wait list	900
% admitted from wait list	10

FRESHMAN PROFILE
Range SAT Verbal	580-670
Average SAT Verbal	628
Range SAT Math	540-640
Average SAT Math	591
Projected Range SAT Writing	620-680
Range ACT Composite	24-28
Average ACT Composite	26
Minimum Paper TOEFL	550
Minimum Computer Based TOEFL	213
Average HS GPA	3.53
% graduated top 10% of class	32
% graduated top 25% of class	77
% graduated top 50% of class	99

DEADLINES
Regular application deadline	1/15
Regular notification	4/1
Nonfall registration?	yes

FINANCIAL FACTS
Financial Aid Rating	**87**
Annual tuition	$22,976
Room & Board	$10,118
Books and supplies	$680
Required fees	$579
% frosh rec. need-based scholarship or grant aid	50
% UG rec. need-based scholarship or grant aid	42
% frosh rec. need-based self-help aid	57
% UG rec. need-based self-help aid	51
% frosh rec. any financial aid	78
% UG rec. any financial aid	68
Avg. frosh grant	$13,126
Avg. frosh loan	$3,062

EMMANUEL COLLEGE

CAMPUS LIFE
Quality of Life Rating	**92**
Fire Safety Rating	**97**
Type of school	private
Affiliation	Roman Catholic
Environment	metropolis

STUDENTS
Total undergrad enrollment	1,881
% male/female	25/75
% from out of state	23
% from public high school	71
% live on campus	65
% African American	8
% Asian	4
% Caucasian	63
% Hispanic	4
% international	3
# of countries represented	39

ACADEMICS

Academic Rating	**82**
Calendar	semester
Student/faculty ratio	16:1
Professors Interesting Rating	87
Professors Accessible Rating	89
% professors teaching UG courses	100
Most common lab size	10-19 students
Most common regular class size	10-19 students

MOST POPULAR MAJORS
business administration and management
elementary education and teaching
psychology

SELECTIVITY

Admissions Selectivity Rating	**78**
# of applicants	2,664
% of applicants accepted	64
% of acceptees attending	27
# of early decision applicants	1
% accepted early decision	100

FRESHMAN PROFILE

Range SAT Verbal	480-580
Average SAT Verbal	530
Range SAT Math	460-570
Average SAT Math	515
Projected Range SAT Writing	540-620
Range ACT Composite	18-26
Minimum Paper TOEFL	500
Minimum Computer Based TOEFL	173
Average HS GPA	3.24
% graduated top 10% of class	14
% graduated top 25% of class	38
% graduated top 50% of class	75

DEADLINES

Early decision application deadline	11/1
Regular notification	rolling
Nonfall registration?	yes

FINANCIAL FACTS

Financial Aid Rating	**73**
Annual tuition	$21,900
Room & Board	$9,700
Books and supplies	$750
Required fees	$400
% frosh rec. need-based scholarship or grant aid	75
% UG rec. need-based scholarship or grant aid	68
% frosh rec. need-based self-help aid	83
% UG rec. need-based self-help aid	66
% frosh rec. any financial aid	87
% UG rec. any financial aid	78
Avg. frosh grant	$11,149
Avg. frosh loan	$3,299

EUGENE LANG COLLEGE/ NEW SCHOOL UNIVERSITY

CAMPUS LIFE

Quality of Life Rating	**83**
Fire Safety Rating	**60**
Type of school	private

STUDENTS

Total undergrad enrollment	887
% male/female	31/69
% from out of state	69
% from public high school	64
% live on campus	30
% African American	5
% Asian	3
% Caucasian	55
% Hispanic	6
% international	2
# of countries represented	15

ACADEMICS

Academic Rating	**87**
Calendar	semester
Student/faculty ratio	16:1
Professors Interesting Rating	83
Professors Accessible Rating	80
% professors teaching UG courses	100
% classes taught by TAs	25
Most common lab size	10-19 students

MOST POPULAR MAJORS
area, ethnic, cultural, and gender studies
creative writing
social sciences

SELECTIVITY

Admissions Selectivity Rating	**83**
# of applicants	854
% of applicants accepted	68
% of acceptees attending	40

FRESHMAN PROFILE

Range SAT Verbal	540-660
Average SAT Verbal	610
Range SAT Math	470-590
Average SAT Math	570
Projected Range SAT Writing	590-670
Range ACT Composite	20-26
Average ACT Composite	27
Minimum Paper TOEFL	550
Average HS GPA	3.06
% graduated top 10% of class	13
% graduated top 25% of class	51
% graduated top 50% of class	90

DEADLINES

Early decision application deadline	11/15
Regular application deadline	2/1
Regular notification	rolling
Nonfall registration?	yes

FINANCIAL FACTS

Financial Aid Rating	**66**
Annual tuition	$24,920
Room & Board	$10,810
Books and supplies	$918
Required fees	$550
% frosh rec. need-based scholarship or grant aid	66
% UG rec. need-based scholarship or grant aid	63
% frosh rec. need-based self-help aid	60
% UG rec. need-based self-help aid	57
Avg. frosh grant	$10,906
Avg. frosh loan	$3,125

FAIRFIELD UNIVERSITY

CAMPUS LIFE

Quality of Life Rating	**81**
Fire Safety Rating	**88**
Type of school	private
Affiliation	Roman Catholic-Jesuit
Environment	town

STUDENTS

Total undergrad enrollment	3,552
% male/female	43/57
% from out of state	75
% from public high school	50
% live on campus	80
% African American	2
% Asian	3
% Caucasian	81
% Hispanic	5
% international	1
# of countries represented	42

ACADEMICS

Academic Rating	**81**
Calendar	semester
Student/faculty ratio	13:1
Professors Interesting Rating	83
Professors Accessible Rating	80
% professors teaching UG courses	100
Most common lab size	20-29 students
Most common regular class size	10-19 students

MOST POPULAR MAJORS
communications studies/speech
communication and rhetoric
English language and literature
marketing/marketing management

SELECTIVITY

Admissions Selectivity Rating	**89**
# of applicants	7,136
% of applicants accepted	64
% of acceptees attending	19
# accepting a place on wait list	1,715

% admitted from wait list	5
# of early decision applicants	140
% accepted early decision	72

FRESHMAN PROFILE

Range SAT Verbal	540-630
Average SAT Verbal	592
Range SAT Math	560-650
Average SAT Math	608
Projected Range SAT Writing	590-650
Range ACT Composite	23-27
Average ACT Composite	26
Minimum Paper TOEFL	550
Minimum Computer Based TOEFL	213
Average HS GPA	3.0
% graduated top 10% of class	32
% graduated top 25% of class	73
% graduated top 50% of class	99

DEADLINES

Early decision application deadline	11/15
Regular application deadline	1/15
Regular notification	4/1
Nonfall registration?	no

FINANCIAL FACTS

Financial Aid Rating	**74**
Annual tuition	$27,450
Room & Board	$9,270
Books and supplies	$500
Required fees	$485
% frosh rec. need-based scholarship or grant aid	46
% UG rec. need-based scholarship or grant aid	44
% frosh rec. need-based self-help aid	42
% UG rec. need-based self-help aid	41
% frosh rec. any financial aid	80
% UG rec. any financial aid	78
Avg. frosh grant	$14,548
Avg. frosh loan	$3,435

FORDHAM UNIVERSITY

CAMPUS LIFE

Quality of Life Rating	**75**
Fire Safety Rating	**89**
Type of school	private
Affiliation	Roman Catholic
Environment	metropolis

STUDENTS

Total undergrad enrollment	7,391
% male/female	40/60
% from out of state	43
% from public high school	47
% live on campus	59
% African American	5
% Asian	6
% Caucasian	57

% Hispanic	11
% international	1
# of countries represented	50

ACADEMICS

Academic Rating	**84**
Calendar	semester
Student/faculty ratio	13:1
Professors Interesting Rating	77
Professors Accessible Rating	78
Most common lab size	10-19 students

MOST POPULAR MAJORS
business administration/management
communications and media studies
English language and literature

SELECTIVITY

Admissions Selectivity Rating	**90**
# of applicants	14,261
% of applicants accepted	50
% of acceptees attending	24
# accepting a place on wait list	2,117
% admitted from wait list	20

FRESHMAN PROFILE

Range SAT Verbal	550-650
Average SAT Verbal	606
Range SAT Math	540-640
Average SAT Math	606
Projected Range SAT Writing	600-670
Range ACT Composite	23-28
Average ACT Composite	27
Minimum Paper TOEFL	575
Minimum Computer Based TOEFL	231
Average HS GPA	3.64
% graduated top 10% of class	34
% graduated top 25% of class	72
% graduated top 50% of class	95

DEADLINES

Regular application deadline	1/15
Regular notification	4/1
Nonfall registration?	yes

FINANCIAL FACTS

Financial Aid Rating	**71**
Annual tuition	$26,200
Room & Board	$10,248
Books and supplies	$725
Required fees	$821
% frosh rec. need-based scholarship or grant aid	63
% UG rec. need-based scholarship or grant aid	62
% frosh rec. need-based self-help aid	55
% UG rec. need-based self-help aid	54
% frosh rec. any financial aid	67
% UG rec. any financial aid	62
Avg. frosh grant	$16,052
Avg. frosh loan	$2,792

FRANKLIN & MARSHALL COLLEGE

CAMPUS LIFE

Quality of Life Rating	**71**
Fire Safety Rating	**88**
Type of school	private
Environment	town

STUDENTS

Total undergrad enrollment	1,931
% male/female	54/46
% from out of state	65
% from public high school	62
% live on campus	66
% African American	2
% Asian	4
% Caucasian	77
% Hispanic	3
% international	8
# of countries represented	63

ACADEMICS

Academic Rating	**88**
Calendar	semester
Student/faculty ratio	11:1
Professors Interesting Rating	94
Professors Accessible Rating	92
% professors teaching UG courses	100
Most common lab size	20-29 students
Most common regular class size	10-19 students

MOST POPULAR MAJORS
business administration/management
political science and government
psychology

SELECTIVITY

Admissions Selectivity Rating	**91**
# of applicants	4,070
% of applicants accepted	49
% of acceptees attending	26
# of early decision applicants	245
% accepted early decision	72

FRESHMAN PROFILE

Range SAT Verbal	580-670
Average SAT Verbal	623
Range SAT Math	590-690
Average SAT Math	636
Projected Range SAT Writing	620-680
Minimum Paper TOEFL	600
Minimum Computer Based TOEFL	250
% graduated top 10% of class	46
% graduated top 25% of class	77
% graduated top 50% of class	97

DEADLINES

Early decision application deadline	11/15
Regular application deadline	2/1

Regular notification 4/1
Nonfall registration? yes

FINANCIAL FACTS
Financial Aid Rating **97**
Annual tuition $30,390
Room & Board $7,540
Books and supplies $650
Required fees $50
% frosh rec. need-based scholarship
  or grant aid 41
% UG rec. need-based scholarship
  or grant aid 37
% frosh rec. need-based self-help aid 41
% UG rec. need-based self-help aid 40
% frosh rec. any financial aid 66
% UG rec. any financial aid 62
Avg. frosh grant $14,292
Avg. frosh loan $3,625

FRANKLIN W. OLIN COLLEGE OF ENGINEERING

CAMPUS LIFE
Quality of Life Rating **99**
Fire Safety Rating **94**
Type of school private
Environment town
STUDENTS
Total undergrad enrollment 216
% male/female 55/45
% from out of state 90
% from public high school 76
% live on campus 100
% African American 3
% Asian 9
% Caucasian 64
% Hispanic 4
% international 1
# of countries represented 8

ACADEMICS
Academic Rating **98**
Calendar semester
Student/faculty ratio 7:1
Professors Interesting Rating 99
Professors Accessible Rating 99
% professors teaching UG courses 100
Most common lab size 20-29 students
MOST POPULAR MAJORS
computer engineering
engineering
mechanical engineering

SELECTIVITY
Admissions Selectivity Rating **99**
# of applicants 546
% of applicants accepted 23

% of acceptees attending 58
# accepting a place on wait list 20
% admitted from wait list 50
FRESHMAN PROFILE
Range SAT Verbal 710-770
Average SAT Verbal 740
Range SAT Math 710-800
Average SAT Math 750
Projected Range SAT Writing 700-740
Range ACT Composite 31-34
Average ACT Composite 32
DEADLINES
Regular application deadline 1/6
Regular notification 3/21
Nonfall registration? no

FINANCIAL FACTS
Financial Aid Rating **99**
Annual tuition $29,400
Room & Board $10,720
Books and supplies $750
Required fees $100
% frosh rec. need-based scholarship
  or grant aid 20
% UG rec. need-based scholarship
  or grant aid 8
% frosh rec. any financial aid 100
% UG rec. any financial aid 100
Avg. frosh grant $30,786

GEORGETOWN UNIVERSITY

CAMPUS LIFE
Quality of Life Rating **85**
Fire Safety Rating **89**
Type of school private
Affiliation Roman Catholic
Environment metropolis
STUDENTS
Total undergrad enrollment 6,282
% male/female 46/54
% from out of state 98
% from public high school 45
% live on campus 78
% African American 7
% Asian 10
% Caucasian 69
% Hispanic 6
% international 4
# of countries represented 81

ACADEMICS
Academic Rating **93**
Calendar semester
Student/faculty ratio 11:1
Professors Interesting Rating 82
Professors Accessible Rating 81
% professors teaching UG courses 100

% classes taught by TAs 8
Most common lab size 10-19 students
Most common
  regular class size fewer than 10 students
MOST POPULAR MAJORS
finance
international relations and affairs
political science and government

SELECTIVITY
Admissions Selectivity Rating **98**
# of applicants 14,855
% of applicants accepted 22
% of acceptees attending 47
# accepting a place on wait list 1,901
% admitted from wait list 1
FRESHMAN PROFILE
Range SAT Verbal 640-740
Range SAT Math 640-730
Projected Range SAT Writing 660-720
Range ACT Composite 27-32
Minimum Paper TOEFL 200
% graduated top 10% of class 90
% graduated top 25% of class 98
% graduated top 50% of class 100
DEADLINES
Regular application deadline 1/10
Regular notification 4/1
Nonfall registration? no

FINANCIAL FACTS
Financial Aid Rating **94**
Annual tuition $29,808
Room & Board $10,554
Books and supplies $960
Required fees $355
% frosh rec. need-based scholarship
  or grant aid 42
% UG rec. need-based scholarship
  or grant aid 37
% frosh rec. need-based self-help aid 37
% UG rec. need-based self-help aid 37
% frosh rec. any financial aid 44
% UG rec. any financial aid 43
Avg. frosh grant $18,464
Avg. frosh loan $2,010

THE GEORGE WASHINGTON UNIVERSITY

CAMPUS LIFE
Quality of Life Rating **76**
Fire Safety Rating **60**
Type of school private
Environment metropolis
STUDENTS
Total undergrad enrollment 10,563
% male/female 44/56

% from out of state	98
% from public high school	70
% live on campus	67
% in (# of) fraternities	16 (12)
% in (# of) sororities	13 (9)
% African American	6
% Asian	10
% Caucasian	66
% Hispanic	5
% international	4
# of countries represented	101

ACADEMICS
Academic Rating	**82**
Calendar	semester
Student/faculty ratio	13:1
Professors Interesting Rating	70
Professors Accessible Rating	68
% professors teaching UG courses	67
% classes taught by TAs	3
Most common lab size	10-19 students
Most common regular class size	20-29 students

SELECTIVITY
Admissions Selectivity Rating	**94**
# of applicants	20,159
% of applicants accepted	38
% of acceptees attending	35
# accepting a place on wait list	2,284
% admitted from wait list	8
# of early decision applicants	1,176
% accepted early decision	63

FRESHMAN PROFILE
Range SAT Verbal	590-690
Average SAT Verbal	620
Range SAT Math	590-680
Average SAT Math	620
Projected Range SAT Writing	620-690
Range ACT Composite	25-30
Average ACT Composite	26
Minimum Paper TOEFL	550
Minimum Computer Based TOEFL	300
% graduated top 10% of class	59
% graduated top 25% of class	80
% graduated top 50% of class	99

DEADLINES
Early decision application deadline	12/1
Regular application deadline	1/15
Regular notification	3/15
Nonfall registration?	yes

FINANCIAL FACTS
Financial Aid Rating	**91**
Annual tuition	$34,000
Room & Board	$11,470
Books and supplies	$850
Required fees	$30

% frosh rec. need-based scholarship or grant aid	39
% UG rec. need-based scholarship or grant aid	38
% frosh rec. need-based self-help aid	35
% UG rec. need-based self-help aid	35
Avg. frosh grant	$11,800
Avg. frosh loan	$3,000

GETTYSBURG COLLEGE

CAMPUS LIFE
Quality of Life Rating	**87**
Fire Safety Rating	**60**
Type of school	private
Affiliation	Lutheran
Environment	village

STUDENTS
Total undergrad enrollment	2,453
% male/female	50/50
% from out of state	72
% from public high school	70
% live on campus	94
% in (# of) fraternities	40 (10)
% in (# of) sororities	26 (5)
% African American	4
% Asian	1
% Caucasian	92
% Hispanic	2
% international	2
# of countries represented	32

ACADEMICS
Academic Rating	**91**
Calendar	semester
Student/faculty ratio	11:1
Professors Interesting Rating	89
Professors Accessible Rating	91
% professors teaching UG courses	100
Most common lab size	10-19 students

MOST POPULAR MAJORS
business administration/management
political science and government
psychology

SELECTIVITY
Admissions Selectivity Rating	**94**
# of applicants	4,839
% of applicants accepted	46
% of acceptees attending	32
# of early decision applicants	232
% accepted early decision	77

FRESHMAN PROFILE
Range SAT Verbal	600-670
Average SAT Verbal	630
Range SAT Math	600-670
Average SAT Math	630
Projected Range SAT Writing	630-680

Average ACT Composite	28
Minimum Paper TOEFL	570
Minimum Computer Based TOEFL	290
% graduated top 10% of class	62
% graduated top 25% of class	84
% graduated top 50% of class	99

DEADLINES
Early decision application deadline	11/15
Regular notification	4/1
Nonfall registration?	yes

FINANCIAL FACTS
Financial Aid Rating	**98**
Annual tuition	$29,990
Room & Board	$7,906
Books and supplies	$500
Required fees	$250
% frosh rec. need-based scholarship or grant aid	57
% UG rec. need-based scholarship or grant aid	57
% frosh rec. need-based self-help aid	50
% UG rec. need-based self-help aid	50
% frosh rec. any financial aid	57
% UG rec. any financial aid	57
Avg. frosh grant	$23,640
Avg. frosh loan	$3,500

GORDON COLLEGE

CAMPUS LIFE
Quality of Life Rating	**96**
Fire Safety Rating	**60**
Type of school	private
Affiliation	Protestant
Environment	village

STUDENTS
Total undergrad enrollment	1,614
% male/female	36/64
% from out of state	71
% from public high school	70
% live on campus	88
% African American	1
% Asian	2
% Caucasian	88
% Hispanic	2
% international	2
# of countries represented	25

ACADEMICS
Academic Rating	**87**
Calendar	semester
Student/faculty ratio	14:1
Professors Interesting Rating	86
Professors Accessible Rating	83
% professors teaching UG courses	100
Most common lab size	10-19 students

Most common
regular class size   10-19 students

MOST POPULAR MAJORS

business administration/management
communications studies/speech communication and rhetoric
English language and literature

SELECTIVITY

Admissions Selectivity Rating   88

# of applicants	987
% of applicants accepted	81
% of acceptees attending	50
# of early decision applicants	119
% accepted early decision	94

FRESHMAN PROFILE

Range SAT Verbal	550-670
Average SAT Verbal	611
Range SAT Math	540-650
Average SAT Math	594
Projected Range SAT Writing	600-680
Range ACT Composite	23-29
Average ACT Composite	26
Minimum Paper TOEFL	550
Minimum Computer Based TOEFL	213
Average HS GPA	3.6
% graduated top 10% of class	33
% graduated top 25% of class	69
% graduated top 50% of class	87

DEADLINES

Early decision application deadline	12/1
Regular notification	rolling
Nonfall registration?	yes

FINANCIAL FACTS

Financial Aid Rating   72

Annual tuition	$21,930
Room & Board	$6,270
Books and supplies	$800
Required fees	$994
% frosh rec. need-based scholarship or grant aid	64
% UG rec. need-based scholarship or grant aid	68
% frosh rec. need-based self-help aid	54
% UG rec. need-based self-help aid	63
Avg. frosh grant	$13,852
Avg. frosh loan	$3,095

GOUCHER COLLEGE

CAMPUS LIFE

Quality of Life Rating	**86**
Fire Safety Rating	**60**
Type of school	private
Environment	city

STUDENTS

Total undergrad enrollment	1,345
% male/female	32/68
% from out of state	73
% from public high school	64
% live on campus	80
% African American	5
% Asian	3
% Caucasian	65
% Hispanic	3
% international	1

ACADEMICS

Academic Rating   86

Calendar	semester
Student/faculty ratio	10:1
Professors Interesting Rating	87
Professors Accessible Rating	87
% professors teaching UG courses	100
Most common lab size	10-19 students

MOST POPULAR MAJORS

communications studies/speech
communication and rhetoric
English language and literature
psychology

SELECTIVITY

Admissions Selectivity Rating   88

# of applicants	2,870
% of applicants accepted	68
% of acceptees attending	21
# accepting a place on wait list	355
% admitted from wait list	3

FRESHMAN PROFILE

Range SAT Verbal	560-660
Average SAT Verbal	607
Range SAT Math	530-630
Average SAT Math	581
Projected Range SAT Writing	600-670
Range ACT Composite	23-27
Average ACT Composite	26
Minimum Paper TOEFL	550
Minimum Computer Based TOEFL	230
Average HS GPA	3.21
% graduated top 10% of class	28
% graduated top 25% of class	63
% graduated top 50% of class	91

DEADLINES

Regular application deadline	2/1
Regular notification	4/1
Nonfall registration?	yes

FINANCIAL FACTS

Financial Aid Rating   77

Annual tuition	$27,100
Room & Board	$5,625
Books and supplies	$800
Required fees	$425
% frosh rec. need-based scholarship or grant aid	47

% UG rec. need-based scholarship or grant aid	53
% frosh rec. need-based self-help aid	41
% UG rec. need-based self-help aid	54
% frosh rec. any financial aid	83
% UG rec. any financial aid	92
Avg. frosh grant	$15,734
Avg. frosh loan	$3,895

GROVE CITY COLLEGE

CAMPUS LIFE

Quality of Life Rating	**77**
Fire Safety Rating	**73**
Type of school	private
Affiliation	Presbyterian
Environment	rural

STUDENTS

Total undergrad enrollment	2,318
% male/female	51/49
% from out of state	48
% from public high school	85
% live on campus	90
% in (# of) fraternities	13 (8)
% in (# of) sororities	16 (8)
% Asian	2
% Caucasian	96
% international	1
# of countries represented	12

ACADEMICS

Academic Rating   84

Calendar	semester
Student/faculty ratio	16:1
Professors Interesting Rating	80
Professors Accessible Rating	88
% professors teaching UG courses	100
Most common lab size	20-29 students
Most common regular class size	20-29 students

MOST POPULAR MAJORS

business administration/management
elementary education and teaching

SELECTIVITY

Admissions Selectivity Rating   95

# of applicants	2,091
% of applicants accepted	47
% of acceptees attending	62
# accepting a place on wait list	938
% admitted from wait list	4
# of early decision applicants	303
% accepted early decision	47

FRESHMAN PROFILE

Range SAT Verbal	575-696
Average SAT Verbal	635
Range SAT Math	578-688
Average SAT Math	636

Projected Range SAT Writing	620-700
Range ACT Composite	25-30
Average ACT Composite	28
Minimum Paper TOEFL	550
Minimum Computer Based TOEFL	213
Average HS GPA	3.73
% graduated top 10% of class	61
% graduated top 25% of class	89
% graduated top 50% of class	97

DEADLINES

Early decision application deadline	11/15
Regular application deadline	2/1
Regular notification	3/15
Nonfall registration?	yes

FINANCIAL FACTS

Financial Aid Rating	**62**
Annual tuition	$10,440
Room & Board	$5,344
Books and supplies	$900
% frosh rec. need-based scholarship or grant aid	42
% UG rec. need-based scholarship or grant aid	36
% frosh rec. need-based self-help aid	25
% UG rec. need-based self-help aid	25
Avg. frosh grant	$4,887
Avg. frosh loan	$6,055

HAMILTON COLLEGE

CAMPUS LIFE

Quality of Life Rating	**74**
Fire Safety Rating	**60**
Type of school	private
Environment	town

STUDENTS

Total undergrad enrollment	1,762
% male/female	50/50
% from out of state	62
% from public high school	60
% live on campus	98
% in (# of) fraternities	34 (7)
% in (# of) sororities	20 (3)
% African American	4
% Asian	5
% Caucasian	77
% Hispanic	4
% Native American	1
% international	5
# of countries represented	40

ACADEMICS

Academic Rating	**95**
Calendar	semester
Student/faculty ratio	9:1
Professors Interesting Rating	96
Professors Accessible Rating	91

% professors teaching UG courses	100
Most common lab size	10-19 students
Most common regular class size	10-19 students

MOST POPULAR MAJORS
economics
political science and government
psychology

SELECTIVITY

Admissions Selectivity Rating	**95**
# of applicants	4,445
% of applicants accepted	34
% of acceptees attending	30
# accepting a place on wait list	529
% admitted from wait list	14
# of early decision applicants	230
% accepted early decision	47

FRESHMAN PROFILE

Range SAT Verbal	620-710
Average SAT Verbal	661
Range SAT Math	640-710
Average SAT Math	668
Projected Range SAT Writing	650-700
Minimum Paper TOEFL	600
Minimum Computer Based TOEFL	250
% graduated top 10% of class	68
% graduated top 25% of class	91
% graduated top 50% of class	99

DEADLINES

Early decision application deadline	11/15
Regular application deadline	1/1
Regular notification	4/1
Nonfall registration?	yes

FINANCIAL FACTS

Financial Aid Rating	**95**
Annual tuition	$33,150
Room & board	$8,310
% frosh rec. need-based scholarship or grant aid	50
% UG rec. need-based scholarship or grant aid	54
% frosh rec. need-based self-help aid	34
% UG rec. need-based self-help aid	39

HAMPSHIRE COLLEGE

CAMPUS LIFE

Quality of Life Rating	**80**
Fire Safety Rating	**83**
Type of school	private
Environment	village

STUDENTS

Total undergrad enrollment	1,344
% male/female	43/57
% from out of state	84
% from public high school	70

% live on campus	93
% African American	3
% Asian	4
% Caucasian	72
% Hispanic	5
% international	3
# of countries represented	26

ACADEMICS

Academic Rating	**88**
Calendar	4-1-4
Student/faculty ratio	12:1
Professors Interesting Rating	87
Professors Accessible Rating	84
% professors teaching UG courses	100
Most common lab size	10-19 students
Most common regular class size	fewer than 10 students

MOST POPULAR MAJORS
liberal arts and sciences/liberal studies
social sciences
visual and performing arts

SELECTIVITY

Admissions Selectivity Rating	**87**
# of applicants	2,180
% of applicants accepted	59
% of acceptees attending	29
# accepting a place on wait list	436
% admitted from wait list	15
# of early decision applicants	38
% accepted early decision	62

FRESHMAN PROFILE

Range SAT Verbal	610-700
Average SAT Verbal	651
Range SAT Math	550-660
Average SAT Math	601
Projected Range SAT Writing	640-700
Range ACT Composite	25-29
Average ACT Composite	27
Minimum Paper TOEFL	577
Minimum Computer Based TOEFL	233
Average HS GPA	3.28
% graduated top 10% of class	26
% graduated top 25% of class	33
% graduated top 50% of class	88

DEADLINES

Early decision application deadline	11/15
Regular application deadline	1/15
Regular notification	4/1
Nonfall registration?	yes

FINANCIAL FACTS

Financial Aid Rating	**92**
Annual tuition	$31,939
Room & Board	$8,519
Books and supplies	$500
Required fees	$580

% frosh rec. need-based scholarship
or grant aid 58
% UG rec. need-based scholarship
or grant aid 56
% frosh rec. need-based self-help aid 58
% UG rec. need-based self-help aid 56
% frosh rec. any financial aid 70
% UG rec. any financial aid 61
Avg. frosh grant $19,785
Avg. frosh loan $2,625

HARTWICK COLLEGE

CAMPUS LIFE
Quality of Life Rating **75**
Fire Safety Rating **60**
Type of school private
Environment town
STUDENTS
Total undergrad enrollment 1,455
% male/female 43/57
% from out of state 64
% live on campus 88
% in (# of) fraternities 15 (5)
% in (# of) sororities 17 (4)
% African American 5
% Asian 1
% Caucasian 63
% Hispanic 4
% Native American 1
% international 3
# of countries represented 34

ACADEMICS
Academic Rating **83**
Calendar 4-1-4
Student/faculty ratio 12:1
Professors Interesting Rating 87
Professors Accessible Rating 86
% professors teaching UG courses 100
Most common lab size 10-19 students
Most common
regular class size 10-19 students
MOST POPULAR MAJORS
business administration/management
psychology

SELECTIVITY
Admissions Selectivity Rating **74**
# of applicants 2,055
% of applicants accepted 88
% of acceptees attending 25
FRESHMAN PROFILE
Range SAT Verbal 510-600
Average SAT Verbal 565
Range SAT Math 520-610
Average SAT Math 567
Projected Range SAT Writing 570-630

Average ACT Composite 2
Minimum Paper TOEFL 550
Minimum Computer Based TOEFL 213
% graduated top 10% of class 20
% graduated top 25% of class 46
% graduated top 50% of class 83
DEADLINES
Regular application deadline 2/15
Regular notification 3/7
Nonfall registration? yes

FINANCIAL FACTS
Financial Aid Rating **89**
Annual tuition $26,190
Room & Board $7,250
Books and supplies $700
Required fees $400
% frosh rec. need-based scholarship
or grant aid 69
% UG rec. need-based scholarship
or grant aid 71
% frosh rec. need-based self-help aid 69
% UG rec. need-based self-help aid 71
% frosh rec. any financial aid 95
Avg. frosh grant $22,211

HARVARD COLLEGE

CAMPUS LIFE
Quality of Life Rating **89**
Fire Safety Rating **60**
Type of school private
Environment metropolis
STUDENTS
Total undergrad enrollment 6,649
% male/female 53/47
% from out of state 84
% from public high school 65
% live on campus 96
% African American 8
% Asian 18
% Caucasian 42
% Hispanic 8
% Native American 1
% international 7

ACADEMICS
Academic Rating **96**
Calendar semester
Student/faculty ratio 8:1
Professors Interesting Rating 79
Professors Accessible Rating 71
% professors teaching UG courses 100
Most common lab size fewer than
10 students
Most common
regular class size fewer than 10 students

MOST POPULAR MAJORS
economics
political science and government
psychology

SELECTIVITY
Admissions Selectivity Rating **99**
# of applicants 19,609
% of applicants accepted 11
% of acceptees attending 79
FRESHMAN PROFILE
Range SAT Verbal 700-800
Range SAT Math 700-790
Projected Range SAT Writing 700-760
Range ACT Composite 30-34
% graduated top 10% of class 90
% graduated top 25% of class 98
% graduated top 50% of class 100
DEADLINES
Regular application deadline 1/1
Regular notification 4/1
Nonfall registration? no

FINANCIAL FACTS
Financial Aid Rating **95**
Annual tuition $26,066
Room & Board $8,868
Books and supplies $2,522
Required fees $2,994
% frosh rec. need-based scholarship
or grant aid 47
% UG rec. need-based scholarship
or grant aid 48
% frosh rec. need-based self-help aid 34
% UG rec. need-based self-help aid 41
Avg. frosh grant $23,750
Avg. frosh loan $1,100

HAVERFORD COLLEGE

CAMPUS LIFE
Quality of Life Rating **98**
Fire Safety Rating **72**
Type of school private
Environment town
STUDENTS
Total undergrad enrollment 1,172
% male/female 47/53
% from out of state 81
% from public high school 57
% live on campus 99
% African American 6
% Asian 13
% Caucasian 71
% Hispanic 6
% Native American 1
% international 3
# of countries represented 38

ACADEMICS
Academic Rating   **98**
Calendar   semester
Student/faculty ratio   8:1
Professors Interesting Rating   95
Professors Accessible Rating   98
% professors teaching UG courses   100
Most common lab size   10-19 students
Most common
    regular class size   fewer than 10 students

MOST POPULAR MAJORS
economics
English language and literature

SELECTIVITY
Admissions Selectivity Rating   **97**
# of applicants   3,035
% of applicants accepted   29
% of acceptees attending   37
# accepting a place on wait list   831
# of early decision applicants   102
% accepted early decision   44

FRESHMAN PROFILE
Range SAT Verbal   640-740
Range SAT Math   640-720
Projected Range SAT Writing   660-720
Minimum Paper TOEFL   600
Minimum Computer Based TOEFL   250
% graduated top 10% of class   79
% graduated top 25% of class   93
% graduated top 50% of class   100

DEADLINES
Early decision application deadline   11/15
Regular application deadline   1/15
Regular notification   4/15
Nonfall registration?   no

FINANCIAL FACTS
Financial Aid Rating   **80**
Annual tuition $29,990
Room & Board $9,420
Books and supplies $1,028
Required fees $280
% frosh rec. need-based scholarship
    or grant aid   40
% UG rec. need-based scholarship
    or grant aid   40
% frosh rec. need-based self-help aid   38
% UG rec. need-based self-help aid   38
% frosh rec. any financial aid   41
% UG rec. any financial aid   40
Avg. frosh grant $21,762
Avg. frosh loan $5,575

HOBART AND WILLIAM SMITH COLLEGES

CAMPUS LIFE
Quality of Life Rating   **74**
Fire Safety Rating   **96**
Type of school   private
Environment   village

STUDENTS
Total undergrad enrollment   1,825
% male/female   46/54
% from out of state   53
% from public high school   65
% live on campus   90
% in (# of) fraternities   15 (5)
% African American   4
% Asian   2
% Caucasian   87
% Hispanic   4
% international   2
# of countries represented   18

ACADEMICS
Academic Rating   **87**
Calendar   semester
Student/faculty ratio   11:1
Professors Interesting Rating   87
Professors Accessible Rating   85
% professors teaching UG courses   100
Most common lab size   10-19 students

MOST POPULAR MAJORS
economics
English language and literature
history

SELECTIVITY
Admissions Selectivity Rating   **87**
# of applicants   3,266
% of applicants accepted   63
% of acceptees attending   23
# accepting a place on wait list   338
% admitted from wait list   7
# of early decision applicants   106
% accepted early decision   79

FRESHMAN PROFILE
Range SAT Verbal   540-630
Average SAT Verbal   550
Range SAT Math   545-640
Average SAT Math   600
Projected Range SAT Writing   590-650
Range ACT Composite   24-27
Minimum Paper TOEFL   550
Minimum Computer Based TOEFL   220
Average HS GPA   3.23
% graduated top 10% of class   31
% graduated top 25% of class   55
% graduated top 50% of class   95

DEADLINES
Early decision application deadline   11/15
Regular application deadline   2/1
Regular notification   4/1
Nonfall registration?   no

FINANCIAL FACTS
Financial Aid Rating   **92**
Annual tuition $30,076
Room & Board $7,987
Books and supplies $850
Required fees $567
% frosh rec. need-based scholarship
    or grant aid   59
% UG rec. need-based scholarship
    or grant aid   61
% frosh rec. need-based self-help aid   48
% UG rec. need-based self-help aid   53
% frosh rec. any financial aid   74
% UG rec. any financial aid   64
Avg. frosh grant $23,902
Avg. frosh loan $2,356

HOFSTRA UNIVERSITY

CAMPUS LIFE
Quality of Life Rating   **62**
Fire Safety Rating   **85**
Type of school   private
Environment   city

STUDENTS
Total undergrad enrollment   8,869
% male/female   47/53
% from out of state   27
% live on campus   44
% in (# of) fraternities   5 (18)
% in (# of) sororities   6 (10)
% African American   10
% Asian   4
% Caucasian   62
% Hispanic   8
% international   2
# of countries represented   61

ACADEMICS
Academic Rating   **76**
Calendar   4-1-4
Student/faculty ratio   14:1
Professors Interesting Rating   68
Professors Accessible Rating   64
% professors teaching UG courses   79
Most common lab size   10-19 students
Most common
    regular class size   10-19 students

MOST POPULAR MAJORS
accounting
marketing/marketing management
psychology

SELECTIVITY
Admissions Selectivity Rating   **84**

# of applicants	11,503
% of applicants accepted	67
% of acceptees attending	23
# accepting a place on wait list	623
% admitted from wait list	59

FRESHMAN PROFILE
Range SAT Verbal	520-610
Average SAT Verbal	567
Range SAT Math	530-620
Average SAT Math	577
Projected Range SAT Writing	570-640
Range ACT Composite	21-27
Average ACT Composite	24
Minimum Paper TOEFL	550
Minimum Computer Based TOEFL	213
Average HS GPA	3.22
% graduated top 10% of class	22
% graduated top 25% of class	54
% graduated top 50% of class	84

DEADLINES
Regular notification	rolling
Nonfall registration?	yes

FINANCIAL FACTS
Financial Aid Rating   **67**

Annual tuition	$19,010
Room & Board	$9,000
Books and supplies	$900
Required fees	$1,002
% frosh rec. need-based scholarship or grant aid	61
% UG rec. need-based scholarship or grant aid	57
% frosh rec. need-based self-help aid	31
% UG rec. need-based self-help aid	31
% frosh rec. any financial aid	89
% UG rec. any financial aid	75
Avg. frosh grant	$9,569
Avg. frosh loan	$2,787

HOOD COLLEGE

CAMPUS LIFE
Quality of Life Rating   **84**
Fire Safety Rating   **80**

Type of school	private
Environment	town

STUDENTS
Total undergrad enrollment	976
% male/female	18/82
% from out of state	19
% live on campus	53
% African American	12
% Asian	2
% Caucasian	70

% Hispanic	2
% international	4
# of countries represented	27

ACADEMICS
Academic Rating   **86**

Calendar	semester
Student/faculty ratio	11:1
Professors Interesting Rating	89
Professors Accessible Rating	86
% professors teaching UG courses	100
Most common lab size	10-19 students
Most common regular class size	10-19 students

MOST POPULAR MAJORS
biology/biological sciences
kindergarten/preschool education and teaching
psychology

SELECTIVITY
Admissions Selectivity Rating   **87**

# of applicants	1,474
% of applicants accepted	55
% of acceptees attending	30

FRESHMAN PROFILE
Range SAT Verbal	490-620
Average SAT Verbal	555
Range SAT Math	490-590
Average SAT Math	541
Projected Range SAT Writing	550-650
Range ACT Composite	20-25
Average ACT Composite	23
Minimum Paper TOEFL	550
Minimum Computer Based TOEFL	215
Average HS GPA	3.57
% graduated top 10% of class	32
% graduated top 25% of class	61
% graduated top 50% of class	93

DEADLINES
Regular application deadline	2/1
Regular notification	3/15
Nonfall registration?	yes

FINANCIAL FACTS
Financial Aid Rating   **86**

Annual tuition	$22,000
Room & Board	$7,750
Books and supplies	$800
Required fees	$335
% frosh rec. need-based scholarship or grant aid	76
% UG rec. need-based scholarship or grant aid	81
% frosh rec. need-based self-help aid	55
% UG rec. need-based self-help aid	58
% frosh rec. any financial aid	98
% UG rec. any financial aid	95

Avg. frosh grant	$15,628
Avg. frosh loan	$5,257

HOUGHTON COLLEGE

CAMPUS LIFE
Quality of Life Rating   **89**
Fire Safety Rating   **81**

Type of school	private
Affiliation	Wesleyan
Environment	rural

STUDENTS
Total undergrad enrollment	1,428
% male/female	33/67
% from out of state	38
% from public high school	65
% live on campus	82
% African American	2
% Asian	2
% Caucasian	87
% Hispanic	1
% international	3
# of countries represented	23

ACADEMICS
Academic Rating   **84**

Calendar	semester
Student/faculty ratio	14:1
Professors Interesting Rating	89
Professors Accessible Rating	87
% professors teaching UG courses	100
Most common lab size	10-19 students
Most common regular class size	10-19 students

MOST POPULAR MAJORS
business administration and management
elementary education and teaching
psychology

SELECTIVITY
Admissions Selectivity Rating   **82**

# of applicants	1,044
% of applicants accepted	89
% of acceptees attending	35

FRESHMAN PROFILE
Range SAT Verbal	540-660
Average SAT Verbal	591
Range SAT Math	530-630
Average SAT Math	579
Projected Range SAT Writing	590-670
Range ACT Composite	23-29
Average ACT Composite	25
Minimum Paper TOEFL	550
Minimum Computer Based TOEFL	213
Average HS GPA	3.16
% graduated top 10% of class	30
% graduated top 25% of class	62
% graduated top 50% of class	89

DEADLINES

Regular notification	rolling
Nonfall registration?	yes

FINANCIAL FACTS

Financial Aid Rating   **71**

Annual tuition	$18,660
Room & Board	$6,320
Books and supplies	$750
% frosh rec. need-based scholarship or grant aid	92
% UG rec. need-based scholarship or grant aid	67
% frosh rec. need-based self-help aid	78
% UG rec. need-based self-help aid	59
% frosh rec. any financial aid	92
% UG rec. any financial aid	68
Avg. frosh grant	$11,337
Avg. frosh loan	$3,306

HOWARD UNIVERSITY

CAMPUS LIFE

Quality of Life Rating	**66**
Fire Safety Rating	**60**
Type of school	private

STUDENTS

Total undergrad enrollment	7,063
% male/female	33/67
% from out of state	90
% from public high school	80
% live on campus	59
% in (# of) fraternities	2 (10)
% in (# of) sororities	1 (8)
% African American	84
% international	7
# of countries represented	85

ACADEMICS

Academic Rating   **83**

Calendar	semester
Student/faculty ratio	8:1
Professors Interesting Rating	70
Professors Accessible Rating	67
Most common lab size	fewer than 10 students
Most common regular class size	10-19 students

MOST POPULAR MAJORS
biology/biological sciences
journalism
radio and television

SELECTIVITY

Admissions Selectivity Rating   **88**

# of applicants	8,860
% of applicants accepted	47
% of acceptees attending	35

FRESHMAN PROFILE

Range SAT Verbal	430-690
Average SAT Verbal	544
Range SAT Math	450-680
Average SAT Math	538
Projected Range SAT Writing	500-690
Range ACT Composite	18-29
Average ACT Composite	22
Minimum Paper TOEFL	550
Minimum Computer Based TOEFL	213
Average HS GPA	3.2
% graduated top 10% of class	23
% graduated top 25% of class	49
% graduated top 50% of class	81

DEADLINES

Regular application deadline	2/15
Regular notification	rolling
Nonfall registration?	yes

FINANCIAL FACTS

Financial Aid Rating   **68**

Annual tuition	$10,840
Room & Board	$5,870
Books and supplies	$1,020
Required fees	$805
% frosh rec. need-based scholarship or grant aid	37
% UG rec. need-based scholarship or grant aid	29
% frosh rec. need-based self-help aid	49
% UG rec. need-based self-help aid	35
% frosh rec. any financial aid	67
% UG rec. any financial aid	51
Avg. frosh grant	$4,475
Avg. frosh loan	$9,457

IMMACULATA UNIVERSITY

CAMPUS LIFE

Quality of Life Rating	**88**
Fire Safety Rating	**77**
Type of school	private
Affiliation	Roman Catholic
Environment	town

STUDENTS

Total undergrad enrollment	2,850
% male/female	17/83
% from out of state	17
% from public high school	65
% live on campus	75
% African American	7
% Asian	1
% Caucasian	87
% Hispanic	2
% international	1
# of countries represented	13

ACADEMICS

Academic Rating   **72**

Calendar	semester
Student/faculty ratio	11:1
Professors Interesting Rating	87
Professors Accessible Rating	88
% professors teaching UG courses	100
Most common lab size	10-19 students

MOST POPULAR MAJORS
business administration/management
psychology

SELECTIVITY

Admissions Selectivity Rating   **60**

# of applicants	595
% of applicants accepted	89
% of acceptees attending	27

FRESHMAN PROFILE

Range SAT Verbal	420-520
Average SAT Verbal	481
Range SAT Math	450-550
Average SAT Math	502
Projected Range SAT Writing	490-570
Minimum Paper TOEFL	550
Minimum Computer Based TOEFL	20
Average HS GPA	3.08

DEADLINES

Regular application deadline	8/15
Regular notification	rolling
Nonfall registration?	yes

FINANCIAL FACTS

Financial Aid Rating   **74**

Annual tuition	$18,000
Room & board	$8,250
Books and supplies	$1,100
% frosh rec. any financial aid	69
Avg. frosh grant	$9,000
Avg. frosh loan	$2,625

INDIANA UNIVERSITY OF PENNSYLVANIA

CAMPUS LIFE

Quality of Life Rating	**72**
Fire Safety Rating	**81**
Type of school	public
Environment	village

STUDENTS

Total undergrad enrollment	11,861
% male/female	44/56
% from out of state	3
% from public high school	95
% live on campus	32
% in (# of) fraternities	10 (19)
% in (# of) sororities	11 (14)
% African American	6

% Asian 1
% Caucasian 81
% Hispanic 1
% international 2
# of countries represented 74

ACADEMICS
Academic Rating 74
Calendar semester
Student/faculty ratio 17:1
Professors Interesting Rating 77
Professors Accessible Rating 77
% professors teaching UG courses 100
Most common lab size 20-29 students

MOST POPULAR MAJORS
communications studies/speech
communication and rhetoric
criminology
elementary education and teaching

SELECTIVITY
Admissions Selectivity Rating 79
of applicants 8,836
% of applicants accepted 55
% of acceptees attending 54

FRESHMAN PROFILE
Range SAT Verbal 480-570
Average SAT Verbal 543
Range SAT Math 470-560
Average SAT Math 534
Projected Range SAT Writing 540-610
Minimum Paper TOEFL 500
Minimum Computer Based TOEFL 300
Average HS GPA 3.36
% graduated top 10% of class 16
% graduated top 25% of class 35
% graduated top 50% of class 74

DEADLINES
Regular notification rolling
Nonfall registration? yes

FINANCIAL FACTS
Financial Aid Rating 73
Annual in-state tuition $4,598
Annual out-of-state tuition $11,496
Room & Board $4,702
Books and supplies $800
Required fees $1,187
% frosh rec. need-based scholarship
 or grant aid 51
% UG rec. need-based scholarship
 or grant aid 50
% frosh rec. need-based self-help aid 63
% UG rec. need-based self-help aid 60
% frosh rec. any financial aid 81
% UG rec. any financial aid 77
Avg. frosh grant $3,935
Avg. frosh loan $2,896

IONA COLLEGE
CAMPUS LIFE
Quality of Life Rating 72
Fire Safety Rating 96
Type of school private
Affiliation Roman Catholic
Environment town
STUDENTS
Total undergrad enrollment 3,413
% male/female 46/54
% from out of state 18
% live on campus 30
% in (# of) fraternities 2 (4)
% in (# of) sororities 4 (7)
% African American 7
% Asian 1
% Caucasian 69
% Hispanic 11
% international 2
# of countries represented 51

ACADEMICS
Academic Rating 77
Calendar semester
Student/faculty ratio 15:1
Professors Interesting Rating 78
Professors Accessible Rating 83
% professors teaching UG courses 100
Most common lab size 20-29 students
Most common
 regular class size 10-19 students

MOST POPULAR MAJORS
business administration/management
criminal justice/law enforcement
administration
mass communications/media studies

SELECTIVITY
Admissions Selectivity Rating 85
of applicants 4,501
% of applicants accepted 60
% of acceptees attending 33
# accepting a place on wait list 122
% admitted from wait list 2

FRESHMAN PROFILE
Range SAT Verbal 515-610
Average SAT Verbal 540
Range SAT Math 530-620
Average SAT Math 541
Projected Range SAT Writing 570-640
Average ACT Composite 23
Minimum Paper TOEFL 550
Minimum Computer Based TOEFL 213
Average HS GPA 3.4
% graduated top 10% of class 29
% graduated top 25% of class 51
% graduated top 50% of class 94

DEADLINES
Regular application deadline 2/15
Regular notification rolling
Nonfall registration? yes

FINANCIAL FACTS
Financial Aid Rating 62
Annual tuition $18,990
Room & Board $9,698
Books and supplies $700
Required fees $540
% frosh rec. need-based scholarship
 or grant aid 26
% UG rec. need-based scholarship
 or grant aid 29
% frosh rec. need-based self-help aid 58
% UG rec. need-based self-help aid 56
% frosh rec. any financial aid 96
% UG rec. any financial aid 86
Avg. frosh grant $11,129
Avg. frosh loan $9,571

ITHACA COLLEGE
CAMPUS LIFE
Quality of Life Rating 77
Fire Safety Rating 74
Type of school private
Environment village
STUDENTS
Total undergrad enrollment 6,005
% male/female 43/57
% from out of state 55
% from public high school 73
% live on campus 70
% in (# of) fraternities 1 (1)
% in (# of) sororities 1 (1)
% African American 2
% Asian 3
% Caucasian 87
% Hispanic 3
% international 3
# of countries represented 70

ACADEMICS
Academic Rating 81
Calendar semester
Student/faculty ratio 12:1
Professors Interesting Rating 80
Professors Accessible Rating 79
% professors teaching UG courses 99
% classes taught by TAs 1
Most common lab size 10-19 students
Most common
 regular class size fewer than 10 students

business administration/management
music/music and performing arts studies
radio and television

SELECTIVITY

Admissions Selectivity Rating	**86**
# of applicants	10,401
% of applicants accepted	67
% of acceptees attending	21
# of early decision applicants	132
% accepted early decision	50

FRESHMAN PROFILE

Range SAT Verbal	540-640
Average SAT Verbal	594
Range SAT Math	550-640
Average SAT Math	596
Projected Range SAT Writing	590-660
Minimum Paper TOEFL	550
Minimum Computer Based TOEFL	213
% graduated top 10% of class	33
% graduated top 25% of class	71
% graduated top 50% of class	97

DEADLINES

Early decision application deadline	11/1
Regular application deadline	2/1
Regular notification	rolling
Nonfall registration?	yes

FINANCIAL FACTS

Financial Aid Rating	**80**
Annual tuition	$25,194
Room & Board	$9,950
Books and supplies	$968
% frosh rec. need-based scholarship or grant aid	67
% UG rec. need-based scholarship or grant aid	66
% frosh rec. need-based self-help aid	63
% UG rec. need-based self-help aid	62
% frosh rec. any financial aid	88
% UG rec. any financial aid	86
Avg. frosh grant	$14,103
Avg. frosh loan	$5,007

JOHNS HOPKINS UNIVERSITY

CAMPUS LIFE

Quality of Life Rating	**66**
Fire Safety Rating	**60**
Type of school	private
Environment	metropolis

STUDENTS

Total undergrad enrollment	4,201
% male/female	56/44
% from out of state	85
% from public high school	60
% live on campus	50

% in (# of) fraternities	22 (11)
% in (# of) sororities	20 (7)
% African American	5
% Asian	22
% Caucasian	62
% Hispanic	5
% international	5
# of countries represented	52

ACADEMICS

Academic Rating	**86**
Calendar	semester
Student/faculty ratio	9:1
Professors Interesting Rating	63
Professors Accessible Rating	63
% professors teaching UG courses	96
Most common lab size	10-19 students
Most common regular class size	10-19 students

biology/biological sciences
biomedical/medical engineering
international relations and affairs

SELECTIVITY

Admissions Selectivity Rating	**98**
# of applicants	11,102
% of applicants accepted	30
% of acceptees attending	32
# accepting a place on wait list	1,612
% admitted from wait list	8
# of early decision applicants	362
% accepted early decision	59

FRESHMAN PROFILE

Range SAT Verbal	640-730
Average SAT Verbal	680
Range SAT Math	660-760
Average SAT Math	706
Projected Range SAT Writing	660-720
Range ACT Composite	27-32
Average ACT Composite	29
Minimum Paper TOEFL	600
Minimum Computer Based TOEFL	250
Average HS GPA	3.67
% graduated top 10% of class	80
% graduated top 25% of class	96
% graduated top 50% of class	99

DEADLINES

Early decision application deadline	11/15
Regular application deadline	1/1
Regular notification	4/1
Nonfall registration?	no

FINANCIAL FACTS

Financial Aid Rating	**89**
Annual tuition	$30,140
Room & Board	$9,516
Books and supplies	$850

Required fees	$500
% frosh rec. need-based scholarship or grant aid	39
% UG rec. need-based scholarship or grant aid	38
% frosh rec. need-based self-help aid	45
% UG rec. need-based self-help aid	41
% frosh rec. any financial aid	51
% UG rec. any financial aid	45
Avg. frosh grant	$22,893
Avg. frosh loan	$2,712

JUNIATA COLLEGE

CAMPUS LIFE

Quality of Life Rating	**85**
Fire Safety Rating	**84**
Type of school	private
Affiliation	Church of Brethren
Environment	village

STUDENTS

Total undergrad enrollment	1,378
% male/female	46/54
% from out of state	30
% from public high school	89
% live on campus	84
% African American	1
% Asian	1
% Caucasian	91
% Hispanic	1
% international	4
# of countries represented	26

ACADEMICS

Academic Rating	**88**
Calendar	semester
Student/faculty ratio	13:1
Professors Interesting Rating	88
Professors Accessible Rating	91
% professors teaching UG courses	100
Most common lab size	10-19 students
Most common regular class size	10-19 students

biology/biological sciences
business administration/management
education

SELECTIVITY

Admissions Selectivity Rating	**88**
# of applicants	1,761
% of applicants accepted	74
% of acceptees attending	30
# of early decision applicants	112
% accepted early decision	85

FRESHMAN PROFILE

Range SAT Verbal	530-630
Average SAT Verbal	580

Range SAT Math 540-630
Average SAT Math 582
Projected Range SAT Writing 580-650
Minimum Paper TOEFL 550
Minimum Computer Based TOEFL 213
Average HS GPA 3.76
% graduated top 10% of class 38
% graduated top 25% of class 76
% graduated top 50% of class 99

DEADLINES

Early decision application deadline 11/15
Regular application deadline 3/15
Regular notification rolling
Nonfall registration? yes

FINANCIAL FACTS

Financial Aid Rating 76
Annual tuition $25,260
Room & Board $7,240
Books and supplies $600
Required fees $630
% frosh rec. need-based scholarship
  or grant aid 74
% UG rec. need-based scholarship
  or grant aid 75
% frosh rec. need-based self-help aid 57
% UG rec. need-based self-help aid 62
% frosh rec. any financial aid 99
% UG rec. any financial aid 96
Avg. frosh grant $16,246
Avg. frosh loan $3,195

KEENE STATE COLLEGE

CAMPUS LIFE

Quality of Life Rating 70
Fire Safety Rating 81
Type of school public
Environment town

STUDENTS

Total undergrad enrollment 4,362
% male/female 42/58
% from out of state 47
% live on campus 55
% in (# of) fraternities 2 (4)
% in (# of) sororities 4 (3)
% Asian 1
% Caucasian 94
% Hispanic 1
% international 1
# of countries represented 11

ACADEMICS

Academic Rating 74
Calendar semester
Student/faculty ratio 18:1
Professors Interesting Rating 74
Professors Accessible Rating 81

% professors teaching UG courses 100
Most common lab size 10-19 students

MOST POPULAR MAJORS

business administration/management
elementary education and teaching
psychology

SELECTIVITY

Admissions Selectivity Rating 73
# of applicants 4,239
% of applicants accepted 75
% of acceptees attending 34

FRESHMAN PROFILE

Range SAT Verbal 460-550
Average SAT Verbal 504
Range SAT Math 450-550
Average SAT Math 499
Projected Range SAT Writing 530-600
Range ACT Composite 18-21
Average ACT Composite 20
Minimum Paper TOEFL 500
Minimum Computer Based TOEFL 173
Average HS GPA 2.99
% graduated top 10% of class 4
% graduated top 25% of class 21
% graduated top 50% of class 66

DEADLINES

Regular application deadline 4/1
Regular notification rolling
Nonfall registration? yes

FINANCIAL FACTS

Financial Aid Rating 70
Annual in-state tuition $5,060
Annual out-of-state tuition $11,500
Room & Board $5,966
Books and supplies $600
Required fees $1,860
% frosh rec. need-based scholarship
  or grant aid 36
% UG rec. need-based scholarship
  or grant aid 33
% frosh rec. need-based self-help aid 49
% UG rec. need-based self-help aid 49

KUTZTOWN UNIVERSITY OF PENNSYLVANIA

CAMPUS LIFE

Quality of Life Rating 72
Fire Safety Rating 60
Type of school public
Environment rural

STUDENTS

Total undergrad enrollment 8,141
% male/female 42/58
% from out of state 9

% from public high school 99
% live on campus 42
% in (# of) fraternities 4 (5)
% in (# of) sororities 4 (6)
% African American 7
% Asian 1
% Caucasian 86
% Hispanic 3
% international 1
# of countries represented 11

ACADEMICS

Academic Rating 73
Calendar semester
Student/faculty ratio 20:1
Professors Interesting Rating 74
Professors Accessible Rating 79
% professors teaching UG courses 99
Most common lab size 20-29 students

MOST POPULAR MAJORS

business administration/management
commercial and advertising art
criminal justice/safety studies

SELECTIVITY

Admissions Selectivity Rating 73
# of applicants 8,198
% of applicants accepted 64
% of acceptees attending 39

FRESHMAN PROFILE

Range SAT Verbal 450-540
Average SAT Verbal 495
Range SAT Math 450-540
Average SAT Math 491
Projected Range SAT Writing 520-590
Minimum Paper TOEFL 500
Minimum Computer Based TOEFL 173
Average HS GPA 3.02
% graduated top 10% of class 6
% graduated top 25% of class 20
% graduated top 50% of class 64

DEADLINES

Regular notification rolling
Nonfall registration? yes

FINANCIAL FACTS

Financial Aid Rating 78
Annual in-state tuition $4,810
Annual out-of-state tuition $12,026
Room & Board $5,274
Books and supplies $1,100
Required fees $1,446
% frosh rec. need-based scholarship
  or grant aid 47
% UG rec. need-based scholarship
  or grant aid 42
% frosh rec. need-based self-help aid 54
% UG rec. need-based self-help aid 49

Avg. frosh grant $3,791
Avg. frosh loan $2,508

LA ROCHE COLLEGE

CAMPUS LIFE
Quality of Life Rating **71**
Fire Safety Rating **88**
Type of school private
Affiliation Roman Catholic
Environment city
STUDENTS
Total undergrad enrollment 1,355
% male/female 36/64
% from out of state 6
% from public high school 79
% live on campus 35
% African American 4
% Asian 1
% Caucasian 84
% Hispanic 1
% Native American 1
% international 9
# of countries represented 28

ACADEMICS
Academic Rating **67**
Calendar semester
Student/faculty ratio 11:1
Professors Interesting Rating 68
Professors Accessible Rating 74
% professors teaching UG courses 98
Most common lab size 10-19 students
Most common
  regular class size fewer than 10 students

MOST POPULAR MAJORS
business administration/management
design and visual communications
elementary education and teaching

SELECTIVITY
Admissions Selectivity Rating **74**
# of applicants 528
% of applicants accepted 69
% of acceptees attending 62
FRESHMAN PROFILE
Range SAT Verbal 430-540
Average SAT Verbal 490
Range SAT Math 470-560
Average SAT Math 510
Projected Range SAT Writing 500-590
Range ACT Composite 19-22
Average ACT Composite 21
Average HS GPA 3.2
% graduated top 10% of class 12
% graduated top 25% of class 26
% graduated top 50% of class 57

DEADLINES
Regular application deadline 8/26
Regular notification rolling
Nonfall registration? yes

FINANCIAL FACTS
Financial Aid Rating **76**
Annual tuition $15,982
Room & board $6,962
Books and supplies $800
% frosh rec. need-based scholarship
  or grant aid 60
% UG rec. need-based scholarship
  or grant aid 51
% frosh rec. need-based self-help aid 74
% UG rec. need-based self-help aid 59
% frosh rec. any financial aid 98
% UG rec. any financial aid 95
Avg. frosh grant $7,193
Avg. frosh loan $2,886

LABORATORY INSTITUTE OF MERCHANDISING

CAMPUS LIFE
Quality of Life Rating **71**
Fire Safety Rating **60**
Type of school proprietary
Environment metropolis
STUDENTS
Total undergrad enrollment 608
% male/female 3/97
% from out of state 52
% from public high school 76
% live on campus 14
% African American 10
% Asian 6
% Caucasian 68
% Hispanic 15
% international 1
# of countries represented 8

ACADEMICS
Academic Rating **64**
Calendar semester
Student/faculty ratio 9:1
Professors Interesting Rating 76
Professors Accessible Rating 73
% professors teaching UG courses 100

SELECTIVITY
Admissions Selectivity Rating **73**
# of applicants 428
% of applicants accepted 63
% of acceptees attending 58
FRESHMAN PROFILE
Range SAT Verbal 430-520
Average SAT Verbal 476

Range SAT Math 400-490
Average SAT Math 462
Projected Range SAT Writing 500-570
Minimum Paper TOEFL 550
Minimum Computer Based TOEFL 213
Average HS GPA 2.8
% graduated top 10% of class 9
% graduated top 25% of class 18
% graduated top 50% of class 53
DEADLINES
Regular notification rolling
Nonfall registration? yes

FINANCIAL FACTS
Financial Aid Rating **90**
Annual tuition $16,600
Room & Board $11,000
Books and supplies $600
Required fees $450
% frosh rec. need-based scholarship
  or grant aid 63
% UG rec. need-based scholarship
  or grant aid 51
% frosh rec. need-based self-help aid 63
% UG rec. need-based self-help aid 51
% UG rec. any financial aid 85
Avg. frosh grant $4,500
Avg. frosh loan $4,000

LAFAYETTE COLLEGE

CAMPUS LIFE
Quality of Life Rating **70**
Fire Safety Rating **60**
Type of school private
Affiliation Presbyterian
Environment village
STUDENTS
Total undergrad enrollment 2,251
% male/female 53/47
% from out of state 70
% from public high school 68
% live on campus 96
% in (# of) fraternities 26 (7)
% in (# of) sororities 45 (6)
% African American 5
% Asian 2
% Caucasian 85
% Hispanic 3
% international 5
# of countries represented 46

ACADEMICS
Academic Rating **89**
Calendar semester
Student/faculty ratio 11:1
Professors Interesting Rating 78
Professors Accessible Rating 86

% professors teaching UG courses	100
Most common lab size	10-19 students
Most common regular class size	10-19 students

SELECTIVITY
Admissions Selectivity Rating	**95**
# of applicants	5,835
% of applicants accepted	36
% of acceptees attending	28
# accepting a place on wait list	1,697
% admitted from wait list	5
# of early decision applicants	244
% accepted early decision	66

FRESHMAN PROFILE
Range SAT Verbal	570-660
Average SAT Verbal	620
Range SAT Math	610-710
Average SAT Math	665
Projected Range SAT Writing	610-670
Range ACT Composite	25-29
Average ACT Composite	28
Minimum Paper TOEFL	550
Average HS GPA	3.8
% graduated top 10% of class	59
% graduated top 25% of class	89
% graduated top 50% of class	100

DEADLINES
Early decision application deadline	2/15
Regular application deadline	1/1
Regular notification	4/1
Nonfall registration?	yes

FINANCIAL FACTS
Financial Aid Rating	**95**
Annual tuition	$27,178
Room & Board	$8,418
Books and supplies	$600
Required fees	$150
% frosh rec. need-based scholarship or grant aid	49
% UG rec. need-based scholarship or grant aid	51
% frosh rec. need-based self-help aid	33
% UG rec. need-based self-help aid	38
Avg. frosh grant	$20,552
Avg. frosh loan	$3,500

LANCASTER BIBLE COLLEGE

CAMPUS LIFE
Quality of Life Rating	**91**
Fire Safety Rating	**60**
Type of school	private
Affiliation	nondenominational
Environment	village

STUDENTS
Total undergrad enrollment	641

% male/female	47/53
% from out of state	25
% live on campus	49
% African American	3
% Caucasian	93
% Hispanic	1
% Native American	1
% international	1

ACADEMICS
Academic Rating	**83**
Calendar	semester
Student/faculty ratio	15:1
Professors Interesting Rating	93
Professors Accessible Rating	87
% professors teaching UG courses	100
Most common lab size	fewer than 10 students
Most common regular class size	10-19 students

MOST POPULAR MAJORS
Bible/biblical studies
elementary education and teaching

SELECTIVITY
Admissions Selectivity Rating	**80**
# of applicants	244
% of applicants accepted	51
% of acceptees attending	100

FRESHMAN PROFILE
Range SAT Verbal	480-580
Average SAT Verbal	520
Range SAT Math	460-570
Average SAT Math	480
Projected Range SAT Writing	540-620
Range ACT Composite	19-23
Average ACT Composite	20
Minimum Paper TOEFL	550
Minimum Computer Based TOEFL	213
Average HS GPA	3.25
% graduated top 10% of class	15
% graduated top 25% of class	32
% graduated top 50% of class	65

DEADLINES
Regular notification	rolling
Nonfall registration?	yes

FINANCIAL FACTS
Financial Aid Rating	**69**
Annual tuition	$10,560
Room & Board	$5,010
Books and supplies	$700
Required fees	$215
% frosh rec. need-based scholarship or grant aid	53
% UG rec. need-based scholarship or grant aid	51
% frosh rec. need-based self-help aid	69

% UG rec. need-based self-help aid	65
Avg. frosh grant	$3,005
Avg. frosh loan	$5,227

LEBANON VALLEY COLLEGE

CAMPUS LIFE
Quality of Life Rating	**77**
Fire Safety Rating	**60**
Type of school	private
Affiliation	Methodist
Environment	rural

STUDENTS
Total undergrad enrollment	1,668
% male/female	42/58
% from out of state	21
% from public high school	95
% live on campus	67
% in (# of) fraternities	11 (4)
% in (# of) sororities	10 (3)
% African American	2
% Asian	2
% Caucasian	91
% Hispanic	1

ACADEMICS
Academic Rating	**82**
Calendar	semester
Student/faculty ratio	13:1
Professors Interesting Rating	77
Professors Accessible Rating	84
% professors teaching UG courses	100
Most common lab size	10-19 students
Most common regular class size	10-19 students

MOST POPULAR MAJORS
business administration/management
elementary education and teaching

SELECTIVITY
Admissions Selectivity Rating	**80**
# of applicants	2,114
% of applicants accepted	73
% of acceptees attending	27
# accepting a place on wait list	2

FRESHMAN PROFILE
Range SAT Verbal	500-610
Average SAT Verbal	547
Range SAT Math	510-610
Average SAT Math	563
Projected Range SAT Writing	560-640
Range ACT Composite	20-25
Minimum Paper TOEFL	550
Minimum Computer Based TOEFL	213
% graduated top 10% of class	29
% graduated top 25% of class	71
% graduated top 50% of class	94

Regular notification — rolling
Nonfall registration? — yes

FINANCIAL FACTS
Financial Aid Rating — **82**
Annual tuition — $22,950
Room & Board — $6,590
Books and supplies — $750
Required fees — $650
% frosh rec. need-based scholarship
  or grant aid — 82
% UG rec. need-based scholarship
  or grant aid — 76
% frosh rec. need-based self-help aid — 64
% UG rec. need-based self-help aid — 65
% frosh rec. any financial aid — 99
% UG rec. any financial aid — 97
Avg. frosh grant — $11,925
Avg. frosh loan — $3,831

LEHIGH UNIVERSITY

CAMPUS LIFE
Quality of Life Rating — **64**
Fire Safety Rating — **80**
Type of school — private
Environment — city

STUDENTS
Total undergrad enrollment — 4,553
% male/female — 59/41
% from out of state — 71
% from public high school — 64
% live on campus — 67
% in (# of) fraternities — 33 (23)
% in (# of) sororities — 39 (9)
% African American — 3
% Asian — 6
% Caucasian — 78
% Hispanic — 2
% international — 3
# of countries represented — 43

ACADEMICS
Academic Rating — **77**
Calendar — semester
Student/faculty ratio — 9:1
Professors Interesting Rating — 77
Professors Accessible Rating — 84
% professors teaching UG courses — 100
Most common lab size — 10-19 students
Most common
  regular class size — 10-19 students

MOST POPULAR MAJORS
finance
mechanical engineering
psychology

SELECTIVITY
Admissions Selectivity Rating — **96**
# of applicants — 9,847
% of applicants accepted — 38
% of acceptees attending — 28
# accepting a place on wait list — 1,270
% admitted from wait list — 10
# of early decision applicants — 403
% accepted early decision — 56

FRESHMAN PROFILE
Range SAT Verbal — 600-670
Average SAT Verbal — 631
Range SAT Math — 640-710
Average SAT Math — 671
Projected Range SAT Writing — 630-680
Minimum Paper TOEFL — 570
Minimum Computer Based TOEFL — 230
% graduated top 10% of class — 74
% graduated top 25% of class — 98
% graduated top 50% of class — 100

DEADLINES
Early decision application deadline — 11/15
Regular application deadline — 1/1
Regular notification — 4/1
Nonfall registration? — yes

FINANCIAL FACTS
Financial Aid Rating — **88**
Annual tuition — $29,140
Room & Board — $8,230
Books and supplies — $800
Required fees — $200
% frosh rec. need-based scholarship
  or grant aid — 48
% UG rec. need-based scholarship
  or grant aid — 43
% frosh rec. need-based self-help aid — 47
% UG rec. need-based self-help aid — 44
% frosh rec. any financial aid — 51
% UG rec. any financial aid — 48
Avg. frosh grant — $19,980
Avg. frosh loan — $3,214

LESLEY COLLEGE

CAMPUS LIFE
Quality of Life Rating — **70**
Fire Safety Rating — **60**
Type of school — private
Environment — metropolis

STUDENTS
Total undergrad enrollment — 1,032
% male/female — 19/81
% from out of state — 41
% from public high school — 80
% live on campus — 66
% African American — 7

% Asian — 5
% Caucasian — 63
% Hispanic — 4
% international — 5
# of countries represented — 12

ACADEMICS
Academic Rating — **77**
Calendar — semester
Student/faculty ratio — 10:1
Professors Interesting Rating — 78
Professors Accessible Rating — 73
% professors teaching UG courses — 100
Most common lab size — 10-19 students

MOST POPULAR MAJORS
counseling psychology
elementary education and teaching

SELECTIVITY
Admissions Selectivity Rating — **77**
# of applicants — 885
% of applicants accepted — 78
% of acceptees attending — 34

FRESHMAN PROFILE
Range SAT Verbal — 480-600
Average SAT Verbal — 535
Range SAT Math — 440-550
Average SAT Math — 517
Projected Range SAT Writing — 540-630
Minimum Paper TOEFL — 500
Minimum Computer Based TOEFL — 173
Average HS GPA — 3.0
% graduated top 10% of class — 20
% graduated top 25% of class — 43
% graduated top 50% of class — 83

DEADLINES
Regular notification — rolling
Nonfall registration? — yes

FINANCIAL FACTS
Financial Aid Rating — **72**
Annual tuition — $22,600
Room & Board — $9,950
Books and supplies — $700
Required fees — $250
% frosh rec. need-based scholarship
  or grant aid — 78
% UG rec. need-based scholarship
  or grant aid — 69
% frosh rec. need-based self-help aid — 78
% UG rec. need-based self-help aid — 69
% frosh rec. any financial aid — 88
% UG rec. any financial aid — 82
Avg. frosh grant — $10,049
Avg. frosh loan — $5,512

LOYOLA COLLEGE IN MARYLAND

CAMPUS LIFE
Quality of Life Rating	89
Fire Safety Rating	85
Type of school	private
Affiliation	Roman Catholic
Environment	village

STUDENTS
Total undergrad enrollment	3,414
% male/female	41/59
% from out of state	81
% from public high school	50
% live on campus	79
% African American	5
% Asian	2
% Caucasian	87
% Hispanic	2
% international	1
# of countries represented	22

ACADEMICS
Academic Rating	83
Calendar	semester
Student/faculty ratio	13:1
Professors Interesting Rating	84
Professors Accessible Rating	86
% professors teaching UG courses	72
Most common lab size	20-29 students
Most common regular class size	10-19 students

MOST POPULAR MAJORS
business administration/management
communications studies/speech
communication and rhetoric

SELECTIVITY
Admissions Selectivity Rating	89
# of applicants	6,979
% of applicants accepted	71
% of acceptees attending	19
# accepting a place on wait list	1,454
% admitted from wait list	33

FRESHMAN PROFILE
Range SAT Verbal	560-650
Average SAT Verbal	606
Range SAT Math	570-650
Average SAT Math	610
Projected Range SAT Writing	600-670
Range ACT Composite	24-29
Average ACT Composite	26
Minimum Paper TOEFL	550
Minimum Computer Based TOEFL	213
Average HS GPA	3.0
% graduated top 10% of class	40
% graduated top 25% of class	77
% graduated top 50% of class	94

DEADLINES
Regular application deadline	1/15
Regular notification	4/1
Nonfall registration?	yes

FINANCIAL FACTS
Financial Aid Rating	93
Annual tuition	$29,500
Room & board	$8,560
% frosh rec. need-based scholarship or grant aid	38
% UG rec. need-based scholarship or grant aid	32
% frosh rec. need-based self-help aid	48
% UG rec. need-based self-help aid	41
% frosh rec. any financial aid	68
% UG rec. any financial aid	65
Avg. frosh grant	$13,370
Avg. frosh loan	$5,370

LYCOMING COLLEGE

CAMPUS LIFE
Quality of Life Rating	84
Fire Safety Rating	72
Type of school	private
Affiliation	Methodist
Environment	town

STUDENTS
Total undergrad enrollment	1,486
% male/female	45/55
% from out of state	23
% live on campus	83
% in (# of) fraternities	14 (5)
% in (# of) sororities	17 (5)
% African American	2
% Asian	1
% Caucasian	96
% Hispanic	1
% international	1
# of countries represented	9

ACADEMICS
Academic Rating	82
Calendar	semester
Student/faculty ratio	13:1
Professors Interesting Rating	83
Professors Accessible Rating	88
% professors teaching UG courses	100
Most common lab size	10-19 students
Most common regular class size	10-19 students

MOST POPULAR MAJORS
biology/biological sciences
business administration/management
psychology

SELECTIVITY
Admissions Selectivity Rating	80
# of applicants	1,651
% of applicants accepted	76
% of acceptees attending	32

FRESHMAN PROFILE
Range SAT Verbal	500-610
Average SAT Verbal	540
Range SAT Math	490-600
Average SAT Math	540
Projected Range SAT Writing	560-640
Average ACT Composite	22
Minimum Paper TOEFL	500
Minimum Computer Based TOEFL	173
Average HS GPA	3.2
% graduated top 10% of class	19
% graduated top 25% of class	54
% graduated top 50% of class	72

DEADLINES
Regular application deadline	7/1
Regular notification	rolling
Nonfall registration?	yes

FINANCIAL FACTS
Financial Aid Rating	75
Annual tuition	$22,336
Room & Board	$6,242
Books and supplies	$600
Required fees	$390
% frosh rec. need-based scholarship or grant aid	83
% UG rec. need-based scholarship or grant aid	82
% frosh rec. need-based self-help aid	73
% UG rec. need-based self-help aid	74
% frosh rec. any financial aid	95
% UG rec. any financial aid	95
Avg. frosh grant	$13,404
Avg. frosh loan	$4,116

MANHATTAN COLLEGE

CAMPUS LIFE
Quality of Life Rating	72
Fire Safety Rating	76
Type of school	private
Affiliation	Roman Catholic
Environment	village

STUDENTS
Total undergrad enrollment	2,905
% male/female	50/50
% from out of state	15
% from public high school	60
% live on campus	70
% in (# of) fraternities	8 (3)
% in (# of) sororities	7 (2)
% African American	5

% Asian	4
% Caucasian	65
% Hispanic	11
% international	2
# of countries represented	11

ACADEMICS
Academic Rating	**63**
Calendar	semester
Student/faculty ratio	13:1
Professors Interesting Rating	75
Professors Accessible Rating	78
% professors teaching UG courses	100
Most common lab size	20-29 students
Most common	
regular class size	10-19 students

MOST POPULAR MAJORS
civil engineering
marketing/marketing management
special education and teaching

SELECTIVITY
Admissions Selectivity Rating	**60**
# of applicants	4,227
% of applicants accepted	59
% of acceptees attending	26
# accepting a place on wait list	178
% admitted from wait list	3
# of early decision applicants	35
% accepted early decision	85

FRESHMAN PROFILE
Range SAT Verbal	620-490
Average SAT Verbal	546
Range SAT Math	640-490
Average SAT Math	566
Projected Range SAT Writing	650-550
Minimum Paper TOEFL	550
Minimum Computer Based TOEFL	213
Average HS GPA	3.4

DEADLINES
Early decision application deadline	11/15
Regular notification	rolling
Nonfall registration?	yes

FINANCIAL FACTS
Financial Aid Rating	**65**
Annual tuition	$18,600
Room & Board	$8,400
Books and supplies	$250
Required fees	$1,400
% frosh rec. need-based scholarship	
or grant aid	57
% UG rec. need-based scholarship	
or grant aid	60
% frosh rec. need-based self-help aid	63
% UG rec. need-based self-help aid	61
% frosh rec. any financial aid	92
% UG rec. any financial aid	88

Avg. frosh grant	$6,245
Avg. frosh loan	$2,425

MANHATTANVILLE COLLEGE

CAMPUS LIFE
Quality of Life Rating	**80**
Fire Safety Rating	**60**
Type of school	private
Environment	village

STUDENTS
Total undergrad enrollment	1,533
% male/female	31/69
% from out of state	34
% live on campus	75
% African American	7
% Asian	3
% Caucasian	62
% Hispanic	17
% Native American	1
% international	9
# of countries represented	48

ACADEMICS
Academic Rating	**77**
Calendar	semester
Student/faculty ratio	11:1
Professors Interesting Rating	76
Professors Accessible Rating	73
% professors teaching UG courses	100
Most common lab size	10-19 students

MOST POPULAR MAJORS
business administration/management
psychology
sociology

SELECTIVITY
Admissions Selectivity Rating	**83**
# of applicants	3,061
% of applicants accepted	57
% of acceptees attending	25
# accepting a place on wait list	100
# of early decision applicants	22
% accepted early decision	40

FRESHMAN PROFILE
Range SAT Verbal	480-610
Average SAT Verbal	560
Range SAT Math	470-600
Average SAT Math	550
Projected Range SAT Writing	540-640
Range ACT Composite	20-24
Average ACT Composite	24
Minimum Paper TOEFL	550
Minimum Computer Based TOEFL	217
Average HS GPA	3.0
% graduated top 10% of class	21
% graduated top 25% of class	47
% graduated top 50% of class	77

DEADLINES
Early decision application deadline	12/1
Regular application deadline	3/1
Regular notification	rolling
Nonfall registration?	yes

FINANCIAL FACTS
Financial Aid Rating	**75**
Annual tuition	$23,620
Room & Board	$10,130
Books and supplies	$800
Required fees	$950
% frosh rec. need-based scholarship	
or grant aid	57
% UG rec. need-based scholarship	
or grant aid	54
% frosh rec. need-based self-help aid	58
% UG rec. need-based self-help aid	55
% frosh rec. any financial aid	85
% UG rec. any financial aid	89
Avg. frosh grant	$15,500
Avg. frosh loan	$3,108

MARIST COLLEGE

CAMPUS LIFE
Quality of Life Rating	**84**
Fire Safety Rating	**87**
Type of school	private
Environment	city

STUDENTS
Total undergrad enrollment	4,686
% male/female	43/57
% from out of state	40
% from public high school	75
% live on campus	56
% in (# of) fraternities	1 (3)
% in (# of) sororities	3 (5)
% African American	4
% Asian	2
% Caucasian	79
% Hispanic	6

ACADEMICS
Academic Rating	**82**
Calendar	semester
Student/faculty ratio	15:1
Professors Interesting Rating	81
Professors Accessible Rating	84
% professors teaching UG courses	97
Most common lab size	20-29 students
Most common	
regular class size	20-29 students

MOST POPULAR MAJORS
business administration/management
communications studies/speech
communication and rhetoric
psychology

SELECTIVITY

Admissions Selectivity Rating	**89**
# of applicants	7,034
% of applicants accepted	49
% of acceptees attending	28
# accepting a place on wait list	985
% admitted from wait list	6

FRESHMAN PROFILE

Range SAT Verbal	550-620
Average SAT Verbal	580
Range SAT Math	550-630
Average SAT Math	589
Projected Range SAT Writing	600-650
Range ACT Composite	23-27
Average ACT Composite	26
Minimum Paper TOEFL	550
Minimum Computer Based TOEFL	213
Average HS GPA	3.3
% graduated top 10% of class	24
% graduated top 25% of class	70
% graduated top 50% of class	94

DEADLINES

Regular application deadline	2/15
Regular notification	3/15
Nonfall registration?	yes

FINANCIAL FACTS

Financial Aid Rating	**71**
Annual tuition	$20,535
Room & Board	$9,218
Books and supplies	$1,150
Required fees	$480
% frosh rec. need-based scholarship or grant aid	63
% UG rec. need-based scholarship or grant aid	59
% frosh rec. need-based self-help aid	50
% UG rec. need-based self-help aid	53
% frosh rec. any financial aid	87
% UG rec. any financial aid	83
Avg. frosh grant	$8,712
Avg. frosh loan	$3,477

MARLBORO COLLEGE

CAMPUS LIFE

Quality of Life Rating	**86**
Fire Safety Rating	**60**
Type of school	private
Environment	rural

STUDENTS

Total undergrad enrollment	357
% male/female	45/55
% from out of state	90
% from public high school	65
% live on campus	86
% African American	1

% Asian	1
% Caucasian	88
% Hispanic	1
% Native American	1
% international	1
# of countries represented	10

ACADEMICS

Academic Rating	**99**
Calendar	semester
Student/faculty ratio	8:1
Professors Interesting Rating	99
Professors Accessible Rating	98
% professors teaching UG courses	100
Most common lab size	fewer than 10 students
Most common regular class size	fewer than 10 students

MOST POPULAR MAJORS
English language and literature
social sciences
visual and performing arts

SELECTIVITY

Admissions Selectivity Rating	**88**
# of applicants	367
% of applicants accepted	67
% of acceptees attending	45
# of early decision applicants	10
% accepted early decision	71

FRESHMAN PROFILE

Range SAT Verbal	590-690
Average SAT Verbal	660
Range SAT Math	510-650
Average SAT Math	590
Projected Range SAT Writing	620-690
Range ACT Composite	26-32
Average ACT Composite	28
Minimum Paper TOEFL	550
Minimum Computer Based TOEFL	213
Average HS GPA	3.2
% graduated top 10% of class	42
% graduated top 25% of class	50
% graduated top 50% of class	85

DEADLINES

Early decision application deadline	11/15
Regular application deadline	2/15
Regular notification	rolling
Nonfall registration?	yes

FINANCIAL FACTS

Financial Aid Rating	**75**
Annual tuition	$26,940
Room & Board	$8,190
Books and supplies	$600
Required fees	$850
% frosh rec. need-based scholarship or grant aid	58

% UG rec. need-based scholarship or grant aid	62
% frosh rec. need-based self-help aid	54
% UG rec. need-based self-help aid	72
% frosh rec. any financial aid	67
% UG rec. any financial aid	82
Avg. frosh grant	$20,907
Avg. frosh loan	$2,483

MARYLAND INSTITUTE COLLEGE OF ART

CAMPUS LIFE

Quality of Life Rating	**79**
Fire Safety Rating	**85**
Type of school	private
Environment	metropolis

STUDENTS

Total undergrad enrollment	1,399
% male/female	38/62
% from out of state	83
% from public high school	65
% live on campus	88
% African American	4
% Asian	8
% Caucasian	68
% Hispanic	5
% Native American	1
% international	6
# of countries represented	48

ACADEMICS

Academic Rating	**89**
Calendar	semester
Student/faculty ratio	10:1
Professors Interesting Rating	83
Professors Accessible Rating	69
% professors teaching UG courses	95
Most common lab size	10-19 students

MOST POPULAR MAJORS
illustration
intermedia/multimedia
painting

SELECTIVITY

Admissions Selectivity Rating	**90**
# of applicants	2,456
% of applicants accepted	44
% of acceptees attending	37
# of early decision applicants	34
% accepted early decision	94

FRESHMAN PROFILE

Range SAT Verbal	540-660
Average SAT Verbal	600
Range SAT Math	510-620
Average SAT Math	570
Projected Range SAT Writing	590-670
Minimum Paper TOEFL	550

Minimum Computer Based TOEFL	213
Average HS GPA	3.55
% graduated top 10% of class	32
% graduated top 25% of class	62
% graduated top 50% of class	87

DEADLINES

Early decision application deadline	11/15
Regular application deadline	3/1
Regular notification	3/15
Nonfall registration?	yes

FINANCIAL FACTS

Financial Aid Rating	**71**
Annual tuition	$24,474
Room & Board	$7,080
Books and supplies	$1,400
Required fees	$730
% frosh rec. need-based scholarship or grant aid	59
% UG rec. need-based scholarship or grant aid	62
% frosh rec. need-based self-help aid	52
% UG rec. need-based self-help aid	55
% frosh rec. any financial aid	81
% UG rec. any financial aid	74
Avg. frosh grant	$8,027
Avg. frosh loan	$3,237

MARYMOUNT COLLEGE OF FORDHAM UNIVERSITY (NY)

CAMPUS LIFE

Quality of Life Rating	**65**
Fire Safety Rating	**60**
Type of school	private
Affiliation	Roman Catholic
Environment	village

STUDENTS

Total undergrad enrollment	1,021
% male/female	3/97
% from out of state	26
% from public high school	79
% live on campus	63
% African American	17
% Asian	5
% Caucasian	39
% Hispanic	14
% international	2
# of countries represented	23

ACADEMICS

Academic Rating	**84**
Calendar	semester
Student/faculty ratio	10:1
Professors Interesting Rating	78
Professors Accessible Rating	82
% professors teaching UG courses	100

Most common lab size	10-19 students
Most common regular class size	10-19 students

MOST POPULAR MAJORS
business/commerce
elementary education and teaching
psychology

SELECTIVITY

Admissions Selectivity Rating	**78**
# of applicants	1,542
% of applicants accepted	78
% of acceptees attending	21

FRESHMAN PROFILE

Range SAT Verbal	450-550
Average SAT Verbal	507
Range SAT Math	430-540
Average SAT Math	483
Projected Range SAT Writing	520-600
Range ACT Composite	19-24
Average ACT Composite	22
Minimum Paper TOEFL	520
Minimum Computer Based TOEFL	190
Average HS GPA	2.9
% graduated top 10% of class	24
% graduated top 25% of class	57
% graduated top 50% of class	86

DEADLINES

Regular application deadline	8/31
Regular notification	rolling
Nonfall registration?	yes

FINANCIAL FACTS

Financial Aid Rating	**70**
Annual tuition	$19,100
Room & Board	$9,760
Books and supplies	$750
Required fees	$602
% frosh rec. need-based scholarship or grant aid	90
% UG rec. need-based scholarship or grant aid	61
% frosh rec. need-based self-help aid	69
% UG rec. need-based self-help aid	49
% frosh rec. any financial aid	70
% UG rec. any financial aid	71
Avg. frosh grant	$16,003
Avg. frosh loan	$4,211

MASSACHUSETTS INSTITUTE OF TECHNOLOGY

CAMPUS LIFE

Quality of Life Rating	**88**
Fire Safety Rating	**89**
Type of school	private
Environment	city

STUDENTS

Total undergrad enrollment	4,132
% male/female	57/43
% from out of state	91
% from public high school	71
% live on campus	93
% in (# of) fraternities	48 (27)
% in (# of) sororities	26 (5)
% African American	6
% Asian	28
% Caucasian	35
% Hispanic	12
% Native American	2
% international	7
# of countries represented	78

ACADEMICS

Academic Rating	**96**
Calendar	4-1-4
Student/faculty ratio	7:1
Professors Interesting Rating	75
Professors Accessible Rating	76
% professors teaching UG courses	100
% classes taught by TAs	1
Most common lab size	fewer than 10 students
Most common regular class size	10-19 students

MOST POPULAR MAJORS
business administration/management
electrical, electronics, and communications engineering
mechanical engineering

SELECTIVITY

Admissions Selectivity Rating	**99**
# of applicants	10,466
% of applicants accepted	16
% of acceptees attending	65
# accepting a place on wait list	604

FRESHMAN PROFILE

Range SAT Verbal	680-760
Average SAT Verbal	712
Range SAT Math	730-800
Average SAT Math	755
Projected Range SAT Writing	680-740
Range ACT Composite	31-34
Average ACT Composite	32
Average HS GPA	4.1
% graduated top 10% of class	97
% graduated top 25% of class	99
% graduated top 50% of class	100

DEADLINES

Regular application deadline	1/1
Regular notification	3/25
Nonfall registration?	no

FINANCIAL FACTS
Financial Aid Rating	**96**
Annual tuition	$30,600
Room & Board	$9,100
Books and supplies	$1,050
Required fees	$200
% frosh rec. need-based scholarship or grant aid	63
% UG rec. need-based scholarship or grant aid	59
% frosh rec. need-based self-help aid	53
% UG rec. need-based self-help aid	54
% frosh rec. any financial aid	79
% UG rec. any financial aid	78
Avg. frosh grant	$23,645
Avg. frosh loan	$3,123

MERCYHURST COLLEGE

CAMPUS LIFE
Quality of Life Rating	**76**
Fire Safety Rating	**60**
Type of school	private
Environment	village

STUDENTS
Total undergrad enrollment	3,537
% male/female	38/62
% from out of state	34
% from public high school	78
% live on campus	58
% African American	3
% Caucasian	84
% Hispanic	1
% international	3

ACADEMICS
Academic Rating	**82**
Calendar	trimester
Student/faculty ratio	19:1
Professors Interesting Rating	84
Professors Accessible Rating	81
% professors teaching UG courses	100
Most common lab size	fewer than 10 students
Most common regular class size	10-19 students

SELECTIVITY
Admissions Selectivity Rating	**79**
# of applicants	2,647
% of applicants accepted	81
% of acceptees attending	34

FRESHMAN PROFILE
Range SAT Verbal	490-590
Average SAT Verbal	545
Range SAT Math	500-590
Average SAT Math	545
Projected Range SAT Writing	550-620
Range ACT Composite	20-25
Average ACT Composite	22
Minimum Paper TOEFL	550
Minimum Computer Based TOEFL	300
Average HS GPA	3.4
% graduated top 10% of class	18
% graduated top 25% of class	48
% graduated top 50% of class	87

DEADLINES
Regular notification	rolling
Nonfall registration?	yes

FINANCIAL FACTS
Financial Aid Rating	**90**
Annual tuition	$17,740
Room & Board	$7,074
Books and supplies	$750
Required fees	$1,353
% frosh rec. need-based scholarship or grant aid	78
% UG rec. need-based scholarship or grant aid	75
% frosh rec. need-based self-help aid	75
% UG rec. need-based self-help aid	73
Avg. frosh grant	$4,530
Avg. frosh loan	$2,387

MERRIMACK COLLEGE

CAMPUS LIFE
Quality of Life Rating	**76**
Fire Safety Rating	**98**
Type of school	private
Affiliation	Roman Catholic
Environment	village

STUDENTS
Total undergrad enrollment	2,232
% male/female	47/53
% from out of state	28
% from public high school	60
% live on campus	73
% in (# of) fraternities	3 (3)
% in (# of) sororities	5 (3)
% African American	1
% Asian	1
% Caucasian	59
% Hispanic	2
% international	1
# of countries represented	17

ACADEMICS
Academic Rating	**77**
Calendar	semester
Student/faculty ratio	12:1
Professors Interesting Rating	74
Professors Accessible Rating	75
% professors teaching UG courses	100
Most common lab size	10-19 students

Most common regular class size   fewer than 10 students

MOST POPULAR MAJORS
business administration/management
communications studies/speech
communication and rhetoric
psychology

SELECTIVITY
Admissions Selectivity Rating	**82**
# of applicants	3,547
% of applicants accepted	64
% of acceptees attending	23
# accepting a place on wait list	350
% admitted from wait list	34

FRESHMAN PROFILE
Range SAT Verbal	500-590
Average SAT Verbal	540
Range SAT Math	510-590
Average SAT Math	555
Projected Range SAT Writing	560-620
Range ACT Composite	20-23
Average ACT Composite	22
Minimum Paper TOEFL	550
Minimum Computer Based TOEFL	230
Average HS GPA	3.3
% graduated top 10% of class	20
% graduated top 25% of class	45
% graduated top 50% of class	83

DEADLINES
Regular application deadline	2/1
Regular notification	4/1
Nonfall registration?	yes

FINANCIAL FACTS
Financial Aid Rating	**84**
Annual tuition	$24,200
Room & board	$11,055
Books and supplies	$800
% frosh rec. need-based scholarship or grant aid	78
% UG rec. need-based scholarship or grant aid	59
% frosh rec. need-based self-help aid	73
% UG rec. need-based self-help aid	59
% frosh rec. any financial aid	86
% UG rec. any financial aid	73
Avg. frosh grant	$12,500
Avg. frosh loan	$6,000

MESSIAH COLLEGE

CAMPUS LIFE
Quality of Life Rating	**89**
Fire Safety Rating	**62**
Type of school	private
Affiliation	Interdenominational Christian
Environment	village

STUDENTS

Total undergrad enrollment	2,887
% male/female	37/63
% from out of state	48
% from public high school	80
% live on campus	86
% African American	3
% Asian	2
% Caucasian	90
% Hispanic	2
% international	2
# of countries represented	29

ACADEMICS

Academic Rating	**84**
Calendar	semester
Student/faculty ratio	13:1
Professors Interesting Rating	83
Professors Accessible Rating	84
% professors teaching UG courses	100
Most common lab size	20-29 students
Most common regular class size	10-19 students

MOST POPULAR MAJORS
elementary education and teaching
nursing/registered nurse training (RN, ASN, BSN, MSN)
psychology

SELECTIVITY

Admissions Selectivity Rating	**88**
# of applicants	2,050
% of applicants accepted	83
% of acceptees attending	40
# accepting a place on wait list	8

FRESHMAN PROFILE

Range SAT Verbal	540-660
Average SAT Verbal	602
Range SAT Math	540-650
Average SAT Math	589
Projected Range SAT Writing	590-670
Range ACT Composite	23-28
Average ACT Composite	26
Minimum Paper TOEFL	550
Minimum Computer Based TOEFL	213
Average HS GPA	3.73
% graduated top 10% of class	39
% graduated top 25% of class	69
% graduated top 50% of class	92

DEADLINES

Regular notification	rolling
Nonfall registration?	yes

FINANCIAL FACTS

Financial Aid Rating	**71**
Annual tuition	$20,120
Room & Board	$6,560
Books and supplies	$810

Required fees	$670
% frosh rec. need-based scholarship or grant aid	62
% UG rec. need-based scholarship or grant aid	64
% frosh rec. need-based self-help aid	62
% UG rec. need-based self-help aid	65
% frosh rec. any financial aid	97
% UG rec. any financial aid	96
Avg. frosh grant	$9,971
Avg. frosh loan	$8,918

MIDDLEBURY COLLEGE

CAMPUS LIFE

Quality of Life Rating	**98**
Fire Safety Rating	**60**
Type of school	private
Environment	village

STUDENTS

Total undergrad enrollment	2,357
% male/female	48/52
% from out of state	93
% from public high school	52
% live on campus	97
% African American	3
% Asian	7
% Caucasian	70
% Hispanic	5
% international	8
# of countries represented	71

ACADEMICS

Academic Rating	**99**
Calendar	4-1-4
Student/faculty ratio	11:1
Professors Interesting Rating	99
Professors Accessible Rating	96
% professors teaching UG courses	100
Most common lab size	10-19 students
Most common regular class size	10-19 students

MOST POPULAR MAJORS
economics
English language and literature
psychology

SELECTIVITY

Admissions Selectivity Rating	**98**
# of applicants	5,122
% of applicants accepted	26
% of acceptees attending	44
# accepting a place on wait list	1,266
% admitted from wait list	6
# of early decision applicants	283
% accepted early decision	38

FRESHMAN PROFILE

Range SAT Verbal	690-750

Average SAT Verbal	720
Range SAT Math	690-750
Average SAT Math	710
Projected Range SAT Writing	690-730
Range ACT Composite	28-32
Average ACT Composite	30
% graduated top 10% of class	77
% graduated top 25% of class	96
% graduated top 50% of class	99

DEADLINES

Early decision application deadline	11/15
Regular application deadline	1/1
Regular notification	4/1
Nonfall registration?	yes

FINANCIAL FACTS

Financial Aid Rating	**95**
Comprehensive fee	$40,400
Books and supplies	$750
% frosh rec. need-based scholarship or grant aid	37
% UG rec. need-based scholarship or grant aid	42
% frosh rec. need-based self-help aid	37
% UG rec. need-based self-help aid	42
% frosh rec. any financial aid	37
% UG rec. any financial aid	42
Avg. frosh grant	$20,161
Avg. frosh loan	$5,377

MONMOUTH UNIVERSITY (NJ)

CAMPUS LIFE

Quality of Life Rating	**73**
Fire Safety Rating	**60**
Type of school	private
Environment	village

STUDENTS

Total undergrad enrollment	4,448
% male/female	41/59
% from out of state	8
% from public high school	82
% live on campus	43
% in (# of) fraternities	8 (7)
% in (# of) sororities	9 (6)
% African American	5
% Asian	2
% Caucasian	78
% Hispanic	4

ACADEMICS

Academic Rating	**75**
Calendar	semester
Student/faculty ratio	14:1
Profs interesting rating	75
Profs accessible rating	78
% profs teaching UG courses	85
Most common reg class size	10-19 students

SELECTIVITY

Admissions Rating	**75**
# of applicants	5,279
% of applicants accepted	66
% of acceptees attending	27
# accepting a place on wait list	548
% admitted from wait list	2
# of early decision applicants	128
% accepted early decision	83

FRESHMAN PROFILE

Range SAT Verbal	480-560
Average SAT Verbal	525
Range SAT Math	490-570
Average SAT Math	534
Projected Range SAT Writing	540-600
Range ACT Composite	21-24
Average ACT Composite	23
Minimum Paper TOEFL	525
Minimum Computer Based TOEFL	197
Average HS GPA	3.0
% graduated top 10% of class	9
% graduated top 25% of class	30
% graduated top 50% of class	60

DEADLINES

Early decision application deadline	12/1
Early decision notification	1/1
Regular application deadline	3/1
Regular notification	prior to 4/1
Nonfall registration?	yes

FINANCIAL FACTS

Financial Aid Rating	**70**
Annual tuition	$19,108
Room & Board	$7,911
Books and supplies	$900
Required fees	$596
% frosh rec. need-based scholarship or grant aid	27
% UG rec. need-based scholarship or grant aid	28
% frosh rec. need-based self-help aid	50
% UG rec. need-based self-help aid	52
% frosh rec. any financial aid	95
% UG rec. any financial aid	88
Avg. frosh grant	$8,277
Avg. frosh loan	$10,461

MOORE COLLEGE OF ART & DESIGN

CAMPUS LIFE

Quality of Life Rating	**74**
Fire Safety Rating	**60**
Type of school	private
Environment	metropolis

STUDENTS

Total undergrad enrollment	501
% male/female	0/100
% from out of state	41
% from public high school	72
% live on campus	31
% African American	7
% Asian	5
% Caucasian	77
% Hispanic	3
% international	2
# of countries represented	8

ACADEMICS

Academic Rating	**71**
Calendar	semester
Student/faculty ratio	9:1
Professors Interesting Rating	88
Professors Accessible Rating	69
% professors teaching UG courses	100
Most common lab size	10-19 students

MOST POPULAR MAJORS
fashion/apparel design
fine/studio arts
graphic design

SELECTIVITY

Admissions Selectivity Rating	**60**
# of applicants	305
% of applicants accepted	62
% of acceptees attending	44
# of early decision applicants	17
% accepted early decision	85

FRESHMAN PROFILE

Average SAT Verbal	512
Average SAT Math	506
Average ACT Composite	19
Minimum Paper TOEFL	527
Minimum Computer Based TOEFL	197
Average HS GPA	3.06

DEADLINES

Early decision application deadline	11/15
Regular application deadline	9/15
Regular notification	rolling
Nonfall registration?	yes

FINANCIAL FACTS

Financial Aid Rating	**62**
Annual tuition	$22,091
Room & Board	$8,654
Books and supplies	$2,160
Required fees	$795
% frosh rec. need-based scholarship or grant aid	65
% UG rec. need-based scholarship or grant aid	75
% frosh rec. need-based self-help aid	57
% UG rec. need-based self-help aid	70
Avg. frosh grant	$7,989
Avg. frosh loan	$11,419

MORAVIAN COLLEGE

CAMPUS LIFE

Quality of Life Rating	**85**
Fire Safety Rating	**86**
Type of school	private
Affiliation	Moravian
Environment	city

STUDENTS

Total undergrad enrollment	1,828
% male/female	39/61
% from out of state	39
% from public high school	77
% live on campus	69
% in (# of) fraternities	14 (3)
% in (# of) sororities	22 (4)
% African American	2
% Asian	2
% Caucasian	81
% Hispanic	3
% international	1
# of countries represented	14

ACADEMICS

Academic Rating	**84**
Calendar	semester
Student/faculty ratio	12:1
Professors Interesting Rating	83
Professors Accessible Rating	86
% professors teaching UG courses	100
Most common lab size	10-19 students
Most common regular class size	10-19 students

MOST POPULAR MAJORS
business administration/management
psychology
sociology

SELECTIVITY

Admissions Selectivity Rating	**81**
# of applicants	1,954
% of applicants accepted	63
% of acceptees attending	31
# accepting a place on wait list	187
% admitted from wait list	12
# of early decision applicants	103
% accepted early decision	71

FRESHMAN PROFILE

Range SAT Verbal	510-600
Average SAT Verbal	563
Range SAT Math	510-610
Average SAT Math	569
Projected Range SAT Writing	570-630
Minimum Paper TOEFL	550
Minimum Computer Based TOEFL	213
% graduated top 10% of class	27
% graduated top 25% of class	57
% graduated top 50% of class	93

DEADLINES

Early decision application deadline	1/15
Regular application deadline	3/1
Regular notification	3/15
Nonfall registration?	yes

FINANCIAL FACTS

Financial Aid Rating	**75**
Annual tuition	$24,813
Room & Board	$7,530
Books and supplies	$760
Required fees	$450
% frosh rec. need-based scholarship or grant aid	79
% UG rec. need-based scholarship or grant aid	75
% frosh rec. need-based self-help aid	69
% UG rec. need-based self-help aid	67
% frosh rec. any financial aid	95
% UG rec. any financial aid	92
Avg. frosh grant	$12,467
Avg. frosh loan	$3,445

MOUNT HOLYOKE COLLEGE

CAMPUS LIFE

Quality of Life Rating	**90**
Fire Safety Rating	**60**
Type of school	private
Environment	village

STUDENTS

Total undergrad enrollment	2,095
% male/female	0/100
% from out of state	74
% from public high school	65
% live on campus	93
% African American	4
% Asian	11
% Caucasian	52
% Hispanic	5
% Native American	1
% international	14
# of countries represented	69

ACADEMICS

Academic Rating	**95**
Calendar	semester
Student/faculty ratio	9:1
Professors Interesting Rating	96
Professors Accessible Rating	90
% professors teaching UG courses	100
Most common lab size	10-19 students
Most common regular class size	10-19 students

MOST POPULAR MAJORS
biology/biological sciences
English language and literature
psychology

SELECTIVITY

Admissions Selectivity Rating	**93**
# of applicants	2,912
% of applicants accepted	56
% of acceptees attending	35
# accepting a place on wait list	264
% admitted from wait list	20
# of early decision applicants	158
% accepted early decision	61

FRESHMAN PROFILE

Range SAT Verbal	610-700
Average SAT Verbal	648
Range SAT Math	580-680
Average SAT Math	625
Projected Range SAT Writing	640-700
Range ACT Composite	26-30
Average ACT Composite	28
Minimum Paper TOEFL	600
Minimum Computer Based TOEFL	250
Average HS GPA	3.59
% graduated top 10% of class	54
% graduated top 25% of class	79
% graduated top 50% of class	98

DEADLINES

Early decision application deadline	11/15
Regular application deadline	1/15
Regular notification	4/1
Nonfall registration?	yes

FINANCIAL FACTS

Financial Aid Rating	**98**
Annual tuition	$32,430
Room & Board	$9,550
Books and supplies	$750
Required fees	$168
% frosh rec. need-based scholarship or grant aid	61
% UG rec. need-based scholarship or grant aid	62
% frosh rec. need-based self-help aid	58
% UG rec. need-based self-help aid	62
% frosh rec. any financial aid	62
% UG rec. any financial aid	65
Avg. frosh grant	$22,357
Avg. frosh loan	$3,321

MUHLENBERG COLLEGE

CAMPUS LIFE

Quality of Life Rating	**75**
Fire Safety Rating	**91**
Type of school	private
Affiliation	Lutheran
Environment	city

STUDENTS

Total undergrad enrollment	2,378
% male/female	42/58

% from out of state	69
% from public high school	77
% live on campus	91
% in (# of) fraternities	19 (4)
% in (# of) sororities	20 (4)
% African American	2
% Asian	2
% Caucasian	91
% Hispanic	4
% international	1

ACADEMICS

Academic Rating	**86**
Calendar	semester
Student/faculty ratio	12:1
Professors Interesting Rating	82
Professors Accessible Rating	84
% professors teaching UG courses	100
Most common lab size	10-19 students
Most common regular class size	10-19 students

MOST POPULAR MAJORS
business administration/management
communications studies/speech
communication and rhetoric
psychology

SELECTIVITY

Admissions Selectivity Rating	**93**
# of applicants	4,040
% of applicants accepted	45
% of acceptees attending	31
# accepting a place on wait list	1,306
% admitted from wait list	1
# of early decision applicants	263
% accepted early decision	71

FRESHMAN PROFILE

Range SAT Verbal	560-660
Average SAT Verbal	608
Range SAT Math	560-660
Average SAT Math	612
Projected Range SAT Writing	600-670
Minimum Paper TOEFL	550
Minimum Computer Based TOEFL	213
Average HS GPA	3.52
% graduated top 10% of class	43
% graduated top 25% of class	76
% graduated top 50% of class	97

DEADLINES

Early decision application deadline	1/15
Regular application deadline	2/15
Regular notification	3/15
Nonfall registration?	yes

FINANCIAL FACTS

Financial Aid Rating	**94**
Annual tuition	$26,570
Room & Board	$7,025

Books and supplies	$1,000
Required fees	$230
% frosh rec. need-based scholarship or grant aid	46
% UG rec. need-based scholarship or grant aid	43
% frosh rec. need-based self-help aid	32
% UG rec. need-based self-help aid	30
% frosh rec. any financial aid	75
% UG rec. any financial aid	78
Avg. frosh grant	$12,827
Avg. frosh loan	$3,138

NAZARETH COLLEGE OF ROCHESTER

CAMPUS LIFE
Quality of Life Rating	**96**
Fire Safety Rating	**60**
Type of school	private
Environment	village

STUDENTS
Total undergrad enrollment	1,905
% male/female	24/76
% from out of state	6
% from public high school	90
% live on campus	57
% African American	4
% Asian	2
% Caucasian	88
% Hispanic	2

ACADEMICS
Academic Rating	**87**
Calendar	semester
Student/faculty ratio	13:1
Professors Interesting Rating	95
Professors Accessible Rating	97
% professors teaching UG courses	97
Most common lab size	10-19 students
Most common regular class size	10-19 students

MOST POPULAR MAJORS
business administration/management
education
psychology

SELECTIVITY
Admissions Selectivity Rating	**81**
# of applicants	1,627
% of applicants accepted	83
% of acceptees attending	28
# of early decision applicants	51
% accepted early decision	89

FRESHMAN PROFILE
Range SAT Verbal	515-615
Average SAT Verbal	569

Range SAT Math	510-610
Average SAT Math	562
Projected Range SAT Writing	570-650
Range ACT Composite	22-27
Average ACT Composite	25
Minimum Paper TOEFL	550
Minimum Computer Based TOEFL	213
Average HS GPA	3.39
% graduated top 10% of class	26
% graduated top 25% of class	63
% graduated top 50% of class	91

DEADLINES
Early decision application deadline	11/15
Regular application deadline	2/15
Regular notification	rolling
Nonfall registration?	yes

FINANCIAL FACTS
Financial Aid Rating	**89**
Annual tuition	$18,040
Room & Board	$7,700
Books and supplies	$700
Required fees	$534
% frosh rec. need-based scholarship or grant aid	79
% UG rec. need-based scholarship or grant aid	80
% frosh rec. need-based self-help aid	68
% UG rec. need-based self-help aid	72
Avg. frosh grant	$10,802
Avg. frosh loan	$2,964

NEUMANN COLLEGE

CAMPUS LIFE
Quality of Life Rating	**69**
Fire Safety Rating	**92**
Type of school	private
Affiliation	Roman Catholic
Environment	town

STUDENTS
Total undergrad enrollment	2,197
% male/female	33/67
% from out of state	27
% from public high school	60
% live on campus	48
% African American	13
% Asian	1
% Caucasian	74
% Hispanic	1
% international	1
# of countries represented	7

ACADEMICS
Academic Rating	**66**
Calendar	semester
Student/faculty ratio	16:1
Professors Interesting Rating	70

Professors Accessible Rating	66
% professors teaching UG courses	98
Most common lab size	20-29 students
Most common regular class size	20-29 students

MOST POPULAR MAJORS
criminal justice/law enforcement administration
liberal arts and sciences/liberal studies
nursing/registered nurse training
(RN, ASN, BSN, MSN)

SELECTIVITY
Admissions Selectivity Rating	**65**
# of applicants	1,741
% of applicants accepted	94
% of acceptees attending	28

FRESHMAN PROFILE
Range SAT Verbal	400-480
Average SAT Verbal	440
Range SAT Math	400-470
Average SAT Math	430
Projected Range SAT Writing	470-540
Minimum Paper TOEFL	550
Minimum Computer Based TOEFL	213
Average HS GPA	3.0
% graduated top 10% of class	1
% graduated top 25% of class	16
% graduated top 50% of class	51

DEADLINES
Regular notification	once information is received
Nonfall registration?	yes

FINANCIAL FACTS
Financial Aid Rating	**82**
Annual tuition	$16,590
Room & Board	$7,740
Books and supplies	$1,400
Required fees	$600
% frosh rec. need-based scholarship or grant aid	76
% UG rec. need-based scholarship or grant aid	75
% frosh rec. need-based self-help aid	76
% UG rec. need-based self-help aid	75
% frosh rec. any financial aid	95
% UG rec. any financial aid	90
Avg. frosh grant	$15,000
Avg. frosh loan	$6,500

NEW JERSEY INSTITUTE OF TECHNOLOGY

CAMPUS LIFE
Quality of Life Rating	**61**
Fire Safety Rating	**60**
Type of school	public
Environment	metropolis

STUDENTS

Total undergrad enrollment	4,944
% male/female	81/19
% from out of state	9
% from public high school	80
% live on campus	28
% in (# of) fraternities	7 (19)
% in (# of) sororities	5 (8)
% African American	10
% Asian	22
% Caucasian	35
% Hispanic	13
% international	6
# of countries represented	98

ACADEMICS

Academic Rating	**70**
Calendar	semester
Student/faculty ratio	13:1
Professors Interesting Rating	61
Professors Accessible Rating	61
% professors teaching UG courses	70
Most common lab size	10-19 students

MOST POPULAR MAJORS
architecture
(BArch, BA/BS, MArch, MA/MS, PhD)
computer and information sciences
information technology

SELECTIVITY

Admissions Selectivity Rating	**80**
# of applicants	2,538
% of applicants accepted	58
% of acceptees attending	46
# accepting a place on wait list	25
% admitted from wait list	44

FRESHMAN PROFILE

Range SAT Verbal	490-600
Average SAT Verbal	544
Range SAT Math	560-660
Average SAT Math	608
Projected Range SAT Writing	550-630
Minimum Paper TOEFL	550
Minimum Computer Based TOEFL	213
% graduated top 10% of class	24
% graduated top 25% of class	57
% graduated top 50% of class	86

DEADLINES

Regular application deadline	4/1
Regular notification	rolling
Nonfall registration?	yes

FINANCIAL FACTS

Financial Aid Rating	**78**
Annual in-state tuition	$7,918
Annual out-of-state tuition	$13,716
Room & Board	$8,242
Books and supplies	$1,200

Required fees	$1,262
% frosh rec. need-based scholarship or grant aid	55
% UG rec. need-based scholarship or grant aid	43
% frosh rec. need-based self-help aid	47
% UG rec. need-based self-help aid	29
Avg. frosh grant	$4,400
Avg. frosh loan	$2,500

NEW YORK UNIVERSITY

CAMPUS LIFE

Quality of Life Rating	**81**
Fire Safety Rating	**64**
Type of school	private
Environment	metropolis

STUDENTS

Total undergrad enrollment	19,826
% male/female	39/61
% from out of state	65
% from public high school	69
% live on campus	54
% in (# of) fraternities	5 (14)
% in (# of) sororities	3 (13)
% African American	5
% Asian	14
% Caucasian	43
% Hispanic	7
% international	4
# of countries represented	143

ACADEMICS

Academic Rating	**85**
Calendar	semester
Student/faculty ratio	12:1
Professors Interesting Rating	74
Professors Accessible Rating	67
Most common lab size	10-19 students
Most common regular class size	20-29 students

MOST POPULAR MAJORS
drama and dramatics/theater arts
finance
liberal arts and sciences/liberal studies

SELECTIVITY

Admissions Selectivity Rating	**95**
# of applicants	34,457
% of applicants accepted	35
% of acceptees attending	38
# accepting a place on wait list	2,078
% admitted from wait list	8
# of early decision applicants	1,210
% accepted early decision	42

FRESHMAN PROFILE

Range SAT Verbal	610-700
Average SAT Verbal	658

Range SAT Math	610-710
Average SAT Math	660
Projected Range SAT Writing	640-700
Range ACT Composite	27-31
Average ACT Composite	29
Minimum Paper TOEFL	600
Minimum Computer Based TOEFL	250
Average HS GPA	3.6
% graduated top 10% of class	63
% graduated top 25% of class	91
% graduated top 50% of class	99

DEADLINES

Early decision application deadline	11/1
Regular application deadline	1/15
Regular notification	4/1
Nonfall registration?	yes

FINANCIAL FACTS

Financial Aid Rating	**75**
Annual tuition	$28,328
Room & Board	$11,210
Books and supplies	$700
Required fees	$1,766
% frosh rec. need-based scholarship or grant aid	54
% UG rec. need-based scholarship or grant aid	53
% frosh rec. need-based self-help aid	52
% UG rec. need-based self-help aid	50
% frosh rec. any financial aid	62
% UG rec. any financial aid	64
Avg. frosh grant	$13,629
Avg. frosh loan	$4,351

NIAGARA UNIVERSITY

CAMPUS LIFE

Quality of Life Rating	**69**
Fire Safety Rating	**60**
Type of school	private
Affiliation	Roman Catholic
Environment	town

STUDENTS

Total undergrad enrollment	2,825
% male/female	39/61
% from out of state	7
% live on campus	54
% in (# of) fraternities	4 (3)
% in (# of) sororities	2 (2)
% African American	5
% Asian	1
% Caucasian	77
% Hispanic	2
% Native American	1
% international	5
# of countries represented	12

ACADEMICS

Academic Rating	**71**
Calendar	semester
Student/faculty ratio	16:1
Professors Interesting Rating	68
Professors Accessible Rating	72
% professors teaching UG courses	97
Most common lab size	10-19 students
Most common regular class size	10-19 students

MOST POPULAR MAJORS
business/commerce
criminal justice/law enforcement administration
teacher education, multiple levels

SELECTIVITY

Admissions Selectivity Rating	**75**
# of applicants	2,946
% of applicants accepted	80
% of acceptees attending	31

FRESHMAN PROFILE

Range SAT Verbal	480-570
Average SAT Verbal	521
Range SAT Math	470-580
Average SAT Math	522
Projected Range SAT Writing	540-610
Range ACT Composite	19-26
Average ACT Composite	22
Minimum Paper TOEFL	500
Minimum Computer Based TOEFL	173
Average HS GPA	3.3
% graduated top 10% of class	14
% graduated top 25% of class	40
% graduated top 50% of class	73

DEADLINES

Regular application deadline	8/1
Regular notification	rolling
Nonfall registration?	yes

FINANCIAL FACTS

Financial Aid Rating	**78**
Annual tuition	$18,000
Room & Board	$8,450
Books and supplies	$700
Required fees	$800
% frosh rec. need-based scholarship or grant aid	80
% UG rec. need-based scholarship or grant aid	78
% frosh rec. need-based self-help aid	80
% UG rec. need-based self-help aid	77
Avg. frosh grant	$11,691
Avg. frosh loan	$2,088

NORTHEASTERN UNIVERSITY

CAMPUS LIFE

Quality of Life Rating	**82**
Fire Safety Rating	**83**
Type of school	private
Environment	metropolis

STUDENTS

Total undergrad enrollment	14,618
% male/female	49/51
% from out of state	65
% in (# of) fraternities	4 (11)
% in (# of) sororities	4 (7)
% African American	6
% Asian	7
% Caucasian	67
% Hispanic	5
% international	5
# of countries represented	123

ACADEMICS

Academic Rating	**79**
Calendar	semester
Student/faculty ratio	16:1
Professors Interesting Rating	64
Professors Accessible Rating	65
% professors teaching UG courses	100
Most common lab size	10-19 students

MOST POPULAR MAJORS
business/commerce
engineering
health services/allied health

SELECTIVITY

Admissions Selectivity Rating	**92**
# of applicants	24,436
% of applicants accepted	42
% of acceptees attending	27
# accepting a place on wait list	1,045
% admitted from wait list	49

FRESHMAN PROFILE

Range SAT Verbal	550-650
Average SAT Verbal	596
Range SAT Math	570-660
Average SAT Math	615
Projected Range SAT Writing	600-670
Range ACT Composite	24-28
Average ACT Composite	26
Minimum Paper TOEFL	550
Minimum Computer Based TOEFL	213
Average HS GPA	3.52
% graduated top 10% of class	36
% graduated top 25% of class	67
% graduated top 50% of class	93

DEADLINES

Regular application deadline	2/1

Regular notification	3/15, 4/1
Nonfall registration?	yes

FINANCIAL FACTS

Financial Aid Rating	**65**
Annual tuition	$26,750
Room & Board	$10,180
Books and supplies	$900
Required fees	$330
% frosh rec. need-based scholarship or grant aid	67
% UG rec. need-based scholarship or grant aid	60
% frosh rec. need-based self-help aid	60
% UG rec. need-based self-help aid	57
% frosh rec. any financial aid	87
% UG rec. any financial aid	72
Avg. frosh grant	$13,965
Avg. frosh loan	$3,588

PACE UNIVERSITY

CAMPUS LIFE

Quality of Life Rating	**74**
Fire Safety Rating	**60**
Type of school	private
Environment	metropolis

STUDENTS

Total undergrad enrollment	8,044
% male/female	39/61
% from out of state	17
% from public high school	70
% live on campus	29
% in (# of) fraternities	5 (8)
% in (# of) sororities	5 (9)
% African American	10
% Asian	12
% Caucasian	45
% Hispanic	12
% international	4
# of countries represented	39

ACADEMICS

Academic Rating	**74**
Calendar	semester
Student/faculty ratio	15:1
Professors Interesting Rating	65
Professors Accessible Rating	66
% professors teaching UG courses	76
Most common lab size	10-19 students
Most common regular class size	fewer than 10 students

MOST POPULAR MAJORS
accounting
finance
information science/studies

SELECTIVITY

Admissions Selectivity Rating	**79**

# of applicants	8,853
% of applicants accepted	70
% of acceptees attending	24

FRESHMAN PROFILE

Range SAT Verbal	480-580
Average SAT Verbal	539
Range SAT Math	500-590
Average SAT Math	548
Projected Range SAT Writing	540-620
Range ACT Composite	21-26
Average ACT Composite	21
Minimum Paper TOEFL	450
Minimum Computer Based TOEFL	133
Average HS GPA	3.2
% graduated top 10% of class	19
% graduated top 25% of class	47
% graduated top 50% of class	86

DEADLINES

Regular notification	rolling
Nonfall registration?	yes

FINANCIAL FACTS

Financial Aid Rating	**67**
Annual tuition	$20,540
Room & Board	$8,400
Books and supplies	$800
Required fees	$612
% frosh rec. need-based scholarship or grant aid	68
% UG rec. need-based scholarship or grant aid	69
% frosh rec. need-based self-help aid	58
% UG rec. need-based self-help aid	60
% frosh rec. any financial aid	94
% UG rec. any financial aid	93
Avg. frosh grant	$10,237
Avg. frosh loan	$4,309

PENN STATE—UNIVERSITY PARK

CAMPUS LIFE

Quality of Life Rating	**83**
Fire Safety Rating	**60**
Type of school	public
Environment	village

STUDENTS

Total undergrad enrollment	33,958
% male/female	53/47
% from out of state	23
% live on campus	38
% in (# of) fraternities	13 (55)
% in (# of) sororities	10 (25)
% African American	4
% Asian	6
% Caucasian	84

% Hispanic	3
% international	2

ACADEMICS

Academic Rating	**75**
Calendar	semester
Student/faculty ratio	17:1
Professors Interesting Rating	65
Professors Accessible Rating	66
Most common lab size	20-29 students
Most common regular class size	20-29 students

SELECTIVITY

Admissions Selectivity Rating	**90**
# of applicants	30,122
% of applicants accepted	58
% of acceptees attending	34

FRESHMAN PROFILE

Range SAT Verbal	530-630
Average SAT Verbal	593
Range SAT Math	560-660
Average SAT Math	617
Projected Range SAT Writing	580-650
Minimum Paper TOEFL	550
Average HS GPA	3.56
% graduated top 10% of class	41
% graduated top 25% of class	80
% graduated top 50% of class	98

DEADLINES

Regular notification	rolling
Nonfall registration?	yes

FINANCIAL FACTS

Financial Aid Rating	**64**
Annual in-state tuition	$9,374
Annual out-of-state tuition	$19,286
Room & Board	$6,230
Books and supplies	$992
Required fees	$448
% frosh rec. need-based scholarship or grant aid	27
% UG rec. need-based scholarship or grant aid	30
% frosh rec. need-based self-help aid	40
% UG rec. need-based self-help aid	43
Avg. frosh grant	$2,800
Avg. frosh loan	$3,193

POLYTECHNIC UNIVERSITY— BROOKLYN

CAMPUS LIFE

Quality of Life Rating	**72**
Fire Safety Rating	**60**
Type of school	private
Environment	metropolis

STUDENTS

Total undergrad enrollment	1,543
% male/female	81/19
% from out of state	4
% from public high school	82
% live on campus	8
% in (# of) fraternities	3 (3)
% in (# of) sororities	4 (1)
% African American	11
% Asian	35
% Caucasian	29
% Hispanic	9
% international	8
# of countries represented	44

ACADEMICS

Academic Rating	**72**
Calendar	semester
Student/faculty ratio	12:1
Professors Interesting Rating	63
Professors Accessible Rating	72
% professors teaching UG courses	100
Most common lab size	20-29 students
Most common regular class size	10-19 students

MOST POPULAR MAJORS
computer and information sciences
computer engineering
electrical, electronics, and communications engineering

SELECTIVITY

Admissions Selectivity Rating	**87**
# of applicants	1,158
% of applicants accepted	69
% of acceptees attending	41

FRESHMAN PROFILE

Range SAT Verbal	490-600
Average SAT Verbal	545
Range SAT Math	580-680
Average SAT Math	630
Projected Range SAT Writing	550-630
Minimum Paper TOEFL	550
Minimum Computer Based TOEFL	217
Average HS GPA	3.2
% graduated top 10% of class	40
% graduated top 25% of class	77
% graduated top 50% of class	92

DEADLINES

Regular notification	rolling
Nonfall registration?	yes

FINANCIAL FACTS

Financial Aid Rating	**79**
Annual tuition	$26,200
Room & Board	$8,000
Books and supplies	$750
Required fees	$970

% frosh rec. need-based scholarship
or grant aid 81
% UG rec. need-based scholarship
or grant aid 75
% frosh rec. need-based self-help aid 58
% UG rec. need-based self-help aid 64
% frosh rec. any financial aid 99
% UG rec. any financial aid 96
Avg. frosh grant $18,466
Avg. frosh loan $6,339

PRINCETON UNIVERSITY

CAMPUS LIFE
Quality of Life Rating **98**
Fire Safety Rating **88**
Type of school private
Environment village
STUDENTS
Total undergrad enrollment 4,678
% male/female 53/47
% from out of state 85
% from public high school 55
% live on campus 98
% African American 8
% Asian 13
% Caucasian 63
% Hispanic 7
% Native American 1
% international 8

ACADEMICS
Academic Rating **88**
Calendar semester
Student/faculty ratio 5:1
Professors Interesting Rating 85
Professors Accessible Rating 95
% professors teaching UG courses 56
MOST POPULAR MAJORS
English language and literature
history
political science and government

SELECTIVITY
Admissions Selectivity Rating **99**
# of applicants 13,695
% of applicants accepted 13
% of acceptees attending 68
# accepting a place on wait list 1,045
% admitted from wait list 8
# of early decision applicants 581
% accepted early decision 32
FRESHMAN PROFILE
Range SAT Verbal 680-770
Range SAT Math 690-790
Projected Range SAT Writing 680-740
Average HS GPA 3.83
% graduated top 10% of class 94

% graduated top 25% of class 99
% graduated top 50% of class 100
DEADLINES
Early decision application deadline 11/1
Regular application deadline 11/1
Regular notification 4/4
Nonfall registration? no

FINANCIAL FACTS
Financial Aid Rating **99**
Annual tuition $31,450
Room & Board $8,763
Books and supplies $990
% frosh rec. need-based scholarship
or grant aid 52
% UG rec. need-based scholarship
or grant aid 49
% frosh rec. need-based self-help aid 52
% UG rec. need-based self-help aid 49
% frosh rec. any financial aid 52
% UG rec. any financial aid 50
Avg. frosh grant $26,500

PROVIDENCE COLLEGE

CAMPUS LIFE
Quality of Life Rating **72**
Fire Safety Rating **96**
Type of school private
Affiliation Roman Catholic
Environment city
STUDENTS
Total undergrad enrollment 4,125
% male/female 43/57
% from out of state 81
% from public high school 57
% live on campus 75
% African American 2
% Asian 2
% Caucasian 82
% Hispanic 2
% international 1
# of countries represented 18

ACADEMICS
Academic Rating **83**
Calendar semester
Student/faculty ratio 12:1
Professors Interesting Rating 79
Professors Accessible Rating 80
% professors teaching UG courses 100
Most common lab size 10-19 students
Most common
regular class size 10-19 students
MOST POPULAR MAJORS
business administration/management
marketing/marketing management
special education

SELECTIVITY
Admissions Selectivity Rating **92**
# of applicants 7,827
% of applicants accepted 54
% of acceptees attending 25
# accepting a place on wait list 1,526
% admitted from wait list 14
FRESHMAN PROFILE
Range SAT Verbal 550-640
Average SAT Verbal 597
Range SAT Math 560-650
Average SAT Math 604
Projected Range SAT Writing 600-660
Range ACT Composite 23-27
Average ACT Composite 25
Minimum Paper TOEFL 550
Minimum Computer Based TOEFL 213
Average HS GPA 3.42
% graduated top 10% of class 42
% graduated top 25% of class 82
% graduated top 50% of class 98
DEADLINES
Regular application deadline 1/15
Regular notification 4/1
Nonfall registration? yes

FINANCIAL FACTS
Financial Aid Rating **73**
Annual tuition $24,800
Room & Board $9,270
Books and supplies $750
Required fees $510
% frosh rec. need-based scholarship
or grant aid 51
% UG rec. need-based scholarship
or grant aid 55
% frosh rec. need-based self-help aid 54
% UG rec. need-based self-help aid 62
% frosh rec. any financial aid 78
% UG rec. any financial aid 75
Avg. frosh grant $11,000
Avg. frosh loan $4,625

QUINNIPIAC UNIVERSITY

CAMPUS LIFE
Quality of Life Rating **77**
Fire Safety Rating **60**
Type of school private
Environment town
STUDENTS
Total undergrad enrollment 5,329
% male/female 39/61
% from out of state 70
% from public high school 80
% live on campus 70
% in (# of) fraternities 6 (2)

% in (# of) sororities	8 (3)
% African American	2
% Asian	2
% Caucasian	77
% Hispanic	4
% international	1
# of countries represented	20

ACADEMICS

Academic Rating	**81**
Calendar	semester
Student/faculty ratio	15:1
Professors Interesting Rating	80
Professors Accessible Rating	79
% professors teaching UG courses	88
Most common lab size	10-19 students
Most common regular class size	10-19 students

MOST POPULAR MAJORS
communications technologies and support services
physical therapy/therapist
psychology

SELECTIVITY

Admissions Selectivity Rating	**87**
# of applicants	10,624
% of applicants accepted	55
% of acceptees attending	23
# accepting a place on wait list	1,020
% admitted from wait list	15

FRESHMAN PROFILE

Range SAT Verbal	520-580
Average SAT Verbal	555
Range SAT Math	540-600
Average SAT Math	560
Projected Range SAT Writing	570-620
Range ACT Composite	22-27
Average ACT Composite	24
Minimum Paper TOEFL	550
Minimum Computer Based TOEFL	213
Average HS GPA	3.4
% graduated top 10% of class	21
% graduated top 25% of class	55
% graduated top 50% of class	89

DEADLINES

Regular notification	rolling
Nonfall registration?	yes

FINANCIAL FACTS

Financial Aid Rating	**65**
Annual tuition	$23,360
Room & Board	$10,300
Books and supplies	$800
Required fees	$980
% frosh rec. need-based scholarship or grant aid	60

% UG rec. need-based scholarship or grant aid	57
% frosh rec. need-based self-help aid	53
% UG rec. need-based self-help aid	52
% frosh rec. any financial aid	70
% UG rec. any financial aid	68
Avg. frosh grant	$13,019
Avg. frosh loan	$2,625

RAMAPO COLLEGE OF NEW JERSEY

CAMPUS LIFE

Quality of Life Rating	**83**
Fire Safety Rating	**84**
Type of school	public
Environment	village

STUDENTS

Total undergrad enrollment	4,833
% male/female	40/60
% from out of state	9
% live on campus	61
% in (# of) fraternities	8 (10)
% in (# of) sororities	5 (10)
% African American	7
% Asian	4
% Caucasian	77
% Hispanic	8
% international	4
# of countries represented	60

ACADEMICS

Academic Rating	**77**
Calendar	semester
Student/faculty ratio	17:1
Professors Interesting Rating	72
Professors Accessible Rating	73
% professors teaching UG courses	100
Most common lab size	20-29 students
Most common regular class size	10-19 students

MOST POPULAR MAJORS
business administration and management
communications studies/speech
communication and rhetoric
psychology

SELECTIVITY

Admissions Selectivity Rating	**89**
# of applicants	4,669
% of applicants accepted	40
% of acceptees attending	40
# accepting a place on wait list	299
% admitted from wait list	15

FRESHMAN PROFILE

Range SAT Verbal	530-610
Average SAT Verbal	580
Range SAT Math	540-620

Average SAT Math	237
Projected Range SAT Writing	580-640
Minimum Paper TOEFL	550
Minimum Computer Based TOEFL	213
Average HS GPA	3.5
% graduated top 10% of class	32
% graduated top 25% of class	71
% graduated top 50% of class	98

DEADLINES

Regular application deadline	3/1
Regular notification	3/1
Nonfall registration?	yes

FINANCIAL FACTS

Financial Aid Rating	**70**
Annual in-state tuition	$5,640
Annual out-of-state tuition	$10,192
Room & Board	$8,208
Books and supplies	$1,000
Required fees	$2,441
% frosh rec. need-based scholarship or grant aid	25
% UG rec. need-based scholarship or grant aid	25
% frosh rec. need-based self-help aid	34
% UG rec. need-based self-help aid	39
% frosh rec. any financial aid	88
% UG rec. any financial aid	81
Avg. frosh grant	$10,501
Avg. frosh loan	$2,614

REGIS COLLEGE

CAMPUS LIFE

Quality of Life Rating	**79**
Fire Safety Rating	**82**
Type of school	private
Affiliation	Roman Catholic
Environment	village

STUDENTS

Total undergrad enrollment	897
% male/female	3/97
% from out of state	11
% from public high school	75
% live on campus	46
% African American	11
% Asian	5
% Caucasian	40
% Hispanic	9
% international	1
# of countries represented	8

ACADEMICS

Academic Rating	**83**
Calendar	semester
Student/faculty ratio	13:1
Professors Interesting Rating	83
Professors Accessible Rating	88

% professors teaching UG courses	86	
Most common lab size	10-19 students	
Most common		
regular class size	10-19 students	

MOST POPULAR MAJORS
communications studies/speech
communication and rhetoric
English language and literature
nursing/registered nurse training
(RN, ASN, BSN, MSN)

SELECTIVITY
Admissions Selectivity Rating 72
# of applicants 603
% of applicants accepted 81
% of acceptees attending 32

FRESHMAN PROFILE
Range SAT Verbal 410-520
Average SAT Verbal 470
Range SAT Math 420-510
Average SAT Math 466
Projected Range SAT Writing 480-570
Minimum Paper TOEFL 550
Minimum Computer Based TOEFL 213
Average HS GPA 2.92
% graduated top 10% of class 14
% graduated top 25% of class 39
% graduated top 50% of class 77

DEADLINES
Regular notification rolling
Nonfall registration? yes

FINANCIAL FACTS
Financial Aid Rating 68
Annual tuition $21,525
Room & Board $9,825
Books and supplies $900
% frosh rec. need-based scholarship
or grant aid 77
% UG rec. need-based scholarship
or grant aid 69
% frosh rec. need-based self-help aid 83
% UG rec. need-based self-help aid 78
% frosh rec. any financial aid 87
% UG rec. any financial aid 60
Avg. frosh grant $10,347
Avg. frosh loan $4,625

RENSSELAER POLYTECHNIC INSTITUTE

CAMPUS LIFE
Quality of Life Rating 61
Fire Safety Rating 92
Type of school private
Environment city

STUDENTS
Total undergrad enrollment 4,888

% male/female	75/25
% from out of state	49
% from public high school	79
% live on campus	56
% in (# of) fraternities	39 (31)
% in (# of) sororities	18 (4)
% African American	4
% Asian	12
% Caucasian	70
% Hispanic	5
% international	4
# of countries represented	70

ACADEMICS
Academic Rating 76
Calendar semester
Student/faculty ratio 14:1
Professors Interesting Rating 61
Professors Accessible Rating 66
% professors teaching UG courses 100
Most common lab size 20-29 students
Most common
regular class size 20-29 students

MOST POPULAR MAJORS
business, management, marketing, and
related support services
computer and information sciences
electrical, electronics, and communications
engineering

SELECTIVITY
Admissions Selectivity Rating 91
# of applicants 5,406
% of applicants accepted 75
% of acceptees attending 27
# accepting a place on wait list 266
% admitted from wait list 26
# of early decision applicants 152
% accepted early decision 84

FRESHMAN PROFILE
Range SAT Verbal 580-690
Average SAT Verbal 633
Range SAT Math 640-730
Average SAT Math 687
Projected Range SAT Writing 620-690
Range ACT Composite 24-28
Average ACT Composite 26
Minimum Paper TOEFL 570
Minimum Computer Based TOEFL 230
% graduated top 10% of class 63
% graduated top 25% of class 94
% graduated top 50% of class 99

DEADLINES
Early decision application deadline 11/15
Regular application deadline 1/1
Regular notification 3/31
Nonfall registration? yes

FINANCIAL FACTS
Financial Aid Rating 89
Annual tuition $31,000
Room & Board $9,506
Books and supplies $1,722
Required fees $857
% frosh rec. need-based scholarship
or grant aid 72
% UG rec. need-based scholarship
or grant aid 72
% frosh rec. need-based self-help aid 47
% UG rec. need-based self-help aid 47
% frosh rec. any financial aid 94
% UG rec. any financial aid 87
Avg. frosh grant $20,299
Avg. frosh loan $5,959

RICHARD STOCKTON COLLEGE OF NEW JERSEY

CAMPUS LIFE
Quality of Life Rating 73
Fire Safety Rating 95
Type of school public
Environment town

STUDENTS
Total undergrad enrollment 6,309
% male/female 42/58
% from out of state 3
% from public high school 74
% live on campus 32
% in (# of) fraternities 3 (9)
% in (# of) sororities 3 (9)
% African American 7
% Asian 4
% Caucasian 82
% Hispanic 6
% international 1
# of countries represented 67

ACADEMICS
Academic Rating 75
Calendar semester
Student/faculty ratio 19:1
Professors Interesting Rating 77
Professors Accessible Rating 72
% professors teaching UG courses 97
Most common lab size 20-29 students
Most common
regular class size fewer than 10 students

MOST POPULAR MAJORS
business administration/management
psychology

SELECTIVITY
Admissions Selectivity Rating 83
# of applicants 3,729

% of applicants accepted		51
% of acceptees attending		44
# accepting a place on wait list		400
% admitted from wait list		16

FRESHMAN PROFILE

Range SAT Verbal	490-570
Average SAT Verbal	561
Range SAT Math	480-590
Average SAT Math	572
Projected Range SAT Writing	550-610
Range ACT Composite	19-23
Average ACT Composite	25
Minimum Paper TOEFL	550
Minimum Computer Based TOEFL	217
Average HS GPA	3.2
% graduated top 10% of class	15
% graduated top 25% of class	56
% graduated top 50% of class	95

DEADLINES

Regular application deadline	5/1
Regular notification	rolling
Nonfall registration?	yes

FINANCIAL FACTS

Financial Aid Rating	**77**
Annual in-state tuition	$5,091
Annual out-of-state tuition	$8,256
Room & Board	$7,252
Books and supplies	$825
Required fees	$2,112
% frosh rec. need-based scholarship or grant aid	28
% UG rec. need-based scholarship or grant aid	29
% frosh rec. need-based self-help aid	45
% UG rec. need-based self-help aid	43
% frosh rec. any financial aid	81
% UG rec. any financial aid	70
Avg. frosh grant	$6,346
Avg. frosh loan	$2,603

RIDER UNIVERSITY

CAMPUS LIFE

Quality of Life Rating	**71**
Fire Safety Rating	**85**
Type of school	private
Environment	village

STUDENTS

Total undergrad enrollment	4,038
% male/female	40/60
% from out of state	24
% from public high school	80
% live on campus	56
% in (# of) fraternities	12 (8)
% in (# of) sororities	12 (7)
% African American	8

% Aslan	3
% Caucasian	75
% Hispanic	5
% international	1
# of countries represented	12

ACADEMICS

Academic Rating	**78**
Calendar	semester
Student/faculty ratio	13:1
Professors Interesting Rating	79
Professors Accessible Rating	81
% professors teaching UG courses	95
Most common lab size	10-19 students
Most common regular class size	10-19 students

MOST POPULAR MAJORS

business administration/management
elementary education and teaching
finance

SELECTIVITY

Admissions Selectivity Rating	**74**
# of applicants	4,197
% of applicants accepted	85
% of acceptees attending	25

FRESHMAN PROFILE

Range SAT Verbal	470-570
Average SAT Verbal	530
Range SAT Math	470-580
Average SAT Math	529
Projected Range SAT Writing	530-610
Minimum Paper TOEFL	550
Minimum Computer Based TOEFL	213
Average HS GPA	3.12
% graduated top 10% of class	13
% graduated top 25% of class	36
% graduated top 50% of class	70

DEADLINES

Regular notification	within 3 to 4 weeks of receipt of application
Nonfall registration?	yes

FINANCIAL FACTS

Financial Aid Rating	**72**
Annual tuition	$22,910
Room & Board	$8,840
Books and supplies	$1,000
Required fees	$560
% frosh rec. need-based scholarship or grant aid	71
% UG rec. need-based scholarship or grant aid	67
% frosh rec. need-based self-help aid	60
% UG rec. need-based self-help aid	53
% frosh rec. any financial aid	72
% UG rec. any financial aid	69

Avg. frosh grant	$11,949
Avg. frosh loan	$3,535

ROBERTS WESLEYAN COLLEGE

CAMPUS LIFE

Quality of Life Rating	**87**
Fire Safety Rating	**87**
Type of school	private
Affiliation	Methodist
Environment	city

STUDENTS

Total undergrad enrollment	1,376
% male/female	33/67
% from out of state	12
% live on campus	70
% African American	6
% Asian	1
% Caucasian	74
% Hispanic	3
% international	3

ACADEMICS

Academic Rating	**82**
Calendar	semester
Student/faculty ratio	17:1
Professors Interesting Rating	87
Professors Accessible Rating	87
% professors teaching UG courses	84
Most common lab size	10-19 students
Most common regular class size	20-29 students

SELECTIVITY

Admissions Selectivity Rating	**80**
# of applicants	703
% of applicants accepted	82
% of acceptees attending	45

FRESHMAN PROFILE

Range SAT Verbal	520-610
Average SAT Verbal	570
Range SAT Math	510-610
Average SAT Math	564
Projected Range SAT Writing	570-640
Range ACT Composite	21-27
Average ACT Composite	24
Minimum Paper TOEFL	550
Minimum Computer Based TOEFL	213
Average HS GPA	3.2
% graduated top 10% of class	26
% graduated top 25% of class	56
% graduated top 50% of class	85

DEADLINES

Regular application deadline	rolling
Regular notification	rolling
Nonfall registration?	yes

FINANCIAL FACTS
Financial Aid Rating   **74**

Annual tuition	$17,183
Room & Board	$6,603
Books and supplies	$650
Required fees	$911
% frosh rec. need-based scholarship or grant aid	87
% UG rec. need-based scholarship or grant aid	87
% frosh rec. need-based self-help aid	82
% UG rec. need-based self-help aid	80
% frosh rec. any financial aid	94
% UG rec. any financial aid	94
Avg. frosh grant	$10,789
Avg. frosh loan	$6,850

ROCHESTER INSTITUTE OF TECHNOLOGY

CAMPUS LIFE
Quality of Life Rating   **68**
Fire Safety Rating   **99**

Type of school	private
Environment	city

STUDENTS
Total undergrad enrollment	11,750
% male/female	71/29
% from out of state	45
% from public high school	85
% live on campus	60
% in (# of) fraternities	5 (19)
% in (# of) sororities	5 (10)
% African American	5
% Asian	7
% Caucasian	71
% Hispanic	3
% international	4
# of countries represented	90

ACADEMICS
Academic Rating   **79**

Calendar	quarter
Student/faculty ratio	14:1
Professors Interesting Rating	65
Professors Accessible Rating	63
% professors teaching UG courses	95
Most common lab size	10-19 students
Most common regular class size	10-19 students

MOST POPULAR MAJORS
computer and information sciences
information technology
photography

SELECTIVITY
Admissions Selectivity Rating   **88**

# of applicants	9,108

% of applicants accepted	67
% of acceptees attending	37
# accepting a place on wait list	150
% admitted from wait list	17
# of early decision applicants	713
% accepted early decision	76

FRESHMAN PROFILE
Range SAT Verbal	540-640
Range SAT Math	570-670
Projected Range SAT Writing	590-660
Range ACT Composite	23-28
Minimum Paper TOEFL	550
Minimum Computer Based TOEFL	215
Average HS GPA	3.7
% graduated top 10% of class	31
% graduated top 25% of class	66
% graduated top 50% of class	92

DEADLINES
Early decision application deadline	12/1
Regular application deadline	2/1
Regular notification	rolling
Nonfall registration?	yes

FINANCIAL FACTS
Financial Aid Rating   **91**

Annual tuition	$21,447
Room & Board	$8,136
Books and supplies	$600
Required fees	$357
% frosh rec. need-based scholarship or grant aid	67
% UG rec. need-based scholarship or grant aid	67
% frosh rec. need-based self-help aid	63
% UG rec. need-based self-help aid	63
% frosh rec. any financial aid	81
% UG rec. any financial aid	75
Avg. frosh grant	$10,300
Avg. frosh loan	$4,400

ROGER WILLIAMS UNIVERSITY

CAMPUS LIFE
Quality of Life Rating   **74**
Fire Safety Rating   **94**

Type of school	private
Environment	village

STUDENTS
Total undergrad enrollment	4,188
% male/female	50/50
% from out of state	86
% from public high school	84
% live on campus	79
% African American	1
% Asian	2
% Caucasian	81

% Hispanic	2
% international	2
# of countries represented	37

ACADEMICS
Academic Rating   **77**

Calendar	4-1-4
Student/faculty ratio	16:1
Professors Interesting Rating	75
Professors Accessible Rating	78
% professors teaching UG courses	100
Most common lab size	20-29 students
Most common regular class size	20-29 students

MOST POPULAR MAJORS
architecture
(BArch, BA/BS, MArch, MA/MS, PhD)
business administration/management
criminal justice/law enforcement administration

SELECTIVITY
Admissions Selectivity Rating   **79**

# of applicants	5,819
% of applicants accepted	78
% of acceptees attending	23
# accepting a place on wait list	110
% admitted from wait list	2
# of early decision applicants	172
% accepted early decision	95

FRESHMAN PROFILE
Range SAT Verbal	480-570
Average SAT Verbal	533
Range SAT Math	490-590
Average SAT Math	540
Projected Range SAT Writing	540-610
Range ACT Composite	21-25
Average HS GPA	3.06
% graduated top 10% of class	13
% graduated top 25% of class	45
% graduated top 50% of class	73

DEADLINES
Early decision application deadline	12/1
Regular notification	rolling
Nonfall registration?	yes

FINANCIAL FACTS
Financial Aid Rating   **82**

Annual tuition	$21,848
Room & Board	$10,237
Books and supplies	$700
Required fees	$1,018
% frosh rec. need-based scholarship or grant aid	57
% UG rec. need-based scholarship or grant aid	37
% frosh rec. need-based self-help aid	57
% UG rec. need-based self-help aid	38

% frosh rec. any financial aid	63
% UG rec. any financial aid	42
Avg. frosh grant	$8,100
Avg. frosh loan	$3,500

ROSEMONT COLLEGE

CAMPUS LIFE
Quality of Life Rating	**73**
Fire Safety Rating	**60**
Type of school	private
Affiliation	Roman Catholic
Environment	village

STUDENTS
Total undergrad enrollment	651
% male/female	9/91
% from out of state	35
% from public high school	61
% live on campus	70
% in (# of) sororities	2
% African American	30
% Asian	6
% Caucasian	49
% Hispanic	6
% international	2
# of countries represented	21

ACADEMICS
Academic Rating	**79**
Calendar	semester
Student/faculty ratio	8:1
Professors Interesting Rating	73
Professors Accessible Rating	77
% professors teaching UG courses	100
Most common lab size	10-19 students

MOST POPULAR MAJORS
English language and literature
psychology
social sciences

SELECTIVITY
Admissions Selectivity Rating	**82**
# of applicants	885
% of applicants accepted	78
% of acceptees attending	34

FRESHMAN PROFILE
Range SAT Verbal	480-600
Average SAT Verbal	520
Range SAT Math	440-550
Average SAT Math	500
Projected Range SAT Writing	540-630
Minimum Paper TOEFL	500
Average HS GPA	3.0
% graduated top 10% of class	57
% graduated top 25% of class	43
% graduated top 50% of class	83

DEADLINES
Regular notification	rolling
Nonfall registration?	yes

FINANCIAL FACTS
Financial Aid Rating	**77**
Annual tuition	$19,450
Room & Board	$7,700
Books and supplies	$800
Required fees	$865
% frosh rec. need-based scholarship or grant aid	50
% UG rec. need-based scholarship or grant aid	68
% frosh rec. need-based self-help aid	90
% UG rec. need-based self-help aid	69
Avg. frosh grant	$17,427
Avg. frosh loan	$4,914

ROWAN UNIVERSITY

CAMPUS LIFE
Quality of Life Rating	**61**
Fire Safety Rating	**92**
Type of school	public
Environment	town

STUDENTS
Total undergrad enrollment	7,970
% male/female	45/55
% from out of state	3
% live on campus	36
% in (# of) fraternities	12 (13)
% in (# of) sororities	8 (12)
% African American	9
% Asian	3
% Caucasian	79
% Hispanic	6

ACADEMICS
Academic Rating	**73**
Calendar	semester
Student/faculty ratio	15:1
Professors Interesting Rating	67
Professors Accessible Rating	65
% professors teaching UG courses	95
Most common lab size	20-29 students

MOST POPULAR MAJORS
business administration/management
communications, journalism, and
related fields
elementary education and teaching

SELECTIVITY
Admissions Selectivity Rating	**86**
# of applicants	6,250
% of applicants accepted	52
% of acceptees attending	39
# accepting a place on wait list	145

FRESHMAN PROFILE
Range SAT Verbal	500-590
Average SAT Verbal	541
Range SAT Math	510-610
Average SAT Math	556
Projected Range SAT Writing	560-620
Minimum Paper TOEFL	550
Minimum Computer Based TOEFL	213
Average HS GPA	3.74
% graduated top 10% of class	18
% graduated top 25% of class	53
% graduated top 50% of class	88

DEADLINES
Regular application deadline	3/15
Regular notification	rolling
Nonfall registration?	yes

FINANCIAL FACTS
Financial Aid Rating	**66**
Annual in-state tuition	$5,828
Annual out-of-state tuition	$11,656
Room & Board	$7,242
Books and supplies	$800
Required fees	$2,142
% frosh rec. need-based scholarship or grant aid	53
% UG rec. need-based scholarship or grant aid	57
% frosh rec. need-based self-help aid	45
% UG rec. need-based self-help aid	54
% frosh rec. any financial aid	80
% UG rec. any financial aid	74
Avg. frosh grant	$5,064
Avg. frosh loan	$2,364

RUTGERS, THE STATE UNIVERSITY OF NEW JERSEY— NEW BRUNSWICK/ PISCATAWAY CAMPUS

CAMPUS LIFE
Quality of Life Rating	**64**
Fire Safety Rating	**84**
Type of school	public
Environment	town

STUDENTS
Total undergrad enrollment	26,366
% male/female	48/52
% from out of state	8
% live on campus	47
% African American	9
% Asian	22
% Caucasian	55
% Hispanic	8
% international	2

ACADEMICS
Academic Rating — **72**

Calendar	semester
Student/faculty ratio	14:1
Professors Interesting Rating	61
Professors Accessible Rating	62
% professors teaching UG courses	70
% classes taught by TAs	20
Most common lab size	10-19 students
Most common regular class size	20-29 students

SELECTIVITY
Admissions Selectivity Rating — **87**

# of applicants	24,434
% of applicants accepted	61
% of acceptees attending	32

FRESHMAN PROFILE

Range SAT Verbal	540-640
Range SAT Math	570-670
Projected Range SAT Writing	590-660
Minimum Paper TOEFL	550
% graduated top 10% of class	39
% graduated top 25% of class	80
% graduated top 50% of class	99

DEADLINES

Regular notification	2/28
Nonfall registration?	yes

FINANCIAL FACTS
Financial Aid Rating — **75**

Annual in-state tuition	$6,793
Annual out-of-state tuition	$13,828
Room & Board	$8,357
Books and supplies	$800
Required fees	$1,771
% frosh rec. need-based scholarship or grant aid	35
% UG rec. need-based scholarship or grant aid	34
% frosh rec. need-based self-help aid	46
% UG rec. need-based self-help aid	44
% frosh rec. any financial aid	54
% UG rec. any financial aid	51
Avg. frosh grant	$7,585
Avg. frosh loan	$2,881

SACRED HEART UNIVERSITY

CAMPUS LIFE
Quality of Life Rating — **73**
Fire Safety Rating — **99**

Type of school	private
Affiliation	Roman Catholic
Environment	town

STUDENTS

Total undergrad enrollment	912
% male/female	31/69
% from out of state	53
% from public high school	67
% live on campus	69
% in (# of) fraternities	6 (4)
% in (# of) sororities	4 (6)
% African American	26
% Asian	6
% Caucasian	376
% Hispanic	25
% Native American	1
% international	5
# of countries represented	38

ACADEMICS
Academic Rating — **76**

Calendar	semester
Student/faculty ratio	13:1
Professors Interesting Rating	73
Professors Accessible Rating	72
% professors teaching UG courses	89
Most common lab size	10-19 students

MOST POPULAR MAJORS
business administration/management
criminal justice/law enforcement administration
psychology

SELECTIVITY
Admissions Selectivity Rating — **80**

# of applicants	4,971
% of applicants accepted	71
% of acceptees attending	25
# accepting a place on wait list	210
% admitted from wait list	8
# of early decision applicants	137
% accepted early decision	67

FRESHMAN PROFILE

Range SAT Verbal	490-570
Average SAT Verbal	527
Range SAT Math	490-580
Average SAT Math	533
Projected Range SAT Writing	550-610
Range ACT Composite	19-24
Average ACT Composite	22
Minimum Paper TOEFL	500
Minimum Computer Based TOEFL	170
Average HS GPA	3.3
% graduated top 10% of class	15
% graduated top 25% of class	45
% graduated top 50% of class	81

DEADLINES

Early decision application deadline	10/1
Regular notification	rolling
Nonfall registration?	yes

FINANCIAL FACTS
Financial Aid Rating — **72**

Annual tuition	$21,990
Room & Board	$9,464
Books and supplies	$700
% frosh rec. need-based scholarship or grant aid	71
% UG rec. need-based scholarship or grant aid	68
% frosh rec. need-based self-help aid	64
% UG rec. need-based self-help aid	60
% frosh rec. any financial aid	86
% UG rec. any financial aid	85
Avg. frosh grant	$8,972
Avg. frosh loan	$2,533

SAINT ANSELM COLLEGE

CAMPUS LIFE
Quality of Life Rating — **75**
Fire Safety Rating — **60**

Type of school	private
Affiliation	Roman Catholic
Environment	village

STUDENTS

Total undergrad enrollment	1,960
% male/female	42/58
% from out of state	77
% from public high school	65
% live on campus	86
% African American	1
% Asian	1
% Caucasian	78
% Hispanic	1
% international	1
# of countries represented	15

ACADEMICS
Academic Rating — **85**

Calendar	semester
Student/faculty ratio	14:1
Professors Interesting Rating	85
Professors Accessible Rating	85
% professors teaching UG courses	100
Most common lab size	10-19 students
Most common regular class size	10-19 students

MOST POPULAR MAJORS
business administration/management
nursing
psychology

SELECTIVITY
Admissions Selectivity Rating — **85**

# of applicants	3,214
% of applicants accepted	66
% of acceptees attending	25
# accepting a place on wait list	425
% admitted from wait list	31
# of early decision applicants	66
% accepted early decision	81

FRESHMAN PROFILE

Range SAT Verbal	520-600
Average SAT Verbal	551
Range SAT Math	510-600
Average SAT Math	556
Projected Range SAT Writing	570-630
Range ACT Composite	22-26
Average ACT Composite	23
Minimum Paper TOEFL	550
Minimum Computer Based TOEFL	213
Average HS GPA	3.14
% graduated top 10% of class	18
% graduated top 25% of class	56
% graduated top 50% of class	88

DEADLINES

Early decision application deadline	11/15
Regular notification	rolling
Nonfall registration?	yes

FINANCIAL FACTS

Financial Aid Rating	**74**
Annual tuition	$22,700
Room & Board	$8,580
Books and supplies	$750
Required fees	$750
% frosh rec. need-based scholarship or grant aid	74
% UG rec. need-based scholarship or grant aid	71
% frosh rec. need-based self-help aid	68
% UG rec. need-based self-help aid	67
Avg. frosh grant	$7,696
Avg. frosh loan	$2,427

SAINT JOSEPH COLLEGE (CT)

CAMPUS LIFE

Quality of Life Rating	**75**
Fire Safety Rating	**93**
Type of school	private
Affiliation	Roman Catholic
Environment	city

STUDENTS

Total undergrad enrollment	1,115
% male/female	0/100
% from out of state	23
% from public high school	79
% live on campus	48
% African American	11
% Asian	1
% Caucasian	50
% Hispanic	6

ACADEMICS

Academic Rating	**78**
Calendar	semester
Student/faculty ratio	12:1
Professors Interesting Rating	82

Professors Accessible Rating	76
% professors teaching UG courses	75
Most common lab size	10-19 students
Most common regular class size	10-19 students

SELECTIVITY

Admissions Selectivity Rating	**69**
# of applicants	789
% of applicants accepted	70
% of acceptees attending	35
# of early decision applicants	3
% accepted early decision	100

FRESHMAN PROFILE

Range SAT Verbal	460-550
Range SAT Math	440-510
Projected Range SAT Writing	530-600
Minimum Paper TOEFL	530
Minimum Computer Based TOEFL	250
% graduated top 10% of class	6
% graduated top 25% of class	27
% graduated top 50% of class	54

DEADLINES

Regular notification	rolling
Nonfall registration?	yes

FINANCIAL FACTS

Financial Aid Rating	**63**
Annual tuition	$21,370
Room & Board	$9,225
Books and supplies	$850
Required fees	$600

SAINT JOSEPH'S UNIVERSITY (PA)

CAMPUS LIFE

Quality of Life Rating	**78**
Fire Safety Rating	**90**
Type of school	private
Affiliation	Roman Catholic-Jesuit
Environment	metropolis

STUDENTS

Total undergrad enrollment	4,823
% male/female	48/52
% from out of state	45
% from public high school	43
% live on campus	59
% in (# of) fraternities	8 (3)
% in (# of) sororities	13 (3)
% African American	7
% Asian	2
% Caucasian	80
% Hispanic	2
% international	1
# of countries represented	48

ACADEMICS

Academic Rating	**80**
Calendar	semester
Student/faculty ratio	15:1
Professors Interesting Rating	79
Professors Accessible Rating	81
% professors teaching UG courses	81
Most common lab size	20-29 students
Most common regular class size	10-19 students

MOST POPULAR MAJORS

finance/marketing/marketing management
specialized merchandising, sales, and related
marketing operations

SELECTIVITY

Admissions Selectivity Rating	**90**
# of applicants	7,949
% of applicants accepted	48
% of acceptees attending	32
# accepting a place on wait list	2,611

FRESHMAN PROFILE

Range SAT Verbal	540-620
Average SAT Verbal	585
Range SAT Math	540-630
Average SAT Math	590
Projected Range SAT Writing	590-650
Range ACT Composite	22-27
Average ACT Composite	27
Minimum Paper TOEFL	550
Minimum Computer Based TOEFL	213
Average HS GPA	3.4
% graduated top 10% of class	30
% graduated top 25% of class	85
% graduated top 50% of class	100

DEADLINES

Regular notification	rolling
Nonfall registration?	yes

FINANCIAL FACTS

Financial Aid Rating	**74**
Annual tuition	$25,770
Room & Board	$9,610
Books and supplies	$1,250
Required fees	$135
% frosh rec. need-based scholarship or grant aid	44
% UG rec. need-based scholarship or grant aid	40
% frosh rec. need-based self-help aid	44
% UG rec. need-based self-help aid	49
% frosh rec. any financial aid	80
% UG rec. any financial aid	80
Avg. frosh grant	$8,325
Avg. frosh loan	$4,215

SAINT MICHAEL'S COLLEGE

CAMPUS LIFE

Quality of Life Rating	**95**
Fire Safety Rating	**69**
Type of school	private
Affiliation	Roman Catholic
Environment	town

STUDENTS

Total undergrad enrollment	1,930
% male/female	45/55
% from out of state	77
% from public high school	68
% live on campus	92
% African American	1
% Asian	1
% Caucasian	94
% Hispanic	1
% international	2
# of countries represented	18

ACADEMICS

Academic Rating	**87**
Calendar	semester
Student/faculty ratio	12:1
Profs interesting rating	94
Profs accessible rating	88
% profs teaching UG courses	100
Most common lab size	10-19 students
Most common reg class size	10-19 students

MOST POPULAR MAJORS
business administration/management
English language and literature
psychology

SELECTIVITY

Admissions Rating	**85**
# of applicants	2,755
% of applicants accepted	70
% of acceptees attending	27
# accepting a place on wait list	271
% admitted from wait list	3

FRESHMAN PROFILE

Range SAT Verbal	520-610
Average SAT Verbal	563
Range SAT Math	520-610
Average SAT Math	561
Projected Range SAT Writing	570-640
Range ACT Composite	21-25
Minimum Paper TOEFL	550
Minimum Computer Based TOEFL	213
Average HS GPA	3.46
% graduated top 10% of class	19
% graduated top 25% of class	55
% graduated top 50% of class	88

DEADLINES

Regular application deadline	2/1
Regular notification	4/1
Nonfall registration?	yes

FINANCIAL FACTS

Financial Aid Rating	**79**
Annual tuition	$26,550
Room & Board	$6,560
Books and supplies	$1,200
Required fees	$220
% frosh rec. need-based scholarship or grant aid	64
% UG rec. need-based scholarship or grant aid	63
% frosh rec. need-based self-help aid	59
% UG rec. need-based self-help aid	60
% frosh rec. any financial aid	81
% UG rec. any financial aid	86
Avg. frosh grant	$13,255
Avg. frosh loan	$4,175

SALISBURY UNIVERSITY

CAMPUS LIFE

Quality of Life Rating	**81**
Fire Safety Rating	**77**
Type of school	public
Environment	town

STUDENTS

Total undergrad enrollment	6,022
% male/female	44/56
% from out of state	14
% from public high school	85
% live on campus	46
% in (# of) fraternities	5 (6)
% in (# of) sororities	6 (5)
% African American	8
% Asian	3
% Caucasian	80
% Hispanic	2
% international	1
# of countries represented	27

ACADEMICS

Academic Rating	**76**
Calendar	4-1-4
Student/faculty ratio	16:1
Professors Interesting Rating	77
Professors Accessible Rating	78
% professors teaching UG courses	100
% classes taught by TAs	2
Most common lab size	20-29 students
Most common regular class size	20-29 students

MOST POPULAR MAJORS
business administration/management
communications studies/speech
communication and rhetoric
elementary education and teaching

SELECTIVITY

Admissions Selectivity Rating	**83**
# of applicants	5,067
% of applicants accepted	61
% of acceptees attending	32

FRESHMAN PROFILE

Range SAT Verbal	510-590
Average SAT Verbal	553
Range SAT Math	530-610
Average SAT Math	568
Projected Range SAT Writing	570-620
Minimum Paper TOEFL	550
Minimum Computer Based TOEFL	213
Average HS GPA	3.45
% graduated top 10% of class	18
% graduated top 25% of class	50
% graduated top 50% of class	87

DEADLINES

Regular notification	3/15
Nonfall registration?	yes

FINANCIAL FACTS

Financial Aid Rating	**66**
Annual in-state tuition	$4,546
Annual out-of-state tuition	$12,124
Room & Board	$7,050
Books and supplies	$900
Required fees	$1,430
% frosh rec. need-based scholarship or grant aid	26
% UG rec. need-based scholarship or grant aid	18
% frosh rec. need-based self-help aid	28
% UG rec. need-based self-help aid	34
% frosh rec. any financial aid	70
% UG rec. any financial aid	82
Avg. frosh grant	$4,589
Avg. frosh loan	$3,543

SALVE REGINA UNIVERSITY

CAMPUS LIFE

Quality of Life Rating	**81**
Fire Safety Rating	**60**
Type of school	private
Affiliation	Roman Catholic
Environment	city

STUDENTS

Total undergrad enrollment	2,039
% male/female	29/71
% from out of state	82
% from public high school	65
% live on campus	60
% African American	1
% Asian	2
% Caucasian	84
% Hispanic	2

% international 1
# of countries represented 14

ACADEMICS
Academic Rating **80**
Calendar semester
Student/faculty ratio 13:1
Professors Interesting Rating 75
Professors Accessible Rating 73
% professors teaching UG courses 95
Most common lab size 10-19 students
Most common
regular class size fewer than 10 students

MOST POPULAR MAJORS
business administration/management
criminal justice/law enforcement
administration
special education

SELECTIVITY
Admissions Selectivity Rating **85**
# of applicants 4,468
% of applicants accepted 56
% of acceptees attending 22
# accepting a place on wait list 564
% admitted from wait list 3

FRESHMAN PROFILE
Range SAT Verbal 500-580
Average SAT Verbal 539
Range SAT Math 500-570
Average SAT Math 540
Projected Range SAT Writing 560-620
Range ACT Composite 22-26
Average ACT Composite 23
Minimum Paper TOEFL 500
Minimum Computer Based TOEFL 173
Average HS GPA 3.28
% graduated top 10% of class 16
% graduated top 25% of class 49
% graduated top 50% of class 87

DEADLINES
Regular notification rolling
Nonfall registration? yes

FINANCIAL FACTS
Financial Aid Rating **70**
Annual tuition $23,500
Room & board $9,500
Books and supplies $750
% frosh rec. need-based scholarship
or grant aid 65
% UG rec. need-based scholarship
or grant aid 62
% frosh rec. need-based self-help aid 65
% UG rec. need-based self-help aid 64
Avg. frosh grant $13,237
Avg. frosh loan $3,724

SARAH LAWRENCE COLLEGE

CAMPUS LIFE
Quality of Life Rating **68**
Fire Safety Rating **91**
Type of school private
Environment metropolis

STUDENTS
Total undergrad enrollment 1,185
% male/female 27/73
% from out of state 82
% from public high school 65
% live on campus 86
% African American 5
% Asian 4
% Caucasian 77
% Hispanic 3
% Native American 1
% international 2
# of countries represented 32

ACADEMICS
Academic Rating **96**
Calendar semester
Student/faculty ratio 6:1
Professors Interesting Rating 98
Professors Accessible Rating 94
% professors teaching UG courses 100
Most common lab size 10-19 students

SELECTIVITY
Admissions Selectivity Rating **93**
# of applicants 2,558
% of applicants accepted 44
% of acceptees attending 29
# accepting a place on wait list 539
# of early decision applicants 89
% accepted early decision 44

FRESHMAN PROFILE
Range SAT Verbal 620-710
Range SAT Math 550-640
Projected Range SAT Writing 650-700
Range ACT Composite 25-30
Minimum Paper TOEFL 600
Minimum Computer Based TOEFL 250
Average HS GPA 3.6
% graduated top 10% of class 39
% graduated top 25% of class 75
% graduated top 50% of class 95

DEADLINES
Early decision application deadline 11/15
Regular application deadline 1/1
Regular notification 4/1
Nonfall registration? no

FINANCIAL FACTS
Financial Aid Rating **87**
Annual tuition $30,120

Room & Board $10,394
Books and supplies $600
Required fees $704
% frosh rec. need-based scholarship
or grant aid 44
% UG rec. need-based scholarship
or grant aid 46
% frosh rec. need-based self-help aid 45
% UG rec. need-based self-help aid 45
% frosh rec. any financial aid 49
% UG rec. any financial aid 48
Avg. frosh grant $20,874
Avg. frosh loan $2,438

SETON HALL UNIVERSITY

CAMPUS LIFE
Quality of Life Rating **62**
Fire Safety Rating **60**
Type of school private
Affiliation Roman Catholic
Environment village

STUDENTS
Total undergrad enrollment 5,009
% male/female 48/52
% from out of state 25
% from public high school 70
% live on campus 42
% in (# of) fraternities 13 (11)
% in (# of) sororities 8 (12)
% African American 11
% Asian 8
% Caucasian 53
% Hispanic 9
% international 2
# of countries represented 49

ACADEMICS
Academic Rating **74**
Calendar semester
Student/faculty ratio 15:1
Professors Interesting Rating 64
Professors Accessible Rating 66
% professors teaching UG courses 65
% classes taught by TAs 1
Most common lab size 10-19 students
Most common
regular class size 10-19 students

MOST POPULAR MAJORS
communications studies/speech
communication and rhetoric
criminal justice/safety studies
nursing/registered nurse training
(RN, ASN, BSN, MSN)

SELECTIVITY
Admissions Selectivity Rating **80**
# of applicants 5,750

% of applicants accepted	82
% of acceptees attending	27
# accepting a place on wait list	960
% admitted from wait list	62

FRESHMAN PROFILE

Range SAT Verbal	490-600
Average SAT Verbal	549
Range SAT Math	500-610
Average SAT Math	553
Projected Range SAT Writing	550-630
Minimum Paper TOEFL	550
Minimum Computer Based TOEFL	213
Average HS GPA	3.3
% graduated top 10% of class	26
% graduated top 25% of class	54
% graduated top 50% of class	85

DEADLINES

Regular notification	rolling
Nonfall registration?	yes

FINANCIAL FACTS

Financial Aid Rating	**66**
Annual tuition	$19,530
Room & Board	$8,550
Books and supplies	$1,200
Required fees	$2,050
% frosh rec. need-based scholarship or grant aid	35
% UG rec. need-based scholarship or grant aid	34
% frosh rec. need-based self-help aid	52
% UG rec. need-based self-help aid	48
% frosh rec. any financial aid	88
% UG rec. any financial aid	77

SETON HILL UNIVERSITY

CAMPUS LIFE

Quality of Life Rating	**70**
Fire Safety Rating	**81**
Type of school	private
Affiliation	Roman Catholic
Environment	village

STUDENTS

Total undergrad enrollment	1,347
% male/female	30/70
% from out of state	17
% live on campus	70
% African American	6
% Asian	1
% Caucasian	88
% Hispanic	1
% international	2
# of countries represented	15

ACADEMICS

Academic Rating	**77**
Calendar	semester

Student/faculty ratio	15:1
Professors Interesting Rating	75
Professors Accessible Rating	73
% professors teaching UG courses	100
Most common lab size	10-19 students

MOST POPULAR MAJORS
business administration/management
fine/studio arts
psychology

SELECTIVITY

Admissions Selectivity Rating	**75**
# of applicants	1,463
% of applicants accepted	77
% of acceptees attending	27

FRESHMAN PROFILE

Range SAT Verbal	460-570
Range SAT Math	450-560
Projected Range SAT Writing	530-610
Minimum Paper TOEFL	500
Minimum Computer Based TOEFL	173
Average HS GPA	3.2
% graduated top 10% of class	14
% graduated top 25% of class	38
% graduated top 50% of class	73

DEADLINES

Regular application deadline	8/15
Regular notification	rolling
Nonfall registration?	yes

FINANCIAL FACTS

Financial Aid Rating	**74**
Annual tuition	$20,630
Room & Board	$7,000
Books and supplies	$1,000
% frosh rec. need-based scholarship or grant aid	91
% UG rec. need-based scholarship or grant aid	85
% frosh rec. need-based self-help aid	75
% UG rec. need-based self-help aid	72
% frosh rec. any financial aid	95
% UG rec. any financial aid	80
Avg. frosh grant	$14,400
Avg. frosh loan	$3,600

SHIPPENSBURG UNIVERSITY OF PENNSYLVANIA

CAMPUS LIFE

Quality of Life Rating	**72**
Fire Safety Rating	**80**
Type of school	public
Environment	village

STUDENTS

Total undergrad enrollment	6,496
% male/female	48/52

% from out of state	6
% from public high school	90
% live on campus	39
% in (# of) fraternities	7 (12)
% in (# of) sororities	9 (10)
% African American	4
% Asian	1
% Caucasian	89
% Hispanic	1

ACADEMICS

Academic Rating	**74**
Calendar	semester
Student/faculty ratio	19:1
Professors Interesting Rating	75
Professors Accessible Rating	76
% professors teaching UG courses	95
Most common lab size	20-29 students
Most common regular class size	10-19 students

MOST POPULAR MAJORS
criminal justice/safety studies
elementary education and teaching
journalism

SELECTIVITY

Admissions Selectivity Rating	**76**
# of applicants	6,460
% of applicants accepted	64
% of acceptees attending	35

FRESHMAN PROFILE

Range SAT Verbal	480-570
Average SAT Verbal	521
Range SAT Math	480-570
Average SAT Math	529
Projected Range SAT Writing	540-610
Minimum Paper TOEFL	550
Minimum Computer Based TOEFL	213
Average HS GPA	3.2
% graduated top 10% of class	9
% graduated top 25% of class	34
% graduated top 50% of class	72

DEADLINES

Regular notification	rolling
Nonfall registration?	yes

FINANCIAL FACTS

Financial Aid Rating	**70**
Annual in-state tuition	$5,986
Annual out-of-state tuition	$13,252
Room & board	$8,762
Books and supplies	$1,000
% frosh rec. need-based scholarship or grant aid	38
% UG rec. need-based scholarship or grant aid	38
% frosh rec. need-based self-help aid	44
% UG rec. need-based self-help aid	44

% frosh rec. any financial aid	74
% UG rec. any financial aid	72
Avg. frosh grant	$3,448
Avg. frosh loan	$4,049

SIENA COLLEGE

CAMPUS LIFE

Quality of Life Rating	**76**
Fire Safety Rating	**98**
Type of school	private
Affiliation	Roman Catholic
Environment	town

STUDENTS

Total undergrad enrollment	3,213
% male/female	43/57
% from out of state	12
% live on campus	70
% African American	2
% Asian	3
% Caucasian	88
% Hispanic	3

ACADEMICS

Academic Rating	**76**
Calendar	semester
Student/faculty ratio	14:1
Professors Interesting Rating	71
Professors Accessible Rating	80
% professors teaching UG courses	100
Most common lab size	20-29 students
Most common regular class size	10-19 students

MOST POPULAR MAJORS
biology/biological sciences
marketing/marketing management
psychology

SELECTIVITY

Admissions Selectivity Rating	**84**
# of applicants	4,145
% of applicants accepted	60
% of acceptees attending	29
# accepting a place on wait list	494
% admitted from wait list	11
# of early decision applicants	48
% accepted early decision	59

FRESHMAN PROFILE

Range SAT Verbal	510-590
Average SAT Verbal	554
Range SAT Math	520-610
Average SAT Math	569
Projected Range SAT Writing	570-620
Range ACT Composite	23-26
Average ACT Composite	25
Minimum Paper TOEFL	550
Minimum Computer Based TOEFL	213
Average HS GPA	3.6

% graduated top 10% of class	10
% graduated top 25% of class	61
% graduated top 50% of class	94

DEADLINES

Early decision application deadline	12/1
Regular application deadline	3/1
Regular notification	3/15
Nonfall registration?	yes

FINANCIAL FACTS

Financial Aid Rating	**72**
Annual tuition	$20,100
Room & Board	$7,985
Books and supplies	$875
Required fees	$175
% frosh rec. need-based scholarship or grant aid	72
% UG rec. need-based scholarship or grant aid	70
% frosh rec. need-based self-help aid	55
% UG rec. need-based self-help aid	56
% frosh rec. any financial aid	84
% UG rec. any financial aid	84
Avg. frosh grant	$11,000
Avg. frosh loan	$2,800

SIMMONS COLLEGE

CAMPUS LIFE

Quality of Life Rating	**86**
Fire Safety Rating	**60**
Type of school	private
Environment	city

STUDENTS

Total undergrad enrollment	1,294
% male/female	0/100
% from out of state	43
% from public high school	81
% live on campus	75
% African American	6
% Asian	6
% Caucasian	68
% Hispanic	3
% international	4
# of countries represented	26

ACADEMICS

Academic Rating	**85**
Calendar	semester
Student/faculty ratio	12:1
Professors Interesting Rating	84
Professors Accessible Rating	83
% professors teaching UG courses	100
Most common lab size	10-19 students

MOST POPULAR MAJORS
communications studies/speech
communication and rhetoric
nursing/registered nurse training
(RN, ASN, BSN, MSN)

SELECTIVITY

Admissions Selectivity Rating	**84**
# of applicants	2,041
% of applicants accepted	67
% of acceptees attending	30
# accepting a place on wait list	46
% admitted from wait list	4

FRESHMAN PROFILE

Range SAT Verbal	510-610
Average SAT Verbal	558
Range SAT Math	500-590
Average SAT Math	539
Projected Range SAT Writing	570-640
Average ACT Composite	24
Minimum Paper TOEFL	560
Minimum Computer Based TOEFL	220
Average HS GPA	3.16
% graduated top 10% of class	20
% graduated top 25% of class	56
% graduated top 50% of class	89

DEADLINES

Regular application deadline	2/1
Regular notification	4/15
Nonfall registration?	yes

FINANCIAL FACTS

Financial Aid Rating	**77**
Annual tuition	$24,680
Room & Board	$10,200
Books and supplies	$800
Required fees	$760
% frosh rec. need-based scholarship or grant aid	83
% UG rec. need-based scholarship or grant aid	78
% frosh rec. need-based self-help aid	70
% UG rec. need-based self-help aid	71
% frosh rec. any financial aid	83
% UG rec. any financial aid	78
Avg. frosh grant	$9,177
Avg. frosh loan	$3,127

SIMON'S ROCK COLLEGE OF BARD

CAMPUS LIFE

Quality of Life Rating	**70**
Fire Safety Rating	**86**
Type of school	private
Environment	village

STUDENTS

Total undergrad enrollment	370

% male/female	42/58
% from out of state	80
% live on campus	85
% African American	2
% Asian	4
% Caucasian	48
% Hispanic	2
% Native American	1
% international	1

ACADEMICS

Academic Rating	**77**
Calendar	semester
Student/faculty ratio	8:1
Professors Interesting Rating	91
Professors Accessible Rating	87
% professors teaching UG courses	100
Most common lab size	10-19 students
Most common	
regular class size	fewer than 10 students

MOST POPULAR MAJORS
cell/cellular biology and histology
creative writing
psychology

SELECTIVITY

Admissions Selectivity Rating	**60**
# of applicants	247
% of applicants accepted	79
% of acceptees attending	72

FRESHMAN PROFILE

Range SAT Verbal	600-700
Average SAT Verbal	650
Range SAT Math	570-660
Average SAT Math	615
Projected Range SAT Writing	630-700
Range ACT Composite	24-30
Average ACT Composite	27
Minimum Paper TOEFL	550
Minimum Computer Based TOEFL	200

DEADLINES

Regular application deadline	7/1
Nonfall registration?	yes

FINANCIAL FACTS

Financial Aid Rating	**70**
Annual tuition	$30,687
Room & Board	$8,088
Books and supplies	$2,000
Required fees	$500
% frosh rec. need-based scholarship	
or grant aid	55
% UG rec. need-based scholarship	
or grant aid	48
% frosh rec. need-based self-help aid	46
% UG rec. need-based self-help aid	41
% frosh rec. any financial aid	78
% UG rec. any financial aid	71

Avg. frosh grant	$19,644
Avg. frosh loan	$2,625

SKIDMORE COLLEGE

CAMPUS LIFE

Quality of Life Rating	**85**
Fire Safety Rating	**60**
Type of school	private
Environment	town

STUDENTS

Total undergrad enrollment	2,609
% male/female	41/59
% from out of state	70
% from public high school	60
% live on campus	76
% African American	3
% Asian	5
% Caucasian	73
% Hispanic	4
% international	1
# of countries represented	28

ACADEMICS

Academic Rating	**89**
Calendar	semester
Student/faculty ratio	9:1
Professors Interesting Rating	84
Professors Accessible Rating	87
% professors teaching UG courses	100
Most common lab size	10-19 students
Most common	
regular class size	10-19 students

MOST POPULAR MAJORS
business administration/management
English language and literature
psychology

SELECTIVITY

Admissions Selectivity Rating	**93**
# of applicants	6,032
% of applicants accepted	48
% of acceptees attending	24
# accepting a place on wait list	996
# of early decision applicants	246
% accepted early decision	60

FRESHMAN PROFILE

Range SAT Verbal	580-670
Average SAT Verbal	626
Range SAT Math	580-670
Average SAT Math	624
Projected Range SAT Writing	620-680
Range ACT Composite	26-29
Average ACT Composite	27
Minimum Paper TOEFL	580
Minimum Computer Based TOEFL	243
Average HS GPA	3.32
% graduated top 10% of class	49

% graduated top 25% of class	81
% graduated top 50% of class	97

DEADLINES

Early decision application deadline	11/15
Regular application deadline	1/15
Regular notification	4/1
Nonfall registration?	yes

FINANCIAL FACTS

Financial Aid Rating	**93**
Annual tuition	$30,800
Room & Board	$8,710
Books and supplies	$750
Required fees	$308
% frosh rec. need-based scholarship	
or grant aid	40
% UG rec. need-based scholarship	
or grant aid	43
% frosh rec. need-based self-help aid	40
% UG rec. need-based self-help aid	43
% frosh rec. any financial aid	40
% UG rec. any financial aid	43
Avg. frosh grant	$21,445
Avg. frosh loan	$2,724

SLIPPERY ROCK UNIVERSITY OF PENNSYLVANIA

CAMPUS LIFE

Quality of Life Rating	**71**
Fire Safety Rating	**60**
Type of school	public
Environment	rural

STUDENTS

Total undergrad enrollment	6,889
% male/female	44/56
% from out of state	4
% from public high school	80
% live on campus	38
% in (# of) fraternities	2 (12)
% in (# of) sororities	2 (9)
% African American	4
% Asian	1
% Caucasian	89
% Hispanic	1
% international	2
# of countries represented	47

ACADEMICS

Academic Rating	**73**
Calendar	semester
Student/faculty ratio	20:1
Professors Interesting Rating	73
Professors Accessible Rating	75
% professors teaching UG courses	100
Most common lab size	20-29 students

Most common regular class size	20-29 students	% male/female	0/100	

Most common
regular class size   20-29 students

MOST POPULAR MAJORS
business/managerial operations
elementary education and teaching
health and physical education

SELECTIVITY
Admissions Selectivity Rating	**75**
# of applicants	4,310
% of applicants accepted	54
% of acceptees attending	64

FRESHMAN PROFILE
Range SAT Verbal	450-540
Average SAT Verbal	495
Range SAT Math	440-540
Average SAT Math	495
Projected Range SAT Writing	520-590
Range ACT Composite	19-23
Average ACT Composite	21
Minimum Paper TOEFL	500
Minimum Computer Based TOEFL	173
Average HS GPA	3.11
% graduated top 10% of class	7
% graduated top 25% of class	26
% graduated top 50% of class	63

DEADLINES
Regular application deadline	6/1
Regular notification	rolling
Nonfall registration?	yes

FINANCIAL FACTS
Financial Aid Rating	**86**
Annual in-state tuition	$4,598
Annual out-of-state tuition	$11,496
Room & Board	$4,542
Books and supplies	$1,000
Required fees	$1,203
% frosh rec. need-based scholarship or grant aid	51
% UG rec. need-based scholarship or grant aid	45
% frosh rec. need-based self-help aid	57
% UG rec. need-based self-help aid	52
% frosh rec. any financial aid	86
% UG rec. any financial aid	75
Avg. frosh grant	$2,907
Avg. frosh loan	$2,434

SMITH COLLEGE

CAMPUS LIFE
Quality of Life Rating	**95**
Fire Safety Rating	**73**
Type of school	private
Environment	town

STUDENTS
Total undergrad enrollment	2,692

% male/female	0/100
% from out of state	72
% from public high school	74
% live on campus	87
% African American	6
% Asian	10
% Caucasian	54
% Hispanic	6
% Native American	1
% international	7
# of countries represented	65

ACADEMICS
Academic Rating	**94**
Calendar	semester
Student/faculty ratio	9:1
Professors Interesting Rating	94
Professors Accessible Rating	88
% professors teaching UG courses	100
Most common lab size	10-19 students
Most common regular class size	10-19 students

MOST POPULAR MAJORS
political science and government
psychology
visual and performing arts

SELECTIVITY
Admissions Selectivity Rating	**94**
# of applicants	2,993
% of applicants accepted	57
% of acceptees attending	41
# accepting a place on wait list	255
# of early decision applicants	156
% accepted early decision	81

FRESHMAN PROFILE
Range SAT Verbal	590-700
Average SAT Verbal	640
Range SAT Math	570-670
Average SAT Math	620
Projected Range SAT Writing	620-700
Range ACT Composite	25-30
Average ACT Composite	27
Minimum Paper TOEFL	600
Minimum Computer Based TOEFL	250
Average HS GPA	3.8
% graduated top 10% of class	59
% graduated top 25% of class	90
% graduated top 50% of class	99

DEADLINES
Early decision application deadline	11/15
Regular application deadline	1/15
Regular notification	4/1
Nonfall registration?	no

FINANCIAL FACTS
Financial Aid Rating	**96**
Annual tuition	$27,330

Room & Board	$9,490
Books and supplies	$1,500
Required fees	$214
% frosh rec. need-based scholarship or grant aid	61
% UG rec. need-based scholarship or grant aid	60
% frosh rec. need-based self-help aid	61
% UG rec. need-based self-help aid	60
% frosh rec. any financial aid	63
% UG rec. any financial aid	74
Avg. frosh grant	$22,721
Avg. frosh loan	$2,109

ST. BONAVENTURE UNIVERSITY

CAMPUS LIFE
Quality of Life Rating	**69**
Fire Safety Rating	**60**
Type of school	private
Affiliation	Roman Catholic
Environment	rural

STUDENTS
Total undergrad enrollment	2,170
% male/female	50/50
% from out of state	24
% from public high school	70
% live on campus	79
% African American	2
% Asian	1
% Caucasian	54
% Hispanic	1
% international	2
# of countries represented	22

ACADEMICS
Academic Rating	**77**
Calendar	semester
Student/faculty ratio	15:1
Professors Interesting Rating	83
Professors Accessible Rating	83
% professors teaching UG courses	100
Most common lab size	10-19 students
Most common regular class size	10-19 students

MOST POPULAR MAJORS
business administration/management
elementary education and teaching
journalism

SELECTIVITY
Admissions Selectivity Rating	**74**
# of applicants	1,834
% of applicants accepted	85
% of acceptees attending	37

FRESHMAN PROFILE
Range SAT Verbal	480-580

Average SAT Verbal 524
Range SAT Math 490-590
Average SAT Math 535
Projected Range SAT Writing 540-620
Range ACT Composite 19-24
Average ACT Composite 22
Minimum Paper TOEFL 550
Minimum Computer Based TOEFL 213
Average HS GPA 3.1
% graduated top 10% of class 11
% graduated top 25% of class 36
% graduated top 50% of class 71

DEADLINES
Regular application deadline 4/15
Regular notification rolling
Nonfall registration? yes

FINANCIAL FACTS
Financial Aid Rating 78
Annual tuition $18,650
Room & Board $6,910
Books and supplies $600
Required fees $835
% frosh rec. need-based scholarship
  or grant aid 75
% UG rec. need-based scholarship
  or grant aid 71
% frosh rec. need-based self-help aid 64
% UG rec. need-based self-help aid 60
Avg. frosh grant $10,928
Avg. frosh loan $3,410

ST. JOHN'S COLLEGE (MD)

CAMPUS LIFE
Quality of Life Rating 93
Fire Safety Rating 87
Type of school private
Environment town

STUDENTS
Total undergrad enrollment 473
% male/female 55/45
% from out of state 85
% from public high school 58
% live on campus 73
% African American 1
% Asian 2
% Caucasian 89
% Hispanic 3
% Native American 1
% international 1
# of countries represented 12

ACADEMICS
Academic Rating 98
Calendar semester
Student/faculty ratio 9:1
Professors Interesting Rating 97
Professors Accessible Rating 94
% professors teaching UG courses 100
Most common lab size 10-19 students

MOST POPULAR MAJORS
liberal arts and sciences studies
and humanities

SELECTIVITY
Admissions Selectivity Rating 90
# of applicants 535
% of applicants accepted 67
% of acceptees attending 38

FRESHMAN PROFILE
Range SAT Verbal 660-760
Range SAT Math 600-690
Projected Range SAT Writing 670-740
Minimum Paper TOEFL 600
Minimum Computer Based TOEFL 250
% graduated top 10% of class 47
% graduated top 25% of class 74
% graduated top 50% of class 93

DEADLINES
Regular notification 2 weeks after completed
application is received
Nonfall registration? yes

FINANCIAL FACTS
Financial Aid Rating 76
Annual tuition $30,570
Room & Board $7,610
Books and supplies $275
Required fees $200
% frosh rec. need-based scholarship
  or grant aid 44
% UG rec. need-based scholarship
  or grant aid 50
% frosh rec. need-based self-help aid 59
% UG rec. need-based self-help aid 54
% frosh rec. any financial aid 60
% UG rec. any financial aid 60
Avg. frosh grant $16,498
Avg. frosh loan $3,125

ST. JOHN'S UNIVERSITY

CAMPUS LIFE
Quality of Life Rating 66
Fire Safety Rating 80
Type of school private
Affiliation Roman Catholic
Environment metropolis

STUDENTS
Total undergrad enrollment 12,302
% male/female 42/58
% from out of state 10
% live on campus 17
% in (# of) fraternities 8 (23)
% in (# of) sororities 7 (23)
% African American 17
% Asian 15
% Caucasian 41
% Hispanic 15
% international 3
# of countries represented 130

ACADEMICS
Academic Rating 70
Calendar semester
Student/faculty ratio 18:1
Professors Interesting Rating 61
Professors Accessible Rating 62
% professors teaching UG courses 91
Most common lab size 20-29 students
Most common
  regular class size 20-29 students

MOST POPULAR MAJORS
criminal justice/law enforcement
administration
finance
pharmacy (PharMD, BS/BPharM)

SELECTIVITY
Admissions Selectivity Rating 82
# of applicants 17,632
% of applicants accepted 62
% of acceptees attending 27

FRESHMAN PROFILE
Range SAT Verbal 460-570
Average SAT Verbal 516
Range SAT Math 470-590
Average SAT Math 535
Projected Range SAT Writing 530-610
Minimum Paper TOEFL 500
Minimum Computer Based TOEFL 173
Average HS GPA 3.5
% graduated top 10% of class 23
% graduated top 25% of class 51
% graduated top 50% of class 80

DEADLINES
Nonfall registration? yes

FINANCIAL FACTS
Financial Aid Rating 72
Annual tuition $22,800
Room & Board $11,000
Books and supplies $1,000
Required fees $480
% frosh rec. need-based scholarship
  or grant aid 75
% UG rec. need-based scholarship
  or grant aid 72
% frosh rec. need-based self-help aid 80
% UG rec. need-based self-help aid 79
% frosh rec. any financial aid 96
% UG rec. any financial aid 91

Avg. frosh grant	$11,852
Avg. frosh loan	$4,081

ST. LAWRENCE UNIVERSITY

CAMPUS LIFE

Quality of Life Rating	**76**
Fire Safety Rating	**67**
Type of school	private
Environment	village

STUDENTS

Total undergrad enrollment	2,102
% male/female	48/52
% from out of state	50
% from public high school	68
% live on campus	95
% in (# of) fraternities	12 (3)
% in (# of) sororities	21 (4)
% African American	2
% Asian	1
% Caucasian	69
% Hispanic	3
% international	4
# of countries represented	24

ACADEMICS

Academic Rating	**88**
Calendar	semester
Student/faculty ratio	11:1
Professors Interesting Rating	87
Professors Accessible Rating	88
% professors teaching UG courses	98
Most common lab size	10-19 students
Most common regular class size	10-19 students

MOST POPULAR MAJORS
English language and literature
political science and government
psychology

SELECTIVITY

Admissions Selectivity Rating	**89**
# of applicants	2,985
% of applicants accepted	61
% of acceptees attending	31
# accepting a place on wait list	312
% admitted from wait list	8
# of early decision applicants	122
% accepted early decision	75

FRESHMAN PROFILE

Range SAT Verbal	530-630
Average SAT Verbal	583
Range SAT Math	540-620
Average SAT Math	580
Projected Range SAT Writing	580-650
Range ACT Composite	23-27
Average ACT Composite	25
Minimum Paper TOEFL	600

Minimum Computer Based TOEFL	250
Average HS GPA	3.43
% graduated top 10% of class	37
% graduated top 25% of class	73
% graduated top 50% of class	95

DEADLINES

Early decision application deadline	11/15
Regular application deadline	2/15
Regular notification	3/30
Nonfall registration?	yes

FINANCIAL FACTS

Financial Aid Rating	**86**
Annual tuition	$30,270
Room & Board	$7,755
Books and supplies	$650
Required fees	$210
% frosh rec. need-based scholarship or grant aid	66
% UG rec. need-based scholarship or grant aid	67
% frosh rec. need-based self-help aid	61
% UG rec. need-based self-help aid	62
% frosh rec. any financial aid	84
% UG rec. any financial aid	83
Avg. frosh grant	$18,835
Avg. frosh loan	$4,448

ST. MARY'S COLLEGE OF MARYLAND

CAMPUS LIFE

Quality of Life Rating	**91**
Fire Safety Rating	**70**
Type of school	public
Environment	rural

STUDENTS

Total undergrad enrollment	1,858
% male/female	42/58
% from out of state	18
% from public high school	79
% live on campus	81
% African American	7
% Asian	4
% Caucasian	80
% Hispanic	3
% international	1
# of countries represented	29

ACADEMICS

Academic Rating	**86**
Calendar	semester
Student/faculty ratio	13:1
Professors Interesting Rating	89
Professors Accessible Rating	93
% professors teaching UG courses	100
Most common lab size	10-19 students

Most common regular class size	10-19 students

MOST POPULAR MAJORS
economics
English language and literature
psychology

SELECTIVITY

Admissions Selectivity Rating	**89**
# of applicants	2,321
% of applicants accepted	57
% of acceptees attending	32
# accepting a place on wait list	340
% admitted from wait list	5
# of early decision applicants	176
% accepted early decision	69

FRESHMAN PROFILE

Range SAT Verbal	580-690
Average SAT Verbal	631
Range SAT Math	570-660
Average SAT Math	616
Projected Range SAT Writing	620-690
Minimum Paper TOEFL	550
Minimum Computer Based TOEFL	260
Average HS GPA	3.45
% graduated top 10% of class	39
% graduated top 25% of class	70
% graduated top 50% of class	90

DEADLINES

Early decision application deadline	12/1
Regular application deadline	1/15
Regular notification	4/1
Nonfall registration?	yes

FINANCIAL FACTS

Financial Aid Rating	**82**
Annual in-state tuition	$9,063
Annual out-of-state tuition	$17,940
Room & Board	$7,980
Books and supplies	$1,000
Required fees	$1,833
% frosh rec. need-based scholarship or grant aid	19
% UG rec. need-based scholarship or grant aid	19
% frosh rec. need-based self-help aid	19
% UG rec. need-based self-help aid	19
% frosh rec. any financial aid	59
% UG rec. any financial aid	62
Avg. frosh grant	$6,495
Avg. frosh loan	$2,625

STEVENS INSTITUTE OF TECHNOLOGY

CAMPUS LIFE

Quality of Life Rating	**75**
Fire Safety Rating	**98**

Type of school	private
Environment	village

STUDENTS

Total undergrad enrollment	1,726
% male/female	76/24
% from out of state	35
% from public high school	80
% live on campus	75
% in (# of) fraternities	34 (10)
% in (# of) sororities	31 (3)
% African American	4
% Asian	16
% Caucasian	53
% Hispanic	9
% international	7
# of countries represented	52

ACADEMICS

Academic Rating	72
Calendar	semester
Student/faculty ratio	9:1
Professors Interesting Rating	61
Professors Accessible Rating	61
% professors teaching UG courses	100
Most common lab size	10-19 students
Most common regular class size	10-19 students

MOST POPULAR MAJORS
computer and information sciences
computer engineering
mechanical engineering

SELECTIVITY

Admissions Selectivity Rating	89
# of applicants	2,195
% of applicants accepted	53
% of acceptees attending	38
# accepting a place on wait list	220
% admitted from wait list	5
# of early decision applicants	87
% accepted early decision	83

FRESHMAN PROFILE

Range SAT Verbal	560-670
Range SAT Math	630-720
Projected Range SAT Writing	600-680
Range ACT Composite	25-30
Minimum Paper TOEFL	550
Minimum Computer Based TOEFL	213
Average HS GPA	3.8
% graduated top 10% of class	52
% graduated top 25% of class	32
% graduated top 50% of class	98

DEADLINES

Early decision application deadline	11/15
Regular application deadline	2/15
Regular notification	3/15
Nonfall registration?	no

FINANCIAL FACTS

Financial Aid Rating	71
Annual tuition	$27,300
Room & Board	$8,930
Books and supplies	$900
Required fees	$250
% frosh rec. need-based scholarship or grant aid	56
% UG rec. need-based scholarship or grant aid	54
% frosh rec. need-based self-help aid	58
% UG rec. need-based self-help aid	60
% frosh rec. any financial aid	83
% UG rec. any financial aid	76
Avg. frosh grant	$24,523
Avg. frosh loan	$3,748

STONEHILL COLLEGE

CAMPUS LIFE

Quality of Life Rating	88
Fire Safety Rating	84
Type of school	private
Affiliation	Roman Catholic
Environment	village

STUDENTS

Total undergrad enrollment	2,401
% male/female	40/60
% from out of state	40
% from public high school	71
% live on campus	82
% African American	3
% Asian	3
% Caucasian	90
% Hispanic	3
% international	1
# of countries represented	8

ACADEMICS

Academic Rating	87
Calendar	semester
Student/faculty ratio	14:1
Professors Interesting Rating	82
Professors Accessible Rating	87
% professors teaching UG courses	100
Most common lab size	20-29 students
Most common regular class size	20-29 students

MOST POPULAR MAJORS
biology/biological sciences
communications studies/speech communication and rhetoric
psychology

SELECTIVITY

Admissions Selectivity Rating	92
# of applicants	4,651
% of applicants accepted	57
% of acceptees attending	23
# accepting a place on wait list	637
% admitted from wait list	29
# of early decision applicants	53
% accepted early decision	65

FRESHMAN PROFILE

Range SAT Verbal	550-630
Average SAT Verbal	590
Range SAT Math	550-630
Average SAT Math	590
Projected Range SAT Writing	600-650
Range ACT Composite	23-27
Average ACT Composite	25
Minimum Paper TOEFL	550
Minimum Computer Based TOEFL	213
Average HS GPA	3.56
% graduated top 10% of class	49
% graduated top 25% of class	88
% graduated top 50% of class	100

DEADLINES

Early decision application deadline	11/1
Regular application deadline	1/15
Regular notification	4/1
Nonfall registration?	yes

FINANCIAL FACTS

Financial Aid Rating	73
Annual tuition	$24,160
Room & Board	$10,564
Books and supplies	$1,200
% frosh rec. need-based scholarship or grant aid	64
% UG rec. need-based scholarship or grant aid	63
% frosh rec. need-based self-help aid	59
% UG rec. need-based self-help aid	60
% frosh rec. any financial aid	91
% UG rec. any financial aid	92
Avg. frosh grant	$11,267
Avg. frosh loan	$4,605

SUFFOLK UNIVERSITY

CAMPUS LIFE

Quality of Life Rating	91
Fire Safety Rating	98
Type of school	private
Environment	metropolis

STUDENTS

Total undergrad enrollment	4,244
% male/female	42/58
% from out of state	18
% from public high school	66
% live on campus	18
% African American	3
% Asian	7
% Caucasian	61

% Hispanic 5
% international 10
# of countries represented 100

ACADEMICS
Academic Rating **73**
Calendar semester
Student/faculty ratio 12:1
Professors Interesting Rating 81
Professors Accessible Rating 76
% professors teaching UG courses 90
% classes taught by TAs 1
Most common lab size 20-29 students
Most common
regular class size 10-19 students
MOST POPULAR MAJORS
business administration/management
communications studies/speech
communication and rhetoric
sociology

SELECTIVITY
Admissions Selectivity Rating **70**
# of applicants 5,006
% of applicants accepted 85
% of acceptees attending 24
# accepting a place on wait list 60
% admitted from wait list 13

FRESHMAN PROFILE
Range SAT Verbal 450-550
Average SAT Verbal 506
Range SAT Math 450-550
Average SAT Math 497
Projected Range SAT Writing 520-600
Range ACT Composite 17-22
Minimum Paper TOEFL 525
Minimum Computer Based TOEFL 197
Average HS GPA 2.92
% graduated top 10% of class 5
% graduated top 25% of class 25
% graduated top 50% of class 63

DEADLINES
Regular notification rolling
Nonfall registration? yes

FINANCIAL FACTS
Financial Aid Rating **66**
Annual tuition $21,140
Room & Board $10,020
Books and supplies $1,000
Required fees $80
% frosh rec. need-based scholarship
or grant aid 51
% UG rec. need-based scholarship
or grant aid 47
% frosh rec. need-based self-help aid 57
% UG rec. need-based self-help aid 53
% frosh rec. any financial aid 77

% UG rec. any financial aid 70
Avg. frosh grant $6,175
Avg. frosh loan $3,615

SUNY AT ALBANY

CAMPUS LIFE
Quality of Life Rating **61**
Fire Safety Rating **81**
Type of school public
Environment city

STUDENTS
Total undergrad enrollment 10,968
% male/female 50/50
% from out of state 5
% live on campus 58
% in (# of) fraternities 2 (19)
% in (# of) sororities 5 (15)
% African American 8
% Asian 6
% Caucasian 62
% Hispanic 7
% international 2
# of countries represented 87

ACADEMICS
Academic Rating **65**
Calendar semester
Student/faculty ratio 19:1
Professors Interesting Rating 61
Professors Accessible Rating 61
% professors teaching UG courses 93
% classes taught by TAs 13
Most common lab size 20-29 students
Most common
regular class size 10-19 students
MOST POPULAR MAJORS
business administration/management
English language and literature
psychology

SELECTIVITY
Admissions Selectivity Rating **85**
# of applicants 17,171
% of applicants accepted 56
% of acceptees attending 21

FRESHMAN PROFILE
Range SAT Verbal 510-600
Range SAT Math 530-620
Projected Range SAT Writing 570-630
Minimum Paper TOEFL 550
Minimum Computer Based TOEFL 213
Average HS GPA 3.37
% graduated top 10% of class 20
% graduated top 25% of class 57
% graduated top 50% of class 95

DEADLINES
Regular application deadline 3/1

Regular notification rolling
Nonfall registration? yes

FINANCIAL FACTS
Financial Aid Rating **71**
Annual in-state tuition $4,350
Annual out-of-state tuition $10,610
Room & Board $7,540
Books and supplies $800
Required fees $1,460
% frosh rec. need-based scholarship
or grant aid 50
% UG rec. need-based scholarship
or grant aid 50
% frosh rec. need-based self-help aid 45
% UG rec. need-based self-help aid 46
% frosh rec. any financial aid 63
% UG rec. any financial aid 60
Avg. frosh grant $5,312
Avg. frosh loan $3,334

SUNY AT BINGHAMTON

CAMPUS LIFE
Quality of Life Rating **62**
Fire Safety Rating **63**
Type of school public
Environment town

STUDENTS
Total undergrad enrollment 10,898
% male/female 51/49
% from out of state 6
% from public high school 87
% live on campus 58
% in (# of) fraternities 8 (20)
% in (# of) sororities 7 (15)
% African American 5
% Asian 17
% Caucasian 52
% Hispanic 6
% international 4
# of countries represented 87

ACADEMICS
Academic Rating **75**
Calendar semester
Student/faculty ratio 22:1
Professors Interesting Rating 63
Professors Accessible Rating 62
% professors teaching UG courses 90
% classes taught by TAs 9
Most common lab size 20-29 students
Most common
regular class size 20-29 students
MOST POPULAR MAJORS
business administration/management
English language and literature
psychology

SELECTIVITY

Admissions Selectivity Rating	**92**
# of applicants	20,116
% of applicants accepted	44
% of acceptees attending	24
# accepting a place on wait list	622
% admitted from wait list	34

FRESHMAN PROFILE

Range SAT Verbal	570-650
Average SAT Verbal	607
Range SAT Math	600-690
Average SAT Math	643
Projected Range SAT Writing	610-670
Range ACT Composite	24-28
Average ACT Composite	26
Minimum Paper TOEFL	550
Minimum Computer Based TOEFL	213
Average HS GPA	3.6
% graduated top 10% of class	40
% graduated top 25% of class	83
% graduated top 50% of class	99

DEADLINES

Regular notification	rolling
Nonfall registration?	yes

FINANCIAL FACTS

Financial Aid Rating	**83**
Annual in-state tuition	$4,350
Annual out-of-state tuition	$10,610
Room & Board	$7,710
Books and supplies	$800
Required fees	$1,406
% frosh rec. need-based scholarship or grant aid	41
% UG rec. need-based scholarship or grant aid	44
% frosh rec. need-based self-help aid	43
% UG rec. need-based self-help aid	46
% frosh rec. any financial aid	81
% UG rec. any financial aid	72
Avg. frosh grant	$4,415
Avg. frosh loan	$3,291

SUNY AT BUFFALO

CAMPUS LIFE

Quality of Life Rating	**70**
Fire Safety Rating	**70**
Type of school	public
Environment	metropolis

STUDENTS

Total undergrad enrollment	17,509
% male/female	54/46
% from out of state	2
% live on campus	38
% in (# of) fraternities	2 (19)
% in (# of) sororities	4 (14)

% African American	7
% Asian	9
% Caucasian	65
% Hispanic	4
% international	6
# of countries represented	113

ACADEMICS

Academic Rating	**70**
Calendar	semester
Student/faculty ratio	15:1
Professors Interesting Rating	62
Professors Accessible Rating	62
% professors teaching UG courses	73
% classes taught by TAs	12
Most common lab size	20-29 students
Most common regular class size	20-29 students

MOST POPULAR MAJORS
business administration/management
mechanical engineering
psychology

SELECTIVITY

Admissions Selectivity Rating	**86**
# of applicants	18,207
% of applicants accepted	56
% of acceptees attending	31
# accepting a place on wait list	1,000
% admitted from wait list	10
# of early decision applicants	406
% accepted early decision	74

FRESHMAN PROFILE

Range SAT Verbal	520-610
Average SAT Verbal	556
Range SAT Math	550-640
Average SAT Math	584
Projected Range SAT Writing	570-640
Range ACT Composite	24-28
Average ACT Composite	24
Minimum Paper TOEFL	550
Minimum Computer Based TOEFL	213
Average HS GPA	3.1
% graduated top 10% of class	24
% graduated top 25% of class	62
% graduated top 50% of class	94

DEADLINES

Early decision application deadline	11/1
Regular notification	rolling
Nonfall registration?	yes

FINANCIAL FACTS

Financial Aid Rating	**78**
Annual in-state tuition	$4,350
Annual out-of-state tuition	$10,610
Room & Board	$8,086
Books and supplies	$795
Required fees	$1,616

% frosh rec. need-based scholarship or grant aid	35
% UG rec. need-based scholarship or grant aid	33
% frosh rec. need-based self-help aid	52
% UG rec. need-based self-help aid	50
% frosh rec. any financial aid	67
% UG rec. any financial aid	75
Avg. frosh grant	$3,282
Avg. frosh loan	$3,414

SUNY AT STONY BROOK

CAMPUS LIFE

Quality of Life Rating	**62**
Fire Safety Rating	**60**
Type of school	public
Environment	town

STUDENTS

Total undergrad enrollment	13,694
% male/female	51/49
% from out of state	4
% from public high school	90
% live on campus	59
% in (# of) fraternities	1 (16)
% in (# of) sororities	1 (16)
% African American	10
% Asian	23
% Caucasian	36
% Hispanic	8
% international	5
# of countries represented	90

ACADEMICS

Academic Rating	**73**
Calendar	semester
Student/faculty ratio	14:1
Professors Interesting Rating	61
Professors Accessible Rating	61
% professors teaching UG courses	88
Most common lab size	10-19 students
Most common regular class size	20-29 students

MOST POPULAR MAJORS
biology/biological sciences
health professions and related sciences
psychology

SELECTIVITY

Admissions Selectivity Rating	**89**
# of applicants	17,701
% of applicants accepted	49
% of acceptees attending	25

FRESHMAN PROFILE

Range SAT Verbal	510-620
Average SAT Verbal	565
Range SAT Math	560-660
Average SAT Math	611

Projected Range SAT Writing	570-650
Minimum Paper TOEFL	550
Minimum Computer Based TOEFL	213
Average HS GPA	3.6
% graduated top 10% of class	33
% graduated top 25% of class	69
% graduated top 50% of class	97

DEADLINES

Regular notification	2/1
Nonfall registration?	yes

FINANCIAL FACTS

Financial Aid Rating	**67**
Annual in-state tuition	$4,350
Annual out-of-state tuition	$10,610
Room & Board	$7,730
Books and supplies	$900
Required fees	$1,039
% frosh rec. need-based scholarship or grant aid	53
% UG rec. need-based scholarship or grant aid	53
% frosh rec. need-based self-help aid	44
% UG rec. need-based self-help aid	47
% frosh rec. any financial aid	76
% UG rec. any financial aid	72
Avg. frosh grant	$5,548
Avg. frosh loan	$2,905

SUNY COLLEGE AT BROCKPORT

CAMPUS LIFE

Quality of Life Rating	**74**
Fire Safety Rating	**79**
Type of school	public
Environment	village

STUDENTS

Total undergrad enrollment	6,854
% male/female	43/57
% from out of state	1
% live on campus	36
% in (# of) sororities	1 (4)
% African American	5
% Asian	1
% Caucasian	79
% Hispanic	3
% international	1
# of countries represented	30

ACADEMICS

Academic Rating	**74**
Calendar	semester
Student/faculty ratio	18:1
Professors Interesting Rating	65
Professors Accessible Rating	67
% professors teaching UG courses	95

Most common lab size	20-29 students
Most common regular class size	20-29 students

MOST POPULAR MAJORS

business administration/management
physical education teaching and coaching
psychology

SELECTIVITY

Admissions Selectivity Rating	**79**
# of applicants	7,283
% of applicants accepted	50
% of acceptees attending	29

FRESHMAN PROFILE

Range SAT Verbal	500-580
Average SAT Verbal	550
Range SAT Math	480-560
Average SAT Math	520
Projected Range SAT Writing	560-620
Range ACT Composite	20-25
Minimum Paper TOEFL	530
Minimum Computer Based TOEFL	197
Average HS GPA	3.3
% graduated top 10% of class	13
% graduated top 25% of class	34
% graduated top 50% of class	86

DEADLINES

Regular notification	rolling
Nonfall registration?	yes

FINANCIAL FACTS

Financial Aid Rating	**86**
Annual in-state tuition	$4,350
Annual out-of-state tuition	$10,300
Room & Board	$7,226
Books and supplies	$900
Required fees	$913
% frosh rec. need-based scholarship or grant aid	65
% UG rec. need-based scholarship or grant aid	50
% frosh rec. need-based self-help aid	62
% UG rec. need-based self-help aid	56
% frosh rec. any financial aid	62
% UG rec. any financial aid	76
Avg. frosh grant	$2,667
Avg. frosh loan	$3,191

SUNY COLLEGE AT FREDONIA

CAMPUS LIFE

Quality of Life Rating	**69**
Fire Safety Rating	**60**
Type of school	public
Environment	rural

STUDENTS

Total undergrad enrollment	4,824
% male/female	41/59

% from out of state	2
% from public high school	75
% live on campus	49
% in (# of) fraternities	5 (4)
% in (# of) sororities	3 (3)
% African American	1
% Asian	1
% Caucasian	94
% Hispanic	2
% Native American	1
% international	1
# of countries represented	8

ACADEMICS

Academic Rating	**77**
Calendar	semester
Student/faculty ratio	17:1
Professors Interesting Rating	65
Professors Accessible Rating	62
% professors teaching UG courses	100
Most common lab size	fewer than 10 students
Most common regular class size	20-29 students

MOST POPULAR MAJORS

business administration/management
elementary education and teaching
music teacher education

SELECTIVITY

Admissions Selectivity Rating	**82**
# of applicants	5,887
% of applicants accepted	56
% of acceptees attending	32
# accepting a place on wait list	307
% admitted from wait list	9
# of early decision applicants	54
% accepted early decision	75

FRESHMAN PROFILE

Range SAT Verbal	510-590
Average SAT Verbal	554
Range SAT Math	510-590
Average SAT Math	560
Projected Range SAT Writing	570-620
Range ACT Composite	21-26
Average ACT Composite	24
Minimum Paper TOEFL	500
Minimum Computer Based TOEFL	173
Average HS GPA	3.34
% graduated top 10% of class	15
% graduated top 25% of class	45
% graduated top 50% of class	90

DEADLINES

Early decision application deadline	11/1
Regular notification	rolling
Nonfall registration?	yes

FINANCIAL FACTS
Financial Aid Rating   **86**

Annual in-state tuition	$4,350
Annual out-of-state tuition	$10,300
Room & Board	$7,120
Books and supplies	$620
Required fees	$1,112
% frosh rec. need-based scholarship or grant aid	60
% UG rec. need-based scholarship or grant aid	55
% frosh rec. need-based self-help aid	54
% UG rec. need-based self-help aid	52
Avg. frosh grant	$2,581
Avg. frosh loan	$2,944

SUNY COLLEGE AT GENESEO

CAMPUS LIFE
Quality of Life Rating   **72**
Fire Safety Rating   **65**

Type of school	public
Environment	rural

STUDENTS

Total undergrad enrollment	5,375
% male/female	39/61
% from out of state	1
% from public high school	80
% live on campus	55
% in (# of) fraternities	10 (8)
% in (# of) sororities	12 (11)
% African American	2
% Asian	5
% Caucasian	83
% Hispanic	3
% international	2
# of countries represented	34

ACADEMICS
Academic Rating   **78**

Calendar	semester
Student/faculty ratio	19:1
Professors Interesting Rating	73
Professors Accessible Rating	73
% professors teaching UG courses	100
Most common lab size	20-29 students

MOST POPULAR MAJORS
biology/biological sciences
business administration/management
education

SELECTIVITY
Admissions Selectivity Rating   **93**

# of applicants	8,661
% of applicants accepted	44
% of acceptees attending	27
# accepting a place on wait list	1,314
% admitted from wait list	2

# of early decision applicants	107
% accepted early decision	58

FRESHMAN PROFILE

Range SAT Verbal	600-670
Average SAT Verbal	621
Range SAT Math	600-670
Average SAT Math	631
Projected Range SAT Writing	630-680
Range ACT Composite	26-28
Average ACT Composite	27
Minimum Paper TOEFL	525
Minimum Computer Based TOEFL	197
Average HS GPA	3.7
% graduated top 10% of class	50
% graduated top 25% of class	86
% graduated top 50% of class	99

DEADLINES

Early decision application deadline	11/15
Regular application deadline	1/15
Regular notification	rolling
Nonfall registration?	yes

FINANCIAL FACTS
Financial Aid Rating   **60**

Annual in-state tuition	$4,350
Annual out-of-state tuition	$10,610
Room & Board	$6,820
Books and supplies	$700
Required fees	$1,085
% frosh rec. need-based scholarship or grant aid	40
% UG rec. need-based scholarship or grant aid	47
% frosh rec. need-based self-help aid	40
% UG rec. need-based self-help aid	47
% frosh rec. any financial aid	65
% UG rec. any financial aid	76
Avg. frosh grant	$1,900
Avg. frosh loan	$3,200

SUNY COLLEGE AT NEW PALTZ

CAMPUS LIFE
Quality of Life Rating   **77**
Fire Safety Rating   **60**

Type of school	public
Environment	rural

STUDENTS

Total undergrad enrollment	6,169
% male/female	32/68
% from out of state	3
% from public high school	92
% live on campus	49
% in (# of) fraternities	3 (10)
% in (# of) sororities	2 (14)
% Asian	4
% Caucasian	58

% Hispanic	9
% international	2

ACADEMICS
Academic Rating   **77**

Calendar	semester
Student/faculty ratio	16:1
Professors Interesting Rating	71
Professors Accessible Rating	72
% professors teaching UG courses	98
Most common lab size	10-19 students
Most common regular class size	10-19 students

MOST POPULAR MAJORS
business administration/management
sociology
special education

SELECTIVITY
Admissions Selectivity Rating   **87**

# of applicants	11,359
% of applicants accepted	40
% of acceptees attending	19
# accepting a place on wait list	300
% admitted from wait list	1

FRESHMAN PROFILE

Range SAT Verbal	500-600
Average SAT Verbal	545
Range SAT Math	510-600
Average SAT Math	551
Projected Range SAT Writing	560-630
Minimum Paper TOEFL	550
Minimum Computer Based TOEFL	213
Average HS GPA	3.3
% graduated top 10% of class	17
% graduated top 25% of class	60
% graduated top 50% of class	95

DEADLINES

Regular application deadline	3/31
Regular notification	rolling
Nonfall registration?	no

FINANCIAL FACTS
Financial Aid Rating   **72**

Annual in-state tuition	$4,350
Annual out-of-state tuition	$10,300
Room & Board	$6,860
Books and supplies	$1,100
Required fees	$870
% frosh rec. need-based scholarship or grant aid	50
% UG rec. need-based scholarship or grant aid	49
% frosh rec. need-based self-help aid	49
% UG rec. need-based self-help aid	47
Avg. frosh grant	$2,205
Avg. frosh loan	$2,149

SUNY COLLEGE AT OSWEGO

CAMPUS LIFE

Quality of Life Rating	**71**
Fire Safety Rating	**68**
Type of school	public
Environment	village

STUDENTS

Total undergrad enrollment	6,945
% male/female	46/54
% from out of state	2
% live on campus	57
% in (# of) fraternities	7 (17)
% in (# of) sororities	6 (12)
% African American	4
% Asian	2
% Caucasian	89
% Hispanic	4
% international	1
# of countries represented	30

ACADEMICS

Academic Rating	**72**
Calendar	semester
Student/faculty ratio	18:1
Professors Interesting Rating	67
Professors Accessible Rating	67
% professors teaching UG courses	93
Most common lab size	20-29 students
Most common	
regular class size	10-19 students

MOST POPULAR MAJORS
business administration/management
communications studies/speech
communication and rhetoric
elementary education and teaching

SELECTIVITY

Admissions Selectivity Rating	**80**
# of applicants	7,466
% of applicants accepted	57
% of acceptees attending	32
# of early decision applicants	73
% accepted early decision	66

FRESHMAN PROFILE

Range SAT Verbal	500-580
Average SAT Verbal	543
Range SAT Math	520-590
Average SAT Math	546
Projected Range SAT Writing	560-620
Range ACT Composite	21-25
Average ACT Composite	23
Minimum Paper TOEFL	550
Minimum Computer Based TOEFL	213
Average HS GPA	3.22
% graduated top 10% of class	10
% graduated top 25% of class	50
% graduated top 50% of class	84

DEADLINES

Early decision application deadline	11/15
Regular notification	rolling
Nonfall registration?	yes

FINANCIAL FACTS

Financial Aid Rating	**78**
Annual in-state tuition	$4,350
Annual out-of-state tuition	$10,610
Room & Board	$7,890
Books and supplies	$800
Required fees	$888
% frosh rec. need-based scholarship or grant aid	62
% UG rec. need-based scholarship or grant aid	61
% frosh rec. need-based self-help aid	57
% UG rec. need-based self-help aid	59
Avg. frosh grant	$2,300
Avg. frosh loan	$2,625

SUNY—PURCHASE COLLEGE

CAMPUS LIFE

Quality of Life Rating	**62**
Fire Safety Rating	**60**
Type of school	public
Environment	town

STUDENTS

Total undergrad enrollment	3,344
% male/female	45/55
% from out of state	17
% live on campus	65
% African American	8
% Asian	4
% Caucasian	62
% Hispanic	10
% international	2
# of countries represented	33

ACADEMICS

Academic Rating	**79**
Calendar	semester
Student/faculty ratio	14:1
Professors Interesting Rating	80
Professors Accessible Rating	67
% professors teaching UG courses	100
% classes taught by TAs	1
Most common lab size	10-19 students
Most common	
regular class size	10-19 students

MOST POPULAR MAJORS
liberal arts and sciences/liberal studies
psychology
visual and performing arts

SELECTIVITY

Admissions Selectivity Rating	**85**
# of applicants	6,899
% of applicants accepted	29
% of acceptees attending	32
# of early decision applicants	6
% accepted early decision	75

FRESHMAN PROFILE

Range SAT Verbal	520-620
Average SAT Verbal	576
Range SAT Math	490-590
Average SAT Math	543
Projected Range SAT Writing	570-650
Minimum Paper TOEFL	550
Minimum Computer Based TOEFL	213
Average HS GPA	3.04
% graduated top 10% of class	9
% graduated top 25% of class	40
% graduated top 50% of class	74

DEADLINES

Early decision application deadline	11/1
Regular notification	5/1
Nonfall registration?	yes

FINANCIAL FACTS

Financial Aid Rating	**66**
Annual in-state tuition	$4,350
Annual out-of-state tuition	$10,610
Room & Board	$7,540
Books and supplies	$1,100
Required fees	$1,092
% frosh rec. need-based scholarship or grant aid	40
% UG rec. need-based scholarship or grant aid	38
% frosh rec. need-based self-help aid	52
% UG rec. need-based self-help aid	50
% frosh rec. any financial aid	80
% UG rec. any financial aid	66
Avg. frosh grant	$5,285
Avg. frosh loan	$3,305

SUSQUEHANNA UNIVERSITY

CAMPUS LIFE

Quality of Life Rating	**79**
Fire Safety Rating	**70**
Type of school	private
Affiliation	Lutheran
Environment	village

STUDENTS

Total undergrad enrollment	1,972
% male/female	44/56
% from out of state	40
% from public high school	85
% live on campus	77
% in (# of) fraternities	21 (5)
% in (# of) sororities	24 (4)
% African American	2
% Asian	2

% Caucasian	93
% Hispanic	2
% international	1
# of countries represented	9

ACADEMICS
Academic Rating	**81**
Calendar	semester
Student/faculty ratio	14:1
Professors Interesting Rating	83
Professors Accessible Rating	87
% professors teaching UG courses	100
Most common lab size	20-29 students
Most common	
regular class size	10-19 students

MOST POPULAR MAJORS
biology/biological sciences
business administration/management
communications studies/speech
communication and rhetoric

SELECTIVITY
Admissions Selectivity Rating	**84**
# of applicants	2,464
% of applicants accepted	70
% of acceptees attending	31
# accepting a place on wait list	305
% admitted from wait list	2
# of early decision applicants	150
% accepted early decision	85

FRESHMAN PROFILE
Range SAT Verbal	530-620
Range SAT Math	540-630
Projected Range SAT Writing	580-650
Minimum Paper TOEFL	550
Minimum Computer Based TOEFL	213
% graduated top 10% of class	35
% graduated top 25% of class	69
% graduated top 50% of class	95

DEADLINES
Early decision application deadline	11/15
Regular application deadline	3/1
Regular notification	rolling
Nonfall registration?	yes

FINANCIAL FACTS
Financial Aid Rating	**77**
Annual tuition	$24,810
Room & Board	$6,840
Books and supplies	$700
Required fees	$315
% frosh rec. need-based scholarship	
or grant aid	63
% UG rec. need-based scholarship	
or grant aid	63
% frosh rec. need-based self-help aid	53
% UG rec. need-based self-help aid	53
% frosh rec. any financial aid	92

% UG rec. any financial aid	92
Avg. frosh grant	$14,380
Avg. frosh loan	$3,140

SWARTHMORE COLLEGE

CAMPUS LIFE
Quality of Life Rating	**87**
Fire Safety Rating	**78**
Type of school	private
Environment	metropolis

STUDENTS
Total undergrad enrollment	1,459
% male/female	48/52
% from out of state	85
% from public high school	57
% live on campus	94
% in (# of) fraternities	7 (2)
% African American	6
% Asian	16
% Caucasian	50
% Hispanic	9
% Native American	1
% international	6
# of countries represented	46

ACADEMICS
Academic Rating	**99**
Calendar	semester
Student/faculty ratio	8:1
Professors Interesting Rating	96
Professors Accessible Rating	95
% professors teaching UG courses	100
Most common lab size	10-19 students
Most common	
regular class size	fewer than 10 students

MOST POPULAR MAJORS
biology/biological sciences
economics
political science and government

SELECTIVITY
Admissions Selectivity Rating	**98**
# of applicants	3,680
% of applicants accepted	38
% of acceptees attending	26
# of early decision applicants	141
% accepted early decision	45

FRESHMAN PROFILE
Range SAT Verbal	680-770
Average SAT Verbal	719
Range SAT Math	670-760
Average SAT Math	711
Projected Range SAT Writing	680-740
% graduated top 10% of class	89
% graduated top 25% of class	97
% graduated top 50% of class	100

DEADLINES
Early decision application deadline	11/15
Regular application deadline	1/1
Regular notification	4/1
Nonfall registration?	no

FINANCIAL FACTS
Financial Aid Rating	**97**
Annual tuition	$29,782
Room & Board	$9,314
Books and supplies	$982
Required fees	$312
% frosh rec. need-based scholarship	
or grant aid	53
% UG rec. need-based scholarship	
or grant aid	48
% frosh rec. need-based self-help aid	52
% UG rec. need-based self-help aid	46
% frosh rec. any financial aid	53
% UG rec. any financial aid	51
Avg. frosh grant	$24,421
Avg. frosh loan	$2,047

SYRACUSE UNIVERSITY

CAMPUS LIFE
Quality of Life Rating	**64**
Fire Safety Rating	**97**
Type of school	private
Environment	city

STUDENTS
Total undergrad enrollment	10,750
% male/female	44/56
% from out of state	55
% from public high school	80
% live on campus	73
% in (# of) fraternities	12 (22)
% in (# of) sororities	16 (19)
% African American	6
% Asian	6
% Caucasian	71
% Hispanic	4
% international	3
# of countries represented	65

ACADEMICS
Academic Rating	**83**
Calendar	semester
Student/faculty ratio	12:1
Professors Interesting Rating	71
Professors Accessible Rating	74
% professors teaching UG courses	95
% classes taught by TAs	6
Most common lab size	fewer than 10 students
Most common	
regular class size	20-29 students

MOST POPULAR MAJORS
marketing/marketing management
political science and government
psychology

SELECTIVITY
Admissions Selectivity Rating	**91**
# of applicants	16,019
% of applicants accepted	59
% of acceptees attending	28
# accepting a place on wait list	883
% admitted from wait list	18
# of early decision applicants	477
% accepted early decision	63

FRESHMAN PROFILE
Range SAT Verbal	570-650
Range SAT Math	580-670
Projected Range SAT Writing	610-670
Minimum Paper TOEFL	550
Minimum Computer Based TOEFL	213
Average HS GPA	3.6
% graduated top 10% of class	44
% graduated top 25% of class	80
% graduated top 50% of class	98

DEADLINES
Early decision application deadline	11/15
Regular application deadline	1/1
Regular notification	3/15
Nonfall registration?	yes

FINANCIAL FACTS
Financial Aid Rating	**86**
Annual tuition	$25,720
Room & Board	$9,970
Books and supplies	$1,190
Required fees	$1,112
% frosh rec. need-based scholarship or grant aid	54
% UG rec. need-based scholarship or grant aid	52
% frosh rec. need-based self-help aid	51
% UG rec. need-based self-help aid	51
% frosh rec. any financial aid	75
% UG rec. any financial aid	75
Avg. frosh grant	$14,588
Avg. frosh loan	$4,100

TEMPLE UNIVERSITY

CAMPUS LIFE
Quality of Life Rating	**83**
Fire Safety Rating	**60**
Type of school	public
Environment	metropolis

STUDENTS
Total undergrad enrollment	22,780
% male/female	43/57
% from out of state	23
% from public high school	79
% live on campus	22
% in (# of) fraternities	1 (13)
% in (# of) sororities	1 (12)
% African American	20
% Asian	8
% Caucasian	57
% Hispanic	3
% international	3
# of countries represented	124

ACADEMICS
Academic Rating	**78**
Calendar	semester
Student/faculty ratio	17:1
Professors Interesting Rating	72
Professors Accessible Rating	73
Most common lab size	10-19 students
Most common regular class size	20-29 students

MOST POPULAR MAJORS
elementary education and teaching
journalism
psychology

SELECTIVITY
Admissions Selectivity Rating	**82**
# of applicants	16,681
% of applicants accepted	63
% of acceptees attending	36

FRESHMAN PROFILE
Range SAT Verbal	490-590
Range SAT Math	500-600
Projected Range SAT Writing	550-620
Range ACT Composite	19-24
Minimum Paper TOEFL	525
Minimum Computer Based TOEFL	195
Average HS GPA	3.24
% graduated top 10% of class	17
% graduated top 25% of class	50
% graduated top 50% of class	90

DEADLINES
Regular application deadline	4/1
Regular notification	rolling
Nonfall registration?	yes

FINANCIAL FACTS
Financial Aid Rating	**78**
Annual in-state tuition	$8,622
Annual out-of-state tuition	$15,788
Room & Board	$7,522
Books and supplies	$800
Required fees	$480
% frosh rec. need-based scholarship or grant aid	70
% UG rec. need-based scholarship or grant aid	67
% frosh rec. need-based self-help aid	60
% UG rec. need-based self-help aid	58
% frosh rec. any financial aid	86
% UG rec. any financial aid	89
Avg. frosh grant	$5,010
Avg. frosh loan	$2,778

THIEL COLLEGE

CAMPUS LIFE
Quality of Life Rating	**70**
Fire Safety Rating	**96**
Type of school	private
Affiliation	Lutheran
Environment	rural

STUDENTS
Total undergrad enrollment	1,217
% male/female	51/49
% from out of state	27
% from public high school	88
% live on campus	78
% in (# of) fraternities	12 (4)
% in (# of) sororities	22 (4)
% African American	6
% Asian	1
% Caucasian	74
% Hispanic	1
% international	5
# of countries represented	14

ACADEMICS
Academic Rating	**76**
Calendar	semester
Student/faculty ratio	16:1
Professors Interesting Rating	78
Professors Accessible Rating	75
% professors teaching UG courses	100
Most common lab size	10-19 students
Most common regular class size	fewer than 10 students

MOST POPULAR MAJORS
biology/biological sciences
business administration/management
psychology

SELECTIVITY
Admissions Selectivity Rating	**71**
# of applicants	1,981
% of applicants accepted	79
% of acceptees attending	24

FRESHMAN PROFILE
Range SAT Verbal	420-530
Average SAT Verbal	485
Range SAT Math	420-533
Average SAT Math	488
Projected Range SAT Writing	490-580
Range ACT Composite	18-22
Average ACT Composite	20
Minimum Paper TOEFL	450

Minimum Computer Based TOEFL	173
Average HS GPA	3.0
% graduated top 10% of class	9
% graduated top 25% of class	22
% graduated top 50% of class	58

DEADLINES

Regular application deadline	8/15
Regular notification	rolling
Nonfall registration?	yes

FINANCIAL FACTS

Financial Aid Rating	**74**
Annual tuition	$16,200
Room & Board	$6,990
Books and supplies	$700
Required fees	$1,390
% frosh rec. need-based scholarship or grant aid	86
% UG rec. need-based scholarship or grant aid	86
% frosh rec. need-based self-help aid	86
% UG rec. need-based self-help aid	86
% frosh rec. any financial aid	98
% UG rec. any financial aid	96
Avg. frosh grant	$9,986
Avg. frosh loan	$4,500

TOWSON UNIVERSITY

CAMPUS LIFE

Quality of Life Rating	**70**
Fire Safety Rating	**85**
Type of school	public
Environment	metropolis

STUDENTS

Total undergrad enrollment	13,627
% male/female	39/61
% from out of state	19
% live on campus	24
% in (# of) fraternities	2 (12)
% in (# of) sororities	3 (10)
% African American	10
% Asian	3
% Caucasian	74
% Hispanic	2
% international	2

ACADEMICS

Academic Rating	**71**
Calendar	semester
Student/faculty ratio	17:1
Professors Interesting Rating	69
Professors Accessible Rating	70
Most common lab size	20-29 students
Most common regular class size	10-19 students

MOST POPULAR MAJORS

business administration/management
elementary education and teaching
mass communications/media studies

SELECTIVITY

Admissions Selectivity Rating	**81**
# of applicants	10,663
% of applicants accepted	67
% of acceptees attending	29

FRESHMAN PROFILE

Range SAT Verbal	490-580
Range SAT Math	500-590
Projected Range SAT Writing	550-620
Range ACT Composite	19-23
Average HS GPA	3.46
% graduated top 10% of class	17
% graduated top 25% of class	48
% graduated top 50% of class	90

DEADLINES

Regular application deadline	2/15
Regular notification	rolling
Nonfall registration?	yes

FINANCIAL FACTS

Financial Aid Rating	**69**
Annual in-state tuition	$5,180
Annual out-of-state tuition	$14,114
Room & Board	$6,828
Books and supplies	$800
Required fees	$1,916
% frosh rec. need-based scholarship or grant aid	22
% UG rec. need-based scholarship or grant aid	25
% frosh rec. need-based self-help aid	32
% UG rec. need-based self-help aid	31
% frosh rec. any financial aid	58
% UG rec. any financial aid	66
Avg. frosh grant	$5,275
Avg. frosh loan	$5,930

TRINITY COLLEGE (CT)

CAMPUS LIFE

Quality of Life Rating	**63**
Fire Safety Rating	**60**
Type of school	private
Environment	metropolis

STUDENTS

Total undergrad enrollment	2,145
% male/female	49/51
% from out of state	78
% from public high school	43
% live on campus	92
% in (# of) fraternities	20 (7)
% in (# of) sororities	16 (7)
% African American	5

% Asian	6
% Caucasian	66
% Hispanic	5
% international	2
# of countries represented	28

ACADEMICS

Academic Rating	**89**
Calendar	semester
Student/faculty ratio	10:1
Professors Interesting Rating	80
Professors Accessible Rating	83
% professors teaching UG courses	100
Most common lab size	10-19 students
Most common regular class size	20-29 students

MOST POPULAR MAJORS

economics
history
political science and government

SELECTIVITY

Admissions Selectivity Rating	**94**
# of applicants	5,510
% of applicants accepted	36
% of acceptees attending	28
# accepting a place on wait list	1,377
% admitted from wait list	1
# of early decision applicants	271
% accepted early decision	60

FRESHMAN PROFILE

Range SAT Verbal	590-700
Average SAT Verbal	650
Range SAT Math	620-710
Average SAT Math	660
Projected Range SAT Writing	620-700
Range ACT Composite	25-29
Average ACT Composite	27
Minimum Paper TOEFL	550
Minimum Computer Based TOEFL	210
% graduated top 10% of class	51
% graduated top 25% of class	81
% graduated top 50% of class	95

DEADLINES

Early decision application deadline	11/15
Regular application deadline	1/15
Regular notification	4/1
Nonfall registration?	no

FINANCIAL FACTS

Financial Aid Rating	**94**
Annual tuition	$28,740
Room & Board	$7,810
Books and supplies	$850
Required fees	$1,490
% frosh rec. need-based scholarship or grant aid	43

% UG rec. need-based scholarship
or grant aid | 45
% frosh rec. need-based self-help aid | 37
% UG rec. need-based self-help aid | 38
Avg. frosh grant | $25,000
Avg. frosh loan | $3,521

TUFTS UNIVERSITY

CAMPUS LIFE
Quality of Life Rating | **90**
Fire Safety Rating | **97**
Type of school | private
Environment | town
STUDENTS
Total undergrad enrollment | 4,888
% male/female | 47/53
% from out of state | 74
% from public high school | 60
% live on campus | 75
% in (# of) fraternities | 15 (11)
% in (# of) sororities | 4 (3)
% African American | 7
% Asian | 13
% Caucasian | 56
% Hispanic | 8
% international | 6
# of countries represented | 65

ACADEMICS
Academic Rating | **89**
Calendar | semester
Student/faculty ratio | 10:1
Professors Interesting Rating | 87
Professors Accessible Rating | 84
% professors teaching UG courses | 100
% classes taught by TAs | 1
Most common lab size | 10-19 students
Most common
regular class size | 10-19 students

MOST POPULAR MAJORS
economics
English language and literature
international relations and affairs

SELECTIVITY
Admissions Selectivity Rating | **97**
# of applicants | 14,728
% of applicants accepted | 27
% of acceptees attending | 32
# of early decision applicants | 551
% accepted early decision | 45

FRESHMAN PROFILE
Range SAT Verbal | 640-730
Range SAT Math | 650-740
Projected Range SAT Writing | 660-720
Range ACT Composite | 27-32
Minimum Paper TOEFL | 200

Minimum Computer Based TOEFL | 300
% graduated top 10% of class | 74
% graduated top 25% of class | 94
% graduated top 50% of class | 99
DEADLINES
Early decision application deadline | 11/15
Regular application deadline | 1/1
Regular notification | 4/1
Nonfall registration? | no

FINANCIAL FACTS
Financial Aid Rating | **94**
Annual tuition | $28,859
Room & Board | $8,640
Books and supplies | $800
Required fees | $734
% frosh rec. need-based scholarship
or grant aid | 36
% UG rec. need-based scholarship
or grant aid | 37
% frosh rec. need-based self-help aid | 34
% UG rec. need-based self-help aid | 37
% frosh rec. any financial aid | 39
% UG rec. any financial aid | 40
Avg. frosh grant | $20,049
Avg. frosh loan | $2,911

UNION COLLEGE (NY)

CAMPUS LIFE
Quality of Life Rating | **70**
Fire Safety Rating | **86**
Type of school | private
Environment | town
STUDENTS
Total undergrad enrollment | 2,144
% male/female | 55/45
% from out of state | 56
% from public high school | 70
% live on campus | 88
% in (# of) fraternities | 29 (9)
% in (# of) sororities | 27 (3)
% African American | 3
% Asian | 6
% Caucasian | 84
% Hispanic | 4
% international | 2
# of countries represented | 18

ACADEMICS
Academic Rating | **90**
Calendar | trimester
Student/faculty ratio | 11:1
Professors Interesting Rating | 88
Professors Accessible Rating | 92
% professors teaching UG courses | 100
Most common lab size | 10-19 students

Most common
regular class size | 10-19 students
MOST POPULAR MAJORS
economics
political science and government
psychology

SELECTIVITY
Admissions Selectivity Rating | **94**
# of applicants | 4,060
% of applicants accepted | 49
% of acceptees attending | 28
# accepting a place on wait list | 681
% admitted from wait list | 15
# of early decision applicants | 165
% accepted early decision | 68

FRESHMAN PROFILE
Range SAT Verbal | 570-660
Average SAT Verbal | 610
Range SAT Math | 590-680
Average SAT Math | 640
Projected Range SAT Writing | 610-670
Average ACT Composite | 27
Minimum Paper TOEFL | 600
Minimum Computer Based TOEFL | 250
Average HS GPA | 3.48
% graduated top 10% of class | 59
% graduated top 25% of class | 83
% graduated top 50% of class | 98
DEADLINES
Early decision application deadline | 11/15
Regular application deadline | 1/15
Regular notification | 4/1
Nonfall registration? | no

FINANCIAL FACTS
Financial Aid Rating | **96**
Comprehensive fee | $38,703
Books and supplies | $450
% frosh rec. need-based scholarship
or grant aid | 48
% UG rec. need-based scholarship
or grant aid | 48
% frosh rec. need-based self-help aid | 40
% UG rec. need-based self-help aid | 45
% frosh rec. any financial aid | 58
% UG rec. any financial aid | 53
Avg. frosh grant | $18,404
Avg. frosh loan | $2,848

UNITED STATES COAST GUARD ACADEMY

CAMPUS LIFE
Quality of Life Rating | **63**
Fire Safety Rating | **83**
Type of school | public
Environment | town

STUDENTS

Total undergrad enrollment	994
% male/female	71/29
% from out of state	94
% from public high school	77
% live on campus	100
% African American	3
% Asian	4
% Caucasian	85
% Hispanic	5
% Native American	1
% international	1
# of countries represented	15

ACADEMICS

Academic Rating	**87**
Calendar	semester
Student/faculty ratio	9:1
Professors Interesting Rating	70
Professors Accessible Rating	90
% professors teaching UG courses	100
Most common lab size	10-19 students
Most common	
regular class size	fewer than 10 students

MOST POPULAR MAJORS
business administration and management
engineering
political science and government

SELECTIVITY

Admissions Selectivity Rating	**96**
# of applicants	1,848
% of applicants accepted	22
% of acceptees attending	78

FRESHMAN PROFILE

Range SAT Verbal	580-670
Average SAT Verbal	621
Range SAT Math	620-680
Average SAT Math	649
Projected Range SAT Writing	620-680
Range ACT Composite	25-30
Average ACT Composite	27
Minimum Paper TOEFL	560
Minimum Computer Based TOEFL	220
Average HS GPA	3.64
% graduated top 10% of class	56
% graduated top 25% of class	90
% graduated top 50% of class	100

DEADLINES

Regular application deadline	1/31
Regular notification	rolling
Nonfall registration?	no

FINANCIAL FACTS

Financial Aid Rating	**99**
Annual in-state tuition	$0
Annual out-of-state tuition	$0

UNITED STATES MERCHANT MARINE ACADEMY

CAMPUS LIFE

Quality of Life Rating	**66**
Fire Safety Rating	**60**
Type of school	public
Environment	village

STUDENTS

Total undergrad enrollment	1,007
% male/female	86/14
% from out of state	87
% from public high school	70
% live on campus	100
% international	2
# of countries represented	3

ACADEMICS

Academic Rating	**81**
Calendar	trimester
Student/faculty ratio	11:1
Professors Interesting Rating	61
Professors Accessible Rating	76
Most common lab size	10-19 students
Most common	
regular class size	10-19 students

MOST POPULAR MAJORS
Engineering
naval architecture and marine engineering
transportation and materials moving services

SELECTIVITY

Admissions Selectivity Rating	**94**
# of applicants	1,797
% of applicants accepted	21
% of acceptees attending	77
# accepting a place on wait list	283
% admitted from wait list	1

FRESHMAN PROFILE

Range SAT Verbal	570-690
Average SAT Verbal	630
Range SAT Math	590-670
Average SAT Math	625
Projected Range SAT Writing	610-690
Range ACT Composite	25-31
Average ACT Composite	28
Minimum Paper TOEFL	550
Minimum Computer Based TOEFL	213
Average HS GPA	3.6
% graduated top 10% of class	26
% graduated top 25% of class	64
% graduated top 50% of class	96

DEADLINES

Early decision application deadline	11/1
Regular application deadline	3/1
Regular notification	rolling
Nonfall registration?	no

FINANCIAL FACTS

Financial Aid Rating	**98**
Annual in-state tuition	$0
Annual out-of-state tuition	$0
Required fees	$3,500
% frosh rec. need-based scholarship	
or grant aid	18
% UG rec. need-based scholarship	
or grant aid	6
% frosh rec. need-based self-help aid	23
% UG rec. need-based self-help aid	8
Avg. frosh grant	$2,229
Avg. frosh loan	$2,625

UNITED STATES MILITARY ACADEMY

CAMPUS LIFE

Quality of Life Rating	**65**
Fire Safety Rating	**60**
Type of school	public
Environment	village

STUDENTS

Total undergrad enrollment	4,175
% male/female	85/15
% from out of state	92
% from public high school	86
% live on campus	100
% African American	7
% Asian	7
% Caucasian	77
% Hispanic	6
% Native American	1
% international	1
# of countries represented	16

ACADEMICS

Academic Rating	**97**
Calendar	semester
Student/faculty ratio	7:1
Professors Interesting Rating	88
Professors Accessible Rating	98
% professors teaching UG courses	100
Most common lab size	10-19 students
Most common	
regular class size	10-19 students

SELECTIVITY

Admissions Selectivity Rating	**96**
# of applicants	10,843
% of applicants accepted	13
% of acceptees attending	84
# accepting a place on wait list	684
% admitted from wait list	53

FRESHMAN PROFILE

Range SAT Verbal	570-660
Average SAT Verbal	627

Range SAT Math	600-690
Average SAT Math	641
Projected Range SAT Writing	610-670
Range ACT Composite	26-30
Average ACT Composite	28
Average HS GPA	3.67
% graduated top 10% of class	50
% graduated top 25% of class	81
% graduated top 50% of class	97

DEADLINES

Regular application deadline	2/28
Regular notification	rolling
Nonfall registration?	no

FINANCIAL FACTS

Financial Aid Rating	**99**
Annual in-state tuition	$0
Annual out-of-state tuition	$0
Books and supplies	$664

UNITED STATES NAVAL ACADEMY

CAMPUS LIFE

Quality of Life Rating	**90**
Fire Safety Rating	**86**
Type of school	public
Environment	village

STUDENTS

Total undergrad enrollment	4,349
% male/female	83/17
% from out of state	94
% from public high school	60
% live on campus	100
% African American	7
% Asian	5
% Caucasian	77
% Hispanic	9
% Native American	2
% international	1
# of countries represented	21

ACADEMICS

Academic Rating	**92**
Calendar	semester
Student/faculty ratio	7:1
Professors Interesting Rating	82
Professors Accessible Rating	99
% professors teaching UG courses	100
Most common lab size	20-29 students

MOST POPULAR MAJORS

economics
political science and government
systems engineering

SELECTIVITY

Admissions Selectivity Rating	**96**
# of applicants	14,423

% of applicants accepted	10
% of acceptees attending	84

FRESHMAN PROFILE

Range SAT Verbal	580-680
Average SAT Verbal	648
Range SAT Math	610-710
Average SAT Math	670
Projected Range SAT Writing	620-680
Minimum Paper TOEFL	200
% graduated top 10% of class	54
% graduated top 25% of class	81
% graduated top 50% of class	96

DEADLINES

Regular application deadline	1/31
Regular notification	rolling
Nonfall registration?	no

FINANCIAL FACTS

Financial Aid Rating	**99**
Annual in-state tuition	$0
Annual out-of-state tuition	$0

UNITY COLLEGE

CAMPUS LIFE

Quality of Life Rating	**68**
Fire Safety Rating	**60**
Type of school	private
Environment	rural

STUDENTS

Total undergrad enrollment	512
% male/female	69/31
% from out of state	64
% from public high school	98
% live on campus	80
% African American	1
% Caucasian	98
% international	1

ACADEMICS

Academic Rating	**62**
Calendar	semester
Student/faculty ratio	14:1
Professors Interesting Rating	70
Professors Accessible Rating	73
% professors teaching UG courses	100

SELECTIVITY

Admissions Selectivity Rating	**69**
# of applicants	500
% of applicants accepted	92
% of acceptees attending	34

FRESHMAN PROFILE

Range SAT Verbal	480-500
Average SAT Verbal	510
Range SAT Math	500-510
Average SAT Math	480
Projected Range SAT Writing	540-560

Minimum Paper TOEFL	500
Minimum Computer Based TOEFL	1
Average HS GPA	2.7
% graduated top 10% of class	3
% graduated top 25% of class	13
% graduated top 50% of class	48

DEADLINES

Regular notification	rolling
Nonfall registration?	yes

FINANCIAL FACTS

Financial Aid Rating	**86**
Annual tuition	$12,330
Room & Board	$5,300
Books and supplies	$450
Required fees	$560
% frosh rec. need-based scholarship or grant aid	75
% UG rec. need-based scholarship or grant aid	67
% frosh rec. need-based self-help aid	78
% UG rec. need-based self-help aid	74
Avg. frosh grant	$5,973
Avg. frosh loan	$6,499

UNIVERSITY OF THE ARTS

CAMPUS LIFE

Quality of Life Rating	**72**
Fire Safety Rating	**60**
Type of school	private
Environment	metropolis

STUDENTS

Total undergrad enrollment	1,939
% male/female	44/56
% from out of state	60
% from public high school	85
% live on campus	36
% African American	9
% Asian	3
% Caucasian	71
% Hispanic	4
% international	2
# of countries represented	40

ACADEMICS

Academic Rating	**78**
Calendar	semester
Student/faculty ratio	9:1
Professors Interesting Rating	82
Professors Accessible Rating	63
% professors teaching UG courses	90
Most common lab size	10-19 students

MOST POPULAR MAJORS

drama and dramatics/theater arts
graphic design
photography

SELECTIVITY

Admissions Selectivity Rating 80

# of applicants	1,951
% of applicants accepted	51
% of acceptees attending	48
# accepting a place on wait list	38
% admitted from wait list	21

FRESHMAN PROFILE

Range SAT Verbal	470-580
Average SAT Verbal	540
Range SAT Math	440-560
Average SAT Math	520
Projected Range SAT Writing	530-620
Range ACT Composite	18-25
Minimum Paper TOEFL	500
Minimum Computer Based TOEFL	173
Average HS GPA	2.87
% graduated top 10% of class	10
% graduated top 25% of class	37
% graduated top 50% of class	70

DEADLINES

Regular notification	rolling
Nonfall registration?	yes

FINANCIAL FACTS

Financial Aid Rating 74

Annual tuition	$22,060
Room & Board	$7,800
Books and supplies	$2,000
Required fees	$850
% frosh rec. need-based scholarship or grant aid	43
% UG rec. need-based scholarship or grant aid	40
% frosh rec. need-based self-help aid	65
% UG rec. need-based self-help aid	90
% frosh rec. any financial aid	87
% UG rec. any financial aid	90
Avg. frosh grant	$6,000
Avg. frosh loan	$3,000

UNIVERSITY OF CONNECTICUT

CAMPUS LIFE

Quality of Life Rating 65
Fire Safety Rating 96

Type of school	public
Environment	town

STUDENTS

Total undergrad enrollment	15,260
% male/female	48/52
% from out of state	30
% from public high school	85
% live on campus	72
% in (# of) fraternities	10 (14)
% in (# of) sororities	7 (9)

% African American	5
% Asian	7
% Caucasian	75
% Hispanic	4
% international	1
# of countries represented	109

ACADEMICS

Academic Rating 76

Calendar	semester
Student/faculty ratio	17:1
Professors Interesting Rating	63
Professors Accessible Rating	69
% professors teaching UG courses	76
% classes taught by TAs	24
Most common lab size	10-19 students
Most common regular class size	20-29 students

MOST POPULAR MAJORS
nursing/registered nurse training
(RN, ASN, BSN, MSN)
political science and government
psychology

SELECTIVITY

Admissions Selectivity Rating 88

# of applicants	18,466
% of applicants accepted	50
% of acceptees attending	35
# accepting a place on wait list	2,734
% admitted from wait list	1

FRESHMAN PROFILE

Range SAT Verbal	530-630
Average SAT Verbal	580
Range SAT Math	550-640
Average SAT Math	597
Projected Range SAT Writing	580-650
Range ACT Composite	22-27
Minimum Paper TOEFL	550
Minimum Computer Based TOEFL	213
% graduated top 10% of class	35
% graduated top 25% of class	79
% graduated top 50% of class	98

DEADLINES

Regular application deadline	2/1
Regular notification	rolling
Nonfall registration?	yes

FINANCIAL FACTS

Financial Aid Rating 72

Annual in-state tuition	$6,096
Annual out-of-state tuition	$18,600
Room & Board	$7,848
Books and supplies	$725
Required fees	$1,816
% frosh rec. need-based scholarship or grant aid	35

% UG rec. need-based scholarship or grant aid	36
% frosh rec. need-based self-help aid	39
% UG rec. need-based self-help aid	40
% frosh rec. any financial aid	48
% UG rec. any financial aid	48
Avg. frosh grant	$6,377
Avg. frosh loan	$2,445

UNIVERSITY OF DELAWARE

CAMPUS LIFE

Quality of Life Rating 77
Fire Safety Rating 87

Type of school	public
Environment	town

STUDENTS

Total undergrad enrollment	16,023
% male/female	42/58
% from out of state	58
% from public high school	80
% live on campus	45
% in (# of) fraternities	13 (15)
% in (# of) sororities	13 (15)
% African American	6
% Asian	3
% Caucasian	85
% Hispanic	4
% international	1
# of countries represented	100

ACADEMICS

Academic Rating 79

Calendar	4-1-4
Student/faculty ratio	13:1
Professors Interesting Rating	72
Professors Accessible Rating	74
% professors teaching UG courses	95
% classes taught by TAs	5
Most common lab size	20-29 students
Most common regular class size	10-19 students

MOST POPULAR MAJORS
biology/biological sciences
elementary education and teaching
psychology

SELECTIVITY

Admissions Selectivity Rating 92

# of applicants	22,208
% of applicants accepted	45
% of acceptees attending	35
# accepting a place on wait list	3,038
% admitted from wait list	3
# of early decision applicants	615
% accepted early decision	38

FRESHMAN PROFILE

Range SAT Verbal	540-630

Range SAT Math | 560-650
Projected Range SAT Writing | 590-650
Range ACT Composite | 24-28
Minimum Paper TOEFL | 550
Minimum Computer Based TOEFL | 213
Average HS GPA | 3.5
% graduated top 10% of class | 38
% graduated top 25% of class | 76
% graduated top 50% of class | 97

DEADLINES
Early decision application deadline | 11/1
Regular application deadline | 1/15
Regular notification | 3/15
Nonfall registration? | yes

FINANCIAL FACTS
Financial Aid Rating | **78**
Annual in-state tuition | $6,304
Annual out-of-state tuition | $15,990
Room & Board | $6,458
Books and supplies | $800
Required fees | $650
% frosh rec. need-based scholarship
or grant aid | 36
% UG rec. need-based scholarship
or grant aid | 30
% frosh rec. need-based self-help aid | 31
% UG rec. need-based self-help aid | 27

UNIVERSITY OF MAINE

CAMPUS LIFE
Quality of Life Rating | **76**
Fire Safety Rating | **60**
Type of school | public
Environment | village

STUDENTS
Total undergrad enrollment | 8,397
% male/female | 49/51
% from out of state | 12
% live on campus | 30
% African American | 1
% Asian | 1
% Caucasian | 93
% Hispanic | 1
% Native American | 2
% international | 2
# of countries represented | 67

ACADEMICS
Academic Rating | **74**
Calendar | semester
Student/faculty ratio | 15:1
Professors Interesting Rating | 68
Professors Accessible Rating | 71
% professors teaching UG courses | 73
% classes taught by TAs | 9
Most common lab size | 10-19 students

Most common
regular class size | 10-19 students
MOST POPULAR MAJORS
business administration/management
education
engineering

SELECTIVITY
Admissions Selectivity Rating | **78**
# of applicants | 5,622
% of applicants accepted | 79
% of acceptees attending | 38

FRESHMAN PROFILE
Range SAT Verbal | 480-590
Average SAT Verbal | 539
Range SAT Math | 480-600
Average SAT Math | 543
Projected Range SAT Writing | 540-620
Range ACT Composite | 20-26
Average ACT Composite | 24
Minimum Paper TOEFL | 530
Minimum Computer Based TOEFL | 197
Average HS GPA | 3.21
% graduated top 10% of class | 21
% graduated top 25% of class | 51
% graduated top 50% of class | 88

DEADLINES
Regular notification | rolling
Nonfall registration? | yes

FINANCIAL FACTS
Financial Aid Rating | **75**
Annual in-state tuition | $5,520
Annual out-of-state tuition | $15,660
Room & Board | $6,732
Books and supplies | $700
Required fees | $1,390
% frosh rec. need-based scholarship
or grant aid | 57
% UG rec. need-based scholarship
or grant aid | 45
% frosh rec. need-based self-help aid | 59
% UG rec. need-based self-help aid | 53
% frosh rec. any financial aid | 83
% UG rec. any financial aid | 81
Avg. frosh grant | $5,760
Avg. frosh loan | $4,172

UNIVERSITY OF MAINE— FORT KENT

CAMPUS LIFE
Quality of Life Rating | **72**
Fire Safety Rating | **60**
Type of school | public
Environment | rural

STUDENTS
Total undergrad enrollment | 926
% male/female | 36/64
% from out of state | 31
% from public high school | 96
% live on campus | 13
% in (# of) fraternities | 5
% in (# of) sororities | 2 (1)
% Caucasian | 8
% international | 3

ACADEMICS
Academic Rating | **71**
Calendar | semester
Student/faculty ratio | 18:1
Professors Interesting Rating | 79
Professors Accessible Rating | 83
% professors teaching UG courses | 100
Most common lab size | 10-19 students
MOST POPULAR MAJORS
business administration/management
elementary education and teaching
nursing/registered nurse training
(RN, ASN, BSN, MSN)

SELECTIVITY
Admissions Selectivity Rating | **62**
# of applicants | 260
% of applicants accepted | 93
% of acceptees attending | 54

FRESHMAN PROFILE
Average SAT Verbal | 450
Range SAT Math
Average SAT Math | 420
Projected Range SAT Writing
Minimum Paper TOEFL | 500
Average HS GPA | 2.72
% graduated top 10% of class | 11
% graduated top 25% of class | 25
% graduated top 50% of class | 59

DEADLINES
Regular notification | starts in 12/1
Nonfall registration? | yes

FINANCIAL FACTS
Financial Aid Rating | **73**
Annual in-state tuition | $4,290
Annual out-of-state tuition | $10,380
Room & Board | $4,000
Books and supplies | $900
Required fees | $554
Avg. frosh grant | $3,440
Avg. frosh loan | $2,923

UNIVERSITY OF MARYLAND—BALTIMORE COUNTY

CAMPUS LIFE

Quality of Life Rating	**70**
Fire Safety Rating	**88**
Type of school	public
Environment	metropolis

STUDENTS

Total undergrad enrollment	9,668
% male/female	53/47
% from out of state	9
% from public high school	87
% live on campus	33
% in (# of) fraternities	4 (12)
% in (# of) sororities	4 (9)
% African American	14
% Asian	19
% Caucasian	55
% Hispanic	3
% international	4
# of countries represented	106

ACADEMICS

Academic Rating	**76**
Calendar	4-1-4
Student/faculty ratio	19:1
Professors Interesting Rating	70
Professors Accessible Rating	65
% professors teaching UG courses	100
% classes taught by TAs	2
Most common lab size	10-19 students
Most common regular class size	10-19 students

MOST POPULAR MAJORS
information technology
psychology
visual and performing arts

SELECTIVITY

Admissions Selectivity Rating	**86**
# of applicants	5,446
% of applicants accepted	70
% of acceptees attending	37
# accepting a place on wait list	90
% admitted from wait list	6

FRESHMAN PROFILE

Range SAT Verbal	540-640
Average SAT Verbal	597
Range SAT Math	580-670
Average SAT Math	624
Projected Range SAT Writing	590-660
Range ACT Composite	22-28
Average ACT Composite	25
Minimum Paper TOEFL	550
Minimum Computer Based TOEFL	220
Average HS GPA	3.5

% graduated top 10% of class	30
% graduated top 25% of class	58
% graduated top 50% of class	86

DEADLINES

Regular application deadline	2/1
Regular notification	rolling
Nonfall registration?	yes

FINANCIAL FACTS

Financial Aid Rating	**71**
Annual in-state tuition	$8,020
Annual out-of-state tuition	$15,620
Room & board	$7,845
Books and supplies	$1,000
% frosh rec. need-based scholarship or grant aid	27
% UG rec. need-based scholarship or grant aid	27
% frosh rec. need-based self-help aid	45
% UG rec. need-based self-help aid	44
% frosh rec. any financial aid	53
% UG rec. any financial aid	53
Avg. frosh grant	$6,000
Avg. frosh loan	$2,500

UNIVERSITY OF MARYLAND—COLLEGE PARK

CAMPUS LIFE

Quality of Life Rating	**69**
Fire Safety Rating	**68**
Type of school	public
Environment	metropolis

STUDENTS

Total undergrad enrollment	24,590
% male/female	51/49
% from out of state	24
% live on campus	33
% in (# of) fraternities	11 (30)
% in (# of) sororities	11 (26)
% African American	12
% Asian	14
% Caucasian	58
% Hispanic	6
% international	2
# of countries represented	169

ACADEMICS

Academic Rating	**76**
Calendar	semester
Student/faculty ratio	18:1
Professors Interesting Rating	69
Professors Accessible Rating	66
Most common lab size	20-29 students
Most common regular class size	20-29 students

MOST POPULAR MAJORS
computer and information sciences
criminology
political science and government

SELECTIVITY

Admissions Selectivity Rating	**93**
# of applicants	22,292
% of applicants accepted	52
% of acceptees attending	37
# accepting a place on wait list	2,530
% admitted from wait list	7

FRESHMAN PROFILE

Range SAT Verbal	560-670
Range SAT Math	590-700
Projected Range SAT Writing	600-680
Minimum Paper TOEFL	575
Minimum Computer Based TOEFL	233
Average HS GPA	3.85
% graduated top 10% of class	53
% graduated top 25% of class	87
% graduated top 50% of class	99

DEADLINES

Regular application deadline	1/20
Regular notification	4/1
Nonfall registration?	yes

FINANCIAL FACTS

Financial Aid Rating	**65**
Annual in-state tuition	$6,200
Annual out-of-state tuition	$17,500
Room & Board	$7,791
Books and supplies	$909
Required fees	$1,210
% frosh rec. need-based scholarship or grant aid	26
% UG rec. need-based scholarship or grant aid	27
% frosh rec. need-based self-help aid	24
% UG rec. need-based self-help aid	28
% frosh rec. any financial aid	70
% UG rec. any financial aid	60
Avg. frosh grant	$5,826
Avg. frosh loan	$4,691

UNIVERSITY OF MASSACHUSETTS—AMHERST

CAMPUS LIFE

Quality of Life Rating	**68**
Fire Safety Rating	**72**
Type of school	public
Environment	village

STUDENTS

Total undergrad enrollment	18,378
% male/female	50/50
% from out of state	15
% from public high school	90

% live on campus	61
% in (# of) fraternities	3 (17)
% in (# of) sororities	7 (15)
% African American	4
% Asian	7
% Caucasian	75
% Hispanic	3
% international	1
# of countries represented	98

ACADEMICS

Academic Rating	**69**
Calendar	semester
Student/faculty ratio	17:1
Professors Interesting Rating	64
Professors Accessible Rating	66
% professors teaching UG courses	87
% classes taught by TAs	13
Most common lab size	20-29 students
Most common regular class size	20-29 students

MOST POPULAR MAJORS
communications studies/speech
communication and rhetoric
psychology

SELECTIVITY

Admissions Selectivity Rating	**78**
# of applicants	17,930
% of applicants accepted	81
% of acceptees attending	29
# accepting a place on wait list	200
% admitted from wait list	50

FRESHMAN PROFILE

Range SAT Verbal	510-610
Average SAT Verbal	561
Range SAT Math	520-630
Average SAT Math	576
Projected Range SAT Writing	570-640
Minimum Paper TOEFL	550
Minimum Computer Based TOEFL	213
Average HS GPA	3.29
% graduated top 10% of class	15
% graduated top 25% of class	45
% graduated top 50% of class	84

DEADLINES

Regular application deadline	1/15
Regular notification	rolling
Nonfall registration?	yes

FINANCIAL FACTS

Financial Aid Rating	**71**
Annual in-state tuition	$1,714
Annual out-of-state tuition	$9,937
Room & Board	$6,189
Books and supplies	$1,000
Required fees	$7,294
% frosh rec. need-based scholarship or grant aid	36
% UG rec. need-based scholarship or grant aid	47
% frosh rec. need-based self-help aid	34
% UG rec. need-based self-help aid	46
% frosh rec. any financial aid	61
% UG rec. any financial aid	76
Avg. frosh grant	$5,931
Avg. frosh loan	$7,052

UNIVERSITY OF MASSACHUSETTS—BOSTON

CAMPUS LIFE

Quality of Life Rating	**71**
Fire Safety Rating	**60**
Type of school	public

STUDENTS

Total undergrad enrollment	8,666
% male/female	42/58
% from out of state	4
% African American	11
% Asian	8
% Caucasian	35
% Hispanic	5
% international	3
# of countries represented	64

ACADEMICS

Academic Rating	**65**
Calendar	semester
Student/faculty ratio	14:1
Professors Interesting Rating	78
Professors Accessible Rating	70
% professors teaching UG courses	100
Most common lab size	10-19 students
Most common regular class size	fewer than 10 students

MOST POPULAR MAJORS
business/commerce
education
social sciences

SELECTIVITY

Admissions Selectivity Rating	**60**
# of applicants	2,903
% of applicants accepted	53
% of acceptees attending	36

FRESHMAN PROFILE

Range SAT Verbal	460-570
Average SAT Verbal	515
Range SAT Math	470-570
Average SAT Math	531
Projected Range SAT Writing	530-610
Minimum Paper TOEFL	500
Average HS GPA	3.0

DEADLINES

Regular application deadline	11/1
Regular notification	rolling
Nonfall registration?	yes

FINANCIAL FACTS

Financial Aid Rating	**84**
Annual in-state tuition	$1,714
Annual out-of-state tuition	$9,758
Required fees	$6,310
% frosh rec. need-based scholarship or grant aid	52
% UG rec. need-based scholarship or grant aid	50
% frosh rec. need-based self-help aid	35
% UG rec. need-based self-help aid	47
Avg. frosh grant	$4,421
Avg. frosh loan	$2,896

UNIVERSITY OF MASSACHUSETTS—LOWELL

CAMPUS LIFE

Quality of Life Rating	**65**
Fire Safety Rating	**89**
Type of school	public
Environment	city

STUDENTS

Total undergrad enrollment	6,343
% male/female	58/42
% from out of state	11
% from public high school	98
% live on campus	33
% African American	4
% Asian	8
% Caucasian	68
% Hispanic	5
% international	2
# of countries represented	73

ACADEMICS

Academic Rating	**76**
Calendar	semester
Student/faculty ratio	15:1
Professors Interesting Rating	66
Professors Accessible Rating	62
% professors teaching UG courses	90
Most common lab size	fewer than 10 students

MOST POPULAR MAJORS
business administration/management
criminal justice/law enforcement
administration
electrical, electronics, and communications
engineering

SELECTIVITY

Admissions Selectivity Rating	**78**

# of applicants	3,935
% of applicants accepted	66
% of acceptees attending	40

FRESHMAN PROFILE

Range SAT Verbal	490-580
Average SAT Verbal	534
Range SAT Math	500-610
Average SAT Math	557
Projected Range SAT Writing	550-620
Minimum Paper TOEFL	500
Minimum Computer Based TOEFL	213
Average HS GPA	3.09
% graduated top 10% of class	13
% graduated top 25% of class	39
% graduated top 50% of class	79

DEADLINES

Regular notification	rolling
Nonfall registration?	yes

FINANCIAL FACTS

Financial Aid Rating 89

Annual in-state tuition	$1,454
Annual out-of-state tuition	$8,567
Room & Board	$6,011
Books and supplies	$500
Required fees	$6,437
% frosh rec. need-based scholarship or grant aid	39
% UG rec. need-based scholarship or grant aid	36
% frosh rec. need-based self-help aid	34
% UG rec. need-based self-help aid	38
% frosh rec. any financial aid	98
% UG rec. any financial aid	98
Avg. frosh grant	$3,580
Avg. frosh loan	$2,117

UNIVERSITY OF NEW HAMPSHIRE

CAMPUS LIFE

Quality of Life Rating	**69**
Fire Safety Rating	**78**
Type of school	public
Environment	village

STUDENTS

Total undergrad enrollment	10,942
% male/female	43/57
% from out of state	41
% from public high school	78
% live on campus	56
% in (# of) fraternities	4 (9)
% in (# of) sororities	5 (5)
% African American	1
% Asian	2
% Caucasian	87
% Hispanic	1

% international	1
# of countries represented	28

ACADEMICS

Academic Rating 73

Calendar	semester
Student/faculty ratio	14:1
Professors Interesting Rating	63
Professors Accessible Rating	65
% professors teaching UG courses	90
% classes taught by TAs	1
Most common lab size	10-19 students
Most common regular class size	20-29 students

MOST POPULAR MAJORS

business administration/management
English language and literature
psychology

SELECTIVITY

Admissions Selectivity Rating 80

# of applicants	11,587
% of applicants accepted	68
% of acceptees attending	31
# accepting a place on wait list	347
% admitted from wait list	9

FRESHMAN PROFILE

Range SAT Verbal	500-610
Average SAT Verbal	550
Range SAT Math	510-620
Average SAT Math	561
Projected Range SAT Writing	560-640
Minimum Paper TOEFL	550
Minimum Computer Based TOEFL	213
% graduated top 10% of class	22
% graduated top 25% of class	63
% graduated top 50% of class	97

DEADLINES

Regular application deadline	2/1
Regular notification	4/15
Nonfall registration?	yes

FINANCIAL FACTS

Financial Aid Rating 71

Annual in-state tuition	$7,210
Annual out-of-state tuition	$18,240
Room & Board	$6,612
Books and supplies	$1,400
Required fees	$2,016
% frosh rec. need-based scholarship or grant aid	42
% UG rec. need-based scholarship or grant aid	36
% frosh rec. need-based self-help aid	56
% UG rec. need-based self-help aid	55
% frosh rec. any financial aid	83
% UG rec. any financial aid	78

Avg. frosh grant	$6,966
Avg. frosh loan	$6,203

UNIVERSITY OF PENNSYLVANIA

CAMPUS LIFE

Quality of Life Rating	**75**
Fire Safety Rating	**60**
Type of school	private
Environment	metropolis

STUDENTS

Total undergrad enrollment	9,719
% male/female	50/50
% from out of state	81
% from public high school	53
% live on campus	64
% in (# of) fraternities	24 (33)
% in (# of) sororities	18 (12)
% African American	6
% Asian	18
% Caucasian	49
% Hispanic	6
% international	9
# of countries represented	113

ACADEMICS

Academic Rating 92

Calendar	semester
Student/faculty ratio	6:1
Professors Interesting Rating	73
Professors Accessible Rating	75
% professors teaching UG courses	100
% classes taught by TAs	6
Most common lab size	fewer than 10 students

MOST POPULAR MAJORS

business administration/management
economics
finance

SELECTIVITY

Admissions Selectivity Rating 99

# of applicants	18,282
% of applicants accepted	21
% of acceptees attending	63
# accepting a place on wait list	1,149
% admitted from wait list	7
# of early decision applicants	1,120
% accepted early decision	34

FRESHMAN PROFILE

Range SAT Verbal	650-740
Average SAT Verbal	694
Range SAT Math	680-760
Average SAT Math	718
Projected Range SAT Writing	670-720
Range ACT Composite	28-33
Average ACT Composite	30

Minimum Paper TOEFL	550
Minimum Computer Based TOEFL	220
Average HS GPA	3.84
% graduated top 10% of class	94
% graduated top 25% of class	99
% graduated top 50% of class	100

DEADLINES

Early decision application deadline	11/1
Regular application deadline	1/1
Regular notification	4/1
Nonfall registration?	no

FINANCIAL FACTS

Financial Aid Rating	**94**
Annual tuition	$27,544
Room & Board	$8,918
Books and supplies	$830
Required fees	$3,172
% frosh rec. need-based scholarship or grant aid	42
% UG rec. need-based scholarship or grant aid	40
% frosh rec. need-based self-help aid	45
% UG rec. need-based self-help aid	44
% frosh rec. any financial aid	62
% UG rec. any financial aid	58
Avg. frosh grant	$26,256
Avg. frosh loan	$3,001

UNIVERSITY OF PITTSBURGH AT BRADFORD

CAMPUS LIFE

Quality of Life Rating	**77**
Fire Safety Rating	**72**
Type of school	public
Environment	village

STUDENTS

Total undergrad enrollment	1,239
% male/female	43/57
% from out of state	12
% live on campus	47
% in (# of) fraternities	8 (3)
% in (# of) sororities	8 (3)
% African American	3
% Asian	1
% Caucasian	90
% Hispanic	1

ACADEMICS

Academic Rating	**75**
Calendar	semester
Student/faculty ratio	15:1
Professors Interesting Rating	80
Professors Accessible Rating	78
% professors teaching UG courses	100
Most common lab size	10-19 students

Most common regular class size	10-19 students

MOST POPULAR MAJORS
business administration/management
criminal justice/law enforcement administration
nursing/registered nurse training
(RN, ASN, BSN, MSN)

SELECTIVITY

Admissions Selectivity Rating	**70**
# of applicants	687
% of applicants accepted	91
% of acceptees attending	51

FRESHMAN PROFILE

Range SAT Verbal	450-550
Average SAT Verbal	502
Range SAT Math	450-560
Average SAT Math	506
Projected Range SAT Writing	520-600
Range ACT Composite	18-23
Average ACT Composite	20
Minimum Paper TOEFL	550
Minimum Computer Based TOEFL	213
Average HS GPA	3.04
% graduated top 10% of class	5
% graduated top 25% of class	21
% graduated top 50% of class	61

DEADLINES

Regular notification	rolling
Nonfall registration?	yes

FINANCIAL FACTS

Financial Aid Rating	**73**
Annual in-state tuition	$9,330
Annual out-of-state tuition	$19,200
Room & Board	$6,344
Books and supplies	$800
Required fees	$650
% frosh rec. need-based scholarship or grant aid	58
% UG rec. need-based scholarship or grant aid	59
% frosh rec. need-based self-help aid	68
% UG rec. need-based self-help aid	76
% frosh rec. any financial aid	76
% UG rec. any financial aid	82
Avg. frosh grant	$3,000
Avg. frosh loan	$2,625

UNIVERSITY OF PITTSBURGH AT JOHNSTOWN

CAMPUS LIFE

Quality of Life Rating	**83**
Fire Safety Rating	**60**
Type of school	public
Environment	city

STUDENTS

Total undergrad enrollment	3,196
% male/female	49/51
% from out of state	1
% live on campus	76
% in (# of) fraternities	3 (4)
% in (# of) sororities	2 (4)
% African American	1
% Asian	1
% Caucasian	96
% Hispanic	1

ACADEMICS

Academic Rating	**75**
Calendar	semester
Student/faculty ratio	20:1
Professors Interesting Rating	82
Professors Accessible Rating	77
% professors teaching UG courses	100
Most common lab size	20-29 students
Most common regular class size	10-19 students

SELECTIVITY

Admissions Selectivity Rating	**71**
# of applicants	3,018
% of applicants accepted	95
% of acceptees attending	30

FRESHMAN PROFILE

Range SAT Verbal	470-560
Average SAT Verbal	508
Range SAT Math	470-570
Average SAT Math	519
Projected Range SAT Writing	530-600
Range ACT Composite	18-23
Average ACT Composite	21
Minimum Paper TOEFL	550
Minimum Computer Based TOEFL	213
Average HS GPA	3.2
% graduated top 10% of class	12
% graduated top 25% of class	33
% graduated top 50% of class	70

DEADLINES

Regular notification	rolling
Nonfall registration?	yes

FINANCIAL FACTS

Financial Aid Rating	**63**
Annual in-state tuition	$9,330
Annual out-of-state tuition	$19,200
Room & board	$6,310
% frosh rec. need-based scholarship or grant aid	59
% UG rec. need-based scholarship or grant aid	55
% frosh rec. need-based self-help aid	89
% UG rec. need-based self-help aid	70
% frosh rec. any financial aid	74

% UG rec. any financial aid 67
Avg. frosh grant $4,295
Avg. frosh loan $2,843

UNIVERSITY OF PITTSBURGH—PITTSBURGH

CAMPUS LIFE
Quality of Life Rating 80
Fire Safety Rating 60
Type of school public
STUDENTS
Total undergrad enrollment 16,677
% male/female 48/52
% from out of state 6
% live on campus 36
% in (# of) fraternities 8 (15)
% in (# of) sororities 7 (11)
% African American 9
% Asian 4
% Caucasian 82
% Hispanic 1
% international 1
# of countries represented 48

ACADEMICS
Academic Rating 81
Calendar semester
Student/faculty ratio 16:1
Professors Interesting Rating 72
Professors Accessible Rating 80
Most common lab size 10-19 students
Most common
  regular class size 20-29 students

MOST POPULAR MAJORS
finance
marketing/marketing management
speech and rhetorical studies

SELECTIVITY
Admissions Selectivity Rating 89
# of applicants 18,973
% of applicants accepted 49
% of acceptees attending 32
FRESHMAN PROFILE
Range SAT Verbal 560-660
Average SAT Verbal 610
Range SAT Math 580-670
Average SAT Math 621
Projected Range SAT Writing 600-670
Range ACT Composite 24-28
Average ACT Composite 26
Minimum Paper TOEFL 550
Minimum Computer Based TOEFL 213
% graduated top 10% of class 46
% graduated top 25% of class 83
% graduated top 50% of class 98

DEADLINES
Regular notification rolling
Nonfall registration? yes

FINANCIAL FACTS
Financial Aid Rating 78
Annual in-state tuition $8,218
Annual out-of-state tuition $17,098
Room & Board $7,090
Books and supplies $700
Required fees $700
% frosh rec. need-based scholarship
  or grant aid 41
% UG rec. need-based scholarship
  or grant aid 36
% frosh rec. need-based self-help aid 54
% UG rec. need-based self-help aid 41

UNIVERSITY OF RHODE ISLAND

CAMPUS LIFE
Quality of Life Rating 64
Fire Safety Rating 84
Type of school public
Environment rural
STUDENTS
Total undergrad enrollment 10,957
% male/female 44/56
% from out of state 39
% from public high school 90
% live on campus 39
% in (# of) fraternities 9 (9)
% in (# of) sororities 10 (8)
% African American 4
% Asian 3
% Caucasian 76
% Hispanic 4

ACADEMICS
Academic Rating 61
Calendar semester
Student/faculty ratio 19:1
Professors Interesting Rating 62
Professors Accessible Rating 61
% professors teaching UG courses 83
% classes taught by TAs 8
Most common lab size 20-29 students
Most common
  regular class size 10-19 students

MOST POPULAR MAJORS
communications studies/speech
communication and rhetoric
nursing/registered nurse training
(RN, ASN, BSN, MSN)
psychology

SELECTIVITY
Admissions Selectivity Rating 60
# of applicants 13,110
% of applicants accepted 70
% of acceptees attending 29
FRESHMAN PROFILE
Range SAT Verbal 510-600
Average SAT Verbal 556
Range SAT Math 520-610
Average SAT Math 568
Projected Range SAT Writing 570-630
Average ACT Composite 24
Minimum Paper TOEFL 550
Minimum Computer Based TOEFL 213
% graduated top 10% of class 18
% graduated top 50% of class 89

DEADLINES
Regular application deadline 2/1
Regular notification rolling
Nonfall registration? yes

FINANCIAL FACTS
Financial Aid Rating 65
Annual in-state tuition $4,680
Annual out-of-state tuition $16,266
Room & Board $7,810
Books and supplies $800
Required fees $2,072
% frosh rec. need-based scholarship
  or grant aid 51
% UG rec. need-based scholarship
  or grant aid 51
% frosh rec. need-based self-help aid 47
% UG rec. need-based self-help aid 48
% frosh rec. any financial aid 51
% UG rec. any financial aid 52
Avg. frosh grant $5,481
Avg. frosh loan $5,178

UNIVERSITY OF ROCHESTER

CAMPUS LIFE
Quality of Life Rating 78
Fire Safety Rating 60
Type of school private
Environment village
STUDENTS
Total undergrad enrollment 4,449
% male/female 53/47
% from out of state
% live on campus 87
% African American 4
% Asian 11
% Caucasian 64
% Hispanic 4
% international 4

ACADEMICS
Academic Rating	**88**
Calendar	semester
Student/faculty ratio	9:1
Professors Interesting Rating	78
Professors Accessible Rating	77
Most common lab size	10-19 students

SELECTIVITY
Admissions Selectivity Rating	**96**
# of applicants	11,052
% of applicants accepted	48
% of acceptees attending	18
# accepting a place on wait list	1,123
% admitted from wait list	14
# of early decision applicants	231
% accepted early decision	44

FRESHMAN PROFILE
Range SAT Verbal	600-700
Average SAT Verbal	665
Range SAT Math	630-710
Average SAT Math	687
Projected Range SAT Writing	630-700
Range ACT Composite	27-32
Average ACT Composite	30
Minimum Paper TOEFL	550
Average HS GPA	3.75
% graduated top 10% of class	76
% graduated top 25% of class	95

DEADLINES
Early decision application deadline	11/1
Regular application deadline	1/20
Regular notification	rolling
Nonfall registration?	yes

FINANCIAL FACTS
Financial Aid Rating	**85**
Annual tuition	$28,250
Room & Board	$9,845
Books and supplies	$550
Required fees	$732
% frosh rec. need-based scholarship or grant aid	56
% UG rec. need-based scholarship or grant aid	55
% frosh rec. need-based self-help aid	41
% UG rec. need-based self-help aid	43

THE UNIVERSITY OF SCRANTON

CAMPUS LIFE
Quality of Life Rating	**83**
Fire Safety Rating	**77**
Type of school	private
Affiliation	Roman Catholic
Environment	city

STUDENTS
Total undergrad enrollment	3,982
% male/female	43/57
% from out of state	49
% from public high school	55
% live on campus	52
% African American	1
% Asian	2
% Caucasian	83
% Hispanic	4
% international	1

ACADEMICS
Academic Rating	**82**
Calendar	semester
Student/faculty ratio	13:1
Professors Interesting Rating	81
Professors Accessible Rating	83
% professors teaching UG courses	98
Most common lab size	10-19 students
Most common regular class size	10-19 students

MOST POPULAR MAJORS
communications studies/speech communication and rhetoric
elementary education and teaching
marketing/marketing management

SELECTIVITY
Admissions Selectivity Rating	**84**
# of applicants	6,133
% of applicants accepted	75
% of acceptees attending	21
# accepting a place on wait list	798
% admitted from wait list	5

FRESHMAN PROFILE
Range SAT Verbal	510-600
Average SAT Verbal	559
Range SAT Math	510-610
Average SAT Math	562
Projected Range SAT Writing	570-630
Minimum Paper TOEFL	500
Minimum Computer Based TOEFL	173
Average HS GPA	3.33
% graduated top 10% of class	22
% graduated top 25% of class	61
% graduated top 50% of class	93

DEADLINES
Regular application deadline	3/1
Regular notification	rolling
Nonfall registration?	yes

FINANCIAL FACTS
Financial Aid Rating	**70**
Annual tuition	$22,214
Room & Board	$9,524
Books and supplies	$900
Required fees	$260
% frosh rec. need-based scholarship or grant aid	68
% UG rec. need-based scholarship or grant aid	64
% frosh rec. need-based self-help aid	63
% UG rec. need-based self-help aid	57
% frosh rec. any financial aid	90
% UG rec. any financial aid	83
Avg. frosh grant	$12,130
Avg. frosh loan	$3,688

UNIVERSITY OF SOUTHERN MAINE

CAMPUS LIFE
Quality of Life Rating	**72**
Fire Safety Rating	**60**
Type of school	public
Environment	village

STUDENTS
Total undergrad enrollment	6,842
% male/female	39/61
% from out of state	10
% live on campus	21
% in (# of) fraternities	2 (4)
% in (# of) sororities	2 (4)
% African American	1
% Asian	1
% Caucasian	95
% Hispanic	1
% Native American	1

ACADEMICS
Academic Rating	**74**
Calendar	semester
Student/faculty ratio	13:1
Professors Interesting Rating	71
Professors Accessible Rating	66
% professors teaching UG courses	90
Most common lab size	10-19 students
Most common regular class size	fewer than 10 students

MOST POPULAR MAJORS
business/commerce
psychology
surgical nurse/nursing

SELECTIVITY
Admissions Selectivity Rating	**74**
# of applicants	3,743
% of applicants accepted	75
% of acceptees attending	34

FRESHMAN PROFILE
Range SAT Verbal	470-570
Average SAT Verbal	524
Range SAT Math	470-570
Average SAT Math	519
Projected Range SAT Writing	530-610

Range ACT Composite 17-20
Average ACT Composite 19
Minimum Paper TOEFL 550
Minimum Computer Based TOEFL 213
Average HS GPA 3.0
% graduated top 10% of class 11
% graduated top 25% of class 34
% graduated top 50% of class 74

DEADLINES
Regular application deadline rolling
Regular notification rolling
Nonfall registration? yes

FINANCIAL FACTS
Financial Aid Rating **72**
Annual in-state tuition $4,620
Annual out-of-state tuition $12,780
Room & Board $5,315
Books and supplies $800
Required fees $715
% frosh rec. need-based scholarship
  or grant aid 55
% UG rec. need-based scholarship
  or grant aid 57
% frosh rec. need-based self-help aid 62
% UG rec. need-based self-help aid 69
% frosh rec. any financial aid 70
% UG rec. any financial aid 79
Avg. frosh grant $3,897
Avg. frosh loan $7,305

UNIVERSITY OF VERMONT

CAMPUS LIFE
Quality of Life Rating **82**
Fire Safety Rating **80**
Type of school public
Environment town

STUDENTS
Total undergrad enrollment 8,143
% male/female 45/55
% from out of state 63
% from public high school 70
% live on campus 52
% in (# of) fraternities 7 (8)
% in (# of) sororities 6 (5)
% African American 1
% Asian 2
% Caucasian 93
% Hispanic 2
% international 1
# of countries represented 40

ACADEMICS
Academic Rating **77**
Calendar semester
Student/faculty ratio 15:1
Professors Interesting Rating 76

Professors Accessible Rating 76
% professors teaching UG courses 85
% classes taught by TAs 2
Most common lab size 10-19 students
Most common
  regular class size 10-19 students

MOST POPULAR MAJORS
business administration/management
psychology

SELECTIVITY
Admissions Selectivity Rating **79**
# of applicants 11,384
% of applicants accepted 76
% of acceptees attending 23
# accepting a place on wait list 977
% admitted from wait list 9

FRESHMAN PROFILE
Range SAT Verbal 530-620
Average SAT Verbal 577
Range SAT Math 530-630
Average SAT Math 578
Projected Range SAT Writing 580-650
Range ACT Composite 22-27
Average ACT Composite 24
Minimum Paper TOEFL 550
Minimum Computer Based TOEFL 213
% graduated top 10% of class 23
% graduated top 25% of class 57
% graduated top 50% of class 93

DEADLINES
Regular application deadline 1/15
Regular notification 3/31
Nonfall registration? yes

FINANCIAL FACTS
Financial Aid Rating **79**
Annual in-state tuition $9,088
Annual out-of-state tuition $22,728
Room & Board $7,016
Books and supplies $832
Required fees $1,138
% frosh rec. need-based scholarship
  or grant aid 52
% UG rec. need-based scholarship
  or grant aid 50
% frosh rec. need-based self-help aid 48
% UG rec. need-based self-help aid 47
% frosh rec. any financial aid 81
% UG rec. any financial aid 77
Avg. frosh grant $10,721
Avg. frosh loan $6,059

URSINUS COLLEGE

CAMPUS LIFE
Quality of Life Rating **88**
Fire Safety Rating **93**

Type of school private
Environment metropolis

STUDENTS
Total undergrad enrollment 1,481
% male/female 47/53
% from out of state 36
% from public high school 61
% live on campus 93
% in (# of) fraternities 17 (7)
% in (# of) sororities 28 (7)
% African American 7
% Asian 4
% Caucasian 79
% Hispanic 3
% international 2

ACADEMICS
Academic Rating **92**
Calendar semester
Student/faculty ratio 11:1
Professors Interesting Rating 88
Professors Accessible Rating 86
% professors teaching UG courses 100
Most common lab size fewer than
  10 students
Most common
  regular class size 10-19 students

MOST POPULAR MAJORS
economics
English language and literature

SELECTIVITY
Admissions Selectivity Rating **89**
# of applicants 1,801
% of applicants accepted 73
% of acceptees attending 30
# accepting a place on wait list 67
% admitted from wait list 27
# of early decision applicants 131
% accepted early decision 80

FRESHMAN PROFILE
Range SAT Verbal 550-660
Average SAT Verbal 605
Range SAT Math 560-660
Average SAT Math 609
Projected Range SAT Writing 600-670
Range ACT Composite 22-28
Average ACT Composite 26
Minimum Paper TOEFL 500
Minimum Computer Based TOEFL 173
Average HS GPA 3.5
% graduated top 10% of class 48
% graduated top 25% of class 75
% graduated top 50% of class 94

DEADLINES
Early decision application deadline 1/15
Regular application deadline 2/15

Regular notification	4/1
Nonfall registration?	yes

FINANCIAL FACTS
Financial Aid Rating **89**

Annual tuition	$31,450
Room & Board	$7,350
Books and supplies	$600
% frosh rec. need-based scholarship or grant aid	82
% UG rec. need-based scholarship or grant aid	83
% frosh rec. need-based self-help aid	82
% UG rec. need-based self-help aid	83
% frosh rec. any financial aid	82
% UG rec. any financial aid	83
Avg. frosh grant	$18,117
Avg. frosh loan	$4,018

VASSAR COLLEGE

CAMPUS LIFE
Quality of Life Rating **79**
Fire Safety Rating **89**

Type of school	private
Environment	town

STUDENTS
Total undergrad enrollment	2,428
% male/female	40/60
% from out of state	73
% from public high school	65
% live on campus	95
% African American	5
% Asian	9
% Caucasian	75
% Hispanic	5
% international	5
# of countries represented	49

ACADEMICS
Academic Rating **95**

Calendar	semester
Student/faculty ratio	8:1
Professors Interesting Rating	90
Professors Accessible Rating	89
% professors teaching UG courses	100
Most common lab size	10-19 students
Most common regular class size	10-19 students

MOST POPULAR MAJORS
English language and literature
political science and government
psychology

SELECTIVITY
Admissions Selectivity Rating **97**

# of applicants	6,193
% of applicants accepted	29
% of acceptees attending	37

# accepting a place on wait list	1,014
# of early decision applicants	247
% accepted early decision	44

FRESHMAN PROFILE
Range SAT Verbal	660-740
Average SAT Verbal	698
Range SAT Math	660-720
Average SAT Math	679
Projected Range SAT Writing	670-720
Range ACT Composite	28-32
Average ACT Composite	30
Minimum Paper TOEFL	600
Minimum Computer Based TOEFL	250
Average HS GPA	3.8
% graduated top 10% of class	68
% graduated top 25% of class	95
% graduated top 50% of class	100

DEADLINES
Early decision application deadline	11/15
Regular application deadline	1/1
Regular notification	4/1
Nonfall registration?	no

FINANCIAL FACTS
Financial Aid Rating **98**

Annual tuition	$30,895
Room & Board	$7,680
Books and supplies	$820
Required fees	$455
% frosh rec. need-based scholarship or grant aid	50
% UG rec. need-based scholarship or grant aid	52
% frosh rec. need-based self-help aid	50
% UG rec. need-based self-help aid	53
% frosh rec. any financial aid	50
% UG rec. any financial aid	52
Avg. frosh grant	$22,009
Avg. frosh loan	$1,890

VILLANOVA UNIVERSITY

CAMPUS LIFE
Quality of Life Rating **82**
Fire Safety Rating **87**

Type of school	private
Affiliation	Roman Catholic
Environment	village

STUDENTS
Total undergrad enrollment	6,892
% male/female	49/51
% from out of state	71
% from public high school	55
% live on campus	75
% in (# of) fraternities	18 (9)
% in (# of) sororities	28 (9)
% African American	3

% Asian	6
% Caucasian	82
% Hispanic	5
% international	2
# of countries represented	30

ACADEMICS
Academic Rating **82**

Calendar	semester
Student/faculty ratio	12:1
Professors Interesting Rating	78
Professors Accessible Rating	80
% professors teaching UG courses	100
Most common lab size	10-19 students
Most common regular class size	10-19 students

MOST POPULAR MAJORS
finance
nursing/registered nurse training
(RN, ASN, BSN, MSN)

SELECTIVITY
Admissions Selectivity Rating **92**

# of applicants	9,175
% of applicants accepted	58
% of acceptees attending	31
# accepting a place on wait list	2,084

FRESHMAN PROFILE
Range SAT Verbal	580-660
Average SAT Verbal	605
Range SAT Math	600-680
Average SAT Math	633
Projected Range SAT Writing	620-670
Range ACT Composite	27-30
Average ACT Composite	27
Minimum Paper TOEFL	550
Minimum Computer Based TOEFL	213
Average HS GPA	3.67
% graduated top 10% of class	48
% graduated top 25% of class	72
% graduated top 50% of class	98

DEADLINES
Regular application deadline	1/7
Regular notification	4/1
Nonfall registration?	no

FINANCIAL FACTS
Financial Aid Rating **71**

Annual tuition	$27,175
Room & Board	$9,067
Books and supplies	$950
Required fees	$550
% frosh rec. need-based scholarship or grant aid	43
% UG rec. need-based scholarship or grant aid	41
% frosh rec. need-based self-help aid	46
% UG rec. need-based self-help aid	41

% frosh rec. any financial aid 66
% UG rec. any financial aid 63
Avg. frosh grant $18,298
Avg. frosh loan $3,089

WAGNER COLLEGE

CAMPUS LIFE
Quality of Life Rating **70**
Fire Safety Rating **60**
Type of school private
Affiliation Lutheran
Environment metropolis
STUDENTS
Total undergrad enrollment 1,929
% male/female 39/61
% from out of state 51
% live on campus 76
% in (# of) fraternities 10 (7)
% in (# of) sororities 11 (7)
% African American 5
% Asian 3
% Caucasian 79
% Hispanic 5

ACADEMICS
Academic Rating **77**
Calendar semester
Student/faculty ratio 16:1
Professors Interesting Rating 73
Professors Accessible Rating 76
% professors teaching UG courses 100
Most common lab size 10-19 students
Most common
  regular class size 10-19 students
MOST POPULAR MAJORS
business administration/management
drama and dramatics/theater arts
psychology

SELECTIVITY
Admissions Selectivity Rating **79**
# of applicants 2,516
% of applicants accepted 67
% of acceptees attending 29
# accepting a place on wait list 93
% admitted from wait list 13
# of early decision applicants 30
% accepted early decision 37
FRESHMAN PROFILE
Range SAT Verbal 530-620
Average SAT Verbal 560
Range SAT Math 530-630
Average SAT Math 560
Projected Range SAT Writing 580-650
Range ACT Composite 23-28
Average ACT Composite 26
Minimum Paper TOEFL 550

Minimum Computer Based TOEFL 217
% graduated top 10% of class 12
% graduated top 25% of class 61
% graduated top 50% of class 91
DEADLINES
Early decision application deadline 1/1
Regular application deadline 3/15
Regular notification rolling
Nonfall registration? yes

FINANCIAL FACTS
Financial Aid Rating **70**
Annual tuition $23,900
Room & Board $7,500
Books and supplies $701
% frosh rec. need-based scholarship
  or grant aid 63
% UG rec. need-based scholarship
  or grant aid 57
% frosh rec. need-based self-help aid 48
% UG rec. need-based self-help aid 44
% frosh rec. any financial aid 89
% UG rec. any financial aid 80
Avg. frosh grant $11,941
Avg. frosh loan $3,508

WASHINGTON & JEFFERSON COLLEGE

CAMPUS LIFE
Quality of Life Rating **68**
Fire Safety Rating **68**
Type of school private
Environment village
STUDENTS
Total undergrad enrollment 1,344
% male/female 52/48
% from out of state 22
% from public high school 86
% live on campus 81
% in (# of) fraternities 47 (7)
% in (# of) sororities 44 (4)
% African American 2
% Asian 1
% Caucasian 87
% Hispanic 1

ACADEMICS
Academic Rating **80**
Calendar 4-1-4
Student/faculty ratio 12:1
Professors Interesting Rating 77
Professors Accessible Rating 82
% professors teaching UG courses 100
Most common lab size 10-19 students
Most common
  regular class size 10-19 students

MOST POPULAR MAJORS
accounting
business/commerce
English language and literature

SELECTIVITY
Admissions Selectivity Rating **89**
# of applicants 4,412
% of applicants accepted 39
% of acceptees attending 27
# accepting a place on wait list 155
% admitted from wait list 24
# of early decision applicants 12
% accepted early decision 21
FRESHMAN PROFILE
Range SAT Verbal 515-610
Average SAT Verbal 570
Range SAT Math 530-630
Average SAT Math 580
Projected Range SAT Writing 570-640
Range ACT Composite 22-26
Average ACT Composite 25
Minimum Paper TOEFL 500
Minimum Computer Based TOEFL 267
Average HS GPA 3.31
% graduated top 10% of class 32
% graduated top 25% of class 65
% graduated top 50% of class 94
DEADLINES
Early decision application deadline 12/1
Regular application deadline 3/1
Regular notification rolling
Nonfall registration? yes

FINANCIAL FACTS
Financial Aid Rating **71**
Annual tuition $24,220
Room & Board $6,710
Books and supplies $600
Required fees $400
% frosh rec. need-based scholarship
  or grant aid 77
% UG rec. need-based scholarship
  or grant aid 75
% frosh rec. need-based self-help aid 68
% UG rec. need-based self-help aid 50
% frosh rec. any financial aid 97
% UG rec. any financial aid 95
Avg. frosh grant $12,719
Avg. frosh loan $2,974

WASHINGTON COLLEGE

CAMPUS LIFE
Quality of Life Rating **71**
Fire Safety Rating **60**
Type of school private
Environment rural

STUDENTS

Total undergrad enrollment	1,335
% male/female	38/62
% from out of state	44
% from public high school	71
% live on campus	80
% in (# of) fraternities	20 (3)
% in (# of) sororities	20 (3)
% African American	4
% Asian	1
% Caucasian	81
% Hispanic	1
% international	4

ACADEMICS

Academic Rating	**84**
Calendar	semester
Student/faculty ratio	12:1
Professors Interesting Rating	87
Professors Accessible Rating	88
% professors teaching UG courses	98
Most common lab size	10-19 students
Most common regular class size	10-19 students

MOST POPULAR MAJORS
business administration/management
English/language arts teacher education
environmental studies

SELECTIVITY

Admissions Selectivity Rating	**90**
# of applicants	2,114
% of applicants accepted	61
% of acceptees attending	28
# accepting a place on wait list	520
# of early decision applicants	36
% accepted early decision	95

FRESHMAN PROFILE

Range SAT Verbal	540-630
Average SAT Verbal	571
Range SAT Math	520-620
Average SAT Math	555
Projected Range SAT Writing	590-650
Range ACT Composite	23-27
Minimum Paper TOEFL	500
Average HS GPA	3.44
% graduated top 10% of class	46
% graduated top 25% of class	77
% graduated top 50% of class	94

DEADLINES

Early decision application deadline	11/15
Regular application deadline	3/15
Regular notification	rolling
Nonfall registration?	yes

FINANCIAL FACTS

Financial Aid Rating	**87**
Annual tuition	$28,230
Room & board	$6,200
% frosh rec. need-based scholarship or grant aid	50
% UG rec. need-based scholarship or grant aid	49
% frosh rec. need-based self-help aid	51
% UG rec. need-based self-help aid	50
Avg. frosh grant	$14,707
Avg. frosh loan	$3,825

WEBB INSTITUTE

CAMPUS LIFE

Quality of Life Rating	**97**
Fire Safety Rating	**60**
Type of school	private
Environment	village

STUDENTS

Total undergrad enrollment	72
% male/female	79/21
% from out of state	68
% from public high school	88
% live on campus	100
% African American	1
% Asian	3
% Caucasian	96

ACADEMICS

Academic Rating	**96**
Calendar	semester
Student/faculty ratio	7:1
Professors Interesting Rating	72
Professors Accessible Rating	98
% professors teaching UG courses	100
Most common lab size	10-19 students

SELECTIVITY

Admissions Selectivity Rating	**98**
# of applicants	103
% of applicants accepted	32
% of acceptees attending	79
# of early decision applicants	8
% accepted early decision	33

FRESHMAN PROFILE

Range SAT Verbal	640-710
Average SAT Verbal	670
Range SAT Math	700-760
Average SAT Math	720
Projected Range SAT Writing	660-700
Average HS GPA	3.9
% graduated top 10% of class	83
% graduated top 25% of class	100
% graduated top 50% of class	100

DEADLINES

Early decision application deadline	10/15
Regular application deadline	2/15
Regular notification	3/15-4/30
Nonfall registration?	no

FINANCIAL FACTS

Financial Aid Rating	**83**
Annual tuition	$0
Room & Board	$7,550
Books and supplies	$600
% frosh rec. need-based scholarship or grant aid	4
% UG rec. need-based scholarship or grant aid	3
Avg. frosh grant	$2,750
Avg. frosh loan	$2,625

WELLESLEY COLLEGE

CAMPUS LIFE

Quality of Life Rating	**96**
Fire Safety Rating	**60**
Type of school	private
Environment	town

STUDENTS

Total undergrad enrollment	2,229
% male/female	0/100
% from out of state	84
% from public high school	63
% live on campus	97
% African American	6
% Asian	28
% Caucasian	43
% Hispanic	6
% international	8
# of countries represented	66

ACADEMICS

Academic Rating	**98**
Calendar	semester
Student/faculty ratio	9:1
Professors Interesting Rating	99
Professors Accessible Rating	98
% professors teaching UG courses	100
Most common lab size	10-19 students
Most common regular class size	10-19 students

MOST POPULAR MAJORS
economics
English language and literature
psychology

SELECTIVITY

Admissions Selectivity Rating	**97**
# of applicants	3,944
% of applicants accepted	37
% of acceptees attending	42
# accepting a place on wait list	920
# of early decision applicants	133
% accepted early decision	61

FRESHMAN PROFILE

Range SAT Verbal	640-740
Average SAT Verbal	689

Range SAT Math | 640-720
Average SAT Math | 678
Projected Range SAT Writing | 660-720
Range ACT Composite | 27-31
Average ACT Composite | 29
Minimum Paper TOEFL | 600
Minimum Computer Based TOEFL | 270
% graduated top 10% of class | 75
% graduated top 25% of class | 95
% graduated top 50% of class | 100

DEADLINES
Early decision application deadline | 11/1
Regular application deadline | 1/15
Regular notification | 4/1
Nonfall registration? | no

FINANCIAL FACTS
Financial Aid Rating | **80**
Room & Board | $9,202
Books and supplies | $800
Required fees | $620
% frosh rec. need-based scholarship
  or grant aid | 55
% UG rec. need-based scholarship
  or grant aid | 57
% frosh rec. need-based self-help aid | 51
% UG rec. need-based self-help aid | 54
% frosh rec. any financial aid | 57
% UG rec. any financial aid | 59
Avg. frosh grant | $24,015
Avg. frosh loan | $2,488

WELLS COLLEGE

CAMPUS LIFE
Quality of Life Rating | **73**
Fire Safety Rating | **85**
Type of school | private
Environment | rural

STUDENTS
Total undergrad enrollment | 384
% male/female | 0/100
% from out of state | 31
% from public high school | 88
% live on campus | 87
% African American | 5
% Asian | 3
% Caucasian | 67
% Hispanic | 4
% Native American | 1
% international | 2
# of countries represented | 5

ACADEMICS
Academic Rating | **88**
Calendar | semester
Student/faculty ratio | 8:1
Professors Interesting Rating | 93

Professors Accessible Rating | 81
% professors teaching UG courses | 100
Most common lab size | 10-19 students

MOST POPULAR MAJORS
psychology
visual and performing arts

SELECTIVITY
Admissions Selectivity Rating | **88**
# of applicants | 381
% of applicants accepted | 77
% of acceptees attending | 30
# of early decision applicants | 11
% accepted early decision | 100

FRESHMAN PROFILE
Range SAT Verbal | 520-640
Average SAT Verbal | 580
Range SAT Math | 470-590
Average SAT Math | 530
Projected Range SAT Writing | 570-660
Range ACT Composite | 20-28
Average ACT Composite | 24
Minimum Paper TOEFL | 550
Minimum Computer Based TOEFL | 213
Average HS GPA | 3.5
% graduated top 10% of class | 45
% graduated top 25% of class | 76
% graduated top 50% of class | 91

DEADLINES
Early decision application deadline | 12/15
Regular application deadline | 3/1
Regular notification | 4/1
Nonfall registration? | no

FINANCIAL FACTS
Financial Aid Rating | **84**
Annual tuition | $14,000
Room & Board | $7,000
Books and supplies | $700
Required fees | $900
% frosh rec. need-based scholarship
  or grant aid | 73
% UG rec. need-based scholarship
  or grant aid | 72
% frosh rec. need-based self-help aid | 73
% UG rec. need-based self-help aid | 72
% frosh rec. any financial aid | 66
% UG rec. any financial aid | 274
Avg. frosh grant | $12,595
Avg. frosh loan | $2,626

WENTWORTH INSTITUTE OF TECHNOLOGY

CAMPUS LIFE
Quality of Life Rating | **70**
Fire Safety Rating | **60**

Type of school | private
Environment | metropolis

STUDENTS
Total undergrad enrollment | 3,367
% male/female | 81/19
% from out of state | 40
% live on campus | 41
% African American | 5
% Asian | 6
% Caucasian | 81
% Hispanic | 4
% international | 3
# of countries represented | 44

ACADEMICS
Academic Rating | **70**
Calendar | semester
Student/faculty ratio | 24:1
Professors Interesting Rating | 64
Professors Accessible Rating | 67
% professors teaching UG courses | 100
Most common lab size | 20-29 students
Most common
  regular class size | 10-19 students

MOST POPULAR MAJORS
architecture
(BArch, BA/BS, MArch, MA/MS, PhD)
computer and information sciences
engineering technology

SELECTIVITY
Admissions Selectivity Rating | **74**
# of applicants | 3,699
% of applicants accepted | 63
% of acceptees attending | 47

FRESHMAN PROFILE
Range SAT Verbal | 550-450
Average SAT Verbal | 510
Range SAT Math | 590-480
Average SAT Math | 553
Projected Range SAT Writing | 600-520
Minimum Paper TOEFL | 525
Minimum Computer Based TOEFL | 197
Average HS GPA | 3.0
% graduated top 10% of class | 2
% graduated top 25% of class | 21

DEADLINES
Regular application deadline | 2/15
Regular notification | rolling
Nonfall registration? | yes

FINANCIAL FACTS
Financial Aid Rating | **61**
Annual tuition | $18,500
Room & Board | $9,000
Books and supplies | $1,000
Required fees | $350

% frosh rec. need-based scholarship or grant aid	23
% UG rec. need-based scholarship or grant aid	11
% frosh rec. need-based self-help aid	58
% UG rec. need-based self-help aid	37
% frosh rec. any financial aid	78
% UG rec. any financial aid	78
Avg. frosh grant	$8,443
Avg. frosh loan	$3,076

WESLEYAN UNIVERSITY

CAMPUS LIFE
Quality of Life Rating	**82**
Fire Safety Rating	**60**
Type of school	private
Environment	town

STUDENTS
Total undergrad enrollment	2,755
% male/female	48/52
% from out of state	92
% from public high school	56
% live on campus	92
% in (# of) fraternities	3 (9)
% in (# of) sororities	1 (4)
% African American	7
% Asian	9
% Caucasian	62
% Hispanic	7
% international	6
# of countries represented	48

ACADEMICS
Academic Rating	**93**
Calendar	semester
Student/faculty ratio	9:1
Professors Interesting Rating	84
Professors Accessible Rating	81
% professors teaching UG courses	100
% classes taught by TAs	1
Most common lab size	10-19 students
Most common regular class size	10-19 students

SELECTIVITY
Admissions Selectivity Rating	**97**
# of applicants	6,538
% of applicants accepted	28
% of acceptees attending	40
# accepting a place on wait list	1,000
% admitted from wait list	4
# of early decision applicants	283
% accepted early decision	48

FRESHMAN PROFILE
Range SAT Verbal	660-750
Average SAT Verbal	700
Range SAT Math	650-740
Average SAT Math	700
Projected Range SAT Writing	670-730
Range ACT Composite	28-32
Average ACT Composite	32
Minimum Paper TOEFL	600
Minimum Computer Based TOEFL	250
% graduated top 10% of class	66
% graduated top 25% of class	95
% graduated top 50% of class	99

DEADLINES
Early decision application deadline	11/15
Regular application deadline	1/1
Regular notification	4/1
Nonfall registration?	no

FINANCIAL FACTS
Financial Aid Rating	**96**
Annual tuition	$32,976
Room & Board	$8,932
Books and supplies	$2,310
Required fees	$214
% frosh rec. need-based scholarship or grant aid	45
% UG rec. need-based scholarship or grant aid	45
% frosh rec. need-based self-help aid	47
% UG rec. need-based self-help aid	48
% UG rec. any financial aid	43
Avg. frosh grant	$23,645
Avg. frosh lban	$2,466

WEST CHESTER UNIVERSITY OF PENNSYLVANIA

CAMPUS LIFE
Quality of Life Rating	**74**
Fire Safety Rating	**60**
Type of school	public
Environment	village

STUDENTS
Total undergrad enrollment	10,181
% male/female	39/61
% from out of state	11
% from public high school	65
% live on campus	30
% in (# of) fraternities	8 (10)
% in (# of) sororities	8 (13)
% African American	8
% Asian	2
% Caucasian	90
% Hispanic	2

ACADEMICS
Academic Rating	**72**
Calendar	semester
Student/faculty ratio	18:1
Professors Interesting Rating	66

Professors Accessible Rating	71
% professors teaching UG courses	100
Most common lab size	20-29 students
Most common regular class size	20-29 students

MOST POPULAR MAJORS
elementary education and teaching
health and physical education
psychology

SELECTIVITY
Admissions Selectivity Rating	**80**
# of applicants	10,401
% of applicants accepted	51
% of acceptees attending	36
# accepting a place on wait list	750
% admitted from wait list	10

FRESHMAN PROFILE
Range SAT Verbal	490-570
Average SAT Verbal	529
Range SAT Math	490-570
Average SAT Math	532
Projected Range SAT Writing	550-610
Minimum Paper TOEFL	550
Minimum Computer Based TOEFL	213
Average HS GPA	3.32
% graduated top 10% of class	12
% graduated top 25% of class	37
% graduated top 50% of class	82

DEADLINES
Regular notification	rolling
Nonfall registration?	yes

FINANCIAL FACTS
Financial Aid Rating	**60**
Annual in-state tuition	$4,810
Annual out-of-state tuition	$12,026
Room & Board	$5,782
Books and supplies	$1,000
Required fees	$1,196
% frosh rec. need-based scholarship or grant aid	32
% UG rec. need-based scholarship or grant aid	29
% frosh rec. any financial aid	55
% UG rec. any financial aid	56
Avg. frosh grant	$1,063
Avg. frosh loan	$1,919

WESTMINSTER COLLEGE (PA)

CAMPUS LIFE
Quality of Life Rating	**78**
Fire Safety Rating	**60**
Type of school	private
Affiliation	Presbyterian
Environment	village

STUDENTS

Total undergrad enrollment	1,261
% male/female	34/66
% from out of state	21
% from public high school	90
% live on campus	78
% in (# of) fraternities	50 (5)
% in (# of) sororities	50 (5)
% African American	3
% Caucasian	81

ACADEMICS

Academic Rating	**82**
Calendar	semester
Student/faculty ratio	12:1
Professors Interesting Rating	80
Professors Accessible Rating	85
% professors teaching UG courses	100
Most common lab size	10-19 students
Most common regular class size	10-19 students

MOST POPULAR MAJORS
biology/biological sciences
business administration/management
education

SELECTIVITY

Admissions Selectivity Rating	**80**
# of applicants	1,444
% of applicants accepted	75
% of acceptees attending	32

FRESHMAN PROFILE

Range SAT Verbal	490-590
Average SAT Verbal	544
Range SAT Math	480-600
Average SAT Math	543
Projected Range SAT Writing	550-620
Range ACT Composite	20-26
Average ACT Composite	24
Minimum Paper TOEFL	500
Average HS GPA	3.3
% graduated top 10% of class	20
% graduated top 25% of class	55
% graduated top 50% of class	87

DEADLINES

Early decision application deadline	11/15
Regular application deadline	4/15
Regular notification	rolling
Nonfall registration?	no

FINANCIAL FACTS

Financial Aid Rating	**84**
Annual tuition	$21,700
Room & Board	$6,600
Required fees	$980
% frosh rec. need-based scholarship or grant aid	66
% UG rec. need-based scholarship or grant aid	68
% frosh rec. need-based self-help aid	57
% UG rec. need-based self-help aid	61
Avg. frosh grant	$7,500
Avg. frosh loan	$3,100

WHEATON COLLEGE (MA)

CAMPUS LIFE

Quality of Life Rating	**69**
Fire Safety Rating	**60**
Type of school	private
Environment	village

STUDENTS

Total undergrad enrollment	1,524
% male/female	37/63
% from out of state	65
% from public high school	61
% live on campus	97
% African American	3
% Asian	3
% Caucasian	78
% Hispanic	4
% international	3
# of countries represented	31

ACADEMICS

Academic Rating	**91**
Calendar	semester
Student/faculty ratio	11:1
Professors Interesting Rating	87
Professors Accessible Rating	84
% professors teaching UG courses	100
Most common lab size	10-19 students
Most common regular class size	10-19 students

MOST POPULAR MAJORS
economics
English language and literature
psychology

SELECTIVITY

Admissions Selectivity Rating	**92**
# of applicants	3,460
% of applicants accepted	45
% of acceptees attending	28
# accepting a place on wait list	763
% admitted from wait list	3
# of early decision applicants	202
% accepted early decision	86

FRESHMAN PROFILE

Range SAT Verbal	560-650
Average SAT Verbal	620
Range SAT Math	580-650
Average SAT Math	610
Projected Range SAT Writing	600-670
Range ACT Composite	24-30
Average ACT Composite	27
Minimum Paper TOEFL	550
Minimum Computer Based TOEFL	213
Average HS GPA	3.45
% graduated top 10% of class	42
% graduated top 25% of class	76
% graduated top 50% of class	93

DEADLINES

Early decision application deadline	11/15
Regular application deadline	1/15
Regular notification	4/1
Nonfall registration?	yes

FINANCIAL FACTS

Financial Aid Rating	**83**
Annual tuition	$30,355
Room & Board	$7,580
Books and supplies	$940
Required fees	$225
% frosh rec. need-based scholarship or grant aid	47
% UG rec. need-based scholarship or grant aid	49
% frosh rec. need-based self-help aid	47
% UG rec. need-based self-help aid	49
% frosh rec. any financial aid	62
% UG rec. any financial aid	63
Avg. frosh grant	$16,678
Avg. frosh loan	$3,568

WIDENER UNIVERSITY

CAMPUS LIFE

Quality of Life Rating	**61**
Fire Safety Rating	**60**
Type of school	proprietary
Environment	town

STUDENTS

Total undergrad enrollment	2,501
% male/female	50/50
% from out of state	45
% from public high school	55
% live on campus	61
% in (# of) fraternities	12 (7)
% in (# of) sororities	11 (3)
% African American	12
% Asian	2
% Caucasian	73
% Hispanic	2
% international	2
# of countries represented	38

ACADEMICS

Academic Rating	**76**
Calendar	semester
Student/faculty ratio	12:1
Professors Interesting Rating	75
Professors Accessible Rating	80

% professors teaching UG courses 70
Most common lab size 10-19 students
Most common
regular class size fewer than 10 students

MOST POPULAR MAJORS
business administration/management
civil engineering
nursing/registered nurse training
(RN, ASN, BSN, MSN)

SELECTIVITY
Admissions Selectivity Rating 70
# of applicants 3,115
% of applicants accepted 80
% of acceptees attending 29

FRESHMAN PROFILE
Range SAT Verbal 440-560
Average SAT Verbal 500
Range SAT Math 430-540
Average SAT Math 515
Projected Range SAT Writing 510-600
Minimum Paper TOEFL 500
Minimum Computer Based TOEFL 173
% graduated top 10% of class 13
% graduated top 25% of class 33
% graduated top 50% of class 62

DEADLINES
Regular notification 2/15
Nonfall registration? yes

FINANCIAL FACTS
Financial Aid Rating 73
Annual tuition $22,800
Room & Board $8,100
Books and supplies $840
Required fees $200
% frosh rec. need-based scholarship
or grant aid 86
% UG rec. need-based scholarship
or grant aid 74
% frosh rec. need-based self-help aid 79
% UG rec. need-based self-help aid 70

WILKES UNIVERSITY

CAMPUS LIFE
Quality of Life Rating 61
Fire Safety Rating 60
Type of school private
Environment city

STUDENTS
Total undergrad enrollment 2,069
% male/female 48/52
% from out of state 16
% from public high school 90
% live on campus 39
% African American 2

% Asian 2
% Caucasian 94
% Hispanic 2

ACADEMICS
Academic Rating 71
Calendar semester
Student/faculty ratio 15:1
Professors Interesting Rating 74
Professors Accessible Rating 71
% professors teaching UG courses 100
Most common lab size 20-29 students
Most common
regular class size 10-19 students

MOST POPULAR MAJORS
business administration/management
pharmacy (PharMD, BS/BPharM)
psychology

SELECTIVITY
Admissions Selectivity Rating 73
# of applicants 2,593
% of applicants accepted 79
% of acceptees attending 27

FRESHMAN PROFILE
Range SAT Verbal 478-580
Average SAT Verbal 526
Range SAT Math 470-600
Average SAT Math 537
Projected Range SAT Writing -620
Minimum Paper TOEFL 500
Minimum Computer Based TOEFL 183
% graduated top 10% of class 19
% graduated top 25% of class 50
% graduated top 50% of class 86

DEADLINES
Regular notification rolling
Nonfall registration? yes

FINANCIAL FACTS
Financial Aid Rating 75
Annual tuition $19,428
Room & Board $8,924
Books and supplies $900
Required fees $980
% frosh rec. need-based scholarship
or grant aid 81
% UG rec. need-based scholarship
or grant aid 82
% frosh rec. need-based self-help aid 72
% UG rec. need-based self-help aid 74
% frosh rec. any financial aid 93
% UG rec. any financial aid 91

WILLIAM PATERSON UNIVERSITY

CAMPUS LIFE
Quality of Life Rating 61
Fire Safety Rating 60
Type of school public
Environment town

STUDENTS
Total undergrad enrollment
% from out of state 2
% from public high school 86
% live on campus 24
% in (# of) fraternities 2 (8)
% in (# of) sororities 3 (11)

ACADEMICS
Academic Rating 66
Calendar semester
Student/faculty ratio 15:1
Professors Interesting Rating 62
Professors Accessible Rating 61
% professors teaching UG courses 100
Most common lab size 20-29 students

MOST POPULAR MAJORS
business administration/management
communications studies/speech
communication and rhetoric
psychology

SELECTIVITY
Admissions Selectivity Rating 70
# of applicants 5,552
% of applicants accepted 66
% of acceptees attending 42
# accepting a place on wait list 80
% admitted from wait list 31

FRESHMAN PROFILE
Range SAT Verbal 450-530
Average SAT Verbal 532
Range SAT Math 450-540
Average SAT Math 529
Projected Range SAT Writing 520-580
Minimum Paper TOEFL 550
Minimum Computer Based TOEFL 213
% graduated top 10% of class 9
% graduated top 25% of class 29
% graduated top 50% of class 70

DEADLINES
Regular application deadline 5/1
Regular notification rolling
Nonfall registration? yes

FINANCIAL FACTS
Financial Aid Rating 69
Annual in-state tuition $7,952
Annual out-of-state tuition $12,690

Room & Board $8,340
Books and supplies $880
% frosh rec. need-based scholarship
  or grant aid 4
% UG rec. need-based scholarship
  or grant aid 29
% frosh rec. need-based self-help aid 5
% UG rec. need-based self-help aid 38
% frosh rec. any financial aid 69
% UG rec. any financial aid 58
Avg. frosh grant $6,361
Avg. frosh loan $3,782

WILLIAMS COLLEGE

CAMPUS LIFE
Quality of Life Rating **96**
Fire Safety Rating **94**
Type of school private
Environment village
STUDENTS
Total undergrad enrollment 1,931
% male/female 50/50
% from out of state 84
% from public high school 54
% live on campus 93
% African American 10
% Asian 9
% Caucasian 67
% Hispanic 8
% international 6
# of countries represented 63

ACADEMICS
Academic Rating **99**
Calendar 4-1-4
Student/faculty ratio 7:1
Professors Interesting Rating 96
Professors Accessible Rating 91
% professors teaching UG courses 100
Most common lab size fewer than
 10 students

Most common
 regular class size 10-19 students
MOST POPULAR MAJORS
art/art studies
economics
political science and government

SELECTIVITY
Admissions Selectivity Rating **98**
# of applicants 5,705
% of applicants accepted 19
% of acceptees attending 49
# of early decision applicants 214
% accepted early decision 38
FRESHMAN PROFILE
Range SAT Verbal 660-760

Average SAT Verbal 705
Range SAT Math 670-760
Average SAT Math 708
Projected Range SAT Writing 670-740
Average ACT Composite 32
% graduated top 10% of class 85
% graduated top 25% of class 97
% graduated top 50% of class 100
DEADLINES
Early decision application deadline 11/10
Regular application deadline 1/1
Regular notification 4/9
Nonfall registration? no

FINANCIAL FACTS
Financial Aid Rating **99**
Annual tuition $29,786
Room & Board $8,110
Books and supplies $800
Required fees $204
% frosh rec. need-based scholarship
  or grant aid 41
% UG rec. need-based scholarship
  or grant aid 40
% frosh rec. need-based self-help aid 41
% UG rec. need-based self-help aid 42
% frosh rec. any financial aid 64
% UG rec. any financial aid 70
Avg. frosh grant $26,700
Avg. frosh loan $2,468

WORCESTER POLYTECHNIC INSTITUTE

CAMPUS LIFE
Quality of Life Rating **77**
Fire Safety Rating **79**
Type of school private
Environment city
STUDENTS
Total undergrad enrollment 2,805
% male/female 76/24
% from out of state 38
% live on campus 60
% in (# of) fraternities 38 (12)
% in (# of) sororities 28 (2)
% African American 2
% Asian 6
% Caucasian 8
% Hispanic 3
% Native American 1
% international 4
# of countries represented 70

ACADEMICS
Academic Rating **85**
Calendar quarter

Student/faculty ratio 13:1
Professors Interesting Rating 74
Professors Accessible Rating 81
% professors teaching UG courses 100
Most common lab size fewer than
 10 students
Most common
 regular class size 10-19 students
MOST POPULAR MAJORS
computer and information sciences
electrical, electronics, and communications
engineering
mechanical engineering

SELECTIVITY
Admissions Selectivity Rating **91**
# of applicants 3,708
% of applicants accepted 75
% of acceptees attending 28
# accepting a place on wait list 107
# of early decision applicants 165
% accepted early decision 84
FRESHMAN PROFILE
Range SAT Verbal 570-670
Average SAT Verbal 620
Range SAT Math 630-720
Average SAT Math 674
Projected Range SAT Writing 610-680
Range ACT Composite 24-29
Average ACT Composite 29
Minimum Paper TOEFL 550
Minimum Computer Based TOEFL 213
Average HS GPA 3.6
% graduated top 10% of class 55
% graduated top 25% of class 86
% graduated top 50% of class 99
DEADLINES
Early decision application deadline 11/15
Regular application deadline 2/1
Regular notification 4/1
Nonfall registration? yes

FINANCIAL FACTS
Financial Aid Rating **80**
Annual tuition $30,990
Room & board $9,460
% frosh rec. need-based scholarship
  or grant aid 73
% UG rec. need-based scholarship
  or grant aid 71
% frosh rec. need-based self-help aid 58
% UG rec. need-based self-help aid 65
% frosh rec. any financial aid 91
% UG rec. any financial aid 89
Avg. frosh grant $12,121
Avg. frosh loan $4,620

WORCESTER STATE COLLEGE

CAMPUS LIFE
Quality of Life Rating	**66**
Fire Safety Rating	**60**
Type of school	public
Environment	city

STUDENTS
Total undergrad enrollment	3,858
% male/female	40/60
% from out of state	3
% live on campus	25
% African American	4
% Asian	3
% Caucasian	78
% Hispanic	4
% international	5
# of countries represented	47

ACADEMICS
Academic Rating	**70**
Calendar	semester
Student/faculty ratio	17:1
Professors Interesting Rating	68
Professors Accessible Rating	62
% professors teaching UG courses	79
Most common lab size	20-29 students
Most common regular class size	10-19 students

MOST POPULAR MAJORS
business administration/management
communications and media studies
psychology

SELECTIVITY
Admissions Selectivity Rating	**75**
# of applicants	2,972
% of applicants accepted	56
% of acceptees attending	38

FRESHMAN PROFILE
Range SAT Verbal	450-540
Average SAT Verbal	498
Range SAT Math	460-550
Average SAT Math	507
Projected Range SAT Writing	520-590
Range ACT Composite	18-23
Average ACT Composite	20
Minimum Paper TOEFL	550
Minimum Computer Based TOEFL	213
Average HS GPA	2.97
% graduated top 10% of class	10
% graduated top 25% of class	29
% graduated top 50% of class	72

DEADLINES
Regular application deadline	6/1
Regular notification	rolling
Nonfall registration?	yes

FINANCIAL FACTS
Financial Aid Rating	**78**
Annual in-state tuition	$970
Annual out-of-state tuition	$7,050
Room & Board	$6,896
Books and supplies	$984
Required fees	$3,609
% frosh rec. need-based scholarship or grant aid	42
% UG rec. need-based scholarship or grant aid	34
% frosh rec. need-based self-help aid	48
% UG rec. need-based self-help aid	42
% frosh rec. any financial aid	49
% UG rec. any financial aid	39
Avg. frosh grant	$1,717
Avg. frosh loan	$1,022

YALE UNIVERSITY

CAMPUS LIFE
Quality of Life Rating	**93**
Fire Safety Rating	**60**
Type of school	private

STUDENTS
Total undergrad enrollment	5,294
% male/female	50/50
% from out of state	87
% from public high school	53
% live on campus	87
% African American	8
% Asian	13
% Caucasian	52
% Hispanic	6
% Native American	1
% international	9
# of countries represented	82

ACADEMICS
Academic Rating	**97**
Calendar	semester
Student/faculty ratio	6:1
Professors Interesting Rating	84
Professors Accessible Rating	81
% classes taught by TAs	12
Most common lab size	10-19 students

SELECTIVITY
Admissions Selectivity Rating	**99**
# of applicants	17,735
% of applicants accepted	11
% of acceptees attending	68
# accepting a place on wait list	998
% admitted from wait list	1
# of early decision applicants	646
% accepted early decision	16

FRESHMAN PROFILE
Range SAT Verbal	690-790
Range SAT Math	690-790
Projected Range SAT Writing	690-750
Range ACT Composite	30-34
Minimum Paper TOEFL	600
% graduated top 10% of class	95
% graduated top 25% of class	99
% graduated top 50% of class	100

DEADLINES
Early decision application deadline	11/1
Regular application deadline	12/31
Regular notification	4/1
Nonfall registration?	no

FINANCIAL FACTS
Financial Aid Rating	**97**
Annual tuition	$29,820
Room & Board	$9,030
Books and supplies	$2,650
% frosh rec. need-based scholarship or grant aid	43
% UG rec. need-based scholarship or grant aid	40
% frosh rec. need-based self-help aid	43
% UG rec. need-based self-help aid	40

PART 4: INDEX BY STATE

CONNECTICUT
Central Connecticut State University 64, 471
Connecticut College 100, 477
Fairfield Univeristy 128, 485
Quinnipiac University 256, 513
Sacred Heart University 280, 519
Saint Joseph College (CT) 284, 520
Trinity College (CT) 362, 537
United States Coast Guard Academy 368, 538
University of Connecticut 380, 541
Wesleyan University 438, 554
Yale University 458, 558

DELAWARE
University of Delaware 382, 541

DISTRICT OF COLUMBIA
American University 20, 461
Catholic University of America 62, 471
George Washington University, The 138, 487
Georgetown University 136, 487
Howard University 166, 494

MAINE
Bates College 36, 465
Bowdoin College 46, 467
Colby College 84, 474
College of the Atlantic 88, 475
Unity College 376, 540
University of Maine 384, 542
University of Maine—Fort Kent 386, 542
University of Southern Maine 414, 548

MARYLAND
Goucher College 144, 489
Hood College 162, 493
Johns Hopkins University 176, 496

Loyola College in Maryland 198, 501
Maryland Institute College of Art 210, 503
Salisbury University 290, 521
St. John's College (MD) 316, 527
St. Mary's College of Maryland 322, 528
Towson University 360, 537
United States Naval Academy 374, 540
University of Maryland—Baltimore County 388, 543
University of Maryland—College Park 390, 543
Washington College 428, 551

MASSACHUSETTS

Amherst College 22, 462
Art Institute of Boston at Lesley University, The................... 26, 463
Assumption College 28, 463
Babson College 30, 463
Bentley College 40, 466
Boston College 42, 466
Boston University 44, 467
Brandeis University.. 48, 467
Clark University 80, 473
College of the Holy Cross 90, 475
Emerson College 122, 484
Emmanuel College 124, 484
Franklin W. Olin College of Engineering 134, 487
Gordon College... 142, 488
Hampshire College 150, 490
Harvard College 154, 491
Lesley College at Lesley University 196, 500
Massachusetts Institute of Technology 214, 504
Merrimack College 218, 505
Mount Holyoke College 230, 508
Northeastern University 244, 511
Regis College 260, 514
Simmons College.. 304, 524
Simon's Rock College of Bard.. 306, 524
Smith College 312, 526
Stonehill College 346, 529
Suffolk University... 348, 529
Tufts University 364, 538
University of Massachusetts—Amherst 392, 543

University of Massachusetts—Boston 394, 544
University of Massachusetts—Lowell 396, 544
Wellesley College 432, 552
Wentworth Institute of Technology 436, 553
Wheaton College (MA) 444, 555
Williams College 452, 557
Worcester Polytechnic Institute 454, 557
Worcester State College 456, 558

NEW HAMPSHIRE
Dartmouth College 106, 480
Keene State College 180, 497
Saint Anselm College 282, 519
University of New Hampshire 398, 545

NEW JERSEY
Drew University 112, 482
Monmouth University (NJ) 224, 506
New Jersey Institute of Technology 238, 509
Princeton University 252, 513
Ramapo College of New Jersey 258, 514
Richard Stockton College of New Jersey 264, 515
Rider University 266, 516
Rowan University 276, 518
Rutgers, The State University of New Jersey—
   New Brunswick 278, 518
Seton Hall University 296, 522
Stevens Institute of Technology 344, 528
The College of New Jersey 96, 476
William Paterson University 450, 556

NEW YORK
Adelphi University 12, 460
Alfred University 16, 460
Bard College 32, 464
Barnard College 34, 464
City University of New York—Baruch College 72, 479
City University of New York—Brooklyn College 74, 479
City University of New York—Hunter College 76, 480
City University of New York—Queens College 78, 480

Clarkson Univeristy 82, 473
Colgate University 86, 474
College of Mount Saint Vincent 94, 476
Columbia University—Columbia College 98, 477
Cooper Union 102, 478
Cornell University 104, 478
Elmira College 120, 483
Eugene Lang College/New School University 126, 485
Fordham University 130, 486
Hamilton College 148, 490
Hartwick College 152, 491
Hobart and William Smith Colleges 158, 492
Hofstra University 160, 492
Houghton College 164, 493
Iona College 172, 495
Ithaca College 174, 495
Laboratory Institute of Merchandising 186, 498
Manhattan College 202, 501
Manhattanville College 204, 502
Marist College 206, 502
Marymount College of Fordham University 212, 504
Nazareth College of Rochester 234, 509
New York University 240, 510
Niagara University 242, 510
Pace University 246, 511
Polytechnic University—Brooklyn 250, 512
Rensselaer Polytechnic Institute 262, 515
Roberts Wesleyan College 268, 516
Rochester Institute of Technology 270, 517
Sarah Lawrence College 294, 522
Siena College 302, 524
Skidmore College 308, 525
St. Bonaventure University 314, 526
St. John's University (Queens) 318, 527
St. Lawrence University 320, 527
State University of New York at Albany 324, 530
State University of New York at Binghamton 326, 530
State University of New York at Buffalo 328, 531
State University of New York at Stony Brook 330, 531
State University of New York College at Brockport 332, 532
State University of New York College at Fredonia 334, 532

State University of New York College at Geneseo 336, 533

State University of New York College at New Paltz 338, 533

State University of New York College at Oswego 340, 533

State University of New York College at Purchase 342, 534

Syracuse University 354, 535

Union College (NY) 366, 538

United States Merchant Marine Academy 370, 539

United States Military Academy 372, 539

University of Rochester 410, 547

Vassar College 420, 550

Wagner College 424, 551

Webb Institute 430, 552

Wells College 434, 553

PENNSYLVANIA

Albright College 14, 460

Allegheny College 18, 461

Arcadia University (formerly Beaver College) 24, 462

Bryn Mawr College 54, 469

Bucknell University 56, 469

California University of Pennsylvania 58, 470

Carnegie Mellon University 60, 470

Chatham College 66, 472

Chestnut Hill College 68, 472

Cheyney University of Pennsylvania 70, 472

College Misericordia 92, 475

Delaware Valley College 108, 481

Dickinson College 110, 481

Drexel University 114, 482

Duquesne University 116, 483

Elizabethtown College 118, 483

Franklin & Marshall College 132, 486

Gettysburg College 140, 488

Grove City College 146, 489

Haverford College 156, 491

Immaculata University 168, 494

Indiana University of Pennsylvania 170, 494

Juniata College 178, 496

Kutztown University of Pennsylvania 182, 497

La Roche College 184, 498

Lafayette College 188, 498

Lancaster Bible College 190, 499

Lebanon Valley College 192, 499

Lehigh University 194, 500

Lycoming College 200, 501

Mercyhurst College 216, 505

Messiah College 220, 505

Moore College of Art & Design 226, 507

Moravian College 228, 507

Muhlenberg College 232, 508

Neumann College 236, 509

Pennsylvania State University—University Park 248, 512

Rosemont College 274, 518

Saint Joseph's University (PA) 286, 520

Seton Hill University 298, 523

Shippensburg University of Pennsylvania 300, 523

Slippery Rock University of Pennsylvania 310, 525

Susquehanna University 350, 534

Swarthmore College 352, 535

Temple University 356, 536

Thiel College 358, 536

University of Pennsylvania 400, 545

University of Pittsburgh at Bradford 402, 546

University of Pittsburgh at Johnstown 404, 546

University of Pittsburgh—Pittsburgh 406, 547

University of Scranton, The 412, 548

University of the Arts 378, 540

Ursinus College 418, 549

Villanova University 422, 550

Washington & Jefferson College 426, 551

West Chester University of Pennsylvania 440, 554

Westminster College (PA) 442, 554

Widener University 446, 555

Wilkes University 448, 556

RHODE ISLAND

Brown University 50, 468
Bryant University 52, 468
Providence College 254, 513
Roger Williams University 272, 517
Salve Regina University 292, 521
University of Rhode Island 408, 547

VERMONT

Bennington College 38, 465
Marlboro College 208, 503
Middlebury College 222, 506
Saint Michael's College 288, 520
University of Vermont 416, 549

NOTES

NOTES

NOTES

ABOUT THE AUTHORS

Robert Franek is a graduate of Drew University and has been a member of The Princeton Review Staff for four years. Robert comes to The Princeton Review with an extensive admissions background, most recently at Wagner College in Staten Island, New York. In addition, he owns a walking tour business and leads historically driven, yet not boring, tours of his home town!

Tom Meltzer is a graduate of Columbia University. He has taught for The Princeton Review since 1986 and is the author or co-author of seven TPR titles, the most recent of which is *Illustrated Word Smart*, which Tom co-wrote with his wife, Lisa. He is also a professional musician and songwriter. A native of Baltimore, Tom now lives in Hillsborough, North Carolina.

Christopher Maier is a graduate of Dickinson College. During the past five years, he's lived variously in New York City, coastal Maine, western Oregon, central Pennsylvania, and eastern England. Now he's at an oasis somewhere in the midwestern cornfields—the University of Illinois—where he's earning his MFA in fiction. Aside from writing for magazines, newspapers, and The Princeton Review, he's worked as a radio disc jockey, a helping hand in a bakery, and a laborer on a highway construction crew. He's trying to avoid highway construction these days.

Julie Doherty is a freelance writer, Web designer, and preschool teacher. She lives in Mexico City.

Andrew Friedman graduated in 2003 from Stanford University, where he was a President's Scholar. He lives in New York City.

MORE BOOKS FOR YOUR
COLLEGE SEARCH

Best 361 Colleges
2006 Edition
0-375-76483-6 • $21.95/C$29.95

Colleges with a Conscience
0-375-76480-1 • $16.95/C$23.95

Complete Book of Colleges
2006 Edition
0-375-76482-8 • $26.95/C$37.95

Guide to College Majors
2005 Edition
0-375-76469-0 • $21.00/C$28.00

The Internship Bible
10th Edition
0-375-76468-2 • $25.00/C$35.00

The Princeton Review